Standard Catalog of®

MILITARY FIREARMS

The Collector's Price and Reference Guide

6TH EDITION

PHILLIP PETERSON

Published by

Gun Digest® Books, an imprint of F+W Media, Inc.
Krause Publications • 700 East State Street • Iola, WI 54990-0001
715-445-2214 • 888-457-2873
www.krausebooks.com

To order books or other products call toll-free 1-800-258-0929
or visit us online at www.krausebooks.com, www.gundigeststore.com
or www.Shop.Collect.com

Cover images courtesy of
Hermann Historica auctioneers, Munich
hermann-historica.com

ISBN-13: 978-1-4402-1451-6
ISBN-10: 1-4402-1451-4

Cover & Design by Tom Nelsen
Edited by Dan Shideler

Printed in the United States of America

Dedication

For the gun collectors of America.

CONTENTS

DIRECTORY

ACKNOWLEDGMENTS

Orval Reichert is a collector of WWII-era semi-automatic pistols, especially the P38, and has been an invaluable help in sorting out a sometimes confusing array of pistol variations. He can be reached at P.O. Box 67, Vadar, WA, 98593.

Joe Gaddini, of SWR, has provided invaluable technical assistance on Class III firearms and suppressors. He can be reached at 119 Davis Road, Suite G-12, Martinez, GA, 30907.

Thanks to Eric M. Larsen for his information concerning Federal firearms laws.

Special thanks go to Simeon Stoddard, former curator of the Cody Firearms Museum, for his research into and contributions concerning the M1 Garand rifle.

Nick Tilotta is an expert on Thompson submachine guns. He helped to explain the subtle differences between models and can be reached at P.O. Box 451, Grapevine, TX, 76099.

Don Westmoreland is a serious student of Japanese and German WWII automatic weapons. His knowledge was extremely valuable.

Gunsmith Stan Andrewski can be reached at 603-746-4387 and is recommended to anyone needing firtst-class work on Class III weapons.

Dan Shea, editor and publisher of *Small Arms Review*, lent his mastery of Class III firearms.

Ted Dawidowicz of Dalvar USA lent numerous photos of imported Polish military firearms. He may be reached at 702-558-6707.

Jim Alley (937-773-4203) of IDSA Books was most generous in granting use of his extensive personal library.

Blake Stevens (905-342-3434) of Collector Grade Publications shared his vast knowledge as well as select photographs from his personal collection.

The suggestions of Ricky Kumor, Sr., and J. B. Wood contributed much to earlier editions of this book – and to this one as well.

The assistance of small arms expert James Rankin is gratefully acknowledged.

Mark Keefe, editor of *American Rifleman*, contributed valuable information on Lee-Enfield rifles.

Richard Wray and Ken Keilholz shared their encyclopedic knowledge and photographs of Class III firearms, without which this would be a lesser book.

J. R. Moody was generous in his assistance concerning Class III and sniper weapons.

Thanks go out to Pedro Bello for sharing his extensive knowledge of machine pistols.

Charlie Cutshaw provided valuable information on rare and hard-to-find military weapons.

Paul Miller and John M. Miller, CWO, U. S. Army (Ret.), generously shared their deep knowledge of military weapons.

Bob Naess is an expert of machine guns and their values, and he kindly lent his assistance to this volume.

Mike LaPlante generously straightened out the maze of variations found in the AR-15 and M16 family of weapons.

And, finally, our thanks go to Ned Schwing, former editor of this volume.

PHOTO CREDITS

Many of the full-format photos appearing in this book were taken by photographer extraordinaire Paul Goodwin.

A special acknowledgment to Kris Leinicke, curator of the Rock Island Arsenal Museum, for providing full access to the museum's outstanding firearms collection.

Karl Karash supplied photos from his personal collection of Colt 1911s.

Jim Rankin shared many photos from his vast personal collection.

Robert Fisch, curator of the museum at the United States Military Academy at West Point, was most generous in sharing the museum's treasure trove of historically significant firearms.

Blake Stevens of Collector Grade Publications shared numerous photos from his outstanding and comprehensive books.

Roberty Segel supplied many beautiful photos of his superb collection of vintage machine guns.

Charles Kenyon lent outstanding Luger photographs, many of which appear in his landmark book, *Lugers at Random*.

Chuck Karwan shared many photos from his extensive photo archives of military weapons.

Ricky Kumor, Sr., went out of his way to photograph many of the fine military firearms that pass through his shop.

Tom Nelson of Ironside International Publishers kindly allowed us to reprint some of his photos of rare weapons from his outstanding series of books on automatic weapons.

John M. Miller helpfully supplied photos of early military firearms.

Paul Scarlata was generous with photos not only of military firearms but of other fascinating historical subjects.

Ryerson Knight was most helpful with photos of pocket pistols.

And, finally, thanks to Dr. Leonardo M. Antaris for the use of the outstanding photos from his book, *Star Firearms*.

INTRODUCTION TO THE 6TH EDITION

Welcome to the 6th edition of *Standard Catalog of Military Firearms*. This is my third time as "author" of this title, although I tend to see myself as more of a reporter or compiler.

The layout and format of this book were pretty much established in editions one through three. Each time out I have attempted to add some new information and pricing that expands the scope and usefulness of this book, to give the readers something new that makes buying the next edition hard to resist. Since there are few "new" models of old military guns to add to the listings, I decided to branch out to include data and values for firearm-related items that many collectors and firearms owners encounter.

With the fourth edition bayonets were added to the listings. This was the first time since the 1970s that a book published in the U.S. had identification and value information for bayonets. Of course there is not enough room in this book to give full coverage to bayonets. There are other books published that are as big as SCMF that focus solely on bayonets. We recommend *Bayonets from Janzen's Notebook*. While not every bayonet variation can be included, we do try to give collectors an idea what might have been issued with their rifles as well as collector pricing.

For the fifth edition we added images and value data on magazines from the vintage handguns listed within. To our knowledge there had never been any reference published that featured the magazines of collectible firearms. This is important as one will often encounter guns with a non-original magazine installed. This certainly affects value of a firearm as many vintage magazines are nearly impossible to find and cost many times what an after market replacement does.

Now for the 6th edition we offer two new groups of listings: Pre-cartridge era rifles and military holsters.

Pre-Cartridge Era Rifles

This includes percussion smoothbore muskets and rifles as well as a few flintlock muskets. These firearms are usually called muzzle loaders by noncollectors. We are trying to go back to 1800 or so for these listings; however it is proving difficult to gather information and images for some of these firearms.

The sister publication to *SCMF*, *Standard Catalog of Firearms*, had continued to include national listings of antique military long guns through the 2010 edition. Two years ago I suggested to *SCF* editor Dan Shideler that we needed to move these listings of military long arms to SCMF and he agreed. So we now have listings and some images of antique weapons for Austria, France, Great Britain, and United States. These were transferred straight from SCF and value information was updated.

Of course that left us short of information about muzzle loaders from other countries. With the help of my friend Paul Bunin, listings were compiled for Belgium, Germany, Japan, Russia and a few others. Paul is a long-time collector and dealer in antique military weaponry and he was of immense help in deciding what to include as well as pricing. We are not claiming this to be comprehensive listing of every model and variation, but a sample of things a collector might encounter. Many of these pre cartridge arms have never been imported to the U.S. in any quantity.

There are two principal ways European rifles ended up in North America. The first is the U.S. Civil War 1861-1865. Early in the conflict both sides had arms buyers scouring Europe for arms to purchase for the war. Hundreds of thousands of English, German, French, and Belgian rifles were used in the war then later sold or scrapped when American made arms were plentiful.

The second way these foreign weapons got here was importation by commercial resellers. Francis Bannerman of New York is probably the largest and most well known. From the late 1800s through the 1930s, Bannerman imported tons of military surplus from all corners of the globe. Their catalog is actually one of the sources we used to identify what models of guns were available on the U.S. market.

Of course some individual examples of other arms might have been carried home by U.S. veterans returning from WWI or WWII but most of these guys were looking for more portable souvenirs. Carrying around a 50-inch long musket would be a bit of a problem to a soldier on the move around Europe for several months.

Military Holsters

Holsters are a very popular accessory item for military handguns. This fascinating corner of the weapons collectors world is virtually ignored by other firearms reference and value guides. There are a few reference works available that go into far more detail than we can include here, but they do not feature pricing. What we do provide are examples of common military holsters including a price range. Now an owner of a 1917 Luger with holster and spare magazine can get an idea what his magazine and holster add to the value of his piece.

As always, if you have comments or suggestions concerning this edition of *Standard Catalog of Military Firearms*, I invite you to contact me at the address below.

Until next time, happy collecting!

Phillip Peterson
0771 S 500 E
Avilla, IN 46710

BASIC MAGAZINE NOMENCLATURE

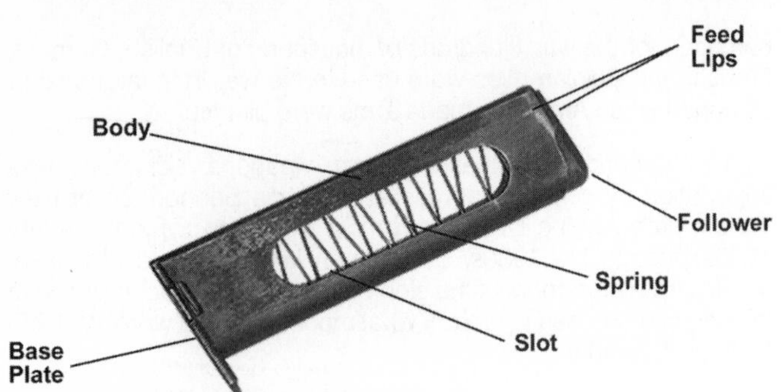

Here are some details to observe when examining a magazine:

- The shape of the follower and feed lips;
- The number and placement of holes or slots in the magazine body:
- The shape of the floor plate and how it is attached to the magazine body;
- Blued, phosphate, nickel, or a combination? Some original magazines have a different finish than the gun they came with.
- Condition. Look for dents in the body that might interfere with filling it, or inserting it in the gun, and for damage to the locking slot. Also check the feed lips for any bends or cracks.
- Markings-. Many original issue magazines have no markings. Some military issue magazines have added markings that are

BASIC BAYONET NOMENCLATURE

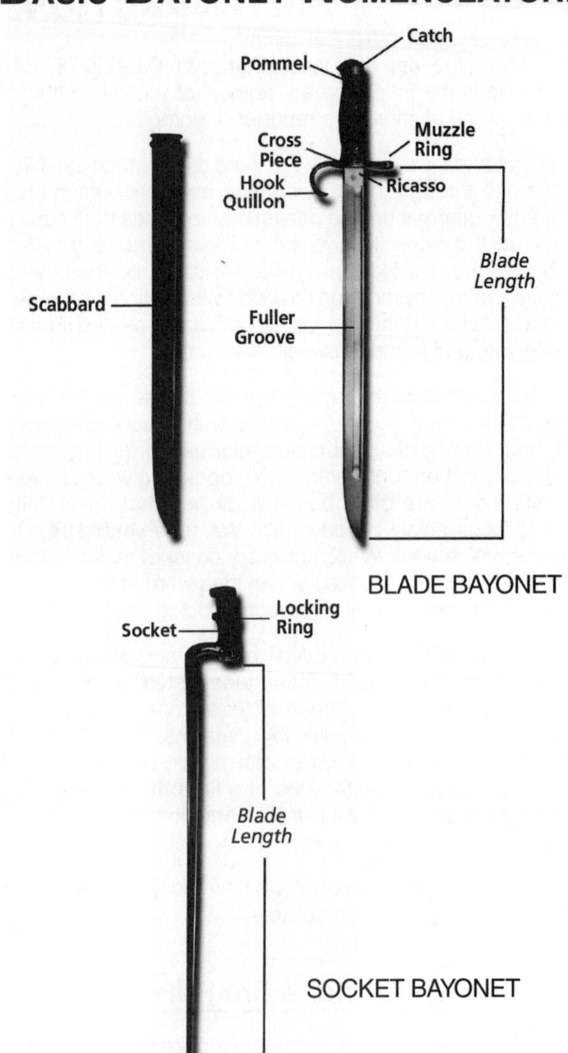

MARKET TRENDS

The 2008 presidential election contributed to a surge in the demand for semi automatic military type firearms. Much of the firearms industry has coasted through 2009 and early 2010 with strong sales. Despite the struggling economy and growing unemployment levels business was brisk.

Fear of impending bans spurned buyers to pay above MSRP for current production models. Manufacturers were leaving their phones off the hook so they could try to fill the increased orders for product. It was common for AR-15 type rifle makers to tell their customers to expect delivery of ordered items in six to 12 months.

When the expected ban failed to materialize, the industry caught up with the backorders and as of early 2011 there is a slump in the sales of many models. There are so many companies currently making AR-15s that prices have fallen by up to $500 for certain models.

Sales of some collectible firearms have slowed as well.

As we gathered pricing data of realized prices from auctions, internet sales and some observed traffic at gun shows, it is clear that there has been a slight drift downward in the selling price of collectible military firearms. The biggest hit has been in what I call mid-range collectibles in the $250 to $750 range. Our read on this is that the working class segment of collectors and accumulators are the ones who have been affected most by down economy. Fewer new collectors are entering the market and the more common items have fallen in value as the existing collectors already have them. There are fewer sales to "non collector" buyers of old military guns who were buying in the past because they were cheap.

The market continues to see strong sales activity at the specialty auction houses such as Rock Island Auctions, Greg Martin, Bonhams and others. RIA had an auction in December 2010 that brought in over $9.7 million in sales from over 3700 lots. There is still no shortage of buyers with deep pockets for excellent condition military weaponry. The upward price trend with excellent plus items has slowed since the collector boom period in the early 2000s but it does continue.

AUCTION HOUSE CREDITS

The following auction houses were kind enough to allow the Catalog to report unusual firearms from their sales. The directors of these auction concerns are acknowledged for their assistance and support.

Amoskeag Auction Company, Inc.
250 Commercial Street, Unit #3011
Manchester, NH 03101
Attention: Jason or Melissa Devine
603-627-7383
603-627-7384 FAX

Bonhams & Butterfield
220 San Bruno Avenue
San Francisco, CA 94103
Attention: James Ferrell
415-861-7500 ext. 3332
415-861-8951 FAX

Old Town Station Ltd.
P.O. Box 15351
Lenexa, KS 66285
Attention: Jim Supica
913-492-3000
913-492-3022 FAX

Rock Island Auction Company
1050 36th Avenue
Moline, IL 61265
Attention: Patrick Hogan
800-238-8022
309-797-1655 FAX

Greg Martin Auctions
660 Third Street, Suite 100
San Francisco, CA 94107
800-509-1988
415-522-5706 FAX

Little John's Auction Service, Inc.
1740 W. La Veta
Orange, CA 92868
Attention: Carol Watson
714-939-1170
714-939-7955 FAX

CONTRIBUTING EDITORS

Bob Ball
Springfield Armory & Mauser rifles
P.O. Box 562
Unionville, CT 06085

Bailey Brower
Savage military pistols
P.O. Box 111
Madison, NJ 07940

Jim Cate
J.P. Sauer pistols
406 Pine Bluff Dr.
Chattanooga, TN 37412
423-892-6320

Jason Devine
Winchester lever actions
250 Commercial Street, Unit #3011
Manchester, NH 03101
603-627-7383
603-627-7384 FAX

Gene Guilaroff
Modern military firearms
P.O. Box 173
Alvaton, KY 42122
270-622-7309
e-mail: arclight@nctc.com

Karl Karash
Colt Model 1911 & 1911A1
288 Randall Road
Berlin, MA 01503
978-838-9401
987-589-2060 FAX

Chuck Karwan
Colt New Service, Browning High-Power, Lee-Enfield, Webley revolvers
958 Cougar Creek Road
Oakland, OR 97462
541-459-4134

Richard M. Kumor Sr.
c/o Ricky's Gun Room
WWII era military firearms
P.O. Box 286
Chicopee, MA 01021
413-592-5000
413-594-5700 FAX
e-mail: Rickysinc@aol.com
Web site: rickysinc.com

Gale Morgan
Luger and Mauser pistols
Pre-World War I pistols
P.O. Box 72
Lincoln, CA 95648
916-645-1720

Robert E. Naess
Class III guns of all types
P.O. Box 471
Cavendish, VT 05142
802-226-7204
e-mail: margoc@mail.tds.net

Jerry Prasser
Recon Ordnance Company
Class III & military weapons
P.O. Box 829
Fond du Lac, WI 54936
920-922-1515
920-922-0737 FAX

Jim Rankin
Walther pistols & pre-war auto pistols
3615 Anderson Road
Coral Gables, FL 33134
305-446-1792

Orvel Reichert
World War II-era semiautomatic pistols
P.O. Box 67
Vader, WA 98593
360-245-3492
e-mail: mr.p38@localaccess.com

Joe Schroeder
Steye/Mannlicher pistols
P.O. Box 406
Glenview, IL 60025
847-724-8816
847-657-6500
847-724-8831 FAX

John Stimson Jr.
High Standard pistols
540 W. 92nd St.
Indianapolis, IN 46260
317-831-2990

Simeon Stoddard
Swiss, Swedish, and Finnish rifles
P.O. Box 2283
Cody, WY 82414

Jim Supica
Smith & Wesson
P.O. Box 15351
Lenexa, KS 66285
913-492-3000

Nick Tilotta
Western Firearms Co.
Thompson submachine guns
P.O. Box 451
Grapevine, TX 76099
817-481-6616
817-251-5136 FAX
www.westernfirearms.com

Denis Todd
M16s
239 Baltimore Pike
Springfield, PA 19064
610-543-7300
dtoddmg@aol.com

Michael Wamsher
World War I & II Weapons
17732 West 67th Street
Shawnee, KS 66217
913-631-0686

PRICING

The firearms prices listed in this book are RETAIL PRICES, that is, the prices at which you can reasonably expect to buy firearms from a dealer or collector. Any firearm can bring more or less depending on many variables. If you choose to sell your gun to a dealer, you will not receive the retail price but instead a wholesale price based on the markup that particular dealer needs to operate.

Also, in certain cases there will be no price indicated under a particular condition but rather the notation "N/A" or the symbol "—". This indicates that there is no known price available for that gun in that condition or the sales for that particular model are so few that a reliable price cannot be given. This can happen with recent production items that are not old enough to be in fair or poor condition.

The prices listed here come from a variety of sources: retail stores, gun shows, individual collectors, and auction houses. Due to the nature of business, one will usually pay higher prices at a retail store than at a gun show. In some cases, internet auctions will produce excellent buys or extravagant prices, depending on any given situation.

In recent years, internet sales of collectible firearms have become a major factor in this market. Auction sites such as www.GunBroker.com have nearly overtaken storefront or gun show purchases for many collectors. In our own business, we find that the auction sites bring me more buyers with more money than we ever had from traditional venues. I usually set up at gun shows to buy merchandise then sell it on line so as to reach more buyers. The better-quality military arms we find rarely ever get displayed on my gun show table; they sell online first – frequently for more than they will bring locally.

The downside of this for those not participating in the internet revolution is that they are missing out on a lot of interesting historical firearms that will never be offered through any other venue. This internet selling has leveled out the market. Any pricing found online is going to reflect a nationwide trend. In the "old days" one could find seasonal and regional differences in the prices of collectibles. A small gun or pawn shop in the middle of farm country might have had a matching Luger priced at $550 sit on the shelf for years. The local buyers weren't interested because they purchased their firearms for hunting, not collecting. Now these local dealers need only offer these slow-selling guns on the internet and they suddenly have the entire country as potential customers.

Collectors will sometimes pay higher prices for a firearm that they need to fill out their collection, when in other circumstances they will not be willing to pay market price if they don't need to have the gun. The point here is that the price paid for firearms is an ever-changing affair based on a large number of variables. The prices in this book are a GENERAL GUIDE as to what a willing buyer and willing seller might agree on. You may find the item for less, and then again you may have to pay more depending on the variables of your particular situation. There is a saying among collectors that goes "I didn't pay too much for this gun, I bought it too soon." This reflects a solid trend with collectible firearms that the prices continue to rise with each year.

Some factors are unique when attempting to set a price on a collectible military firearm, for example the presence of import markings or matching numbers. Both of these can have an impact on the value of a collectible firearm. How much? Good question.

Import Markings

Under the terms of the Gun Control Act of 1968, all firearms imported to the U.S. must be marked with certain information. This includes importer, model, country of origin and caliber. While this does not have any effect on new sporting firearms, it does add non-original markings to vintage military guns. In 1986, when military surplus firearms were once again legal for importation, most importers put all the required information in a very small stamping on the side of the barrel. In the mid-1990s, the government established new size criteria for the markings and most importers had to enlarge them. They also required that military surplus firearms be marked with a unique serial number on the receiver. This was because it was discovered that original serial numbers could have been duplicated on similar models. This new number is the one that gets recorded in the transfer records for a particular firearm.

In cases where identical models were imported in both pre-1968 and post-1986 eras, the non import marked examples might bring a higher price to some collectors.

To further confuse the issue, some importers recently started using a dot matrix import marking on the receivers of their products. They put all the required information on the receiver, not just the serial number. In some cases this is placed over the original markings. Now, to me, that does have an impact on the value. Since many collectors seek out examples based on unique markings, having those marks covered with new ones must reduce the desirability of these arms. Again, there is no set amount to discount these "billboard" marked guns; just be aware that many buyers will pass by such items.

Matching Numbers

Many foreign military firearms had all or part of the serial number stamped on the main pieces of the gun. The Germans were particularly fond of the practice. A Luger P-08 pistol or 98K Mauser rifle has the last two digits of the serial number stamped on almost every piece of the gun that is large enough for it to fit. Other manufacturers might only number main components. Some did not number anything but the receiver or barrel. Each country and maker had their own practice. Some entries in this edition will list parts numbering practices for the item. Some do not. I tried including the information when I began this project but found it took up too much space and time to go into such detail for each item. Suffice it to say that if you are examining a military firearm and any major part bears a number different than the one on other major parts, it is probably mismatched.

How much a mismatched part on a gun might affect the price is another factor that is impossible to include in the listings. If a major part such as the bolt is not matching, many collectors would not be interested in an item at any price. A bargain shopper looking for a shootable example of an item might not care that no two pieces on a gun have matched numbers. A good thing to remember is that higher the collector demand and price of an item, the more a mismatched part will impact the price.

Luckily for the collectors of U.S. military firearms, we seldom used the practice of numbering any parts but the receiver. There might be assembly or contractor numbers but not serial numbers. Only some early 1911 pistols numbered the slides internally.

Many items that were imported in the 1950s and 60s have not been brought in since the 1986 lifting of the ban on imported military surplus. In these cases there is no accurate way to determine how many of a particular model was imported in the pre-GCA 1968 days. Detailed records of the old imports were not usually kept. Many of the companies of that era no longer exist. Likewise, there are some models and variations listed in this book that have never been imported to this country in quantity. I still needed to apply some sort of price information for these, even if I could find no actual examples of pricing during research for this edition. In such cases I have simply made an educated guess. This is based on personal experience with similar models and my assumptions of demand and scarcity of a given model. In some cases I may be wrong. A serious collector who has been searching for a particular variation to fill a void in his collection may very well be willing to spend much more than any price given in this book.

The price ranges listed in these pages come from the author's personal experience, observations of vendors at gun shows and online, and opinions of some collectors whose items were photographed for use in this book. With some items, no example could be found for sale. In these cases the price range given is the author's best guess. There will, of course, be examples that the reader might find that are outside the price range included here. In the final analysis, the prices listed herein are given to assist the shooter and collector in pursuing their hobby with a better understanding of what is going on in the marketplace. If this book can expand one's knowledge, then it will have fulfilled its purpose.

GRADING SYSTEM

In the opinion of the editor all grading systems are subjective. It is our task to offer the collector and dealer a measurement that most closely reflects a general consensus on condition. The system we present seems to come closest to describing a firearm in universal terms. We strongly recommend that the reader acquaint himself with this grading system before attempting to determine the correct price for a particular firearm's condition. Remember, in most cases, condition determines price.

NIB—New in Box

This category can sometimes be misleading. It means that the firearm is in its original factory carton with all of the appropriate papers. It also means the firearm is new; that it has not been fired and has no wear. This classification brings a substantial premium for both the collector and shooter. The NIB category will not be included with most listings in SCMF as few military issue firearms can be found in NIB condition. The only exceptions are a few commercial versions of military firearms that are included in the book because no genuine examples exist on the U.S. market.

Excellent

Collector quality firearms in this condition are highly desirable. The firearm must be in at least 98 percent condition with respect to blue wear, stock or grip finish, and bore. The firearm must also be in 100 percent original factory condition without refinishing, repair, alterations, or additions of any kind. Sights must be factory original as well. This grading classification includes both modern and antique (manufactured prior to 1898) firearms.

Very Good

Firearms in this category are also sought after both by the collector and shooter. Firearms must be in working order and retain approximately 92 percent metal and wood finish. It must be 100 percent factory original, but may have some small repairs, alterations, or non-factory additions. No refinishing is permitted in this category. Both modern and antique firearms are included in this classification.

Good

Modern firearms in this category may not be considered to be as collectable as the previous grades, but antique firearms are considered desirable. Modern firearms must retain at least 80 percent metal and wood finish, but may display evidence of old refinishing. Small repairs, alterations, or non-factory additions are sometimes encountered in this class. Factory replacement parts are permitted. The overall working condition of the firearm must be good as well as safe. The bore may exhibit wear or some corrosion, especially in antique arms. Antique firearms may be included in this category if their metal and wood finish is at least 50 percent original factory finish.

Fair

Firearms in this category should be in satisfactory working order and safe to shoot. The overall metal and wood finish on the modern firearm must be at least 30 percent and antique firearms must have at least some original finish or old re-finish remaining. Repairs, alterations, nonfactory additions, and recent refinishing would all place a firearm in this classification. However, the modern firearm must be in working condition, while the antique firearm may not function. In either case, the firearm must be considered safe to fire if in a working state.

Poor

Neither collectors nor shooters are likely to exhibit much interest in firearms in this condition. Modern firearms are likely to retain little metal or wood finish. Pitting and rust will be seen in firearms in this category. Modern firearms may not be in working order and may not be safe to shoot. Repairs and refinishing would be necessary to restore the firearm to safe working order. Antique firearms will have no finish and will not function. In the case of modern firearms, their principal value lies in spare parts. On the other hand, antique firearms in this condition may be used as "wall hangers" or as an example of an extremely rare variation or have some kind of historical significance.

HOW DID THEY GET HERE?

by Phillip Peterson

Most of the firearms contained in this book were made for military use in another country. Yet there are millions of these weapons in the hands of American shooters and collectors. It really would be impossible to get an accurate number. How did they get here? Well, that becomes an interesting bit of history.

Veteran Bring-Backs

The big prize! Weapons have been desirable war booty throughout history. Veterans from any foreign war in which the United States has participated carted home untold numbers of firearms in their duffle bags, foot lockers or pockets. The most common would have to be handguns because of their size and ease of transportation. Rifles present a slight problem due to their length. Examples will be encountered in which the stock is "duffle cut." This means the rifle was taken apart and the stock was cut in two pieces so they would fit in a duffle bag, foot locker or mailing carton. If the soldier was smart, he made the cut under a barrel band so the cut could be hidden when the rifle was reassembled. However he got it home, the soldier still had to carry the item with him for days or months before it could be sent home.

I do not know if there was any official regulation about war souvenir firearms during WWI. In those days, firearms were not such controversial items. Look at the numbers of WWI-vintage Maxim machine guns that exist today. Imagine a soldier trying to figure a way to bring one of those home – yet some managed to do it. Even small cannon found their way here. In many cases it would have to be an officer or person involved in logistics to arrange transport of large, heavy items that would not fit in an individual soldier's kit. Some machine guns or cannon were brought home as unit trophies by the regiment that captured it. These were later sold off by VFW posts after the memory of the capture died off along with the aging veterans.

During WWII there were some regulations in effect that required servicemen to have "capture papers" to possess enemy equipment, including firearms. These rules were enforced only by some, not all, commanders. I have spoken to many WWII veterans who shipped or carried home single guns or a foot locker full of stuff without any official permission or documentation. Others tell stories of officers "seizing" their trophy Luger or other prize, while leaving other less desirable items alone. One has to wonder where those seized items ended up? There was a form in use that was issued to servicemen who followed the official process. Any war souvenir firearm accompanied with an original capture paper is now a highly desirable item. In fact such a paper can add 25 – 50% to the price of the gun over what it would be without it. This paper proves a link to the past.

Similar regulations were in effect during Korea and Viet Nam. After the passage of the Gun Control Act of 1968, which changed federal regulations for importation of firearms, the military authorities required service persons bringing home any captured firearms to go through an import process set forth in that law. However, since the GCA '68 also banned the importation of military surplus firearms, and most firearms captured in a war were of course military in nature, it effectively ended the ability of veterans to bring home captured firearms. Still, some pre-1899 antique firearms along with parts, magazines and accessories from newer weapons were permitted. Some small firearms were simply brought home hidden in luggage or equipment. The first Soviet Makarov pistol I ever saw was at a gun show in 1983. It was being sold by a soldier just home from the U.S. action in Grenada. (I passed on it because the 9x18mm ammunition was unavailable.)

A few well-publicized cases of smuggling after the Grenada action and the first Gulf War have totally ended any legal way for service persons to bring or send home ANY captured firearm or even part of one. In one example, a general had sent home several full automatic AK-47s that had been disabled simply by removing the firing pin. This was a violation of federal law as the receivers of these guns were intact and they could be easily repaired. Then there were several instances where illegal firearms and explosive munitions were hidden inside military vehicles by persons involved in transporting them back to the states after the conflict. The actions of a few have ruined things for everyone.

At this time the official military policy is to destroy any captured enemy equipment that is not of use by us or our allies. This means that collectible Mauser and Enfield bolt action rifles are being blown up in Iraq. I've read that original cases of unissued Mausers have been destroyed along with tons of antique machine guns and other munitions. Individual soldiers are strictly forbidden from possessing any non-issue firearms, magazines or ammunition. Attempts to ship home contraband items through the Army Post Office system are prosecuted. Some soldiers have been put in federal prison for attempting to smuggle back illegal firearms.

Importation: The "Good Old Days"

After WWII there were literally tons of military firearms of every kind left lying around many nations. Barges of equipment were dumped in the oceans to get them out of the way. Some countries, their economies decimated by years of war, had very little in the way of commodities that could be sold for cold hard cash. They did have the tons of firearms and other surplus material that they no longer needed. Enter Sam Cummings, founder of Interarms, and other entrepreneurs like him. Deals were cut and ships were loaded. From the late 1940s until 1968 they imported the surplus weaponry from WWII and earlier and sold it here in the USA.

A primary market for these firearms was the veterans who had learned to shoot during the war. Many of the military rifles were purchased to provide cheap hunting guns. Unfortunately, many of these simply had the stocks chopped to make the gun look more like a hunting rifle. Others went to gunsmiths who stripped them for the action, which was rebarreled in a new caliber. A few articles appeared in firearms magazines dealing with the foreign firearms but most of those either questioned the quality of manufacture or told of how to convert or "sporterize" the inexpensive guns. Pistols were bought by the veterans who never got them as souvenirs while in the service.

In the 1960s some baby boomers who had grown up in the shadow of the "greatest generation" and saw all the war movies popular in the post war years started collecting these pieces of history. This period was the beginning of gun collecting as we know it today. This first generation of gun collectors had almost no reference material about the firearms they were collecting. No Standard Catalogue of Military Firearms back then! There had been a few articles published in military manuals and magazines during the war about the equipment the enemy used. These had only a small part of the information that the new collectors wanted. They pooled information with other collectors about the guns they had, and they learned about production numbers and variations. Some even traveled overseas and contacted the makers to ask for production data. Not that it was very easy to find. Much of the information about Axis weaponry had been destroyed during the war. Often makers were reluctant to discuss their participation in arming the enemies of the USA. As the knowledge base expanded, books were written and collecting clubs were formed.

End of the Line?

The end of the first era of firearm importation came with the passage of the Gun Control Act of 1968. This law banned the importation of military surplus firearms and established the "sporting use" criteria for new guns that is still applied to firearm imports today. The import ban was actually supported by much of the U.S. sporting arms industry. The publicly stated reason was concern about the quality and safety of the old military guns made in other nations under questionable conditions. In fact, they did not like the competition from lower priced firearms that were, in some cases, of better quality than the stuff they were making here.

Of course, there were already millions of foreign military firearm here. Over the next 16 years the supply dwindled but never quite ran out. A few small lots of police-issued surplus firearms were permitted in if it could be proved that they were not used by any military force. During this time, the number of collector publications and clubs expanded. More shooters got interested in the military firearms as historical items rather than as inexpensive guns to be used for hunting.

Another Golden Era Begins!

In 1984, Republican Senator Robert Dole inserted an amendment into a Trade and Tariff Act as it worked its way through congress. The "Dole Amendment" changed U.S. Code to allow the importation of firearms listed by the Secretary of the Treasury (BATF) as curios and relics. The C&R designation includes firearms 50 or more years old as well as some newer items, if they are ruled to be of interest to collectors or museums. Unfortunately, machine guns were not included in the new imports to be permitted. They did retain the sporting use criteria for handguns, which imposes size requirements that a gun must meet to be importable. Thus, original WWII Walther PPKs and other small pistols remain banned from importation. But the larger Colt 1911s, Lugers and Walther PPs qualify. The only downside to the new imports is that they must be marked by the importer under terms of the GCA 1968. These marks separate the recent import firearms from those that were here prior to 1968. This can be a factor in the price that some collectors will pay for an item. Of course, many models and variations were never imported to the U.S. before 1968 so an import stamped gun might be the only option available.

The first decade of "new" surplus imports brought us many of the firearms that today are hard to find and bring several times what they sold for when the importers had them. Swedish M1896, 96-38 and 1938 Mausers, Finnish M 27, 28, 28-30, 39 Mosin Nagants, Hakims, Rashids, FN 1949s, M-1 Garands and Carbines, German WWII 98K Mausers, G-43s, Lugers, P-38s, Makarovs, and many others are now the focus of many collections. As this is written, we have Yugoslavian Mausers and SKS, Russian 91-30, 1938, 1944 Mosin Nagants, and Turkish Mausers.

What will tomorrow bring? Since before 1968, it has been said that they must be running out of firearms to import but importers keep finding them. The firearms keep turning up in remote nations eager for U.S. dollars to support their sagging economies. Of course these foreign governments are no longer giving their stuff away at bargain prices. They have seen what old firearms sell for in America and adjust their price upwards.

The era of high-quality European sources for excellent condition Mausers, Lugers and other arms is probably gone. These easy sources were harvested in the pre-1968 days and again since 1984. The fall of Russian communism opened the armories of our former adversaries, and right now there is a surplus of surplus Mosin Nagants. Another fact is that in the 1950s most nations adopted "assault weapons" capable of fully automatic function as their main military issue weapons. These will never be allowed importation for average citizens.

There is a bit of good news for those who like the select-fire designs. Since the 2004 expiration of the Clinton-era ban on many semi-automatic firearms, a new industry has been born. There are currently several small manufacturers of semi-automatic versions of select-fire weapons. In some cases only a few hundred of a model are being offered to buyers on a pre-pay basis. These firearms are not inexpensive. For instance, there are a couple of makers of semi-automatic German WWII-type MG-34 and MG-42 machine guns that are priced in the $5,000 range. These small makers and the models they offer are too numerous and ever-changing to include every one in this edition. I suggest that those interested in such items search the internet or look in the pages of Gun Digest Magazine.

At some point the supply of items legal for importation will slow to a trickle, then dry up. Or, an anti-gun administration will simply close the door to importing firearms for good. It could happen. Keep this in mind when you vote. Your participation might be key to your continued enjoyment of this fascinating hobby.

CLASS III (FULL-AUTO AND SELECT-FIRE) WEAPONS

In order to better understand the pricing structure of NFA weapons, it is necessary to understand the different chronological sequences of NFA weapons.

by Ned Schwing

Pre-1968: The Gun Control Act of 1968 was one of the most crucial. Pursuant to NFA weapons, the 1968 Act stipulated that no more imported machine guns could be brought into the system. As a result, pre-1968 imported guns command a premium because of their original manufacture. During 1968, the NFA branch of the ATF allowed a one-month amnesty period so that returning servicemen from Vietnam could register their war trophies. It was during this period that many AK47s, PPSH41s, and MP40 machine guns were put into the system. Many more U.S. and foreign manufactured guns were also registered at this time as well. All of these guns command a premium because of their originality and registration.

Pre-1986 conversions or guns with newly manufactured receivers: Domestic production of NFA weapons continued until 1986, when the Hughes amendment to the 1986 Firearms Owners Protection Act prohibited the registration of domestic machine guns. Thus the door was closed to any further production of machine guns available to individuals. NFA weapons already registered could remain in the system and be transferred to qualified individuals. This situation drove prices higher and continues to do so. This group of weapons consists of many desirable semi-automatics that were legally converted into fully-automatic weapons. These include the AR-15 converted to M-16, HK94s converted to the MP5, the HK91s converted to the G3, and the HK93 converted to the HK33.

There is another classification of Class III guns that are not original guns but are instead referred to as "side plate guns." A newly manufactured side plate is registered as the receiver on these guns. These include belt-fed Browning Model 1917s, 1919s, M-2 .50-cal., Vickers, and a few others. There are also re-welds or rewats. These are guns that were deactivated and then reactivated. Pricing for these categories can be confusing, and it is suggested that the collector or shooter seek expert advice before a purchase.

Most pre-1968 imports and all pre-1986 domestically made machine guns are transferrable to individuals, if they live in a state that allows individuals to possess them.

Pre-1986 Dealer Samples: Those individuals who wish to be Class III dealers in machine guns have many more NFA weapons to choose from, especially the newer, more contemporary designs. Pre-1986 dealer samples, imported before 1986, can be transferred between dealers only and retained personally by them after they surrender their Class III licenses. These dealer samples can be transferred only to other dealers.

Post-1986 dealer samples are even more restrictive. Only dealers wishing to demonstrate these weapons and who can produce a law enforcement letter can obtain them. Unlike the pre-1986 samples, these post-1986 samples cannot be retained after the registrant's license is surrendered.

For those readers who are interested in advancing their knowledge and understanding of Class III firearms, it is recommended that they subscribe to *Small Arms Review*, a first rate publication that has many informative and useful features. There are sections on the law, new products, and illuminating articles on all aspects of NFA weapons and their history. *Small Arms Review* may be contacted at Moose Lake Publishing, 223 Sugar Hill Rd., Harmony, ME 04942. Telephone 207-683-2959 or FAX 203-683-2172. E-mail SARreview@aol.com. Web site: www.smallarmsreview.com.

NOTE: *The prices listed for Class III firearms reflect the most current information as of publication date. Prices for Class III firearms are very volatile with rapid and sudden price changes. It is highly recommended that the latest market prices be verified in a particular market prior to a purchase.*

DEWAT (Deactivated War Trophy) MACHINE GUNS: Mention should be made that these guns, which have been rendered inactive according to BATF regulations, have a general value that is a rough percentage of the value of their active counterparts of approximately 85 percent. This percentage is only an approximation because of a wide range of factors ranging from who performed the deactivation, the extent of the work, how difficult it would be to reactivate the gun, and whether or not the work could be done without altering the basic look and function of the original. The collector should note that very rare machine guns, DEWAT or not, will bring the same price.

Thompson Model 1921A DEWAT • Courtesy Amoskeag Auction Company

An M-3 submachine gun registered as a DEWAT • Courtesy Amoskeag Auction Company

The Argentine Republic, located in southern South America, has an area of 1,073,518 sq. mi. (3,761,274 sq. km.) and an estimated population of 37.03 million. Capital: Buenos Aires. Its varied topography ranges from the subtropical lowlands of the north to the towering Andean Mountains in the west and the wind-swept Patagonian steppe in the south. The rolling, fertile pampas of central Argentina are ideal for agriculture and grazing, and support most of the republic's population. Meatpacking, flour milling, textiles, sugar refining and dairy products are the principal industries. Oil is found in Patagonia, but most mineral requirements must be imported.

Argentina was discovered in 1516 by the Spanish navigator Juan de Solis. A permanent Spanish colony was established at Buenos Aires in 1580, but the colony developed slowly. When Napoleon conquered Spain, the Argentines set up their own government on May 25, 1810. Independence was formally declared on July 9, 1816. A strong tendency toward local autonomy, fostered by difficult transportation, resulted in a federalized union.

NOTE: Argentine manufactures most of its small arms in government factories located in different locations around the country. This factory is known as the *Fabrica Militar de Armas Portatiles "Domingo Matheu"* (FMAP "DM"). It is located in Rosario.

HANDGUNS

Nagant M 1893 revolver by Simson & Co. Suhl

A six shot revolver chambered for 11mm German revolver cartridge. Based on the Belgian large frame Nagant revolver.

Exc.	V.G.	Good	Fair	Poor
850	675	500	300	200

Simson& Co. Suhl, Nagant Revolver

Steyr Mannlicher Model 1905

A semi-automatic pistol chambered in 7.65mm Mannlicher. It has a six-inch barrel. Made in Austria by Waffenfabrik Steyr. The first self-loading pistol used by the Argentine military. Manufactured with the Argentine crest on the left side of the frame cover. The crest was ground off the pistols sold as surplus in the 1960s. Frequently found in excellent condition, these pistols saw little use.

Steyr Mannlicher M1905 pistol *• courtesy Rock Island Auctions*

Exc.	V.G.	Good	Fair	Poor
700	575	425	300	200

NOTE: Add 100 percent for pistols with intact Argentine crest.

Colt Model 1911 A1

Argentina purchased several thousand Model 1911 a1 pistols from Colt before tooling up to manufacture their own. See listings under United States, handguns.

Argentine D. G. F. M. Sistema 1927 (Colt 1911A1 type)

(Direccion General de Fabricaciones Militares.) Made at the F.M.A.P. (Fabrica Militar de Arms Portatiles [Military Factory of Small Arms]. Licensed Colt copies with a SN range of 24,000 to 112,494 The parts are generally interchangeable with those of the Colt 1911A1. Most pistols were marked "D.G.F.M. - (F.M.A.P.) Sist Colt Cal. 11.25mm MOD 1927". Late pistols were marked FM within a cartouche on the right side of the slide. These pistols are found both with and without import markings, often in excellent condition, currently more often in refinished condition, and with

Argentine Hi-Power *• Courtesy Blake Stevens, from The Browning High-Power Automatic Pistol, Stevens*

a seemingly endless variety of slide markings. None of these variations have yet achieved any particular collector status or distinction. Price for pistol with matching frame, slide and barrel. Deduct 25 percent for mismatch.

Exc.	V.G.	Good	Fair	Poor
750	500	400	275	225

Courtesy Karl Karash collection

Argentine D.G.F.M. Sistema 1927 .22LR Conversion

A Systema 1927 pistol converted to fire .22LR. This uses a floating chamber system similar to the Colt Ace. Standard issue guns were converted. Marked on the slide "Transe A Cal 22 POR EST Venturini S.A." There are two variations which are similar but parts and magazines are not interchangeable. Several hundred of these were imported in the 1990s. All were re-finished when the conversion was done.

Exc.	V.G.	Good	Fair	Poor
700	500	400	275	225

Argentine Made Ballester Molina

Unlicensed, Argentine redesigned versions (parts are NOT interchangeable with Colt except for the barrel and magazine). These pistols are found both with and without U.S. import markings. Many of the imported pistols have been re-blued or parkerized. Pistols without import markings usually have an extra "B" prefix number and are often in Excellent to Unissued condition. These Ballester Molinas were acquired by Great Britain during WWII and might bear "Not English Make" and other English proof marks. Add 50 percent for English marked pistols. Ballester Rigaud was another Argentine manufacturer; not as common as Ballester Molina. Add 10 percent for Ballester Rigaud made pistols.

Exc.	V.G.	Good	Fair	Poor
550	400	300	250	200

Note: Argentine made magazines for the System 1927 and Ballester Molina have a serial number stamped on the base. Add 10% for a matching magazine.

FN Model 1935 GP

Postwar contract production for Argentine military and police. Argentine crest on top of slide. Produced before licensed production by FM in Argentina was begun in 1969. Some were imported to U.S. in the early 1990s. Frequently found in well-used condition; many were refinished in Argentina. Price for pistol with matching frame, slide and barrel. Deduct 25 percent for mismatch. Refinished = Good price.

Exc.	V.G.	Good	Fair	Poor
750	600	450	350	300

FM Model 1935 GP/Browning Pistol PD

Designated by the Argentine military as the "Browning Pistol PD." Licensed from FN and manufactured by FMAP "DM." Since 1969, Argentina has built about 185,000 of these pistols, some of which have been sold commercially. This 9x19 caliber pistol is marked on the left side of the slide, ***"Fabrica Militar De Armas Portatiles "D.M." Rosario, D.G.F.M., Licencia F N Browning, Industrai Argentina."*** Some have been imported for commercial sale.

Exc.	V.G.	Good	Fair	Poor
450	350	275	225	175

Star

Argentina used a small number of Star selective fire pistols for its special forces. See Spain, Handguns, Star Model M.

SUBMACHINE GUNS

Shortly after World War II, Argentina purchased a number of Beretta Model 38A2 directly from Beretta. The Argentine military also used the Sterling Mark 4

Bayonet for 1891 Mauser Rifle

Courtesy Rock Island Auction Company

and the Sterling Mark 5 (silenced version) purchased directly from Sterling against British forces during the Falkland War. The Argentine Coast Guard purchased HK MP5A2 and MP5A3 guns from Germany.

Argentina has also produced a number of submachine guns of its own design and manufacture. The PAM 1, PAM 2, the FMK series, and the Mems series were, or are, all Argentine submachine guns. It is doubtful if any of these guns were imported into the U.S. prior to 1968 and are therefore not transferable.

RIFLES

Argentine Pre-Cartridge Era Rifles:

Prior to the adoption of the Model 1879 Remington Rolling block, Argentina used a variety of European manufactured percussion rifles.

REMINGTON

Model 1879 Rolling Block

Argentina purchased about 75,000 rifles from Remington in 11.15x58Rmm (.43 Spanish). They have an octagon barrel behind the rear sight, and will be marked "Argentino Modello 1879 EN" on the top flat. Many Argentine M1879 Rolling Blocks were re-finished by the Argentine arsenals before they were sold. Use the Good-Very Good prices for a re-finished example.

Exc.	*V.G.*	*Good*	*Fair*	*Poor*
750	625	500	400	300

Bayonet for Remington Model 1879

Brass handle. Muzzle ring. Hook quillion. 18.3" single edge blade. Maker marked "W.R. Kirschbaum Solingen" on the ricasso. Other side is marked "RA" (Republica Argentina) Brass tipped leather scabbard. Price range 150 – 250.

MAUSER

M1891 Rifle

This rifle was made in Germany with a 29.1" barrel and 5-round magazine. Full stock with straight grip with half-length upper handguard. Rear sight V-notch. Chambered for the 7.65x53mm cartridge. Weight is about 8.8 lbs. Marked with Argentine crest on receiver ring. Most Model 1891 Mauser rifles found in the U.S. will have the Argentine crest ground off the top of the receiver. This was done by Argentina when they were sold as surplus in the 1960s. Many are in excellent condition and were probably never issued. Price for rifle with matching receiver, barrel, bolt, magazine and stock. Deduct 30 percent for mismatch.

Exc.	*V.G.*	*Good*	*Fair*	*Poor*
400	300	250	175	150

Add 100 percent for rifles with an intact Argentine crest.

Note: Model 1891 rifles and carbines made by Ludwig Lowe Co. of Berlin are considered antiques under U.S. law. Guns made by DWM are considered modern since some were made after 1898. There might be a slight premium for the Lowe guns since they can be sold freely.

Bayonet for 1891 Mauser Rifle

Aluminum or brass grips. 15.75" single edge blade. Made in Germany by Weyersburg, Kirschbaum & Co. Solingen; so marked on the ricasso. Argentine crest below "Modelo Argentino 1891" on the other side. Some had the Argentine crest ground off when sold as surplus. Serial number on blade and scabbard. Price range 85-35.

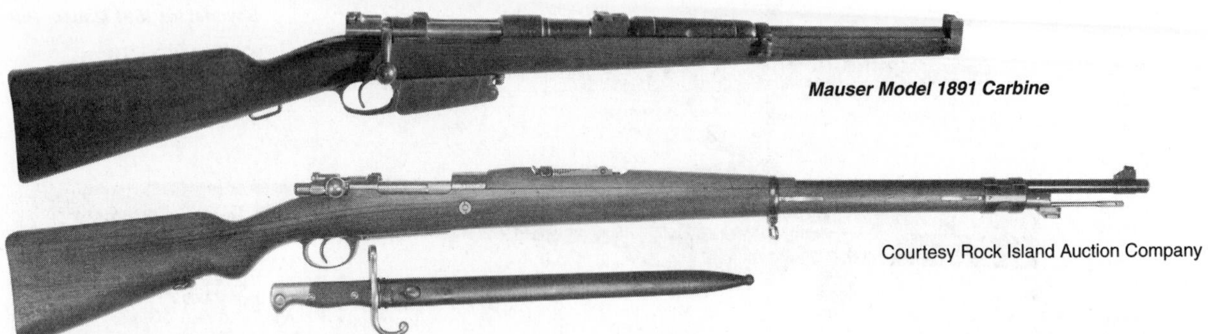

Mauser Model 1891 Carbine

Courtesy Rock Island Auction Company

ARGENTINA

M1891 Carbine

Full stock with straight grip. Front sight protectors and sling loops attached to bottom of stock behind the triggerguard. Turned down bolt. Barrel length is 17.6". Caliber is 7.65x53mm. Weight is about 7.2 lbs. Most 1891 Carbines will have an intact Argentine crest. They were sold after Argentina stopped grinding the crests. Price for rifle with matching receiver, barrel, bolt, magazine and stock. Deduct 30 percent for mismatch.

Exc.	V.G.	Good	Fair	Poor
550	400	300	200	150

M1891 Engineers Carbine

Same as 1891 carbine with added barrel bands with bayonet lug. Some were imported to the U.S. in the 1990s.

Exc.	V.G.	Good	Fair	Poor
550	400	300	200	150

Bayonet for M1891 Engineers Carbine

Brass grips. No barrel ring. Made from shortened M1879 Rolling block bayonets. Price range 250 – 85.

M1909 Rifle

Based on the German Gew-98 design and fitted with a 29-inch barrel and tangent rear sight graduated to 2000 meters. Almost full stock with pistol grip. The 5-round magazine fits in a flush box magazine with hinged floor plate. Chambered for the 7.65x53mm cartridge. Weight is about 9 lbs. Made in Germany by DWM. Argentine crest on receiver ring. Some 1909s will be found with a ground off crest. Deduct 20 percent for ground crest examples. Price for rifle with matching receiver, barrel, bolt, magazine and stock. Deduct 30 percent for mismatch.

Exc.	V.G.	Good	Fair	Poor
550	425	375	250	175

Model 1909 with close-up of receiver ring showing Argentine crest • *Courtesy Stoddard Martial collection, Paul Goodwin photo*

M1909 Sniper Rifle, Without Scope

Same as above but with bent bolt and scope. Some telescopes were German-made for the Argentine army.

Exc.	V.G.	Good	Fair	Poor
700	600	500	350	250

NOTE: Add $1000 for a sniper rifle with scope and mount.

M1909 Cavalry Carbine

Built by the German company DWM and in Argentina by D.G.F.M. This 7.65x53mm rifle has a full-length stock with straight grip and 21.5-inch barrel. Upper handguard is 2/3 length. Bayonet fittings. Weight is about 8.5 lbs. About 19,000 of these carbines were produced in Argentina between 1947 and 1959. Deduct 10% for Argentine manufactured gun. Price for rifle with matching receiver, barrel, bolt, magazine and stock. Deduct 30 percent for mismatch.

Exc.	V.G.	Good	Fair	Poor
575	425	300	225	150

M1909 Mountain Carbine

Sometimes referred to as the Engineers model. This is a cut-down Model 1909 rifle with 21.25-inch barrel with bayonet lug. Rear sight graduated to 1400 meters. Weight is about 8.5 lbs.

Exc.	V.G.	Good	Fair	Poor
500	400	300	225	150

Bayonet for Argentine 1909 Mauser Rifle and Carbine

Wood grips. 15.75-inch single edge blade. Maker marked on the ricasso "Weyersburg, Kirschbaum & Co. Solingen" or domestically made by "Fabrica Militar

Model 49 built for Argentina • Courtesy Stoffard Martial collection, Paul Goodwin photo

De Armas Portatiles". Argentine crest below "Modelo Argentino 1909" on the opposite side. Might be found with a ground crest. Serial number on blade and scabbard. Price range 90 – 35.

FN FAL (Argentine Manufacture)

Current issue for the Argentine military. It is assumed there are no select-fire versions available on the U.S. market. A number of these have been imported into the U.S. in semi-automatic configuration. Marked, "Fabrica Militar De Armas Portatiles-Rosario, Industrai Argentina."

Exc.	*V.G.*	*Good*	*Fair*	*Poor*
1000	900	750	—	—

FN Model 1949

Semi-automatic rifle sold to Argentina after WWII. Argentine crest on receiver. Originally, it was chambered for the 7.65x53mm Mauser cartridge and had a fixed 10-round magazine. Later, nearly all were converted for the Argentine navy. These will be marked "ARA." A new 7.62x51 NATO/.308 barrel was installed and a detachable magazine system was added. The magazines held 20 rounds and were unique to the design. Some Argentine Navy FN 1949s were imported to the U.S. in the 1990s and the magazines were shortened to 10 rounds to comply with the 1994 "Assault weapon" law. After this law expired in 2004, some unaltered 20-round magazines appeared on the market.

FN 1949 rifle, original configuration, in 7.65x53mm with fixed magazine. Very rare. No known U.S. importation. Price for rifle with matching receiver, barrel, bolt, carrier and top cover. Deduct 20 percent for mismatch.

Exc.	*V.G.*	*Good*	*Fair*	*Poor*
2500	1700	1200	900	700

FN 1949 Rifle, Argentine Navy Conversion to 7.62mm with one 20 round magazine. Deduct $30 for a 10-round magazine.

Exc.	*V.G.*	*Good*	*Fair*	*Poor*
1000	850	750	500	400

Bayonet for Argentine FN 1949

Wood handle. 9.25-inch double edge blade. No makers mark. Navy version is marked "ARA" See listing under Belgium, Rifles for image. Price range 80 – 35.

SHOTGUNS

Mossberg Model 500

In 1976, the Argentine navy acquired the Mossberg Model 500 in 12 gauge. It is unknown if any Argentine contract guns have ever been sold on the U.S. market. Price assumes an original Argentine contract example.

Exc.	*V.G.*	*Good*	*Fair*	*Poor*
600	500	400	200	100

MACHINE GUNS

The Argentine military has used a wide variety of machine guns from various sources. Obsolete guns include the Browning Model 1917 water-cooled gun. More current machine guns are the Browning .50 caliber M2 HB, the FN MAG, the French AAT-52, and the MG3.

Argentine Maxim Model 1895

This gun was sold to Argentina from both British and German sources. Standard pattern early Maxim gun with smooth brass water jacket and brass feed plates. Most likely chambered for the 7.65x53mm Mauser cartridge. Rate of fire was about 400 rounds per minute. Weight of the gun was approximately 60 lbs. Marked in Spanish on the receiver as well as the country of manufacture.

NOTE: According to Dolf Goldsmith, author of *The Devil's Paintbrush*, some 55 of these guns are in private hands in the U.S.

Pre-1968 (Rare)

Exc.	*V.G.*	*Fair*
40000	35000	30000

Pre-1986 manufacture with new side plate

Exc.	*V.G.*	*Fair*
28000	25000	20000

British Maxim Nordenfelt M1895 in 7.65mm • Courtesy private NFA collection, Paul Goodwin photo

ARGENTINA

AUSTRALIA

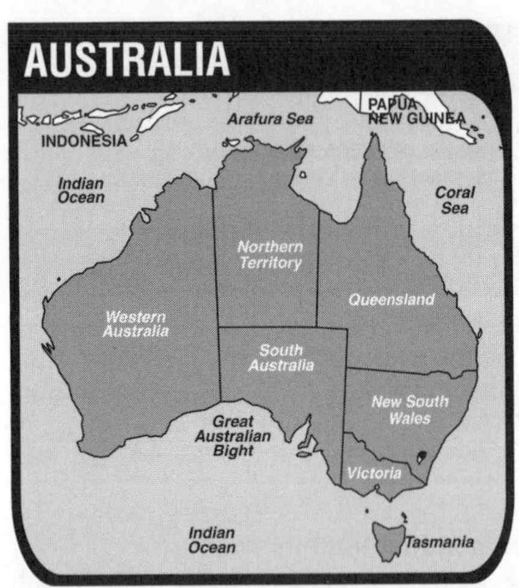

The Commonwealth of Australia, the smallest continent in the world, is located south of Indonesia between the Indian and Pacific oceans. It has an area of 2,967,893 sq. mi. (7,686,850 sq. km.) and an estimated population of 18.84 million. Capital: Canberra. Due to its early and sustained isolation, Australia is the habitat of such curious and unique fauna as the kangaroo, koala, platypus, wombat, echidna and frilled-necked lizard. The continent possesses extensive mineral deposits, the most important of which are iron ore, coal, gold, silver, nickel, uranium, lead and zinc. Raising livestock, mining and manufacturing are the principal industries. Chief exports are wool, meat, wheat, iron ore, coal and nonferrous metals.

The first Caucasians to see Australia probably were Portuguese and Spanish navigators of the late 16th century. In 1770, Captain James Cook explored the east coast and annexed it for Great Britain. Following the loss of British North America, New South Wales was established as a penal colony by Captain Arthur Phillip on January 26, 1788, a date now celebrated as Australia Day. Dates of creation of the six colonies that now comprise the states of the Australian Commonwealth are: New South Wales, 1823; Tasmania, 1825; Western Australia, 1838; South Australia, 1842; Victoria, 1851; Queensland, 1859. The British Parliament approved a constitution providing for the federation of the colonies in 1900. The Commonwealth of Australia came into being in 1901. Australia passed the Statute of Westminster Adoption Act on October 9, 1942, which officially established Australia's complete autonomy in external and internal affairs, thereby formalizing a situation that had existed for years.

Australia is a founding member of the Commonwealth of Nations. Elizabeth II is the Head of State as Queen of Australia; the Prime Minister is Head of Government.

HANDGUNS

The Australian military currently uses the Browning Model 1935 designated the L9A1. These guns were manufactured by Inglis during World War II and since by FN. Chambered for 9mm cartridge. The first FN built pistols were purchased in 1963.

Prior to the L9A1, Australia used assorted Webley revolvers in .455 and the Mk IV revolver in .38/200 procured from Great Britain. In the 1940s WWII they also received some S&W "Victory" revolvers in .38/200. These have some Australian markings but are otherwise identical to the English version. See listings under ***Great Britain***.

Australian Model L9A1 Pistol

This model is the standard British issue 9mm Model 1935 pistol built by FN under contract. Marked, "pistol, self-loading" instead of "pistol, automatic." First ordered in June of 1963. None have been imported to the U.S.

Exc.	V.G.	Good	Fair	Poor
800	650	500	300	250

SUBMACHINE GUNS

Australian military forces currently use its own designed and produced F1 submachine gun as well as the HK MP5 and MP5SD. The Sterling L34A1 silenced version is also used by special operations units.

Owen

This Australian submachine gun is chambered for the 9mm Parabellum cartridge. It features a top mounted 33-round magazine and quick release barrel attachment. The barrel is 9.75" long and the rate of fire is 700 rounds per minute. Weight is about 9.25 lbs. It was produced from 1941 to 1944. Marked "owen 9mm mki lysaght pk Australia patented 22/7/41" on the right side of the frame.

Austen Submachine Gun • *Courtesy Thomas Nelson, from **The World's Submachine Guns, Vol. 1***

Pre-1968

Exc.	V.G.	Fair
17500	15000	12000

Pre-1986 manufacture with new receiver or re-weld

Exc.	V.G.	Fair
12000	9000	N/A

Austen Mark I

Introduced in 1943 this gun is a take-off on the British Sten with a folding butt similar to the MP40. Chambered for the 9mm Parabellum cartridge and fitted with an 8-inch barrel with forward grip. Uses a 28-round box magazine. Rate of fire is approximately 500 rounds per minute. Weight is about 9 lbs. About 20,000 were produced between 1943 and 1945 by Diecasters and Carmichael in Australia.

Pre-1968

Exc.	V.G.	Fair
17500	15000	12000

Owen • *Paul Goodwin photo*

Pre-1986 manufacture with new receiver or re-weld

Exc.	V.G.	Fair
N/A	N/A	N/A

F-1

First introduced in 1962, this submachine gun was built by the Australian arsenal at Lithgow. Chambered for the 9mm Parabellum cartridge and fitted with an 8-inch barrel, this gun has a round receiver with a wooden buttstock with pistol grip and perforated barrel jacket. The 34-round magazine is top mounted. Weight is about 7 lbs. Rate of fire is approximately 600 rounds per minute.

NOTE: It is not known how many, if any, of these guns are in the U.S. and are transferable. Prices listed below are estimates only.

Pre-1968

Exc.	V.G.	Fair
18000	15000	12000

RIFLES

In 1985 the Australian Defense Ministry adopted the Steyr AUG 5.56mm F8 rifle as its service rifle. Australia also uses the British Parker Hale M82 Sniper Rifle, as well as the U.S. M16A1 rifle.

Australian Pre Cartridge Era and Early Breech Loading Rifles

Australia was armed with a variety of English percussion rifles, most of which were made by Enfield. Cartridge rifles supplied by the British include the Snider and Martini series. Models and values are found in the ***Great Britain*** chapter.

Martini Cadet Rifle cal. .310

Made in England by the Birmingham Small Arms Co. This small scale Martini in marked on the side "Commonwealth of Australia" and has a kangaroo monogram on the receiver. It was intended for use by youth cadet trainees. The barrel is inches long. Many of these were imported prior to 1968 and many have been converted into sporting guns. Price is for unaltered example. These sometimes have had the chamber lengthened slightly to allow firing of .32-20 Winchester ammunition. This does not reduce the value to most collectors.

Exc.	V.G.	Good	Fair	Poor
600	500	350	200	150

No. 1 SMLE Mark III

Made in Australia by M.A. Lithgow 1914-1945. This is the same as the English made SMLE #1 Mk III and is chambered in .303 British. It has a 10-round detachable magazine. Many were imported to the U.S. in the 1990s. Serial number is usually found on the receiver, bolt, nose cap and fore stock. Deduct 20 percent for MM parts.

Exc.	V.G.	Good	Fair	Poor
500	375	250	175	125

No. 1 SMLE Mark III* H

Built only at Lithgow arsenal in Australia and features a heavier barrel marked with an "h" near the receiver.

Exc.	V.G.	Good	Fair	Poor
550	425	300	200	150

Bayonet for Australian No. 1 SMLE Mark III

Same as the English Pattern 1907 bayonet. Wood grips. 15-inch single edge blade. Marked "M.A." or "MA

1918 Lithgow marking; WWII rifles do not have the shield.

AUSTRALIA

Bayonet for Australian No. 1 SMLE Mark III

***Australian L1A1 Rifle** • Courtesy Blake Stevens, The FAL Rifle*

Lithgow." Scabbards sometimes marked "Mangrove." Price range 125 – 50.

Bolo Bayonet for No. 1 SMLE Mark III

Wood grip. 11.5-inch single edge bolo shaped blade. Made in limited quantities during WW2. Price range 750 – 450.

No. 1 Mark III* H.T. (Australian) Sniper

Introduced toward the end of World War II, this rifle used mostly rebuilt Mark III actions dating to between 1915 and 1918. Fitted with both high and low mounts. The standard bracket telescope tube is marked, "SIGHT TELESCOPE PATT 1918 (AUS)." These rifles are fitted with a heavy barrel. Only about 1,500 of these rifles were converted.

SCOPE NOTE: The No. 32 (Marks 1-3) scope was the most commonly used on British-made guns. The No. 32 and the Alaskan are not the same scope. About 100 Lyman Alaskan scopes were fitted to Long Branch No. 4 Mark 1*(T) rifles in 1944-1945. In addition to the British-made scopes, R.E.I. Ltd. in Canada made its own version of the No. 32 and these are usually found on Long Branch guns. The No. 67 scope, used on about 100 Long Branch (T)s was made by R.E.I. and differs from the design of the No. 32.

Exc.	V.G.	Good	Fair	Poor
3500	2800	1800	—	—

Rifle No. 6 Mark I & Mark I/I (AUST)

This model was essentially a trials rifle built in Australia at Lithgow. Similar to the No. 5 but with a No. 1 receiver. Metal components have been milled for lightening. Barrel length is 20.5" with flash hider. The Mark I differs from the Mark I/I in rear sight. Rear sight is open and graduated to 2,000 yards on the Mark I and the Mark I/I uses an aperture sight graduated from 200 to 800 yards. Both models have serial numbers with an "XP" prefix. Each model has two variations of buttplates: one standard brass and the other composition padded with hinges at bottom for trap access.

NOTE: Beware of fakes. Seek expert advice prior to a sale.

Exc.	V.G.	Good	Fair	Poor
2500	2200	1500	900	600

L1A1 Rifle

This is the British version of the FN-FAL in the "inch" or Imperial pattern. Most of these rifles were semi-automatic only. This rifle was the standard service rifle for the British Army from about 1954 to 1988. The rifle was made in Lithgow, Australia, under license from FN. The configurations for the L1A1 rifle are the same as the standard FN-FAL Belgium rifle. Only a few of these rifles were imported into the U.S. They are very rare. This "inch" pattern British gun will also be found in other Commonwealth countries such as Australia, New Zealand, Canada, and India.

NOTE: Only about 180 Australian L1A1s were imported into the U.S. prior to 1989. These are rare and in great demand.

Exc.	V.G.	Good	Fair	Poor
7500	6000	5000	—	—

MACHINE GUNS

Between 1925 and 1930 the Australian firm of Lithgow built the Vickers machine gun. Later, between 1938 and 1940, the same company built the Bren gun in .303 caliber. Approximately 12,000 Vickers and 17,000 Bren guns were built in Australia during this period. After World War II the Australian military adopted the U.S. M60 machine gun, the Browning 1919A4, and the .50 caliber Browning M2HB. More recently, that country's military uses the Belgian FN MAG, and the German MG3.

Australian Bren

This is a slightly modified version of the MK I built by the Small Arms Factory, Lithgow, beginning in 1940. Marked "MA" and "LITHGOW" on the right side of the receiver. A total of 17,429 guns were produced when production stopped August 13, 1945.

Pre-1968 (Extremely Rare)

Exc.	V.G.	Fair
40000	37500	30000

Australian Vickers

Manufactured by the Small Arms Factory in Lithgow beginning in 1929. The gun was last built in 1945. Serial numbers began with the number 1 and went to 9,999. From then on the prefix "B" was added. Highest serial number recorded is B2344.

Pre-1968

Exc.	V.G.	Fair
N/A	—	—

Pre-1986 conversions (side-plate using Colt 1915 or 1918 plates)

Exc.	V.G.	Fair
17500	15000	12500

The Republic of Austria, a parliamentary democracy located in mountainous central Europe, has an area of 32,374 sq. mi. (83,850 sq. km.) and a population of 8.08 million. Capital: Wien (Vienna). Austria is primarily an industrial country. Machinery, iron, steel, textiles, yarns and timber are exported.

The territories later to be known as Austria were overrun in pre-Roman times by various tribes, including the Celts. Upon the fall of the Roman Empire, the country became a margravate of Charlemagne's Empire. Premysl II of Otakar, King of Bohemia, gained possession in 1252, only to lose the territory to Rudolf of Habsburg in 1276. Thereafter, until World War I, the story of Austria was conducted by the ruling Habsburgs.

During the 17th century, Austrian coinage reflected the geo-political strife of three wars. From 1618-1648, the Thirty Years' War between northern Protestants and southern Catholics produced low quality, "kipperwhipper" strikes of 12, 24, 30, 60, 75 and 150 Kreuzer. Later, during the Austrian-Turkish War, 1660-1664, coinages used to maintain soldier's salaries also reported the steady division of Hungarian territories. Finally, between 1683 and 1699, during the second Austrian-Turkish conflict, new issues of 3, 6 and 15 Kreuzers were struck, being necessary to help defray mounting expenses of the war effort.

During World War I, the Austro-Hungarian Empire was one of the Central Powers with Germany, Bulgaria and Turkey. At the end of the war, the Empire was dismembered and Austria established as an independent republic. In March 1938, Austria was incorporated into Hitler's short-lived Greater German Reich. Allied forces of both East and West occupied Austria in April 1945, and subsequently divided it into 4 zones of military occupation. On May 15, 1955, the 4 powers formally recognized Austria as a sovereign independent democratic state.

HANDGUNS

Model 1870

This revolver is built on a Lefaucheux-Francotte double action solid frame with fixed cylinder with mechanical rod ejection. It is chambered for the 11.3mm cartridge and fitted with a 7.3-inch round barrel. The non-fluted cylinder holds 6 rounds. The frame and barrel were iron, not steel. Checkered wooden grips with lanyard loop. Built by the Austrian firm of Leopold Gasser, and marked "L.GASSER, WIEN, PATENT, OTTAKRING." Weight is about 53 oz., or 3.3 lbs., making it one of the heaviest military service revolvers of its time. When the Model 1878 was introduced and adopted by the Austro-Hungarian army, the Model 1870 was sold to the Balkan States and was sometimes referred to as the "Montenegrin" revolver.

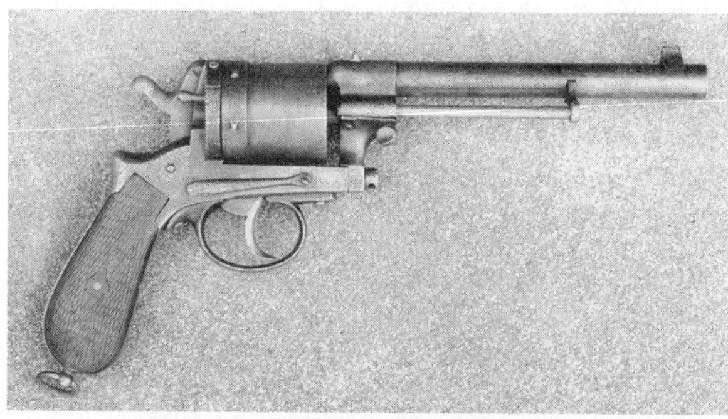

Model 1870 • *Courtesy J. B. Wood*

Military Unit Marked

Exc.	*V.G.*	*Good*	*Fair*	*Poor*
1250	750	400	250	150

Non-Unit Marked

Exc.	*V.G.*	*Good*	*Fair*	*Poor*
900	600	350	225	150

Model 1870/74 Gasser Trooper's Model

Similar to the above model but built with cast steel instead of iron. It was issued from 1874 to 1919. Built by the Austrian firm of Leopold Gasser. Weight is still about 53 oz.

Military Unit Marked

Exc.	*V.G.*	*Good*	*Fair*	*Poor*
1250	750	400	250	150

Non-Unit Marked

Exc.	*V.G.*	*Good*	*Fair*	*Poor*
900	600	350	225	150

Model 1878 Officer's Model

Because the Model 1870 revolver was so heavy and large, Johann Gasser, Leopold's younger brother, designed a smaller version chambered for the 9mm (9x26) cartridge. The barrel length was 4.8 inches and the overall length was reduced as well. The weight of this revolver was about 27 oz.

Exc.	*V.G.*	*Good*	*Fair*	*Poor*
850	600	350	200	150

Model 1898 Rast & Gasser

This model was built on the Schmidt-Galand double action solid frame with 8-round cylinder with loading gate and mechanical ejection rod. Chambered for the 8mm cartridge and fitted with a 4.5-inch round barrel. The caliber was too light to be effective as a military sidearm. The firing pin was a spring-loaded frame-mounted plunger instead of the more common hammer-mounted type. Checkered wooden grips with lanyard loop. In service from 1898 to 1938. Weight is about 33 oz.

Short Grip

Exc.	*V.G.*	*Good*	*Fair*	*Poor*
600	450	300	200	125

Short Barrel

Exc.	*V.G.*	*Good*	*Fair*	*Poor*
3000	2200	1500	900	350

Model 1898 • Paul Goodwin photo

STEYR

Osterreichische Waffenfabrik Gesellschaft GmbH, Steyr (1869-1919)
Steyr-Werke AG (1919-1934)
Steyr-Daimler-Puch, Steyr (1934-1990)
Steyr-Mannlicher GmbH, Steyr (1990-)

Steyr Model 1893 Gas Seal Test Revolver

Chambered for the 8mm cartridge this 7-shot 5.5-inch barrel revolver was built by Steyr as a prototype for the Austrian army. Fewer than 100 were built. Several different variations. It is recommended that an expert be consulted prior to a sale.

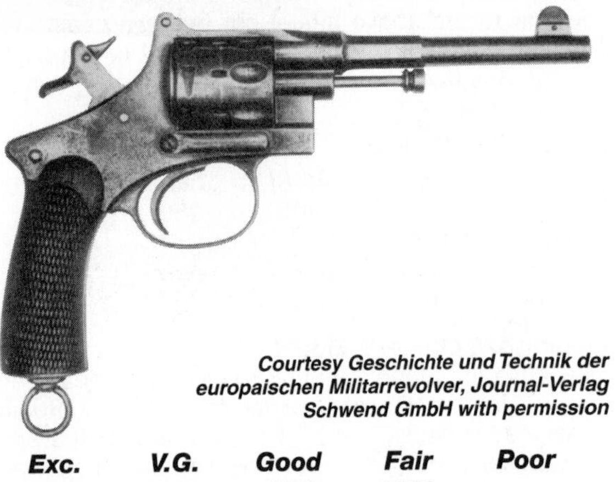

Courtesy Geschichte und Technik der europaischen Militarrevolver, Journal-Verlag Schwend GmbH with permission

Exc.	V.G.	Good	Fair	Poor
15000	9000	5000	2000	—

Roth Steyr Model 1907

Based on the patents granted to Karel Krnka and Georg Roth, the 8mm Model 1907 had a rotating barrel locking system and was the first self-loading pistol adopted by the Austro-Hungarian army. It was also the first successful double action automatic pistol. Add 20 percent for early Steyr examples without a large pin visible on right side of frame, or for those made in Budapest instead of Steyr.

Courtesy Joseph Schroeder

Exc.	V.G.	Good	Fair	Poor
900	750	550	375	250

Holster for Steyr Model 1907

Leather construction. Top flap. Separate pouch for clips on the Left side. Single belt loop on back. A scarce holster.

Steyr Model 1907 holster

Exc.	V.G.	Good	Fair	Poor
500	350	200	125	50

Steyr Hahn Model 1911

The Steyr Hahn was originally introduced as a commercial pistol but was quickly adopted by the Austro-Hungarian, Chilean, and Romanian militaries. Magazine capacity is 8 rounds. Weight is about 30 oz. Commercial examples were marked "Osterreichische Waffenfabrik Steyr M1911 9m/m" on the slide, have a laterally adjustable rear sight, and are rare. Austrian militaries are marked simply "STEYR" and the date of manufacture, while those made for Chile and Romania bear their respective crests. Some of the Romanian or Chilean contract pistols have been imported to the U.S. recently. These were refinished and had the crests ground off.

During WWII the Germans rebarreled a number of Steyr Hahns to 9mm Parabellum for police use, adding "P.08" to the slide along with appropriate Waffenamt markings. The German army designation for this pistol was "Pistole Mod 12(o)."

Steyr Hahn Model 1911 with Chilean crest • Courtesy Orvel Reichert

Commercially Marked

Exc.	V.G.	Good	Fair	Poor
1250	900	700	500	350

P.08 Marked Slides, see entry under *Germany*

Austrian Military

Exc.	V.G.	Good	Fair	Poor
550	450	400	300	200

Romanian or Chilean contract, original finish with intact crest

Exc.	V.G.	Good	Fair	Poor
500	400	300	250	200

Romanian or Chilean contract, refinished with ground crest

Exc.	V.G.	Good	Fair	Poor
N/A	N/A	250	200	150

Close-up of slide showing conversion number "08" for 9x19 caliber • *Courtesy Orvel Reichert*

FEG (Frommer) Stop Model 1912

Introduced in 1912 and took a whole new approach compared to any of the pistols this company had produced to that point. It is still unconventional as it uses two recoil springs in a tube above the barrel and resembles an air pistol in this way. It is chambered for 7.65mm or 9mm short and has a 3.75-inch barrel. The detachable magazine holds 7 rounds, and the sights are fixed. This locked-breech action, semi-automatic pistol was a commercial success. It was used widely by the Austro-Hungarian military during WWI. It was manufactured between 1912 and 1920.

Courtesy James Rankin

Exc.	V.G.	Good	Fair	Poor
500	350	275	175	125

Glock 17

Adopted by the Austrian military in 1983. This model is chambered for the 9mm Parabellum cartridge. It is a double action only semi-automatic that has a 4.49-inch barrel and a 17-shot detachable magazine. The empty weight of this pistol is 21.91 oz. It is not

believed that any Austrian-issue Glocks have been imported to the U.S. This pistol was introduced on the U.S. civilian market in 1985 and is still currently produced. See ***Standard Catalog of Firearms*** for commercial prices.

SUBMACHINE GUNS

Steyr-Solothurn MP 30

Introduced in 1930 and built at the Steyr plant under license from the Swiss firm, Solothurn. It was adopted by the Austrian police. Chambered for the 9x23 Steyr cartridge and fitted with a 7.8-inch jacketed barrel. It is fed by a 32-round magazine and has a rate of fire of about 500 rounds per minute. Wood buttstock with unusual upswept appearance. It is select fire. Weight is about 9.5 lbs. Produced from 1930 to 1935 with approximately 6,000 manufactured.

Pre-1968

Steyr Model 1930 • *Courtesy Thomas Nelson, from **World's Submachine Guns, Vol. I***

Exc.	V.G.	Fair
15000	12500	10000

Pre-1986 reweld

Exc.	V.G.	Fair
8500	7500	N/A

Steyr-Solothurn S1-100 [MP 34(o)]

This gun machine was designed in Germany, perfected in Switzerland, and built in Austria. Steyr-Solothurn was a shell company established to enable the German company Rheinmetall to evade the restrictions of the Versailles Treaty that prevented them from producing military small arms. The gun was used by the Austrian army as well as the German army. It is chambered for the 9x23 Steyr cartridge as well as others. The German army used them in 9mm Parabellum while Austrian troops used the gun chambered for the 9mm Mauser cartridge. The gun was also sold to Portugal where it was designated the Model 42. Barrel length is almost 7.8 inches. Magazine capacity is 32 rounds. Rate of fire is about 500 rounds per minute. Fixed

MP 34 • *Paul Goodwin photo*

wooden butt and forearm. Weight is approximately 9.5 lbs. Produced from 1934 to 1939. On this gun, a magazine loading device is built into the magazine housing.

Pre-1968

Exc.	V.G.	Fair
15000	12500	10000

Pre-1986 reweld

Exc.	V.G.	Fair
8500	7500	N/A

Steyr MPi69

Built in Austria, this submachine gun is chambered for the 9mm cartridge. It was adopted by the Austrian army in 1969. The gun features a 10-inch barrel and 25- or 32-round magazine. It has a rate of fire of 550 rounds per minute. It is marked "STEYR-DAIMLER-PUCH AG MADE IN AUSTRIA" on top of the receiver. The folding stock is metal. The gun weighs about 7 lbs. Production stopped in 1990.

Pre-1968 (Rare)

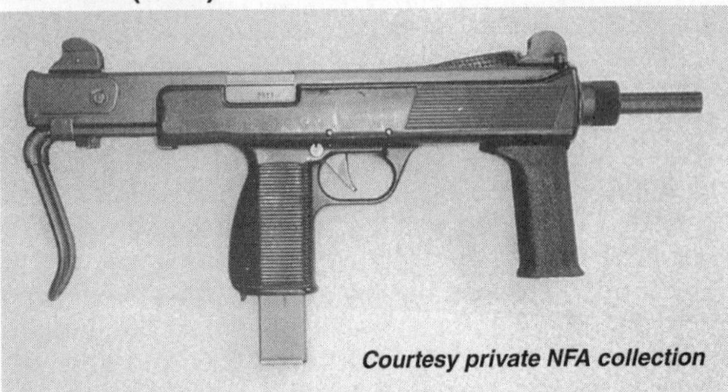

Courtesy private NFA collection

Exc.	V.G.	Fair
12500	10000	8500

RIFLES

Austrian Pre-Cartridge Era Rifles

The end of the Napoleonic Wars found the army of the Austria Hungarian Empire armed with a variety of flintlock firearms. The foot troops carried either the M1798 or the M1807 musket or the M1807 yager rifle. The mounted forces were armed with either the M1798 dragoon carbine, the M1798 Hussarcarbine, the M1798 rifled cavalry carbine, the M1781 Cuirassier musketoon, and the M1798 pistol. In 1828 a new flintlock musket superseded the M1798 pattern, only to be modified again in 1835. In the latter years, however, the Austrian military also began experimenting with a variation of the percussion system invented by Giuseppe Console, utilizing a small elongated copper cylinder filled with fulminate. In 1840, the flintlock muskets adopted in 1835 were adapted to a variation of this percussion system as modified by Baron von Augustin. This system was made army-wide in 1842 with the adoption of a new musket and yager rifle with locks specifically manufactured for the Augustin tubelocks. In 1849, a new rifle replaced the M1842 pattern; both of these rifles were based on the Devilgne chambered breech. In 1850, a cavalry carbine and a horse pistol were added to the tubelock series. All of these arms were either .69 or .71 caliber. The tubelock, however, was short-lived; in 1854, Austria abandoned the tubelock system in favor of standard percussion cap then widely used by the armies of Europe. At the same time it adopted a new smaller caliber (.54) which it applied to the new M1854 rifle-musket and the M1855 yager rifle. A horse pistol based on the same system (Lorenz's compressed, elongated ball) was adopted in 1859.

Large numbers of the Austrian longarms were imported to the United States in the first two years of the American Civil War. Beginning in 1863, the Confederate States also imported large numbers of the M1854 series rifle-muskets. Most of the tubelocks first being modified to standard percussion in Belgium before importation, arms of prime interest to American collectors, accordingly demand higher prices.

In 1867, the Austria-Hungarian Empire adopted two different breechloading mechanisms and the self-contained metallic cartridge. Those muzzleloading arms deemed acceptable for alteration (the M1854 series of rifle-muskets and rifles) were adapted to the Wanzel system. Newly made arms (the M1867 rifle) were made in conformity with Werndl's breechloading design.

Austrian arms were generally made on contract with the major gun makers in and near Vienna ("Wien" in Austrian). These makers usually marked their products with their name upon the barrel of the arm, near the breech. The major makers included BENTZ, FERD. FRUWIRTH (who also simply marked his arms "F. F."), CARL HEISER, JOSEF JESCHER, ANNA OSTERLIEN, PIRKO, TH. ROTTME, G. SCHLAGER, TH. SEDERE, F. UMFAURER, WANZEL, and ZEILINGER (with the "Z" usually backwards). Lockplates were marked with the government ownership mark (a small double-headed eagle) and the date of manufacture (deleting the number "1" from the year, such as "847" for "1847".) Since the arms were not interchangeable, mating numbers are usually found on all the metal parts.

Austrian Musket, M1828

Overall length 57-3/4 inches; barrel length 42-1/2 inches; caliber .69. Basically following the pattern of the French M1822 musket, this arm still accepted the quadrangular M1799 bayonet, distinguished by having a solid socket with a hook ring at its rear, like the Prussian bayonet for the M1808 musket.

Exc.	V.G.	Good	Fair	Poor
—	2000	1650	950	400

Austrian Musket, M1835

Overall length 57-3/4 inches; barrel length 42-1/2 inches; caliber .69. The M1835 musket follows the pattern of the Austrian M1807 musket, but is adapted for the Consule tubelock percussion system, which essentially replaced the frizzen and pan with a hinged tube retainer. This arm still uses the M1799 quadrangular bayonet.

Exc.	V.G.	Good	Fair	Poor
—	2500	2000	1200	450

Austrian Musket, M1840

Overall length 57-3/4 inches; barrel length 42-1/2 inches; caliber .69. The M1840 musket was manufactured in flint. Its primary differences from the M1828 musket lie in its furniture (mainly the front band) and the bayonet attachment, which consists of a lug beneath the barrel and an elongated hook projecting from the forend of the stock to accept the new M1840 quadrangular bayonet. The bayonet is distinguished by having a straight slot in its socket, closed by a bridge.

Exc.	V.G.	Good	Fair	Poor
—	2500	1800	1100	450

Austrian Musket, M1842

Overall length 57-3/4 inches; barrel length 42-1/2 inches; caliber .69 (.71). The M1842 musket was manufactured in Augustin tubelock. Its main distinction from the M1840 flintlock musket is the lock, which in addition to having the integral hinged tubelock mechanism in lieu of the frizzen, has a distinctly rounded rear tail. Although 25,000 of these muskets were imported into the United States for use by Fremont's forces in Missouri in 1861, many were subsequently altered to percussion. The Cincinnati contractors, Hall, Carroll & Co. or Greenwood & Co. accounted for 10,000 of these arms, all of which were altered to percussion by means of the cone-in-barrel system. These were also rifled and a portion of them sighted with a long range rear sight similar to the Enfield P1853 rifle-musket. Many of the balance were subsequently sent to the Frankfort Arsenal in Philadelphia, where they were subcontracted to Henry Leman of Lancaster for alteration to standard percussion. Those altered by Leman are distinguished by having a new breechpiece with integral bolster, the latter with a cleanout screw through its face. In addition to the 25,000 imported for Fremont, the firm of H. Boker & Co. of New York imported approximately 8,000 Austrian M1842 muskets which it had altered to percussion in Belgium. The French method of adding a reinforced bolster to the top right-hand side of the barrel was used. Many of those were also rifled and sighted in the manner of the French adaptations fashionable in Europe. George Heydecker of New York City imported another 4,000 in 1863 that were seized in transit to Canada, reputedly for delivery to Mexican republican forces.

In original tubelock

Exc.	V.G.	Good	Fair	Poor
—	3500	2500	1500	600

Altered to percussion (Cincinnati contractors)

Exc.	V.G.	Good	Fair	Poor
—	2000	1500	800	300

Altered to percussion (Leman)

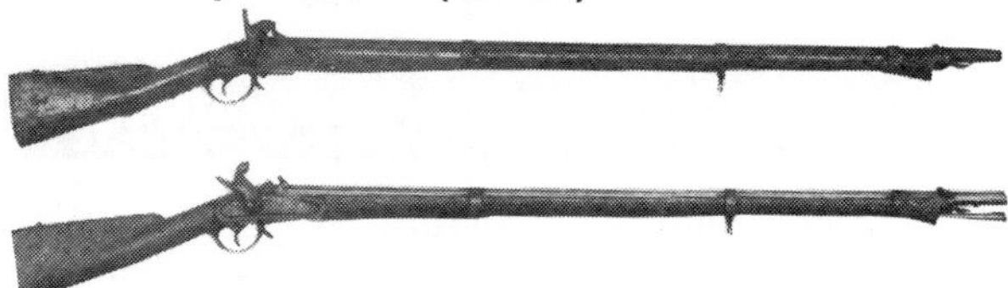

Exc.	V.G.	Good	Fair	Poor
—	2000	1500	800	350

Altered to percussion and rifled (Boker)

Exc.	V.G.	Good	Fair	Poor
—	2000	1500	800	350

Austrian M1844 "Extra Corps" Musketoon

Overall length 48-3/8 inches; barrel length 33-1/2 inches; caliber .69 (.71). Is essentially a shortened version of the Austrian M1842 musket. In original Augustin tubelock, it is virtually unknown. Most of the production is thought to have been purchased by arms speculators at the beginning of the American Civil War and altered to standard percussion in Liege, Belgium. The Belgian alteration followed the second pattern adopted by that government to alter arms to percussion and consisted of brazing a "lump" of metal to the upper right-hand side of the barrel, into which a cone was threaded. The arms so altered were also rifled and sighted. The sights either copied the Austrian M1854 rifle-musket folding sight or the French "ladder" rear sight using the pattern utilized on the M1829 rifled cavalry musketoon. Over 10,000 of these arms were imported into the United States in 1861-1862 by Herman Boker & Co. of New York City.

Altered to percussion and rifled (Boker)

Exc.	V.G.	Good	Fair	Poor
—	2250	1750	950	400

Austrian M1842 Yager rifle

Overall length 48-1/4 inches; barrel length 33-1/4 inches; caliber .69/.71. The Austrian M1842 yager rifle ("Kammer Busche") was originally manufactured in tubelock for the rifle battalions of the Austrian Army. Its bore terminated in a Delvigne breech, i.e. a chamber of lesser diameter than the caliber whose lip served as a base for disfiguring the projectile to fill the rifling. Made obsolete by the Thouvenin and Minie systems, many M1842 yager rifles were altered in 1860 in Belgium to standard percussion and sold to the Italian revolutionaries led by Giuseppe Garibaldi, giving the gun that nickname. Two methods of alteration were applied. One, the "Belgian" system, brazed a "lump" of iron to the upper right surface of the breech, which was tapped for a standard percussion cone. The other, the "Prussian," involved fitting the breech with a new barrel section incorporating a new bolster. At least 500 of these altered arms were imported into the United States during the American Civil War, where they (and the M1849 yager rifles similarly altered) were called "Garibaldi Rifles."

Exc.	V.G.	Good	Fair	Poor
—	2500	1750	1000	350

Austrian M1849 Yager rifle

Overall length 48 inches; barrel length 33-1/4 inches; caliber .71. The successor to the M1842 Austrian "Kammer Busche," the M1849 model is distinguished by having its barrel wedge fastened rather than retained by bands. Both the M1842 and the M1849 yager rifles were adapted to socket bayonets having long straight knife blades; both socket types were slotted. That of the M1842 was secured to the barrel by the same method as the M1842 Austrian musket; that of the M1849, however, locked onto a lug on the right side of the barrel and was secured by a rotating ring on the back of the socket. Adapted to standard percussion in the same manner as the M1842 yager rifles, more than 25,000 were sold to the U.S. War Department in 1862 and 1863.

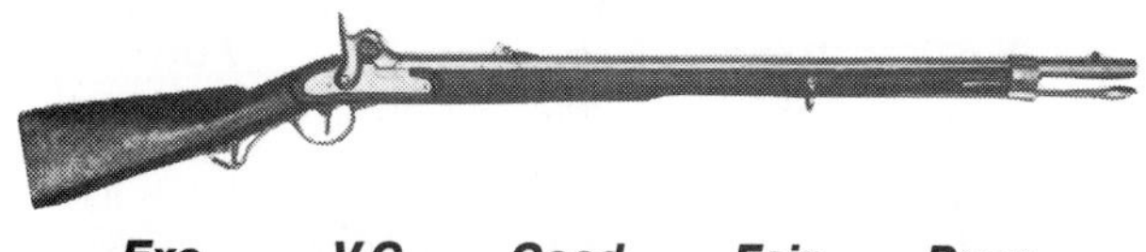

Exc.	V.G.	Good	Fair	Poor
—	2500	1750	1000	350

Austrian M1850 Horse Pistol

Overall length 16 inches; barrel length 8-7/8 inches; caliber .69. A bulky brass mounted pistol with lanyard ring, this arm was made originally in tubelock. However, a small quantity appear to have been altered to standard percussion locks in Liege, Belgium. In the process the double-strapped front bands of the original were removed and the forestock cut away to adapt the stock to an iron ramrod. (In Austrian service the ramrod was hung from the crossbelt of the mounted trooper.) Quantities imported into the United States are uncertain but may have been included among the 346 foreign horse pistols purchased by the U.S. War Department from P.S. Justice in 1861.

Exc.	*V.G.*	*Good*	*Fair*	*Poor*
—	2650	1800	800	400

Austrian M1850 Carbine

Overall length 30 inches; barrel length 14-1/2 inches; caliber .71. Originally manufactured in tubelock for Austrian cavalry service, this large caliber, short-barreled rifled carbine (12-groove rifling) saw service in the United States when 10,000 were purchased by U.S. purchasing agent George Schuyler in 1861. Those purchased for U.S. service, however, had been altered in Liege, Belgium for standard percussion locks in the same manner that the Austrian M1842 and M1849 yager rifles had been altered.

Exc.	*V.G.*	*Good*	*Fair*	*Poor*
—	2250	1650	1000	450

M1854 Rifle-Musket (The "Lorenz")

Overall length 52 inches; barrel length 37-1/4 inches; caliber .54 (and .58). Adopted in 1854 as a replacement for its smoothbore muskets, the Austrian M1854 rifle-musket was made in three variants. The standard infantry arm had a simple block sight for mass volley fire. The rifles for the "rear rank" men were similar but with a folding leaf sight with windows graduated to 900 paces. A similar sight was also applied to the rifles for sharpshooter battalions, which also had a cheekpiece built into the buttstock. The quadrangular socket bayonet locked onto the front sight, whose sides were angled to accept the diagonal slot in the bayonet's socket. The Austrian M1854 rifle-musket was the second most prolifically imported arm during the American Civil War, with some 89,000 being imported into the Confederacy and more than 175,000 into the Union. Thousands of the latter were bored up to .58 caliber before being imported.

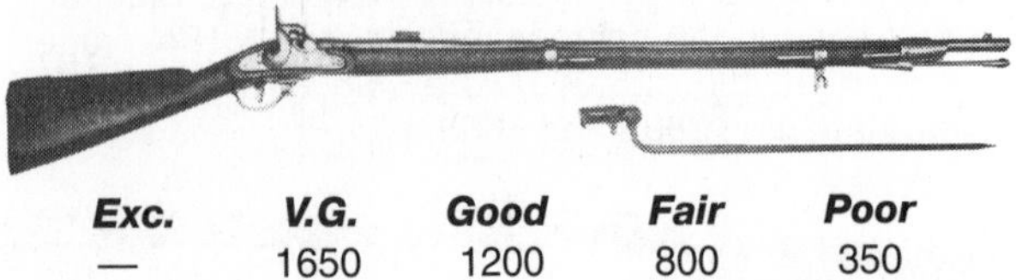

Exc.	*V.G.*	*Good*	*Fair*	*Poor*
—	1650	1200	800	350

M1854 Yager Rifle

Overall length 43 inches; barrel length 28 inches; caliber .54. Designed for the rifle battalions of the Austrian army to replace the M1842 and M1849 rifles, the M1854 yager rifles are distinguished by having an octagonal, wedge-fastened barrel turned round near the muzzle to accept a socket bayonet with a long straight knife blade. An angled lug on the turned section engaged the diagonal slot in the bayonet's socket. The rear sight for these rifles is unusual, consisting of a curved slide that traverses two upright walls and can be locked with a turn key on its right side for various ranges up to 900 paces. These rifles were made for Austrian service without provision for a ramrod (that device being affixed to a crossbelt of the individual soldier). But the approximately 2,500 that were imported for U.S. service during the American Civil War were adapted for a ramrod by inletting a channel under the forestock.

Exc.	*V.G.*	*Good*	*Fair*	*Poor*
—	2500	1850	1200	500

Austrian M1859 Horse Pistol

Overall length 16 inches (less stock); barrel length 10-3/8 inches; caliber .54. The M1850 tubelock pistol was replaced in the Austrian service in 1859 with a new standard percussion rifled horse pistol firing the Lorenz "compression" elongated ball. Like the U.S. M1855 horse pistol, this new pistol had a detachable shoulder stock so that it could be used as a carbine. Like its predecessors, no provision was made for a ramrod, which continued to be attached to a belt crossing the trooper's torso.

Exc.	*V.G.*	*Good*	*Fair*	*Poor*
—	2500	1800	900	500

Austrian M1854/67 "Wanzel" Alteration to Breechloader

Overall length 52-1/4 inches; barrel (bore) length; 34-1/2 inches; caliber .54. The "Wanzel" breechloading mechanism applied to the Austrian M1854 rifle-muskets is much like the Allin "trapdoor" applied in the U.S. to long arms during the period 1865-1873. A breech block that hinges forward upon the barrel is released by a lever on the right side of the block, permitting insertion of a brass cartridge. In the process of altering these arms to breechloaders the sling swivels were moved from the middle band and trigger guard bow to the middle of the forestock and the buttstock.

Exc.	*V.G.*	*Good*	*Fair*	*Poor*
—	1750	1250	750	350

AUSTRIAN CARTRIDGE LONG ARMS

Werndl Model 1867 Infantry Rifle

This is a single shot rotary breech block action with external side hammer. It is full stocked with exposed muzzle and bayonet fitting. Chambered for the 11.15x58R Werndl cartridge. Barrel length is 33.6 inches. Weight is about 9.75 lbs. About 600,000 Model 1867 rifles were built.

Exc.	*V.G.*	*Good*	*Fair*	*Poor*
600	500	350	200	125

Werndl Model 1867 Carbine

Similar to the rifle above but with a 22.4-inch barrel. Chambered for the 11x36R Werndl cartridge. Weight is approximately 7 lbs. About 11,000 carbines were produced.

Exc.	*V.G.*	*Good*	*Fair*	*Poor*
750	600	400	250	150

Werndl Model 1873 Infantry Rifle

This model is an improved version of the Model 1867 with central exposed hammer. Caliber is 11x41RM Werndl. Barrel length is 33.2 inches. Weight is about 9.25 lbs. Total production was about 400,000.

Exc.	*V.G.*	*Good*	*Fair*	*Poor*
600	500	350	200	125

Werndl Model 1873 Carbine

Similar to the M1873 rifle but with a 22.8-inch barrel. Chambered for the 11x36R Werndl cartridge. Weight is about 7 lbs. Total production for this model was about 100,000 carbines.

Exc.	*V.G.*	*Good*	*Fair*	*Poor*
650	550	400	250	150

Werndl Model 1867/77 Rifles and Carbines

This model was the Model 1873 but redesigned for the 11x58R cartridge with a modified rear sight graduated from 200 to 2100 steps.

Exc.	*V.G.*	*Good*	*Fair*	*Poor*
500	400	300	200	100

Bayonet for Werndl Rifles and Carbines

Checkered hard rubber grip. Muzzle ring with lock screw. Hook quillon. 18.6-inch single edge yatagan style blade. Sometimes marked "OEWG" with Austrian eagle along with various unit marks. Steel scabbard. Price range 250 – 125.

MANNLICHER

Built by Steyr & Fegyvergyar

Model 1885

This was the first magazine rifle used by Austria-Hungary and the first straight-pull rifle used as a general issue shoulder arm. This model required that a clip be used to load the box magazine, loose cartridges could not be loaded. Like the U.S. M1 Garand, clips were ejected up from the receiver when empty. Chambered for the 11.15mmx58R black powder cartridge. Barrel length is 31" with two barrel bands. Box magazine held 5 clip loaded rounds. Weight was about 10 lbs. Only about 1500 of these rifles were built.

Exc.	*V.G.*	*Good*	*Fair*	*Poor*
1250	950	750	500	300

Model 1886

This rifle was produced in large numbers and adopted for general service use. This model is similar to the Model 1885 but unlike the M85, the clip of this rifle ejected out of the bottom of the magazine. Still chambered for the 11.15mmx58R black powder cartridge. Barrel length was 30 inches. After 1888 most of these rifles were converted to 8x50R smokeless powder. Two barrel bands with pistol grip stock. This rifle was made at Steyr. Weight was slightly under 10 lbs. Price for M 1886 in 11.15mm.58R. Many of the 1886 Steyr rifles found in the U.S. were imported from Chile and are in fair to good condition.

Austrian infantryman with Model 1886 rifle with bayonet • *Courtesy Paul S. Scarlata from Mannlicher Military Rifles, Andrew Mobray Publishers*

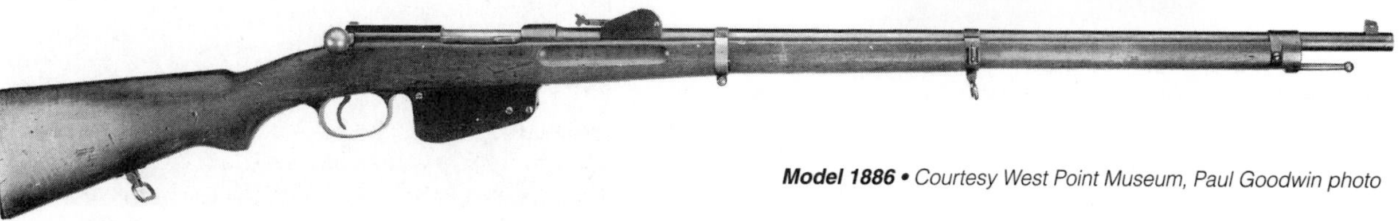

Model 1886 • *Courtesy West Point Museum, Paul Goodwin photo*

AUSTRIA/HUNGARY & AUSTRIA

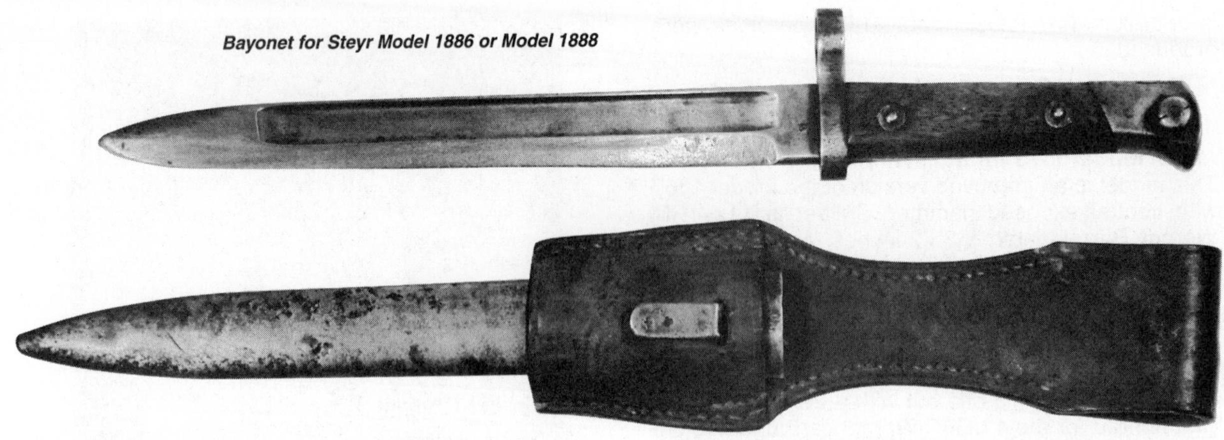
Bayonet for Steyr Model 1886 or Model 1888

Exc.	V.G.	Good	Fair	Poor
750	600	375	250	175

Bayonet for Steyr Model 1886 or 1888

Wood grips. Muzzle ring. 9.6-inch single edge blade with the cutting edge down. Steel scabbard. These are basically the same bayonet with the muzzle opening being larger for the M1886. Price range 125 – 75.

Model 1888

This model is the same as the Model 1886 except chambered for the 8x50R black powder cartridge.

Exc.	V.G.	Good	Fair	Poor
650	500	350	200	125

Model 1888/1890

This variation is the result of the change-over from black powder to smokeless. This model was chambered for the 8x50R smokeless powder cartridge with a stronger bolt locking wedge. Barrel length was 30 inches. New sights were added to accommodate the new cartridge. These sights were graduated. This model was also made at Steyr. A number of these were sold to Bulgaria, Greece, and Chile. A number of these rifles were used during WWI and some were found in irregular units during WWII.

Exc.	V.G.	Good	Fair	Poor
750	600	400	200	125

Model 1890 Carbine

This model represented a departure from previous models, not only in design, but incorporated a stronger action to better handle the 8x50R smokeless cartridge. On this model the bolt head contained the extractor. The result of this new design was that the trigger was behind the end of the bolt handle. Barrel length was 19.5 inches with a single barrel band and no handguard. There is no bayonet lug on this rifle. The box magazine capacity was 5 rounds of clip-loaded ammunition. Weight is about 7 lbs.

Exc.	V.G.	Good	Fair	Poor
750	625	500	300	175

Model 1895 Infantry Rifle

Chambered for the 8x50R cartridge, this straight pull bolt action rifle was fitted with a 30" barrel with an integral clip loaded magazine and wooden handguard. This model has essentially the same action as the Model 1890 Carbine. Fitted with leaf sights. Weight is about 8 lbs. Produced from 1895 to about 1918 both at Steyr and Budapest. The rifle was marked with either of these two locations on top of the receiver ring along with "M95."

This was the primary shoulder arm of the Austro-Hungarian army during WWI and was made in huge quantities. The rifle was also used by Bulgaria and Greece. Many of these models were used in Italy during WWII, as well as the Balkans during that same period of time.

NOTE: In the 1930s, both Austria and Hungary converted large numbers of these rifles to 8x56Rmm. Many of these rifles were converted to carbines at the same time. Converted rifles will have an "S" or "H" stamped over the chamber. Many of the Model 1895 rifles and carbines imported recently have been re-finished. Use the very good column for the re-finished guns.

Steyr M1895 Rifle original configuration in 8x50Rmm.

Exc.	V.G.	Good	Fair	Poor
500	400	300	175	125

Model 1888/1890 • *Courtesy West Point Museum, Paul Goodwin photo*

Austrian soldiers with Model 95 rifles *• Courtesy Paul S. Scarlata from Mannlicher Military Rifles, Andrew Mobray Publishers*

Steyr M1895 Rifle converted to 8x56Rmm

Exc.	V.G.	Good	Fair	Poor
350	275	200	150	100

Model 1895 Sharpshooter's Rifle

Same configuration as the Infantry rifle except for the addition of double set triggers. Rare.

Exc.	V.G.	Good	Fair	Poor
1000	850	600	350	200

Model 1895 Sniper Rifle

Same as the Sharpshooter's rifle but fitted with a telescope sight. Extremely rare. Deduct 50 percent if there is no scope.

Exc.	V.G.	Good	Fair	Poor
5000	4000	3000	—	—

Model 1895 Cavalry Carbine

Essentially the same as the Infantry rifle with a shorter barrel. Barrel length is 19.5 inches. The sling swivels are located on the side on the stock and there is no bayonet lug or stacking hook. Weight is about 7 lbs. Produced until 1918.

1895 Carbine in the original 8x50Rmm.

Exc.	V.G.	Good	Fair	Poor
425	350	250	150	100

Model 1895 Short Rifle (Stuzen M95)

This model was designed for non-cavalry use as it was fitted with a bayonet lug and sling swivels on the underside of the rifle. It was also fitted with a stacking hook attached to the barrel band. When the bayonet is attached, a blade sight is integral with the bayonet barrel ring for sighting purposes. Weight is about 7.5 lbs.

1895 Short Rifle in the original 8x50Rmm

Exc.	V.G.	Good	Fair	Poor
350	275	200	150	100

1895 Short Rifle converted to 8x56Rmm and re-finished.

Many were imported in the last few years, resulting in a stale market.

Exc.	V.G.	Good	Fair	Poor
200	150	100	80	60

Bayonets for Steyr 1895 Series

Wood grips. 9.8-inch blade, cutting edge is to the top. Muzzle ring. Carbine model has a front sight blade on top of barrel ring. Made with or without a hook quillon. Crosspiece has two rivets. Ricasso can be marked "OEWG" or "FGGY" with an Austrian eagle. Refinished examples have been imported with the reworked rifles. They have electropenciled numbers. Price range 100 – 40.

Ersatz Bayonets for Steyr 1895 Series

During WWI, Austria copied the German practice of making substitute bayonets for their 1895 rifles and carbines. The two shown are examples only. Other types exist. Metal handle. Muzzle ring. 10" single edge blade. Steel scabbard. Twisted handle with riveted muzzle ring. Blade length 9.75" Steel scabbard. Price range 175 – 75.

Close-up of receiver ring of Model 1895 Steyr Rifle

Model 1895 Steyr Cavalry Carbine *• Courtesy West Point Museum, Paul Goodwin photo*

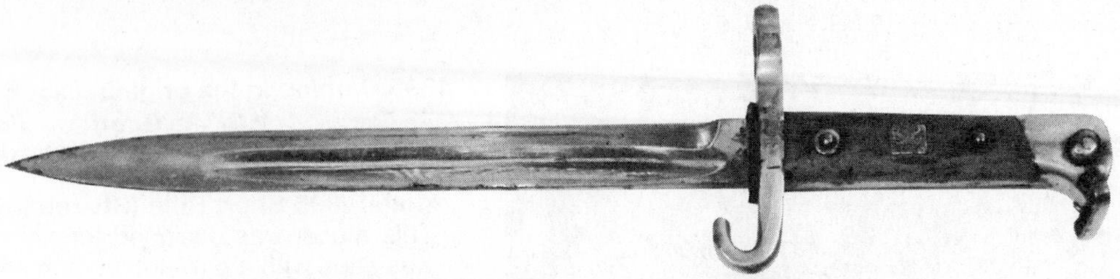

Bayonets for the Steyr 1895 Series

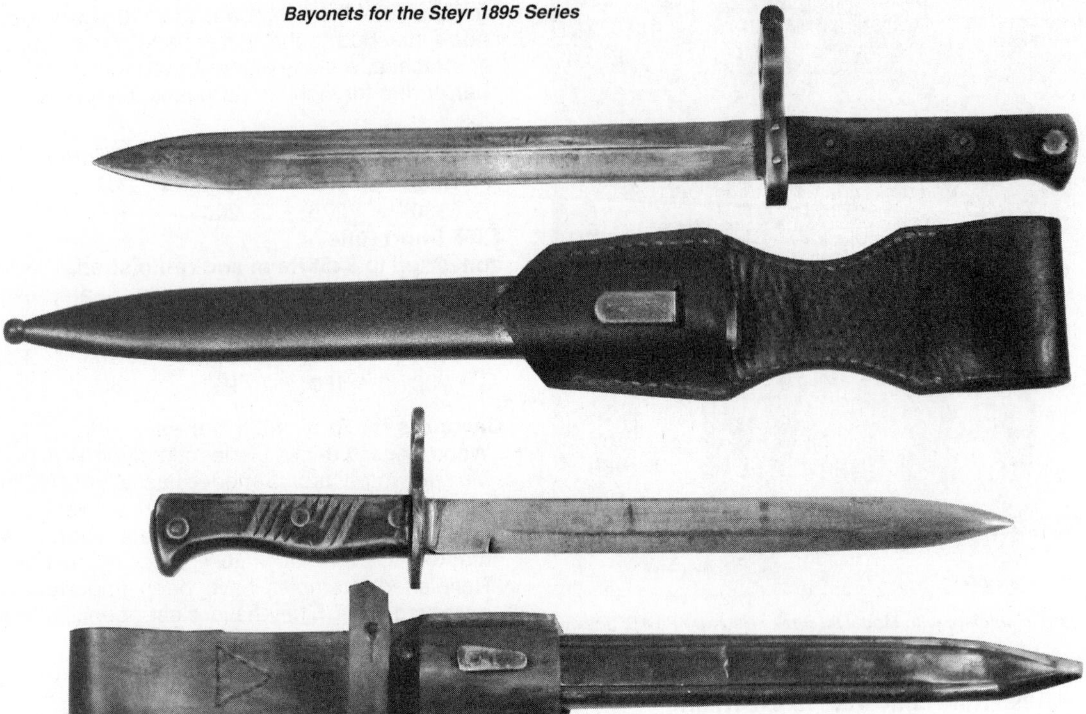

Ersatz bayonets for the Steyr 1895 Series

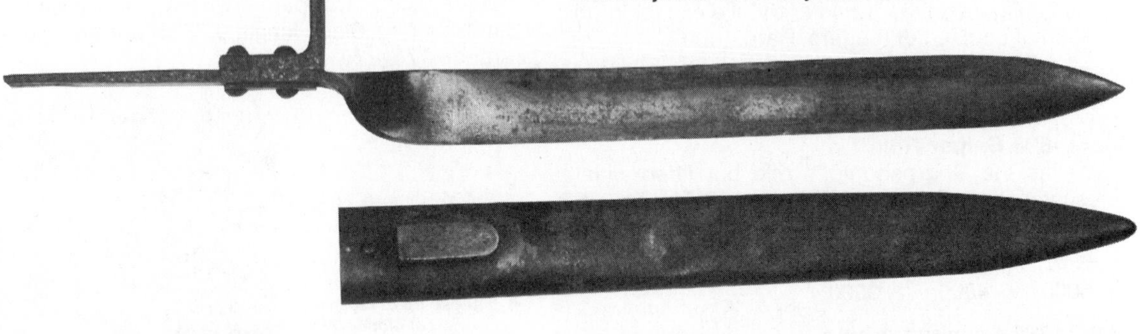

STEYR

Osterreichische Waffenfabrik Gesellschaft GmbH, Steyr (1869-1919)

Steyr-Werke AG (1919-1934)
Steyr-Daimler-Puch, Steyr (1934-1990)
Steyr-Mannlicher GmbH, Steyr (1990-)

Model 95 Rifle (Model 31)

A number of Model 95 rifles and short rifles were modified to accept the 8x56Rmm cartridge after World War I. The letter "H" is stamped on the barrel or the receiver. This is a straight pull rifle with 19.6-inch barrel and a 5-round fixed magazine. Weight is approximately 7.5 lbs.

Exc.	V.G.	Good	Fair	Poor
350	275	200	150	100

Mannlicher Schonauer Model 1903

Built for Greece in 6.5x54mm. This rifle uses the unique rotary magazine. Some were imported in the pre 1968 era but the action for this model was popular for building custom rifles. Many Greek military were destroyed to get the actions.

Courtesy Paul S. Scarlata from Mannlicher Military Rifles, Andrew Mobray Publishers

Exc.	V.G.	Good	Fair	Poor
650	500	350	200	100

NOTE: For Carbine version add a 50 percent premium.

Model 1904

Similar to the Dutch Model 1895 but chambered for 8x57mm rimless cartridge. Many of

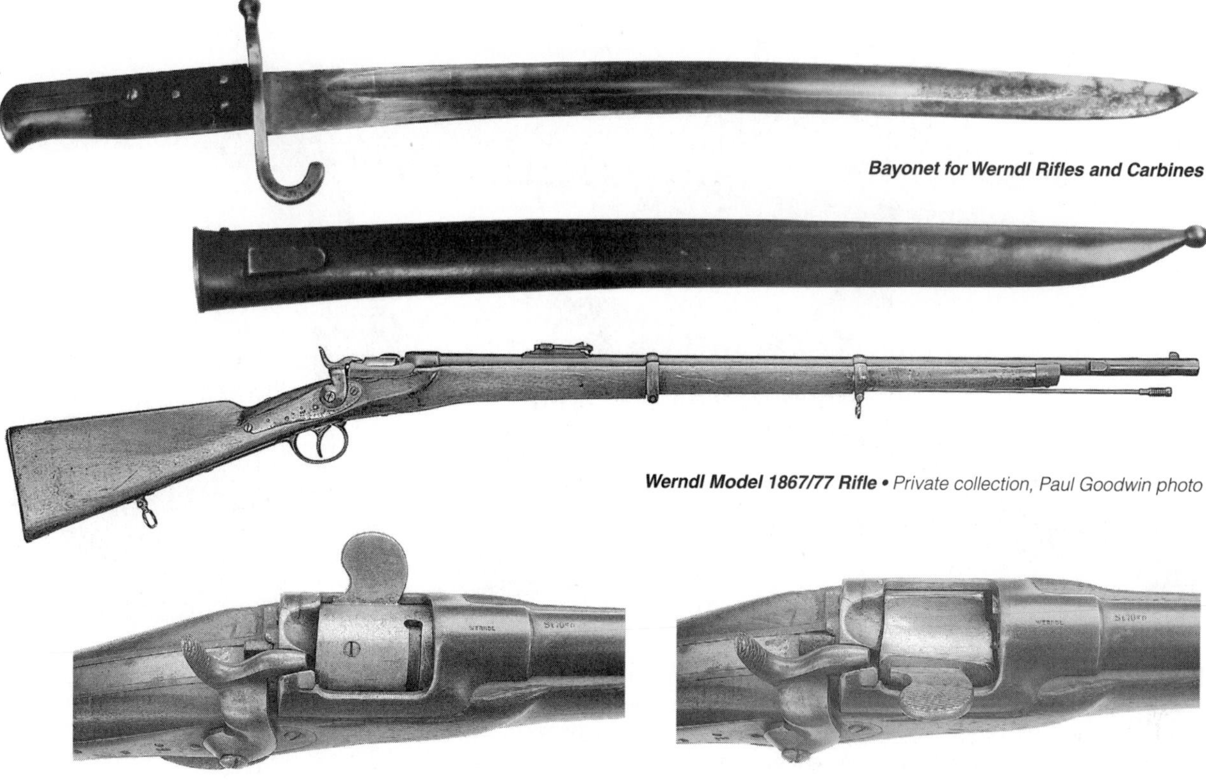

Bayonet for Werndl Rifles and Carbines

Werndl Model 1867/77 Rifle • Private collection, Paul Goodwin photo

these rifles were sold to China and about 11,000 were sold to the Irish Ulster Volunteer Force.

Exc.	V.G.	Good	Fair	Poor
500	350	275	175	125

NOTE: For Irish Ulster marked versions add a 30 percent premium.

Model SSG-PI

This model features a black synthetic stock originally designed as a military sniper rifle. Fitted with a cocking indicator, single or double set trigger, 5-round rotary magazine or 10-round magazine. Receiver is milled to NATO specifications for Steyr ring mounts. Barrel length is 26 inches. Rifle weighs about 9 lbs. Offered in 7.62 NATO.

NOTE: This model was originally called the SSG 69.

Exc.	V.G.	Good	Fair	Poor
1700	1300	1000	—	—

Steyr AUG (Armee Universal Gewehr)

Produced by Steyr-Mannlicher beginning in 1978, this rifle is chambered for the 5.56x45mm cartridge. It is a bullpup design with a number of different configurations. Barrel lengths are 13.6 inches in submachine gun configuration, 16.3 inches in carbine, 19.8 inches in rifle, and 24.2 inches in a heavy barrel sniper configuration. Magazine is 30 or 42 rounds. Carry handle is an optic sight of 1.5 power. Adopted by Austrian army and still in production. Weight is 7.7 lbs. in rifle configuration. Rate of fire is about 650 rounds per minute.

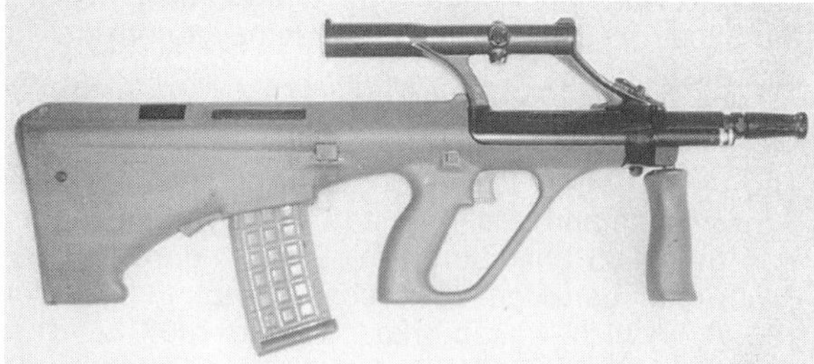

Steyr AUG • Courtesy Private NFA collection

Pre-1986 full-auto conversions of semi-automatic version

Exc.	V.G.	Good
15000	12500	10000

Steyr AUG (Semi-automatic Version)

As above but in semi-automatic only. Two models, the first with green furniture and fitted with a 20-inch barrel. The second with black furniture and fitted with a 16" barrel.

First Model

Exc.	V.G.	Good	Fair	Poor
5000	3500	3000	—	—

Second Model

Exc.	V.G.	Good	Fair	Poor
5500	3500	3000	—	—

MAUSER

M1914 Rifle

This rifle is identical to the Model 1912. Austrian rifles are fitted with large sling swivels in order to accommodate the Austrian sling. Some of these rifles are unit marked on the buttplate or buttplate tang.

Exc.	V.G.	Good	Fair	Poor
750	600	450	250	150

Model 07/12 Schwarzlose *• Private NFA collection, Paul Goodwin photo*

MACHINE GUNS

Austria-Hungary also used the Maxim, having purchased some in 1889. These guns were designated the Model 89/1, then with modifications called the M89/04. Austrian Hungary used their own design, the Skoda M1893, but this gun was never considered successful.

Model 07/12 Schwarzlose

The gun was designed by Andreas Wilhelm Schwarzlose and built in Austria by Steyr. First model was the 1905 chambered for the standard military 8x50Rmm cartridge. Successor was the Model 1907/12 which was marked as the M07/12. The gun was built until 1918 in 8x50R. The Czechs built a version called the M7/24 chambered for the 7.92 cartridge. The Romanians converted Steyr M07/12s to 7.92 with lengthened water jackets. The gun was also manufactured by the Dutch, Swedish, and Hungarians. It was adopted by Austria-Hungary in 1905. It was also sold to the Dutch, Greeks, and Germans as well. It saw use in WWI. Barrel length was 24.4 inches and rate of fire was about 500 rounds per minute. Fed by a 250-round cloth belt. The gun was produced until 1918. Marked "MG SCHWARZLOSE M7/12" on the rear of the receiver. Weight is about 44 lbs. Italy used this gun, as part of World War I reparations, through World War II.

Aircraft versions with modified internals to increase the rate of fire were marked M7/12 (16/A) and M7/12 (16/R), and these have no jackets on the barrel. Note that the gun marked "MG SCHWARZLOSE M7/12," which is correct, but the other side is marked "WAFFENFABRIK STEYR" with the date of manufacture underneath.

No factory Schwarzloses were built with ventilated shrouds. They were either fitted with water-jackets or had bare exposed barrels for aircraft use. No doubt there were field expedients of various sorts, but there is no evidence of any factory ventilated shrouds.

NOTE: The predecessor to this gun was the Model 1905. Its rate of fire was about 350 rounds per minute, and it was fitted with a smaller oil reservoir. An aircraft version of the Model 07/12 was the Model 07/16, which had a rate of fire of about 600 rounds per minute. Early versions were water-cooled, later versions were air-cooled. Last version had no jacket.

Pre-1968

Exc.	*V.G.*	*Fair*
30000	27500	25000

Pre-1986 conversions (reweld)

Exc.	*V.G.*	*Fair*
22000	20000	18000

An unusual machine gun placement; a Schwarlose in a tree *• Courtesy Paul S. Scarlata*

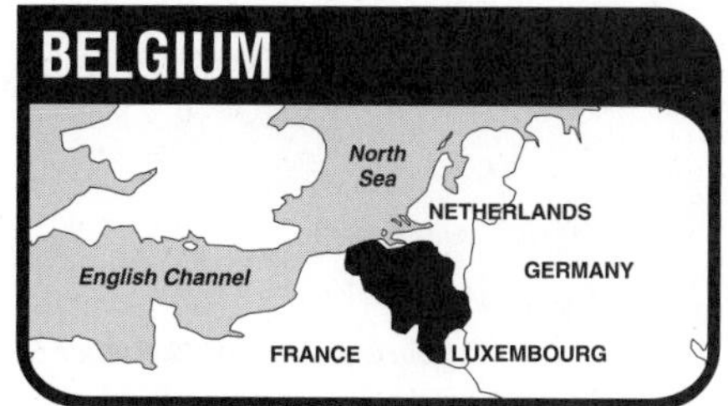

The Kingdom of Belgium, a constitutional monarchy in northwest Europe, has an area of 11,780 sq. mi. (30,519 sq. km.) and a population of 10.1 million, chiefly Dutch-speaking Flemish and French-speaking Walloons. Capital: Brussels. Agriculture, dairy farming, and the processing of raw materials for re-export are the principal industries. Beurs voor Diamant in Antwerp is the world's largest diamond trading center. Iron and steel, machinery motor vehicles, chemicals, textile yarns and fabrics comprise the principal exports.

At the Congress of Vienna in 1815 the area was reunited with the Netherlands, but in 1830 independence was gained and the constitutional monarchy of Belgium was established. A large part of the Duchy of Luxembourg was incorporated into Belgium and the first king was Leopold I of Saxe-Coburg-Gotha. It was invaded by the German Army in August, 1914 and the German forces carried on a devastating occupation of most of the territory until the Armistice. Belgium joined the League of Nations. On May 10, 1940 it was invaded again by the German army. The Belgian and Allied forces were quickly overwhelmed and were evacuated through Dunkirk. Allied troops reached Belgium again in Sept. 1944. Prince Charles, Count of Flanders, assumed King Leopold's responsibilities until liberation by the U.S. Army in Austria on May 8, 1945. As of January 1, 1989, Belgium became a federal kingdom.

BIBLIOGRAPHICAL NOTES: The best overview of Belgian military firearms are two books by Claude Gaier; *FN 100 Years, The Story of the Great Liege Company, 1889-1989*, 1989, and *Four Centuries of Liege Gunmaking*, 1985.

HNADGUNS

E. & L. NAGANT

Model 1878 Officer's Revolver (Fluted Cylinder)

This 6-shot double action centerfire revolver is chambered for the 9mm cartridge. Solid frame with fixed cylinder sliding rod ejection. Octagon barrel is 5.5 inches. Issued to Belgian officers, it is marked with the Nagant address and logo. Wooden checkered grips with lanyard loop. Weight is about 33 oz. Produced from 1878 to 1886.

Courtesy Geschichte und Technik der europaischen Militarrevolver, Journal-Verlag Schwend GmbH with permission

Exc.	V.G.	Good	Fair	Poor
1750	900	500	300	200

Model 1883 Revolver (Non-Fluted Cylinder)

This model was also chambered for the 9mm centerfire cartridge. Fitted with a 5.5-inch octagon barrel. Wooden checkered grips with lanyard loop. A simplified version of the Model 1878 Officer's revolver. This model was used by NCOs, artillery, and troops in the Belgian army from 1883 to 1940.

Courtesy Geschichte und Technik der europaischen Militarrevolver, Journal-Verlag Schwend GmbH with permission

Exc.	V.G.	Good	Fair	Poor
1250	750	400	275	150

Model 1878/86 Officer's Revolver (Fluted Cylinder)

This 6-shot revolver was issued to officers in the Belgian army. Chambered for the 9mm cartridge and fitted with a 5.5-inch octagon barrel. Checkered wooden grips with lanyard loop. Produced from 1886 to 1940.

Courtesy Geschichte und Technik der europaischen Militarrevolver, Journal-Verlag Schwend GmbH with permission

Exc.	V.G.	Good	Fair	Poor
1500	850	450	300	175

Model 1883/86 Revolver

Similar to the Model 1878/86 Officer's but issued to NCOs as a regular sidearm. Cylinder is non-fluted. The hammer rebounds slightly after the revolver has been fired.

Courtesy Geschichte und Technik der europaischen Militarrevolver, Journal-Verlag Schwend GmbH with permission

Exc.	V.G.	Good	Fair	Poor
1250	750	400	275	150

BELGIUM

GAVAGE, ARMAND

A 7.65mm caliber semi-automatic pistol with a fixed barrel and a concealed hammer. Similar in appearance to the Clement. Markings with "AG" molded into the grips. Some (1,500 est.) have been found bearing German Waffenamts. Manufactured from 1930s to 1940s. Add 100 percent for German marked pistols.

Gavage 7.65mm pistol with German markings

Exc.	V.G.	Good	Fair	Poor
500	425	300	175	150

FABRIQUE NATIONALE

NOTE: For historical and technical information, see Blake Stevens, The Browning High Power Automatic Pistol, Collector Grade Publications, 1990.

Model 1903

A considerable improvement over the Model 1900. It is also a blowback-operated semi-automatic; but the recoil spring is located under the barrel, and the firing pin travels through the slide after being struck by a hidden hammer. The barrel is held in place by five locking lugs that fit into five grooves in the frame. This pistol is chambered for the 9mm Browning long cartridge and has a 5-inch barrel. The finish is blued with molded plastic grips, and the detachable magazine holds 7 rounds. There is a detachable shoulder stock/holster along with a 10-round magazine that was available for this model. These accessories are extremely rare and if present would make the package worth approximately five times that of the pistol alone. There were approximately 58,000 manufactured between 1903 and 1939. This model was one of the Browning patents that the Eibar Spanish gunmakers did so love to copy because of the simplicity of the design.

It should be noted that during WWI the Spanish supplied almost one million Model 1903 copies for the French army.

Production Note: FN had a number of contract sales to foreign countries from 1907 to about 1928. These countries are:

Sweden: 1907-1908	10,000
Russia: 1908-1910	8,200
Ottoman Empire: 1908-1923	8,000
England: 1914	100
Holland: 1922	80
Estonia: 1922-1928	4616
El Salvador: 1927-	?
Paraguay: 1927	324

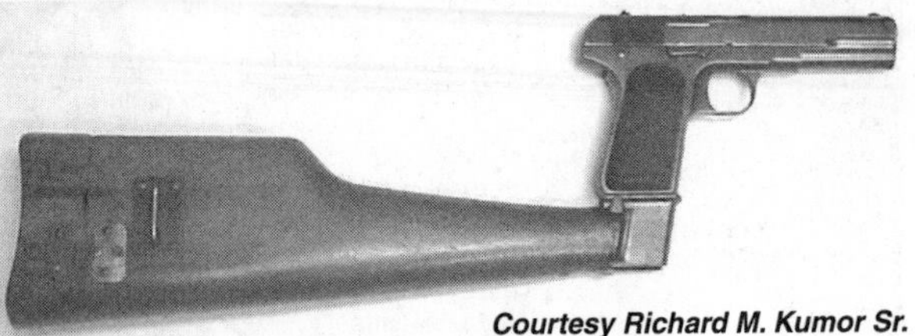

Courtesy Richard M. Kumor Sr.

Exc.	V.G.	Good	Fair	Poor
800	650	500	300	200

Model 1910 "New Model"

Chambered for 7.65mm and 9mm short. It has a 3.5-inch barrel, is blued, and has molded plastic grips. The principal difference between this model and its predecessors is that the recoil spring on the Model 1910 is wrapped around the barrel. This gives the slide a more graceful tubular appearance instead of the old slab-sided look. This model has the triple safety features of the 1906 Model 2nd variation and is blued with molded plastic grips. This model was adopted by police forces around the world. It was manufactured between 1912 and 1954.

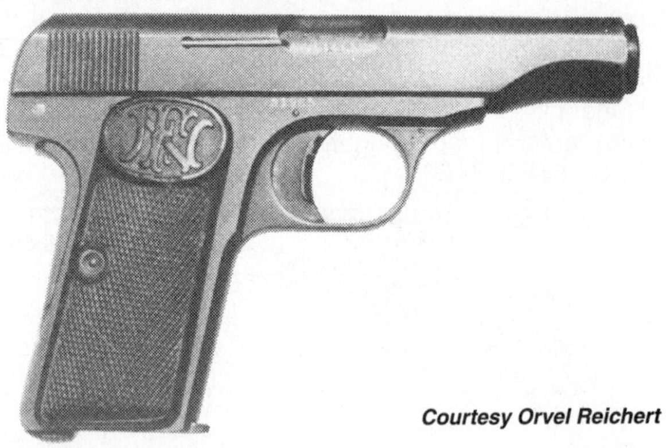

Courtesy Orvel Reichert

Exc.	V.G.	Good	Fair	Poor
500	300	250	175	125

Model 1922

Similar to the Model 1910, with a longer 4.5-inch barrel and correspondingly longer slide. This model was a military success, and approximately 200,000 were produced during the WWII German occupation of Belgium in 1940-1944. These pistols that bear the Waffenamt acceptance marks are known as the "Pistole Modell 626(b)," and are chambered for 7.65mm only. The Germans also had a 9mm version designated the "Pistole Modell 641(b)." These pistols

Model 1922 • *Paul Goodwin photo*

would bring a 25 percent premium. There were approximately 360,000 of these pistols produced during the German occupation. There are a number of subvariations that may effect value. See listings under Netherlands and Yugoslavia for their M 1922 contract pistols. They were manufactured between 1912 and 1959.

Exc.	V.G.	Good	Fair	Poor
450	275	200	125	100

Model 1935

The last design from John Browning and was developed between 1925 and 1935. This pistol is known as the Model 1935, the P-35, High-Power or HP, and also as the GP (which stood for "Grand Puissance") and was referred to by all those names at one time or another. The HP is essentially an improved version of the Colt 1911 design. The swinging link was replaced with a fixed cam, which was less prone to wear. It is chambered for the 9mm Parabellum and has a 13-round detachable magazine. The only drawback to the design is that the trigger pull is not as fine as that of the 1911, as there is a transfer bar instead of a stirrup arrangement. This is necessary due to the increased magazine capacity resulting in a thicker grip. The barrel is 4.75 inches in length. It has an external hammer with a manual and a magazine safety, was available with various finishes and sight options, and was furnished with a shoulder stock. The Model 1935 was used by many countries as their service pistol; as such there are many variations. We list these versions and their approximate values. There are books available specializing in this model, and it would be beneficial to gain as much knowledge as possible if one contemplates acquisition of this fine and highly collectible pistol.

Prewar Commercial Model

Found with either a fixed sight or a sliding tangent rear sight and is slotted for a detachable shoulder stock. It was manufactured from 1935 until 1940. Wood holster stock, add 50 percent.

Fixed Sight Version

Exc.	V.G.	Good	Fair	Poor
900	725	500	375	275

Tangent Sight Version

Exc.	V.G.	Good	Fair	Poor
1100	850	700	550	400

Prewar & WWII Military Contract

The Model 1935 was adopted by many countries as a service pistol, and some of them are as follows:

Belgium

Exc.	V.G.	Good	Fair	Poor
1200	1050	900	600	375

Canada and China
(See John Inglis & Company)

Denmark (See Denmark)

Great Britain

Exc.	V.G.	Good	Fair	Poor
1150	1000	850	550	325

Estonia

Exc.	V.G.	Good	Fair	Poor
1200	1050	900	600	375

Holland

Exc.	V.G.	Good	Fair	Poor
1250	1100	950	650	400

Latvia

Exc.	V.G.	Good	Fair	Poor
1500	1350	1050	775	500

Lithuania

Exc.	V.G.	Good	Fair	Poor
1250	1100	950	650	400

Romania

Exc.	V.G.	Good	Fair	Poor
1500	1350	1050	775	500

German Military Pistole Modell 640(b)

In 1940 Germany occupied Belgium and took over the FN plant. The production of the Model 1935 continued, with Germany taking the output. The FN plant was assigned the production code "ch," and many thousands were produced. The finish on these Nazi guns runs from as fine, as the Prewar Commercial series, to downright crude, and it is possible to see how the war was progressing for Germany by the finish on their weapons. One must be cautious with some of these guns, as there have been fakes noted with their backstraps cut for shoulder stocks, producing what would appear to be a more expensive variation. Individual appraisal should be secured if any doubt exists.

Paul Goodwin photo

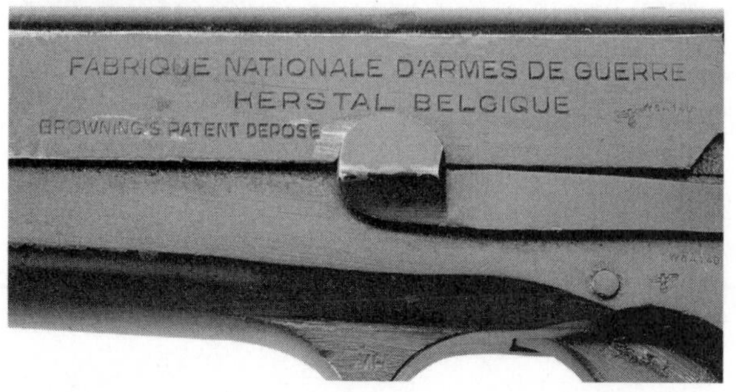

Fixed Sight Model

Exc.	V.G.	Good	Fair	Poor
750	600	500	300	250

Courtesy Orvel Reichert

Courtesy Orvel Reichert

Tangent Sight Model

50,000 manufactured.

Exc.	*V.G.*	*Good*	*Fair*	*Poor*
900	775	700	550	400

Captured Prewar Commercial Model

These pistols were taken over when the plant was occupied. They are slotted for stocks and have tangent sights. There were few produced between serial number 48,000 and 52,000. All noted have the "WaA613" Nazi proof mark. Beware of fakes!

Exc.	*V.G.*	*Good*	*Fair*	*Poor*
1500	1400	1150	750	500

Nazi Holster for FN 1935 Pistol

Leather construction. Brown or black color. German codes and dated on back. Some are not marked. Price range: 300 – 150.

Nazi Holster for FN 1935 Pistol

Postwar Military Contract

Manufactured from 1946, and they embody some design changes—such as improved heat treating and barrel locking. Pistols produced after 1950 do not have barrels that can interchange with the earlier model pistols. The earliest models have an "A" prefix on the serial number and do not have the magazine safety. These pistols were produced for many countries, and there were many thousands manufactured.

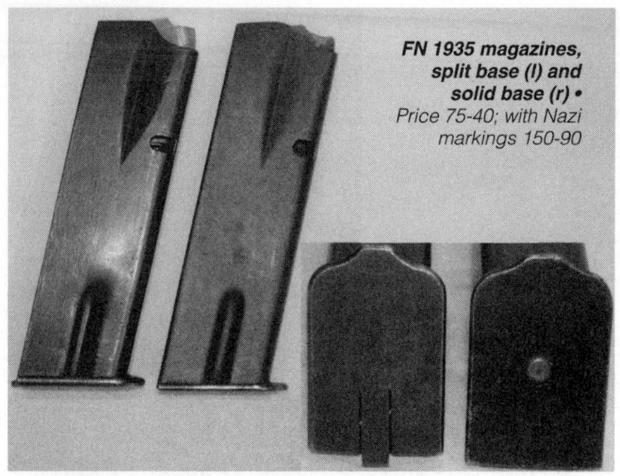

FN 1935 magazines, split base (l) and solid base (r) • *Price 75-40; with Nazi markings 150-90*

Fixed Sight

Exc.	*V.G.*	*Good*	*Fair*	*Poor*
600	500	400	300	250

Tangent Sight

Exc.	*V.G.*	*Good*	*Fair*	*Poor*
750	675	575	400	300

Slotted and Tangent Sight

Exc.	*V.G.*	*Good*	*Fair*	*Poor*
1500	1250	750	500	400

Sultan of Oman

This is the only post war Hi-Power that is designated a Curio and Relic pistol. It has a tangent sight. The grip is slotted to accept a shoulder stock which is a legal accessory to this model. Fewer than 50 of these pistols were brought into the U.S. These were from a canceled contract for Oman. Very rare.

NIB	*Exc.*	*V.G.*	*Good*	*Fair*	*Poor*
6000	5750	4500	—	—	—

NOTE: For pistols with no shoulder stock deduct $1,000.

SUBMACHINE GUNS

Prior to 1940, Belgium used the MP28 (Model 34) as its standard military submachine gun. FN also manufactured, under license from Israeli Military Industries (IMI), a copy of the UZI submachine gun.

Vigneron M2

This subgun was issued to the Belgian army in 1953. It was also used by those same forces in the Belgian Congo. Many of these guns were taken by Congo forces after independence. A number of Vigneron guns may be found over much of Central Africa. The gun is chambered for the 9mm cartridge and has a wire folding stock. Barrel length is 11.75 inches with the rear portion of the barrel finned. A muzzle compensator is also standard. Magazine capacity is 32 rounds. Rate of fire is about 600 rounds per minute. Capable of select fire. Markings are found on the right side of the magazine housing and read, "ABL52 VIG M1." Also on the right side of the receiver is stamped "LICENCE VIGNERON." Weight is about 7.25 lbs. The gun was in production from 1952 to 1962.

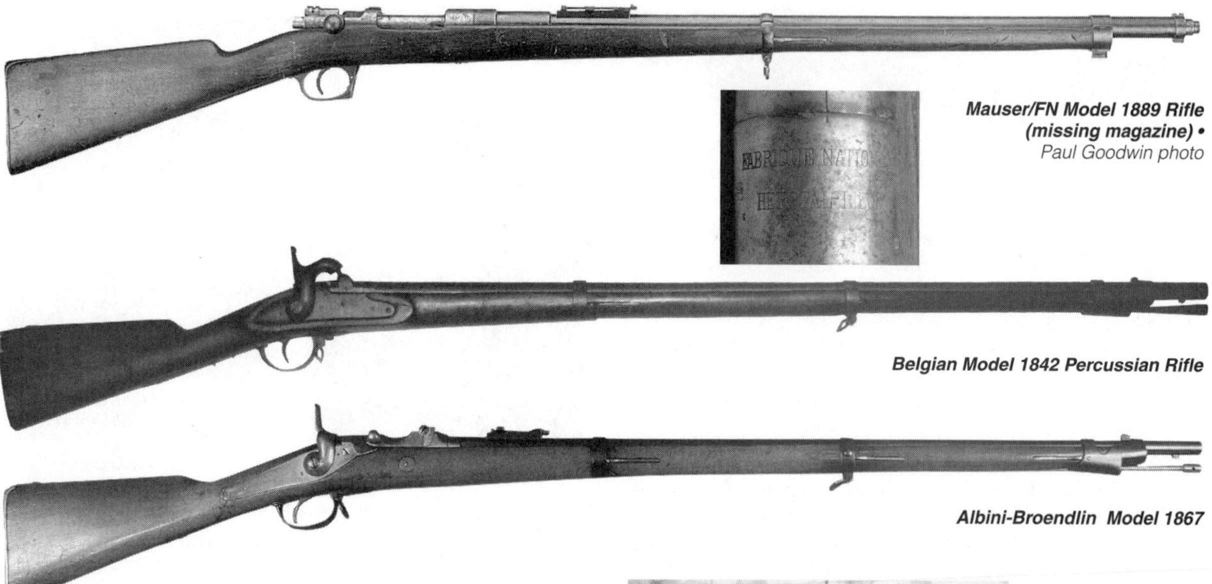

Mauser/FN Model 1889 Rifle (missing magazine) • *Paul Goodwin photo*

Belgian Model 1842 Percussian Rifle

Albini-Broendlin Model 1867

Pre-1968

Exc.	V.G.	Fair
15000	12500	10000

RIFLES

Belgian Pre-Cartridge Era Rifles

Leige, Belgium was an early arms manufacturing center. Numerous models were produced at several factories. Many were copies of English or French patterns. They were exported all around the globe. Belgian made rifles were the most prolific foreign made arm imported to North America by both sides of the U.S. Civil War. There are far too many contracts and variations to list here. Below is an example of the typical Belgian import.

Belgian Model 1842 Percussian Rifle

Caliber 69; 40.5-inch barrel. A copy of the French Mle 1842 rifle. The example shown was made by A. Francotte. Add 10-25% for a U.S. Civil War example. Add 100+% for Confederate examples. Beware of fakes.

Exc.	V.G.	Good	Fair	Poor
800	650	450	250	150

Albini-Broendlin Model 1867

A breech loading conversion of earlier Belgian issue rifles. Models include the M1841/67 and the 1853/67. A new 32-inch barrel was installed. Caliber is 11x50Rmm. Utilizes a front hinged lifting breechblock similar to the U.S. Trapdoor series.

Exc.	V.G.	Good	Fair	Poor
1500	950	700	300	200

MAUSER (FN)

Model 1889 Rifle

The Mauser rifle that Fabrique Nationale was incorporated to manufacture. It is chambered for 7.65mm and has a 30.5-inch barrel. The magazine holds 5 rounds. The unique feature that sets the Belgian rifle apart from the Mausers made by other countries is the thin steel tube that encases the barrel. This was the first Mauser to use a charger loaded detachable box magazine. The sights are of the military type. The finish is blued, with a walnut stock. This rifle was also made by the American firm of Hopkins and Allen (rare).

Model 1889 Rifle • *Courtesy Paul S. Scarlata*

Exc.	V.G.	Good	Fair	Poor
750	600	450	250	150

NOTE: For the Hopkins and Allen examples, add a premium of 100 percent.

Bayonets for Model 1889 Mauser

Wood grips. Muzzle ring. Hook quillon. These were made in long and short single edge blade styles. The appearance of the long version is similar to the Argentine 1909 bayonet. Long model might be marked "Hopkins & Allen" on the ricasso. Steel scabbard. Price range 250 – 100 Add 100 percent for H&A marked examples.

M1889 Carbine

Barrel length is 21 inches. Fitted for a bayonet. Weight is about 7.5 lbs.

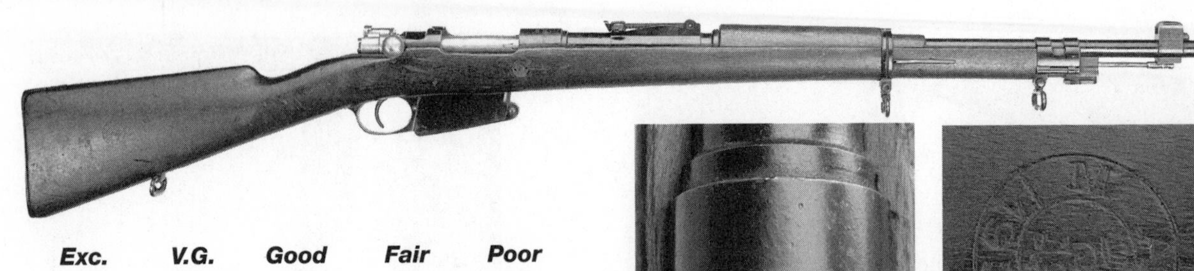

Exc.	V.G.	Good	Fair	Poor
800	600	450	200	150

M1889 Carbine Lightened

Fitted with a 15.75-inch barrel and turned down bolt. A slotted sling bracket mounted on left side of buttstock.

Exc.	V.G.	Good	Fair	Poor
750	600	450	200	150

M1889 Carbine Lightened

Same as above but with longer stock. A unique bayonet, handle has no guard and frequently having a double curved blade, was also issued with this carbine. No examples of this bayonet could be found to list here.

Exc.	V.G.	Good	Fair	Poor
750	600	450	200	150

M1890 Turkish Rifle

Captured Turkish Model 1890 rifles with Belgian rear sight similar to the Model 1889 rifle. No handguard. Original Turkish markings remain. Belgian proofs.

Exc.	V.G.	Good	Fair	Poor
750	550	375	250	150

M1916 Carbine

Similar to the Model 1889 but with different bracket on buttstock.

Exc.	V.G.	Good	Fair	Poor
750	600	450	175	150

M1935 Short Rifle

This model is very similar to the German Kar 98k and uses the M98 bolt system. It is fitted with a 5-round flush magazine. Chambered for 7.65mm Mauser cartridge. Barrel length is 23.5 inches. Weight is about 9 lbs.

Exc.	V.G.	Good	Fair	Poor
750	600	450	250	175

M1889/36 Short Rifle

This model is a converted Model 1889 with a 23.5-inch barrel with wooden handguard. The upper barrel band and front sight are of the Model 1935 type. The bolt system appears similar to the Model 98. Chambered for the 7.65mm Mauser cartridge. Weight is about 9 lbs.

Exc.	V.G.	Good	Fair	Poor
575	475	350	200	150

Belgian Model 1889/36 Short Rifle • *Courtesy West Point Museum, Paul Goodwin photo*

Belgian M1916/24 Bayonet for Mausers

Belgium used a variety of bayonets of the patten shown. Wood grips. Muzzle ring. The common infantry version shown has a 17.6-inch double edge blade. The Gendarmerie version has a single edge T-shaped blade. There are also versions with shortened blade lengths of 12.3 inches – 13.8 inches. Price range 225 – 100.

M50 Short Rifle

Post war surplus rifle converted to .30-06 caliber. Barrel length is 23.2 inches. Tangent leaf rear sight graduated to 2000 meters. Marked "B/ABL/[DATE]." Weight is approximately 9 lbs.

Exc.	V.G.	Good	Fair	Poor
650	500	400	250	150

M35/46 Short Rifle

Similar to the M50 short rifle.

Exc.	V.G.	Good	Fair	Poor
550	425	350	175	150

M24/30 .22 Caliber Training Rifle–Army

This is a military training rifle in .22 caliber built for the Belgian army after WWII.

Exc.	V.G.	Good	Fair	Poor
750	600	450	300	200

M24/30 .22 Caliber Training Rifle–Navy

Same as above but for the Belgian navy.

Exc.	V.G.	Good	Fair	Poor
750	600	450	300	200

FN M30 Postwar Short Rifle (M24/30, M35/46)

Built after WWII for the Belgian army. It uses the standard M98 action. Converted from Model 1935 rifle to .30-06 caliber. Barrel length is 23.3". Weight is about 9 lbs. Magazine capacity is 5-round in an integral box.

Exc.	V.G.	Good	Fair	Poor
600	450	300	175	150

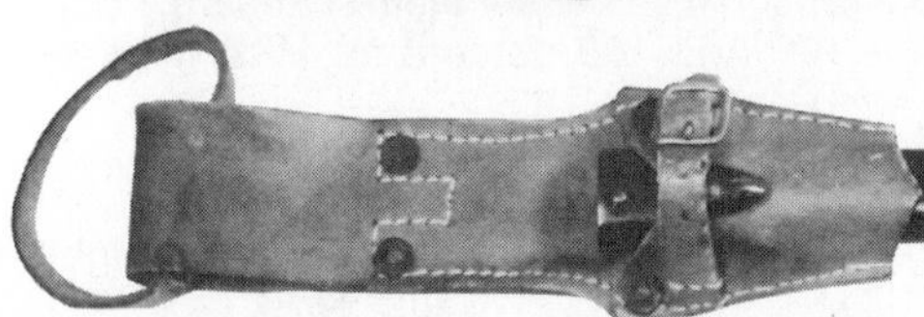

Belgian M1916/24 Bayonet for Mausers

Model 30 Postwar Short Rifle •
Courtesy Daniel Rewers Collection, Paul Goodwin photo

Model 1924/30 Export Bayonets for Mausers

Wood handle. Muzzle ring. 15- or 9.5-inch single edge blade. No markings except possibly a serial number on the end of the pommel. Sold with the M1924 Mauser rifles to many nations. Price range 80 – 40.

FABRIQUE NATIONALE

Model 1949 or SAFN 49

A gas-operated semi-automatic rifle chambered for 7x57, 7.92mm, and .30-06. It has a 23" barrel and military-type sights. The fixed magazine holds 10 rounds. The finish is blued, and the stock is walnut. This is a well-made gun that was actually designed before WWII. When the Germans were in the process of taking over Belgium, a group of FN engineers fled to England and took the plans for this rifle with them, preventing the German military from acquiring a very fine weapon. This model was introduced in 1949, after hostilities had ceased. This model was sold on contract to Egypt, chambered for 7.92mm; to Venezuela, chambered for 7x57; and to Argentina, Colombia, Indonesia, Belgium, and Luxembourg chambered for the .30-06. Argentina models were chambered for the 7.65x53mm as well as the Argentina navy which had its rifles chambered for the 7.62 NATO cartridge. The FN 1949 bears serial numbers on the receiver, top cover, bolt and bolt carrier. Deduct 25 percent for any MM parts.

Courtesy Richard M. Kumor Sr.

Belgium military issue

Cal. 30-06. Receiver marked "ABL". No Belgian issue FN 1949s have been legally imported as they have the slot in the receiver to allow installation of a select-fire trigger group. This makes it a machine gun under BATFE regulations. There might be a handful of pre-1968 imports but none could be found while preparing this edition. They would need to registered with the NFA to be legal.

Exc.	V.G.	Good	Fair	Poor
n/a	n/a	n/a	n/a	n/a

Columbian contract

Cal. 30-06. Receiver marked with Columbian crest.

Exc.	V.G.	Good	Fair	Poor
1150	900	750	450	300

Luxemborg contract

Cal. 30-06. Receiver marked "AL".

Exc.	V.G.	Good	Fair	Poor
1100	900	750	400	300

Egyptian contract: See Egypt.

Venezualan contract

Cal. 7x57mm. Receiver marked with Venezuelan crest. The only FN-49 that was issued with a flash hider.

Exc.	V.G.	Good	Fair	Poor
900	750	550	300	250

Argentine contract: See Argentina.

Bayonet for FN Model 1949, Type 1

Wood grips. 9-1/4 inch double edge blade. National versions have slightly different marks. The Belgian is marked "SA .30" and is numbered on the pommel and the scabbard. The Egyptian has Farsi numbers on the end of the handle. Some versions have no markings at all. Pricing is the same. Price range 75 – 30.

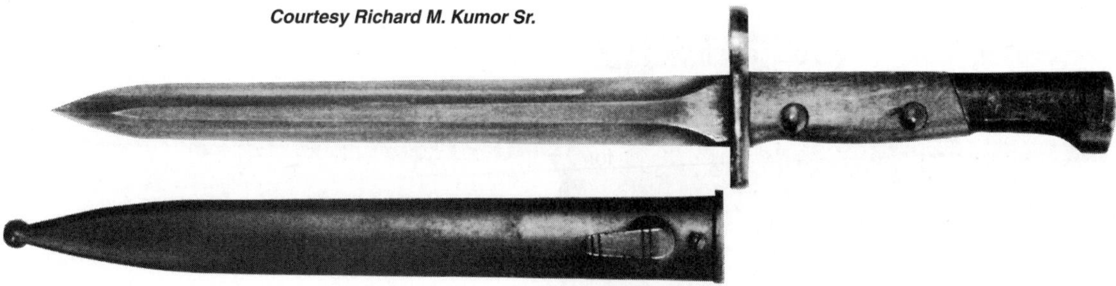

Bayonet for FN Model 1949, Type 1

Bayonet for FN Model 1949, Type 2

BELGIUM

Bayonet for FN Model 1949, Type 2

This bayonet was made for the Venezuelan 7mm rifle. Wood grips. 15 inch single edge blade. This is the same as the FN Model 1924 long export bayonet that has the muzzle ring enlarged to .715 inch to fit over the flash hider on the FN 1949. The only marking is a serial number on the end of the pommel. Price range 80 – 40.

Model 30-11 Sniper Rifle

Chambered for the 7.62 NATO cartridge. It has a 20-inch heavy barrel and Anschutz sights. There is a flash suppressor mounted on the muzzle. It is built on a highly precision-made Mauser bolt action fed by a 9-round, detachable box magazine. The walnut stock is rather unique in that the butt is made up of two parts, with the rear half being replaceable to suit the needs of different-sized shooters. It is issued with a shooting sling, bipod, and a foam-lined carrying case. This is a rare firearm on the commercial market as it was designed and sold to the military and police markets.

Exc.	V.G.	Good	Fair	Poor
5000	4500	3500	2750	2000

FN-FAL

A gas-operated, semi-automatic version of the famous FN battle rifle. This weapon has been adopted by more free world countries than any other rifle. It is chambered for the 7.62 NATO or .308 and has a 21" barrel with an integral flash suppressor. The sights are adjustable with an aperture rear, and the detachable box magazine holds 20 rounds. The stock and forearm are made of wood or a black synthetic. This model has been discontinued by the company and is no longer manufactured.

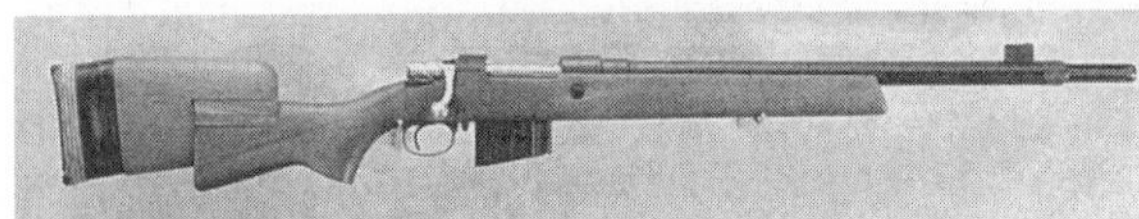
Courtesy Jim Supica, Old Town Station

The models listed below are for the metric pattern Type 2 and Type 3 receivers, those marked "FN MATCH." The models below are for semi-automatic rifles only. FN-FAL rifles in the "inch" pattern are found in the British Commonwealth countries of Australia, India, Canada, and of course, Great Britain. These rifles are covered separately under their own country headings.

50.00–21" Rifle Model

NIB	Exc.	V.G.	Good	Fair	Poor
3500	3000	2500	2000	N/A	N/A

50.63–18" Paratrooper Model

NIB	Exc.	V.G.	Good	Fair	Poor
4000	3500	3000	2750	N/A	N/A

50.64–21" Paratrooper Model

NIB	Exc.	V.G.	Good	Fair	Poor
4000	3500	3000	2750	N/A	N/A

50.41–Synthetic Butt H-Bar

NIB	Exc.	V.G.	Good	Fair	Poor
3250	2800	2500	2000	N/A	N/A

50.42–Wood Butt H-Bar

NIB	Exc.	V.G.	Good	Fair	Poor
4000	3500	3000	2750	N/A	N/A

NOTE: There are a number of U.S. companies that built FN-FAL receivers and use military surplus parts. These rifles have only limited collector value as of yet.

18" Para Model •
Courtesy Blake Stevens, from ***The FAL Rifle***

21" Para Model •
Courtesy Blake Stevens, from ***The FAL Rifle***

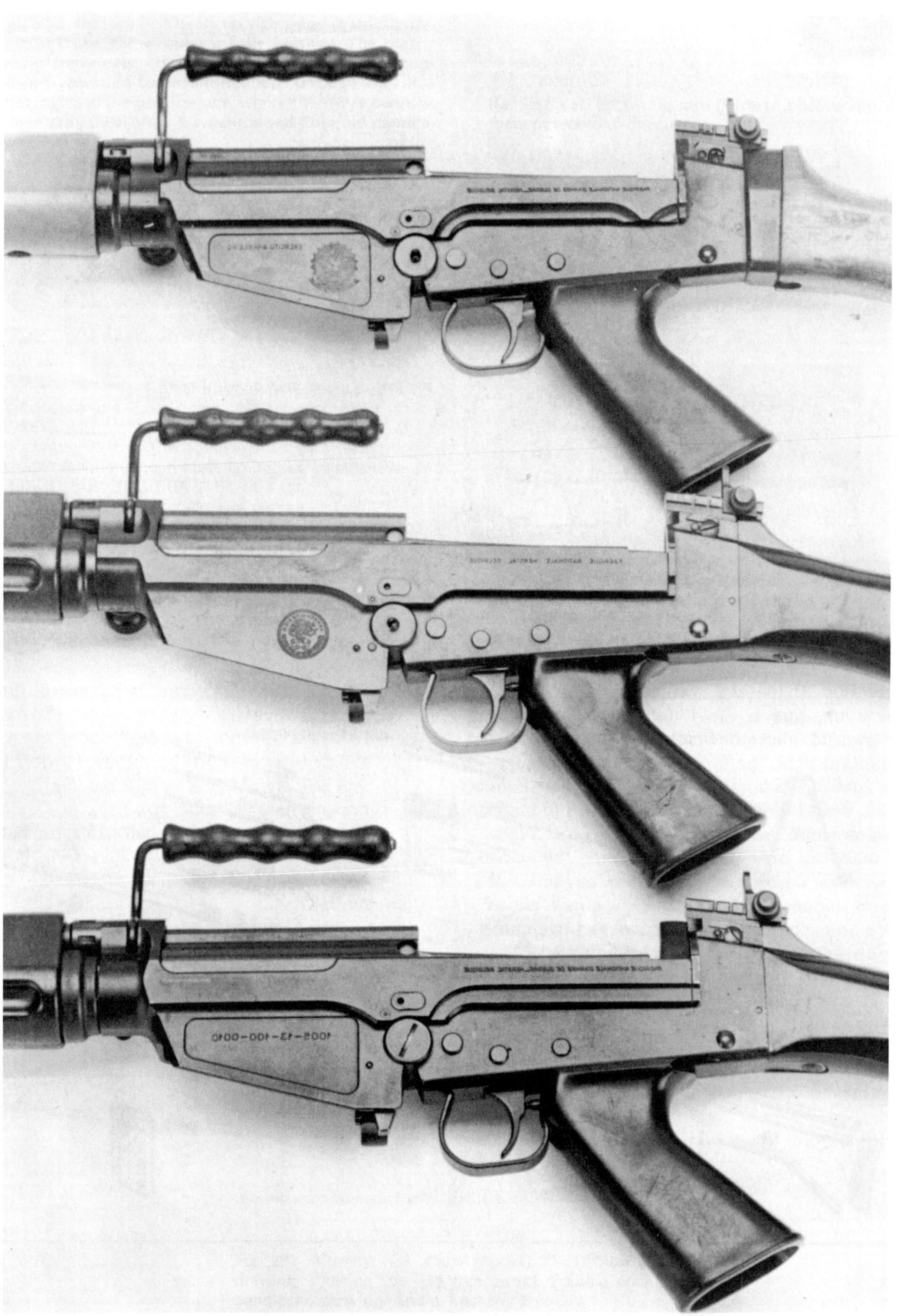

FAL Receivers: Top - Type 2; Middle - Type 3; Bottom - Type 1 • *Courtesy Blake Stevens*

FN Heavy Barrel Model •
Courtesy Blake Stevens, from The FAL Rifle

Courtesy FN

FN FAL "G" Series (Type 1 Receiver)

The first FAL to be imported to the U.S. The receivers are capable of accepting select-fire parts. These rifles are subject to interpretation by the BATF as to their legal status. A list of BATF legal serial numbers is available. This information should be referenced prior to a purchase. There were 1,848 legal "G" Series FN FAL rifles imported into this country. All were "grandfathered" and remain legal to posess.

Standard

NIB	*Exc.*	*V.G.*	*Good*	*Fair*	*Poor*
7500	6500	5000	3000	N/A	N/A

Lightweight

NIB	*Exc.*	*V.G.*	*Good*	*Fair*	*Poor*
7500	6500	5000	3000	N/A	N/A

FN FAL–Select Fire Assault Rifle

First produced in 1953, this 7.62x51mm select fire rifle has been used worldwide. It is fitted with a 20.8-inch barrel and a magazine that holds 20 rounds. It is available in several different configurations. Weight is about 9.8 lbs. Marked "FABRIQUE NATIONALE HERSTAL." Markings will also indicate many other countries made this rifle under license from FN.

Pre-1968 (Rare)

Exc.	*V.G.*	*Fair*
18500	15000	12000

Pre-1986 full-auto conversions of semi-automatic model

Exc.	*V.G.*	*Fair*
15000	12500	10000

Bayonets for FN FAL

There are two primary patterns for this rifle. Many were exported along with the FAL rifles. Type 1 has wood, metal or plastic grips. Muzzle ring with flash hider prongs. 7.75" single edge blade. Steel scabbard. Price range 60 – 25. Type 2 has a tubular handle that fits over the flash hider. 6.3" double edge blade. Steel or plastic scabbard. Price range 60 – 25.

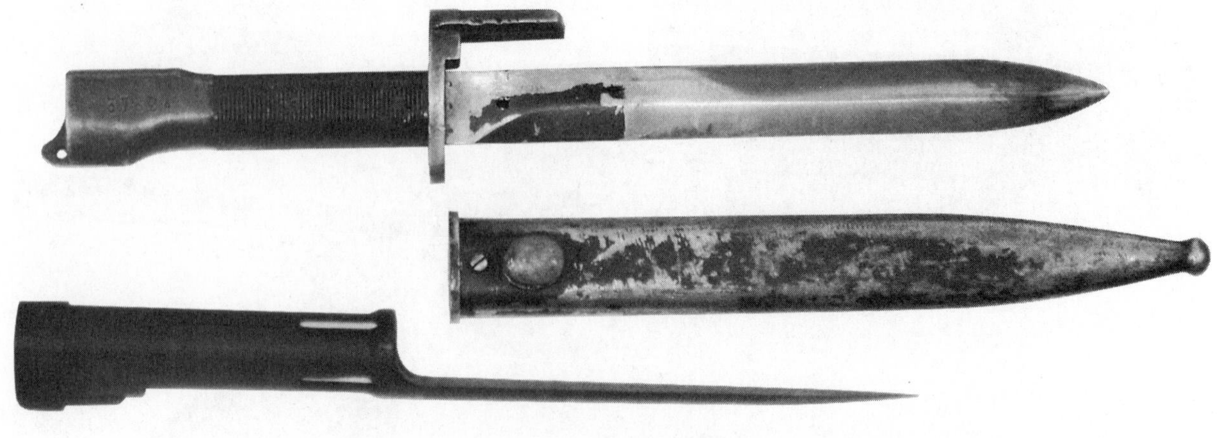

Bayonets for FN FAL

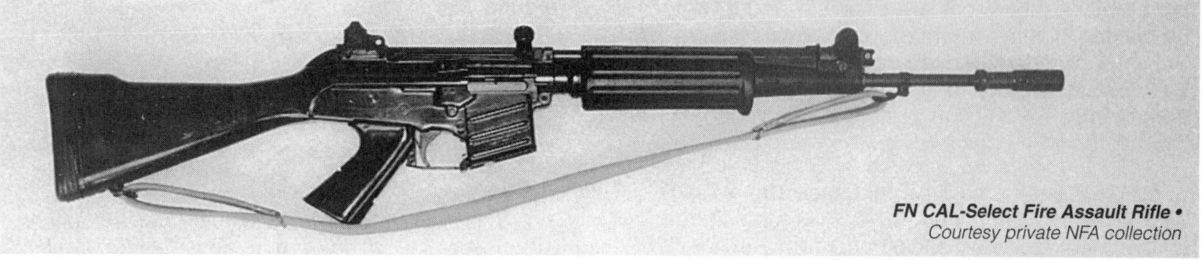
FN CAL-Select Fire Assault Rifle • Courtesy private NFA collection

FN CAL

Chambered for the 5.56x45mm cartridge and designed with a rotary bolt. It is fitted with an 18.2-inch barrel and has a magazine capacity of 20 or 30 rounds. Weight is about 6 lbs. With folding stock. Produced from 1966 to 1975 and is marked "FABRIQUE NATIONALE HERSTAL MOD CAL 5.56MM" on the left side of the receiver. This rifle was not widely adopted. A rare rifle. Only about 20 of these rifles were imported into the U.S.

NIB	Exc.	V.G.	Good	Fair	Poor
7000	6500	5000	3000	—	—

FN CAL-Select Fire Assault Rifle

Chambered for the 5.56x45mm cartridge and designed with a rotary bolt. It is fitted with an 18.2-inch barrel and has a magazine capacity of 20 or 30 rounds. Its rate of fire is 650 rounds per minute. Weight is about 6 lbs. With folding stock. Produced from 1966 to 1975 and is marked "FABRIQUE NATIONALE HERSTAL MOD CAL 5.56MM" on the left side of the receiver. This rifle was not widely adopted.

Pre-1968 (Rare)

Exc.	V.G.	Fair
15000	12500	10000

FNC

A lighter-weight assault-type rifle chambered for the 5.56mm cartridge. It is a gas-operated semi-automatic with an 18- or 21-inch barrel. It has a 30-round box magazine and is black, with either a fixed or folding stock. This model was also discontinued by FN.

Standard

Fixed stock, 16- or 18-inch barrel.

NIB	Exc.	V.G.	Good	Fair	Poor
3800	3500	2750	2000	N/A	N/A

Paratrooper Model

Folding stock, 16- or 18-inch barrel.

NIB	Exc.	V.G.	Good	Fair	Poor
3800	3500	2750	2000	N/A	N/A

NOTE: The above prices are for Belgian-made guns only.

FN FNC-Select Fire Assault Rifle

This model, introduced in 1979, took the place of the CAL. Chambered for the 5.56x45mm cartridge and fitted with a 17.5-inch barrel, it weighs about 8.4 lbs. It has a 30-round magazine capacity. Rate of fire is 700 rounds per minute. Fitted with a metal folding stock. This model will accept M16 magazines. Marked "FNC 5.56" on left side of receiver. This rifle was adopted by the Belgian, Indonesian, and Swedish militaries.

Pre-1986 full-auto conversions of semi-automatic model

Exc.	V.G.	Fair
8000	6000	4500

FN BAR Model D (Demontable)

This was the FN version of the Browning automatic rifle. It is fitted with a quick change barrel and pistol grip. It was offered in a variety of calibers from 6.5 Swedish Mauser to the 7.92x57mm Mauser. It is fitted with a 19.5-inch barrel and has a rate of fire of either 450 or 650 rounds per minute. Weight is about 20 lbs. Marked "FABRIQUE NATIONALE D'ARMES DE GUERRE HERSTAL-BELGIQUE" on left side of receiver.

FN sold about 700 Model Ds to Finland in 1940 which the Finns used during their "Winter War" with the Russians. These Finnish BARs were chambered for the 7.63x54R cartridge. Also a small number of FN guns were sold to China (2,000) and Ethiopia in the 1930s. These BARs were chambered for the 7.92x57mm Mauser cartridge. After World War II FN sold its Model 30 BAR to a number of countries around the world.

Courtesy Jim Thompson

Pre-1968 (Very Rare)

Exc.	V.G.	Fair
37500	32500	27500

Pre-1986 manufacture with new receiver or re-weld

Exc.	V.G.	Fair
25000	20000	18000

MACHINE GUNS

Fabrique Nationale has a long history of manufacturing John M. Browning's firearms. These firearms include the Browning Model 1917, M1919, and .50 caliber heavy gun. The light machine guns were chambered in a variety of calibers and sold around the world by FN. During WWII the FN factory was occupied by German troops, but after the war in 1945 when production finally returned to normal levels, the Belgians produced the air-cooled Browning guns in 7.62x63mm (.30-06) for the Belgian army. When NATO adopted the 7.62x51mm cartridge, FN designed and built the FN MAG machine gun.

FN MAG (Mitrailleuse d'Appui Generale) (M240)

First produced in Belgium in 1955, this machine gun is chambered for the 7.62x51mm cartridge. It is fitted with a 21.3-inch quick change barrel and has an adjustable rate of fire of 700 to 1000 rounds per minute. It is belt-fed with metal links. The basic configuration uses a wooden buttstock, smooth barrel with bipod attached to gas cylinder, pistol grip, and slotted flash hider. The gun can also be attached to a tripod as well as used with an anti-aircraft mount. Weight is about 22 lbs. Marked "FABRIQUE NATIONALE D'ARMES DE GUERRE HERSTAL BELGIUM" on the right side of the receiver. This gun is still in production and is in use by over 80 countries worldwide.

There is an aircraft version of this gun designated as Model 60-30 (single mount) or 60-40 (twin mount). The gun can also be mounted in a coaxial configuration such as a tank or armored vehicle.

Pre-1968 (Very Rare)

Exc.	*V.G.*	*Fair*
125000+	—	—

Pre-1986 conversions

Side-plates, 65 registered.

Exc.	*V.G.*	*Fair*
80000	75000	67500

NOTE: This is an extremely rare machine gun with prices based on scarcity and demand. It is possible for prices to exceed $125,000 under certain conditions.

FN Minimi (M249)

Designed as a squad automatic weapon (SAW) and chambered for the 5.56x45mm cartridge, this machine gun has a rate of fire of 700 to 1,000 rounds per minute and is equipped with a 30-round box magazine or 100 to 200-round boxed belts. Rate of fire with box magazine is higher than when using belt. The quick change barrel length is 18" and weight is about 15 lbs. Marked "fn minimi 5.56" on the left side of the receiver. First produced in 1982, this gun is called the M249 machine gun in the U.S. Army. It is also in service in a number of other countries such as Canada, Australia, and Italy.

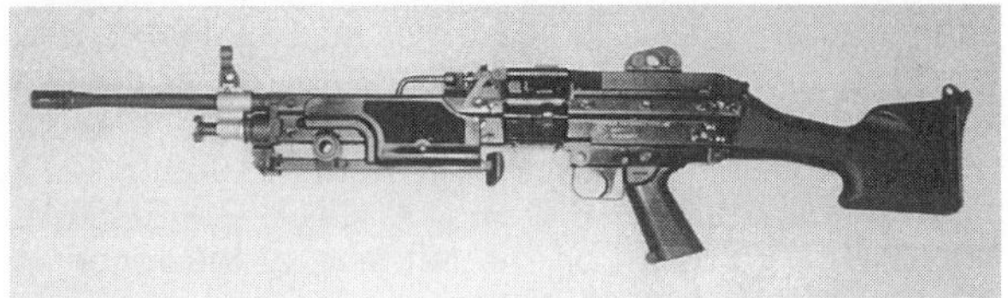

Courtesy private NFA collection

Pre-1986 transferable

Extremely rare, 1 known.

Exc.	*V.G.*	*Fair*
150000+	—	—

FN MAG (Mitrailleuse d'Appui Generale) (M240) •
Courtesy Amoskeag Auction Company

The Federative Republic of Brazil, which comprises half the continent of South America and is the only Latin American country deriving its culture and language from Portugal, has an area of 3,286,488 sq. mi. (8,511,965 sq. km.) and a population of *169.2 million. Capital: Brasilia. The economy of Brazil is as varied and complex as any in the developing world. Agriculture is a mainstay of the economy, while only 4 percent of the area is under cultivation. Known mineral resources are almost unlimited in variety and size of reserves. A large, relatively sophisticated industry ranges from basic steel and chemical production to finished consumer goods. Coffee, cotton, iron ore and cocoa are the chief exports.

Brazil was discovered and claimed for Portugal by Admiral Pedro Alvares Cabral in 1500. Portugal established a settlement in 1532 and proclaimed the area a royal colony in 1549. During the Napoleonic Wars, Dom Joao VI established the seat of Portuguese government in Rio de Janeiro. When he returned to Portugal, his son Dom Pedro I declared Brazil's independence on Sept. 7, 1822, and became emperor of Brazil. The Empire of Brazil was maintained until 1889 when the federal republic was established. The Federative Republic was established in 1946 by terms of a constitution drawn up by a constituent assembly. Following a coup in 1964 the armed forces retained overall control under a dictatorship until civilian government was restored on March 15, 1985. The current constitution was adopted in 1988.

HANDGUNS

NOTE: Brazil used a number of Colt Model 1911A1 pistols (Pst M1911A1). These pistols are still in service in second line units. Mauser shipped a few hundred Model 1912/14 pistols to Brazil. In the 1930s about 500 Mauser Schnellfeuer pistols were purchased and a few are still in service. Brazil has also purchased the Beretta Model 92 from Italy. In the 1980s Brazil began to produce its own version of the Colt 1911A1 known as the Imbel M973. Other variations of this pistol have been produced in 9x19, 9x17, and .38 Super. No examples of these pistols are known in the U.S.

Smith & Wesson Model 1917

Similar the U.S. Model 1917 revolver. Chambered for the .45 automatic cartridges. 25,000 were produced with the Brazilian crest and date 1937 on the frame. Many Brazilian contract guns were imported since 1986. Some were in well used condition.

Exc.	***V.G.***	***Good***	***Fair***	***Poor***
650	525	400	325	250

SUBMACHINE GUNS

Brazil has used or is using in second line units the U.S. M3 gun, the Beretta Model 12, the H&K MP5 and MP5SD. Brazil has additionally issued the Walther MPK. A few Thompson M1s and U.S. Reisings are used as well.

URU Model 2

Chambered for the 9mm parabellum cartridge and fitted with a 7" barrel with slotted barrel jacket. Made of stampings with round receiver. Forward magazine acts as a handgrip. Magazine capacity is 30 rounds. Detachable wooden butt or steel single strut stock. Rate of fire is about 750 rounds per minute. Weight is about 6.5 lbs. Produced in Brazil at Bilbao SA in Sao Paulo.

Pre-1968

Exc.	***V.G.***	***Fair***
N/A	N/A	N/A

RIFLES

Brazil uses the HK 33E, the M16 (Model 614), the M16A2, and the FN FAL and variations, built under license from FN. The Brazilian military also uses the U.S. M1 rifle converted to 7.62 NATO caliber.

MAUSER

M1894 Rifle

Similar to the Spanish Model 1893 but with a cylindrical bolt head. Barrel length is 29 inches. Chambered for the 7x57 cartridge. Magazine is flush mounted and has a 5-round capacity. Adjustable rear sight from 400 to 2,000 meters. Brazilian crest on receiver ring. Produced by DWM and FN.

Exc.	***V.G.***	***Good***	***Fair***	***Poor***
600	475	250	175	125

M1894 Carbine

As above but with 18-inch barrel and adjustable rear sight to 1,400 meters. No bayonet lug.

Exc.	***V.G.***	***Good***	***Fair***	***Poor***
650	500	300	175	125

M1904 Mauser-Verueiro Rifle

Chambered for the 6.5x58Pmm cartridge, this model was fitted with a 29-inch barrel. Tangent sight graduated to 2,000 meters. Brazilian crest on receiver ring. Produced by DWM.

Exc.	***V.G.***	***Good***	***Fair***	***Poor***
700	550	400	250	150

M1907 Rifle

Built by DWM from 1904 to 1906. Sold to Brazil in 1907. Chambered for the 7x57mm cartridge. Pistol grip stock. Fitted with a 29-inch barrel. Tangent rear sight graduated to 2,000 meters. Built by DWM. Brazilian crest on receiver ring.

Exc.	***V.G.***	***Good***	***Fair***	***Poor***
600	475	250	175	125

M1907 Carbine

As above with shorter barrel. Produced from 1907 to 1912 by DWM.

Exc.	***V.G.***	***Good***	***Fair***	***Poor***
600	475	250	175	125

M1908 Rifle

Similar in appearance to the Gew 98. Chambered for the 7x57mm cartridge. Built by DWM between 1908

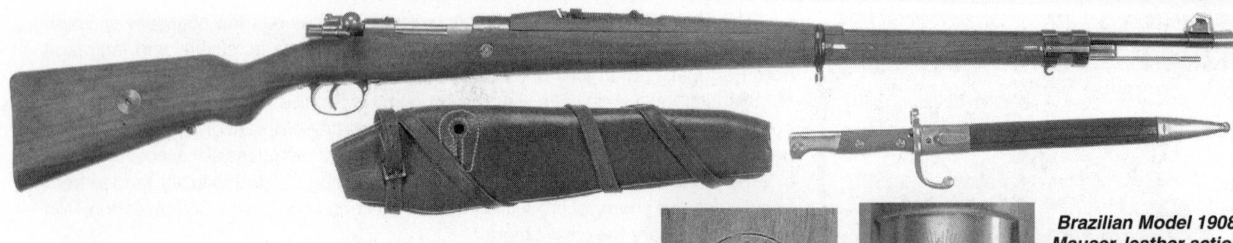

Brazilian Model 1908 Mauser, leather action cover and bayonet. Stock cartouche and receiver crest shown • *Courtesy Rock Island Auction Company*

and 1914. Fitted with a 29.25-inch barrel. Magazine capacity is 5 rounds. Tangent rear sight graduated to 2,000 meters. Brazilian crest on receiver ring.

Exc.	V.G.	Good	Fair	Poor
600	425	250	175	125

M1908 Short Rifle

Same as the Model 1908 rifle but with a 22-inch barrel.

Exc.	V.G.	Good	Fair	Poor
600	425	250	175	125

Bayonet for Brazilian Mauser

Wood grips. 11.75-inch single edge blade. Made by Weyersberg, Kischbaum & Co. Solingen. Leather scabbard with brass fittings. Price range 75 – 25.

M1922 Carbine

Chambered for the 7x57mm cartridge and fitted with a 19.5-inch barrel. Magazine capacity is 5 rounds. Tangent rear sight graduated to 1,400 meters. Built by FN. Weight is about 6.5 lbs.

Exc.	V.G.	Good	Fair	Poor
650	500	300	175	125

VZ 24 Short Rifle

This rifle was built in Czechoslovakia and sold to Brazil in 1932. Bent bolt handle with flat bolt knob. Finger grooves in forend. Czech markings (BRNO). About 15,000 sold to Brazil.

Exc.	V.G.	Good	Fair	Poor
800	675	400	250	150

M1935 Mauser Banner Rifle

Chambered for the 7x57mm cartridge. Fitted with a 28.75-inch barrel. Magazine capacity is 5 rounds. Tangent rear sight graduated to 2,000 meters. Brazilian crest on receiver ring. Finger grooves in forend. Weight is about 10 lbs.

Exc.	V.G.	Good	Fair	Poor
750	525	350	175	125

M1935 Mauser Banner Carbine

As above but with 21.5-inch barrel. Rear sight graduated to 1,400 meters. Bent bolt handle. Stock cut to accommodate the downturn of the bolt handle. Mauser banner logo on the receiver ring. Brazilian crest on receiver ring. Weight is about 9 lbs.

Exc.	V.G.	Good	Fair	Poor
800	650	400	250	150

M1908/34 Short Rifle

Built in Brazil at Itajuba. The stock for this model used local wood and not European walnut. Chambered for the .30-06 cartridge. Fitted with a 23.5" barrel. Tangent rear sight graduated to 2,000 meters. Weight is about 9.75 lbs. Brazilian crest on receiver ring. Manufacturer's markings on side rail.

Exc.	V.G.	Good	Fair	Poor
500	375	250	175	125

M1954 Caliber .30-06 Short Rifle

This model was also built in Brazil and chambered for the .30-06 cartridge. Fitted with a 23.25" barrel. Tangent rear sight graduated to 2,000 meters. Pistol grip stock with finger grooves. Nose cap fitted with a bayonet lug. Weight is about 8.75 lbs. Brazilian crest on receiver ring.

Exc.	V.G.	Good	Fair	Poor
500	375	250	175	125

MACHINE GUNS

The Brazilian military uses a wide variety of machine guns. They are: the FN MAG, Browning M1919A4, the Browning .50 M2 HB, the Danish Madsen converted to .30 caliber, and even the Hotchkiss LMG in 7mm. The Brazilian military has also developed, in the 1990s, its own design called the Uirapuru GPMG in 7.62x51mm.

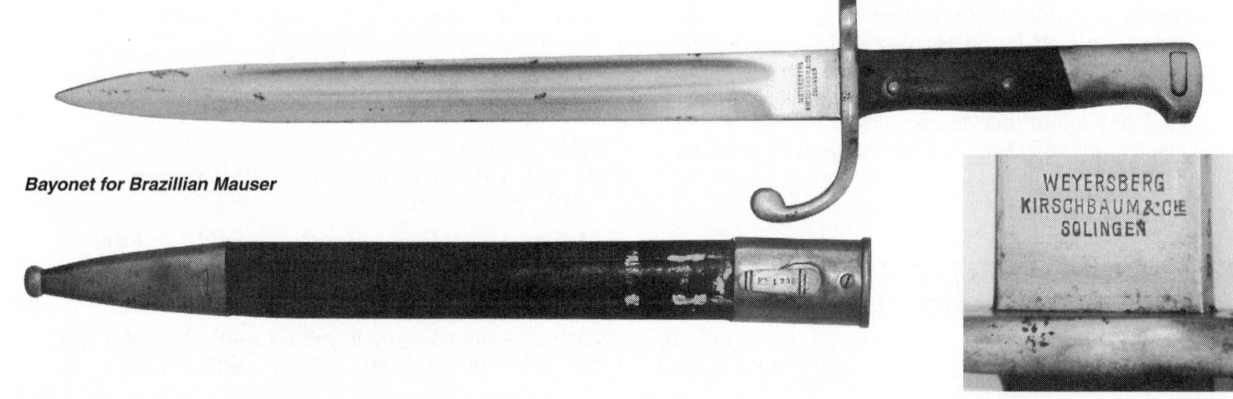

Bayonet for Brazillian Mauser

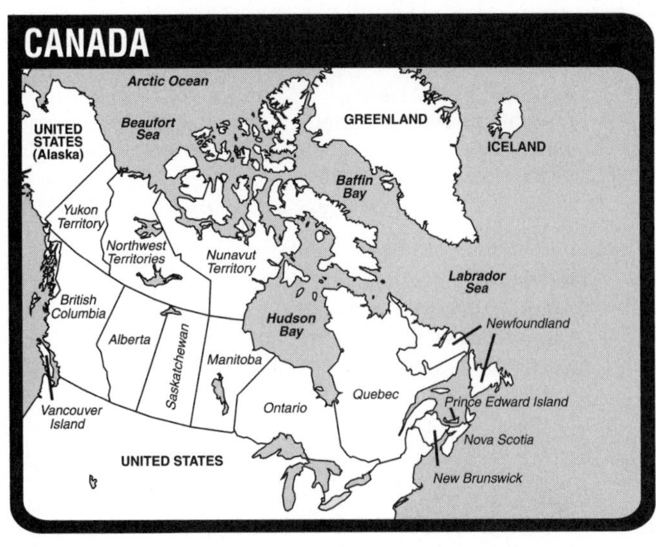

Canada is located to the north of the United States, and spans the full breadth of the northern portion of North America from Atlantic to Pacific oceans, except for the State of Alaska. It has a total area of 3,850,000 sq. mi. (9,971,550 sq. km.) and a population of 30.29 million. Capital: Ottawa.

Jacques Cartier, a French explorer, took possession of Canada for France in 1534, and for more than a century the history of Canada was that of a French colony. Samuel de Champlain helped to establish the first permanent colony in North America, in 1604 at Port Royal, Acadia – now Annapolis Royal, Nova Scotia. Four years later he founded the settlement in Quebec.

The British settled along the coast to the south while the French, motivated by a grand design, pushed into the interior. France's plan for a great American empire was to occupy the Mississippi heartland of the country, and from there to press in upon the narrow strip of English coastal settlements from the west. Inevitably, armed conflict erupted between the French and the British; consequently, Britain acquired Hudson Bay, Newfoundland and Nova Scotia from the French in 1713. British control of the rest of New France was secured in 1763, largely because of James Wolfe's great victory over Montcalm near Quebec in 1759.

During the American Revolution, Canada became a refuge for great numbers of American Royalists, most of whom settled in Ontario, thereby creating an English majority west of the Ottawa River. The ethnic imbalance contravened the effectiveness of the prevailing French type of government, and in 1791 the Constitutional act was passed by the British parliament, dividing Canada at the Ottawa River into two parts, each with its own government: Upper Canada, chiefly English and consisting of the southern section of what is now Ontario; and Lower Canada, chiefly French and consisting principally of the southern section of Quebec. Subsequent revolt by dissidents in both sections caused the British government to pass the Union Act, July 23, 1840, which united Lower and Upper Canada (as Canada East and Canada West) to form the Province of Canada, with one council and one assembly in which the two sections had equal numbers.

The union of the two provinces did not encourage political stability; the equal strength of the French and British made the task of government all but impossible. A further change was made with the passage of the British North American Act, which took effect on July 1, 1867, and established Canada as the first federal union in the British Empire. Four provinces entered the union at first: Upper Canada as Ontario, Lower Canada as Quebec, Nova Scotia and New Brunswick. The Hudson Bay Company's territories were acquired in 1869 out of which were formed the provinces of Manitoba, Saskatchewan and Alberta. British Columbia joined in 1871 and Prince Edward Island in 1873. Canada took over the Arctic Archipelago in 1895. In 1949 Newfoundland came into the confederation.

Canada is a member of the Commonwealth of Nations. Elizabeth II is Head of State as Queen of Canada.

As a member of the British Commonwealth, Canada has primarily used English-made firearms. Several models have been produced by Canadian companies.

CANADA

HANDGUNS

INGLIS, JOHN & COMPANY

This firm manufactured Browning Pattern .35 semi-automatic pistols for the Canadian, Chinese, and British governments. Pistols are parkerized dark gray and include black plastic grips and a lanyard ring. Premium paid for pistols which still display the Canadian "Lend-Lease" decal on the front grip strap. Fewer than 160,000 pistols were manufactured between 1943 and 1945. Add $350 for original Canadian-produced wood stocks.

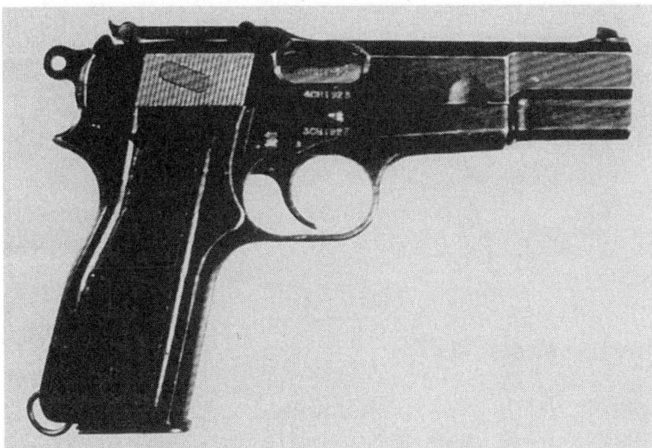

NOTE: The correct magazine for the Inglis produced pistols will have a split back base and will bear the initialed "JI" on the front. See magazine image under Belgium FN 1935.

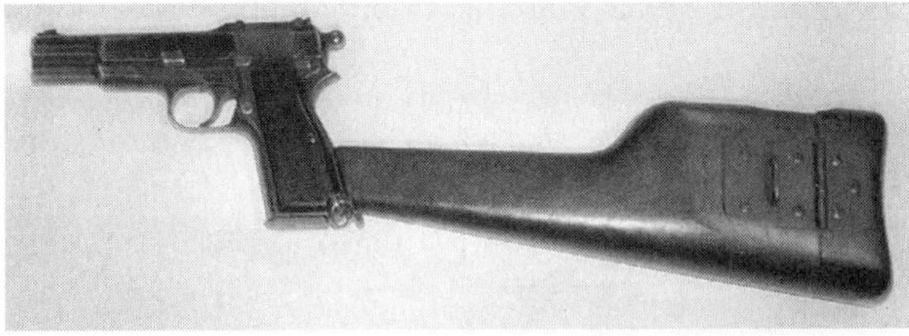

Courtesy Richard M. Kumor Sr.

Mk. 1 No. 1 (Chinese Marked)

The first 4,000 pistols destined for the Chinese government included a six character Chinese marking on the slide, as well as a serial number which incorporated the letters "CH." Includes a tangent rear sight and a stock slot.

Exc.	V.G.	Good	Fair	Poor
1000	850	700	400	300

Mk. 1 No. 1

Identical to the Chinese-marked model but without the Chinese characters.

Exc.	V.G.	Good	Fair	Poor
1000	850	500	350	275

CANADA

Mk. 1 No. 1*

Externally identical to the No. 1 Mk. 1 but the slide includes the marking Mk. 1*. This mark may be factory applied, or applied in the field after conversion.

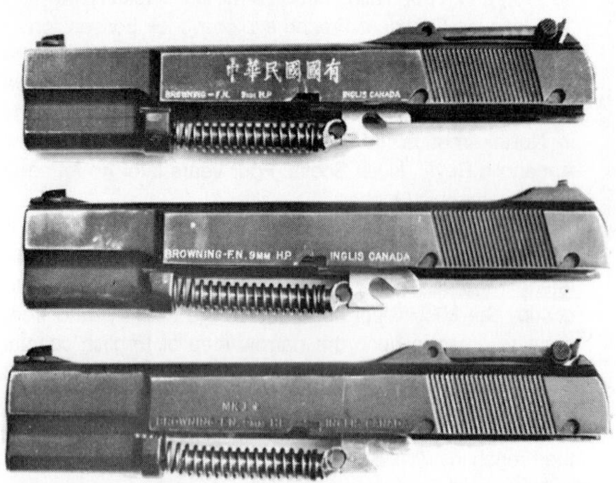

*Inglis slides from top to bottom: Chinese pattern No. 1 Mk.1, Canadian forces No. 2 Mk.1, later Chinese-type No. 1 Mk. 1** • *Courtesy Blake Stevens, The Browning High-Power, Stevens*

Exc.	V.G.	Good	Fair	Poor
750	600	500	350	275

No. 2 Mk. 1

The first 10,000 pistols made for Canada/Britain display the standard slide legend, fixed rear sight in the distinctive Inglis "hump," and no stock slot. All No. 2 type pistols will incorporate the letter "T" within the serial number.

Exc.	V.G.	Good	Fair	Poor
1000	925	850	350	250

No. 2 Mk. 1*

Identical to the No. 2 Mk. 1 externally but the slide includes the marking Mk. 1*. This mark may be factory applied, or applied in the field after conversion. Some examples imported from England or New Zealand may include the "No. 2" stamped or engraved on the slide.

Paul Goodwin photo

Exc.	V.G.	Good	Fair	Poor
750	600	500	425	375

No. 2 Mk. 1* Slotted

A small quantity of pistols, mostly in the 3Txxx range, were made up from Chinese frames and include the stock slot. Beware of fakes.

Exc.	V.G.	Good	Fair	Poor
1500	1250	925	625	500

DP Pistols

Approximately 150 No. 1 type pistols, some with the Chinese inscription, were made up as display and presentation pistols. Serial numbers will range from approximately DP1 to DP150.

Exc.	V.G.	Good	Fair	Poor
2500	2000	1750	1450	1200

Inglis Diamond

In the last week of production, Inglis marked a small quantity of pistols with their trademark, the word Inglis within a diamond. Both the No. 1 and No. 2-style pistols were so marked. Some pistols remained in the white while others were parkerized. It is believed that fewer than 50 pistols were marked.

Exc.	V.G.	Good	Fair	Poor
2500	2250	1900	1650	1200

New Zealand Issue

Only 500 pistols were acquired by New Zealand in the 1960s. A small quantity was modified and marked by the NZ Special Air Service.

Exc.	V.G.	Good	Fair	Poor
1250	950	700	575	525

British Issue

A large quantity of pistols have been imported from the British Ministry of Defense over the past several years. These pistols often display a black "paint" finish and may be marked "FTR" (Factory Thorough Repair) or "AF" (meaning unknown).

Exc.	V.G.	Good	Fair	Poor
600	525	400	325	250

Dutch Issue

The Netherlands used over 10,000 Inglis pistols. Early versions display a small crown over W mark on the rear sight while later models will have Dutch serial numbers, Belgian proofs, and Belgian barrels.

Exc.	V.G.	Good	Fair	Poor
2500	2300	2100	1800	1600

Belgian Issue

Belgium received 1,578 pistols as aid from Canada in the 1950s. These remained in use with the Gendarmerie until recently. Some pistols will display a gray "paint" finish and have numbered magazines. These have been wrongly identified as Danish navy in the past.

Exc.	V.G.	Good	Fair	Poor
3000	2500	2300	2100	1700

SAVAGE

Savage Model 1907

Canada purchased 500 Model 1907 pistols sometime during World War I. Chambered for 7.65mm. These pistols were later redirected to England but most

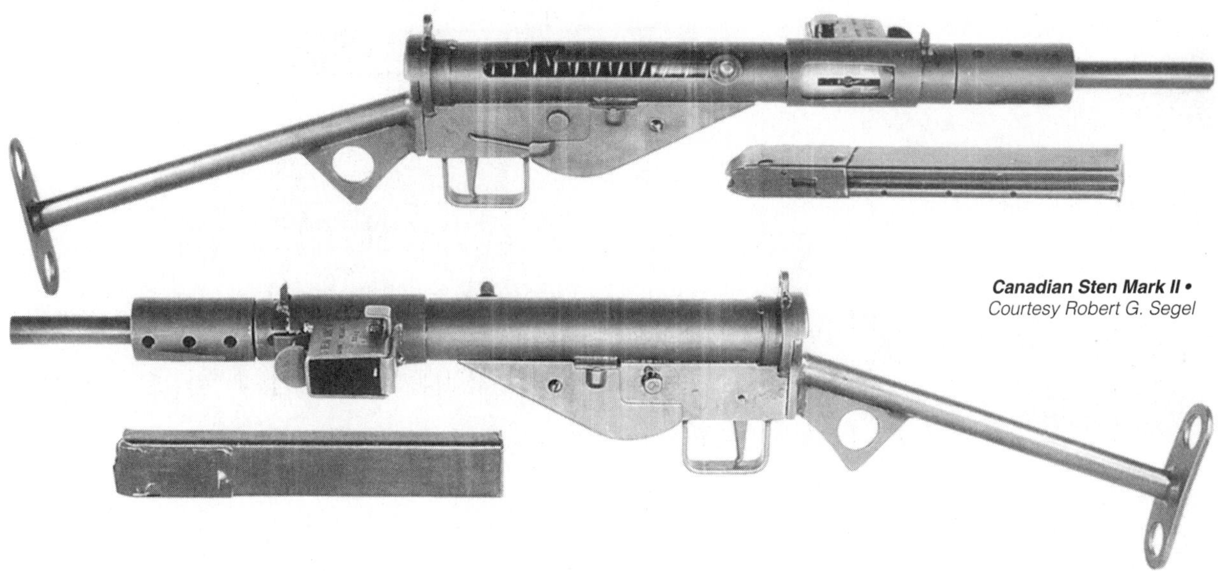

Canadian Sten Mark II • *Courtesy Robert G. Segel*

will have the Canadian Broad Arrow stamped on the frame near the safety.

Exc.	V.G.	Good	Fair	Poor
750	600	400	200	150

SUBMACHINE GUNS

Canadian Sten MK II

These are Canadian built Sten MK II guns built at Long Branch between February 1942 and September 1945. A total of 133,497 guns were produced in this interval. Canadian built Stens are marked "LONG BRANCH" on the magazine housing with the date of manufacture.

NOTE: Canadian Stens do not bring a premium over British-made Stens.

Pre-1968

Exc.	V.G.	Fair
6500	5000	4000

Pre-1986 manufacture with U.S.-manufactured receivers

Exc.	V.G.	Fair
3500	3000	2000

Sterling-Canadian C1

Chambered for the 9mm cartridge, this submachine gun features a 7.75" barrel and collapsible metal stock. The rate of fire is 550 rounds per minute. Weight is about 6 lbs. Produced from 1953 to 1988. Still made in India under license. Marked "smg 9mm c1" on the magazine housing.

The Canadian version of the Sterling is much like the British except for a 30-round magazine without rollers as followers, a different type bayonet (FAL), and internal modifications. A 10-round magazine is also available. Designated the "C1" by the Canadian military. It was first produced in Canada in the late 1950s.

Courtesy private NFA collection

Pre-1968 (Very Rare)

Exc.	V.G.	Fair
15000	12500	9000

Pre-1986 manufacture with new receiver or re-weld

Exc.	V.G.	Fair
7500	6500	5500

RIFLES

Canadian Pre-Cartridge Era Rifles

As an English colony during the 19th century, Canada was issued with the typical British-made long arms found throughout the realm. See listings in the Great Britain chapter.

PEABODY

Canadian Rifle Musket (1867)

Chambered for the .50-60 Peabody rimfire cartridge and fitted with a 36-inch barrel. Blued barrel with case hardened furniture. "CM" marked on right side of buttstock and "DWB" on left wrist. Canada purchased 3,000 of these rifles but a total of 5,000 were produced.

Exc.	V.G.	Good	Fair	Poor
1800	1500	1000	500	200

ROSS RIFLE CO.

Designed in 1896 by Sir Charles Ross, this straight pull rifle was manufactured in a variety of styles. Due to problems with the bolt design, it never proved popular and was discontinued in 1915.

Mark I

This rifle was adopted by the Canadian military in 1903. Barrel length is 28 inches. Chambered for .303 caliber with a "Harris Controlled Platform Magazine"

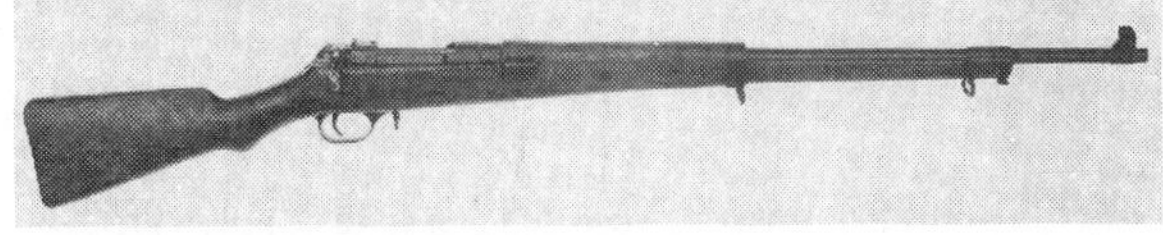

Courtesy Buffalo Bill Historical Center, Cody, Wyoming

Ross .22 single-shot rifle. Close-up of "broad arrow" on buttstock and receiver markings • *Courtesy Stoddard Martial collection, Paul Goodwin photo*

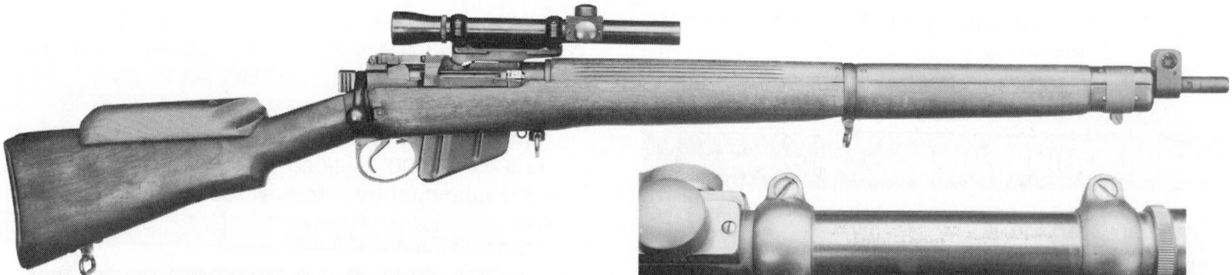

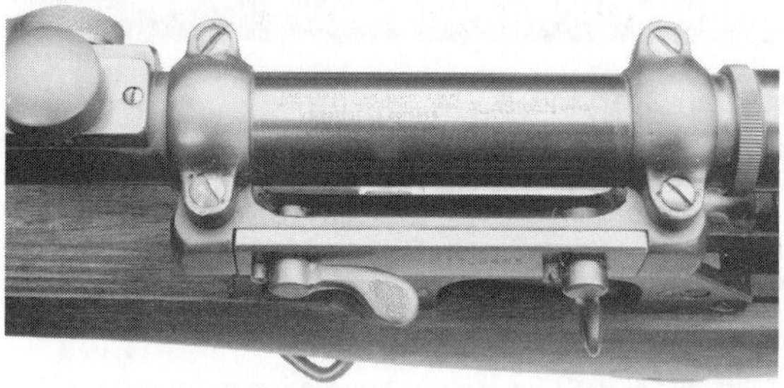

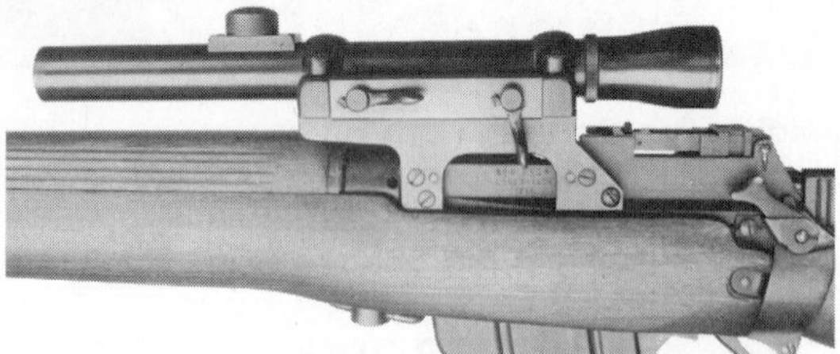

Canadian No. 4 Mk1 T "Long Branch" with original Lyman Alaskan scope set. Scope is mounted on a Griffin & Howe type base and mount. All numbers match on this rifle. Notice the broad arrow mark on the base of the top turret • *Courtesy Michael Wamsher, Paul Goodwin photo*

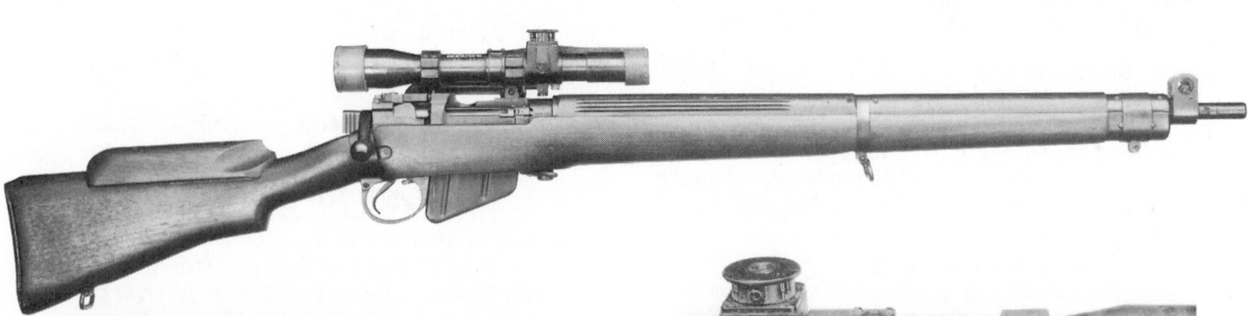

Canadian No. 4 Mk1 T "Long Branch" Sniper with original matching Canadian "R.E.L." scope set (No. 32 Mk3). All numbers match on this rifle. Notice the broad arrow on the left side of the scope • *Courtesy Michael Wamsher, Paul Goodwin photo*

that can be depressed by an external lever to facilitate loading. Magazine capacity is 5 rounds. Marked "ROSS RIFLE COM. QUEBEC CANADA" on left side of receiver. About 5,000 of these rifles were built.

Exc.	V.G.	Good	Fair	Poor
850	650	500	350	250

Mark I Carbine

As above, with a 26-inch barrel without bayonet lug.

Exc.	V.G.	Good	Fair	Poor
950	750	550	350	250

Mark II

Introduced in 1905 with a modified rear sight, longer handguard, no receiver bridge. Marked "ROSS RIFLE CO. QUEBEC CANADA 1905."

Courtesy Paul S. Scarlata from *Mannlicher Military Rifles*, **Andrew Mobray Publishers**

NOTE: Some Ross Mk IIs were sold to the U.S. for training use during WWI. These will have a U.S. mark and ordnance bomb cartouche in the grip area behind the trigger guard. Add up to 30% for U.S. marked guns.

Exc.	V.G.	Good	Fair	Poor
750	600	450	300	200

Mark III

Built between 1910 and 1916 with improved lockwork and stripper clip guides. Extended single column 5-round box magazine. Barrel length is 30 inches. Marked "ROSS RIFLE CO." over "CANADA" over "M10" on receiver ring. About 400,000 of these rifles were produced with about 67,000 sent to the British Army.

Mark III Ross rifle • *Courtesy Paul S. Scarlata*

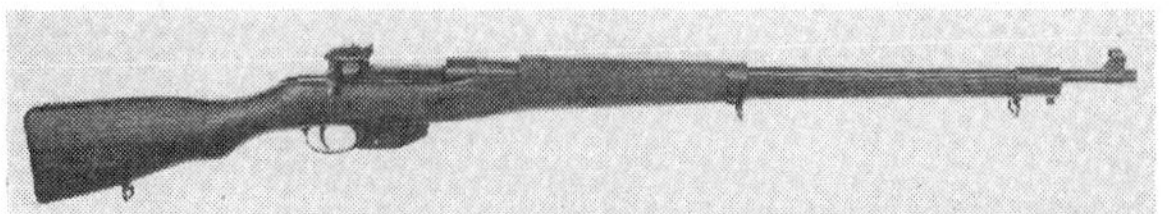

Courtesy Buffalo Bill Historical Center, Cody, Wyoming

Exc.	V.G.	Good	Fair	Poor
700	550	450	300	200

Mark III*

As above, with a magazine cutoff.

Exc.	V.G.	Good	Fair	Poor
700	550	450	300	200

Bayonet for Ross Rifles

Wood handle. Muzzle ring. 10-inch single edge blade. The blade tip was recut after 1915 to make a sharper point. Leather scabbard. Some will be seen with U.S. markings, but they usually do not alter the value. Price range 150 – 75.

Ross Military Match Rifle

A .280 Ross or .303 caliber straight pull military-style rifle with a 30" barrel having peep sights. Blued with a walnut stock. Similar in appearance to the Mark III except for flush magazine with .280 version.

Exc.	V.G.	Good	Fair	Poor
850	700	575	400	250

Ross Military Training Rifle

Chambered for the .22 caliber cartridge, this straight pull rifle is single shot only.

Exc.	V.G.	Good	Fair	Poor
800	600	500	300	200

LEE ENFIELD

Long Branch

Rifle No. 4 Mark I & Mark I*

Same as the English No.4 Mk 1 in .303 British. 10 round detachable magazine. Some have walnut stocks. Serial numbers should appear on the receiver, bolt and fore stock. These have a slight premium over the English-made rifles.

Exc.	V.G.	Good	Fair	Poor
500	350	200	150	125

Bayonet for Ross Rifles

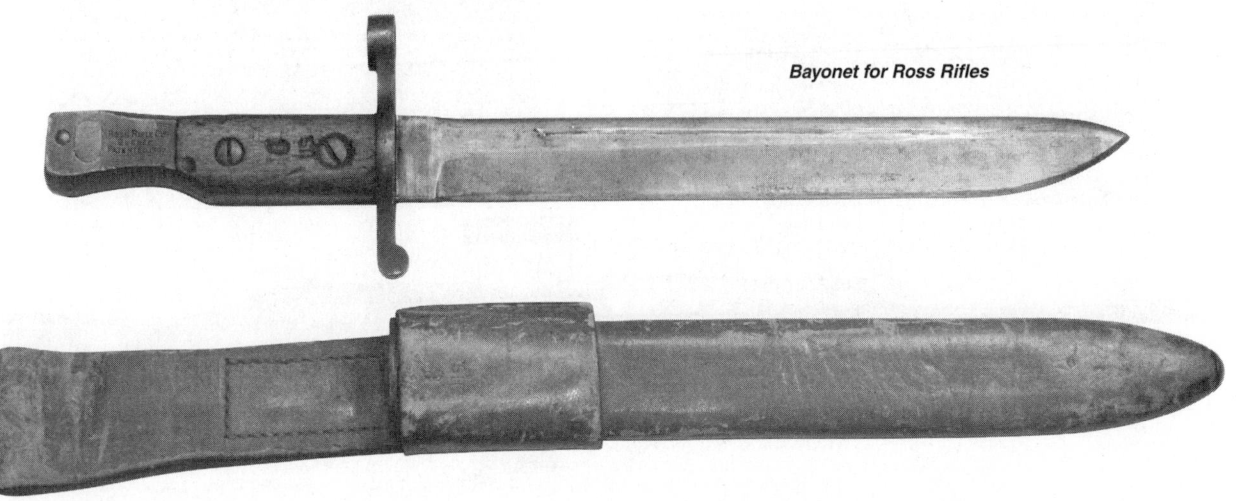

Winchester Model 1894 Carbine • *Courtesy Rock Island Auction Company*

Rifle No. 4 Mark I (T) & Mark I* (T)

These are sniper versions of the No. 4 Mark I and the Mark I*. Fitted with scope mounts on the left side of the receiver and a wooden cheekpiece screwed to the buttstock. A No. 32 or a No. 67 (Canadian) telescope was issued with these rifles. A few, estimated to be about 100, were fitted with U.S. Lyman scopes. Many of these rifles were converted by Holland & Holland. About 25,000 rifles using various telescopes were converted.

Exc.	***V.G.***	***Good***	***Fair***	***Poor***
3500	2800	2500	1500	1000

NOTE: Prices above are for rifles in original wood case and scope numbered to the rifle. Deduct 10 percent if scope mount does not match the rifle. For rifles without case deduct 10 percent. For a rifle without the scope and rings but with cheek piece and scope bases deduct 75 percent.

Winchester Model 1894 Carbine

This is the Canadian military version of the Winchester saddle ring carbine. Fitted with a 20-inch barrel and chambered for the .30-30 cartridge. Extra set of sling swivels added to left side of buttstock and forearm. Stamped with the Canadian "Broad Arrow" (an arrow inside the letter C).

Exc.	V.G.	Good	Fair	Poor
1750	1500	950	450	250

FABRIQUE NATIONALE

C1/C1A1 (FN FAL)

Canada was one of the first countries to adopt the FN-FAL rifle. This is a semi-automatic version with 21-inch barrel. Twenty-round box magazine. The rear sight on the C1 is a revolving disk with five different sized openings. Ranges calibrated from 200 to 600 yards; numbered 2 to 6 on the sight. The sight may be folded when not in use. Weight is about 9.5 lbs. About 1959 the C1 was modified to use a 2-piece firing pin and a plastic carry handle replaced the wooden type. Both types of rifles utilize the long prong flash hider on the muzzle. The author could find no indication that any of these were ever legally imported to the U.S. as a semi-automatic. It would have to be in the same class as the FN FAL "G" series as the receiver is capable of accepting select fire parts.

For C1/C1A1 registered as NFA firearms:

Pre-1986

Exc.	***V.G.***	***Fair***
18500	15000	10000

C2/C2A1

This is Canada's version of the FN heavy barrel Squad Light Automatic Rifle. Select fire with a rate of fire of about 700 rounds per minute. Barrel length is 21 inches. Magazine capacity is 30 rounds. Weight is approximately 15 lbs. Built by Long Branch Arsenal, Ontario.

Pre-1986

Exc.	***V.G.***	***Fair***
18500	15000	12500

C7/C8 (M16A2)

In 1985 the Canadian firm of Diemaco began producing a Canadian version of the Colt M16A2 rifle. There are differences between the Colt-built M16

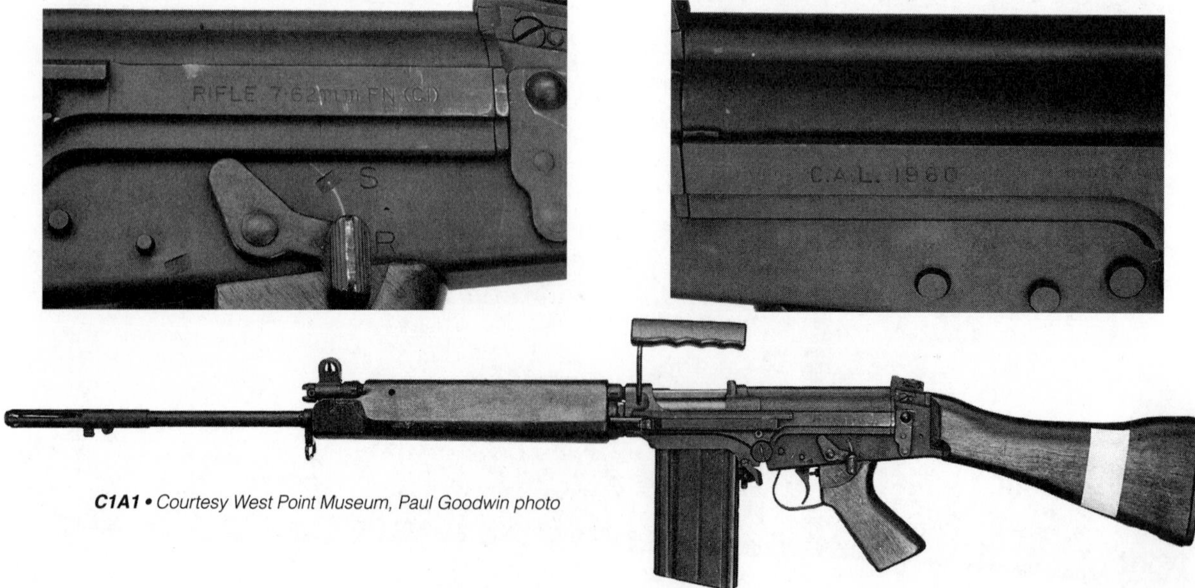

C1A1 • *Courtesy West Point Museum, Paul Goodwin photo*

Inglis Bren Mk I • *Courtesy Blake Stevens, The Bren Gun Saga, Dugelby*

and the Diemaco version. However, due to import restrictions on Class 3 weapons, no Diemaco M16s were imported into the U.S. for transferable civilian sale. Therefore, no Diemaco lowers are available to the civilian collector. There are Diemaco uppers in the U.S. that will fit on Colt lowers. The 20-inch rifle version is designated the C7 while the 16-inch carbine version is called the C8. There are a number of other Diemaco Canadian uppers that may be seen in the U.S., such as the LMG and 24-inch barreled versions. Values should be comparable to those of Colt uppers.

MACHINE GUNS

NOTE: Canada used the Lewis and Vickers machine guns during World War II. The Toronto firm of John Inglis produced Mark I and Mark II Bren guns in .303 caliber in large quantities for British and Canadian troops. Beginning in 1943 Canada produced almost 60 percent of the total Bren gun production for World War II. This amounted to about 186,000 guns produced during the war. Canada also uses the Browning Model 1919A4, called the C1 machine gun in 7.62mm (.308) as its primary light machine gun.

See Great Britain Machine Guns, Bren.

Canadian Bren Mk I and Mk II

The first examples of the Canadian Bren were built in 1940 by the Inglis Company. A total of 186,000 Brens were built in Canada with 56,000 going to the Canadian army. Marked with the date and manufacturer (Inglis) on the right side of the receiver.

Pre-1968

Exc.	*V.G.*	*Fair*
45000	42500	40000

Pre-1986 mfg with reweld receiver

Exc.	*V.G.*	*Fair*
25000	22500	20000

Canadian Chinese Bren Mk II

Full production of Mk II Bren guns in 7.62x57mm began in January of 1944 and ended in 1945. These guns were produced under a Chinese contract. About 39,300 of these guns are marked with Chinese characters and Inglis with the date of manufacture. Some 3,700 guns were sent to resistance groups in Europe. These were not marked in Chinese, but marked with "CH" prefix serial numbers. A few of these guns were converted to .308 for Canadian use.

Pre-1968 (Very Rare)

Exc.	*V.G.*	*Fair*
45000	42500	40000

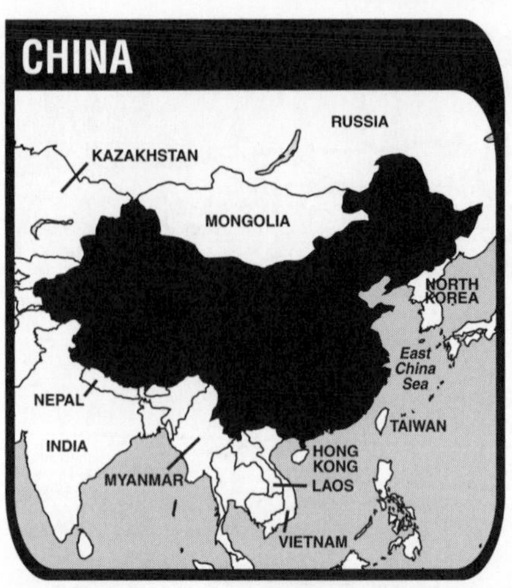

The Peoples Republic of China, located in eastern Asia, has an area of 3,696,100 sq. mi. (9,596,960 sq. km.) (including Manchuria and Tibet) and a population of *1.20 billion. Capital: Peking (Beijing). The economy is based on agriculture, mining, and manufacturing. Textiles, clothing, metal ores, tea and rice are exported.

China's ancient civilization began in east-central Henan's Huayang county, 2800-2300 B.C. The warring feudal states comprising early China were first united under Emperor Ch'in Shih (246-210 B.C.) who gave China its name and first central government. Subsequent dynasties alternated brilliant cultural achievements with internal disorder until the Empire was brought down by the revolution of 1911, and the Republic of China installed in its place. Chinese culture attained a pre-eminence in art, literature and philosophy, but a traditional backwardness in industry and administration ill prepared China for the demands of 19th century Western expansionism which exposed it to military and political humiliations, and mandated a drastic revision of political practice in order to secure an accommodation with the modern world.

The Republic of 1911 barely survived the stress of World War I, and was subsequently all but shattered by the rise of nationalism and the emergence of the Chinese Communist movement. Moscow, which practiced a policy of cooperation between Communists and other parties in movements for national liberation, sought to establish an entente between the Chinese Communist Party and the Kuomintang ('National Peoples Party') of Sun Yat-sen. The ensuing cooperation was based on little more than the hope each had of using the other.

An increasingly uneasy association between the Kuomintang and the Chinese Communist Party developed and continued until April 12, 1927, when Chiang Kai-shek, Sun Yat-sen's political heir, instituted a bloody purge to stamp out the Communists within the Kuomintang and the government and virtually paralyzed their ranks throughout China. Some time after the mid-1927 purges, the Chinese Communist Party turned to armed force to resist Chiang Kai-shek and during the period of 1930-34 acquired control over large parts of Kiangsi (Jiangxi), Fukien (Fujian), Hunan and Hupeh (Hubei). The Nationalist Nanking government responded with a series of campaigns against the soviet power bases and, by October of 1934, succeeded in driving the remnants of the Communist army to a refuge in Shensi (Shaanxi) Province. There the Communists reorganized under the leadership of Mao Tse-tung, defeated the Nationalist forces, and on Sept. 21, 1949, established the Peoples Republic of China. Thereafter relations between Russia and Communist China steadily deteriorated until 1958, when China emerged as an independent center of Communist power.

HANDGUNS

MAUSER

Mauser C96

Between the two world wars, the Chinese military purchased a number of Mauser 1896 pistols directly from Mauser and other commercial sources. These purchases consisted mainly of Bolos and Model 1930s. Some of these pistols are marked with Chinese characters; many are not. The Chinese government purchased a large quantity of Mauser pistols directly from Mauser and continued to do so until they began purchasing Browning Hi-Power pistols from FN in the mid 1930s.

The Chinese also made their own copies of Mauser broomhandles as well as Spanish copies. Some of the more commonly encountered varieties are listed here. In addition to these purchases, China made its own copies of the Mauser broomhandle as well as the Astra. See Germany, Handguns, Mauser for more detailed descriptions and prices.

Taku Naval Dockyard Model • *Private collection, Paul Goodwin photos*

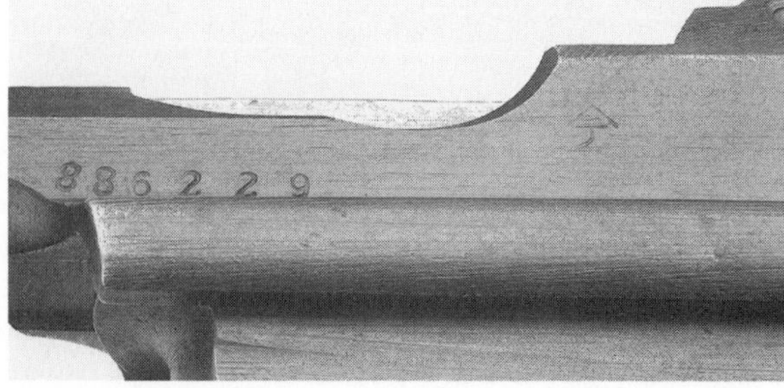

Chinese contract Mauser 1896 and 1930, standard or bolo frame. With or without Chinese markings

Many thousands of these were imported in the late 1980s and early 1990s. Many are in fair or poor condition. Bores are usually a rusted hole that a .30 caliber bullet will drop through. A few specimans in Good or VG condition might be seen. Many were rebuilt and re-finished by importers or other companies. For a re-built gun with new 7.63 or 9mm barrel, use the Good value.

Exc.	*V.G.*	*Good*	*Fair*	*Poor*
1000	600	450	300	200

Chinese Marked, Handmade Copies

Crude copies of the Model 96; unsafe to fire.

Exc.	V.G.	Good	Fair	Poor
500	400	350	250	175

Taku-Naval Dockyard Model

Approximately 6,000 copies of the Model 96 were made at the Taku-Naval Dockyard. Values listed below include a correct shoulder stock/holder.

Exc.	V.G.	Good	Fair	Poor
2500	1500	1000	500	400

Shansei Arsenal Model

Approximately 8,000 Model 96 pistols were manufactured in .45 ACP caliber at the Shansei Province Arsenal in 1929. Magazine capacity is 10 rounds.

NOTE: It has been reported that some newly made copies of the Shansei .45 were recently exported from China. Proceed with caution.

NOTE: Copies of the Model 96 were made by Unceta (Astra), Eulogio Arostegui (Azul), and Zulaica y Cia (Royal) and marketed by the firm of Beistegui Hermanos. These copies are covered in their own sections of this text.

Note the difference in size...

Standard Mauser (Small Ring)

Exc.	V.G.	Good	Fair	Poor
2000	1500	1250	800	500

CHINA STATE ARSENALS

Type 51/54 Pistol (TT33)

A 7.62mm semi-automatic pistol with a 4.5-inch barrel and 8-shot magazine. There is no safety. This model

From top to bottom: M20 export model, K54, K51 • *Courtesy Chuck Karwan*

was produced in a number of communist countries. It is essentially a Soviet Tokarev TT-33.

Exc.	V.G.	Good	Fair	Poor
650	500	400	300	200

NOTE: For cutaways add 200 percent.

Type 51/54 Pistol by Norinco

A 7.62mm semi-automatic pistol with a 4.5" barrel and 8-shot magazine. Made in the 1990s by Norinco for export to the U.S. A safety was added to comply with U.S. regulations. Also offered in 9mm or as a convertible model that came with 7.62 and 9mm barrel and magazines. Add 25 percent for two barrel set.

Exc.	V.G.	Good	Fair	Poor
275	200	175	150	125

Type 59 Makarov by Norinco

This semi-automatic pistol is similar in appearance to the Walther PP pistol and is chambered for the 9mm Makarov (9x18mm) cartridge. It has a double-action trigger and is fitted with fixed sights. Barrel length is 3.6 inches and overall length is 6.4 inches. Weight is approximately 25 oz. Magazine capacity is 8 rounds. Made for export by Norinco and imported in the early 1990s. No original Chinese issue Type 59s have been imported. If there are any here, it is

CHINA/PEOPLE'S REPUBLIC

***North Vietnamese Type 50 M** • Paul Goodwin photo*

likely they were vet "bringbacks" from Viet Nam or a later conflict.

Exc.	V.G.	Good	Fair	Poor
325	250	200	175	150

Add 100 percent for Chinese issue Type 59 without Norinco markings.

Type 80

A Chinese version of the Mauser 96 pistol chambered for the 7.63x25mm cartridge. Fitted with a 7-inch barrel and detachable 10- or 20-round magazine, this pistol is capable of select fire. Weight is approximately 40 oz. See Mauser Schnellfeuer.

SUBMACHINE GUNS

Type 43/53

This is a Chinese copy of a Soviet PPS 43 built during the Korean War.

Pre-1968

Exc.	V.G.	Fair
18500	15000	12500

Type 50

This model is a Chinese copy of the Soviet PPSh-41 submachine gun. It is chambered for the 7.62 Soviet pistol cartridge. Barrel is 10.5" and magazine capacity is 25, 32, or 40 rounds. Rate of fire is 600 rounds per minute. Weight is approximately 7.5 lbs. Markings are located on top of the receiver.

Pre-1968

Exc.	V.G.	Fair
18500	15500	12500

North Vietnamese K-50M

Similar to the Type 50 but unlike the Soviet model, this gun features a telescoping metal stock and no muzzle compensator.

Pre-1968

Exc.	V.G.	Fair
18500	15000	13000

RIFLES

Chinese Pre-Cartridge Era Rifles

Imperial Chinese Arsenals were copying European firearms since the early 1800s. There is very little information available on Chinese arms production of this era. Much Chinese territory was held as colonies by European powers and the weapons used would have been those from the parent nation.

MAUSER

Mauser Rifles

The Chinese used a wide variety of Mauser rifles from the Gew 71 to the Chinese Model 1924. Some of these are marked with Chinese characters and others are not. Many thousands of Mausers were imported from China in the 1980s and early 1990s. Most of the variations listed here were included in the importation. Most of these were in Fair or Poor condition. They have been used a lot in the 50 or more years in Chinese service. Any Chinese contract Mauser in Very Good or better condition is a rare item.

For in-depth information on Chinese Mausers, see Robert W.D. Ball's, ***Mauser Military Rifles of the World***, Krause Publications.

G71 Rifle

This rifle is identical to the German model of the same designation.

Exc.	V.G.	Good	Fair	Poor
900	700	500	250	150

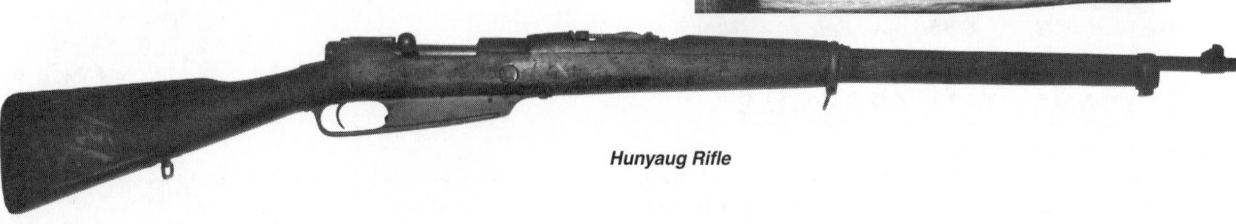

Hunyaug Rifle

K71 Carbine

This carbine is identical to the German model of the same designation.

Exc.	V.G.	Good	Fair	Poor
1250	1000	800	500	250

M1895 Rifle

This model is identical to the Chilean Model 1895 rifle.

Exc.	V.G.	Good	Fair	Poor
700	500	300	150	100

Hunyaug Rifle

This is a Chinese made rifle chambered for 8x57mm Mauser. It is a copy of the Gew-1888. The rifle does not have the barrel jacket. It was the first bolt action design manufactured in China.

Exc.	V.G.	Good	Fair	Poor
500	300	175	130	90

M1907 Rifle

This model is based on the German Model 1904. Chambered for the 7.92x57mm cartridge. Fitted with a 29-inch barrel and 5-round magazine. Tangent rear sight to 2,000 meters. Made with a pistol grip stock and upper handguard. On the receiver ring two superposed diamonds are marked with the Chinese date for rifles made in China. German built rifles will have Mauser or DWM stamped on them. Weight is about 8.25 lbs.

Exc.	V.G.	Good	Fair	Poor
800	500	250	150	100

M1907 Carbine

As above but with 21.75-inch barrel and tangent sight to 1,400 meters. Turned down bolt handle and full stock. No bayonet. Weight is about 8 lbs.

Exc.	V.G.	Good	Fair	Poor
800	500	250	150	100

M1912 Steyr Rifle

Chambered for the 7x57mm cartridge and fitted with a 28.75-inch barrel. Weight is about 9 lbs. Built in Austria.

Exc.	V.G.	Good	Fair	Poor
800	500	250	150	100

M98/22 Rifle

Manufactured by CZ in BRNO, this rifle is based on the Mexican Model 1912 with a Model 98 action. It is half cocked with a full-length upper handguard with pistol grip. Chambered for the 7.92x57mm Mauser cartridge. Barrel length is 29 inches with a 5-round integral magazine. Weight is about 9.5 lbs. China purchased about 70,000 of these rifles.

Exc.	V.G.	Good	Fair	Poor
650	450	350	200	150

FN M24 and 30 Short Rifles

Exc.	V.G.	Good	Fair	Poor
600	400	250	150	100

M21 Short Rifle

A Chinese copy of the FN Model 30 Short Rifle. Pistol grip stock with upper handguard from receiver to upper band. Chambered for the 7.92x57mm cartridge and fitted with a 23.6" barrel. Tangent rear sight to 2,000 meters. Weight is about 8.5 lbs. Chinese characters marked on the receiver ring.

Exc.	V.G.	Good	Fair	Poor
350	250	150	100	75

Chiang Kai-shek Short Rifle

Chambered for the 7.92x57mm cartridge. Fitted with a 23.6-inch barrel. Tangent rear sight to 2,000 meters. Magazine capacity is 5 rounds in a flush mounted box magazine. Weight is approximately 8.75 lbs. Chinese markings on the receiver ring. Manufactured between 1936 and 1949, this rifle became the standard issue for Chinese troops.

Exc.	V.G.	Good	Fair	Poor
500	250	150	100	75

VZ24 Short Rifle

This is the Czech Model 24 short rifle purchased from Czechoslovakia in the mid-1930s. Approximately 100,000 were purchased and all have a "P" prefix in the serial number. All are dated 1937. Many of these rifles were captured by the Japanese during World War II and issued to Japanese troops. After the war these rifles were reissued to Chinese troops.

Exc.	V.G.	Good	Fair	Poor
600	400	250	150	100

M1933 Standard Model Short Rifle

Chambered for the 7.92x57mm cartridge and fitted with a 23.6-inch barrel. Magazine capacity is 5 rounds in a flush-mounted box magazine. Tangent rear sight to 2,000 meters. Mauser banner trademark is marked on the receiver ring. Weight is about 8.75 lbs. Stock has a pistol grip and upper handguard. Straight bolt handle.

Exc.	V.G.	Good	Fair	Poor
800	600	350	175	125

M1933 Standard Model Carbine

As above but with turned down bolt handle and sling swivels mounted on left side of stock. Chambered for the 7.92x57mm cartridge but also offered in 7.65x53mm and 7x57mm. Mauser trademark on receiver ring. Weight is about 8.5 lbs.

Exc.	V.G.	Good	Fair	Poor
800	600	350	175	125

Bayonets for Chinese Mausers

China acquired bayonets along with the rifles they purchased from foreign makers. Look in the appropriate nations' listings for bayonet specifics. ***Janzens Notebook*** mentions they made some domestically but none could be documented at the time of this writing.

VZ24 with Japanese Folding Bayonet (Chinese copy)

A copy of the VZ24 and fitted with a Japanese Model 44 folding bayonet. Pistol grip stock and straight bolt handle. Barrel length is 23 inches. Chambered for the 7.92x57mm cartridge. Rear tangent sight to 2,000 meters. Chinese markings on the receiver. Weight is about 9 lbs.

Exc.	V.G.	Good	Fair	Poor
1000	700	400	250	150

Manchurian Mauser Rifle (Mukden Arsenal)

See Japan, Rifles.

Type 53 Rifle • *Courtesy West Point Museum, Paul Goodwin photo*

ARISAKA

In 1946 the Chinese obtained large numbers of Japanese Type 99 rifles. These rifles were altered to 7.92x57mm, 8x57mm, or 7.62x39mm calibers. Original Type 99 barrels were cut and re-chambered. Most parts were refinished.

Exc.	***V.G.***	***Good***	***Fair***	***Poor***
350	250	200	150	125

Type 53

This is a Chinese copy of the Soviet Model 1944 Mosin-Nagant carbine. Production began in 1953. Early models up to 1959 have Chinese characters for the model designation stamped on the receiver. Rifles made after 1959 do not have these characters. Production ended sometime in the early 1960s. Type 53s have the bolt, magazine, floorplate, and buttplate serial-numbered to the rifle. Deduct 25% for mismatched parts.

Exc.	***V.G.***	***Good***	***Fair***	***Poor***
300	225	150	75	50

Type 56 Carbine (SKS)

A 7.62x39mm semi-automatic rifle with a 20.5-inch barrel and 10-shot fixed magazine. Blued with oil finished stock. The early Chinese military issue Type 56 rifles came with a blade bayonet. Later models had the spike bayonet. Price listed is for used Type 56 made for the Chinese military. Some were brought back from Viet Nam, others were imported in the late 1980s. Add 25% for non import marked rifles.

Exc.	***V.G.***	***Good***	***Fair***	***Poor***
400	325	275	200	150

Norinco SKS

Same as above, but made for export sales to the U.S. Will have "Norinco" or other importer's name on the receiver. They have a orange-colored wood stock. At first they were imported with a spike bayonet, then the U.S. government ruled that the attached bayonet violated the "Sporting use" definition in federal law. Later importation had no mounting bracket for the bayonet.

Exc.	***V.G.***	***Good***	***Fair***	***Poor***
325	275	200	N/A	N/A

Bayonets for Type 56 SKS

After the U.S. government prohibited importation of SKS rifles with bayonets installed, the importers simply brought them in separately. Value for blade or spike is the same. Price range 25 – 10.

North Korean Type 56 Carbine (SKS)

Same overall design as the Chinese version but with high quality fit and finish. Has a gas shut off valve on the gas block. This was to allow use of a grenade launcher. Reddish-brown laminated stock. Rare.

Exc.	***V.G.***	***Good***	***Fair***	***Poor***
1400	1000	800	600	300

Chinese Type 56 Rifle

A close copy of the AK-47 and first produced in 1958, this select fire rifle is chambered for the 7.62x39mm

SKS Carbine • *Paul Goodwin photo*

Chinese Type 56-1 • *Paul Goodwin photo*

cartridge. It is fitted with a 16-inch barrel and has a magazine capacity of 30 rounds. This model has a folding bayonet hinged below the muzzle. Weight is about 8.4 lbs. Rate of fire is 600 rounds per minute. Markings on left side of receiver. Still in production. This rifle was adopted by Chinese forces and was seen in Cambodia as well.

There are a number of subvariations of the Type 56. Early guns had machined receivers with Chinese characters for selector markings, some of which are marked "M22" to designate export sales. Another style is fitted with a folding spike bayonet as well as a machined receiver. Still another style has a stamped receiver, Chinese characters for selector markings, and a folding spike bayonet. All are direct copies of the Soviet model AK-47.

Another variation of the Type 56 was the Type 56-1, which featured prominent rivets on a folding metal butt. No bayonet. Other variants of the Type 56-1 are fitted with a folding spike bayonet and folding metal buttstock. The Type 56-2 has a skeleton tubular stock which folds to the right side of the receiver with no bayonet. There is also the Type 56-C with plastic furniture, side folding butt with cheekpiece, and improved sights with no bayonet.

NOTE: Type 56 rifles manufactured by China North Industries (NORINCO) will have stamped on the left side of the receiver the number "66" in a triangle.

Pre-1968

Exc.	V.G.	Fair
32500	30000	28000

Pre-1986 conversions

Exc.	V.G.	Fair
15000	14000	13000

Type 56 (AK Clone semi-automatic versions)

Imported from China in semi-automatic versions and built by Poly Tech and Norinco in different styles and configurations, some of which are listed below. Pre-1990 imports with standard stocks, not the thumbhole "sporter" versions.

Milled Receiver—Poly Tech

Exc.	V.G.	Good	Fair	Poor
1500	1200	800	N/A	N/A

Stamped Receiver—Poly Tech

Exc.	V.G.	Good	Fair	Poor
1100	800	500	N/A	N/A

Stamped Receiver—Norinco

Exc.	V.G.	Good	Fair	Poor
950	700	450	N/A	N/A

NOTE: For folding stock version add 20 percent.

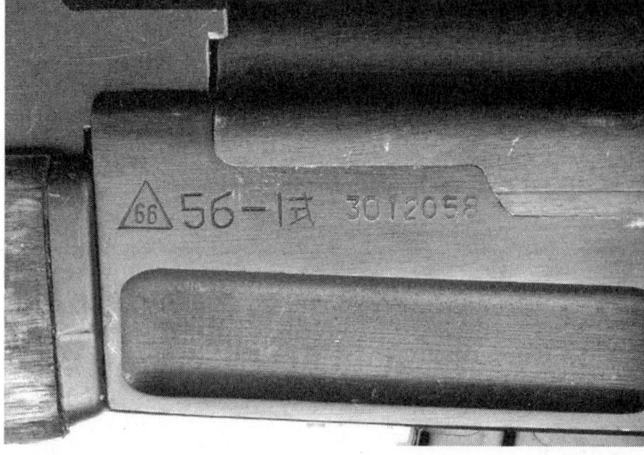

Type 79

A Chinese copy of the Soviet Dragunov SVD sniper rifle.

Exc.	V.G.	Good	Fair	Poor
3000	2500	1500	N/A	N/A

MACHINE GUNS

NOTE: See also Great Britain, Machine Guns, Bren MK2.

Type 24

A Chinese copy of the German Model 1909 commercial Maxim built under the supervision of German engineers.

Pre-1968

Exc.	V.G.	Fair
25000	18500	15000

Pre-1986 manufacture with new side plate

Exc.	V.G.	Fair
12500	11000	10000

Type 26

Czech VZ26 purchased in the 1930s.

Pre-1968

Exc.	V.G.	Fair
28000	26000	24000

Pre-1986 manufacture with new receiver or re-weld

Exc.	V.G.	Fair
20000	17500	15000

Type 53

Chinese copy of the Soviet DPM machine gun.

Pre-1968

Exc.	V.G.	Fair
20000	18000	16000

Type 53 • *Courtesy West Point Museum, Paul Goodwin photo*

Pre-1986 manufacture with new receiver or re-weld

Exc.	*V.G.*	*Fair*
10000	9000	8000

Type 54

Chinese-made variation of the Soviet DShK 38/46.

Pre-1968

Exc.	*V.G.*	*Fair*
—	35000	30000

Type 57 with mount • *Courtesy West Point Museum, Paul Goodwin photo*

Type 58 • Courtesy West Point Museum, Paul Goodwin photo

Type 56

Chinese copy of the Soviet Model RPD light machine gun.

Pre-1968 (Rare)

Exc.	V.G.	Fair
45000	37500	35000

Pre-1986 manufacture with new receiver or re-weld

Exc.	V.G.	Fair
35000	27500	25000

Type 57

Chinese copy of the Soviet SG-43.

Pre-1968

Exc.	V.G.	Fair
35000	28000	25000

Pre-1986 manufacture with new receiver or re-weld

Exc.	V.G.	Fair
28000	25000	20000

Type 58

Licensed Chinese-made copy of the Soviet RP-46.

Pre-1968

Exc.	V.G.	Fair
25000	23000	21000

Pre-1986 manufacture with new receiver or re-weld

Exc.	V.G.	Fair
10000	9000	8000

CZECHOSLOVAKIA

The Republic of Czechoslovakia, founded at the end of World War I, was part of the old Austrian-Hungarian Empire. It had an area of 49,371 sq. mi. (127,870 sq. km.) and a population of 15.6 million. Capital: Prague (Praha).

Czechoslovakia proclaimed itself a republic on Oct. 28, 1918, with Tomas G. Masaryk as President. Hitler's rise to power in Germany provoked Czechoslovakia's German minority in the Sudetenland to agitate for autonomy. At Munich (Munchen) in Sept. of 1938, France and Britain, seeking to avoid World War II, forced the cession of the Sudetenland to Germany. In March, 1939, Germany invaded Czechoslovakia and established the "protectorate of Bohemia and Moravia". Bohemia is a historic province in northwest Czechoslovakia that includes the city of Prague, one of the oldest continually occupied sites in Europe. Moravia is an area of considerable mineral wealth in central Czechoslovakia. Slovakia, a province in southeastern Czechoslovakia under Nazi influence was constituted as a republic. The end of World War II saw the re-established independence of Czechoslovakia, while bringing it within the Russian sphere of influence. On Feb. 23-25, 1948, the Communists seized control of the government in a coup d'etat, and adopted a constitution making the country a 'people's republic'. A new constitution adopted June 11, 1960, converted the country into a 'socialist republic', which lasted until 1989. On Nov. 11, 1989, demonstrations against the communist government began and in Dec. of that same year, communism was overthrown, and the Czech and Slovak Federal Republic was formed. In 1993 the CSFR split into the Czech Republic and The Republic of Slovakia.

NOTE: The term "VZ" stands for model (*Vzor*) in Czech. This abbreviation is used in place of the English word Model. The author has sometimes used both terms but never together.

HANDGUNS

Most Czech handguns are of Czech design and manufacture. See below.

Army Pistole 1922

Semi-automatic pistol chambered for the .380 ACP (9x17mm short) cartridge. Barrel length is 3.5 inches. Magazine capacity is 8 rounds. Weight is approximately 22 oz. Adopted by the Czech army in 1922 and called the M22. This was the first Czech designed and manufactured service semi-automatic pistol. It was based on a German locked breech design and made under license from Mauser. Blued with checkered plastic grips. Manufactured between 1921 and 1923. Because of production difficulties, only about 22,000 were built.

Exc.	V.G.	Good	Fair	Poor
700	550	350	200	150

CZ M1922 magazine (l) and CZ 1927 magazine marked "P Mod 27" (r). • *Price 70-30*

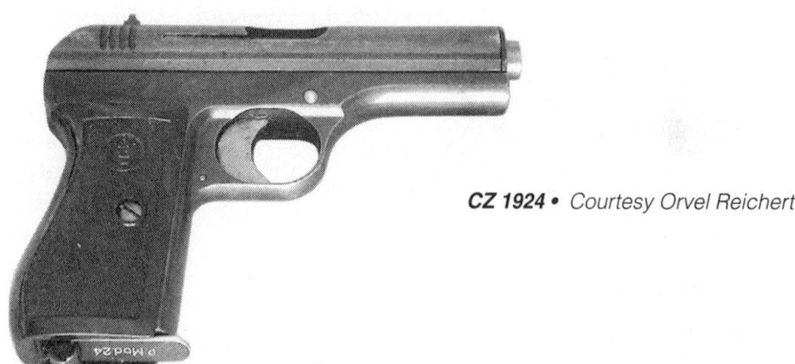

CZ 1924 • Courtesy Orvel Reichert

CZ 1924

The first large production military pistol produced by CZ. It is a locked-breech pistol with a 3.5" rotating barrel chambered for the 9mm short cartridge, external hammer, and a magazine safety. It features a rounded slide and is blued with a wrap-around walnut grip. Magazine capacity is 8 rounds. The slide is marked "Ceska Zbrojovka A.S. v Praze." Weight is approximately 24 oz. About 170,000 of these pistols were produced between 1922 and 1938.

NOTE: A limited number of pistols have been noted marked "CZ 1925" and "CZ 1926." There are various minor design changes on each model, and it is conjectured that they were prototypes that were manufactured on the road to the production of the less complicated, blowback-operated CZ 1927 pistol.

Exc.	V.G.	Good	Fair	Poor
700	475	300	200	100

NOTE: For Nazi-proofed add 50 percent.

CZ 1927

A semi-automatic pistol chambered for the 7.65mm cartridge (.32 ACP), marked the same as the CZ 1924, but the cocking grooves on the slide are cut vertically instead of sloped as on the earlier model. This model was blued with checkered, wrap-around, plastic grips. These early guns were beautifully made and marked "CESKA ZBROJOVKA AS V PRAZE."

This version remained in production during the German occupation of Czechoslovakia between 1939 and 1945. Occupation pistols are marked, "BOHMISCHE WAFFENFABRIK IM PRAG." The Germans used the code "fnh" on these wartime pistols and designated the model the "Pistole Mod 27(t)." The finish declined as the war progressed, with the very late guns rough but functional. There are several subvariations of this pistol that may affect value. A total of about 450,000 were produced during the German occupation. After the war, these pistols continued in production until 1951. There were almost 700,000 manufactured.

Early CZ 27 with Nazi production markings • Courtesy Orvel Reichert

Early CZ 27 with Nazi production markings • Courtesy Orvel Reichert

Exc.	V.G.	Good	Fair	Poor
500	375	250	200	150

NOTE: For Nazi-proofed add 25 percent.

NOTE: Some of these pistols were made with an extended barrel for the use of a silencer. This variation brings a large premium. Fewer than 10 CZ 27s were made in .22 caliber.

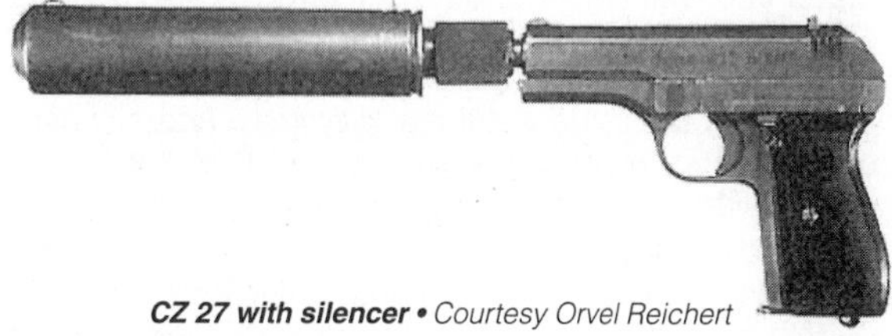

CZ 27 with silencer • Courtesy Orvel Reichert

Holster for CZ-27

WWII vintage leather construction. Magazine pouch on front. Wide belt loop on back. Black or brown. Some have Nazi markings on the inside of the flap. Add 50% for Nazi markings.

Exc.	V.G.	Good	Fair	Poor
100	75	50	25	n/a

Holster for CZ-27

Wartime CZ 27 with Nazi production markings • *Courtesy Orvel Reichert*

CZ 1938

It is chambered for the 9mm short cartridge (.380 Auto) and has a 4.65-inch barrel. Except for a few examples with a conventional sear and slide safety, it is double action-only with exposed hammer, and difficult to fire accurately. It utilizes a 9-round, detachable box magazine; and the slide is hinged at the muzzle to pivot upward for ease of cleaning and disassembly. It is well made and well finished, but is as large in size as most 9mm Parabellum pistols. Production began in 1938, and the Germans adopted it as the "Pistole Mod 39" on paper; but it is doubtful that any were actually used by the German army. It now appears that the P39(t), which is the Nazi designation, were all sent to Finland and a large number with "SA" (Finnish) markings have recently been surplused along with their holsters. A few SA marked guns have been modified by the Finnish army to function single or double action. About 40,000 of these pistols were manufactured.

Exc.	V.G.	Good	Fair	Poor
750	600	450	250	175

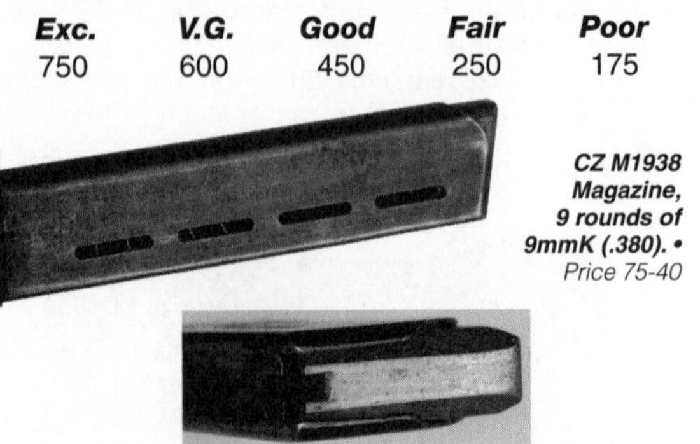

CZ M1938 Magazine, 9 rounds of 9mmK (.380). • *Price 75-40*

CZ 1938 Nazi-Proofed (P39[t])

Fewer than 1,000 of these pistols were Nazi-proofed late in the war. E/WaA76 acceptance stamp on left frame and barrel.

Exc.	V.G.	Good	Fair	Poor
1900	1600	1250	600	300

CZ 1950

This is a blowback-operated, semi-automatic, double action pistol chambered for the 7.65mm cartridge with a 3.75-model barrel. Magazine capacity is 8 rounds. Weight is about 23 oz. It is patterned after the Walther Model PP with a few differences. The safety catch is located on the frame instead of the slide; and the triggerguard is not hinged, as on the Walther. It is dismantled by means of a catch on the side of the frame. Although intended to be a military pistol designed by the Kratochvil brothers, it proved to be underpowered and was adopted by the police. There were few released on the commercial market.

CZ 1950 • *Courtesy Chuck Karwan*

Exc.	V.G.	Good	Fair	Poor
300	200	150	100	75

Model 1970

This model was an attempt to correct dependability problems with the Model 50. There is little difference to see externally between the two except for markings and the grip pattern. Markings are "VZOR 70 CAL 7.65." Production began during the 1960s and ended in 1983.

CZ M1970 • *Courtesy Rock Island Auction Company*

Exc.	V.G.	Good	Fair	Poor
275	200	150	100	75

CZ 1952

Since the Czechoslovakian army was not happy with the underpowered CZ 1950 pistol, they began using Soviet weapons until 1952, when this model was designed. It was designed for a new cartridge known as the 7.62mm M48. It was similar to the Soviet cartridge but loaded to a higher velocity. This is a single action, semi-automatic pistol with a 4.5-inch barrel. It has a locked breech that utilizes two roller cams. Magazine capacity is 8 rounds. Many refurbished and original pistols were imported into the U.S. beginning around 2004.

Exc.	V.G.	Good	Fair	Poor
300	125	100	75	65

CZ 75

Introduced in 1975. 4.5-inch barrel. 9mm 15 round magazine. Offered in both commercial and military versions the CZ 75 is used by more than 60 countries around the world in 9mm. Approximately 1,250,000 military pistols are in service. The Czechs use the pistol in their Special Forces units. The CZ-75 was banned from import to the U.S. until 1994 when the U.S. relaxed the ban on imports of firearms from former communist countries. A few early commercial models were imported by law enforcement officers before 1994, thanks to an exception in the import rules. These brought a premium price at the time. Frequently in the 700-800 range. The popularity of the CZ-75 design inspired copies to be made in Switzerland, Italy and Israel. These were imported to the U.S. beginning in the mid 1980s. To the author's knowledge, no military issue CZ-75s have appeared on the U.S. market. Price for current commercial CZ-75B, basic model. Black finish, fixed sights. Many options and finishes are available.

NIB	Exc.	V.G.	Good	Fair	Poor
500	400	350	N/A	N/A	N/A

CZ 82/83

This is a fixed-barrel .380 caliber pistol. It features an ambidextrous safety and magazine catch behind the triggerguard. The pistol is stripped by means of a hinged triggerguard. Barrel length is 3.8 inches, overall length is 6.8 inches, and weight is about 23 oz.

The Model 82 designation is the military model, while the Model 83 is the commercial version. The Model 83 is offered in two calibers: 9x18 Makarov, and .380. The military Model 82 is offered in only one caliber, the 9mm Makarov. The Model 82 is the side arm of the Czech army. The Model 82 is no longer in production, but the Model 83 is currently manufactured.

NIB	Exc.	V.G.	Good	Fair	Poor
350	250	200	175	150	125

SUBMACHINE GUNS

The Czechs built the CZ 247 and the CZ 47 after World War II, but did not adopt these guns for their own military use. Instead they were exported to South America and other countries. These submachine guns are chambered for the 9mm Parabellum cartridge and are similar in appearance to the CZ 1938 gun but with a 40-round magazine.

CZ 23/25

The Model 23 has a wooden stock while the Model 25 has a folding metal stock; otherwise all other dimensions are the same. Introduced in 1948, this submachine gun is chambered for the 9mm cartridge. Magazine capacity is 25- or 40-round box type. Rate of fire is about 600 rounds per minute. Weight is approximately 8 to 8.5 lbs., depending on model. This gun introduced the hollow bolt that allows for the short length of the gun (17.5 inches with butt folded, 27 inches with butt extended) and was copied in the Uzi. The magazine well is located in the pistol grip, another feature copied by the UZI. The trigger mechanism is designed so that light pressure gives semi-automatic fire while full trigger pressure gives full automatic fire. Weight of the gun is about 7 lbs. A variation of this model is called the Model 24/26 and is the same except for the caliber: 7.62mm.

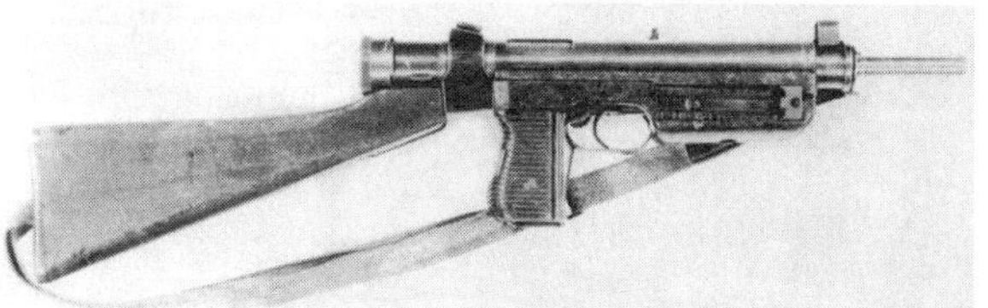

Courtesy Thomas Nelson, *The World's Submachine Guns, Vol. 1*

NOTE: Prices listed are estimates only.

Pre-1968

Exc.	V.G.	Fair
12500	11000	10000

ZK 383

This submachine gun was first introduced in 1933. It is chambered for the 9mm Parabellum cartridge and fitted with a 12.8-inch quick change barrel with jacket. Adjustable rate of fire from 500 to 700 rounds per minute by means of a removable insert in the bolt. This model was fitted with a bipod. Rear sight is a V-notch tangent graduated to 800 meters. Weight is about 9.5 lbs. This gun was sold to Bulgaria, some South American countries, and was used by the German army from 1938 to 1945.

ZK 383 • *Courtesy Thomas Nelson, The World's Submachine Guns, Vol. 1*

A variation of this model called the ZK 383P was used by police units and does not have a bipod or quick change barrel. The ZK 383H was a limited production version with a folding magazine housing fitted to the bottom of the gun rather than the side.

Pre-1968

Exc.	***V.G.***	***Fair***
14000	13000	12000

Skorpion Samopal VZ61

Introduced in 1960 this weapon is sometimes referred to as a machine pistol because of its size. Chambered for the 7.65x17SR Browning (.32 ACP) cartridge. Export models of this gun are chambered for the 9x17mm (.380 ACP[VZ63]), 9x18mm Makarov (VZ64), and the 9x19mm Parabellum (VZ68). The gun has a 4.5-inch barrel and is fitted with a wooden pistol grip. Overall length with butt folded is 10.5 inches; with butt extended 20.5 inches. Weight is approximately 3 lbs. Rate of fire is about 700 rounds per minute. A licensed copy made in Yugoslavia is called the Model 84. No transferable examples known.

Pre-1968

Exc.	***V.G.***	***Fair***
N/A	N/A	N/A

CZ USA Vz 61 Skorpion semi automatic handgun

New commercial production semi automatic version of the Vz-61 using some original parts as well as American made parts. Cal. 7.65mm/.32 automatic. 4.5-inch barrel.

Exc.	***V.G.***	***Good***	***Fair***	***Poor***
800	700	500	n/a	n/a

RIFLES

Immediately after WWI the Czechs continued to use the Mannlicher Model 1895 rifle until 1924 when they began production of their own Mauser action rifles.

Mauser

Ceskoslovensha Zbrojovaka (ZB), Brno

NOTE: In 1924 the Czechs began to manufacture a number of Mauser-designed rifles for export, and for its own military use. Czech Mausers were based on the Model 98 action. Many of these rifles were sold to other

Skorpion • *Courtesy West Point Museum,* Paul Goodwin photo

countries and will be found under Germany, Mauser, Rifles.

NOTE: Prices are for rifles with matching numbers and original markings. Most recent imports have mismatched bolts. Many have receiver markings ground off. Deduct 50 percent for mismatch or recent ground imports.

M1898/22 Rifle

Manufactured by CZ in Brno this rifle is based on the Mexican Model 1912 with a Model 98 action. It is half stocked with a full-length upper handguard with pistol grip. Chambered for the 7.92x57mm Mauser cartridge. Barrel length is 29 inches with a 5-round integral magazine. Weight is about 9.5 lbs. This rifle was used by Turkey as well as other countries.

Courtesy Rock Island Auction Company

Exc.	V.G.	Good	Fair	Poor
600	400	250	150	100

VZ23 Short Rifle

Used by the Czech army this 7.92x57mm rifle was fitted with a 21.5-inch barrel and 5-round magazine. Tangent leaf rear sight graduated to 2,000 meters. Most were marked, "CZECHOSLOVAKIAN FACTORY FOR ARMS MANUFACTURE, BRNO" on the receiver ring. Weight is about 9 lbs.

Exc.	V.G.	Good	Fair	Poor
800	600	350	175	100

VZ12/33 Carbine

This rifle was produced primarily for export. It has a pistol grip stock with ¾-length upper handguard and two barrel bands fairly close together. Bolt handle is bent down. Barrel length is 21.5-inch with 5-round magazine. Rear leaf sight is graduated to 1,400 meters. Weight is about 8 lbs. Country crest stamped on receiver.

Exc.	V.G.	Good	Fair	Poor
800	650	400	250	100

VZ16/33 Carbine

Designed for paramilitary units this rifle has a 19.25-inch barrel. Chambered for the 7.92x57mm cartridge as well as other calibers depending on country. Magazine capacity is 5 rounds. Tangent rear leaf sight graduated to 1,000 meters. Czech crest stamped on receiver ring. This rifle formed the basis on the German Model 33/40 paratroop carbine used during WWII.

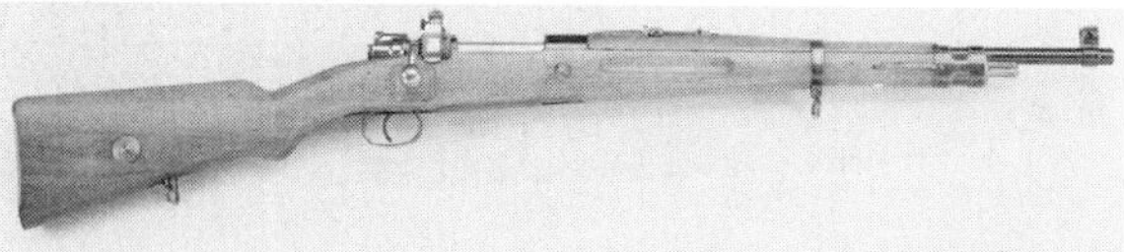

Courtesy Cherry's Fine Guns

Exc.	V.G.	Good	Fair	Poor
950	800	650	300	200

CZECH STATE

Ceskoslovenska Zbrojovka Brno (BRNO) was established in 1919 as the state arms factory. It was originally state owned but later, in 1924, was reorganized as a limited liability company.

M1895

The Czechs built about 5,000 of these Mannlicher rifles.

Exc.	V.G.	Good	Fair	Poor
600	400	250	150	100

Model 24 (VZ24)

This rifle marks the first Czech produced military rifle for the Czech army. It was based on the Mauser 98 action. The rifle was in wide use by other countries such as Germany prior to WWII. Chambered for the 7.92mm cartridge and fitted with a 23-inch barrel, this model had a 5-round non-detachable box magazine. The rear sight was graduated from 300 to 2,000 meters in 100 meter increments. Weight is about 9 lbs.

Exc.	V.G.	Good	Fair	Poor
650	450	275	150	100

Bayonet for Czech VZ 24 and other Mausers

Wood handle. 11.75-inch single edge blade. The cutting edge is to the top. Most have a muzzle ring, but these were sometimes removed. Cross piece has two rivets. Marked on the blade "CSZ" and possibly a Czech lion and date. Price range 60 – 20.

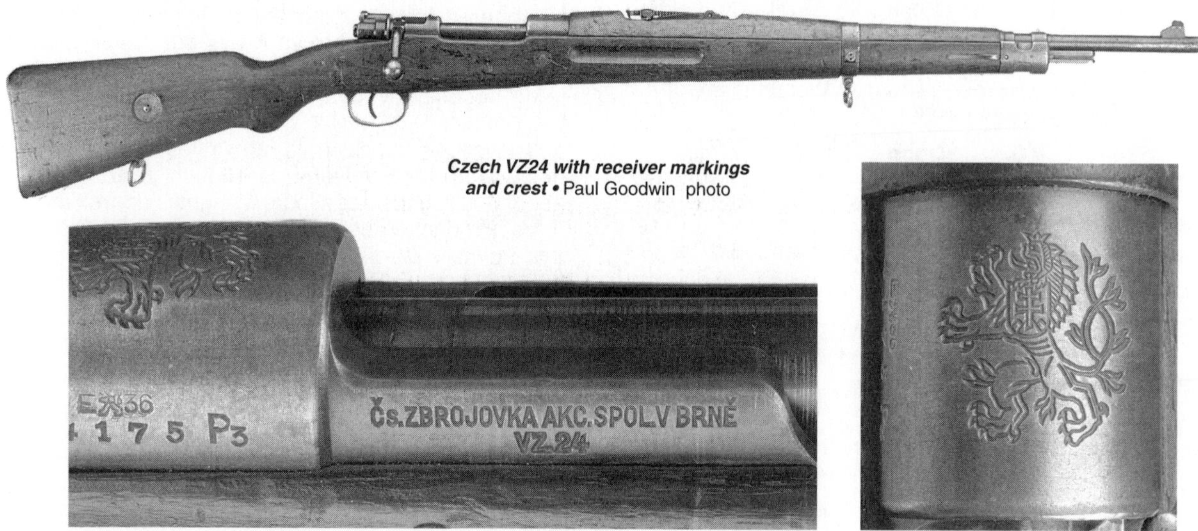

Czech VZ24 with receiver markings and crest • Paul Goodwin photo

CZECHOSLOVAKIA

Bayonet for Czech VZ24

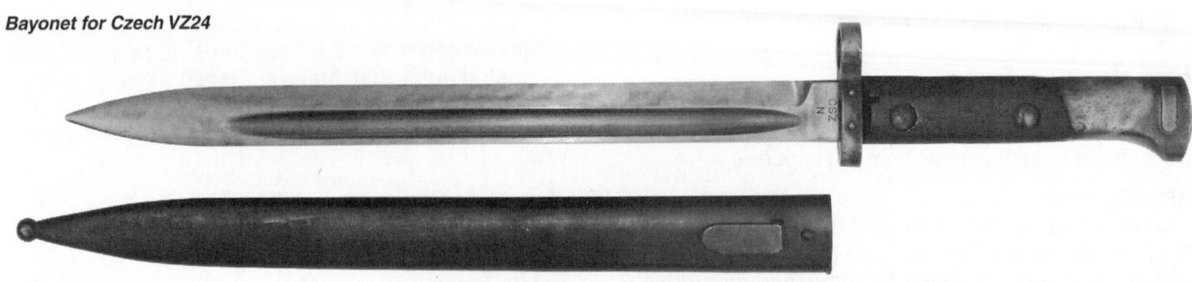

Model ZH29

Introduced in 1929, this semi-automatic rifle was designed by Emmanuel Holek of CZ at Brno. It is chambered for the 7.92x57mm cartridge and is fitted with a 21.5-inch barrel with aluminum cooling jacket. Fitted with a bayonet lug. The detachable box magazine has a 10- or 25-round capacity. Weight is about 10 lbs. Exported to Thailand and Ethiopia. Very rare.

Courtesy Thomas Nelson, *The World's Submachine Guns, Vol. 1*

Exc.	V.G.	Good	Fair	Poor
13500	10500	7500	—	—

Model ZK420S

Chambered for the 7.92x57mm cartridge this rifle was first introduced in 1942 but did not appear in its final form until 1946. It was also offered in 7mm, .30-06, and 7.5mm Swiss. This was a gas operated semi-automatic rifle with 21-inch barrel and upper handguard. The detachable magazine has a 10-round capacity. Front sight is hooded. Rear sight is notched tangent with ramp. Weight is about 10 lbs. Not adopted by Czech military but tested by many countries. Built by CZ Brno in limited numbers. Very rare.

Exc.	V.G.	Good	Fair	Poor
10500	9000	8000	—	—

Model 52

Chambered for 7.62x45 caliber, this gas operated semi-automatic rifle is fitted with a 20.5-inch barrel. This model has a full stock with pistol grip. Folding non-detachable bayonet. Hooded front sight and notched tangent rear sight with ramp. Detachable box magazine with 10-round capacity. Weight is about 9.7 lbs. First produced in 1952.

Exc.	V.G.	Good	Fair	Poor
500	400	350	275	225

Model 52/57

Similar to the Model 52 except chambered for the 7.62x39 cartridge.

Courtesy Thomas Nelson, *The World's Submachine Guns, Vol. 1*

Exc.	V.G.	Good	Fair	Poor
750	600	450	300	250

Model 1957 Sniper Rifle

This rifle, introduced in 1954, is built on a Mosin Nagant 1891/30 action and fitted with a 28.7-inch barrel chambered for the 7.62x54mmR cartridge. Magazine capacity is 5 rounds. Half stock with pistol grip and handguard. Rifle is supplied with a 2.5x telescope. Weight is approximately 9.5 lbs. Built by CZ in Brno. Production ended in 1957. Deduct 50 percent if there is no scope.

Exc.	V.G.	Good	Fair	Poor
1250	1000	850	600	400

VZ58

First produced in 1959, this select fire assault rifle is chambered for the 7.62x39mm Soviet cartridge. Its appearance is similar to an AK-47 but it is an entirely different design. It is gas operated but the bolt is locked to the receiver by a vertically moving block similar to the Walther P-38 pistol. Early rifles were fitted with a plastic fixed stock while later rifles used a folding metal stock. Barrel length is 16-inch. Rate of fire is about 800 rounds per minute. Weight is approximately 7 lbs. Production ceased in 1980. Made at CZ Brno and Povaske Strojarne. The two versions of this gun are designated the VZ58P with fixed stock and the VZ58V for metal folding stock.

Pre-1968

Exc.	V.G.	Fair
18000	15000	12000

VZ 58 Military Sporter, semi-automatic

Limited importation by CZ USA. Offered with standard or folding stock.

Exc.	V.G.	Good	Fair	Poor
1000	800	700	n/a	n/a

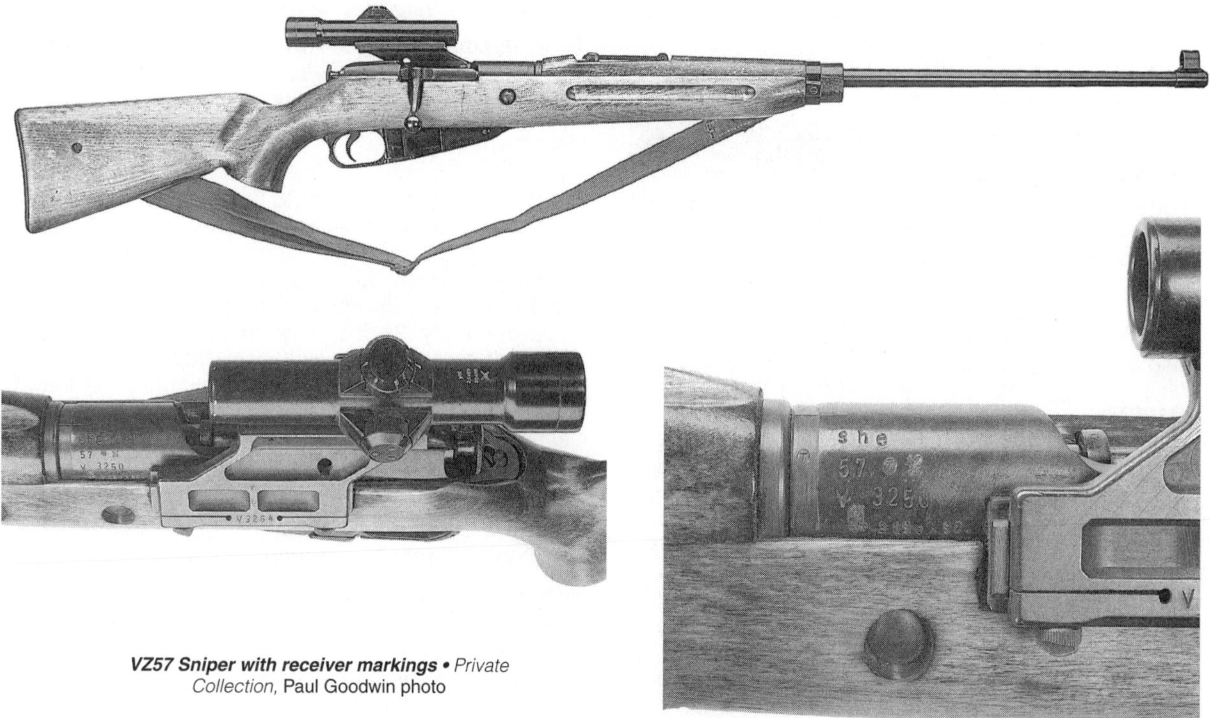

VZ57 Sniper with receiver markings • *Private Collection,* Paul Goodwin photo

VZ58 with receiver markings • *Courtesy West Point Museum,* Paul Goodwin photo

CZECHOSLOVAKIA

VZ 58 semi-automatic (new production)

Limited production by Ohio Ordnance Works. Built from original parts on a U.S.-made semi-automatic receiver.

Exc.	*V.G.*	*Good*
1500	1250	N/A

MACHINE GUNS

The Czechs used the Steyr-built Schwarzlose Model 7/24 adopted to 7.92mm immediately after World War I. Czechoslovakia has also used the Soviet SG43 and the Soviet DT. Today the Czech army uses the ZB 59 as its primary machine gun. The ZB 59 is called a universal machine gun when mounted on a bipod. It is also used by the Czech military with a light barrel.

ZB VZ26

Manufactured by CZ Brno, this weapon is a light air-cooled gas-operated select-fire machine gun chambered for the 7.92x57mm Mauser cartridge. Fitted with a 23.7-inch finned barrel, it has a rate of fire of 500 rounds per minute. It is fed by a 20- or 30-round box magazine. Bipod and carry handle standard. Wooden butt with pistol grip. Quick change barrel. It was adopted by over two dozen countries around the world. It was the forerunner of the famous British Bren gun (model designation ZGB33). Produced from 1925 to 1945. On left side of receiver marked "brno," and on right side marked "LEHKY KULOMET ZB VZ26." Weight is about 21 lbs. This gun was, and still is, used in large numbers throughout the world.

ZB made small improvements to the VZ26 along with the date of the improvements. These guns are essentially the same as the ZB 26, but are known as the ZB VZ27 and VZ28.

Pre-1968

Exc.	*V.G.*	*Fair*
35000	32500	30000

Pre-1986 manufacture with new receiver or re-weld

Exc.	*V.G.*	*Fair*
25000	23000	20000

ZB VZ30

This weapon has an outward appearance almost identical to that of the VZ26 but with the exception of a new bolt movement design different from the VZ26. It has a 26.5" finned barrel and uses a 30-round top mounted straight box magazine. The rate of fire is about 600 rounds per minute. Weight of the gun is approximately 21 lbs. This model was adopted by China, Spain, and Iran. Between 1939 and 1945 it was also used by the German army. A variation of the ZB VZ30 is the ZB VZ30J (Yugoslavian or Venezuelan) similar to the VZ30 but with a heavy knurled portion of the barrel at the breech end.

Pre-1968

Exc.	*V.G.*	*Fair*
20000	18500	17000

ZGB VZ30 (VZ32/33/34)

Same as the VZ30 but modified to fire the British .303 cartridge. Uses a curved 20-round magazine to accommodate the .303 cartridge. Improved versions of this gun are known as the VZ32, the VZ33, and the VZ34. These later versions use a 30-round magazine and a slightly shorter barrel. Reduced rate of fire to 500 rounds per minute.

Pre-1968

Exc.	*V.G.*	*Fair*
25000	20000	18000

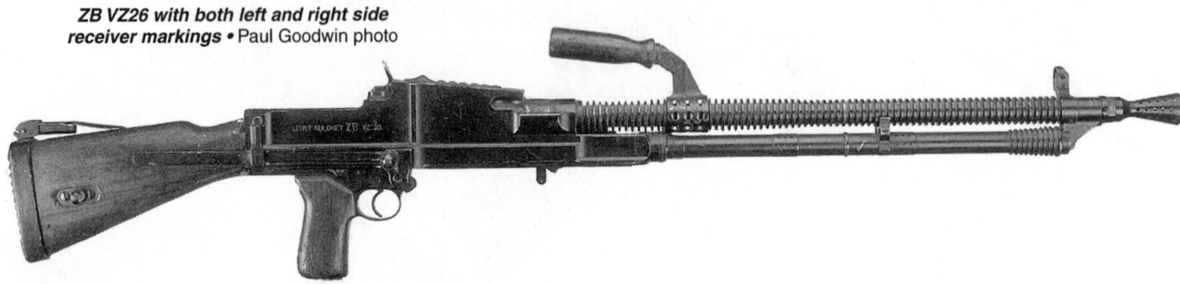

ZB VZ26 with both left and right side receiver markings • Paul Goodwin photo

ZB VZ37 (Model 53 for export)

Introduced in 1937 this gun was designed as a medium air-cooled machine gun chambered for the 7.92x57mm cartridge. The finned barrel was 26.5 inches in length. Uses a 100- or 200-round metal belt. Grips mounted under the receiver with trigger. Rate of fire was either 500 or 700 rounds per minute. Weight is approximately 40 lbs. This gun is usually tripod mounted. A number of these guns were supplied to Viet Cong and North Vietnamese forces during the 1960s. Some 4,000 were sold to Israel in 1949. Many more were exported to the Middle East and Africa.

Pre-1968 (Very Rare)

Exc.	*V.G.*	*Fair*
30000	25000	22000

ZB 39

In 1939 the Czechs exported a small number (est. fewer than 100) of this gun to Bulgaria in 8x56R Austrian Mannlicher caliber. This gun is stamped with the Bulgarian crest and other markings. The gun is fitted with a forward sling swivel, a ring-mounted extension around the wrist of the stock, and a different compact sight mounting system is used. Some examples are found in .303 caliber and it is thought that these examples come from South Africa.

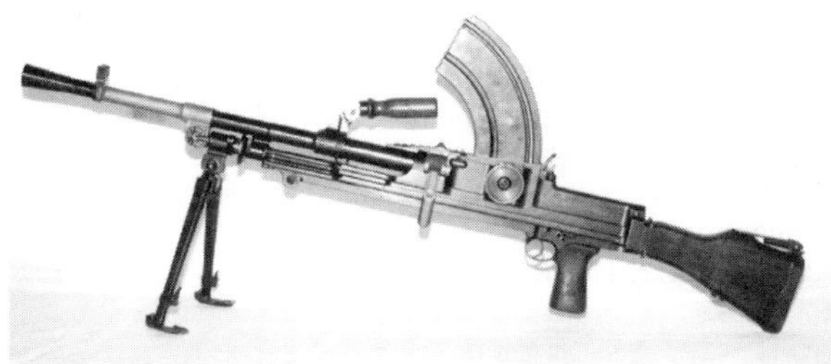

VZ39 Export Gun • *Courtesy Robert E. Naess*

Pre-1968

Extremely rare; only one transferable example known.

VZ52/57

This gun is based on the ZB VZ30. It is chambered for the 7.62x39 rimless cartridge (Warsaw Pact). The gun was originally chambered for the 7.62x45 rimless cartridge (VZ52). Barrel length is 27 inches and is quick-change. It is fed by a 100-round belt or 25-round detachable box magazine. Rate of fire is 900 rounds per minute with box magazine and about 1,100 rounds per minute with belt. Weight is about 17.5 lbs. with bipod. This is a select-fire weapon with the finger pressure on the trigger determining full auto or single-round fire. The gun was introduced in 1952. This gun is often seen in Central America.

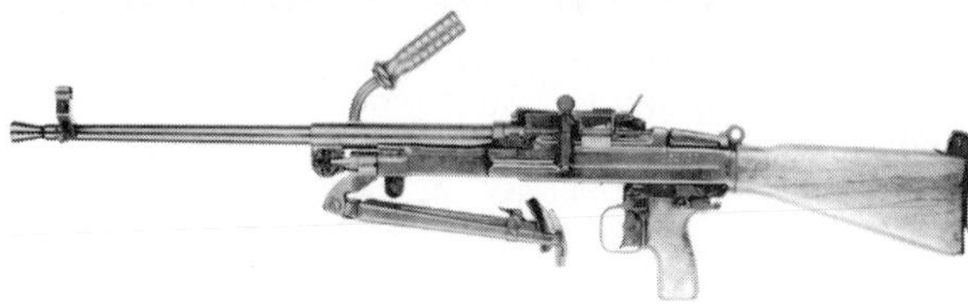

Pre-1968 (Very Rare)

Exc.	*V.G.*	*Fair*
40000	35000	25000

Model 07/24 Schwarzlose

This is a Czech-built Schwarzlose chambered for the 7.92 cartridge.

Pre-1968

Extremely rare; only one transferable example known.

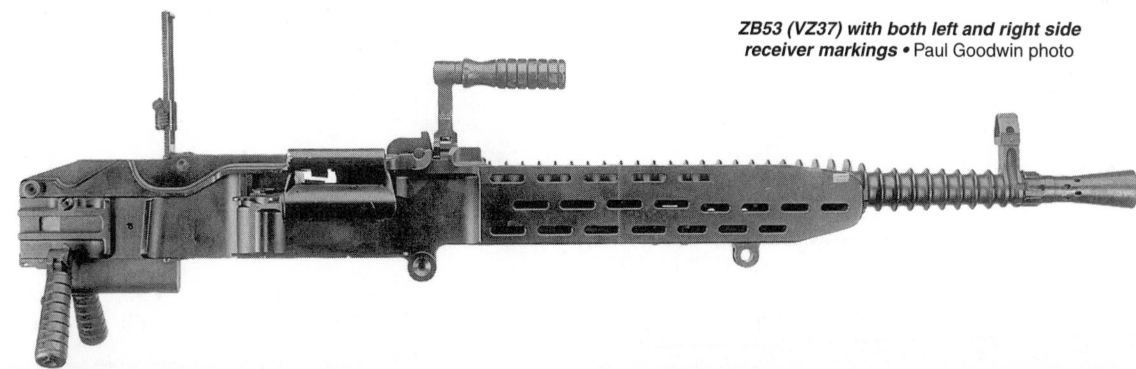

ZB53 (VZ37) with both left and right side receiver markings • Paul Goodwin photo

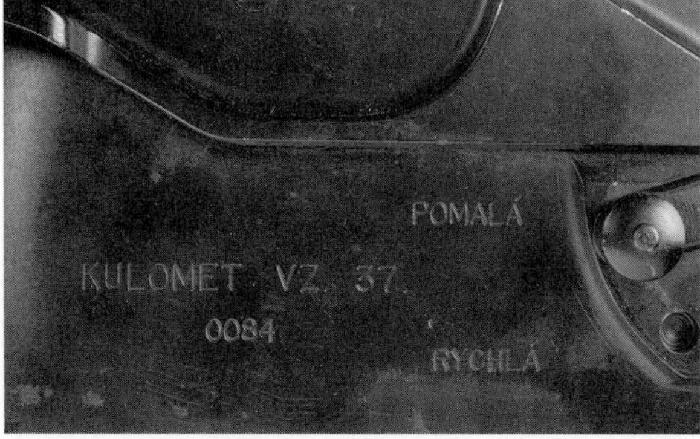

The Kingdom of Denmark (Danmark), a constitutional monarchy located at the mouth of the Baltic Sea, has an area of 16,639 sq. mi. (43,070 sq. km.) and a population of 5.2 million. Capital: Copenhagen. Most of the country is arable. Agriculture, is conducted by large farms served by cooperatives. The largest industries are food processing, iron and metal, and shipping. Machinery, meats (chiefly bacon), dairy products and chemicals are exported.

Denmark, a great power during the Viking period of the 9th-11th centuries, conducted raids on western Europe and England, and in the 11th century united England, Denmark and Norway under the rule of King Canute. Despite a struggle between the crown and the nobility (13th-14th centuries) which forced the King to grant a written constitution, Queen Margaret (Margrethe) (1387-1412) succeeded in uniting Denmark, Norway, Sweden, Finland and Greenland under the Danish crown, placing all of the Nordic countries under the rule of Denmark. An unwise alliance with Napoleon caused the loss of Norway to Sweden in 1814. In the following years a liberal movement was fostered, which succeeded in making Denmark a constitutional monarchy in 1849.

DENMARK

HANDGUNS

In addition to the handguns listed below, the Danes used the Browning Hi-Power 9mm pistol designated the Model 46. They also used the Swedish Model 40 Lahti, called the Model 40S by the Danes. In the late 1940s the Danes adopted the SIG 9mm Model 47/8 pistol (P-210-2).

Model 1871

This 6-shot revolver was built on a Lefaucheux-Francotte solid frame fixed cylinder with non-mechanical ejection. This is an 11mm pinfire revolver. Octagon barrel length is 5 inches. Weight is about 34 oz. Smooth wooden grips with lanyard loop. Built by the Belgian firm of Auguste Francotte. Issued to the Danish navy from 1871 to 1882.

Courtesy Geschichte und Technik der europaischen Militarrevolver, Journal-Verlag Schwend GmbH with permission

Exc.	V.G.	Good	Fair	Poor
850	600	400	200	125

Model 1871/81

This model is a Model 1871 converted to centerfire 11mm. The conversion was done at the Danish navy yard in Copenhagen in 1881. All other specifications are the same as those for the Model 1871.

Exc.	V.G.	Good	Fair	Poor
750	500	300	150	75

Courtesy Geschichte und Technik der europaischen Militarrevolver, Journal-Verlag Schwend GmbH with permission

Model 1865/97

This revolver is built on the Chamelot-Delvigne solid-frame, fixed-cylinder action with non-mechanical ejection. It was originally issued to the Danish navy in 1865 as an 11mm pinfire sidearm and was later converted in Kronberg to 11.45mm centerfire revolver. The revolver is fitted with a lever-type safety that blocks the hammer from the cylinder when engaged. Barrel length is 5 inches. Checkered wood grips with lanyard loop located behind the hammer. Weight is about 30 oz. Issued to the Danish navy from 1897 to 1919.

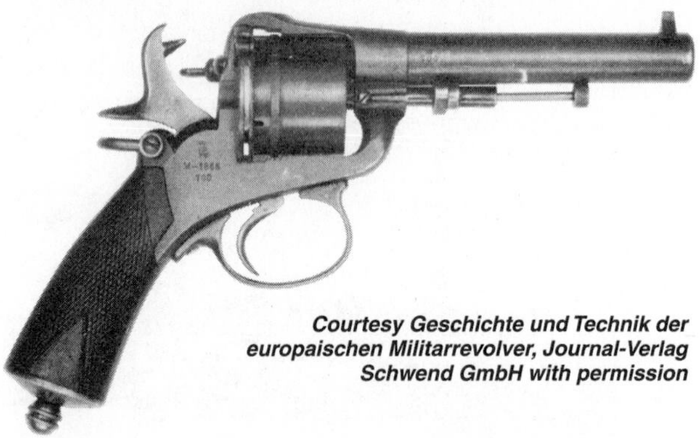

Courtesy Geschichte und Technik der europaischen Militarrevolver, Journal-Verlag Schwend GmbH with permission

Exc.	V.G.	Good	Fair	Poor
1750	1000	600	350	200

Courtesy Geschichte und Technik der europaischen Militarrevolver, Journal-Verlag Schwend GmbH with permission

Model 1882

This revolver was built on the Lefaucheux-Francotte solid-frame fixed cylinder with non-mechanical ejection. Capacity was 6 rounds and the gun was chambered for the 9mm cartridge. The half-round half-octagon barrel was 5.5 inches. This revolver was issued to Danish NCOs from 1888 to 1919.

Exc.	V.G.	Good	Fair	Poor
1200	650	400	200	125

Model 1886

This revolver was chambered for the 9.5mm cartridge and fitted with a 3-inch barrel. Built by Auguste Francotte in Liege, Belgium, and issued to military police units in the Danish army beginning in 1886.

Courtesy Geschichte und Technik der europaischen Militarrevolver, Journal-Verlag Schwend GmbH with permission

Exc.	V.G.	Good	Fair	Poor
850	600	400	250	75

Model 1891

This revolver employed a top-break, hinged frame with latch and was chambered for the 9mm cartridge and fitted with a 6.3-inch half-round half-octagon barrel. Checkered wooden grips with lanyard loop. Built by J.B. Ronge fils of Liege, Belgium. Weight is about 33 oz. Issued to Danish navy units from 1891 to 1941.

NOTE: A training version of this revolver was also used by the Danish navy and was chambered for the 5.1mm cartridge. All other specifications are the same.

Standard Model

Courtesy Geschichte und Technik der europaischen Militarrevolver, Journal-Verlag Schwend GmbH with permission

Exc.	V.G.	Good	Fair	Poor
1200	650	400	250	150

Model 1891/96 Training Version

Courtesy Geschichte und Technik der europaischen Militarrevolver, Journal-Verlag Schwend GmbH with permission

Exc.	V.G.	Good	Fair	Poor
3500	1750	800	500	300

Bergmann-Bayard Model 1908

Built by the Belgium firm of Pieper SA from 1908 to about 1914. Caliber is 9x23mm Bergman-Bayard with 4-inch barrel. Many foreign contracts were built in this model.

Exc.	V.G.	Good	Fair	Poor
1250	950	700	400	200

Courtesy Rock Island Auction Company

Bergmann-Bayard Model 1910-21

After WWI Pieper could no longer supply Bergmann-Bayard pistols to the Danish army, so Denmark made their own at their two national arsenals, Haerens Rustkammer and Haerens Tojus as the Model 1910-21. Most pre-war Pieper-made pistols were modified to 1910-21 configuration during the postwar years.

Courtesy Rock Island Auction Company

Exc.	V.G.	Good	Fair	Poor
1500	1100	850	700	300

Danish Holster for Bergman-Bayard Model 1910-21

Leather construction with carrying strap. Price range: 250 – 100.

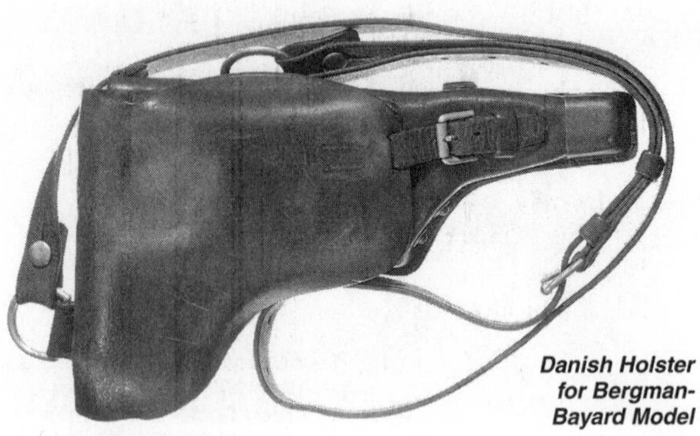

Danish Holster for Bergman-Bayard Model

Model 46

This is the Danish designation for the postwar Browning Hi-Power. Marked "M 1946 HV" on the left side of the frame. Fixed sights.

Exc.	V.G.	Good	Fair	Poor
1350	1100	950	650	400

P210 (Model 49)

See Switzerland, Handguns, SIG.

SUBMACHINE GUNS

The Danish military has also used the Finnish Suomi MP41, the Swedish Model 37/39, and the HK MP5A2 and MP5A3 submachine guns.

Danish Hovea M49

Introduced in 1949 this submachine gun is chambered for the 9mm Parabellum cartridge and fitted with an 8.5-inch barrel. Folding metal butt. Magazine capacity

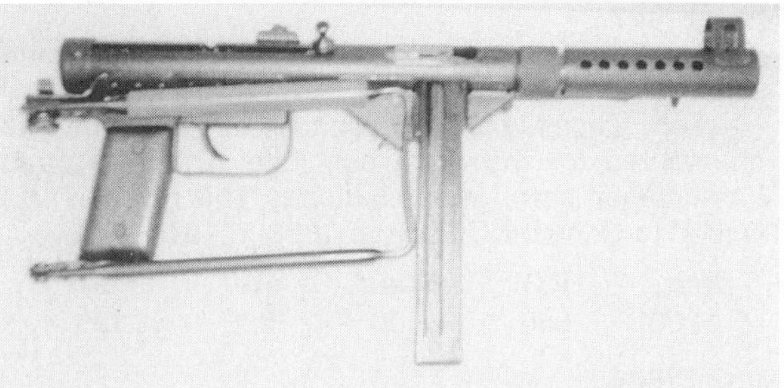

Courtesy private NFA collection

is 35 rounds. Rate of fire is about 600 rounds per minute. Weight is approximately 7.5 lbs. This gun was originally developed by Husqvarna for the Swedish army. Denmark purchased the rights and built the gun for its own forces.

Pre-1968

Exc.	V.G.	Fair
20000	18000	16000

Madsen M50

This submachine gun was produced from 1945 to 1953 by the Danes. It is chambered for the 9mm cartridge and is fitted with a 7.8-inch barrel. Its rate of fire is about 500 rounds per minute. Marked "MADSEN" on the right side of receiver. Weight is approximately 7 lbs.

This gun has some unusual features, such as a flat receiver with barrel attached with locking nut that when unscrewed allows the left side of the receiver to fold back to expose the right side, which contains all the moving parts. Fitted with a quick change barrel. Very simple design allows for fast and economical construction.

Courtesy private NFA collection

Pre-1968

Exc.	V.G.	Fair
8000	7000	6000

Pre-1986 manufacture or re-weld

Exc.	V.G.	Fair
4000	3500	3000

RIFLES

More recently, Danish military forces have used the U.S. M16A1 rifle, the HK G3, the M1 Garand, and the Enfield Model 1917 rifle.

REMINGTON ROLLING BLOCK

Model 1867 Rifle

This rifle was modified from rimfire to centerfire. Chambered for the 11.7x42R Danish/Remington cartridge. Fitted with a 35.7-inch barrel. Weight is approximately 9.25 lbs. Full stocked with exposed

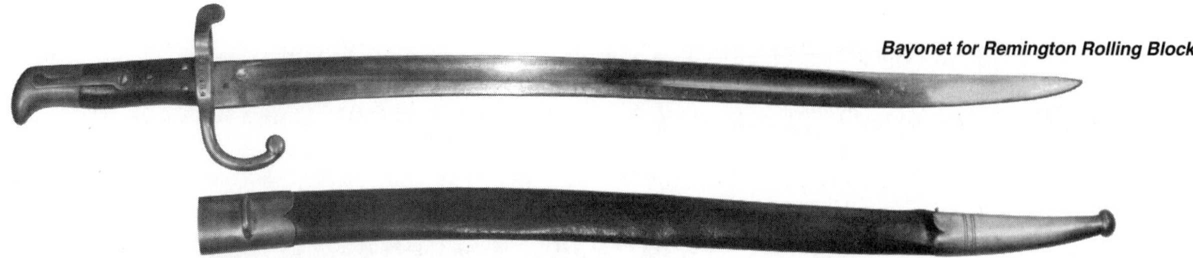
Bayonet for Remington Rolling Block

muzzle and bayonet bar with lug on right side. Three barrel bands. On the left side of the receiver is marked "M.1867" with the Danish Crown. The upper tang is marked with either "REMINGTON" or "KJOBENHAVN" with the year of manufacture.

Exc.	V.G.	Good	Fair	Poor
700	625	450	350	250

Bayonet for Remington Rolling Block

Hard rubber grips. Muzzle ring. Hook quillon. 21.6-inch single edge yatagan-style blade. Steel tipped leather scabbard. Marked on ricasso "GEBR WEYERSBERG SOLINGEN." Price range 250 – 125.

Model 1867 Carbine

Similar to the rifle but with half length walnut stock with one barrel band and 21-inch barrel. Three variations were produced: Artillery, Engineer, and Cavalry. Weight is approximately 7 lbs.

Exc.	V.G.	Good	Fair	Poor
850	700	550	400	300

Model 1867/93 Marine Rifle

This rifle was built in Denmark at Kjobenhavn Arsenal. It was essentially a Model 1867 rifle rebuilt to fire the 8x58R Danish Krag cartridge. Barrel length is 21 inches and weight is about 7 lbs. Nose cap has bayonet fittings.

Exc.	V.G.	Good	Fair	Poor
750	600	500	400	300

Model 1867/96 Cavalry Carbine

This model was also built in Denmark and was a Model 1867 carbine rechambered for the 11.7x51R Danish cartridge.

Exc.	V.G.	Good	Fair	Poor
750	625	500	375	250

MAUSER

The rifles listed below are war surplus captured from the Germans at the end of World War II. These rifles were converted by the Danes to military target rifles.

G98 Action Military Target Rifle (Model 52)

Exc.	V.G.	Good	Fair	Poor
750	500	350	250	150

K98k Action Military Target Rifle (Model 58)

Exc.	V.G.	Good	Fair	Poor
750	500	350	250	150

KRAG JORGENSEN

The Krag rifle was developed in Norway and first adopted by Denmark. It was standard issue in some form through WWII. For a list of U.S. models and prices see United States, Rifles, Krag Jorgensen. For those collectors who are interested in the Danish Krags, the only major difference, other than caliber, lies in the operation of the loading gate. Prices listed below are for unaltered Danish Krags. The forerunner of the U.S. Krags was the Model 1889 rifle.

NOTE: All Danish Krags are chambered for the 8x58Rmm cartridge.

Danish Model 1889

This rifle was developed by Ole Krag and Eric Jorgensen. It used a single forward bolt locking lug plus a bolt guide rib. Chambered for the 8x58Rmm cartridge, the rifle was fitted with a 33-inch barrel with full stock and no pistol grip. The barrel is fitted with a full-length metal handguard. A flush loose-loaded box magazine was used. The bolt handle was straight. There were a number of different carbine versions but all of these were full stocked and fitted with 23.5-inch barrel with bayonet lugs on all but one variation: the artillery carbine (see below). These guns are marked prior to 1910 "GEVAERFABRIKEN KJOBENHAVN" [date] over "M89" on the left side of the receiver. Approximately 140,000 of these rifles and carbines were manufactured prior to 1930. During the German occupation in WWII, the Germans reintroduced the rifle for its own use.

Exc.	V.G.	Good	Fair	Poor
750	625	500	400	250

Bayonet for 1889 Krag rifle

Checkered hard rubber grips. 9.1-inch single edge blade. Steel tipped leather scabbard. Example shown is marked on ricasso "Alex Coppel Solingen." Price range 175 – 100.

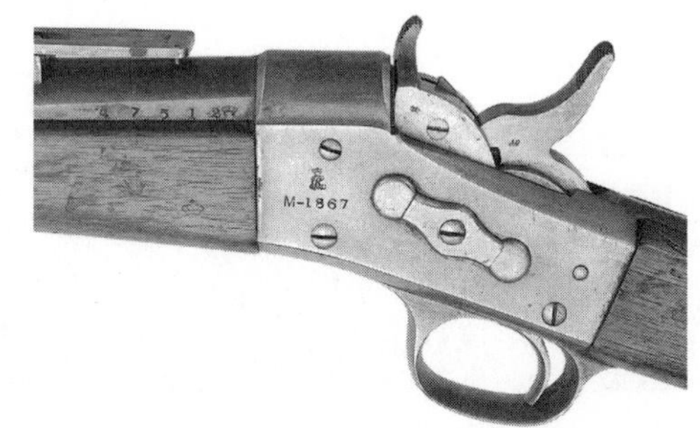

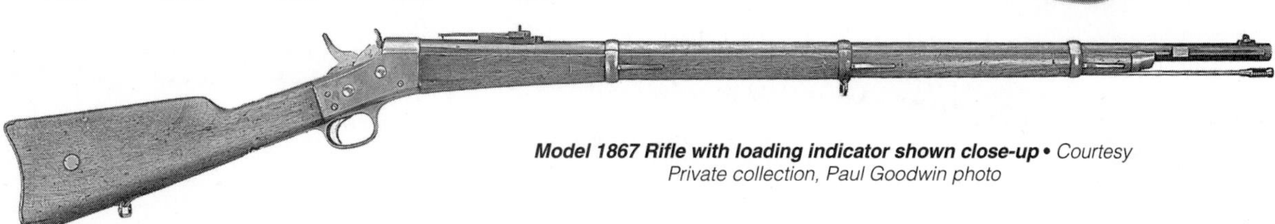
Model 1867 Rifle with loading indicator shown close-up • Courtesy Private collection, Paul Goodwin photo

Bayonet for 1889 Krag Rifle

Model 1889 Infantry Carbine

Introduced in 1924, this model is a converted Model 1889 rifle with metal barrel jacket and bayonet stud. Barrel length is 24 inches. Tangent rear sight. Magazine capacity is 5 rounds. Weight is about 8.5 lbs. Marked "F" before the serial number.

Exc.	*V.G.*	*Good*	*Fair*	*Poor*
850	700	550	350	200

Model 1889 Artillery Carbine

Similar to the Infantry carbine and also introduced in 1924, this model features a turn down bolt handle, a triangle shaped upper sling swivel, and a hanger stud on the left side of the stock.

Exc.	*V.G.*	*Good*	*Fair*	*Poor*
850	700	550	350	200

Model 1889 Engineer Carbine

This model was introduced in 1917. It is fitted with a wooden handguard and a slightly shorter barrel, about ½ inch. Marked with "I" before the serial number.

Exc.	*V.G.*	*Good*	*Fair*	*Poor*
850	700	550	350	200

Model 1889 Cavalry Rifle

Introduced in 1914, this model is fitted for a bayonet. Straight bolt handle. Marked with "R" before the serial number.

Exc.	*V.G.*	*Good*	*Fair*	*Poor*
800	650	450	300	200

Bayonet for 1889 Krag carbine

Wood grips. Muzzle ring. 17.6-inch single edge T-shaped blade. Steel tipped leather scabbard. Price range 175 – 100.

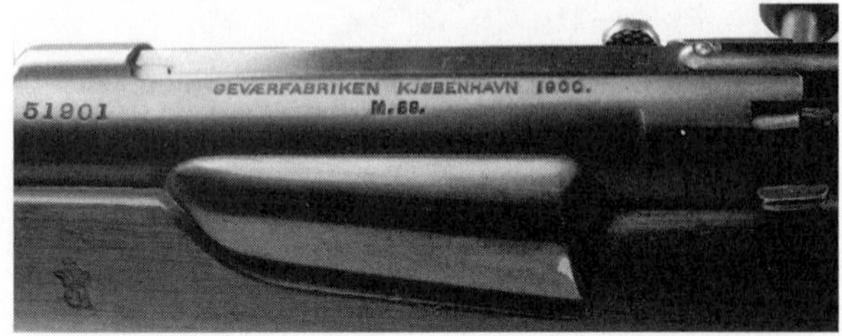

Danish troops with their Krags • Courtesy Paul S. Scarlata

Model 1928 Sniper Rifle

This model is based on the Model 1889 with half stock but fitted with a 26-inch heavy barrel, micrometer rear sight, and hooded front sight. Wooden handguard. Turned down bolt. Similar in appearance to the U.S. 30 caliber-style "T" rifle. Weight is approximately 11.5 lbs.

Exc.	*V.G.*	*Good*	*Fair*	*Poor*
1500	1100	800	500	200

MADSEN

Model 47

Sometimes referred to as the Madsen light military rifle, this post-WWII bolt-action rifle was sold to Colombia in limited quantities of 5,000 guns. Some rifles will have a metal disk on the left side bearing the seal of Columbia. These might bring $50-100 more. Fitted with a rubber buttplate. Chambered in .30-06. Other calibers were listed in the Madsen catalogue but the only order received was from Columbia. Barrel length was 23 inches with a magazine capacity of 5 rounds. Weight was about 8 lbs.

Exc.	*V.G.*	*Good*	*Fair*	*Poor*
750	600	450	325	250

NOTE: Add $150 for rifles with numbered matching bayonet.

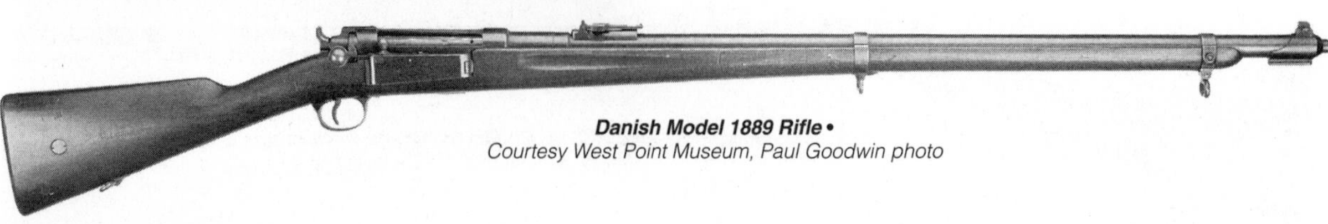

Danish Model 1889 Rifle •
Courtesy West Point Museum, Paul Goodwin photo

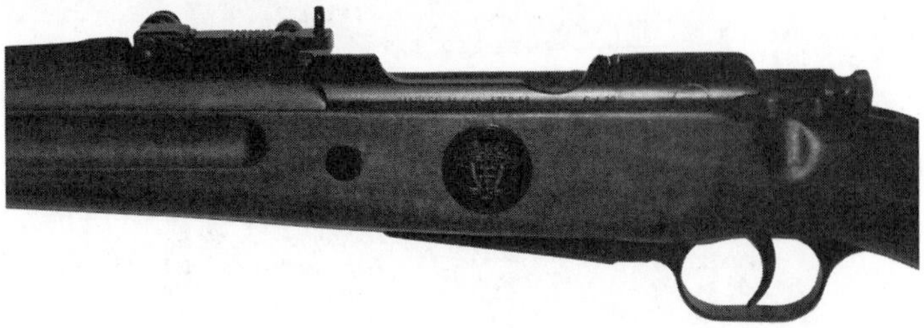

Madsen M1947, Columbian Armed Forces disk on left side

Bayonet for 1889 Krag Carbine

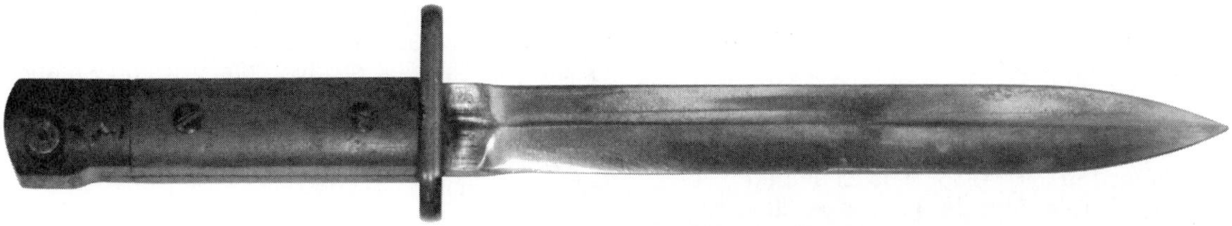

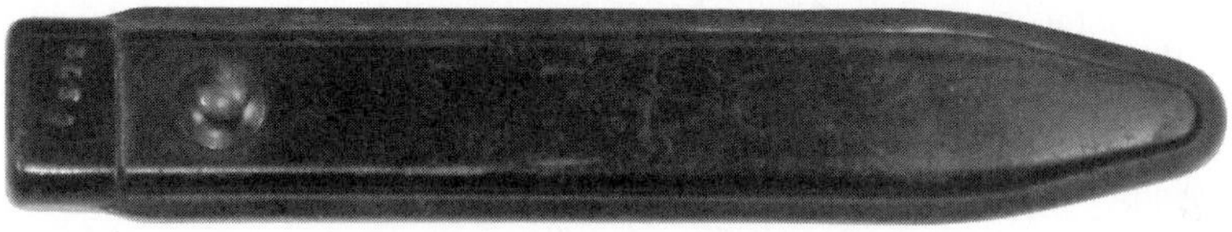

Bayonet for Madsen M 47

Bayonet for Madsen M 47

Wood handle. 8.25-inch inch double edge blade. Steel scabbard. The only marking is a serial number. Price range 150 – 70.

Bayonets for M-1 Garand

Denmark made their own M-1 and M-5 type bayonets for the M-1 Garand rifles they received from the U.S. The dimensions are the same as the U.S. versions. They have Danish markings. The scabbards are plastic and have a simulated wood appearance. Price range M-1: 125 – 60. Price range M-5: 100 – 50.

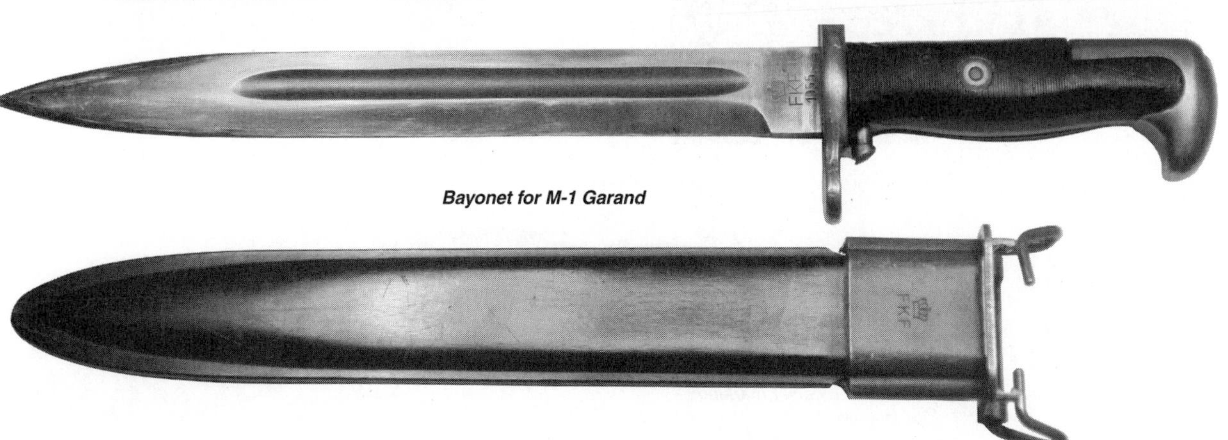

Bayonet for M-1 Garand

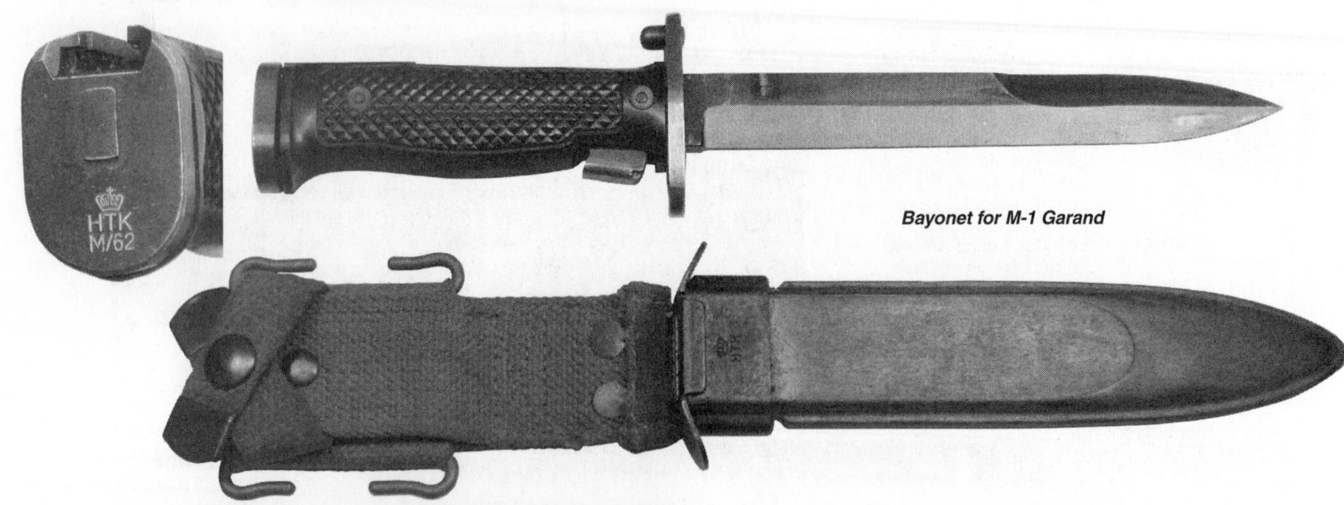

Bayonet for M-1 Garand

MACHINE GUNS

After WWII Denmark used the British Bren gun chambered for the .303 caliber, the Swedish Model 37 6.5mm gun, the U.S. Model 1919A4 and A5 versions, and the .50 M2 Browning. More recently the Danes used the German MG 42/59.

Madsen

This was the first practical light machine gun. It was produced from 1897 to 1955. It is chambered for several calibers from 6mm to 8mm. It is fitted with a 22.7-inch barrel and a top feeding 25-, 30-, or 40-round magazine. Rate of fire is 450 rounds per minute. Its weight is approximately 20 lbs. Marked "MADSEN MODEL" on the right side of the receiver. Found all over the world during a 50-year period.

Pre-1968

Exc.	*V.G.*	*Fair*
12000	11000	10000

Madsen-Satter

First produced in 1952, this belt-fed machine gun is chambered for the 7.62x51mm NATO cartridge. Designed to be used on a tripod for sustained fire, it had a rate of fire of 650 to 1000 rounds per minute (adjustable). Fitted with a 22-inch barrel. Weight is approximately 23.4 lbs. Marked "MADSEN-SETTER" on left front side of receiver. Many South American countries used this gun, as do many other countries around the world. Production stopped on this gun in 1960 in Denmark but continued under license to Indonesia until the 1970s.

Courtesy private NFA collection

Pre-1968 (Very Rare)

Exc.	*V.G.*	*Fair*
25000	23000	22000

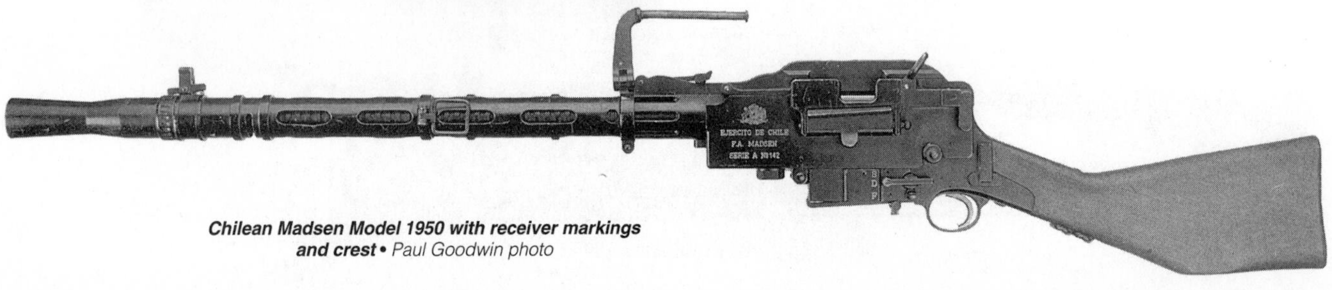

Chilean Madsen Model 1950 with receiver markings and crest • Paul Goodwin photo

EGYPT

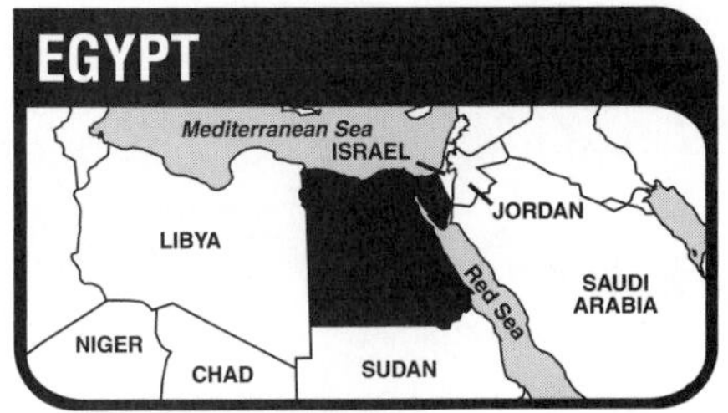

The Arab Republic of Egypt, located on the northeastern corner of Africa, has an area of 385,229 sq. mi. (1,1001,450 sq. km.) and a population of 62.4 million. Capital: Cairo. Although Egypt is an almost rainless expanse of desert, its economy is predominantly agricultural. Cotton, rice and petroleum are exported. Other main sources of income are revenues from the Suez Canal, remittances of Egyptian workers abroad and tourism.

Egyptian history dates back to about 3000 B.C. when the empire was established by uniting the upper and lower kingdoms. Following its 'Golden Age' (16th to 13th centuries B.C.), Egypt was conquered by Persia (525 B.C.) and Alexander the Great (332 B.C.). The Ptolemies, descended from one of Alexander's generals, ruled until the suicide of Cleopatra (30 B.C.) when Egypt became the private domain of the Roman emperor, and subsequently part of the Byzantine world. Various Muslim dynasties ruled Egypt from 641 on, including Ayyubid Sultans to 1250 and Mamluks to 1517, when it was conquered by the Ottoman Turks, interrupted by the occupation of Napoleon (1798-1801). A semi-independent dynasty was founded by Muhammad Ali in 1805 which lasted until 1952. Turkish rule became increasingly casual, permitting Great Britain to inject its influence by purchasing shares in the Suez Canal. British troops occupied Egypt in 1882, becoming the de facto rulers. On Dec. 14, 1914, Egypt was made a protectorate of Britain. British occupation ended on Feb. 28, 1922, when Egypt became a sovereign, independent kingdom. The monarchy was abolished and a republic proclaimed on June 18, 1953.

On Feb. 1, 1958, Egypt and Syria formed the United Arab Republic. Yemen joined on March 8 in an association known as the United Arab States. Syria withdrew from the United Arab Republic on Sept. 29, 1961, and on Dec. 26 Egypt dissolved its ties with Yemen in the United Arab States. On Sept. 2, 1971, Egypt finally shed the name United Arab Republic in favor of the Arab Republic of Egypt.

HANDGUNS

Helwan

Egyptian made copy of the Beretta Model 1951. Chambered for 9mm. 4.5-inch barrel. 8-round magazine. Fixed sights. Weight is about 31 oz. Many Helwans have been imported commercially to the U.S.

Exc.	*V.G.*	*Good*	*Fair*	*Poor*
250	225	75	125	100

SUBMACHINE GUNS

Port Said

This is a copy of the Swedish K. Chambered for 9mm Parabellum. The barrel is 8.25 inches in length. Weight is about 8 lbs. Rate of fire is about 600 rounds per minute.

Pre-1968

Exc.	*V.G.*	*Fair*
12500	8000	5000

Pre-1986 manufacture with new receiver

Exc.	*V.G.*	*Fair*
7500	5000	3500

RIFLES

Remington Rolling Block Model 1870

Made by Remington for Egypt. 60,000 were purchased between 1870-1876. Chambered for 11.43x50Rmm. Identified by the Farsi markings on the barrel and rear sight. Many have been imported to the U.S. Some were used as training rifles and had the firing pins and extractors missing. Usually found in Fair-Poor condition.

Exc.	*V.G.*	*Good*	*Fair*	*Poor*
700	550	300	175	150

Fabrique National Model 1949 or SAFN 49

A gas-operated semi-automatic rifle chambered for 7.92mm. It has a 23-inch barrel and military-type sights. The fixed magazine holds 10 rounds. Egyptian crest on top of receiver.

Exc.	*V.G*	*Good*	*Fair*	*Poor*
800	650	450	300	250

NOTE: Many Egyptian FN 1949s were restocked and reblued by Century Arms in the early 1990s. The new stock is a light colored wood that is stained to resemble walnut. Brass or plastic buttplate. Deduct 25 percent for a restocked rifle.

Bayonet for Egyptian FN 1949

FN made bayonet with Farsi numbers on the pommel. See listing in Belgium, Fabrique National for information and image. Price range 75 – 40.

Hakim

A semi-automatic rifle chambered in 8x57mm Mauser. It has a 24-inch barrel that ends with a large recoil compensator. 10-round detachable magazine. This is

Bayonet for Hakim

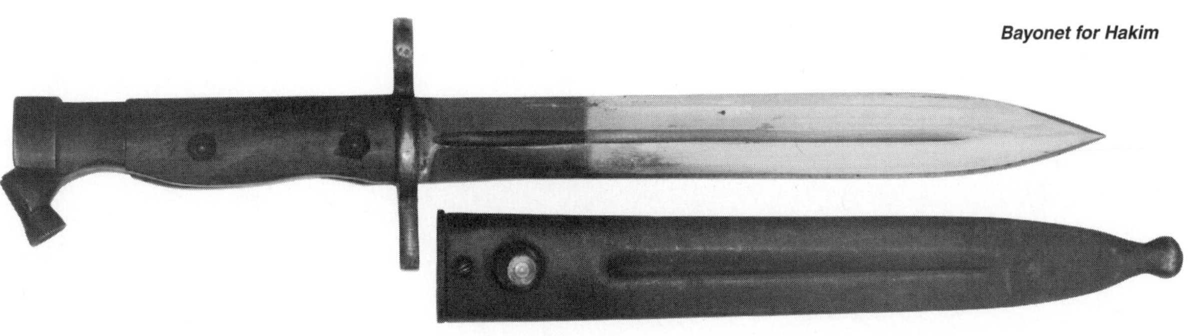

EGYPT

Egyptian-made Hakim rifle

Rashid

a copy of the Swedish AG-42b rifle and was designed with the help of Swedish engineers. Made at the Maadi factory. Many were imported in the late 1980s.

Exc.	V.G.	Good	Fair	Poor
550	450	400	300	200

Hakim Training Rifle .22LR

A semi-automatic rifle chambered in .22LR that is patterned after the Hakim. Marked "Made in Italy." A few came in with the regular Hakims.

Exc.	V.G.	Good	Fair	Poor
500	450	400	300	200

Bayonet for Hakim

Wood handle. Muzzle ring. 8.25-inch double edge blade. A close copy of the Swedish 1896 Mauser bayonet except for the wood handle. Steel scabbard. Price range 80 – 40.

Rashid

This is a native Egyptian design, basically a scaled-down Hakim chambered in 7.62x39mm. It uses a 10-round detachable magazine. A folding bayonet is attached to the barrel, similar to the Soviet SKS. About 8000 were made in the 1960s. Some were imported to the U.S. in the 1990s.

Exc.	V.G.	Good	Fair	Poor
700	550	450	350	250

AKM

Maadi semi-automatic, pre-1994

A close copy of the Soviet AKM series. Chambered in 7.62x39mm. Two semi-automatic versions have been imported to the U.S. One was the first semi-automatic Kalashnikov offered on the U.S. market. These appeared in the early 1980s and were imported by Steyr.

Exc.	V.G.	Good	Fair	Poor
1250	950	800	—	—

Maadi semi-automatic, sporter

The second was imported after passage of the 1994 "assault weapons" law and had a thumbhole sporter type stock installed to comply with the terms of that law. The importer called these the MISR (Maadi Industries Sporting Rifle).

Exc.	V.G.	Good	Fair	Poor
600	500	400	—	—

FINLAND

The Republic of Finland, the third northernmost state of the European continent, has an area of 130,559 sq. mi. (338,127 sq. km.) and a population of 5.1 million. Capital: Helsinki. Lumbering, shipbuilding, metal and woodworking are the leading industries. Paper, timber, wood pulp, plywood and metal products are exported.

The Finns, who probably originated in the Volga region of Russia, took Finland from the Lapps late in the 7th century. They were conquered in the 12th century by Eric IX of Sweden, and brought into contact with Western Christendom. In 1809, Sweden was conquered by Alexander I of Russia, and the peace terms gave Finland to Russia which became a grand duchy, with autonomy, within the Russian Empire until Dec. 6, 1917, when, shortly after the Bolshevik revolution it declared its independence. After a brief but bitter civil war between the Russian communists and Finnish nationalists in which the Whites (nationalists) were victorious, a new constitution was adopted, and on Dec. 6, 1917 Finland was established as a republic. In 1939 Soviet troops attacked Finland over disputed territorial concessions which were later granted in the peace treaty of 1940. When the Germans invaded Russia, Finland became involved and in the Armistice of 1944 lost the Petsamo area to the Soviets.

HANDGUNS

During the 1920s and 1930s the Finnish army relied primarily on the Model 1895 Russian Nagant revolver and the Spanish 7.65mm self-loading pistols, the Ruby (Model 19). During World War I the Finns were supplied with the Mauser M1896 Broomhandle in a late wartime commercial configuration. In the early 1920s the Finns adopted a commercial model of the DWM Luger, called by the Finns the Model 23. By the late 1920s the Finnish military decided to adopt and domestically produce a 9mm self-loading pistol of their own. It was called the Lahti.

The Finns, more recently, have used the FN M1935 in 9mm and the French MAB PA-15 pistol in 9mm.

M35 Lahti

This 9x19mm semi-automatic pistol was adopted in 1935 and built at VKT. This pistol is a locked-breech semi-automatic that features a bolt accelerator that does much to make this a reliable firearm. This pistol is the same as the Swedish Model 40 Lahti, with a 4.7-inch barrel and 8-round magazine, except that it has a loaded chamber indicator on top of the pistol, a different assembled recoil spring, and the Finnish pistol's grips are marked "VKT." Finnish army markings on top of slide. This pistol was designed to function in extreme cold and has a reputation for reliability. About 5,700 wartime Lahti pistols were produced.

Exc.	V.G.	Good	Fair	Poor
1250	1000	800	550	300

Finnish M35 Lahti • *Courtesy J.B. Wood*

SUBMACHINE GUNS

The first Finnish submachine gun was developed by Aimo Lahti in 1922. This gun later became the Model 1926 with only about 200 built in 7.65mm caliber. A perfected design was later built called the Model 1931

Model 1931 • *Paul Goodwin photo*

FINLAND

Suomi. Since the end of World War II the Finns have used the Sten Mark II and Mark III guns.

Suomi Model 1931

First produced in Finland in 1931, this submachine gun is chambered for the 9mm cartridge. It was widely used by Scandinavian armies as well as several countries in South America. It features a 12.25-inch barrel with wooden stock and 71-round drum magazine. Box magazine capacity is 20 or 50 rounds. Rate of fire is 900 rounds per minute. Weight is about 10 lbs. Marked on the end cap and left side of the receiver. Production stopped in 1944. A total of about 80,000 were produced by Tikka.

This gun was also made in Sweden where it was designated the Model 37-39. In Switzerland it was called the Model 43/44. In Denmark it was made by Madsen.

Pre-1968

Exc.	*V.G.*	*Fair*
16000	14500	13000

Suomi Model 1944

This Finnish gun is based on the Russian Model PPS-43, but the Model 1944 fires the 9mm cartridge. It is fitted with a 9.66-inch barrel and accepts a 36-round box magazine or 71-round drum magazine. Rate of fire is 650 rounds per minute. Weight is about 6.35 lbs. Production stopped in 1945. Marked on left side of receiver. TIKKA built about 10,000 of these guns.

Pre-1968

Exc.	*V.G.*	*Fair*
16000	14500	13000

RIFLES

Prior to 1917, Finland was part of Russia. All Finnish military bolt action rifles are built on Mosin Nagant actions. There are a number of sub-variations of Finnish Mosin Nagants that are beyond the scope of this book and may be of interest to the collector. A website that gives excellent information for all Mosin Nagant rifles is www.mosinnagant.net. The beginner can get a lot of basic information from Terence Lapin's ***The Mosin-Nagant Rifle,*** and Doug Bowers' ***Rifles of the White Death***.

My thanks to Fred Schrope for providing more detailed information on the Finnish Mosin Nagant series.

Note: Unusual markings or serial numbers on any Finnish rifle may greatly increase the price.

Model 1891 (Finnish Army Variation)

Many were simply reconditioned Russian Model 1891s, but had the sights calibrated to meters, the trigger may be modified to two stage pull, and are frequently fitted with two piece Finnish made stocks with sling swivels. Many were fitted with Tikkakoski and VKT barrels which were made in Finland. All the barrels are about 31.6 inches in length. Built through 1944.

Exc.	*V.G.*	*Good*	*Fair*	*Poor*
400	300	250	150	100

Model 1891 Dragoon (Finnish Army Variation)

Basically a Russian Model 1891 Dragoon rifle modified as above with a side mounted Mauser Kar 98-type sling. Barrel length is 28.8 inches. About 19,000 of these rifles were produced.

Exc.	*V.G.*	*Good*	*Fair*	*Poor*
500	350	275	150	100

Model 91/24 Civil Guard Infantry Rifle

This model was assembled in the Civil Guard work shop and was basically, an M1891 that was fitted with

Model 1891 Finnish Army rifle with close-up of barrel markings. From the top: "B" indicates Belgian made; "VKT" indicates state factory at Jyvaskyla; "D" indicates re-chambered for "D46&D166" ammunition • *Courtesy Stoddard Martial collection, Paul Goodwin photo*

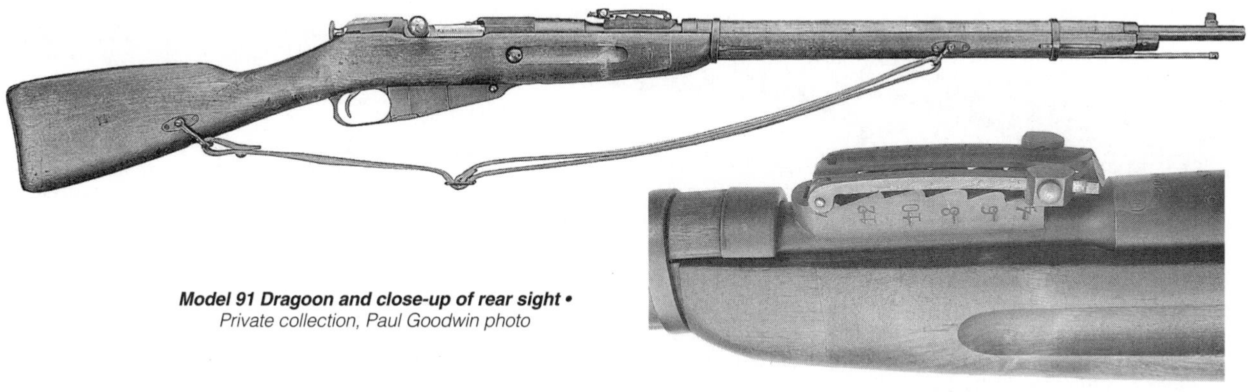

Model 91 Dragoon and close-up of rear sight • *Private collection, Paul Goodwin photo*

Model 91/24 with SIG heavy stepped barrel for bayonet attachment. Close-up of barrel markings indicate armor's notation that the barrel has been shortened and re-chambered • *Courtesy Stoddard Martial collection, Paul Goodwin photo*

a new barrel made by SIG or Böhler-Stahl. With the exception of the first 3000 SIGs, all the barrels were of a larger diameter with a step at the muzzle to allow the use of the Russian bayonet. The main identifying mark is the Civil Guard Crest stamped on the top of the barrel chamber. For the SIG barrels, the SIG logo is imprinted on the right side of the barrel chamber just above the wood line.

Exc.	***V.G.***	***Good***	***Fair***	***Poor***
450	350	250	150	100

Model 91/24 Civil Guard Carbine

As above but with 24-inch barrel. It is estimated that 650 of these carbines were produced. Very Rare.

Exc.	***V.G.***	***Good***	***Fair***	***Poor***
900	650	400	300	150

Model 1927 Army Short Rifle

This rifle used a 27-inch barrel made mainly by Tikkakoski with a very few by VKT. They had a nearly full stock with a bayonet lug on the front band. The rear sight was the same as used on the M1891. The front sight was of a new design that had protective ears. Most of the stocks were made from shortened M1891 Russian stocks. Many had new forends affixed by the Finnish Finger-joint system. All M1927s have the date and barrel maker stamped on top of the barrel chamber, 1927-1940. Serial numbers range

Model 1927 rifle with 1st style barrel band. This band was modified in 1937 • *Courtesy Simeon Stoddard collection, Paul Goodwin photo*

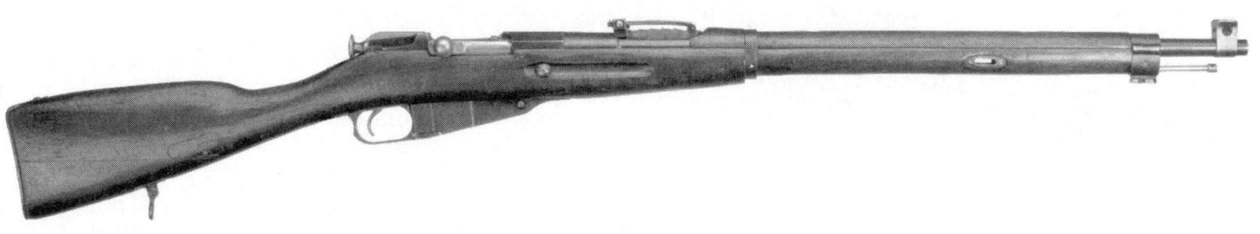

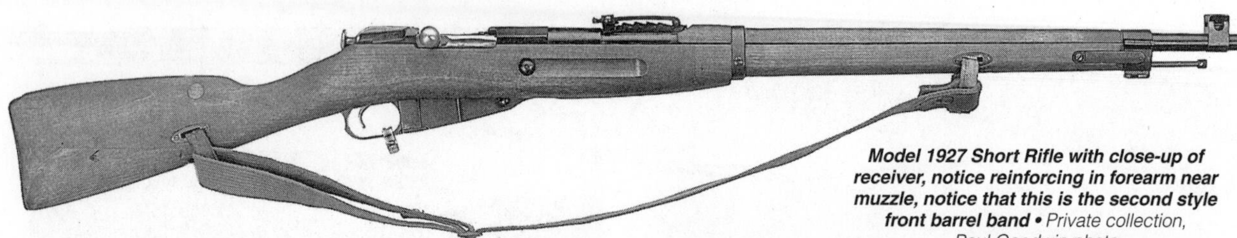

Model 1927 Short Rifle with close-up of receiver, notice reinforcing in forearm near muzzle, notice that this is the second style front barrel band • *Private collection, Paul Goodwin photo*

from 20000 to 87500. All years after 1935 are quite rare. About 1936, the army improved the front band by attaching extensions rearward. This was to prevent stock breakage from bayonet usage. Most of the earlier models were fitted with this type of band upon being arsenal rebuilt.

Exc.	V.G.	Good	Fair	Poor
500	400	325	250	150

Model 1927/91-30 Modified Rifle

During the Winter War with Russia, any rifle that could shoot was needed by the Finnish army. Many Model 1927 rifles were restocked with Model 91-30 stocks to make them useable.

Exc.	V.G.	Good	Fair	Poor
500	400	325	250	150

Model 1927rv Cavalry Carbine

Similar to the Model 1927 rifle but fitted with a 24-inch barrel and turned-down bolt. Side mounted sling. Weight is approximately 8.75 lbs. About 2,500 were produced with serial numbers between 72,800 and 74,900. Very rare, as most were lost during WWII. The remainder were imported into the U.S. in the 1960s - about 300.

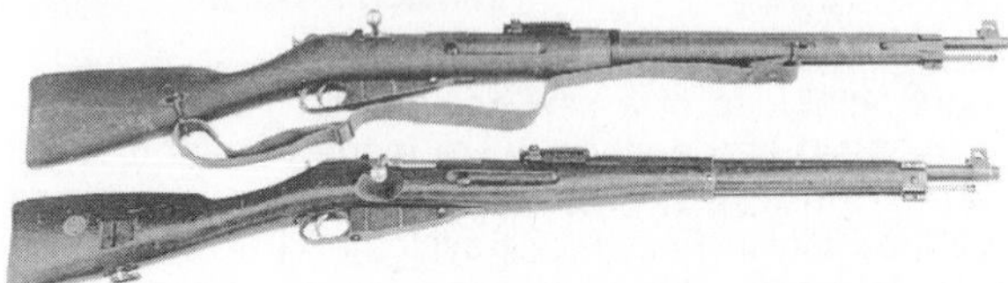

M27 Rifle on top and M27 Carbine at bottom • *Courtesy Chuck Karwan*

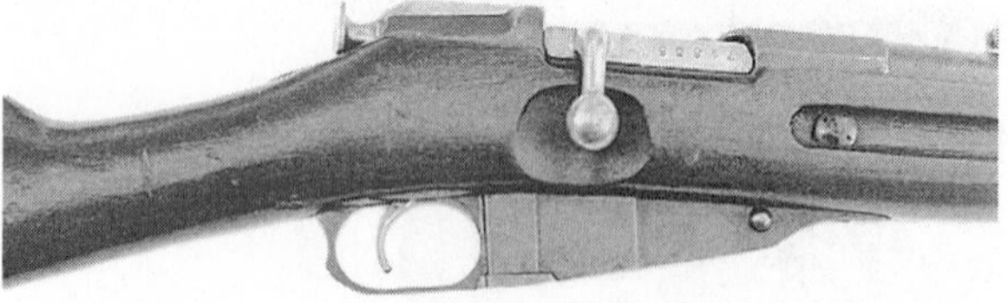

M27 Carbine action • *Courtesy Chuck Karwan*

Exc.	V.G.	Good	Fair	Poor
2000	1500	1000	500	350

Model 1928 Civil Guard Short Rifle

Similar to the Model 1927 except with minor differences such as a non-hinged front barrel band that was stronger and a fore stock enlarged in diameter to help prevent splitting. The letters "SY" are stamped on the top of the barrel chamber. The first 20000 had SIG barrels, and the final 13000 had Tikkakoski barrels. The SIG barrels are marked on the right side of the barrel chamber under the wood line. The Tikkakoski's have the triangle T on top of the chamber. There is no visible date stamped on the barrel chamber. Serial numbers range from 0 to 33016.

Exc.	V.G.	Good	Fair	Poor
550	450	375	250	150

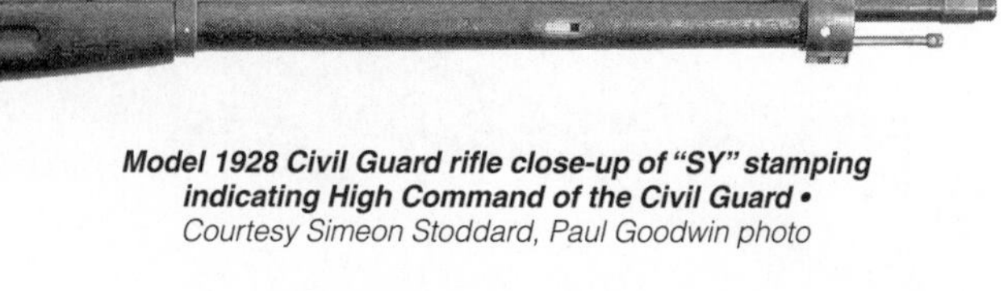

Model 1928 Civil Guard rifle close-up of "SY" stamping indicating High Command of the Civil Guard • *Courtesy Simeon Stoddard, Paul Goodwin photo*

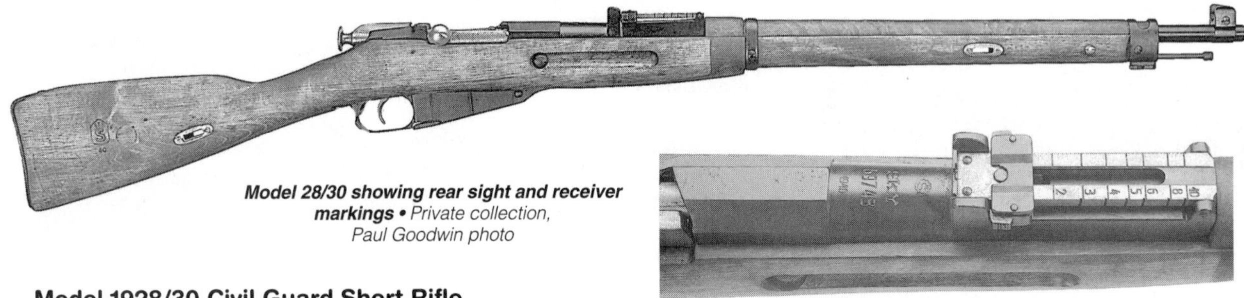

***Model 28/30 showing rear sight and receiver markings** • Private collection, Paul Goodwin photo*

Model 1928/30 Civil Guard Short Rifle

This is the same as the Model 1928 Short Rifle but with an improved magazine and different rear sight graduated to 2,000 meters. The barrels were made by SAKO and have the SAKO gear and the date stamped on top of the barrel chamber - 1934-1940. 1933 models do not have the date stamp and have the same front sight as the M1928s. Serial numbers range from 33017 to 72900.

Exc.	*V.G.*	*Good*	*Fair*	*Poor*
575	450	350	250	150

Bayonet for Finnish M-27, 28, 28/30 Mosin Nagants

Wood grips. Muzzle ring. Straight quillon bent slightly forward. 11.8-inch single edge blade. Maker marked on ricasso "Fiskars" or "Hackman & Co." Steel scabbard. These are very scarce in the U.S. and sometimes will sell for as much as the rifles they fit. Price range 300 – 125.

Finnish Model 91/30

This was a Finnish-manufactured rifle produced by Tikka in 1943 and 1944. About 24,000 were built. Most of these rifles were not used in WWII but kept in storage until 1986 when sold as surplus. Barrel length is 28.7 inches, caliber is 7.62x53R and sights are calibrated from 100 to 2,000 meters. Weight is about 8.75 lbs.

Exc.	*V.G.*	*Good*	*Fair*	*Poor*
300	250	200	150	125

Bayonet for Finnish 91/30

This is a Russian-made 91/30 bayonet with the added "SA" property mark. See Russia chapter for bayonet information. Price range 100 – 50.

***Model 91/30 rifle with close-up of barrel markings indicating Tikka manufacture** • Courtesy Stoddard Martial collection, Paul Goodwin photo*

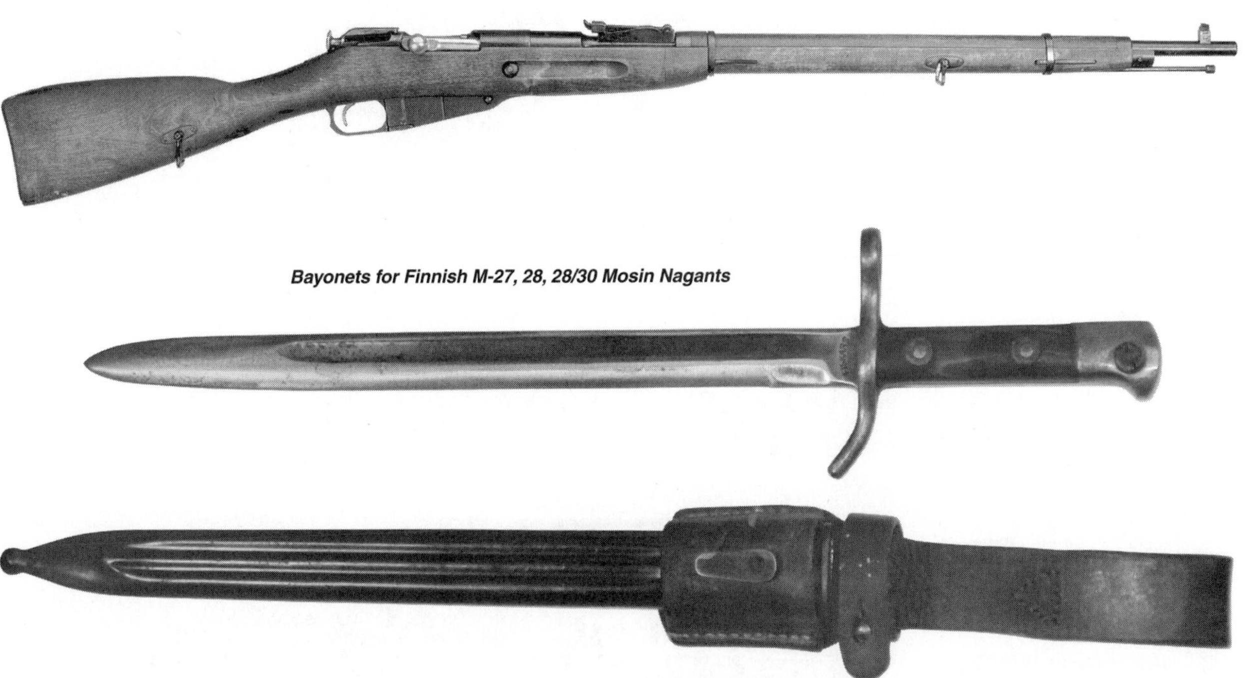

Bayonets for Finnish M-27, 28, 28/30 Mosin Nagants

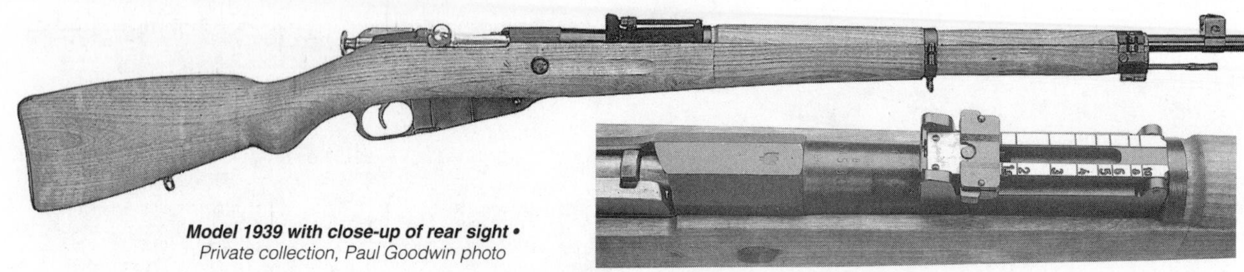

Model 1939 with close-up of rear sight •
Private collection, Paul Goodwin photo

Model 1939 Short Rifle (Army and Civil Guard)

Similar to the Model 1928-30 with identical sights except that a 150 meter marking was added. The stock was a completely new design with all but a few having a pistol grip. Barrel length is 27 inches, but is of a smaller diameter than the Model 1928-30. Wartime models were produced by Sako and VKT. Tikkakoski and. "B" barrels were produced postwar. SAKO serial numbers range from 200000 to 260000. VKTs range from 20000 to 77000, but there are examples outside this range. The Civil Guard (SkY) serial numbers range from 500000 to 511000.

Exc.	*V.G.*	*Good*	*Fair*	*Poor*
375	300	250	175	125

NOTE: Add a 25 percent premium for SAKO-built rifles. Rifles marked "Sk.Y" (Civil Guard) will command a 100 percent premium.

Bayonet for Model 1939

Wood handle. Muzzle ring. Crosspiece bent slightly forward. Marked "SKY" on one side of ricasso and "Veljekset Kulmala" on the other. 7.5-inch single edge blade. These have been reproduced recently and the example shown here is a reproduction. The reproductions run $70-40 retail. Original specimans do not have a blued blade. Price range 275 – 150.

Model 28/76 Target Rifle

This is a M-28 that was modified for target shooting. Made in the mid-1970s from m-28/30 rifles. Features a turned down bolt handle, target type peep sight and globe front sight. The original barrel was left intact. A new target type stock is installed. Several hundred were imported in the mid 2000's.

Exc.	*V.G.*	*Good*	*Fair*	*Poor*
1000	750	600		

Swedish Model 1896 Rifle

Used by the Finns without modifications, these rifles have "SA" Finnish army property markings on the receiver. Some of these rifles were lent to the Finnish government, some were sold to them.

Exc.	*V.G.*	*Good*	*Fair*	*Poor*
600	450	350	200	150

Italian Model 1938 Carcanco 7.35mm

Marked with the "SA" property marking on the rear left side of the barrel. These are more common than the Italian issue M-38s without the SA marking.

Exc.	*V.G.*	*Good*	*Fair*	*Poor*
275	200	150	125	100

FINNISH SNIPER RIFLES

In 1937 the Finns began to develop a sniper rifle built around the Mosin-Nagant rifle. Approximately 400 M39 sniper rifles were built with a 3X Physica telescope.

Finnish army ownership marking on a Sweedish Model 1896 •
Courtesy Stoddard Martial collection, Paul Goodwin photo

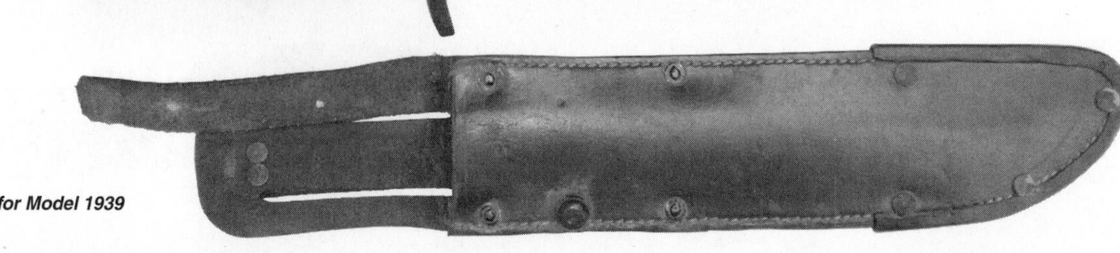

Bayonet for Model 1939

These scopes were a prismatic box design for use, not only on rifles, but on machine guns and mortars as well. During World War II the Finns used the Model 39 rifle with German Ajacks scope. About 500 of these rifles were built, and were known as the Model 39/43. Finland also used Soviet scopes on its rifles with Ajacks mounts. These Soviet scopes were designated the PE and PEM. The only difference was that the PEM scope has no focusing ring on the eyepiece.

NOTE: There are no known examples of Finnish sniper rifles in the U.S.

TRG-21

The receiver is similar to the TRG-S, but the polyurethane stock features a unique design. The trigger is adjustable for length and two-stage pull and also for horizontal or vertical pitch. This model also has several options that would affect the price: muzzle brake, one-piece scope mount, bipod, quick detachable sling swivels, and military nylon sling. The rifle is offered in 7.62 NATO only. It is fitted with a 25.75-inch barrel and weighs 10.5 lbs.

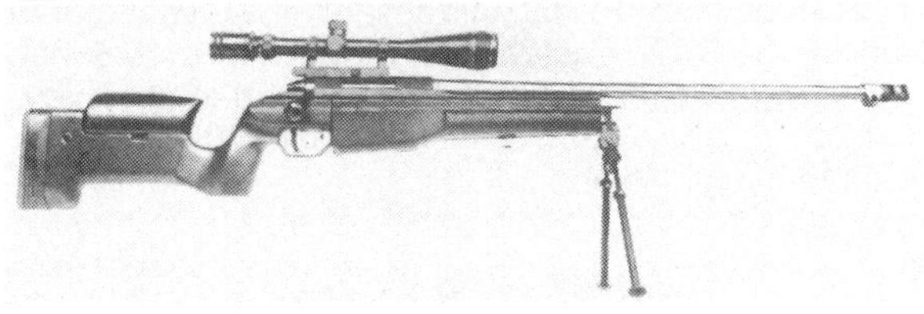

NIB	Exc.	V.G.	Good	Fair	Poor
3500	2750	1850	—	—	—

TRG-22

This model is similar to the TRG-21 but meets Finnish military requirements. Introduced in 2000.

NIB	Exc.	V.G.	Good	Fair	Poor
2700	2000	—	—	—	—

TRG-41

Exactly the same as the TRG-21 except chambered for the .338 Lapua Magnum cartridge.

NIB	Exc.	V.G.	Good	Fair	Poor
4350	3500	2500	1500	—	—

TRG-42

This model is similar to the TRG-41 but meets Finnish military requirements. Introduced in 2000.

NIB	Exc.	V.G.	Good	Fair	Poor
3100	2300	—	—	—	—

Valmet M62

Based on the third model AK-47 but with internal differences built by Valmet. SAKO also built many of these rifles. Machined receiver. Perforated plastic forend and handguard. Tube butt. Barrel length is 16.5 inches. Magazine is 30 rounds. Rate of fire is about 650 rounds per minute. Weight is about 9 lbs. Production in Finland began in 1965. Rifles produced from 1965 to 1969 were designated "M 62 PT." PT stands for day sight. In 1969 Model 62s were produced with folding night sights. Beginning in 1972 these night sights were fitted with tritium inserts.

NOTE: There are a number of different versions of this rifle: the M62-76–a Finnish AKM; the M62-76M plastic stock; M62-76P wood stock; M62-76T tubular steel folding stock.

Pre-1968

Exc.	V.G.	Fair
N/A	N/A	N/A

Pre-1986 conversions of semi-automatic model

Exc.	V.G.	Fair
10000	8500	N/A

Valmet M62S

A semi-automatic version of the M62 imported for sale in the U.S. by Interarms. Offered in both 7.62x39mm and 5.56x45mm.

NIB	Exc.	V.G.	Good	Fair	Poor
3000	2800	2300	900	750	500

Valmet M71

A different version of the M62 with solid plastic butt and rear sight in front of chamber. Sheet metal receiver.

Right and left side of M62 • *Courtesy Blake Stevens, Kalashnikov, **The Arms and the Man**, Collector Grade Publications*

Chambered for the 7.62x39mm and the 5.56x45mm cartridges. Weight reduced to 8 lbs.

Pre-1968

Exc.	*V.G.*	*Fair*
N/A	N/A	N/A

Pre-1986 conversions of semi-automatic version

Exc.	*V.G.*	*Fair*
10000	8500	N/A

Valmet M71S

A semi-automatic version of the M71 imported for sale in the U.S. by Interarms.

Model 71S • *Courtesy Blake Stevens, Kalashnikov: Arms and the Man, Ezell*

NIB	*Exc.*	*V.G.*	*Good*	*Fair*	*Poor*
1750	1250	1000	750	n/a	n/a

Valmet M76

This model has a number of fixed or folding stock options. It is fitted with a 16.3-inch barrel and has a magazine capacity of 15, 20, or 30 rounds. Its rate of fire is 700 rounds per minute. It is chambered for the 7.62x39mm Soviet cartridge or the 5.56x45mm cartridge. Weight is approximately 8 lbs. Marked "VALMET JYVAKYLA M78" on the right side of the receiver. Produced from 1978 to 1986.

There are 10 variants of this model.

Pre-1968

Exc.	*V.G.*	*Fair*
N/A	N/A	N/A

Pre-1986 conversions of semi-automatic version

Exc.	*V.G.*	*Fair*
12500	10000	N/A

NOTE: For rifles in 7.62x39mm caliber add a 20 percent premium. For rifles chambered for .308 caliber deduct $2,500.

Model 78 (Semi-automatic)

As above, in 7.62x51mm, 7.62x39mm, or .223 with a 24.5" heavy barrel, wood stock, and integral bipod. Semi-automatic-only version.

Valmet Model 78 • *Courtesy Chuck Karwan*

NIB	*Exc.*	*V.G.*	*Good*	*Fair*	*Poor*
1750	1350	1000	850	600	300

MACHINE GUNS

During the early years the Finns used the Maxim Model 09, Maxim Model 21 and the Maxim Model 09-32, all chambered for the 7.62mm cartridge.

Model 76 (stamped receiver) • *Courtesy Blake Stevens, Kalashnikov: Arms and the Man, Ezell*

Lahti Saloranta Model 26

Designed and built as a light machine gun this model was chambered for the 7.62mm rimmed cartridge. Fitted with a 20-round box magazine or a 75-round drum magazine. The rate of fire was about 500 rounds per minute. Weight is approximately 23 lbs. This gun was also chambered for the 7.92mm cartridge for sale to the Chinese prior to WWII.

Pre-1968

Exc.	*V.G.*	*Fair*
Too Rare To Price		

Valmet M62 (AK)

First introduced in 1962, this assault rifle is chambered for the 7.62x39mm cartridge. Fitted with a 16.5-inch barrel. Plastic forend with single strut butt. Thirty-round magazine. Rate of fire is about 650 rounds per minute. Weight is about 9 lbs.

Pre-1968

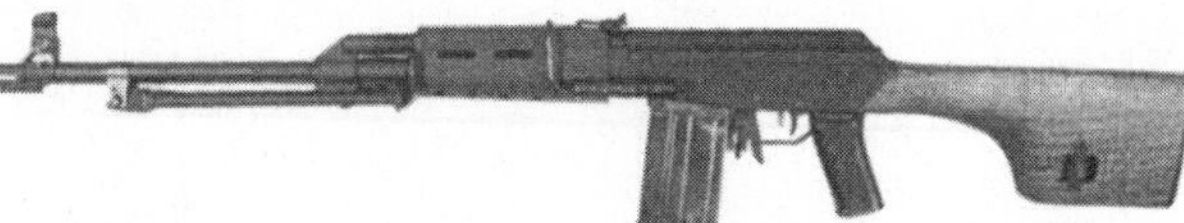

Model 62 • *Courtesy Blake Stevens, Kalashnikov: Arms and the Man, Ezell*

Exc.	*V.G.*	*Fair*
N/A	N/A	N/A

Pre-1986 conversions of semi-automatic version

Exc.	*V.G.*	*Fair*
12000	9500	N/A

Valmet M78

This model is a heavy-barrel version of the Valmet M76. Barrel length is 18.75 inches. It is offered in 7.62x39mm and 5.56x45mm calibers as well as few in 7.62 NATO. Marked "VALMET Jyvaskyla M78" on the right side of the receiver. Rate of fire is about 650 rounds per minute and magazine capacity is 15 or 30 rounds. Weight is about 10.3 lbs. Produced from 1978 to 1986.

Courtesy private NFA collection

Pre-1968

Exc.	*V.G.*	*Fair*
N/A	N/A	N/A

Pre-1986 conversions of semi-automatic version

Exc.	*V.G.*	*Fair*
12000	9500	N/A

NOTE: For guns chambered for 7.62x39 add 20 percent.

The French Republic, largest of the West European nations, has an area of 210,026 sq. mi. (547,030 sq. km.) and a population of 58.1 million. Capital: Paris. Agriculture, manufacturing, tourist industry and financial services are the most important elements of France's diversified economy. Textiles and clothing, steel products, machinery and transportation equipment, chemicals, pharmaceuticals, nuclear electricity, agricultural products and wine are exported.

The monarchy was ousted by the Revolution of 1848 and the Second Republic proclaimed. Louis Napoleon Bonaparte (nephew of Napoleon I) was elected president of the Second Republic. He was proclaimed emperor in 1852. As Napoleon III, he gave France two decades of prosperity under a stable, autocratic regime, but led it to defeat in the Franco-Prussian War of 1870, after which the Third Republic was established.

The Third Republic endured until 1940 and the capitulation of France to the swiftly maneuvering German forces. Marshal Philippe Petain formed a puppet government that sued for peace and ruled unoccupied France until 1942 from Vichy. Meanwhile, General Charles de Gaulle escaped to London where he formed a wartime government in exile and the Free French army. De Gaulle's provisional exile government was officially recognized by the Allies after the liberation of Paris in 1944, and De Gaulle, who had been serving as head of the provisional government, tacitly maintained that position. In October 1945, the people overwhelmingly rejected a return to the prewar government, thus paving the way for the formation of the Fourth Republic in 1947 just after the dismissal of De Gaulle, at grips with a coalition of rival parties, the Communists especially.

In actual operation, the Fourth Republic was remarkably like the Third, with the National Assembly the focus of power causing a constant governmental instability. The later years of the Fourth Republic were marked by a burst of industrial expansion unmatched in modern French history. The growth rate, however, was marred by a two colonial wars, nagging inflationary trend that weakened the franc and undermined the betterment of the people's buying power. This and the Algerian conflict led to the recall of De Gaulle to power, the adoption of a new constitution vesting strong powers in the executive, and the establishment in 1959 of the current Fifth Republic.

HANDGUNS

Bibliographical Note: For additional historical information, technical data, and photos, see Eugene Medlin and Jean Huon, ***Military Handguns of France, 1858-1958***, Excalibur Publications, 1993.

Model 1870 Navy (Navy Contract)

This 6-shot solid-frame fixed-cylinder revolver uses a mechanical ejection system. Chambered for the 11mm cartridge and fitted with a 4.7-inch round barrel. Smooth wooden grips with lanyard loop. Adopted by the French navy in 1870 and remained in service until 1900. Built by the French firm "LEFAUCHEUX" in Paris. Marked "E LEFAUCHEUX" on the top of the frame, and on the right side "BVT. S.G.D.G. PARIS" with a naval anchor on the butt cap of the grip. This revolver was the first centerfire handgun to be adopted by any nation's military. About 6,000 revolvers were built under contract.

A modified version of this pistol was built by the French arsenal at St. Etienne (MAS) designated the Model 1870N. About 4,000 of these revolvers were produced and are marked, "MODEL 1870" on the top strap and "MODIFIE N" on the right side of the sighting groove. The military arsenal proof of MAS is on the cylinder and the underside of the barrel.

Revolvers fitted with military extractors have the extractor located along the barrel while civilian revolvers have the extractor located offset from the barrel.

Model 1873 with barrel and frame markings •
Paul Goodwin photo

FRANCE

Military Extractor

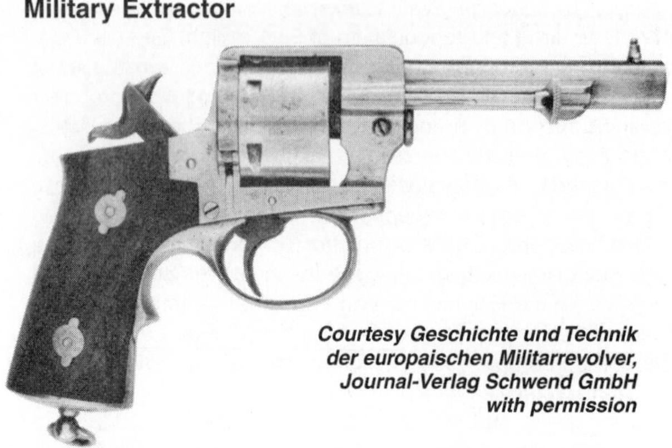

Courtesy Geschichte und Technik der europaischen Militarrevolver, Journal-Verlag Schwend GmbH with permission

Exc.	V.G.	Good	Fair	Poor
3500	2000	1500	800	500

Civilian Extractor

Exc.	V.G.	Good	Fair	Poor
2500	1500	1000	600	400

Model 1873

Built on a Chamelot-Delvigne type locking system with a solid frame, fixed cylinder, and mechanical rod ejection. Chambered for the 11mm cartridge and fitted with a 4.7-inch half-round half-octagon barrel. Non-fluted cylinder. It is both a single- and double-action revolver. Finish was left in the white. Marked "MRE D'ARMES ST. ETIENNE" on the right side of the frame. On top of the barrel marked "MLE 1873" There are many other small markings on the revolver as well. Weight is approximately 36 oz. Built by French military armory at St. Etienne. Between 1873 and 1886 approximately 350,000 of these revolvers were produced.

"Mle 1873"

Exc.	V.G.	Good	Fair	Poor
650	500	350	250	175

Army

Exc.	V.G.	Good	Fair	Poor
650	500	350	250	175

Navy, marked "Mle 1873 M"

Exc.	V.G.	Good	Fair	Poor
950	600	500	300	175

French Holster for 1873 Revolver

Clamshell design. Leather construction. Beware of reproductions. Price range: 250 – 100.

French Holster for 1873 Revolver

Model 1874

The Model 1874 was essentially the same as the Model 1873 but with a fluted cylinder and blued finish. Used by French naval officers from 1878 to 1945. Between 1874 and 1886 approximately 36,000 of these revolvers were produced.

Army

Exc.	V.G.	Good	Fair	Poor
800	600	400	300	175

Navy

Exc.	V.G.	Good	Fair	Poor
2500	1500	750	350	200

Model 1892

Chambered for an 8mm centerfire cartridge and has a 4.6-inch barrel with a 6-shot cylinder. Weight is about 30 oz. It is erroneously referred to as a "Lebel"; there is no certainty that Nicolas Lebel had anything to do with its design or production but he was the chairman

Model 1892 with frame markings • *Paul Goodwin photo*

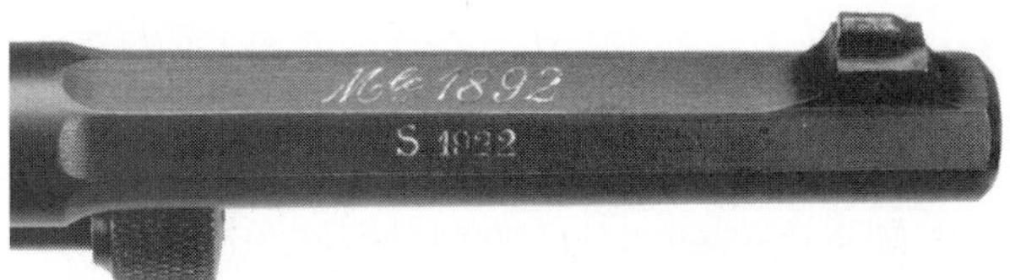

***Close-up of the barrel marking indicating year of manufacture on Model 1892** • Courtesy Stoddard Martial collection, Paul Goodwin photo*

of the selection board that chose the design. This revolver is a simple double action, with a swing-out cylinder that swings to the right side for loading. The design of this weapon is similar to that of the Italian Model 1889. There is one redeeming feature on this revolver, and that is a hinged side plate on the left side of the frame that could be swung away after unlocking so that repairs or cleaning of the lockwork could be performed with relative simplicity. The cartridge for which this weapon was chambered was woefully inadequate. This revolver remained in use from its introduction in 1893 until the end of WWII in 1945, mainly because the French never got around to designing a replacement.

NOTE: There are a number of commercial variations of this revolver, some of which are Spanish-made copies and others are St. Etienne commercial examples.

Navy (anchor on butt)

Exc.	V.G.	Good	Fair	Poor
600	500	400	275	200

Army

Exc.	V.G.	Good	Fair	Poor
450	325	275	200	150

Model 1892 "A Pompe"

As above, except that the cylinder latch is a sleeve around the ejector rod that can be moved forward to release the cylinder.

Exc.	V.G.	Good	Fair	Poor
750	550	300	150	100

Holster for Mle 1892 Revolver

Leather costruction with top flap. Ammo pouch under flap has three loops for feed strips that held six cartridges each. Two belt loops on the back and some have shoulder strap loops as well.

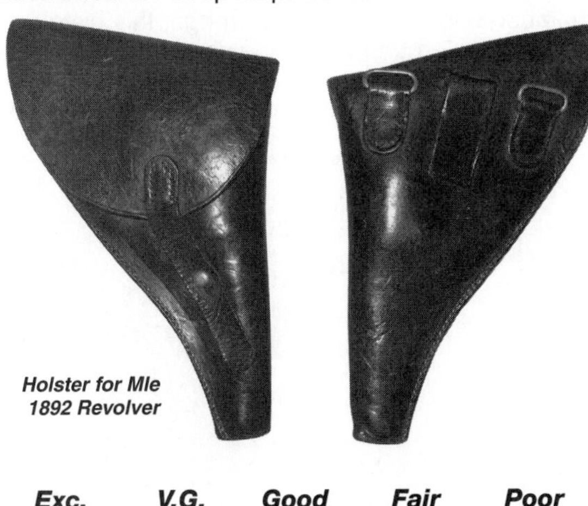

Holster for Mle 1892 Revolver

Exc.	V.G.	Good	Fair	Poor
150	100	75	40	25

Le Francais Model 28 Type Armee

A unique pistol chambered for the 9mm Browning cartridge. It is a large pistol with a 5-inch barrel that was hinged with a tip-up breech. This is a blowback-operated semi-automatic pistol that has no extractor. The empty cases are blown out of the breech by gas pressure. The one feature about this pistol that is desirable is that it is possible to tip the barrel breech forward like a shotgun and load cartridges singly, while holding the contents of the magazine in reserve. This weapon has fixed sights and a blued finish, with checkered walnut grips. It was manufactured in 1928 and built by Manufrance. This pistol was submitted to the French government for military issue but was not accepted. Only a few pistols were purchased by the French government for trials.

Exc.	V.G.	Good	Fair	Poor
1250	950	750	500	200

Model 1935A

A 7.65mm French Long caliber semi-automatic pistol with a 4.3-inch barrel. Magazine capacity is 8 rounds. Fixed sights. Weight is about 26 oz. Eventually became known as the Model 1935A. This pistol was designed and built for the French military and about 10,000 were produced up to June 20, 1940, when the factory, SACM (Societe Alsacienne des Constructions Mecaniques, Cholet, France), was occupied by

***Model 1935A** • Courtesy private collection*

FRANCE

German troops. About 24,000 were built and used by the German army during World War II.

German Waffenamt Model (7.65mm Pistole 625f)

Exc.	V.G.	Good	Fair	Poor
475	350	275	200	150

Standard Model

Exc.	V.G.	Good	Fair	Poor
300	200	150	125	100

Model 1935S

As above, with an enlarged chamber area that locked into the ejection port and a 4.3" barrel. Built by MAC Chatellerault, MAS, SAGEM, and MF (Manufrance). About 85,000 pistols were produced between 1939 and 1953. The French Foreign Legion used this pistol in fighting in Indo-China in 1953 and 1954. It was also used by French forces during the Algerian Rebellion between 1954 and 1962.

Model 1935S • Courtesy Richard M. Kumor Sr.

Exc.	V.G.	Good	Fair	Poor
300	300	150	125	100

MAB Model D

This semi-automatic pistol is built along the lines of the FN Model 1910. Built in Bayonne, France (MAB). Chambered for the 7.65mm cartridge. Early examples had a steel frame and later ones had an alloy frame. German army test and acceptance marks stamped on pistol. About 50,000 were produced during World War II.

Exc.	V.G.	Good	Fair	Poor
475	400	300	300	150

Standard model without German WW II marks

Many were imported in the 1980s and these have an adjustable rear sight made of plastic and replacement left grip with thumb rest. Both were added to make the pistol compliant with the GCA 1968 import rules.

Exc.	V.G.	Good	Fair	Poor
200	175	150	125	100

MAC/MAS Model 1950

A 9mm Parabellum caliber semi-automatic pistol with a 9-shot magazine. Barrel length is 4.4". Weight is about 34 oz. Blued, with ribbed plastic grips. The pistol's design was strongly influenced by the Model 1935S. The Model 1950 was used by all of the French military forces as the standard issue sidearm, including nations that were former French colonies. Approximately less than 350,000 Model 1950s were produced.

Exc.	V.G.	Good	Fair	Poor
750	550	400	275	200

MAS G1

This is a Beretta 92G, which is a double action 9mm pistol with decocking lever. Barrel length is 4.9 inches. Magazine capacity is 15 rounds. Weight is about 34 oz. Military marked. No known U.S. imports.

Exc.	V.G.	Good	Fair	Poor
N/A	—	—	—	—

MAB PA-15

This pistol is a French military version of the commercial Unique Model R Para. Chambered for the 9mm Parabellum cartridge and fitted with a 4.5" barrel. Magazine capacity is 15 rounds. Weight is about 38 oz. This pistol was officially adopted by the French military. A target version of this pistol, the F1 Target, was adopted by the French air force and army.

MAS Model 1950 • Private collection, Paul Goodwin photo

Exc.	V.G.	Good	Fair	Poor
600	450	350	200	100

UNIQUE

When the French Vichy government signed an armistice with Germany in 1940, the Germans occupied Handaye in France, the site of Manufacture D'Armes Des Pyrenees. This factory then produced for the German army the Model 16 and Model 17.

Model 16

Chambered for the 7.65mm cartridge, this pistol was fitted with a 7-round magazine. German army proof test and acceptance stamp. Hard rubber grips. About 2,000 were built under German supervision.

Model 16 • Courtesy Orvel Reichert

Exc.	V.G.	Good	Fair	Poor
550	450	300	175	100

Model 17

Similar to the above but with a 9-shot magazine. About 30,000 of these pistols were built under German control.

Exc.	*V.G.*	*Good*	*Fair*	*Poor*
500	425	275	175	100

Unique Kriegsmodell

This is an improved Model 17 with exposed hammer. Approximately 18,000 were manufactured under German occupation.

Exc.	*V.G.*	*Good*	*Fair*	*Poor*
600	450	300	200	100

SAVAGE

Model 1907 (French Model 1907-13)

A .32 or .380 semi-automatic pistol with a 3.75- or 4.25-inch barrel, depending upon caliber, and a 9- or 10-shot magazine. Blued with hard rubber grips. The .380 caliber model is worth approximately 30 percent more than the values listed below. This pistol was sold to the French government during World War I and used by the French military. These guns were not stamped with French acceptance marks. The first shipment was made in 1914. Most of these pistols were fitted with a lanyard ring. French contract Model 1907 pistols were chambered for the 7.65mm cartridge and are fitted with a chamber indicator. Most French pistols will have the caliber designation in both ".32 CAL" and "7.65MM" stamped on the slide. Approximately 30,000 to 40,000 of these pistols were sold to France. Serial number ranges for these pistols are 105,000 to 130,000 and 136,000 to 167,000. There are a few in the 80,000 to 90,000 serial number range. There were fewer than 50 experimental Savage pistols numbered 000xx-A. These rare pistols will bring a substantial premium.

Courtesy Orvel Reichert

Exc.	*V.G.*	*Good*	*Fair*	*Poor*
850	600	450	300	150

NOTE: It is very rare to find a military Savage in very good or better condition. Beware refinished pistols.

SUBMACHINE GUNS

The French used the German 9mm Erma submachine gun prior to WWII. The first French-designed and -built submachine gun was the MAS 35, designated the SE-MAS Type L, chambered for the 7.65 Long pistol cartridge and built at Manufacture d'Armes de St. Etienne, St. Etienne, France. This gun was quickly superseded by the more common MAS 38.

MAS 35 SE

This model is the forerunner of the MAS 38. Chambered for the 7.65mm long cartridge. Barrel length is 8.8 inches. Rate of fire is approximately 600 rounds per minute. Full auto fire only. Fed by a 32-round box magazine. Rear sight has 100 and 200 meter settings. Weight is about 6.25 lbs.

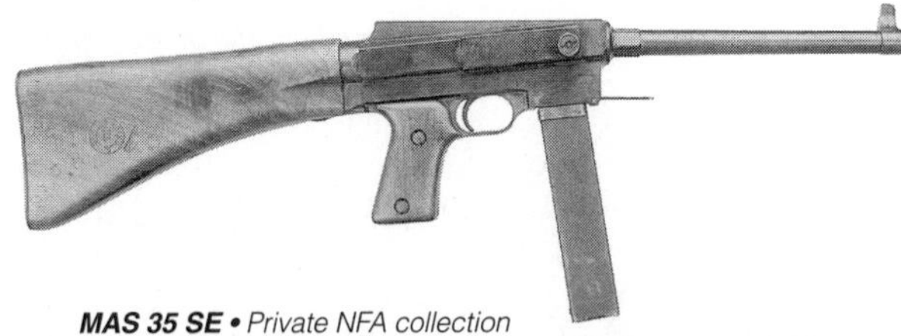

MAS 35 SE • *Private NFA collection*
Paul Goodwin photo

Pre-1968

Exc.	*V.G.*	*Fair*
7500	6500	5500

MAS 38

Built in France and chambered for the 7.65mm French Long cartridge. Fitted with an 8.75-inch barrel and a magazine capacity of 32 rounds. Fitted with a fixed wooden butt. Rate of fire is about 650 rounds per minute. Uses a folding trigger for safety. Weight is approximately 6.5 lbs. On the left side of the receiver marked "CAL 7.65 L MAS 1938." Produced from 1938 to 1946.

Pre-1968

Exc.	*V.G.*	*Fair*
7000	6000	5500

MAT 49

This French submachine gun was first produced in 1949 and is no longer in production. Built at the French arsenal at Tulle using a stamped steel frame and receiver, it is chambered for the 9mm cartridge and fitted with a 9-inch barrel. The magazine housing acts as a forward grip and folds forward under the barrel. Fitted with an ejection port cover. It was used by French forces and is still found in former French colonies. The magazine capacity is 32 rounds and the weight is about 8 lbs. Rate of fire is 600 rounds per minute. Markings are "M.A.T. MLE 49 9M/M" on the left side of the receiver.

FRANCE

MAS 38 • Courtesy West Point Museum, Paul Goodwin photo

MAT 49 with receiver markings • Paul Goodwin photo

Pre-1968

Exc.	V.G.	Fair
18000	15000	12500

Pre 1986 manufacture with new receiver or re-weld

Exc.	V.G.	Fair
14000	12000	10000

Hotchkiss Type Universal

Introduced in 1949 and intended as a police weapon. Select-fire. It is a basic blowback design and chambered for the 9mm Parabellum cartridge. Fitted with a 10.8-inch barrel. Magazine capacity is 32 rounds. Rate of fire is about 650 rounds per minute.

The gun is made so that it can be folded to a very compact size. The stock, magazine, and barrel collapse to make the overall length of the gun only

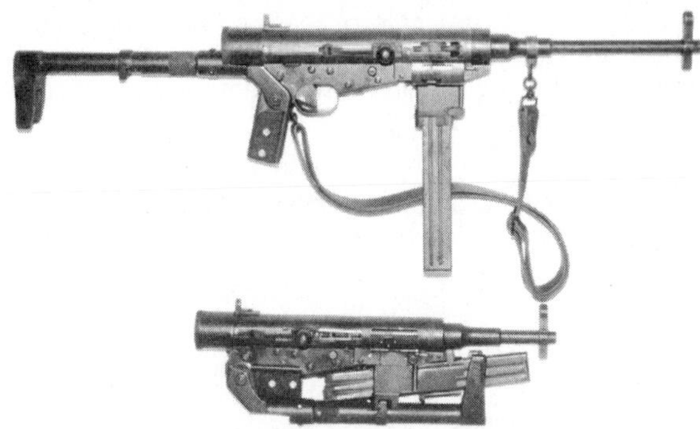

17.2 inches. Weight is approximately 7.5 lbs. This submachine gun saw limited use in Indo-China and a small number of guns were sold to Venezuela in the early 1950s.

Pre-1968 (Extremely rare; only one transferable sample known)

Exc.	V.G.	Fair
20000	—	—

FRENCH Pre-Cartridge Era Rifles

(including copies made in Liege, Belgium)
Charleville, St. Etienne, Chatellrault, Mutzig and Tulle Armories

Most of these firearms were the products of five major armories, the old Charleville Armory and St. Etienne works, and the newer armories at Chatellrault, Mutzig, and Tulle. The armory of manufacture was invariably inscribed in script upon the lock, usually preceded by an abbreviation "MANUFACTIRE ROY LE DE" or "M RE R LE DE" until 1848, "M RE N LE DE" from 1848 until 1852, and "M RE IMP ALE DE" after 1852, respectively representing, "The Royal Manufactory at," "The National Manufactory at," and "The Imperial Manufactory at ...." In addition to these lock markings, the specific model year was usually marked on the barrel tang, preceded by an "M." If the model had been altered, a "T" (for "transformed") was added after the date, and if subsequently remodeled, the script ("BIS" was added after that (for "again"). Date of manufacture usually appears upon the barrel, and also within the pressed circle surrounding the "touch mark" on the right side of the buttstock. Numerous inspection marks also appear on the metal parts of the gun.

The arms manufactured for the French military were widely copied in Europe's major firearms center, Liege, Belgium. The Liege gun trade, however, was based on the "factory" system. Each specialist, working out of his own cottage, manufactured one type of part on subcontract and delivered it to an assembler. Many of the final assemblers in Liege did not mark their products or did so only with crowned initials. Those that did usually marked their "products" upon the lockplates. Among the better known Liege assemblers' marks during the middle of the 19th century were ANCION & CIE/A LIEGE, A F (A. Francofte), B F (Beuret Freres), C D (probably for Charles Dandoy), D (anchor) C (probably Dejerdine & Co., Demousse & Co., or DeFooz & Co.), D L (DeLoneux) C. DANDOY/A LIEGE, A. & CH DE LONEUX DRISKET & WAROUX, G M (Gulikers Marquinay), V. GULIKERS/A LIEGE, J L (Joseph LeMille), L (anchor) C or L. LAMBIN & CIE/ LIEGE, LE MILLE/A LIEGE, P.J. MALHEREBE & CIE/ LIEGE, E. MUNSEUR/LIEGE, J.A. PETRY/A LIEGE, G. SCHOPEN/A LEIGE, TANNER & CIE., T. TILKEN/ A/LIEGE, AND V P (Vivario-Plombeur). It should be noted, however, that these makers produced not only copies of French arms, but also accepted contracts for arms from other European powers, notably Russia, Spain, the Piedmont, Saxony, and England. Whether marked on the lock or not, all Liege barrels were required to pass a proof of strength, and having done so were marked near their breech with a small tower and the Liege black powder proof, an oval encompassing the letters "E/LG/"(star). The main French firearms produced or copied during the muzzleloading era included the following:

French M1777 Flintlock Musket (for Infantry/Light Infantry)

Overall length 58-1/8 to 56 inches; barrel length 42-7/8 to 40-1/2 inches; caliber .69. Frequently called a Charleville musket as this was the main builder.

Exc.	V.G.	Good	Fair	Poor
—	4500	2850	1250	600

French M1816 Flintlock Musket (for Infantry/Light Infantry)

Overall length 58-1/8 to 56 inches; barrel length 42-7/8 to 40-1/2 inches; caliber .69. This musket is basically the French M1777 musket with minor improvements. Although the French did not subsequently alter this model to percussion, the Kingdom of Wurtemberg obtained several thousand from the Charleville Armory, which were altered to percussion and then rifled and sighted after their own models of 1842 and 1855, the barrel receiving a long-range French-style rear sight after rifling. As many as 2,000 of these may have been imported into the United States in 1862 by Marcellus Hartley.

In flintlock

Exc.	V.G.	Good	Fair	Poor
—	3500	1850	1000	500

Altered to percussion, rifled and sighted

Exc.	V.G.	Good	Fair	Poor
—	1450	800	450	250

French M1822 Flintlock Musket (for Infantry/Light Infantry)

Overall length 58 to 55-7/8 inches; barrel length 42-5/8 to 40-5/8 inches (40-5/8 inches for both types if "T

FRANCE

BIS"); caliber .69 (.71 for rifled versions). The French M1822 musket in either full infantry length or the shorter version for light infantry (***voltiguers***), set the pattern for most of the muskets subsequently adopted by the European powers during the second quarter of the 19th Century.

In the 1840s many were "transformed," i.e. altered to percussion by adding a convex bolster to the upper right side of the barrel near the breech for a cone and replacing the flintlock battery with a percussion hammer. With the adoption of the Minie ball projectile, it was determined to further upgrade these arms; however, because a new caliber had been adopted, the old barrels were deemed too thin to both enlarge and rifle. Accordingly, new barrels were made in .71 caliber. The percussion version was copied in Liege (by Ancion, Francotte, and Falise & Trapmann) for the Kingdom of Piedmont as its M1844 musket and M1860 rifle musket. These are distinguished by the enlarged tip of the hammer spur, a peculiar rear sight added to the breech and tang, and Liege markings.

In flintlock

Exc.	V.G.	Good	Fair	Poor
—	3500	1750	900	400

Altered to percussion, and rifled

Exc.	V.G.	Good	Fair	Poor
—	1250	800	450	250

French M1822 Cavalry and Lancer Flintlock Musketoons (and "T")

Overall length 34-5/8 inches; barrel length 19-5/8 inches; caliber .69. The main difference between the carbines carried by the cavalry and that of the lancers was the manner of slinging, with the latter having sling rings attached to the upper band and to a projection set into the buttstock. The ramrod was carried separately, consequently there was no inletting of the forestock. After 1842, both types were altered to percussion in the same manner as the M1822 muskets and pistols.

In flintlock

Exc.	V.G.	Good	Fair	Poor
—	1800	950	675	300

In percussion and rifled

Exc.	V.G.	Good	Fair	Poor
—	1250	650	400	150

French M1829 Artillery Flintlock Carbine (and "T BIS")

Overall length 37-1/4 to 38-1/4 inches (for "T BIS"); barrel length 23-5/8 inches; caliber .69/.71 (for "T BIS"). The carbine for artillerists was similar in configuration to that for the cavalry and lancers, differing primarily in having a ramrod in a channel below the barrel. After 1841, these arms were altered to percussion and after 1846 a bayonet lug with long guide was added to the right side of the barrel to accommodate the French M1847 yatagan saber bayonet. At the same time, a number of these arms were sighted, rifled, and a "tige" (a metal column or pillar) was inserted into the breech of the bore that permitted the arm to fire the Thouvenin projectile. After 1857 new barrels were manufactured that permitted the introduction of the standard Minie projectile of .71 caliber.

Exc.	V.G.	Good	Fair	Poor
—	1750	900	575	250

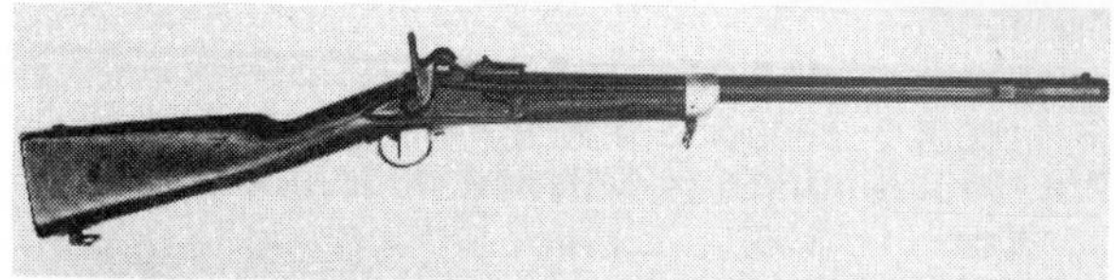

In percussion and rifled

Exc.	V.G.	Good	Fair	Poor
—	1000	600	350	150

French M1837 Rifle ("Carbine a la Poncharra")

Overall length 51-5/8 inches; barrel length 34-1/4 inches; caliber .69. The first of the French percussion arms for the general services, the M1837 rifle was designed on the Poncharra system. In this system, a chamber of lesser diameter than the bore was affixed to the barrel. A projectile of the diameter across the lands and its "sabot" was rammed into the barrel, and upon striking the lip of the chamber theoretically expanded into the rifling.

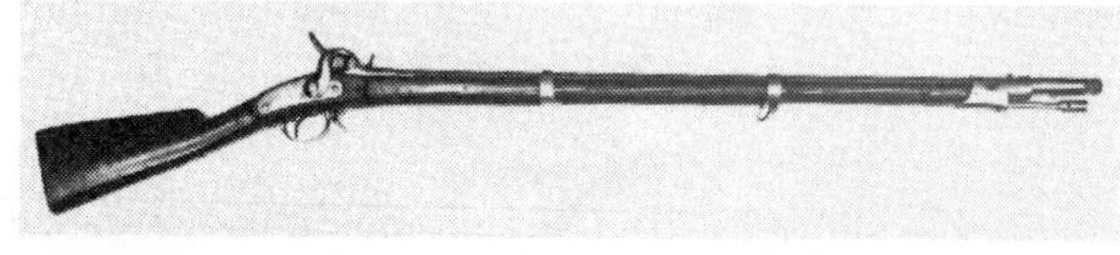

Exc.	V.G.	Good	Fair	Poor
—	2100	1250	650	250

French M1840 Rifle ("Carbine de Munition")

Overall length 48-1/8 inches; barrel 32-5/8 inches; caliber .71. After the success of the M1837 carbine, the rifle went into production at the armories at Mutzig and Chatellrault as the M1840 "carbine Tierry" or "carbine de munition." It was modified in 1842. The design was modified by adding a projection to the lower end of the buttplate. Herman Boker of New York City imported 25,000 of the M1840 rifles in 1862, but the slow twist of the rifling caused them to be classified as "4th class" weapons and none were issued.

Exc.	V.G.	Good	Fair	Poor
—	1750	900	450	200

French M1840 and M1842 Percussion Muskets (Infantry/Light Infantry)

Overall length 58-1/4 to 55-1/4 inches; barrel length 42-5/8 to 40-1/2 inches; caliber .71. The M1840 and M1842 muskets were the first percussion arms adopted for general infantry service in the French army, both being distinguished by employing back action percussion locks. The M1840 was distinguished from the M1842 by having a screwed in "patent" breech integrating the bolster, while the bolster of the M1842 musket was forged integral to the barrel, both flush with the right side of the barrel. The M1842 musket was later "transformed" to the M1842T by rifling the

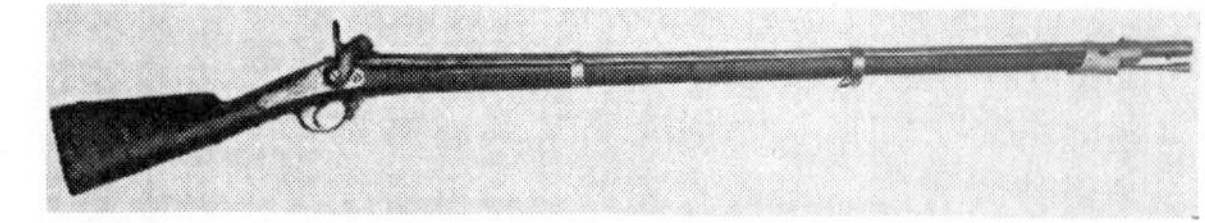

barrel with four broad grooves. The Belgian gun trade copied the M1842T both with and without the block rear sight that stood on the breechplug tang.

Exc.	V.G.	Good	Fair	Poor
—	1750	900	550	250

French M1853 Musket, M1853 "T" and M1857 Rifle-Muskets

Overall length 58-1/8 inches (M1853 infantry musket only) to 55-1/4 inches; barrels 42-5/8 (M1853 only) to 40-1/2 inches; caliber .71. In 1853, the M1842 series of arms was modified slightly, the most visible difference being the right face of the bolster, which stands away from the right side of the barrel. After the adoption of the "Minie ball" as the main projectile of the French army, the new M1857 rifle musket was introduced. It was essentially the same as the M1853 "T" light infantry musket but its bore was rifled with four broad grooves.

Exc.	V.G.	Good	Fair	Poor
—	1450	850	450	200

French M1846 and M1853 Rifles ("Carbine a tige")

Overall length 49-1/4 inches; barrel length 34-1/4"; caliber .71. In 1846 the French abandoned the Delvigne chamber rifles in favor of a different method of compressing the projectile into the rifling, that of M. Thouvenin. In Thouvenin's system, the chamber with a lip was replaced with a metal column or pillar "a tige" extending from the breechplug into the bore. After the powder settled around the "tige" the bullet was rammed into the bore and compressed against the tige to expand it into the rifling. The rifle adopted in 1853 differed from the original model adopted in 1846 only in the bolster configuration, the latter extending away from the right side of the barrel. At least a thousand Belgian made "carbines a tige" were imported into the Confederacy in 1861. Accordingly, Belgian "tige" rifles with proven Southern usage should command a premium over those without such history.

Exc.	V.G.	Good	Fair	Poor
—	1750	900	550	250

French M1853 "T" and M1859 Rifles ("Carbine de Vincennes")

Overall length 49-1/4 inches; barrel length 34-1/4 inches; caliber .71. With the adoption of the self expanding "Minie ball" in 1857, the French ordnance soon adopted a rifle which was suitable for it, the M1859 "carbine de Vincennes." Beginning in 1860, the M1853 "tige" rifles were "transformed" by the removal of the pillars from the breechplugs and fitting them with the rear sight leaves of the M1859 rifle. The M1853 "T" and M1859 French rifle was widely copied in Liege, and thousands were exported to the United States during the American Civil War, while most of the French made M1859 rifles reposed in French arsenals. Like the M1840 and M1846 and M1853 rifles, the M1859 rifle took a long yatagan blade saber bayonet that was affixed to a lug with a guide on the right side of the barrel.

Exc.	V.G.	Good	Fair	Poor
—	1750	950	550	250

RIFLES

CHASSEPOT

Model 1866 Rifle

This needle gun, bolt-action, single-shot model was an improvement over the German Dreyse. Chambered for the 11mm nitrated paper or cloth cartridge with an internal priming pellet. Barrel length is 32.5" with full stock with two barrel bands. These rifles were adopted by the French military in 1866. The rifle was made by a number of different French arsenals as well as contractors in England, Belgium, Spain, and Austria. About 600,000 of these rifles were captured by the Germans during the Franco-Prussian War in 1870-71. Some of these were converted to 11x50.2R Bavarian Werder cartridge and stamped with German acceptance marks. Some rifles were then later converted to the 11.15x60R Mauser cartridge. A total of 1,000,000 rifles were built by 1870.

Exc.	V.G.	Good	Fair	Poor
900	750	500	300	150

Model 1866 Carbines

Several different variations of carbines were built on the Chassepot action. Some were half stocked and others had full stocks. Some were fitted with brass buttplates, triggerguards, and barrel bands.

Exc.	V.G.	Good	Fair	Poor
1150	900	750	450	300

Bayonet for 1866 Chassepot

Brass handle. Muzzle ring. Hook quillon. 22.5-inch single edge yatagan blade. Steel scabbard. Makers name and date engraved in cursive on top of blade. Price range 175 – 75.

***MAS 38** • Courtesy Rock Island Auction Company*

Bayonet for Model 1866 Chassepot

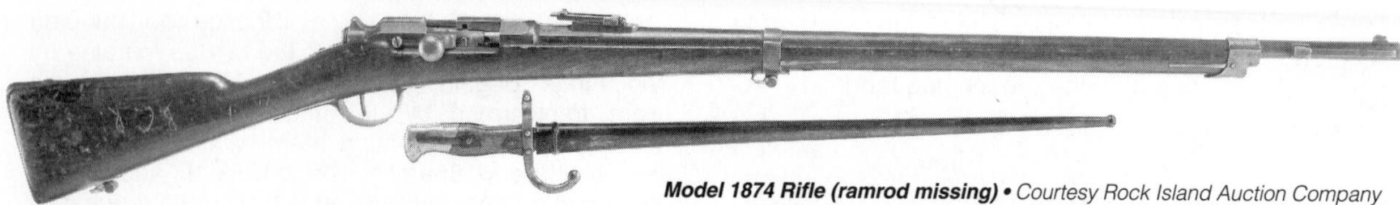

Model 1874 Rifle (ramrod missing) • Courtesy Rock Island Auction Company

PEABODY

Spanish Rifle (1869)

Identical to the Spanish Rifle. Chambered for the .43 Spanish centerfire cartridge and fitted with a 33-inch barrel. Full stock with two barrel bands. Blued barrel and case hardened furniture. About 33,000 rifles were produced for the French government.

Exc.	V.G.	Good	Fair	Poor
950	650	500	300	250

GRAS

Model 1874 & M1874/M14 & M80

An 11x59Rmm caliber bolt action single shot rifle with a 32-inch barrel with a walnut stock, two iron barrel bands, and a metal tip. The bayonet is a spike blade with a wood handle and a brass butt cap. Many of these rifles were converted early in WWI to 8x50.5Rmm Lebel caliber by sleeving the barrel and re-chambering. This converted rifle was designated the 1874/ M14. Many of the conversions were fitted with wooden handguards. The rifle was built at Chatellerault, Mutzig, Tulle and so marked.

There was a Musketoon version, model designation M1874, with 27-inch barrel and three brass barrel bands. The Musketoon did not have a bayonet lug. It was made at St. Chatellerault and so marked.

A Carbine version was also built at St. Etienne and so marked. It was designated the M80 and was fitted with a 20-inch barrel with two brass barrel bands.

Rifle

Exc.	V.G.	Good	Fair	Poor
800	650	500	250	150

Musketoon

Exc.	V.G.	Good	Fair	Poor
1000	850	600	350	200

Carbine

Exc.	V.G.	Good	Fair	Poor
1000	850	600	350	200

Bayonet for Gras Model 1874

Wood grips with brass pommel. 20.5-inch single edge blade that is a tapered T shape with the flat edge on top. Hooked quillon. Manufacturers name and year are engraved on the top of the blade. Serial numbered on the quillon and scabbard. Price range 125 – 50.

Model 1878 & 1878/M84 Navy

This rifle was produced at Steyr on contract with the French navy and marines. It was fitted with a 29-inch barrel and chambered for the 11x59R Gras cartridge. It has a 6-round magazine tube in the forend. The rifle was loaded through the action with the bolt open. These rifles will probably be marked "STEYR MLE. 1878 MARINE" on the left side of the receiver.

The 1878/M84 variation had the magazine extending slightly beyond the forend cap. The 1878/84 was produced at Chatellerault and St. Etienne. It was not made by Steyr.

Exc.	V.G.	Good	Fair	Poor
850	650	400	200	150

LEBEL

The Lebel system was invented by Nicolas Lebel in 1886. The French replaced the single-shot Gras Model 1874 rifle with this weapon. This was the first successful smallbore rifle and sent the rest of the European continent into a dash to emulate it. The Lebel was chambered for the 8mm Lebel cartridge with smokeless powder. The Lebel system was used until World War I when it was supplemented by the Berthier rifle.

Model 1886 "Lebel"

Chambered for the 8mm Lebel cartridge. While the cartridge was the first to use smokeless powder, the rifle was based on the old Gras Model 1874. It has a 31-inch barrel and holds 8 shots in a tubular magazine that runs beneath the barrel. This design is long and heavy and was not in use for long before being replaced by the more efficient box magazine weapons, such as those from Mauser. This rifle has a two-piece stock with no upper handguard. It is held on by two barrel bands, and a cruciform bayonet could be fixed under the muzzle. Weight of the rifle was

Bayonet for Gras Model 1874

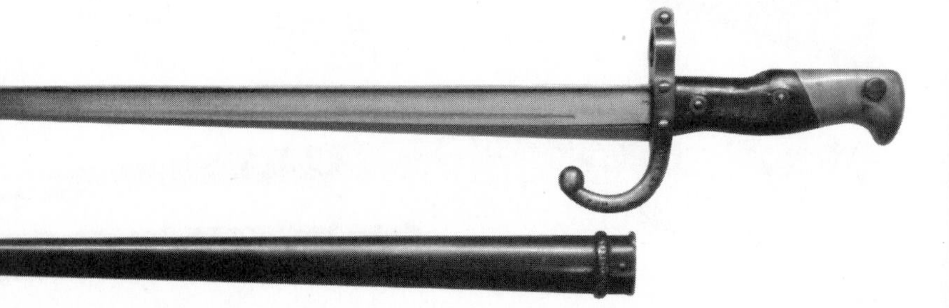

about 9.5 lbs. Although this rifle was made obsolete rather quickly, it did have the distinction of being the first successful smokeless powder smallbore rifle; there were shortened examples in use until the end of WWII. This rifle was made at Chatellerault, St. Etienne, and Tulle arsenals and so marked.

Exc.	V.G.	Good	Fair	Poor
750	550	450	350	250

Model 1886/M93/R35

A shorter version of the above. Fitted with a 17.7" barrel and a 3-round tubular magazine. Weight was about 7.8 lbs. Issued in 1935.

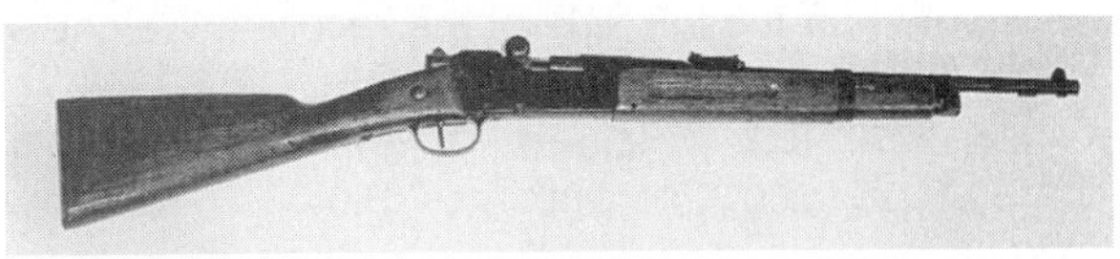

Exc.	V.G.	Good	Fair	Poor
550	450	375	300	250

NOTE: Add 50 percent for Nazi marked models.

Bayonets for Lebel and Berthier Rifles

Aluminum or brass handle with 15.75-inch inch spike blade. The early version, Model 1886, has a hook quillon. The quillon was eliminated during WWI with the Mle. 1886/15. The long thin blade and scabbard was found to be easily bent. The last version, Mle. 1886/35, had the blade shortened to 13.25 inches. Price range 100 – 40.

BERTHIER-MANNLICHER

Adolph Berthier was a French army officer. He developed his new design to accommodate the new, more modern 8mm cartridge. His bolt action rifles employed Mannlicher-style clips which were used to form part of the box magazine design. These clips fell out of the bottom of the action when the last round was chambered. The early models of Berthier rifles used 3-round clips. During WWI, a 5-round clip was adopted and many of the 3-shot models were modified to take the larger clips. Most Berthiers are numbered on the barrel, bolt, trigger guard and stock. Deduct 25% for mismatched parts.

Model 1890 Cavalry Carbine

This bolt action model has sling swivels mounted on the left side of the stock. The carbines did not have a bayonet lug. One-piece stock had a straight

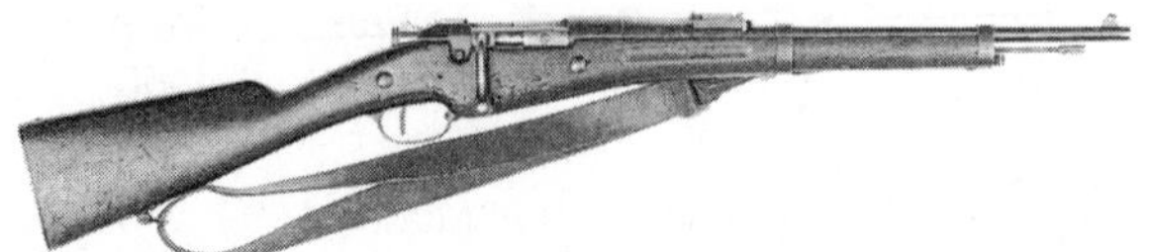

Courtesy Paul S. Scarlata, Collecting Classic Bolt Action Military Rifles

grip without a handguard. The stock just forward of the triggerguard was swelled, giving a potbelly appearance. This swell contained the magazine. Stock had two cross bolts. Bolt handle was extra long. Barrel length was 17.7 inches. Weight was approximately 6.8 lbs. These carbines were built at Chatellerault and St. Etienne arsenals and so marked in script on the left side of the receiver.

Exc.	V.G.	Good	Fair	Poor
600	475	300	150	100

Model 1892 Artillery

This model was similar in appearance to the Model 1890 carbine with the exception that it was fitted with a bayonet lug and bottom sling swivels. No handguard.

Exc.	V.G.	Good	Fair	Poor
550	400	300	150	100

Model 1892 Carbine

Chambered for the 8x50.5Rmm Lebel cartridge and fitted with a 17.5-inch barrel. One-piece stock bellied forward to fully enclose a box magazine with a 5-round capacity. Original Model 1892 carbine were not fitted with upper handguards, but conversions were so fitted. Turned-down bolt handle. Marked "MLE. 1892" on the left side of the receiver.

FRANCE

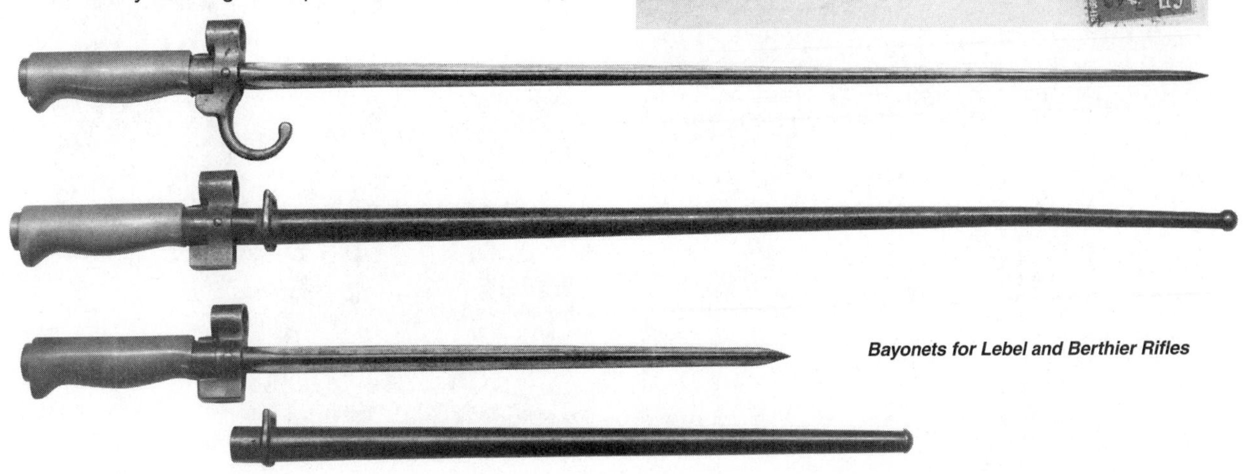

Bayonets for Lebel and Berthier Rifles

Exc.	V.G.	Good	Fair	Poor
650	500	400	200	150

Model 1892/M16

This is a conversion of the Model 1892 with the addition of a 5-round extended magazine and upper handguard. Conversion was done during WWI, hence the 1916 designation.

Exc.	V.G.	Good	Fair	Poor
450	325	250	150	100

NOTE: For rifles originally chambered for .22 rimfire add 100 percent.

Bayonet for 1892 and 1916 Berthier Carbine

Wood grips. Cross piece has two rivets. Barrel ring is cut out for the front sight. Hook quillon. 15.25-inch single edge blade. The upper edge of the blade has a short fuller at the tip, an unusual feature. Price range 80 – 40.

Model 1902

This model was based on the Model 1890 and 1892 carbines. It was designed for use by colonial troops in Indo-China. It was fitted with a 25-inch barrel with no upper handguard. One piece stock with straight grip with swell for magazine in front of triggerguard. Long bolt handle. Two crossbolts. These rifles were built at Chatellerault, St. Etienne, and Tulle arsenals, and so marked on the left side of the receiver. Weight was about 8 lbs.

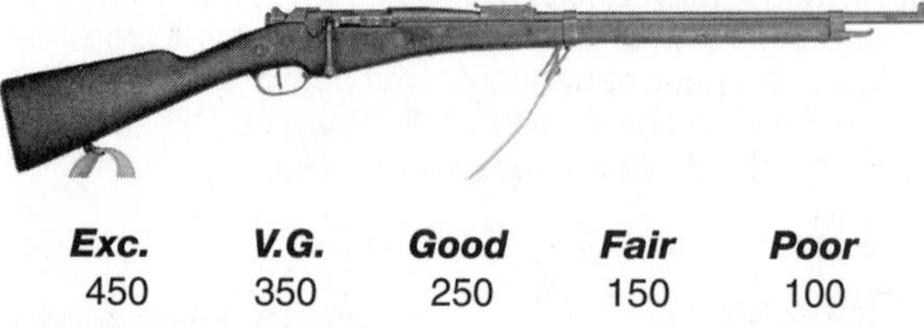

Exc.	V.G.	Good	Fair	Poor
450	350	250	150	100

Model 1907

Similar to the Model 1902 but with a 31.5-inch barrel. No upper handguard. Other specifications the same as the Model 1902 except weight was about 8.5 lbs.

Exc.	V.G.	Good	Fair	Poor
450	350	250	150	100

Model 1907/15

Similar to the Model 1907 except for a straight bolt design. Barrel length was 31.5 inches with upper handguard. Besides being built at the three French arsenals, this rifle was also made by Remington-UMC on contract in 1914 and 1915. These examples are so marked on the left side of the receiver. Weight is about 8.25 lbs.

Exc.	V.G.	Good	Fair	Poor
400	300	200	150	100

NOTE: Add 100 percent for Remington-built rifles.

Model 1916 Rifle

Similar to the Model 1907/15 except fitted with a 5-round extended magazine.

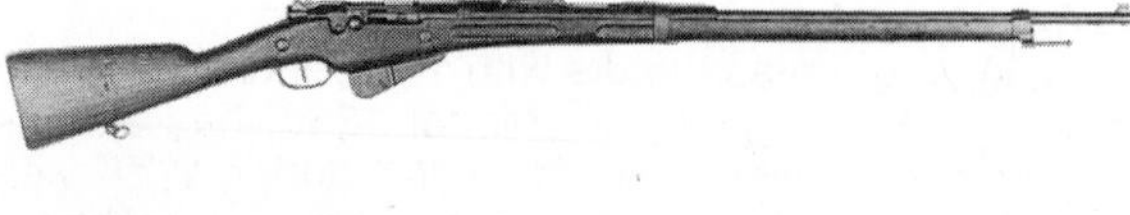

Exc.	V.G.	Good	Fair	Poor
450	300	200	150	100

Model 1916 Carbine

This is a Model 1916 rifle with a 17.7-inch barrel and 5-round magazine. Weight is about 7 lbs.

Exc.	V.G.	Good	Fair	Poor
400	275	200	150	100

Model 1907/15-M34

This model was fitted with a 23-inch barrel and a new Mauser-type 5-round staggered column magazine. Clips were no longer needed in this design. It was chambered for the 7.5x54 rimless cartridge. Weight is about 8 lbs. Some of these rifles were used during WWII.

Exc.	V.G.	Good	Fair	Poor
650	500	350	250	100

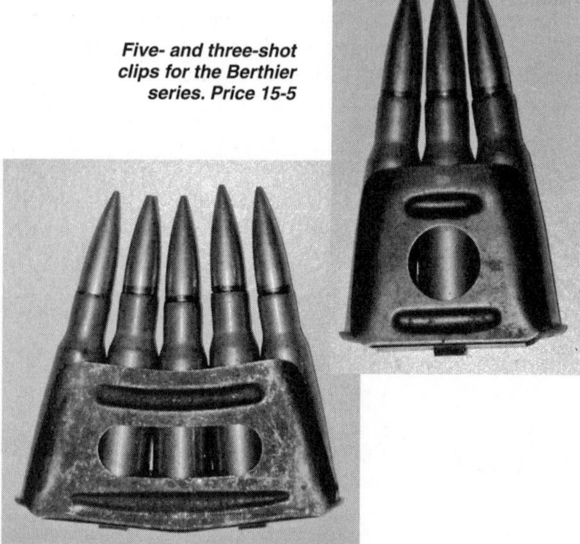

Five- and three-shot clips for the Berthier series. Price 15-5

Model 1907/15 • *Courtesy West Point Museum, Paul Goodwin photo*

MAS Model 1917 • *Courtesy West Point Museum, Paul Goodwin photo*

Model 1886/74/1917 Signal Rifle

A scarce variation of the military issue rifle.

Courtesy Richard M. Kumor Sr.

Exc.	V.G.	Good	Fair	Poor
950	700	400	200	100

MAUSER

Post-WWII Modified K98k Carbine

Exc.	V.G.	Good	Fair	Poor
550	450	350	175	100

DAUDETEAU

St. Denis

Model 71/94 Dovitis Rifle and Carbine

A Mauser Model 1871 action rebarreled to the 6.5x53.5SRmm Daudeteau No. 12 cartridge. Single shot. Made for Uruguay in the 1890s. Model 1871 rifles and carbines were converted in France at the St. Denis arsenal. The military officer who ordered the model was named Dovitis, and his name became associated with the model.

Exc.	V.G.	Good	Fair	Poor
450	375	300	225	150

Model 1896

Chambered for the 6.5x53.5SRmm Daudeteau No. 12 cartridge. Fitted with a 32.5" barrel. Fixed box charger-loaded magazine with 5-round capacity as part of triggerguard. Full stock with half length upper handguard. Weight is approximately 8.5 lbs. Several thousand rifles were made for military trials. All of these rifles were produced between 1896 and 1897.

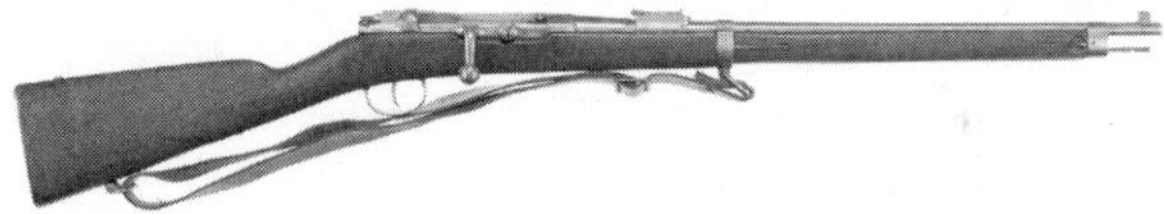

Courtesy Rock Island Auction Company

Exc.	V.G.	Good	Fair	Poor
750	550	350	250	150

FRENCH STATE ARSENALS

MAS, MAT

Model 1917

An 8x50mm Lebel caliber semi-automatic gas operated rifle with a 31.4-inch barrel, 5-shot half-oval charger loaded magazine, and full-length walnut stock with cleaning rod. Weight is about 11.5 lbs. Produced by MAT.

Exc.	V.G.	Good	Fair	Poor
1800	1500	1200	800	500

Model 1918

As above in an improved version, with a 23.1-inch barrel. Uses a standard cartridge charger. Weight is about 10.5 lbs.

Exc.	V.G.	Good	Fair	Poor
1800	1500	1200	800	500

NOTE: This note applies to both the Models 1917 and 1918. These rifles were unsatisfactory in service during WWI and some consider them to be unsafe to fire. After the war, they had their gas systems deactivated before being sold as surplus or issued to colonial troops as straight pull bolt actions. Others were demilled by cutting

MAS Model 1918 with missing handguard •
Courtesy private collection, Paul Goodwin photo

the barrel under the rear barrel band and grinding the firing pin. Deduct 50 percent for these examples.

MAS 36

A 7.5x54mm caliber bolt action rifle with a 22.6" barrel and 5-shot magazine. Bolt handle slants forward. Blued with a 2-piece walnut stock. Weight is about 8.25 lbs. The standard French service rifle from 1936 to 1949. This was the last bolt action general service rifle to be adopted by a major military power. The rifles made 1936-39 have a black laquer finish and are sought after by collectors. Most are numbered on the receiver, bolt, trigger guard, floor plate and stock. Deduct 25% for miss-matched parts.

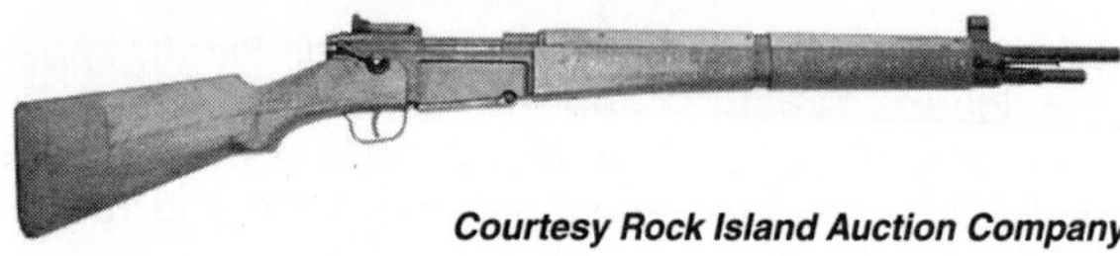

Courtesy Rock Island Auction Company

Exc.	V.G.	Good	Fair	Poor
500	350	225	150	100

MAS 1936 Post-WWII Issue

Many were imported in the 1990s and are in unissued condition. These postwar and arsenal reworked rifles have a gray parkerized finish.

Exc.	V.G.	Good	Fair	Poor
300	175	150	100	75

MAS 36 LG48 or 36/51

This is a MAS 36 rifle with a grenade launcher built into the barrel of the rifle. A folding sight arm was located on the left side of the barrel. Grenade range was varied by rotating the collar around the muzzle. Produced from about 1948 to 1951 and used extensively by the French army in Indo-China. Many were imported in the 1990s and are in unissued condition.

Exc.	V.G.	Good	Fair	Poor
300	225	150	125	100

Bayonet for MAS 36, 36-51, MAS 44 Semi-automatic

A 17-inch steel spike with the back end knurled. Stores backwards in a tube beneath the rifle's barrel. Price range 45 – 25.

MAS 36 CR39

As above, with an aluminum folding stock and 17.7-inch barrel. Weight is about 8 lbs. Designed for parachute and mountain troops. This is a rare variation.

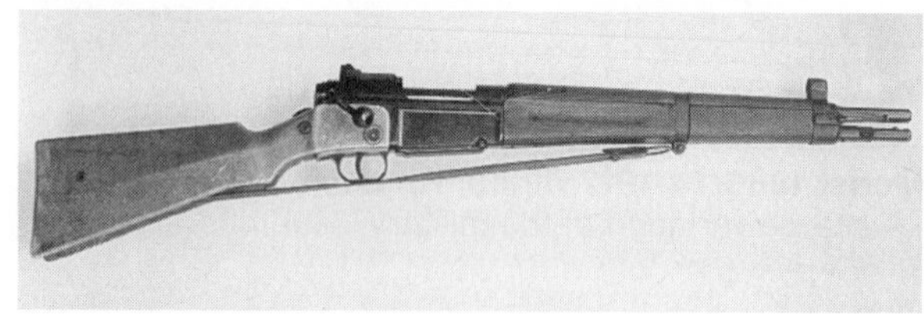

Courtesy Richard M. Kumor Sr.

MAS 36 Para rifle in arsenal refinish with wooden stock •
Courtesy Richard M. Kumor Sr.

Exc.	V.G.	Good	Fair	Poor
1500	1200	900	600	300

MAS 36 Sub-Caliber

This variation is a MAS 36 but with a special cartridge case designed for .22 caliber long rifle ammunition. Marked "5.5 REDUCED CALIBER" on the receiver.

Exc.	V.G.	Good	Fair	Poor
750	600	500	400	300

MAS 36 LG48 with grenade launcher built into barrel •
Courtesy private collection, Paul Goodwin photo

Close-up of the MAS 36 .22 caliber training rifle • *Courtesy private collection, Paul Goodwin photo*

Bayonet for MAS 36, 36-51, MAS 44 Semi-automatic

MAS 44

This model was the first semi-automatic adopted by the French military. It is gas operated and chambered for the 7.5x54mm cartridge and used a detachable 10 round magazine. It later developed into the Model 49.

Courtesy Richard M. Kumor Sr.

Exc.	V.G.	Good	Fair	Poor
750	600	450	300	250

MAS 45

This is a bolt action military training rifle chambered for the .22 caliber cartridge. Many were imported in the 1990s and are in unissued condition.

Exc.	V.G.	Good	Fair	Poor
500	375	300	175	150

MAS 49

Introduced in 1949, this model is a 7.5x54mm gas-operated semi-automatic rifle with a 22.6-inch barrel and full-length walnut stock. It has a grenade launcher built into the front sight. Fitted with a 10-round magazine. No bayonet fittings. Weight is about 9 lbs.

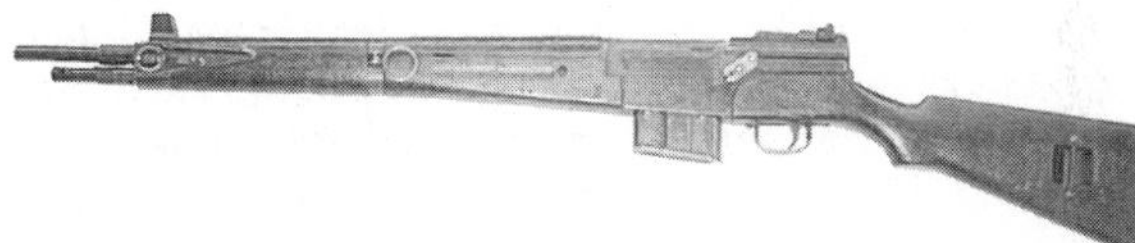

Courtesy Richard M. Kumor Sr.

Exc.	V.G.	Good	Fair	Poor
700	550	450	275	225

MAS 1949/56

This model is a modification of the Model 49. It is fitted with a 20.7-inch barrel. Principal modification is with NATO standard grenade launcher. A special grenade sight is also fitted. This model has provisions to fit a bayonet. Weight is about 8.5 lbs. Many were imported in the 1990s and are in unissued condition.

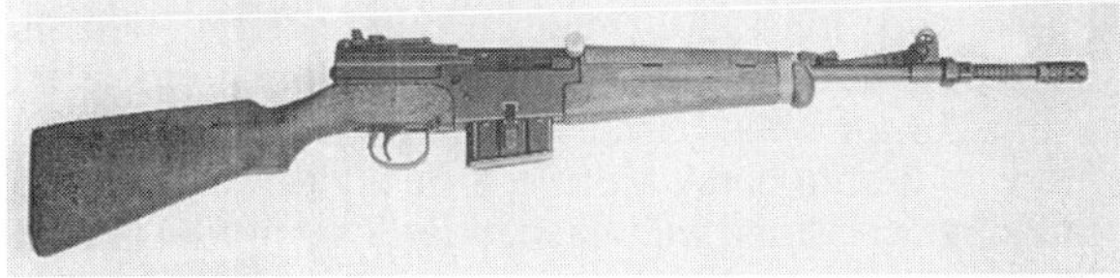

Courtesy Richard M. Kumor Sr.

Exc.	V.G.	Good	Fair	Poor
450	375	300	225	175

MAS 45 with close-up of receiver marking • *Courtesy Daniel Rewers, Paul Goodwin photo*

Bayonet for MAS 1949/56

FRANCE

Bayonet for MAS 1949/56

Plastic grips. Two muzzle rings. 7.9-inch single edge blade. Steel scabbard. Price range 75 – 35.

Model FR-F 1 Sniper Rifle

Introduced in 1964, this 7.5x54mm rifle is based on the MAS 36 and uses the same style two-piece stock with pistol grip. Barrel length is 22 inches with bipod attached to forend. Barrel is fitted with a muzzle brake. Fitted with open sights but 3.8 power telescope often used. Magazine capacity is 10 rounds. Many of these rifles were converted to 7.62mm caliber.

Exc.	V.G.	Good	Fair	Poor
5500	4500	4000	—	—

Model FR-F 2 Sniper Rifle

A 1984 improved version of the F 1 rifle. The forearm has a plastic covering. The bipod is attached to a yoke around the barrel, and the barrel is covered with a thermal sleeve to reduce heat. The features and dimensions the same as the F 1.

Exc.	V.G.	Good	Fair	Poor
6500	5500	5000	—	—

FAMAS F1 Assault Rifle

Introduced in 1980, this bullpup design rifle is chambered for the 5.56x45mm cartridge and fitted with a 19.2 inches barrel with fluted chamber. Select fire with 3-shot burst. Muzzle is designed for grenade launcher and fitted with flash hider. This model is also fitted for a bayonet and a bipod. Magazine capacity is 25 rounds. Rate of fire is about 950 rounds per minute. Weight is approximately 8 lbs. No transferable examples exist in the U.S.

Pre-1968

Exc.	V.G.	Fair
N/A	N/A	N/A

FAMAS F1 Rifle, semi automatic

Same as above but in semi-automatic version only. Approximately 100 were imported by Century Arms in the 1980s. Scarce.

Exc.	V.G.	Good	Fair	Poor
9500	8000	6000	N/A	N/A

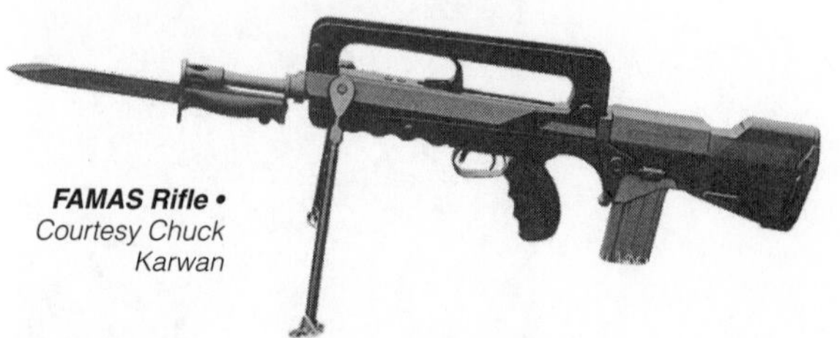
FAMAS Rifle • Courtesy Chuck Karwan

Bayonet for FAMAS

Plastic grip. Two muzzle rings. 7.9-inch single edge blade. Steel scabbard. This bayonet looks like the MAS 49/46 bayonet but the scabbard has a flat tip instead of pointed. Price range 150 – 75.

MACHINE GUNS

Model 1907 St. Etienne

Built by the French arsenal MAS, this is a reversed gas-action gun chambered for the 8x50R Lebel cartridge. It was an unsuccessful attempt to improve on the Hotchkiss gun. The rate of fire is between 400 and 500 rounds per minute and is regulated by changing the gas cylinder volume. Barrel jacket is half-length over a 28-inch barrel. Fitted with spade grips with trigger. Fed by 24- or 30-round metal strips. Weight is approximately 57 lbs. with tripod. This gun was not able to withstand the rigors of trench warfare and was withdrawn from combat in Europe.

Model 1907 St. Etienne • Robert G. Segel collection

Pre-1968

Exc.	V.G.	Fair
40000	—	—

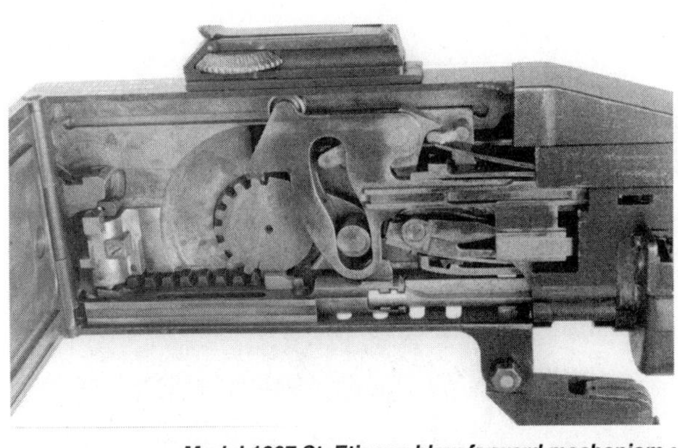

Model 1907 St. Etienne blow forward mechanism • *Robert G. Segel collection*

Model 52 (AAT Mle. 52)

Introduced in 1952 as a general purpose machine gun with light 19-inch quick-change barrel with flash hider and bipod. This gun employs a blowback operation with two-piece bolt and fluted chamber. Chambered for the 7.62mm cartridge. The buttstock is a single-piece metal folding type. Rate of fire is about 700 rounds per minute and is belt-fed from the left side. Weight is about 21 lbs.

A heavy barrel version of this gun is built around a 23.5-inch barrel. Weight is about 24 lbs. Gun is usually placed on a U.S. M2 tripod. All other specifications same as light barrel version.

Pre-1968

Exc.	*V.G.*	*Fair*
25000	23000	20000

Hotchkiss Model 1914

This model is an improvement over the original Model 1897 gun but with steel cooling fins instead of brass. Otherwise it remains an air-cooled gun chambered for the 8x50R Lebel cartridge. It is fed by a 24- or 30-round metal strips or by a 250-round belt. Its rate of fire is about 500 rounds per minute. Barrel length is 31" and weight is about 55 lbs. The tripod for the Hotchkiss weighed another 55 lbs. by itself. In production from 1914 to 1930. Marked "MITRAILLEUSE AUTOMATIQUE HOTCHKISS M1914 SDGD CALIBERE ——" on left side of receiver. The gun was used by the French army in both WWI and WWII. During WWI it was used by a number of Allied forces as well. As a matter of fact, American forces used the Hotchkiss more widely than any other machine gun. After World War II the gun appeared with French forces in Indo-China, where the Viet Minh and later the Viet Cong used the gun.

NOTE: An earlier version of this gun, the Model 1909, was fitted with brass cooling fins instead of steel. The original design of the Hotchkiss was the Model 1897. This gun was fed by 30 round metal strips and had a rate of fire of about 600 rounds per minute. Similar in appearance to the Model 1909. This gun was very popular with the Japanese who used it during the Russo-Japanese War of 1904-1905. This led the Japanese to develop the Type 92 for Japan's use during World War II.

Model 1914 Hotchkiss • *Robert G. Segel collection*

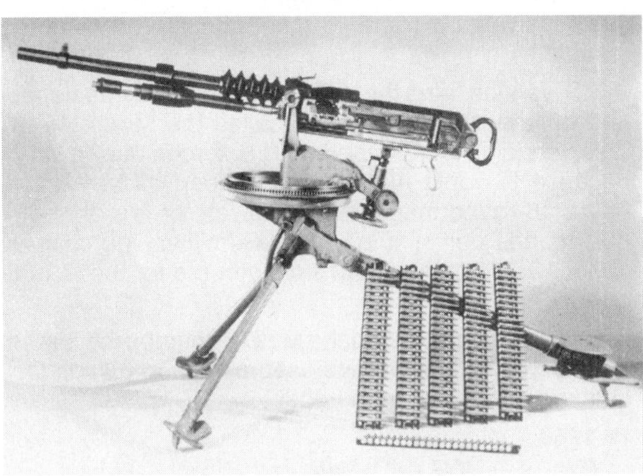

A Von Karner modified Model 1914 rechambered for the 7.62x54Rmm Russian cartridge. Modified for the Dutch government prior to World War II for use in the East Indies against Japanese forces. Most were sunk by Japanese subs before reaching their destination • *Courtesy John M. Miller*

Model 1914 Hotchkiss with receiver markings • *Paul Goodwin photo*

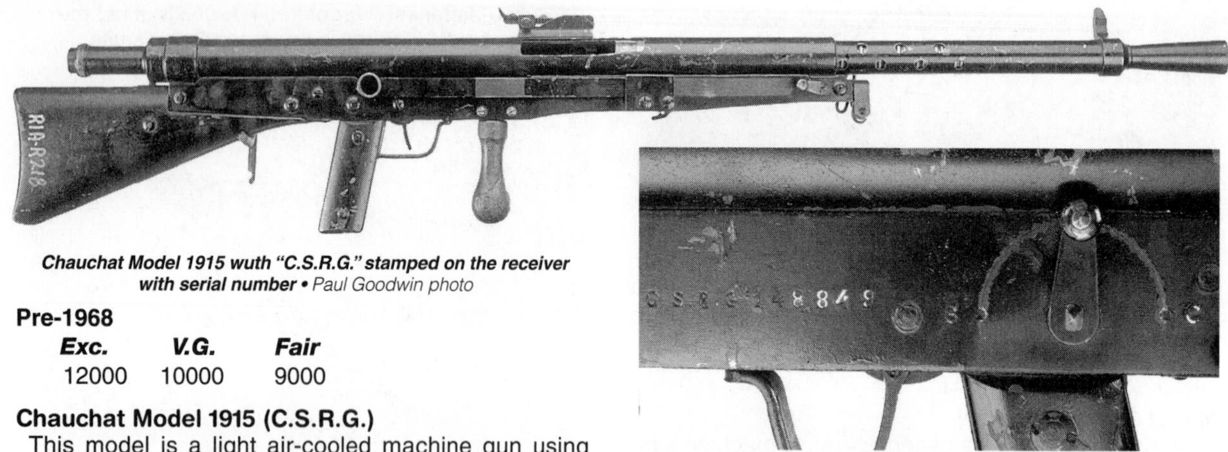

Chauchat Model 1915 wuth "C.S.R.G." stamped on the receiver with serial number • *Paul Goodwin photo*

Pre-1968

Exc.	*V.G.*	*Fair*
12000	10000	9000

Chauchat Model 1915 (C.S.R.G.)

This model is a light air-cooled machine gun using a long recoil operation with a rotating bolt. It is chambered for the 8x50R Lebel and features an 18.5-inch barrel with barrel jacket. The 20-round magazine is a semi-circular type located under the receiver. Wooden buttstock and bipod. Rate of fire is about 250 rounds per minute. Used during WWI. The gun was inexpensively built and was not considered combat-reliable.

A U.S. version firing the .30-06 cartridge was designed and built by the French and called the Model 1918. This version was not used by U.S. forces during WWI because it would not function properly. The M1918 has a 16-round magazine and a rate of fire of about 300 rounds per minute. The U.S. military purchased about 19,000 of these guns chambered for the .30-06 cartridge.

After WWI Belgium used the M1918 chambered for the 7.65mm cartridge. Greece used a version (Gladiator) chambered for the 8mm Lebel.

Pre-1968

Exc.	*V.G.*	*Fair*
4500	4000	3500

Pre-1986 Rewat

Exc.	*V.G.*	*Fair*
4000	3000	2500

NOTE: For U.S. versions add 100 percent.

Chatellerault M1924/M29

This is an air-cooled light gas piston machine gun that the French referred to as an automatic rifle. It is chambered for the 7.5x54mm French cartridge. Fitted with a 19.7-inch barrel with flash hider and bipod. Wooden butt and forearm. Select fire with two triggers. Fed by a 25-round detachable top-mounted box magazine. Rate of fire is about 500 rounds per minute. Weight is approximately 24 lbs. with bipod. Introduced in 1929, the gun was used extensively in combat by French troops.

Another version of this model is known as the M1931A introduced in 1931. It is essentially an M1924/29 for use on a tank as a fixed place machine gun with tripod. Fitted with a 23-inch heavy barrel. The gun can use a 36-round box magazine or 150-round drum, both of which attach to the right side of the gun. Its rate of fire is 750 rounds per minute.

Pre-1968

Exc.	*V.G.*	*Fair*
17500	12500	10000

Pre-1986 manufacture with new receiver or re-weld

Exc.	*V.G.*	*Fair*
11400	10000	12000

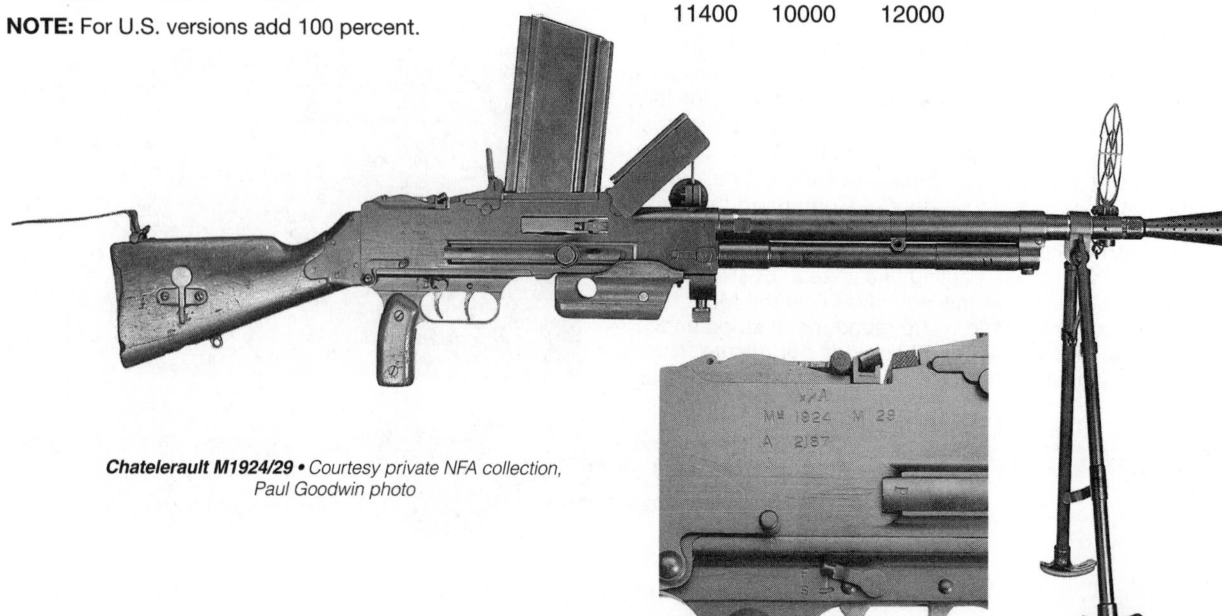

Chatelerault M1924/29 • *Courtesy private NFA collection, Paul Goodwin photo*

Although the origin of the German Empire can be traced to the Treaty of Verdun that ceded Charlemagne's lands east of the Rhine to German Prince Louis, it was for centuries little more than a geographic expression, con- sisting of hundreds of effectively autonomous big and little states. Nominally the states owed their allegiance to the Holy Roman Emperor, who was also a German king, but as the Emperors exhibited less and less concern for Germany the actual power devolved on the lords of the individual states. The fragmentation of the empire climaxed with the tragic denouement of the Thirty Years War, 1618-48, which devastated much of Germany, destroyed its agriculture and medieval commercial eminence and ended the attempt of the Hapsburgs to unify Germany. Deprived of administrative capacity by a lack of resources, the imperial authority became utterly powerless. At this time Germany contained an estimated 1,800 individual states, some with a population of as little as 300. The German Empire of recent history (the creation of Bis- marck) was formed on April 14, 1871, when the king of Prussia became German Emperor William I. The new empire comprised 4 kingdoms, 6 grand duchies, 12 duchies and principalities, 3 free cities and the nonautonomous province of Alsace-Lorraine. The states had the right to issue gold and silver coins of higher value than 1 Mark; coins of 1 Mark and under were general issues of the empire.

A nation of north-central Europe which from 1871 to 1945 was, successively, an empire, a republic and a totalitarian state, attained its territorial peak as an empire when it comprised a 208,780 sq. mi. (540,740 sq. km.) homeland and an overseas colonial empire.

As the power of the Roman Empire waned, several war-like tribes residing in northern Germany moved south and west, invading France, Belgium, England, Italy and Spain. In 800 A.D. the Frankish king Charlemagne, who ruled most of France and Germany, was crowned Emperor of the Holy Roman Empire, a loose federation of an estimated 1,800 German States that lasted until 1806. Modern Germany was formed from the eastern part of Charlemagne's empire.

After 1812, the German States were reduced to a federation of 32, of which Prussia was the strongest. In 1871, Prussian chancellor Otto von Bismarck united the German States into an empire ruled by William I, the Prussian king. The empire initiated a colonial endeavor and became one of the world's greatest powers. Germany disintegrated as a result of World War I.

It was reestablished as the Weimar Republic. The humiliation of defeat, economic depression, poverty and discontent gave rise to Adolf Hitler, 1933, who reconstituted Germany as the Third Reich and after initial diplomatic and military triumphs, expanded his goals beyond Europe into Africa and USSR which led it into final disaster in World War II, ending on VE Day, May 7, 1945.

HANDGUNS

Bibliographical Note: For information on a wide variety of German military handguns, see Jan Still, ***Axis Pistols***, 1986.

REICHSREVOLVER

Germany

There are two basic versions of the German Standard Service Revolver designed by the Small Arms Commission of the Prussian army in the 1870s. Revolvers of this type were produced by the Erfurt Royal Arsenal, F. Dreyse of Sommerda, Sauer & Sohn, Spangenberg & Sauer, and C.H. Haenel of Suhl. Normally, the maker's initials can be found on an oval above the triggerguard.

Model 1879

A 10.55mm caliber revolver with a 7.2-inch stepped octagon barrel, 6-shot cylinder and fixed sights. Standard finish is browned with smooth walnut grips having a lanyard ring at the base. Weight is about 36 oz. Regimental markings are on the butt crown plate. These revolvers are fitted with a safety catch. There is no provision for cartridge ejection. Each empty shell is removed with the cylinder axis pin. In use from 1882 until 1919.

Exc.	*V.G.*	*Good*	*Fair*	*Poor*
1200	850	500	300	200

NOTE: Add 20 percent for Mauser-built revolvers.

Model 1883

As above with a 5-inch stepped octagon barrel and round bottom grips with lanyard loop. Weight is about 32 oz. The finish on early production guns was browned, and on the balance of production the finish was blued. Regimental markings are located on the backstrap. In use from 1885 until 1919. Mauser-built M1883s are rare.

Exc.	*V.G.*	*Good*	*Fair*	*Poor*
850	600	400	250	175

NOTE: For Mauser-built revolvers add 250 percent.

STEYR

Steyr Hahn Model 1911

The Steyr Hahn was originally introduced as a commercial pistol but was quickly adopted by the Austro-Hungarian, Chilean, and Romanian militaries. During WWII the Germans rebarreled a number of Steyr Hahns to 9mm Parabellum for police use, adding "P.08" to the slide along with appropriate Waffenamt markings.

Courtesy Orvel Reichert

German WWII Issue (P.08 marked)

Exc.	V.G.	Good	Fair	Poor
900	700	450	200	125

DREYSE

Dreyse 7.65mm

Chambered for the 7.65mm cartridge, with a 3.6-inch barrel and a 7-shot magazine. Blowback and striker fired. The slide is marked "Dreyse Rheinmetall Abt. Sommerda." Blued with plastic grips. Weight is about 25 oz. Originally intended for commercial sales, this model was issued to staff officers and rear area troops in 1917.

Exc.	V.G.	Good	Fair	Poor
400	250	175	100	75

Dreyse 9mm

As above, but chambered for the 9mm cartridge with a 5-inch barrel and an 8-shot magazine. The slide marked "Rheinische Mettellwaaren Und Maschinenfabrik, Sommerda." Blued with plastic grips. Weight is about 37 oz. Used by troops in World War I but not officially adopted by the German military.

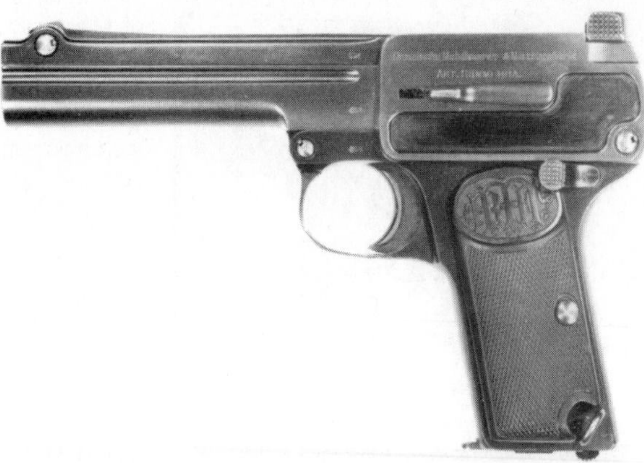

Courtesy James Rankin

Exc.	V.G.	Good	Fair	Poor
3000	2000	800	450	300

BERGMANN, THEODOR

Gaggenau, Germany

Bergmann Model 1910-21

See Denmark.

MAUSER

Model 1896 "Broomhandle Mauser Pistol"

Manufactured from 1896 to 1939, the Model 1896 Pistol was produced in a wide variety of styles as listed below. It is recommended that those considering the purchase of any of the following models should consult Breathed & Schroeder's ***System Mauser***, Chicago, 1967, as it provides detailed descriptions and photographs of the various models. See also Wayne Erickson and Charles Pate, ***The Broomhandle Pistol, 1896-1936***, 1985.

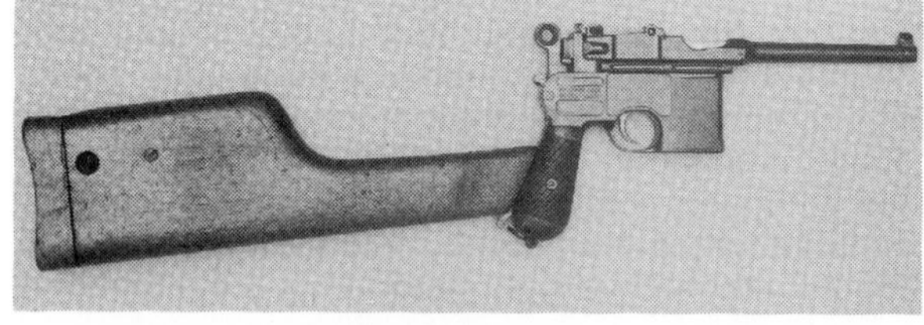

Courtesy Wallis & Wallis, Lewes, Sussex, England

NOTE: A correct, matching stock/holster will add approximately 40 percent to value of each category.

"BUYER BEWARE" ALERT BY GALE MORGAN: In the 1980s and 1990s large quantities of "Broomhandle" Mausers and Astra "copies" were imported into the United States from China. Generally these were in Poor or Fair condition and offered for sale in the $125 to $300 price range, primarily as shooters or parts guns. In recent years a cottage industry has sprung up where these very common pistols have been "converted" to "rare, exotic, near mint, original" specimens selling well into the four figure price range. I have personally seen English Crest, the U.S. Great Seal, unheard-of European dealers, aristocratic Coats-of-Arms, and Middle East Medallions beautifully photo-etched into the magazine wells and rear panels of some really common wartime commercials with price tags that have been elevated to $2,500 plus. They are quite eye-catching and if they are sold as customized/modified Mausers, the seller can price the piece at whatever the market will bear. However, if sold as a factory original–BUYER BEWARE.

Turkish Contract Cone Hammer

Chambered for 7.63mm Mauser cartridge and fitted with a 5.5-inch barrel. Rear sight is marked in Farsi characters. Grips are grooved walnut with 21 grooves. Proof mark is a 6-pointed star on both sides of the chamber. Marked in Turkish script and bearing the crest of Sultan Abdul-Hamid II on the frame. Approximately 1,000 were sold to Turkey.

Courtesy Joe Schroeder

Courtesy Gale Morgan

Exc.	V.G.	Good	Fair	Poor
10000	7500	5000	3000	2000

Contract Transitional Large Ring Hammer

This variation has the same characteristics of the "Standard Cone Hammer" except the hammer has a larger, open ring. It is fitted with a 5.5-inch barrel and an adjustable sight marked from 50 to 500 meters. Grips are walnut with 23 grooves. Some of these pistols were issued to the German army for field testing.

Exc.	V.G.	Good	Fair	Poor
3500	2800	2500	1150	800

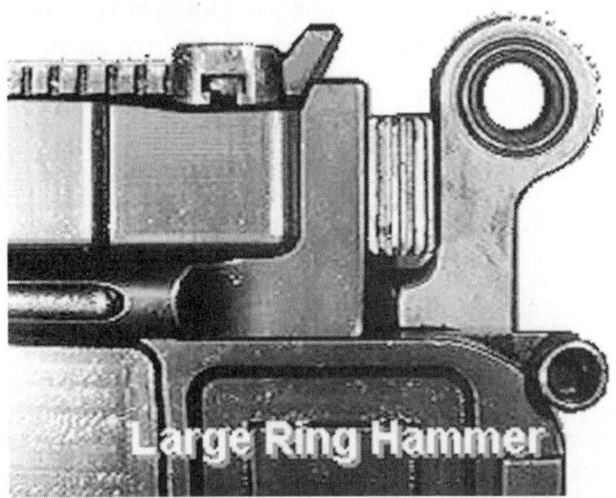

Courtesy Gale Morgan

Model 1899 Flat Side–Italian Contract

Similar to the above, with a 5.5-inch barrel, adjustable rear sight, and the frame sides milled flat. Left flat of chamber marked with "DV" proof. A "crown over AV" is stamped on the bottom of the barrel. All parts are serial numbered. Approximately 5,000 were manufactured in 1899.

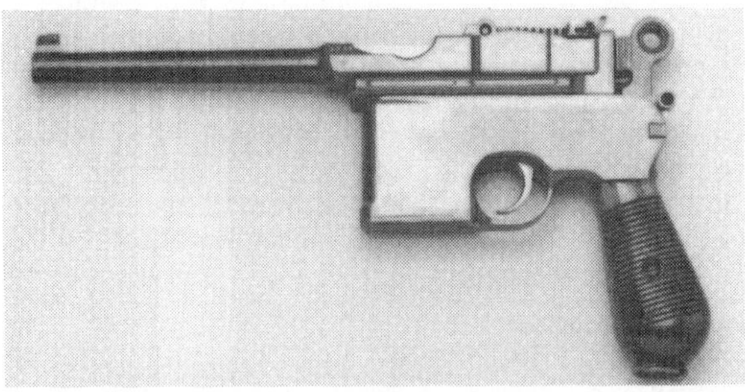

Courtesy Butterfield & Butterfield, San Francisco, California

Exc.	V.G.	Good	Fair	Poor
4250	3000	1500	1200	900

Contract Flat Side

Fitted with a 5.5-inch barrel with adjustable rear sight marked 50 to 500 meters. Grips are walnut with 23 grooves. The proof mark is the German military acceptance proofs. This model was used for field testing by the German army in 1899 or 1900. Number of pistols is unknown but most likely very small.

Exc.	V.G.	Good	Fair	Poor
2700	2200	1500	1000	750

Persian Contract

Persian rising sun on left rear barrel extension. Persian Lion crest in center of rear frame panel. Barrel length is 5.5 inches and grips are walnut with 34 grooves. Adjustable rear sight marked from 50 to 1,000 meters. Prospective purchasers should secure a qualified appraisal prior to acquisition. Serial numbers in the 154000 range.

Exc.	V.G.	Good	Fair	Poor
4200	3500	2250	1400	1000

Standard Wartime Commercial

Identical to the prewar Commercial Model 96, except that it has 30-groove walnut grips and the rear of the hammer is stamped "NS" for new safety. A number of these have the Austrian military acceptance marks in addition to the German commercial proofs. These pistols were also used by the German army as well.

Courtesy Gale Morgan

Exc.	V.G.	Good	Fair	Poor
1750	1200	800	500	350

9mm Parabellum Military Contract

As above, in 9mm Parabellum caliber with 24-groove grips, stamped with a large "9" filled with red paint. Rear sights are adjustable with 50 to 500 meter markings. This model has German military acceptance marks on the right side of the chamber. Fit and finish on these pistols are poor. Some examples have the Imperial German Eagle on the front of the magazine well. About 150,000 of these pistols were built for the German government.

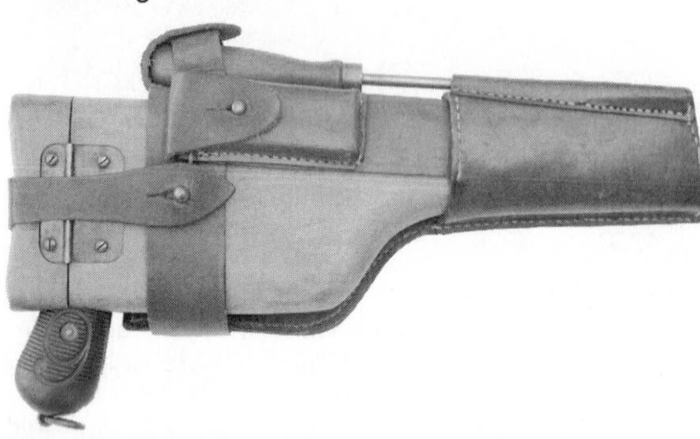

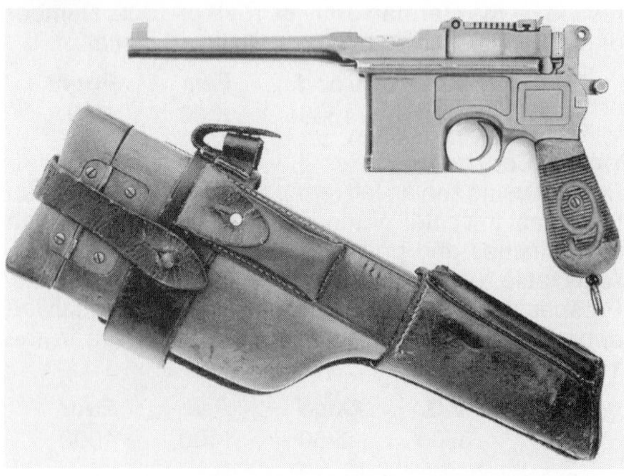

Mauser 9mm military contract "red nine" rig • *Courtesy Gale Morgan*

Exc.	V.G.	Good	Fair	Poor
2250	1600	900	700	450

1920 Rework

A Model 96 modified to a barrel length of 3.9 inches and in 7.63mm Mauser or 9mm Parabellum caliber. Rear sight on this model is fixed. German military acceptance marks are located on the right side of the chamber. Often encountered with police markings.

Courtesy Gale Morgan

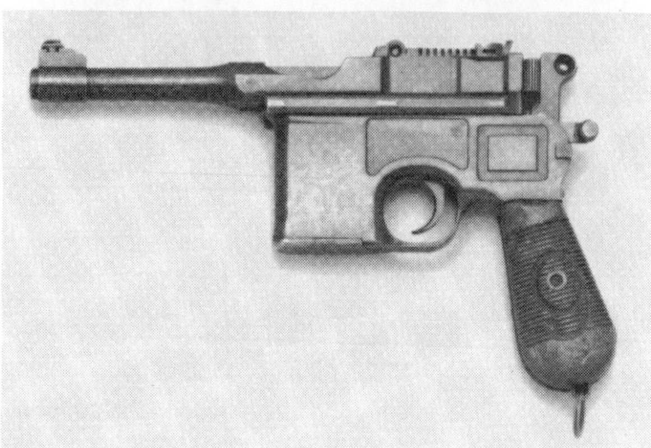

Courtesy Butterfield & Butterfield, San Francisco, California

Exc.	V.G.	Good	Fair	Poor
1250	1000	600	400	350

Late Postwar Bolo Model

Chambered for the 7.63mm Mauser cartridge and fitted with a 3.9-inch barrel. Rear sight marked for 50 to 500 meters or 50 to 1,000 meters. Grips are walnut with 22 grooves. Some of these pistols bear Chinese characters. The Mauser banner trademark is stamped on the left rear panel.

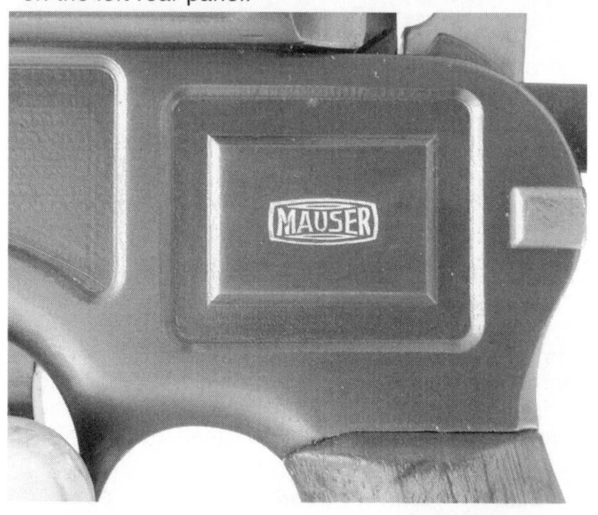

Courtesy Gale Morgan

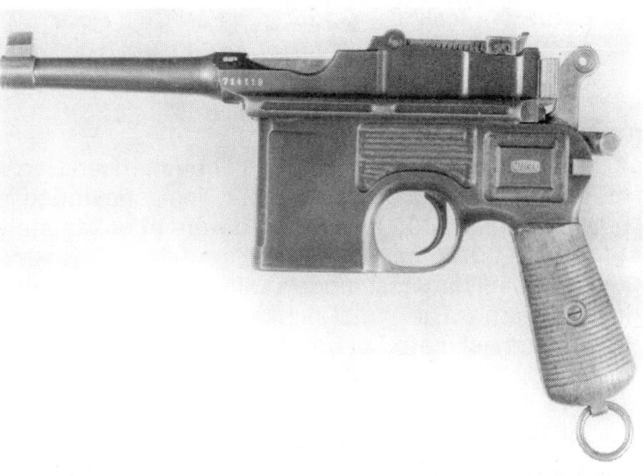

Courtesy Gale Morgan

Exc.	V.G.	Good	Fair	Poor
2200	1200	700	400	200

Early Model 1930

A 7.63mm caliber Model 96 with a 5.2-inch stepped barrel, 12-groove walnut grips and late style safety. The rear adjustable sight is marked in 50 to 1,000 meters. Some of these pistols have Chinese characters on the left side of the magazine well.

Courtesy Gale Morgan

Courtesy Gale Morgan

Exc.	V.G.	Good	Fair	Poor
2000	1500	1100	650	400

Late Model 1930

Identical to the above, except for solid receiver rails.

Exc.	V.G.	Good	Fair	Poor
2000	1500	1100	650	400

Model 1930 Removable Magazine

Similar to the above, but with a detachable magazine. Very rare. Limited production in the 84,000-88,000 SN range. Beware of fakes assembled using Model 712 parts with the full auto parts openings welded up.

Exc.	V.G.	Good	Fair	Poor
20000	15000	10000	6500	3000

Mauser Schnellfeuer (Model 712 or Model 32)

This is not a submachine gun but rather a machine pistol. Chambered for 7.63mm Mauser cartridge. Barrel length is 5.5 inches and rear sight is adjustable from 50 meters to 1,000 meters. Walnut grips with 12 grooves. Magazine capacity is 10 or 20 rounds with a detachable magazine. This pistol is often encountered with Chinese markings as it was very popular in the Orient. Approximately 100,000 were produced. Rate of fire is between 900 and 1,100 rounds per minute. It should be noted that the Model 712 was used to some limited extent by the Waffen SS during World War II as well as the German Luftwaffe. Stamped with army test proof.

NOTE: The prices listed below are for guns with commercial markings and correct Mauser Schnellfeuer stock. Schnellfeuer stocks are cut larger inside to accommodate selector switch. For German army acceptance stamped pistols add 5-10 percent depending on condition. For pistols without stock or incorrect stock deduct $750 to $1,000.

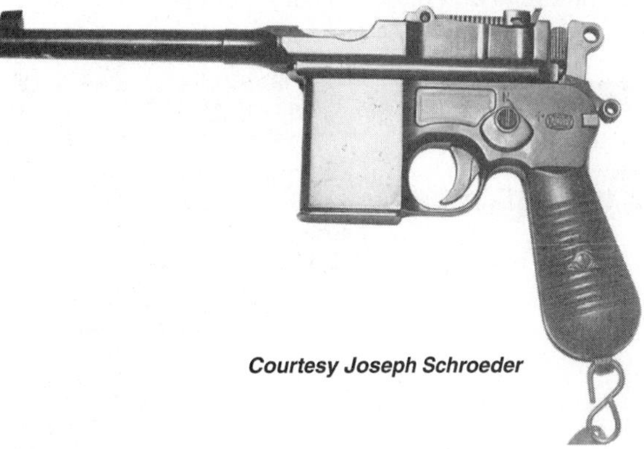

Courtesy Joseph Schroeder

Pre-1968

Exc.	V.G.	Fair
20000	15000	12500

Mauser Model 712 semi automatic, with U.S. Made receiver

Built by U.S. importer Navy Arms, Federal Ordnance, and possibly other companies. This pistol features a 712 upper assembly and a new semi automatic frame that accepts the Schnellfeuer 10 and 20 round magazines.

Exc.	V.G.	Good	Fair	Poor
850	700	600	N/A	N/A

LUGER

Bibliographical Note: See Charles Kenyon's ***Lugers at Random***, Handgun Press, 1969, for historical information, technical data, and photos. See also Jan Still, ***Axis Pistols***, 1986.

GERMANY

Just before the turn of the 20th century, Georg Luger (1849-1923) redesigned the Borchardt semi-automatic pistol so that its mainspring was housed in the rear of the grip. The resulting pistol, the German army's Pistole '08, was to prove extremely successful and his name has become synonymous with the pistol, despite the fact his name never appeared on it.

The following companies manufactured Luger pattern pistols at various times:

1. DWM–Deutsch Waffen und Munitions – Karlsruhe, Germany
2. The Royal Arsenal of Erfurt, Germany
3. Simson & Company – Suhl, Germany
4. Mauser – Oberndorf, Germany
5. Vickers Ltd. – England
6. Waffenfabrik Bern – Bern, Switzerland, see Switzerland, Handguns, Luger.
7. Heinrich Krieghoff – Suhl, Germany

NOTE: The model listings below contain the commonly accepted Lugers that are considered military issue. It should be pointed out that in wartime, commercial pistols were often diverted to military use if necessary.

DEUTSCHE WAFFEN UND MUNITIONS

1900 Swiss Contract

4.75-inch barrel, 7.65mm caliber. The Swiss Cross in Sunburst is stamped over the chamber. The military serial number range is 2001-5000; the commercial range, 01-21250. There were approximately 2,000 commercial and 3,000 military models manufactured.

Paul Goodwin photo

Swiss Cross & Sunburst • *Courtesy Gale Morgan*

Exc.	*V.G.*	*Good*	*Fair*	*Poor*
5500	4000	2000	1500	1000

NOTE: Wide trigger add 20 percent.

1900 American Eagle

4.75-inch barrel, 7.65mm caliber. The American Eagle crest is stamped over the chamber. The serial range is between 2000-200000, and there were approximately 11,000-12,000 commercial models marked "Germany" and 1,000 military test models without the commercial import stamp. The serial numbers of this military lot have been estimated at between 6100-7100.

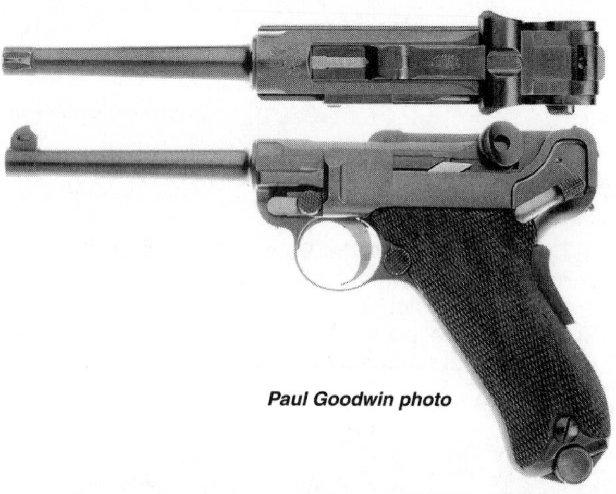

Paul Goodwin photo

Exc.	*V.G.*	*Good*	*Fair*	*Poor*
5500	3200	1500	900	800

NOTE: add 50% for U.S. test model, SN range 6000-7500. Has no "Germany" or proof marks.

1900 Bulgarian Contract

An old model, 1900 Type, with no stock lug. It has a 4.75-inch barrel and is chambered for the 7.65mm cartridge. The Bulgarian crest is stamped over the chamber, and the safety is marked in Bulgarian letters. The serial range is 20000-21000, with 1,000 manufactured. This is a military test model and is quite rare as most were rebarreled to 9mm during the time they were used. Even with the 9mm versions, approximately 10 are known to exist. It was the only variation to feature a marked safety before 1904.

Paul Goodwin photo

Exc.	*V.G.*	*Good*	*Fair*	*Poor*
12000	8000	4000	2500	1800

1902 American Eagle Cartridge Counter

As above, with a "Powell Indicating Device" added to the left grip, a slotted magazine with a numbered window that allows visual access to the number of cartridges remaining. There were 50 Lugers altered in this way at the request of the U.S. Board of Ordnance, for U.S. army evaluation. The serial numbers are 22401-22450. Be especially wary of fakes!

Paul Goodwin photo

Exc.	V.G.	Good	Fair	Poor
32500	25000	16000	6000	3500

1904 Navy

6-inch heavy barrel, 9mm caliber. The chamber area is blank, and the extractor is marked "Geladen." The safety is marked "Gesichert." There were approximately 1,500 manufactured in the one- to four-digit serial range, for military sales to the German navy. The toggle has a "lock" comparable to 1900 types.

Paul Goodwin photo

Exc.	V.G.	Good	Fair	Poor
40000	30000	16000	6000	4500

1906 U.S. Army Test Luger .45 Caliber

5-inch barrel, .45 ACP caliber. Sent to the United States for testing in 1907. The chamber is blank; the extractor is marked "Loaded," and the frame is polished under the safety lever. The trigger on this model has an odd hook at the bottom. Only five of these pistols were manufactured.

Too Rare To Price

1906 Swiss Military

Same as the Swiss Commercial, with the Geneva Cross in shield appearing on the chamber.

Courtesy Rock Island Auction Company

Exc.	V.G.	Good	Fair	Poor
3500	2800	2000	900	700

1906 Swiss Police Cross in Shield

As above, with a shield replacing the sunburst on the chamber marking. There were 10,215 of both models combined. They are in the 5000-15215 serial number range.

1906 Swiss Police Cross in Shield • Courtesy Gale Morgan

Paul Goodwin photo

Exc.	V.G.	Good	Fair	Poor
3500	2800	2000	900	700

1906 Dutch Contract

4-inch barrel, 9mm caliber. It has no stock lug, and the chamber is blank. The extractor is marked "GELADEN" on both sides, and the safety is marked "RUST" with a curved upward pointing arrow. This pistol was manufactured for military sales to the Netherlands, and a date will be found on the barrel of most examples encountered. The Dutch refinished their pistols on a regular basis and marked the date on the barrels. There were approximately 4,000 manufactured, serial numbered between 1 and 4000.

Courtesy Gale Morgan

Paul Goodwin photo

Exc.	*V.G.*	*Good*	*Fair*	*Poor*
3000	2250	1500	800	600

NOTE: add 100% for non-refinished example.

1906 Royal Portuguese Navy

4-inch barrel, 9mm caliber, and has no stock lug. The Royal Portuguese naval crest, an anchor under a crown, is stamped above the chamber. The extractor is marked "CARREGADA" on the left side. The frame under the safety is polished. There were approximately 1,000 manufactured with one- to four-digit serial numbers.

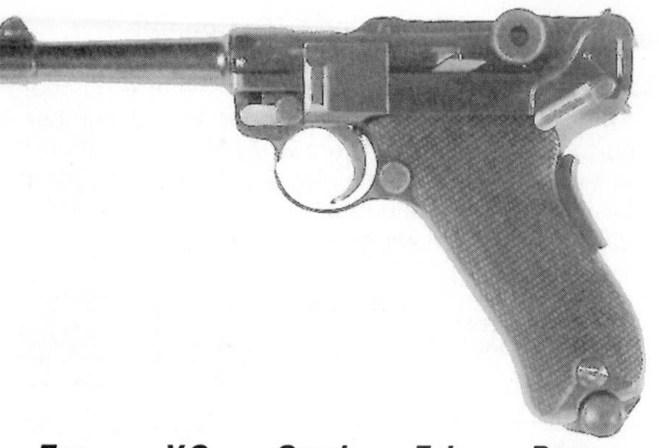

Exc.	*V.G.*	*Good*	*Fair*	*Poor*
10000	8000	6500	4000	2500

1906 Royal Portuguese Army (M2)

4.75-inch barrel, 7.65mm caliber. It has no stock lug. The chamber area has the Royal Portuguese crest of Manuel II stamped upon it. The extractor is marked "CARREGADA." There were approximately 5,000 manufactured, with one- to four-digit serial numbers.

Portuguese Army "M2" • *Courtesy Gale Morgan*

Exc.	*V.G.*	*Good*	*Fair*	*Poor*
3000	2700	1200	600	500

1906 Republic of Portugal Navy

4-inch barrel, 9mm caliber. It has no stock lug, and the extractor was marked "CARREGADA." This model was made after 1910, when Portugal had become a republic. The anchor on the chamber is under the letters "R.P." There were approximately 1,000 manufactured, with one- to four-digit serial numbers.

Exc.	*V.G.*	*Good*	*Fair*	*Poor*
11000	9000	5500	3500	2500

1906 Brazilian Contract

4.75-inch barrel, 7.65mm caliber. It has no stock lug, and chamber area is blank. The extractor is marked "CARREGADA," and the frame under the safety is polished. There were approximately 5,000 manufactured for military sales to Brazil.

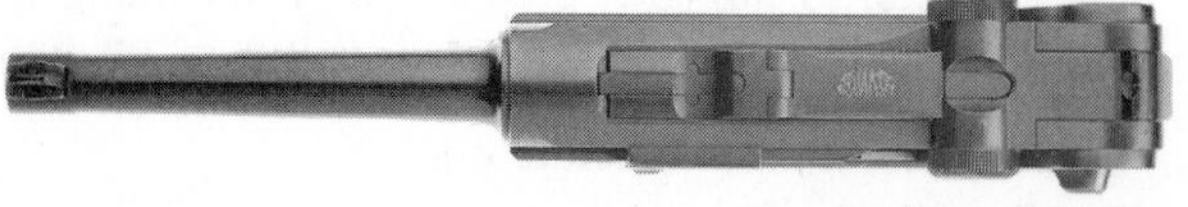

Paul Goodwin photo

Paul Goodwin photo

Exc.	V.G.	Good	Fair	Poor
3000	2250	1100	750	450

1906 Bulgarian Contract

4.75-inch barrel, 7.65mm caliber. It has no stock lug, and the extractor and safety are marked in cyrillic letters. The Bulgarian crest is stamped above the chamber. Nearly all of the examples located have the barrels replaced with 4-inch 9mm units. This was done after the later 1908 model was adopted. Some were refurbished during the Nazi era, and these pistols bear Waffenamts and usually mismatched parts. There were approximately 1,500 manufactured, with serial numbers of one to four digits.

Courtesy Rock Island Auction Company

Exc.	V.G.	Good	Fair	Poor
7500	6500	5000	3500	1500

1906 Russian Contract

4-inch barrel, 9mm caliber. It has no stock lug, and the extractor and safety are marked with cyrillic letters. Crossed Nagant rifles are stamped over the chamber. There were approximately 1,000 manufactured, with one- to four-digit serial numbers; but few survive. This is an extremely rare variation, and caution should be exercised before purchase.

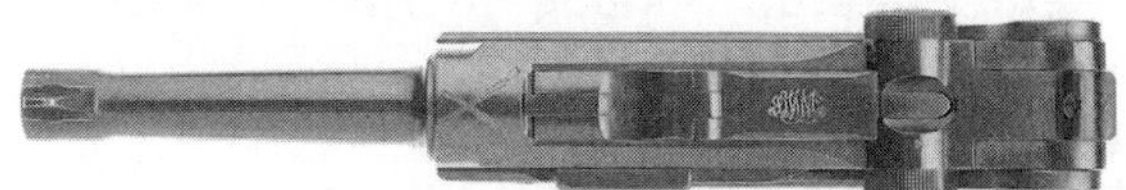

Paul Goodwin photo

Exc.	V.G.	Good	Fair	Poor
18000	15000	9500	4500	2500

Paul Goodwin photo

Close-up of 1906 Russian Contract • Courtesy Gale Morgan

1906 Navy 1st Issue

6-inch barrel, 9mm caliber. The safety and extractor are both marked in German, and the chamber area is blank. There is a stock lug, and the unique two-position sliding navy sight is mounted on the rear toggle link. There were approximately 12,000 manufactured for the German navy, with serial numbers of one to five digits. The wooden magazine bottom features concentric rings.

Paul Goodwin photo

Close-up of 1906 Navy 1st Issue • Courtesy Gale Morgan

NOTE: Many of these pistols had their safety changed so that they were "safe" in the lower position. Known as "1st issue altered." Value at approximately 20 percent less.

Exc.	V.G.	Good	Fair	Poor
7000	5500	3000	1300	950

1906 Navy 2nd Issue

As above, but manufactured to be safe in the lower position. Approximately 11,000 2nd Issue Navies manufactured, with one- to five-digit serial numbers—some with an "a" or "b" suffix. They were produced for sale to the German navy.

Paul Goodwin photo

Exc.	V.G.	Good	Fair	Poor
6500	4750	2500	1000	750

1908 Navy

As above, with the "Crown M" military proof. They may or may not have the concentric rings on the magazine bottom. There were approximately 40,000 manufactured, with one- to five-digit serial numbers with an "a" or "b" suffix. These Lugers are quite scarce as many were destroyed during and after WWI.

Exc.	V.G.	Good	Fair	Poor
6500	5000	3000	1100	800

1914 Navy

Similar to the above, but stamped with the dates from 1914-1918 above the chamber. Most noted are dated 1916-1918. There were approximately 30,000 manufactured, with one- to five-digit serial numbers with an "a" or "b" suffix. They are scarce as many were destroyed or altered as a result of WWI, even though about 40,000 were built.

Paul Goodwin photo

Exc.	V.G.	Good	Fair	Poor
5000	3500	2500	950	700

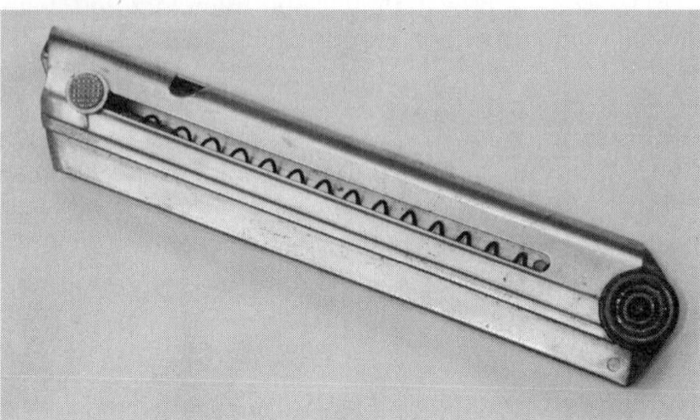

Navy Luger magazine, wood base with concentric circles. Price 250-100

1908 Military 1st Issue

4-inch barrel, 9mm caliber. This was the first Luger adopted by the German army. It has no stock lug or hold open. The extractor and safety are both marked in German. The chamber is blank. There were approximately 20,000 manufactured, with one- to five-digit serial numbers—some with an "a" suffix.

Exc.	V.G.	Good	Fair	Poor
1500	1250	800	500	350

1908 Military Dated Chamber (1910-1913)

As above, with the date of manufacture stamped on the chamber.

Exc.	V.G.	Good	Fair	Poor
1250	950	750	500	350

DWM Military dated 1914-1918

The standard P-08 used during WW1. 9mm with a 4-inch barrel. Year of manufacture stamped on chamber. Same as the Model 1908 1st issue but has a stock lug and hold-open.

Exc.	V.G.	Good	Fair	Poor
1500	1000	750	500	350

1914 Artillery dated 1914 - 1918

Fitted with an 8-inch barrel and chambered for the 9mm Parabellum cartridge, it features a nine-position adjustable sight that has a base that is an integral part of the barrel. This model has a stock lug and was furnished with a military-style flat board stock and holster rig. The chamber is dated from 1914-1918, and the safety and extractor are both marked. This model was developed for artillery and machine gun crews; and many thousands were manufactured, with one- to five-digit serial numbers—some have letter suffixes. This model is quite desirable from a collector's standpoint and is rarer than its production figures would indicate. After the war many were destroyed as the allies deemed them more insidious than other models for some reason.

Courtesy Rock Island Auction Company

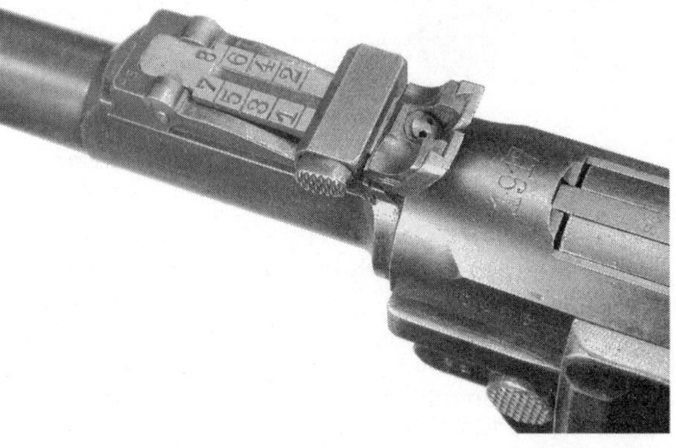

Close-up of rear sight on 1914 Artillery • *Courtesy Gale Morgan*

Exc.	***V.G.***	***Good***	***Fair***	***Poor***
3000	2000	1200	900	600

NOTE: For models stamped with 1914 date add 50 percent.

DWM Double Dated

Has a 4-inch barrel, 9mm cartridge. The date 1920 or 1921 is stamped over the original chamber date of 1910-1918, hence the double-date nomenclature. These are arsenal-reworked WWI military pistols and were then issued to the German military and/ or police units within the provisions of the Treaty of Versailles. Many thousands of these Lugers were produced.

Courtesy Rock Island Auction Company

Courtesy Rock Island Auction Company

Exc.	***V.G.***	***Good***	***Fair***	***Poor***
1000	800	650	400	300

1920 Police/Military Rework

As above, except that the original manufacture date was removed before the rework date was stamped. There were many thousands of these produced.

Exc.	***V.G.***	***Good***	***Fair***	***Poor***
900	750	600	350	300

1920 Navy Carbine

Cal. 7.65mm, 11-3/4-inch barrel. Assembled from surplus navy parts with the distinctive two-position, sliding navy sight on the rear toggle link. Most are marked with the export stamp (GERMANY) and have the naval military proofmarks still in evidence. The safety and extractor are marked, and rarely one is found chambered for the 9mm cartridge. Few were manufactured.

Close-up of rear sight on 1914 Artillery • *Courtesy Gale Morgan*

Exc.	***V.G.***	***Good***	***Fair***	***Poor***
6500	5500	3000	1800	900

1923 Dutch Commercial & Military

Fitted with a 4-inch barrel, 9mm caliber. It has a stock lug, and the chamber area is blank. The extractor is marked in German, and the safety is marked "RUST" with a downward pointing arrow. This model was sold commercially and to the military in the Netherlands. There were approximately 1,000 manufactured in the one- to three-digit serial range, with no letter suffix.

Exc.	***V.G.***	***Good***	***Fair***	***Poor***
3500	2400	1000	850	550

Royal Dutch Air Force

Fitted with a 4-inch barrel, 9mm caliber. Marked with the Mauser Oberndorf proofmark and serial numbered in the 10000 to 14000 range. The safety marked "RUST."

Exc.	V.G.	Good	Fair	Poor
4000	2500	1000	800	550

VICKERS LTD.

1906 Vickers Dutch

Has a 4-inch barrel, 9mm caliber. There is no stock lug, and it uses a grip safety. The chamber is blank, and the extractor is marked "Geladen." "Vickers Ltd." is stamped on the front toggle link. The safety is marked "RUST" with an upward pointing arrow. Examples have been found with an additional date as late as 1933 stamped on the barrel. These dates indicate arsenal refinishing and in no way detract from the value of this variation. Arsenal reworks are matte finished, and the originals are a higher polished rust blue. There were approximately 10,000 manufactured in the 1-10100 serial number range.

Paul Goodwin photo

Exc.	V.G.	Good	Fair	Poor
3500	2800	1800	1200	750

ERFURT ROYAL ARSENAL

1908 Erfurt

Has a 4-inch barrel, 9mm caliber. It has no stock lug, and the year of manufacture, from 1910-1913, is stamped above the chamber. The extractor and safety are both marked in German, and "ERFURT" under a crown is stamped on the front toggle link. There were many thousands produced as Germany was involved in WWI. They are found in the one- to five-digit serial number range, sometimes with a letter suffix.

Exc.	V.G.	Good	Fair	Poor
1400	950	600	400	350

1914 Erfurt Military

Has a 4-inch barrel, 9mm caliber. It has a stock lug and the date of manufacture over the chamber, 1914-1918. The extractor and safety are both marked in German, and the front link is marked "ERFURT" under a crown. The finish on this model is rough; and as the war progressed in 1917 and 1918, the finish got worse. There were many thousands produced with one- to five-digit serial numbers, some with letter suffixes.

Courtesy Rock Island Auction Company

Exc.	V.G.	Good	Fair	Poor
1250	900	600	400	350

1914 Erfurt Artillery

Fitted with an 8-inch barrel, 9mm caliber. It has a stock lug and was issued with a flat board-type stock and other accessories, which will be covered in the section of this book dealing with same. The sight is a nine-position adjustable model. The chamber is dated 1914-1918, and the extractor and safety are both marked in German. "ERFURT" under a crown is stamped on the front toggle link. There were a great many manufactured with one- to five-digit serial numbers, some with a letter suffix. This model is similar to the DWM Artillery except that the finish is not as fine.

Paul Goodwin photo

Exc.	V.G.	Good	Fair	Poor
2900	1850	1200	800	600

Double Date Erfurt

Has a 4-inch barrel, 9mm caliber. The area above the chamber has two dates: the original 1910-1918, and the date of rework, 1920 or 1921. The extractor and safety are both marked in German, and this model can be found with or without a stock lug. "ERFURT" under a crown is stamped on the front toggle link. Police or military unit markings are found on the front of the grip straps more often than not. Thousands of these were produced.

Exc.	V.G.	Good	Fair	Poor
900	750	600	400	350

WAFFENFABRIK BERN

See Swiss, Handguns, Bern.

SIMSON & CO.

SUHL, GERMANY

Simson & Co. Rework

Fitted with a 4-inch barrel, and chambered for either the 7.65 or 9mm caliber. The chamber is blank, but some examples are dated 1917 or 1918. The forward toggle link is stamped "SIMSON & CO. Suhl." The extractor and safety are marked in German. Most examples have stock lugs; some have been noted without them. The only difference between military models and commercial models is the proofmarks.

Exc.	V.G.	Good	Fair	Poor
1400	1100	900	600	500

Simson Dated Military

Has 4-inch barrel, 9mm caliber. There is a stock lug, and the year of manufacture from 1925-1928 is stamped above the chamber. The extractor and the safety are both marked in German. The checkered walnut grips of Simson-made Lugers are noticeably thicker than others. This is an extremely rare variation. Approximately 2,000 were manufactured with one- to three-digit serial numbers, and few seem to have survived.

Paul Goodwin photo

Exc.	V.G.	Good	Fair	Poor
4500	2750	1800	850	550

Simson S Code

Has a 4-inch barrel, 9mm caliber. The forward toggle link is stamped with a Gothic "S". It has a stock lug, and the area above the chamber is blank. The extractor and the safety are both marked. The grips are also thicker. There were approximately 12,000 manufactured with one- to five-digit serial numbers—some with the letter "a" suffix. This pistol is quite rare on today's market.

Paul Goodwin photo

Exc.	V.G.	Good	Fair	Poor
4500	3000	1800	1000	750

EARLY NAZI ERA REWORKS MAUSER

Produced between 1930 and 1933, and normally marked with Waffenamt markings.

Death's Head Rework

Has a 4-inch barrel, 9mm caliber. It has a stock lug, and a skull and crossbones are stamped, in addition to the date of manufacture, on the chamber area. This date was from 1914-1918. The extractor and safety are both marked. The Waffenamt proof is present. It is thought that this variation was produced for the 1930-1933 era "SS" division of the Nazi Party. Mixed serial numbers are encountered on this model and do not lower the value. This is a rare Luger on today's market, and caution should be exercised before purchase. Beware of fakes.

Exc.	V.G.	Good	Fair	Poor
2800	1750	950	600	450

Kadetten Institute Rework

4-inch barrel, 9mm caliber. It has a stock lug, and the chamber area is stamped "K.I." above the 1933 date. This stood for Cadets Institute, an early "SA" and "SS" officers' training school. The extractor and safety are both marked, and the Waffenamt is present. There were only a few hundred reworked, and the variation is quite scarce. Beware of fakes.

Exc.	V.G.	Good	Fair	Poor
3200	2750	1250	800	600

Mauser Unmarked Rework

4-inch barrel, 9mm caliber. The entire weapon is void of identifying markings. There is extensive refurbishing, removal of all markings, rebarreling, etc. The stock lug is present, and the extractor and safety are marked. The Waffenamt proofmark is on the right side of the receiver. The number manufactured is not known.

Exc.	V.G.	Good	Fair	Poor
1450	1000	850	600	450

GERMANY

MAUSER-MANUFACTURED LUGERS

Mauser Oberndorf DWM Marked

4-inch barrel, 9mm caliber. It has a stock lug, blank chamber area, and a marked extractor and safety. This is an early example of Mauser Luger, and the front toggle link is still marked "DWM" as leftover parts were intermixed with new Mauser parts in the production of this pistol. This is one of the first Lugers to be finished with the "salt blue" process. There were approximately 500 manufactured with one- to four-digit serial numbers with the letter "v" suffix. This is a rare variation.

Exc.	V.G.	Good	Fair	Poor
5000	3200	2000	1500	900

1935/06 Portuguese "GNR"

4.75-inch barrel, 7.65mm caliber. It has no stock lug but has a grip safety. The chamber is marked "GNR," representing the Republic National Guard. The extractor is marked "Carregada"; and the safety, "Seguranca." The Mauser banner is stamped on the front toggle link. There were exactly 564 manufactured according to the original contract records that the Portuguese government made public. They all have four-digit serial numbers with a "v" suffix.

Exc.	V.G.	Good	Fair	Poor
3500	2700	1600	900	750

Paul Goodwin photo

S/42 K Date

4-inch barrel, 9mm caliber. It has a stock lug, and the extractor and safety are marked. This was the first Luger that utilized codes to represent maker and date of manufacture. The front toggle link is marked "S/42" in either Gothic or script; this was the code for Mauser. The chamber area is stamped with the letter "K," the code for 1934, the year of manufacture. Approximately 10,500 were manufactured with one- to five-digit serial numbers—some with letter suffixes.

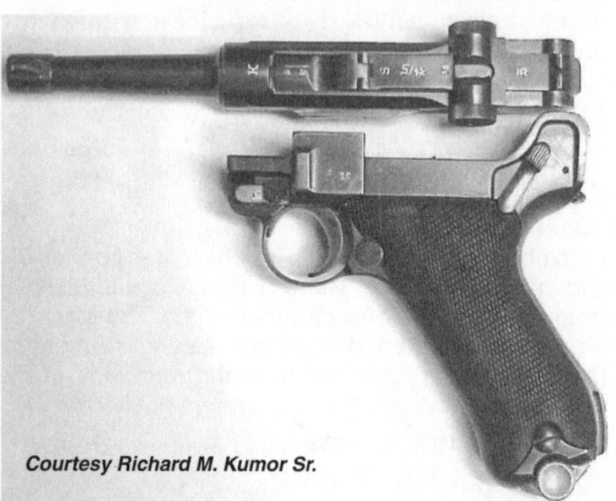

Courtesy Richard M. Kumor Sr.

Exc.	V.G.	Good	Fair	Poor
6000	4000	2200	1200	1000

S/42 G Date

As above, with the chamber stamped "G," the code for the year 1935. The Gothic lettering was eliminated, and many thousands of this model were produced.

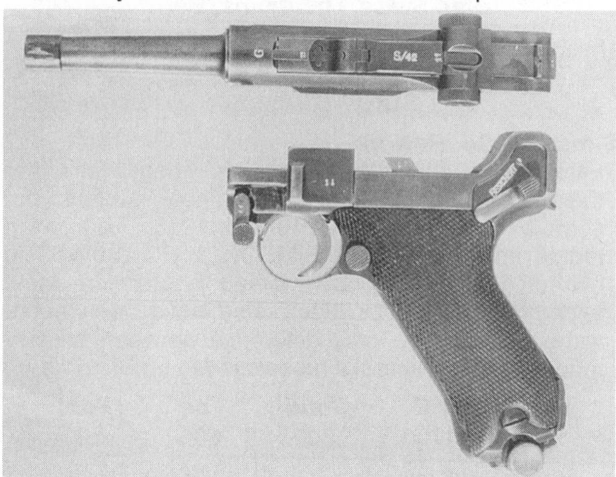

Courtesy Orvel Reichert

Exc.	V.G.	Good	Fair	Poor
2800	2000	1000	650	450

Dated Chamber S/42

4-inch barrel, 9mm caliber. The chamber area is dated 1936-1940, and there is a stock lug. The extractor and safety are marked. In 1937 the rust blue process was eliminated entirely, and all subsequent pistols were salt blued. Many thousands were manufactured with one- to five-digit serial numbers—some with a letter suffix.

Exc.	V.G.	Good	Fair	Poor
1750	1300	850	500	400

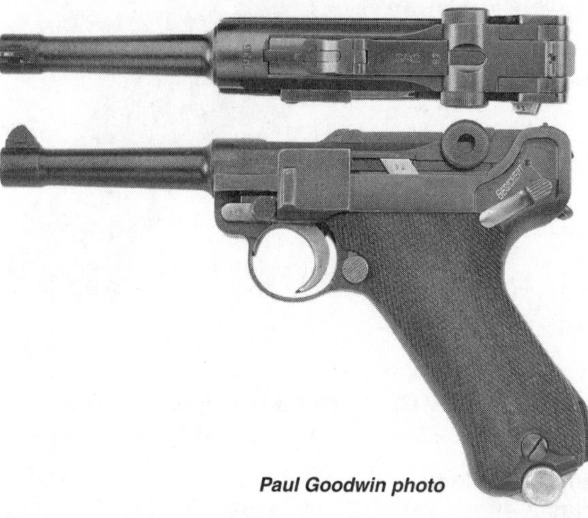

Paul Goodwin photo

NOTE: Rarest variation is early 1937 with rust blued and strawed parts, add 20 percent.

Code 42 Dated Chamber

4-inch barrel, 9mm caliber. The new German code for Mauser, the number 42, is stamped on the front toggle link. There is a stock lug. The chamber area is dated 1939 or 1940. There were at least 50,000 manufactured with one- to five-digit serial numbers—some have letter suffixes.

Exc.	V.G.	Good	Fair	Poor
1650	1200	800	400	350

41/42 Code

As above, except that the date of manufacture is represented by the final two digits (e.g. 41 for 1941). There were approximately 20,000 manufactured with the one- to five-digit serial number range.

Exc.	V.G.	Good	Fair	Poor
1850	1500	1000	700	500

byf Code

As above, with the "byf" code stamp on the toggle link. The year of manufacture, either 41 or 42, is stamped on the chamber. This model was also made with black plastic, as well as walnut grips. There were many thousands produced with the one- to five-digit serial numbers—some with a letter suffix.

Exc.	V.G.	Good	Fair	Poor
1500	1100	800	450	350

Paul Goodwin photo

WWII P-08 Magazines left, milled steel, marked "fxo", aluminum base with SN. Center, extruded steel, un-marked, un-numbered black plastic base. Right, extruded stainless steel body, marked "Haenel Schmeisser," aluminum base.

Luger Magazine 1937-1945

Steel body. Aluminum or plastic base. Add 25% for fxo marked

Exc.	V.G.	Good	Fair	Poor
150	125	90	50	35

Persian Contract 4"

4" barrel, 9mm caliber. It has a stock lug, and the Persian crest is stamped over the chamber. All identifying markings on this variation—including extractor, safety, and toggle—are marked in Farsi, the

Persian Contract 4" • *Paul Goodwin photo*

Persian alphabet. There were 1,000 manufactured. The serial numbers are also in Farsi.

Exc.	V.G.	Good	Fair	Poor
4500	3000	2000	1200	750

Persian Contract Artillery

As above, with an 8-inch barrel and nine-position adjustable sight on the barrel. This model is supplied with a flat board stock. 1,000 were manufactured and sold to Persia.

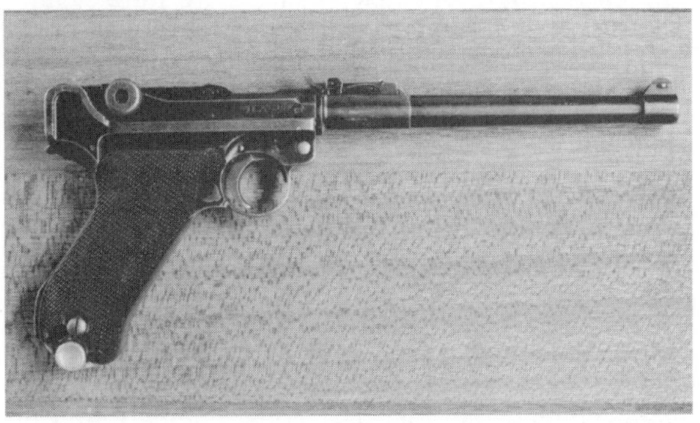

Persian Contract 4" • *Paul Goodwin photo*

Exc.	V.G.	Good	Fair	Poor
4800	3500	2500	1300	1000

1934 Mauser Dutch Contract

4-inch barrel, 9mm caliber. The year of manufacture, 1936-1939, is stamped above the chamber. The extractor is marked "Geladen," and the safety is marked "RUST" with a downward pointing arrow. The Mauser banner is stamped on the front toggle link. Checkered walnut grips. This was a military contract sale, and approximately 1,000 were manufactured with four-digit serial numbers with a letter "v" suffix.

Paul Goodwin photo

Exc.	V.G.	Good	Fair	Poor
3500	3000	2000	1100	850

1934 Mauser Swedish Contract

4.75-inch barrel, 9mm or 7.65mm caliber. The chamber is dated 1938 or 1939. The extractor and safety are both marked in German, and there is a stock lug. The front toggle link is stamped with the Mauser banner. There were only 275 dated 1938 and 25 dated 1939 in 9mm. There were only 30 chambered for 7.65mm dated 1939. The serial number range is four digits with the letter "v" suffix.

Exc.	V.G.	Good	Fair	Poor
3750	3250	2000	1250	900

1934 Mauser German Contract

4-inch barrel, 9mm caliber. The chamber is dated 1936-1942, and the front toggle link is stamped with the Mauser banner. There is a stock lug, and the extractor and safety are both marked. The grips are either walnut or black plastic. There were several thousand manufactured with one- to five-digit serial numbers—some with letter suffixes. They were purchased for issue to police or paramilitary units.

Exc.	V.G.	Good	Fair	Poor
3000	2300	1500	800	550

Austrian Bundes Heer (Federal Army)

4-inch barrel, 9mm caliber. The chamber is blank, and there is a stock lug. The extractor and safety are marked in German, and the Austrian federal army proof is stamped on the left side of the frame above the triggerguard. There were approximately 200 manufactured with four-digit serial numbers and no letter suffix.

Exc.	V.G.	Good	Fair	Poor
2800	2000	1500	700	500

Mauser 2-Digit Date

4-inch barrel, 9mm caliber. The last two digits of the year of manufacture—41 or 42—are stamped over the chamber. There is a stock lug, and the Mauser banner is on the front toggle link. The extractor and safety are both marked, and the proofmarks were commercial. Grips are either walnut or black plastic. There were approximately 2,000 manufactured for sale to Nazi political groups. They have one- to five-digit serial numbers—some have the letter suffix.

Exc.	V.G.	Good	Fair	Poor
2800	2200	1500	900	650

KRIEGHOFF-MANUFACTURED LUGERS

S Code Krieghoff

4-inch barrel, 9mm caliber. The Krieghoff trademark is stamped on the front toggle link, and the letter "S" is stamped over the chamber. There is a stock lug, and the extractor and safety are both marked. The grips are brown checkered plastic. There were approximately 4,500 manufactured for the Luftwaffe with one- to four-digit serial numbers.

Courtesy Rock Island Auction Company

Exc.	V.G.	Good	Fair	Poor
5000	3750	2500	1000	750

Grip Safety Krieghoff

4-inch barrel, 9mm caliber. The chamber area is blank, and the front toggle link is stamped with the Krieghoff trademark. There is a stock lug and a grip safety. The extractor is marked "Geleden," and the safety is marked "FEUER" (fire) in the lower position. The grips are checkered brown plastic. This is a rare Luger, and the number produced is not known.

Exc.	V.G.	Good	Fair	Poor
7500	5000	3750	1500	900

36 Date Krieghoff

4-inch barrel, 9mm caliber. It has a stock lug and the Krieghoff trademark on the front toggle link. The safety and extractor are marked, and the grips are brown plastic. The two-digit year of manufacture, 36, is stamped over the chamber. There were approximately 700 produced in the 3800-4500 serial number range.

Exc.	V.G.	Good	Fair	Poor
4500	3500	2750	1500	950

Paul Goodwin photo

4-Digit Dated Krieghoff

As above, with the date of production, 1936-1945, stamped above the chamber. There were approximately 9,000 manufactured within the 4500-14000 serial number range.

Exc.	V.G.	Good	Fair	Poor
4500	3750	2200	1500	950

NOTE: add 100% for 1944 or 1945 date.

LUGER ACCESSORIES

Detachable Carbine Stocks

Approximately 13 inches in length, with a sling swivel and horn buttplate.

Exc.	V.G.	Good	Fair	Poor
4500	3500	1500	700	500

Artillery Stock with Holster

The artillery stock is of a flat board style approximately 13.75 inches in length. There is a holster and magazine pouches with straps attached. This is a desirable addition to the Artillery Luger.

Exc.	V.G.	Good	Fair	Poor
1500	1000	550	400	300

Navy Stock without Holster

As above, but 12.75 inches in length with a metal disc inlaid on the left side.

Exc.	V.G.	Good	Fair	Poor
3000	1500	1000	500	400

NOTE: With holster add 100 percent.

Ideal Stock/Holster with Grips

A telescoping metal tube stock with an attached leather holster. It is used in conjunction with a metal-backed set of plain grips that correspond to the metal hooks on the stock and allow attachment. The Ideal stock is U.S. patented and is so marked.

Exc.	V.G.	Good	Fair	Poor
2000	1400	1000	700	450

Drum Magazine 1st Issue

A 32-round, snail-like affair that is used with the Artillery Luger. It is also used with an adapter in the German 9mm submachine gun. The 1st Issue has a telescoping tube that is used to wind the spring. There is a dust cover that protects the interior from dirt. Price for functional magazine with dust cover.

Exc.	V.G.	Good	Fair	Poor
1800	1000	750	500	300

Drum Magazine 2nd Issue

As above, with a folding spring winding lever.

Exc.	V.G.	Good	Fair	Poor
1500	900	850	500	300

Drum Magazine Loading Tool

This tool is slipped over the magazine and allows the spring to be compressed so that cartridges could be inserted.

Exc.	V.G.	Good	Fair	Poor
800	550	500	300	200

Drum Magazine Unloading Tool

The origin of this tool is unknown and caution should be exercised before purchase.

Drum Carrying Case

The same caveat as above applies.

Exc.	V.G.	Good	Fair	Poor
250	200	125	100	50

Luger Holster

Common design with top flap. Spare magazine pouch on the right side. Two belt loops on back. The same basic pattern was used throughout the P-08's service life. Most will bear a maker's name and date. Brown or black leather.

Exc.	V.G.	Good	Fair	Poor
450	300	150	60	50

GERMANY

LANGENHAN, FRIEDRICH

Langenhan Army Model

A blowback-operated semi-automatic pistol chambered for the 7.65mm Auto Pistol cartridge. It has a 4-inch barrel and a detachable magazine that holds 8 rounds. Weight is about 24 oz. The pistol was made with a separate breechblock that is held into the slide by a screw. This feature doomed this pistol to eventual failure as when this screw became worn, it could loosen when firing and allow the breechblock to pivot upwards—and the slide would then be propelled rearward and into the face of the shooter. This is not a comforting thought. This pistol was produced and used in WWI only and was never offered commercially. It is marked "F.L. Selbstlade DRGM." The finish is blued, and the grips are molded rubber, with "F.L." at the top.

CAUTION: As noted above, this is an unsafe weapon to fire.

Courtesy James Rankin

Exc.	V.G.	Good	Fair	Poor
300	225	200	150	100

P.38: GERMAN WWII SERVICE PISTOL

Walther developed its German military service pistol, the P.38 or Model HP (Heerespistole), in 1937. It was adopted by the German military as its primary handgun in 1938. The background behind this adoption by the German military is an interesting one. In the 1930s, the German Army High Command wanted German arms manufacturers to develop a large-caliber semi-automatic pistol to replace the Luger, which was difficult and costly to manufacture. The army wanted a pistol that was easy to manufacture as well as simple to assemble and disassemble. It also required a pistol that could be produced by several manufacturers if necessary and one whose parts would be interchangeable among manufacturers. Walther had just completed its Model HP for worldwide distribution and had the advantage over the other German companies. The German High Command approved Walther's design with only a few mechanical changes. This designation, the P.38, was not used by Walther on its commercial guns. Production began in late 1939 for both civilian and military use. Both military and commercial versions were produced throughout the war years. The civilian pistol was referred to as the MOD HP until late in the war, when a few were marked "MOD P.38" to take advantage of the identity of the military pistol. In late 1942, Mauser and Spreewerke began production of the P.38. Mauser was assigned the code "BYF" and in 1945 the code was changed to "SVW." Spreewerke's code was "CYQ." Late in the war the die stamp broke and the code appears as "CVQ."

The P.38 is a double-action semi-automatic pistol that is short-recoil operated and fires from a locked breech by means of an external hammer. It is chambered for the 9mm Parabellum and has a 5" barrel. The detachable magazine holds 8 cartridges and the front sight is adjustable for windage. Initially the finish was a high quality blue, but when the war effort increased, less time was spent on the finish. The P.38 was equipped with two styles of plastic grips. Early pistols have a checkered grip and later grips are the military ribbed variety; the later style is much more common. The P.38 was produced by three companies and each had its own distinct markings and variations as outlined below. Despite the large number of variations that the P.38 collector will encounter, it is important for him to be aware that there are no known documented examples of P.38s that are factory engraved, nickel-plated, have barrels that are longer or shorter than standard, or built as military presentation pistols.

Collectors should be made aware of a final note. The P.38 pistol was first adopted more than 50 years ago. During that period of time the pistol has seen use all over the world. After the end of WWII several governments came into possession of fairly large quantities of P.38s and used them in their own military and police agencies. Many countries have reworked these older P.38s with both original and new component parts. The former U.S.S.R. is the primary source of reworked P.38s. Many of these pistols have been completely refinished and re-proofed by a number of countries. The collector should be aware of the existence of reworked P.38s and examine any P.38 carefully to determine if the pistol is original German military issue. These reworked pistols bring substantially lower prices than original P.38s.

Walther Commercial

The Commercial version of the P.38 is identified by commercial proofmarks of a crown over N or an eagle over N. Production started at around serial number 1000 and went through serial number 26659. This was the first of the commercial pistols and was a high-quality, well-made gun with a complete inscription on the left slide. A few of these early pistols were equipped with checkered wooden grips. The quality decreased as the war progressed. There are many variations of these commercial models and values can vary from $1,000 to $16,000. It is suggested that these pistols be appraised and evaluated by an expert.

A few of the Walther commercial model variations follow:

MOD HP–Early w/High Gloss Blue

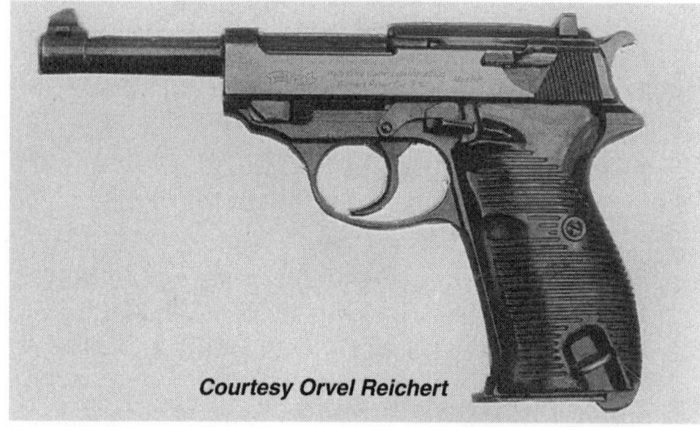

Courtesy Orvel Reichert

Exc.	V.G.	Good	Fair	Poor
3000	1750	750	600	400

MOD HP–Early w/High Gloss Blue & Alloy Frame

Courtesy Orvel Reichert

Exc.	V.G.	Good	Fair	Poor
10000	6500	3500	2000	1000

MOD HP–Late w/Military Blue Finish

Courtesy Orvel Reichert

Exc.	V.G.	Good	Fair	Poor
2000	1400	750	550	350

NOTE: Add $500 for "Eagle/359" on right side.

MOD P38–Late with Military Blue

1,800 produced.

Courtesy Orvel Reichert

Exc.	V.G.	Good	Fair	Poor
2700	1400	750	600	400

Walther Military Zero Series

This was the first of the military P.38s and they are well made with a high polish finish. These pistols have the Walther banner and the designation P.38. The serial number began with 01 and went through about 013714. The First Zero Series has a concealed extractor and rectangular firing pin. About 1,000 First Zero Series were built. The Second Zero Series has a rectangular firing pin and standard extractor, with a production of about 2,300. The Third Zero Series has a standard firing pin and standard extractor and has the highest production with 10,000 built.

First Issue Zero Series

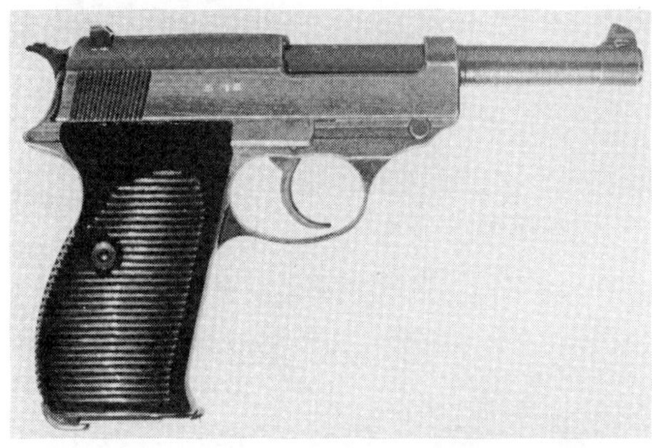

Courtesy Orvel Reichert

Exc.	V.G.	Good	Fair	Poor
9000	7500	4500	2500	1500

Courtesy Orvel Reichert

Second Issue Zero Series

Courtesy Orvel Reichert

Exc.	V.G.	Good	Fair	Poor
7500	4500	3250	2000	1000

GERMANY

Third Issue Zero Series

Courtesy Orvel Reichert

Exc.	*V.G.*	*Good*	*Fair*	*Poor*
3500	2200	1250	800	500

480 CODE

This code was utilized by Walther in late 1940 and represents the first true military contract pistols. There were approximately 7,250 guns produced under this code. There are two subvariations: one with a round lanyard loop and the other with a rectangular lanyard loop.

Courtesy Orvel Reichert

Exc.	*V.G.*	*Good*	*Fair*	*Poor*
7500	5500	3000	1750	1000

"AC" CODES

This variation follows the 480 code.

"ac" (no date)

This variation has on the slide "P.38ac" then the serial number only. This is the first use of the "ac" code by Walther. There were approximately 2,700 pistols produced with this code and this is the rarest of all military P.38s.

Exc.	*V.G.*	*Good*	*Fair*	*Poor*
8000	6000	4250	2800	1500

"ac40"

There are two types of "ac40s." The first variation is the ac with the 40 added, that is the "40" was hand stamped below the "ac". There are about 6,000 of these produced. The second variation is the "ac40" rolled on together. There are also about 14,000 of these produced as well. The "ac" 40 added is more valuable than the standard "ac40."

"ac40" (added)

Courtesy Orvel Reichert

Courtesy Orvel Reichert

Exc.	*V.G.*	*Good*	*Fair*	*Poor*
3750	2500	1750	1000	600

"ac40" (standard)

Courtesy Orvel Reichert

Exc.	*V.G.*	*Good*	*Fair*	*Poor*
2500	1200	950	700	500

"ac41"

There are three variations of the "ac41." The first variation has "ac" on left triggerguard and features a high gloss blue. About 25,000 of this variation were made. The second variation, about 70,000 were produced, also has a high gloss blue but does not have "ac" on the triggerguard. The third variation features a military blue rather than a high gloss blue and had a production run of about 15,000 pistols.

"ac41" (1st variation)

Exc.	*V.G.*	*Good*	*Fair*	*Poor*
2200	1100	700	500	350

"ac41" (2nd variation)

Exc.	V.G.	Good	Fair	Poor
1500	750	600	450	300

ac41 (1st variation) • Courtesy Orvel Reichert

ac41 (2nd variation) • Courtesy Orvel Reichert

"ac41" (3rd variation)

Courtesy Orvel Reichert

Exc.	V.G.	Good	Fair	Poor
1400	650	500	400	300

"ac42"

There are two variations of the "ac42" code. The first has an eagle over 359 stamped on all small parts as do all preceding variations and a production of 21,000 pistols. The second variation does not have the eagle over 359 stamped on small parts. This second variation has a large production run of 100,000 pistols.

"ac42" (1st variation)

Exc.	V.G.	Good	Fair	Poor
1300	650	500	350	275

ac42 (1st variation) • Courtesy Orvel Reichert

"ac42" (2nd variation)

Exc.	V.G.	Good	Fair	Poor
1200	600	500	300	250

"ac43"

This code has three variations. The first is a standard date with "ac" over "43". It has an early frame and extractor cut. The second variation has the late frame and extractor cut. Both variations are frequently encountered because approximately 130,000 were built.

"ac43" (1st variation)

Courtesy Orvel Reichert

Exc.	V.G.	Good	Fair	Poor
900	675	500	250	200

"ac43" (2nd variation)

Exc.	V.G.	Good	Fair	Poor
700	600	500	250	200

"ac43" single line slide

This variation represents the beginning of the placement of the date on the same line with the production code. There were approximately 20,000 built in this variation.

Courtesy Orvel Reichert

Exc.	V.G.	Good	Fair	Poor
900	650	500	350	250

"ac44"

This variation also has the date stamped beside "ac" and is fairly common. About 120,000 were produced.

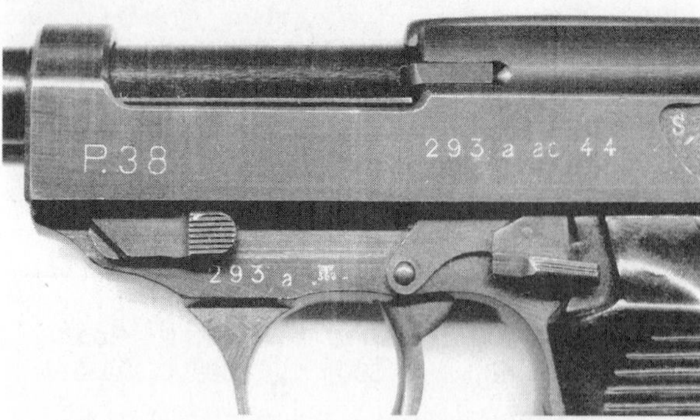

Courtesy Orvel Reichert

ac44 FN Slide left and right sides • *Courtesy Orvel Reichert*

Exc.	V.G.	Good	Fair	Poor
750	600	500	250	200

NOTE: Add $300 for FN frame (Eagle/140).

"ac45"

This code has three variations. The first has all matching numbers on a plum colored frame. About 32,000 of this first variation were produced. The second variation has a capital "A" in place of the lowercase "a." The third variation has all major parts with factory mismatched numbers, with a single eagle over 359 on the slide. The first variation is the most common of this code.

"ac45" (1st variation)

Exc.	V.G.	Good	Fair	Poor
800	650	500	250	200

"ac45" (2nd variation)

Exc.	V.G.	Good	Fair	Poor
950	700	500	300	250

"ac45" (3rd variation)

Exc.	V.G.	Good	Fair	Poor
750	650	500	250	200

NOTE: Add $200 for pistols with Czech barrels; barrel code "fnh."

ac45 (1st variation) • *Courtesy Orvel Reichert*

ac45 (2nd variation) • *Courtesy Orvel Reichert*

ac45 (3rd variation) • *Courtesy Orvel Reichert*

"ac45" Zero Series

This is a continuation of the commercial pistols with a military marked slide. This series has "ac45" plus the 0 prefix serial number on the left side as well as the usual P.38 roll stamp. It may or may not have commercial proofmarks. A total of 1,200 of these "ac45" Zero Series guns were produced in 1945. They are often seen with a plum colored slide.

Exc.	V.G.	Good	Fair	Poor
2800	1750	850	500	400

MAUSER MILITARY

The following P.38s were produced by Mauser and are identified by various Mauser codes.

GERMANY

Courtesy Orvel Reichert

"byf42"

Approximately 19,000 P.38s were manufactured in this variation. Some of these pistols will have a flat blue finish.

Courtesy Orvel Reichert

Exc.	V.G.	Good	Fair	Poor
2200	1250	750	500	300

"byf43"

A common variation of the P.38 with approximately 140,000 produced.

Courtesy Orvel Reichert

Exc.	V.G.	Good	Fair	Poor
850	650	500	250	200

"byf44"

Another common variation with a total production of about 150,000 guns.

Exc.	V.G.	Good	Fair	Poor
850	550	500	250	200

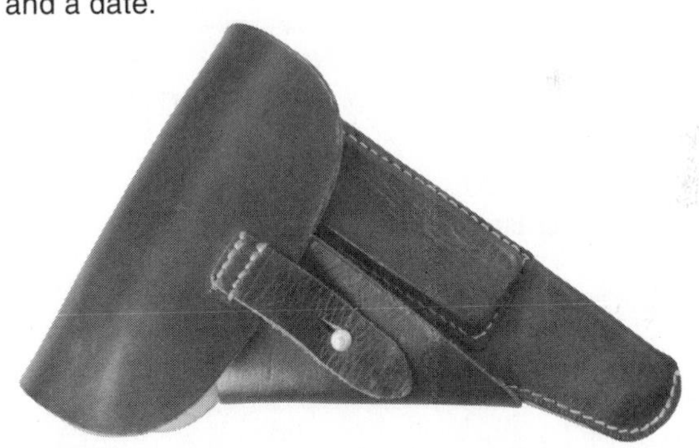

Courtesy Orvel Reichert

NOTE: Add $100 for dual tone finish that is a combination of blue and gray components.

Leather holster for P-38

Similar to the Luger holster. It has the magazine pouch on the front or right side. Most will have makers code and a date.

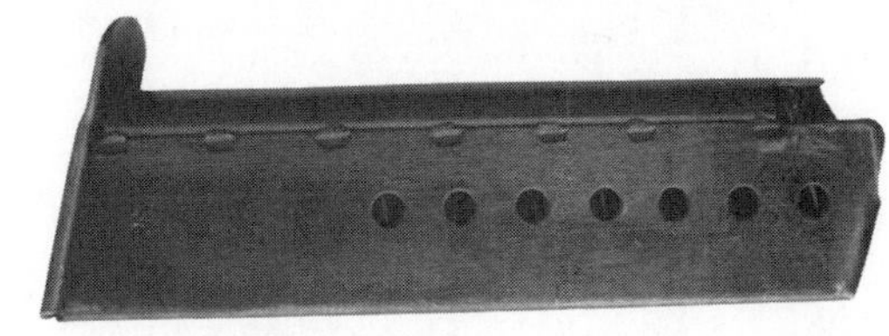

Exc.	V.G.	Good	Fair	Poor
200	150	100	50	25

P-38 Magazine

Steel construction. Most are marked P38 on the side. Those marked on the back spine with an eagle 135 waffen mark are from Mauser. Those with a tiny eagle 359 waffen mark and WaA706 are from Walther. Jvd marking is a contractor. Unmarked magazines are Spreewerke or sub contractor manufacture.

Exc.	V.G.	Good	Fair	Poor
100	75	60	40	25

GERMANY

AC43/44-FN slide

Courtesy Orvel Reichert

Exc.	V.G.	Good	Fair	Poor
2000	1200	725	600	450

"svw45"

The Mauser code is changed from "byf" to "svw." This variation was produced until the end of the war when France took over production and continued through 1946. French-produced guns will have a 5-point star on the right side of the slide. A large number of these French pistols have been imported thereby depressing values.

"svw45"-German Proofed

Courtesy Orvel Reichert

Exc.	V.G.	Good	Fair	Poor
2200	1200	725	550	400

"svw45"-French Proofed

Courtesy Orvel Reichert

Exc.	V.G.	Good	Fair	Poor
650	400	475	250	200

Courtesy Orvel Reichert

"svw46"-French Proofed

Exc.	V.G.	Good	Fair	Poor
700	550	450	300	250

MAUSER "POLICE" P.38

Mauser produced the only Nazi-era Police P.38 during the 1943 to 1945 period. It is generally believed that only 8,000 guns were serially produced, although a few oddballs show up beyond that range.

Police guns are easily recognized by the appearance of a commercial proof (eagle over N) instead of the Military proof (eagle over swastika). They also have a civilian (Police) acceptance stamp (either an Eagle L or Eagle F).

The guns have a stacked code with date below the code. Earliest guns were coded "byf" over "43" and later, "byf" over "44". In the late 1944 production, a group of slides manufactured for Walther at the FN plant in Belgium were received and used. These slides all have the "ac" over "43" or "ac" over "44" code. Finally, in 1945, a few "svw" over "45" coded guns were made. These Walther coded slides are hard to find, and the 1945 guns are quite rare.

Because of the increased value of these guns, it is wise to have them examined by an expert before purchase.

"byf/43"

Exc.	V.G.	Good	Fair	Poor
2500	1700	1200	800	500

"byf/44"

Exc.	V.G.	Good	Fair	Poor
2500	1700	1200	800	500

"ac/43"

Exc.	V.G.	Good	Fair	Poor
5000	3500	2000	1250	800

"ac/44"

Exc.	V.G.	Good	Fair	Poor
5000	3500	2000	1250	800

"svw/45"

Exc.	V.G.	Good	Fair	Poor
6000	4500	2500	1600	1000

SPREEWERKE MILITARY

Production of the P.38 began at Spreewerk in late 1942 and Spreewerke used the code "cyq" that had been assigned to it at the beginning of the war.

"cyq"

Eagle/211 on frame, two examples known.

Exc.	V.G.	Good	Fair	Poor
5000	—	—	—	—

"cyq" (1st variation)

The first 500 of these guns have the eagle over 359 on some small parts and command a premium. Value depends on markings and an expert should be consulted for values.

Exc.	V.G.	Good	Fair	Poor
1400	1000	750	600	500

"cyq" (standard variation)

There were approximately 300,000 of these pistols produced in this variation, which makes them the most common of all P.38 variations.

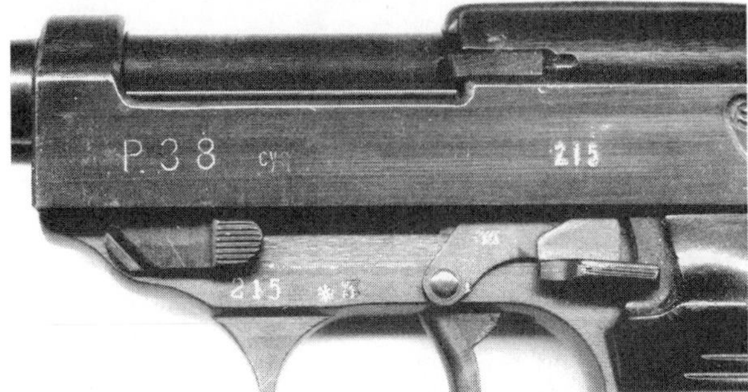

Courtesy Orvel Reichert

Courtesy Orvel Reichert

Courtesy Orvel Reichert

Exc.	V.G.	Good	Fair	Poor
650	550	475	250	200

NOTE: If "A" or "B" prefix add $250.

"cyq" Zero Series

This variation features a Zero ahead of the serial number and only about 5,000 of these guns were produced.

Exc.	V.G.	Good	Fair	Poor
1250	750	500	350	275

Courtesy Orvel Reichert

NOTE: Add $250 for a cyq P-38 with a AC43 or AC44 marked "FN" slide.

P-38 postwar Soviet rework

Recent importation from former Soviet bloc countries. Some are collectible variations, that have matching numbers. Others were repaired and assembled with renumbered parts. All have been refinished and have importer markings. There might be a slight premium for the rare models; however they are refinished and many collectors consider them to be worth less than original examples.

Exc.	V.G.	Good	Fair	Poor
650	550	450	—	—

Walther Model P-1

This is a postwar P.38. It has an alloy frame. This model was adopted by the German army as the standard sidearm in 1957, and remained in service until 1980. Many were imported recently and they are common. Most are in VG or excellent condition. Note: carefully examine the alloy frame for cracking along the slide rails.

Exc.	V.G.	Good	Fair	Poor
450	350	250	—	—

MAUSER POCKET PISTOLS

Model 1914

A 7.65mm caliber semi-automatic pistol with a 3.5-inch barrel, fixed sights, and wrap-around walnut grips. The slide marked "Waffenfabrik Mauser A.G. Oberndorf A.N. Mauser's Patent." The frame has the Mauser banner stamped on its left side. Manufactured between 1914 and 1934. Almost all Model 1914 pistols built between serial numbers 40,000 and 180,000 will be seen with German military acceptance stamps. A few will have the Prussian Eagle stamped on the front of the triggerguard.

Courtesy Ryerson Knight

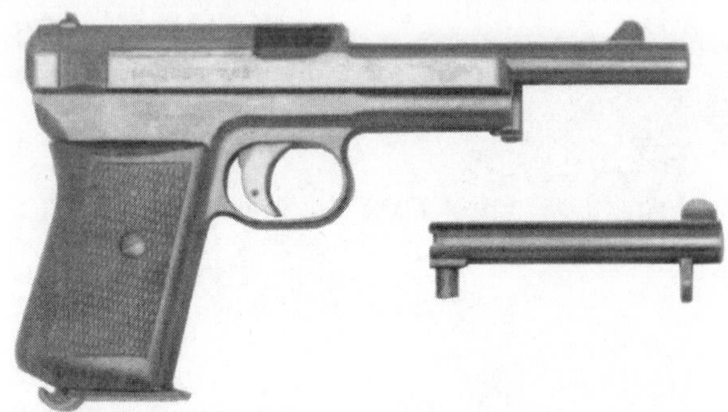

Courtesy Butterfield & Butterfield, San Francisco, California

Exc.	V.G.	Good	Fair	Poor
500	400	250	150	100

NOTE: add 25% for German or Prussian military marks.

Model 1934

Similar to the Model 1910 and Model 1914, with the slide marked "Mauser-Werke A.G. Oberndorf A. N." It has the Mauser banner stamped on the frame. The reverse side is marked with the caliber and "D.R.P. u A.P." Manufactured between 1934 and 1939. Those with Nazi Waffenamt markings are worth approximately 20 percent more than the values listed below. Those marked with an eagle over the letter "M" (navy marked) are worth approximately 100 percent more than the values listed below.

Courtesy Ryerson Knight

Courtesy Gale Morgan

Exc.	V.G.	Good	Fair	Poor
550	425	300	150	100

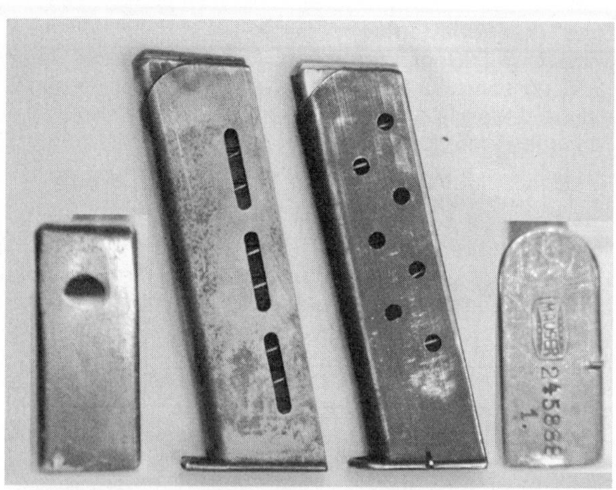

Mauser M1914 (left) and M1934 (r) magazines. Price 60-30

Model HSC

A 7.65mm or 9mm short caliber double action semi-automatic pistol with a 3.4" barrel, 7- or 8-shot magazine and fixed sights. Introduced in 1938 and produced in the variations listed below.

Low Grip Screw Model

As above, with screws that attach the grip located near the bottom of the grip. Highly polished blue, checkered walnut grips, and the early address without the lines and has the Eagle N proof. Some have been observed with Nazi Kreigsmarine markings. Approximately 2,000 were manufactured.

Exc.	V.G.	Good	Fair	Poor
4500	3000	1500	750	600

Early Commercial Model

A highly-polished blued finish, checkered walnut grips, the standard Mauser address on the slide, and the Eagle N proofmark. The floorplate of the magazine stamped with the Mauser banner.

Early Commercial model with magazine stamping • *Courtesy Ryerson Knight*

Exc.	V.G.	Good	Fair	Poor
650	500	400	275	175

Transition Model

As above, but not as highly finished.

Exc.	V.G.	Good	Fair	Poor
550	450	350	225	175

Early Nazi Army Model

Highly polished with Waffenamt No. 135 or 655 markings. Checkered walnut grips. Acceptance marks are located on the left side of the triggerguard.

Courtesy Orvel Reichert • Close-up courtesy Ryerson Knight

Exc.	V.G.	Good	Fair	Poor
650	575	500	250	175

Late Nazi Army Model

Blued or parkerized, with walnut or plastic grips, and the 135 acceptance mark only. It also has the Eagle N proof.

Exc.	V.G.	Good	Fair	Poor
550	475	400	225	175

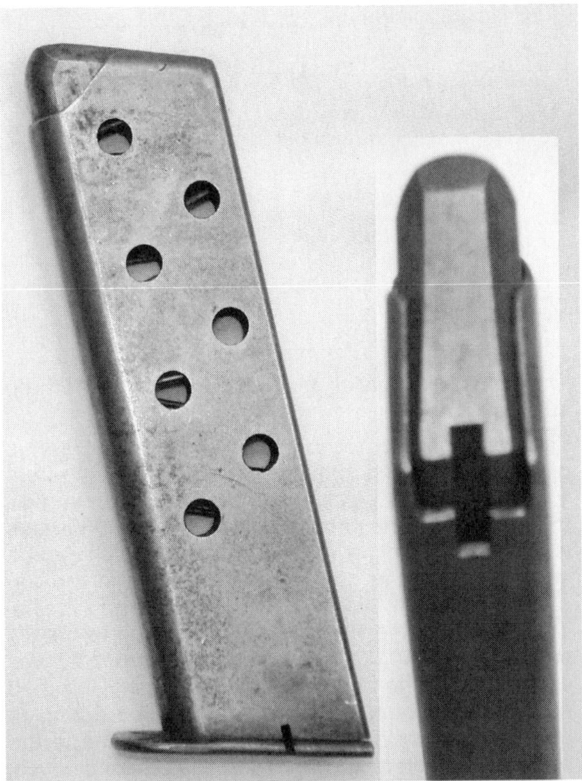

Magazine for Mauser HSc. Price 50-30

Early Nazi Navy Model

Highly polished with checkered walnut grips and the eagle over "M" marking on the front grip strap.

Courtesy Ryerson Knight

Exc.	V.G.	Good	Fair	Poor
1000	800	600	400	300

Wartime Nazi Navy Model

Similar to the above, with the navy acceptance mark on the side of the triggerguard. Blued, with either checkered walnut or plastic grips. It has the standard Mauser address and banner and also the Eagle N proof.

Exc.	V.G.	Good	Fair	Poor
750	600	500	400	200

Early Nazi Police Model

Identical to the Early Commercial Model with an eagle over "L" mark on the left side of the triggerguard.

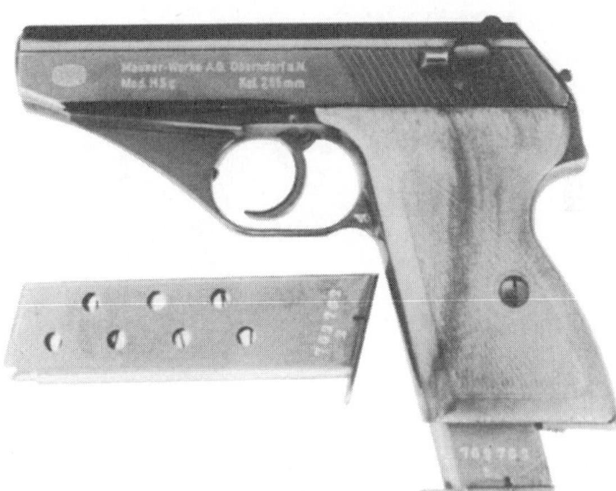

Courtesy Ryerson Knight

Exc.	V.G.	Good	Fair	Poor
650	550	475	250	175

Wartime Nazi Police Model

As above, with a three-line Mauser address.

Exc.	V.G.	Good	Fair	Poor
575	475	450	250	175

Wartime Commercial Model

As above, without acceptance markings on the triggerguard.

Exc.	V.G.	Good	Fair	Poor
500	400	350	200	125

French Manufactured Model

Blued or parkerized with walnut or plastic grips and

the triggerguard marked on the left side with the monogram "MR."

Exc.	V.G.	Good	Fair	Poor
375	300	250	150	100

SAUER, J. P. & SON

Text and prices by Jim Cate.

Sauer Model 1913

FIRST SERIES: incorporates an extra safety button on the left side of the frame near the trigger and the rear sight, a simple milled recess in the cocking knob itself. The serial number range runs from 1 to approximately 4750 and this first series is found only in 7.65mm caliber. All were for commercial sales as far as can be determined. Some were tested by various militaries, no doubt.

A. European variation—all slide legends are in the German language.

B. English Export variation—slide legends are marked J.P. Sauer & Son, Suhl - Prussia, "Sauer's Patent" Pat'd May 20 1912.

Both were sold in thick paper cartons or boxes with the color being a reddish purple with gold colored letters, etc. Examples of the very early European variation are found with the English language brochure or manual as well as an extra magazine, cleaning brush, and grease container. These were shipped to England or the U.S. prior to Sauer producing the English Export variation.

A. European variation

Exc.	V.G.	Good	Fair	Poor
1100	900	650	400	250

B. English Export variation

Exc.	V.G.	Good	Fair	Poor
1450	1150	800	500	300

Original box with accessories and manual: Add $500 if complete and in very good to excellent condition.

SECOND SERIES: extra safety button eliminated, rear sight acts as cocking knob retainer.

A. Commercial variation

Normal European/German slide markings are normally found; however, it has been called to my attention that there are English Export pistols in this SECOND SERIES which have the English markings on the slide which are similar to those found on the FIRST SERIES of the Model 1913. This is applicable to both the 7.65mm and 6.35mm model pistols. These are exceptionally scarce pistols and should command at least a 50 percent premium, perhaps more due to their rarity. This commercial variation had factory manuals printed in English, Spanish, and German which came with the cardboard boxed pistols. With the original Sauer box accessories and manual: Add $300 if in very good to excellent condition.

Caliber 7.65mm variation

Exc.	V.G.	Good	Fair	Poor
450	375	300	250	100

Caliber 7.65mm variation with all words in English (i.e. Son, Prussia, etc.)

Exc.	V.G.	Good	Fair	Poor
700	575	450	300	200

Caliber 6.35mm variation

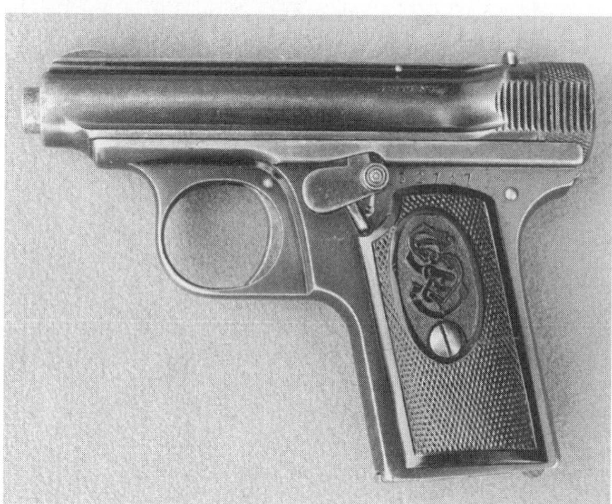

This particular pistol must be divided into three subvariations.

This variation appears to be in a serial number range of its own. The first subvariation appears to run from 1 to 40,000. It is highly doubtful if this quantity was manufactured. The second subvariation incorporates a Zusatzsicherung or Additional Safety which can be seen between the normal safety lever and the top of the left grip. It locked the trigger bar when in use. This second range appears to run from approximately serial number 40,000 to 51,000, which probably was continuous in the number produced. Lastly, the third subvariation examples were manufactured during or after 1926. The triggerguard has a different shape; the slide has a greater area of vertical milled finger grooves; the added Additional Safety (Zusatzsicherung) now acts as the hold open device as well. These are found up to approximately 57,000. Then a few examples of the first subvariation are found from 57,000 up to about 62,500. This was, no doubt, usage of remaining parts.

Caliber 6.35mm first subvariation

Exc.	V.G.	Good	Fair	Poor
350	300	250	150	75

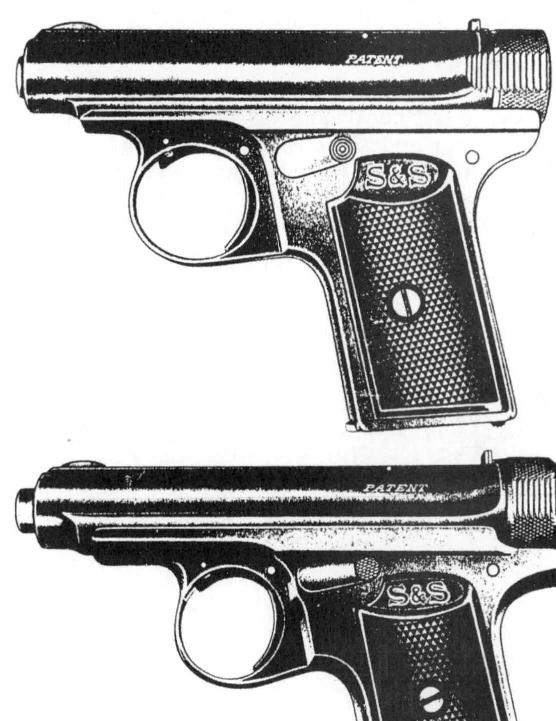

Caliber 6.35mm second subvariation

Exc.	V.G.	Good	Fair	Poor
350	300	250	150	75

Caliber 6.35mm third subvariation

Exc.	V.G.	Good	Fair	Poor
450	375	300	200	100

Caliber 6.35mm English export variation (all words in English; i.e. Son, Prussia, etc.)

Very rare; only one example known.

Exc.	V.G.	Good	Fair	Poor
1000	700	500	300	200

NOTE: that any commercial pistol could be special ordered with a factory nickel finish, special grip material (pearl, wood, etc.), as well as different types of engraving. It would be in your best interest to have these pistols examined by an expert.

B. Police variations

These will be of the standard German Commercial configuration but nearly always having the Zusatzsicherung (Additional Safety) added to the pistol. This safety is found between the regular safety lever and the top of the left grip. Police used both calibers, 7.65mm and 6.35mm, but the 7.65 was predominant. After the early part of the 1930s the 6.35 was not available to police departments. Thus the 6.35mm police marked Sauer is rather scarce in relation to the 7.65mm caliber. A few in 7.65mm are dated 1920 on the left side of the frame and were used by auxiliary policemen in Bavaria. Normal police property markings are on the front or rear grip-straps. Most were originally issued with at least two magazines and a police accepted holster. The magazines were usually numbered and the holsters are found with and without pistol numbers.

Caliber 6.35mm police marked but without Zusatzsicherung

Exc.	V.G.	Good	Fair	Poor
450	350	275	200	100

Caliber 6.35mm police marked with Zusatzsicherung

Exc.	V.G.	Good	Fair	Poor
450	375	275	200	100

Caliber 7.65mm police marked without Zusatzsicherung

Exc.	V.G.	Good	Fair	Poor
375	325	275	175	125

Caliber 7.65mm police marked with Zusatzsicherung

Exc.	V.G.	Good	Fair	Poor
400	350	275	175	125

NOTE: Add 10 percent for one correctly numbered magazine, or 20 percent if found with both correctly numbered magazines. Add 30 percent if found with correct holster and magazines.

C. R.F.V. (Reich Finanz Verwaltung)

This Sauer variation is rarely found in any condition. The R.F.V. markings and property number could be 1 to 4 digits. This variation is found in both calibers and was used by the Reich's Customs and Finance Department personnel.

Caliber 6.35mm R.F.V. marked pistols

Exc.	V.G.	Good	Fair	Poor
800	650	500	350	250

Caliber 7.65mm R.F.V. marked pistols

Exc.	V.G.	Good	Fair	Poor
750	600	400	300	200

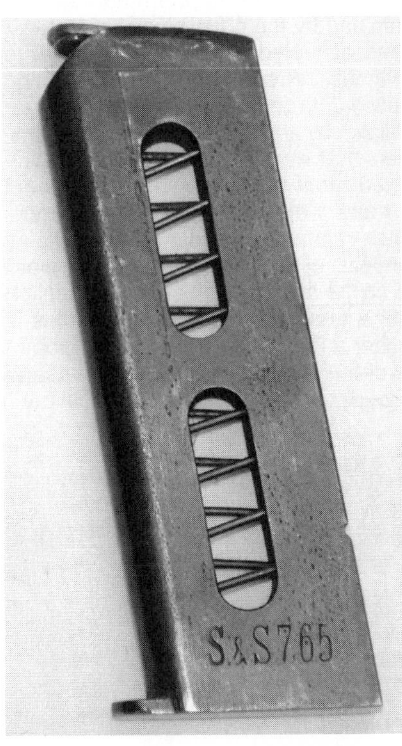

JP Sauer M1913 magazine marked "S&S 7,65". Price 55-30

GERMANY

D. Imperial Military variations

These were normal German commercial variations of the time period having either the Imperial Eagle acceptance marking applied on the front of the triggerguard and having the small Imperial Army inspector's acceptance marking (crown over a scriptic letter) on the right side of the frame close to the Nitro proof; or having just the Imperial Army inspector's marking alone. Usually these pistols are found in the 40,000 to 85,000 range. However, the quantity actually Imperial Military accepted is quite low even though thousands were privately purchased by the officer corps. There are examples in 6.35mm which are Imperial Military accepted but these are very scarce.

Caliber 7.65mm Imperial Military accepted pistols

Exc.	V.G.	Good	Fair	Poor
550	475	400	275	150

Caliber 6.35mm Imperial Military accepted pistols

Exc.	V.G.	Good	Fair	Poor
750	575	450	300	150

E. Paramilitary marked Sauer pistols, of the 1925-35 period

A very few of the Model 1913 pistols will have been marked by paramilitary groups or organizations of this period. Usually this marking is no more than a series of numbers above another series of numbers, such as 23 over 12. These are found usually on the left side of the frame next to the left grip. Most of these numbers are indicative of property numbers assigned to a particular pistol's belonging to a particular SA Group, Stahlhelm, or an organization such as the Red Front (early communist). Any pistol of this type should be examined by an expert to determine if it is an original example.

Exc.	V.G.	Good	Fair	Poor
500	425	350	200	100

F. Norwegian police usage, post-World War II

After the war was over many surplus German weapons were put back into use by the government of Norway. The Germans had occupied this country and large numbers of weapons remained when the fighting ended. This included a large number of surplus Sauer pistols being utilized by the police (POLITI) forces. Most of the Sauers that were used by the Politi which have been imported into the U.S. have been the Model 1913; however, there were a number of the Model 1930 pistols which reached our country as well. All examples, regardless of the model, have the word POLITI stamped on the slide as well as a rampant lion on a shield under a crown marking. Following this is the property number and this number is also stamped into the left side of the frame. Most saw much usage during the postwar period. All are in 7.65mm caliber.

Exc.	V.G.	Good	Fair	Poor
500	425	350	200	100

Model 38 and 38-H

(H Model) Variations

A. Model 38

This pistol started at 260,000. It is Crown N Nitro proofed, has a cocking/decocking lever, and a loaded indicator pin, and is double action. It has a high polish blue; is in 7.65mm (the standard production pistol); is found without the thumbsafety on the slide; with a pinned mag release. VERY RARE.

1. One Line Slide Legend variation

About 250 produced.

Exc.	V.G.	Good	Fair	Poor
2500	1600	1200	600	300

2. Two Line Slide Legend variation C/N proofs

Blued, with pinned magazine release. About 850 produced.

Exc.	V.G.	Good	Fair	Poor
1850	1400	1000	500	275

3. Two Line Slide Legend variation C/N proofs

Blued, magazine release button retained by a screw.

Exc.	V.G.	Good	Fair	Poor
1000	850	600	400	275

NOTE: Add $250 for factory nickel; $350 for factory chrome; $1000 for engraving; $500 for NIROSTA marked barrel.

4. SA der NSDAP Gruppe Thuringen marked variation

Blued, C/N proofs, with mag release button held by a screw. VERY RARE.

Exc.	V.G.	Good	Fair	Poor
3000	2000	1000	500	275

B. Model 38-H or H Model

This model has a thumb safety on the slide, Crown N Nitro proof, high polish blued finish, a cocking/decocking lever, double action, and is found in 7.65mm caliber as the standard production pistol. This model is found only with the two line slide legend or logo. Type 1, variation 2.

1. Standard Commercial variation as described above

Exc.	V.G.	Good	Fair	Poor
850	700	475	300	175

NOTE: Add $100 for factory nickel (factory chromed has not been identified); $1000 for factory engraving; $250 for exotic grip material; $500 for NIROSTA marked stainless barrel.

2. SA der NSDAP Gruppe Thuringia variation

Same as 1 above except having SA markings on slide, with blued finish.

Exc.	V.G.	Good	Fair	Poor
2500	1800	600	350	200

NOTE: Add $700 for SA marked ankle holster in excellent condition.

3. L.M. MODEL

(Leicht Model–lightweight model); frame and slide made of DURAL (Duraluminum), in the 264800 range, with thumb safety, and regular black bakelite grips. RARE.

Exc.	V.G.	Good	Fair	Poor
3850	3250	2500	1500	850

4. Police accepted variation

Found with Police Eagle C acceptance on left triggerguard and having Crown N proofs.

Exc.	V.G.	Good	Fair	Poor
850	700	500	300	175

Type Two Model 38-H (H Model)

There are no Model 38 pistols in the Type Two description, only the H Model with thumbsafety. These begin at serial number 269100 and have the Eagle N Nitro proofs, with a blued high polish finish and black bakelite grips. The normal caliber is 7.65mm.

A. H Model

1. Standard Commercial

Exc.	V.G.	Good	Fair	Poor
750	550	475	300	200

NOTE: Add $1500 for boxed examples complete with factory manual, clean ring rod, all accessories, extra magazine, etc. $250 for factory nickel, $350 for factory chrome, $1000 for factory engraving.

2. .22 Caliber variation, found in 269900 range

Slide and magazines are marked CAL. .22 LANG. (Some with steel frame and slides; some with Dural frames and slides.) VERY RARE.

Exc.	V.G.	Good	Fair	Poor
4500	2800	1800	500	250

3. Jager Model

A special order pistol in .22 caliber similar in appearance to Walther's 1936 Jagerschafts pistol. VERY RARE, and watch for fakes.

Exc.	V.G.	Good	Fair	Poor
2500	1850	1200	600	250

4. Police Eagle C and Eagle F acceptance variations

These are the first Eagle N (post January 1940) police accepted pistols and are found in the 270000 to 276000 ranges.

Exc.	V.G.	Good	Fair	Poor
650	500	400	325	200

NOTE: Add 25 percent for E/F.

5. German Military variation

This is the first official military accepted range of 2000 pistols. It is in a TEST range found between 271000 and 273000. Two Eagle 37 military acceptance marks are found on the trigger guard.

Exc.	V.G.	Good	Fair	Poor
1200	900	675	475	300

6. Second Military variation

These pistols are found with the high polish finish but have only one Eagle 37 acceptance mark. The letter H is found on all small parts.

Exc.	V.G.	Good	Fair	Poor
600	425	350	275	175

7. Police Eagle C acceptance variation

This variation includes the remainder of the high polish blued police accepted pistols.

Exc.	V.G.	Good	Fair	Poor
575	425	350	275	175

Type Three 38-H Model

(H Model)

This terminology is used because of the change of the exterior finish of the Sauer pistols. Due to the urgency of the war, the order was received to not polish the exterior surfaces of the pistols as had been done previously. There was also a change in the formulation of the grip's material. Later in this range there will be found stamped parts, zinc triggers and magazine bottoms, etc. used to increase the pistol's production. Type Three has a full slide legend.

A. H Model

1. Military accepted with one Eagle 37 Waffenamt mark

Exc.	V.G.	Good	Fair	Poor
550	475	400	275	150

2. Commercial, with only Eagle N Nitro proofmarks

Exc.	V.G.	Good	Fair	Poor
475	400	350	250	150

NOTE: See Type Two Commercial info, prices apply here also.

3. Police accepted with the Police Eagle C acceptance

Exc.	V.G.	Good	Fair	Poor
600	525	400	250	150

NOTE: See Type Two Police info, prices apply here also.

Type Four 38-H Model

(H Model)

This is a continuation of the pistol as described in Type Three except the J.P. Sauer & Sohn, Suhl legend is dropped from the slide and only CAL. 7.65 is found on the left side. The word PATENT may or may not appear on the right side. Many are found with a zinc trigger.

A. H Model

1. Military accepted with one Eagle 37 Waffenamt mark

Exc.	V.G.	Good	Fair	Poor
575	475	400	275	150

2. Commercial, having only the Eagle N Nitro proofs

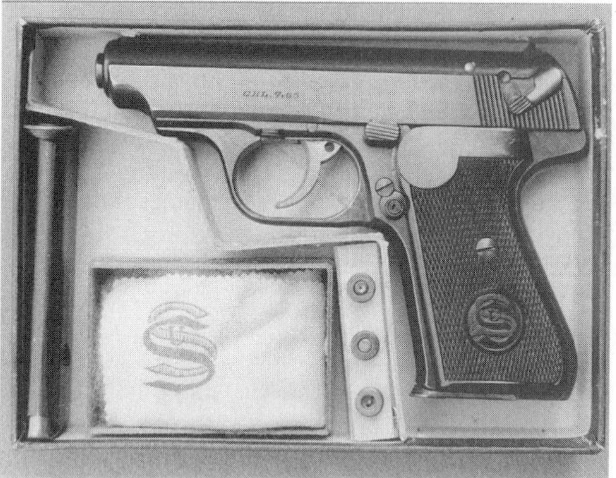

Exc.	V.G.	Good	Fair	Poor
450	400	350	250	150

NOTE: See Type Two Commercial info, prices apply here also.

3. Police accepted with the Police Eagle C acceptance

Exc.	V.G.	Good	Fair	Poor
600	525	400	250	150

NOTE: See Type Two price info, prices apply here also.

WALTHERS

Collecting the Military Models PP and PPK and their earlier cousins

James Rankin

If you are a firearms collector or entertain the idea of becoming one, the collecting of Walther manufactured firearms is a very exciting and rewarding one. With Walthers you have a wide range of firearms that the Walther Company manufactured or is manufacturing from which to choose. There are rifles, shotguns, pistols and flare and air guns. All have different models, variations of the models, calibers and gauges. Second, if you become knowledgeable in the field your purchases should increase in value not only allowing you to have the excitement of collecting, but the accumulation of equity in your collection.

The Walther Company, led by its family members, have been manufacturing, firearms since 1886 when Carl Walther founded a gun shop in the town of Zella, which was later incorporated into the town of Zella-Mehlis, Germany. At first, Walther produced shotguns and rifles, Later, Fritz Walther, Carl's oldest son, joined the firm and brought his genius for design to the company and it expanded its production into pistols.

Although the Walther Company has produced many types of pistols from the early 1900s, the Models PP and PPK were latecomers on the automatic pistol scene when compared to such pistol manufacturers such as Mauser, Luger and Colt as they did not make their appearance till 1929. However, shortly thereafter they were being sold in all parts of the world. These beautifully made pistols were the first of the original double-action blowback semi-automatic pistols. They had a successful commercial design with a high polished blue finish that was second to none.

A few years after the Models PP and PPK appearance on the world's firearm market, Adolf Hitler and the National Socialist German Workers Party took over the reigns of the German government, the military and the police. It was then that a majority of the Walther production was contracted for by the NSDAP, German army and the national police.

With the emergence of the NSDAP as the power in Germany, the increase in military power was ordered, and the Army High Command-OKH-Heereswaffenamt began placing contracts with the Walther Company for both the Walther Models PP and PPK. Most of the models were contracted for in caliber 7.65mm. There were contracts for a smaller amount in the Model PP in caliber 9mm Kurz and even less in the Model PPK in the same caliber. Depending on their serial number range these pistols showed Crown over N. or Eagle over N. nitro proofing on the right side of the pistol's slide, barrel and chamber. The military acceptance proofs, Eagle over 359 and Eagle over WaA359 were placed on the left side of the pistol's slide and frame to the rear of the model designation and the to the rear of the trigger on the frame.

The Models PP and PPK with the Waffenamt proofs began with a high polished blue finish on each pistol. But as the years progressed toward the end of World War II and the labor diminished these models showed a milled finish. The following is a short description of the Models PP and PPK bearing the Waffenamt proofs.

The first of the Models PP and PPK with the high polished blue finish had the Eagle over

Walther Model PP

Continued

GERMANY

Walther Model PPK
with Party Leader Grips

359 proof on the left side of the slide and frame with an occasional proof on the left rear of the slide at the tang. Grips were black on the Model PP and brown on the Model PPK.

The second series of proofs was the Eagle over WaA359. These too were found on high polished Models PP and PPK except there was no proof on the rear of the slide at the tang. Grips were black and brown respectively.

The third series was the Eagle over WaA359 found on the milled finish models till the end of World War II. On these later pistols the proofs remained in the same location on the pistols with some changes in the pistols themselves. On the Model PP you will find the standard two-piece black grips as well as reddish colored grips. Near the end of World War II there pressed wood grips with the Walther Banner. On some of the late PP models there will be an AC proof on the right side of the slide in conjunction with the serial number. Some of the late Waffenamt Model PPs will have no legends or inscriptions on the left side of the slide. These models have flat frames with no step at the trigger guard hinge, and some have no indicator pin. On the Model PPK the pistol will have the standard brown one piece wrap around Walther grips and will be found with grayish grips as well as black ones.

The Model PP and PPK in 9mm Kurz are both fairly rare pistols. With Waffenamt proofs they are even rarer. These pistols usually have bottom magazine releases. Their magazines will have the Walther Banner and Cal. 9mm on the left side of the magazine. Many of the 9mm Kurz models had the magazines numbered to the serial number on the pistol. These 9mm Kurz models all had a high polished finish.

There were earlier manufactured Walthers that were used by the military. Walther began to manufacture pistols in 1908 with their production of the Model 1. The Model 4 produced in 1910 was their first really successful pistol. This semiautomatic was the approximate size of the Model PPK saw use in World War I although there are no records showing that the German military placed a contract with the Walther Company. Most were carried as side arms by officers of the German Imperial Army. The Model 6 was basically a large Model 4 in caliber 9mm Parabellum. It was designed for the German Imperial Army in 1915. It was the first pistol that Walther designed and produced for the military and the first Walther in 9mm parabellum. It was produced for a period of two years and there were probably less than 1500 manufactured. After the war some Model 6s remained at the factory. They were proofed "Made in Germany" and exported, some to the United States. In the United States the Model 6 is quite rare and commands a high price.

The Model 7 was a small version of the Model 6 in 6.35mm. Walther produced these pistols for the military for about six months. They were carried by many German officers. Although in 6.35mm it was the largest 6.35mm pistol produced by Walther at the time.

In 1920 and 1921 Walther produce both the Models 8 and 9 for commercial sales. They were the first of the modern Walthers with many features seen later in the Models PP and PPK. Both these pistols were favorites of German officers in World War II as hide out pistols. However, the Model 8 was carried by many officers in a holster on their belt.

The military Model PPK is more difficult to find than the Model PP. The high polished pistols in both models are both fairly rare. It will take sometime for a collector to put a collection of Waffenamt Models PP and PPK together, but with perseverance one should be quite pleased with his or her collection. One should remember in the collecting of firearms, Walthers or any other maker, condition is everything.

Walther Model 6

4. Eigentum NSDAP SA Gruppe Alpenland slide marked pistols

These unique pistols are found in the 456000 and 457000 serial number ranges. They have thumb safety levers on the slides.

Exc.	V.G.	Good	Fair	Poor
3200	2200	1000	575	325

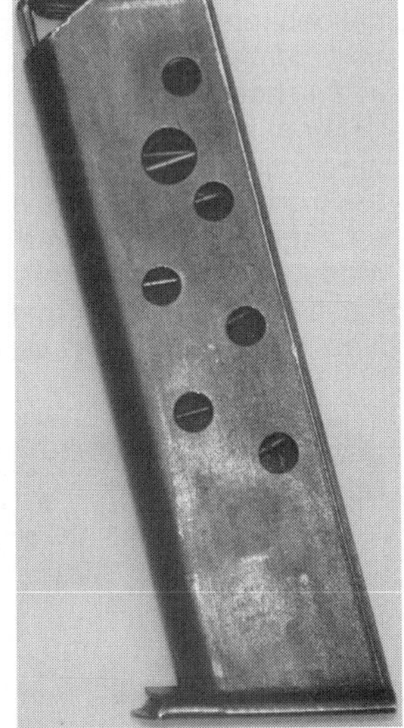

Late wartime Sauer 38H magazine. Early examples have alloy base with Sauer monogram. Price 65-40

5. NSDAP SA Gruppe Alpenland slide marked pistols

These unique pistols are found in the 465000 serial number range. They have thumb safety levers on the slide.

Exc.	V.G.	Good	Fair	Poor
2800	1800	1000	450	250

6. H. Himmler Presentation Pistols

These desirable pistols have a high polish finish with DEM SCHARFSCHUTZEN - H. HIMMLER on the left side of the slide (with no other markings), and J.P. SAUER & SOHN over CAL.7.65 on the right side (opposite of normal). These pistols came in imitation leather cover metal cases with cloth interiors having a cleaning brush, extra magazine and cartridges.

Exc.	V.G.	Good	Fair	Poor
15000	12000	8500	3500	1000

B. Model 38

To speed up production even more, the thumb safety (Handsicherung-Hammer safety) was eliminated. The side continues to be marked only with CAL. 7.65. The frame's serial number changes from the right side to the left side at 472000 with overlaps up to 489000.

1. Military accepted with one Eagle 37 Waffenamt mark

Exc.	V.G.	Good	Fair	Poor
500	425	375	250	175

2. Commercial, having only the Eagle N Nitro proofs

Exc.	V.G.	Good	Fair	Poor
450	400	350	250	175

NOTE: See Type Two Commercial info, prices apply here also.

3. Police accepted with the Police Eagle C acceptance

Exc.	V.G.	Good	Fair	Poor
575	450	400	300	200

4. Police accepted with the Police Eagle F acceptance

GERMANY

Exc.	V.G.	Good	Fair	Poor
500	425	350	250	175

NOTE: (3&4) See Type Two Police info above, prices apply here also.

Type Five Model 38

(& H Model Pistols)

There are two different basic variations of the Type Five Sauer pistols. Either may or may not have a thumb safety lever on the slide. The main criteria is whether the frame is factory numbered as per normal and follows the chronological sequence of those pistols in the preceding model. After the frames were used, which were already numbered and finished upon the arrival of the U.S. army, the last variation came about. Neither variation has any Nitro proofmarks.

A. First variation

Factory numbered sequential frames starting on or near serial number 506800. Slides and breech blocks may or may not match.

Exc.	V.G.	Good	Fair	Poor
475	350	275	225	100

B. Second variation

Started with serial number 1; made from mostly rejected parts, generally have notched triggerguards, may or may not be blued, no Nitro proofs, slides may or may not have factory legends, etc. Approximately 300 assembled.

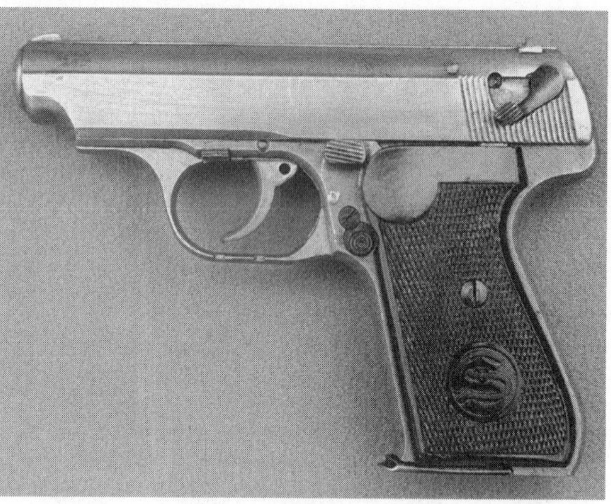

Exc.	V.G.	Good	Fair	Poor
750	500	300	200	100

NOTE: There are some pistols which have postwar Russian Crown N Nitro proofs. The Russians may have assembled a very few pistols after the U.S. army left this section after the war. Several have been found with newly made barrels in 7.65mm with a C/N proof.

WALTHER

Bibliographical Note: For technical details, historical information, and photos see James Rankin, ***Walther, Volumes I, II, and III***, 1974-1981.

Model 6

A 9mm semi-automatic pistol. The largest of the Walther numbered pistols. Approximately 1,500 manufactured. Blued with checkered hard rubber grips with the Walther logo on each grip. Sometimes seen with plain checkered wood grips. Introduced 1915.

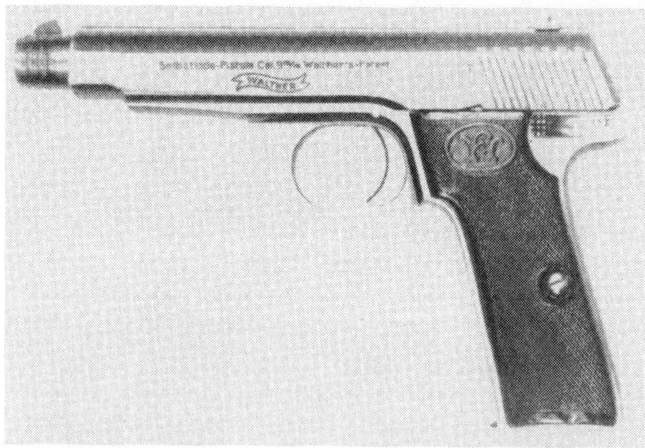

Courtesy James Rankin

Exc.	V.G.	Good	Fair	Poor
7500	5500	3000	1500	700

Model PP

A semi-automatic pistol in .22, .25, .32, and .380 caliber. Introduced in 1928. It was the first successful commercial double action pistol. It was manufactured in finishes of blue, silver, and gold, and with three different types of engraving. Grips were generally two-piece black or white plastic with the Walther banner on each grip. Grips in wood or ivory are seen, but usually on engraved guns. There are many variations of the Model PP and numerous NSDAP markings seen on the pre-1946 models that were produced during the Nazi regime. All reflect various prices.

Courtesy James Rankin

Model PP .22 Caliber

Exc.	V.G.	Good	Fair	Poor
900	700	450	250	150

Model PP .25 Caliber

Exc.	V.G.	Good	Fair	Poor
4800	4000	2500	1500	600

Model PP .32 Caliber High Polished Finish

Exc.	V.G.	Good	Fair	Poor
650	575	500	225	175

Model PP .32 Caliber Milled Finish

Exc.	V.G.	Good	Fair	Poor
550	450	400	200	125

GERMANY

Model PP .380 Caliber

Exc.	V.G.	Good	Fair	Poor
950	750	550	475	350

Model PP .32 Caliber with Duraluminum Frame

Exc.	V.G.	Good	Fair	Poor
800	675	550	400	200

Model PP .32 Caliber with Bottom Magazine Release

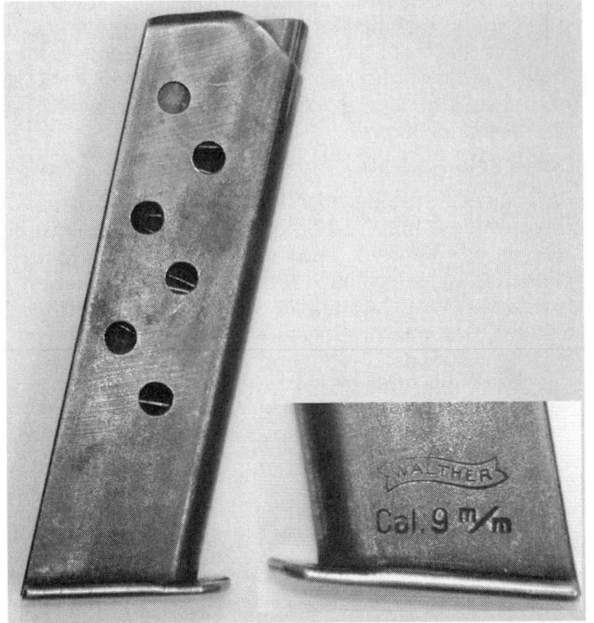

Early bottom release Walther PP 9mm Short magazine (.380). Price 150-75

Exc.	V.G.	Good	Fair	Poor
1100	800	600	400	200

Model PP .32 Caliber with Verchromt Finish

Exc.	V.G.	Good	Fair	Poor
2000	1450	1000	700	400

Courtesy Orvel Reichert

Model PP .32 Caliber in Blue, Silver, or Gold Finish and Full Coverage Engraving

Blue

Exc.	V.G.	Good	Fair	Poor
5000	3500	3000	1200	700

Silver

Exc.	V.G.	Good	Fair	Poor
6000	4000	3000	1200	700

Gold

Exc.	V.G.	Good	Fair	Poor
6500	4500	3500	1500	700

NOTE: Add $250 for ivory grips with any of the three above. Add $700 for leather presentation cases. Add $500 for .22 caliber. Add $1000 for .380 caliber.

Model PP .32 Caliber, Allemagne Marked

Exc.	V.G.	Good	Fair	Poor
1200	900	650	325	250

Model PP .32 Caliber, A.F. Stoeger Contract

Exc.	V.G.	Good	Fair	Poor
2500	1750	1050	700	400

Model PP .32 Caliber with Waffenamt Proofs, High Polished Finish

The Waffenamt proofs were the military eagle over 359 on the early models. Military eagle over WaA359 on later models. The Waffenamt proof was on the left side of the frame to the rear of the trigger and on the left side of the slide in front of the slide serrations. The 9mmk models have a bottom magazine release. Rare in both .22 LR and 9mmk calibers.

Model PP Waffenamt • Courtesy James Rankin

Exc.	V.G.	Good	Fair	Poor
1200	800	450	275	150

Model PP .32 Caliber with Waffenamt Proofs Milled Finish

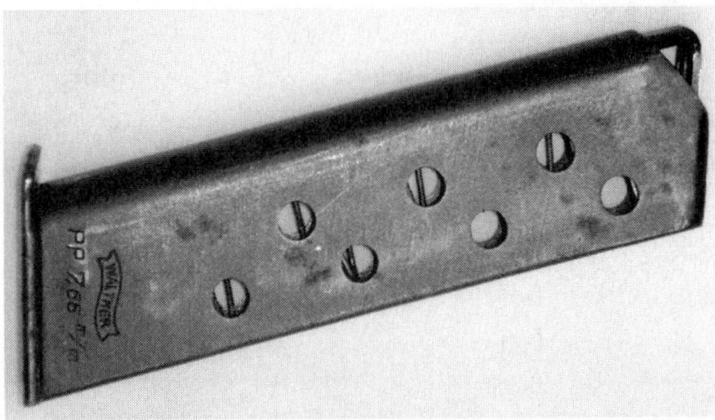

Walther PP 7.65m/m magazine, German, WWII. Price 75-35

Exc.	V.G.	Good	Fair	Poor
650	550	400	250	150

Model PP .32 Caliber, Police Eagle/C Proofed, High Polished Finish

The police proofs were the police eagle over the swastika with the letter "C" to the right of the swastika. Later models have the eagle over the swastika with the letter "F" (see below). The police proof was on the left side of the frame to the rear of the trigger.

GERMANY

Model PP Police • Courtesy James Rankin

Exc.	V.G.	Good	Fair	Poor
1200	800	550	300	200

Model PP .32 Caliber, Police Eagle/C and Police Eagle/F Proofed, Milled Finish

Exc.	V.G.	Good	Fair	Poor
900	750	500	300	200

Holster for Walther PP

This style of holster was used for the PP as well as several other 7,65mm automatics. The basic pattern is the same. Spare magazine pouch on the front. Single wide belt loop on the back. Brown or black leather. Many were not marked. Marked examples are worth 50 – 100% more.

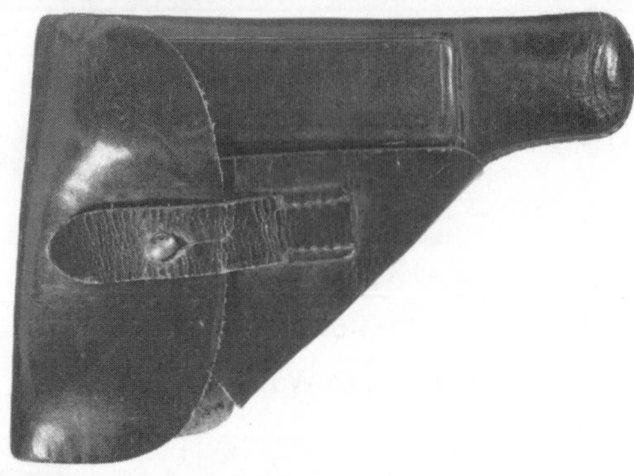

Exc.	V.G.	Good	Fair	Poor
150	100	50	35	20

Model PP .32 Caliber, NSKK Marked On the Slide

The NSKK, National Sozialistisches Kraftfahr Korps, Transport Corps. These pistols were issued to officers in the corps. The NSKK emblem is on the left side of the frame in front of the slide serrations.

Model PP NSKK Marked • Courtesy James Rankin

Exc.	V.G.	Good	Fair	Poor
2500	2000	850	550	300

NOTE: Add $500 for proper NSKK DRGM AKAH holster.

Model PP .32 Caliber, NSDAP Gruppe Markings

The SA, Sturm Abteilung, was comprised of various districts throughout Germany and each was separately named. The proof was SA der NSDAP on the top line with the name of the district below. These proofs were found on the front grip strap. Some later models had the SA proof on the rear grip strap. A few SA models had a two-digit number following the district name. The .22 LR model is rare.

Listed below are the SA districts:

Alpenland, Berlin-Brandenburg, Bayerische Ostmark, Bayerwald, Donau, Eibe, Franken, Hansa, Hessen, Hochland, Kurpflaz, Mitte, Mittelrhein, Neckar, Nordsee, Neiderrhein, Neidersachsen, Nilfswerk, Nordwest, Oder, Ostmark, Osterreich, Oberrhein, Ostland, Pommern, Schlesien, Sachsen, Sudmark, Sudeten, Sudwest, Tannengberg, Thuringen, Standarte Feldherrnhalle, Weichsel, Westfalen, Westmark.

Model PP NSPAD Marked • Courtesy James Rankin

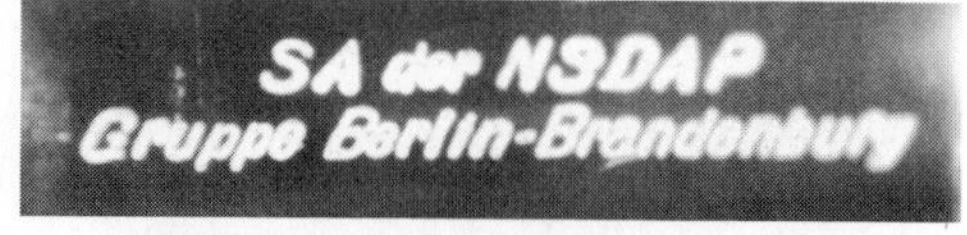

Model PP NSPAD Marked • Courtesy James Rankin

Exc.	V.G.	Good	Fair	Poor
2000	1500	1000	500	300

NOTE: Add $500 for proper SA DRGM AKAH holster.

Model PP .32 Caliber PDM Marked with Bottom Magazine Release

Model PP PDM marked • Courtesy James Rankin

The PDM, Polizei Direktion Munchen, Police Department Munich. The PDM mark was placed on equipment belonging to the Munich police. It can be found on the left side of the frame behind the trigger and is followed by one to four numbers. The PDM pistol has a bottom magazine release.

Exc.	V.G.	Good	Fair	Poor
850	700	550	475	300

Model PP .32 Caliber RJ Marked

The RJ, Reich Jugend, Hitler Youth Organization. The RJ proof is on front grip strap. Some models are in .22 caliber.

Model PP RJ marked • Courtesy James Rankin

Exc.	V.G.	Good	Fair	Poor
850	675	550	400	150

Model PP .32 Caliber. RFV Marked. High Polished or Milled Finish

Model PP RFV marked • Courtesy James Rankin

Exc.	V.G.	Good	Fair	Poor
850	675	550	400	150

Model PP .32 Caliber RBD Munster Marked

The RBD Munster, State Railway Directorate Munster in Westfalen. The RBD Munster is on the front grip strap followed by (Westf.).

Model PP RBD • Courtesy James Rankin

Exc.	V.G.	Good	Fair	Poor
2200	1750	1200	650	400

Model PP .32 Caliber RpLt Marked

The RpLt, Rigspoliti, Danish State Police, is on the left side of the frame directly above the forward part of the triggerguard. The RpLt is followed by "Nr". The number is from one to four digits, and is an inventory number within the police department.

Model PP RpLt marked • Courtesy James Rankin

Exc.	V.G.	Good	Fair	Poor
950	750	475	375	200

Model PP .32 Caliber RZM Marked

The RZM, Reichs Zueg Meisterei, was the equipment office of the NSDAP, and the RZM model of the PP was carried by the NSDAP member who was awarded the use of the pistol. The RZM emblem is on the left side of the slide in front of the slide serrations. Rare.

Exc.	V.G.	Good	Fair	Poor
2500	2000	1250	600	300

Model PP .32 Caliber Statens Vattenfallsverk Marked

The Statens Vattenfallsverk was contracted by Sweden for use in hydro-electric plant security. The Staten Vattenfallsverk is on the right side of the slide to the front of the slide serrations. There is an "Nr" above each inscription for inventory control. Some of these pistols have Duraluminum frames.

Model PP Statens Vattenfallsverk • Courtesy James Rankin

Exc.	V.G.	Good	Fair	Poor
1000	800	550	375	200

Model PP .32 Caliber AC Marked

The Model AC was a late wartime pistol with a milled finish. The AC proofmark was usually found on either side of the slide. These pistols sometimes did not have the Walther inscription or trademark. Wood grips replaced the plastic.

Model PP AC marked • Courtesy James Rankin

Exc.	V.G.	Good	Fair	Poor
675	550	450	250	150

Model PP .32 Caliber, Duraluminum Frame

Exc.	V.G.	Good	Fair	Poor
750	600	500	400	150

Model PP .380 Caliber, Bottom Magazine Release and Waffenamt Proofs

Exc.	V.G.	Good	Fair	Poor
2000	1500	700	500	300

Model PP Persian Contract

This model was contracted by Persia for its police units. It is a bottom magazine release model with the Persian Royal Crest and Farsi inscription on the left side of the slide, and the Walther Banner and inscription on the right side of the slide.

Model PP Persian Contract • Courtesy James Rankin

Exc.	V.G.	Good	Fair	Poor
3500	2950	2250	1000	500

Model PPK

A semi-automatic pistol in .22, .25, .32, and .380 caliber. Introduced six months after the Model PP in 1929. A more compact version of the Model PP with one less round in the magazine and one-piece wrap-around checkered plastic grips in brown, black, and white with the Walther banner on each side of the grips. The Model PPK will be found with the same types of finishes as the Model PP as well as the same styles of engraving. Grips in wood or ivory are seen with some of the engraved models. As with the Model PP there are many variations of the Model PPK and numerous NSDAP markings seen on the pre-1946 models that were produced during the Nazi regime. All reflect various prices.

Courtesy Orvel Reichert

Courtesy James Rankin

Model PPK .22 Caliber

Exc.	V.G.	Good	Fair	Poor
1750	1200	900	500	300

Model PPK .25 Caliber

Exc.	V.G.	Good	Fair	Poor
7000	4500	2500	1200	500

Model PPK .32 Caliber, High Polished Finish

Exc.	V.G.	Good	Fair	Poor
650	550	425	250	150

Model PPK .32 Caliber, Milled Finish

Exc.	V.G.	Good	Fair	Poor
575	450	350	250	150

Model PPK .380 Caliber

Courtesy Orvel Reichert

Exc.	V.G.	Good	Fair	Poor
2200	1750	1300	750	375

Model PPK .32 Caliber with Duraluminum Frame

Exc.	V.G.	Good	Fair	Poor
1250	900	675	450	300

Model PPK .32 Caliber with Verchromt Finish

Exc.	V.G.	Good	Fair	Poor
2500	1800	1200	700	350

Model PPK .32 Caliber in Blue, Silver, or Gold Finish and Full Coverage Engraving

Blue

Exc.	V.G.	Good	Fair	Poor
5000	3500	2500	1200	700

Silver

Exc.	V.G.	Good	Fair	Poor
6000	4000	3000	1200	700

Gold

Exc.	V.G.	Good	Fair	Poor
6500	4500	3500	1500	700

NOTE: Add $750 for ivory grips with any of the three above. Add $700 for leather presentation cases. Add $500 for .22 caliber. Add $1000 for .380 caliber.

Model PPK .32 Caliber Marked Mod. PP on Slide

Exc.	V.G.	Good	Fair	Poor
3000	2000	1600	1000	600

Model PPK .32 Caliber with Panagraphed Slide

Exc.	V.G.	Good	Fair	Poor
650	550	450	300	200

Model PPK .32 Caliber, Czechoslovakian Contract

Exc.	V.G.	Good	Fair	Poor
1550	1200	800	450	300

Model PPK .32 Caliber. Allemagne Marked

Exc.	V.G.	Good	Fair	Poor
1250	900	750	400	300

Model PPK .32 Caliber with Waffenamt Proofs and a High Polished Finish

The Waffenamt proofs were the military eagle over 359 on the early models. Military eagle over WaA359 on later models. The Waffenamt proof was on the left side of the frame to the rear of the trigger and on the left side of the slide in front of the slide serrations. The 9mmk models have a bottom magazine release. Rare in both .22 LR and 9mmk calibers.

Exc.	V.G.	Good	Fair	Poor
1800	1000	775	400	250

Model PPK .32 Caliber with Waffenamt Proofs and a Milled Finish

Exc.	V.G.	Good	Fair	Poor
1100	800	550	400	300

Model PPK .32 Caliber. Police Eagle/C Proofed, High Polished Finish

Exc.	V.G.	Good	Fair	Poor
1500	975	675	425	350

Model PPK .32 Caliber. Police Eagle/C Proofed, Milled Finish

The police proofs were the police eagle over the swastika with the letter "C" to the right of the swastika. Later models have the eagle over the swastika with the letter "F" (see below). The police proof was on the left side of the frame to the rear of the trigger.

Exc.	V.G.	Good	Fair	Poor
1250	800	650	400	300

Model PPK .32 Caliber. Police Eagle/F Proofed, Duraluminum Frame. Milled Finish

Exc.	V.G.	Good	Fair	Poor
1500	1100	750	575	350

Model PPK .22 Caliber. Late War, Black Grips

Exc.	V.G.	Good	Fair	Poor
1200	750	600	450	300

Model PPK .32 Caliber, Party Leader Grips, Brown

The Party Leader-gripped PPK was the honor weapon of the NSDAP and was given to political leaders from the Fuhrer. The Party Leader grip is usually mottled brown plastic with the NSDAP eagle holding a swastika circled by a wreath on each side of the grip. Near the end of WWII a small number of Party Leader grips were black

Exc.	V.G.	Good	Fair	Poor
5000	4250	3000	1800	900

Model PPK .32 Caliber, Party Leader Grips, Black

Courtesy Rock Island Auction Company

Exc.	V.G.	Good	Fair	Poor
3250	3000	2750	2550	2500

NOTE: If grips are badly cracked or damaged on the two Party Leaders above, reduce each valuation by 50%. BEWARE! There are reproduction Party Leader grips on the market.

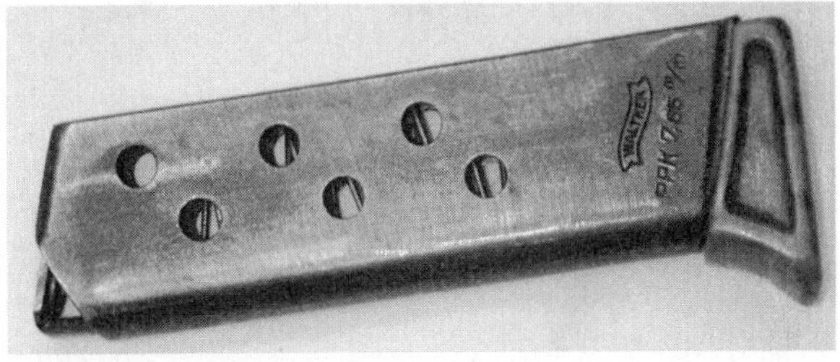

Walther PPK 7.65m/m magazine, early finger rest. Price 200-100, without rest 125-60

GERMANY

Model PPK .32 Caliber RZM Marked

Courtesy Rock Island Auction Company

Exc.	V.G.	Good	Fair	Poor
2500	1800	1100	500	300

NOTE: Add 100% for RZM PPK with party leader grips.

Model PPK .32 Caliber PDM Marked with Duraluminum Frame and Bottom Magazine Release

The PDM, Polizei Direktion Munchen, Police Department Munich. The PDM mark was placed on equipment belonging to the Munich police. It can be found on the left side of the frame behind the trigger and is followed by one to four numbers. The PDM pistol has a bottom magazine release. This model is much rarer than the PP version.

Exc.	V.G.	Good	Fair	Poor
2500	1800	1150	750	450

Model PPK .32 Caliber. RFV Marked

Exc.	V.G.	Good	Fair	Poor
1700	1500	900	650	300

Model PPK .32 Caliber. DRP Marked

The DRP, Deutsche Reichs Post, German Postal Service. The DRP is found on the left side of the frame behind the trigger.

Model PPK DRP marked • Courtesy James Rankin

Exc.	V.G.	Good	Fair	Poor
1850	1575	1000	700	375

Model PPK .32 Caliber. Statens Vattenfallsverk

The Statens Vattenfallsverk was contracted by Sweden for use in hydro-electric plant security. The Staten Vattenfallsverk is on the right side of the slide to the front of the slide serrations. There is an "Nr" above each inscription for inventory control. Some of these pistols have Duraluminum frames.

Exc.	V.G.	Good	Fair	Poor
1400	1200	700	450	300

HECKLER & KOCH

VP 70Z

This is a blowback-operated semi-automatic chambered for the 9mm Parabellum cartridge. It is striker-fired and double action only. The barrel is 4.5 inches long, and the double-column magazine holds 18 rounds. The finish is blued, and the receiver and grips are molded from plastic. This model was discontinued in 1986.

NIB	Exc.	V.G.	Good	Fair	Poor
550	450	350	300	N/A	N/A

VP 70M

This is similar to the VP 70Z except for a very important feature: When a shoulder stock is added, the internal mechanism is altered to fire full automatic 3-round burst. When the shoulder stock is removed, the pistol reverts back to semi-automatic. The rate of fire is a very high 2,200 rounds per minute. This version has no safety devices. First produced in 1972 and discontinued in 1986.

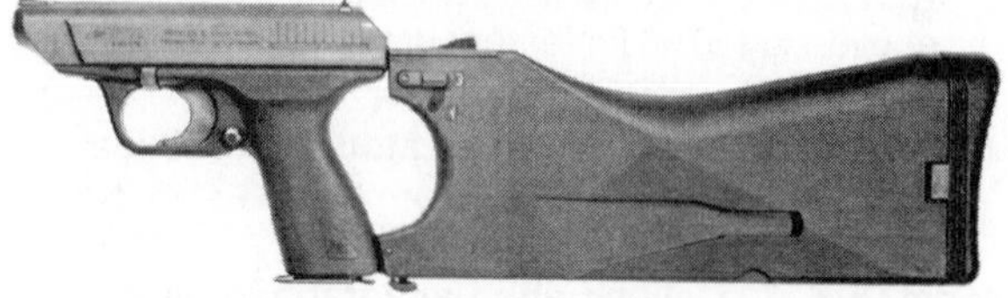

H&K VP 70M • Courtesy Thomas Nelson, World's Machine Pistols, Vol. II

Pre-1968

Exc.	V.G.	Fair
N/A	N/A	N/A

P9

This is a single action, delayed-blowback semiautomatic pistol chambered for 9mm or 7.65mm

Parabellum. The action is based on the G-3 rifle mechanism and is single action only. The barrel is 4 inches in length, and the pistol has an internal hammer and a thumb-operated hammer drop and decocking lever. There is also a manual safety and a loaded-chamber indicator. The finish is parkerized, and the grips are molded plastic and well contoured. It has fixed sights. This model was manufactured between 1977 and 1984. This model is rarer than the P9S model. This was H&K's first military pistol.

NIB	*Exc.*	*V.G.*	*Good*	*Fair*	*Poor*
1500	1200	850	500	N/A	N/A

SUBMACHINE GUNS

MP18/1 (WWI)

This was the first German submachine gun and it was designed by Hugo Schmeisser in 1916. It was used by German military forces in WWI. The gun was chambered for the 9mm Parabellum cartridge. The barrel length is 7.5 inches and the snail magazine holds 32 rounds. The rate of fire is about 450 rounds per minute. Markings are "MP 18 L" above the chamber and "C.G HANEL WAFFENFABRIK SUHL" on the left side of the receiver. Weight is about 9 lbs.

Pre-1968

Exc.	*V.G.*	*Fair*
25000	17500	12000

Pre-1986 manufacture with new receiver or re-weld

Exc.	*V.G.*	*Fair*
15000	12500	10000

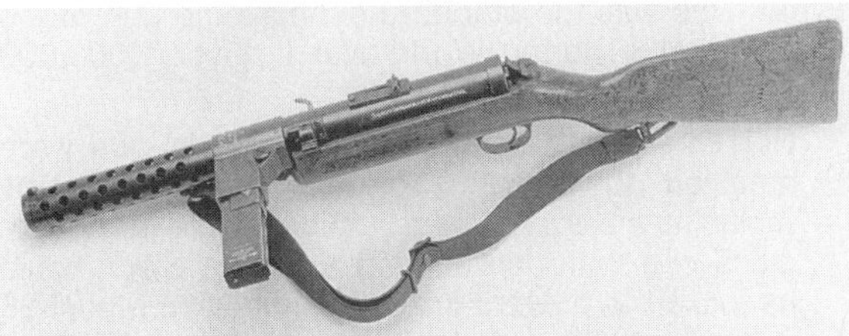

***Private NFA collection** • Gary Gelson photo*

MP18/1 (Postwar)

Introduced into combat by German troops in 1918. Designed by Hugo Schmeisser and built by Bergmann. Chambered for 9mm cartridge. In place of the 32-round snail drum, a box magazine holds 20 or 32 rounds. The magazine is essentially the only difference between the WWI guns and the postwar examples. Barrel length is 8 inches. Rate of fire is about 400 rounds per minute. Was in use from 1918 to 1930s. Weight is about 9 lbs.

Pre-1968

Exc.	*V.G.*	*Fair*
22500	17000	12000

Pre-1986 manufacture with new receiver or re-weld

Exc.	*V.G.*	*Fair*
15000	12500	10000

Bergman MP28

This model is an improved version of the MP18. It is fitted with a tangent sight and straight magazine. It also has a selector switch to allow for semi-auto fire. Rate of fire is approximately 500 rounds per minute. Chambered for a variety of calibers including 9mm Parabellum, 9mm Bergmann, 7.65mm Parabellum, 7.63mm, and .45 ACP. Magazine capacity is 20, 32, or 50 rounds with special 25-round magazine for .45 ACP models. Built in Belgium by Pieper. Many of these guns were sold to South American countries. They were also used by German Police units including SS units. It was never adopted by the German army. Markings over the chamber are "MP 28 II SYSTEM SCHMEISSER PATENT." Weight is 8.8 lbs.

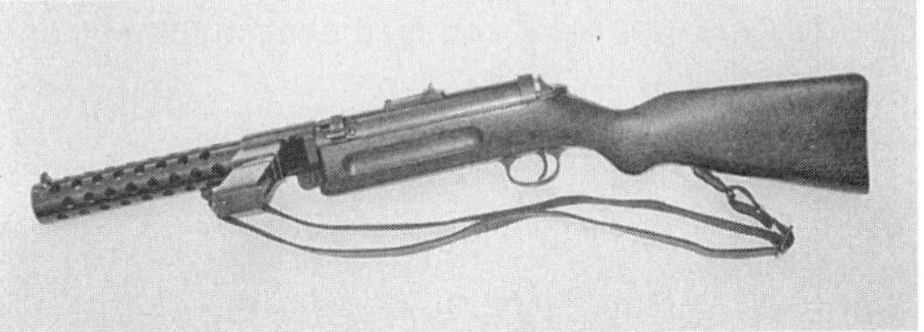

Courtesy Richard M. Kumor Sr.

Pre-1968

Exc.	*V.G.*	*Fair*
18500	15000	10000

Pre-1986 manufacture with new receiver or re-weld

Exc.	*V.G.*	*Fair*
9500	7500	6500

Erma EMP

First developed in Germany in 1934, this submachine gun was chambered for the 9mm cartridge. It was fitted with a wooden vertical fore-grip. The gun was fitted with a 9.75-inch barrel with a 20- or 32-round magazine. The rate of fire was 500 rounds per minute.

***MP 18/1 with markings** • Paul Goodwin Photo*

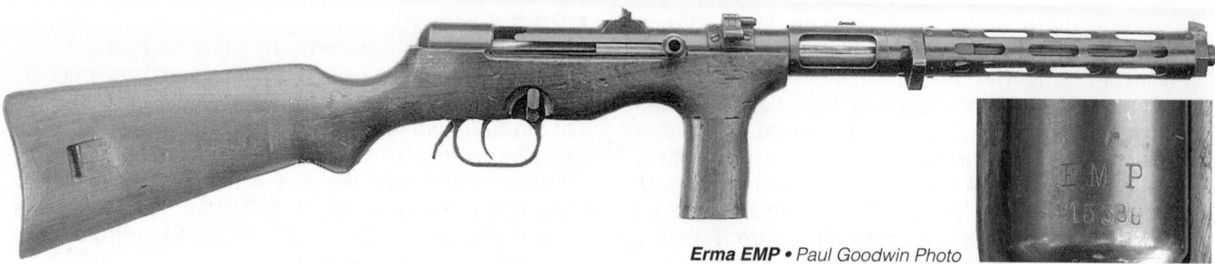

Erma EMP • *Paul Goodwin Photo*

The weight was about 8.25 lbs. Marked "EMP" on rear receiver cap. Production ceased in 1945. This gun was used extensively in the Spanish Civil War.

Pre-1968

Exc.	*V.G.*	*Fair*
18000	15000	12000

Pre-1986 manufacture with new receiver or re-weld

Exc.	*V.G.*	*Fair*
7500	5500	4500

GERMANY

Steyr-Solothurn (Solothurn SI-100 or MP34[o])

See Austria, Submachine Guns, Steyr.

MP34/I & MP35/I

Similar in appearance to the MP28, and produced in Germany by Walther in Zella Mehlis. Chambered for the 9mm cartridge and fitted with a 7.8- or 12.6-inch barrel. Other calibers were offered such as the 9mm Bergmann, 9mm Mauser, .45 ACP, and 7.63 Mauser. Rear sight had a V-notch tangent graduated to 1,000 meters. The gun had a cocking handle much like that of a rifle located at the rear of the receiver. Fitted with two triggers, the outer one fired semi-automatic and the inner one fired full automatic. The 24- or 32-round magazine fed from the right side. Rate of fire was about 650 rounds per minute and weight is approximately 9 lbs. The MP35/I was a modified MP34/I and was used by the German SS. Built by Junker & Ruh. Many more MP35/I guns were built than MP34/I.

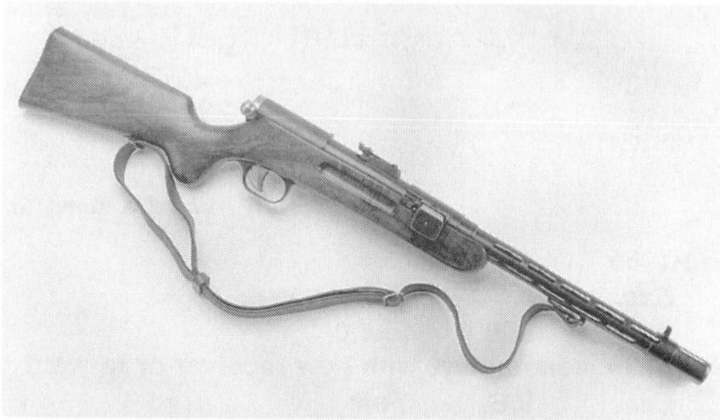

Private NFA collection, Gary Gelson photo

Pre-1968

Exc.	*V.G.*	*Fair*
18000	15000	12500

NOTE: For "SS" marked MP35 guns add $3,000.

MP38

This German submachine gun was first produced in 1938. It is often called the Schmeisser but that is incorrect. It was designed by Vollmer and built by the Erma company. It is chambered for the 9mm cartridge and is fitted with a 9.75" barrel. It has a folding stock and a magazine capacity of 32 rounds. Its rate of fire is 500 rounds per minute. Full automatic fire only. Weight is approximately 9 lbs. Marked "mp38" on the rear receiver cap. Production ceased in 1940. Produced by Erma. This was the standard submachine gun of the German army during World War II. Over 1,000,000 were produced.

NOTE: In 1940 and 1941 some Model 38s were modified to prevent accidental discharges, by replacing the one-piece retracting handle with a two-piece one that incorporated a cut-out which could be locked to prevent firing. This modified Model 38 is designated the Model 38/40.

Pre-1968 (Rare)

Exc.	*V.G.*	*Fair*
25000	22500	17500

Pre-1986 manufacture with new receiver or re-weld

Exc.	*V.G.*	*Fair*
8500	7500	6500

MP38 • *Paul Goodwin photo*

MP40 • *Paul Goodwin photo*

MP41 • *Private NFA collection, Gary Gelson photo*

German Manufacturing Codes for the MP38 & MP40:

Erma	1938 to 1940	"27"
Erma	1940 to 1944	"afy"
Haenal	1938 to 1940	"122"
Haenal	1940 to 1944	"fxo"
Steyr	1939 to 1940	"660"
Steyr	1940 to 1944	"bnz"

MP40

This model was the successor to the MP38 with more quickly manufactured components. The steel receivers are pressed with a corrugated magazine housing. The grip frame is pressed steel as well. Weight and barrel length are the same as the MP38 as is magazine capacity and rate of fire. This model was produced from 1940 to 1945 by Erma. Marked "MP40" on the rear receiver cap. Approximately 1,000,000 of these guns were produced.

NOTE: There is a rare modification of this submachine gun designated the MP40/II, which is fitted with a magazine housing that holds two magazines. These magazines fit in an oversized sliding housing that moves laterally, allowing a full magazine to be moved into place when the first magazine becomes empty. Not developed until late 1943. Not considered a successful attempt to increase ammunition capacity.

Pre-1968

Exc.	*V.G.*	*Fair*
18500	15000	10000

Pre-1986 manufacture with new receiver or re-weld

Exc.	*V.G.*	*Fair*
8500	5000	N/A

MP41

This model was built by Schmeisser to compete with the official adopted military MP40. The gun was not adopted by the German army. The result is that very few of these guns exist. The MP40-style receiver and barrel were fitted to a wooden buttstock and a select fire mechanism was added. Weight is about 8 lbs. Marked "MP41 PATENT SCHMEISSER C.G.HAENEL SUHL" on the top of the receiver. About 27,500 of these guns were built between 1941 and 1945.

Pre-1968 (Rare)

Exc.	*V.G.*	*Fair*
19500	16000	12000

Pre-1986 manufacture with new receiver or re-weld

Exc.	*V.G.*	*Fair*
8500	5000	N/A

Walther MPK and MPL

This German submachine gun was first produced in 1963. The MPK is a short barrel (6.7 inches) version and the MPL is the long barrel (10.14 inches) version. Magazine capacity is 32 rounds of 9mm. Rate of fire is 55 rounds per minute. Weight empty is 6.1 lbs. Markings are on the left side of the receiver. Production of this model ceased in 1985.

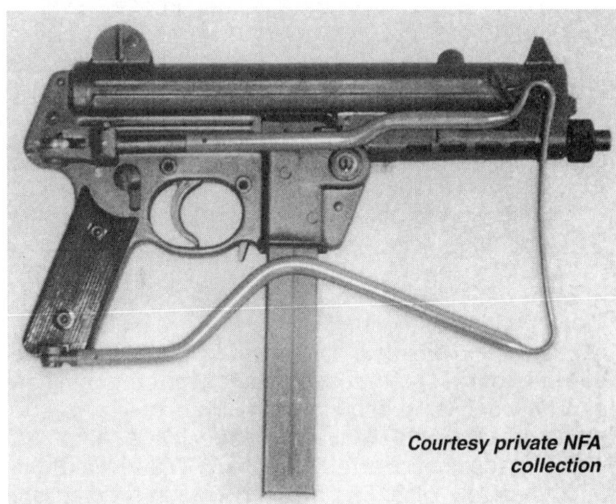

Courtesy private NFA collection

Pre-1968 (Rare)

Exc.	*V.G.*	*Fair*
18000	15000	N/A

HK MP5

First produced in 1965, this submachine gun is quite popular worldwide, being in service in a number of

Courtesy Richard M. Kumor Sr.

countries. It is produced in 9mm, .40 S&W, and 10mm. It is offered in a number of variations. The basic model is fitted with an 8.75-inch barrel with retractable stock. Magazine capacity is 15 or 30 rounds. Rate of fire is 800 rounds per minute. Weight is approximately 5.5 lbs. Marked "MP5 KAL 9MMX19" on top rib of receiver.

Pre-1968 (Rare)

Exc.	*V.G.*	*Fair*
19500	17500	16000

Pre-1986 conversions of semi-automatic version

Exc.	*V.G.*	*Fair*
14500	13000	12000

NOTE: Add 15 percent for registered receiver using OEM parts.

HK MP5 K

This model is essentially the same as the MP5 with the exception of a 4.5-inch barrel. Weight is about 4.4 lbs.

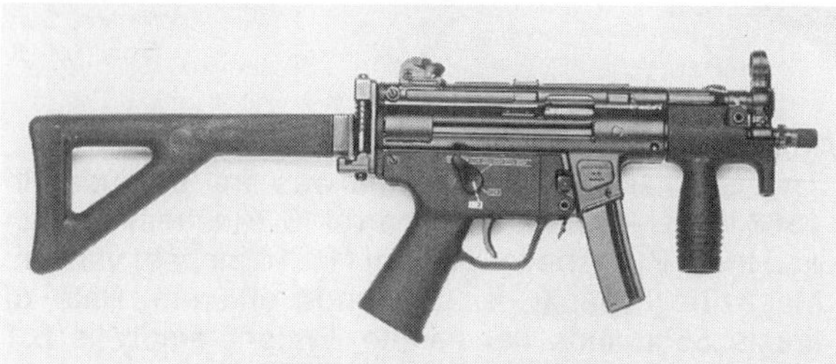

Courtesy Heckler & Koch

Pre-1968 (Rare)

Exc.	*V.G.*	*Fair*
N/A	N/A	N/A

Pre-1986 conversions of semi-automatic model

Exc.	*V.G.*	*Fair*
15000	12500	N/A

NOTE: Add 15 percent for registered receiver using OEM parts.

HK MP5 SD

This variation of the MP5 uses a suppressor, making it one of the quietest submachine guns ever. The barrel is ported so that supersonic 9mm ammunition can be used at subsonic levels. Rate of fire is 800 rounds per minute. Magazine capacity is 15 or 30 round magazines. Barrel length is 7.7" and weight is approximately 7 lbs. This model comes in six different configurations that may affect price.

Courtesy Heckler & Koch

Pre-1968

Exc.	*V.G.*	*Fair*
N/A	N/A	N/A

Pre-1986 conversions of semi-automatic model

Exc.	*V.G.*	*Fair*
20000	17500	N/A

NOTE: Add 15 percent for registered receiver using OEM parts.

HK 53

This submachine gun fires the 5.56x45mm cartridge. It is fitted with an 8.25-inch barrel and retractable stock. Magazine capacity is 25 rounds. Rate of fire is about 700 rounds per minute. Weight is approximately 6.7 lbs. Marked "MP53 KAL 5.56X45" on top rib of receiver. The gun is in service in several military and police units around the world.

Pre-1968

Exc.	*V.G.*	*Fair*
N/A	N/A	N/A

Pre-1986 conversions of HK 93

Exc.	*V.G.*	*Fair*
15000	12000	N/A

Courtesy Heckler & Koch

HK 53 in firing port configuration • *Paul Goodwin Photo*

RIFLES

German Pre-Cartridge Era Rifles

Germany did not exist as a single nation until 1871. It was made of at least 26 nation-states, principalities, and city-states that unified into a single confederation called the ***German Empire*** at that time. Prior to unification, each of these individual states purchased their own arms and it is not possible to list more than a sample here. Prussia was the largest and most prominent of these states and it is their arms that are listed here.

Prussian Model 1809 Flintlock Musket

Usually referred to as a Postdam musket, and that name is sometimes found on the lock plate. Total length of 56-1/2 inches with a 41-inch barrel. .75 caliber, smooth bore. Weight is about 9 lbs. This is similar to the M 1777 muskets used by the Hessians in the U.S. Revolution. A pre-1800 example would bring 25-50% more.

Exc.	*V.G.*	*Good*	*Fair*	*Poor*
2250	1600	1250	650	400

Prussian M1809 Conversion to Percussion

Sometimes referred to as a 1809/39.

Exc.	*V.G.*	*Good*	*Fair*	*Poor*
1250	900	750	450	250

Prussian M1839 Percussion Musket

As above but manufactured as a percussion firearm. .71 caliber.

Exc.	*V.G.*	*Good*	*Fair*	*Poor*
1250	900	750	450	250

NOTE: Some Prussian muskets were issued to Northern regiments early in the American Civil War. Add 100% to any 1809/39 or 1839 musket with unit or state markings.

Dreyse Needle Gun

The Dreyse needle-gun was a military breechloading rifle, famous as the main infantry weapon of the Prussians, who adopted it for service in 1841 as the **Dreyse Zündnadelgewehr**, or ***Prussian Model 1841***. Its name comes from its 0.5-inch (13 mm) needle-like firing pin, which passed through the paper cartridge case to impact a percussion cap seated in the base of the bullet. The Dreyse rifle was also the first breech-loading rifle to use a bolt to open and close the chamber, executed by turning and pulling a bolt handle. The gun was the invention of the gunsmith Johann Nikolaus von Dreyse.

Prussian M1841 Dreyse Needle Gun

Caliber 15.4mm. Total length of 53 inches. Barrel length is 33-1/2 inches. The weight is about 10 ½ lb.

Exc.	*V.G.*	*Good*	*Fair*	*Poor*
3000	2250	1600	900	450

Prussian M 1857 Dreyse Needle Carbine

Caliber 15.4mm. Total length of 31-1/2 inches. The barrel is 15 inches. Weight is about 6-1/2 lbs. Stocked to the muzzle with a shoulder strap ring under the wrist of the stock.

Exc.	*V.G.*	*Good*	*Fair*	*Poor*
3500	2700	1850	1000	575

Prussian M1862 Dreyse Needle Rifle

An improved version of the 1841 with a shorter barrel.

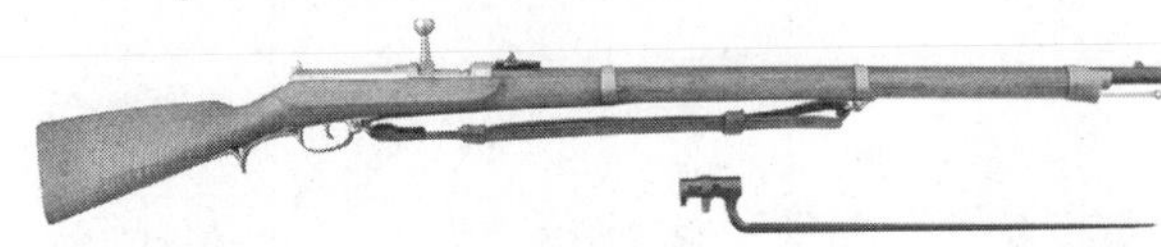

Exc.	*V.G.*	*Good*	*Fair*	*Poor*
2500	1750	1250	750	500

Bayonets for Dreyse Rifles

There were a few patterns of socket bayonet made for the Dreyse rifles, as shown in the images above. Price range 250-150.

MAUSER MILITARY BOLT ACTION RIFLES

FOR COUNTRIES NOT LISTED UNDER SEPARATE HEADING

NOTE: Many of these models have never been imported to the U.S. in quantity. In some cases only a handful of a given model exist and no recent sales activity could be documented to establish a price range. In these cases, the prices listed are educated estimates.

Argentina

See Argentina, Rifles, Mauser.

Austria

See Austria, Rifles, Mauser.

Belgium

See Belgium, Rifles, Mauser.

Bolivia

M1895 Rifle

Exc.	*V.G.*	*Good*	*Fair*	*Poor*
500	350	250	150	100

M1907 Rifle

Exc.	*V.G.*	*Good*	*Fair*	*Poor*
550	375	250	150	100

M1907 Short Rifle

Exc.	*V.G.*	*Good*	*Fair*	*Poor*
550	375	250	150	100

VZ24 Short Rifle

Exc.	V.G.	Good	Fair	Poor
650	500	300	225	125

M1933 Standard Model Export Model Short Rifle

Exc.	V.G.	Good	Fair	Poor
800	575	400	250	150

M1950 Series B-50 Rifle

Exc.	V.G.	Good	Fair	Poor
600	450	375	225	125

Brazil

See Brazil, Rifles, Mauser.

Chile

Courtesy Rock Island Auction Company

M1893 Rifle

Exc.	V.G.	Good	Fair	Poor
500	375	250	150	100

M1895 Rifle

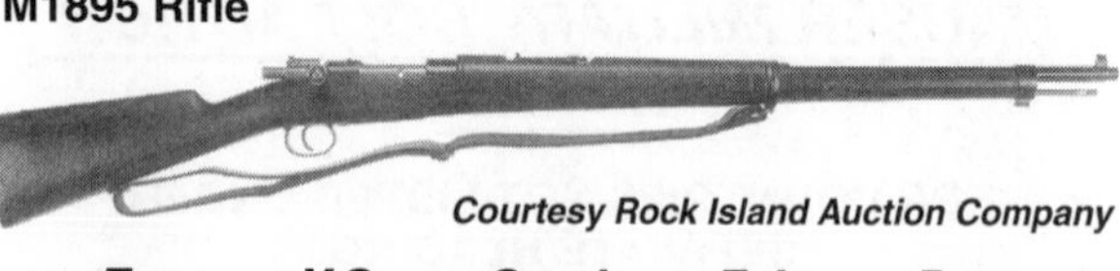

Courtesy Rock Island Auction Company

Exc.	V.G.	Good	Fair	Poor
550	425	275	150	100

M1895/61 7.62 NATO Conversion

Exc.	V.G.	Good	Fair	Poor
400	300	250	175	125

M1895 Short Rifle

Exc.	V.G.	Good	Fair	Poor
550	425	300	150	100

Bayonet for Chilean Model 1895 Mauser

Wood grips. 9.8-inch single edge blade. Muzzle ring. Chilean Star in shield marking on one side of ricasso. Maker marked Weyersberg, Kirschbaun & Co. Solingen. SN: on cross piece and scabbard frog stud. Price range 45 – 20.

M1896 Carbine

Exc.	V.G.	Good	Fair	Poor
600	425	250	150	100

M1912 Steyr Rifle

Courtesy Rock Island Auction Company

Exc.	V.G.	Good	Fair	Poor
650	475	300	175	100

M1912 Steyr Short Rifle

Exc.	V.G.	Good	Fair	Poor
650	475	300	175	100

M1912/61 7.62 NATO Conversion

Exc.	V.G.	Good	Fair	Poor
400	325	250	150	100

Bayonet for Chilean Model 1912 Mauser

Wood grips. 9.8-inch single edge blade. Muzzle ring. Made in Austria by Steyr. Marked OEWG. Steel scabbard that is the same style as the M1895 bayonet comes in. Price range 70 – 35.

M1935 Carabineros Carbine

Exc.	V.G.	Good	Fair	Poor
800	650	450	300	150

China

See China, Rifles, Mauser.

Colombia

M1891 Rifle (Argentine Pattern)

Exc.	V.G.	Good	Fair	Poor
550	400	275	150	100

M1904 Rifle

Exc.	V.G.	Good	Fair	Poor
700	525	300	175	100

M1912 Steyr Rifle

Exc.	V.G.	Good	Fair	Poor
650	475	300	175	100

VZ23 Short Rifle

Exc.	V.G.	Good	Fair	Poor
700	550	300	175	100

Steyr-Solothurn A-G M1929 Short Rifle

Exc.	V.G.	Good	Fair	Poor
750	550	300	175	100

FN M24 and 30 Short Rifles

Exc.	V.G.	Good	Fair	Poor
750	575	350	175	100

VZ12/33 Carbine

Exc.	V.G.	Good	Fair	Poor
800	625	450	275	150

FN M1950 Short Rifle

Exc.	V.G.	Good	Fair	Poor
700	525	350	200	100

Costa Rica

M1895 Rifle

Exc.	V.G.	Good	Fair	Poor
550	400	250	150	90

M1910 Rifle

Exc.	V.G.	Good	Fair	Poor
600	475	300	175	100

FN M24 Short Rifle

Exc.	V.G.	Good	Fair	Poor
700	475	300	175	100

Czechoslovakia

See Czechoslovakia, Rifles, Mauser.

Denmark

See Denmark, Rifles, Mauser.

Dominican Republic

M1953 Rifle

Exc.	V.G.	Good	Fair	Poor
600	425	300	150	125

M1953 Short Rifle

Exc.	V.G.	Good	Fair	Poor
650	425	250	150	100

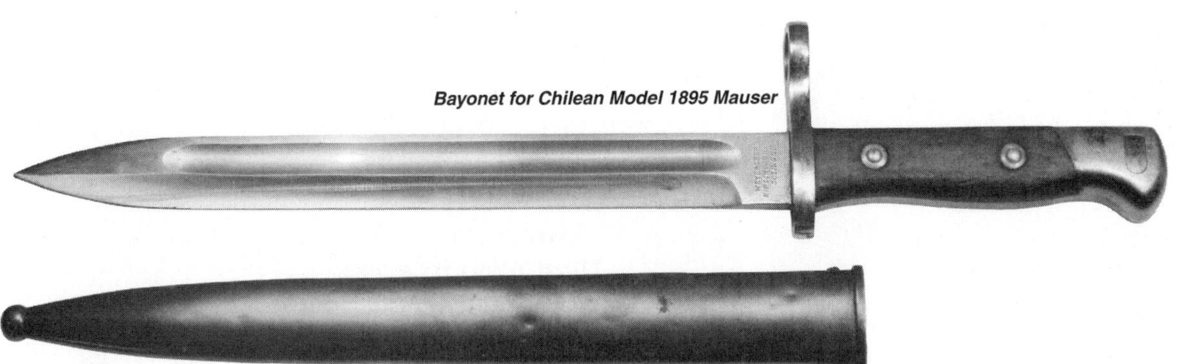
Bayonet for Chilean Model 1895 Mauser

Ecuador

M71/84 Rifle

Exc.	V.G.	Good	Fair	Poor
850	650	500	325	250

M1891 Rifle (Argentine Pattern)

Exc.	V.G.	Good	Fair	Poor
650	425	275	150	100

M1907 Rifle

Exc.	V.G.	Good	Fair	Poor
700	550	350	175	100

M1910 Rifle

Exc.	V.G.	Good	Fair	Poor
700	500	300	175	100

VZ24 Short Rifle

Exc.	V.G.	Good	Fair	Poor
700	500	300	175	100

VZ12/33 Carbine

Exc.	V.G.	Good	Fair	Poor
800	575	350	200	150

FN M30 Short Rifle

Exc.	V.G.	Good	Fair	Poor
750	550	300	175	100

El Salvador

M1895 Rifle

Exc.	V.G.	Good	Fair	Poor
550	400	250	150	100

VZ12/33 Carbine

Exc.	V.G.	Good	Fair	Poor
750	525	400	250	150

Estonia

Czech Model L Short Rifle

Exc.	V.G.	Good	Fair	Poor
850	725	550	250	150

Ethiopia

FN M24 Carbine

Exc.	V.G.	Good	Fair	Poor
800	650	400	200	100

M1933 Standard Model Short Rifle

Exc.	V.G.	Good	Fair	Poor
850	700	550	250	150

M1933 Standard Model Carbine

Exc.	V.G.	Good	Fair	Poor
850	600	400	250	150

France

See France, Rifles, Mauser.

Greece

M1930 Short Rifle

Exc.	V.G.	Good	Fair	Poor
750	575	400	250	150

M1930 Carbine

Exc.	V.G.	Good	Fair	Poor
750	575	400	300	150

Guatemala

M1910 Rifle

Exc.	V.G.	Good	Fair	Poor
550	400	300	150	100

M1935 Carabineros Carbine • Courtesy Rock Island Auction Company

Bayonet for Chilean Model 1912 Mauser

VZ25 Short Rifle (Model 24)

Exc.	V.G.	Good	Fair	Poor
550	400	325	175	100

VZ33 Carbine

Exc.	V.G.	Good	Fair	Poor
750	575	350	200	150

Haiti

FN M24/30 Short Rifle

Exc.	V.G.	Good	Fair	Poor
750	525	350	175	100

Honduras

G 71 Rifle

Exc.	V.G.	Good	Fair	Poor
850	650	500	350	200

M1895 Rifle (Chilean Pattern)

Exc.	V.G.	Good	Fair	Poor
550	400	300	150	100

M1933 Standard Model Short Rifle

Exc.	V.G.	Good	Fair	Poor
700	500	350	175	100

Iraq

Post-WWII-style Carbine

Exc.	V.G.	Good	Fair	Poor
450	325	250	150	100

Ireland

G 71 Rifle

Exc.	V.G.	Good	Fair	Poor
800	650	450	275	150

Israel

See Israel, Rifles, Mauser.

Japan

See Japan, Rifles, Mauser.

Latvia

VZ24 Short Rifle

Exc.	V.G.	Good	Fair	Poor
850	700	550	350	200

Liberia

FN M24 Short Rifle

Exc.	V.G.	Good	Fair	Poor
600	475	300	175	100

Lithuania

FN M30 Short Rifle

Exc.	V.G.	Good	Fair	Poor
850	700	450	250	150

FN M24 Short Rifle

Exc.	V.G.	Good	Fair	Poor
800	575	400	250	150

Luxembourg

M1900 Rifle

Exc.	V.G.	Good	Fair	Poor
850	650	475	300	150

FN M24/30 Short Rifle

Exc.	V.G.	Good	Fair	Poor
700	575	350	175	100

Manchuria

See Japan, Rifles.

Mexico

See Mexico, Rifles, Mauser.

Morocco

Post-WWII FN Carbine

Made in .30-06 and 7.62mm. FN address only. No crest. A small quantity were mported in the 1990s.

Exc.	V.G.	Good	Fair	Poor
650	475	350	200	100

Netherlands

See Netherlands, Rifles, Mauser.

Nicaragua

VZ23 Short Rifle

Exc.	V.G.	Good	Fair	Poor
650	500	350	175	100

VZ12/33 Carbine

Exc.	V.G.	Good	Fair	Poor
750	600	450	200	125

Norway

See Norway, Rifles, Mauser.

Orange Free State

M1895 Rifle

Exc.	V.G.	Good	Fair	Poor
800	625	450	225	150

M1895 Chilean-marked Rifle

Exc.	V.G.	Good	Fair	Poor
750	550	400	225	150

M1896 Loewe & Co. Rifle

Exc.	V.G.	Good	Fair	Poor
800	600	400	225	150

M1897 DWM Rifle

Exc.	V.G.	Good	Fair	Poor
800	600	450	250	150

Paraguay

M1895 Rifle (Chilean Pattern)

Exc.	V.G.	Good	Fair	Poor
550	400	275	150	100

M1907 Rifle

Exc.	V.G.	Good	Fair	Poor
650	475	300	175	100

M1907 Carbine

Exc.	V.G.	Good	Fair	Poor
650	475	300	175	100

M1909 Haenel Export Model Rifle

Exc.	V.G.	Good	Fair	Poor
750	600	450	175	100

M1927 Rifle

Exc.	V.G.	Good	Fair	Poor
550	375	250	150	100

M1927 Short Rifle

Exc.	V.G.	Good	Fair	Poor
550	375	250	150	100

FN M24/30 Short Rifle

Exc.	V.G.	Good	Fair	Poor
750	525	350	175	100

Persian M98/29 Long Rifle • Courtesy Rock Island Auction Company

M1933 Standard Model Short Rifle

Exc.	V.G.	Good	Fair	Poor
750	575	400	250	125

M1933 Standard Model Carbine

Exc.	V.G.	Good	Fair	Poor
750	575	400	250	125

Persia/Iran

M1895 Rifle

Exc.	V.G.	Good	Fair	Poor
650	475	325	150	100

FN M24/30 Short Rifle

Exc.	V.G.	Good	Fair	Poor
700	475	350	175	100

M98/29 Long Rifle

Exc.	V.G.	Good	Fair	Poor
500	425	300	175	100

VZ24 Short Rifle

Exc.	V.G.	Good	Fair	Poor
750	550	350	175	100

M30 Carbine

Exc.	V.G.	Good	Fair	Poor
700	500	300	175	100

M49 Carbine

Exc.	V.G.	Good	Fair	Poor
600	475	300	175	100

Peru

M1891 Rifle M1891 Carbine

Exc.	V.G.	Good	Fair	Poor
450	325	250	150	100

M1895 Rifle

Exc.	V.G.	Good	Fair	Poor
450	325	250	150	100

M1909 Rifle

Exc.	V.G.	Good	Fair	Poor
800	650	400	175	100

VZ24 Short Rifle

Exc.	V.G.	Good	Fair	Poor
700	475	300	175	100

VZ33 Carbine

Exc.	V.G.	Good	Fair	Poor
600	475	300	175	100

M1935 Short Rifle (converted to .30-06)

Exc.	V.G.	Good	Fair	Poor
450	325	250	150	100

M1935 Short Rifle

Courtesy Rock Island Auction Company

Exc.	V.G.	Good	Fair	Poor
600	475	300	175	100

Poland

See Poland, Rifles, Mauser.

Portugal

See Portugal, Rifles, Mauser.

Romania

See Romania, Rifles.

Saudi Arabia

FN M30 Short Rifle

Exc.	V.G.	Good	Fair	Poor
700	550	400	250	150

Serbia/Yugoslavia

See Yugoslavia, Rifles, Mauser.

Slovak Republic

VZ24 Short Rifle

Exc.	V.G.	Good	Fair	Poor
600	475	300	175	100

South Africa

M1896 ZAR Rifle

Exc.	V.G.	Good	Fair	Poor
750	625	350	175	100

ZAE M1896 B Series Rifle

Exc.	V.G.	Good	Fair	Poor
750	625	350	175	100

M1896 ZAR Loewe Long Rifle

Exc.	V.G.	Good	Fair	Poor
750	650	400	200	100

M1895/1896 C Series

Exc.	V.G.	Good	Fair	Poor
700	600	375	175	100

Spain

See Spain, Rifles, Mauser.

Sweden

See Sweden, Rifles, Mauser.

Syria

M1948 Short Rifle

Courtesy Rock Island Auction Company

Exc.	V.G.	Good	Fair	Poor
400	325	250	125	100

Thailand/Siam

G 71 Rifle

Exc.	V.G.	Good	Fair	Poor
850	600	400	300	150

M1903 (Type 45) Rifle

Made in Japan at the Koishikowa arsenal.

Exc.	V.G.	Good	Fair	Poor
450	325	250	150	100

M1904 Rifle

Exc.	V.G.	Good	Fair	Poor
450	325	250	150	100

M1923 (Type 66) Short Rifle

Exc.	V.G.	Good	Fair	Poor
450	325	250	150	100

Transvaal

G 71 Rifle

Exc.	V.G.	Good	Fair	Poor
850	675	500	300	150

Turkey

See Turkey, Rifles, Mauser.

Uruguay

G 71 Rifle

Exc.	V.G.	Good	Fair	Poor
850	650	500	300	150

M1895 Rifle

Exc.	V.G.	Good	Fair	Poor
550	375	250	150	100

M1908 Rifle

Exc.	V.G.	Good	Fair	Poor
600	400	250	150	100

M1908 Short Rifle

Exc.	V.G.	Good	Fair	Poor
600	400	250	150	100

FN M24 Short Rifle

Exc.	V.G.	Good	Fair	Poor
700	525	350	175	100

VZ37 (937) Short Rifle

Exc.	V.G.	Good	Fair	Poor
700	550	300	175	100

VZ37 (937) Carbine

Exc.	V.G.	Good	Fair	Poor
700	550	300	175	100

Venezuela

G 71/84 Rifle

Exc.	V.G.	Good	Fair	Poor
850	650	500	350	200

M1910 Rifle

Exc.	V.G.	Good	Fair	Poor
575	450	300	150	100

VZ24 Short Rifle

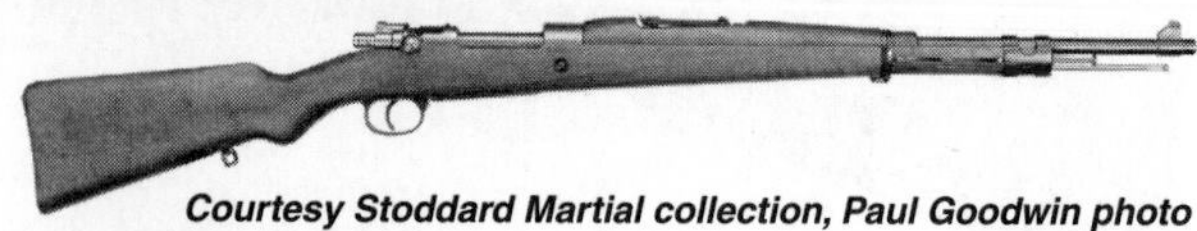

Courtesy Stoddard Martial collection, Paul Goodwin photo

Exc.	V.G.	Good	Fair	Poor
750	500	375	200	100

FN M24/30 Short Rifle

Courtesy Cherry's Fine Guns

Exc.	V.G.	Good	Fair	Poor
750	500	375	200	100

FN M24/30 Carbine

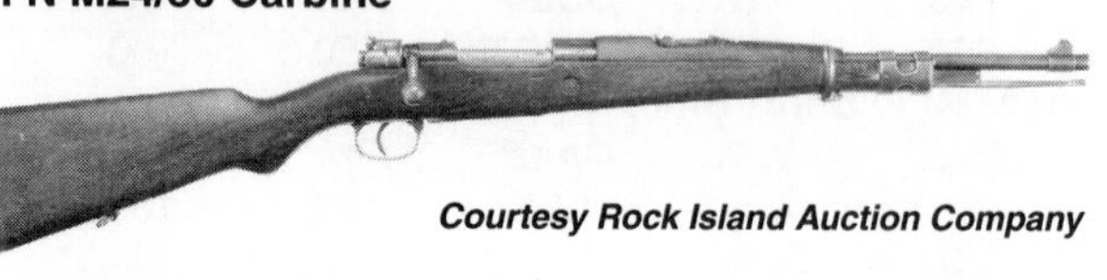

Courtesy Rock Island Auction Company

Exc.	V.G.	Good	Fair	Poor
850	650	375	200	100

FN M24/30 Military Target Rifle

Exc.	V.G.	Good	Fair	Poor
900	750	550	175	100

Yemen

FN M30 Short Rifle

Exc.	V.G.	Good	Fair	Poor
750	550	400	175	100

MAUSER

GERMAN ISSUE RIFLES

Established in 1869 by Peter and Wilhelm Mauser, this company came under the effective control of Ludwig Loewe and Company of Berlin in 1887. In 1896 the latter company was reorganized under the name Deutsches Waffen und Munition or, as it is better known, DWM.

For history and technical details, see Robert W.D. Ball's ***Mauser Military Rifles of the World***, Krause Publications.

Model 1871

This was the first German metallic cartridge rifle. It was a 11x60Rmm caliber single shot bolt action rifle with a 33.5-inch barrel with bayonet lug, full-length stock secured by two barrel bands, and a cleaning rod. There is no upper handguard on this model. This model did not have an ejector so empty shells had to be removed manually. The rear sight was a leaf type with graduations out to 1,600 meters. Weight was about 10 lbs. The barrel was marked "Mod. 71" together with the year of production and the manufacturer's name, of which there were several. First produced in 1875. Blued with a walnut stock.

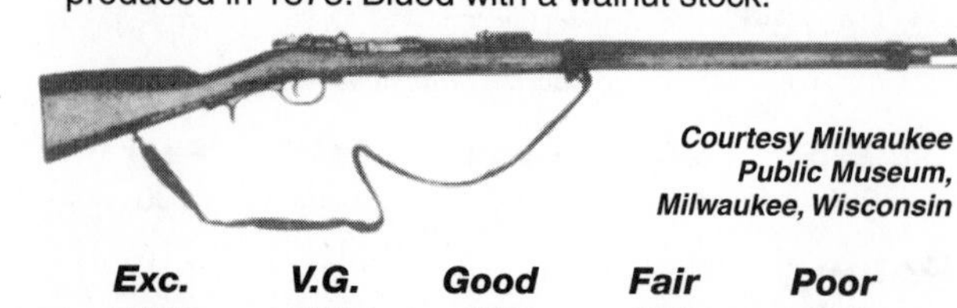

Courtesy Milwaukee Public Museum, Milwaukee, Wisconsin

Exc.	V.G.	Good	Fair	Poor
1100	850	600	300	150

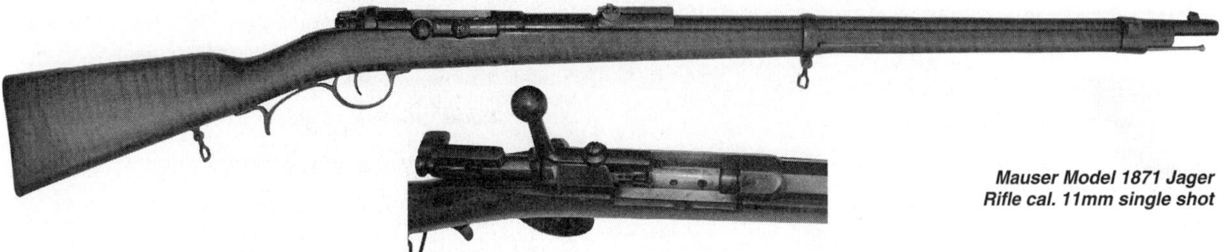

Mauser Model 1871 Jager Rifle cal. 11mm single shot

Model 1871 Jaeger Rifle

As above, with a 29.4-inch barrel and finger grip extension behind the triggerguard. Weight is about 10 lbs.

Exc.	V.G.	Good	Fair	Poor
1250	900	650	450	300

Bayonet for Mauser Model 1871

Brass handle. Muzzle ring. S shaped quillon. 18.3-inch single edge blade. Brass tipped leather scabbard. Makers mark on speciman shown "Gebr Weyersberg, Solingen." Price range 300 – 175.

Pioneer Bayonet for 1871 Mauser

Brass handle. Muzzle ring. S shaped quillon. 20-inch heavy blade with saw back. Brass-tipped leather scabbard. Rare. Issued to engineer units only. Price range 800 – 400.

Model 1871 Carbine

As above, with a 20-inch barrel and no bayonet lug. Full stocked to the muzzle. Weight is about 7.5 lbs.

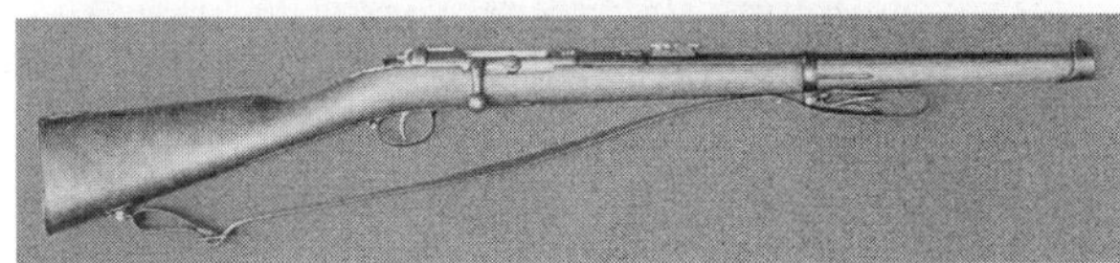

***1871 Mauser Carbine, Kar 71** • Courtesy Bob Ball*

Exc.	V.G.	Good	Fair	Poor
1500	950	700	350	225

Model 1871 Short Rifle

As above, but with upper and lower barrel bands and bayonet lug.

Exc.	V.G.	Good	Fair	Poor
1150	875	650	350	225

Model 79 G.A.G. Rifle (Grenz-Aufsichts-Gewehr)

Fitted with a 25-inch barrel and built by Haenel in Suhl and so marked. It is also marked "G.A.G." Used by German border guards. It is full stock almost to the muzzle. It is chambered for the 11x37.5mm cartridge. Weight is about 7 lbs. Single shot.

Exc.	V.G.	Good	Fair	Poor
1000	750	550	300	200

Model 71/84 Rifle

The Model 71 modified by the addition of a tubular 8-round magazine. This model was fitted with an ejector. Barrel length 31.5 inches. Weight is approximately 10 lbs. Issued in 1886. About 900,000 were produced. Marked "I.G.MOD.71/84" on the left side of the receiver.

Exc.	V.G.	Good	Fair	Poor
1000	800	650	350	275

Bayonet for Mauser 71/84

Wood grips. Muzzle ring. 10-inch single edge blade. Steel scabbard. This was the first standard issue knife type bayonet. Also used on the Gew-1888 rifle. These are somewhat rare as many were converted for use on the Gew-98 during WWI. Price range 250 – 125.

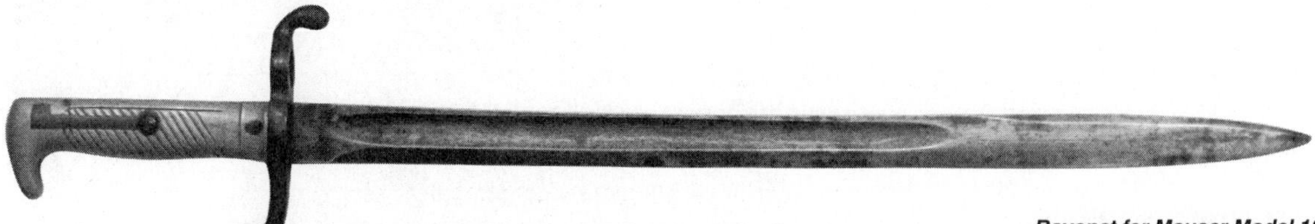

Bayonet for Mauser Model 1871

Pioneer Bayonet for Mauser Model 1871

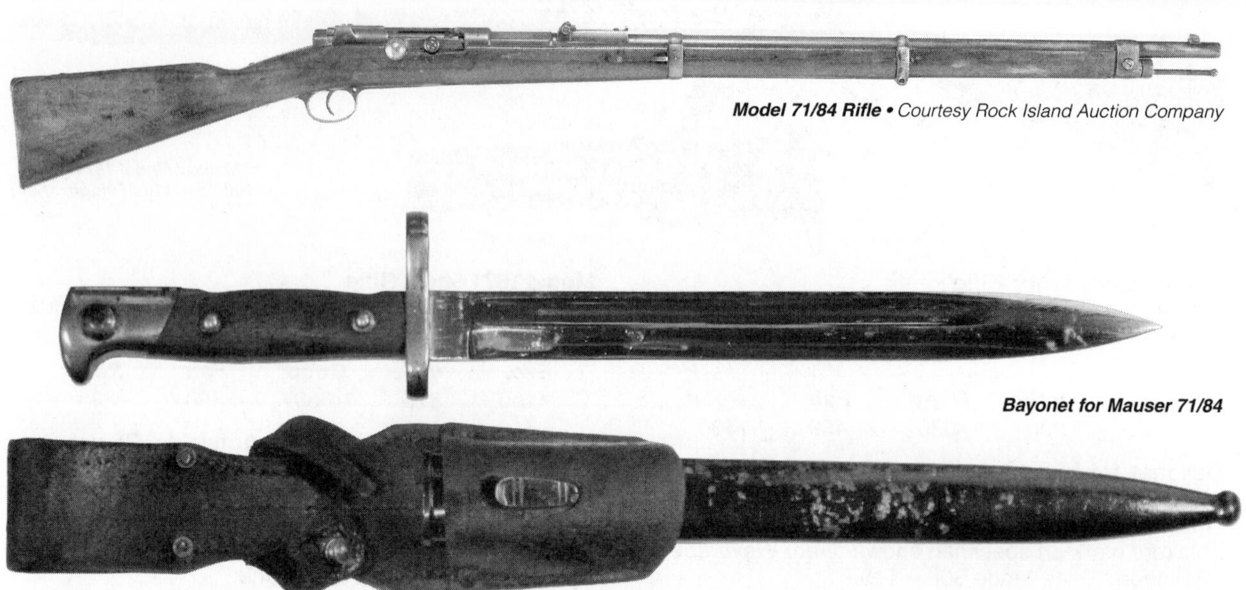

Model 71/84 Rifle • *Courtesy Rock Island Auction Company*

Bayonet for Mauser 71/84

Model 88 Commission Rifle

A 7.92x57mm caliber bolt action rifle with a 29-inch barrel that is covered with a hollow steel tube. 5-shot magazine that requires Mannlicher type clips, full-length stock, bayonet lug, and cleaning rod. Marked "GEW. 88" together with the year of manufacture and the maker's name. This was the first military rifle to take a rimless cartridge. Weight is about 9 lbs. About 1,000,000 of these rifles were produced. Many of these rifles were later modified to feed without the Mannlicher clip. This model is known as a M-88/05. Used in World War I by the German, Austro-Hungarian, Bulgarian, and Turkish armies. Original Commission 88 rifles are uncommon.

Exc.	V.G.	Good	Fair	Poor
750	500	350	150	125

Model 88 Turkish Rework

Germany provided many Model 1888's to Turkey who used them in WW1 and later. They were reworked to the 88-05 pattern and usually have a rear sight marked with Farsi numerals. Most have a small crescent marking on the receiver ring. Parts will have mixed serial numbers. Many of these were imported with the Turkish Mausers in the 1990's.

Exc.	V.G.	Good	Fair	Poor
250	200	150	100	75

Model 88 Commission Rifle • *Courtesy Paul S. Scarlata*

Model 88 Commission Carbine

A 7.92x57mm caliber bolt action rifle with a 20-inch barrel, 5-shot magazine, full-length stock. Marked "Kar. 88" together with the year of manufacture and the maker's name.

Exc.	V.G.	Good	Fair	Poor
800	650	500	350	250

Kar.88 Carbine

Clip for Gew-1888 Rifle or Kar-88 Carbine. Not needed on the 88/05

Model 98 Rifle (Gewehr 98)

The best known of all Mauser rifles. A 7.92mm bolt action rifle with a 29-inch barrel, 5-shot flush fitting magazine, full-length stock, half-length handguard, cleaning rod, and bayonet lug. Pre-1915 versions had a steel grommet through the buttstock and finger grooves on the forend. These early guns also were fitted with a V-notch rear sight adjustable from 400 to 2,000 meters. This sight was called a "Lange Vizier". It is known to U.S. collectors as the "roller coaster" sight. Rifles built

Gew 1888 • *Courtesy Paul S. Scarlata*

Mauser Gew 98 with trench cover •
Courtesy John M. Miller

after World War I were fitted with tangent rear sights graduated from 100 to 2,000 meters. Marked "GEW. 98" together with the date of manufacture and maker's name. Weight is about 9 lbs. About 3,500,000 of these rifles were built from its introduction in 1898 to 1918.

This rifle was built by the following government arsenals and commercial firms: Amberg, Danzig, Erfurt, Spandau, Mauser, DWM, J.P. Sauer & Sohn, V. Chr. Schilling, C.G. Haenel, Simson & Co., and Waffenwerke Oberspree Kornbusch & Co. Nearly all parts have the last 2 digits of the serial number. Price assumes matching numbers. Deduct 25-75% for miss match.

Exc.	V.G.	Good	Fair	Poor
850	675	450	200	125

Bayonet for Gew 1898 Mauser

Wood grip. No muzzle ring. 20.6-inch thin blade with single edge. Also made in a sawback version that was issued to noncommissioned officers. Maker's name on ricasso. Dated on top of blade in front of crosspiece. Steel tipped leather or all steel scabbards were made. This is the first bayonet issued for the Gew-98. The design was dropped when it was discovered that the thin blade could be easily bent or broken in service. Price range standard blade version 225 – 125. Price range sawback version 400 – 200.

Model 98 Carbine

17-inch barrel and full stock to the muzzle without handguard. Turned-down bolt with a spoon shaped handle, as on the Kar-88. The rear sight resembles a shorter version of the Gew-98 sight, graduated to 1800 meters. Not fitted for a bayonet. Produced at the Erfurt arsenal from 1900 to 1902. About 3,000 were produced. In 1902 the Model 98A, with bayonet bar and cleaning rod, was also produced at Erfurt until 1905. Weight was about 7.5 lbs. Very rare. Only a few examples survive.

Exc.	V.G.	Good	Fair	Poor
2500	2000	1500	1000	500

Model 98 AZ Carbine/Model 98a

This model has the same stock as the Model Gew 98 but with a slot through the buttstock. Barrel length was 24". Bolt handle was turn down type and the full stock

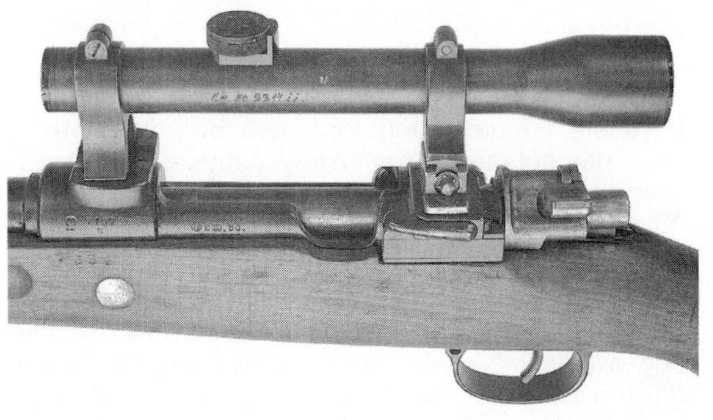

Bayonets for Gew 1898 Mauser: sawback (top) and standard

World War I Gew 98 Sniper with offset claw mount • *Private Collection, Paul Goodwin photo*

Model 98 AZ • *Courtesy West Point Museum, Paul Goodwin photo*

went to the muzzle with full upper handguard. Fitted with a bayonet stud and curved stacking bar on the forearm cap. Magazine capacity is 5 rounds. Weight is about 8 lbs. Introduced in 1908 with about 1,500,000 total production. Stamped "kar 98" on the left side of the receiver. After WWI these rifles were renamed the Model 98a. Fitted with a small ring receiver. Nearly all parts have the last 2 digits of the serial number. Price assumes matching numbers. Deduct 25-75% for miss match.

Exc.	*V.G.*	*Good*	*Fair*	*Poor*
850	600	450	250	150

German Bayonets of WWI

Germany used a wide variety of bayonets on the Mauser Gew-8 and Kar-98 rifles. They entered the war issuing the 1898/05 or "Butcher blade" model. As the war progressed the shorter blade types and the ersatz models were introduced.

A whole chapter could be devoted to the German WWI bayonets. We have room for only a few types here. A small percentage of German bayonets were made with a sawback. They were issued only to noncommissioned officers or pioneer troops. The German model designations are used in the headings.

S98/05

Wood handle. Swept back quillon. 14.5-inch single edge "butcher" style blade. Maker marked on the ricasso. Dated on top of the blade in front of the cross

Mauser 98 AZ • *Courtesy Paul S. Scarlata*

piece. Some early versions have the saw back. This was phased out during the war due to negative allied propaganda. Most had the saw back ground off and were re-issued. The first scabbards were leather with steel fittings, followed by all steel.

Price ranges:

98/05 with saw back 250 – 125.

98/05 with saw back removed 175 – 75.

98/05 made without saw back 150 – 50.

S84/98 WWI Version

This was made by converting the 71/84 Mauser bayonets. The muzzle ring was removed and the "T" slot was lengthened. 9.8-inch single edge blade. They are found with sawback, removed sawback and no sawback. Price range 200 – 80, with sawback versions bringing the higher pricing.

Bayonet for S98/05

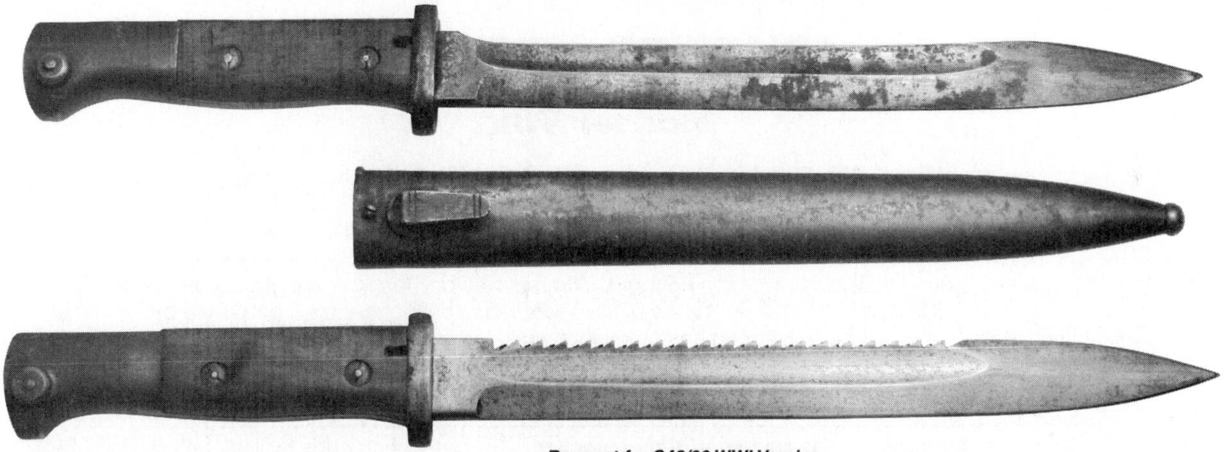

Bayonet for S48/98 WWI Version

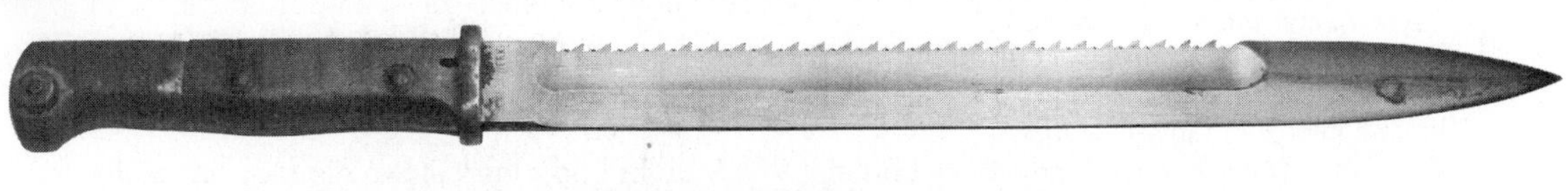

Bayonet for S98/14

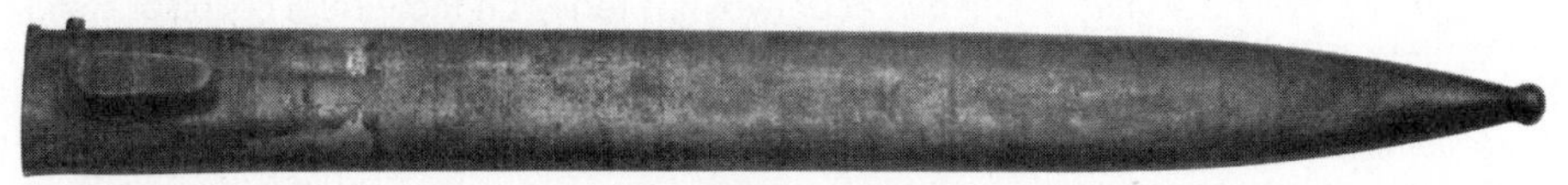

Ersatz Bayonets

Ersatz Bayonet, Crank Handle Version

GERMANY

S98/14

Wood handle. No quillon. 12.1" single edge blade. Made with and without the sawback.

Price Range 250-125

Ersatz bayonets

Germany made substitute or ersatz bayonets during WWI. They are of lower quality in materials and worksmanship. These are easily identified by the metal handles. They usually do not have maker's marks. Made in various blade lengths. Most have a muzzle ring. Some made for use on the 98az carbine have the ring removed. Due to the wide variety that will be observed, the price range is wide. Many of those found in the U.S. came from Turkey, where the blades were shortened. (See Turkey chapter.)

COLLECTOR SPOTLIGHT

Mauser 98k

The Mauser K98 rifle used by Germany during the second world war is one of the most collected military firearms today. Adopted in 1935 and produced through the war's end in 1945, the K98 Mauser offers collectors numerous possible variations and collecting levels. More than 11 million K98s were made in the 10 years they were used by Germany. There is far too much information available on the K98 to include in this book. For more detailed information I suggest *Mauser Military Rifles of the World* by Robert Ball, published by Krause Publications, and *Backbone of the Wehrmacht* by Richard Law, published by Collector Grade Publications. The Ball book gets into fine detail that will be of interest to advanced collectors, such as production data from individual makers and the huge variety of markings found on individual parts.

Two main factors that affect the price of a K98 are:

Maker: The Mauser K98 was made by nine manufacturers during its service life. The top of the receiver is marked with a production code and year of manufacture. The production code system was devised by Germany in the 1930s to conceal the names of firms involved in the production of arms and was used throughout the war. Some makers made far fewer rifles than others and the lower production figures will make a rifle worth more to a collector looking for that particular maker or date. The manufacturers and the codes they used are:

Mauser Werke AG Oberndorf aN: S/42K, S/42G, S/42, 42, byf, SVW
JP Sauer & Sohn, Suhl: S/147, S/147K, S/147G, 147, ce
Gustloff-Werke Weimar: bcd, 337
Mauser-Werke AG Berlin Borsigwalde: S/243G, S/243, 243, ar
Waffenfabrik Brunn AG Brno or Bystrica: 945, dot, dou, swp
Steyr-Daimler Puch: 660, bnz
Berlin-Lubecker Maschinenfabrik: S/237, 237
Erfurter Maschinenfabrik (ERMA): S/27, 27, ax
Berlin-Suhler Waffenwerke: *bsw*

Matching Numbers: Nearly every part of a 98k Mauser bears the last two digits of the serial number found on the receiver. Even a single mismatched screw or barrel band can reduce the value of a rifle to a collector examining a specimen being sold as collector grade. There is no set percentage to reduce the price if a 98k has a mismatched part or two. It is really an individual collector's choice whether to add such a firearm to the collection or not.

Phillip Peterson

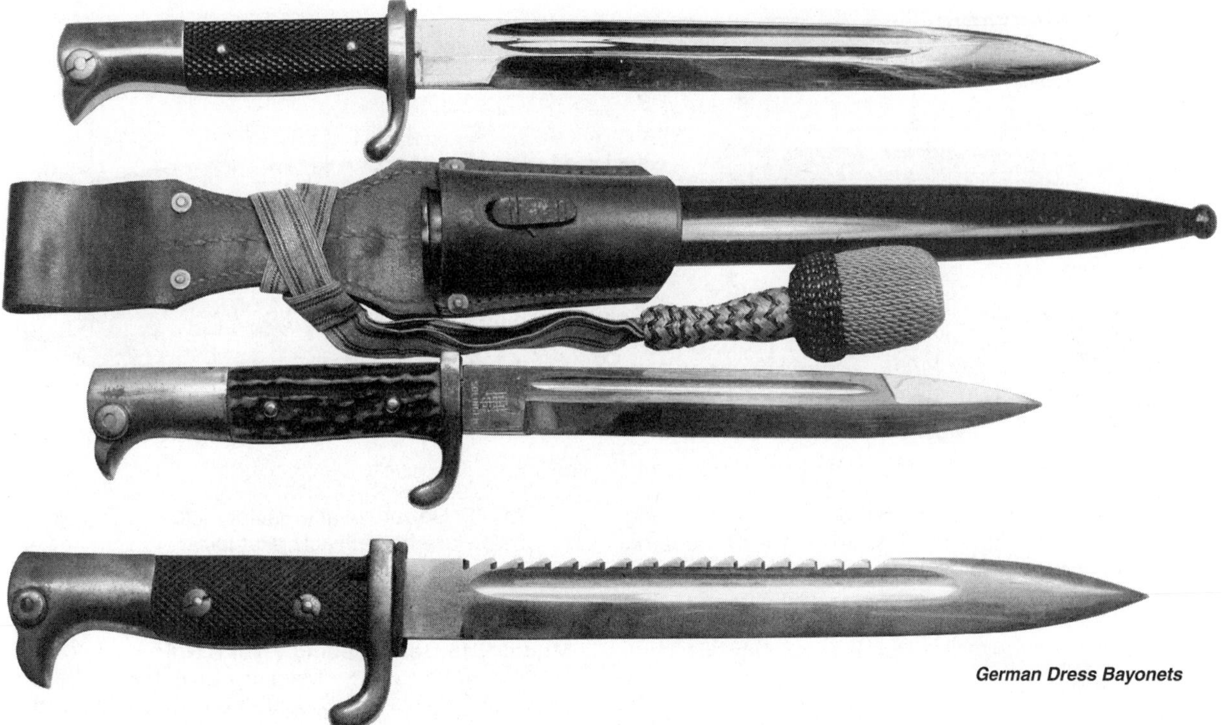

German Dress Bayonets

The crank handle version shown is one of the more desirable models and has been reproduced recently. Price range 400 – 75.

German Dress or Parade Bayonets (Kurzes)

Checkered hard rubber or bone handles. Chrome plated pommel, cross piece and blade. The blades come in a variety of lengths. Scabbards are painted gloss black. These interesting bayonets were made as replacements for swords. They appeared before WWI and were made through WWII. Some were carried to the front, but they were really purchased as dress items to be worn while on leave or at military ceremonies. They are listed here because they are frequently seen in the U.S. There are also knives that look the same but lack the attaching slot or lock. Price range 300 – 50, with the WWII Nazi-marked versions bringing the higher pricing.

Model 98 Transitional Rifle

As a result of the armistice, Model 98 rifles were modified with a simple tangent rear sight, the markings were ground off, and they were arsenal refinished.

Exc.	V.G.	Good	Fair	Poor
600	450	350	150	100

Model 98 KAR 98b Rifle

Also a product of the armistice the Model 98 rifle was altered with the addition of a flat tangent rear sight, removed stacking hook, and a slot was cut for a sling in the buttstock. The bolt handle was bent. Otherwise this is a Model 98 rifle.

Exc.	V.G.	Good	Fair	Poor
600	450	350	200	150

Model 98k Carbine (Short Rifle)

This was the standard shoulder arm of the German military during WWII. Introduced in 1935 about 11,000,000 were produced. Barrel length is 23.6". Magazine capacity is 5 rounds of 7.92mm. Rear sight was a tangent leaf graduated to 2,000 meters. Weight is about 8.5 lbs. Produced by a number of German arsenals using a variety of different identifying codes.

Model 98k

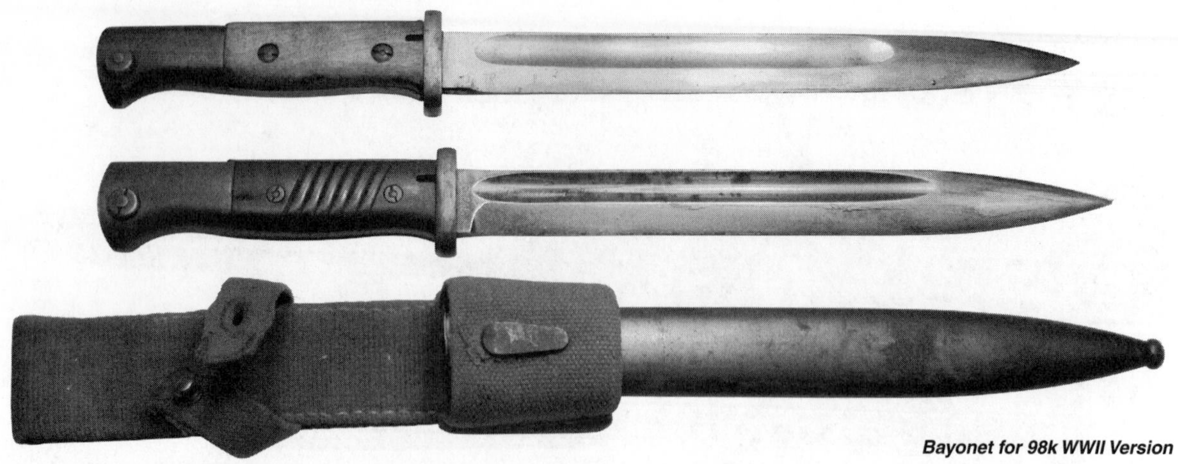

Bayonet for 98k WWII Version

GERMANY

Date of production is found on the receiver ring. Nearly all parts have the last two digits of the serial number. Price assumes matching numbers. Deduct 25-75% for mismatch.

Courtesy Buffalo Bill Historical Center, Cody, Wyoming

Exc.	V.G.	Good	Fair	Poor
1000	750	600	350	200

Model 98k Carbine (Short Rifle) Russian Capture

Mauser 98ks captured by Russia during WWII. They re-worked and refinished them after the war. Few will have any originally matching parts. The bolt and some major parts were re-numbered to match the receiver with an electric pencil by the Russians. The Nazi era markings are usually intact. Sometimes the swastikas were removed by the Russians or other nations that re-used the 98k.

Exc.	V.G.	Good	Fair	Poor
400	300	250	200	150

Bayonet for 98k (84/98) WWII Version

The standard bayonet for the K98k Mauser rifle. Smooth wood grips are found on early examples. Later production has composite grips. The 9.8" single edge blade has a blued or phosphate finish. Made by several contractors. Wartime production has a manufacturers code and a two digit date. Usually has a serial number on the ricasso and scabbard. They seldom are found that match. Collectors will pay up to a 100 percent premium for matching specimens or rare makers and dates. Price range 250 – 50.

Model 98k Carbine (Short Rifle with extended magazine)

This model is a 98k with a non-removable 25-round magazine. It was an attempt to solve the problem of the limited magazine capacity of the standard 98k. This magazine could be filled singly or with 5-round clips.

Courtesy Amoskeag Auction Company

NOTE: Beware of after-factory add-ons. Prices listed below are for verifiable examples.

Exc.	V.G.	Good	Fair	Poor
5000	3500	3000	1800	950

Model 1916 Self-Loading Flyer's Rifle

First built in 1916 by Mauser at Oberndorf, this is a semi-automatic recoil operated rifle chambered for the 7.92x57mm cartridge. Fitted with a 26-inch barrel. Some sources list the magazine capacity at 25 rounds, others at 20 rounds. The magazine is slightly curved. Weight of rifle is about 10.5 lbs. The rifle was issued with 10 magazines. It is estimated that somewhere between 1,000 and 2,000 were produced. The rifle was designed to be used by airborne gunners during WWI. Very Rare.

Exc.	V.G.	Good	Fair	Poor
25000	20000	17500	12000	7500

DSM 34 Training Rifle

A single shot rifle chambered for .22LR. Resembles a K98k Mauser. Introduced in the 1930s and used for training by various German government and para military organizations. Made by several companies including: Mauser, Walther, Geco, BSW, Erma and Simson. Most have the bolts serial numbered to the rifle.

NOTE: there is a large variety of variations of these .22 Trainers. Each company that produced the DSM 34 pattern rifles used their own action design. Some makers and variations will command higher prices from collectors. This entry is for the military stocked models only. There are also many different sporter-stocked .22s that are generally worth less. See ***Mauser Smallbore Trainers*** by Collector Grade Publications for very detailed information about these training rifles.

Exc	V.G.	Good	Fair	Poor
1250	900	650	300	200

ERMA, Erfurt 22 Conversion Unit for K98k Mauser

This includes a .22LR barreled action that installs in the standard K98k. Uses a 7-round detachable magazine. Issued in a wooden storage case. Deduct 25% if no case.

Exc	VG	Good	Fair	Poor
1000	850	700	400	300

Mauser DSM-34 .22LR action

German Sniper Rifles

The German sniper rifle used the K98k rifle as its foundation from 1914 to the end of WWII, although other models such as the G41 and G43 were as employed in that role later in World War II. To simplify a somewhat complex subject, German Sniper rifles are separated into five distinct types. These varieties are based on the type of telescope sight used on the rifle.

- The 1st Type is the short rail system.
- The 2nd type is the ZF41 and ZF41/1 scopes.
- The 3rd type is the turret mount system in both low and high variations.
- The 4th type is the long rail system.
- The 5th type is the claw mount system.

Different systems were used at different times and often overlap each other. Each system has its own varieties of telescopes made by different manufacturers. Some scopes are numbered to the rifle while others are not. Some rifles and scopes bear the markings of the Waffen-SS, and these will bring a premium.

There were a number of different manufacturers of sniper scopes during the period between 1914 and 1945, and each of these manufacturers was assigned a production code. For example, Schneider & Co. was "dkl". These codes and other pertinent information, including historical information, data, and photos, can be seen in The German Sniper, 1914-1945, Peter R. Senich, Paladin Press, 1982.

NOTE: Prices listed below are for the rifle and the correct scope and base, i.e. verifiable examples. Sometimes the scope and base are not numbered. It is recommended that an expert opinion be sought before purchase. It should be noted that the prices for German sniper rifles are subject to variations with different scope and mount combinations. Proceed with caution.

Model 98k Sniper Rifle (High Turret Model)

A sniper version of the 98k with different manufactured scopes. This variation has a 6.35mm recess depth

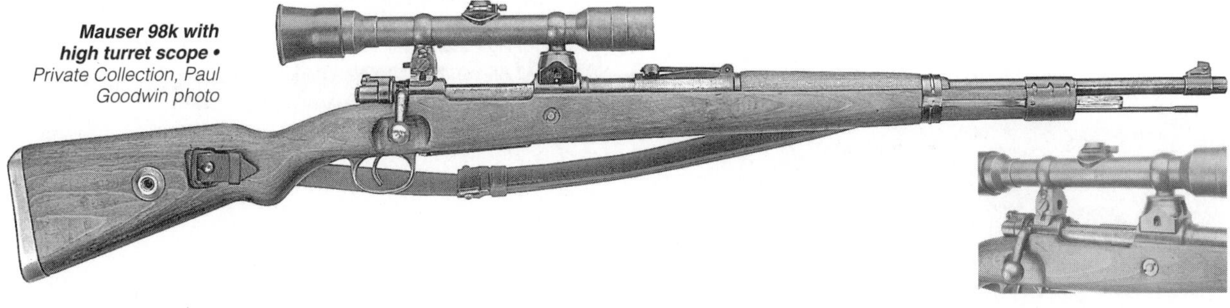

Mauser 98k with high turret scope • *Private Collection, Paul Goodwin photo*

Mauser 98k Short Rail Sniper Rifle •
Courtesy Amoskeag Auction Company

greater in the front base cone than the low turret mount. Thus the distinguishing feature in these sniper rifles is the mount, although high-quality German-made scopes will bring a premium.

Exc.	***V.G.***	***Good***	***Fair***	***Poor***
12500	7500	5000	2000	1000

Model 98k Sniper Rifle (Low Turret Model)

As above but with a lower front base cone than the high turret mount.

Courtesy Rock Island Auction Company

Exc.	***V.G.***	***Good***	***Fair***	***Poor***
12500	7500	5000	2000	1000

Model K98k Sniper Rifle (Short Rail System)

This mounting system was originally intended for police use during the mid-1930s. Beginning in 1941 this mounting was adopted for general combat use with 98k rifles. Ajack, Zeiss, Hensoldt, and Kahles in 4x are the often-encountered scopes on these mounts. Some of these short rail models were produced specifically for the Waffen-SS and these will command a considerable premium for correctly marked rifles and scopes.

Exc.	***V.G.***	***Good***	***Fair***	***Poor***
8000	5000	3000	2000	1000

Model K98k Sniper Rifle (Long Rail System)

This mounting system was not utilized in the German military until 1944. This system required that the 98k rifle be modified by having an enlarged receiver flat machined to accommodate the mounting base. This receiver flat has three large tapped screw holes and two smaller holes for tapered pins. It should be noted that these are very valuable and collectable rifles that are subject to fakes. Consult an expert prior to a purchase.

Exc.	***V.G.***	***Good***	***Fair***	***Poor***
12500	7500	5000	2000	1000

Model K98k Sniper Rifle (Claw Mount System)

According to Senich about 10,000 "bnz" code 98k rifles were produced with claw mounts from late in 1943 to 1944. Various 4x scopes were used on these mounts but the most often encountered is the Hensoldt, Wetzlar (code "bmj"). Original issue rifles will have the rifle, base, and scope with matching numbers.

Exc.	***V.G.***	***Good***	***Fair***	***Poor***
12500	7500	5000	2000	1000

Model K98k Sniper Rifle (ZF41)

This version of the 98k is fitted with a ZF41 scope (1.5x). It is not, in the true sense of the word, a

Mauser 98k Short Rail Sniper Rifle •
Courtesy Amoskeag Auction Company

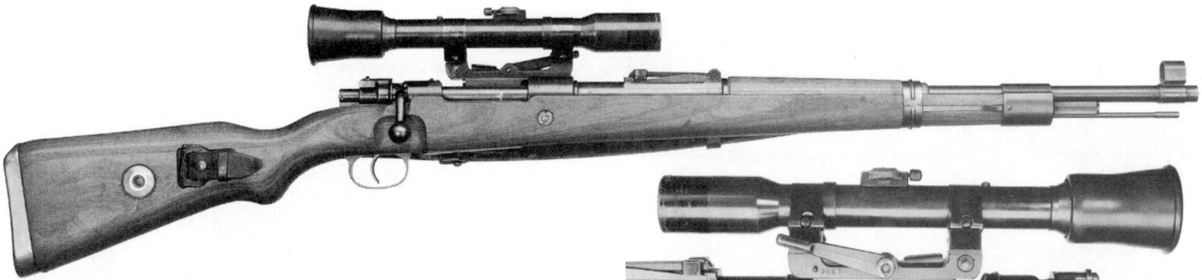

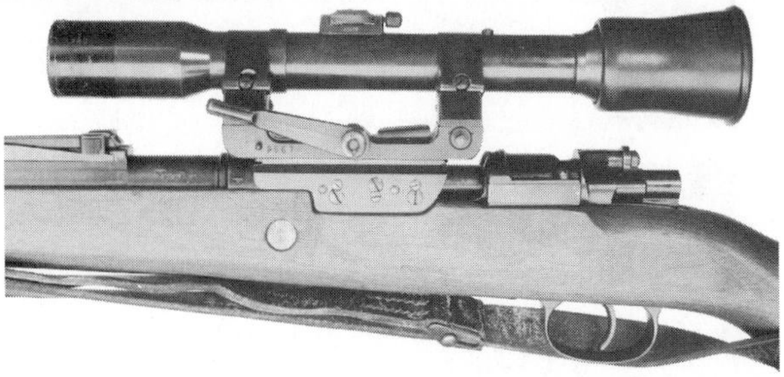

German "bcd4" Long Rail Sniper. This is the blued variation with flat ground safety • *Courtesy Michael Wamsher, Paul Goodwin photo*

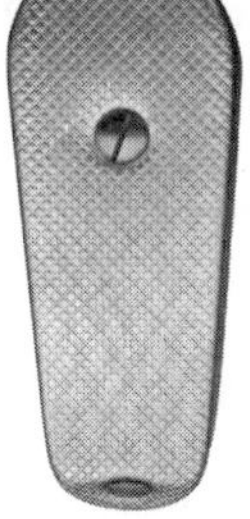

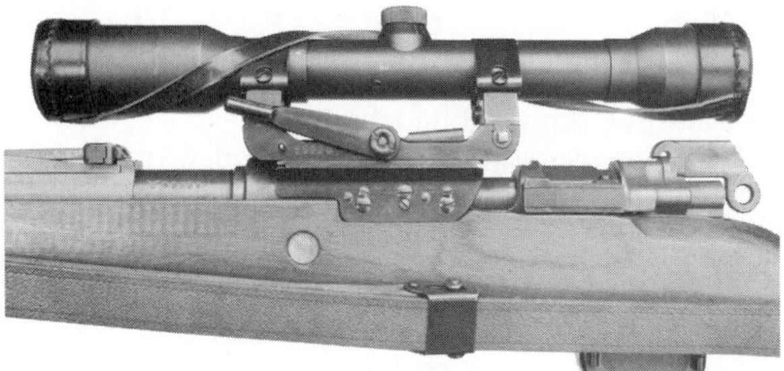

German "bcd4" Long Rail Sniper with later phosphate finish with "key" safety. Note the original checkered butt plate • *Courtesy Michael Wamsher, Paul Goodwin photo*

GERMANY

German "bcz" Single Claw Sniper Rifle. Hensold-Wetzar coded "bmj" scope with winter "t" • *Courtesy Rock Island Auction Company*

Mauser K98k with ZF41 scope • *Private Collection, Paul Goodwin photo*

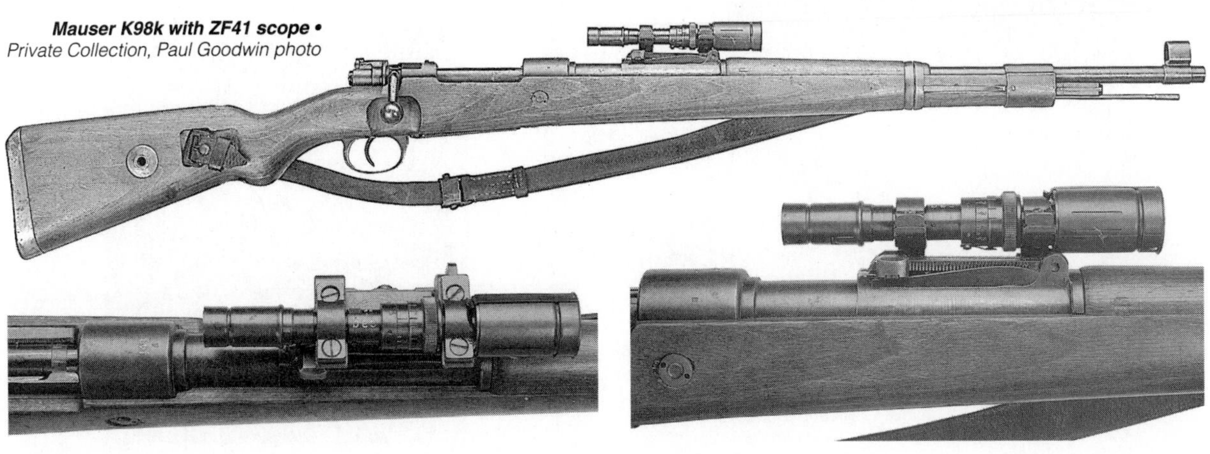

Model 1933 Standard Model • *Courtesy West Point Museum, Paul Goodwin photo*

GERMANY

sniper rifle but rather the scope is fitted as an aid to marksmanship. More than 300,000 were produced in this configuration between 1941 and 1945.

Exc.	*V.G.*	*Good*	*Fair*	*Poor*
3500	2500	1250	750	400

Model K98k Sniper Rifle (Dual Rail)

This sniper version is fitted with a dual rail scope mount. It is estimated that only about 25 of these rifles were built using this sight system.

Exc.	*V.G.*	*Good*	*Fair*	*Poor*
Too Rare To Price				

Model 1933 Standard Model Short Rifle

Introduced in 1933 and fitted with a 23.6-inch barrel full stock with pistol grip and finger grooves in forend. Short upper handguard. Weight is about 8.75 lbs. Used extensively by the German Condor Legion in the Spanish Civil War, 1936 to 1939. Stamped with Mauser banner on receiver ring with date of manufacture.

Exc.	*V.G.*	*Good*	*Fair*	*Poor*
1200	900	750	350	250

Model 1933 Standard Model Carbine

Similar to the Model 98k but forearm has finger grooves. Mauser banner stamped on top of receiver ring with date of manufacture. Weight is about 8.5 lbs.

Exc.	*V.G.*	*Good*	*Fair*	*Poor*
1250	1000	800	400	300

Model 33/40 Carbine

This carbine was made in Brno in Czechoslovakia during World War II after it was occupied by the German army. This model featured a laminated stock with full upper handguard. Fitted with a 19.2" barrel and marked "G. 33/40" together with the year of production and the maker's code. Marked "dot" over the date or "945" over the date. Weight is about 8 lbs.

Model 33/40 • *Courtesy West Point Museum, Paul Goodwin photo*

Waffen SS and their Gew 33/40 rifles • *Courtesy Paul S. Scarlata*

Exc.	V.G.	Good	Fair	Poor
1500	1000	850	400	250

Model 29/40 Rifle (G29o)

This rifle was built by Steyr for the German Luftwaffe. It has a bent bolt and an "L" marked stock. There is some confusion over the origins of this model and its correct designations and configurations. Consult an expert prior to a sale.

Exc.	V.G.	Good	Fair	Poor
1000	800	500	300	200

Model 24 (t) Rifle

This is the German version of the Czech VZ24 rifle built during the German occupation of that country during WWII.

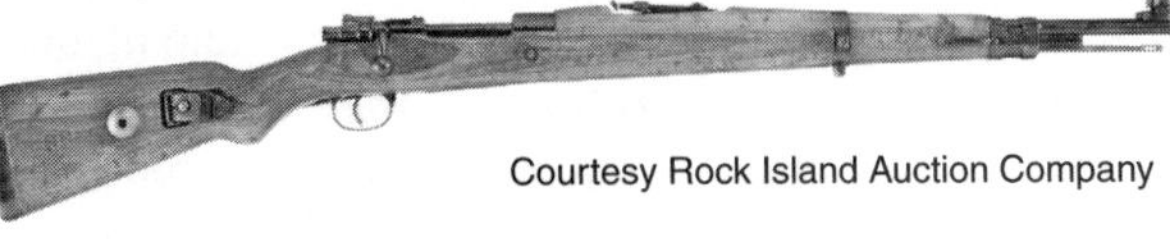

Courtesy Rock Island Auction Company

Exc.	V.G.	Good	Fair	Poor
950	750	500	250	150

Model VG-98

These are crude half-stocked 7.92mm weapons produced near the end of the war to arm the German population. Barrel length is about 21inches and some use a 10-round magazine while other examples are single shot. Weight is about 7 lbs. It is made from parts of older, often unserviceable Mausers. Will command premium prices.

Exc.	V.G.	Good	Fair	Poor
9000	6000	4000	1800	1000

Model VG-1 (Volksturm Gewehr)

This rifle was made in the last days of WWII and is crudely made. It used the magazine of a semi-automatic Model 43 rifle. Beware of firing this weapon. It is roughly made but because of historical interest and high demand, prices command a premium.

Exc.	V.G.	Good	Fair	Poor
9000	7500	5500	3000	1500

Model VG-2

Chambered for the 7.9mm cartridge and fitted with a 10-round G43 magazine. This bolt action rifle has a 21-inch barrel with no bayonet lug. Cheaply built. Receiver is a "U" shaped stamping. Rare.

Exc.	V.G.	Good	Fair	Poor
9000	7500	5500	3000	1500

Model VG-5

Another last-ditch, locally produced rifle made at the very end of World War II. Chambered for the 7.92x33mm Kurz cartridge. Stamped receiver. Magazine is MP44 type. Simply and roughly made.

Exc.	V.G.	Good	Fair	Poor
20000	15000	10000	5000	3000

Model 1918 Anti-Tank Rifle

Chambered for the 13x92SR cartridge, this was the first Mauser anti-tank rifle. Barrel length is 39 inches and weight is about 37 lbs. The Mauser banner is stamped on the upper receiver over the date "1918." Used successfully by the Germans against Allied tanks during WWI.

Exc.	V.G.	Good	Fair	Poor
7500	6000	5000	3500	2000

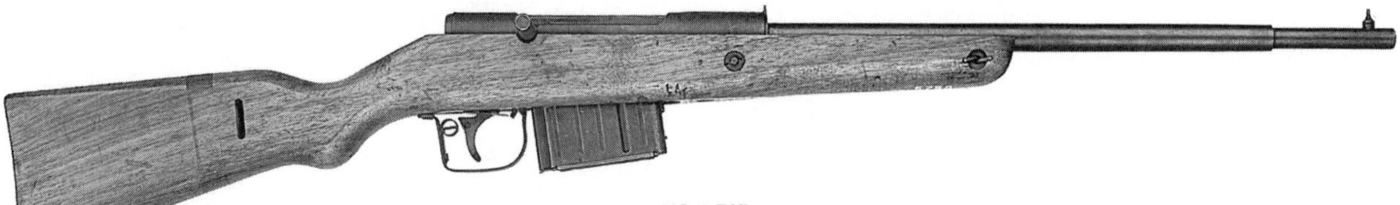

VG-1 Rifle •
Courtesy West Point Museum, Paul Goodwin photo

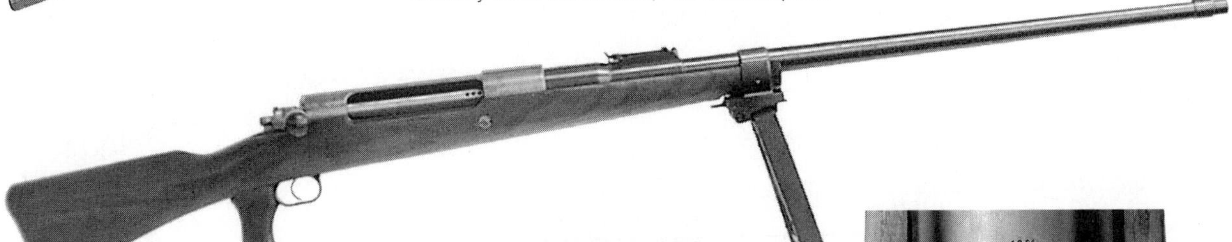

Model 1918 Anti-Tank Rifle •
Courtesy Amoskeag Auction Company

GERMAN WWII MILITARY RIFLES

Model G 41 Rifle(M)

First produced in 1941. Built by Mauser (code S42). Not a successful design and very few of these rifles were produced. These are extremely rare rifles today. Chambered for the 7.92mm Mauser cartridge. semi-automatic gas operated with rotating bolt. It was full stocked with a 10-round box magazine. Barrel length is 21.5 inches and weight is about 11 lbs. The total produced of this model is estimated at 20,000 rifles.

Courtesy Richard M. Kumor Sr.

Exc.	*V.G.*	*Good*	*Fair*	*Poor*
9500	8000	6500	4000	1800

Model G 41(W)

Similar to the above model but designed by Walther and produced by "duv" (Berlin-Lubeck Machine Factory) in 1941. This rifle was contracted for 70,000 units in 1942 and 1943. Correct examples will command a premium price.

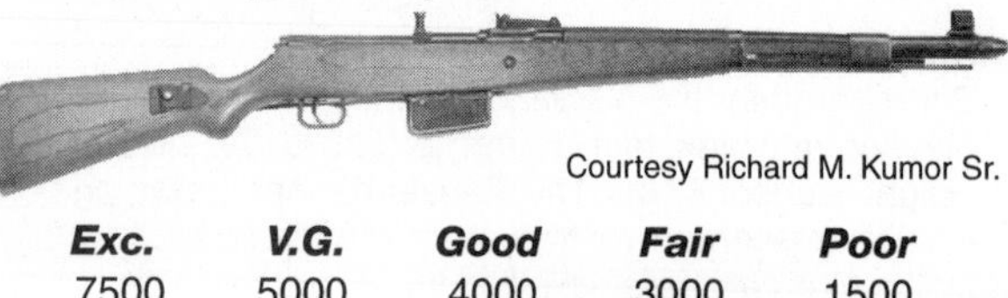

Courtesy Richard M. Kumor Sr.

Exc.	*V.G.*	*Good*	*Fair*	*Poor*
7500	5000	4000	3000	1500

Model G 43(W) (K43)

An improved version of the G 41(W), introduced in 1943, with a modified gas system that was the more typical gas and piston design. Built by Carl Walther (code "ac"). Full stocked with full-length handguard. Laminated Wood stock. Receiver has a dovetail for telescope sight on the right side. Barrel length is 22 inches and magazine capacity is 10 rounds. Weight is approximately 9.5 lbs. It is estimated that some 500,000 of these rifles were produced. Used by German sharpshooters during World War II and also by the Czech army after WWII.

Exc.	*V.G.*	*Good*	*Fair*	*Poor*
2500	1750	1000	800	500

Model G 43(W) (K43) Sniper Rifle

A G-43 or K-43 issued with a ZF-4 scope and mount.

Exc.	*V.G.*	*Good*	*Fair*	*Poor*
6000	5000	4000	3000	2000

Model FG 42 (Fallschirmjager Gewehr)

This select fire 7.92x57mm rifle was adopted by the Luftwaffe for its airborne troops. It was designed to replace the rifle, light machine gun, and submachine gun. It incorporates a number of features including straight line stock and muzzle brake, reduced recoil mechanism, closed-bolt semi-automatic fire, and open-bolt full-auto fire. Rate of fire is about 750 rounds per minute. It had a mid-barrel bipod on early (1st Models, Type "E") models and front mounted barrel bipod on later (2nd Models, Type "G") models. Barrel attachment

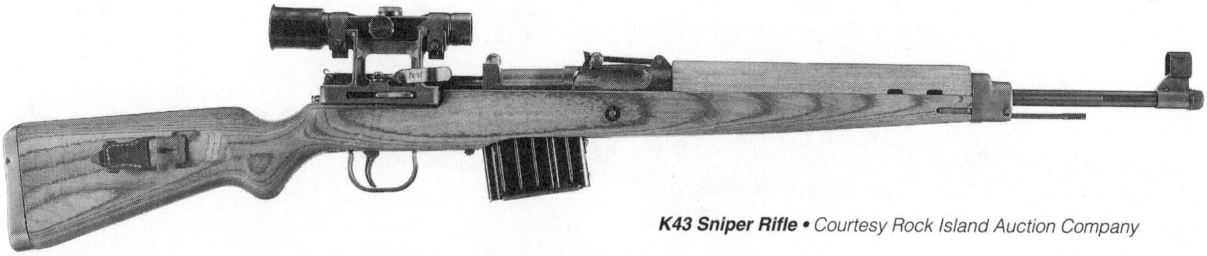

K43 Sniper Rifle • *Courtesy Rock Island Auction Company*

Model G 43 left side with receiver markings, note rough finish • *Paul Goodwin photo*

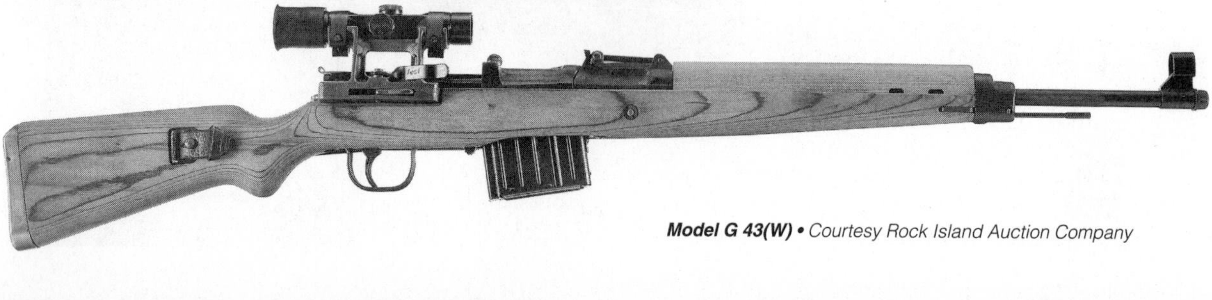

Model G 43(W) • *Courtesy Rock Island Auction Company*

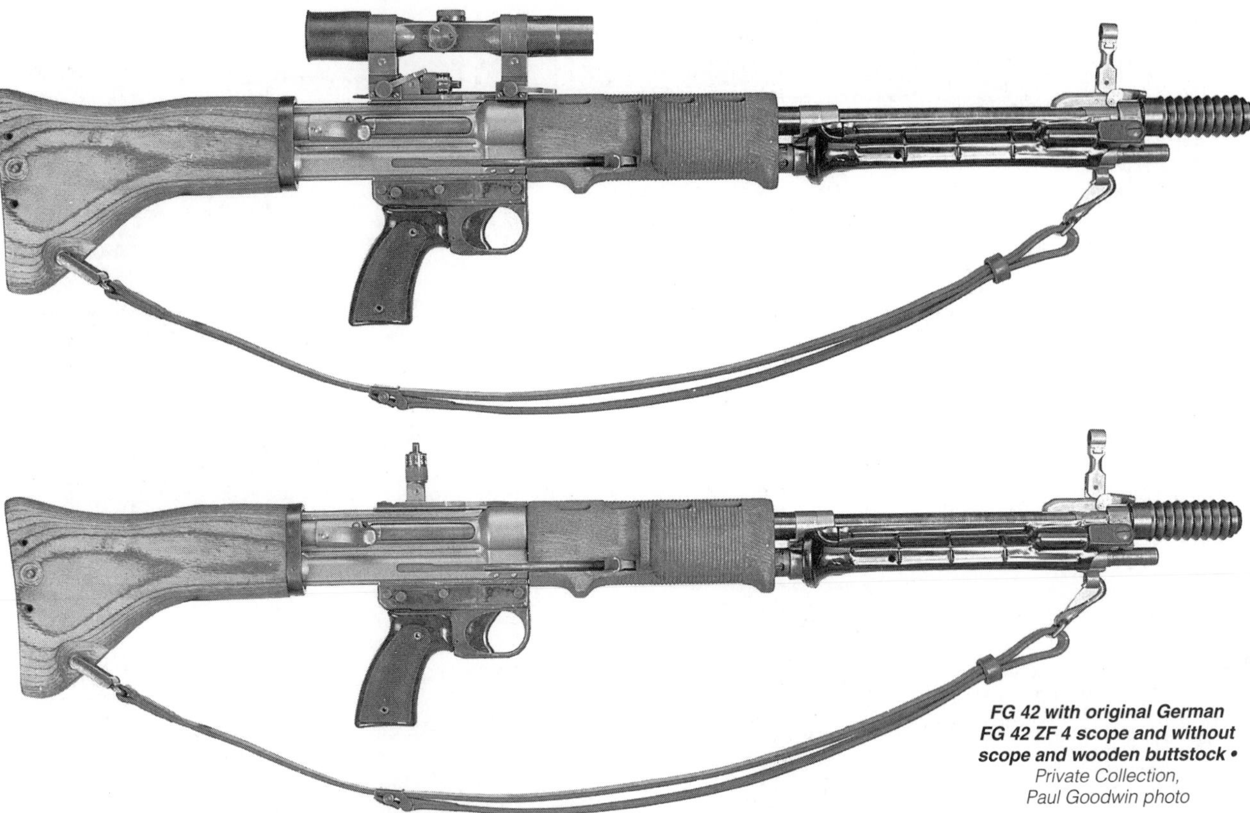

FG 42 with original German FG 42 ZF 4 scope and without scope and wooden buttstock • *Private Collection, Paul Goodwin photo*

for pike-style bayonet. First Models were fitted with steel buttstocks, sharply raked pistol grips, and 2nd Models with wooden stocks and more vertical pistol grips. The 20-round magazine is left side mounted. Fitted with a 21.5-inch barrel, the rifle weighs about 9.5 lbs. This breech mechanism was to be used years later by the U.S. in its M60 machine gun.

Pre-1968

Exc.	*V.G.*	*Fair*
45000	35000	25000

NOTE: For rifles fitted with original German FG 42 scopes add between $5,000 and $10,000 depending on model. Consult an expert prior to a purchase.

STURMGEWEHR GROUP

Because the German military thought the 7.92x57mm cartridge too powerful for its needs, a new cartridge was developed to provide less recoil, lighter weight, and less expensive production. This new cartridge, developed in the mid 1930s by Gustav Genschow, Polte, and others, was called the 7.92x33mm Kurtz (Short) cartridge. The entire cartridge was 1.89 inches in length and had a bullet weight of 125 grains. This new cartridge was introduced in 1943 and spawned a new series of firearms designed for that cartridge.

Bibliographical Note: For a complete and exhaustive account of the Sturmgewehr rifles see Hans-Dieter Handrich's ***Sturmgewehr: From Firepower to Striking Power***, Collector Grade Publications, 2004.

MKb42(W)

This select-fire open bolt machine carbine built by Walther was used on the Russian front. It was fitted with a 30-round box magazine and 16-inch barrel. Rate of fire was about 600 rounds per minute. It was fitted with a wooden stock and metal forearm. The rest of the weapon, with the exception of the barrel and bolt, was made from sheet metal to save cost and weight. Weight was about 9.75 lbs. A total of about 8,000 of these weapons were built by Walther. This model was not selected by the German Army because, according to Handrich's book, the front sight was too wide, and covered the target at 300m. The construction was too complex, which resulted in lack of reliability. Trigger pull was excessive for accurate fire.

Pre-1968 (Very Rare)

Exc.	*V.G.*	*Fair*
25000	18500	15000

GERMANY

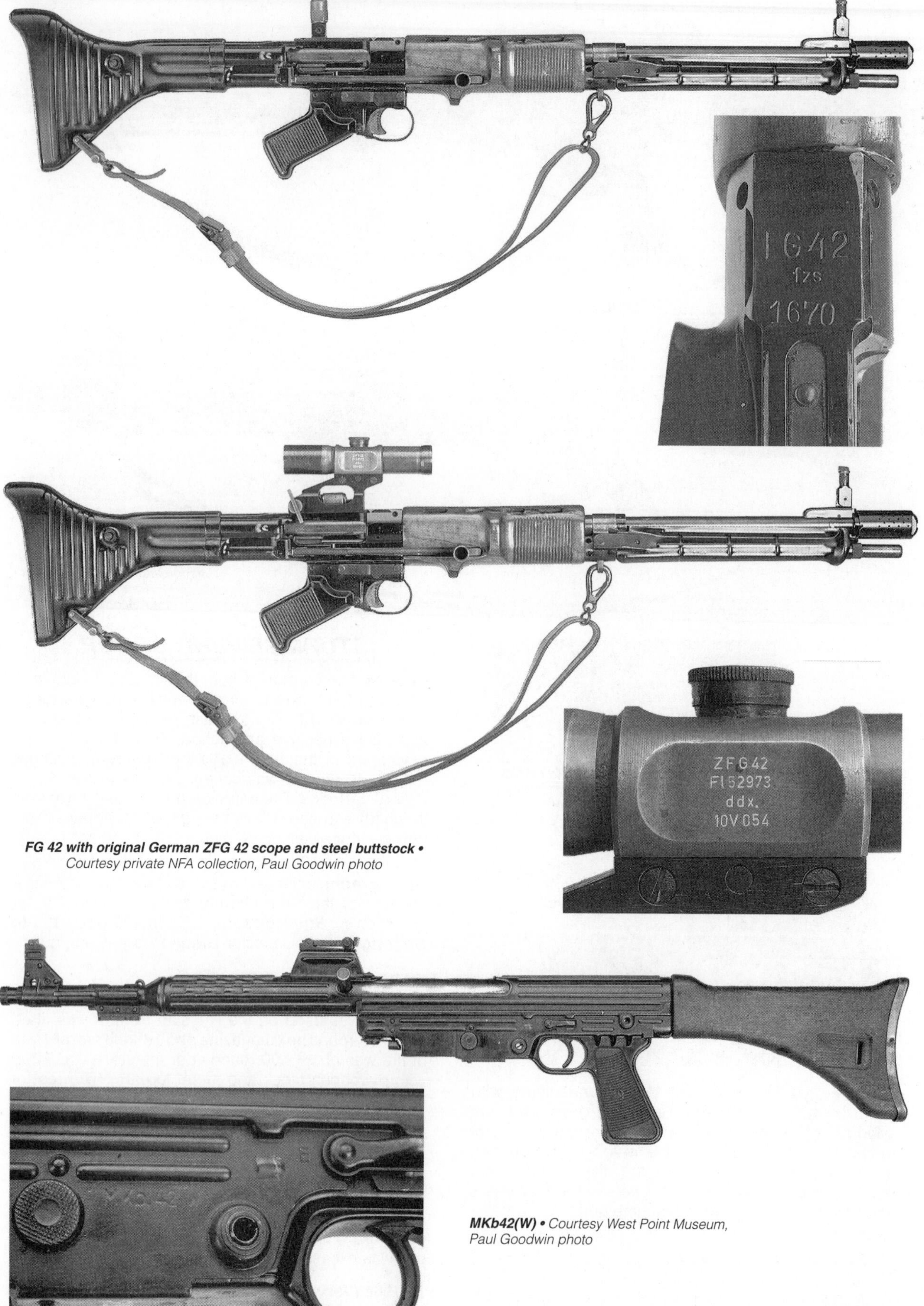

FG 42 with original German ZFG 42 scope and steel buttstock • *Courtesy private NFA collection, Paul Goodwin photo*

***MKb42(W)* •** *Courtesy West Point Museum, Paul Goodwin photo*

MKb42(H) • *Courtesy West Point Museum, Paul Goodwin photo*

MKb42(H)

This was a design similar to the Walther version (open bolt) except for a 14.5-inch barrel and other internal differences. It was built by Haenel, and also saw extensive use on the Eastern Front. This version proved to be better than the Walther design. Its rate of fire was a somewhat slower 500 rounds per minute. Weight was approximately 11 lbs. Some 8,000 of these weapons were also produced. Handrich states that the advantages of the Haenel model were simple, reliable construction, greater sight radius for more accurate fire, good front sight, and uniform trigger pull.

NOTE: Some MKb42(H) rifles had bayonet lugs while others did not. All of these rifles were fitted with mounting rails for a telescope sight.

Pre-1968

Exc.	*V.G.*	*Fair*
25000	18500	12500

MP43 • *Paul Goodwin photo*

DEWAT MP44 • *Courtesy Amoskeag Auction Company*

MP43, MP43/1

With some redesign this model was a newer MKb42(H). This weapon was adopted by the Waffenamt as standard issue in 1944. Originally built by Haenel, it was later produced by Mauser and Erma. This model was the forerunner of the MP44 and StG44. The MP43 had a stepped barrel while the MP43/1 had a straight barrel.

Pre-1968

Exc.	V.G.	Fair
18500	14500	9500

Pre-1986 manufacture with new receiver or re-weld

Exc.	V.G.	Fair
7500	5500	4000

MP44

This German automatic rifle was first produced in 1943 and chambered for the 7.92x33 Kurz cartridge. Fitted with a solid stock and 16.3" barrel, it has a magazine capacity of 30 rounds. The rate of fire is 500 rounds per minute. Weight is about 11.5 lbs. Marked "mp44" on top of the receiver. Production ceased in 1945. This rifle was used extensively on the Eastern Front during World War II.

Pre-1968

Exc.	V.G.	Fair
18500	15000	13000

Pre-1986 manufacture with new receiver or re-weld

Exc.	V.G.	Fair
7500	6500	5500

StG44

This version of the MP43-MP44 series is nothing more than a name change from the MP44.

Pre-1968

Exc.	V.G.	Fair
18500	15000	12500

Pre-1986 manufacture with new receiver or re-weld

Exc.	V.G.	Fair
7500	6500	5000

Stg44 & G43 in combat • Courtesy Paul S. Scarlata

Model 86 SR

Introduced in 1993, this bolt action 7.62 NATO is sometimes referred to as the Specialty Rifle. Fitted with a laminated wood and special match thumbhole stock or fiberglass stock with adjustable cheekpiece. Stock has rail in forearm and an adjustable recoil pad. Magazine capacity is 9 rounds. Finish is a non-glare blue. The barrel length with muzzle brake is 28.8 inches. Many special features are found on this rifle, from adjustable trigger weight to silent safety. Mauser offers many options on this rifle as well that will affect the price. Weight is approximately 11 lbs.

NIB	Exc.	V.G.	Good	Fair	Poor
3300	2950	2500	1750	1250	750

Model 93 SR

Introduced in 1996, this is a tactical semi-automatic rifle chambered for the .300 Win. Mag. or the .338 Lapua cartridge. Barrel length is 25.5 inches with an overall length of 48.4 inches. Barrel is fitted with a muzzle brake. Magazine capacity is 6 rounds for .300 and 5 rounds for .338 caliber. Weight is approximately 13 lbs.

NIB	Exc.	V.G.	Good	Fair	Poor
N/A	—	—	—	—	—

HECKLER & KOCH

HK G3

Courtesy Heckler & Koch

First adopted by the German army in 1959. Chambered for the 7.62x51mm cartridge and fitted with a 17.5-inch barrel. Solid wooden stock on early models and plastic stock on later models (A3). Folding stock (A2) also offered. Magazine capacity is 20 rounds with a rate of fire of 550 rounds per minute. Weight is about 9.7 lbs. Marked "G3 HK" on left side of magazine housing. This select-fire rifle has seen service with as many as 60 military forces around the world. There are several variations of this model.

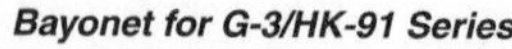

Bayonet for G-3/HK-91 Series

Model 94

Pre-1968

Exc.	V.G.	Fair
15000	14000	9000

Pre-1986 conversions of semi-automatic version

Exc.	V.G.	Fair
8500	7500	7000

Bayonet for G-3/HK-91 series

Ribbed round plastic handle. Latch stud in back of pommel inserts into the plug adapter below the front sight. Muzzle ring. 6.5-inch double edge blade. Plastic scabbard with simulated wood grain appearance. Price range 150 – 50.

Model 91

This rifle is recoil-operated, with a delayed-roller lock bolt. It is chambered for the .308 Winchester cartridge and has a 17.7-inch barrel with military-style aperture sights. It is furnished with a 20-round detachable magazine and is finished in matte black with a black plastic stock. This model is a semi-automatic version of the select fire G3 rifle.

Exc.	V.G.	Good	Fair	Poor
2750	2300	1550	1200	800

Model 91 A3

This model is simply the Model 91 with a retractable metal stock.

Exc.	V.G.	Good	Fair	Poor
3000	2500	1600	1300	900

Model 93

This model is similar to the Model 91 except that it is chambered for the .223 cartridge and has a 16.4-inch barrel. The magazine holds 25 rounds, and the specifications are the same as for the Model 91. This is a semi-automatic version of the select fire HK33 rifle.

Exc.	V.G.	Good	Fair	Poor
2750	2300	1500	1200	800

Model 93 A3

This is the Model 93 with the retractable metal stock.

Exc.	V.G.	Good	Fair	Poor
3000	2500	1650	1300	900

Model 94

This is a carbine version chambered for the 9mm Parabellum cartridge, with a 16.5" barrel. It is a smaller-scaled weapon that has a 15-shot magazine.

Exc.	V.G.	Good	Fair	Poor
3850	3300	2750	2200	1500

Model 94 A3

This model is a variation of the Model 94 with the addition of a retractable metal stock.

Exc.	V.G.	Good	Fair	Poor
3900	3400	2900	2300	1500

HK 33

This model is a reduced caliber version of the standard HK G3. First produced in 1968 this model is chambered for the 5.56x45mm NATO cartridge (.223 caliber). This rifle is available in several variants, namely a sniper version with set trigger, telescope sight and bipod; a retractable stock version (A3); and a carbine version (12.68"). The HK 33 features a 15.35-inch barrel without flash hider, and a magazine capacity of 25 or 40 rounds. The rate of fire is 750 rounds per minute.

HK 33 K • Courtesy Heckler & Koch

Model 94 A3

The rifle is marked "HK 33 5.56MM" with serial number on the left side of the magazine housing. The rifle is still in production and is in service in Chile, Brazil, various countries in southeast Asia, and Africa. Weight is approximately 8 lbs. for standard model.

Pre-1968

Exc.	*V.G.*	*Fair*
18500	15000	12000

Pre-1986 conversions of semi-automatic version

Exc.	*V.G.*	*Fair*
8500	8000	N/A

NOTE: The HK 33 K is the same as the HK 33 with the exception of a 13" barrel. Prices may differ slightly for the HK 33 K version.

HK G41

First produced in 1983, this 5.56x45mm chambered select-fire rifle is fitted with a 17.5-inch barrel and has a magazine capacity of 30 rounds. Rate of fire is about 850 rounds per minute. Marked "HK G41 5.56MM" on the left side of the magazine housing. This model will accept M16 magazines. This model is also available with fixed or retractable stock. Weight is 9.7 lbs. No known examples in the U.S.

HK G41 • Courtesy Heckler & Koch

Pre-1968

Exc.	*V.G.*	*Fair*
N/A	N/A	N/A

PSG-1

This rifle is a high-precision sniping rifle that features the delayed-roller semi-automatic action. It is chambered for the 7.62 NATO (.308 Winchester) cartridge and has a 5-shot magazine. Barrel length is 25.6 inches. It is furnished with a complete array of accessories including a 6x42-power illuminated Hensoldt scope. Rifle weighs 17.8 lbs.

NIB	*Exc.*	*V.G.*	*Good*	*Fair*	*Poor*
14500	12500	9000	7500	6000	4000

SHOTGUNS

SAUER, J.P. & SON

Luftwaffe Survival Drilling

A double barrel 12 gauge by 9.3x74R combination shotgun/rifle with 28-inch barrels. Blued with a checkered walnut stock and marked with Nazi

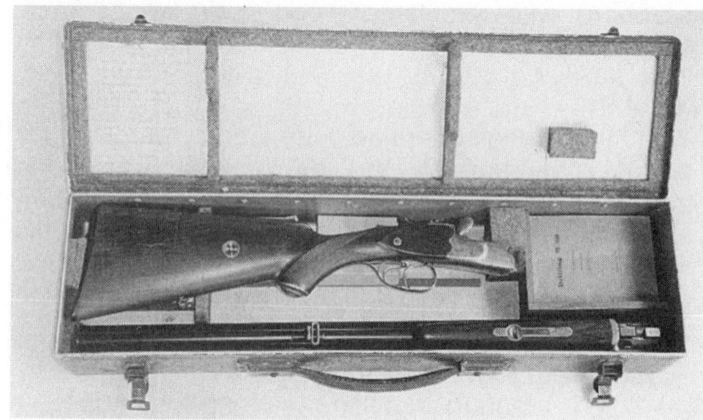

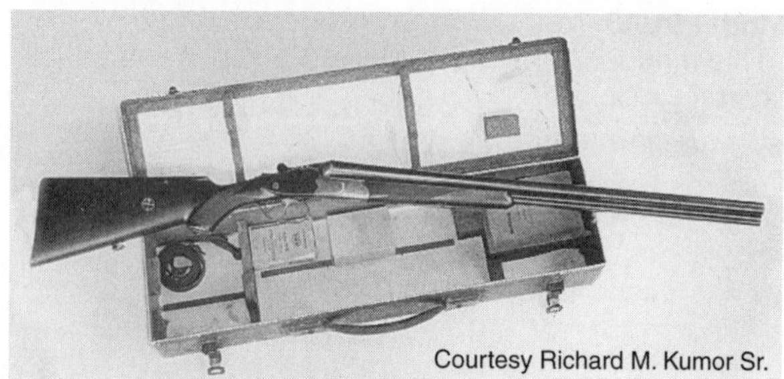

Courtesy Richard M. Kumor Sr.

Model PSG-1

inspection. Stampings on the stock and barrel breech. Normally furnished with an aluminum case.

Exc.	***V.G.***	***Good***	***Fair***	***Poor***
6000	5500	3800	2500	—

NOTE: Add 50 percent to prices for case.

MACHINE GUNS

Germany adopted the Maxim gun and designated it the MG 01, which was built on the Belgian Maxim pattern Model 1900. It was not until 1908 that Germany produced its own version of the Maxim called the MG 08.

Bibliographical Note: For information on a wide variety of German machine guns, see Daniel D. Musgrave, ***German Machineguns***, 2nd edition, Ironside International Publishers, 1992. Also Folke Myrvang, M***G 34-MG42, German Universal Machineguns***, Collector Grade Publications, 2002. Dolf L. Goldsmith, ***The Devil's Paintbrush***, (the Maxim Gun) Collector Grade Publications, 2002.

Maxim '08 (MG 08)

Germany adopted this gun at the turn of the 20th century. In 1908 they began to produce the gun themselves. This was the standard German heavy machine gun during WWI. Chambered for the 7.92x57mm cartridge this gun had a rate of fire of 400 to 500 rounds per minute from its 28-inch barrel. It

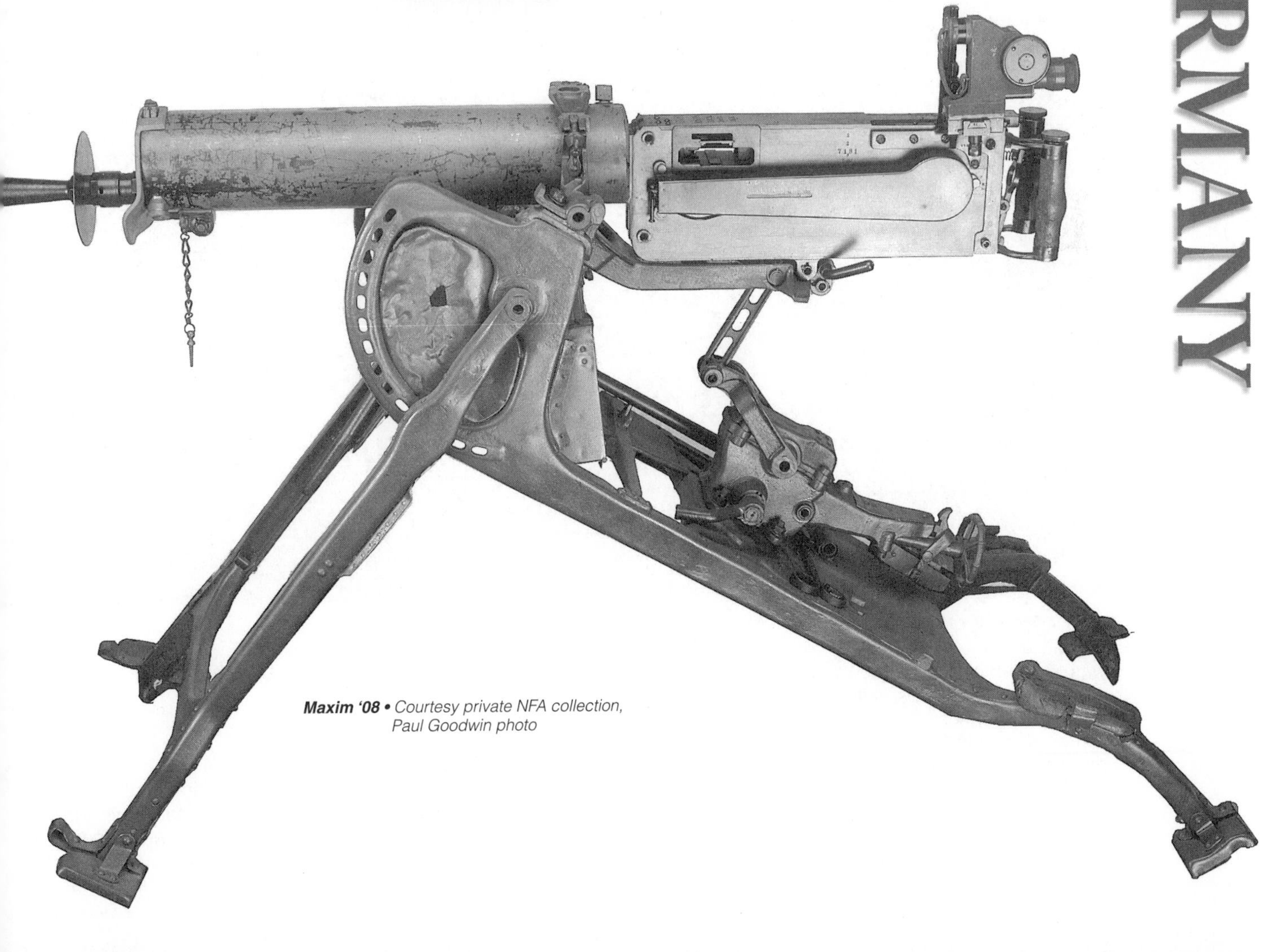

Maxim '08 • *Courtesy private NFA collection, Paul Goodwin photo*

MG 08/15 • *Courtesy West Point Museum, Paul Goodwin photo*

MG 08/15 September 1939 in Poland • *Courtesy Blake Stevens, The Devil's Paintbrush, Collector Grade Publications*

was fed with a 100- or 250-round fabric belt. The gun weighed about 41 lbs. with a sled mount weighing about 83 pounds. The gun was marked "deutche waffen und munitionsfabriken berlin" with the year of production on the left side of the receiver. The serial number was located on the top of the receiver. The gun was produced from 1908 to about 1918.

Pre-1968

Exc.	*V.G.*	*Fair*
25000	18000	15000

Pre-1986 manufacture with new side plate

Exc.	*V.G.*	*Fair*
15000	10000	N/A

Maxim '08/15

A more movable version of the Maxim Model '08. Chambered for the 7.92x57mm Mauser cartridge and fitted with a 28-inch water-cooled barrel with bipod, it weighs about 31 lbs. It is fed by a 100-round cloth belt housed inside of a special drum with a rate of

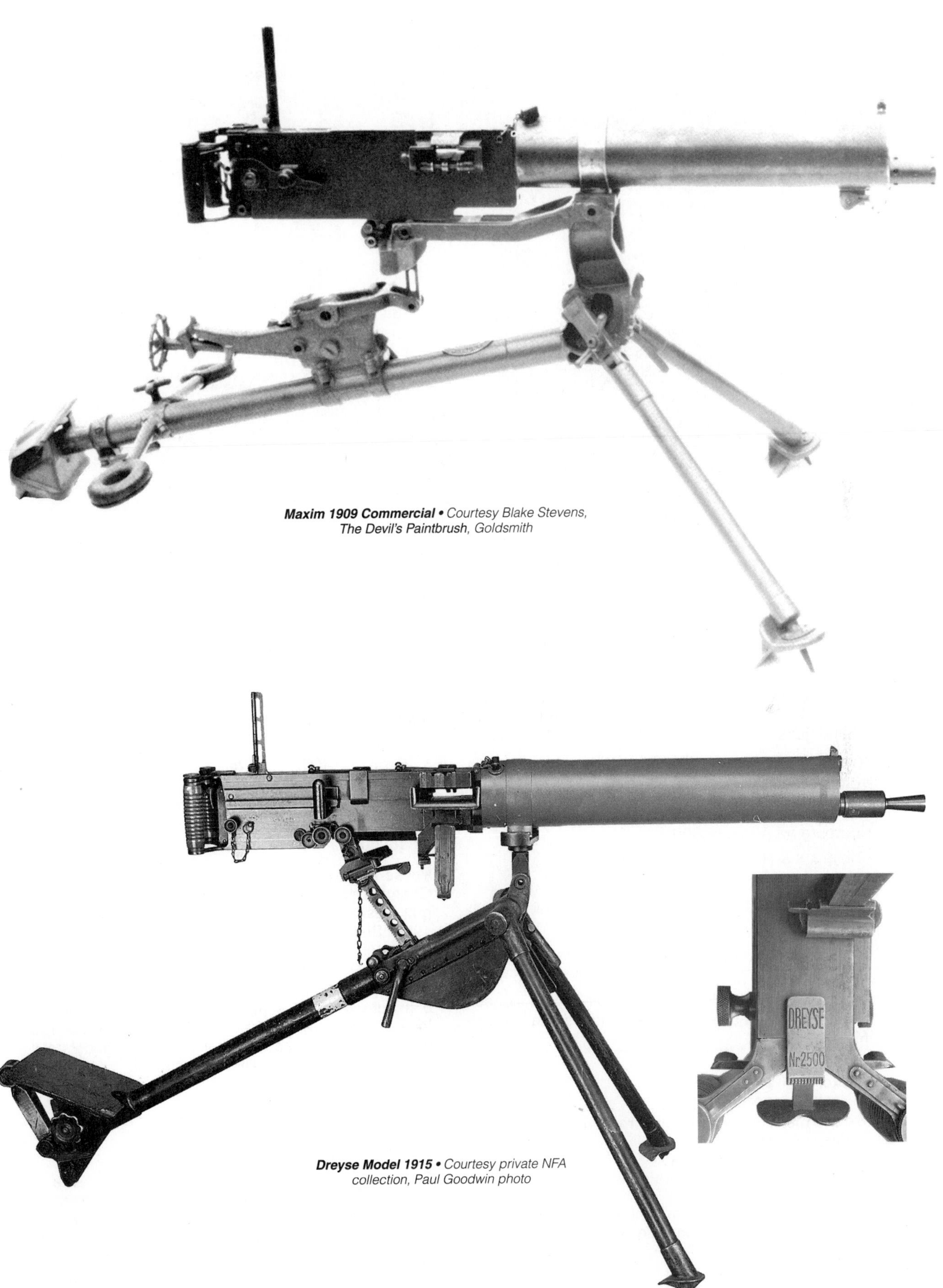

Maxim 1909 Commercial • *Courtesy Blake Stevens, The Devil's Paintbrush, Goldsmith*

Dreyse Model 1915 • *Courtesy private NFA collection, Paul Goodwin photo*

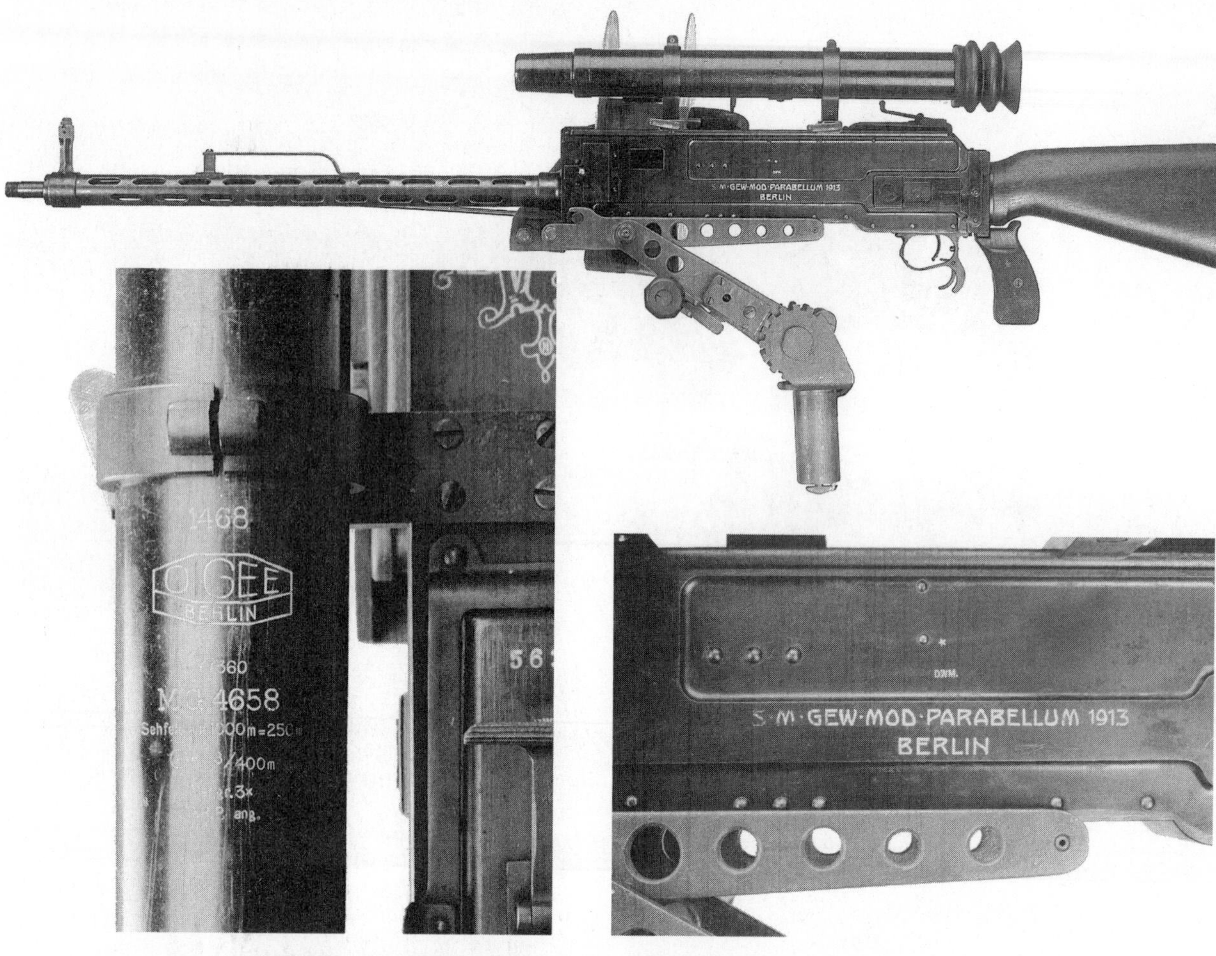

Parabellum with original scope • *Courtesy private NFA collection, Paul Goodwin photo*

fire of 500 rounds per minute. Marked "LMG 09/15 SPANDAU" on top of the receiver. Spandau produced 50,000 guns.

Other manufacturers of the gun were:

- Erfurt–33,000
- Maschinen Fabrik Augsburg,

Nurnburg (M.A.N.)–14,000

- Siemens & Halske (S&H)–13,000
- J.P. Sauer & Sohn, Suhl–11,000
- Rheinsche Maschinen & Metallwaren Fabrik
- (Rh.M. & M.F)–7,000
- Deutche Waffen und Munitions Fabriken (D.W. & M.F.)–2,000

Another version of this gun with an air-cooled slotted barrel jacket was used in aircraft and was called the IMG 08/15.

Pre-1968

Exc.	V.G.	Fair
18500	15000	12000

Pre-1986 manufacture with new receiver or re-weld

Exc.	V.G.	Fair
12500	10000	N/A

Model 1909

A DWM commercial version of the Model 1908 built for export. Fitted with a muzzle booster. Some were sent to Costa Rica as well as Brazil, Mexico, Romania, Switzerland, Belgium, China, and Persia. Some of these countries, like Switzerland and China, built their own military versions of the DWM 1909 commercial. A seldom-seen variation.

Pre-1968

Exc.	V.G.	Fair
22500	18000	12500

Pre-1986 manufacture with new receiver or re-weld

Exc.	V.G.	Fair
15000	11500	10500

Dreyse Model 1910/15

Chambered for the 7.92x57mm Mauser cartridge, this gun was based on the Louis Schmeisser patents of 1907. Built by Rheinmetall in Sommerda, Germany. Named in honor of Johann Niklaus von Dreyse who died in 1875. This is a water-cooled gun designed for sustained fire. Rate of fire is about 550 to 600 rounds a minute. Weight is approximately 37 lbs. Most of these guns were converted by Germany to MG 13s during the 1930s, so few original Dreyse models still survive. Very rare in unaltered condition.

Pre-1968

Exc.	V.G.	Fair
28000	25000	20000

Parabellum MG 14

Chambered for the 7.9mm cartridge, this was a water-cooled light machine gun. There was also an air-cooled version with a slotted water jacket. Barrel length is 27.75 inches. Rate of fire is about 700 rounds per minute. Weight is about 21.5 lbs. This gun was derived from the Maxim but the main spring is located behind the receiver and is compressed during recoil.

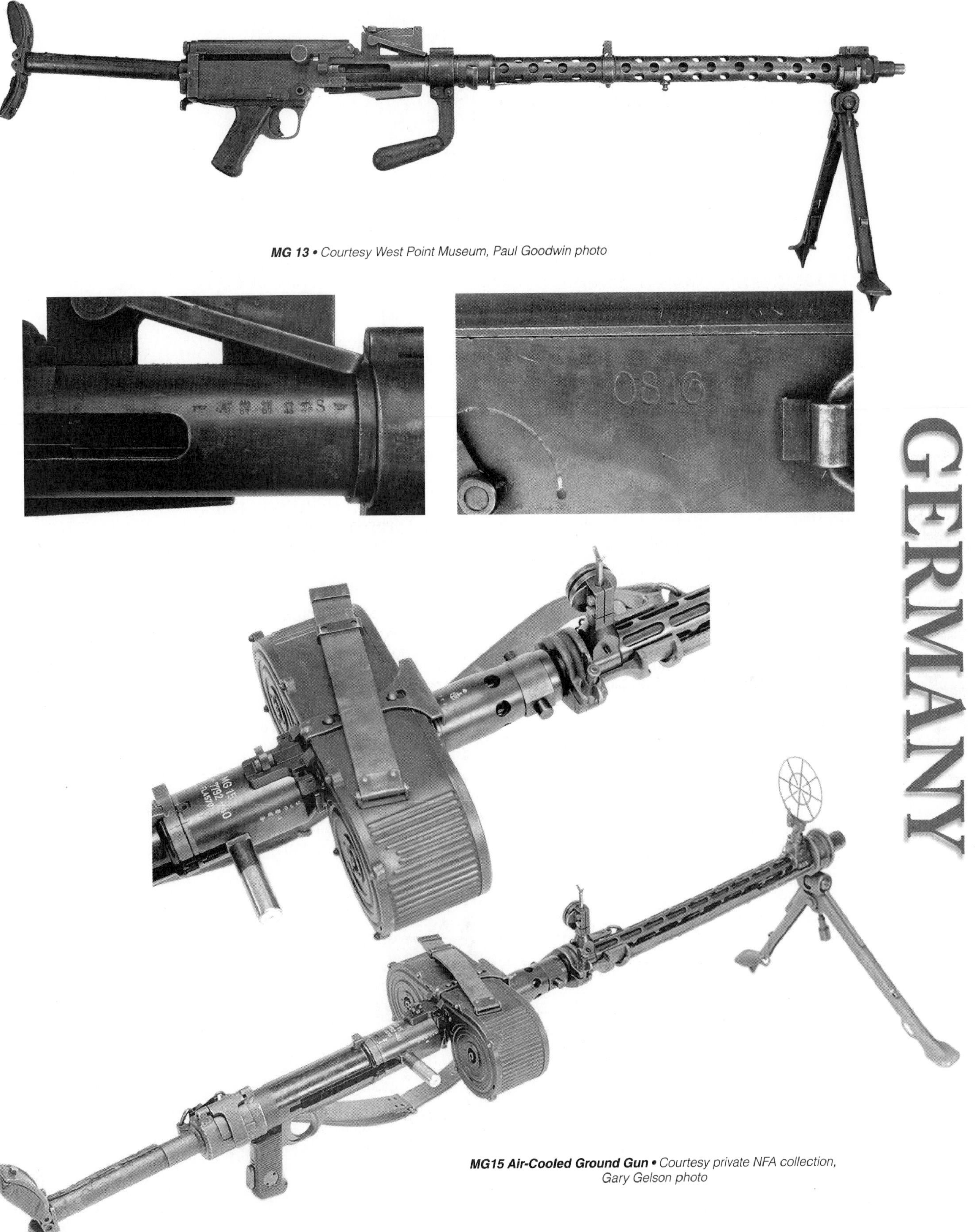

MG 13 • *Courtesy West Point Museum, Paul Goodwin photo*

MG15 Air-Cooled Ground Gun • *Courtesy private NFA collection, Gary Gelson photo*

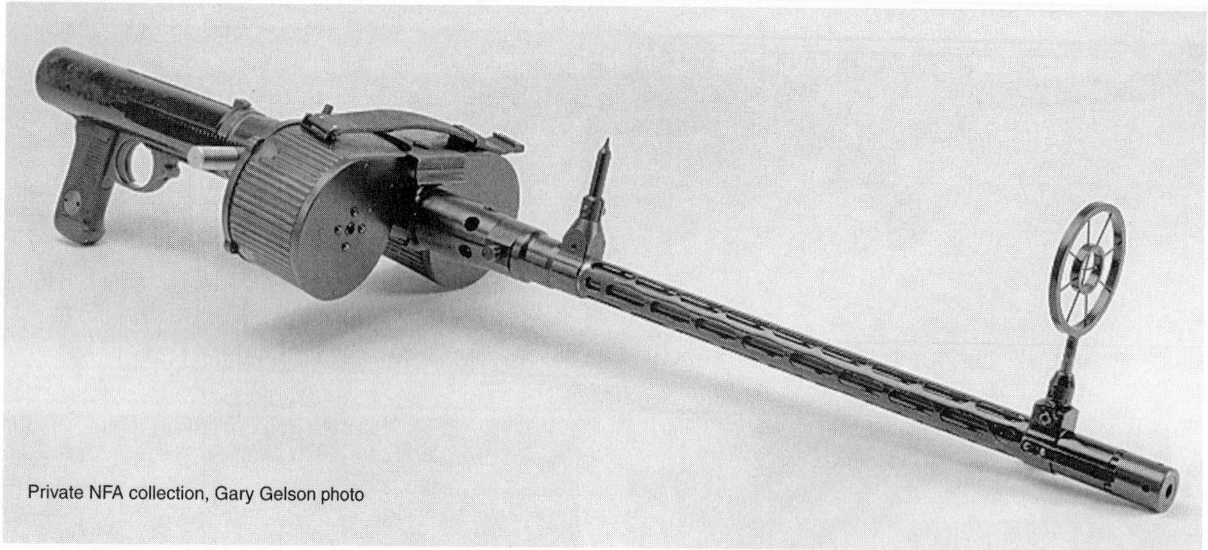

Private NFA collection, Gary Gelson photo

GERMANY

The gun was much lighter than the Maxim. Also, the Parabellum has no dead stop on the crank handle. The gun was the standard observer's machine gun in German two-seat aircraft during World War I. The gun was also used in Zeppelins as well as a ground gun. Built by DWM.

Pre-1968

Exc.	***V.G.***	***Fair***
Too Rare To Price.		

MG 13

In 1932 the German army adopted the MG 13 as its standard machine gun. Chambered for the 7.92x57mm cartridge and fitted with a 28-inch air-cooled barrel, this gun is recoil operated. The butt is a single arm metal type with pistol grip. The bipod is attached close to the muzzle. A 25-round box magazine or a 75-round saddle drum magazine can be used. Weight is about 25 lbs. with bipod. Who manufactured the gun is unclear, but Simson of Suhl, Germany, is often reported to be the manufacturer, perhaps because the company was the only legal machine gun manufacturer under the Versailles Treaty. Evidence suggests that the gun was made at Sommerda by Rheinmetall.

NOTE: The 75-round drum for use with the MG 13 is rare because it uses an MG15 drum with a special magazine extension to fit into the side of the MG 13 magazine well.

Pre-1968

Exc.	***V.G.***	***Fair***
22500	18500	15000

Pre-1986 manufacture with new receiver or re-weld

Exc.	***V.G.***	***Fair***
15000	13000	11000

MG15 Aircraft Gun

Used by the German air force in its bombers, this air-cooled gun is chambered for the 7.92x57JS cartridge. Rate of fire is about 850 rounds per minute. Barrel length is 28". Saddle drum magazine with 75-round capacity was used. Weight is about 28 lbs. Built by Krieghoff. Made by Rheinmetall beginning in 1932.

Pre-1968

Exc.	***V.G.***	***Fair***
20000	18000	16500

Pre-1986 manufacture with new receiver or re-weld

Exc.	***V.G.***	***Fair***
15000	13000	12000

Private NFA collection, Gary Gelson photo

MG15 Water-Cooled Ground Gun

A converted aircraft machine gun, this water-cooled model was used by ground forces from 1944 to 1945. Barrel length was 30 inches and weight is about 33 lbs. Chambered for the 7.92x57JS cartridge. Rate of fire is about 750 rounds per minute. Ammunition capacity is a 75-round saddle drum magazine. Built by Krieghoff.

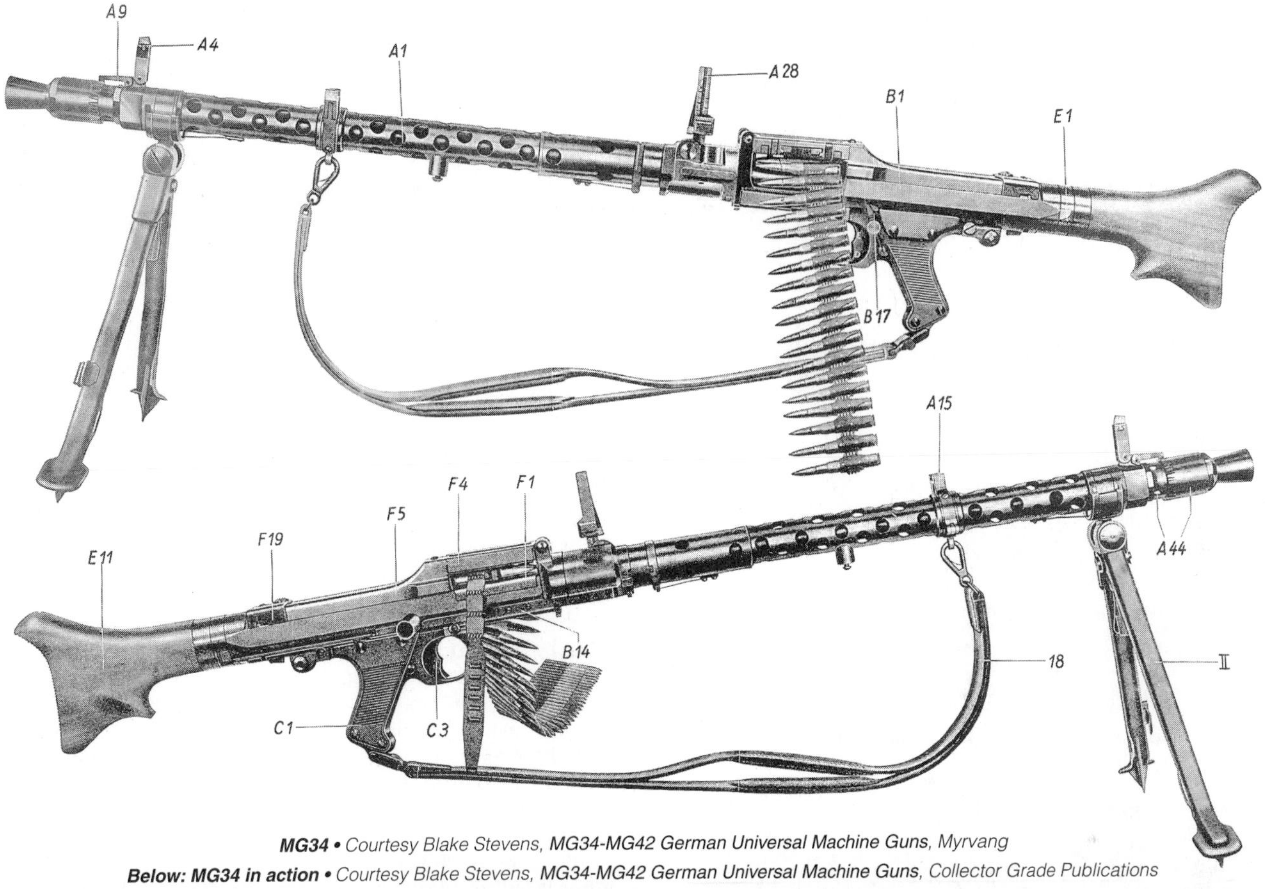

MG34 • *Courtesy Blake Stevens,* ***MG34-MG42 German Universal Machine Guns****, Myrvang*

Below: MG34 in action • *Courtesy Blake Stevens,* ***MG34-MG42 German Universal Machine Guns****, Collector Grade Publications*

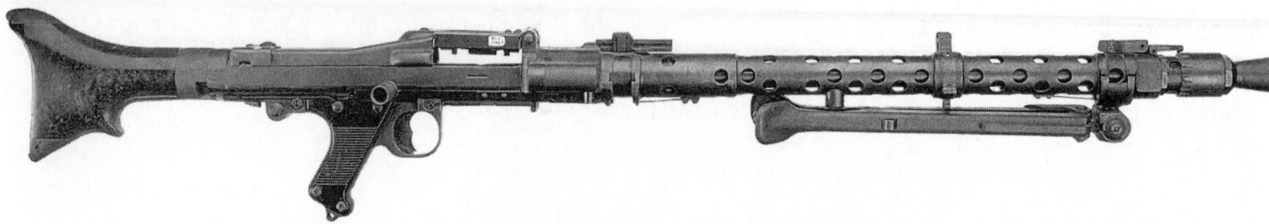

MG34 with receiver markings • *Paul Goodwin photo*

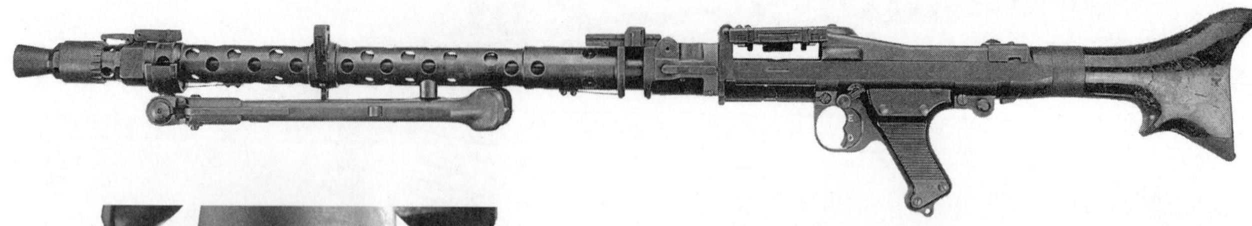

Pre-1968

Exc.	*V.G.*	*Fair*
22500	18000	15000

Pre-1986 manufacture with new receiver or re-weld

Exc.	*V.G.*	*Fair*
15000	13000	12000

MG15 Air-Cooled Ground Gun

Same as the aircraft gun but converted to ground use in 1944 and 1945 by attaching a bipod and single strut buttstock.

Pre-1968

Exc.	*V.G.*	*Fair*
25000	23000	21500

Pre-1986 manufacture with new receiver or re-weld

Exc.	*V.G.*	*Fair*
22000	20000	18500

MG34

Designed and built by Mauser, this was the first general purpose machine gun to be produced in large numbers. It was introduced into the German army in about 1936, and stayed in production until the end of the war in 1945. Chambered for the 7.92x57mm Mauser cartridge, this gun had a 25-inch barrel with a 50-round belt or 75-round saddle drum. Rate of fire was about 800 to 900 rounds per minute. Marked "MG34" with its serial number on top of the receiver. Weight was approximately 26.5 lbs. There were a number of different bipod and tripod mounts for this gun, as well as different gun configurations such as antiaircraft use, use in armored vehicles, and one configuration where only automatic fire was possible. After WWII the gun was used by the Czechs, French, and Israelis, as well as the Viet Cong. Superseded by the MG42.

Pre-1968

Exc.	*V.G.*	*Fair*
38000	35000	30000

Pre-1986 manufacture with new receiver or re-weld

Exc.	*V.G.*	*Fair*
25000	22500	20000

MG42-MG42/59-MG1-MG3

MG3 • Courtesy private NFA collection

This gun replaced the MG34 and was chambered for the 7.92x57mm Mauser cartridge. It has a 20.8-inch quick change barrel and is fed by a 50-round belt. Its rate of fire is about 1,000 to 1,200 rounds per minute. The butt is synthetic with pistol grip. The gun weighs about 25 lbs. Marked "mg42" on the left side of the receiver. This gun was produced from 1938 until the end of the war in 1945. Its design was the result of wartime engineering which used roller locks – at the time a revolutionary design concept.

MG42 in action • *Courtesy Blake Stevens,* ***MG34-MG42 German Universal Machine Guns****, Collector Grade Publications*

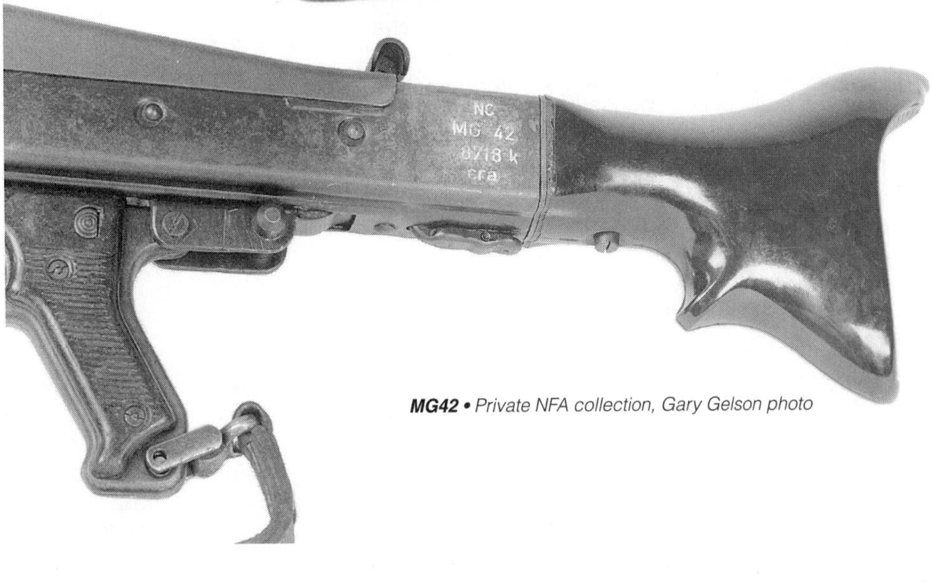

MG42 • *Private NFA collection, Gary Gelson photo*

HK23 • Courtesy Heckler & Koch

GERMANY

Postwar models, the MG42/59 followed by the MG1 then the MG3, are still in use by the German army. These postwar guns are chambered for the 7.62x51mm cartridge. These models utilize many important improvements in manufacturing and design, and are in use by many countries throughout the world. There are a number of licensed versions of the MG42/59 made in Austria, Italy, Spain, Portugal, Turkey, Yugoslavia, and Switzerland.

MG42

Pre-1968

Exc.	*V.G.*	*Fair*
40000	35000	32500

Pre-1986 manufacture with new receiver or re-weld

Exc.	*V.G.*	*Fair*
32500	30000	25000

NOTE: For MG42/5 and MG42/59 add 75 percent premium (eight examples known). For MG3 add 125 percent (three known).

HK11 (HK11A1-HK11E)

Designed as a light air-cooled machine gun chambered for the 7.62x51mm cartridge, this gun uses a roller-delayed bolt. The quick change barrel is 17.7 inches long. Fixed synthetic stock with pistol grip and bipod. Uses a 20-round box magazine or 80 dual drum. Rate of fire is about 850 rounds per minute. Weight is approximately 15 lbs.

NOTE: There is no drum magazine on the HK11A1.

Pre-1968

Exc.	*V.G.*	*Fair*
N/A	N/A	N/A

Pre-1986 manufacture with new receiver or re-weld

Exc.	*V.G.*	*Fair*
16500	14000	12000

HK13 (HK13E)

This gun is similar to the HK11 but is chambered for the 5.56x45mm cartridge. Quick change 17.7-inch barrel. Fed by a 20-, 30-, or 40-round box magazine, or 100-round dual drum. Rate of fire is about 800 rounds per minute. Weight is approximately 12 lbs.

NOTE: There are a number of variants of this model. The HK13C has a baked-on forest camouflage finish. The HK13E is a modernized version with selective improvements, such as a 3-round burst capability. The rifling has been changed to stabilize 62 grain bullets. The HK13E1 is the same as the HK13E with rifling twist to accommodate 54 grain bullets. The HK13S has a baked-on desert camouflage scheme.

NOTE: There is a semi-automatic version of this gun. Value would be around $6,000 for one in excellent condition.

Pre-1968

Exc.	*V.G.*	*Fair*
N/A	N/A	N/A

Pre-1986 manufacture with new receiver or re-weld

Exc.	*V.G.*	*Fair*
15000	13000	11000

HK21 (HK21E-HK23E)

These guns form a series of general purpose machine guns. The 21 series is chambered for the 7.62x51mm cartridge while the 23E is chambered for the 5.56x45mm cartridge. The HK21 is fitted with a 17.5-inch barrel and has a rate of fire of 900 rounds per minute. Its weight is about 17 lbs. Marked on the top of receiver. The HK21 was first produced in 1970 but is no longer in production, while the HK21E and 23E are still produced.

This series of guns has variations similar to the HK13 series of guns.

NOTE: The HK21E and HK23E will bring a premium of 75 percent over the older HK21/2.

Pre-1968 Model 21

Exc.	*V.G.*	*Fair*
20000	17500	16000

Pre-1986 manufacture with new receiver or re-weld

Exc.	*V.G.*	*Fair*
20000	18000	17000

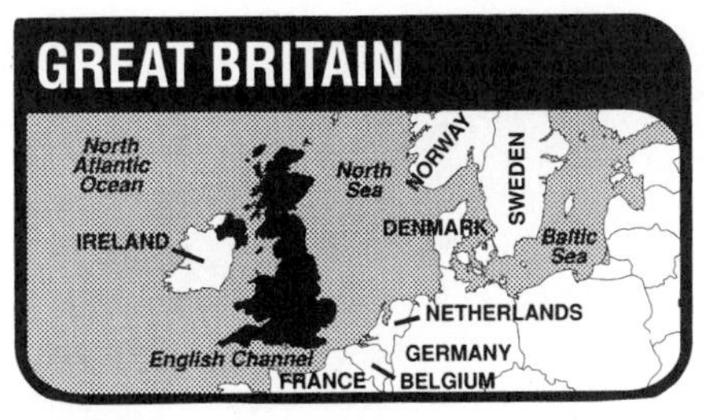

The United Kingdom of Great Britain and Northern Ireland, located off the northwest coast of the European continent, has an area of 94,227 sq. mi. (244,820 sq. km.) and a population of 54 million. Capital: London. The economy is based on industrial activity and trading. Machinery, motor vehicles, chemicals, and textile yarns and fabrics are exported.

After the departure of the Romans, who brought Britain into a more active relationship with Europe, it fell prey to invaders from Scandinavia and the Low Countries who drove the original Britons into Scotland and Wales, and established a profusion of kingdoms that finally united in the 11th century under the Danish King Canute. Norman rule, following the conquest of 1066, stimulated the development of those institutions, which have since distinguished British life. Henry VIII (1509-47) turned Britain from continental adventuring and faced it to the sea - a decision that made Britain a world power during the reign of Elizabeth I (1558-1603). Strengthened by the Industrial Revolution and the defeat of Napoleon, 19th century Britain turned to the remote parts of the world and established a colonial empire of such extent and prosperity that the world has never seen its like. World Wars I and II sealed the fate of the Empire and relegated Britain to a lesser role in world affairs by draining her resources and inaugurating a worldwide movement toward national self-determination in her former colonies.

By the mid-20th century, most of the territories formerly comprising the British Empire had gained independence, and the empire had evolved into the Commonwealth of Nations, an association of equal and autonomous states, which enjoy special trade interests. The Commonwealth is presently composed of 54 member nations, including the United Kingdom. All recognize the British monarch as head of the Commonwealth. Sixteen continue to recognize the British monarch as Head of State. They are: United Kingdom, Antigua and Barbuda, Australia, Bahamas, Barbados, Belize, Canada, Grenada, Jamaica, New Zealand, Papua New Guinea, St. Christopher & Nevis, Saint Lucia, Saint Vincent and the Grenadines, Solomon Islands, and Tuvalu. Elizabeth II is personally, and separately, the Queen of the sovereign, independent countries just mentioned. There is no other British connection between the several individual, national sovereignties, except that High Commissioners represent them each instead of ambassadors in each others' countries.

HANDGUNS

Adams Model 1872 Mark 2, 3, and 4

A .450 caliber double action revolver with a 6-inch octagonal barrel and 6-shot cylinder. Blued with walnut grips. Built by Adams Patent Small Arms Company. Weight was about 40 oz. This was the first breechloading revolver issued to the British mounted units. In service from 1872 to 1919.

Exc.	*V.G.*	*Good*	*Fair*	*Poor*
—	1250	600	400	200

WEBLEY & SCOTT, LTD.

Bibliographical Note: For historical information, technical data, and photos see William Dowell, ***The Webley Story***, Skyrac Press, 1987.

Note on caliber conversion: Many Webley .455 revolvers encountered in the U.S. have had the cylinders shortened to allow use of .45 ACP ammunition in half moon clips, or the .45 Auto Rim revolver ammunition. It is fairly easy to spot the converted guns. First, look at the gap between the cylinder back and the breech face. If it is barely 1/16 inch, it is original. If the gap is 1/8 inch or more, then the cylinder has been shortened for the .45ACP. Another thing to look at is the serial number on the cylinder. It should be on the rear edge. If it looks like the numbers have the bottom third missing, then the gun has been converted. Deduct 25-50 percent for a Webley or Enfield .455 that has been converted.

Mark I

A .455 caliber double action top break revolver with a 4-inch barrel and 6-shot cylinder. Blued with hard rubber grips. Manufactured from 1887 to 1894. Models issued to the Royal Navy have the letter "N" stamped on top of the frame behind the hammer.

NOTE: Military version chambered for .455 cartridge only while commercial versions were chambered for the .442 and .476 cartridges.

Courtesy Faintich Auction Services, Inc., Paul Goodwin photo

Exc.	*V.G.*	*Good*	*Fair*	*Poor*
800	650	500	350	200

Mark II

As above, with a larger hammer spur and improved barrel catch. Manufactured from 1894 to 1897.

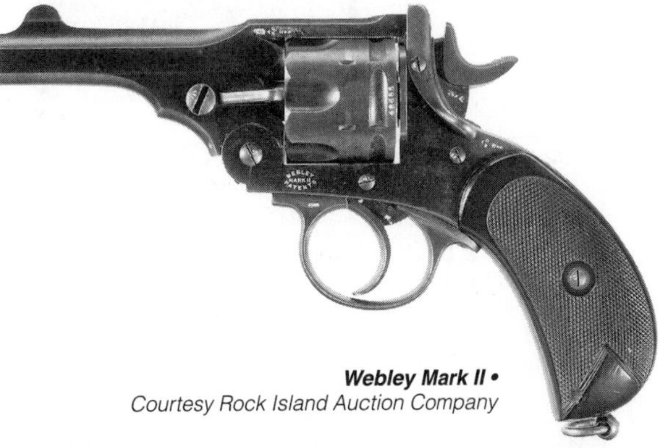

Webley Mark II •
Courtesy Rock Island Auction Company

Exc.	*V.G.*	*Good*	*Fair*	*Poor*
800	650	500	350	200

Mark III

As above, with internal improvements. Introduced in 1897.

GREAT BRITAIN

Webley Mark II markings on the left side • Courtesy Rock Island Auction Company

Courtesy Rock Island Auction Company

Exc.	V.G.	Good	Fair	Poor
800	650	500	350	200

Mark IV

As above, with a .455 caliber and 4- or 6-inch barrel. Sometimes referred to as the "Boer War" model because it was supplied to British troops in South Africa between 1899 and 1902.

Courtesy Faintich Auction Services, Inc., Paul Goodwin photo

Exc.	V.G.	Good	Fair	Poor
800	650	500	350	200

Mark V

As above, with a 4- (standard) or 6-inch barrel. Manufactured from 1913 to 1915.

Exc.	V.G.	Good	Fair	Poor
800	650	500	350	200

Mark IV .380 (.38S&W)

Webley produced a military version of its .38 revolver for military use during World War II. Marked "War Finish" on the frame. This model was intended to

Courtesy Faintich Auction Services, Inc., Photo Paul Goodwin

NOTE: There was also a commercial Mark IV. It was made in .22 caliber with 6-inch barrel, .32 caliber with 3-inch barrel, and .38 caliber with 3-, 4-, or 5-inch barrel. Add 50 percent for .22 or .32 versions.

Exc.	V.G.	Good	Fair	Poor
450	300	225	175	125

Mark VI .455

As above, with 6-inch barrel and square butt. Introduced in 1915 and replaced with the .380 models in 1928.

Courtesy Faintich Auction Services, Inc., Photo Paul Goodwin

Exc.	V.G.	Good	Fair	Poor
700	550	400	250	200

Leather holster for Webley Mk VI

Top flap with strap near the upper edge. This is a WWI era design. Some bear makers name and dates on the back. Single wide belt loop. Some also have loops for chest strap.

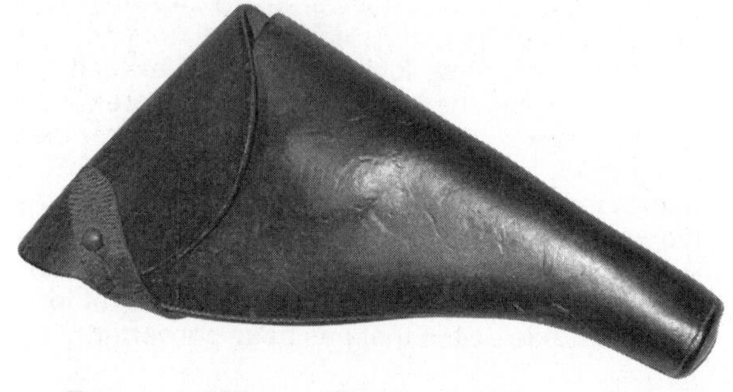

Exc.	V.G.	Good	Fair	Poor
200	150	100	75	40

Model 1913–Semi-automatic Pistol

The Model 1913 was the result of years of development in conjunction with the British government and was finally adopted in 1913 as the Model 1913 MK1N for Royal Navy issue. It has the same breech-locking system as the Model 1910, but has an external hammer and is chambered for the .455 Webley self-loading cartridge. About 1,000 Model 1913s were sold commercially and serial numbered along with the smaller caliber pistols. In 1915, a variation of the Model 1913 with butt slotted for a shoulder stock, an adjustable rear sight, and a hammer safety was adopted for use by the Royal Horse Artillery. Shoulder stocks are very rare, and will double values shown for the RHA model. All militaries were numbered in their own series; about 10,000 made in both variations.

Model 1913

Exc.	*V.G.*	*Good*	*Fair*	*Poor*
1900	1650	1400	1000	750

Model 1913 (RHA model)

Courtesy Joseph Schroeder

Exc.	*V.G.*	*Good*	*Fair*	*Poor*
3500	2750	1800	1100	800

Webley-Fosbery Model 1914

This is an automatic revolver that is recoil-operated by the barrel-cylinder group sliding across the frame to cock the hammer and revolve the cylinder using the zig-zag grooves in the cylinder. Chambered for the .455 cartridge. Cylinder has a 6-round capacity. Barrel length is 6". Weight is about 30 oz. This sidearm was not officially adopted by British forces but was widely used by them during WWI.

Webley-Fosbery Model 1914 • Courtesy Rock Island Auction Company

Webley-Fosbery Model 1914 • Courtesy Rock Island Auction Company

Exc.	*V.G.*	*Good*	*Fair*	*Poor*
7500	5000	3500	1750	1250

ENFIELD ROYAL SMALL ARMS FACTORY

In 1879, the British army needed revolvers, and the Royal Small Arms Factory was commissioned to produce them. The result was that on August 11, 1880, the Enfield Mark 1 was accepted for duty.

Enfield Mark 1 Revolver

A 6-shot, hinged-frame, break-open revolver. It has an odd ejection system—when the barrel is pulled down, the cylinder moves forward; and the extractor plate remains in place, retaining the spent cartridges. This revolver is chambered for the .476 cartridge and has a 6-shot cylinder. The barrel is 6 inches long, and the finish is blued with checkered walnut grips. Weight is about 40 oz.

Exc.	*V.G.*	*Good*	*Fair*	*Poor*
1500	1050	800	500	250

Enfield Mark 2

The Mark 2 is similar externally, with some design improvements—such as a rounded front sight, taper-bored cylinders, an integral top strap, and plain grips. The Mark 2 was introduced in 1881 and was replaced by the Webley Mark I in 1887.

Exc.	V.G.	Good	Fair	Poor
1500	1000	750	500	250

Enfield-Produced Webley Mark 6

This model is identical to the Webley-produced versions. It is of .455 caliber and is stamped "Enfield" on the frame.

Exc.	V.G.	Good	Fair	Poor
750	600	475	250	200

Enfield No. 2 Mark I/Mark 1*

Originally chambered for the .380 (.38 S&W). It is a 6-shot, break-open double action, with a 5" barrel. The finish is blued, with black plastic checkered grips. This model was actually a modified Webley design and was adopted in 1932. In 1938, the bullet was changed from a 200-grain lead "soft-nosed" to a 178-grain jacketed, in response to pressure from the Geneva Conference.

Exc.	V.G.	Good	Fair	Poor
375	275	200	150	100

Enfield No. 2 Mark I*

The same as the Mark I with the hammer spur and single action lockwork omitted in response to the Royal Tank Regiment's fear that the spur would catch on the tank as the crews were entering and exiting their confines.

NOTE: During WWII these pistols were also manufactured by Albion Motors Ltd. of Glasgow, Scotland. These pistols were produced between 1941 and 1943, and approximately 24,000 were made. They are marked "Albion" on the right side of the frame. With some collectors, there might be a small premium on these pistols. Enfield pistols with the marking "SM" or "SSM" will also be noted, and this refers to various parts produced by Singer Sewing Machine Company of England. These pistols were assembled at Enfield. Used until 1957, when the FN-Browning GP35 semi-automatic pistol replaced them.

Enfield No. 2 Mark 1 • Courtesy West Point Museum, Paul Goodwin photo*

Enfield No. 2 Mark 1 • Courtesy West Point Museum, Paul Goodwin photo*

Exc.	V.G.	Good	Fair	Poor
350	250	175	125	100

EIBAR, SPAIN

During WWI, the British government contracted with two Spanish firms to build what was called the Old Pattern No.1 Mark I revolver by Garate y Compania and the Old Pattern No. 2 Mark I revolver by Trocaola, Aranzabal y Compania. Both companies were located in Eibar, Spain. These revolvers were chambered for the .455 caliber cartridge and were fitted with 5" barrels. They will have British proof marks and property marks.

Exc.	V.G.	Good	Fair	Poor
300	250	200	125	100

COLT and SMITH & WESSON

Britain acquired Colt New Service and Smith & Wesson First Model and Second Model Ejector .455 revolvers from the U.S. Approximately 75,000 of these revolvers were sent to England between 1914 and 1916.

Enfield No. 2 Mark 1 • Paul Goodwin photo

GREAT BRITAIN

Colt New Service, .455 with English markings

Exc.	*V.G.*	*Good*	*Fair*	*Poor*
800	600	450	250	150

Smith & Wesson Hand Ejector .455 with English markings

Exc.	*V.G.*	*Good*	*Fair*	*Poor*
750	575	400	225	150

NOTE: Be sure these are in the original .455 caliber. Many seen in the U.S. have had the cylinder shortened to allow use of .45 automatic or .45 Long Colt cartridges. Deduct 25% for an altered revolver.

SUBMACHINE GUNS

NOTE: For historical information and technical details see Laider and Howroyd, ***The Guns of Dagenham; Lanchester, Patchett, Sterling***, Collector Grade Publications, 1999. Laider, ***The Sten Machine Carbine***, Collector Grade Publications, 2000.

Lanchester Mk1/Mk1*

The British submachine gun was produced from 1940 to about 1942. It is chambered for the 9mm cartridge and is fitted with a 7.75-inch barrel. The magazine capacity is 50 rounds. Rate of fire is 600 rounds per minute. Weight is about 9.5 lbs. This British gun is almost an exact copy of the Bergmann MP28. The magazine housing is made of brass. The bayonet lug will accept a Model 1907 pattern bayonet. Most of these weapons were issued to the Royal Navy and stayed in service there until the 1960s. Markings are "LANCHESTER MARK I" on the magazine housing.

The Mk1* has had the fire selector switch in front of the triggerguard removed, thus making the weapon capable of full automatic fire only.

Pre-1968

Exc.	*V.G.*	*Fair*
7000	6500	6000

Lanchester Mark I* • *Courtesy West Point Museum, Paul Goodwin photo*

NOTE: Add a premium of 15 percent for the Mark 1 version.

Sten Mark II

The Mark II is the most common version of the Sten models. It is chambered for the 9mm cartridge and features a removable stock and barrel. The magazine capacity is 32 rounds. Barrel length is 7.66". The rate of fire is 550 rounds per minute. Markings are located on top of the magazine housing and are stamped "sten mk II." Weight is approximately 6.6 lbs. Produced from 1942 to 1944 with about two million built in Britain, Canada, and New Zealand.

NOTE: The Mark II S is the silenced version of the Mark II. Fitted with a canvas foregrip. Weight is about 7.75 lbs. and rate of fire is about 450 rounds per minute.

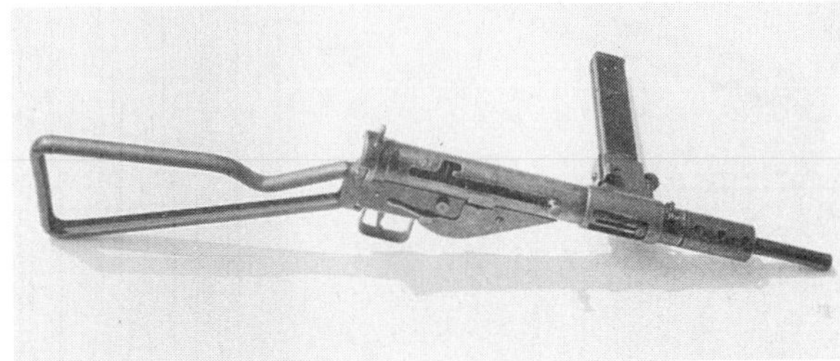

Courtesy Richard M. Kumor Sr.

Pre-1968

Exc.	*V.G.*	*Fair*
5000	4500	4000

Pre-1986 manufacture with new receiver or re-weld

Exc.	*V.G.*	*Fair*
3000	2500	2500

Sten Mark III

This model was a expeditiously built version of the Marks 1 and 2, and featured a one-piece receiver and barrel jacket of welding tubing with a non-removable barrel. No flash hider. Built at Lines and Long Branch arsenals. All other specifications are the same as the Marks I and II.

Pre-1968

Exc.	*V.G.*	*Fair*
5000	4500	4000

Pre-1986 manufacture with new receiver or re-weld

Exc.	*V.G.*	*Fair*
3000	2500	2500

Sten Mark V

This version of the Sten was first produced in 1944. It featured a wooden stock and pistol grip. The barrel could accept a bayonet. Finish was better than

GREAT BRITAIN

Sten Mark III • *Courtesy Robert G. Segel*

Sten Mark V • *Courtesy Robert G. Segel*

standard service of the period. Barrel length was 7.75 inches and magazine capacity was 32 rounds. Rate of fire was 600 rounds per minute. Weight was increased to 8.6 lbs. over the Mark II. Marked "STEN M.C. MK V" on top of the magazine housing. Production ceased on this version in 1946.

NOTE: The Mark VI is the silenced version of the Mark V. Fitted with a long barrel and silencer assembly. Weight is about 9.8 lbs. and rate of fire is about 450 rounds per minute.

Pre-1968

Exc.	*V.G.*	*Fair*
5500	4500	4250

Pre-1986 manufacture with new receiver or re-weld

Exc.	*V.G.*	*Fair*
3500	3000	2500

Sterling Mk 4 (L2A3)

Chambered for the 9mm cartridge this submachine gun features a 7.75" barrel, 34-round side mounted magazine, collapsible metal stock. The last version of the Sterling, the Mk 4, is a result of a long line of improvements to the gun beginning with the Pachett. The Pachett was originally developed during WWII and produced by the Sterling Co. in Dagenham, England and the Royal Ordnance Factory in Fazakerley, England. Next came the Mk 2 and the Mk 3 beginning in 1953 and the Mk 4 during the late 1950s.

It has seen wide use throughout the world having been adopted by the British army, New Zealand and approximately 40 other countries. The rate of fire is 550 rounds per minute. Weight is about 6 lbs. Produced from 1953 to 1988. Still made in India under license. Marked "sterling smg 9mm" on the magazine housing.

Pre-1968 (Rare)

Exc.	*V.G.*	*Fair*
17500	15000	11000

Pre-1986 conversion of semi-automatic version

Exc.	*V.G.*	*Fair*
8000	6000	n/a

Sterling L34A1

This is a silenced version of the L2A3 Mark 4 gun. The silencer is fitted with a short wooden forearm. Barrel length is the same as the unlicensed version. Weight is about 8 lbs.

Pre-1968 (Rare)

Exc.	*V.G.*	*Fair*
18500	15000	11000

Pre-1986 conversions

Exc.	*V.G.*	*Fair*
10000	9000	8000

RIFLES

NOTE: For historical information and technical data see: Reynolds, E.G.B., The Lee-Enfield Rifle, Herbert Jenkins, Ltd., 1960. The Lee-Enfield Story, Ian Skennerton, 1993. Stevens, Blake, UK and Commonwealth FALs, Vol. 2, The FAL Series, Collector Grade Publications, 1980. Skennerton has also written a number of monographs on other British rifles that are well worth study by the collector.

ENGLISH PRE-CARTRIDGE ERA RIFLES

ENFIELD, ENGLAND

Until the establishment of the Royal Armory at Enfield in 1816, the government of England relied solely upon the contract system to obtain small arms for its naval and military forces. Even after the Enfield Armory began is first major production in 1823, the contractors continued to dominate the production of arms for the military. These contractors were concentrated in two major cities, Birmingham and London. Although a number of makers from Birmingham were capable of manufacturing arms, "lock, stock, and barrel," and of assembling them, most of the makers of that city specialized in the making of specific parts, which could be assembled into complete arms on the "factory system" then prevalent in Liege. When the English War Department was the purchaser, the parts were usually delivered to the Tower of London for assembly. Most military arms made in Birmingham accordingly are seldom marked with a single maker's name. Rather they bear the English crown and the name "TOWER" on the lock. Those barrels that passed proof at Birmingham after 1813 were marked with the view and proofmarks derived from Ketland's only proofmarks; these consisted of a pair of crowned, crossed scepters, one pair of which had the letter "V" in the lower quarter and the other of which had the letters "B," "C," and "P" respectively in the left, right, and lower quarters. In contrast, the arms manufactured at London were almost always completed by their manufacturers, and bear their names usually upon the lockplates and barrels. The London gunmakers also marked their barrels with a pair of proofmarks, consisting of a crown over a "V" and a crown over an intertwined "G" and "P." Prominent martial arms makers in the London trade through the 1860s included, "BOND," "BARNETT," "BLISSETT," "GREENER," "HOLLIS & SONS," "LONDON ARMORY CO," "KERR," "PARKER, FIELD & SONS," "PRITCHETT," "POTTS & HUNT," "ROBERT WHEELER," "WILSON & CO.," and "YEOMANS." (It should be noted that most of these London makers also manufactured sporting and other trade arms, which will bear similar marks.) During the period of transition from the contract system to the reliance upon the works at Enfield (roughly 1816 through 1867), the arms themselves underwent major transitions, first from flintlock to percussion ignition systems and then from smoothbore to rifled bore, first in large and then in small bore sizes. The major infantry types include:

New Land Pattern Musket aka *Brown Bess*

Overall length 58-1/2 inches; barrel length 42 inches; caliber .75. The mainstay of the British Army during

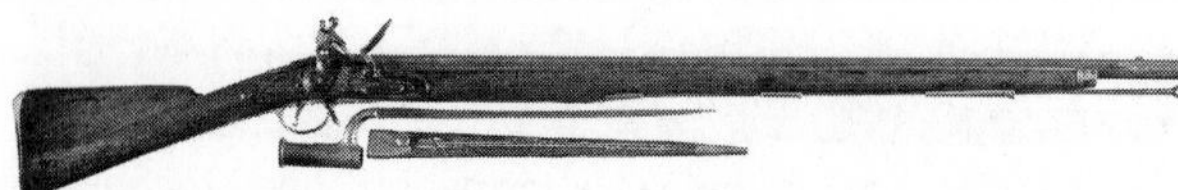

the Napoleonic Wars, this flintlock arm continued, primarily, in service until 1838, with major quantities (5,000 from each) being ordered from Enfield and from the contractors as late as 1823.

Exc.	V.G.	Good	Fair	Poor
—	3250	1800	850	600

Socket Bayonet for Brown Bess

Total length is 22 inches. Triangle shaped blade is 17 inches. As shown in image. Add $100 for intact leather scabbard. Price range 250 – 75.

Pattern of 1839 (P1839) Musket

Overall length 55 inches; barrel length 39 inches; caliber .76. In 1838 the British War Department contracted for the parts for 30,000 new flintlock arms. However, before these arms could be assembled, the War Department adopted the percussion system of ignition and ordered that these arms be made as percussion. Obsolete by 1861, large numbers were purchased by the Southern Confederacy and imported for use in the American Civil War. Arms with firm evidence of Confederate military usage increases the value of the arm considerably.

Exc.	V.G.	Good	Fair	Poor
—	1500	950	500	350

Pattern of 1842 (P1842) Musket (and Rifled Musket)

Overall length 55 inches; barrel length 39-1/4 inches; caliber .75. The first English-made as percussion musket to be issued to the Line Regiments of the British Army, continued in production through the Crimean War. The final production (1851-1855) of 26,400 were made with rifled barrel and a long range rear sight soldered to the barrel, similar in configuration to that of the P1851 rifle-musket. These rifled versions of the P1842 musket will command a premium.

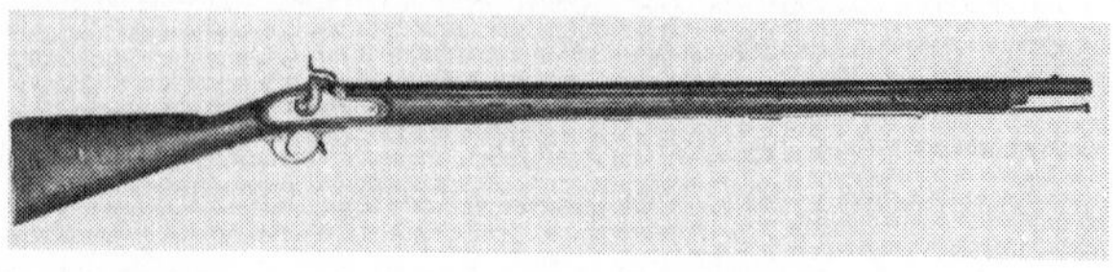

Exc.	V.G.	Good	Fair	Poor
—	1500	950	500	350

Brunswick" Rifles (First Model or P1837) and (Second Model or P1845)

Overall length 46-1/2 inches (P1837), 45-3/4 inches (P1845); barrel length 33 inches (P1837), 30 inches (P1845); caliber .704. The "Brunswick" rifle differed from its predecessor (the "Baker rifle") adopted for the English "Rifle Brigade" in having a large bore cut with only two spiraling grooves. These grooves engaged a specially cast ball having a raised belt circumventing it. The first model of the "Brunswick rifle" adopted in 1837 is primarily distinguished by having a "backaction" percussion lock, which continued in production until 1844 despite having been officially changed to the standard "barlock" in 1841. Those made after 1844 bear the standard percussion lock. The value of these rifles is enhanced by virtue of the importation of at least 2,000 (probably first model variants) into the Southern Confederacy during the American Civil War. (It should be noted that Russia also adopted a variant of the "Brunswick" style rifle, having them made in Liege, Belgium and so marked with Liege proofmarks. These rifles are distinguished by having a distinctive rear sight with an adjustable arcing ladder.)

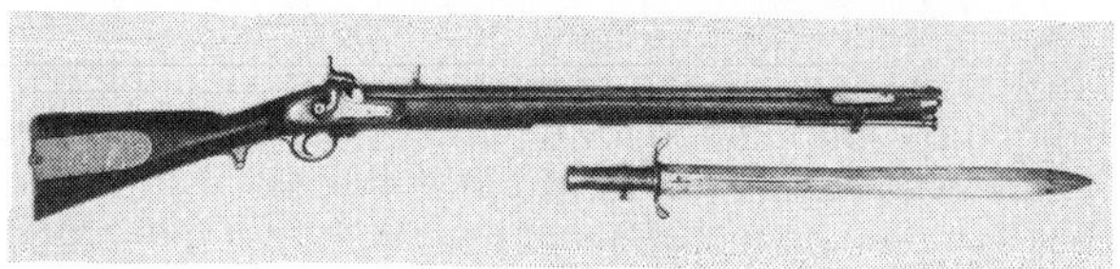

Exc.	V.G.	Good	Fair	Poor
—	2500	1500	700	450

Pattern of 1851 (P1851) Rifle Musket

Overall length 55 inches; barrel length 39 inches; caliber .702. With the success of the "Minie ball" projectile in France, England in 1851 adopted its first production rifle musket. Externally resembling the P1842 musket, the P1851 is distinguished by the long range rear sight soldered to the barrel and its smaller caliber (.70) rifled bore. Approximately 35,000 were manufactured until 1855, with a substantial number being imported to the United States during the early years of the American Civil War.

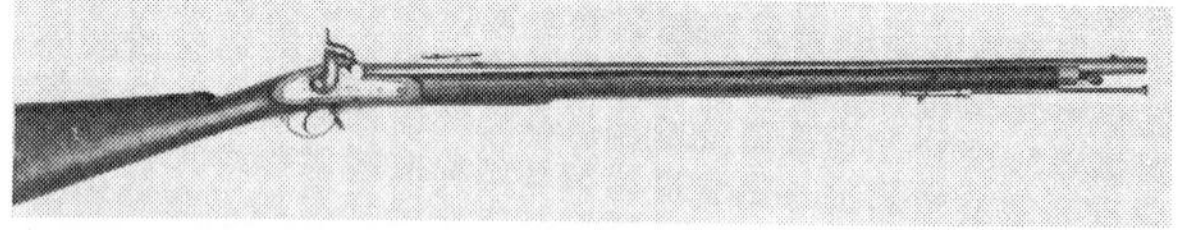

Exc.	V.G.	Good	Fair	Poor
—	2750	1750	800	450

Pattern of 1853 (P1853) Rifle Musket (First Through Fourth Types)

Overall length 55 inches (54 inches on fourth type); barrel length 39 inches; caliber .577. The P1853 rifle musket underwent several changes during the span of its production. The earliest type (first model) was made with clamping bands. Due to problems with the bands slipping, the bands were modified in late 1855 to solid, spring fastened (second model), the upper wider than the other two. However, in 1858 the government reverted to clamping bands continuing production in this style through 1863. Those made at Enfield after 1859 were one inch shorter in the butt stock, but the contractors continued to deliver them in 55-inch length well into the 1860s. The fourth model is distinguished by the "Baddeley patent" clamping barrel bands, wherein the screwheads are recessed into the bands. The third model saw the greatest production, with more than 600,000 being imported into the north and about 300,000 into the south during the American Civil War. P1853 rifle muskets with early Confederate importation marks on the stock and butt plate command a premium if authentic.

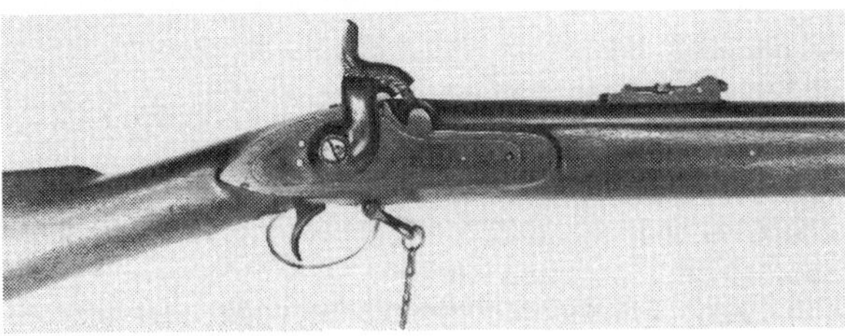

Exc.	V.G.	Good	Fair	Poor
3500	2500	1500	850	400

American-Made Copies of the English P1853 Rifle Musket

Three firms during the period from 1855 through 1862 produced copies of the P1853 rifle musket: Robbins & Lawrence of Windsor, Vermont; Orison Blunt of New York City; and John Moore of New York City. All three types command a premium over the standard imported muskets and can be distinguished as follows:

Robbins & Lawrence P1853 Rifle Muskets

During the Crimean War, Robbins & Lawrence received a contract for 25,000 P1853 rifle muskets of the second model. Due to production delays, the company had delivered only 10,400 when the war ended. Due to the penalties for non-deliveries, Robbins & Lawrence declared bankruptcy. An additional 5,600 arms were made on the firms machinery while in receivership by the "Vermont Arms Co." before the machinery was sold to Sharps and Eli Whitney, Jr. The Robbins & Lawrence-made P1853 rifle muskets are distinguished by the lock marking "WINDSOR" beneath the date (such as "1856") on the forward part of the lock and by non-English proofmarks on the barrel. Many of these arms saw service in the American Civil War, with Alabama obtaining several hundred in 1861. Arms with confirmed southern usage will bring substantial premiums.

Exc.	V.G.	Good	Fair	Poor
—	3000	2000	1250	600

Orison Blunt P1853 Rifle Muskets

At the beginning of the Civil War, Orison Blunt of New York City attempted to produce a copy of the P1853 rifle musket but with a 40-inch barrel and in .58 caliber. After making several hundred, his proposed contract with the U.S. War Department was declined. Nevertheless, in mid-1862, it is thought that about 1,000 of his rifle muskets were purchased by the U.S. government and sent to Illinois to arm volunteers. Blunt "Enfields" are distinguished by two distinct markings. While most lockplates are totally unmarked, a few are known with the mark "UNION" on the forward part of the lockplate and an eagle impressed into the rounded tail. More importantly, Blunt barrels bear an oval with the letters "DP/B" near the breech. (Note: Not all P1853 rifle muskets with 40-inch barrels were made by Blunt; Birmingham and Liege contractors supplied the Spanish government with a 40-inch barrel copy of the P1853 English rifle musket as well, and some of these were diverted to the American market during the Civil War. These are usually distinguished by the letter "C" in a diamond near the breech of the barrel

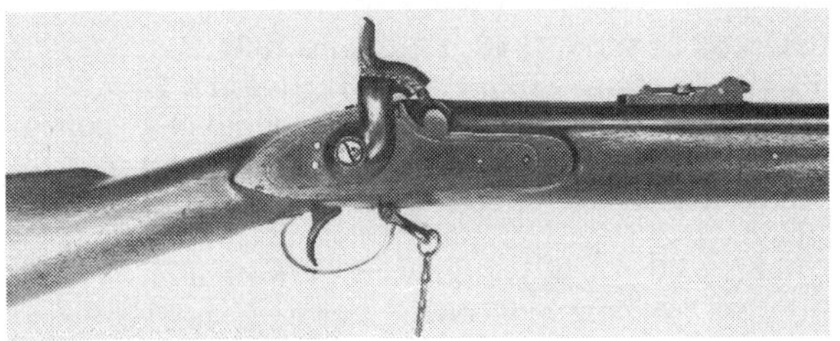

surrounded by proofmarks.)

Exc.	V.G.	Good	Fair	Poor
—	3500	2000	1250	600

John P. Moore P1853 Rifle Muskets

During the American Civil War arms merchant John P. Moore of New York City received a contract for the delivery of 20,000 P1853 rifle muskets, supposedly to be made in the United States. In fact, most of his contract was made in Birmingham, England, with only 1,080 completely made in the United States. These are distinguished by having an unusual script proofmark on the barrel near the breech instead of the standard Birmingham crossed scepters. These script letters have been interpreted as either "V LB" or "EP I" depending on how they are read. All of Moore's P1853 deliveries bear a distinctive lock marking, consisting of the date forward of the hammer ("1861", "1862", or "1863") and an eagle perched on a shield on the tail. The shield bears the letter "M" in its chief. Moore also delivered 999 short rifles (33-inch barrels) with the same lock markings. Likewise, all of the barrels on the Moore P1853 rifle musket contract are serially numbered, either on the forward side near the muzzle or on the side of the bayonet lug/front sight. Because the Moore rifles have been misidentified as a product of a North Carolina arms merchant, they tend to command higher prices than are warranted by their numbers.

Exc.	V.G.	Good	Fair	Poor
—	2700	1850	900	450

"Brazilian Naval Rifle"

Overall length 48 inches; barrel length 32 inches; caliber .58. Markings on lockplate forward of hammer "D (anchor) C"; the same mark stamped in the wood and metal in various places on the rifle; on barrel, same mark and Liege proofmarks (an oval encompassing the letters E/LG/(star). Although neither made for the English government nor in England, this rifle copies so many features of the English P1856 series rifles as to be easily mistaken for it. The major differences consist of a longer (3-3/8 inch) sight base than the English rifles and a front band/nosecap that also serves as the ramrod funnel. These Liege-made rifles were supposedly made for the Brazilian government, but at the beginning of the American Civil War they were diverted to the United States, about 10,000 being imported. To show their new ownership, a brass

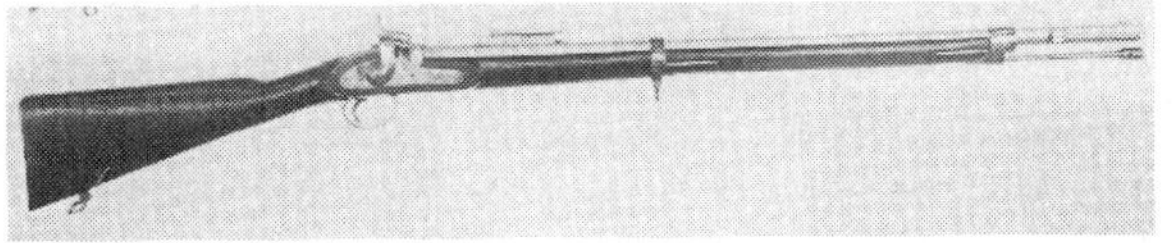

GREAT BRITAIN

shield bearing the U.S. coat of arms was screwed into the wrist of the stock.

Exc.	V.G.	Good	Fair	Poor
—	1800	1250	650	275

Patterns of 1856, 1858, 1860, and 1861 (P1856, P1858, P1860, P1861) Sergeant's Rifles

Overall length 49 inches; barrel length 33"; caliber .577. The four variations of the short rifle adopted for sergeants in the British Army in 1856 are relatively minor. The P1856 is mainly distinguished by having a short (1/2 inch) key forward of the saber bayonet lug on the right side of the barrel. The P1858 rifle moved this lug to the forward band, permitting the extension of the length of the forestock. (A brass furnished rifle also without the key but with the lug on the barrel was also adopted in 1858 for the Navy; it is distinguished by having its rear sling swivel attached to the trigger guard bow instead of the tail of the trigger guard strap.) The P1860 rifle differed from its predecessors by having five groove rifling instead of three groove. The introduction of a new gunpowder in 1861 permitted the resighting of the ladder on the P1861 rifle to 1,250 yards instead of the 1,100 yards that had been previously used. Significant quantities of these rifles were purchased by both belligerents during the American Civil War; those with proven Southern history will command a premium.

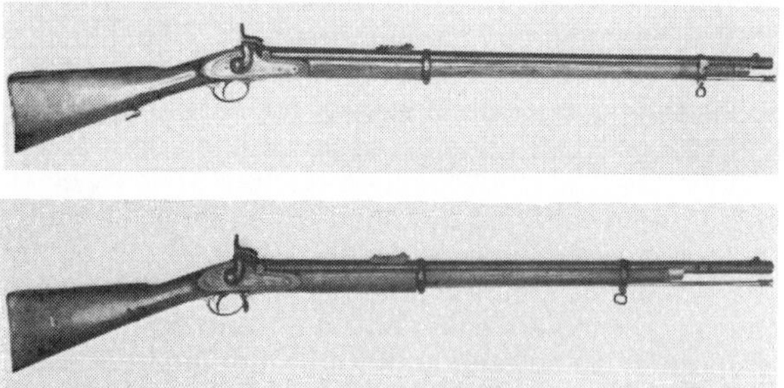

Exc.	V.G.	Good	Fair	Poor
3000	2250	1650	900	450

Pattern of 1853 (P1853) Artillery Carbine (First, Second, and Third Models)

Overall length 40 inches; barrel length 24 inches; caliber .577. Designed for the gunners of the Royal Artillery, this carbine was meant to be slung over the shoulder and accordingly has a sling swivel on the upper band and upon a lug inset into the buttstock. The first model (adopted in 1853), like the sergeant's rifle has a 1-1/2-inch key forward of the saber bayonet lug on the right side of the barrel; in addition to other minor improvements, this key was eliminated in the second model, adopted in 1858. In 1861, a third model was adopted, having five groove rifling and improved rear sight. Approximately 1,000 of the latter type saw service in the American Civil War. Carbines with Confederate stock and buttplate markings will command a premium.

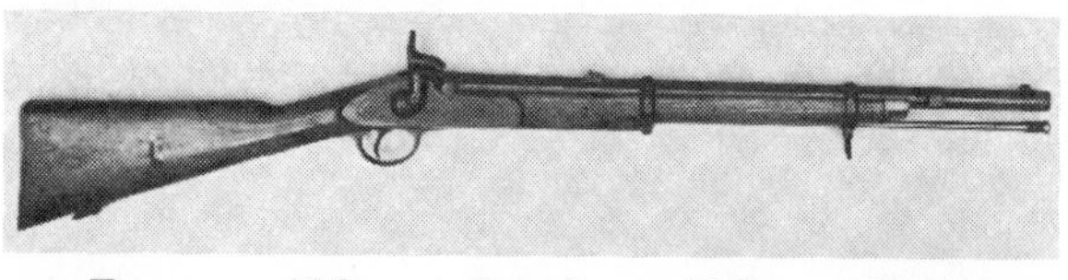

Exc.	V.G.	Good	Fair	Poor
—	2500	1650	850	450

Patterns of 1856 (P1856) and Pattern of 1861 (P1861) Cavalry Carbines

Overall length 37 inches (P1856), 36-1/2 inches (P1861) barrel length 21 inches; caliber .577. Due to inadequacies in the various breechloading carbines tried by the British mounted service, in 1856 the War Department adopted a muzzle-loading carbine incorporating the features of the P1853 series small arms. The earlier version had three groove rifling and a small rear sight with two leaves. In 1861 this was replaced by a larger ladder sight and five groove rifling adopted. More than 6,000 P1856 carbines were imported by the Southern Confederacy during the Civil War to make up for the inadequate supply of carbines. Carbines with verifiable Southern history command a premium.

Exc.	V.G.	Good	Fair	Poor
—	2500	1650	850	450

SNIDER

This design was the invention of Jacob Snider, an American from New York. The idea was to convert, in a simple way, muzzle-loading rifles to cartridge-firing-breech loaders. Snider cut away a rear section of the barrel and inserted a breech block with firing pin hinged at the side so that it could be opened and a cartridge inserted. The rifle was fired by an external hammer. Despite extraction problems, this design was used by the British Army, beginning in 1868 in the Ethiopian campaign, for six years and remained in service in second line units into the 1880s. It was

Courtesy Blake Stevens, *The Guns of Dagenham,* ***Collector Grade Publications***

Pattern 2* • *Courtesy Rock Island Auction Company*

the first general issue breech-loader in the British army, and perhaps more important was the parallel development of the Boxer cartridge for use in this rifle. The Boxer cartridge was a .577 caliber with steel rim and rolled heavy paper cartridge case (factory made, see photo below) that held the powder. The bullet was a soft lead.

NOTE: All Snider rifles and carbines are scarce. Examples in excellent condition are rarely encountered.

Bibliographical Note: It is strongly suggested that the reader interested in the myriad of details and variations of the Snider see Ian Skennerton, ***A Treatise On the Snider***, 1977.

Pattern 1 Rifled Musket

Converted Enfield muzzle-loading rifle. Barrel length is 36.5". Brass furniture with flat hammer face. Rear sight marked to 950 yards. Approved 1866.

Exc.	*V.G.*	*Good*	*Fair*	*Poor*
1750	1200	800	500	300

Pattern 1*

Similar to the Pattern 1 but with a countersunk barrel at the rear of the chamber to accommodate the cartridge rim. The asterisk (*) was marked on top of the receiver to indicate the conversion. Approved in May 1967.

Exc.	*V.G.*	*Good*	*Fair*	*Poor*
1500	1200	800	500	300

Pattern 2*

Similar to the Pattern I* but it is a direct conversion from the muzzle-loading Enfields and not the Pattern I*. The top of the receiver is marked "Mark II*". Also introduced in May 1867.

Exc.	*V.G.*	*Good*	*Fair*	*Poor*
1500	1200	800	500	300

Pattern 2**

This conversion is the most-often-encountered conversion. It has the cartridge recess like the earlier conversion, but also has a cupped hammer face, a better shaped extractor, and a larger breech block face. Introduced in May 1867.

Exc.	*V.G.*	*Good*	*Fair*	*Poor*
1250	1000	650	450	300

Pattern 3

Similar in outward appearance to the earlier conversions but with a flat hammer face and a spring-loaded locking latch on the left side of the breech block. The receiver is marked "III". Introduced in January 1869.

Exc.	*V.G.*	*Good*	*Fair*	*Poor*
1500	1200	800	500	300

Short Enfield Rifle P60 Mark II**

This conversion used an Enfield Pattern 1860 with the barrel cut to 30.5 inches from 33 inches. Cupped hammer face. Two barrel bands, a sword bar, and case hardened furniture. Sling swivels on butt and upper barrel band. Sights marked to 400 yards on the rear sight and 1,000 yards on the leaf sight. Top of the receiver marked "II**". Introduced in March of 1867.

Exc.	*V.G.*	*Good*	*Fair*	*Poor*
1500	1200	800	500	300

Short Enfield Rifle P60 Mark II** Naval Rifle

Similar to the Mark II** army version except that brass furniture is used in place of iron. Some Naval rifles were not fitted with a butt sling swivel. Introduced in August of 1867.

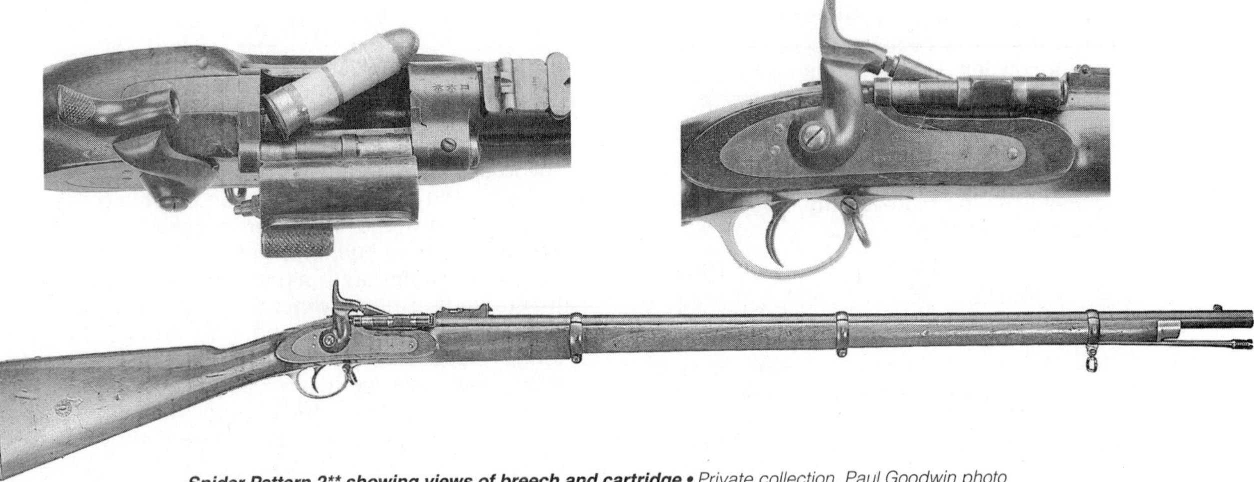

Snider Pattern 2 showing views of breech and cartridge** • *Private collection, Paul Goodwin photo*

Exc.	V.G.	Good	Fair	Poor
1500	1200	800	500	300

Short Enfield Rifle P60 Mark III

When this conversion was introduced in January of 1869, the steel barrel was also introduced, but a few early examples (about 1,200) were fitted with iron barrels. This rifle was actually a newly manufactured gun instead of a conversion of a muzzleloader. The top of the receiver is marked "III".

Exc.	V.G.	Good	Fair	Poor
1500	1200	800	500	300

Mark II Engineers (Lancaster) Carbine**

This is a converted Lancaster rifle with a 29-inch barrel, brass furniture, and cupped hammer face. Two barrel bands with sling swivel on upper band. Butt-mounted rear swivel. "LANCASTER'S PATENT" stamped on the barrel. Rear leaf sight marked to 1,150 yards. Introduced in 1867 with about 5,000 rifles converted.

Exc.	V.G.	Good	Fair	Poor
1850	1450	950	600	350

Artillery Carbine P61 Mark II**

Introduced in May of 1867. It has 2 barrel bands, a sword bar, brass buttplate and trigger guard. The hammer face is cupped. The rear sight has a maximum range of 600 yards. Barrel length is 21.5 inches. Receiver is marked "II**". About 60,000 were converted.

Exc.	V.G.	Good	Fair	Poor
1850	1450	950	600	350

Artillery Carbine P61 Mark III

This was a newly manufactured conversion with a spring loaded locking latch on the left side of the breech block. The barrel is steel and is 21.5 inches long. Brass furniture with flat hammer face. Marked "III" on the top of the action. Introduced in 1869.

Exc.	V.G.	Good	Fair	Poor
1850	1450	950	600	350

Artillery Carbine P61 Mark IV

This rifle uses the Mark III breech and is fitted with a 21.5-inch barrel. Rear sight graduated to 900 yards. Two barrel bands with the stock coming to within 1.125 inches of the muzzle. Brass furniture. Introduced in 1891.

Exc.	V.G.	Good	Fair	Poor
1850	1450	950	600	350

Cavalry Carbine P61 Mark II**

This carbine was fitted with a half stock. The butt was fitted with a trap for a two-piece cleaning rod. Sling bar and ring on left side although some may not have the bar fitted. Brass furniture. Barrel length is 19.25 inches. Rear sight is a ladder type to 600 yards fitted with a leather protector secured by a screw on each side of the stock. A snap cap is secured by a chain screwed into the triggerguard. No sling swivels. Introduced in May of 1867.

Exc.	V.G.	Good	Fair	Poor
1850	1450	950	600	350

Cavalry Carbine Mark III

This is a newly manufactured carbine using the Mark III breech. Only a few early examples used iron barrel; the rest used steel. Brass furniture. Flat hammer face. The stock was newly made. Introduced in January of 1869.

Exc.	V.G.	Good	Fair	Poor
1850	1450	950	600	350

Yeomanry Carbine Mark I

This carbine was converted from Snider long rifles and issued to volunteer cavalry forces. Fitted with a 19.2-inch barrel. Brass furniture. Flat hammer face. The side nail cups are from the long rifle and made of brass instead of steel. Introduced in July of 1880.

Exc.	V.G.	Good	Fair	Poor
1850	1450	950	600	350

Naval Rifle P58

Approved in August 1867 and fitted with a 30.5-inch barrel with brass furniture. Many were not fitted with a lower sling swivel. The receiver is marked, "II**" on the top near the barrel. Leaf sight is graduated to 1,000 yards with a ramp step from 100 to 400 yards. About 53,500 of these rifles were produced.

Exc.	V.G.	Good	Fair	Poor
1500	1200	800	500	300

Irish Constabulary Carbine Mark II P56**

This carbine is a conversion of the Enfield Pattern 1856 short rifle. Barrel length is 22.5 inches. Iron furniture. Cupped hammer face. Sword bar. Two barrel bands. Stock stops 1.4 inches from muzzle. Sling swivels on upper barrel band and butt stock. Brass triggerguard. Stamped "II**" on receiver. Introduced in July of 1867.

Exc.	V.G.	Good	Fair	Poor
1850	1450	950	500	350

Irish Constabulary Carbine Mark III

Similar to the Mark II** but with flat hammer face and spring loaded locking latch on left side of breech block. Fitted with an iron barrel. Rear sight graduated to 900 yards. Introduced in January of 1869.

Exc.	V.G.	Good	Fair	Poor
1850	1450	950	500	300

Convict Civil Guard Carbine P53

This carbine was issued especially for penal service. Rounded forend, two barrel bands, no rear sight or sling swivels. Converted from Pattern 1853 rifle. Stamped II** on breech. Some of these carbines are rifled, while others are smoothbore with choked muzzle for shot cartridges. Introduced September of 1867.

Exc.	V.G.	Good	Fair	Poor
1850	1450	950	600	350

Martini-Henry

This single shot rolling block rifle was built on the Martini block action (a modification of the American Peabody action) and a rifled barrel by Alexander Henry. Early rifles built prior to 1885 used a fragile rolled cartridge case while later post 1885 versions used a solid case. The rifle was chambered for the .577-450 cartridge that used a paper patch bullet. The British army built these rifles with three different buttstock lengths and marked the half-inch-shorter-than-standard rifles with an "S" on the stock while longer stocks were marked with an "L." Standard length buttstocks were not marked. Martini-Henry rifles and carbines were used by British military forces all over the world during the latter quarter of the 19th century. Produced by Enfield, BSA, and LSA.

When 'arf of your bullets fly wide in the ditch,
Don't call your Martini a cross-eyed old bitch;
She's human as you are - you treat her as sich,
An' she'll fight for the young British soldier.
Rudyard Kipling

Martini in action • *Courtesy Paul S. Scarlata*

Mark 1 Rifle

Chambered for the .577-450 Martini-Henry cartridge and fitted with a 33.2-inch barrel, this lever operated single shot rifle was fitted with a steel bayonet and was full stocked with no upper handguard. Weight is about 8.75 lbs. Introduced in 1874.

Exc.	***V.G.***	***Good***	***Fair***	***Poor***
1450	1000	750	400	250

Mark 2 Rifle

Similar to the Mark 1 but with an improved trigger in 1877.

Exc.	***V.G.***	***Good***	***Fair***	***Poor***
1250	900	700	500	250

Mark 3 Rifle

An improved version introduced in 1879 of the Mark 2 with double lump barrel and wider breech block. Weight is slightly heavier than the Marks 1 and 2 at about 9 lbs.

Exc.	***V.G.***	***Good***	***Fair***	***Poor***
1250	900	700	500	250

Mark 4 Rifle

Introduced in 1887, this Mark was fitted with a longer lever, a thinner breech block with modified extractor, narrow buttstock with bayonet fitting to accommodate a P1887 sword bayonet. Weight is about 9.25 lbs.

Exc.	***V.G.***	***Good***	***Fair***	***Poor***
1250	900	700	500	250

Pattern 1887 Bayonet for Martini-Henry

Checkered hard rubber grips. Muzzle ring. 18.3-inch single edge blade. Steel tipped leather scabbard. Ricasso has various English military marks. Price range 275 – 150.

Cavalry Carbine Mark 1

This configuration was introduced in 1877 and is a short version of the rifle with full stock, no handguard, front sight with protectors, and a reduced charge carbine cartridge; the .577-450 Martini-Henry Carbine cartridge. Barrel length is about 21.25 inches. Weight is approximately 7.5 lbs.

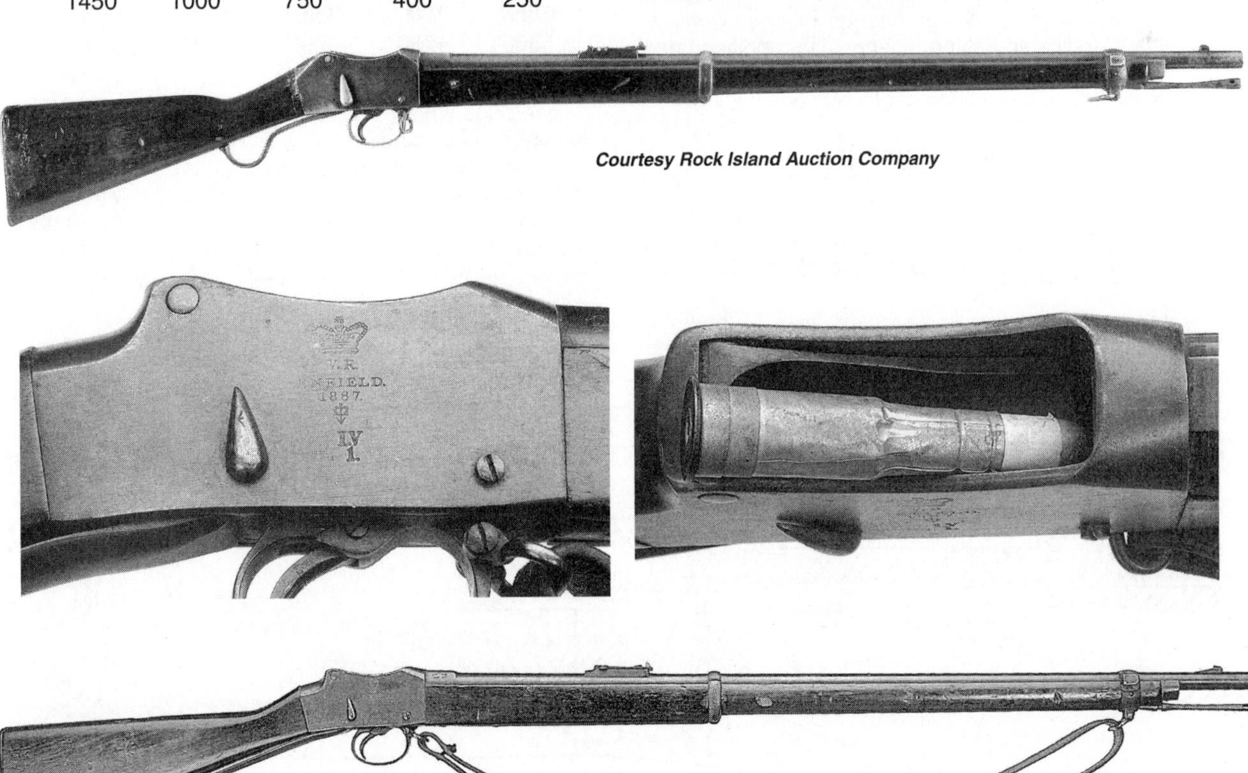

Courtesy Rock Island Auction Company

Martini-Henry Mark IV with close up of receiver and open breech with cartridge • *Private collection, Paul Goodwin photo*

Pattern 1887 Bayonet for Martini-Henry

Exc.	V.G.	Good	Fair	Poor
1500	1250	950	700	350

Artillery Carbine Mark 2

This model is similar to the Cavalry Carbine but with bayonet fittings. Introduced in 1879. Weight is about 7.7 lbs.

Exc.	V.G.	Good	Fair	Poor
1500	1250	950	700	350

NOTE: Many Martini Henrys were converted to .303 British caliber. These conversions will command about the same price as unconverted rifles.

LEE-METFORD

NOTE: The Lee-Metford rifles were produced at the Royal Small Arms Factory, Enfield; the Birmingham Small Arms Co.; Sparkbrook, Vickers, Birmingham, and the London Small Arms Co., and so marked on the right side under the bolt handle for rifles and on the left side for carbines. The British used the MARK and * system to denote improvements. The "MARK" indicated a major design change or improvement. The "*" indicated a minor change. Un-modified Lee-Metford rifles are rare. Most early models were rebuilt into later versions or given to colonial troops.

TRIALS RIFLES

The first trials for magazine rifles for the British army began in 1880. There were a number of initial contenders which will not be covered here. By 1883, the number of serious competitors was reduced to those listed below.

Owen Jones

This model was an adaptation of the Martini action and fitted with a 33-inch barrel chambered for the .402 caliber Enfield-Martini cartridge. Five-round magazine. Folding rear sight graduated to 2,000 yards. Weight is about 10.5 lbs. An unknown number of these rifles were built with different type magazine feeds and styles.

Exc.	V.G.	Good	Fair	Poor
5500	4750	4000	2500	—

Lee-Burton

This rifle used the Lee action, the first British rifle to do so. Chambered for the .402 caliber Enfield-Martini cartridge and fitted with a 30.2-inch barrel. Built by Enfield. Magazine capacity is 5 rounds. Marked "ENFIELD 1886" of left side of the receiver. Weight is about 10 lbs. About 300 were produced.

Exc.	V.G.	Good	Fair	Poor
5500	4750	4000	2500	—

Improved Lee

These rifles were purchased directly from Remington in 1887. Chambered for the .43 caliber Spanish cartridge and fitted with a 32-inch barrel. Folding leaf rear sight was graduated to 1,200 yards. Magazine capacity was 5 rounds. Weighs approximately 10 lbs. Marked with the Remington address on the receiver. About 300 were used in the trials. The only indication

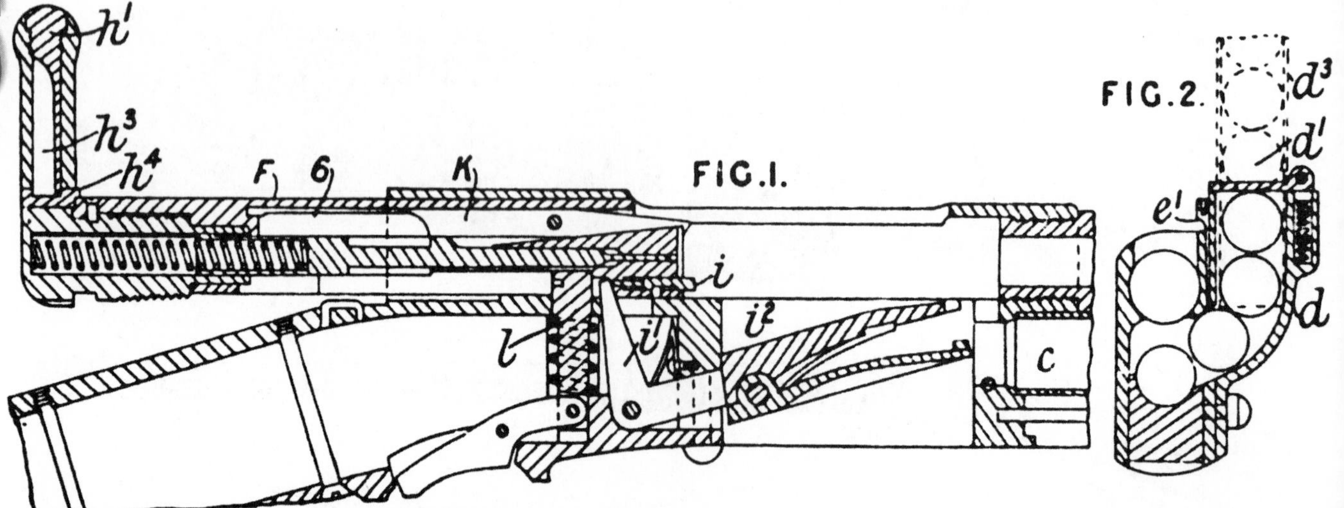

Burton Patent #4046, Oct. 5, 1880, showing receiver and magazine hopper system in FIG. 2 • British Small Arms Patents

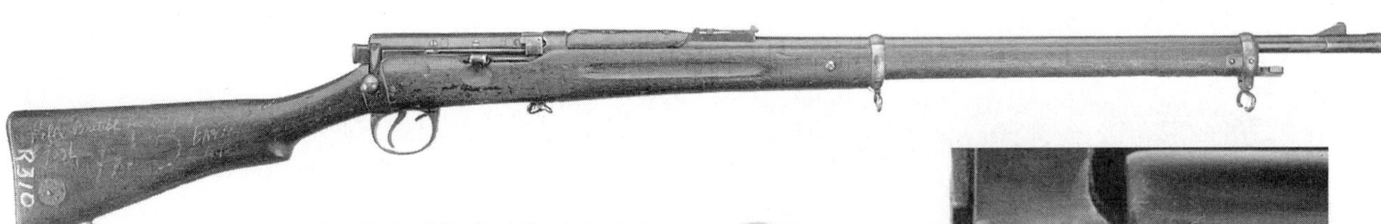

*Lee-Metford 1** • *Paul Goodwin photo*

that this is a trials rifle is the marking "WD" on the right side of the butt.

Exc.	V.G.	Good	Fair	Poor
3750	3000	2500	1500	—

.303 Magazine Rifle-1888 Trials Model

Developed from the Improved Lee but chambered for the .303 cartridge and fitted with a 30.2-inch barrel. No upper handguard. Magazine capacity is 7 rounds. Marked, "ENFIELD 1888." Weight is about 9 lbs. Some 387 of these rifles were produced.

Exc.	V.G.	Good	Fair	Poor
4500	3750	3000	1750	—

Mark I

A bolt action service rifle chambered for the .303 black powder British cartridge. It was designed by James Paris Lee and incorporated rifling developed by William Metford. This rifling was specifically designed to alleviate the problem of black powder fouling. 30.2-inch barrel and an 8-round, detachable box magazine located in front of the triggerguard. Furnished with magazine cutoff, it features military-type sights and a cleaning rod mounted underneath the barrel and a trap in the steel buttplate to house cleaning tools. Finger grooves in forend. The finish is blued, with a full-length walnut stock held on by two barrel bands. Weight is about 10 lbs. It was introduced in 1888. Approximately 358,000 were produced.

Exc.	V.G.	Good	Fair	Poor
900	800	650	400	250

Mark I*

Similar to the Mark 1 except that the safety catch was removed from the cocking piece and a brass disc was inletted into the buttstock for regimental markings. There were a number of internal improvements, as well as the fitting of a different, blade-type front sight and V-notch rear sight graduated to 1,800 yards. This model was fitted with an 8-round magazine. It was introduced in 1892.

Exc.	V.G.	Good	Fair	Poor
900	800	650	400	250

Mark II

Has a modified magazine that holds 10 rounds in a double column. A half-length cleaning rod was located under the 30.2-inch barrel. No finger grooves in forend. Fitted with brass buttplate with long heel tang. Rear leaf sight graduated to 1,800 yards. No butt marking disk. It was introduced in 1892. Weight reduced to 9.25 lbs. About 250,000 were produced.

Exc.	V.G.	Good	Fair	Poor
900	800	650	400	250

Mark II*

Has a lengthened bolt, with the addition of a safety catch. Barrel length is 30.2 inches. No finger grooves in forend. All parts are interchangeable with the Mark II rifle. It was introduced in 1895. About 13,000 were produced.

Exc.	V.G.	Good	Fair	Poor
900	800	650	400	250

Mark I Carbine

Has a 20.75-inch barrel. Rear sight is graduated to 2,000 yards. Buttstock is fitted with a marking disk. No bayonet fittings. Weight was about 7.5 lbs. It was introduced in 1894. Approximately 18,000 were produced.

NOTE: Many Lee-Metford rifles were modified after 1902 to accept a stripper clip guide which required the removal of the dust cover. Such modification results in a deduction of 10 percent from original Lee-Metford rifles.

Exc.	V.G.	Good	Fair	Poor
950	850	700	500	300

Pattern 1888 Bayonet for Lee-Medford & Lee-Enfield

Wood grips. Muzzle ring. 12-inch double edge blade. Steel tipped leather scabbard. These are frequently found without the scabbard. The popular explanation is that many were burned in South Africa after the Boer War. This was done because the leather was

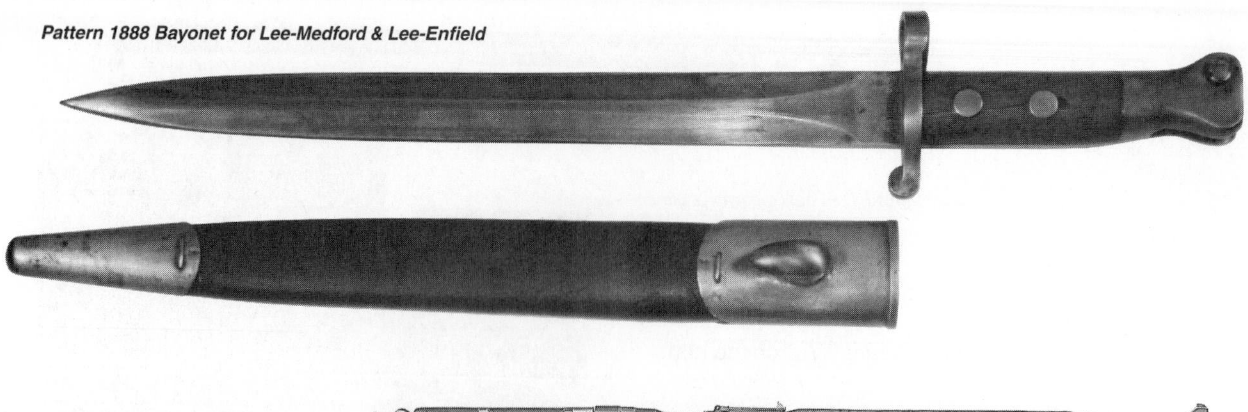
Pattern 1888 Bayonet for Lee-Medford & Lee-Enfield

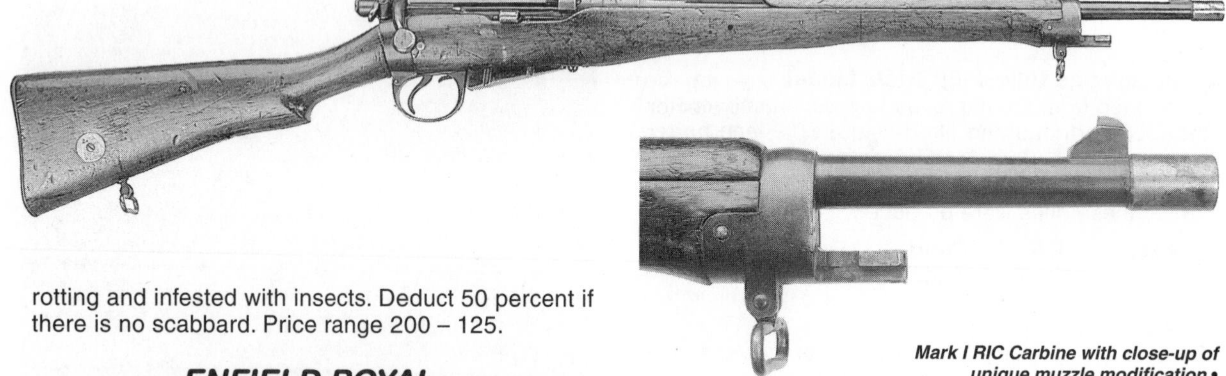
Mark I RIC Carbine with close-up of unique muzzle modification • Private collection, Paul Goodwin photo

GREAT BRITAIN

rotting and infested with insects. Deduct 50 percent if there is no scabbard. Price range 200 – 125.

ENFIELD ROYAL SMALL ARMS FACTORY

NOTE: This series of rifles is marked by the presence of deeper Enfield rifling rather than the shallow Metford rifling. The same manufacturers that built the Lee-Metford built the Lee-Enfield along with Ishapore, India, and Lithgow, Australia.

Lee-Enfield Rifle • Courtesy Paul S. Scarlata

Lee-Enfield Mark I Rifle

Chambered for the .303 cartridge and has a 30-inch barrel. The attached box magazine holds 10 rounds, and the sights are military-styled. Rear leaf sight graduated to 1,800 yards. The stock is full-length walnut, and there is a cleaning rod beneath it. There is a magazine cutoff located on the right side of the receiver. There are two barrel bands and a bayonet lug. The upper handguard extended from the receiver ring to the rear sight. The buttplate is brass with extended upper tang with trap for cleaning equipment. Weight is about 9.25 lbs. This model was manufactured between 1895 and 1899. Approximately 315,000 were manufactured.

Paul Goodwin photo

Exc.	V.G.	Good	Fair	Poor
900	750	600	400	200

Lee-Enfield Mark I* Rifle

No attached cleaning rod, otherwise the same as the Mark I rifle. It was introduced in 1899. Almost 600,000 of these rifles were produced.

Exc.	V.G.	Good	Fair	Poor
900	750	600	400	200

NOTE: Many long Lee-Enfield rifles were modified for charger loading (stripper clip). Prices are 10 percent less than unmodified rifles.

Lee-Enfield Mark I Carbine

This model is the same as the Lee-Metford except for the Enfield rifling and so marked. Slight different

Mark II • *Courtesy West Point Museum, Paul Goodwin photo*

rear sight marked "EC" on bottom right hand corner of leaf. Introduced in 1896. Rear sight leather protector is standard on this carbine. Weight is about 7.5 lbs. Approximately 14,000 were produced.

Exc.	*V.G.*	*Good*	*Fair*	*Poor*
950	750	500	300	150

Lee-Enfield Mark I* Carbine

Same as the Mark I carbine but with no cleaning rod and no left side sling bar. Rear sight leather protector. Introduced in 1899. A little more than 26,000 were produced.

Exc.	*V.G.*	*Good*	*Fair*	*Poor*
1000	750	500	300	150

Lee-Enfield Mark I RIC Carbine

This model was converted from Lee-Enfield carbines and was fitted with a bayonet lug for a Pattern 1888 bayonet. This required a collar to be added at the muzzle to increase the barrel diameter to accept the bayonet ring. It was first converted in 1905 for the Royal Irish Constabulary. About 11,000 were converted.

Exc.	*V.G.*	*Good*	*Fair*	*Poor*
750	600	450	250	150

NO. 1 SMLE SERIES

The SMLEs were not designated No. 1s until the British changed their rifle nomenclature system in 1926. Guns made prior to that date were marked "SMLE," not No. 1.

No. 1 SMLE Mark 1 • *Paul Goodwin photo*

No. 1 Mark III* • *Courtesy West Point Museum, Paul Goodwin photo*

SMLE Trials Rifle

About 1,000 of these rifles were built for trials in 1902. Fitted with a full-length handguard and a charger loading system. Barrel length is 25.2 inches with a .303 chamber. Sheet metal buttplate. Weight is about 8 lbs. A number of different features appeared on this rifle that were later incorporated into the regular production SMLE. Most of these rifles were converted to Aiming Tube Short Rifles in 1906 and are extremely rare.

Exc.	V.G.	Good	Fair	Poor
1500	1150	800	500	200

No. 1 SMLE Mark I

Introduced in 1902 this was the first of the "Short, Magazine Lee-Enfield" or No. 1 series of rifles. It was fitted with a full stock with pistol grip and a 25.2-inch barrel. It also had a full upper handguard. Rear sight is leaf-type graduated to 2,000 yards. The bayonet mountings are integral with the nosecap. Magazine capacity was 10 rounds. Magazine cutoff on right side of receiver. Weight was about 8 lbs. A little more than 360,000 of these rifles were produced.

Exc.	V.G.	Good	Fair	Poor
750	600	400	300	150

No. 1 SMLE Mark I*

A minor modification of the SMLE Mark I. Introduced in 1906. Fitted with a buttplate trap and a new style butt sling swivel. About 60,000 of these rifles were produced.

Exc.	V.G.	Good	Fair	Poor
750	600	400	250	100

No. 1 SMLE Mark II

The Mark I and II Long Lee converted by fitting a shorter and lighter barrel (25.2 inches), modifying the action to accept a stripper clip, and fitting new sights. It was introduced in 1903. Approximately 40,000 Mark IIs were manufactured.

Exc.	V.G.	Good	Fair	Poor
550	375	300	150	100

No. 1 SMLE Mark II*

A modification of the Mark II SMLE to add features from the SMLE Mark III so that it would correspond with that model. Introduced in 1908. About 22,000 were converted.

Exc.	V.G.	Good	Fair	Poor
550	375	300	150	100

No. 1 SMLE Mark III

Chambered for .303 British and has a 25.2-inch barrel with a 10-round magazine. The magazine has a cutoff, and the sights are military-styled with volley sights on the left side and open sights at top rear. The action is

modified to accept a stripper clip and automatically eject it when the bolt is closed. Weight is approximately 8.5 lbs. This model was introduced in 1907. The Mark III was one of the more successful and famous British military rifles. It was used extensively in World War I and World War II. In many areas of the old British Commonwealth it is still used today. Almost 7,000,000 of these were produced. Matching numbers usually found on: receiver, bolt, fore stock, nose cap. Deduct 25% for MM parts.

Courtesy Richard M. Kumor Sr.

Exc.	V.G.	Good	Fair	Poor
500	400	300	150	100

Enfield charger clip with .303 British cartridges

No. 1 Mark III and Mark III* Drill Rifles

These rifles were modified for drill use and stamped "DP." They feature a firing pin with no tip and on occasion a bolt head with the firing pin hole welded closed. Worth more as parts.

Exc.	V.G.	Good	Fair	Poor
100	90	80	60	50

No. 1 Mark III Single Shot Rifles

Converted to single shot at Ishapore, India, and have magazine well filled. Intended for use with "unreliable" Indian troops.

Exc.	V.G.	Good	Fair	Poor
150	125	100	90	75

No. 1 Mark III and Mark III* Grenade Launching Rifles

Built on the standard Mk III and Mk III* rifles with the addition of a wire wrapping on the front of the barrel. These rifles are usually marked "E.Y." to indicate only ball ammunition be used in an emergency. A cup-type grenade launcher was fitted. Add $50 for the grenade launcher.

Exc.	V.G.	Good	Fair	Poor
400	275	200	120	100

Lee-Enfield .410 Musket

Built around the No. 1 Mark III rifle and converted in Ishapore, India to a single shot .410 shotgun. Intended for guard duty. The rifle fired a special .303 case that was not necked down. This model, if in original configuration, will not accept a modern .410 shotshell. Some U.S. importer have lengthened the chamber to 3 inches to allow use of commercial .410 shells. Those rifles that have been altered to accept modern .410 shells will be worth less to some collectors, more to those who want to shoot them.

Exc.	V.G.	Good	Fair	Poor
200	175	150	100	75

GREAT BRITAIN

No. 1 rifle (World War II version) with grenade launcher • *Courtesy private collection, Paul Goodwin photo*

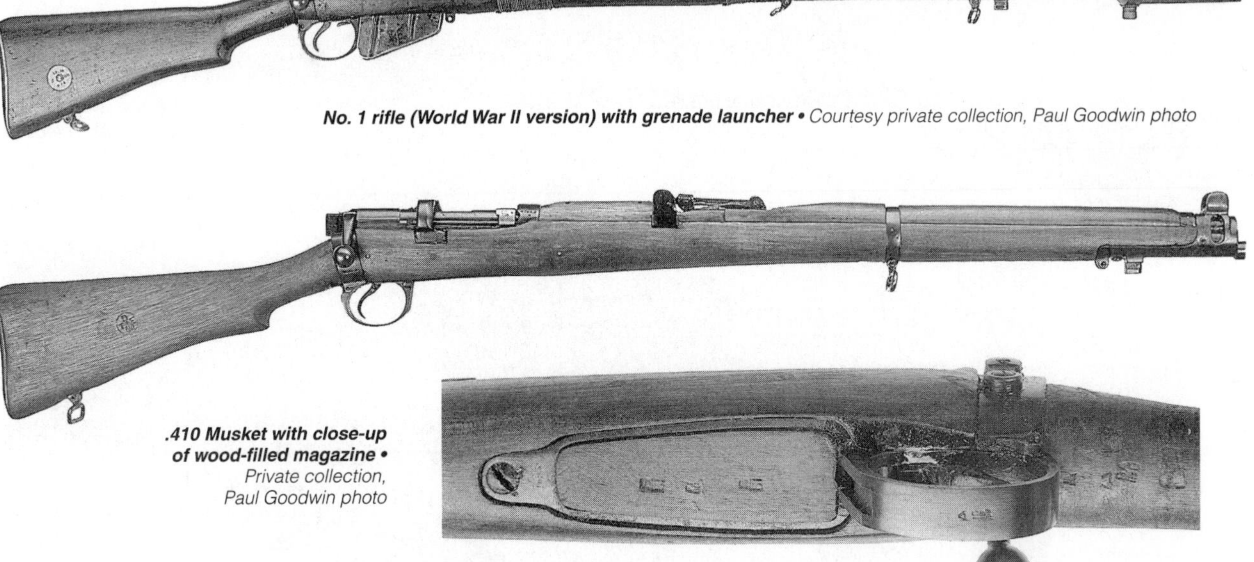

.410 Musket with close-up of wood-filled magazine • *Private collection, Paul Goodwin photo*

GREAT BRITAIN

No. 1 SMLE Mark IV

This model was Lee-Metford and Lee-Enfield rifles converted to Mark III configuration. The receiver was modified for a charger bridge and safety catch. The dust cover lugs were also removed from the bolt. Adopted in 1907. Almost 100,000 of these rifles were converted.

Exc.	V.G.	Good	Fair	Poor
500	325	275	200	100

Rifle Charger Loading Long Lee-Enfield Mark I/I*

These are converted Lee-Enfield rifles adapted to charger loading. Many of these rifles were used in the early days of WWI by the British Royal Navy. Over 180,000 of these rifles were produced.

Exc.	V.G.	Good	Fair	Poor
800	700	550	300	150

No. 1 SMLE Mark III*

This variation does not have a magazine cutoff, the rear sight windage adjustment, left side auxiliary long range sights, a center swivel lug, or a brass buttstock marking disc. Over 2 million of this model were made during World War I. It was last built in England in 1944 by B.S.A. This model was also manufactured in India at Ishapore until 1964, and in Australia at Lithgow through the 1950s, and are so marked. Weight is about 9 lbs.

Exc.	V.G.	Good	Fair	Poor
400	300	225	150	100

NOTE: See Australia for the Lithgow rifles. For rifles built in India deduct 20 percent

No. 1 SMLE Mark V

Similar to the Mark III except for the use of a receiver mounted wide aperture rear sight. The folding sight is graduated from 200 yards to 1,400 yards with even number on the right side and odd on the left. Serial numbers range from 1 to 9999, then an "A" prefix was used. The standard pattern 1907 sword bayonet was issued with the rifle. Between 1922 and 1924 only 20,000 were produced. A scarce model.

Exc.	V.G.	Good	Fair	Poor
975	750	650	450	300

Pattern 1907 Bayonet for SMLE series

Wood grips. Ring for nose cap stud that is below the barrel. 15-inch single edge blade. Steel tipped leather scabbard. Manufactured by several contractors, the most common of which are Wilkinson and Sanderson. Scarcer makers such as Vickers, Remington and Mole might bring a premium to some collectors. This design was originally made with a quillon similar to that found on the Japanese Type 30 bayonet. After the quillon was dropped from production, most of the earlier models had it removed.

Add 200 percent or more for a P1907 bayonet with intact quillon. Reproductions of the quillon model have

SMLE magazine (top pair) - note the tension spring on the lower back. Magazine for #4 or #5 Enfield rifles (bottom pair). Price for each type, 60-30

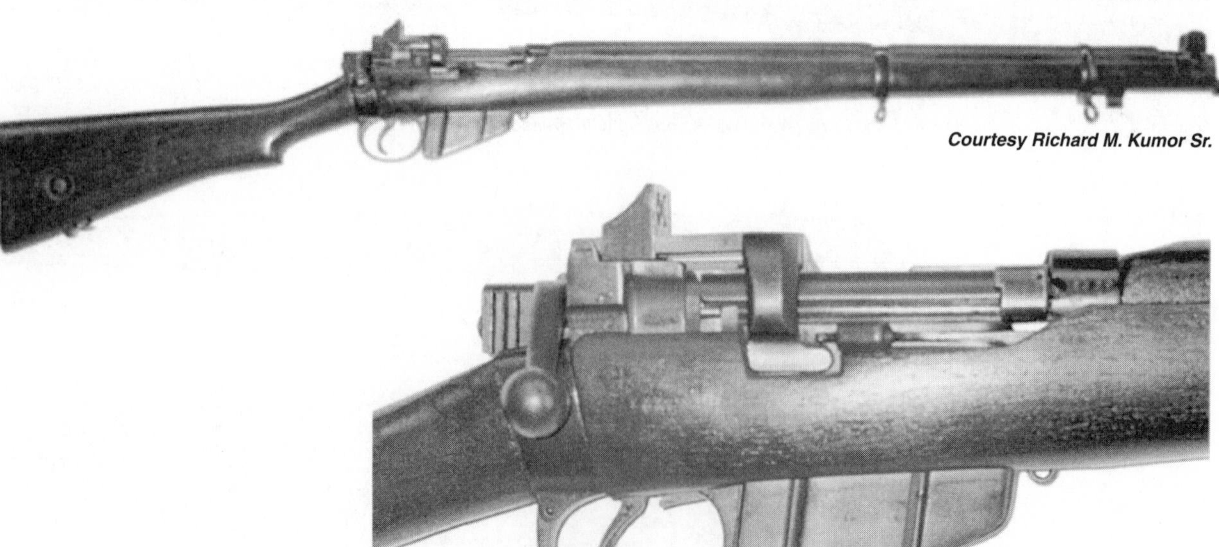

Courtesy Richard M. Kumor Sr.

Close-up of Mark V rear sight • *Courtesy Richard M. Kumor Sr.*

Pattern 1907 Bayonet for SMLE series

appeared in recent years. They are made in India and the quality is poor. Price range 100 – 40.

No. 1 SMLE Mark VI
This model had the rear sight located on the receiver bridge. It also used a heavier barrel, lighter nose cap, and smaller bolt head than previous models. It did have the magazine cutoff. Checkered forend. There were three variants of this rifle: Pattern A introduced in 1926, Pattern B introduced in 1929 to 1931 and Pattern C introduced in 1935. About 1,000 trials rifles were built in Pattern B.

Exc.	V.G.	Good	Fair	Poor
4000	2750	1750	—	—

NO. 4 SERIES

Rifle No. 4 Mark 1 Trials Model
Introduced in 1931 with about 2,500 being produced. This is a No. 1 Mark VI with the exception of the shape of the action, and designation markings. Some had no markings at all. Many were later converted to No. 4 Mark I (T) sniper rifles. Markings are commonly found on the right side of the butt socket.

Exc.	V.G.	Good	Fair	Poor
2500	1750	1100	—	—

Rifle No. 4 Mark I
An improved version of the No. 1 Mark VI that featured a stronger action with an aperture sight. It was issued in 1931. It was redesigned in 1939 for mass production with shortcuts taken for wartime production. Barrel length is 25.2 inches with 10-round magazine. The barrel diameter is larger than the SMLE series and extended almost 3 inches out of the forend. Weight is about 8.75 lbs. This model was used extensively during WWII. It is still in use today. About 2 million of these rifles were produced but none were built at Enfield. Instead they were built at Long Branch in Canada and Savage-Stevens.

Exc.	V.G.	Good	Fair	Poor
500	375	275	150	100

Rifle No. 4 Mark I*
This model was almost identical to the No. 4 Mark I, but was produced in North America during WWII. The principal U.S. producer was Savage-Stevens (marked u.s. property); in Canada marked "LONG BRANCH." The Savage-Stevens guns have a "C" in the serial number for Chicopee Falls and guns with "L" serial numbers were produced at Longbranch. This model differed from the Mark 1 in that the bolt-head catch was eliminated and a cut-out on the bolt head track was used for its removal. Over 2 million were produced during the war.

***No. 4 Enfield in Korea** • Courtesy Paul S. Scarlata*

Exc.	V.G.	Good	Fair	Poor
450	350	275	150	100

Rifle No. 4 Mark 2
This model was fitted with a trigger that was pinned to the receiver rather than the triggerguard. Introduced in 1949. This rifle had a higher quality finish than its wartime predecessors.

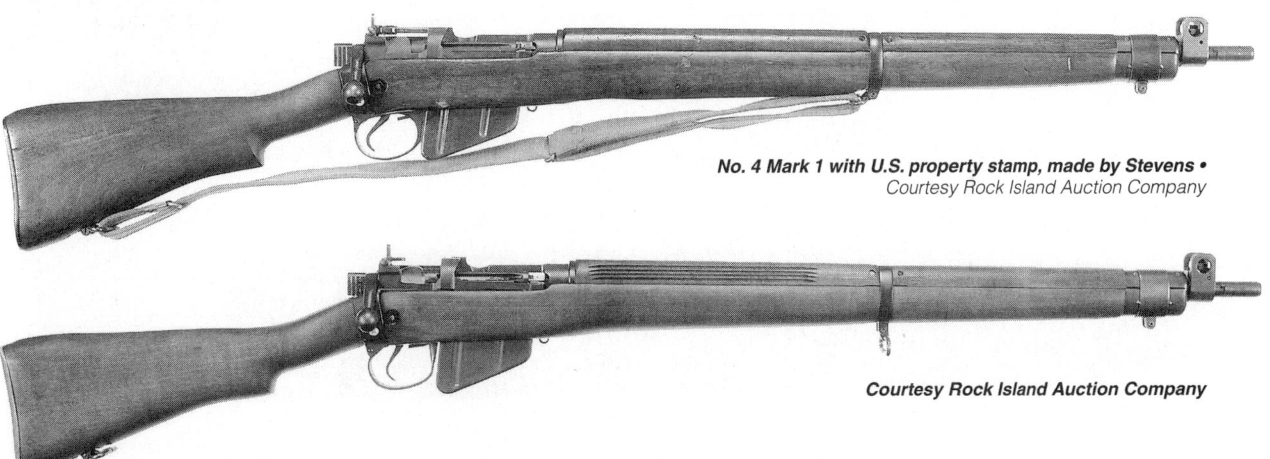
***No. 4 Mark 1 with U.S. property stamp, made by Stevens** • Courtesy Rock Island Auction Company*

Courtesy Rock Island Auction Company

Exc.	V.G.	Good	Fair	Poor
550	375	300	175	100

Rifle No. 4 Mark 1/2 (converted No. 4 Mark I) & No. 4 Mark 1/3 (converted No. 4 Mark I*)

These models have new trigger mechanism installed to more closely emulate the Mark 2 and upgraded components. The conversion required altering the old markings. This was done with an electric pencil instead of a stamp. The result is quite obvious.

Exc.	V.G.	Good	Fair	Poor
450	375	300	175	100

Bayonets for No. 4 Rifle Series

There were three types of bayonets made for the No. 4 rifles. The first style is the spike. The first spike design, the Mk1, has a cruciform blade, which was machined to a + shape when viewed from the end. The Mk.1 is scarce and there have been fakes and reproductions made. The Mk. II was made by the millions and is very common. The spike is simply round with a point machined on the tip. Made by numerous contractors. There are several minor variations in the production methods but none stands out as more valuable than another. The third type is the No. 9 Mk. 1 with a bowie-style blade.

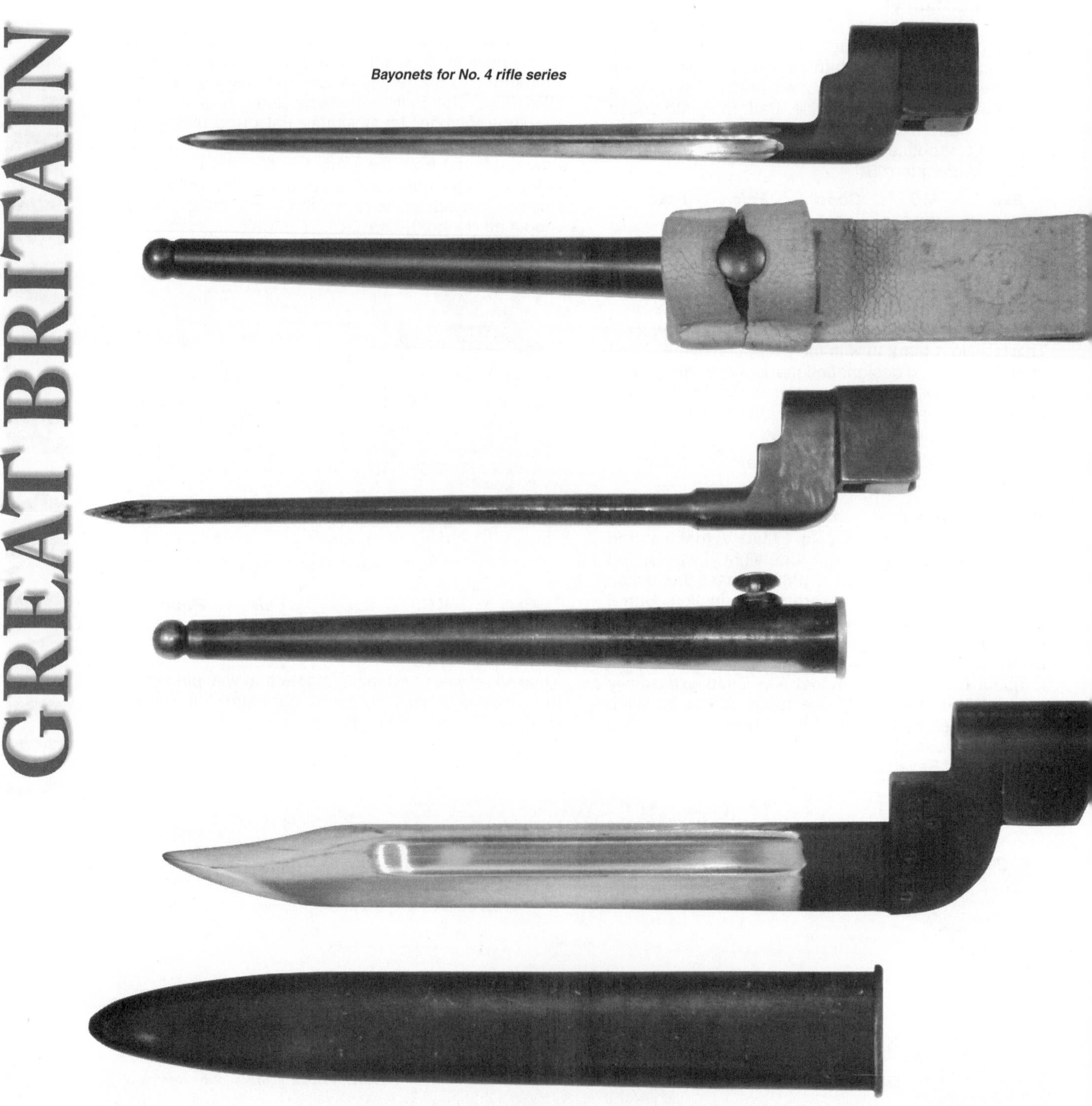

Bayonets for No. 4 rifle series

Mk.1 Spike with cruciform blade.
BEWARE of fakes! Price range 200 – 75.

Mk. II Spike with round blade.
Price range 25 – 10.

No. 9 Mk. 1 bayonet.
This has an 8-inch bowie-style blade. Price range 70 – 30.

JUNGLE CARBINES

No. 1 Shortened & Lightened Rifle
Fitted with a 20-inch barrel and a shortened forend. The rear aperture sight is mounted on the charger bridge and graduated for 200 and 500 yards. Fitted for a blade bayonet. Weight is about 8.75 lbs. About 32 of these rifles were built at Lithgow. The serial number has an "XP" prefix.

NOTE: Extremely rare. Beware of fakes. Seek expert advice prior to purchase.

Exc.	V.G.	Good	Fair	Poor
N/A	—	—	—	—

Rifle No. 5 Mark 1
Also known as the "Jungle Carbine." Introduced in 1944. It is chambered for the .303 British cartridge and has a 20.5-inch barrel with an attached flash suppressor and a shorter forend and handguard. It is furnished with a rubber buttpad and modified rear sight graduated to 800 yards. This was not a popular weapon with the soldiers who carried it, as the recoil was excessive due to the lighter weight. Weight is approximately 7 lbs. About 250,000 were built. This model has its own distinctive knife bayonet.

Courtesy Richard M. Kumor Sr.

Exc.	V.G.	Good	Fair	Poor
550	425	300	175	125

NOTE: add 20% for 1944 or 1945 dated Jungle Carbine

No. 5 Bayonet for Jungle Carbine
Wood grips. Large muzzle ring that fits over the flash hider. 7.9-inch single edge blade. Steel scabbard. English military markings. Some copies have been imported from India that are marked "R.F.I." Deduct 50 percent for Indian mfg. Price range 200 – 100.

No. 7 Bayonet for No. 4 Mk1
Many of the No. 5 bayonets were converted for use on the No. 4 rifles. A pivoting socket was added to the handle that allows it to mount on the barrel. Red plastic grips. Price range 150 – 70.

NOTE: The same steel scabbards were used on the No. 5, No. 7 and No. 9 bayonets. It is common to find any of these without a scabbard. Deduct $30 for no scabbard.

SNIPER RIFLES

NOTE: For Canadian built No. 4 Mk1 T rifles see Canada, Rifles.

SMLE Sniper (Optical Sights)
These rifles are Mark III and Mark III* mounted with optical sights. These sights are comprised of a special front and rear sight that when used together form a telescope with a magnification of 2 to 3 power. About 13,000 of these rifles were fitted with these optical sights. Three different optical makers were used with Lattey being the largest. Conversions were performed by unit armorers beginning in 1915.

NOTE: Beware of fakes. Seek expert advice prior to a purchase.

Exc.	V.G.	Good	Fair	Poor
3500	3000	2000	—	—

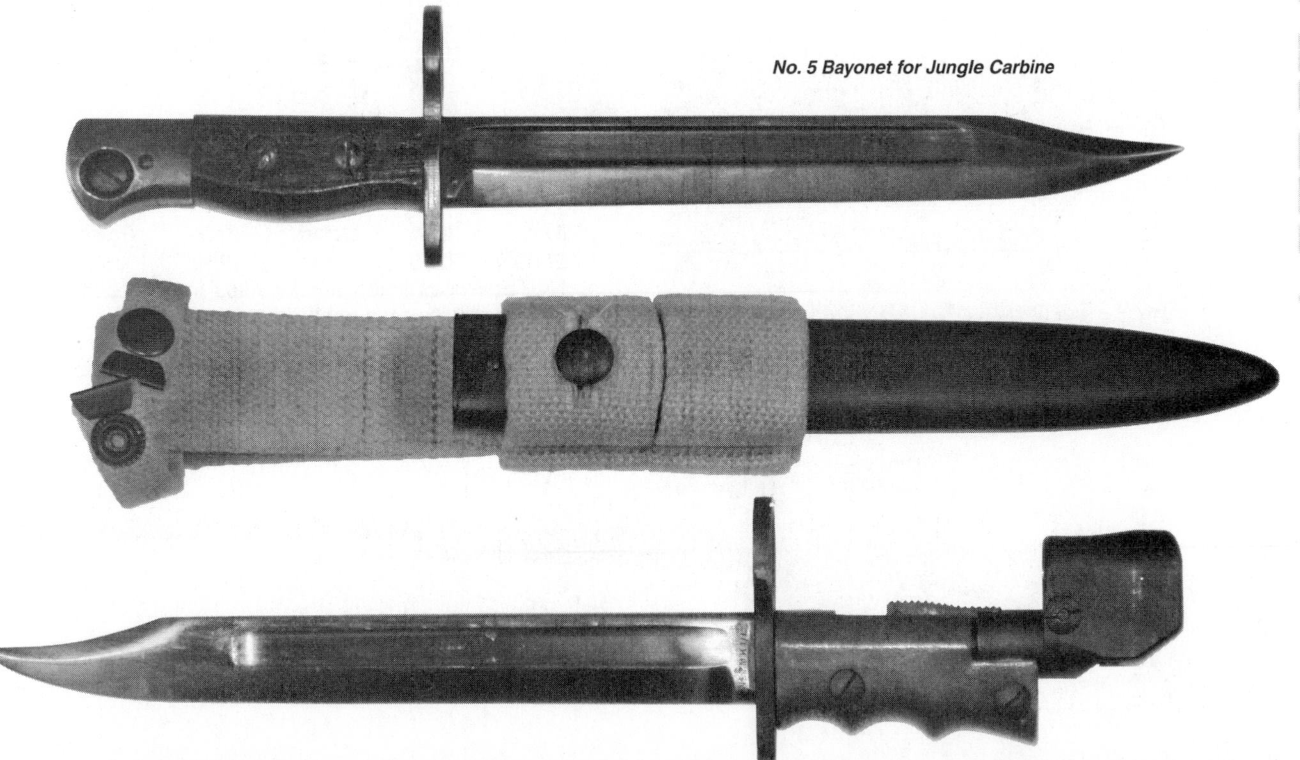

No. 5 Bayonet for Jungle Carbine

GREAT BRITAIN

Early L-42A1 conversion of a No. 4 Mk(T) rifle by Sterling • Private collection, Paul Goodwin photo

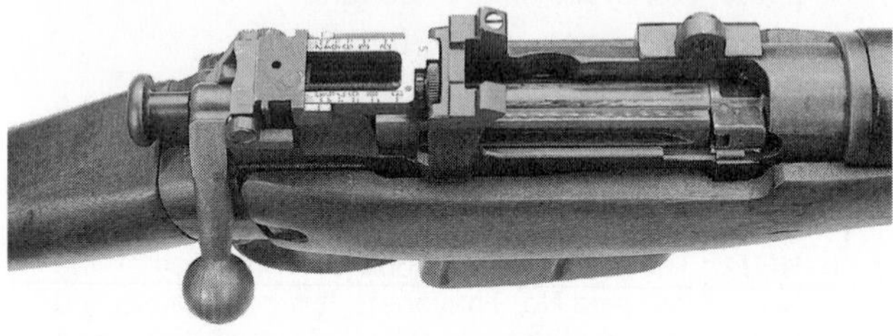

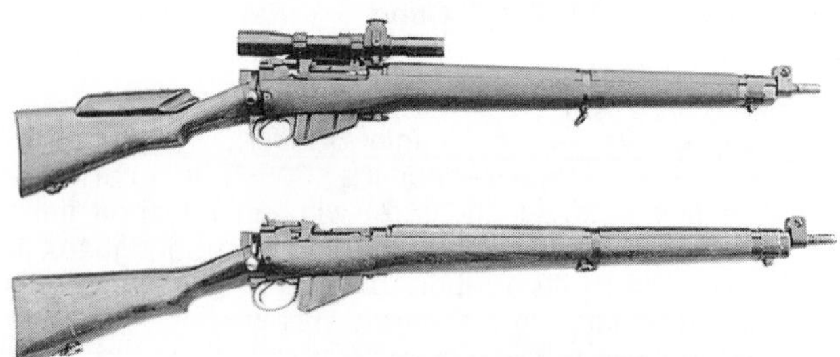

SMLE Sniper (Telescope Sights)

As above, but fitted with conventional telescope sights made by Periscope, Aldis, Winchester, and others. A total of about 9,700 of these rifles were fitted with telescope sights using Mark III and Mark III* rifles during WWI.

NOTE: Beware of fakes. Seek expert advice prior to a sale.

Exc.	V.G.	Good	Fair	Poor
3500	3000	2000	—	—

Rifle No. 4 Mark I (T) & Mark I* (T)

These are sniper versions of the No. 4 Mark I and the Mark1*. Fitted with scope mounts on the left side of the receiver and a wooden cheekpiece screwed to the buttstock. A No. 32 or a No. 67 (Canadian) telescope was issued with these rifles. Many of these rifles were converted by Holland & Holland. About 25,000 rifles using various telescopes were converted.

No. 4 Mark I (T) on top and Standard No. 4 Mark I at bottom • Courtesy Chuck Karwan

No.4 Mark I (T) close-up of action and scope • Courtesy Chuck Karwan

Exc.	V.G.	Good	Fair	Poor
2500	2250	1800	1250	850

NOTE: Prices listed are for rifles in original wood case and scope numbered to the rifle. For rifles without case deduct 10 percent. A subvariation of this model has no scope fitted to the rifle and is not stamped with a "t" on the butt.

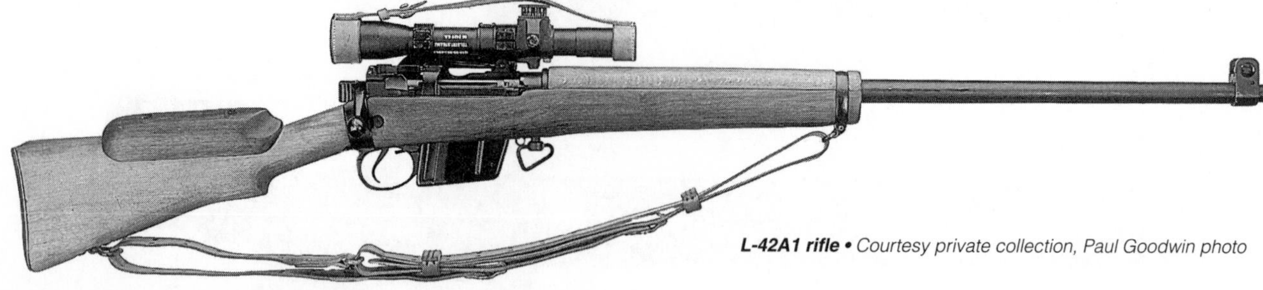

L-42A1 rifle • Courtesy private collection, Paul Goodwin photo

L42A1

Introduced in 1970, this rifle is a converted No. 4 (T) chambered for the 7.62mm cartridge. Half stocked with upper handguard with 27.6-inch heavy barrel. A converted No. 32 Mark 3 scope is used marked, "TEL. STRT. STG. L1A1." Weight is about 12.5 lbs. Some 10,000 were converted at Enfield.

Exc.	*V.G.*	*Good*	*Fair*	*Poor*
2500	2000	1500	700	350

NOTE: Prices listed are for rifles with original wood case.

LEE-ENFIELD .22 CALIBER RIFLES

Short Rifle Mark I

This single-shot .22 caliber model is converted from the Lee-Metford Mark I* rifle but with a 25-inch barrel. Introduced in 1907.

Exc.	*V.G.*	*Good*	*Fair*	*Poor*
650	450	300	200	100

Long Rifle Mark II

This single shot .22 caliber rifle was converted from long Lee-Enfield rifles. Adopted in 1912.

Exc.	*V.G.*	*Good*	*Fair*	*Poor*
650	450	300	200	100

Short Rifle Mark I*

This .22 caliber single shot conversion is modified from the Lee-Metford Mark I* rifle.

Exc.	*V.G.*	*Good*	*Fair*	*Poor*
1200	950	700	500	200

Short Rifle Mark III

This .22 caliber conversion is from the SMLE Mark II and Mark II*. Adopted in 1912.

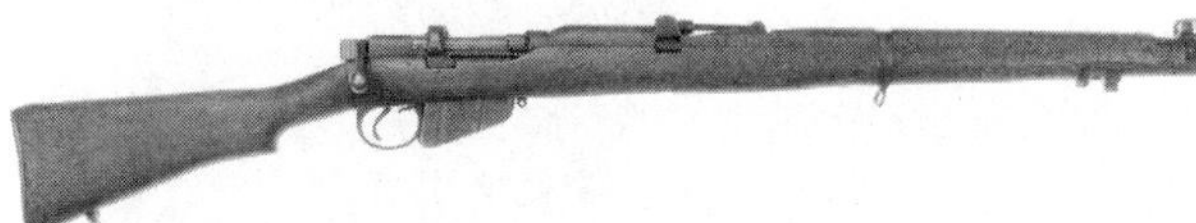

Courtesy Rock Island Auction Company

Exc.	*V.G.*	*Good*	*Fair*	*Poor*
500	400	300	150	100

Rifle No. 2 Mark IV

This model uses converted SMLEs. Some of these conversions are fitted with new .22 caliber barrels and others use .303 barrels with .22 caliber bore liners. These rifles have special bolt heads. Weight is about 9 lbs.

Courtesy Rock Island Auction Company

Exc.	*V.G.*	*Good*	*Fair*	*Poor*
450	350	300	150	100

Rifle No. 2 Mark IV*

A subvariation of Rifle No. 2 Mark IV.

Exc.	*V.G.*	*Good*	*Fair*	*Poor*
450	350	300	150	100

Rifle C No. 7

This model was developed at the Long Branch Canadian arsenal. It is a single shot .22 caliber version of the No. 4. Canadian nomenclature is "Rifle C" No. 7 .22 in Mark I. This model was also made by B.S.A. with a 5-round magazine. About 20,000 were produced.

Exc.	*V.G.*	*Good*	*Fair*	*Poor*
500	400	300	175	125

Rifle No. 7 Mark 1

This is a conversion of the No. 4, not a new rifle. Introduced in 1948. Different bolt from the Canadian version Rifle C No. 7 Mark 1. This rifle was intended for use at 25 yards. About 2,500 were built at BSA.

Exc.	*V.G.*	*Good*	*Fair*	*Poor*
500	400	300	175	125

NOTE: Be aware that A.G. Parker built a commercial version of this rifle. For those models deduct $100.

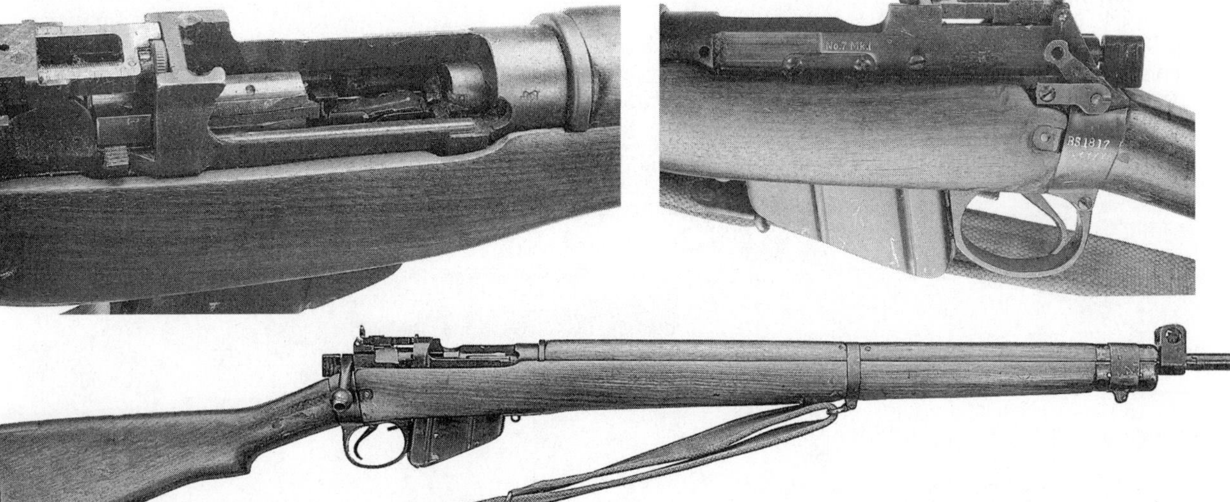

No. 7 Mark 1 with close-up views of receiver • *Private collection, Paul Goodwin photo*

GREAT BRITAIN

No. 5 Trials Rifle

This rifle was the forerunner of the No. 8. It was designed as a competition small bore rifle with special sights and half stock. It is fitted with a No.4 butt that has a checkered grip. The upper handguard is a No. 5 in length. It uses a No. 1 magazine converted to .22 caliber. It could be used as a single shot or magazine feed. Rear sight is micrometer graduated to 100 yards. Target tunnel front sight. Barrel length is 19 inches. Weight is about 8.5 lbs. About 100 of these rifles were built.

Exc.	V.G.	Good	Fair	Poor
1250	900	650	—	—

Rifle No. 8 Mark 1

This rifle was adopted in 1950. This is a single shot rifle with 24-inch barrel fitted with a rear peep sight. Half stocked with three sling swivels, the middle one is attached in front of the triggerguard. Weight is 9 lbs. Approximately 17,000 of these rifles were produced.

***No. 8 Mark 1 rifle** • Private collection, Paul Goodwin photo*

Exc.	V.G.	Good	Fair	Poor
700	550	375	200	100

Rifle No. 9 Mark 1

This .22 caliber single shot conversion was done by Parker Hale using No. 4 rifles. Main differences are the bolt, barrel, magazine, and rear sight. The magazine is an empty case without spring or follower. Weight is about 9.25 lbs. The conversion was done between 1956 and 1960. About 3,000 of these rifles were converted for the Royal Navy.

Exc.	V.G.	Good	Fair	Poor
700	550	375	200	100

7.62x51mm CONVERSIONS & MANUFACTURE

NOTE: The NATO cartridge 7.62x51mm was adopted by NATO in December of 1953. Conversions began soon after.

L8 Series

This series consists of converted No. 4 rifles from .303 to 7.62mm. Conversions involved a new barrel, and a new magazine stamped, "CR12A." The old receiver marks were eliminated and new ones using an electric pencil were substituted. Some rear sights graduated to 1,300 meters, and other graduated to 1,000 meters. Series conversions are as follows:

L8A1 converted from No. 4 MK 2
L8A2 converted from No. 4 MK 1/2
L8A3 converted from No. 4 MK 1/3
L8A4 converted from No. 4 MK I
L8A5 converted from No. 4 MK I*

Exc.	V.G.	Good	Fair	Poor
975	700	500	300	150

L39A1

This conversion uses a No. 4 Mark 2 action and is similar to a L42A1 sniper rifle without the scope. Fitted with target-type front and rear sights. Half stocked. Weight is about 10 lbs.

Exc.	V.G.	Good	Fair	Poor
1500	1100	750	400	200

NOTE: For 7.62 NATO magazine add $75. For English match sights by Parker Hale add $125.

L42A1

See Sniper Rifles.

Rifle 7.62mm 2A and 2A1 (India)

This rifle is based on a No. 1 Mark III* rifle utilizing newly made receivers of stronger steel to handle the higher .308 pressures. The Indians referred to it as "EN" steel. New rear sight graduated to 800 meters. New detachable box magazine with 10-round capacity.

Magazine for Indian-made Enfield 2A rifle, price 60-45

***L39A1 rifle** • Courtesy private collection, Paul Goodwin photo*

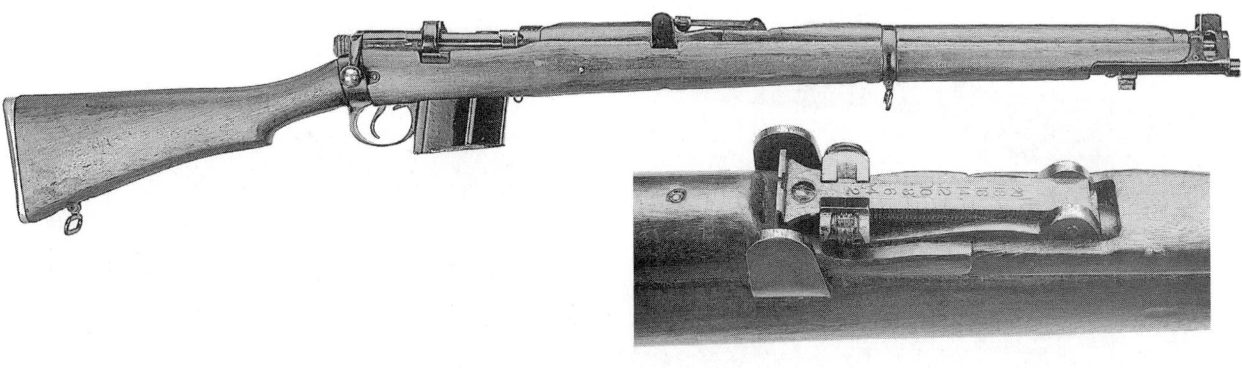

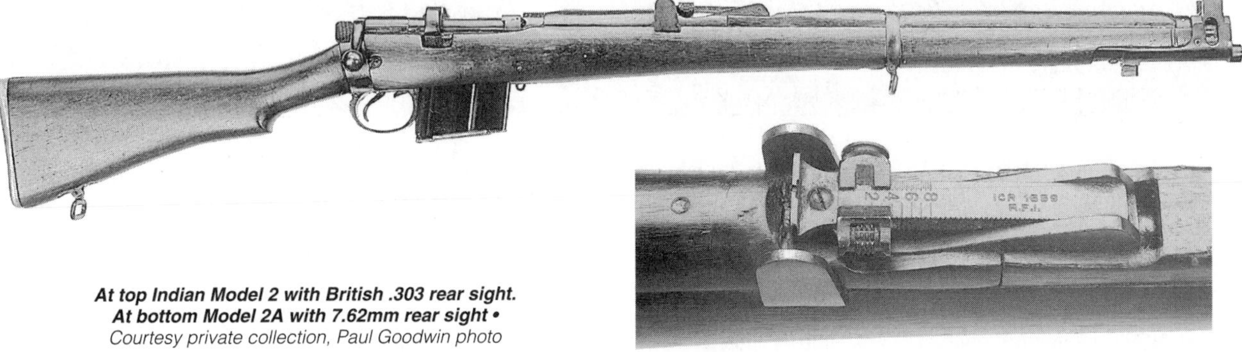

At top Indian Model 2 with British .303 rear sight. At bottom Model 2A with 7.62mm rear sight • *Courtesy private collection, Paul Goodwin photo*

The buttplate is cast alloy. Manufactured in India at Ishapore. Weight is about 9.5 lbs. Most imported rifles are in the 2A1 configuration.

Exc.	V.G.	Good	Fair	Poor
325	275	225	125	100

Enfield Fencing Muskets

These are not firearms but rather fabricated or converted rifles made to look and feel like the real thing. They were used for bayonet practice and drilling practice. There are a large number of variations, at least 17, and to cover each is beyond the scope of this book. The prices listed below only represent a possible range of prices. Some rifles were later converted to fencing muskets.

Exc.	V.G.	Good	Fair	Poor
200	100	75	50	20

OTHER BRITISH RIFLES

Boys Anti-Tank Rifle

Developed in the 1930s, this rifle was chambered for the .55-caliber armor piercing cartridge. It was fitted with a 36-inch barrel with muzzle brake. It had

Boys Anti-Tank Rifle • *Courtesy West Point Museum, Paul Goodwin photo*

GREAT BRITAIN

No. 3 Mark I • Courtesy West Point Museum, Paul Goodwin photo

GREAT BRITAIN

a detachable 5-round box magazine. Weight was approximately 36 lbs. Available in two versions: a long barrel (36 inches) and a short barrel airborne model. Not used much after 1940 due to inability to penetrate modern armor. Some of these rifles were used by the U.S. Marine Corp. in the Pacific during World War II.

NOTE: The .55 caliber Boys Rifle is listed as a destructive device by the ATF and is therefore subject to all NFA rules. Many have been re-barreled to .50 BMG, thus removing them from NFA status.

Exc.	V.G.	Good	Fair	Poor
4000	3000	2500	2000	1000

No. 3 Mark I (Pattern 14)

Built on a modified Mauser-type action and was chambered for the .303 British cartridge. It is fitted with a 26-inch barrel and 5-round magazine. It was a secondary-issue arm during WWI and was simpler to mass-produce than the SMLE. These rifles were produced in the U.S.A. by Remington and Winchester. There are a number of marks for this model divided between Remington, Eddystone, and Winchester.

The Mark Ie was built at Remington Arms at Eddystone, Pennsylvania. The Mark Ir were built at Remington Arms in Ilion, New York. The Mark Iw was built at Winchester Repeating Arms in New Haven, Connecticut. Add 25 percent for Winchester built P-14.

Exc.	V.G.	Good	Fair	Poor
550	425	350	225	150

Pattern 1914 Bayonet for Enfield

Wood grips with two large grooves. Muzzle ring. 15-inch single edge blade. Uses the same steel tipped leather scabbard as the P1907 bayonet. Made in U.S.A. by Remington or Winchester for the Pattern 1914

Pattern 1914 Bayonet for Enfield

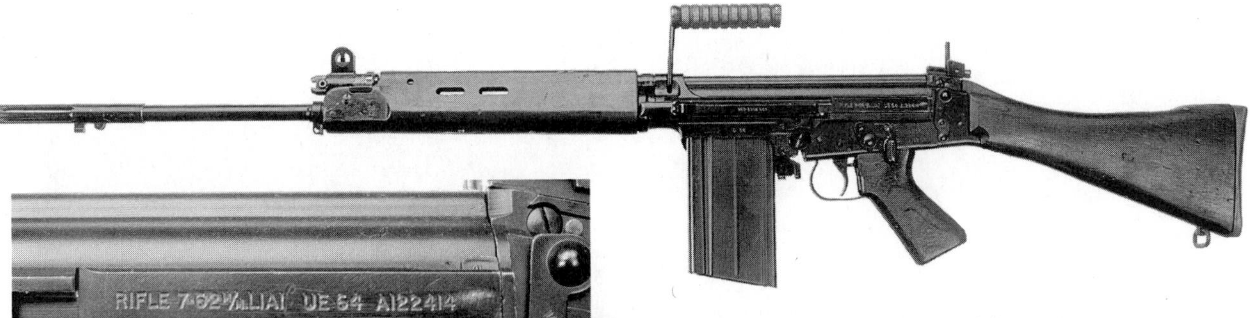

FN-FAL L1A1 rifle • *Paul Goodwin photo*

Enfield rifles produced by the same makers. Marked "Remington" or "W" on one side of the ricasso. The other side has English broad arrow property marks. Some P 1914 bayonets will be found that also bear U.S. M 1917 markings. These were made for Great Britain during WWI but were diverted to American service after the U.S. entered the war. See United States, rifles for the U.S. M 1917 bayonet. Price range 150 – 65. Note: Add 25 percent for Winchester made examples.

No. 3 Mark I* Pattern 14W(F) (T)

This is a No. 3 Mark I that has been converted to a sniper configuration. These rifles were built by Winchester during World War I. The (F) model has a long range aperture and dial sight along with the scope. On the (T) model the long range sights were removed. It is estimated that about 1,500 of these rifles were built. A rare rifle. Caution should be used prior to purchase.

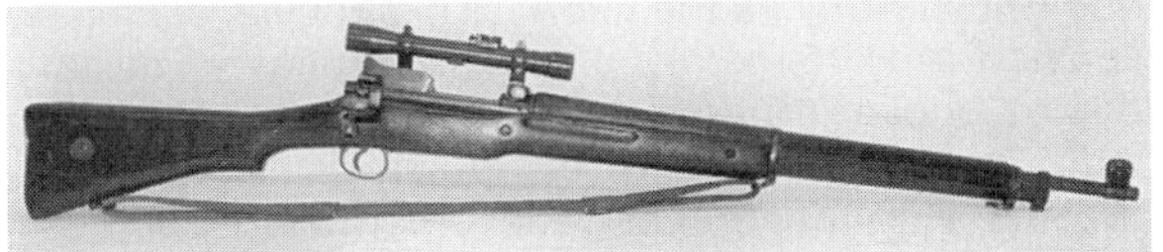

Courtesy Richard M. Kumor Sr.

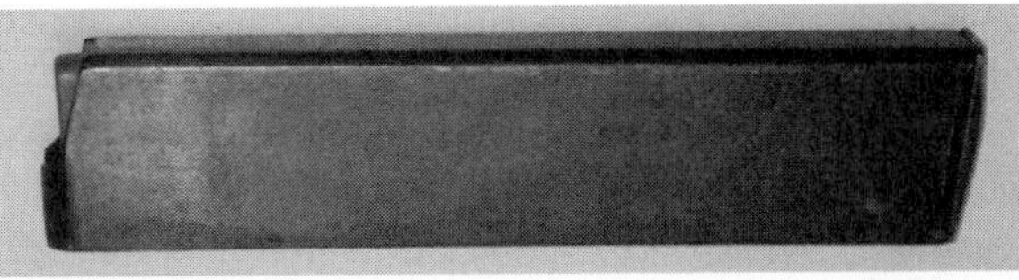

Magazine for S&W Model1940 Light Rifles

Close-up of sniper scope and mount • *Courtesy Richard M. Kumor Sr.*

Exc.	V.G.	Good	Fair	Poor
5000	4500	3500	—	—

SMITH & WESSON

Model 1940 Light Rifle, Mk. 1 and Mk. II

A 9mm semi-automatic rifle with a 9-3/4-inch fluted barrel. It features a tenite stock. Uses 20-round detachable magazine that inserts from the front of the magazine well/ejection chute. Weight was about 8 lbs.

In 1939, Great Britain decided it wanted a semi-automatic carbine in 9mm. Smith & Wesson accepted a $1,000,000 downpayment to design one and begin production. They had the design ready by September, 1940 and initial shipment of about 1000 Mk I rifles was soon delivered. These failed a 5000-round test performed at the Enfield Arsenal. The S&W engineers had designed the gun using U.S.-made 9mm ammunition, which develops less breech pressure than European made 9mm. There were problems with parts breakage and reliability with the overly complicated rifle. The English demanded that changes be made to correct the problems. The Mk II was the result. However, by that time war production

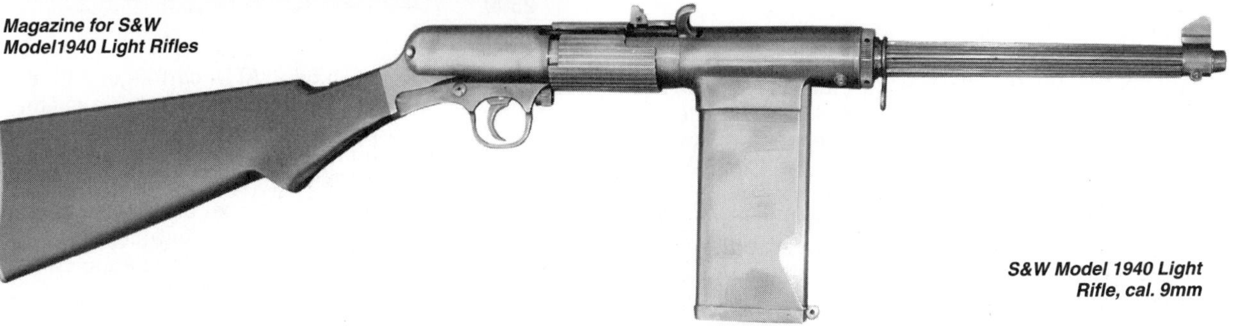

S&W Model 1940 Light Rifle, cal. 9mm

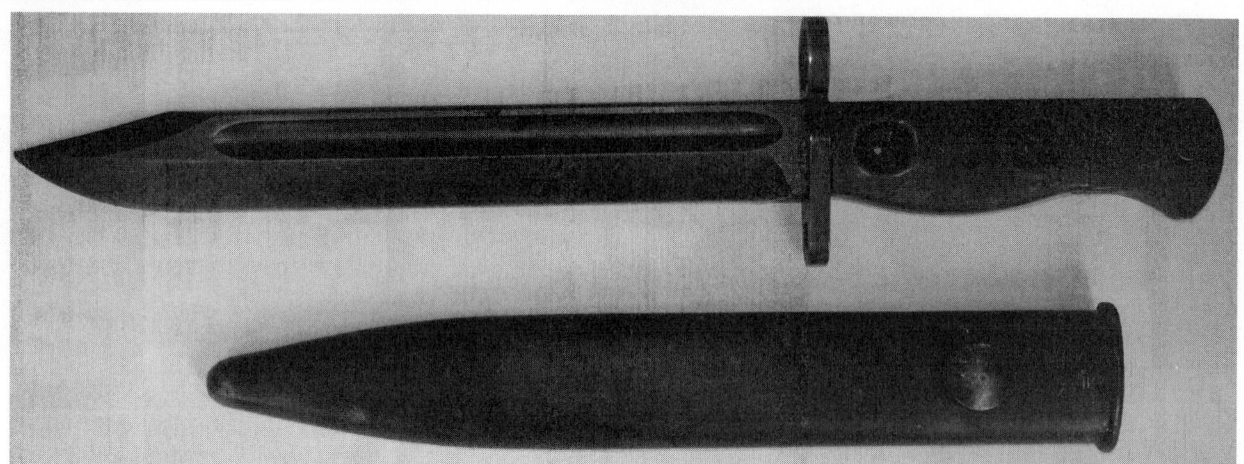

L1A3 Bayonet with metal handle

had reached a critical point and the English gave up on the project. Rather than demand a cash refund from S&W, they accepted several thousand Model 1905 M&P revolvers chambered in the .380 (.38 S&W) cartridge. The rifles they had received were placed in storage. A few might have been issued to home guards and security units. After the war they destroyed all but a few of the 1940 Light Rifles. A few were saved and remain in the Enfield Pattern Room and the Imperial War Museum.

In the 1970s, during a cleanup at the S&W factory in Springfield, Mass., a small lot of 130 Mk I and 80 Mk II Model 1940 rifles was discovered, still packed in their original crates. These were sold to an American arms dealer, who sold them on the U.S. market. Thus, the only Model 1940 Light rifles in private hands reside within the United States.

Exc.	*V.G.*	*Good*	*Fair*	*Poor*
4500	3000	N/A	N/A	N/A

STERLING

De Lisle Carbine

This rifle is built on a Lee-Enfield action with a .45 ACP-caliber barrel fitted inside a large suppressor tube. Barrel length is 8.25 inches. Magazine capacity is 8 rounds using a Colt Model 1911 magazine. Weight is about 7.5 lbs. About 100 to 150 of these rifles were built by Sterling during WWII for use in special operations. Most were destroyed after the war. All NFA rules apply to the purchase of these weapons. Rare.

Exc.	*V.G.*	*Good*	*Fair*	*Poor*
7500	6000	5000	N/A	N/A

L1A1 Rifle

This is the British version of the FN-FAL in the "INCH" or Imperial pattern. Most of these rifles were semi-automatic only. This rifle was the standard service rifle for the British army from about 1954 to 1988. The rifle was made in Great Britain under license from FN. The configurations for the L1A1 rifle is the same as the standard FN-FAL Belgium rifle. Only a few of these rifles were imported into the U.S. They are very rare. This "inch" pattern British gun will also be found in other Commonwealth countries such as Australia, New Zealand, Canada, and India.

NOTE: The only known pre-1986 L1A1 rifles imported into the U.S. are Australian and Canadian. See that country for prices. See also Canada for its C1 and C2 versions of the FN FAL.

L1A1 Rifle with U.S. made receiver

There are a number of U.S. companies that build or import L1A1 rifles (imported rifles are in a sporter configuration) but these have no collector value. Rifles built with military surplus parts and U.S.-made receivers also have no collector value as of yet.

Exc.	*V.G.*	*Good*	*Fair*	*Poor*
800	700	500	N/A	N/A

L1 A3 Bayonet for L1A1 rifle

Metal handle. Price range 75-30.

ACCURACY INTERNATIONAL

Founded in 1980 by Malcom and Sarah Cooper, they designed sniper rifles which were later adopted by the British Army as the L96A1. This English company, located in Portsmouth, provides its rifles to military forces in over 43 countries, and these models have been used in Northern Ireland, Sri Lanka, Somalia, Bosnia, Rwanda, and in Desert Storm. Most of these rifles are currently NATO codified.

Model AE

Chambered for the 7.62x51 cartridge and fitted with a 24-inch heavy barrel. Stock is a black synthetic. Magazine capacity is 5 rounds. Weight is approximately 13.25 lbs.

Exc.	*V.G.*	*Good*	*Fair*	*Poor*
2500	—	—	—	—

Model AW

Chambered for the 5.56 NATO cartridge and the 7.62x51 NATO cartridge, this bolt action rifle is fitted with a 26-inch heavy match grade barrel with muzzle brake. Magazine capacity is 8 rounds for the 5.56 and 10 rounds for the 7.62x51. Olive green or black stock with adjustable buttstock. Optional bipod, scope, and other accessories can be included in a complete kit. Prices below are for rifle only. Weight is about 14.25 lbs.

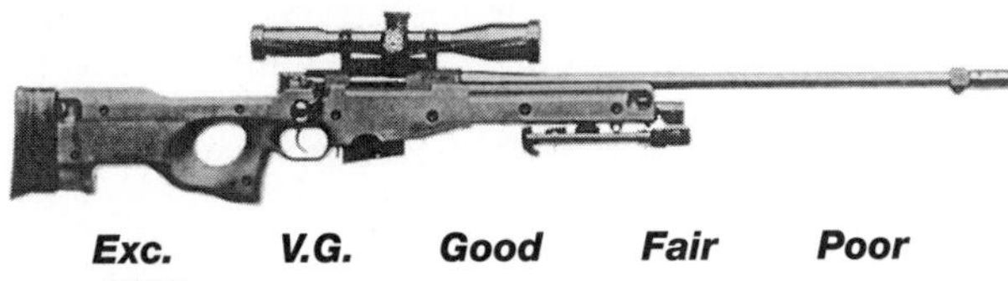

Exc.	V.G.	Good	Fair	Poor
4700	—	—	—	—

Model AWP

Similar to the Model AW but with black stock and metal and 24-inch barrel. Offered in .243 and .308 calibers. Weight is about 14 lbs.

Exc.	V.G.	Good	Fair	Poor
4400	—	—	—	—

Model AWS

A suppressed version of the AW model. Weight is about 13 lbs.

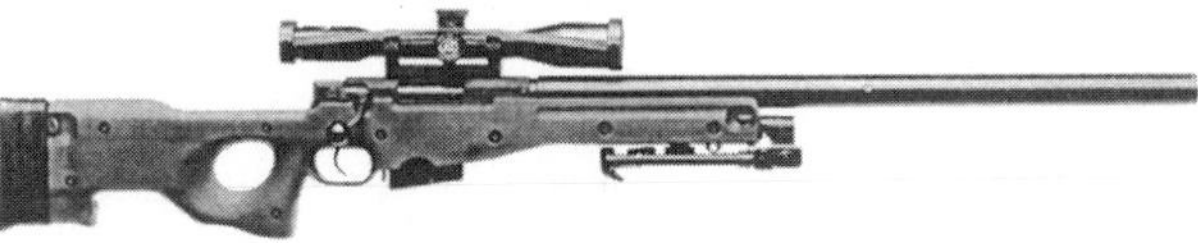

Exc.	V.G.	Good	Fair	Poor
N/A	—	—	—	—

Model AWM

Similar to the Model AW but chambered for the .300 Winchester Magnum or .338 Lapua Magnum cartridge. Fitted with a 26-inch barrel with muzzle brake. Magazine capacity is 5 rounds. Weight is about 15.5 lbs.

Exc.	V.G.	Good	Fair	Poor
5000	—	—	—	—

Model AW 50

Chambered for the .50 caliber Browning cartridge. Barrel length is 27-inch with muzzle brake. Magazine capacity is 5 rounds. Weight is about 33 lbs. Supplied with metal case, spare magazine, carry handle, sling, and tool kit.

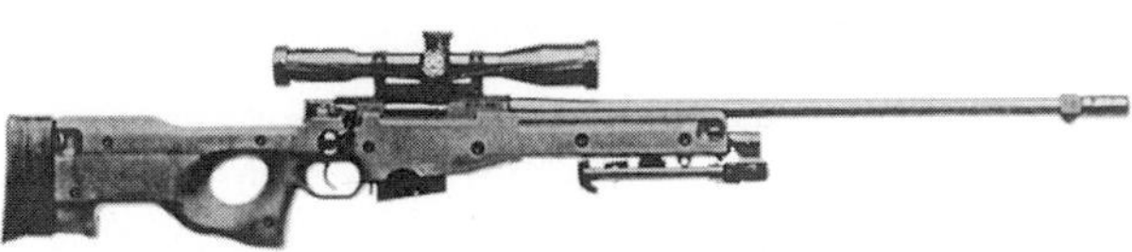

Exc.	V.G.	Good	Fair	Poor
10925	—	—	—	—

PARKER-HALE

Founded in Birmingham, England in 1890, this firm converted Lee-Enfield rifles into sporting guns. During World War II it manufactured military ammunition and repaired service rifles. In 1992, the company was sold to Navy Arms who then established a subsidiary called Gibbs Rifle Co. to produce and sell the Parker-Hale line.

M82

This bolt action rifle uses a Mauser 98 action fitted to a heavy 26-inch barrel chambered for the 7.62x51mm cartridge. Magazine capacity is 4 rounds. Used as a sniper rifle by the Australian, New Zealand, and Canadian military. Marked "PARKER-HALE LTD BIRMINGHAM ENGLAND 7.62 NATO" on top of the barrel. Produced from 1982 to about 1984.

Exc.	V.G.	Good	Fair	Poor
2500	2000	1500	850	—

M85

This is an improved version of the M82 with a Mauser 98 type bolt action designed to compete for a British military contract against the Accuracy International rifle. It did not win the trials. It is fitted with a removable 10-round magazine, 27.5-inch heavy barrel with iron sights, and telescope mounts on the receiver. Rifle is half stocked with adjustable buttplate. Bipod is attached to forend rail. Weight is about 12.5 lbs. with scope. Chambered for the 7.62x51mm NATO round.

Exc.	V.G.	Good	Fair	Poor
3500	3000	2500	1500	—

MACHINE GUNS

NOTE: For historical information and technical details see: Dugelby, The Bren Gun Saga, Collector Grade Publications, 1999. Goldsmith, The Grand Old Lady of No Man's Land, The Vickers Machinegun, Collector Grade Publications, 1994.

Bren MK1

Introduced in 1938 and designed in Czechoslovakia as the ZB vz2,6 this British version is chambered for the .303 British cartridge during the early part of its service. After WWII it was adapted to the 7.62x51mm cartridge. It was fitted with a top mounted magazine of 30 rounds. Rate of fire is 500 rounds per minute. The gun was set up to fire selectively as well. The gun has a 24.8-inch barrel and an empty weight of 22 lbs. The rear sight is an offset drum type. The buttstock has a hand grip and top strap. The bipod has fixed legs, and the cocking handle folds away. Marked "bren mk" on the right side of the receiver.

The Bren MK2 (1941) has a leaf type rear sight and a simplified buttstock. The Bren MK3 (1944) is lighter (19 lbs) and fitted with a shorter barrel (22.2 inches). The Bren MK4 (1944) has minor differences in the buttstock. The L4A1 (1958) is a converted MK3 to 7.62mm caliber. The L4A2 (1958) is a converted MK3 with lighter bipod. The L4A3 is a converted MK2 to 7.62mm caliber: used by navy and RAF. The L4A4 (1960) is similar to the L4A2 except for a chrome-lined barrel. The L4A6 is a converted L4A1 with chrome lined barrel.

In 1941, the MK2 was produced in Canada for the Chinese Nationalist army in 7.92x57mm caliber (see Canada). A .30-06 version was made in Taiwan.

Be aware that there are a number of different mounts for the Bren gun besides the traditional bipod. There is a tripod mount as well as an antiaircraft mount.

NOTE: The Vickers-Berthier gun is similar in external design, caliber, and general appearance as the Bren except it has a distinctive operating mechanism and other significant differences. This gun is made in India and that country used the gun in World War II. It is still in use in that country. This gun is extremely rare as only a few known transferable examples exist. For pre-1968 Vickers-Berthier guns a price of $35,000 in Excellent condition would be a good starting place for value.

Bren MK I • *Courtesy private NFA collection*

Bren MK1

Pre-1968 (Rare)

Exc.	V.G.	Fair
50000	35000	N/A

Pre-1986 manufacture with new receiver or re-weld

Exc.	V.G.	Fair
35000	27500	N/A

Bren MK2

Pre-1968 (Rare)

Exc.	V.G.	Fair
42000	40000	38000

Pre-1986 manufacture with new receiver or re-weld

Exc.	V.G.	Fair
25000	22000	N/A

Lewis 0.303in, Mark 1

This gas-operated machine gun is chambered for the .303 British cartridge. Though perfected by an American army officer, Colonel Isaac Lewis (1858-1931), it was first produced in Belgium in 1912 where it was used extensively by British forces during WWI. In fact, it was the principal British light machine gun used in WWI. It has a 26-inch barrel and a rate of fire of about 550 rounds per minute. Called by the Germans the "Belgian Rattlesnake." Magazine capacity is 47- or 97-round drum. Its weight is approximately 26 lbs. Marked "LEWIS AUTOMATIC MACHINE GUN/MODEL 1914 PATENTED" behind the magazine drum. The gun was produced by BSA and Savage Arms of the U.S. Production stopped in 1925. A number of other countries used the gun as well, such as France, Norway, Japan, Belgium, Honduras, and Nicaragua.

The Lewis MK2 was introduced in 1915 which was a MK1 without the radiator and barrel jacket. The buttstock was removed and spade grips attached for aircraft use. The Lewis MK2* modified the gun to increase the rate of fire to about 800 rounds per minute. See also United States, Machine Guns, Savage-Lewis M1917.

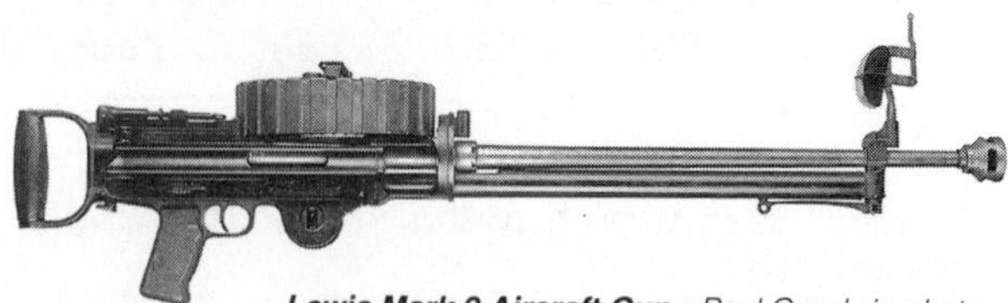

Lewis Mark 2 Aircraft Gun • *Paul Goodwin photo*

Pre-1968

Exc.	V.G.	Fair
25000	18000	12500

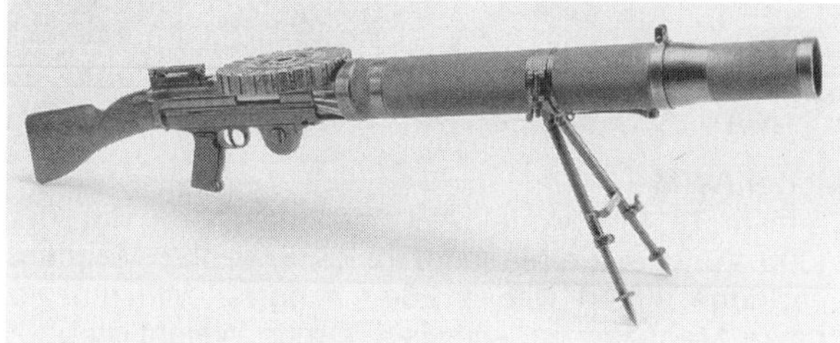

Private NFA collection • *Photo by Gary Gelson*

Vickers Mark 1

This British water-cooled machine gun was first produced in 1912 and chambered for the .303 British cartridge. In essence, an improved Maxim with the action inverted. It has a 28-inch barrel with corrugated water jacket and is fed by a 250-round cloth belt. Its rate of fire is 450 rounds per minute. Its weight is approximately 40 lbs. It was also used in aircraft and stayed in service in various countries until the

Vickers-Berthier • *Courtesy NFA private collection, Paul Goodwin photo*

British Vickers Mark 4 • *Courtesy Blake Stevens, The Grand Old Lady of No Man's Land*

1970s. Besides use in British forces, the gun was sold to South American countries between the two World Wars. Serial number is marked on top rear of water jacket. The Vickers gun was capable of sustained fire of 100,000 rounds without stopping.

Variations of the Vickers Mark 1 are: the Mark 1*, which is an aircraft gun with a pierced and louvered barrel jacket for air-cooling. Some of these guns had a rate of fire of about 850 rounds per minute and marked "SU" for "speeded up." There were several other Vickers aircraft variations which incorporated minor modifications. The Vickers was also used on tanks. These variations were designated the Mark 4A, Mark 4B, Mark 6, Mark 6*, Mark 7. A .50 caliber Vickers was also produced for tank and naval use. These guns are designated the .5 inch Mark 3, and .5 inch Mark 4. These guns had a rate of fire of about 675 rounds per minute and weighed approximately 60 lbs.

NOTE: For the Colt produced version in .30-06 caliber see United States, Machine Guns.

Pre-1968

Exc.	*V.G.*	*Fair*
35000	25000	18000

Pre-1986 manufacture with new receiver or re-weld

Exc.	*V.G.*	*Fair*
18000	15000	N/A

Hotchkiss Mark I

Although a French design, the British army purchased the rights to manufacture the Hotchkiss during WWI. These British guns were known as the Mark 1 and Mark 1* and were built in the Royal Small Arms factory in England. The British Hotchkiss was chambered for the .303 British cartridge. This version was fed by a 30-round metallic strip and had a rate of fire of about 500 rounds per minute. The gun weighed about 27 lbs. Barrel length was 23.5 inches. The British Hotchkiss stayed in service in the British army until 1946. A belt-fed version (Mark I*) for use on tanks used a 250-round belt.

Courtesy Butterfield & Butterfield

Pre-1968

Exc.	*V.G.*	*Fair*
18000	15000	10000

Besa

Introduced in 1939, this gun was a design bought from the Czech's ZB vz53 and produced in Britain by BSA in a slightly modified form. It was used primarily on tanks. It was an air-cooled gun chambered for the 7.92x57mm cartridge. It was gas operated but with a recoiling barrel. It has a rate of fire of approximately 500 or 800 rounds per minute using a selector switch for high or low rate. Weight of the gun is about 48 lbs. Feeds from a 250-round belt.

There are a number of variations of the initial model. The Mark 2 has some minor modifications. The Mark 3 has a single rate of fire of 800 rounds per minute. The Mark 3* has a single rate of fire of 500 rounds per minute.

Pre-1968

Exc.	*V.G.*	*Fair*
35000	28000	20000

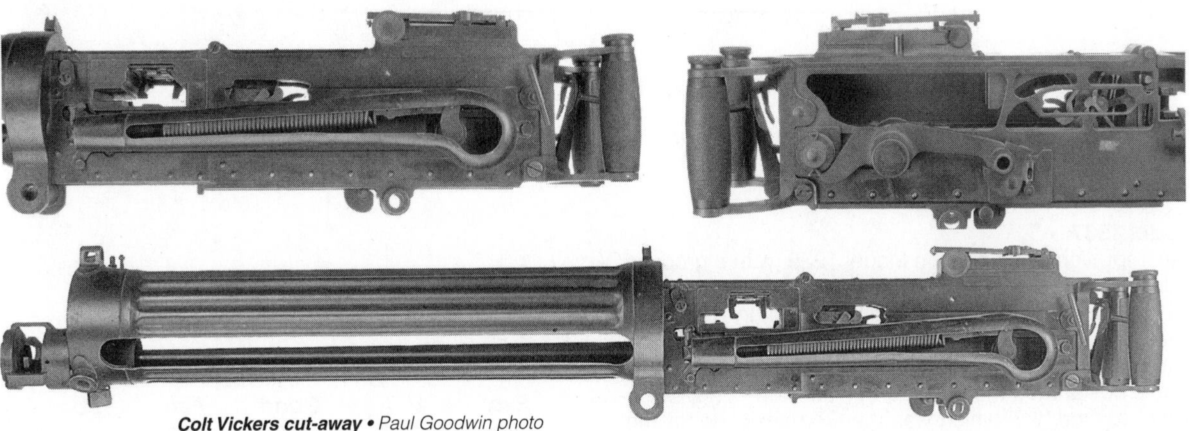

Colt Vickers cut-away • *Paul Goodwin photo*

The Republic of Hungary, located in central Europe, has an area of 35,929 sq. mi. (93,030 sq. km.) and a population of 10.7 million. Capital: Budapest. The economy is based on agriculture, bauxite and a rapidly expanding industrial sector. Machinery, chemicals, iron and steel, and fruits and vegetables are exported.

The ancient kingdom of Hungary, founded by the Magyars in the 9th century, achieved its greatest extension in the mid-14th century when its dominions touched the Baltic, Black and Mediterranean Seas. After suffering repeated Turkish invasions, Hungary accepted Habsburg rule to escape Turkish occupation, regaining independence in 1867 with the Emperor of Austria as king of a dual Austro-Hungarian monarchy.

After World War I, Hungary lost 2/3 of its territory and 1/2 of its population and underwent a period of drastic political revision. The short-lived republic of 1918 was followed by a chaotic interval of communist rule, 1919, and the restoration of the monarchy in 1920 with Admiral Horthy as regent of the kingdom. Although a German ally in World War II, Hungary was occupied by German troops who imposed a pro-Nazi dictatorship, 1944. Soviet armies drove out the Germans in 1945 and assisted the communist minority in seizing power. A revised constitution published on Aug. 20, 1949, established Hungary as a People's Republic' of the Soviet type. On October 23, 1989, Hungary was pro-claimed the Republic of Hungary.

HANDGUNS

STEYR

Osterreichische Waffenfabrik Gesellschaft GmbH, Steyr (1869-1919)

Steyr-Werke AG (1919-1934)
Steyr-Daimler-Puch, Steyr (1934-1990)
Steyr-Mannlicher GmbH, Steyr (1990-)

Model 1929

A blowback-operated semi-automatic chambered for the 9mm short cartridge. It has an external hammer, and the barrel is retained by four lugs. This is a simple and reliable pistol, and it was adopted by the military as a replacement for the Stop. This model was manufactured between 1929 and 1937. About 50,000 pistols were produced. It was also produced in a .22 Long Rifle.

Courtesy James Rankin

Exc.	*V.G.*	*Good*	*Fair*	*Poor*
500	300	200	175	125

Model 1937

An improved version of the Model 1929, with a grooved slide to make cocking easier. It was adopted as the M1937 by the Hungarian Military, and in 1941 the German government ordered 85,000 pistols chambered for 7.65mm to be used by the Luftwaffe. These pistols were designated the "P Mod 37 Kal 7.65." They were also marked "jhv," which was the German code for the Hungarian company. These German pistols also have a manual safety, which is not found on the Hungarian military version and bears the Waffenamt acceptance marks. This model was manufactured from 1937 until the end of WWII.

Nazi Proofed 7.65mm Version (Pistole Modell 37[u])

Exc.	*V.G.*	*Good*	*Fair*	*Poor*
550	400	250	150	100

Courtesy James Rankin

9mm Short Hungarian Military Version

Hungarian Military Model 37 • Courtesy Rock Island Auction Company

Exc.	*V.G.*	*Good*	*Fair*	*Poor*
450	300	175	125	75

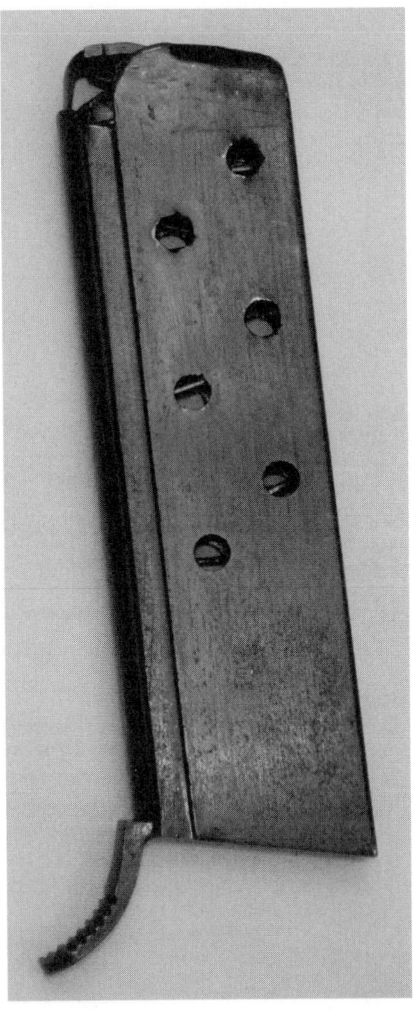
Femaru M37 magazine with finger rest. Marked on bottom " 37 M". Price 75-40

Model 48 (7.62mm)

Hungarian M48 • Courtesy Chuck Karwan

This is a Hungarian copy of the Soviet 7.62mm TT33 pistol. The pistol has molded plastic grips with the Hungarian coat of arms.

Exc.	*V.G.*	*Good*	*Fair*	*Poor*
750	600	450	300	200

Tokagypt

A licensed copy of the TT33 pistol produced by Fegyvergar (FEG) of Hungary. Chambered for the 9mm cartridge, and intended for, but never issued to, the Egyptian army in the 1950s. Barrel length is 4.5" and magazine capacity is 7 rounds. Manual thumb safety. Weight is approximately 32 oz.

Hungarian Tokagypt • Courtesy Chuck Karwan

Exc.	*V.G.*	*Good*	*Fair*	*Poor*
750	650	500	350	150

NOTE: For pistols without markings deduct 25 percent.

PA-63

An aluminum frame copy of the Walther PP in a slightly larger size. Chambered for the 9mm Makarov cartridge. This was the standard Hungarian service pistol until recently. Many have been imported here.

Exc.	*V.G.*	*Good*	*Fair*	*Poor*
200	150	120	90	75

R-61

This model is a smaller version of the PA-63. Chambered for the 9mm Makarov. This model is slightly longer than a Walther PPK and was intended for issue to high-ranking officers, CID, and police units.

Exc.	*V.G.*	*Good*	*Fair*	*Poor*
300	250	200	N/A	N/A

SUBMACHINE GUNS

Model 39

Produced by Danuvia in Budapest, this submachine gun is chambered for the 9x25mm Mauser Export cartridge. It is fitted with a 19.5" barrel and a full stocked rifle-style wooden stock. Magazine capacity is 40 rounds. The magazine folds into a recess in the forward part of the stock. Fitted with a bayonet lug. Gun features a two-part bolt design. Introduced in the late 1930s but not issued until 1941. Weight is about 8 lbs. Rate of fire is approximately 750 rounds per minute. About 8,000 were produced.

NOTE: It is not known how many, if any, of these guns are in the U.S. and are transferable. Prices listed are estimates only.

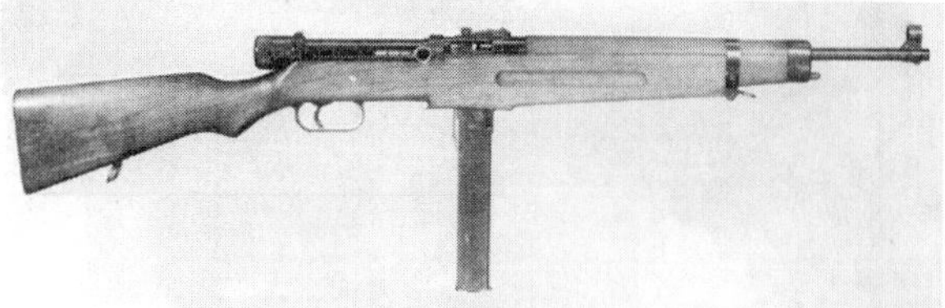

Model 39M • Courtesy Thomas Nelson, *The World's Submachine Guns, Vol. 1*

Pre-1968

Exc.	*V.G.*	*Fair*
15000	6500	6000

Model 43

This model, introduced in 1942, is an improved version of the Model 39. It has a shorter barrel at 16.5", a folding stock, pistol grip, and an improved magazine. Weight is about 8 lbs. Rate of fire and caliber remain the same. Produced until 1945.

NOTE: It is not known how many, if any, of these guns are in the U.S. and are transferable. Prices listed below are estimates only.

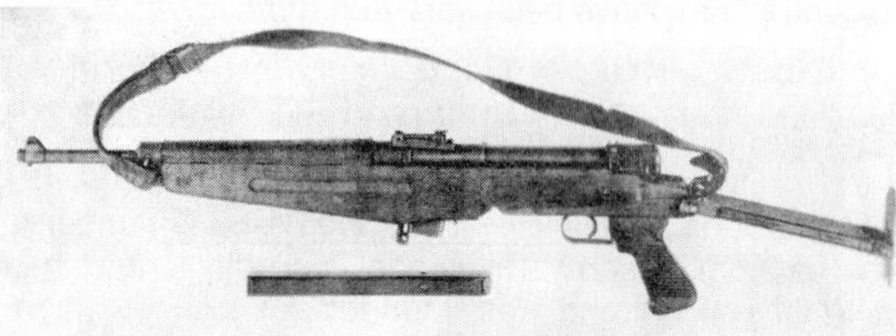

Model 43M • Courtesy Thomas Nelson, *The World's Submachine Guns, Vol. 1*

Pre-1968

Exc.	*V.G.*	*Fair*
12500	10500	9500

Model 48

This is a Hungarian copy of the Soviet PPSh-41 submachine gun. See also *Russia, Submachine Guns.*

Pre-1968

Exc.	*V.G.*	*Fair*
12500	10500	9500

RIFLES

MANNLICHER

Built by Steyr & Fegyvergyar

Model 1935 Short Rifle

This model is based on the Romanian Model 1893. However, it is chambered for the 8x56R Hungarian Mannlicher cartridge. Barrel length is 23.6". Magazine capacity is 5 rounds in a clip loaded box magazine. Full stock with full-length handguard. Weight is approximately 9 lbs.

Exc.	*V.G.*	*Good*	*Fair*	*Poor*
750	600	475	300	175

Model 35 with close-up of receiver ring • Private collection, Paul Goodwin photo

FEGYVERGYAR

Fegyver es Gepgyar Resvenytarsasag, Budapest, (1880-1945)
Femaru es Szersazamgepgyar NV (1945-1985)
FEG Arms & Gas Appliances Factory (1985-)

Model Gewehr 98/40

Built by FEG but with many Mannlicher and Mauser components in its design. Based on Hungarian M1935 short rifle. Chambered for the 7.92x57mm cartridge and Mauser charger loaded. Two-piece stock. Barrel length is 23.6". Weight is about 9 lbs. This rifle was not actually a Hungarian issue weapon but was made for Germany. It takes the standard 98K bayonet.

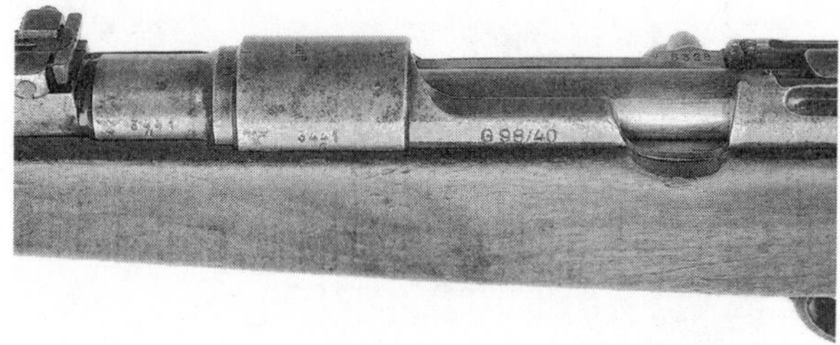

Model 98/40 • Private collection, Paul Goodwin photo

Exc.	*V.G.*	*Good*	*Fair*	*Poor*
900	750	550	300	200

Model 43 Rifle

This is a Model 35 redesigned on the German Model 98/40 and chambered for the 7.92mm cartridge. Barrel length is 23.75". Magazine capacity is 5-rounds fixed box. Rear sight is tangent with notch. Weight is approximately 8.5 lbs. Takes the Hungarian 35M bayonet. Issued to the Hungarian army in 1943.

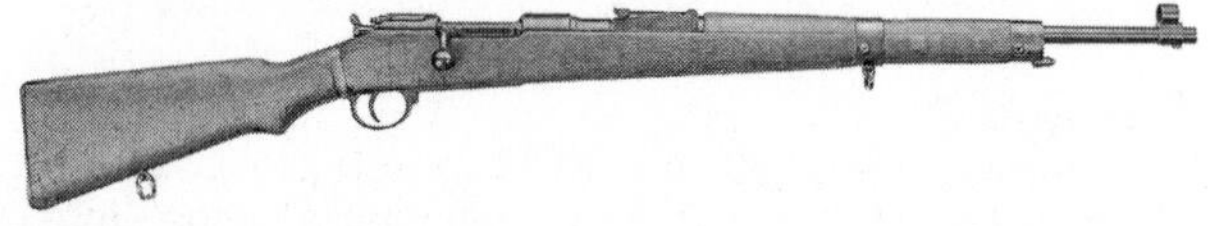

Model 43 rifle • Private collection, Paul Goodwin photo

Exc.	V.G.	Good	Fair	Poor
800	650	500	300	175

Bayonet for 35M and 43M Rifle

Round wood handle. Muzzle ring. 13.3" double edge blade. Steel scabbard. Price range 400 – 200.

44.M (Mosin-Nagant)

This is the Hungarian copy of the Soviet 1944 Mosin-Nagant. Produced in 1952-1955 by FEG. This rifle can be identified by the Communist national crest (a star on top of a globe with a hammer but no sickle) on top of the receiver ring. Stocks are marked with a "B" in a circle and may have "02" on top of the receiver ring that is the code for Hungary. Many have been imported since the mid 1990's.

Exc.	V.G.	Good	Fair	Poor
200	150	100	75	50

48.M (Mosin-Nagant)

This is a Hungarian copy of the M91/30 Mosin Nagant Soviet rifle chambered for the 7.62mm cartridge. Barrel length is 28.5". Five-round magazine. Weight about 8.5 lbs. Exported worldwide.

Exc.	V.G.	Good	Fair	Poor
400	325	250	150	100

48.M (Mosin-Nagant) Sniper Rifle

Same configuration as the Russian M91/30 sniper rifle using a Hungarian made rifle and scope. Before the mass import of Russian 91/30 snipers during the 1990s, the Hungarian-made guns were the only ones seen in the U.S. Some were probably "imported" from Canada in the trunk of a car. Price listed is for rifle and scope.

Exc.	V.G.	Good	Fair	Poor
1000	850	700	500	400

STEYR

Osterreichische Waffenfabrik Gesellschaft GmbH, Steyr (1869-1919)

Steyr-Werke AG (1919-1934)
Steyr-Daimler-Puch, Steyr (1934-1990)
Steyr-Mannlicher GmbH, Steyr (1990-)

Model 95 Rifle (Model 31)

A number of Model 95 rifles and short rifles were modified to accept the 8x56mm cartridge after World War I. The letter "H" is stamped on the barrel or the receiver. This is a straight pull rifle with 19.6" barrel and a 5-round fixed magazine. Weight is approximately 7.5 lbs.

Exc.	V.G.	Good	Fair	Poor
250	150	100	75	50

HUNGARIAN AK CLONES

AKM-63

A close copy of the AKM but with plastic furniture. Fitted with a vertical grip under the forend. Weighs about 1/2 lb. less than the Russian AKM.

Pre-1968

Exc.	V.G.	Fair
18000	15000	13000

Pre-1986 conversions of semi-automatic model

Exc.	V.G.	Fair
8000	7000	600

AKM-63 Semi-automatic Copy

This semi-automatic version of the AKM-63 is in a pre-ban (1994) configuration.

Exc.	V.G.	Good	Fair	Poor
1000	850	750	—	—

NOTE: Add 20 percent for folding stock (AMD65style).

AMD-65

This model is an AKM-63 with a 12.5" barrel, two-port muzzle brake, and a side folding metal butt. Rate of fire is about 600 rounds per minute. Weight is approximately 7 lbs.

Pre-1968

Exc.	V.G.	Fair
25000	22500	20000

Pre-1986 conversion of semi-automatic version

Exc.	V.G.	Fair
15000	13000	11000

AMD-65 semi-automatic, U.S. Made

Recent production using some original AMD-65 parts assembles on a new U.S. made receiver and 16" barrel.

Exc.	V.G.	Good	Fair	Poor
650	600	550	N/A	N/A

NGM

This assault rifle is the Hungarian version of the AK-74 chambered for the 5.56x45mm cartridge. Fitted with a 16.25" barrel. Magazine capacity is a 30-round box type. Rate of fire is about 600 rounds per minute. Weight is approximately 7 lbs.

Pre-1968

Exc.	V.G.	Fair
N/A	N/A	N/A

MACHINE GUNS

Hungary was supplied with a wide variety of Soviet machine guns after World War II from the RPD to the DShK38. Many of these machine guns were later copied by the Hungarians while retaining the Soviet model designations.

Bayonet for 35M and 43M Rifles

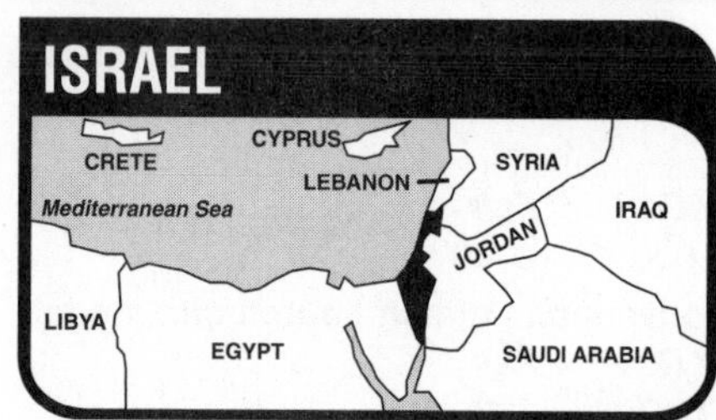

The state of Israel, a Middle Eastern republic at the eastern end of the Mediterranean Sea, bounded by Lebanon on the north, Syria on the northeast, Jordan on the east, and Egypt on the southwest, has an area of 9,000 sq. mi. (20,770 sq. km.) and a population of 6 million. Capital: Jerusalem. Finished diamonds, chemicals, citrus, textiles, minerals, electronic and transportation equipment are exported.

ISRAEL

HANDGUNS

NOTE: Israel has used a number of different handguns during its early fight for independence and in the turbulent years after. These handguns included Enfield and Webley revolvers as well as Browning Hi-power, Lugers and P-38 pistols. They also built a modified copy of the Smith & Wesson Military & Police model chambered for the 9x19 cartridge which required the use of two three-round half-moon clips.

Beretta M1951

This 9mm semi-automatic pistol is the standard Israeli military sidearm. See *Italy, Handguns, Beretta.*

Jericho

A 9mm or .41 Action Express double action semi-automatic pistol with a 4.72" barrel, polygonal rifling, ambidextrous safety and fixed sights. Blued with plastic grips. Weight is approximately 36 oz. Magazine capacity is 16 rounds in 9mm. This pistol is primarily used by the Israeli police and other government agencies, generally in 9mm.

Exc.	*V.G.*	*Good*	*Fair*	*Poor*
600	400	350	300	200

SUBMACHINE GUNS

NOTE: Prior to the development of the UZI the Israelis used British Sten guns and other WWII submachine guns that were available for purchase on the arms market.

UZI

First produced in Israel in 1953, this submachine gun is chambered for the 9mm cartridge. It was designed by Uzi Gal and was based on the Czech designs that were used by Israeli forces in the 1947-48 conflicts. It is fitted with a 10.14" barrel and metal folding stock. It has a magazine capacity of 25, 32, or 40 rounds. Empty weight is about 7.7 lbs. Rate of fire is 600 rounds per minute. This gun enjoys widespread use and is found in military and police units all over the world. Marked "uzi smg 9mm" on left side of receiver.

Pre-1968 (Very Rare)

Exc.	*V.G.*	*Good*
15000	13000	11000

Pre-1986 manufacture with new receiver or reweld

Exc.	*V.G.*	*Good*
8000	6500	5000

Vector UZI pre-1986 conversion

The receiver was produced, marked, and registered by Group Industries, Louisville, KY, prior to May 1986. Receiver fixed parts manufacturing and receiver assembly is done by Vector Arms, Inc. of North Salt Lake, UT. A total of 3,300 receivers built. All parts (South African) interchangeable with original IMI guns. Receiver parkerized. All other specifications same as original UZI.

Pre-1986 conversions

NIB/Exc.	*V.G.*	*Good*
7000	6000	5000

Mini-UZI

First produced in 1987, this is a smaller version of the original UZI. It functions the same as its larger counterpart. Accepts 20-, 25-, and 32-round magazines. Rate of fire is about 900 to 1,100 rounds per minute. Weight is about 6 lbs. Overall length is about 14" with butt retracted and 23" with butt extended.

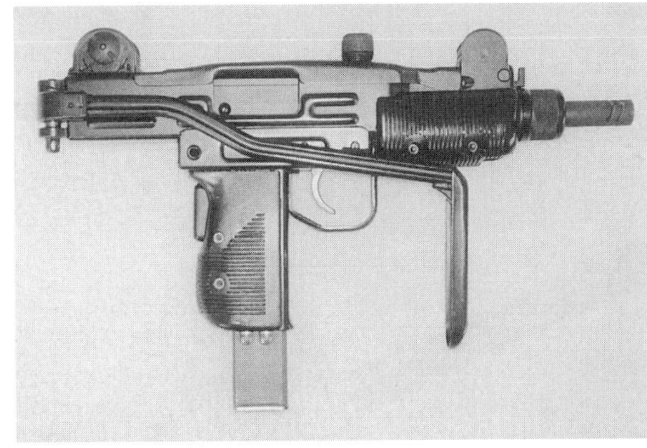

Courtesy private NFA collection

Pre-1986 conversion of semi-automatic version

Exc.	*V.G.*	*Good*
9500	7000	5000

RIFLES

NOTE: During the 1950s, Israel converted Mauser 98 rifles to 7.62mm caliber. Some of these were later sold as surplus. The Israeli military employed a large number, about 150,000 Colt-built M16A1 rifles and M16A1 carbines during the 1970s. This weapon is still popular with the IDF today. They also have used FN-built and IMI-assembled FN-FAL rifles. Israeli military forces were even issued AKM rifles. In 1975 the U.S. government sold about 22,000 M14 rifles to the Israeli military.

Mauser

German 98k, Post-WWII rework

German WW2 issue rifles that were sold to Israel in the late 1940s. The Nazi-era swastika markings are usually ground off, or peened. Most are found with a small Star of David mark on top of the receiver. Originally issued in 8x57mm, most found in the U.S. have been rebarreled to 7.62mm. A "7.62" caliber designation will be stamped on top of the receiver and on the stock. The serial numbers will not match as all were rebuilt.

Exc.	*V.G.*	*Good*	*Fair*	*Poor*
450	375	300	150	100

Model 1949 Bayonet for 98 Mauser

Composite grips. Muzzle ring. 9.7" single edge blade. Dated 1949 with Hebrew markings on ricasso. Steel scabbard with Star of David on frog stud. Some of these were made from German WW2 bayonets that had a new cross piece with muzzle ring installed. Others were of new manufacture. Price range 80 – 35.

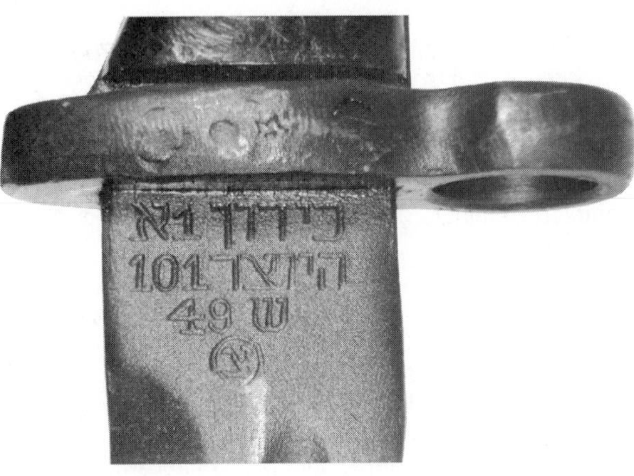

Czech Post-WWII 98k Short Rifle

This model is identical to the German Model K98k with the exception of an oversize triggerguard. Some have been converted to 7.62x51mm.

Exc.	*V.G.*	*Good*	*Fair*	*Poor*
425	375	300	150	100

FN 98k-style Short Rifle 7.62mm

This model was purchased directly from FN in the 1950s and is the same configuration as the German

FN 98k Short Rifle • Private collection, Paul Goodwin photo

Israeli K98 with grenade launcher • Courtesy Stoddard Martial collection, Paul Goodwin photo

Model 98k carbine. It is marked with the Israeli crest on the receiver ring.

Exc.	*V.G.*	*Good*	*Fair*	*Poor*
550	425	350	175	125

Mauser 98 Training Rifle, .22LR

A single-shot rifle featuring a Mauser 1898 action with a new .22-caliber barrel. The barrels are frequently marked Remington, as they used barrels from civilian-purchased guns.

Exc.	*V.G.*	*Good*	*Fair*	*Poor*
650	500	350	200	125

Galil ARM-Select Fire Assault Rifle

This automatic rifle is produced in Israel and is chambered for the 5.56x45mm cartridge. Similar in appearance to the AK-47 this rifle is fitted with an 18" barrel and folding stock. Magazine capacity is 35 or 50 rounds. Rate of fire is 550 rounds per minute. Model markings on the left side of the receiver are in Hebrew. Weight is approximately 8.7 lbs. First produced in 1971. Still in production. No original examples are transferable.

Courtesy private NFA collection

Pre-1986 conversions of semi-automatic model

Exc.	*V.G.*	*Good*
15000	12500	10000

Galil SAR-Select Fire Assault Rifle

Similar to the ARM but with a folding metal stock and a barrel length of 13". Weight of SAR is about 8.25 lbs.

Galil SAR • Courtesy private NFA collection

Pre-1986 conversions of semi-automatic model

Exc.	*V.G.*	*Good*
20000	15000	10000

Model AR

This rifle is an Israeli variant of the AK-47 based on the Valmet. It is also used by the South African military where it is called the R-4 rifle. It is a .223 or .308 caliber semi-automatic rifle with 16" or 19" barrel. Parkerized with the flip "Tritium" night sights and folding stock. The .308 version would bring about a 10 percent premium.

Exc.	*V.G.*	*Good*	*Fair*	*Poor*
2900	2000	1500	N/A	N/A

Model ARM

As above, with a ventilated wood handguard and a folding bipod and carrying handle. The .308 will bring about a 10 percent premium.

Exc.	*V.G.*	*Good*	*Fair*	*Poor*
2800	2000	1500	N/A	N/A

Galil Sniper Rifle

Introduced in 1983 and similar to the above rifle chambered for the 7.62x51 NATO caliber, with a 20" heavy barrel, adjustable wooden stock, and a 6/40 scope is furnished in addition to the Tritium night sights. Supplied to military in semi-automatic version only. Weight is about 14 lbs. Supplied with two 25-shot magazines and a fitted case.

NIB	*Exc.*	*V.G.*	*Good*	*Fair*	*Poor*
8500	7500	6000	4000	N/A	N/A

IDF Mauser Rifle Model 66SP

This is a bolt action rifle chambered for the .308 Win. cartridge. Adjustable trigger for pull and travel. Barrel length is 27". Specially designed stock has broad forend and a thumb hole pistol grip. Cheekpiece is adjustable as is the recoil pad. The rifle is fitted with an original Swarovsky 6x24 BDC Mil-Spec scope. Supplied with case. This rifle is military issue, built by Mauser for the Israel Defense Force in the early

Model ARM Assault Rifle • Courtesy West Point Museum, Paul Goodwin photo

1980s. Fewer than 100 imported into the U.S by Springfield Armory.

Exc.	*V.G.*	*Good*	*Fair*	*Poor*
3000	2500	—	—	—

MACHINE GUNS

Israel uses a variety of foreign-built machine guns from the FN MAG, Browning 1919 and Browning .50 caliber heavy machine gun. There are no known transferable Israeli machine guns in the U.S.

The Italian Republic, a 700-mile-long peninsula extending into the heart of the Mediterranean Sea, has an area of 116,304 sq. mi. (301,230 sq. km.) and a population of 60 million. Capital: Rome. The economy centers around agriculture, manufacturing, forestry and fishing. Machinery, textiles, clothing and motor vehicles are exported.

From the fall of Rome until modern times, 'Italy' was little more than a geographical expression. Although nominally included in the Empire of Charlemagne and the Holy Roman Empire, it was in reality divided into a number of independent states and kingdoms presided over by wealthy families, soldiers of fortune or hereditary rulers. The 19th century unification movement fostered by Mazzini, Garibaldi and Cavour attained fruition in 1860-70 with the creation of the Kingdom of Italy and the installation of Victor Emmanuel, king of Sardinia, as king of Italy. Benito Mussolini came to power during the post-World War I period of economic and political unrest, and installed a Fascist dictatorship with a figurehead king as titular Head of State. Mussolini entered Italy into the German-Japanese anti-comitern pact (Tri-Partite Pact) and withdrew from the League of Nations. The war did not go well for Italy and Germany was forced to assist Italy in its failed invasion of Greece. The Allied invasion of Sicily on July 10, 1943 and bombings of Rome brought the Fascist council to a no vote of confidence on July 23, 1943. Mussolini was arrested but soon escaped and set up a government in Salo. Rome fell to the Allied forces in June, 1944 and the country was allowed the status of cobelligerent against Germany. The Germans held northern Italy for another year. Mussolini was eventually captured and executed by partisans.

Following the defeat of the Axis powers, the Italian monarchy was dissolved by plebiscite, and the Italian Republic proclaimed.

ITALY

HANDGUNS

Modello 1874

This was the first handgun adopted by the Kingdom of Italy's military forces. It was very similar to the French Model 1874 and is chambered for the 10.35mm cartridge. It is fitted with a 6.3" octagon barrel. Cylinder is fluted and grips are checkered wood with lanyard loop. Built by Siderugica Glisenti and others. Weight is about 40 oz. In use by the Italian military from 1872 to 1943.

Exc.	*V.G.*	*Good*	*Fair*	*Poor*
900	600	350	200	125

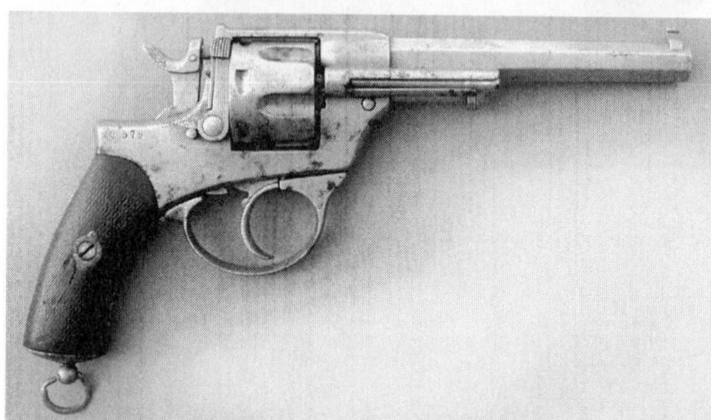

Modello 1874 • Courtesy Supica"s Old Town Station

System Bodeo Modello 1889 (Enlisted Model)

Courtesy Rock Island Auction Company

A 10.4mm caliber revolver with a 4.5" octagonal barrel and 6-shot cylinder. Folding trigger, no trigger guard. Built on a Chamelot-Delvigne frame with loading gate on the right side. This revolver was adopted as the Italian service revolver in 1889 and was replaced by the Glisenti in 1910. Manufactured by various Italian arms companies. This revolver, in different configurations, remained in service until 1945.

Exc.	*V.G.*	*Good*	*Fair*	*Poor*
500	350	250	150	100

Modello 1889 (Officer's Model)

Essentially the same as the enlisted man's model with a round barrel, non-folding trigger, and conventional triggerguard.

Exc.	*V.G.*	*Good*	*Fair*	*Poor*
500	350	250	150	100

Glisenti Model 1910

A 9mm Glisenti caliber semi-automatic pistol with a 3.9" barrel, fixed sights, and 7-shot magazine. Weight is about 30 oz. Manufactured from 1910 to 1915. As many as 100,000 of these pistols were produced and used during World War II.

WARNING: *Standard 9x19 ammo must not be fired in this gun.*

Modello 1889 (Officer's Model) • Courtesy Richard M. Kumor Sr.

Courtesy Faintich Auction Service • Photo Paul Goodwin

Model 1910 with black plastic grips with crown • Courtesy Richard M. Kumor Sr.

Exc.	*V.G.*	*Good*	*Fair*	*Poor*
750	550	400	250	150

BERETTA, PIETRO

Model 1915

A 7.65mm caliber semi-automatic pistol with 3.5" barrel, fixed sights, and 7-shot magazine. Blued with walnut grips. Weight is about 20 oz. The slide is marked "PIETRO BERETTA BRESCIA CASA FONDATA NEL 1680 CAL. 7.65MM BREVETTO 1915." Manufactured between 1915 and 1922.

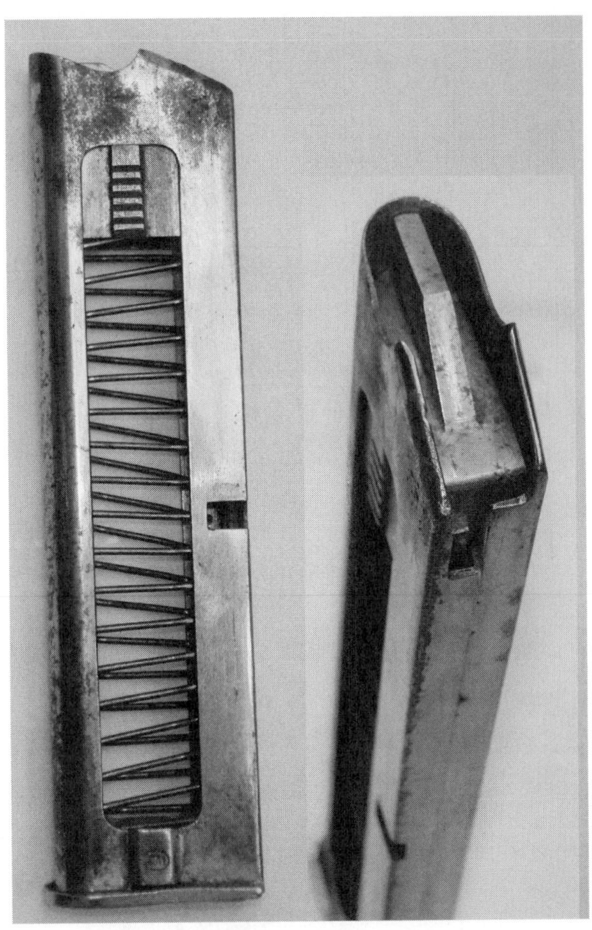

9mm Glisenti M1910 magazine. Price 150-70

Used by the Italian military during WWI and WWII. About 65,000 were produced, most of which were not martially marked.

Courtesy Rock Island Auction Company

Exc.	*V.G.*	*Good*	*Fair*	*Poor*
500	350	225	150	100

Model 1915 2nd Variation

As above, in 9mm Glisenti caliber with 3.75" barrel. Checkered wood grips. Weight is about 32 oz.

Exc.	*V.G.*	*Good*	*Fair*	*Poor*
650	500	400	200	125

Model 1915/1919

This model is an improved version of the above pistol but chambered for the 7.65mm cartridge. It also incorporates a new barrel-mounting method and a longer cutout in the top of the slide. Produced from 1922 to 1931 for the Italian military with about 50,000 manufactured, most without military markings.

Courtesy Orvel Reichert

Exc.	*V.G.*	*Good*	*Fair*	*Poor*
400	300	225	150	100

Beretta Model 1915-1919 magazine 7.65mm. Price 65-40

Model 1923

A 9mm caliber semi-automatic pistol with 4" barrel and 8-shot magazine. Blued with steel grips. The slide is marked "Brev 1915-1919 Mlo 1923." Exposed hammer. Italian army markings on left grip tang. Some pistols are cut for a shoulder stock. Manufactured from 1923 to 1935. Approximately 10,000 manufactured.

Exc.	*V.G.*	*Good*	*Fair*	*Poor*
650	500	350	225	150

Model 1931

A 7.65mm caliber semi-automatic pistol with 3.5" barrel and open-top slide. Blued with walnut grips and marked "RM" separated by an anchor. Issue limited to the Italian navy. Produced from 1931 to 1934 for the Italian navy. Approximately 8,000 manufactured.

Exc.	*V.G.*	*Good*	*Fair*	*Poor*
800	650	400	200	150

Model 1934

As above, with 9mm Corto (Kurz) caliber. The slide is marked, "P. Beretta Cal. 9 Corto-Mo 1934 Brevet

Courtesy Orvel Reichert

Gardone VT." This inscription is followed by the date of manufacture that was given numerically, followed by a Roman numeral that denoted the year of manufacture on the Fascist calendar, which began in 1922. This model was the most common prewar Beretta pistol and was widely used by all branches of the Italian military. Examples are marked "RM" (navy), "RE" (army), "RA" (air force), and "PS" (police). Manufactured between 1934 and 1959.

Courtesy Orvel Reichert

Exc.	*V.G.*	*Good*	*Fair*	*Poor*
500	400	300	150	100

Air Force "RA" marked

Exc.	*V.G.*	*Good*	*Fair*	*Poor*
675	550	400	225	150

Navy "RM" marked

Exc.	*V.G.*	*Good*	*Fair*	*Poor*
750	650	475	250	175

Holster for Beretta Model 1934 and 1935

Leather construction. Top flap. Single magazine pouch on the front. Single belt loop on back. Some WWII era versions were dyed a green color. Price range 150 - 50

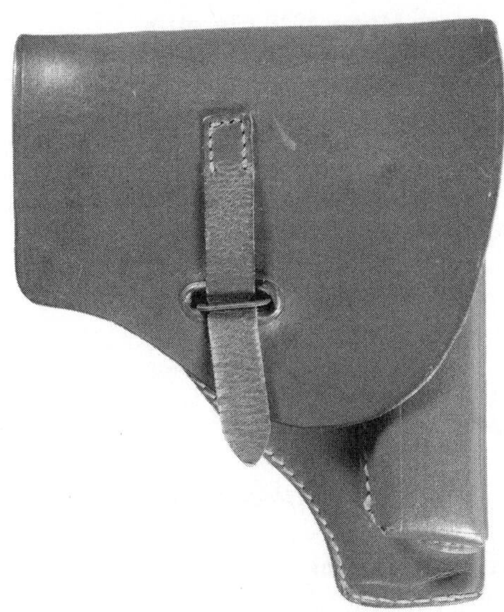

Model 1934 Romanian Contract

See Romania, Handguns.

Model 1935

As above, in 7.65mm caliber. Manufactured from 1935 to 1959. A number of these pistols were built and used by the German army during the occupation of Italy in World War II. Some of these pistols are marked with the German army acceptance stamp. Pistols produced in 1944 and 1945 were likely used by the German army without markings. Some of these wartime pistols are marked with Italian navy or air force markings. Production between 1934 and 1943 was about 200,000 pistols. Production continued after WWII. Deduct 20 percent for post-war dated commercial pistols.

Model 1935 • Courtesy Orvel Reichert

Exc.	*V.G.*	*Good*	*Fair*	*Poor*
550	400	300	150	100

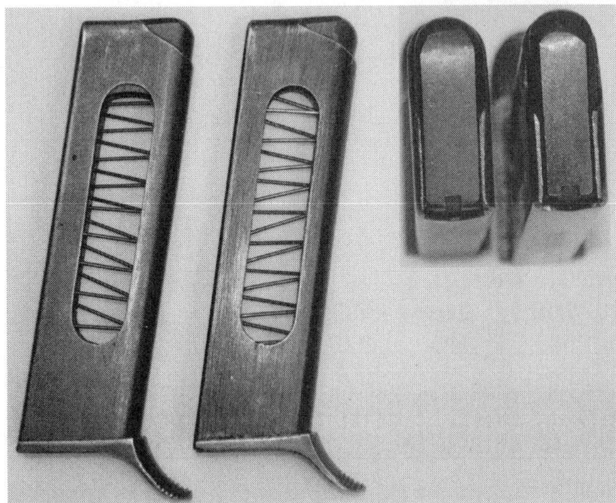

Beretta Models 1934 (l) and 1935 magazines (r). Difference is visible from the top. price 65-30

Model 1951

Chambered for the 7.65 or 9mm cartridges, this model was fitted with a 4.5" barrel and had an 8-round magazine. Fixed sights. Weight was about 31 oz. This pistol was used by the Italian military as well as by Egypt and Israel. Sold commercially under the name "Brigadier."

Exc.	*V.G.*	*Good*	*Fair*	*Poor*
600	475	350	250	175

NOTE: See Egypt, Helwan

ITALY

ITALY

Model 92

A 9mm caliber double action, semi-automatic pistol with a 5" barrel, fixed sights, and a 16-round, double-stack magazine. Blued with plastic grips. Introduced in 1976 and is now discontinued. This model was used by the Italian State Police forces. The U.S. military version, the M9, is based on this series. Price given is for commercial pistols. It is not known if any Italian military issue Beretta 92's have been imported.

NOTE: There are a number of different versions of this pistol. The main differences lie in the safety type and magazine release, barrel length, and magazine capacity.

NIB	Exc.	V.G.	Good	Fair	Poor
500	400	375	300	250	200

SUBMACHINE GUNS

Italy also uses the HK MP5A3 and MP5SD in its police and anti-terrorist units.

Villar Perosa Model 1915

This was the first submachine gun adopted by any military force. Chambered for the 9x19mm Glisenti cartridge. Barrel length is 12.5". Its rate of fire was about 1200 rounds per minute. Fed by a 25-round box top-mounted magazine. This gun was designed to be mounted in pairs on aircraft, various types of vehicles, and from fixed mounts with its spade grip. Weight of pair is about 14 lbs.

Pre-1968 (Very Rare)

Exc.	V.G.	Fair
25000	22500	20000

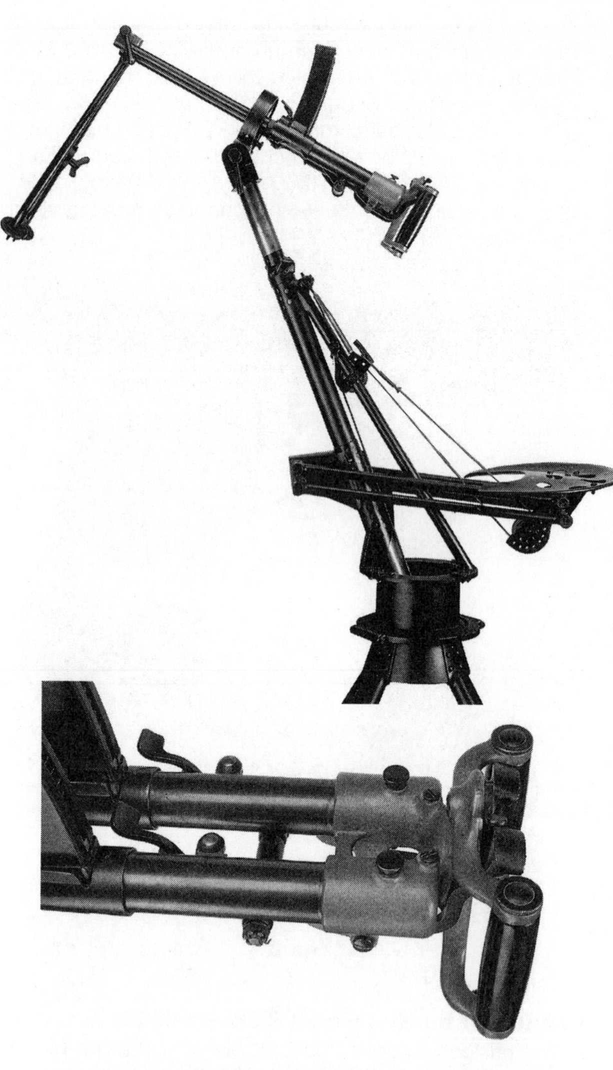

Twin Villar Perosa guns in simulated aircraft mount • Courtesy private NFA collection, Paul Goodwin photo

Villar Perosa Model 1918 (Beretta)

This gun is an adapted Villar Perosa fitted into a wooden stock with new trigger mechanism. Most of the original M1915 Villar Perosa's were converted to the Model 1918. Barrel length is 12.5". Magazine capacity is 25 rounds. Rate of fire is about 900 rounds per minute. Select fire. Weight is about 8 lbs. This gun was used by the Italian army from the end of WWI to WWII.

Beretta Model 1918 • Courtesy Thomas Nelson, *The World's Submachine Guns, Vol. 1*

Pre-1968 (Extremely Rare)

Exc.	V.G.	Fair
9500	9000	8000

Beretta Model 1938A

This Italian-made submachine gun is chambered for the 9mm Parabellum cartridge and was produced from

1938 to about 1950. It was in use by German, Italian, and Romanian armies in different eras. Argentina also purchased a number of Model 38As directly from Beretta. It is fitted with a 12.25" barrel, full rifle-style stock, and has a magazine capacity of 10, 20, 30, or 40 rounds. Its rate of fire is 600 rounds per minute. Markings on top of receiver are "MOSCHETTI AUT-BERETTA MOD 1938A BEREVETTO NO 828 428 GARDONE V.T. ITALIA." This weapon was fitted with two triggers: The front trigger fires in the semi-automatic mode, and the rear trigger fires in the automatic mode. A few early models were fitted with a bayonet lug. Weight is about 9.25 lbs.

Private NFA collection • Photo by Gary Gelson

Pre-1968

Exc.	*V.G.*	*Fair*
12500	10000	7500

Beretta Model 38/42

This is an improved wartime version of the Model 1938 without the barrel shroud. This was a less-well-finished model than the Model 1938A. Barrel length is a little over 8". Rate of fire is about 550 rounds per minute. Magazine capacity is 20 or 40 rounds. Produced from 1943 to about 1975. Weight is approximately 7 lbs. Marked "M.P. BERETTA MOD 38/42 CAL 9" on the top of the receiver. This model was used by Italian and German troops in Italy in the latter stages of World War II. Some of these guns were sold to Romania in 1944.

NOTE: A simplified version of the Model 38/42 is designated the Model 38/44 and features a lighter and more simple bolt design and main operating spring. This main spring is very similar to the one used in the British Sten gun. The Model 38/ 44 was sold to Syria, Pakistan, Iraq, and Costa Rica, among others, following WWII.

Pre-1968

Exc.	*V.G.*	*Fair*
10500	8500	7000

F.N.A.-B Model 1943

This Italian submachine gun was built in 1943 and 1944. It is fitted with a 7.75" shrouded barrel. Chambered for the 9mm cartridge. Magazine capacity is 20 or 40 rounds with a machined magazine housing that folds forward when not in use. Rate of fire is 400 rounds per minute. The gun fires from the closed bolt position. It is made entirely of machined steel. It is estimated that some 7,000 of these guns were produced and were used by both Italian and German troops in WWII.

Pre-1968 (Rare)

Exc.	*V.G.*	*Fair*
12500	11000	10000

Beretta Model 12

Chambered for the 9mm Parabellum cartridge, this sub gun was produced from 1959 to about 1978. It was manufactured basically from steel stampings. Fitted with a bolt that wraps around the barrel. Also fitted with a front vertical hand grip and either a folding metal stock or detachable wood stock. First used by Italian military in 1961. Also used in South America and Africa. Barrel is 7.75" long with a magazine capacity of 20, 30, or 40 rounds. Rate of fire is 500 rounds per minute. Marked "MOD12-CAL9/ M PARABELLUM" on the top of the receiver. Weight is about 6.5 lbs.

Pre-1968 (Rare)

Exc.	*V.G.*	*Fair*
12500	11000	10000

Beretta Model 12S

Similar to the Model 12 but with an improved safety system, sights, and folding stock fixture. Production began in 1978 when it replaced the Model 12.

ITALY

Beretta Model 38/42 • Private NFA collection, Paul Goodwin photo

Courtesy private NFA collection

Pre-1968

Exc.	*V.G.*	*Fair*
12500	11000	10000

Franchi LF-57

First produced in Italy in 1960, this submachine gun is chambered for the 9mm cartridge. It was placed in service with the Italian navy. Produced until 1980. It is fitted with an 8" barrel and has a magazine capacity of 20 or 40 rounds. Equipped with a folding stock. Rate of fire is about 500 rounds per minute. Marked "S P A LUIGI FRANCHI-BRESCIA-CAL9P." Weight is 7 lbs.

Pre-1968

Exc.	*V.G.*	*Fair*
9500	8500	7500

Beretta Model 93R

Built of the Beretta Model 92 frame and slide, this machine pistol is chambered for the 9mm Parabellum cartridge. It is fitted with a 6.1" barrel with muzzle brake and uses a 15- or 20-round magazine. Can be fitted with a shoulder stock. Rate of fire is about 1,100 rounds per minute. Has a 3-round burst mode, and a small swing-down metal foregrip mounted on the front of the triggerguard. Weight is about 2.5 lbs. Used by the Italian anti-terrorist units.

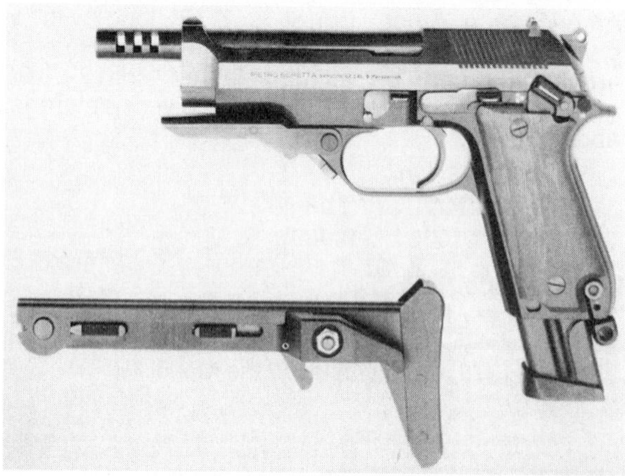

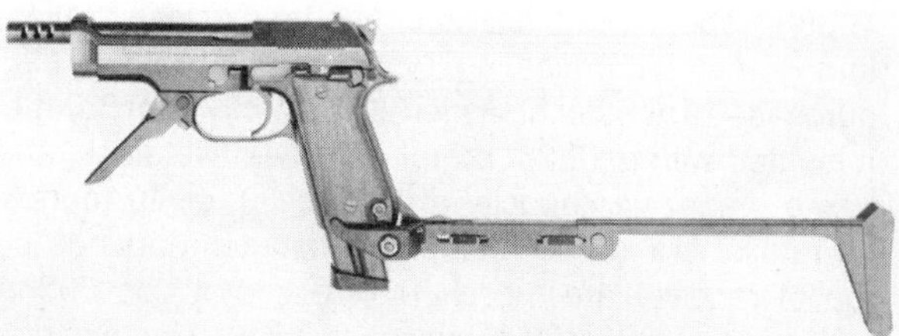

Beretta Model 93R • Courtesy Thomas Nelson, *The World's Machine Pistols, Vol. II*

Pre-1986 conversions

Exc.	*V.G.*	*Fair*
16000	15000	14000

ITALY

RIFLES

Prior to 1965 Italy used the U.S. M1 carbine as well as the M1 Garand. Beretta manufactured a large number of these rifles and many are still in use by some military units. Also used by counter-terrorist units is the HK G3 SG1 sniper rifle and the Mauser Model 66 sniper rifle.

VETTERLI

NOTE: See also Switzerland, Rifles, Vetterli.

Model 1870 Rifle

This rifle was produced at Brescia and Torino arsenals under license from the Swiss firm Vetterli. It was chambered for the 10.35x47Rmm centerfire cartridge. Single shot and full stock. This rifle was fitted with a sheet steel bolt opening cover which rotates left to right to close over the receiver opening. The barrel was 34" in length with the rear portion hexagonal. Marked on the upper left barrel flat with the maker's name and on the left barrel flat, the date. There is also a short barrel (24") version of this rifle. Single-shot Vetterlis are rarely found. Most were converted to the Vitale magazine system.

Exc.	*V.G.*	*Good*	*Fair*	*Poor*
700	600	450	250	150

Model 1870 Carbine

Same as above but fitted with a 17.5" barrel. The stock was half-stocked with brass or steel forearm bands.

Model 1870 Rifle • Private collection, Paul Goodwin photo

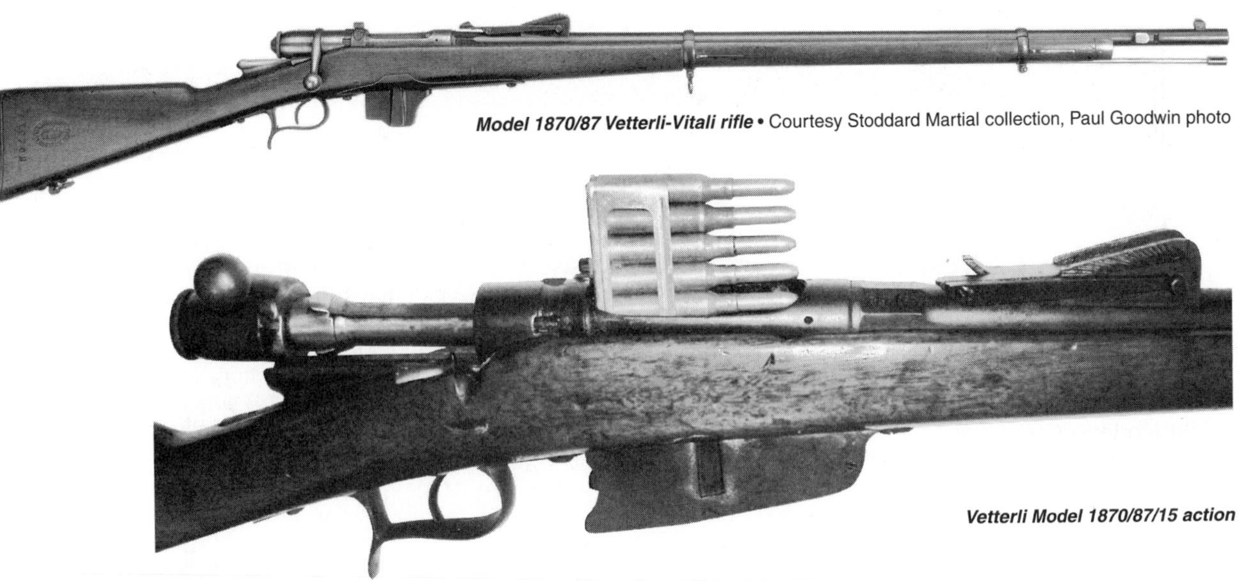

Model 1870/87 Vetterli-Vitali rifle • Courtesy Stoddard Martial collection, Paul Goodwin photo

Vetterli Model 1870/87/15 action

The bayonet folded under the barrel with the blade tip inserted into the forearm.

Exc.	***V.G.***	***Good***	***Fair***	***Poor***
850	650	500	250	150

Model 1882 Naval Rifle

This rifle used the Model 1870 action. Fitted with a 28.75" barrel and chambered for the 10.4x47R Vetterli-Vitali cartridge. Full stocked. Weight is approximately 9 lbs. This model had no loading port but was charged by loading through the open action. The tube held 8 rounds. Made at Turni.

Exc.	***V.G.***	***Good***	***Fair***	***Poor***
850	650	500	250	100

Model 1870/87 Rifle/Carbine (Vetterli-Vitali)

This rifle was the same as the Model 1870 with the important exception of having been converted to magazine feed. The 4-round magazine was developed by Guiseppe Vitali. The magazine is unusual because the charger had to be fully inserted and then withdrawn with a string as the cartridge stripped away. Over 1,000,000 of these rifles were issued. A large number of these converted rifles and carbines were sold to Russia.

Exc.	***V.G.***	***Good***	***Fair***	***Poor***
750	650	500	250	150

Model 1870/87/15 Rifle (Vetterli-Vitali)

During WW1 nearly all the remaining model 1870/87 rifles were converted to use the 6.5x52mm Italian service ammunition. This was done by soldering a liner with 6.5mm bore in the original barrel. A new magazine was installed that allows use of the Mannlicher-Carcano six shot clip. This is the most common Italian Vetterli to be found in the U.S. today.

Exc.	***V.G.***	***Good***	***Fair***	***Poor***
300	250	175	125	100

Bayonets for Vetterli series

Model 1870/87

Wood grips. Muzzle ring. Hook quillon. 22.5" single edge blade. Brass tipped leather scabbard. Frequently found without a scabbard. Price range 200 – 100.

Model 1870/87/15

The model 1870/87 bayonets were converted by shortening the blade to 9.1" and the quillon was removed. The leather scabbards were also shortened. Price range 125 – 60.

Bayonet for Model 1870/87/15

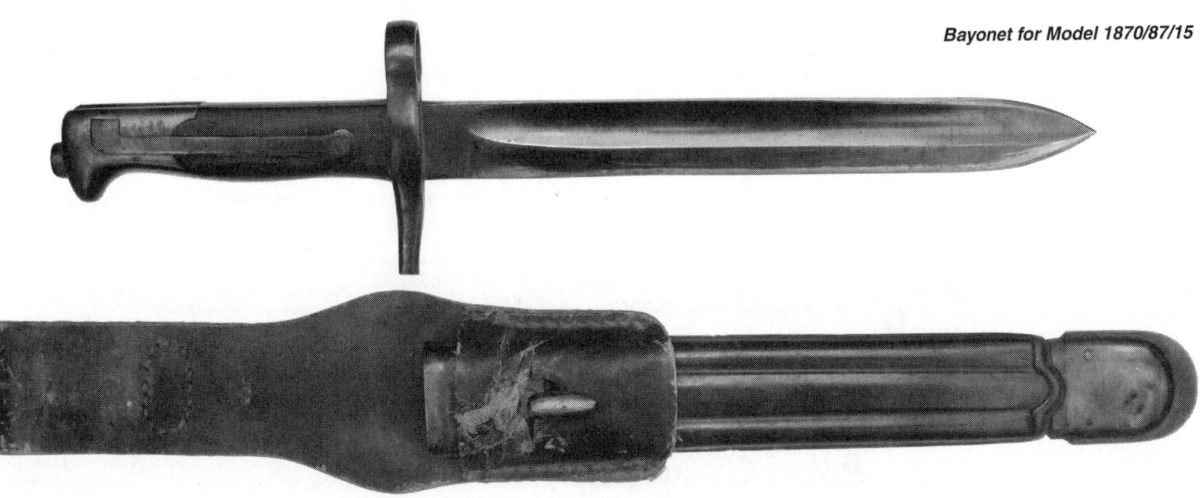

Bayonet for Model 1870/87

CARCANO

NOTE: For drawings, data, and history see *The Carcano: Italy's Military Rifle* by Richard Hobbs, 1997.

Fucile Modello 1891 Rifle

Designed by Salvator Carcano, the Model 1891 was adopted as Italy's standard service rifle in 1892. A 6.5x52mm caliber bolt action rifle with a 30.6" barrel, 6-shot Mannlicher clip loading magazine, full-length stock, split bridge receiver, and a tangent rear sight with a wooden handguard and barrel bands retaining the stock. Fitted for a knife-type bayonet. On early versions the barrel behind the rear sights is octagonal. Weight is about 8.5 lbs. Produced at the Brescia, Terni, Roma, Torino and Beretta arsenals. On post-1922 examples Roman numerals appear on the upper right barrel flat, denoting the year of the Mussolini rule. Adding the Roman numeral to 1922 will provide the year of production. So, a Carcano with the Roman numeral XIV (14) was made in 1936. Many millions of this rifle were produced through WWII.

Italian troops with their Carcano rifles • Courtesy Paul S. Scarlata

Exc.	V.G.	Good	Fair	Poor
400	300	225	175	125

Bayonet for Mannlicher Carcano Models 1891 and 1941

Wood grips. Muzzle ring. 11.8" single edge blade. Early issue pieces came in a brass-tipped leather scabbard. At some point they began making the scabbards from steel. Most of the metal scabbards have a fluted surface, similar to those found on the Finnish Mosin Nagant bayonets. Price range 125 – 50.

Model 1891 Cavalry Carbine (Moshetto)

Same as above but half stocked with an 18" barrel with

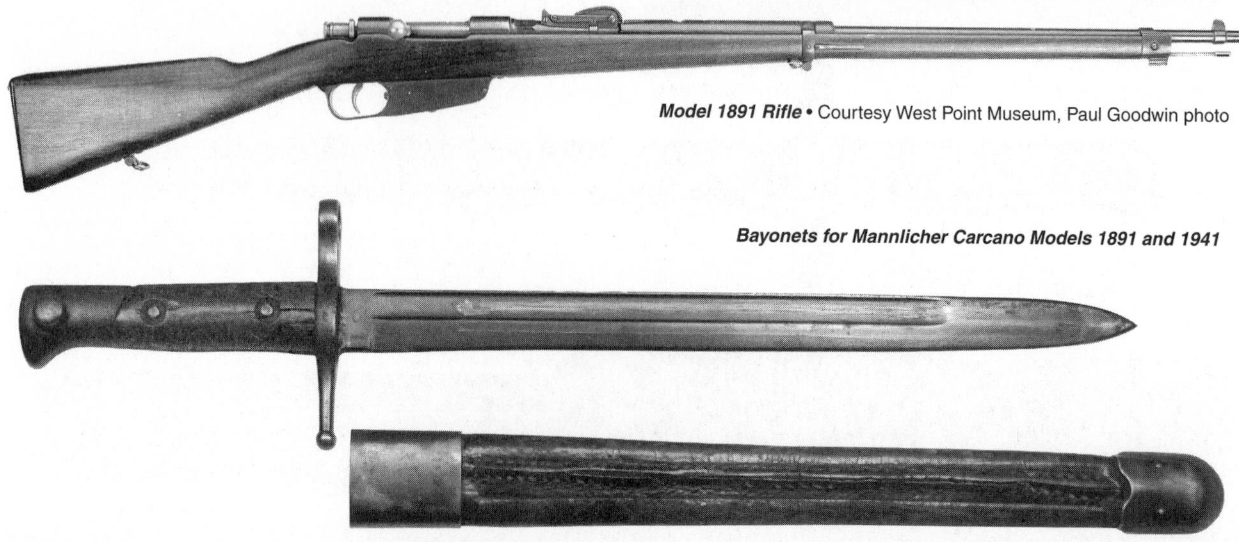

Model 1891 Rifle • Courtesy West Point Museum, Paul Goodwin photo

Bayonets for Mannlicher Carcano Models 1891 and 1941

Model 91 TS Carbine showing bayonet fitting • Private collection, Paul Goodwin photo

folding bayonet attached to the muzzle. Weight is about 6.5 lbs.

Exc.	*V.G.*	*Good*	*Fair*	*Poor*
375	250	200	150	100

Model 1891 TS (Truppe Speciali)

Similar to the Carbine above but without permanently attached bayonet. The original version of the TS pattern takes a unique bayonet. The nose cap has a bayonet lug that is side ways to the barrel. The bayonet slides over the barrel then turns to the side to latch. Later TS versions did away with this bayonet and use the standard 1891 pattern.

Exc.	*V.G.*	*Good*	*Fair*	*Poor*
400	300	250	150	125

Bayonet for Model 1891 T.S.

The same as the 1891 bayonet but has a lateral slot in the top of the pommel for mounting on the T.S. carbine. Discontinued after a short time, these bayonets are rare. Price range 250 – 125.

Model 1891/24 Carbine

Many Model 1891 rifles had the barrels shortened to 18 inches. This model will resemble the TS. The conversion was approved in 1924. They retain the longer rear sight graduated to 2000 meters. Takes the same blade bayonet as the Model 1891 rifle.

Courtesy Richard M. Kumor Sr.

Exc.	*V.G.*	*Good*	*Fair*	*Poor*
350	275	225	150	125

Model 1891/28 Carbine

Similar in appearance to the Model 1891/24 carbine. This version was produced between 1928 and 1938 with barrel dates so stamped. The main difference in in the rear sight, which is adjustable from 600 to

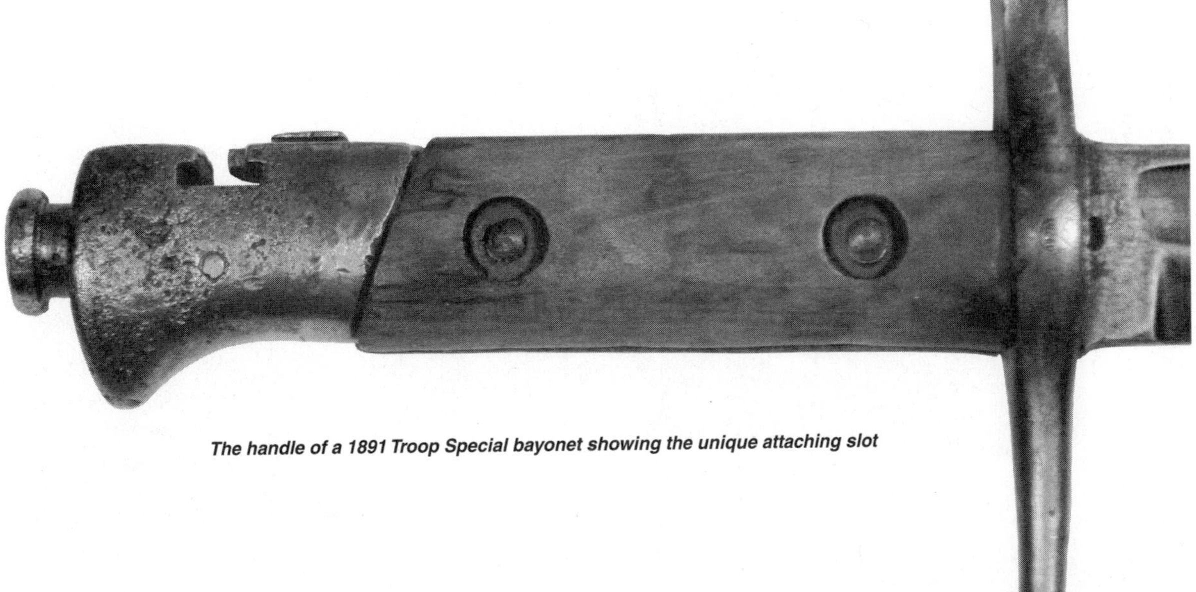

The handle of a 1891 Troop Special bayonet showing the unique attaching slot

1,500 meters. Produced at a number of different Italian arsenals. Weight is about 6.75 lbs.

M91/28 Carbine with grenade launcher • Courtesy Richard M. Kumor Sr.

Exc.	*V.G.*	*Good*	*Fair*	*Poor*
350	275	225	150	125

NOTE: The grenade launcher was called the "Tromboni Launchi Bombe." Add 200 percent for any Carcano with a grenade launcher.

Model 1938 Short Rifle (Prototype)

This model is chambered for the 7.35x51mm cartridge and fitted with a 22" barrel. It has a 6-round detachable box magazine. Bent bolt handle. It is full stocked with one barrel band and exposed barrel and bayonet lug. Long handguard. Simple fixed rear sight. Weight is about 7.5 lbs. Produced at the Terni arsenal. Very rare.

Exc.	*V.G.*	*Good*	*Fair*	*Poor*
N/A	—	—	—	—

Model 1938 Short Rifle (Production version)

As above but with two barrel bands and half-length handguard. The left side of the butt stock is marked in large letters "cal. 7.35." Rear sight is fixed at 200 meters. Weight is about 6.5 lbs.

NOTE: This rifle marked the first new caliber for Italian military rifles, the 7.35mm. When World War II began, about 285,000 rifles had been built in 7.35mm. From then on all Model 1938 Short Rifles and their variants were produced in the older 6.5mm caliber.

Exc.	*V.G.*	*Good*	*Fair*	*Poor*
300	250	175	125	100

Bayonet for Model 1938 Carcano

Wood grips. Muzzle ring. 7" single edge blade. The original version of this bayonet has a folding blade which fit into a groove in the forestock of the rifle. The folding version was costly to produce and the blade lock was found to loosen up with use. A fixed blade version replaced it and many of the folding bayonets were converted to fixed style by changing the cross piece. The fixed blade version was issued in a steel scabbard. Price range, folding model, 250 – 125. Price range, fixed blade, 150 – 60.

Model 1938 Cavalry Carbine

This model has a 17.75" barrel. It is fitted with a folding bayonet that fits under the barrel when not deployed. Chambered for the 7.35x53mm or 6.5mm cartridge. Built by FNA in Brescia and other Italian firms. The rear sight is a fixed 200-meter sight for rifles chambered for the 7.35mm cartridge. Weight is about 6.5lbs. About 100,000 were produced. Original 7.35mm carbines are somewhat scarce and might bring a 25 percent premium.

Model 1938 Carbine • Courtesy West Point Museum, Paul Goodwin photo

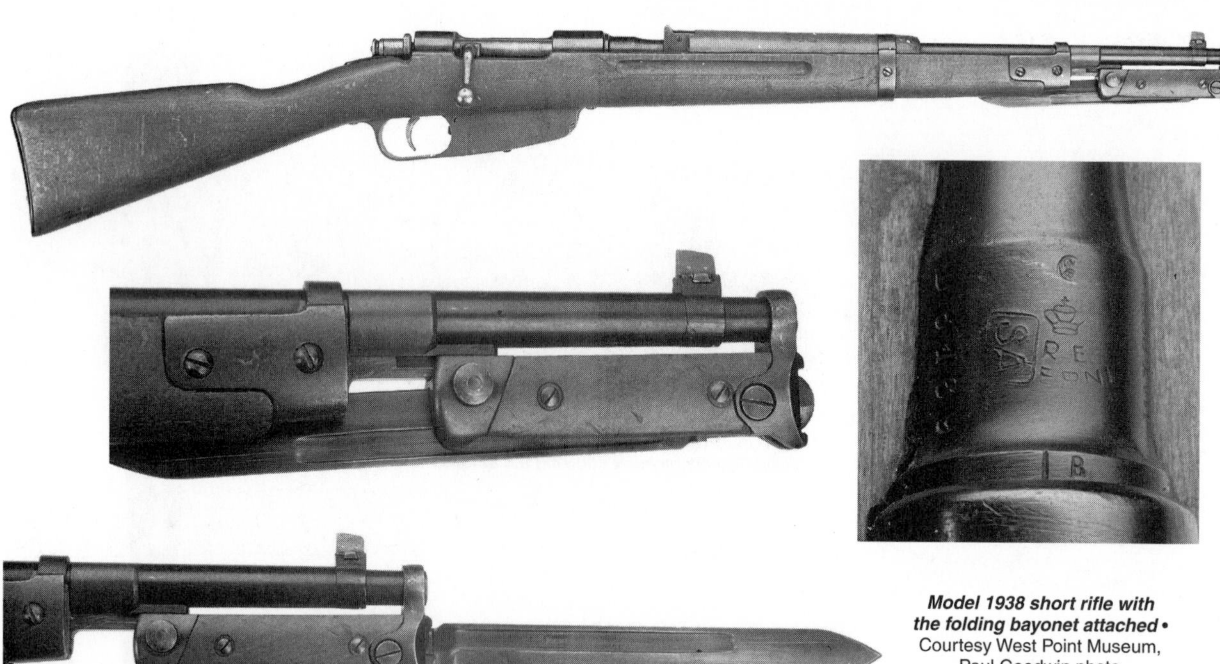

Model 1938 short rifle with the folding bayonet attached • Courtesy West Point Museum, Paul Goodwin photo

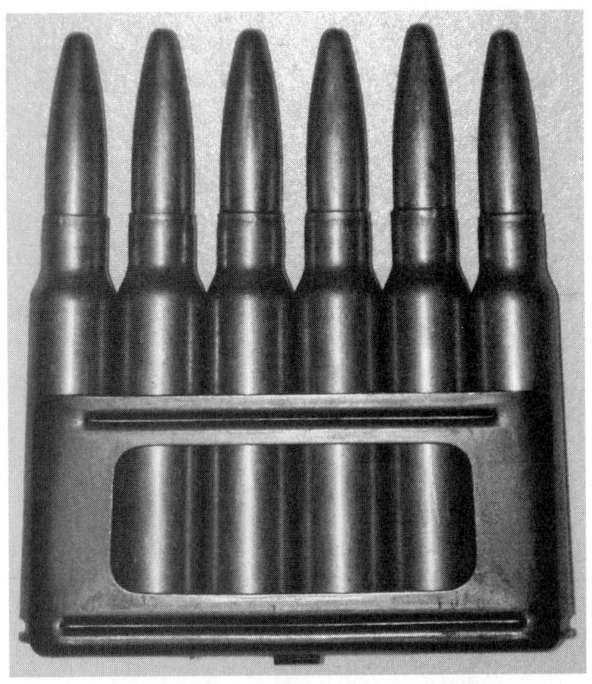

Clip for Mannlicher-Carcano. Brass or steel construction. Works with either 6.5mm or 7.35mm. Price 10-4

Exc.	V.G.	Good	Fair	Poor
300	250	175	125	75

Model 1938 T.S. Carbine

Same as 1891 T.S. carbine but with a fixed rear sight.

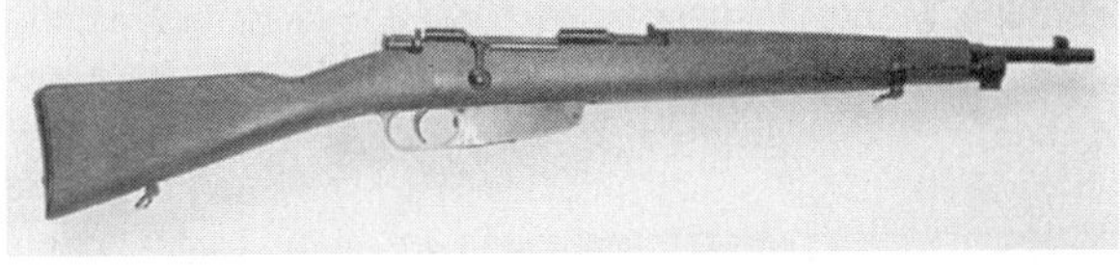

Courtesy Richard M. Kumor Sr.

Exc.	V.G.	Good	Fair	Poor
300	250	200	125	75

NOTE: For original M-38 T.S. carbines in 7.35mm add a premium of 50 percent.

Model 1938/43 Cavalry & T.S. Carbine converted to 7.9x57mm Mauser

During the last months of WWII the Germans converted some Carcanos carbines to use the 7.9 Mauser cartridge. They were not intended for front line service. This was done by boring out the original barrel. "7.9" is marked behind the rear sight. Barrel length is 18". Rear sight is fixed at 200 meters. Though they retain the Carcano magazine system, they were issued as single shots. The 7.9 Mauser cartridge is too large to fit in the Carcdano clip or magazine. The work was done by the H. Kreighoff company. They might bear an HK and German waffen markings. These German conversions are rare.

Exc.	V.G.	Good	Fair	Poor
800	700	600	400	300

Post-WWII conversion to 7.9 Mauser

After WWII, many Carcano carbines were converted to 7.9 Mauser using the same process used by the Germans. History is unclear as to what country these were made for. It is likely they were done in Italy in order to make the tons of surplus Carcanos they had more sellable on the world arms market. Marked with a large "S" on top of the barrel. Some have "7.9" on the rear sight. No HK or other German marks. These are common on the U.S. market and are frequently confused with the much rarer German conversions.

Exc.	V.G.	Good	Fair	Poor
250	175	150	100	75

Model 1941 Rifle (1891/41)

This is a 6.5mm rifle fitted with a 27.25" barrel and 6-round detachable box magazine. Very similar to the Model 1891 but for length and rear sight from 300 to 1,000 meters. Weight about 8.2 lbs. Frequently found in excellent condition as they were un-issued when Italy ended its' participation in WWII. Some were refinished after the war for export sales. They will be marked "Made in Italy" A few of these rifles were sold to Israel and will be marked with the Star of David.

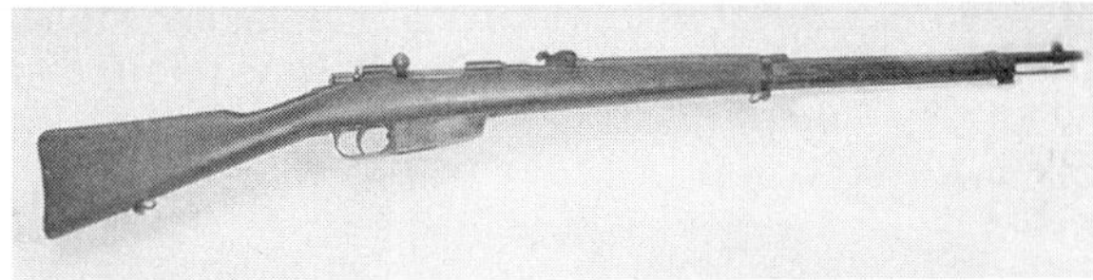

Courtesy Richard M. Kumor Sr.

Exc.	V.G.	Good	Fair	Poor
300	250	175	125	100

Italian Youth Rifle (Moshetto Balia)

Smaller version of the Carcano 1891 Cavalry Carbine, with folding bayonet. Barrel length is 14.4". Used for youth training and as awards in youth fascist groups. Not a real firearm, they were manufactured by toy companies. Although they appear to have a chamber, it is believed only blank cartridges were ever made for them. They would take a small version of the Mannlicher clip, although the clips are rarer than the guns, and none could be found to show in this book.

Courtesy Richard M. Kumor Sr.

Exc.	V.G.	Good	Fair	Poor
500	400	300	250	150

NOTE: Add $75 for dedication plaque.

Breda Model PG

Chambered for the 7x57mm rimless cartridge, this is a gas operated self-loading rifle with an 18" barrel and 20-round detachable box magazine. The particular rifle was made by Beretta for Costa Rica and is marked "GOBIERNO DE COSTA RICA," with the date 1935 and Roman numerals XIII. Weight was about 11.5 lbs. Fitted for a Costa Rican Mauser bayonet. Very rare. Price listed is the author's guess only. None found on the market.

Exc.	V.G.	Good	Fair	Poor
2500	2000	1500	1000	500

Breda Model PG • Paul Goodwin photo

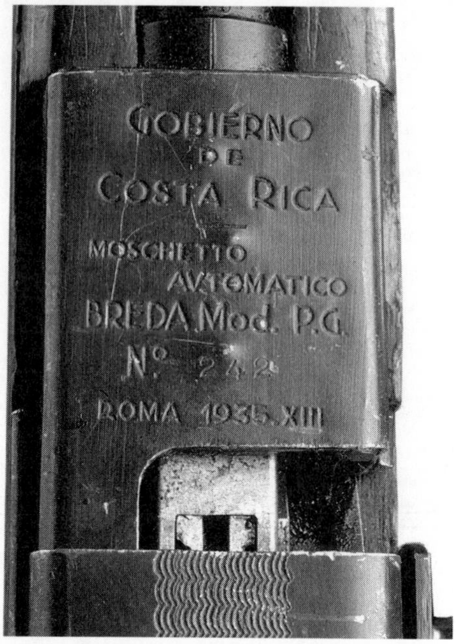

GOBIERNO DE COSTA RICA MOSCHETTO AVTOMATICO BREDA Mod. P.G. Nº 242 ROMA 1935.XIII

Beretta Model BM59-Select Fire Assault Rifle

This select fire rifle closely resembles the U.S. M1 Garand rifle. Chambered for the 7.62x51mm cartridge, it is fitted with a 19" barrel and 20-round magazine. It has a rate of fire of 750 rounds per minute. Weight is about 10 lbs. Marked "P BERETTA BM59" on the top rear of the receiver. Produced from 1961 to 1966. This rifle did see service in the Italian army. There are a number of variations to this rifle, including the BM59 Alpini with folding stock short forearm and bipod for use by Alpine troops, and the BM59 Parachutist Rifle with 18" barrel, folding stock, and detachable muzzle brake (the Italians referred to it as a Tri-Comp).

Pre-1968

Exc.	*V.G.*	*Fair*
8500	7000	5000

Pre-1986 conversions of semi-automatic version

Exc.	*V.G.*	*Fair*
5500	4250	N/A

BM-59 Semi-Automatic

A gas-operated semi-automatic rifle with detachable box magazine. Chambered for .308 cartridge. Walnut stock. Barrel length is 19.3" with muzzle brake. Magazine capacity is 5, 10, or 20 rounds. Weight is about 9.5 lbs.

Exc.	*V.G.*	*Good*	*Fair*	*Poor*
2000	1750	1250	N/A	N/A

Model BM59 • Courtesy West Point Museum, Paul Goodwin photo

Beretta AR70/.223 Select Fire Assault Rifle

Chambered for the 5.56x45mm cartridge, this select fire rifle was fitted with a 17.5" barrel and a 30-round magazine. Most were fitted with a solid buttstock while others were fitted with a folding stock. Weight was about 8.3 lbs. Marked "P BERETTA AR 70/223 MADE IN ITALY" on the left side of the receiver. This rifle was not widely adopted. Produced from 1972 to 1980.

Courtesy private NFA collection

Pre-1968 (Rare)

Exc.	*V.G.*	*Fair*
N/A	N/A	N/A

Pre-1986 conversions of semi-automatic version

Exc.	*V.G.*	*Fair*
10000	7500	5000

Beretta SC 70 Select Fire Assault Rifle

Similar to the AR 70 and chambered for the 5.56x45mm cartridge. It feeds from a 30-round magazine. The SC 70 has a folding stock and is fitted with a 17.5" barrel. Weight is about 8.8 lbs. The SC 70 short carbine also has a folding stock and is fitted with a 13.7" barrel. Weight is about 8.3 lbs. Both of these rifles are still in production and used by the Italian army since approved for service in 1990.

SC 70 Carbine • Courtesy private NFA collection

SC 70 Short Carbine • Courtesy private NFA collection

Pre-1968

Exc.	*V.G.*	*Fair*
N/A	N/A	N/A

Pre-1986 conversions of semi-automatic version

Exc.	*V.G.*	*Fair*
10000	8000	6500

AR-70

A .223 caliber, semi-automatic rifle with a 17.7" barrel, adjustable diopter sights, and an 8- or 30-shot magazine. Black epoxy finish with a synthetic stock. Weight is approximately 8.3 lbs.

NIB	*Exc.*	*V.G.*	*Good*	*Fair*	*Poor*
2500	2200	1900	1500	N/A	N/A

Bayonet for BM-59 and AR-70

This bayonet is a variation on the U.S. M-1 carbine bayonet and the dimensions are the same. It has a hard plastic handle. It is currently used on the Beretta-made rifles. Price range 250 – 100.

SHOTGUNS

Franchi SPAS 12

A 12 gauge slide action or semi-automatic shotgun with a 21.5" barrel and 9-shot magazine. Anodized black finish with a composition folding or fixed stock. Weight is about 9.25 lbs.

NIB	*Exc.*	*V.G.*	*Good*	*Fair*	*Poor*
950	800	600	500	N/A	N/A

Franchi SPAS 15

Similar to the SPAS 12 but with a detachable 6-round box magazine. Tubular steel folding stock and 18" barrel or fixed stock with 21" barrel. Weight is about 8.5 lbs. Very few imported into the U.S.

Exc.	*V.G.*	*Good*	*Fair*	*Poor*
6000	4500	3000	—	—

NOTE: For guns with folding stock and 18" barrel add $1,000.

MACHINE GUNS

Italy used the Maxim Model 1906 and Model 1911. Both of these models were chambered for the 6.5mm cartridge. During WWI, Italy purchased a number of Colt Model 1914 guns (Potato Diggers) chambered for the 6.5mm cartridge. When the war ended, Italy received a large number of Austrian Schwarzlose Model 1907/12 as war reparations. The first Italian light machine gun was the Breda Model 1924, the forerunner of the Breda Model 30.

After WWII, Italy adopted the U.S. Model 1919A4 and .50 NM2 HB guns, as well as the MG42/59, for which several Italian firms make the components under license.

World War I Italian machine gun team with Model 1914 Revelli • Robert G. Segel collection

Revelli Model 1914 • Courtesy private NFA collection, Paul Goodwin photo

Beretta M70/78

Similar to the Model 70/223 but fitted with a heavy 17.5" barrel. Magazine capacity is 30 or 40 rounds. Rate of fire is 700 rounds per minute. Marked "P BERETTA FM 70/78 MADE IN ITALY" on left side of the receiver. First produced in 1978 with production ending in 1983.

Pre-1968

Exc.	*V.G.*	*Fair*
N/A	N/A	N/A

Revelli Model 1914

This was the first Italian-designed medium machine gun to be made in quantity. It was chambered for the 6.5mm cartridge and fitted with a 26" barrel. It was fed by a unique 50-round magazine with 10 compartments holding 5 rounds each. Because of its blowback system where the barrel moved a short distance rearward before the bolt moved away from the breech, there was no extraction system other than to oil the cartridges so that they did not rupture. Rate of fire was about 400 rounds per minute. Weight was 38 lbs. without tripod, 50 lbs. with tripod. The gun was manufactured by Fiat. Many of these guns were used by the Italians in WWII as well as in WWI.

Pre-1968

Exc.	*V.G.*	*Fair*
10000	7500	5000

Fiat Model 1928 (SAFAT)

This is a light version of the Revelli Model 1914. Chambered for the 6.5 Carcano cartridge. Magazine is a 20-round magazine. Rate of fire is about 500 rounds per minute. Weight is approximately 21 lbs. Only a few thousand were manufactured during its limited production. Very rare.

Pre-1968

Exc.	*V.G.*	*Fair*
N/A	N/A	N/A

Revelli/Fiat Model 35

This is a converted Revelli Model 1914 to 8mm. It is an air-cooled gun. It is fed by a 300-round belt. It's fired from a closed bolt. It was not a successful gun. Weight without tripod was 40 lbs.

Pre-1968

Exc.	*V.G.*	*Fair*
6000	5000	4500

Breda Model 30

First produced in Italy in 1930, this machine gun was chambered for the 6.5x52mm cartridge. It is fitted with a 20.3" barrel. Magazine capacity is 20 rounds. Rate of fire is 475 rounds per minute. Marked "MTR LEGG MOD 30....BREDA ROMA" on top of receiver. Weight is about 22 lbs. Production on this model ceased in 1937. This was the primary Italian machine gun of WWII.

NOTE: A number of pre-1968 7mm Costa Rican contract guns are in the U.S. These are valued the same as the 6.5mm guns.

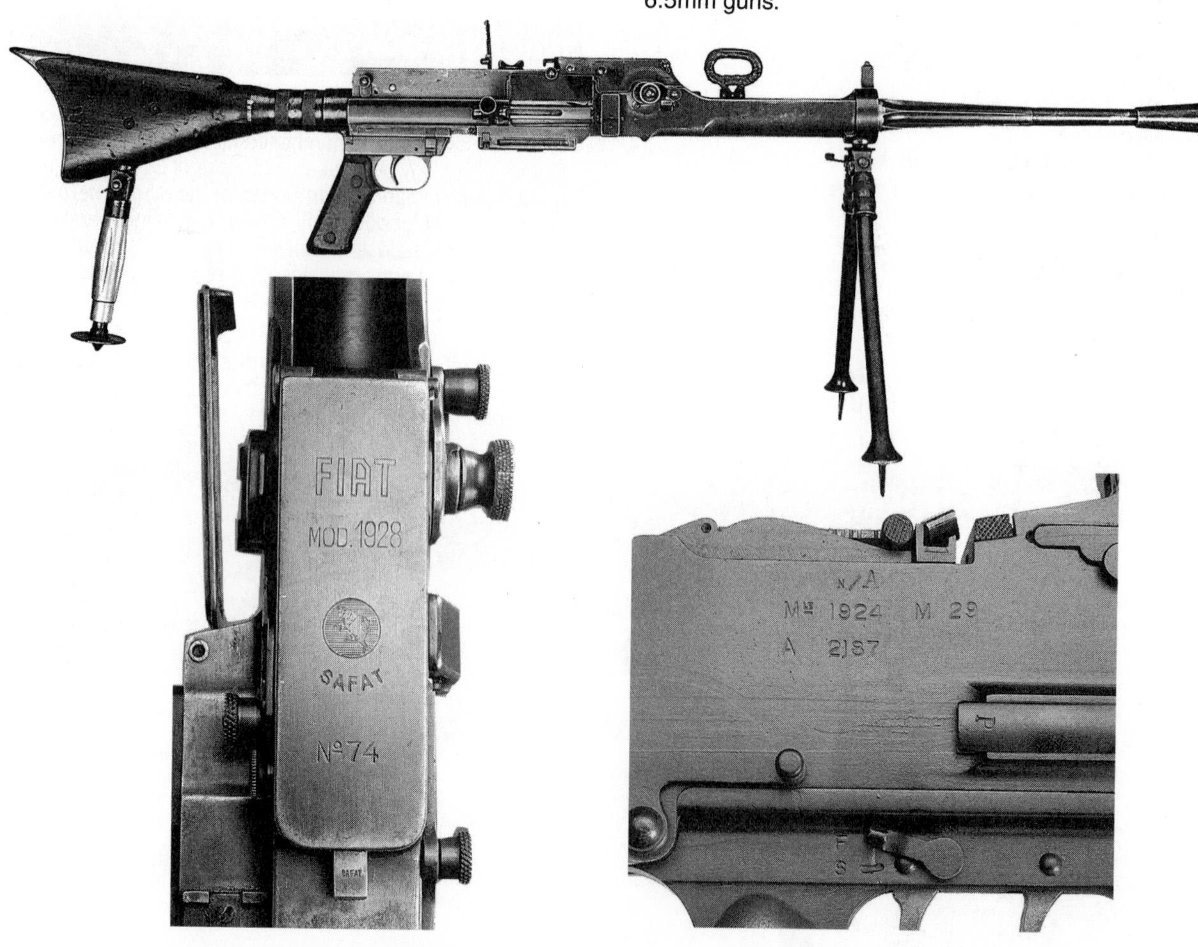

Fiat Model 1928 • Courtesy private NFA collection, Paul Goodwin photo

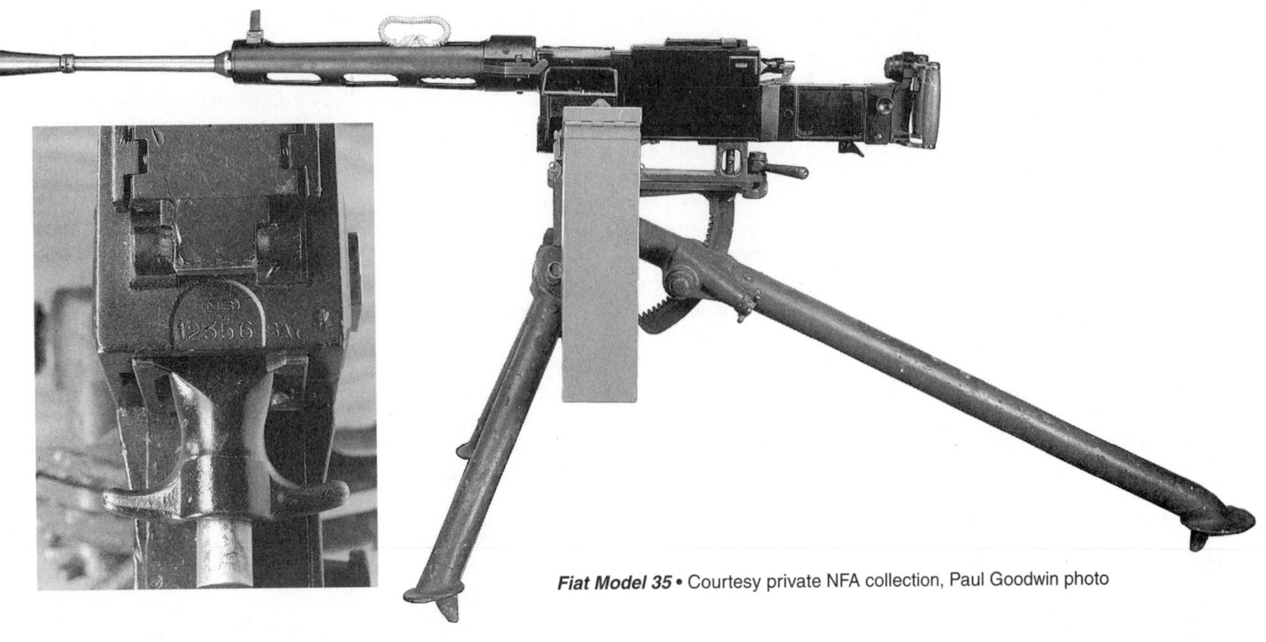

Fiat Model 35 • Courtesy private NFA collection, Paul Goodwin photo

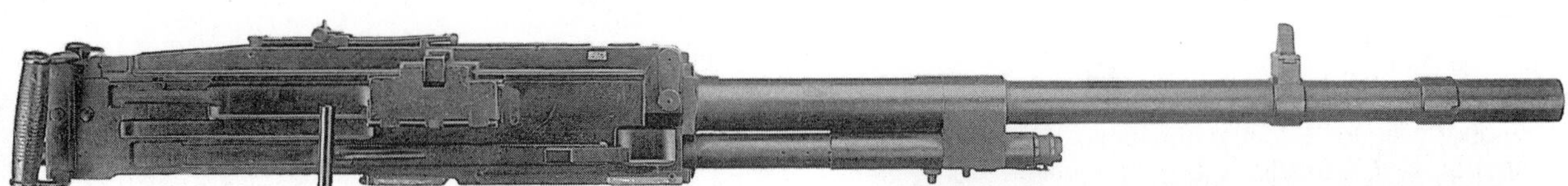

Breda Model 37 with receiver markings • Paul Goodwin photo

Pre-1968

Exc.	*V.G.*	*Fair*
10000	7500	5000

Breda Model 37

Chambered for the 8x59 Breda cartridge, this gas operated machine gun had a rate of fire of 450 rounds per minute. It was fitted with a 26.5" barrel and weighs approximately 43 lbs. It was fed with a 20-round strip. Marked "MITRAGLIATRICE BREDA MOD 37" on the left side of the receiver. Produced from 1936 to 1943, this was the standard heavy machine gun of the Italian army during WWII. The Model 37 was considered to be one of the best Italian machine guns used in WW II, mainly because of its reliability and accuracy.

Pre-1968

Exc.	*V.G.*	*Fair*
28000	25000	18000

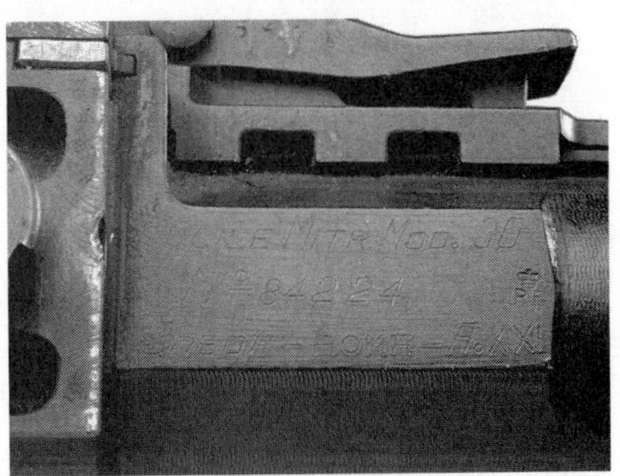

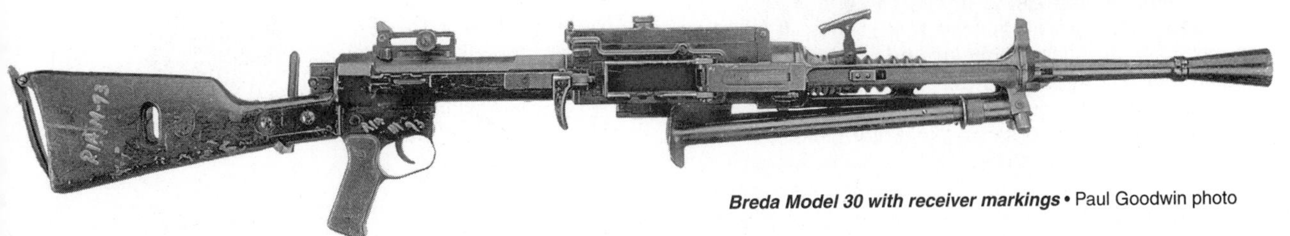

Breda Model 30 with receiver markings • Paul Goodwin photo

Japan, a constitutional monarchy situated off the east coast of Asia, has an area of 145,809 sq. mi. (377,835 sq. km.) and a population of 123.2 million. Capital: Tokyo. Japan, one of the major industrial nations of the world, exports machinery, motor vehicles, electronics and chemicals.

Japan, founded (so legend holds) in 660 B.C. by a direct descendant of the Sun Goddess, was first brought into contact with the west by a storm-blown Portuguese ship in 1542. European traders and missionaries proceeded to enlarge the contact until the Shogunate, sensing a military threat in the foreign presence, expelled all foreigners and restricted relations with the outside world in the 17th century. After Commodore Perry's U.S. flotilla visited in 1854, Japan rapidly industrialized, abolished the Shogunate and established a parliamentary form of government, and by the end of the 19th century achieved the status of a modern economic and military power. A series of wars with China and Russia, and participation with the allies in World War I, enlarged Japan territorially but brought its interests into conflict with the Far Eastern interests of the United States, Britain and the Netherlands, causing it to align with the Axis Powers for the pursuit of World War II. After its defeat in World War II, General Douglas MacArthur forced Japan to renounce military aggression as a political instrument, and he instituted constitutional democratic self-government. Japan quickly gained a position as an economic world power.

HANDGUNS

Bibliographical Note: For technical data, history, and photos see Fred Honeycutt, Jr., *Military Pistols of Japan*, 3rd Ed., Julian Books, 1994.

Type 26 Revolver

A 9mm caliber double action hinged-barrel revolver with a 6-shot cylinder. Because this pistol does not have a hammer spur, it functions only in double action. Fitted with a 4.75" barrel. Checkered beech grips. Grips from later examples have 19 serrations. Weight is about 31 oz. Manufactured from 1893 to 1924 in various government arsenals. Marked on right side of frame. This revolver was used by NCOs during WWII. Fewer than 60,000 of these revolvers were manufactured.

Courtesy Amoskeag Auction Co., Inc.

Exc.	*V.G.*	*Good*	*Fair*	*Poor*
850	650	400	300	150

4th Year Type Nambu Pistol

This is a quality-built semi-automatic pistol chambered for the 8mm cartridge. It is fitted with a 4.7" barrel and has a magazine capacity of 8 rounds. It can be identified by the grip safety located on the front strap and tangent sights. The early models, known as "Grandpa" to collectors, can be identified by a wooden-bottom magazine and stock slot. Later pistols, known as "Papa" Nambu, have aluminum-bottom magazines and only a very few "Papas" were slotted for stocks. The values shown here are only approximate. Different variations may bring different prices and an appraisal is recommended. Pistols with original wooden stocks are worth considerably more.

It is estimated that approximately 8,500 of these pistols were produced.

Grandpa

Grandpa • Courtesy of James Rankin

Exc.	*V.G.*	*Good*	*Fair*	*Poor*
7500	5000	3000	1800	900

NOTE: Add $1,500 for original matching shoulder stock-holster.

Papa

Papa • Courtesy of James Rankin

Exc.	*V.G.*	*Good*	*Fair*	*Poor*
2500	1800	1500	1000	500

Holster for Papa Nambu

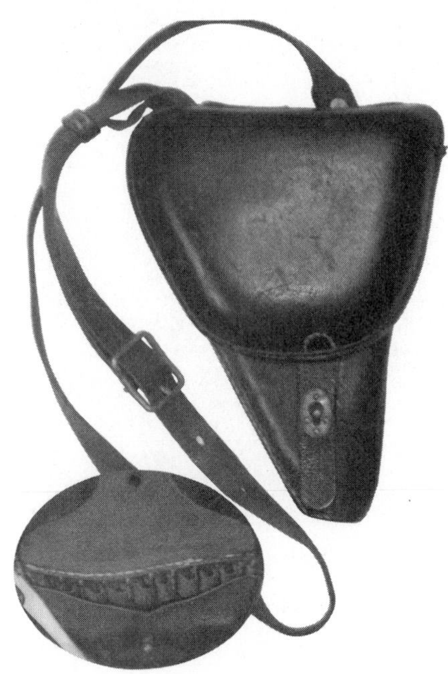

Leather construction. Clamshell type. Similar to the more common Type 14 holster. The major difference is that the Papa holster has cartridge loops in the pouch on the front. Price range: 500 – 250.

Baby Nambu

As above, with a 3.5" barrel. 7mm cartridge is unique to the gun. A much smaller version of the Papa 8mm pistol. It is a well-made piece. Production ceased in 1927 with about 6,500 pistols produced.

Courtesy Rock Island Auction Company

Exc.	*V.G.*	*Good*	*Fair*	*Poor*
4800	3500	2500	1000	750

14th Year Type Nambu Pistol/T-14

Similar to the 4th Year Type but without a grip safety and with grooved grips and a larger triggerguard. Manufactured until 1945. Early guns have a small triggerguard. Later models have a much larger triggerguard. Early guns will bring a premium of 20 percent. The month and year of production are indicated on the right side of the receiver, just below the serial numbers on both the Type 14 and Type 94 pistols. The guns are dated from the beginning of the reign of Hirohito (Sho-wa period), which started in 1925. Thus 3.12 means 1928-Dec. and 19.5 means 1944-May.

From 1926 to 1939 (small triggerguard) about 66,700 pistols were manufactured. From 1939 to 1945 (large triggerguard) approximately 73,000 pistols were produced.

This example features the later large trigger guard •
Courtesy Michael Wamsher, Paul Goodwin photo
T-14 pistol and rig with matching magazines.

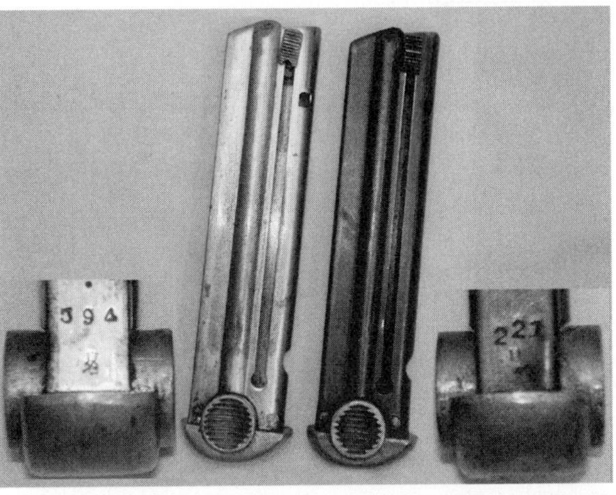

Type 14 8mm Nambu magazines. Price range 150-60

Courtesy Orvel Reichert

Exc.	*V.G.*	*Good*	*Fair*	*Poor*
550	450	350	250	150

Holster for Type 14 Nambu

Clamshell style. Made from leather or rubberized canvas. Most were issued with a carrying strap. Price range: 350 – 100

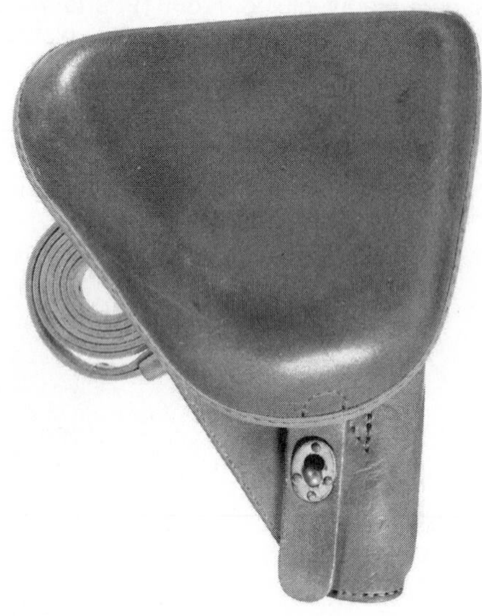

Type 94 Pistol/T-94

An 8mm caliber semi-automatic pistol with a 3.8" barrel and 6shot magazine. Weight is about 27 oz. This was a secondary service pistol issued in WWII. Most late-war examples are poorly constructed and finished. Manufactured from 1935 to 1945. Approximately 70,000 of these pistols were produced.

Courtesy Rock Island Auction Company

Courtesy James Rankin

Magazine for Type 94 Nambu. Price 75-40

Exc.	*V.G.*	*Good*	*Fair*	*Poor*
500	300	250	175	125

Holster for Type 94 Pistol

Leather construction with magazine pouch on front.

Price range: 175 – 75

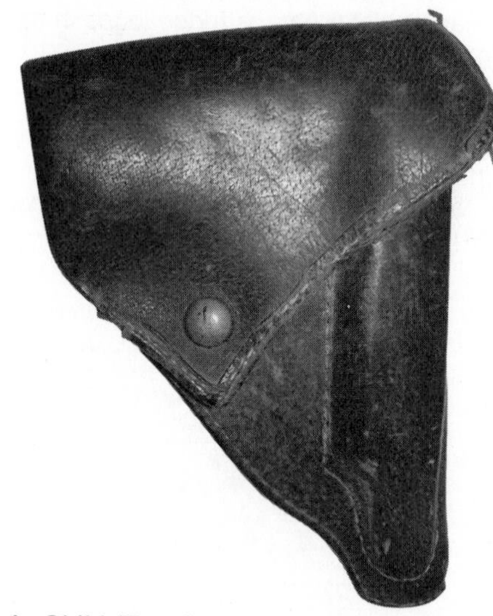

Hamada Skiki (Type) 2

Designed in 1942. There were several variations of this pistol chambered for both 7.65mm and 8mm Nambu. Production started in 1942 and ended in 1945. Probably fewer than 1,500 pistols were assembled. Rare.

Exc.	*V.G.*	*Good*	*Fair*	*Poor*
5000	3500	2500	2000	1500

SUBMACHINE GUNS

The Japanese military used Bergmann submachine guns built by SIG. These guns were similar to the MP 18 but chambered for the 7.63 Mauser cartridge and used a box magazine. These guns were fitted for a bayonet. It was not until the late 1930s that the Japanese began a development program to produce their own submachine gun; the first one was the Type 100/40.

Type 100/40

Adopted for use in 1940, this submachine gun is chambered for the 8x21mm Nambu cartridge and fitted with a 9" barrel with perforated jacket, fitted with a bayonet bar. It is mounted on a wooden half stock with tubular receiver made at the Kokura arsenal. These guns will also be seen with a folding stock made at the Nagoya arsenal. It is estimated that some 10,000 guns were built with fixed stocks and about 6,000 were built with folding stocks. Both types had 30-round box magazines. Rate of fire is approximately 450 rounds per minute. Weight was about 7.5 lbs. This model was issued primarily to paratroopers.

Japanese Type 100/40 • Courtesy Thomas Nelson, *World's Submachine Guns, Vol. I*

Pre-1968

Exc.	*V.G.*	*Fair*
18000	15000	10000

Type 100/44

This model was first produced in Japan in 1944. It is chambered for the 8mm Nambu cartridge. The barrel is 9.2" long with a honeycombed barrel jacket without bayonet bar. The side-mounted magazine capacity is 30 rounds. Markings are in Japanese on the rear of the receiver. Produced until the end of the war. Weight is about 8.5 lbs. Rate of fire is 800 rounds per minute. Approximately 8,000 were produced at the Nagoya arsenal. This improved version was issued to the infantry.

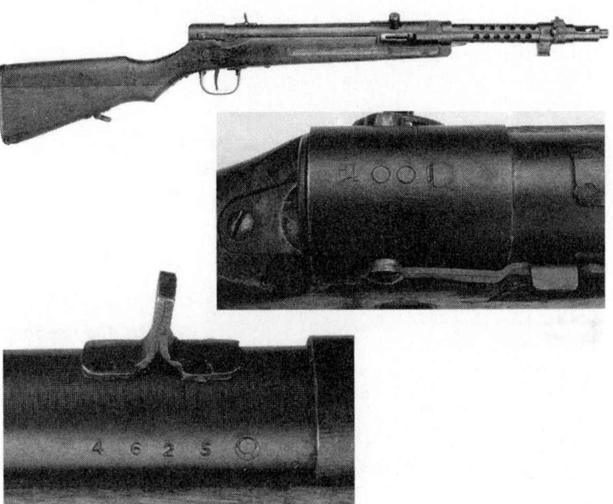

Pre-1968

Exc.	*V.G.*	*Fair*
18000	15000	10000

Type 100 Bayonet

This bayonet was made for use on the Type 100 sub-machine gun and the Arisaka paratrooper rifles. Wood grips. Muzzle ring. No quillon. 7.75" single edge blade. The single maker was Toyoda Loom Co, under Nagoya supervision. The maker's mark appears on the top of the tang, instead of on the ricasso. These have been faked. Beware! Price range 1800 – 1000.

RIFLES

Bibliographical Note: For historical information, technical data and photos see *Military Rifles of Japan*, 4th edition. Fred Honeycutt Jr., 1993.

Japanese Pre-Cartridge Era Rifles

The earliest firearms made by Japan were match lock muskets. These were used in limited quantities through the 1860's. Prior to the 1870s Japan acquired several models of percussion rifles from foreign sources. These include English, French and Dutch models. See listings under country of origin. Japanese marked examples will bring 25-100% more from collectors.

Japanese Manufactured Match Lock (Tanegashima)

Produced from the mid 1500's until the 1870s. Manufacture was not standardized and a variety of types have been observed. Price listed here is for common grade examples. Highly engraved versions with gold inlay can bring many times what plain guns do.

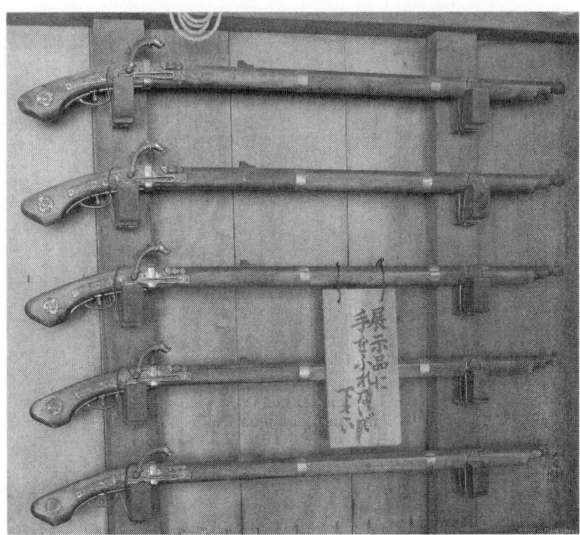

Exc.	*V.G.*	*Good*	*Fair*	*Poor*
2500	1600	1100	750	500

JAPAN

Japanese Manufactured Enfield 1855

The Koishikowa arsenal in Tokyo was founded in 1870. At that time, the Japanese began production of a copy of the English Pattern 1855 Enfield Musket in .577 caliber. It featured a 39-inch barrel, a rifled bore and rifle sights. Made from 1870-1880 it was replaced by the Murata Type 13 series.

Exc.	*V.G.*	*Good*	*Fair*	*Poor*
2000	1500	950	650	350

MARTINI

Model 1874 Peabody-Martini Rifle

Chambered for the .45 Turkish centerfire cartridge and fitted with a 32.5" barrel. Blued barrel and furniture with case hardened or blued receiver. Numbered in Arabic script. About 7,000 built for Japanese Navy.

Exc.	*V.G.*	*Good*	*Fair*	*Poor*
1500	1250	1000	750	400

MURATA

This series of Japanese military rifles was designed by Major Tsuneyoshi, superintendent of Japanese small arms in the late 1870s. These first single-shot bolt action rifles were based on the French Gras design. Later, Murata was influenced by the French Lebel with its tubular magazine. These rifles were built at the Imperial arsenal in Tokyo.

Murata Type 13 (M.1880)

This was the first Japanese-designed bolt action rifle. This was a single-shot rifle with no extractor or safety. Chambered for the 11x60Rmm cartridge with a barrel length of 31.25". One piece full-length stock with two barrel bands. The machinery to build this rifle was purchased from Winchester. The rear barrel flat is stamped with the Imperial chrysanthemum. The left side of the receiver is stamped with Japanese characters.

Exc.	*V.G.*	*Good*	*Fair*	*Poor*
2000	1500	1000	600	400

Murata Type 16

Same as above but fitted with a 25" barrel for cavalry use.

Exc.	*V.G.*	*Good*	*Fair*	*Poor*
2500	1650	1200	700	500

Murata Type 18 (M.1885)

An 11mm caliber bolt-action rifle with a 31.25" barrel, and full-length stock secured by two barrel bands. This was an improved version of the Type 13, which added receiver gas escape ports, a flat-top receiver ring, and a safety. These rifles were used in the Sino-Japanese War of 1894 and the Russo-Japanese War as well.

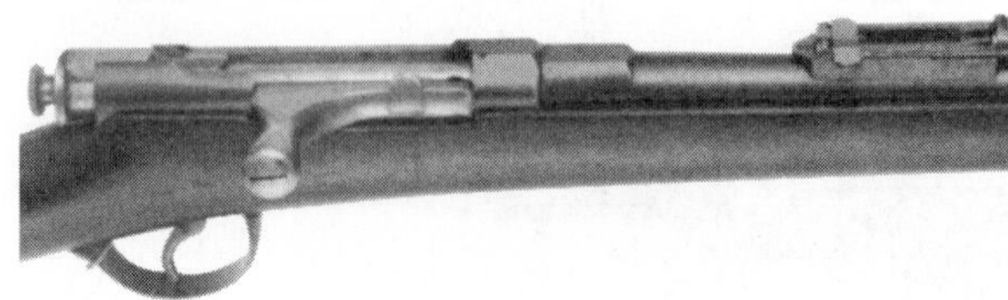

Courtesy Buffalo Bill Historical Center, Cody, Wyoming

Exc.	*V.G.*	*Good*	*Fair*	*Poor*
1750	1200	800	500	350

Bayonet for Type 18 Murata

Wood grips. Muzzle ring. Hook quillon. 18" single edge blade. Has the Imperial Chrysanthemun mark on the cross piece. Steel tipped leather scabbard. Rare. Price range 700 – 400.

Murata Type 22 (M.1889)

Produced circa 1889-1899 in caliber 8x53Rmm. Fitted with a 29.50" barrel with 8-round tubular magazine located in the forearm. This model was full stocked to the muzzle with straight grip. There were two variations of this rifle. The early version had a barrel band forward of the forend band. In the later version, this extra band was eliminated. This was Japan's first smokeless powder military rifle and was the standard rifle issued to Japanese forces in the Sino-Japanese War of 1894.

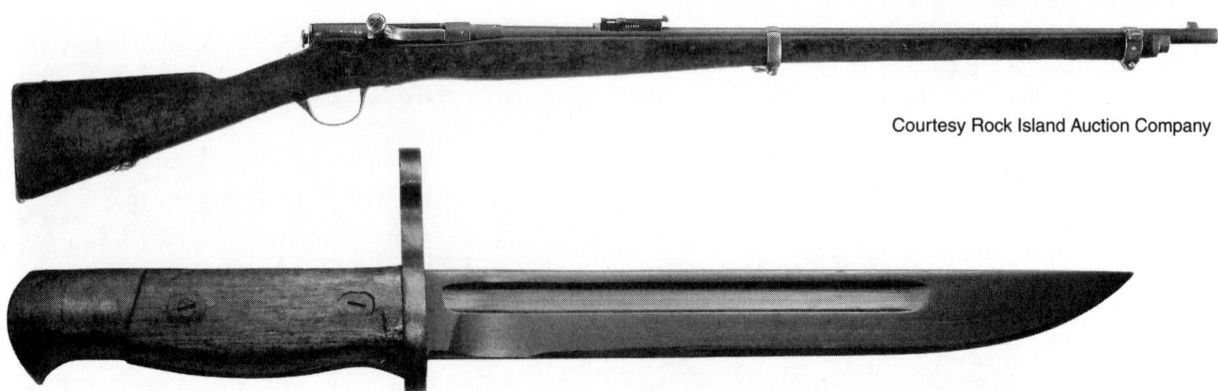

Courtesy Rock Island Auction Company

Type 100 Bayonet

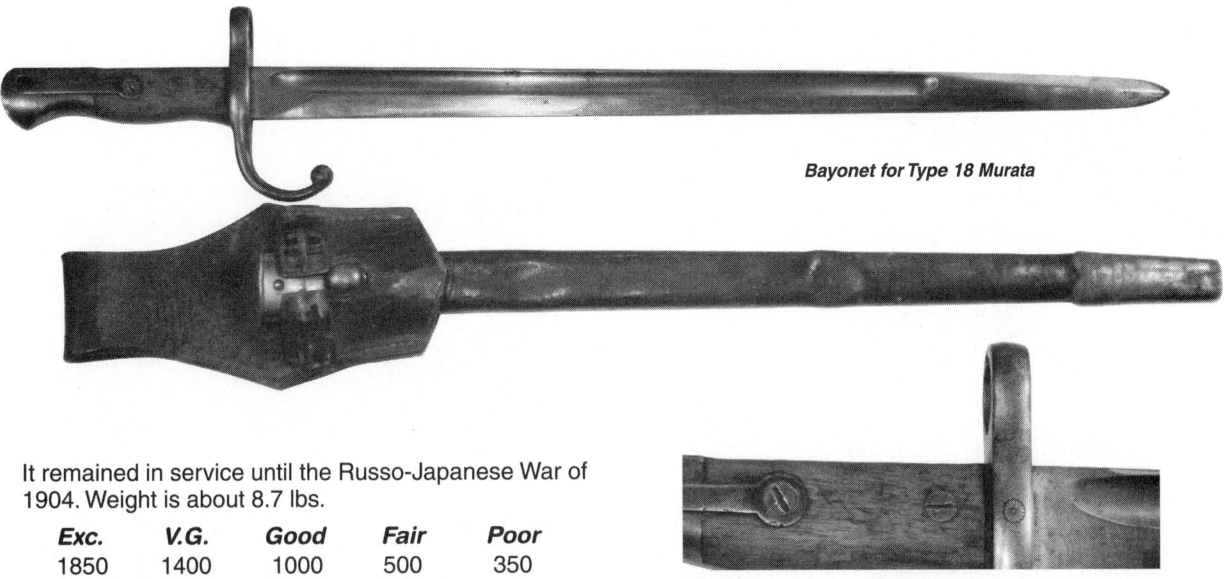

Bayonet for Type 18 Murata

It remained in service until the Russo-Japanese War of 1904. Weight is about 8.7 lbs.

Exc.	*V.G.*	*Good*	*Fair*	*Poor*
1850	1400	1000	500	350

Bayonet for Type 22 Murata

Wood grip. Muzzle ring. Hook quillon. 10.9" single edge blade. Has the Imperial Chrysanthemum mark on the cross piece. There are two versions of this bayonet. The difference is in the length of the handle. Type 1 has a 3" handle and type 2 has a 3.75" handle. Steel scabbard. Rare. Price range 700 – 400.

Murata Type 22 Carbine

Introduced in 1894 and fitted with a 19.5" barrel and 5-round magazine. No bayonet fitting. A rare carbine.

Courtesy Richard M. Kumor Sr.

Exc.	*V.G.*	*Good*	*Fair*	*Poor*
2500	1900	1400	750	500

ARISAKA

This series of Japanese military rifles was developed by Colonel Nariake Arisaka, Superintendent of the Tokyo Arsenal. His task was to find a replacement for the Murata rifles that showed some defects during the Sino-Japanese War of 1894.

A note about the chrysanthemun marking on Arisaka rifles and carbines:

All Arisaka rifles and carbines were manufactured with the Imperial Chrysanthemum, or mum, on the receiver above the Japanese characters indicating the type of rifle. This is the symbol of ownership by the emperor. The only exceptions are rifles made for non-military use or foreign contracts. The mum was usually ground off, or had file marks cut through it, on rifles when they were surrendered at the end of WWII. There are various accounts as to why it was done and who removed them but the end result is

Bayonet for Type 22 Murata

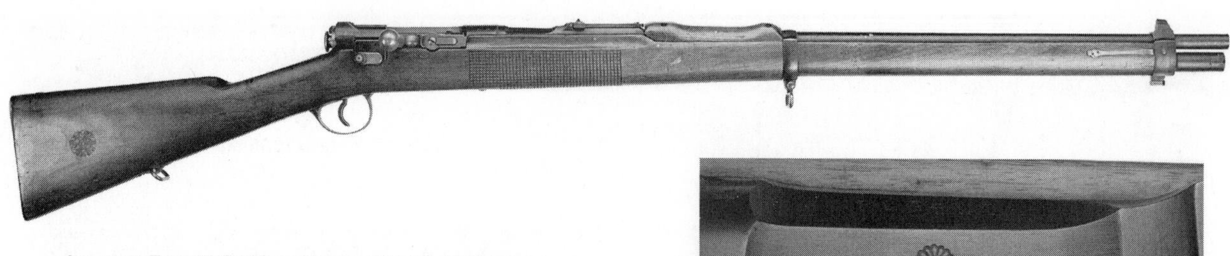

Japanese Type 30 Carbine • Courtesy West Point Museum, Paul Goodwin photo

that many Arisakas seen in the U.S. have the mum removed or damaged. The common belief is that a rifle with an intact mum is a battlefield captured weapon, taken before anyone could destroy the mum. An Arisaka with an intact mum can sell for as much as twice the amount of one with mum removed. The prices given here are for Arisakas with an intact mum. Deduct 25 to 50 percent for rifles without the mum.

Arisaka Type 30 Rifle (aka Hook Safety) (M.1897)

A 6.5x51SRmm Arisaka caliber bolt action rifle with a 31.5" barrel, 5shot magazine and full-length stock secured by two barrel bands and a wooden upper handguard. This was the first box-magazine Mauser-Mannlicher design used by the Japanese military. Straight handle bolt. This was the primary shoulder arm of Japanese troops during the Russo-Japanese War of 1904. Some of these rifles remained in service until WWII. A number of these rifles were sold to Great Britain and Russia during World War I. The Type 30 was also built for Siam (Thailand) and marked by that country's crest on the receiver bridge. It was designed by Nariaki Arisaka. Manufactured from 1897 to 1905. The rifle gets its nickname, "hook-safety," from the prominent hook projecting from the left side of the rear of the bolt.

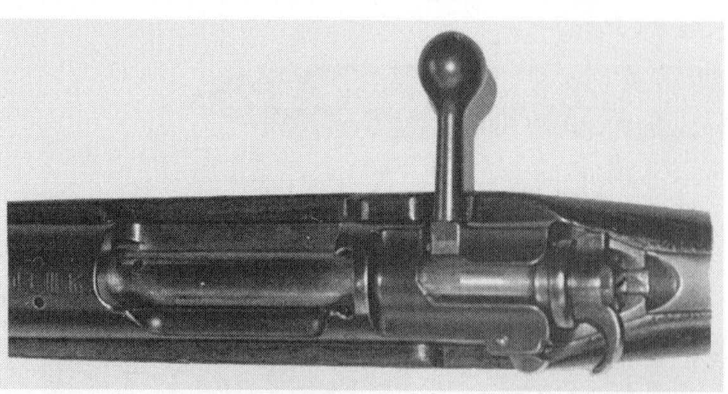

Courtesy Richard M. Kumor Sr.

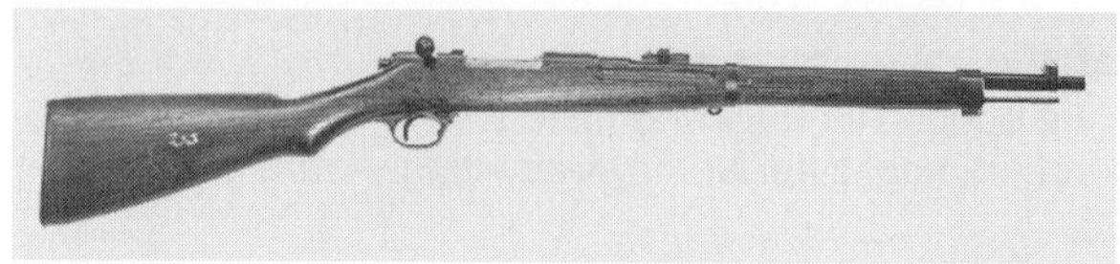

Courtesy Richard M. Kumor Sr.

Exc.	*V.G.*	*Good*	*Fair*	*Poor*
750	600	500	300	200

Arisaka Type 30 Carbine (aka Hook Safety Carbine)

As above, with a 20" barrel and no upper handguard.

Exc.	*V.G.*	*Good*	*Fair*	*Poor*
750	600	500	300	200

Arisaka Type 35 Navy (M.1902)

Adopted by the Japanese navy in 1902, this was an improved version of the Type 30 rifle. Some main differences are that the hook safety was reduced in length and checkered. The receiver included a spring-latched bolt cover. Used during the Russo-Japanese War of 1904. About 40,000 were built. Many of these were sold to Great Britain and Russia during World War I. All dimensions are the same as the Type 30 rifle.

Exc.	*V.G.*	*Good*	*Fair*	*Poor*
600	450	350	250	150

Arisaka Type 38 Rifle (M.1905)

A 6.5mm Arisaka caliber bolt action rifle with a 31.5" barrel, 5shot magazine and large bolt handle. Full-length stock secured by two barrel bands with finger grooves. Weight is about 9 lbs. It was based on the Model 1893 Spanish Mauser. This rifle saw extensive use as late as World War II. Manufactured from 1905 to 1945. Most production switched to the Type 99 in 7.7mm beginning in 1939. This model was built at the Koishikowa, Kokura, Nagoya, and Mukden arsenals. This model was the first issued with a simple sheet steel dust cover that slides

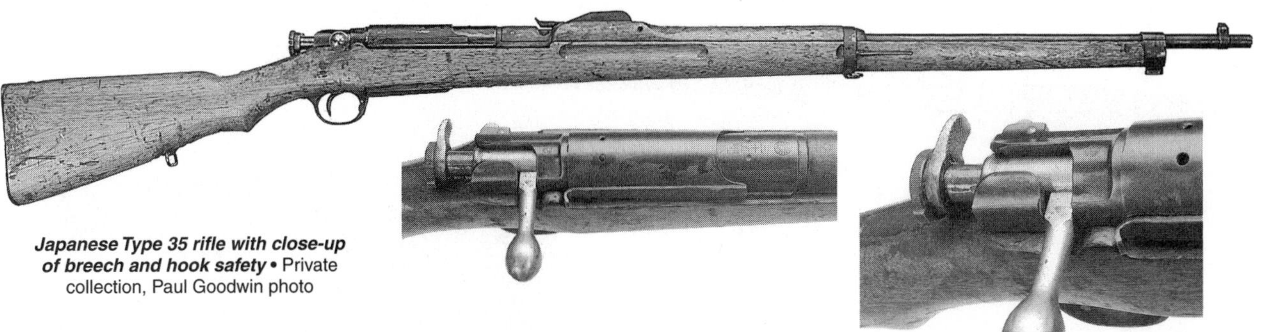

Japanese Type 35 rifle with close-up of breech and hook safety • Private collection, Paul Goodwin photo

COLLECTOR SPOTLIGHT

Markings on Arisaka Rifles and Carbines

The Japanese Arisaka Type 38, 44 and 99 rifles have a following of dedicated collectors. Many will pay prices much higher than those listed in this book for original, matching specimens. There are many factors that determine the desirability of a particular rifle. There is not room in this book to go into the fine detail needed to determine whether a given rifle will be one of the high-price examples. Some of the things that a collector will look for include intact mum, arsenal of manufacture, series and matching numbers. An intact mum is explained at the beginning of this section.

I will attempt to briefly describe what to look when collecting Arisakas. Japanese rifles are a hard field to explain to those not familiar with the following minor differences.

On the left side of the receiver are the serial number and an *arsenal mark*. A list of arsenal marks is shown in this section. Some arsenals made more rifles than others. A *series mark* is a Japanese character in a circle next to the arsenal mark. Early production Arisakas did not use a series mark.

The practice of using series marks started in the 1930s. There were over 30 series marks used. There is not enough room to show them here. There would be SN: 1 to 10,000 of a series made then a new mark was used. Each arsenal used its own block of series marks.

Here are arsenal markings for Japan's Arisaka rifles. No. 1 was used for Tokyo's Koishikawa Arsenal (1870-1935) and the Kokura Arsenal (1935-45). The other arsenal locations and dates are: 2) Nagoya Arsenal, 3) Jinsen Arsenal (Korea) and 4) Mukden Arsenal (Manchuria). Paired markings indicate the supervising arsenal (Kokura or Nagoya) and a second symbol representing the manufacturing company: 5) Tokyo Kogyo, 6) and 7) Tokyo Juki Kogyo, 8) Howa Jyuko and 9) Izawa Jyuko.

Numbering Practices

Early production rifles used a three-digit *assembly number* that is located on the underside of the receiver. Parts were matched to the assembly number, not the serial number. Several other parts can be numbered internally as well. The gun must be dis-assembled to see them. Most sellers will not allow this to be done. If the bolt parts, floor plate and bayonet lug match, it is a somewhat safe bet that the assembly number is the same and the rifle can be called matching. Occasionally, some parts will match the serial number visible on the left side of receiver with others matching the hidden assembly number. Confusing, huh? If there are more than two numbers present (serial and assembly), it can be assumed that the rifle is mismatched. In later production, all parts are matched to the serial number. All but the earliest Type 99s are numbered to match the serial number. Type 99s do not have a numbered floor plate.

There is no set percentage of price to deduct if an Arisaka is mismatched. Few mismatched guns will bring the Excellent or Very Good price, regardless of condition.

So why did I add this information? Just to inform sellers and buyers how to tell if their Arisaka might be in the high-dollar category and therefore justify further research. I suggest using the Honeycutt book and consultation with knowledgeable collectors. Good luck!

Phillip Peterson

Arisaka Type 38 Rifle • Courtesy West Point Museum, Paul Goodwin photo

in grooves in the receiver. The bolt handle sticks through an opening in the cover and the cover moves with the bolt when operated. The dust cover is frequently missing, as it is easy to re-insert the bolt in the action without it. Some of these rifles were made in 7mm Mauser. They were made for Mexico and have the Mexican crest of the receiver. *See: Mexico* for a listing of this variation.

Exc.	V.G.	Good	Fair	Poor
475	350	250	175	125

Arisaka Type 38 Carbine

As above, with a 19" barrel and upper handguard. Equipped for a bayonet. Weight is about 7.25 lbs.

Courtesy Richard M. Kumor Sr.

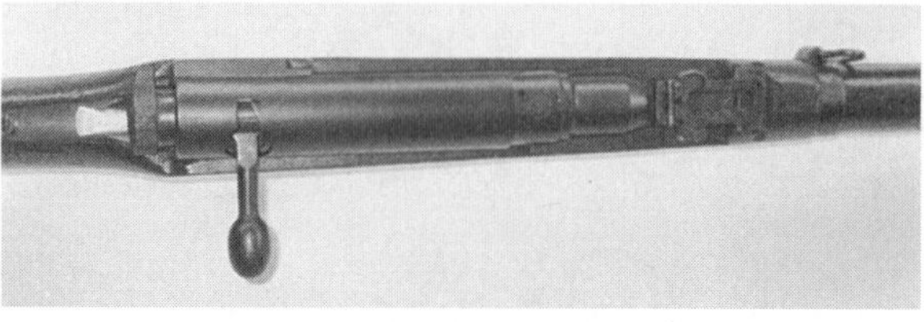

Courtesy Richard M. Kumor Sr.

Exc.	V.G.	Good	Fair	Poor
500	375	300	175	125

Thai Type 38 Conversions

Short Rifle .30-06

Exc.	V.G.	Good	Fair	Poor
600	475	350	250	150

Half-Stock Carbine 6.5mm

Exc.	V.G.	Good	Fair	Poor
550	425	300	200	100

Manchurian Mauser Rifle (Mukden Arsenal)

This rifle has many features from both the Mauser 98 and the Arisaka. Barrel length is 29" and most rifles are chambered for the 7.92x57mm cartridge while some are chambered for the Japanese 6.5mm cartridge. Magazine capacity is 5 rounds. Bolt handle is pear shaped. Marked on top of receiver ring with Mukden arsenal symbol.

Exc.	V.G.	Good	Fair	Poor
700	550	400	250	100

Arisaka Type 44 Carbine

Similar to the Type 38 carbine but with an 18.5" barrel

and folding bayonet that hinged into the forearm. Weight was about 9 lbs.

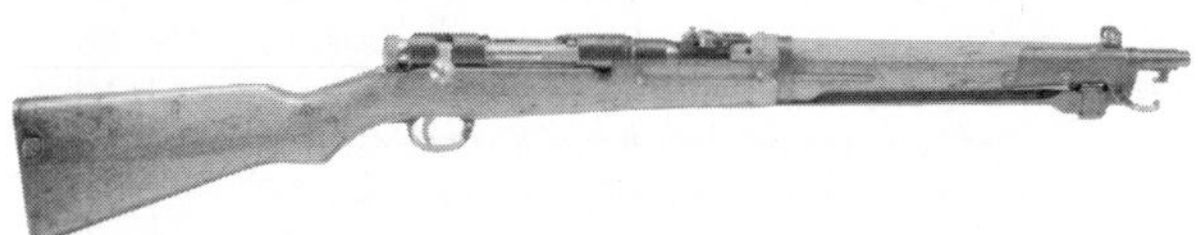

Type 44 Carbine • Courtesy Rock Island Auction Company

Exc.	V.G.	Good	Fair	Poor
800	650	450	300	200

NOTE: Price assumes an intact mum and correctly matching numbers. See the "Collector Spotlight" on Arisaka rifles for numbering practices. Deduct 25-50 percent for ground mum or mismatch.

Arisaka Type 97 "Sniper's Rifle"

The Type 38 with a side-mounted 2.5-power telescope and a bipod. Introduced in 1937. The telescope mounted on each rifle was factory fitted and stamped with the serial number of the rifle. The rear sight was a peep with folding from 400 to 2,200 meters. Weight is approximately 11 lbs. with scope. Deduct 50 percent for a sniper rifle missing the scope.

Exc.	V.G.	Good	Fair	Poor
4000	2500	1200	600	300

Arisaka Type 99 Short Rifle

This model is an improved version of the Type 38 rifle. A 7.7mm caliber bolt action rifle with a 26" barrel and full-length stock secured by two barrel bands. Non-detachable magazine capacity is 5 rounds. Fitted with a folding wire monopod. Weight is about 8.5 lbs. Adopted for military use in 1939. The rear sight on this rifle was a graduated leaf-type with folding arms to help aiming at aircraft. Parts such as floor plate, butt plate, bolt cover, and swivel bands were made from metal stampings. The monopod and anti-aircraft sight were phased out as the war progressed. The first use of this model in combat against U.S. forces was during the Battle of Guadalcanal beginning in August, 1942.

Exc.	V.G.	Good	Fair	Poor
500	375	300	125	75

NOTE: Price assumes an intact mum and correctly matching numbers. See the "Collector Spotlight" on Arisaka rifles for numbering practices. Deduct 25-

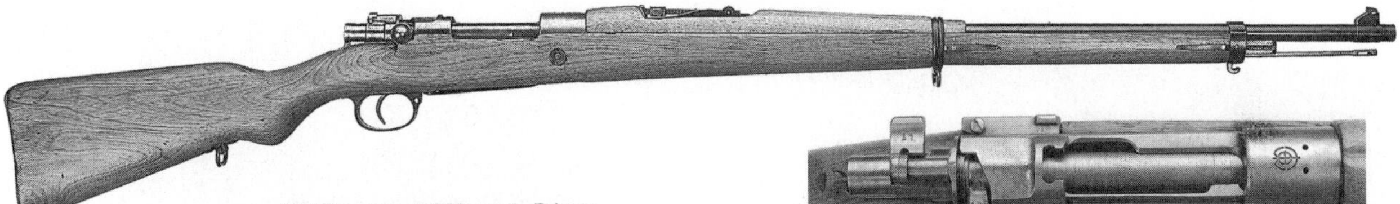

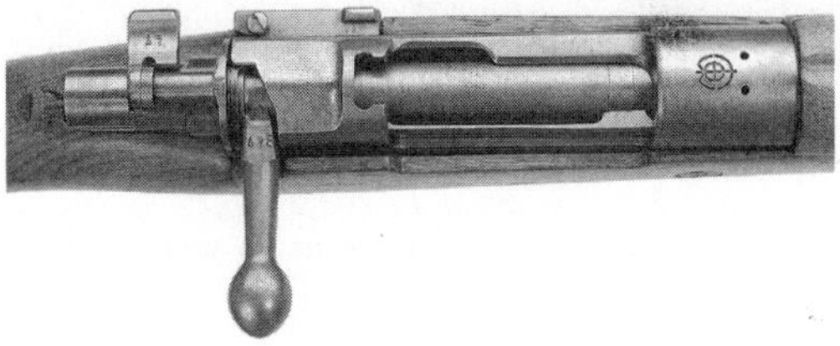

Mukden Arsenal Mauser • Private collection, Paul Goodwin photo

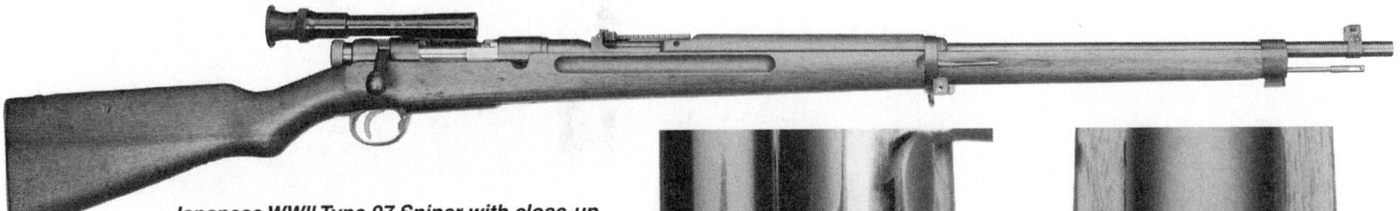

Japanese WWII Type 97 Sniper with close-up of scope and markings. All numbers match. Notice full "Mum" • Courtesy Michael Wamsher, Paul Goodwin photo

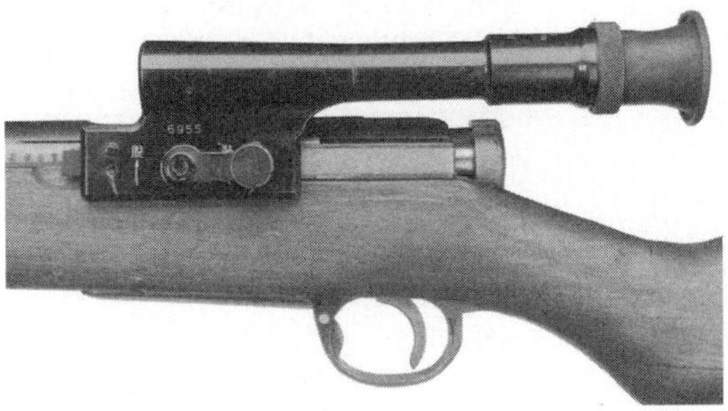

JAPAN

50 percent for ground mum or mismatch. Add 15 percent for monopod.

Arisaka Type 99 Long Rifle

This variation is the same as the above model but fitted with a 31.4" barrel. Weight is about 9 lbs. This is a scarce variation.

Exc.	*V.G.*	*Good*	*Fair*	*Poor*
750	550	450	175	125

NOTE: Price assumes an intact mum and correctly matching numbers. See the "Collector Spotlight" on Arisaka rifles for numbering practices. Deduct 25-50 percent for ground mum or mismatch. Add 30 percent for monopod and dust cover.

Type 30 Bayonet

This bayonet was made for use on all Arisaka rifles and carbines except for the Type 44. It also was used on the Type 96 and 99 light machine guns. The only WWII case where a machine gun could mount a bayonet. Wood grips. Muzzle ring. Some have a hook quillon, others do not. 15.75" single edge blade. Some have a blued blade, others will be polished white. Made by four arsenals: Kokura, Nagoya, Mukden and Jinsen. Also several contractors working under supervision of Kokura or Nagoya. The quality of finish and manufacturing declined as WWII progressed. Late war examples do not have a fuller in the blade and were issued with a wooden scabbard. Price range 175 – 40.

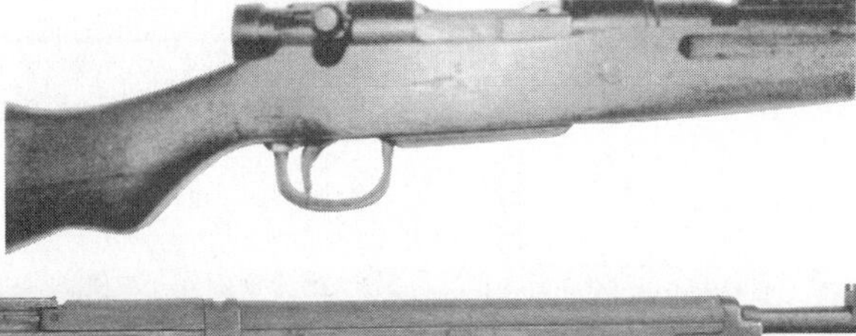

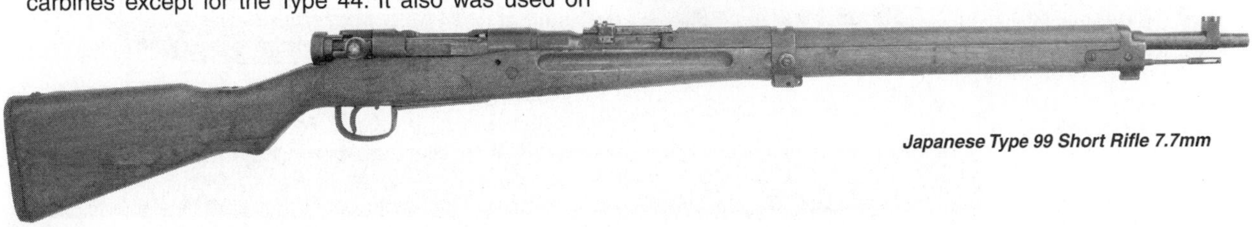

Japanese Type 99 Short Rifle 7.7mm

Courtesy Rock Island Auction Company

Arisaka Flag Pole

This interesting item is included here because it attaches to the bayonet lug of the Arisaka rifles. The owner of the pictured item knows of only a handful in U.S. collections. Price estimation of 2000 – 1000.

Pole Bayonet

Wood handle. No pommel or rifle mounting fixtures.15.2" single edge blade. Late war wood scabbard. Example shown has a Jinsen arsenal marking. This is not actually a bayonet but is made with a bayonet blade, so it is included here. It was a last-ditch weapon intended to mount on a wood or metal pole. The idea was to

JAPAN

Type 30 Bayonets

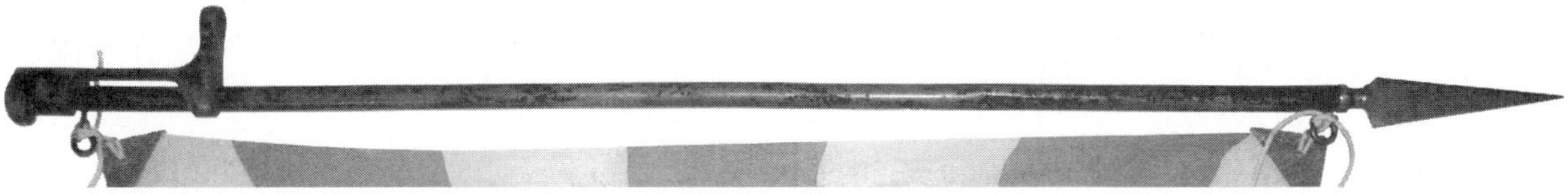

Arisaka Flag Pole, image courtesy Larry Brown collection

Flag Pole Bayonet, image courtesy Larry Brown collection

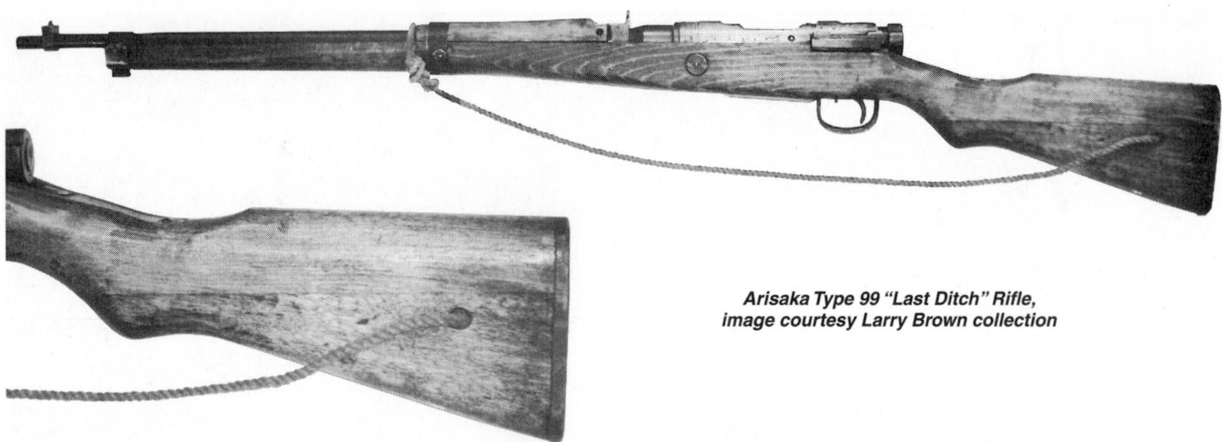

Arisaka Type 99 "Last Ditch" Rifle, image courtesy Larry Brown collection

JAPAN

stab an enemy soldier and take his rifle. Price range 600 – 250.

Arisaka Type 99 "Last Ditch" Rifle

This is a Type 99 simplified for easier production. Typical features include a cylindrical bolt knob, a fixed peep sight, no front sight guards and a wooden buttplate. Not all rifles have each of these features. Some last ditch rifles have a hole in the stock instead of a sling swivel. The hole is for using a piece of rope as a sling. Add 25 percent for a rope sling rifle.

Exc.	V.G.	Good	Fair	Poor
350	250	150	125	100

NOTE: Price assumes an intact mum and correctly matching numbers. See the "Collector Spotlight" on Arisaka rifles for numbering practices. Deduct 25-50 percent for ground mum or mismatch.

Test Type 1 Paratroop Rifle

Bolt action rifle chambered for 6.5mm Japanese. Barrel length is 19". Cleaning rod is 17 3/16" long. The stock is a two-piece buttstock with full-length handguard and a hinge attached at the wrist. Metal finish is blued. Total number produced is approximately 200-300 rifles.

Exc.	V.G.	Good	Fair	Poor
3000	2500	2000	1200	500

Type 100 Paratroop Rifle

Chambered for 7.7mm Japanese cartridge. Barrel length is 25-1/4" long. Blued cleaning rod 21-5/16" long. Rear sight is adjustable from 300 to 1500 meters. Two-piece buttstock with full handguard can be disassembled with an interrupted-thread connector. Bolt handle is detachable. Metal finish is blued. Total number produced is estimated at 500 rifles.

Exc.	V.G.	Good	Fair	Poor
4500	4000	3000	—	—

Type 2 Paratroop Rifle

Similar to the model above but with a different style of takedown. This model uses a wedge and bail wire connector. This rifle production began in late 1943.

Exc.	V.G.	Good	Fair	Poor
2500	1850	1200	500	200

Type 99 "Sniper's Rifle"

The standard Type 99 with a 25.5" barrel and either a 2-1/2 power or 4-power telescope. Deduct 50 percent for a sniper rifle missing the scope.

Exc.	V.G.	Good	Fair	Poor
3000	2500	1800	1200	750

NOTE: The 4x scope is more rare than the 2-1/2 power scope. For 4x scope add $500.

Type 5 Semi-automatic Rifle

A 7.7mm semi-automatic rifle with a 10-round box magazine patterned after the U.S. M1. Made at the Kure

Courtesy Richard M. Kumor Sr.

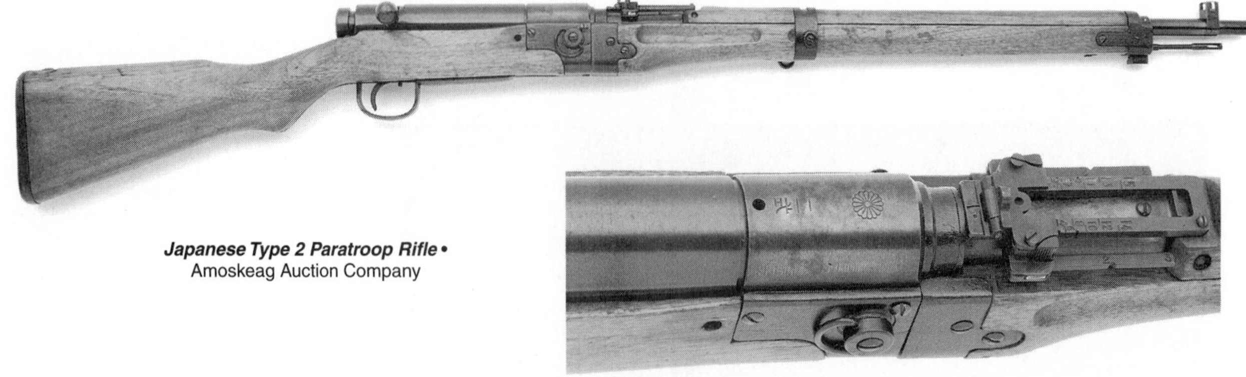

Japanese Type 2 Paratroop Rifle • Amoskeag Auction Company

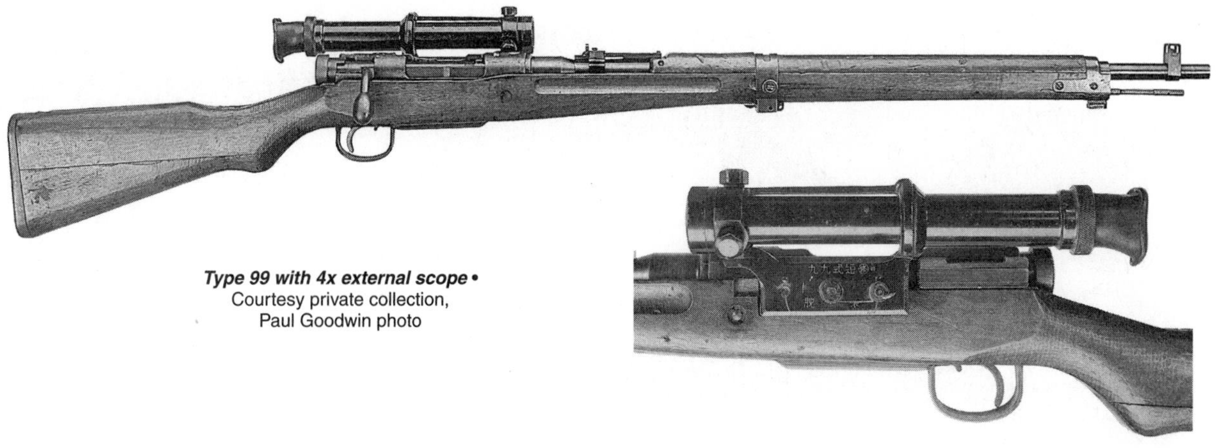

Type 99 with 4x external scope • Courtesy private collection, Paul Goodwin photo

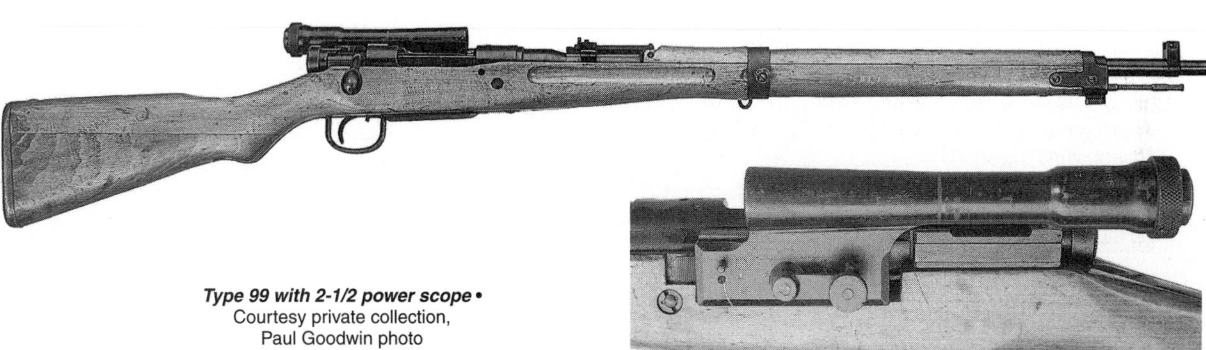

Type 99 with 2-1/2 power scope • Courtesy private collection, Paul Goodwin photo

JAPAN

Naval Arsenal in 1945. It is believed that approximately 20 were made. Prospective purchasers should secure a qualified appraisal.

Action of a Type I Rifle, made in Italy

Exc.	*V.G.*	*Good*	*Fair*	*Poor*
22000	19000	14000	—	—

CARCANO

Type I

Made in Italy, this is a Carcano action coupled with an Arisaka magazine system. Appears similar to the Type 38 rifle. Made under contract in the 1930's. Type I's have no receiver markings except for the serial number.

Exc.	*V.G.*	*Good*	*Fair*	*Poor*
350	275	200	150	100

MAUSER

G 71 Rifle

This is the same rifle as built for the German Empire. Chambered for the 11x60mm cartridge and fitted with a 33.5" barrel. Full stocked. Single shot. Weight is about 10 lbs.

Exc.	*V.G.*	*Good*	*Fair*	*Poor*
750	575	450	300	150

Japanese Training Rifle

Made for training of military recruits and school students. A "non-gun" copy of the Arisaka Type 38 or Type 99 Long Rifle. Not safe to fire. Many were brought home as war souvenirs. These are frequently confused with real rifles by the u-informed. The trainers have no mum, model or arsenal markings. They have a serial number on the receiver and bolt. Some have a maker's logo.

Exc.	*V.G.*	*Good*	*Fair*	*Poor*
175	150	100	50	25

MACHINE GUNS

The Japanese used the Hotchkiss gun during the Russo-Japanese War and later adopted the Model 1914 Hotchkiss. Both of these guns were chambered for the 6.5mm cartridge.

Japanese Type 1

Introduced in 1941 as an improvement over the Type 92. Barrel length is 23" with cooling fins the same diameter through its length. The muzzle is fitted with a flash hider. Fed by a 30-round metal strip and

Japanese Type 11 • Courtesy private NFA collection, Paul Goodwin photo

JAPAN

chambered for the 7.7mm cartridge. Rate of fire is approximately 550 rounds per minute. Weight is about 77 lbs. with tripod.

NOTE: Many of these guns were not stamped "Type 1" but instead "Type 92." The finned barrel is the key feature.

Pre-1968

Exc.	*V.G.*	*Fair*
14000	12500	11000

Japanese Type 3

Medium air-cooled gun chambered for 6.5x51SR Arisaka cartridge and introduced in 1914. The Hotchkiss Model 1897 influenced the design of this gun. Cooling fins on the barrel. Spade grips and tripod mount with sockets for carrying poles. Weight was about 63 lbs. Barrel length was 29.5". Fed from a metal 30-round strip. Rate of fire was about 400 rounds per minute. Introduced in 1914.

Pre-1968

Exc.	*V.G.*	*Fair*
12000	10000	9000

Japanese Type 11

First produced in 1922, this is a light air-cooled machine gun chambered for the 6.5x51SR Arisaka cartridge. The gun utilizes a 30-round hopper feed system. The 19" barrel is finned. Weight is about 22.5 lbs. Rate of fire is 500 rounds per minute. Fitted with a bipod. This was the most widely used machine gun by the Japanese military during combat in China between 1937 and 1939.

Japanese Type 89 Vickers Aircraft • Courtesy Blake Stevens

Pre-1968

Exc.	*V.G.*	*Fair*
9500	8000	7000

Japanese Type 89

This gun was produced in 1929 and is a copy of the British Vickers aircraft gun but chambered for the 7.7x56R (.303 British) cartridge. Weight is about 27 lbs.

Pre-1968

Exc.	*V.G.*	*Fair*
16500	15000	13000

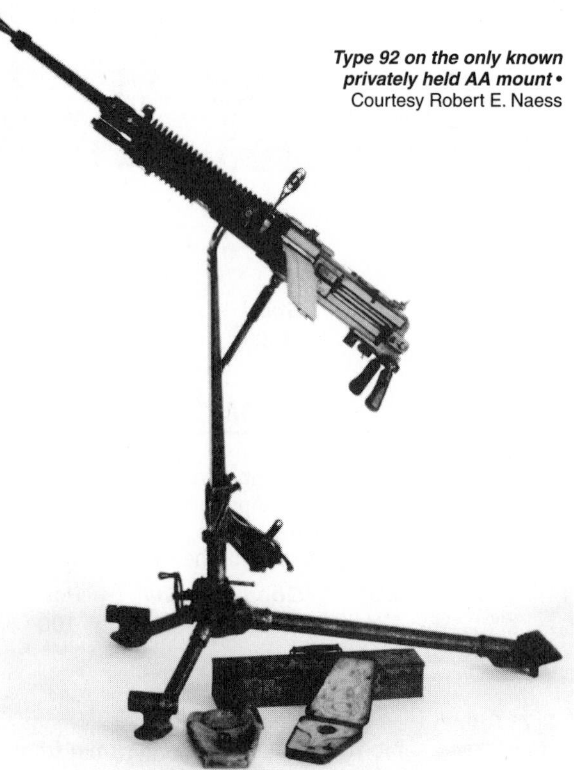

Type 92 on the only known privately held AA mount • Courtesy Robert E. Naess

Japanese Type 92

This is an improved version of the Type 3 gun introduced in 1932. Chambered for the 7.7x58SR cartridge. It was fitted with dropped grips behind and below the receiver instead of spade grips. Barrel length is 28". Fed by a metal 30-round strip. Rate of fire was about 450 rounds per minute. Weight is about 100 lbs. with tripod. Gun alone weighs approximately 60 lbs. The mount was designed so that two men could carry it by means of poles or pipes fitted into the legs of the mount. This was the most widely used Japanese machine gun of WWII.

NOTE: The Type 92 designation was also applied to the Japanese copy of the Lewis gun. See *Great Britain, Machine Guns, Lewis 0.303in, Mark 1*.

Pre-1968

Exc.	*V.G.*	*Fair*
15000	12500	10000

Pre-1986 manufacture with new receiver or reweld

Exc.	*V.G.*	*Fair*
11000	10000	9000

Japanese Type 92 Lewis

This is a licensed copy of the British Lewis gun. Caliber is .303. Built in both ground and aircraft configurations. There are some minor technical differences between the two. Spade grips. The Japanese tripod for this gun is unique to the gun.

NOTE: Prices listed below are for the gun with original Japanese tripod. Deduct $2,500 for no tripod or incorrect tripod.

Type 92 • Private NFA collection, Gary Gelson photo

Pre-1968

Exc.	*V.G.*	*Fair*
11000	10000	9000

Japanese Type 96

Designed by General Kijiro Nambu and introduced in 1936, this light, air-cooled machine gun is chambered for the 6.5mm cartridge. It was considered an improvement over the Model 11. This model has a top-mounted box magazine with a 30-round capacity. The cartridges are oiled when loaded into the magazine by an oiler built into the magazine loader. Barrel length is a finned 22" quick-change affair with carrying handle. The wood buttstock has a pistol grip. Rate of fire is

Japanese Model 96 with plaque that reads, "Presented to U.S.M.A. by two former superintendents: General Douglas MacArthur and Lt. Gen. Robert L. Eichelberger captured at Buna, New Guinea, Dec. 27, 1942" • Courtesy West Point Museum, Paul Goodwin photo

Japanese Type 97 Tank • Courtesy private NFA collection, Paul Goodwin photo

JAPAN

Type 99 • Courtesy private NFA collection, Paul Goodwin photo

Japanese Machine Gun Trainer •
Paul Goodwin photo

about 550 rounds per minute. Weight is approximately 20 lbs. These guns are sometimes seen with a 2.5 power scope fitted on the receiver. This was the standard light machine gun of the Japanese military from 1936 to 1939.

NOTE: Magazines are scarce.

Pre-1968

Exc.	*V.G.*	*Fair*
9500	7000	4500

Japanese Type 97

This model was designed in 1937 to be fired from a tank or aircraft. It was to replace the Type 92 gun and is chambered for the 7.7mm cartridge. Its barrel length is 28" and the barrel is finned for cooling. Design is similar to the Czech VZ26. This was the first Japanese machine gun that did not require oiled ammunition. Weight is about 24 lbs. Rate of fire is approximately 500 rounds per minute. Fed by a 30-round box magazine.

Pre-1968

Exc.	*V.G.*	*Fair*
9000	7000	5000

Japanese Type 98

This is a copy of the German MG 15 ground gun. First used in 1938. Fed by a 75-round saddle drum with a rate of fire of 900 rounds per minute.

Pre-1968

Exc.	*V.G.*	*Fair*
9500	7000	5000

Japanese Type 99

Chambered for the 7.7x58mm Arisaka cartridge, this machine gun was first produced for the Japanese army in 1939, and is an improved version of the Type 96. Although first produced in 1939 it was not issued until 1942 and first used in combat in 1943. It is fitted with a 21.3" quick change barrel and a 30-round top feed magazine. Its rate of fire is 850 rounds per minute. It weighs about 23 lbs. The gun is marked on the right front side of the receiver with date of manufacture and maker's symbols. The gun has a bipod under the barrel and a monopod under the toe of the buttstock. Production ceased with the end of WWII.

Pre-1968

Exc.	*V.G.*	*Fair*
12000	9000	5000

Japanese Machine Gun Trainer

These guns were built in small machine shops all over Japan in the 1930s and 1940s so that young school-age males could be taught the basic techniques and operations of machine guns. Blowback operation. This gun does in fact fire a reduced load of either 6.5mm or 7.7mm cartridges, as well as blanks and is registered as a machine gun under the NFA. These guns, as a group, are different enough so that no two will be exactly the same. Caution: Do not fire this gun. It is unsafe.

Pre-1968

Exc.	*V.G.*	*Fair*
5000	4000	2500

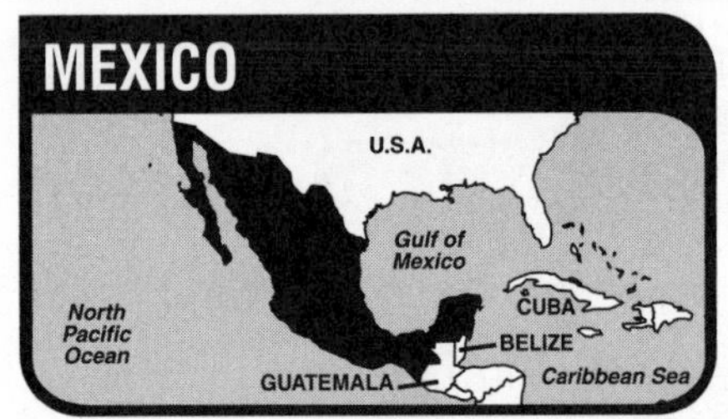

The United States of Mexico, located immediately south of the United States has an area of 759,529 sq. mi. (1,967,183 sq. km.) and an estimated population of 100 million. Capital: Mexico City. The economy is based on agriculture, manufacturing and mining. Oil, cotton, silver, coffee, and shrimp are exported.

Mexico was the site of highly advanced Indian civilizations 1,500 years before conquistador Hernando Cortes conquered the wealthy Aztec empire of Montezuma, 1519-21, and founded a Spanish colony, which lasted for nearly 300 years. During the Spanish period, Mexico, then called New Spain, stretched from Guatemala to the present states of Wyoming and California, its present northern boundary having been established by the secession of Texas during 1836 and the war of 1846-48 with the United States.

Independence from Spain was declared by Father Miguel Hidalgo on Sept. 16, 1810, (Mexican Independence Day) and was achieved by General Agustin de Iturbide in1821. Iturbide became emperor in 1822 but was deposed when a republic was established a year later. For more than fifty years following the birth of the republic, the political scene of Mexico was characterized by turmoil, which saw two emperors (including the unfortunate Maximilian), several dictators and an average of one new government every nine months passing swiftly from obscurity to oblivion. The land, social, economic and labor reforms promulgated by the Reform Constitution of Feb. 5, 1917 established the basis for sustained economic development and participative democracy that have made Mexico one of the most politically stable countries of modern Latin America.

HANDGUNS

NOTE: Other than the Obregon, the Mexican military has relied on foreign purchases of its military handguns. The principal sidearm is the Colt Model 1911 in .45 ACP, purchased from the U.S. government. Mexico has also purchased pistols from Heckler & Koch, the P7M13, and numerous Smith & Wesson revolvers and pistols for its police forces.

OBREGON

Pistola Automatica Sistema Obregon

This is a .45 caliber semi-automatic pistol with a 5-inch barrel. Similar to the Colt M1911A1 but with a combination slide and safety latch on the left side of the frame. The breech is locked by rotating the barrel, instead of the Browning swinging link. This unusual locking system results in a tubular front end appearance to the pistol. Originally designed for the Mexican military, it was not adopted as such and only about 1,000 pistols were produced and sold commercially, mostly to Mexican military officers. The pistol is 8.5 inches long overall and weighs about 40 ozs. The magazine holds seven cartridges. This is a rare pistol.

Exc.	*V.G.*	*Good*	*Fair*	*Poor*
4500	2750	1250	750	400

Colt Model 1911A1

This is the standard service pistol of the Mexican military in .45 ACP.

SUBMACHINE GUNS

NOTE: The Mexican military availed itself of the Thompson submachine gun in various models, from the Model 1921 to the Model M1A1. The Mexican government has also purchased directly from the U.S. government a number of M3A1 .45 ACP submachine guns. From Germany the Mexican government purchased the HK MP5 and the HK 53. The MP5 is currently made in Mexico under license from HK.

Mendoza (HM-3)

Developed by Rafael Mendoza in the 1950s, this submachine gun is produced by Productos Mendoza S.A. in Mexico City. This is a relatively small select-fire gun chambered for the .45 ACP, .38 Super, or 9mm cartridges. Barrel length is 10 inches, although some examples are found with 16 inches barrels in full automatic fire only. The box magazine capacity is 20 rounds. Rate of fire is about 550 rounds per minute. Weight is about 5 lbs. Stock is tubular steel. An unknown number of these guns are used by the Mexican army.

RIFLES

NOTE: Mexico used a number of different models of the Mauser bolt action rifle. Most Mexican military rifles found in the U.S. are in well used condition. They frequently will rate only good, fair or poor condition. An excellent condition example will bring a premium price. Since the end of WWII, the Mexican military has purchased a number of foreign rifles for military use. These consist of U.S. M1 and M2 carbines, Colt M16A1 rifles in the 1970s, FN-FAL rifles, some of which were assembled in Mexico beginning in 1968 with FN supplied parts. In 1979 Mexico began to produce, under license from HK, the G3 rifle (G3A3 and G3A4).

MEXICAN PRE-CARTRIDGE ERA RIFLES

Mexico used a variety of foreign made percussion rifles. Guns from Spain, Belgium, England and the U.S. might be encountered. Most will be in well used condition.

PEABODY

Spanish Rifle (1869)

Chambered for the .43 Spanish centerfire cartridge and fitted with a 33-inch barrel. Full stock with two barrel bands. Blued barrel and case hardened furniture. About 8,500 rifles were produced for the Mexican government.

Exc.	V.G.	Good	Fair	Poor
750	600	450	300	200

WHITNEY

Model 1873 Rifle

This is a rolling block design similar to the Remington. It does not use the hammer to lock the block. Fitted with a 35-inch barrel and full stock with three barrel bands. Chambered for the 11.15x58T Spanish Remington cartridge. Weight is about 9.5 lbs. On the right side of the receiver is the Mexican crest. Upper tang is marked with "Whitney Arms."

Exc.	V.G.	Good	Fair	Poor
1800	1250	1000	600	350

Model 1873 Carbine

Similar to the rifle but with 20.5-inch barrel and two-piece stock. Fitted with cavalry bar sling and ring on stock. Weight is about 7.25 lbs.

Exc.	V.G.	Good	Fair	Poor
1800	1250	1000	600	350

REMINGTON ROLLING BLOCK

Model 1897 Rifle

Chambered for the 7x57mm Spanish Mauser cartridge. Full stocked with two barrel bands. Barrel length is 30 inches. Weight is about 8.5 lbs. Marked Remington on upper tang. Some have the Mexican crest; many do not. Crested rifles will bring up to 25% more. Rear sight is ladder-type marked to 2,300 yards.

Exc.	V.G.	Good	Fair	Poor
700	575	450	350	250

MAUSER

M1895 Rifle

This was the standard rifle for the Mexican army under the Diaz regime. It is similar to the Spanish Model 1893. Fitted with an almost full stock with straight grip with no finger grooves. Barrel length is 29 inches and chambered for the 7x57mm cartridge. Rear leaf sight graduated to 2,000 meters. Bayonet lug. Magazine capacity is 5 rounds. Weight is about 8.5 lbs. Produced by both DWM and the Spanish firm Oviedo. Price assumes matching numbers. Deduct 25-50% for mismatch.

Exc.	V.G.	Good	Fair	Poor
700	500	300	150	100

M1895 Carbine

Similar to the Model 1895 rifle except with 17.25-inch barrel, bent bolt handle, and side-mounted sling. No bayonet fittings. Weight is about 7.5 lbs. Some but not all are marked with Mexican crest on receiver ring. Price assumes matching numbers. Deduct 25-50% for mismatch.

Exc.	V.G.	Good	Fair	Poor
700	500	300	150	100

M1902 Rifle

This model has an improved Model 98 action. Nearly full-length stock with half-length upper handguard. This model was built by DWM and Steyr. Barrel length is 29 inches. Caliber is 7x57mm. Straight bolt handle. Rear sight graduated to 2,000 meters. Mexican crest on receiver ring. Weight is about 8.75 lbs. Price assumes matching numbers. Deduct 25-50% for mismatch.

Exc.	V.G.	Good	Fair	Poor
750	500	300	175	125

M1907 Steyr Rifle

This rifle was fitted with an almost full-length stock with pistol grip. Upper barrel band has a stacking hook. Bayonet lug accepts Model 98 bayonet. Barrel length is 29 inches. Caliber is 7x57mm. Straight bolt. Weight is about 8.75 lbs. Marked, "STEYR.MODEL 1907/[date]" on receiver ring. Price assumes matching numbers. Deduct 25-50% for mismatch.

Exc.	V.G.	Good	Fair	Poor
750	500	300	175	125

M1910 Rifle

This was the first Mauser produced by Mexico at the Fabrica Nacional de Cartuchos and the Fabrica Nacional de Armas in Mexico City. Similar to the Model 1902 rifle. Straight grip stock. Bayonet stud for Model 1895 bayonet. Barrel length is 29 inches and caliber is 7x57mm. Marked on top of receiver ring. Price assumes matching numbers. Deduct 25-50% for mismatch.

Exc.	V.G.	Good	Fair	Poor
600	375	300	200	150

M1910 Carbine

Very similar to the Model 1895 carbine with the addition of the Model 98 action and barley corn front sights. Mexican crest on receiver ring. Weight is about 8 lbs. Barrel length is 17.5 inches and caliber is 7x57mm. Price assumes matching numbers. Deduct 25-50% for mismatch.

Exc.	V.G.	Good	Fair	Poor
650	400	300	200	150

M1912 Steyr Rifle

Mexico bought these rifles directly from Steyr. This model is fitted with a 29-inch barrel and large receiver ring with straight bolt. Nearly full-length stock with pistol grip. Chambered for the 7x57mm cartridge. Receiver ring marked "MODEL 1912" over "STEYR" over the date. Weight is about 8.75 lbs. Price assumes matching numbers. Deduct 25-50% for mismatch.

Exc.	V.G.	Good	Fair	Poor
650	475	350	250	150

M1912 Steyr Short Rifle

This short rifle is the same as the Model 1912 rifle except for turned down bolt handle and barrel length.

Exc.	V.G.	Good	Fair	Poor
650	475	350	250	150

FN M24 Short Rifle

Approximately 25,000 of these rifles were bought from FN by Mexico in 1926 and 1927. This then is the standard FN Model 1924 version with pistol grip stock without finger grooves. Barrel length is 23.5 inches and caliber is 7x57mm. Weight is about 8.5 lbs. Price assumes matching numbers. Deduct 25-50% for mismatch.

Exc.	V.G.	Good	Fair	Poor
700	500	375	250	150

MEXICO

FN M24 Carbine

Same as above but with 16-inch barrel and no bayonet fittings. The barrel length was the shortest ever used on a Mauser rifle. Weight is about 7.5 lbs. Price assumes matching numbers. Deduct 25-50% for mismatch.

Exc.	V.G.	Good	Fair	Poor
850	600	400	250	150

VZ12/33 Carbine

This is the Czech export Model 12/33 carbine. Pistol grip stock. Barrel length is 22 inches and caliber is 7x57mm. Weight is about 8.5 lbs. Marked with Mexican crest on receiver ring. Price assumes matching numbers. Deduct 25-50% for mismatch.

Exc.	V.G.	Good	Fair	Poor
750	575	350	200	150

ARISAKA

Model 1913

Identical to the Japanese service rifle of the same model but chambered for the 7x57mm cartridge. The rear sight has been modified for this cartridge. The nose cap has been modified to accept the standard Mexican bayonet. The Mexican eagle and "REPUBLICA MEXICANA" are marked on the barrel near the breech. About 40,000 rifles were ordered but only 5,000 delivered in 1913. The rest were sold to Russia during WWI. Manufactured in Japan in Koishikawa.

Exc.	V.G.	Good	Fair	Poor
850	600	450	300	200

NOTE: A few carbines were also built. These will bring a premium of 60 percent.

MONDRAGON

Model 1908 & Model 1915

Firearms designed by Manuel Mondragon were produced on an experimental basis first at St. Chamond Arsenal in France and later at SIG in Neuhausen, Switzerland. The latter company was responsible for the manufacture of the two known production models: the Model 1908 and 1915.

The Model 1908 Mondragon semi-automatic rifle holds the distinction of being the first self-loading rifle to be issued to any armed forces. Only about 400 of these rifles were delivered to the Mexican army in 1911 when the revolution broke out. The rifle was chambered for the 7x57mm Mauser cartridge and featured a 24.5-inch barrel. It has an 8-round box magazine. Weight is about 9.5 lbs. SIG had several thousand of these rifles left after the Mexicans were unable to take delivery. When WWI got under way the Swiss firm sold the remaining stocks to Germany. These rifles were called the Model 1915 and they were all identical to the Model 1908 except for the addition of a 30-round drum magazine.

Courtesy Rock Island Auction Company

Exc.	V.G.	Good	Fair	Poor
7500	6000	4500	2750	1500

FABRICA NACIONAL de ARMAS

Mexico City

Model 1936

This bolt action rifle was chambered for the 7mm cartridge and uses a short-type Mauser action. The rifle is of Mexican design and resembles the Springfield Model 1903A1 in appearance. Barrel length is 22 inches; 5-round non-detachable magazine. Tangent rear sight with "V" notch. Weight is about 8.25 lbs.

Exc.	V.G.	Good	Fair	Poor
750	550	400	275	200

Model 1954

This Mexican-produced and designed rifle also uses a Mauser action, but resembles a Springfield Model 1903A3 in appearance. The stock is laminated plywood. Barrel length is 24 inches and chambered for the .30-06 cartridge. Weight is approximately 9 lbs. Some of these rifles may still be in service.

Exc.	V.G.	Good	Fair	Poor
750	550	450	300	200

MACHINE GUNS

NOTE: The Mexican military has used a variety of foreign-built machine guns. The Madsen Model 1934, the Model 1896 Hotchkiss 7mm machine gun, and the Browning Model 1919, as well as the 5.56mm Ameli, the FN MAG, and the HK 21A1, and the Browning .50 M2HB. Mexico also produced its own excellent gun, the Mendoza C-1934 light machine gun and the RM2 gas operated machine gun issued in 1960.

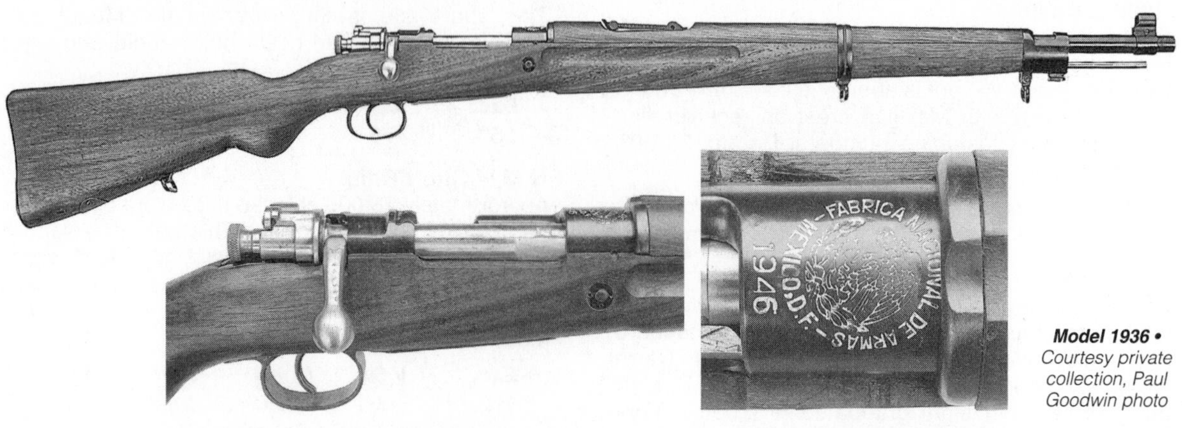

Model 1936 • *Courtesy private collection, Paul Goodwin photo*

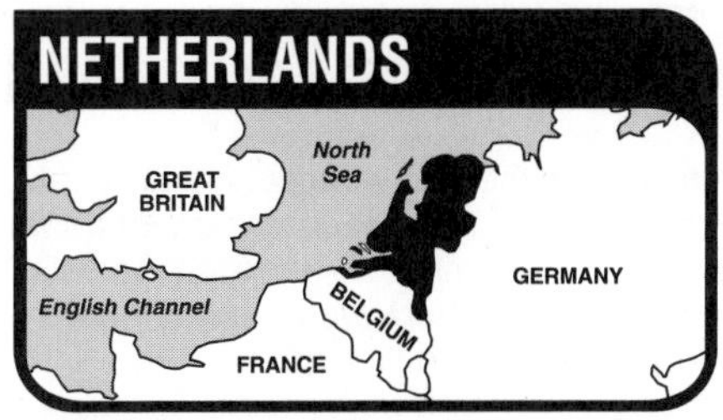

The Kingdom of the Netherlands, a country of western Europe fronting on the North Sea and bordered by Belgium and Germany, has an area of 15,770 sq. mi. (41,500 sq. km.) and a population of 16.1 million. Capital: Amsterdam, but the seat of government is at The Hague. The economy is based on dairy farming and a variety of industrial activities. Chemicals, yarns and fabrics, and meat products are exported.

After being a part of Charlemagne's empire in the 8th and 9th centuries, the Netherlands came under control of Burgundy and the Austrian Hapsburgs, and finally was subjected to Spanish dominion in the 16th century. Led by William of Orange, the Dutch revolted against Spain in 1568. The seven northern provinces formed the Union of Utrecht and declared their independence in 1581, becoming the Republic of the United Netherlands. In the following century, the *Golden Age* of Dutch history, the Netherlands became a great sea and colonial power, a patron of the arts and a refuge for the persecuted. The United Dutch Republic ended in 1795 when the French formed the Batavian Republic. Napoleon made his brother Louis, the King of Holland in 1806, however he abdicated in 1810 when Napoleon annexed Holland. The French were expelled in 1813, and all the provinces of Holland and Belgium were merged into the Kingdom of the United Netherlands under William I, in 1814. The Belgians withdrew in 1830 to form their own kingdom, the last substantial change in the configuration of European Netherlands. German forces invaded in 1940 as the royal family fled to England where a government-in-exile was formed.

HANDGUNS

During WWII, the Dutch also used the Enfield revolver chambered for the .38 Special cartridge, as well as the Webley Model I in .38 Special, the Webley Model VI chambered for the .455 cartridge.

Since the end of WWII, the Dutch have used the Walther P5, the HK P9S, the FN High Power (both Belgian and Canadian built), the Smith & Wesson Model 19, the Colt Python (4"), the Colt Model 1911A1, the FN Model 1910, and the FN Model 1910/22.

Model 1873 (Old Model)

This solid-frame double action revolver is based on the Chamelot Delvigne design. Chambered for the 9.4mm cartridge. Fitted with a 6.3" octagonal barrel. Gate loaded non-fluted cylinder holds 6 rounds. With no ejector rod, a separate rod was required. Smooth wooden grips with lanyard ring. Was issued in 1873 and remained in service through 1945. Built by a number of different companies such as J.F.J. Bar, DeBeaumont, P. Stevens, Hembrug, etc. Military marked. Weight is about 44 oz.

NOTE: An Officer's Model was also used but was not military issue and not military marked. Major differences are fluted cylinder, checkered wooden grips, and 5" barrel.

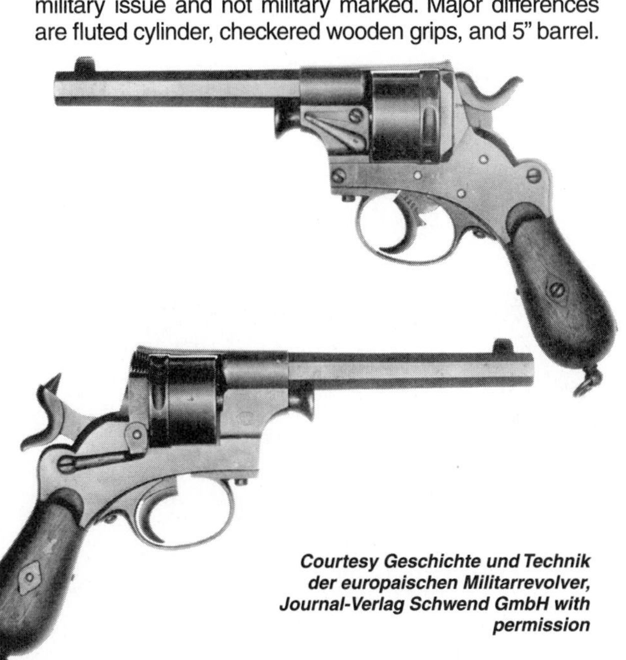

Courtesy Geschichte und Technik der europaischen Militarrevolver, Journal-Verlag Schwend GmbH with permission

Exc.	*V.G.*	*Good*	*Fair*	*Poor*
750	600	500	400	250

Model 1873 (New Model)

Similar to the Old Model but with 6.3" round barrel. First issued in 1909. Built by Hembrug. Military marked.

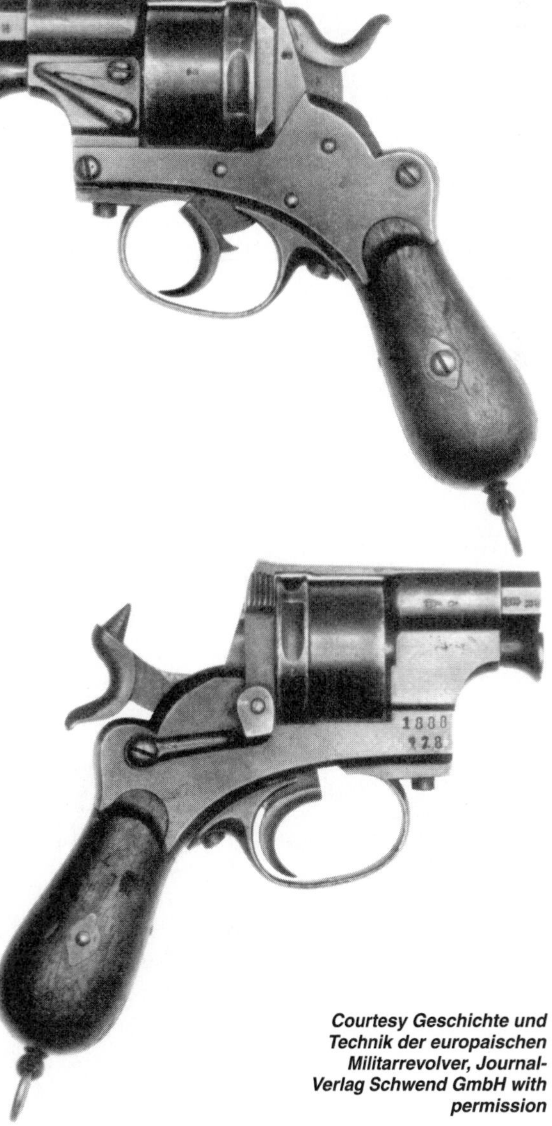

Courtesy Geschichte und Technik der europaischen Militarrevolver, Journal-Verlag Schwend GmbH with permission

Exc.	V.G.	Good	Fair	Poor
750	550	400	300	150

Model 1873/1919

This model is based on the Model 1873 but modified to fire tear gas projectiles. Chambered for the 9.4mm cartridge but with a 12mm caliber barrel. Barrel length was only 1.9" in length with no front sight. Smooth wooden grips with lanyard ring. In service from 1919 to 1945. Built by Hembrug and military marked.

Exc.	V.G.	Good	Fair	Poor
1200	850	550	—	—

Model 94 (Colonial Model)

This double action revolver was first issued to the Dutch Colonial Army in 1894 and remained in service until 1945. Chambered for the 9.4mm cartridge and fitted with a 4.3" barrel. Fluted cylinder holds 6 rounds. Checkered wooden grips with lanyard ring. Built by Hembrug. Military marked.

Courtesy Geschichte und Technik der europaischen Militarrevolver, Journal-Verlag Schwend GmbH with permission

Exc.	V.G.	Good	Fair	Poor
600	400	300	200	100

NETHERLANDS

SUBMACHINE GUNS

The Dutch military uses the UZI submachine gun (IMI), and several variants of the HK MP5. During World War II, the Dutch purchased a number of American made UD submachine guns in 9mm. There were no submachine guns of Dutch design issued to its military.

RIFLES

The Dutch military has used a number of different foreign-made military rifles including: FN FAL, HK PSG 1, HK 33SG1, and the U.S. M1 rifle. During WWII the Dutch used the Johnson semi-automatic rifle in its Far East colonies.

BEAUMONT/VITALI

Model 1871 Rifle

This single shot black powder rifle, chambered for the 11.3x51R cartridge, featured a heavy internally recessed two-piece bolt handle with a V-spring to activate the striker. The bolt head included the extractor. There was no ejector. Barrel length was 32.7". One-piece stock with two barrel bands. Fitted for a socket bayonet. Original rifles were issued in the white. Rear sight graduated to 1,100 meters. Weight is about 9.75 lbs. Nearly all were later converted to the 1871/88 pattern. Unalterd examples are scarce.

Exc.	V.G.	Good	Fair	Poor
800	700	600	300	250

Model 1871 Carbine

Same as above but with 22" barrel. Also fitted for a socket bayonet.

Exc.	V.G.	Good	Fair	Poor
650	550	475	300	200

Model 1871/88

This model was a conversion to the Vitali magazine. It featured a bolt-mounted ejector and a magazine cut-off

Beaumont-Vitali Model 1871/88 • *Private collection, Paul Goodwin photo*

on the left side of the receiver. Magazine capacity is 4 rounds. All other specifications are the same as the Model 1871. Rear sight is graduated to 1,300 meters. Weight is approximately 10 lbs. This rifle was used by the Dutch army and remained in secondary service through WWII.

Exc.	V.G.	Good	Fair	Poor
400	300	200	150	100

Bayonet for Beaumont Rifles

Socket type with a locking ring. 20.1" quadrangular blade. Appears similar to the Swiss Vetterli socket bayonet shown in the *Switzerland, rifles* section. The two are sometimes confused. Price range 170 – 75.

MANNLICHER

NOTE: The many variations of Dutch Model 1895 Mannlicher series is due to the fact that the Netherlands military and the Dutch East Indies each purchased their own versions of this design. All are similar except for differences in barrel band placement, hand guards and bayonet fittings. Some of these rifles have a wooden block covering the left side of the magazine. These were added after 1914 to protect the magazines from damage. Rifles without this modification are referred to as the "Old Model," while rifles with the change are called "New Models." There can be New Models and Old Models of many of these carbines. There are a few more sub-variations that are not given separate entries here. Pricing is generally the same. Some Dutch East Indies guns will bring more due to lower production totals and fact that many were converted to .303 British.

Model 1895 Rifle

This 6.5x53R rifle was produced in two versions. One for the regular army and the other for the Dutch East Indies. The colonial model has two gas escape holes in the receiver ring. The rifle is full-stocked with a half-length handguard. It is fitted with a bayonet bar. Barrel length is 31". Magazine capacity is 5 rounds and is clip loaded. After World War II, many of these rifles were rebored and converted to .303 British. Built by both Steyr and Hembrug. Weight is about 9.5 lbs.

Netherlands Mannlicher Model 1895 Rifle • *Courtesy Paul S. Scarlata from Mannlicher Military Rifles, Andrew Mobray Publishers*

Exc.	V.G.	Good	Fair	Poor
600	425	275	175	150

Model 1895 No. 1 Cavalry Carbine

This model featured a half stock with no handguard and sling bars on the left side. Barrel length is 17.7". Weight is about 6.75 lbs. Built by both Steyr and Hembrug.

Exc.	V.G.	Good	Fair	Poor
500	375	275	175	150

Model 1985 No. 2 Gendarmerie Carbine

This model is a full-stocked version with bayonet fittings. Weight is about 7 lbs.

Exc.	V.G.	Good	Fair	Poor
550	400	275	200	150

Model 1895 No. 3 Engineer & Artillery Carbine

Similar to the No. 2 carbine but with long handguard. Weight is almost 7 lbs.

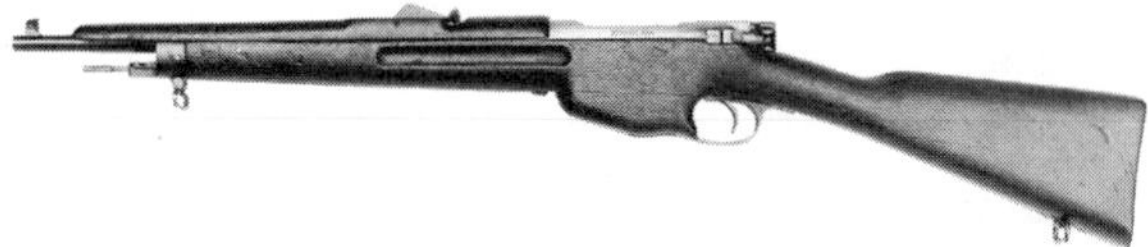

Courtesy Paul S. Scarlata from *Mannlicher Military Rifles,* ***Andrew Mobray Publishers***

Exc.	V.G.	Good	Fair	Poor
550	400	275	200	150

Clip for Netherlands M1895 Mannlicher series

Model 1895 No. 4 Bicycle Troops' Carbine

Similar to the No. 3 carbine but with handguard the same length as the stock.

Courtesy Paul S. Scarlata from *Mannlicher Military Rifles,* ***Andrew Mobray Publishers***

Model 1895 Cavalry Carbine, with side sling swivels

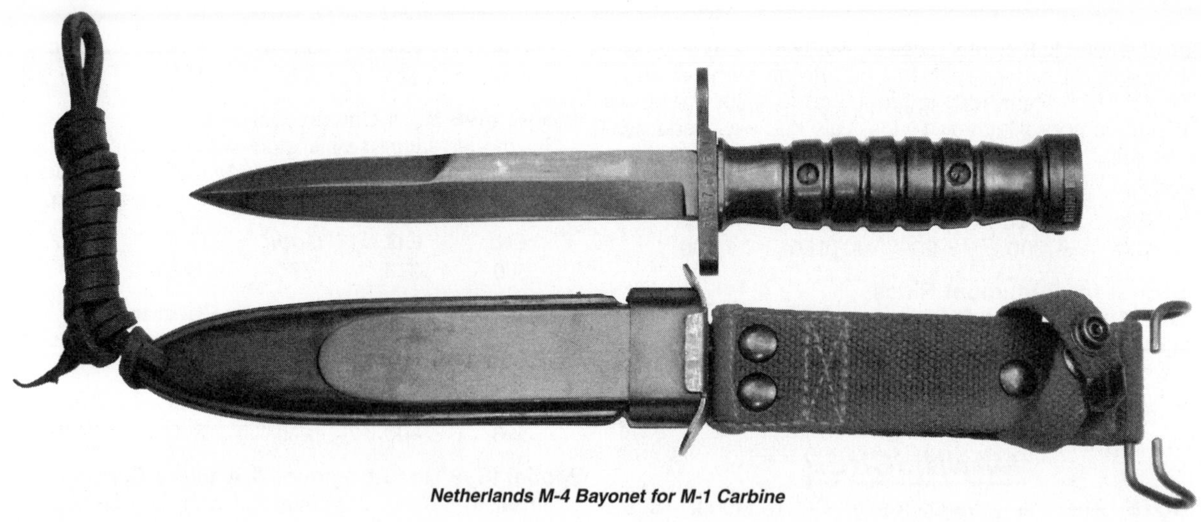

Netherlands M-4 Bayonet for M-1 Carbine

Exc.	*V.G.*	*Good*	*Fair*	*Poor*
500	400	300	225	150

Model 1917

Sometimes called the "machine gunner's rifle" because ammunition was the same as the Dutch Lewis and Schwarzlose machine guns. Chambered for the 8x57 cartridge and fitted with a 31.3" barrel with quadrant sight to 2,000 meters. Similar action to the Model 1895. Weight is about 9.25 lbs. Built by Hembrug.

Exc.	*V.G.*	*Good*	*Fair*	*Poor*
750	500	350	200	150

Model 1895 Carbine No. 5

This model was built by Hembrug beginning in 1930 and is a cut-down version of the Model 1895 rifle. It was issued to the Dutch Air Force. Barrel length is 17.9". Weight is about 7.75 lbs.

Exc.	*V.G.*	*Good*	*Fair*	*Poor*
600	450	300	200	100

Model 1895 No. 5 Carbine, with long hand guard

Model 1895 Military Police Carbine

The "Marechausse" or Dutch Military Police used a carbine that does not have a bayonet mount. Approximately 28,000 were made.

Exc.	*V.G.*	*Good*	*Fair*	*Poor*
600	450	300	200	100

Model 1895 "Marechausse" (Military Police) Carbine

Model 1895, converted to .303 British

The nation of Malaysia includes the territory that was once the Dutch East Indies. They converted many Mannlicher M 1895 rifles and carbines to .303 British. Some of these have a flash hider and rubber recoil pad added. Many of these .303 conversions have been imported to the U.S.

Exc.	*V.G.*	*Good*	*Fair*	*Poor*
500	325	250	175	100

Bayonet for Mannlicher Model 1895 series

Wood grips held on by two large rivets. Pommel resembles that of the English Pattern 1888 bayonet. Muzzle ring. Early version has a hook quillon, later deleted. 14" T shaped blade. Ricasso marked "Hembrug." Leather scabbard. Price range 175 – 75.

MAUSER (FN)

M1948 Carbine

This rifle was built by FN for the Dutch police. Chambered for the 7.9x57mm cartridge and fitted with a 17.3" barrel with bayonet fittings. Full stock with pistol grip and upper handguard. Magazine capacity is 5 rounds. Marked with letter "J" or "W" with crown on receiver ring. Rear sight is V notch graduated from 200 to 1,400 meters. Weight is about 7.5 lbs.

Exc.	*V.G.*	*Good*	*Fair*	*Poor*
1200	850	550	350	250

Netherlands M-4 Bayonet for M-1 Carbine

Post-WWII production for the U.S. M-1 carbines supplied after the war. Same as the U.S. M-4 but has a plastic grip held with two screws. Plastic scabbard has a simulated wood grain finish. Price range 75 – 35.

MACHINE GUNS

In 1908 the Dutch adopted the Schwarzlose machine gun in 7.92Rmm, various Madsen models chambered for the 6.5mm cartridge, the Lewis gun in 6.5mm, and the Vickers Model 1918 in 7.92mm. The Dutch military has also used the FN MAG, the Bren Mark 2 in .303, and the .50 M2 HB. During WWII the Dutch also used the Johnson LMG in .30-06 as well as the Browning Model 1919 variants.

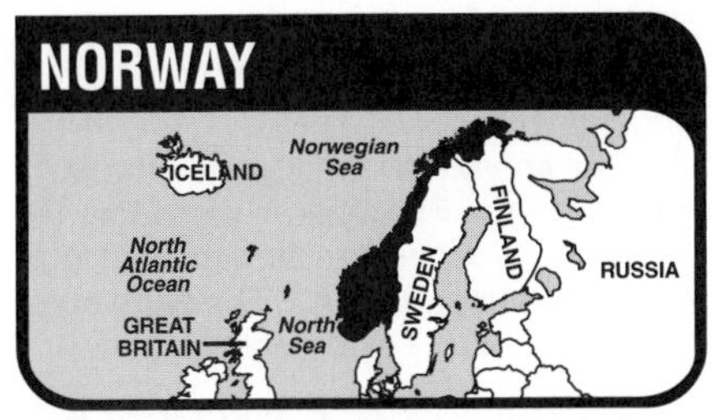

The Kingdom of Norway (*Norge, Noreg*), a constitutional monarchy located in northwestern Europe, has an area of 150,000sq. mi. (324,220 sq. km.), including the island territories of Spitzbergen (Svalbard) and Jan Mayen, and a population of *4.2 million. Capital: Oslo (Christiania). The diversified economic base of Norway includes shipping, fishing, forestry, agriculture, and manufacturing. Nonferrous metals, paper and paperboard, paper pulp, iron, steel and oil are exported.

A united Norwegian kingdom was established in the 9th century, the era of the indomitable Norse Vikings who ranged far and wide, visiting the coasts of northwestern Europe, the Mediterranean, Greenland and North America. In the 13th century the Norse kingdom was united briefly with Sweden, then passed through inheritance in 1380 to the rule of Denmark which was maintained until 1814. In 1814 Norway fell again under the rule of Sweden. The union lasted until 1905 when the Norwegian Parliament arranged a peaceful separation and invited a Danish prince (King Haakon VII) to ascend the throne of an independent Kingdom of Norway.

HANDGUNS

NAGANT

Model 1883 Revolver

Adopted in 1883, this Nagant six-round revolver has a solid frame with loading gate and mechanical rod ejection. Double action. Chambered for the 9x23R Belgian Nagant cartridge. Barrel is part round and part hexagon and is 5.5" long. Fluted cylinder and checkered wood grips with lanyard loop. Weight is about 32 oz. This model stayed in service until 1940. It was issued to both officers and NCOs.

Courtesy Geschichte und Technik der europaischen Militarrevolver, Journal-Verlag Schwend GmbH with permission

Exc.	*V.G.*	*Good*	*Fair*	*Poor*
1250	750	400	275	150

Model 1887/93 Revolver

Similar in appearance to the Model 1883 but chambered for the 7.5x22R Norwegian Nagant cartridge. Barrel length is 4.5". Weight is about 28 oz. In service until 1940.

Courtesy Geschichte und Technik der europaischen Militarrevolver, Journal-Verlag Schwend GmbH with permission

Exc.	*V.G.*	*Good*	*Fair*	*Poor*
1250	750	400	275	150

Model 1912/14

All of the Model 1912/14 pistols were produced by the Norwegian arsenal at Kongsberg Vapenfabrikk. The official designation of the Norwegian Colt pistol was "COLT AUTOMATISK PISTOL, MODEL 1912, CAL. 11.43 M/M." In 1917 the designation changed to "11.25 M/M AUTOMATISK PISTOL MODEL 1914." The new marking began with serial number 96 (see Table 1). For a more detailed explanation of the differences in the Norwegian pistols see Clawson's, *Colt .45 Government Models, 1912 through 1970.*

Kongsberg Vapenfabrikk Model M/1914 (Norwegian) copy SN 1-96

Rarely seen. Condition 99-100 percent add 20-30 percent.

Norwegian slide legend left side • *Courtesy Karl Karash*

Exc.	*V.G.*	*Good*	*Fair*	*Poor*
3500	2200	1150	850	600

Kongsberg Vapenfabrikk Model M/1914 (Norwegian) copy 29614 to 30536

Numbers must match.

Norwegian slide markings right side • *Courtesy Karl Karash*

NORWAY

Exc.	V.G.	Good	Fair	Poor
1400	900	750	600	400

Kongsberg Vapenfabrikk Model M/1914 (Norwegian) copy SN 29,615 to 30,535

Waffenamt marked on slide and barrel. Numbers must match. Waffenamt marked M/1914s outside this range are probably FAKES. Condition 99-100 percent add 20-30 percent.

Exc.	V.G.	Good	Fair	Poor
3000	1900	1150	850	600

Notice the extended slide stop on the left side • Courtesy Karl Karash

Norwegian slide legend left side with extended slide stop • Courtesy Karl Karash

TABLE 1

DATE	SERIAL RANGE	DATE	SERIAL RANGE
1917	1-95	1929	20101-21400
1918	96-600	1932	21441-21940
1919	601-1150	1933	21941-22040
1920	1151-1650	1934	22041-22141
1921	1651-2200	1936	22142-22211
1922	2201-2950	1939	22212-22311
1923	2951-4610	1940	22312-22361
1924	4611-6700	1941	22362-26460
1925	6701-8940	1942	26461-29614
1926	8941-11820	1945	29615-30535
1927	11821-15900	1947	32336-32854
1928	15901-20100		

SUBMACHINE GUNS

Norway used the German MP40, designated the M40, chambered for the 9x19mm Parabellum cartridge. The Norwegian military also issued the British Sten gun, as well as the HK MP5A2 and MP5A3. The Norwegian Marines use the Suomi 37/ 39 submachine gun.

RIFLES

The Norwegian military also uses the HK G3 rifle, the Mauser 98K converted to 7.62x51mm, as well as now-obsolete U.S. M1 Garands and U.S. M1 and M2 carbines.

Model 1842 Kammerlader Percussion Rifle

A unique breech loading percussion fired rifle. Breechblock moves back and upwards by means of a lever on the right side. The hammer is on the underside, just in front of the trigger guard. The original caliber was 17.5mm, with later models being 11.8mm. Several variations were made including some carbines and long versions. Pricing on the U.S. market is about the same for all.

Exc.	V.G.	Good	Fair	Poor
3250	2500	1500	850	600

Model 1860 Rifle

A conversion of the Model 1842 to use a 12.2mm rimfire cartridge.

Exc.	V.G.	Good	Fair	Poor
2500	2000	1200	750	500

REMINGTON ROLLING BLOCK

NOTE: See also U.S. Rifles, Remington, for Remington built rolling block rifles for Norway.

Model 1867 Rifle

Built in Norway by Christiana, Husqvarna, or Kongsberg. Fitted with a 37.3" barrel with three barrel bands and full length stock. Brass buttplate. Chambered for the 12.17x42R Norwegian Remington rimfire cartridge. Weight is about 10 lbs.

Exc.	V.G.	Good	Fair	Poor
850	650	500	300	150

Model 1889 Carbine

This model was essentially a Model 1867 fitted with a 24" barrel chambered for the 8x58R Danish Krag cartridge. Built at Kongsberg. Weight is about 8.5 lbs.

Exc.	V.G.	Good	Fair	Poor
1100	800	650	425	225

JARMANN

Kongsberg

Model 1880-1882 Experimental

In 1880-1882 about 500 Jarmanns were produced in Sweden for use in trials in Norway. This experimental model used a curved 5-round box magazine mounted from the top right side of the receiver forward of the bolt handle. Chambered for the 10.15x61Rmm cartridge and fitted with a 32" barrel. Marked with Carl Gustaf markings.

Exc.	V.G.	Good	Fair	Poor
Too Rare To Price				

Model 1884 Rifle

Bolt action rifle with magazine tube under barrel with 8-round capacity. Chambered for the 10.15x61R Jarmann cartridge. Full stocked with two barrel bands. Fitted with a 32.5" barrel. Weight is about 10 lbs. These rifles made at Kongsberg and marked with a "K" on the receiver ring.

Exc.	V.G.	Good	Fair	Poor
Too Rare To Price				

NOTE: A carbine version was built but never adopted by Norway.

Model 1884/87

Similar to the Model 1884 but with recalibrated rear sight for smokeless powder.

Exc.	V.G.	Good	Fair	Poor
Too Rare To Price				

MAUSER

K98k Reissued Short Rifle (.30-06)

The only difference between this rifle and the standard issue German model is the markings. The Norwegian word "HAER" meaning "Army" is stamped on the receiver ring. A number of other stampings that denote Norwegian military organizations may also be seen, such as: HV=Home Guard; FLY=Air Force; KNM=Navy; K.ART=Coast Artillery; NSB=Government Railway; POLITI=Police.

Exc.	V.G.	Good	Fair	Poor
600	450	375	250	150

K98k Action Military Target Rifle (Model 59)

Exc.	V.G.	Good	Fair	Poor
700	600	500	275	150

Model 84S

This rifle uses a modified Mauser 98 military action with the original markings removed. Chambered for the 7.62mm NATO cartridge and first introduced in 1984. Built by Vapensmia A/S in Norway. Fitted with a heavy barrel by the German company Heym. Has a 5-round detachable magazine. Fitted with a 6x42 Schmidt & Bender scope. Adjustable trigger. Laminated birch stock. This rifle was also sold commercially.

Exc.	V.G.	Good	Fair	Poor
1500	1150	800	500	300

KRAG JORGENSEN

See also *U.S., Rifles, Krag*

NOTE: The Norwegian Krag rifles differ from the U.S. Krags primarily in that it does not have a cartridge cutoff. The Norwegian Krags were used by the Norwegian army as its principal long arm until the Germans occupied Norway in 1940. The majority of these rifles were built at Kongsberg, although some were produced at Steyr and FN Herstal. Norwegian Krags were chambered for the 6.5x55mm Swedish Mauser cartridge.

Model 1894 Rifle

This rifle is full stocked with pistol grip and full-length handguard. Barrel length is 30". Box magazine is located in horizontal position and has a capacity of 5 rounds. Tangent rear sight. Weight is approximately 9 lbs.

Courtesy Paul S. Scarlata, *Collecting Classic Bolt Action Military Rifles*

Exc.	V.G.	Good	Fair	Poor
1000	800	600	400	275

Model 1895 Carbine

This model is half stocked with short handguard and fitted with a 20.5" barrel. Magazine capacity is 5 rounds. Weight is about 7.5 lbs. Very similar in appearance to the U.S. Krag carbine.

Courtesy Paul S. Scarlata, *Collecting Classic Bolt Action Military Rifles*

Exc.	V.G.	Good	Fair	Poor
1500	1000	800	400	275

Model 1897 Carbine

Similar to the Model 1895 carbine except the rear sling swivel is located near the toe of the buttstock.

Exc.	V.G.	Good	Fair	Poor
1500	1000	700	400	275

Model 1904 Carbine

This model has a 20.5" barrel with full stock and upper handguard but no bayonet lug. Weight is about 8.4 lbs. Estimated production is about 2,750.

Exc.	V.G.	Good	Fair	Poor
1500	1100	800	400	275

Model 1906 Boy's Training Rifle

Introduced in 1906 for use at schools and shooting clubs. Chambered for the 6.5x55mm cartridge. Barrel length is about 20.5". Weight is about 7.25 lbs. No upper handguard with shorter stock dimensions. Turned down bolt handle. One barrel band has front swivel. Estimated production is about 3,321. Rare.

Exc.	V.G.	Good	Fair	Poor
1800	1250	1000	500	350

Model 1907 Carbine

Similar to the Model 1907 but with sling swivels located on rear barrel band and buttstock.

Exc.	V.G.	Good	Fair	Poor
1500	1000	700	400	275

Model 1912 Carbine

Full stocked with 24" barrel and 5-round magazine. Fitted with a bayonet lug on nose cap. Weight is about 8.5 lbs. About 30,100 were produced.

Courtesy Paul S. Scarlata, *Collecting Classic Bolt Action Military Rifles*

Exc.	V.G.	Good	Fair	Poor
1200	800	500	300	250

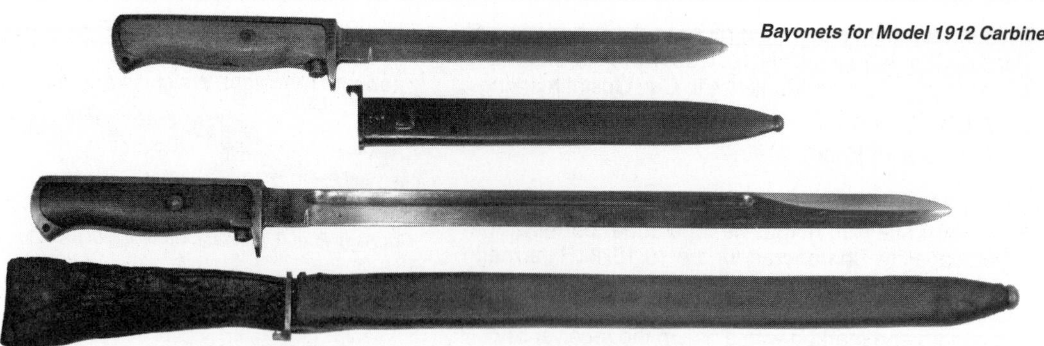
Bayonets for Model 1912 Carbine

Bayonets for Norwegian Krag Jorgensen

Model 1894 Rifle

Wood grip. 8.3" single edge blade. Steel scabbard. Price range 175 – 100.

Model 1912 Carbine

Wood grip. 14.3" single edge blade. Leather scabbard. Price range 175 – 100.

Model 1923 Sniper

This model is fitted with a full stock and checkered pistol grip. Full-length handguard. Heavy barrel length is 26.2". Bayonet fittings on nose cap. Micrometer rear sight with aperture. Marked "M.1894" on receiver. Magazine capacity is 5 rounds. Weight is about 9 lbs. Scarce with total production of about 630 rifles.

Courtesy Paul S. Scarlata, Collecting Classic Bolt Action Military Rifles

Exc.	V.G.	Good	Fair	Poor
4500	4000	3000	2000	800

Model 1925 Sniper

Fitted with a 30" heavy barrel similar to the Model 1894 rifle but with checkered pistol grip and micrometer rear peep sight. Weight is approximately 10 lbs. Scarce.

Exc.	V.G.	Good	Fair	Poor
4500	4000	3000	2000	800

Model 1930 Sniper

This model has a sporter-style half stock with checkered full pistol grip. Heavy 29.5" barrel. No bayonet fittings. Micrometer rear sight. Marked "M/1894/30." Weight is approximately 11.5 lbs. Scarce.

Exc.	V.G.	Good	Fair	Poor
4500	4000	3000	2000	800

Norwegian Modified Bayonets for U.S. M-1 Garand and M-1 Carbine

Shown are a pair of interesting modifications Norway did to make bayonets for the rifles they received from the U.S. after WW2. The German 98K bayonet has a small stud added to fit into the M-1 Garand gas plug. Price range 175 – 75. The Norwegian 1894 Krag bayonet has an added muzzle ring to fit the M-1 Carbine. Price range 150 – 60.

MACHINE GUNS

Norway used the Hotchkiss machine gun, chambered for the 6.5mm cartridge, beginning in 1911, as well as the Model 1914 and Model 1918 Madsen guns. The Browning Model 1917 water-cooled gun was used by the Norwegians and designated the Model 29. After WWII the Norwegian military used the Browning Model 1919A4, as well as the MG 34 and MG 42. Currently Norway has adopted the MG 42/59 as its standard machine gun, designating it the LMG 3.

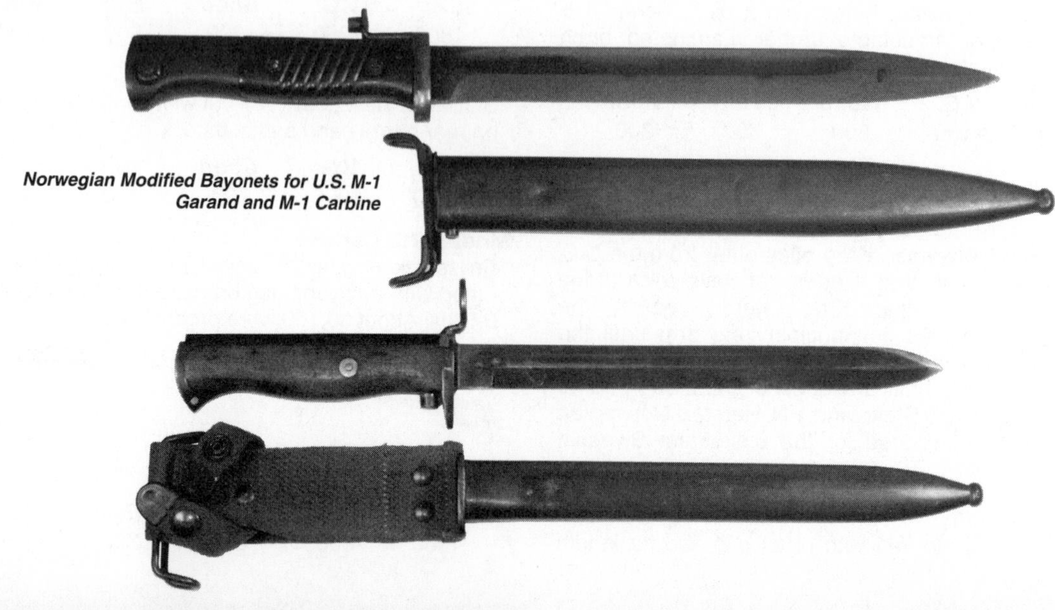
Norwegian Modified Bayonets for U.S. M-1 Garand and M-1 Carbine

The Republic of Poland, located in central Europe, has an area of 120,725 sq. mi. (312,680 sq. km.) and a population of *38.2 million. Capital: Warszawa (Warsaw). The economy is essentially agricultural, but industrial activity provides the products for foreign trade. Machinery, coal, coke, iron, steel and transport equipment are exported.

Poland, which began as a Slavic duchy in the 10th century and reached its peak of power between the 14th and 16th centuries, has had a turbulent history of invasion, occupation or partition by Mongols, Turkey, Transylvania, Sweden, Austria, Prussia and Russia.

The first partition took place in 1772. Prussia took Polish Pomerania, Russia took part of the eastern provinces, and Austria occupied Galicia and its capital city Lwów. The second partition occurred in 1793 when Russia took another slice of the eastern provinces and Prussia took what remained of western Poland. The third partition, 1795, literally removed Poland from the map. Russia took what was left of the eastern provinces. Prussia seized most of central Poland, including Warsaw. Austria took what was left of the south. Napoleon restored to Poland much of the territory lost to Prussia and Austria, but after his defeat another partition returned the Duchy of Warsaw to Prussia, made Kraków into a tiny republic, and declared what remained to be the Kingdom of Poland under the czar and in permanent union with Russia.

Poland re-emerged as an independent state recognized by the Treaty of Versailles on June 28, 1919, and maintained its independence until 1939 when it was invaded by, and partitioned between, Germany and Russia. Poland's present boundaries were determined by the U.S.-British-Russian agreement of Aug. 16, 1945. The Government of National Unity was replaced when the Polish Communist-Socialist faction claimed victory at the polls in 1947 and established a Peoples Democratic Republic' of the Soviet type in 1952. On December 29, 1989 Poland was proclaimed as the Republic of Poland.

POLAND

HANDGUNS

RADOM

(Fabryka Broniw Radomu)

This company was established after WWI and produced military arms for Poland. During WWII the Radom factory was operated by the Nazis. Production was not resumed after the war.

Ng 30

A copy of the Russian Nagant revolver chambered for the 7.62mm Russian cartridge. Approximately 20,000 were manufactured during 1930 and 1936.

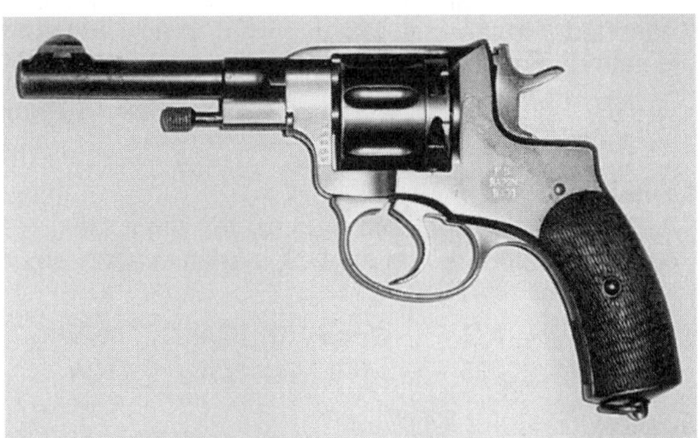

Courtesy Richard M. Kumor Sr.

Exc.	V.G.	Good	Fair	Poor
3000	2300	1500	500	350

VIS-35

A 9mm semi-automatic pistol with a 4.5-inch barrel, fixed sights, and an 8-shot magazine. On this model there is no manual safety; however, a decocking lever is installed that allows the hammer to be safely lowered on a loaded chamber. Versions made prior to WWII are engraved with a Polish eagle on the slide and "FB" and "VIS" are molded into the grips. These prewar pistols are slotted for a holster stock. German production pistols were made without the decocking lever and subsequently without the stripping catch. They also eliminated the stock slot. These pistols were stamped "P35P" and bear the Waffenamt inspector's mark "WaA77." Near the end of the war, the take-down was eliminated and the grips were replaced with crude wooden grips. The slide, barrel, and frame are all numbered to match each other.

NOTE: Prices quoted are for 1939 dated guns. Earlier years bring a significant premium.

Polish Eagle Model-1936 through 1939

Exc.	V.G.	Good	Fair	Poor
3500	2000	1500	750	300

Polish Army issue VIS-35 • *Courtesy Rock Island Auction Company*

Courtesy Richard M. Kumor Sr.

POLAND

Nazi Captured Polish Eagle—Waffenamt Marked

Exc.	V.G.	Good	Fair	Poor
4000	3500	1800	650	300

Nazi Polish Eagle (Navy marked)

Courtesy Richard M. Kumor Sr.

Nazi Production Model (Model 35[p])

Type 1 features 3 levers and stock slot

Exc.	V.G.	Good	Fair	Poor
1200	850	650	200	175

Courtesy Richard M. Kumor Sr.

Type 2 features 3 levers and no stock slot

Exc.	V.G.	Good	Fair	Poor
750	600	500	350	200

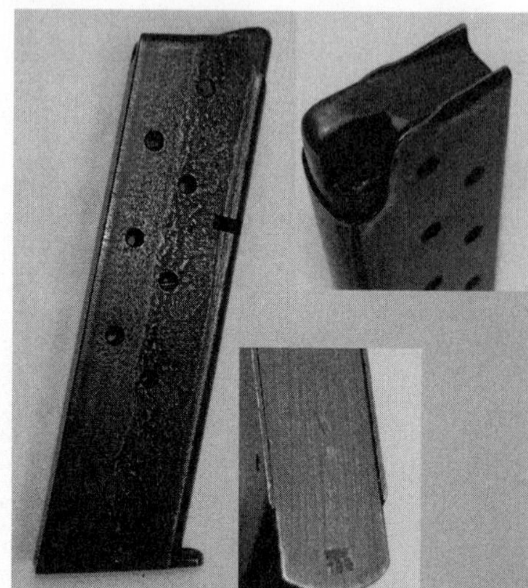

Radom VIS-35 magazine with German marking. Price 150-60

Type3 features 2 levers and no slot

Exc.	V.G.	Good	Fair	Poor
700	550	450	300	200

Nazi Type 3 made by Steyr

Most have grooved wood grips.

Exc.	V.G.	Good	Fair	Poor
1500	1100	850	450	200

Nazi Type 3 "bnz" code

Exc.	V.G.	Good	Fair	Poor
3500	2500	1200	650	500

Leather holster for Radom P-35

Similar to German P-38 type. Top flap. Wartime versions have a single magazine pouch on the front. Pre-war Polish holsters have two magazine pouches. Add 50% for pre-war holster.

Exc.	V.G.	Good	Fair	Poor
250	175	125	100	25

VIS-35 Reissue

This is an exact copy of the original VIS-35 pistol. Limited to 100 pistols with fewer than that number imported into the U.S. The importer, "Dalvar of USA," is stamped on the barrel.

NIB	Exc.	V.G.	Good	Fair	Poor
2300	—	—	—	—	—

Model 64

A PPK size pistol chambered for the 9mm Makarov cartridge. Appeared on the U.S. market in 2005, most in unissued condition.

Exc.	V.G.	Good	Fair	Poor
275	225	175	N/A	N/A

Tokarev (Pistolet TT)

Polish copy with manual safety added to comply with U.S. import regulations.

Exc.	V.G.	Good	Fair	Poor
400	300	250	150	125

NOTE: Add 100% if there is no added safety.

P-83

This pistol is chambered for the 9x18 (Makarov) cartridge. It is fitted with a 3.5-inch barrel and has a double action trigger with decocker. Magazine capacity is 8 rounds. Weight is about 25 oz. Black oxide finish. Developed in the early 1970s, it is similar to a Makarov pistol except it is built from stampings. Used by Polish army and security forces. A small number of commercial pistols was imported in the early 1990s.

NOTE: Several thousand Polish military issue P-83's were imported in 2009 and are currently available on the U.S. market.

Exc.	*V.G.*	*Good*	*Fair*	*Poor*
350	300	275	N/A	N/A

P-93

Similar to the P-83 differing only in cosmetics but chambered for 9mm Makarov only. The decocking lever is on the frame instead of the slide. Barrel length is 3.9 inches. Black oxide finish.

NIB	*Exc.*	*V.G.*	*Good*	*Fair*	*Poor*
450	350	275	—	—	—

MAG-95

This pistol is chambered for the 9mm Parabellum cartridge and fitted with a 4.5-inch barrel. Magazine capacity is 15 rounds. Trigger is double action with external hammer. Weight is about 38 oz. Black oxide finish. Optional 20-round magazine. In use by Polish forces on NATO duty. Limited U.S. importation in the 1990's.

Exc.	*V.G.*	*Good*	*Fair*	*Poor*
550	500	450	—	—

SUBMACHINE GUNS

NOTE: Poland was supplied with Soviet made PPSh M1941 and PPS M1943 submachine guns.

M1943/52

This gun is a Polish-built modification of the Soviet PPS M1943 submachine gun in 7.63mm caliber. It is select fire and is fitted with a 9.5-inch barrel. Magazine capacity is a 35-round box. Rate of fire is about 600 rounds per minute. Weight is approximately 8 lbs. Wooden buttstock.

Pre-1968

Exc.	*V.G.*	*Fair*
20000	17500	15000

WZ-63

Introduced in 1964, this submachine gun is a small, almost pistol-size weapon chambered for the 9x18mm Makarov cartridge. It is fitted with a 6-inch barrel with folding metal butt. The folding is designed to be used as a front vertical grip, if desired. A noticeable spoon-shaped muzzle compensator is used. Magazine is a box type with 15- or 25-round capacity. Rate of fire is about 600 rounds per minute. Weight is approximately 4 lbs.

Pre-1968

Exc.	*V.G.*	*Fair*
20000	17500	15000

RIFLES

MAUSER

NOTE: Poland began producing Mauser rifles and carbines in early 1902 at the Warsaw arsenal.

Polish 98 Mauser • *Courtesy Paul S. Scarlata*

M98 Rifle

This rifle is similar to the German Gew 98 with a tangent rear sight instead of the German style. Nearly full stock with pistol grip and finger grooves on the forend. Half length upper handguard. Many were assembled from German parts. Some will be found with small Polish Eagles stamped on the bolt knob.

Exc.	V.G.	Good	Fair	Poor
650	450	350	175	150

M98AZ Rifle

This rifle is the same as the German Model 98AZ, and was assembled using German WW1 parts. In addition to the standard placement of sling swivels, a sling bar is fitted to the left side of the stock. Polish wood is used on the stock in place of walnut. These are found both with and without Polish markings on the receiver. Price shown assumes Polish markings. An unmarked M98AZ will bring up to 50 percent less.

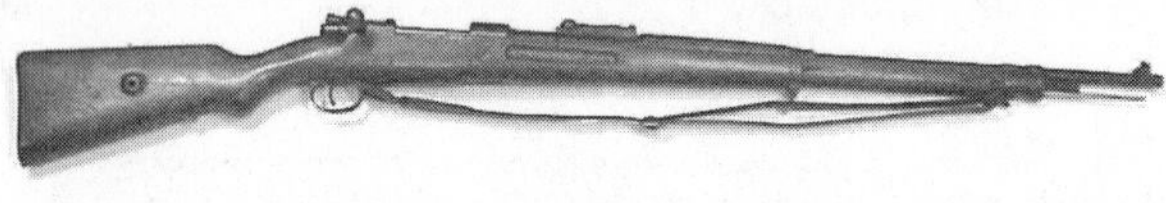

Exc.	V.G.	Good	Fair	Poor
900	750	550	300	150

Wz29 Short Rifle

This rifle was built at the Radom factory. Barrel length is 23.6 inches and caliber is 7.92x57mm. Straight bolt handle. Almost full stock with pistol grip and grasping grooves on the forestock. A sling bar is fitted to the left side of the stock. Tangent leaf rear sight graduated to 2,000 meters. Weight is about 9 lbs.

Exc.	V.G.	Good	Fair	Poor
1000	800	600	400	200

Wz 98a Rifle

Exc.	V.G.	Good	Fair	Poor
1000	800	600	400	200

Wz29 .22 Caliber Training Rifle

Exc.	V.G.	Good	Fair	Poor
2000	1700	1200	750	400

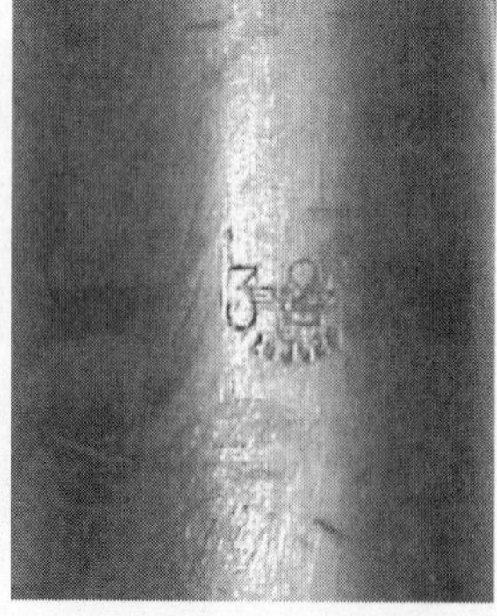

Kbk8 Wz31 .22 Caliber Training Rifle

Exc.	V.G.	Good	Fair	Poor
2000	1700	1200	750	400

Bayonets for Polish Mausers

Poland used German 98-05 bayonets on their Gew-98 rifles. After WWI they produced their own bayonets that are patterned after the German K98 type. They were made by two makers and will bear the maker's name and/or a Polish eagle and a serial number on the ricasso. F.B. Radom was made with a muzzle ring, although the rings were often removed by the Germans during WWII. Perkun made bayonets without the muzzle ring. Price range 175 – 50.

Wz 48 .22 Caliber Training Rifle

Produced after WWII as a training rifle. It is based on the Mosin Nagant Model 1938 but with a longer barrel.

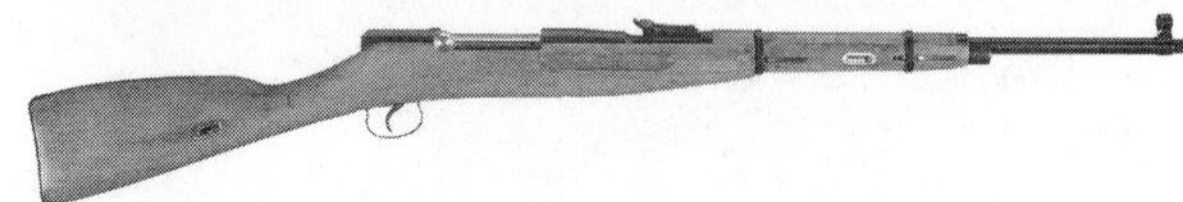

Exc.	V.G.	Good	Fair	Poor
350	250	175	N/A	N/A

Polish Model 1891/30 Sniper Rifle

These are the Soviet rifles used by the Poles but refinished. Polish sniper rifles are identified by the serial numbered mounting rails being the same as the scope.

Exc.	V.G.	Good	Fair	Poor
1200	900	700	N/A	N/A

Model 1891/98/25 Polish Nagant

The production of these rifles started in the early 1920s at the Warsaw arsenal. Chambered for the 7.92mm cartridge but fitted with a bayonet lug and stamped with a small crowned Polish Eagle on receiver and bolt. It has a 23.5-inch barrel with 5-round non-detachable box magazine. Leaf rear sight. Weight is approximately 8 lbs. A very rare variation. Original, unaltered examples will command a premium price. About 77,000 of these rifles were produced.

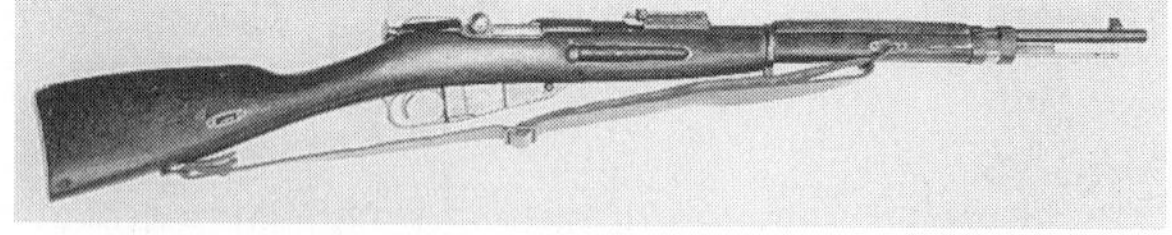

***Polish 1891/98/25 Rifle** • Courtesy Richard M. Kumor Sr.*

Exc.	V.G.	Good	Fair	Poor
1100	900	700	400	200

Polish Model 1944 Nagant

Produced in Poland from 1950 until about 1962. Polish markings on the receiver, stock, and barrel. Poland's factory code 11 on receiver Many of these were

***Polish Wz 29** • Courtesy Richard M. Kumor Sr.*

PMK-DGM • *Courtesy West Point Museum, Paul Goodwin photo*

Bayonet for Polish PMK (AK-47)

imported in recent years. Many were in unissued condition. Examples without import stamps probably came in from Canada in the 1980s.

Exc.	V.G.	Good	Fair	Poor
350	275	200	125	90

KbKg Model 1960 or PMK-DGM and PMKM

All of these rifles are copies of AK-47 variations. Both the PMK and PMKM are sometimes equipped with grenade launchers fitted to the muzzle.

Pre-1968

Exc.	V.G.	Fair
30000	27500	25000

Bayonet for Polish PMK (AK-47)

Red plastic handle. 5.8-inch single edge blade with cutting edge to the top. No serrations on the back. Price range 45 – 20.

MACHINE GUNS

NOTE: Poland used a variety of foreign-built machine guns prior to WWII. Some of these were the Browning Model 1917s and the BAR. Both of these guns were chambered for the 7.92mm cartridge. After the war Poland used Soviet-issued weapons.

Polish BAR (Wz28)

This Polish BAR was chambered for the 7.92x57mm cartridge with skids on its bipod instead of spikes and a bipod attached to the gas regulator instead of the muzzle. Barrel length is 24 inches with AA ring sight base. Approximately 12,000 Polish-built BARs were produced between 1930 and 1939. These guns are marked "R.K.M. BROWNING WZ. 28 P.W.U.F.K. [DATE] [SERIAL NUMBER]" located on the receiver. A number of these guns (est. 500) saw service in the Spanish Civil War and were used by German military forces.

Pre-1968

Exc.	V.G.	Fair
25000	22500	20000

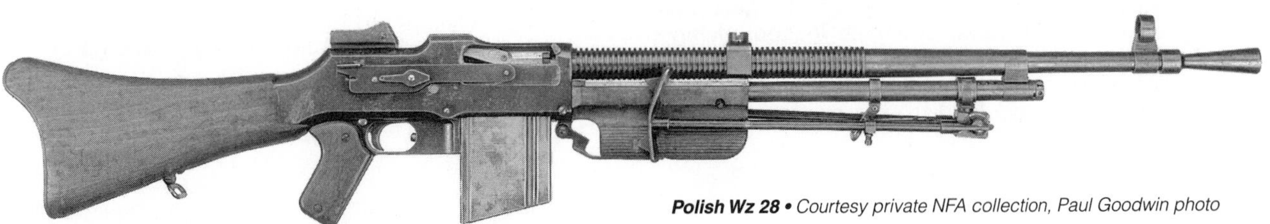

Polish Wz 28 • *Courtesy private NFA collection, Paul Goodwin photo*

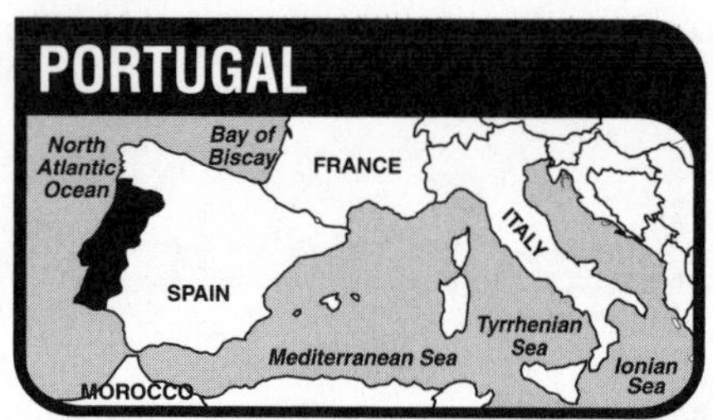

The Portuguese Republic, located in the western part of the Iberian Peninsula in southwestern Europe, has an area of 35,553 sq. mi. (92,080 sq. km.) and a population of *10.5 million. Capital: Lisbon. Portugal's economy is based on agriculture, tourism, minerals, fisheries and a rapidly expanding industrial sector. Textiles account for 33% of the exports and Portuguese wine is world famous. Portugal has become Europe's number one producer of copper and the world's largest producer of cork.

After centuries of domination by Romans, Visigoths and Moors, Portugal emerged in the 12th century as an independent kingdom financially and philosophically prepared for the great period of exploration that would soon follow. Attuned to the inspiration of Prince Henry the Navigator (1394-1460), Portugal's daring explorers of the15th and 16th centuries roamed the world's oceans from Brazil to Japan in an unprecedented burst of energy and endeavor that culminated in 1494 with Portugal laying claim to half the transoceanic world. Unfortunately for the fortunes of the tiny kingdom, the Portuguese population was too small to colonize this vast territory. Less than a century after Portugal laid claim to half the world, English, French and Dutch trading companies had seized the lion's share of the world's colonies and commerce, and Portugal's place as an imperial power was lost forever. The monarchy was overthrown in 1910 and a republic was established.

On April 25, 1974, the government of Portugal was seized by a military junta which reached agreements providing for independence for the Portuguese overseas provinces of Portuguese Guinea (*Guinea-Bissau*), Mozambique, Cape Verde Islands, Angola, and St. Thomas and Prince Islands (*Sao Tome and Principe*).

PORTUGAL

HANDGUNS

Portugal adopted the Walther PP in 7.65x17mm, and the Walther P1 in 9mm. FN provided the machinery to manufacture the FN 35 GP pistol. Heckler & Koch also sold its VP70M to the Portuguese military.

Model 1878 Army

This 9.1x17.5R Portuguese Abadie cartridge officer's revolver was fitted with a 4.5-inch octagon barrel and 6-round fluted cylinder. The revolver was double action with a solid frame and gate loaded. The most unique features is the Abadie system of linking the loading gate to the hammer to prevent accidental discharge while loading. Weight is about 27 oz. This revolver remained in service until 1919.

Courtesy Geschichte und Technik der europaischen Militarrevolver, Journal-Verlag Schwend GmbH with permission

Exc.	V.G.	Good	Fair	Poor
750	600	400	200	150

Model 1886 Army/Navy

This revolver was issued to troopers. Chambered for the 9.35x17.5R Portuguese Abadie cartridge. Double action with solid frame and gate loaded. Octagon barrel is 5.6 inches long. Cylinder is fluted and holds 6 rounds. Weight is about 30 oz. This revolver also employs the Abadie loading gate system. Remained in service until 1910.

Exc.	V.G.	Good	Fair	Poor
750	600	400	200	150

Courtesy Geschichte und Technik der europaischen Militarrevolver, Journal-Verlag Schwend GmbH with permission

Model 1907 Portuguese Contract

Similar to the commercial guns but with a lanyard ring like the French contract model. Chambered for the 7.65mm cartridge. Original Portuguese pistols will have the Portuguese Crest on the grips. Only about 1,150 of these pistols were produced and very few have the original Portuguese grips. Very rare. Proceed with caution.

Exc.	V.G.	Good	Fair	Poor
1500	1000	750	600	300

SUBMACHINE GUNS

The Portuguese military has used a wide variety of submachine guns over the years purchased from other countries. Some of these sub guns are: the Beretta M12, Vigneron, Uzi, Sterling MK4, Ingram M10, the Star Z-45, and the Franchi LF-57.

FBP M948

Produced in Portugal at its government arsenal in 1948. Chambered for the 9mm parabellum cartridge and fitted with a 9.8" barrel. Blowback operation. Sliding wire stock. Cycle rate is about 500 rounds per minute. Magazine capacity is 32 rounds. Weight is about 7.5 lbs. Designed by Major Goncalves Cardoso of the Portuguese Army. Combines features from the German MP40 and the American M3 grease gun.

Pre-1968

Exc.	V.G.	Fair
N/A	N/A	N/A

FBP M976

This is an improved version of the above model. Cyclic

rate is about 600 rounds per minute. A 36-round magazine was also available along with the 32-round type. In service until the 1980s.

Pre-1968

Exc.	V.G.	Fair
N/A	N/A	N/A

Bayonet for FPB submachine gun

Wood grips. Handle resembles a typical Mauser type without muzzle ring. 6.9-inch double edge blade. No markings except a serial number on pommel. Steel scabbard. One of the few bayonets manufactured for a submachine gun. Price range 250 – 125.

RIFLES

Portugal has used the Galil type 5.56mm rifle, the HK33, the FN FAL, small quantities of the AR-10, and the FMBP government arsenal produced G3 rifle.

STEYR

Model 1885 Rifle

Built in Austria for the Portuguese Army this is a single shot block breech action operated by the trigger guard. The action is similar to the English Martini Henry. Full stocked. Chambered for the 8x60R Guedes cartridge. Barrel length is 33.3 inches and weight is about 9 lbs.

Exc.	V.G.	Good	Fair	Poor
800	600	450	300	200

MANNLICHER

Model 1896

Produced by Steyr about 4,200 cavalry carbines were acquired by Portugal in 6.5x53Rmm. Barrel length is 17.7 inches. Five-round clip-loaded magazine. Marked Steyr on the left side of the receiver and the Portuguese crest on the receiver ring. No bayonet attachment.

Exc.	V.G.	Good	Fair	Poor
750	475	275	175	100

MAUSER

Model 1886 (Mauser-Kropatschek)

A copy of the Mauser 71-84 and built by Steyr, this rifle came in three configurations: carbine, short rifle, and rifle. Chambered for the 8x60R (later 8x56R) cartridge. Carbines were fitted with a 20.5" barrel, short rifle with 26-inch barrels, and rifles with 32.25-inch barrels. The short rifle and carbine did not have an upper handguard as did the rifle which was fitted with a clip-on handguard. All three variations had bayonet attachments.

Exc.	V.G.	Good	Fair	Poor
500	400	300	175	25

Bayonet for Model 1885 Guedes and Model 1886 Kropatschek

Wood grips. Muzzle ring. 18.4-inch single edge blade. Marked "Steyr 1886" on top of blade. Steel scabbard. Fits both the M 1885 Guedes single shot and the M 1886 Kropatschek rifles. Price range 125 – 60.

M1904 Mauser-Verueiro Rifle

Chambered for the 6.5x58Rmm cartridge and designed by a Portuguese officer (Vergueiro). Fitted with a 29.1-inch barrel, 5-round flush box magazine. Tangent rear leaf sight to 2,000 meters. Carlos I crest on the receiver ring. Weight is about 8.5 lbs. The stock has an almost superficial pistol grip and upper handguard from the receiver to upper barrel band. The rifle is fitted with a split bridge receiver and modified Mannlicher-Schoenauer bolt.

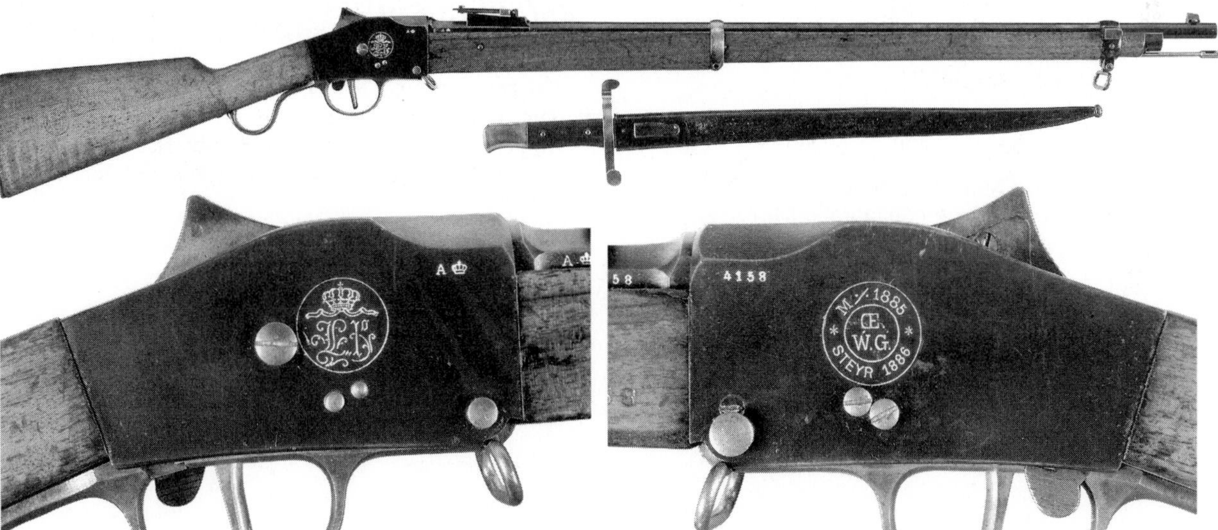

Model 1885 Rifle • *Courtesy Rock Island Auction Company*

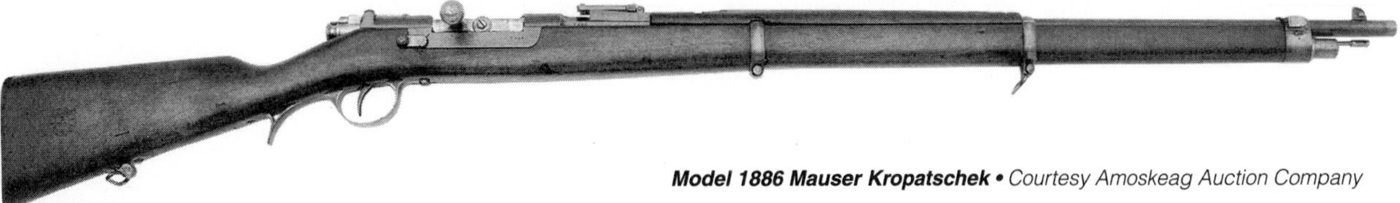

Model 1886 Mauser Kropatschek • *Courtesy Amoskeag Auction Company*

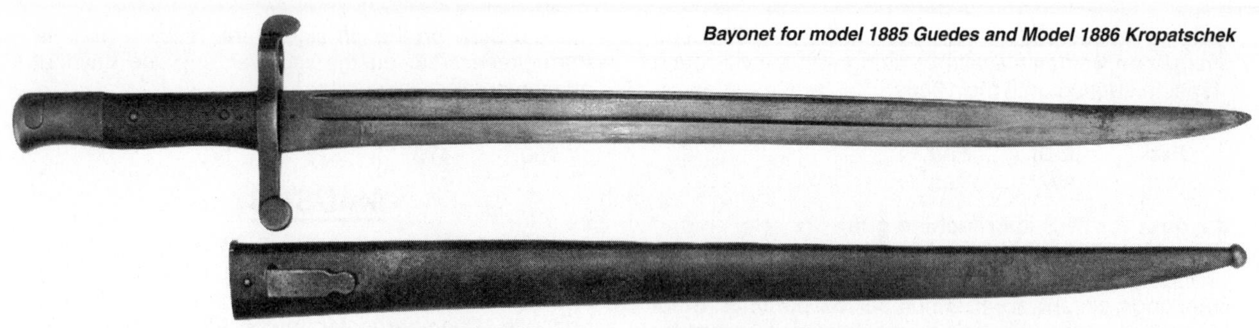

Bayonet for model 1885 Guedes and Model 1886 Kropatschek

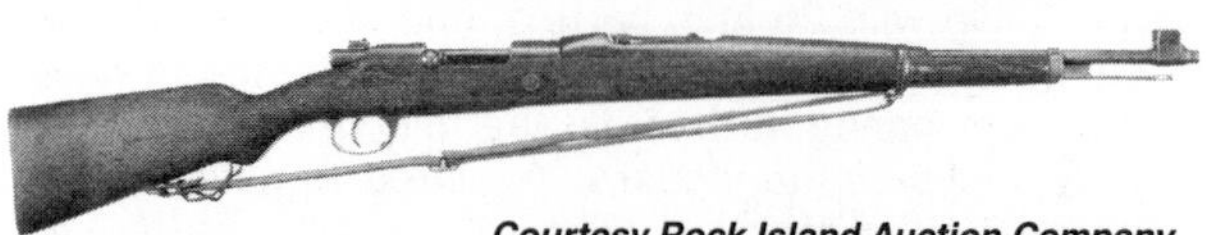

Courtesy Rock Island Auction Company

Exc.	V.G.	Good	Fair	Poor
600	400	275	150	125

M1904/M39 Rifle

This model was the result of a conversion of the Model 1904 to conform to the 1930s Model 1937-A rifle. Rifle was rechambered to 7.92x57mm, the barrel shortened to 23.6 inches. The front sight was fitted with sight protectors. Markings are the same as the Model 1904 rifle. Weight is about 8 lbs. Some were imported in the 1990s.

Exc.	V.G.	Good	Fair	Poor
300	225	175	125	100

Bayonet for 1904 Vergueiro

Wood grips. Muzzle ring. 12-inch single edge blade. Looks the same as numerous Mauser long export bayonets. Unmarked except for SN on pommel. Steel scabbard. Price range 85 – 40.

M1933 Standard Model Short Rifle

Portugal purchased a number of this model directly from Germany. They are standard German export models in every respect.

Exc.	V.G.	Good	Fair	Poor
850	650	400	250	150

M1933 Standard Model Carbine

As above but in carbine configuration.

Exc.	V.G.	Good	Fair	Poor
850	650	400	250	150

M1937-A Short Rifle

This rifle replaced the Model 1904 in 1937. Similar to the German K98k carbine. Chambered for the 7.92x57mm cartridge and fitted with a 23.6-inch barrel. Box magazine holds 5 rounds and is flush with the bottom of the stock. Rear leaf tangent sight to 2,000 meters. Front sight has sight protectors. Portuguese national crest of the receiver ring. Weight is about 8.75 lbs.

Exc.	V.G.	Good	Fair	Poor
900	750	550	250	150

M1941 Short Rifle

The Model 1937-A with updates to make production the same as the German war time K98k. Changes include a cupped buttplate and K98 type sling slot in stock. In 1944 the German government halted arms exports due to wartime shortages. German military markings were added. The rifles, still bearing the Portugese crest, were then issued to the Wehrmacht. Add 50 percent for German marked rifles.

Exc.	V.G.	Good	Fair	Poor
1000	850	700	450	250

MACHINE GUNS

The Portuguese military has used the MG42, HK21, FN MAG, M60D, M219, .50 M2 HB machine guns. The Portuguese purchased in 1938 a number of modified Dreyse Model 1918 machine guns which they Portuguese referred to as the Model 938.

Romania (formerly the Socialist Republic of Romania), a country in southeast Europe, has an area of 91,699 sq. mi. (237,500 sq. km.) and a population of 23.2 million. Capital: Bucharest. Machinery, foodstuffs, raw minerals and petroleum products are exported. Heavy industry and oil have become increasingly important to the economy since 1959.

A new constitution was adopted in 1923. During this period in history, the Romanian government struggled with domestic problems, agrarian reform and economic reconstruction.

On August 23, 1944, King Mihai I proclaimed an armistice with the Allied Forces. The Romanian army drove out the Germans and Hungarians in northern Transylvania, but the country was subsequently occupied by the Soviet army. That monarchy was abolished on December 30, 1947, and Romania became a "People's Republic" based on the Soviet regime. The process of sovietization included Soviet regime. The anti-Communist combative resistance movement developed frequent purges of dissidents: mainly political but also clerical, cultural and peasants. Romanian elite disappeared into the concentration camps. The anti-Communist combative resistance movement developed in spite of the Soviet army presence until 1956. The partisans remained in the mountains until 1964. With the accession of N. Ceausescu to power, Romania began to exercise a considerable degree of independence, refusing to participate in the invasion of Czechoslovakia (August 1968). In 1965, it was proclaimed a "Socialist Republic". After 1977, an oppressed and impoverished domestic scene worsened.

On December 17, 1989, an anti-Communist revolt in Timisoara. On December 22, 1989 the Communist government was overthrown. Ceausescu and his wife were arrested and later executed. The new government established a republic, the constitutional name being Romania.

HANDGUNS

Steyr Hahn Model 1911

Chambered for the 9mm Steyr cartridge, this pistol was made by Steyr for the Romanian military in 1913 and 1914, as well as other military forces. This particular model is marked with Romanian crest over 1912 on left of slide. Some of these pistols were used by Romanian military during WWII.

Exc.	*V.G.*	*Good*	*Fair*	*Poor*
750	575	350	250	150

Beretta Model 1934 Romanian Contract

This model is identical to the Beretta Model 1934 except the slide is marked "9mm Scurt" instead of "9mm Corto." Built for the Romanian military in 1941 with an estimate of approximately 20,000 manufactured in Italy. Some were imported in the late 1990s and have the Century Arms billboard import stamp. Deduct 25 percent for import marked guns.

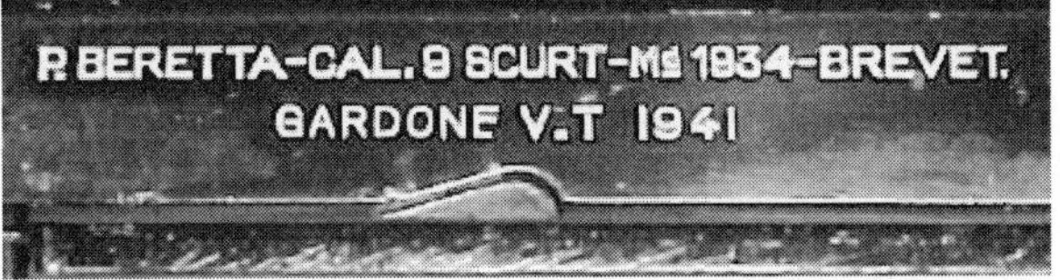

Courtesy Orvel Reichert

Exc.	*V.G.*	*Good*	*Fair*	*Poor*
525	400	300	225	125

Model 74

A Romanian copy of the Walther PP chambered for the 7.65mm (.32 ACP) cartridge. This pistol has an aluminum frame and is similar to the FEG Hungarian R61 with the exception of a heel-type magazine release.

Exc.	*V.G.*	*Good*	*Fair*	*Poor*
250	150	125	100	80

Soviet TT33 Tokarev

A Romanian made copy of the Soviet TT-33. 7.62x25mm No safety.

Exc.	*V.G.*	*Good*	*Fair*	*Poor*
850	700	600	500	300

Romanian TT-33, recent import with added safety and import markings

Exc.	*V.G.*	*Good*	*Fair*	*Poor*
350	300	250	N/A	N/A

SUBMACHINE GUNS

Before 1939 Romania acquired Beretta 9mm Model 1938A submachine guns. After 1939 the Romanian armed forces used the Beretta 38/42 in 9mm Parabellum. Then after the war Romania adopted the Czech VZ24 and VZ26 guns.

Orita M 1941

This gun was manufactured in Romania at Cugir Arsenal. It is similar to the MP 41 but uses magazines that are similar in appearance to the German model but are not interchangeable with it. Fitted with a one-piece wooden stock. Chambered for the 9mm Parabellum cartridge. Semiautomatic or full auto fire. The rear leaf and ramp sight is quite large and located well forward on the barrel. Barrel length is 11.25 inches. Magazine capacity is 25 rounds. The gun has a cycle rate of about 600 rounds per minute. Weight is approximately 7.75 lbs.

RIFLES

PEABODY

Romanian Rifle (1867-1868)

Chambered for the .45 Romanian centerfire cartridge and fitted with a 32.25-inch barrel. Blued barrel with casehardened furniture. Full stock with two barrel bands. Oiled wooden stocks. A total of 25,000 rifles were made in serial range 21,000 to 52,000.

Exc.	*V.G.*	*Good*	*Fair*	*Poor*
—	1500	1000	500	200

PEABODY-MARTINI

Witten, Germany

Model 1879 Peabody-Martini Rifle

Made in Germany and based on the Turkish Model 1874 rifle. Chambered for the 11.43x60R Peabody-Martini cartridge. Fitted with a 33.25-inch barrel. Full stocked with two barrel bands. Weight is about 9.5 lbs.

Exc.	V.G.	Good	Fair	Poor
—	850	500	300	150

MANNLICHER

Model 1892

Introduced in 1892 and built by Steyr, this turn bolt rifle is chambered for the 6.5x53Rmm cartridge. This model is full stocked with straight grip and half-length handguard. Fitted with a cleaning rod and bayonet fittings. Barrel length is 28.5-inch. Leaf rear sight. Clip loaded magazine has a 5-round capacity. Weight is about 9 lbs. Marked "OE" over "W.G." on receiver ring and "MD. 1892" on left side of receiver.

Exc.	V.G.	Good	Fair	Poor
700	500	300	175	150

Model 1893

This is an improved version of the Model 1892 with stacking hook added and bolt modifications to prevent faulty assembly. Other specifications are the same as the Model 1892.

Exc.	V.G.	Good	Fair	Poor
700	450	300	175	150

Model 1893 Carbine

This is a short version of the Model 1893 rifle with 17.7" barrel. No handguard and no bayonet fittings. Weight is approximately 7.25 lbs.

Exc.	V.G.	Good	Fair	Poor
800	650	450	250	150

MAUSER

VZ24 Short Rifle

This model is a copy of the Czech VZ24 Short Rifle. The only difference is the Romanian crest on the receiver ring.

Exc.	V.G.	Good	Fair	Poor
850	650	450	200	125

STATE FACTORIES

Romanian Mosin-Nagant M1944

These rifles are marked on the receiver with a small arrowhead in a triangle below a wreath with the letters "RPR." Romanian stocks are marked with a "C" in a diamond. These rifles were produced in the 1950s. Many have been imported to the U.S.

Exc.	V.G.	Good	Fair	Poor
300	200	150	75	50

PSL Sniper Rifle (misnamed FPK)

This model is chambered for the 7.62x54Rmm cartridge and fitted with a modified AKM-type receiver. Magazine capacity is 10 rounds. Buttstock is similar to the Soviet SVD but with a molded cheekpiece. The muzzle brake is of Romanian design. Equipped with a telescope sight. Weight is about 10.5 lbs. Currently imported.

Exc.	V.G.	Good	Fair	Poor
750	650	500	—	—

SKS

A Romanian-manufactured version of the Russian rifle. Some were imported in the 1990s. Usually found in well-used condition.

Exc.	V.G.	Good	Fair	Poor
500	350	275	200	150

AK-47 (semi-automatic version)

Romanian copy of the Soviet AK-47. Current importation. Scope rail on left side of receiver. Has a SVD type stock made from laminated wood. Several variations have been imported and others were built in the U.S. from imported parts.

Courtesy West Point Museum, Paul Goodwin photo

Exc.	V.G.	Good	Fair	Poor
450	375	300	—	—

AKM

Copy of the Soviet AKM except for a noticeable curved-front vertical foregrip formed as part of the forend.

Pre-1968

Exc.	V.G.	Fair
8500	8000	7500

AKM-R

This is a compact version of the Soviet AKM with an 8-inch barrel and side-folding metal butt. Magazine capacity is 20 rounds. Chambered for the 7.62x39mm cartridge. Rate of fire is about 600 rounds per minute. Weight is approximately 7 lbs.

Pre-1968

Exc.	V.G.	Fair
25000	20000	17500

AK-74 (semi automatic)

Similar to the Soviet rifle in 5.45x39mm. Current importation. Scope rail on left side of receiver. Has a SVD type stock made from laminated wood. Also offered in 5.56mm/.223.

Exc.	V.G.	Good	Fair	Poor
400	300	250	—	—

MACHINE GUNS

The Romanians used Soviet-built RPDs, SGMs, PK, PKB, PKS, PHTs, and the Soviet-made DShK 38/46.

RPK (Romanian Manufacture)

Copy of Soviet RPK.

Romanian Schwarzlose converted to 7.62 caliber with larger waterjacket and metal belt • *Courtesy Robert E. Naess*

Exc.	V.G.	Fair
N/A	N/A	N/A

RUSSIA (U.S.S.R.)

Russia, formerly the central power of the Union of Soviet Socialist Republics and now of the Commonwealth of Independent States occupies the northern part of Asia and the eastern part of Europe, has an area of 17,075,400 sq. km. Capital: Moscow.

The first Russian dynasty was founded in Novgorod by the Viking Rurik in 862 A.D. under Yaroslav the Wise (1019-54). The subsequent Kievan state became one of the great commercial and cultural centers of Europe before falling to the Mongols of the Batu Khan, 13th century, who were suzerains of Russia until late in the 15th century when Ivan III threw off the Mongol yoke. The Russian Empire was enlarged, solidified and Westernized during the reigns of Ivan the Terrible, Peter the Great and Catherine the Great, and by 1881 extended to the Pacific and into Central Asia. Contemporary Russian history began in March of 1917 when Tsar Nicholas II abdicated under pressure and was replaced by a provisional government composed of both radical and conservative elements. This government rapidly lost ground to the Bolshevik wing of the Socialist Democratic Labor Party which attained power following the Bolshevik Revolution which began on Nov. 7, 1917. After the Russian Civil War, the regional governments, national states and armies became federal republics of the Russian Socialist Federal Soviet Republic. These autonomous republics united to form the Union of Soviet Socialist Republics that was established as a federation under the premiership of Lenin on Dec. 30, 1922.

In the fall of 1991, events moved swiftly in the Soviet Union. Estonia, Latvia and Lithuania won their independence and were recognized by Moscow, Sept. 6. The Commonwealth of Independent States was formed Dec. 8, 1991 in Mensk by Belarus, Russia and Ukraine. It was expanded at a summit Dec. 21, 1991 to include 11 of the 12 remaining republics (excluding Georgia) of the old U.S.S.R.

HANDGUNS

NOTE: Russia contracted for a number of Smith & Wesson revolvers over a period of years. The number of these revolvers purchased by Russia was about 350,000. These revolvers were made for the Russian military and are covered under U.S., Handguns, Smith & Wesson.

NAGANT

Model 1895 "Gas Seal" Revolver

A 7.62mm caliber single or double action revolver with a 4.35-inch barrel and 7-shot cylinder. Called a Gas Seal because as the hammer is cocked, the cylinder is moved forward to engage the barrel breech forming a seal between the cylinder and the barrel. Blued with either walnut or plastic grips. Weight was approximately 28 oz. In service from 1895 to approximately 1947.

Early production built by Nagant Brothers in Liege, Belgium.

Exc.	*V.G.*	*Good*	*Fair*	*Poor*
600	500	375	175	100

NOTE: Single action only versions are much less encountered and will command a 50 percent premium.

Imperial Russian production at Tula arsenal. Dated 1897-1917

Exc.	*V.G.*	*Good*	*Fair*	*Poor*
550	425	325	175	100

Nagant Model 1895 • *Paul Goodwin photo*

Soviet era production at Tula arsenal. Dated 1920-1947

Exc.	V.G.	Good	Fair	Poor
450	325	250	150	125

Refinished imports

A large number of Nagant revolvers have been imported to the U.S. in the last few years. They have been refinished and some have plastic grips.

Exc.	V.G.	Good	Fair	Poor
200	175	150	—	—

Model 1895 Nagant .22 Caliber

As above but chambered for .22 caliber cartridges. Converted at the Tula arsenal from surplus 7.62mm revolvers. Used as a training revolver from 1925 to 1947.

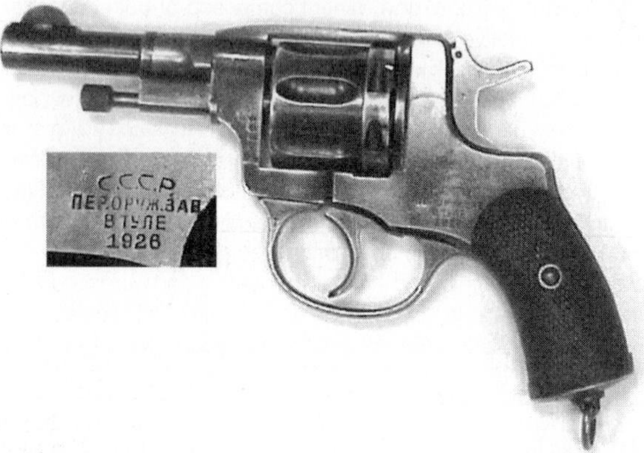

Exc.	V.G.	Good	Fair	Poor
850	600	450	200	100

Model 1895 Nagant (KGB)

This is a standard Nagant with the important exception of a 3.5-inch barrel and shorter grip frame. Used by the Russian secret police during the Stalin years. Extremely rare. Proceed with caution.

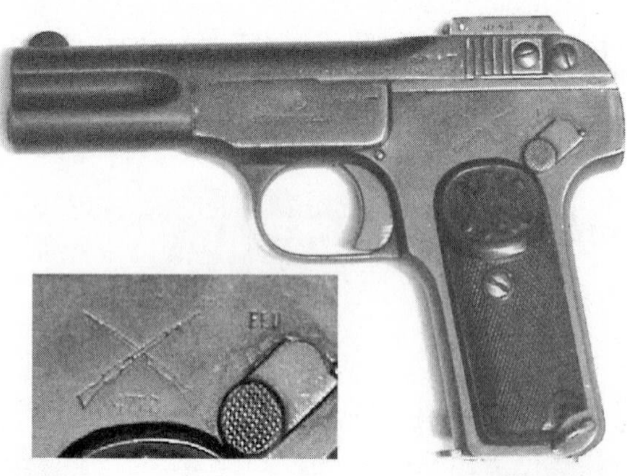

Exc.	V.G.	Good	Fair	Poor
2000	1500	1000	—	—

FN 1900 Russian Contract

An unknown number of these FN pistols were purchased by the Russian government. Little information is known. Proceed with caution.

Exc.	V.G.	Good	Fair	Poor
1000	700	500	300	200

SOVIET STATE FACTORIES

Tokarev TT-30 & TT-33

Fyedor Tokarev was a Russian weapons designer who began his career at the Sestroretsk rifle factory in 1907. He was responsible for the development of machine guns, pistols, and automatic rifles. The TT series of pistols were just some of his designs.

In 1930 the TT-30 was adopted, and in 1933 a slightly modified version, the TT-33, was introduced. A 7.62mm semi-automatic pistol with a 4.5-inch barrel and 8-shot magazine. This model was produced in a number of communist countries. Each country had its own model designation for the pistol. In Poland and Yugoslavia it is called the M57; in Hungary it was known as the M48; in China the M51 and M54; and in North Korea the M68. The North Korean M68 differs from the other Tokarevs in the location of the magazine release and the elimination of the barrel locking link.

Courtesy Richard M. Kumor Sr.

Exc.	V.G.	Good	Fair	Poor
650	475	350	125	100

NOTE: In 1941 the German army captured a number of Russian pistols, namely the TT-33. It was designated the Pistol 615 (r). Add 50 percent for German marked examples. Add 50 percent for TT-30, for cut-aways add 200 percent.

Russian officer with TT33 Tokarev • *Courtesy Paul S. Scarlata*

NOTE: A small quantity of Soviet TT-33 have been imported to the U.S. since the mid 1990s. Most had a safety added to comply with U.S. import regulations. Deduct 25 percent for an import with added safety. A few were brought in by a small importer in 2005 without the added safety and were sold until BATF realized the mistake and seized the remaining pistols until they could have the safeties added.

Russian TT-33 Holster

Leather construction through WWII. Post war they were made from a synthetic material.

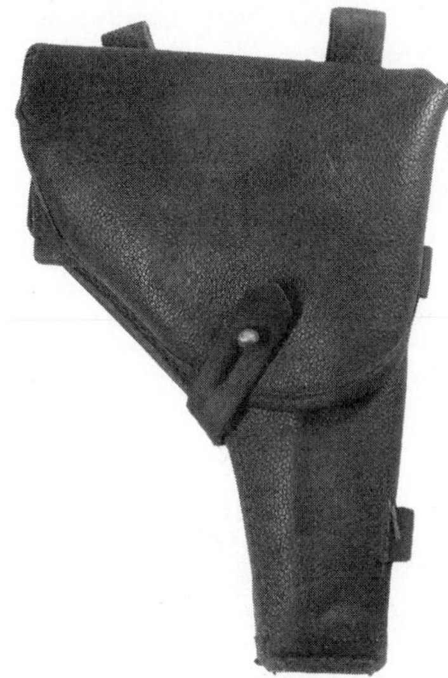

Price range for leather 150 – 50.

Price range for synthetic 70 – 35.

Tokarev Model R-3

A training version of the TT Tokarev pistols chambered for the .22 rimfire cartridge.

Exc.	V.G.	Good	Fair	Poor
800	650	500	300	200

Tokarev Model R-4

A long barrel target version of the TT Tokarev pistol chambered for the .22 rimfire cartridge.

Exc.	V.G.	Good	Fair	Poor
800	650	500	300	200

Courtesy Orvel Reichert

TK TOZ (Tula Korovin)

A .25 caliber pocket pistol produced by the Soviet arsenal at Tula. Fitted with a 2.7-inch fixed barrel. Magazine capacity is 8 rounds. Weight is approximately 14 oz. Used by military officers and police units. Produced from 1926 to about 1935.

Exc.	V.G.	Good	Fair	Poor
650	550	400	250	150

Makarov, Soviet issue

This semi-automatic pistol is similar in appearance to the Walther PP pistol and is chambered for the 9mm Makarov (9x18mm) cartridge. It has a double action trigger and is fitted with fixed sights. Barrel length is 3.6 inches and overall length is 6.4 inches. Weight is approximately 25 oz. Magazine capacity is 8 rounds. Current U.S. government regulations will not permit surplus Makarovs to be imported. A few Soviet issue Makarovs were imported in the 1990s, mixed in with surplus Makarovs from Bulgaria.

Exc.	V.G.	Good	Fair	Poor
500	400	300	200	150

Makarov, commercial production

These were made for export sales to the U.S. and imported in the 1990s. The rules for Russian arms imports were changed and importation was halted. They were offered in 9x18mm Makarov and .380. They come with an adjustable rear sight, required to qualify for importation.

Exc.	V.G.	Good	Fair	Poor
300	250	200	—	—

Stechkin with stock • *Courtesy Thomas Nelson, The World's Machine Pistols, Vol. II*

Stechkin

A select fire pistol chambered for the 9x18 Makarov cartridge. Fitted with a 5.5-inch barrel and a 20-round magazine. Rate of fire is about 750 rounds per minute. Weight is approximately 36 oz. This was the standard service pistol of the Soviet army between 1955 and 1975. A wooden stock/holster is supplied with the pistol.

NOTE: It is not known how many, if any, of these machine pistols are in the U.S. and are transferable. Prices listed below are estimates only.

Pre-1968 (Extremely Rare)

Exc.	*V.G.*	*Fair*
30000+	—	—

SUBMACHINE GUNS

PPD-1934/38 (Pistol Pulyemet Degtyarev)

Introduced in 1938 and based on the Bergman MP28 submachine gun. Select fire. The buttstock is wooden. Barrel is 10.5 inches with perforated barrel jacket and tangent sight. Chambered for the 7.62 Soviet pistol cartridge. Magazine capacity is 25-round box or 71-round drum. Rate of fire is approximately 800 rounds per minute. Weight is about 8.5 lbs.

Pre-1968

Exc.	*V.G.*	*Fair*
17000	15000	13000

PPD-1940

First produced in 1940, this Russian-built submachine gun is chambered for the 7.62 Soviet pistol cartridge. The gun was fitted with a 71-round drum magazine and 10-inch barrel. The rate of fire was 800 rounds per minute. The serial number and factory code are located on top of the receiver. Weight is about 8 lbs. Production ceased in 1941.

Pre-1968

Exc.	*V.G.*	*Fair*
17000	15000	13000

Pre-1986 manufacture with new receiver or re-weld

Exc.	*V.G.*	*Fair*
N/A	5500	5000

PPSh-41 (Pistol Pulyemet Shpagin)

This Russian select fire submachine gun was produced from 1941 until 1947. About five million were built and many were sold throughout the world. Some were converted from the 7.62 pistol cartridge to the 9mm cartridge by Germany. The gun could use a 71-round drum magazine or a 35-round box magazine. Rate of fire was 900 rounds per minute. The barrel was 10.3 inches long with slotted barrel jacket and weighed almost 8 lbs. Early models had a tangent back sight while most were fitted with a two-position, flip-up rear sight. Markings are located on the receiver.

NOTE: A German conversion 9mm kit was made for this gun. The kit uses MP-40 magazines. Too rare to price.

Courtesy Richard M. Kumor Sr.

PPD-1940 • *Courtesy West Point Museum, Paul Goodwin photo*

Pre-1968

Exc.	V.G.	Fair
25000	20000	17500

Pre-1986 manufacture with new receiver or re-weld

Exc.	V.G.	Fair
15000	12500	N/A

PPSh-41 Semi-Automatic

There are currently some U.S. manufacturers offering semi automatic rifle versions of the PPSh. These have 16-inch barrels and fire from a closed bolt.

Exc.	V.G.	Fair
800	650	n/a

PPS 1943 (Pistol Pulyemet Sudaev)

Chambered for the 7.62 pistol cartridge this full automatic only submachine gun is fitted with a 10-inch barrel with slotted barrel jacket and 35-round box magazine. The receiver and jacket are stamped out of one piece of sheet steel. The metal butt folds behind the ejection port. Rate of fire is about 700 rounds per minute. Weight is approximately 7.5 lbs. Introduced in 1943 as an improvement over the PPsh-41.

Courtesy Richard M. Kumor Sr.

Courtesy Richard M. Kumor Sr.

Pre-1968

Exc.	V.G.	Fair
18500	15000	12500

PPS-43 Semi Automatic

There are currently some U.S. manufacturers offering semi automatic rifle or pistol versions of the PPS-43. These rifles have 16 inch barrels and a folding stock. The pistol version has the original 10-inch barrel and has the stock permanently welded in the closed position.

Exc.	V.G.	Fair
750	600	n/a

RIFLES

Russian Pre-Cartridge Era Rifles

Made at Tula, Sestroretsk, Izhevsk.

Model 1808 Musket

A flintlock musket adopted at the beginning of the Napoleonic Wars. A copy of the French Charlliville Mle 1777 Musket. 41.5-inch barrel. Cal. .69/17.5mm. Some shorter barreled versions were also made.

Exc.	V.G.	Good	Fair	Poor
3000	2200	1800	950	550

Model 1808/44 Percussion Conversion

The Model 1808 converted to percussion. 41.5-inch barrel. Cal. .69/17.5mm.

Exc.	V.G.	Good	Fair	Poor
2800	1850	1500	750	350

Model 1845 Percussion Rifle

Cal. 69/ 17.5mm 41.5-inch barrel. The final .69 caliber gun Russia issued.

Exc.	V.G.	Good	Fair	Poor
2800	1850	1500	750	350

Model 1854 Percussion Rifle

.60 cal./15.25mm.

Exc.	V.G.	Good	Fair	Poor
2500	1850	1200	750	350

Model 1856 *Vintovka* (Rifled Musket) Percussion Rifle

A three band rifle similar to the English Pattern 1853 Enfield. It has a 33.6-inch rifled barrel cal. 15.25mm. Total length is 52.7 inches.

Exc.	V.G.	Good	Fair	Poor
2800	1950	1500	750	350

Model 1867 Krnka

A breech loading conversion of the Model 1856 percussion rifle. Chambered for the 15.24x40Rmm

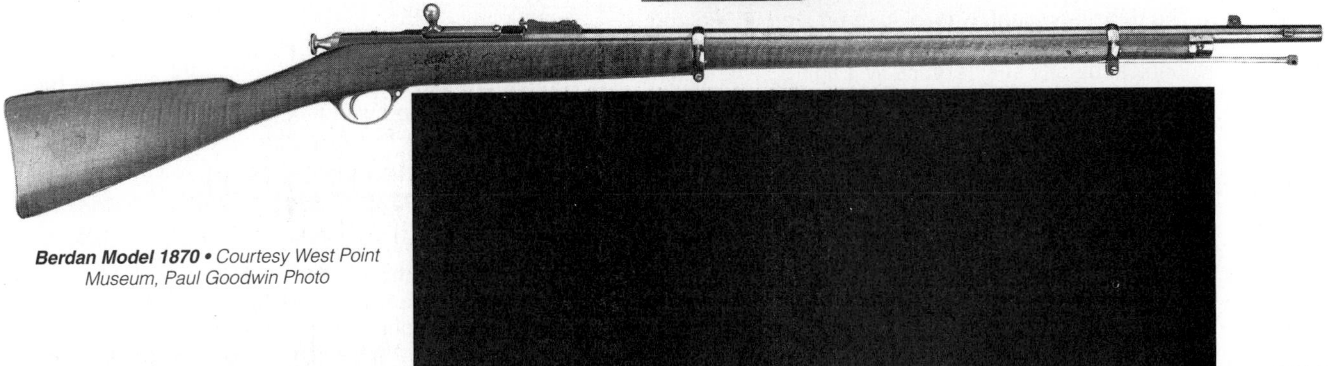

Berdan Model 1870 • Courtesy West Point Museum, Paul Goodwin Photo

Model 1891 • *Courtesy West Point Museum, Paul Goodwin Photo*

cartridge. Approximately 850,000 were issued to Russian troops.

Exc.	V.G.	Good	Fair	Poor
2500	1850	1200	750	350

BERDAN

Berdan Model 1870 (Berdan II)

After Colt had built and supplied the Russians with the first Berdan rifles, BSA of Birmingham, England, produced another 30,000. BSA, in 1871 and 1872, also provided the tooling and machinery so that the Russians could build their own version of the Berdan. A total of 3,500,000 Russian Berdans were built at the arsenals in Ishevsk, Sestroryetsk, and Tula. This single-shot model had an octagon receiver with a short bolt handle. Caliber was 10.66x57Rmm with a barrel length of 32.5". Marked with the Russian arsenal on top of the receiver ring flat. These rifles saw service as late as World War I. Some captured Russian rifles were issued to German units during WWI.

Exc.	V.G.	Good	Fair	Poor
1800	1250	900	500	300

Bayonet for Berdan II

Socket type with locking ring. 20-inch blade. Old-type Tula arsenal mark on socket. Price range 400 –175.

MOSIN-NAGANT

The Mosin-Nagant rifles were developed at Tula by Sergi Mosin. The feed system was developed by Belgian designer Leon Nagant. Russian production began in 1892 and took place at the Imperial ordnance factories at Tula, Sestroryetsk and Izhevsk. Additionally, the French arsenal at Chatelerault made over 500,000 Model 1891 rifles 1892-1895. Most Russian Mosin Nagants bear the serial number on the top of the chamber, bolt, cocking piece, floor plate and butt plate. Deduct 20% for miss matched parts.

The Mosin-Nagant was also produced in Poland, Hungary, Romania, and China. For history and technical details see Terence W. Lapin's, The Mosin-Nagant Rifle, North Cape Publications, 1998.

NOTE: During WWII the Germans captured thousands of Russian weapons. Many of these were Russian Mosin-Nagant rifles. These rifles were reissued with German code numbers to designate them as foreign equipment (Fremdgerat). Part of the code included the lower case (r) denoting that the rifle was Russian. A German marked Russian firearm might bring a 10-25 percent premium from a collector of German weapons.

Model 1891

A 7.62x54Rmm caliber bolt action rifle with a 31.6-inch barrel, 5-shot integral magazine, ladder rear sight, and a full-length stock secured by two barrel bands. Blued with a walnut stock. The Model 1891, before 1918, was fitted with an octagonal receiver ring with a heavyweight rear barrel section behind the rear sight. Pre-1908 version did not have upper handguards. Post-1908 rifles had sling swivels mounted through slots in the butt and forearm. Front sight was an unhooded blade while the rear sight was a ramp and leaf affair. Weight of these rifles was about 9.5 lbs. Used extensively in the Russo-Japanese War of 1904-1905. A total of over 9,000,000 of these rifles were built between 1892 and 1922.

Early production Model 1891 made 1892- 1908. Without handguard.

Exc.	V.G.	Good	Fair	Poor
750	550	350	175	125

WW1 era Czarist production Model 1891, made 1908-1918. With hand guard.

Exc.	V.G.	Good	Fair	Poor
650	475	300	150	100

NOTE: Some Model 1891 rifles captured by Austria were converted to take the 8x50R Austrian cartridge. These examples are extremely rare and command a $300 premium.

Communist era production 1919-1922

Exc.	V.G.	Good	Fair	Poor
650	475	300	150	100

Model 1891 Dragoon Rifle

Same as above but for a 28.75-inch barrel. Fitted with a short handguard with sling slots in buttstock and forend. Weight was reduced to about 8.5 lbs. Replaced the Model 1891 rifle as standard issue after 1920.

German military designation 253 (r)

Exc.	V.G.	Good	Fair	Poor
650	475	300	175	125

Model 1891 Cossack Rifle

This variant is almost identical to the Dragoon Rifle but instead is fitted with a tangent rear sight. The rifle was not issued with a bayonet.

German military designation 254 (r)

Exc.	V.G.	Good	Fair	Poor
650	475	300	175	125

Model 1891/30 Rifle

This is an improved version of the Model 1891 Dragoon rifle. The older octagon receiver is replaced with a cylindrical one. It has a 28.7-inch barrel with metric

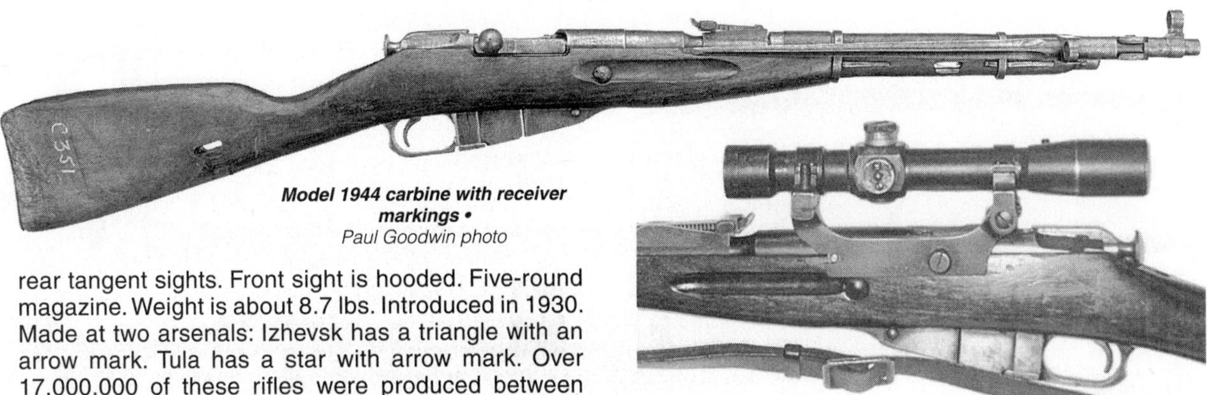

Model 1944 carbine with receiver markings • *Paul Goodwin photo*

Close-up of P.E. scope • *Courtesy Richard M. Kumor Sr.*

rear tangent sights. Front sight is hooded. Five-round magazine. Weight is about 8.7 lbs. Introduced in 1930. Made at two arsenals: Izhevsk has a triangle with an arrow mark. Tula has a star with arrow mark. Over 17,000,000 of these rifles were produced between 1930 and 1944.

1891/30 rifle with original finish

Exc.	*V.G.*	*Good*	*Fair*	*Poor*
300	225	150	100	75

NOTE: Russian Rifles marked "Made in USSR" or "USSR" were sold to Spain during their civil war in the 1930's.

Recent imports

Many 91-30s have been imported in recent years resulting in a stagnant market. Many were refinished by Russia and are usually sold with a sling, bayonet and cleaning kit.

1891/30 reworked rifle

Exc.	*V.G.*	*Good*	*Fair*	*Poor*
125	100	75	n/a	n/a

Bayonets for Mosin Nagant

A 16.9" socket bayonet. The last socket bayonet issued by any nation. The model 1891 has a locking ring. The model 91-30 has a spring catch. They used to be quite scarce but many have been recently imported with the 91-30 rifles. Price range, 1891 with locking ring, 90 – 40. Price range, 91-30 with spring catch, 50 – 20.

1891-30 Bayonet, transitional type

This is the same as the standard 91-30 socket bayonet except that it has a front sight guard. This was made for the early 91-30 rifles that had a blade sight without the round hood. Some call it a "Panshin" bayonet, named for the Russian designer. This is a scarce bayonet. Price range 250 – 125.

Model 1891/30 Sniper Rifle w/3.5 power PU scope

This is a Model 1891/30 with a scope attached to the left of the receiver, and a longer turned-down bolt handle. The serial number sometimes starts with the letters "CH". Also retains the original iron sights.

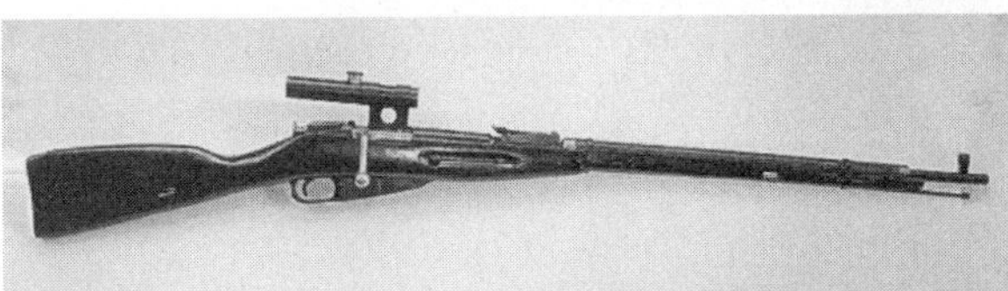

Courtesy Richard M. Kumor Sr.

Exc.	*V.G.*	*Good*	*Fair*	*Poor*
1250	900	750	400	N/A

Model 1891/30 Sniper Rifle, U.S. built with 3.5 power PU scope

There are some U.S. importers that have assembled 1891/30 rifles with post war or recent production PU scopes. If installed correctly, these are hard to spot. Look around the inletting for the scope base.

Exc.	*V.G.*	*Good*	*Fair*	*Poor*
550	450	400	N/A	N/A

Model 1891/30 Sniper Rifle w/4 power P.E. scope

This is a Model 1891/30 with a scope attached. This scope was used until about 1940. Most, but not all, of these scopes are dated 1921 to 1935 and made by Carl Zeiss in Jena, Germany.

Exc.	*V.G.*	*Good*	*Fair*	*Poor*
2250	1700	1100	850	N/A

Model 1907/1910 Carbine

As above, with a 20-inch barrel and modified sights. No bayonet fittings. Leaf sight is graduated in Russian arshins form of measurement from 400 to 2,000. Weight is 7.5 lbs. Very rare.

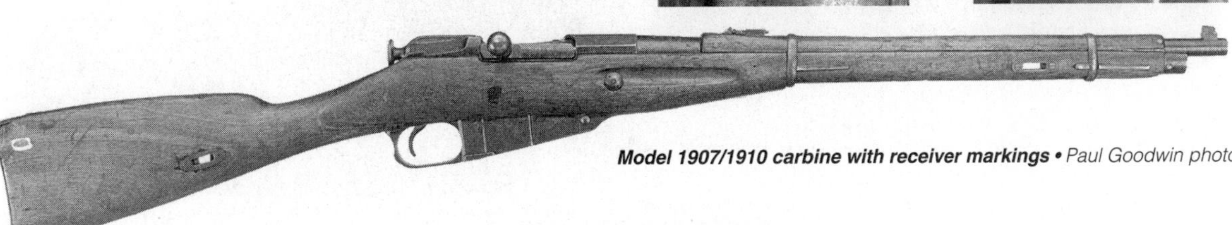

Model 1907/1910 carbine with receiver markings • *Paul Goodwin photo*

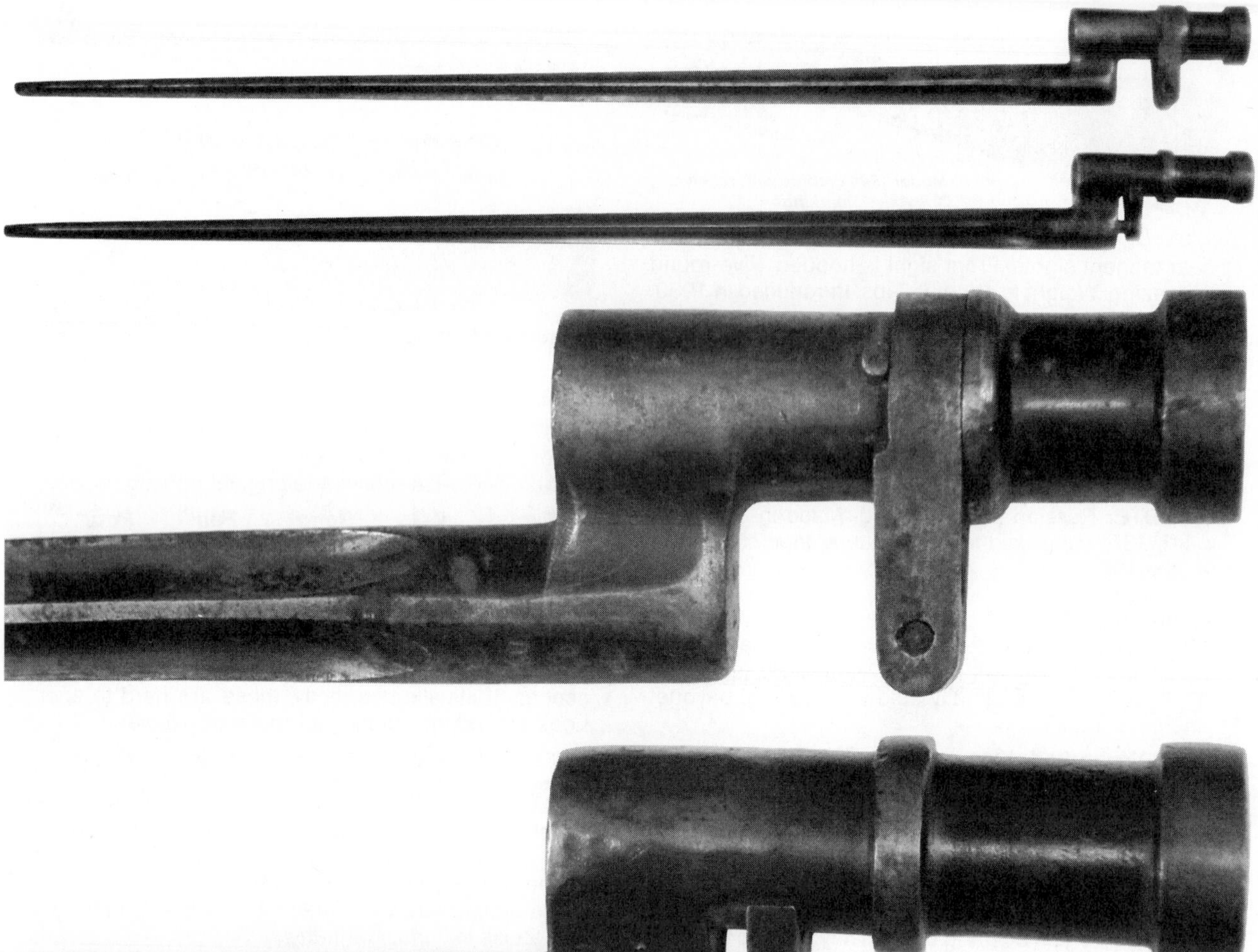

Bayonets for Mosin Nagant

1891-30 Bayonet, transitional type

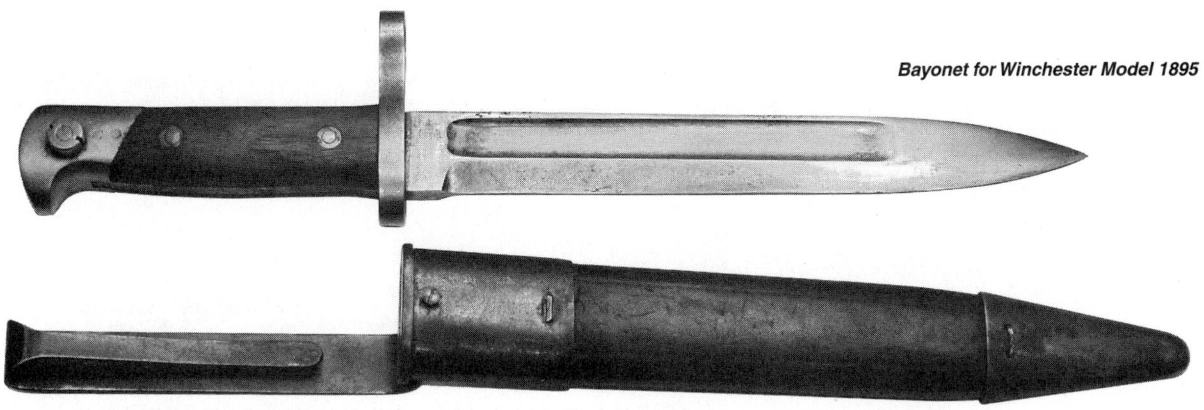
Bayonet for Winchester Model 1895

German military designation 453 (r)

Exc.	V.G.	Good	Fair	Poor
1800	1250	950	500	300

Model 1938 Carbine

This model replaced the Model 1907/1910 carbine. It is fitted with a 20-inch barrel. Rear tangent sight is in meters from 1 through 10. No bayonet fittings. Weight is about 7.5 lbs. Produced from 1939 to 1944. Very few were produced in 1945. About 2,000,000 were produced.

German military designation 454 (r)

Model 1938 Carbine, original finish.

Exc.	V.G.	Good	Fair	Poor
300	225	150	75	50

Many M1938s have been imported in recent years. Many were refinished by Russia and are usually sold with a sling and cleaning kit.

Model 1938 re-worked carbine

Exc.	V.G.	Good	Fair	Poor
175	150	125	N/A	N/A

Some Model 91/30 rifles were arsenal converted to M38 carbine configuration. These may be marked M91/59. Conversions done in Bulgaria, Czechoslovakia, and possibly the Soviet Union. Some of these rifles have been included with the recent re-works imported.

Model 91/59, a shortened 91/30

Exc.	V.G.	Good	Fair	Poor
175	150	125	N/A	N/A

Model 1944 Carbine

This was the last Mosin-Nagant produced by the U.S.S.R. . It was fitted with a folding bayonet hinged at the barrel muzzle. The barrel was about ½ inch longer than the Model 1938 carbine. Rear tangent sight is in meters from 1 through 10. Originally produced with a hardwood stock, after WWII some were fitted with a laminated stock. With the bayonet this carbine weighed about 9 lbs. This model was copied by the Chinese and designated the Type 53. This model was also made in Poland and Romania. The Russian Model 1944 Carbine was used in Afghanistan in the 1980s and by Palestinian guerrilla groups, also in the 1980s.

Model 1944 with original finish, not re-worked.

Exc.	V.G.	Good	Fair	Poor
350	250	175	100	50

Re-worked Model 1944

Many M1944s have been imported in recent years resulting in a stagnant market. Many were refinished by Russia and are usually sold with a sling and cleaning kit.

Exc.	V.G.	Good	Fair	Poor
175	150	125	N/A	N/A

Winchester

Model 1895 Russian Musket

Approximately 294,000 Model 1895 Muskets were sold to the Imperial Russian Government between 1915 and 1916. Fitted with clip guides in the top of the receiver and with bayonet. Chambered for the 7.62x54mm R cartridge. The first 15,000 Russian Muskets had 8-inch knife bayonets, and the rest were fitted with 16" bayonets. Some of these rifles went to Spain in its Civil War in 1936-1939.

Exc.	V.G.	Good	Fair	Poor
4000	2500	1000	500	250

Bayonet for Winchester Model 1895

Wood grips. Muzzle ring. 8.3- or 16-inch single edge blade. Marked "Winchester Repeatings Arms Co." inside face of cross piece beside ricasso. Steel tipped leather scabbard. Price range 500 – 250.

TOKAREV

Fyedo Vassilevich Tokarev designed not only the Tokarev rifle in 1938 and 1940, but the pistol and machine gun that bear his name as well. An experimental model, the Model 1930 was built for military trials. The Model 1935, fitted with a 17.75-inch barrel, was built for trials but was not successful. Only about 500 were produced.

M1938 Sniper • Courtesy Richard M. Kumor Sr.

Courtesy Richard M. Kumor Sr.

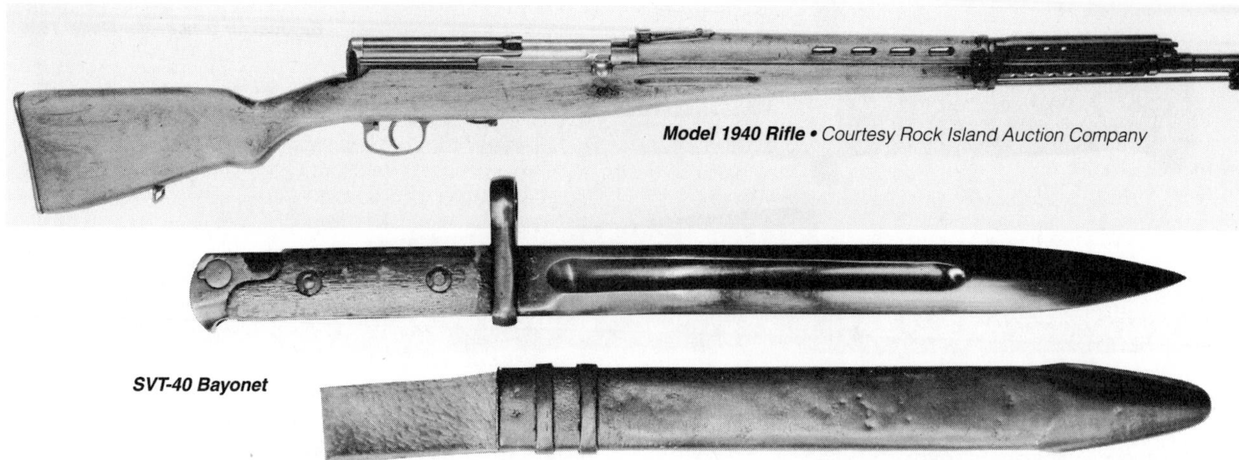

Model 1940 Rifle • Courtesy Rock Island Auction Company

SVT-40 Bayonet

M1938 Rifle (SVT)

A 7.62x54Rmm caliber gas-operated semi-automatic or select fire rifle with a 24-inch barrel with muzzle break and 10-shot magazine (15 rounds in select fire). Cleaning rod in stock. Blued with a two-piece hardwood stock extending the full-length of the rifle. Upper handguard is 3/4 length of barrel. Weight is about 8.5 lbs. Manufactured from 1938 to 1940. Approximately 150,000 of these rifles were manufactured.

Exc.	V.G.	Good	Fair	Poor
2000	1700	1200	750	500

Female Russian soldier with Tokarev rifle • Courtesy Paul S. Scarlata

Courtesy Richard M. Kumor Sr.

NOTE: Add 300 percent for sniper variation with scope.

M1940 Rifle (SVT)

An improved semi-automatic version of the M1938 with half-stock and half-length slotted handguard with a sheet metal handguard and muzzle brake. Ten-round magazine. Weight is about 8.5 lbs. Approximately 2,000,000 were produced.

SVT-40 with original finish, not a re-work

Exc.	V.G.	Good	Fair	Poor
1300	975	800 500	400	

NOTE: Add 300 percent for Sniper variation with scope.

Several thousand SVT-40s were imported in the 1990s. They had been re-worked by Soviet arsenals.

SVT-40, post war re-work

Exc.	V.G.	Good	Fair	Poor
900750	650	n/a	n/a	

CAUTION: All Tokarev SVT carbines (18.5-inch barrel) encountered with "SA" (Finnish) markings were altered to carbine configuration by their importer and have little collector value. It is believed

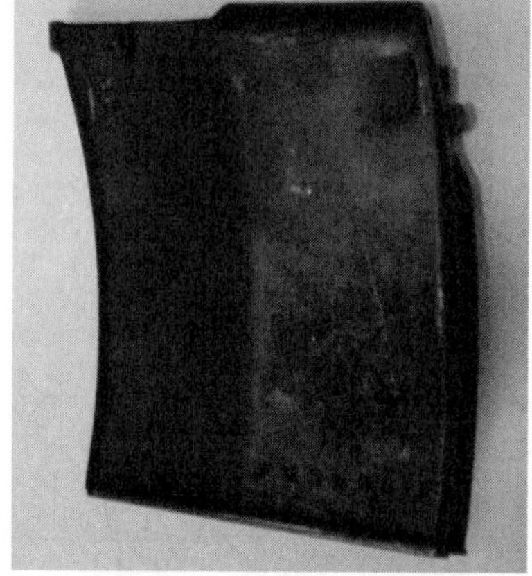

SVT-40 10-round magazine. • Price 100-50

Courtesy Richard M. Kumor Sr.

that few, perhaps 2,000, SVT40 carbines were ever made by the USSR.

Bayonet for SVT-40

Wood grips. Muzzle ring. 9.5-inch single edge blade with the cutting surface down. The earlier SVT-38 bayonet looks the same but has the cutting edge on top of the blade. Steel scabbard. Price range 300 – 175.

DRAGUNOV

Yevgeni Fyordorov Dragunov was born in 1920. He was in the Soviet army from 1939 to 1945. After the war he worked in the Izhevsk rifle factory where he designed and developed the Dragunov rifle.

SVD Sniper Rifle

This model, developed as a replacement for the Mosin-Nagant Model 1891/30 Sniper rifle, was introduced in 1963. It is chambered for the 7.62x54R cartridge. It is fitted with a 24.5-inch barrel with prong-style flash hider and has a skeleton stock with cheek rest and slotted forearm. Semi-automatic with an action closely resembling the AK series of rifles. A PSO-1 telescope sight with illuminated reticle is supplied with the rifle from the factory. This sight is fitted to each specific rifle. Magazine capacity is 10 rounds. Weight is about 9.5 lbs.

A captured Soviet 7.62x54R SVD sniper rifle, Afghanistan • *Courtesy Blake Stevens, **Kalashnikov, The Arms and the Man**, Collector Grade Publications*

Exc.	V.G.	Good	Fair	Poor
4000	3500	3000	—	—

Draganov "Tiger" carbine

A version of the SVD made for the U.S. market in the 1990s. Lacks the flash hider and has a re-designed stock. Currently banned from importation.

Exc.	V.G.	Good	Fair	Poor
2500	1750	1250	n/a	n/a

SIMONOV

Sergei Simonov was born in 1894 and later became a master gunsmith. He worked in a machine gun factory in the 1920s. He designed and developed several different firearm designs including the rifle that bears his name.

Simonov AVS-36

First built in Russia in 1936, this rifle is chambered for the 7.62x54R Soviet cartridge. Fitted with a 24.3-inch barrel with muzzle brake and a 20-round magazine. This automatic rifle has a rate of fire of 600 rounds per minute. It weighs 9.7 lbs. Production ceased in 1938.

AVS-36 • *Courtesy Steve Hill, Spotted Dog Firearms*

RUSSIA

Soviet SVD Sniper • *Courtesy West Point Museum, Paul Goodwin photo*

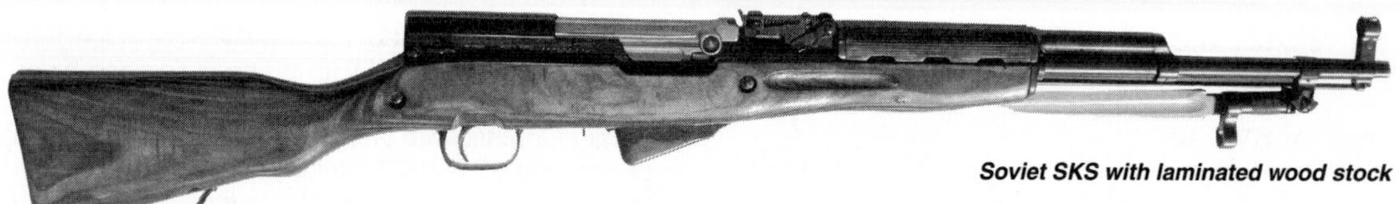
Soviet SKS with laminated wood stock

Pre-1968

Exc.	V.G.	Fair
10000	9000	8000

SKS

Introduced in 1946 this 7.62x39mm semi-automatic rifle is fitted with a 20.5-inch barrel and 10-shot fixed magazine. Blued steel finish. It has a folding blade-type bayonet that folds under the barrel and forearm. Weight is about 8.5 lbs. They were issued with hardwood or laminated stocks. Serial numbers on: receiver, bolt, carrier, top cover, magazine and stock. This rifle was the standard service arm for most Eastern bloc countries prior to the adoption of the AK-47. Approximatly 20,000 Russian SKS were imported in the early 1990s. Price is for these imports. Add 50% for non import marked SKS.

Exc.	V.G.	Good	Fair	Poor
500	425	350	225	150

Deduct 25% for mismatched parts.

NOTE: This rifle was also made in Romania, East Germany, Yugoslavia, and China. See each country for other SKS pricing.

Albanian SKS

As above but manufactured in Albania. It has features slightly different from other SKS's. The hand guard is longer, magazine box has a different shape, and the bolt handle is flat instead of round. A few thousand were imported in the 1990's.

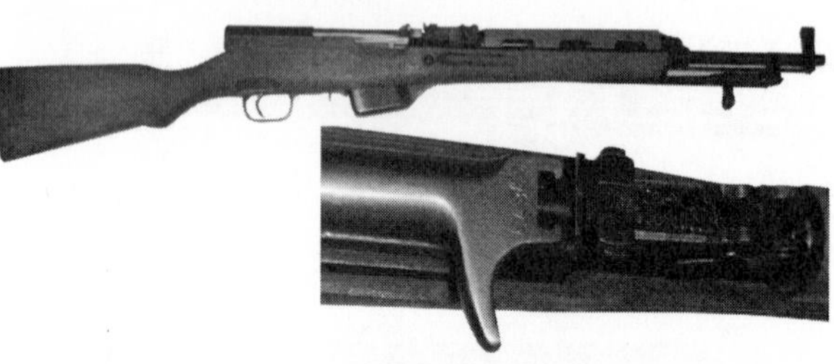

Exc.	V.G.	Good	Fair	Poor
450	375	300	200	150

KALASHNIKOV

Mikhail Kalashnikov was born in 1920. He was drafted into the Soviet army in 1939 and won the Order of the Red Star for bravery in combat during the German invasion of Russia in 1941. He became an amateur gun designer and after several unsuccessful attempts developed the AK series of rifles for the 7.62x39mm cartridge.

Avtomat Kalashnikov AK-47

Designed by Mikhail Kalashnikov and first produced in 1947, the Russian AK-47 is chambered for the 7.62x39mm cartridge and operates on a closed bolt principal. Select fire. The standard model is fitted with a 16-inch barrel and a fixed beech or birch stock. Early rifles have no bayonet fittings. Magazine capacity is 30 rounds. Rate of fire is 700 rounds per minute. Rear sight is graduated to 800 meters. The bolt and carrier are bright steel. Weight is 9.5 lbs. Markings are located on top rear of receiver. This model was the first line rifle for Warsaw Pact. The most widely used assault rifle in the world and still in extensive use throughout the world.

Pre-1968

Exc.	V.G.	Fair
33000	30000	28000

Pre-1986 manufacture with new receiver or re-weld

Exc.	V.G.	Fair
15000	13000	11000

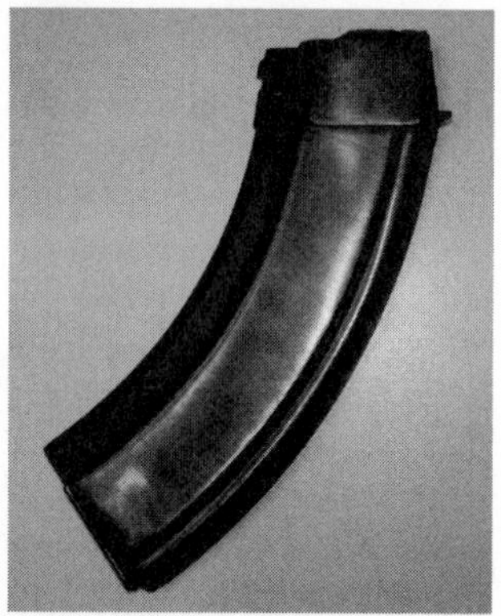
Early Russian AK-47 magazine with flat sides. • Price 50-35

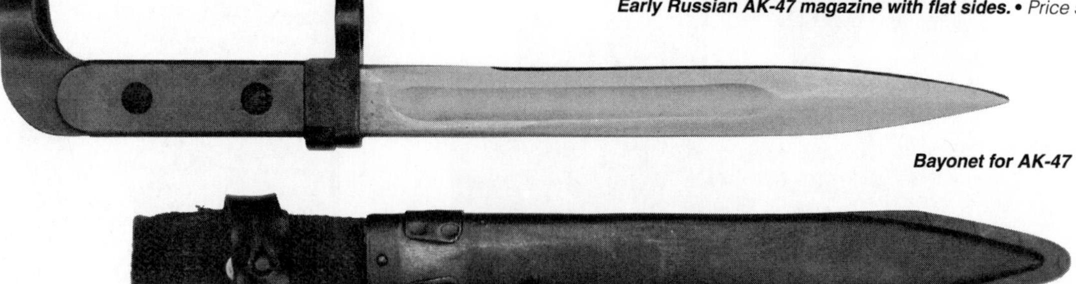
Bayonet for AK-47

RUSSIA

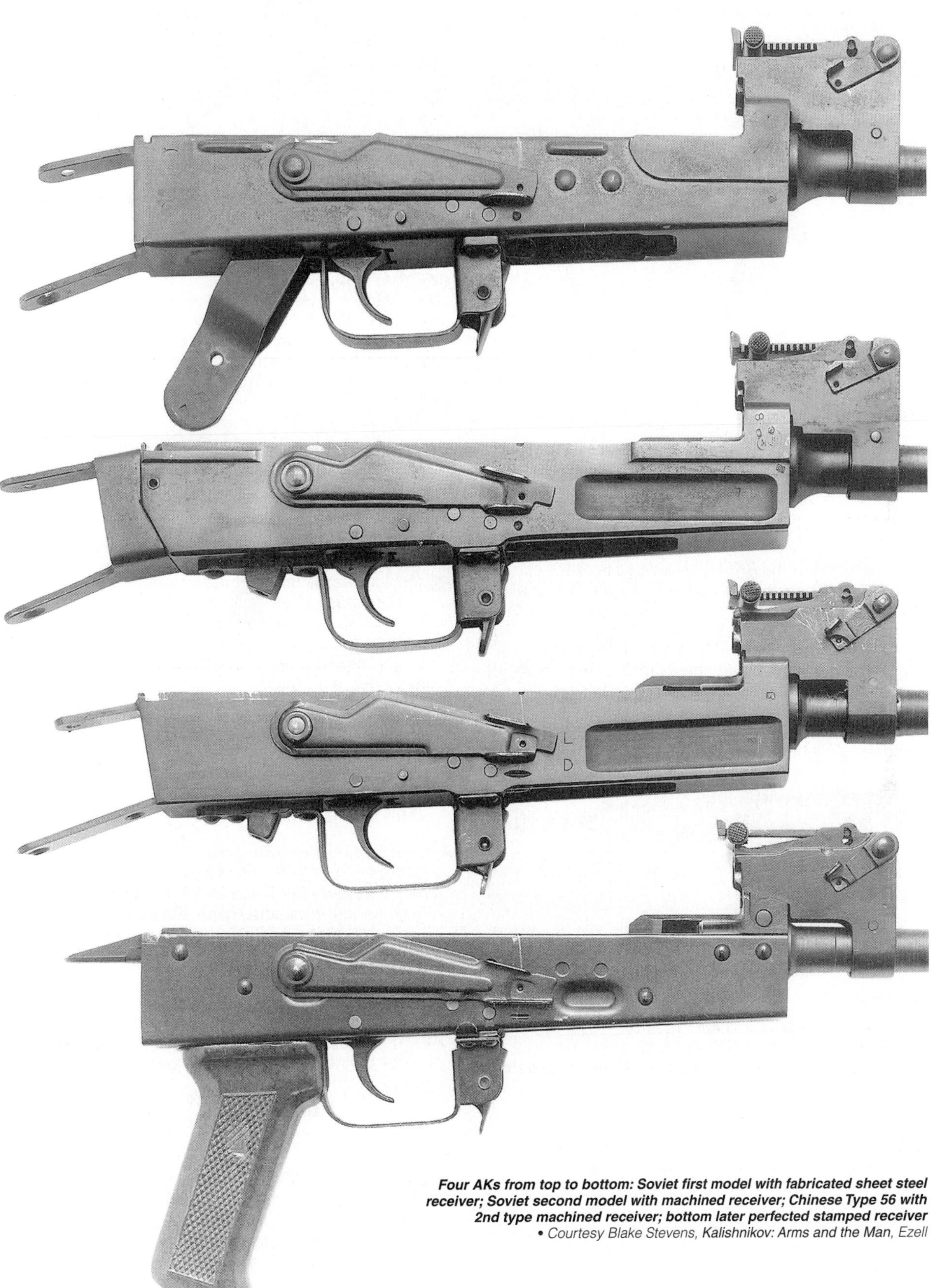

Four AKs from top to bottom: Soviet first model with fabricated sheet steel receiver; Soviet second model with machined receiver; Chinese Type 56 with 2nd type machined receiver; bottom later perfected stamped receiver
• Courtesy Blake Stevens, Kalishnikov: Arms and the Man, Ezell

RUSSIA

RUSSIA

Bayonet for AK-47

Plastic handle. 7.9-inch double edge blade. Price range 40 – 20.

AK-S

A variation of the AK rifle is the AK-S. Introduced in 1950, this rifle features a folding steel buttstock which rests under the receiver.

AK-S • *Courtesy West Point Museum, Paul Goodwin photo*

Pre-1968

Exc.	*V.G.*	*Fair*
33000	30000	28000

Pre-1986 manufacture with new receiver or re-weld

Exc.	*V.G.*	*Fair*
15000	13000	11000

AKM

This variation of the AK-47, introduced in 1959, can be characterized by a small indentation on the receiver above the magazine. Pressed steel receiver with a parkerized bolt and carrier. Laminated wood furniture and plastic grips. The forend on the AKM is a beavertail-style. The rear sight is graduated to 1,000 meters. Barrel length and rate of fire was the same as the AK-47 rifle. Several other internal production changes were made as well. Model number is located on the top rear of the receiver. Weight is approximately 8.5 lbs.

AKM, stock folded • *Courtesy private NFA collection*

Pre-1968

Exc.	*V.G.*	*Fair*
38000	36000	34000

Pre-1986 manufacture with new receiver or re-weld

Exc.	*V.G.*	*Fair*
15000	13000	11000

AKM-S

In 1960 the AKM-S was introduced which featured a steel folding buttstock as seen on the AK-S. Weight is approximately 8 lbs.

Pre-1968

Exc.	*V.G.*	*Fair*
38000	36000	34000

Pre-1986 manufacture with new receiver or re-weld

Exc.	*V.G.*	*Fair*
15000	13000	11000

AKM-S • *Courtesy West Point Museum, Paul Goodwin photo*

Bayonet for AKM

Plastic handle. 5.8-inch blade with fine saw teeth on back edge. Wire cutter stud on scabbard tip. Price range 45 – 25.

AK-74 Assault Rifle

Similar to the AK-47 but chambered for the 5.45x39mm cartridge. Magazine capacity is 30 rounds. Barrel length is 16.35 inches. Select fire with semi-auto, full auto, and 3-shot burst. Weight is about 8.9 lbs. Rate of fire is approximately 650 to 700 rounds per minute.

NOTE: There are no known original Soviet transferable examples in the U.S. Prices below are for pre-1986 conversions only using AKM receiver and original parts.

Courtesy Steve Hill and Doug McBeth, A.S.D. Firearms

Pre-1968

Exc.	*V.G.*	*Fair*
N/A	N/A	N/A

Pre-1986 manufacture with new receiver or re-weld

Exc.	*V.G.*	*Fair*
15000	13000	11000

AK-74 (Semi-automatic only)

Introduced in 1974, this rifle is chambered for a smaller caliber, the 5.45x39.5mm, than the original AK-47 series. It is fitted with a 16-inch barrel with muzzle brake and has a 30-round plastic magazine. The buttstock is wooden. Weight is approximately 8.5 lbs.

In 1974 a folding stock version was called the AKS-74, and in 1980 a reduced caliber version of the AKM-SU called the AK-74-SU was introduced. No original military AK-74s are known to exist in this country.

Exc.	*V.G.*	*Good*	*Fair*	*Poor*
N/A	—	—	—	

AK-47/AKM COPIES

These are copies of the Kalashnikov designs with only minor alterations. Because original military select fire AK assault rifles are so rare this list includes rifles that have never been imported to the U.S.

Note: for a list of semi-automatic variations of the AK available on the American market see ***Gun Digest Buyers Guide to Tactical Rifles,*** Phillip Peterson, 2010.

BULGARIA

AK-47

This is an exact copy of the Russian AK-47. Imported in the late 1980's.

Exc.	V.G.	Good	Fair	Poor
1000	850	750	n/a	n/a

CHINA

See China, Rifles.

EGYPT

See Egypt, Rifles.

EAST GERMANY

MPiK

A copy of the AK-47 without a cleaning rod.

Exc.	V.G.	Good	Fair	Poor
N/A	N/A	N/A	N/A	N/A

MpiKS

A copy of the AKS without cleaning rod.

Exc.	V.G.	Good	Fair	Poor
N/A	N/A	N/A	N/A	N/A

MPiKM

A copy of the AKM with a cleaning rod. Early models used wooden stocks while later ones used plastic. Not fitted with a muzzle compensator.

Courtesy Blake Stevens, *Kalashnikov, The Arms and the Man,* **Collector Grade Publications**

Exc.	V.G.	Good	Fair	Poor
N/A	N/A	N/A	N/A	N/A

MPiKMS

Copy of a AKMS without shaped muzzle.

Exc.	V.G.	Good	Fair	Poor
N/A	N/A	N/A	N/A	N/A

KKMPi69

A version of the MPiKM without the gas cylinder. Chambered for the .22 caliber Long Rifle cartridge and used as a training rifle.

Exc.	V.G.	Good	Fair	Poor
N/A	N/A	N/A	N/A	N/A

HUNGARY

See Hungary, Rifles.

IRAQ

Tabuk

This model is a copy of the Soviet AKM. An export version was built in 5.56mm.

Exc.	V.G.	Good	Fair	Poor
N/A	N/A	N/A	N/A	N/A

NORTH KOREA

Type 58

This model is a copy of the Soviet AK-47 solid receiver without the finger grooves on the forearm.

Courtesy Blake Stevens, *Kalashnikov, The Arms and the Man,* **Collector Grade Publications**

Pre-1968

Exc.	V.G.	Fair
20000	11000	8500

Pre-1986 manufacture with new receiver or re-weld

Exc.	V.G.	Fair
5500	5000	4500

Type 68

This is a copy of the Soviet AKM-S with lightening holes drilled into the folding butt.

Exc.	V.G.	Good	Fair	Poor
N/A	N/A	N/A	N/A	N/A

POLAND

See Poland, Rifles.

ROMANIA

See Romania, Rifles.

YUGOSLAVIA

See Yugoslavia, Rifles.

MACHINE GUNS

NOTE: Russia used early Maxim guns against the Japanese during the Russo-Japanese War of 1904-1905. The Russian military also used the Madsen Model 1902 and the Colt Model 1914 during WWI, as well as the Lewis gun.

Model 1905 Maxim

The first machine gun built in Russia at the Tula arsenal. Based on the Belgian Model 1900 Maxim with 28-inch barrel with smooth bronze water jacket.

World War I Russian machine gun crew with M1905 •
Robert G. Segel collection

Fed by a 250-round belt with a 450 rounds per minute rate of fire. Gun weighs about 40 lbs.

Pre-1968

Exc.	V.G.	Fair
35000	28000	18000

Pre-1986 manufacture with new side-plate

Exc.	V.G.	Fair
22000	18000	12500

Model 1910 Maxim (SPM)

This is a Russian-built water-cooled machine gun chambered for the 7.62x54R cartridge. Early guns use a smooth water jacket while later ones used corrugated type. In 1941 these guns were given a large water-filling cap so that ice and snow could be used in extreme conditions. Barrel length is 28 inches. Fed by a 250-round cloth belt. Rate of fire is approximately 550 rounds per minute. Gun weighs about 52 lbs. and the tripod weighs about 70 lbs.

Pre-1968

Exc.	V.G.	Fair
35000	28000	18000

Pre-1986 manufacture with new sideplate

Exc.	V.G.	Fair
22000	18000	12500

Model DP 28 (Degtyarev Pulyemet)

This was the first original Russian-designed light machine gun. Developed in 1926 by Vasily Degtyarev at the Tula Arms Factory this gun was chambered for the 7.62x54R Russian cartridge. It was an air-cooled gun with 24-inch finned barrel. It was fitted with a rifle-style stock and bipod. It was fed with a 47-round flat drum. Rate of fire is approximately 550 rounds per minute. Weight is about 20 lbs. Designed as a light infantry machine gun. Used by all Warsaw Pact countries.

This was the first in a series of DP variants. The DA is an aircraft mounted machine gun. The DT is a tank-mounted weapon with a 60-round drum. Others are the DPM, the DTM, and the RP46.

Pre-1968

Exc.	V.G.	Fair
22500	20000	17500

Pre-1986 manufacture with new receiver or re-weld

Exc.	V.G.	Fair
18000	16000	14000

DP 28 Semi-Automatic

There are currently some companies making semi automatic DP-28 for the U.S. market. Most are built on new receivers using Russian or Polish parts kits.

Exc.	V.G.	Fair
2500	1850	n/a

Russian Model 1905 in caliber 7.62mm produced at Tula Arsenal •
Courtesy private NFA collection, Paul Goodwin photo

Maxim M1910 • Courtesy private NFA collection, Paul Goodwin photo

RUSSIA

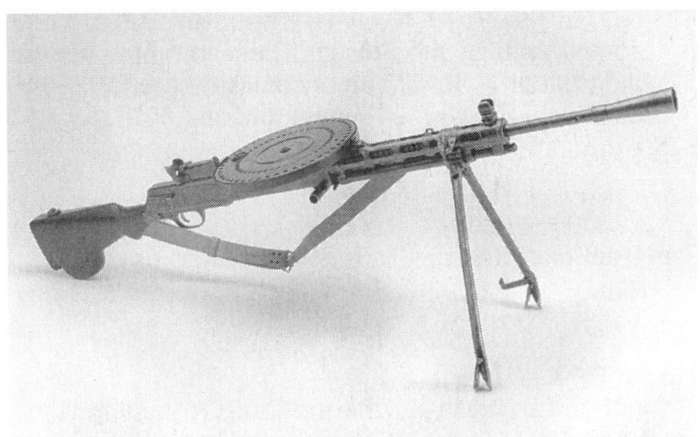
Model DP 28 • Private NFA collection • Gary Gelson photo

Model 1939 DS Gun

A medium machine version of the DP 28. Two rates for fire: 550 rounds per minute and 1100 rounds per minute. Fed by a 250-round cloth belt. Weight is about 26 lbs. Limited production. No known examples in the U.S.

Pre-1968

Exc.	V.G.	Fair
N/A	N/A	N/A

Model DPM

Introduced in 1944, this is a modification of the DP machine gun by placing the return spring in a tube

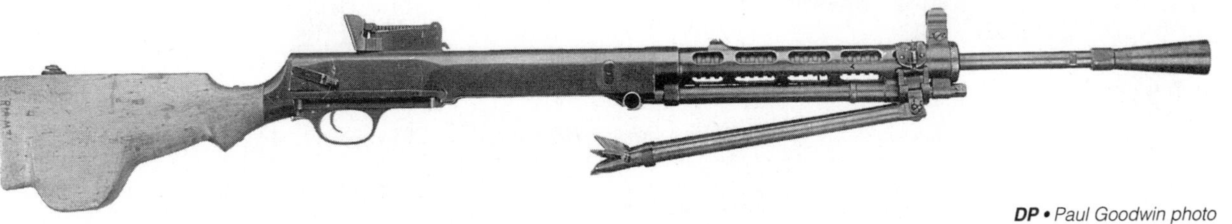
DP • Paul Goodwin photo

Model RPK • *Courtesy West Point Museum, Paul Goodwin photo*

RUSSIA

at the rear of the receiver, sticking out over the butt. A pistol grip was added to facilitate firing. The bipod was attached to the barrel casing. No grip safety but a safety lever in its place. Barrel length is 24 inches and the drum capacity is 47 rounds. Rate of fire is 550 rounds per minute. Weight is approximately 27 lbs.

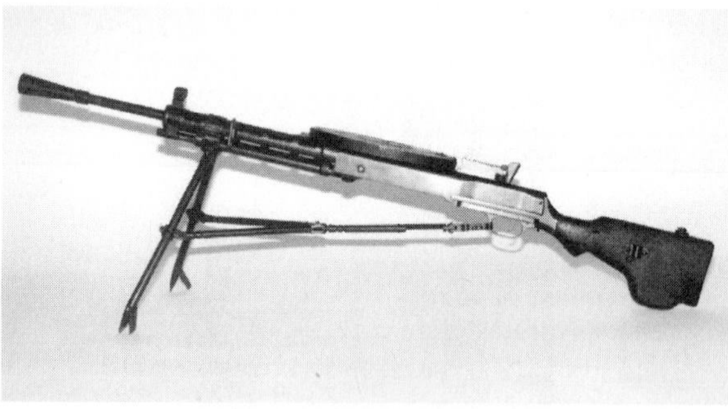

Russian DP with unusual bipod triangulation • *Courtesy Robert E. Naess*

Pre-1968

Exc.	***V.G.***	***Fair***
22500	20000	17500

Pre-1986 manufacture with new receiver or re-weld

Exc.	***V.G.***	***Fair***
10000	8000	6000

Model RP-46

This gun is a version of the DP series of machine guns and is a metallic belt or magazine fed 7.62mm caliber. It was designed to be used as a company-size machine gun and is fitted with a 24-inch quick change heavy barrel. Introduced in 1946. Weight is about 29 lbs. Rate of fire is approximately 650 rounds per minute. The North Koreans use this same gun designated as the Type 64.

NOTE: Many RP-46s were fitted with DP or DPM components by the Soviets. These components are dated prior to 1946. The prices listed are for RP-46 guns with RP-46 (1946) components.

Pre-1968

Exc.	***V.G.***	***Fair***
22000	20000	18000

Pre-1986 manufacture with new receiver or re-weld

Exc.	***V.G.***	***Fair***
19000	17000	16000

Model RPK

Introduced around 1960 this model is the light machine gun equivalent to the AKM assault rifle. It is fitted with a 23-inch non-quick change barrel. It uses either a 75-round drum magazine or a 40-round box magazine. It is also capable of using the 30-round magazine of the AK and AKM rifles. This model replaced the RPD as the squad automatic weapon (SAW) of the Soviet army.

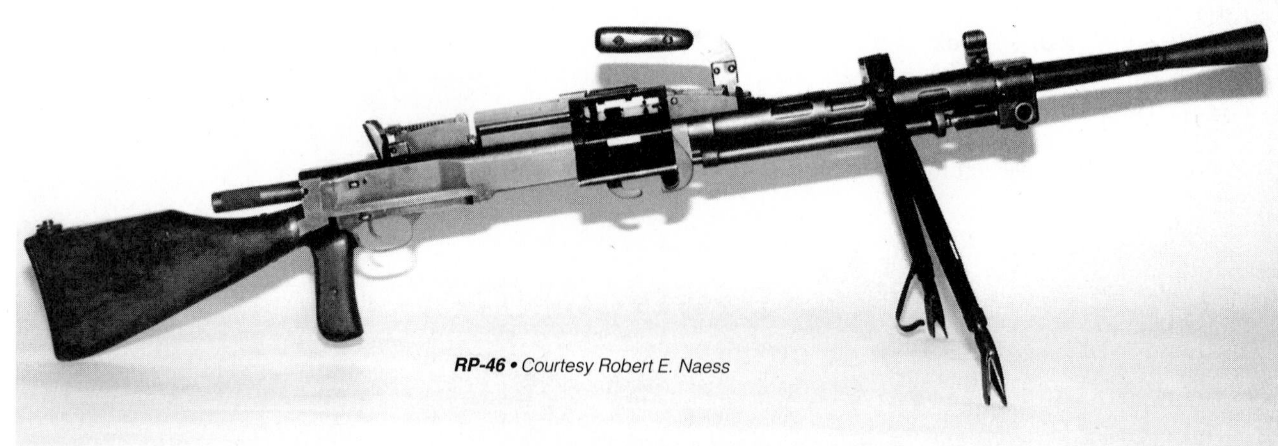

RP-46 • *Courtesy Robert E. Naess*

Pre-1968

Exc.	V.G.	Fair
25000	23000	21000

Pre-1986 manufacture with new receiver or re-weld

Exc.	V.G.	Fair
18000	16000	14000

Model RPKS

This is the Model RPK with a side folding stock. All other dimensions and specifications are the same.

Pre-1968

Exc.	V.G.	Fair
25000	23000	21000

Pre-1986 manufacture with new receiver or re-weld

Exc.	V.G.	Fair
18000	16000	14000

Model RPK-74

Similar to the RPK but chambered for the 5.45x39mm cartridge. Select fire with 4 positions: safe, semi-auto, full auto, and 3-shot burst. Barrel length is 23.6 inches. Magazine capacity is 45-round box magazine. Also uses a 30-round magazine. Weight is about 12 lbs. and rate of fire is approximately 650 to 700 rounds per minute.

NOTE: There are no known original Soviet transferable examples in this country. Prices listed are for conversion using Russian AKM receiver and Russian parts.

Courtesy Steve Hill and Doug McBeth, A.S.D. Firearms

Pre-1968

Exc.	V.G.	Fair
N/A	N/A	N/A

Pre-1986 manufacture with new receiver or re-weld

Exc.	V.G.	Fair
19500	18000	N/A

Model PK/PKS (Pulemet Kalashnikova/Stankovy)

This is a general purpose air-cooled machine gun that is chambered for the 7.62mm Soviet cartridge. When this gun is mounted on a bipod it is designated the Model PK; when mounted on a tripod it is called a Model PKS. The operating system of this gun is the same as the AK series except turned upside down. It is fitted with a 26-inch quick change barrel and can be fed by a 100-, 200-, or 250-round metal belt. The rate of fire is about 700 rounds per minute. Weight is approximately 20 lbs. Introduced in 1963.

The PK, when mounted on tanks, is designated the PKT. The PKM is an improved version of the PK with lighter components. The PKMS is a PKM mounted on a tripod. The PKB is a PKM without butt, bipod, pistol grip, or trigger. Instead, a spade grip with trigger is fitted to the receiver.

Pre-1968

Exc.	V.G.	Fair
N/A	N/A	N/A

Pre-1986 manufacture with new receiver or re-weld

Exc.	V.G.	Fair
—	38000	—

Model DShK M38-M1938/46

Introduced in 1938 this is a heavy air-cooled gas operated machine gun chambered for the 12.7x108mm cartridge. The feed system on the early guns (M1938) uses a rotary mechanism while the later versions (M1939/46) use a conventional lever system. The barrel is 42 inches and finned with muzzle brake. Fed by a 50-round metal belt either from the right or left side. The rate of fire is about 550 rounds per minute. Weight of the gun is approximately 75 lbs. The mount can weigh 250 lbs. This was the primary heavy machine gun in Korea in 1950-1953, and it was used both as a ground gun and as an anti-aircraft gun. The gun is mounted on a wheeled carriage or a heavy tripod.

NOTE: Many M1938/46 guns were converted from M1938 models. It is extremely difficult to determine when the conversion was done and by whom. Proceed with caution.

Pre-1968 (Very Rare)

Exc.	V.G.	Fair
—	45000	42500

Pre-1986 manufacture with new receiver or re-weld

Exc.	V.G.	Fair
—	40000	—

Courtesy Steve Hill, Spotted Dog Firearms

Degtyarev RPD

This is a belt-fed machine gun chambered for the 7.62x39mm cartridge. It has a rate of fire of 700 rounds per minute and is fitted with a 100-round disintegrating belt carried in a drum. It has a 20.5" barrel and weighs about 15.6 lbs. This weapon was at one time the standard squad automatic weapon in the Soviet bloc. It was produced in large numbers and is still in use today in Southeast Asia and Africa.

Pre-1968 (Very Rare)

Exc.	V.G.	Fair
36000	35000	34000

Pre-1986 manufacture with new receiver or re-weld

Exc.	V.G.	Fair
35000	33000	31500

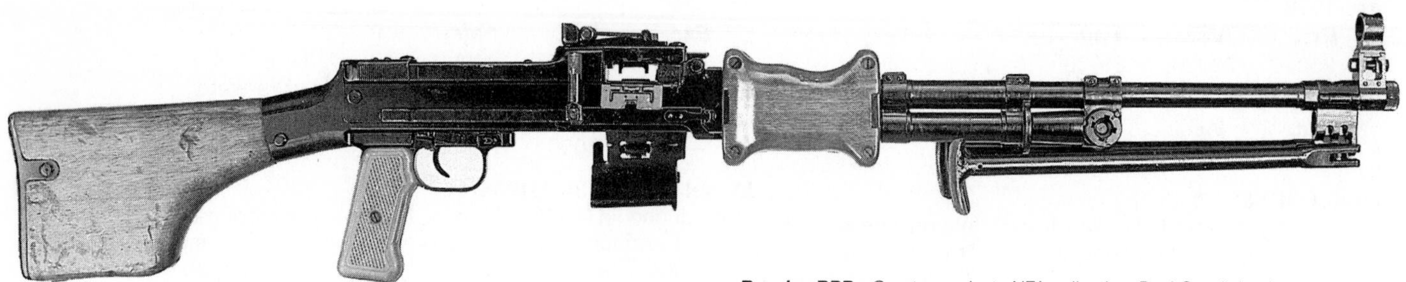
Russian RPD • *Courtesy private NFA collection, Paul Goodwin photo*

Goryunov SG43

This model was the standard Soviet machine gun during WWII. Chambered for the 7.62x54R Soviet cartridge, it is fitted with a 28-inch smooth barrel and is fed with a 250-round metal link belt. Rate of fire is 650 rounds per minute. Its weight is about 30 lbs. Marked on the top of the receiver. In production from 1943 to 1955.

Pre-1968

Exc.	V.G.	Fair
25000	23000	21000

Pre-1986 manufacture with new receiver or re-weld

Exc.	V.G.	Fair
20000	18000	16000

Model SGM

A modified version of the SG43 with fluted barrel and cocking handle on right side of receiver. Dust covers on both feed and ejection ports. Barrel length is 28 inches. Weight is approximately 30 lbs. Fed by 250-round metal link belt. There are variants of the SG43 which are the SGMT, a tank mounted version with electric solenoid. The SGMB is similar to the SGM but with dust covers over feed and ejection ports.

Pre-1968 (Very Rare)

Exc.	V.G.	Fair
25000	23000	21000

RUSSIA

SG 43 • *Courtesy private NFA collection, Paul Goodwin photo*

The Spanish State, forming the greater part of the Iberian Peninsula of southwest Europe, has an area of 195,988 sq. mi. (504,714 sq. km.) and a population of 39.4 million including the Balearic and the Canary Islands. Capital: Madrid. The economy is based on agriculture, industry and tourism. Machinery, fruit, vegetables and chemicals are exported.

Discontent against the mother country increased after 1808 as colonists faced new imperialist policies from Napoleon or Spanish liberals. The revolutionary movement was established which resulted in the eventual independence of the Vice-royalties of New Spain, New Granada and Rio de la Plata within 2 decades.

The doomed republic was trapped in a tug-of-war between the right and left wing forces inevitably resulting in the Spanish Civil War of 1936-38. The leftist Republicans were supported by the U.S.S.R. and the International Brigade, which consisted of mainly communist volunteers from all over the western world. The right wing Nationalists were supported by the Fascist governments of Italy and Germany. Under the leadership of Gen. Francisco Franco, the Nationalists emerged victorious and immediately embarked on a program of reconstruction and neutrality as dictated by the new "Caudillo"(leader) Franco.

The monarchy was reconstituted in 1947 under the regency of General Francisco Franco; the king designate to be crowned after Franco's death. Franco died on Nov. 20, 1975. Two days after his passing, Juan Carlos de Borbon, the grandson of Alfonso XIII, was proclaimed King of Spain.

HANDGUNS

NOTE: Officers in the Spanish military provided their own sidearms during the later half of the 19th century and into the early 20th century. The Spanish government provided guidelines for purchase and many Spanish officers purchased Smith & Wesson and Merwin & Hulbert revolvers. In 1884 the Spanish government directed its military officers corps to purchase the Smith & Wesson .44 Double Action Top Break built by Orbea y Compania of Eibar, Spain. It was designated the Model 1884. There were a number of Spanish gun makers building revolvers during the late 19th century, and many of these handguns were used by the Spanish military but were not marked as such. During WWI Spain provided a number of handguns to Britain, France, and other countries due to the shortage of military sidearms in those countries. We only touch on the more significant models.

IT IS ALSO IMPORTANT TO NOTE THAT VARIOUS SPANISH MANUFACTURERS SOLD ALMOST ONE MILLION COPIES OF THE FN/BROWNING MODEL 1903 TO THE FRENCH DURING WWI.

BIBLIOGRAPHICAL NOTE: For additional historical information, technical data, and photos see Leonardo Antaris, ***Astra Automatic Pistols***, Colorado, 1998.

Bergmann-Bayard Model 1908

Built by the Belgium firm of Pieper SA from 1908 to about 1914. Caliber is 9x23mm Bergman-Bayard with 4-inch barrel. Many foreign contracts were built in this model with Spain being one of the largest. See also Denmark.

Courtesy Rock Island Auction Company

Exc.	*V.G.*	*Good*	*Fair*	*Poor*
1250	950	700	400	200

CAMPO GIRO

Model 1910

Similar to the above, in 9mm Largo. Tested, but not adopted, by the Spanish army.

Exc.	*V.G.*	*Good*	*Fair*	*Poor*
1200	800	650	500	450

Model 1913

An improved version of the above.

Model 1913 *• Courtesy James Rankin*

Exc.	*V.G.*	*Good*	*Fair*	*Poor*
950	750	650	500	450

Model 1913/16

An improved version of the above.

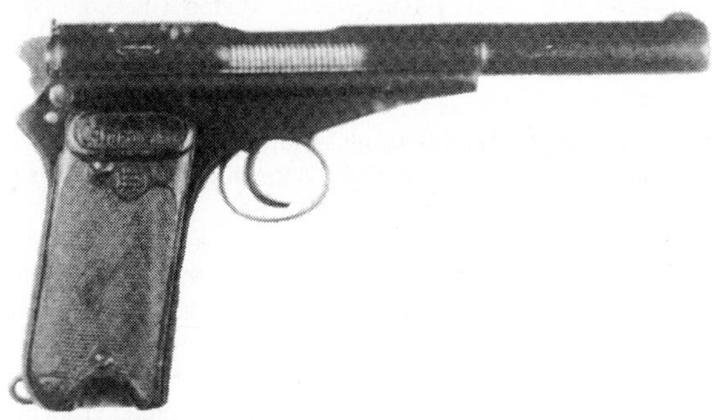

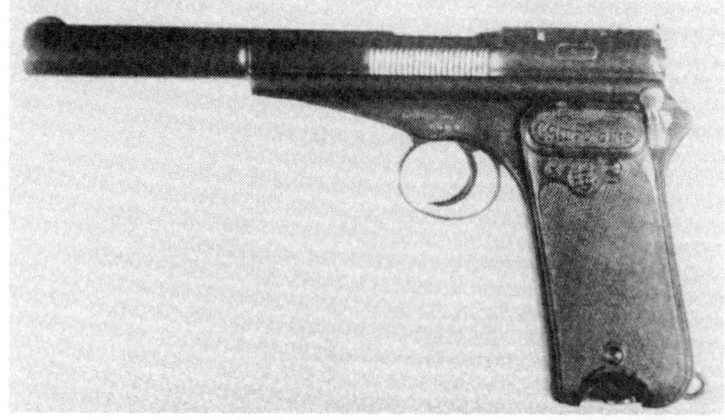

Courtesy James Rankin

Exc.	V.G.	Good	Fair	Poor
650	450	375	300	200

ASTRA-UNCETA SA

During WWII the German army and air force purchased a number of Astra 400 and 600 pistols. They were of excellent quality.

Astra 400 or Model 1921

A 9x23 Bergmann caliber semi-automatic pistol with a 6-inch barrel. Blued with black plastic grips. This model was adopted for use by the Spanish army. Approximately 106,000 were made prior to 1946.

Exc.	V.G.	Good	Fair	Poor
400	275	200	100	75

6,000 Astra 400 pistols were delivered to the German army in 1941. The generally accepted serial number range of the German Astra 400 is 92,850-98,850. Most were not marked with any German acceptance stamps. Beware any Astra 400 with waffenamt markings.

Courtesy Orvel Reichert

German-Issue Astra 400

Exc.	V.G.	Good	Fair	Poor
550	400	275	150	100

Astra 400 Copies (Ascaso, R.E.)

During the Spanish Civil War, the Republican forces were unable to procure enough handguns from established weapons factories as these were in Nationalists' hands. The Republicans built their own factories to produce copies of the Spanish army's Model 1921 Astra 400. These are exact copies except for the markings.

Exc.	V.G.	Good	Fair	Poor
500	350	200	100	75

Astra 300

As above, in 7.65mm or 9mm short. Used during WWII by German forces. Between 1941 and 1944 some 63,000 were produced in 9mm Kurz, and about 22,000 were produced in 7.65mm. The SN of German purchased Astra 300' begins at 540,300 but there are several blocks of numbers rather than a single series. The highest known is in the 620,000 range. Some

9mm short pistols were marked with a WaA251 waffen mark. Others were not. Almost no 7.65mm Astra 300s will be found with Nazi markings. Exercise caution when examining a Nazi marked 7.65mm Model 300.

In total there were approximately 171,000 Astra Model 300s manufactured 1923-1946.

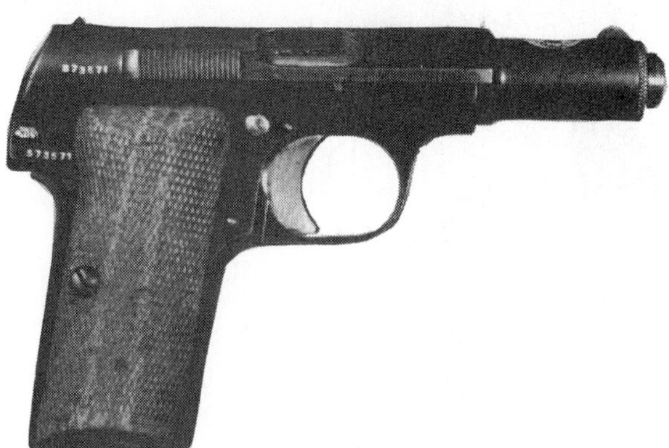

Exc.	*V.G.*	*Good*	*Fair*	*Poor*
550	400	275	150	100

NOTE: Nazi proofed add 25 percent.

Holster for Astra 300

Similar to German holsters for small automatics. Price range: 150 – 50

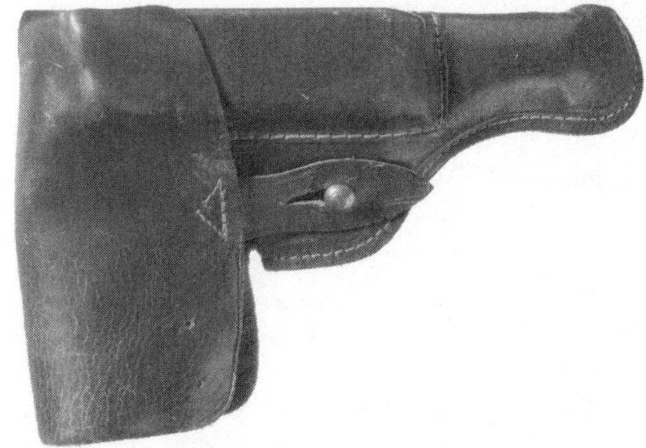

Astra 600

Similar to the Model 400, but in 9mm Parabellum. In 1943 and 1944 approximately 10,500 were manufactured for the German military. SN range 1-10,500. Some of these World War II guns will have Nazi waffenamt or proof marks, others do not.

Exc.	*V.G.*	*Good*	*Fair*	*Poor*
600	475	350	200	150

Post WWII Astra 600, SN above 10,500

An additional 49,000 were made through 1945 and commercially sold. Many went to the West German police in the early 1950s and these were later imported to the U.S.

Exc.	*V.G.*	*Good*	*Fair*	*Poor*
400	325	250	150	100

ASTRA 900 SERIES

The Astra 900 series of pistols were copied from the Mauser Model 1896, but while similar in appearance to the Mauser, the Astra 900 series is mechanically quite different. Many consider the Astra 900 series as good as, or better than, their German equivalent.

Astra Model 900

Courtesy Tom Nelson, *The World's Machine Pistol and Submachine Guns, Vol. IIA,* ***Ironside International Publishers***

Introduced in 1928 this is similar in appearance to the Mauser C96 pistol. Fitted with a 5.5-inch barrel chambered for the 7.63mm cartridge and fitted with a ring hammer. Ten-round box magazine with charger loading. Weight is about 40 oz. Production discontinued in 1955. Between 1928 and 1944 almost 21,000 were manufactured. Some of these pistols (about 1,000) were purchased by the German military in France in 1943. No military acceptance marks but can be identified by serial number (see Still, Axis Pistols). Serial numbers 32788 through 33774 were used by the German army during WWII. These examples will bring a 50 percent premium.

NOTE: A large number of the Astra 900 series were sold to China. Some were imported with the Chinese surplus in the 1990's. They are frequently found in fair to poor condition. They have a small import stamp on the underside of the barrel. Some of these are also marked with Chinese characters.

Exc.	V.G.	Good	Fair	Poor
1800	1250	750	500	250

Astra Model 901

Introduced in 1928, this is similar to the Model 900 (5.5-inch barrel) but with select fire capability. Fixed 10-round magazine. Many of these pistols were sold to China in the 1930s. Rate of fire is about 900 rounds per minute. Weight is about 44 oz. Only about 1,600 of these pistols were produced. Exceedingly rare. Only a tiny number of these pistols are transferable, perhaps fewer than five.

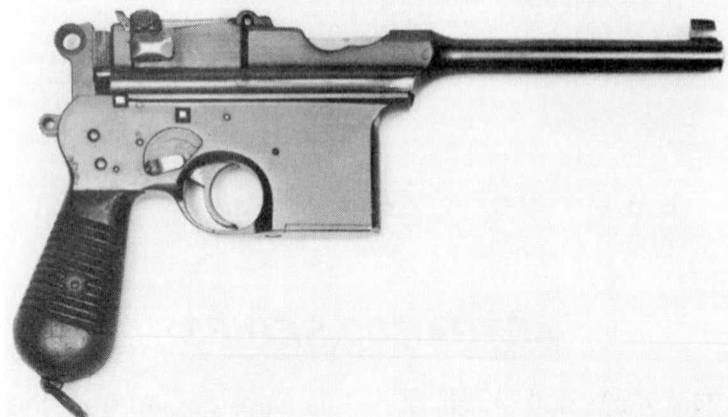

Courtesy Tom Nelson, *The World's Machine Pistol and Submachine Guns, Vol. IIA,* ***Ironside International Publishers***

SPAIN

Pre-1968

Exc.	V.G.	Fair
9500	8000	7500

Astra Model 902

Same as above but with 7-inch barrel. Some went to China with various military units in the 1930s, but most remained in Spain. Weight is approximately 53 oz. About 7,000 of these pistols were built. Very rare in this country for transferable examples. Perhaps fewer than 10 known.

Courtesy Tom Nelson, *The World's Machine Pistol and Submachine Guns, Vol. IIA,* ***Ironside International Publishers***

Pre-1968

Exc.	V.G.	Fair
9500	8000	7500

Astra 903/903E

This is a detachable 10- or 20-round magazine pistol developed in 1932. Fitted with a 6.25-inch barrel. Select fire. Some of these pistols were sold to China and others went to the German army in France in 1941 and 1942. No German acceptance proofs, but can be identified by serial number (see Still). Some 3,000 of this model were produced. It is estimated that fewer than 15 of these pistols are transferable in the U.S.

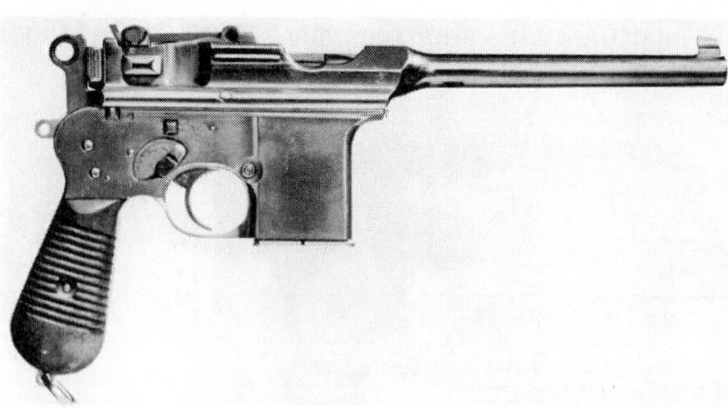

Courtesy Tom Nelson, *The World's Machine Pistol and Submachine Guns, Vol. IIA,* ***Ironside International Publishers***

Pre-1968

Exc.	V.G.	Fair
10000	9000	8500

Astra Model 904 (Model F)

Similar to the other 900 series machine pistols but chambered for the 9mm Largo cartridge and fitted with a rate reducer that reduces the rate of fire from 900 rounds per minute to approximately 350 rounds per minute. Magazine is 10- or 20-round detachable design. The Model 904 was first produced in 1933 and was the prototype of the Model F. Only 9 Model 904s were built. About 1,100 Model F pistols were issued, most of which went to the Spanish Guardia Civil. Perhaps fewer than 10 of these pistols are known to exist on a transferable basis in the U.S.

Astra Model F • *Courtesy Chuck Karwan*

Pre-1968

Exc.	V.G.	Fair
12500	11000	10000

NOTE: Add $800-400 for an original Astra stock/holster with any 900 series pistol. Astra stocks are difficult to locate. Watch out for Chinese made copies. They are made from the same light colored wood found on Chinese SKS and AK rifles. Add $200-100 for a Chinese made stock/holster.

ROYAL

Royal machine pistols were manufactured by Beistegui Hermanos in Eibar, Spain. These were the first machine pistols made in Spain, starting in 1927. These pistols were used extensively by the Chinese during their civil wars in the 1930s and against the Japanese during WWII.

Royal MM31 (1st Model)

First produced in 1927. Chambered for the 7.63mm cartridge. The pistol was capable of selective fire and semi-automatic fire, as well as full automatic fire. Magazine capacity was 10 or 20 rounds in a fixed box magazine. Barrel lengths were 5.5 inches with some made in 6.3 inches and 7 inches. Rear tangent sight. Rate of fire was about 850 rounds per minute. Production stopped on the first model in 1929 with approximately 23,000 pistols built. Extremely rare.

Pre-1968

Exc.	*V.G.*	*Fair*
30000	25000	20000

Royal MM31 (2nd Model)

This model has three variations. All were chambered for the 7.63mm cartridge and all were select fire models. All had a cycle rate of fire of about 850 rounds per minute. Early versions had either a 5.5- or 7-inch barrel. The last version was fitted with a 5.5-inch barrel only. The 1st variation had a fixed 10-round magazine while the 2nd variation had a 20-round fixed magazine. The 3rd version had a detachable 10-, 20-, or 30-round magazine. All variations were marked "MM31" or "ROYAL." Very rare.

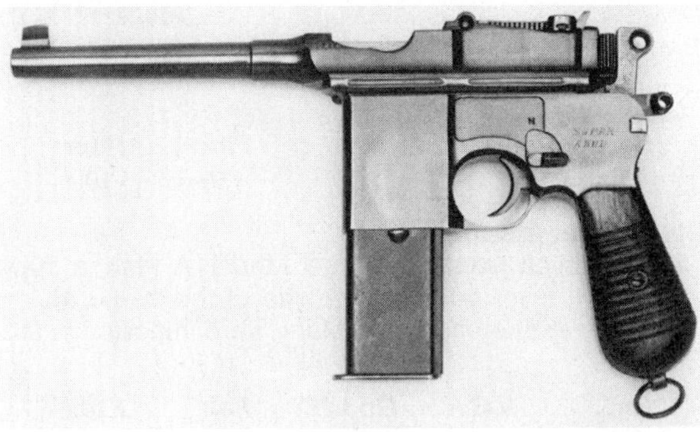

Courtesy Tom Nelson,** The World's Machine Pistol and Submachine Guns, Vol. IIA, **Ironside International Publishers

Pre-1968

Exc.	*V.G.*	*Fair*
9500	8500	8000

Super Azul

This was the 4th variation of the MM31, introduced in 1931, often referred to as the Super Azul or New Model. Chambered for the 7.63mm cartridge, it was also offered in 9mm Bergmann and .38 Colt Super Automatic. Select fire. Fitted with a 5.5" barrel and a detachable magazine with a capacity of 10, 20, or 30 rounds. Magazine will interchange with German Mauser Schnellfeuer pistol. Rate of fire of about 850 rounds per minute. Production ceased in 1936 with the outbreak of the Spanish Civil War.

Pre-1968

Exc.	*V.G.*	*Fair*
9500	8500	8000

Royal MM34

Chambered for the 7.63mm cartridge and fitted with a 7-inch barrel. Fixed magazine capacity of 10 or 20 rounds. Fitted with a rate reducer in the grip. Select fire with full auto fire at various adjustable rates. Marked "MM34" on right side of frame. Extremely rare.

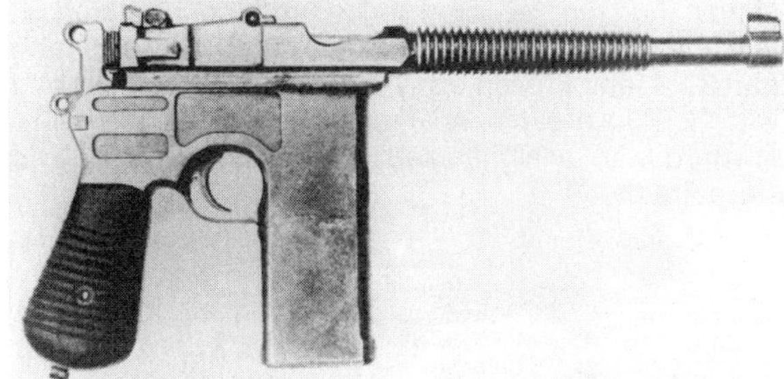

Courtesy Tom Nelson,** The World's Machine Pistol and Submachine Guns, Vol. IIA, **Ironside International Publishers

Pre-1968

Exc.	*V.G.*	*Fair*
9500	8500	8000

LLAMA

Model IX

Chambered for the 7.65mm Para, 9mm Largo, or .45 ACP, this model has a locked breech with no grip safety. Built from 1936 to 1954.

Exc.	*V.G.*	*Good*	*Fair*	*Poor*
400	275	200	150	100

Model IX-A

This version of the Model IX is fitted with a grip safety. Current production models are chambered for the .45 ACP only. Weighs about 30 oz. with 5" barrel.

Exc.	*V.G.*	*Good*	*Fair*	*Poor*
325	225	150	125	100

ECHEVERRIA, STAR-BONIFACIO SA

NOTE: These pistols are stamped with a letter code to denote year built: For 1938 the letter "N," up to 1945 the letter "P."

Bibliographical Note: For photos, production data, and in-depth history, see ***Star Firearms*** by Leonardo M. Antaris. This book is a must for the Spanish handgun collector. The book can be obtained from Firac Publications, 1230 East Rusholme St. #107, Davenport, IA 52803.

Model 1914

Similar to the Model 1908, with a 5-inch barrel and larger grips that have the Star name molded into them. This model was the first to have the six-pointed star surrounded by rays of light (that became the Star trademark) stamped on its slide.

The French Army purchased approximately 20,000 Model 1914s for use during World War I. These

Courtesy Leonardo M. Antaris,** Star Firearms, **with permission

pistols had coarse checkering and no name inset into the grips. Later pistols were fitted with 5.5-inch barrels. Many French army magazines were stamped with "BE" in a circle. All French military pistols were finished with a highly dark blue finish. Small parts were fire blue.

Courtesy Leonardo M. Antaris, *Star Firearms,* **with permission**

Exc.	*V.G.*	*Good*	*Fair*	*Poor*
600	450	300	200	150

Model CO

First produced in 1929 and later dropped from production during the Spanish Civil War, this model was produced again in 1941. About 600 of these pistols were sold to the German military during 1941 and 1942. Chambered for the 6.35mm cartridge and fitted with a 3.3-inch barrel. This model stayed in production until 1956. Prices are for military examples.

Exc.	*V.G.*	*Good*	*Fair*	*Poor*
500	400	325	250	150

Courtesy Leonardo M. Antaris, *Star Firearms,* **with permission**

Star Model A

A modification of the Model 1919, chambered for the 7.63 Mauser, 9mm Largo, and 9mm Luger (scarce), as well as the rarely seen 9mm Steyr. Barrel length is 5 inches. The slide is similar in appearance to the 1911 Colt, and the spur hammer has a small hole in it. Early models had no grip safety, but later production added this feature. Some models are slotted for addition of a shoulder stock. This model was popular with the Spanish Civil Guard as well as the Spanish Air Force (stamped with air force logo).

Courtesy Leonardo M. Antaris, *Star Firearms,* **with permission**

Exc.	*V.G.*	*Good*	*Fair*	*Poor*
400	300	200	150	100

Star Model A Super

An improved version of the Model A with a new takedown lever on the right side of the frame and a loaded chamber indicator. Many were imported in the 1990's.

Exc.	*V.G.*	*Good*	*Fair*	*Poor*
450	325	225	175	125

Courtesy Leonardo M. Antaris, *Star Firearms,* **with permission**

Star Model M (MD)

A select fire version of the Model A. Most were chambered for 9x23mm cartridge while some were chambered for the .45 ACP cartridge. This pistol was built during the 1930s. Some examples were sold to Nicaragua and Argentina. Rate of fire is about 800 rounds per minute. The selector switch is located on the right side of the slide. Several thousand were produced.

Star Model M • *Courtesy Chuck Karwan*

Pre-1968

Exc.	V.G.	Fair
9500	8000	6500

Star Model B

Similar to the Model A. It is chambered for 9mm Parabellum and has a spur hammer with no hole. This model was introduced in 1928. Approximately 20,000 pistols were sold to the German army and about 6,000 to the German navy. These military pistols are stamped with German military acceptance stamps. About 15,000 Model Bs were sold to Bulgaria during 1943 and 1944. Also used by the German Police and the Republic of South Africa.

Courtesy Leonardo M. Antaris, *Star Firearms,* **with permission**

German marked Star Model B

Exc.	V.G.	Good	Fair	Poor
600	475	375	175	125

Model B without German markings

Exc.	V.G.	Good	Fair	Poor
400	250	200	175	125

Star Model B Super

Introduced in 1946, this model features a new takedown system with the lever on the right side of the frame. A loaded chamber indicator was also added. Production ended in 1983. Adopted by the Spanish army in 1946. Many were imported to the U.S. in the 1990's.

Courtesy Leonardo M. Antaris, *Star Firearms,* **with permission**

Exc.	V.G.	Good	Fair	Poor
450	325	250	200	100

Star Model 1941 S

A small frame pistol chambered for 9mm short (.380). This model was purchased by the Spanish air force and is stamped on the right side of the frame with the air force seal. Most of these air force pistols were produced between 1945 and 1947, with a total production of about 9,100 pistols. A small batch was imported here to the U.S. in the early 1990's. A large number of Model S pistols were also sold to police agencies in Spain and elsewhere. The balance of production was sold commercially. Interarms imported commercial Star S pistols in the 1980s and 1990s. Prices listed below are for Spanish air force marked examples. Deduct 50 percent for commercial pistols.

Spanish Air Force Star Model S Pistol • *Courtesy Richard M. Kumor Sr.*

Exc.	V.G.	Good	Fair	Poor
600	400	300	200	100

Star Model SI

Chambered for the 7.65mm cartridge, this pistol was ordered by the Portuguese navy beginning in 1946. Between 1946 and 1948 a total of about 4,900 pistols were ordered for the Portuguese. Also, about 300 pistols were sold to the Chilean navy in 1964. A number of these pistols were also sold to police agencies in Spain and Europe. The balance of the Model SI production was commercial.

Exc.	V.G.	Good	Fair	Poor
450	350	275	200	100

Star Model BM

A steel-framed 9mm that is styled after the Colt 1911. It has an 8-shot magazine and a 4-inch barrel. It was available either blued or chrome-plated. Previously imported by Interarms. Some European police issue Star BM's were imported in the 1990s.

Exc.	V.G.	Good	Fair	Poor
300	250	200	150	125

SPAIN

SUBMACHINE GUNS

The Spanish made a number of submachine guns, both domestic designs and copies of foreign guns. The Spanish MP28 II was a copy of the Bergmann MP28 II in 9mm Bergmann caliber. The Model 1941/44 was a copy of the German Erma. Star made a number of submachine guns in the 1930s that were used on a limited basis in the Spanish Civil War. These were the S135, the RU35, and the TN35, all chambered for the 9x23 Largo cartridge. The first two of these models had adjustable rates of fire and the last, the TN35, had a rate of fire of about 700 rounds per minute. However, these guns were never standard issue in the Spanish army.

Star Z-45

This design is based on the German MP40 but with the cocking handle on the left side. It was fitted with an 8" barrel that was easily removable and covered by a perforated barrel jacket. The gun has a two-stage trigger: pull slightly for single shots and pull more for full automatic fire. Magazine is a 30-round box type. Gun has a rate of fire of about 450 rounds per minute. Weight is approximately 8.5 lbs. Introduced into service in 1944. This weapon is supplied with either a fixed wood stock or folding metal one. The Z-45 was the standard submachine gun of the Spanish army and was sold to Chile, Cuba, Portugal, and Saudi Arabia.

Pre-1968

Exc.	V.G.	Fair
17500	15500	14000

Star Z-62

This select-fire submachine gun was introduced in 1960 and is chambered for the 9mm Largo or 9mm Parabellum cartridge. It has an 8-inch barrel with perforated barrel jacket. Folding metal buttstock. The box magazine has a 20-, 30-, or 40-round capacity. Rate of fire is about 550 rounds per minute. Weight is approximately 6.5 lbs. This gun was issued both to the Spanish army and the Guardia Civil. Marked "STAR EIBAR ESPANA MODEL Z-62" with the serial number

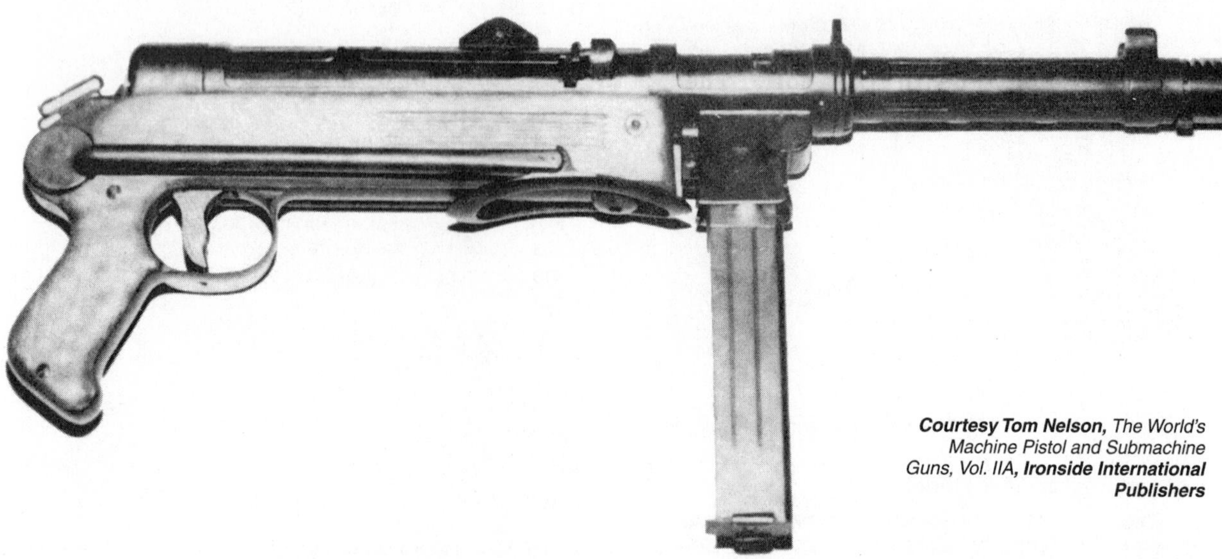

Courtesy Tom Nelson, *The World's Machine Pistol and Submachine Guns, Vol. IIA,* **Ironside International Publishers**

on the left side of the magazine housing. Produced until about 1970.

Pre-1968

Exc.	*V.G.*	*Fair*
17000	15000	13000

Star Z-70

Introduced into the Spanish army in 1971, this select-fire submachine gun is chambered for the 9x19mm cartridge, and is considered an improved version of the Z-62 with new trigger mechanism. It is fitted with an 8-inch barrel and has a rate of fire of 550 rounds per minute. Choice of 20-, 30-, or 40-round magazines. Folding metal stock. Weight is about 6.3 lbs. Built by Star Bonifacio Echeverria in Eibar, Spain. No longer in production. Used mainly by the Spanish armed forces.

Courtesy private NFA collection

Pre-1968

Exc.	*V.G.*	*Fair*
N/A	N/A	N/A

RIFLES

PEABODY

Spanish Rifle (1869)

Chambered for the .43 Spanish centerfire cartridge and fitted with a 33-inch barrel. Full stock with two barrel bands. Blued barrel and case hardened furniture. About 10,000 rifles were produced for the Spanish government.

Exc.	*V.G.*	*Good*	*Fair*	*Poor*
2000	1750	1250	600	400

REMINGTON ROLLING BLOCK

Model 1870 Rifle

This is the standard Remington rolling block single-shot rifle with a 35-inch barrel. Chambered for the 11.15x57R Spanish Remington cartridge. Full stocked with three barrel bands. Weight is about 9.25 lbs. Upper tang marked Remington.

Exc.	*V.G.*	*Good*	*Fair*	*Poor*
1250	850	600	450	250

Model 1870 Carbine

Same as the rifle but with 27-inch barrel and full stock with two barrel bands. Weight is about 8.75 lbs. Made at Oviedo Armoury from 1871 to about 1889.

Exc.	*V.G.*	*Good*	*Fair*	*Poor*
1250	1000	750	450	250

Model 1870 Short Rifle

Similar to the Model 1870 pattern but with 32-inch barrel. Weight is about 8.75 lbs. Manufactured at Oviedo.

Exc.	*V.G.*	*Good*	*Fair*	*Poor*
1000	800	500	350	250

Model 1871 Infantry Rifle

Fitted with a 37-inch barrel and chambered for the 11.15x57R Spanish Remington cartridge. Full stock with three barrel bands. Bayonet fittings. Weight is about 9 lbs. Built at Oviedo and Placencia armories.

Exc.	*V.G.*	*Good*	*Fair*	*Poor*
1050	900	550	350	250

Model 1871 Short Rifle

As above but with 28-inch barrel with full stock and two barrel bands. Weight is about 8.75 lbs. Produced at Placencia Armoury.

Exc.	*V.G.*	*Good*	*Fair*	*Poor*
1050	900	650	450	250

Model 1871 Cavalry Carbine

As above but with 23-inch barrel and half stock with sling swivels and sling bar on left side of stock. Weight is about 7.25 lbs.

Exc.	*V.G.*	*Good*	*Fair*	*Poor*
1250	1000	750	450	250

Model 1871 Artillery Carbine

As above but full stocked with two barrel bands and bayonet fitting.

Exc.	*V.G.*	*Good*	*Fair*	*Poor*
1250	1000	750	450	250

Model 1889 Dragoon Carbine

This model was a short version of the Model 1871 rifle with full stock, two barrel bands, and no bayonet fittings. Barrel length is 31.5 inches. Weight is about 8.75 lbs.

Exc.	*V.G.*	*Good*	*Fair*	*Poor*
1250	1000	750	450	250

MAUSER

M1891 Rifle

Based on the Turkish Model 1890 rifle with full stock and no handguard. Chambered for 7.65x53mm cartridge with barrel length of 29 inches. Exposed 5-round box magazine. Weight is about 9 lbs.

Exc.	*V.G.*	*Good*	*Fair*	*Poor*
1250	850	600	300	200

M1892 Rifle

Similar to the Model 1891 but with internal charger loaded magazine, improved extractor, and removable magazine floor plate. Chambered for 7.65x53mm cartridge. Half-length handguard. Barrel length is 29 inches. Weight is about 9 lbs.

Exc.	*V.G.*	*Good*	*Fair*	*Poor*
1250	850	600	300	200

M1892 Carbine

Same action as the Model 1891 rifle but full stock with nose cap, bent bolt handle, sling bar, and saddle ring. Chambered for 7.65x53mm cartridge. Barrel length is 17.5 inches. Weight is about 7.5 lbs. Built by Loewe.

Bayonet for 1893 Mauser

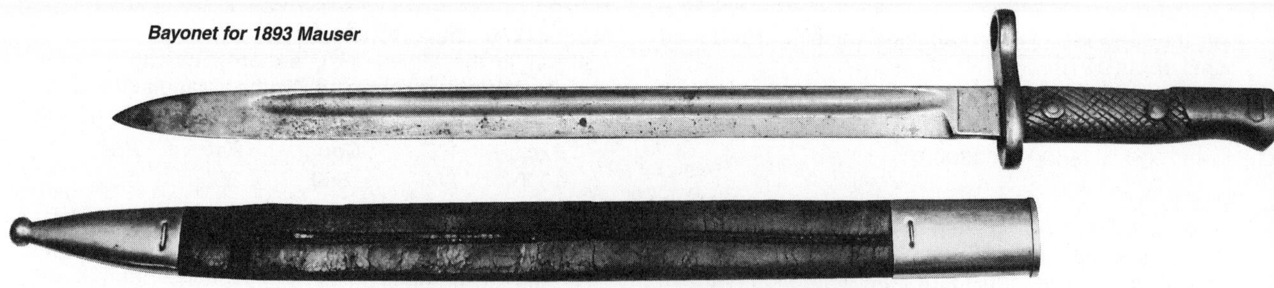

Exc.	V.G.	Good	Fair	Poor
1250	850	600	300	200

M1893 Rifle

Built by Ludwig Lowe, DWM, and Fabrique National. Later made at Oveido, Spain. This model is considered to be the "Spanish Mauser." Chambered for the 7x57mm cartridge and fitted with a 29-inch barrel. Buttstock has straight grip. A charger loading magazine is concealed in the buttstock. The receiver has a charger loading guide in the receiver bridge. Weight is about 8.5 lbs. Serial numbers usually appear on the receiver, bolt, bolt sleeve, safety, trigger guard, and floor plate.

SPAIN

Model 1893 Rifle, made by Lowe, DWM or FN.

Exc.	V.G.	Good	Fair	Poor
750	475	325	150	100

Model 1893 Rifle, made at Oveido, Spain

Courtesy private NFA collection

Exc.	V.G.	Good	Fair	Poor
500	375	250	125	75

M1893 Short Rifle

This is a short version of the Model 1893 rifle with a 21.5-inch barrel. Fitted with bent bolt and half-length handguard. Weight is about 8 lbs.

Exc.	V.G.	Good	Fair	Poor
450	300	225	150	100

NOTE: many Spanish 1893 short rifles have been imported that have no markings except for a serial number. These were re-worked during the Spanish civil war.

M1893 Short Rifle without markings

Exc.	V.G.	Good	Fair	Poor
225	175	150	100	75

Bayonet for 1893 Mauser

Wood handle. Barrel ring. 16.1-inch single edge blade. Usually marked "Artilleria Nacional Toledo" Leather scabbard with steel fittings. There is also a shorter version with a 9.75" blade. Price range 70 – 25.

M1895 Carbine

A full stocked carbine with 17.5-inch barrel. Made by Lowe or Oveido. No bayonet mount. Saddle ring behind trigger guard. Weight is about 7 lbs.

Exc.	V.G.	Good	Fair	Poor
800	575	400	175	125

M1916 Short Rifle 7x57mm

This model was built by Fabrica de Armas in Oviedo, Spain, from 1916 to 1951. A shortened version of the Model 1893 rifle with 21.75-inch barrel and chambered for the 7x57mm cartridge. Rear sight graduated to 2,000 meters. Almost full stock with upper handguard. Sight protectors on front sight. Spanish crest on receiver ring. Some were reworked during the Spanish civil war and had the crest removed. Deduct 50 percent for rifle without Spanish crest. Weight is about 8 lbs.

Exc.	V.G.	Good	Fair	Poor
400	300	275	175	125

M1916 Short Rifle 7.62mm

Many of the 1916 rifles were converted to the 7.62mm CETME cartridge. As these use a Mauser M1893 action, some experts consider these unsafe to fire with .308 Winchester or 7.62 NATO ammunition.

Exc.	V.G.	Good	Fair	Poor
250	175	150	125	100

M1916 Carbine

Produced at the Oviedo arsenal. Fitted with a 17-inch barrel chambered for the 7x57mm cartridge. Straight grip stock with 3/4-length stock and upper handguard. No bayonet fittings. Bent bolt handle. Weight is about 6.75 lbs.

Exc.	V.G.	Good	Fair	Poor
550	325	250	150	125

M1933 Standard Model Short Rifle

This rifle is chambered for the 7x57mm cartridge and fitted with a 22-inch barrel. Straight grip stock with upper handguard. Tangent leaf rear sight graduated to 2,000 meters. Marked with Mauser banner over the date of manufacture on receiver. Weight is about 8.2 lbs.

Exc.	V.G.	Good	Fair	Poor
900	750	575	250	150

M1943 Short Rifle

Uses a Mauser 1898 type action. This model replaced the Model 1916 Short Rifle. Chambered for the 7.92x57mm cartridge and fitted with a 23.6-inch barrel. Stock is 3/4-length with pistol grip. Straight bolt handle. Tangent leaf rear sight graduated to 2,000 meters. Weight is about 8.5 lbs. Marked with Spanish crest on receiver ring.

NOTE: This model was made for the Spanish army and air force. The army model has a bayonet lug while the air force model does not.

Exc.	V.G.	Good	Fair	Poor
300	225	175	125	100

FR 7 Special Purpose Rifle (Training/Reserve)

An arsenal-converted (1950s) Model 1916 short rifle with 18.5-inch CETME barrel. Upper wooden handguard. Chambered for the 7.62x51 CETME cartridge. Weight is about 7.5 lbs.

Exc.	V.G.	Good	Fair	Poor
300	200	150	125	100

FR 8 Special Purpose Rifle (Training/Reserve)

Arsenal-converted Model 43 in the same configuration as the FR 7. Has a Mauser M1898 action.

Exc.	V.G.	Good	Fair	Poor
400	325	275	200	150

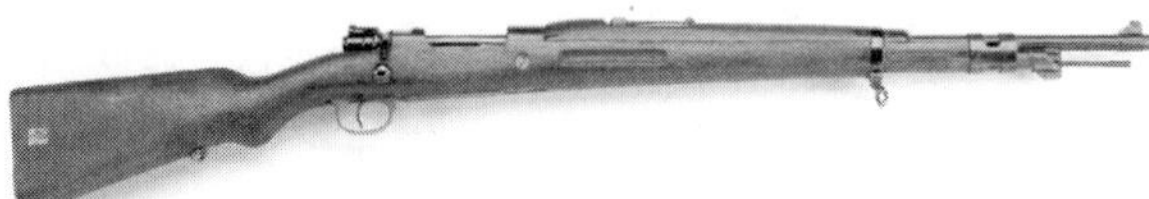

Model 1943 Short Rifle • *Courtesy Cherry's Fine Guns*

CETME

CETME Autoloading Rifle (Sport)

A 7.62mm/.308 caliber semi-automatic rifle with a fluted chamber, a 17.74-inch barrel, an aperture rear sight, and a 20-round detachable magazine. Black with a military-style wood stock. It is similar in appearance to the H&K 91 assault rifle. A few hundred were imported to the U.S. in the 1960's by Mars Equipment Co.

Exc.	V.G.	Good	Fair	Poor
3000	2500	2000	—	—

CETME Semi-Automatic Rifle, U.S. Manufacture

A 7.62mm/.308 caliber semi-automatic rifle with a fluted chamber, a 17.74-inch barrel, an aperture rear sight, and a 20-round detachable magazine. Black with a military-style wood stock. It is similar in appearance to the H&K 91 assault rifle. Several companies have manufactured these using Spanish CETME parts on

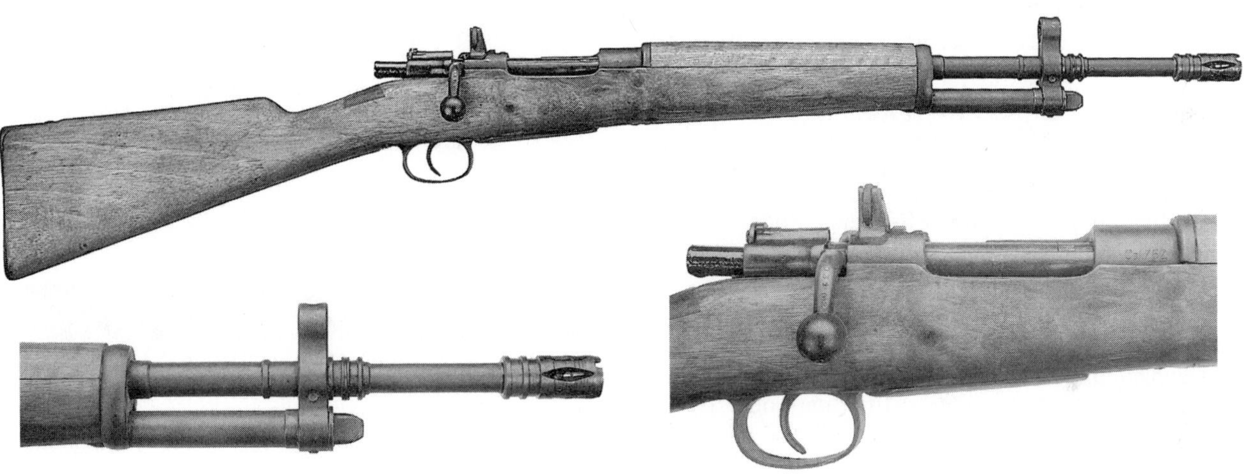

FR 7 • *Courtesy private collection, Paul Goodwin photo*

FR 8 • *Courtesy private collection, Paul Goodwin photo*

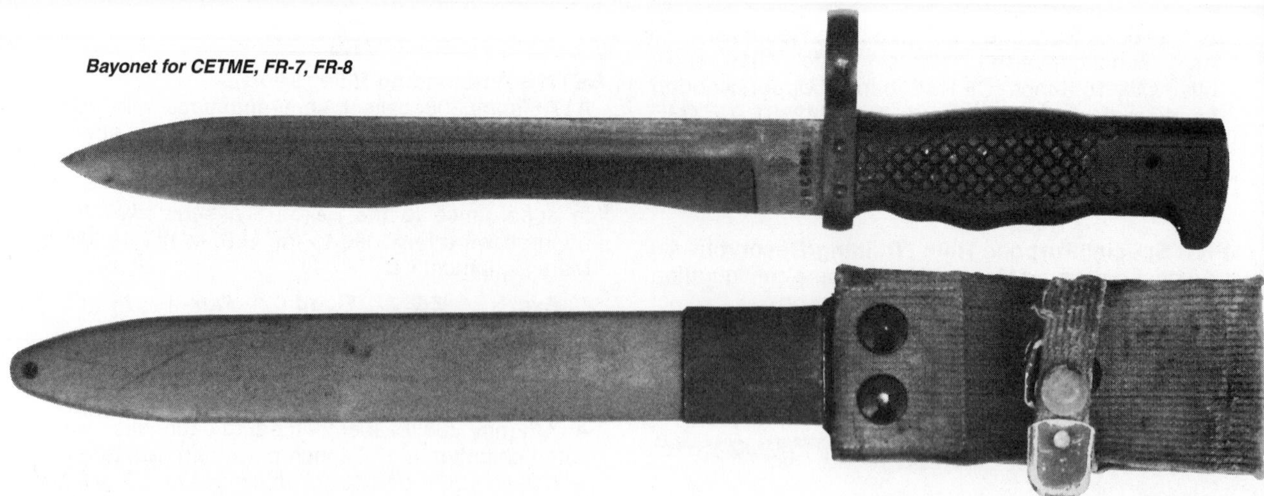
Bayonet for CETME, FR-7, FR-8

new U.S. made receivers. There were quality issues with some makers and buyers should research these before purchasing.

Exc.	V.G.	Good	Fair	Poor
550	450	350	—	—

SPAIN

Bayonet for CETME, FR-7, FR-8

Plastic handle. 8-7/8-inch bolo style blade. Made by Santa Barbara. Fits the CETME rifle but requires an adaptor that inserts in the tube above the barrel. Also fits the Mauser FR-7 and FR-8 rifles. Price range 15 – 35.

Model 58

Introduced in 1958 and manufactured by Centro de Estudios de Materials Especiales (CETME), this Spanish-made rifle is similar to the HK G3 rifle and is chambered for the 7.62x51mm cartridge. This is a select-fire weapon with a rate of fire of about 600 rounds per minute. The bipod, when retracted, acts as a metal forend. Barrel length is 17-inch. Tangent rear sight. Weight is approximately 11 lbs.

Pre-1968

Exc.	V.G.	Fair
6000	5000	4500

Santa Barbara CETME Model L

First produced in 1984, this 5.56x45mm select fire rifle was adopted by the Spanish army. It is fitted with a 15.6-inch barrel and 30-round magazine. It also has a fixed stock. Rate of fire is 650 rounds per minute. Weight is about 7.5 lbs. A short barrel (12.5") carbine version is known as the Model LC. Still in service.

Pre-1968

Exc.	V.G.	Fair
N/A	N/A	N/A

MACHINE GUNS

In 1907, the Spanish used the 7mm Hotchkiss machine gun and later the Model 1914, also in 7mm. The Spanish armed forces also adopted the Madsen Model 1902 and Model 1922 guns. During the Spanish Civil War, large numbers of foreign machine guns were sent to Spain, including the Soviet Maxim Tokarev, Soviet DP guns, Czech VZ26, VZ30, and ZB53 as well as other German and Italian machine guns. At the present time the Spanish army uses the MG 42/59 machine gun.

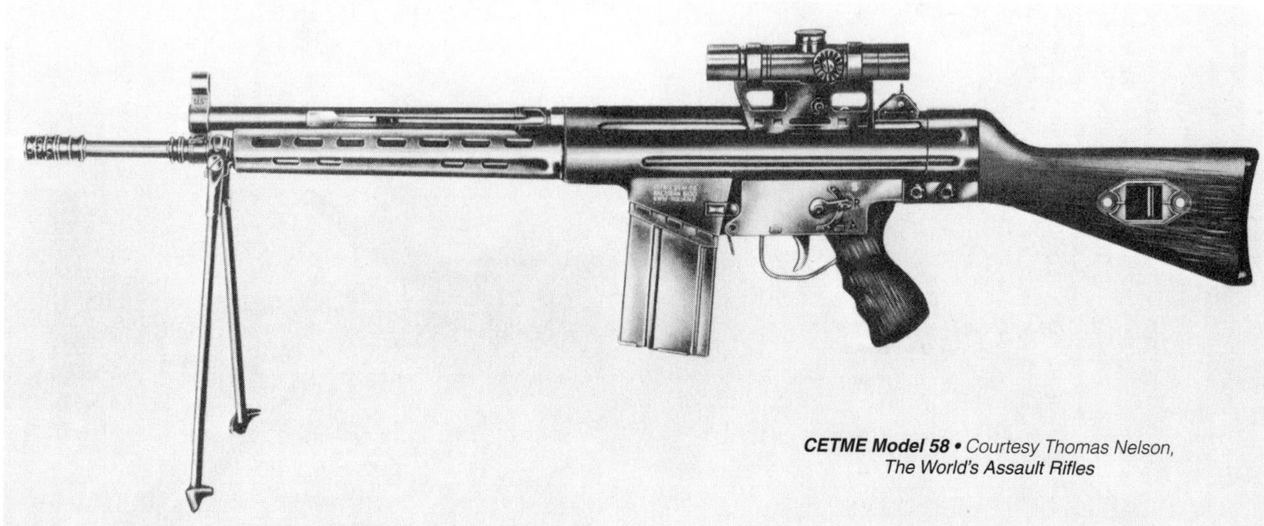
***CETME Model 58** • Courtesy Thomas Nelson, The World's Assault Rifles*

CETME Ameli • *Courtesy Chuck Karwan*

FAO Model 59

This is a Spanish-built gun designed on the Czech ZB26. It is chambered for the 7.62mm cartridge and is belt-fed with 50-round metallic links in a drum. Full automatic fire only. Barrel length is 22" with attached bipod. Gun weighs about 20 lbs. Rate of fire is approximately 650 rounds per minute.

Pre-1968

Exc.	*V.G.*	*Fair*
16500	15500	15000

Pre-1986 manufacture with new receiver or re-weld

Exc.	*V.G.*	*Fair*
14000	13000	11000

ALFA Model 1944

This gun was designed for use as a heavy machine gun. Chambered for the 7.92x57 Mauser cartridge and fitted with a 29.5-inch barrel. Select fire. Fed by a 100-round metallic link belt loaded in a drum. Rate of fire is about 800 rounds per minute. Weight is approximately 28 lbs.

NOTE: The Model 44 was also supplied to Egypt with aluminum cooling fins extending the length of the barrel and large slots in the gas cylinder.

Pre-1968 (Very Rare)

Exc.	*V.G.*	*Fair*
N/A	N/A	N/A

ALFA Model 55

Introduced in 1955, this is an updated version of the Model 44 chambered for the 7.62mm cartridge and fitted with a shorter 24-inch ribbed barrel with a lighter tripod. Rate of fire is about 800 rounds per minute. Weight is approximately 28 lbs.

Pre-1968

Exc.	*V.G.*	*Fair*
N/A	N/A	N/A

Ameli

Introduced in 1980, this is a light air-cooled machine gun chambered for the 5.56x45mm cartridge. It is fitted with a 15.75-inch barrel with slotted jacket, carry handle, and bipod. Barrel is quick change with flash hider. Belt-fed with 100- or 200-round belts. Plastic stock with pistol grip. Rate of fire is about 900 rounds per minute. Weight is approximately 11.5 lbs. Similar in appearance to the MG42 but smaller in size.

Pre-1968

Exc.	*V.G.*	*Fair*
N/A	N/A	N/A

SWEDEN

SWEDEN

The Kingdom of Sweden, a limited constitutional monarchy located in northern Europe between Norway and Finland, has an area of 173,732 sq. mi. (449,960 sq. km.) and a population of *8.5 million. Capital: Stockholm. Mining, lumbering and a specialized machine industry dominate the economy. Machinery, paper, iron and steel, motor vehicles and wood pulp are exported.

Olaf Skottkonung founded Sweden as a Christian stronghold late in the 10th century. After conquering Finland late in the 13th century, Sweden, together with Norway, came under the rule of Denmark, 1397-1523, in an association known as the Union of Kalmar. Modern Sweden had its beginning in 1523 when Gustaf Vasa drove the Danes out of Sweden and was himself chosen king. Under Gustaf Adolphus II and Charles XII, Sweden was one of the great powers of 17th century Europe – until Charles invaded Russia in 1708, and was defeated at the Battle of Pultowa in June, 1709. Early in the 18th century, a coalition of Russia, Poland and Denmark took away Sweden's Baltic empire and in 1809 Sweden was forced to cede Finland to Russia. The Treaty of Kiel ceded Norway to Sweden in January 1814. The Norwegians resisted for a time but later signed the Act of Union at the Convention of Moss in August 1814,The Union was dissolved in 1905 and Norway became independent. A new constitution that took effect on Jan. 1, 1975, restricts the function of the king largely to a ceremonial role.

HANDGUNS

Sweden purchased a small number, about 10,000, of Walther P-38 pistols in 1939, designated the Model 39. Also, a limited number of Walther PP pistols were used by the army as well.

Model 1871

The Swedish military issued the Lefaucheux-Francotte 6-shot revolver built by Auguste Francotte in Liege, Belgium, and also by Husqvarna. The frame was solid with fixed cylinder and no mechanical ejection. Chambered for the 11mm cartridge and fitted with a 5.9-inch round barrel. Checkered wooden grips with lanyard loop. Six-round cylinder is non-fluted. Weight is about 41 oz. First adopted by the cavalry and then included other units as well. In use between 1871 and 1890.

Courtesy Geschichte und Technik der europaischen Militarrevolver, Journal-Verlag Schwend GmbH with permission

Exc.	V.G.	Good	Fair	Poor
1250	750	500	350	200

Model 1863/79

This revolver is a converted pinfire to 11mm centerfire. Octagon barrel is 6.2 inches. Smooth wooden grips with lanyard loop. Built by Lefaucheux in Paris. In use between 1879 and 1890.

Courtesy Geschichte und Technik der europaischen Militarrevolver, Journal-Verlag Schwend GmbH with permission

Exc.	V.G.	Good	Fair	Poor
800	500	300	175	100

Model 1884

In 1884 the Swedish Navy chose the French Model 1873 revolver as its issue sidearm. It was designated the Model 1884. It was chambered for the 11mm cartridge and fitted with a 4.4-inch half-round half-octagon barrel. Checkered wood grips with lanyard loop. It was built in St. Etienne. Used by the navy from 1884 to 1887.

Courtesy Geschichte und Technik der europaischen Militarrevolver, Journal-Verlag Schwend GmbH with permission

Exc.	V.G.	Good	Fair	Poor
650	400	250	175	125

HUSQVARNA

Model 1887 Officer's Model

This double action revolver was chosen by the Swedish army as its official sidearm. It was a 6-shot double action Nagant design chambered for the 7.5mm cartridge with

Left side of Model 1887 Swedish revolver •
Courtesy Daniel Rewers collection, Paul Goodwind photo

fluted cylinder. It was fitted with a 4.5-inch half-round half-octagon barrel. Checkered wood grips with lanyard loop. Weight is about 24 oz. The first of these revolvers were built by the Nagant brothers in Liege beginning in 1887. Husqvarna produced 13,000 Model 1887 revolvers between 1897 and 1905. Some of these revolvers remained in Swedish reserve service until 1947. Many have been imported to the U.S. in VG-Exc condition.

Courtesy Rock Island Auction Company

Exc.	V.G.	Good	Fair	Poor
550	375	250	125	75

Model 1907 (Browning Model 1903)

This pistol is a copy of the FN Browning Model 1903 made for the Swedish army beginning in 1907. Built by Husqvarna. It is chambered for the 9x20 Browning Long cartridge. It is identical in every way to the FN model. This pistol remained in service until 1940. Many were converted to the .380 caliber and imported into the U.S.

Courtesy Orvel Reichert

Exc.	V.G.	Good	Fair	Poor
600	475	350	250	175

NOTE: Deduct 50% if pistol has been modified to fire .380.

Holster for 1907 Husqvarna

Pebble grained leather. Crown mark on flap. Twin magazine pouch on the fromt.

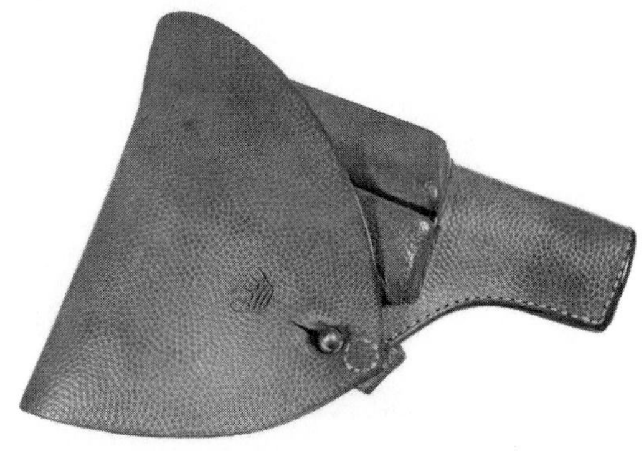

Lahti Model 40

Exc.	V.G.	Good	Fair	Poor
100	75	50	25	n/a

Lahti Model 40

A 9mm caliber semi-automatic pistol with a 5.5-inch barrel and 8-shot magazine. The grip is cut for a shoulder stock. Designed by Aimo Johannes Lahti, built with some alterations to the original design by Husqvarna and adopted as the standard Swedish sidearm in 1942. It differs from the Finnish version in that it does not have a loaded chamber indicator. The front sight is also higher. Production stopped in 1946 with some 84,000 pistols produced.

Exc.	V.G.	Good	Fair	Poor
650	525	400	275	175

SUBMACHINE GUNS

The Swedes used the Thompson submachine gun designated the 11mm Model 40 in limited numbers. They also used the Finnish Suomi (Model 37-39) and the Bergmann Model 34, designated the Swedish Model 39.

Carl Gustav 45

This 9mm weapon was first produced in 1945 in Sweden. This submachine gun is still in use. Models built between 1945 and 1948 are fitted with a 50-round Suomi magazine, while after 1948 guns have a 36-round two column magazine. It is used by the Swedish and Indonesian armies. Some integral silencer versions were used by Special Forces in Vietnam. Barrel is 8.25-inch in length. Fitted with retractable stock. Rate of fire is about 600 rounds per minute. Weight is about 8 lbs. This is the principal submachine gun in use by the Swedish army today.

Courtesy Richard M. Kumor Sr.

Sweedish "K" (M45/B) with integral suppressor • *Courtesy West Point Museum, Paul Goodwin photo*

Carl Gustav M45/B • *Courtesy private NFA collection*

SWEDEN

Pre-1968

Exc.	V.G.	Fair
15000	13000	12000

Pre-1986 mfg with new receiver tube

Exc.	V.G.	Fair
8500	6500	N/A

NOTE: Add 33 percent for M45/B model, which features a different non-removable magazine well, green finish, and improved bolt retention. There is also an M45/C that is fitted with a bayonet lug and a M45/E that is select fire.

RIFLES

REMINGTON

Sweden utilized the Remington rolling block rifles. Some of these were produced by Remington and others by Carl Gustav and Husqvarna.

Model 1867 Rifle

Chambered for the 12.17x42mm rimfire cartridge and fitted with a 35.5" barrel. Full stock with three barrel bands, cleaning rod, and bayonet lug on right side. Weight is about 9.25 lbs.

Exc.	V.G.	Good	Fair	Poor
900	750	600	400	100

Model 1864/68/85 Carbine

Chambered for the 12.7x42mm rimfire cartridge and fitted with a 16.5" barrel. Rear sight graduated from 250 to 800 meters. Full stock with cleaning rod and one barrel band. Built by Carl Gustav.

Exc.	V.G.	Good	Fair	Poor
1100	1000	850	550	200

Model 1870

Built by Carl Gustav and Husqvarna, this model is chambered for the 12.7x42mm rimfire cartridge. Fitted with a 16.5-inch barrel with rear sight graduated from 250 to 900 meters. Full stock with one barrel band at the muzzle. Weight is about 6 lbs.

NOTE: Many of these rifles were later converted to centerfire.

Exc.	V.G.	Good	Fair	Poor
1200	1050	850	550	200

Model 1884 Rifle

Chambered for the 10.15x61Rmm cartridge and fitted with a 31-inch barrel.

Exc.	V.G.	Good	Fair	Poor
900	750	600	400	100

Model 1884 Carbine

As above but with 16.5-inch barrel.

Exc.	V.G.	Good	Fair	Poor
1200	1050	850	550	200

Model 1889

Chambered for the 8x58Rmm Danish Krag cartridge and fitted with a 33-inch barrel with rear sight graduated from 300 to 2,400 meters. Full stock with two barrel bands. Sling swivel on first barrel band and in front of triggerguard. Finger grooves in stock ahead of breech and below rear sight. Bayonet lug.

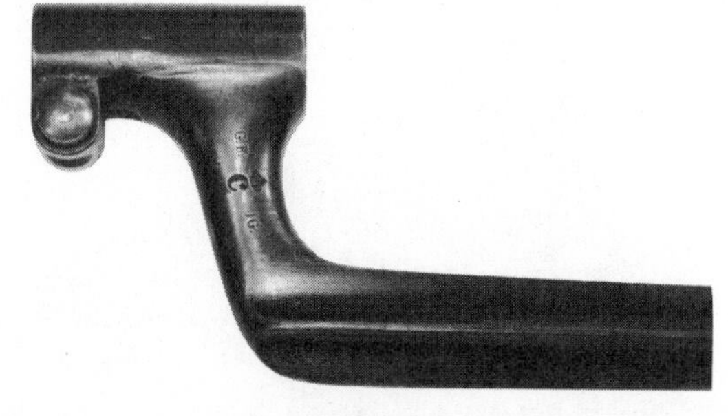
Bayonet for 1889 Rolling Block

Bayonet for 1894/14 Mauser Carbine

Exc.	*V.G.*	*Good*	*Fair*	*Poor*
950	750	600	400	100

Bayonet for 1889 Rolling Block

19.5-inch socket type. Spring button latch. Marked with Swedish crown over C. Price range 150 – 80.

MAUSER

NOTE: These Mauser rifles were built either by Mauser, Carl Gustafs, or Husqvarna. On the right side of the buttstock is frequently seen a tin disk with the unit number and sometimes a capital letter. The letter "I" stands for infantry, "A" for artillery, "T" for reserves, and "K.FL." for marines.

M1894 Carbine

Chambered for the 6.5x55mm cartridge and fitted with a 17.5-inch barrel. Full stocked in European carbine-style with half-length handguard with finger grooves. Turned down bolt. Magazine capacity is 5 rounds. Leaf rear sight graduated from 300 to 1,600 meters. Weight is about 7.5 lbs. About 12,000 of these rifles were built by Mauser, the rest by Carl Gustafs and Husqvarna. Early models had no provision for mounting a bayonet. After the bayonet attachment was added to the nose cap this model was known as a 94/14. Many of the earlier carbines had the new nose cap installed. Values are generally the same. A slightly higher price might be encountered for the Mauser made carbines.

Exc.	*V.G.*	*Good*	*Fair*	*Poor*
1000	750	500	400	200

NOTE: Interarms imported many 1894 Carbines in the 1960s. They ground the date off the receiver then stamped it with "Interarms G 33/50". Deduct 25-50% for an Interarms marked Model 1894 Carbine.

Bayonet for 1894/14 Mauser Carbine

Wood handle. 13-inch double edge blade. Steel scabbard. Price range 150 – 50.

1915 Naval Bayonet for 1894 Mauser Carbine

Wood grips. Ring for stud below barrel. 19.9-inch single edge blade with cutting edge to top. Steel scabbard. A scarce bayonet. Price range 400 – 250.

M1896 Rifle

Action similar to the Model 1894 but with a 29" barrel, full-length stock, half-length upper handguard, and bayonet lug. Rear sight graduated from 300 to 2,000 meters on Mauser and Gustaf built rifles, and 100 to 800 meters on Husqvarna built rifles. Swedish crown over maker and date stamped on receiver ring. Magazine capacity is 5 rounds. Weight is about 9 lbs. Add 25 percent for Husqvarna built M 1896.

NOTE: A number of these rifles were sent to Finland during the early days of WWII to fight the Soviets. A number were also sent to Denmark as well. These Danish rifles have a Danish silver coin in the right side of the buttstock in place of the Swedish marking disk.

Exc.	*V.G.*	*Good*	*Fair*	*Poor*
400	300	200	150	125

M1896 Sniper Rifle/M41 AGA scope

This is a Model 1896 rifle with Model 41 AGA scope mounted.

Exc.	*V.G.*	*Good*	*Fair*	*Poor*
2000	1800	1500	1000	700

M1896 Sniper Rifle/M42 AGA scope

This is a Model 1896 rifle with Model 42 AGA scope mounted.

Exc.	*V.G.*	*Good*	*Fair*	*Poor*
2000	1800	1500	1000	700

Deduct 50 percent for sniper rifles without a scope.

Model 96-38

About 30,000 Model 1896 rifles were shortened to the same overall length as the Model 1938 Short Rifle. The straight bolt handle of the Model 1896 was retained. Weight is about 8.375 lbs.

Exc.	*V.G.*	*Good*	*Fair*	*Poor*
425	350	275	150	125

Model 38 Short Rifle

Similar to the Model 1896 but with turned-down bolt handle and barrel length of 23.5 inches. Designed for mounted troops. Magazine capacity is 5 rounds. Rear sight graduated from 100 to 600 meters. Weight is approximately 9 lbs. Built by Husqvarna.

Exc.	*V.G.*	*Good*	*Fair*	*Poor*
450	375	275	175	125

1915 Naval Bayonet for 1894 Mauser Carbine

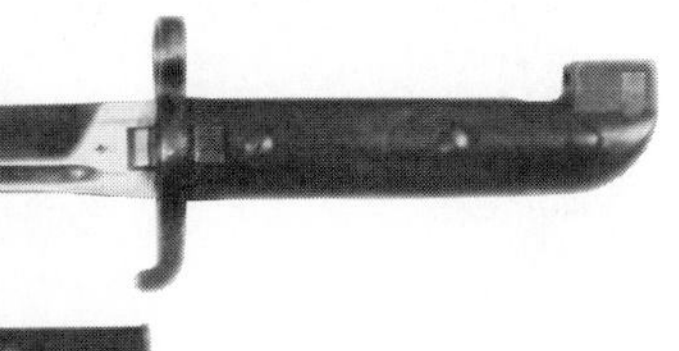

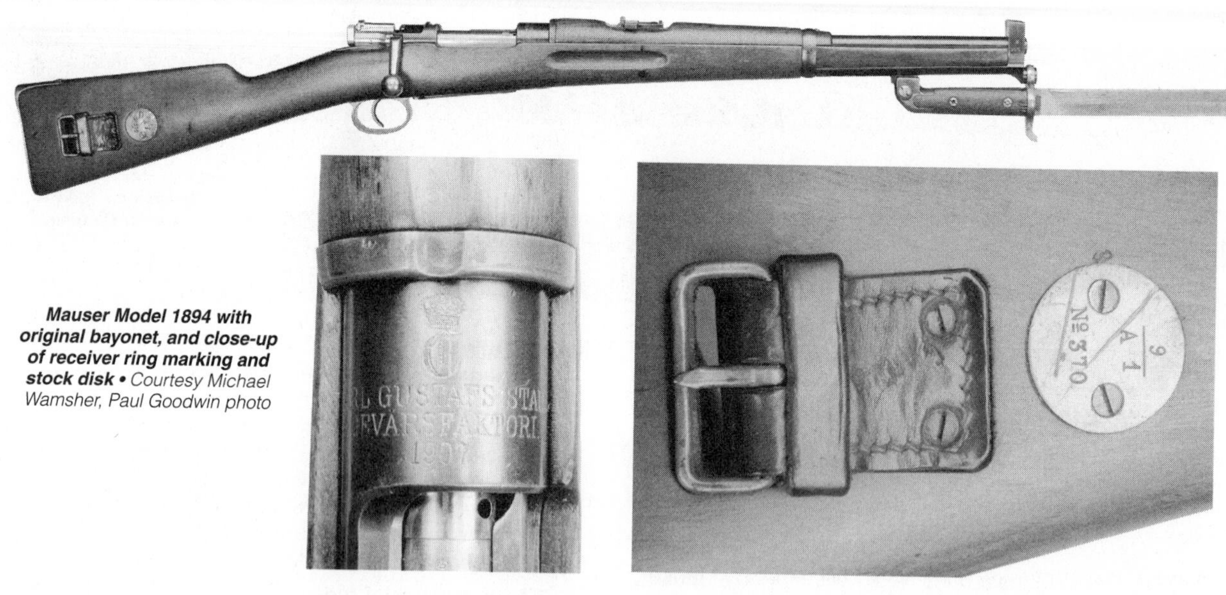

Mauser Model 1894 with original bayonet, and close-up of receiver ring marking and stock disk • *Courtesy Michael Wamsher, Paul Goodwin photo*

Model 1896 Sniper Rifle with M44 Scope • *Courtesy Rock Island Auction Company*

Model 1896 with AGA42 Scope, close-up of scope and markings • *Courtesy Stoddard Martial collection, Paul Goodwin photo*

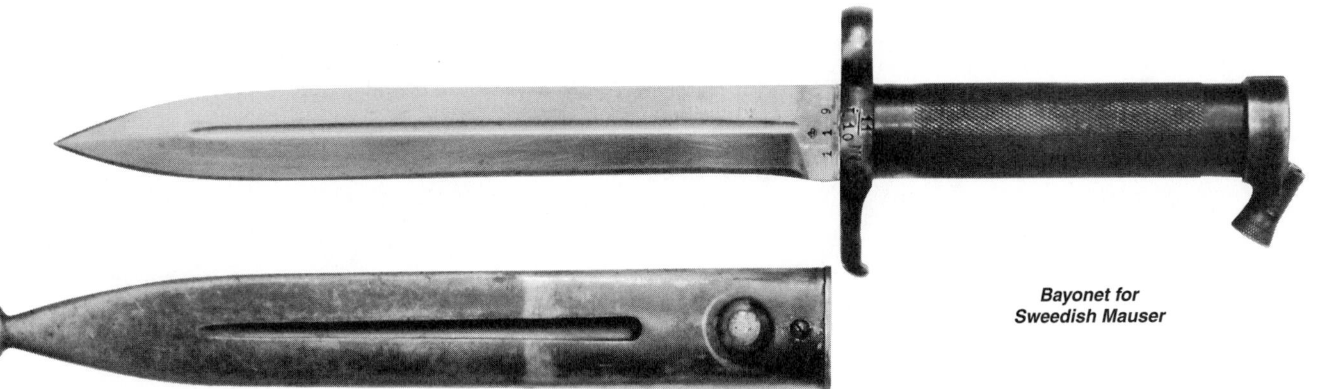

Bayonet for Sweedish Mauser

SWEDEN

Bayonet for Swedish Mauser

Steel handle. 8-3/8-inch double edge blade. Fits the 1896, 96-38, 1938 Mauser rifles and the AG-42b rifle. Price range 60 – 25.

Model 38/22 Training Rifle

Similar to the Model 38 Short Rifle but chambered for the .22 caliber rimfire cartridge.

Exc.	V.G.	Good	Fair	Poor
900	750	600	300	175

M1938/40 Short Rifle (Model 40)

This model is a Swedish modified German Kar. 98k converted to the 8x63mm machine gun cartridge. The rifle was fitted with a muzzle brake to soften recoil but the cartridge was too powerful for the gun. Four-round magazine. Weight is about 9.5 lbs. Very rare. Most were sold as surplus to Israel, where they were rebuilt into 7.62mm rifles.

Exc.	V.G.	Good	Fair	Poor
1800	1400	1000	700	500

M1896 Sniper Rifle/M44 AGA scope (Model 41)

A Model 1896 Rifle fitted with either a Model 44 AGA 3x65 scope, Model 42 AGA 3x65 scope, or Model 41 4x90 ZF Ajack scope.

Exc.	V.G.	Good	Fair	Poor
1500	1200	850	650	500

M1896 Military Target Rifles

A Model 1896 rifle with special micrometer target sights. Many have been imported in the last decade.

Exc.	V.G.	Good	Fair	Poor
600	475	350	—	—

Model CG-63 and CG-80 Target Rifle

Built by Carl Gustav, this rifle was chambered for the .22 rimfire, 6.5x55mm, or 7.62mm cartridge. Fitted with a medium weight 29.1-inch barrel. Half-length stock with half-length upper handguard. The CG-80 was not fitted with a handguard. Five round magazine. It has a turned-down bolt handle flattened on top. Generally fitted with aperture rear sight mounted on receiver bridge. Many minor variations are encountered in this rifle. Weight is approximately 9.5 lbs.

Exc.	V.G.	Good	Fair	Poor
850	700	500	300	200

Ljungman AG-42B

Designed by Eril Eklund and placed in service with the Swedish military in 1942—less than a year after it was designed. The rifle is a direct gas-operated design with no piston or rod. It is chambered for the 6.5mm cartridge and has a 24.5-inch barrel with a 10-round detachable magazine. This rifle has military-type sights and a full-length stock and handguard held on by barrel bands. Rear sight is graduated from 100 to 700 meters. There are provisions for a bayonet. There is also an Egyptian version of this rifle known as the "Hakim." The U.S. AR-15 rifles use the same type of gas system.

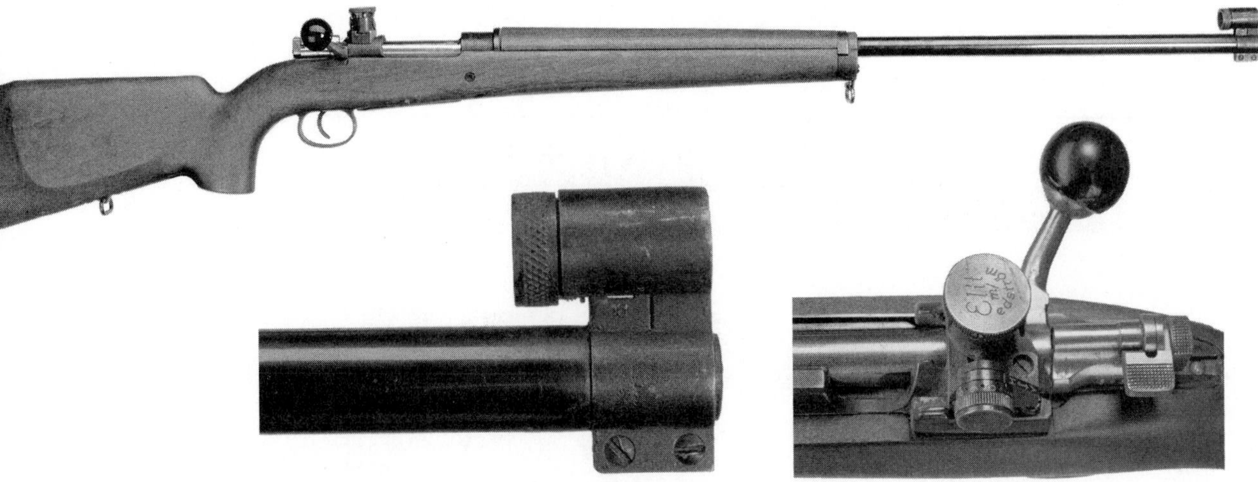

***Model CG-63 Match Rifle with close-ups of front and rear sights** • Courtesy Stoddard Martial collection, Paul Goodwin photo*

SWEDEN

Model 21 Sweedish BAR •
Courtesy private NFA collection, Gary Gelson photo

Sweedish Model 1937 •
Courtesy private NFA collection, Paul Goodwin photo

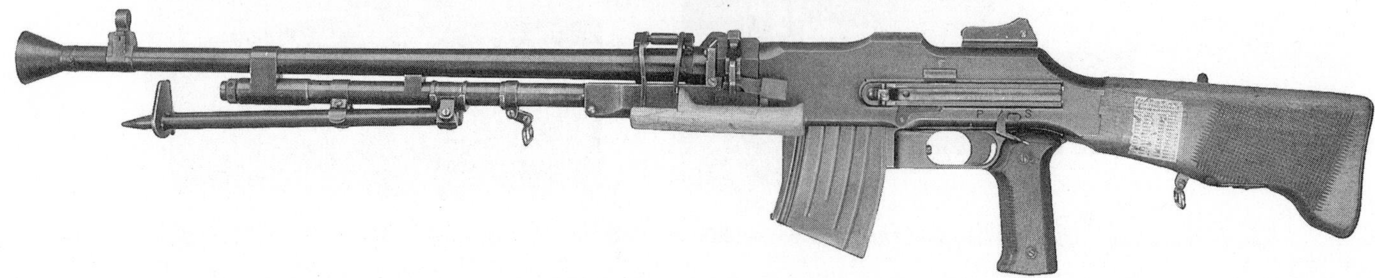

AG-42B action • Courtesy Chuck Karwan

Exc.	V.G.	Good	Fair	Poor
850	675	500	350	250

Swedish mountain troops with M1896 Mausers • Courtesy Paul S. Scarlata

MACHINE GUNS

The Swedish armed forces have utilized a wide variety of machine guns from several countries. Sweden adopted the Schwarzlose Model 14 in 6.5mm caliber, the Browning Model 1917A1 water-cooled gun (Model 36), the Browning Model 1919A6 (Model 42), the Czech VZ26 in 6.5mm caliber (Model 39), and more currently the FN MAG in 7.62mm (Model 58). These early FN MAG guns were chambered for the 6.5x55mm Mauser cartridge.

Swedish Model 36

This is the Swedish version of the Browning Model 1917 water-cooled gun. The gun shown is in a twin anti-aircraft configuration, and is too rare to price.

Pre-1968

Exc.	V.G.	Fair
28000	26000	24000

Swedish BAR Model 21

Designated the Swedish Kg. (Kulsprutegevar, light machine gun) these guns were built in Sweden under license from Colt between 1923 and 1935. Chambered for the Swedish 6.5x55mm cartridge. This model does not have a quick change barrel as originally built. A little over 8,000 of these BARs were built in Sweden during its production life.

Pre-1968

Exc.	V.G.	Fair
25000	23000	21000

Swedish BAR Model 37

The Model 37 Swedish BAR is an improved version of the Model 21 with a screw-on receiver extension that allowed the adoption of a quick change barrel. A total of about 15,000 Model 37s were produced between 1937 and 1944.

NOTE: A number of Model 21s were refitted with quick change barrels and designated the Model 21/37.

Pre-1968 (Very Rare)

Exc.	V.G.	Fair
12000	10000	9000

SWEDEN

Sweedish Model 1936 Twin • Courtesy private NFA collection, Paul Goodwin photo

The Swiss Confederation, located in central Europe north of Italy and south of Germany, has an area of 15,941 sq. mi. (41,290 sq. km.) and a population of *6.6 million. Capital: Bern. The economy centers about a well developed manufacturing industry. Machinery, chemicals, watches and clocks, and textiles are exported.

Switzerland, the habitat of lake dwellers in prehistoric times, was peopled by the Celtic Helvetians when Julius Caesar made it a part of the Roman Empire in 58 B.C. After the decline of Rome, Switzerland was invaded by Teutonic tribes, who established small temporal holdings which in the Middle Ages, became a federation of fiefs of the Holy Roman Empire. As a nation, Switzerland originated in 1291 when the districts of Nidwalden, Schwyz and Uri united to defeat Austria and attain independence as the Swiss Confederation. After acquiring new cantons in the 14th century, Switzerland was made independent from the Holy Roman Empire by the 1648 Treaty of Westphalia. The revolutionary armies of Napoleonic France occupied Switzerland and set up the Helvetian Republic, 1798-1803. After the fall of Napoleon, the Congress of Vienna, 1815, recognized the independence of Switzerland and guaranteed its neutrality. The Swiss Constitutions of 1848 and 1874 established a union modeled upon that of the United States.

HANDGUNS

Model 1872

This Swiss Model 1872 is a 10.4mm rimfire revolver with a 6-shot fluted cylinder. It is fitted with a 5.9-inch octagon barrel. The frame is solid with fixed fluted cylinder and mechanical rod ejection. Checkered wood grips with lanyard loop. The revolver was built by the Belgian firm of Pirlot Freres in Liege. It was issued from 1872 until 1878. Weight is 37 oz. This was the last foreign-built handgun to be issued to the Swiss military.

NOTE: This is a very rare revolver as most were converted to centerfire with the Model 1872/78 in 1878.

Courtesy Geschichte und Technik der europaischen Militarrevolver, Journal-Verlag Schwend GmbH with permission

Exc.	V.G.	Good	Fair	Poor
N/A	—	—	—	—

Model 1872/78

This is a centerfire converted Model 1872 in 10.4mm. This revolver was rarely used by the Swiss military.

Courtesy Geschichte und Technik der europaischen Militarrevolver, Journal-Verlag Schwend GmbH with permission

Exc.	V.G.	Good	Fair	Poor
1500	—	—	—	—

Model 1878

This was the first Swiss-made revolver used by the Swiss military. Made in Bern, this Schmidt-Galand-type revolver was chambered for the 10.4mm cartridge. The frame was solid with fixed cylinder and mechanical rod ejection. 4.5-inch octagon barrel. Checkered grips with the Swiss cross on the left side. Weight was about 35 oz. This revolver was issued to cavalry units with about 6,000 in service.

Courtesy Geschichte und Technik der europaischen Militarrevolver, Journal-Verlag Schwend GmbH with permission

Exc.	V.G.	Good	Fair	Poor
1750	1000	600	350	250

Model 1882

This revolver was similar in appearance to the Model 1878 but was chambered for the smaller 7.5mm cartridge. It was fitted with a 4.5-inch octagon barrel. Early Model 1882 revolvers were fitted with hard rubber checkered grips while later guns will be seen with grooved wooden grips. This revolver was built in

Right side of the Model 1882 Swiss revolver • *Courtesy Rock Island Auction Company*

Switzerland at Bern or SIG. Weight is about 27 oz. This model stayed in use in the Swiss military from 1882 to as late as 1950.

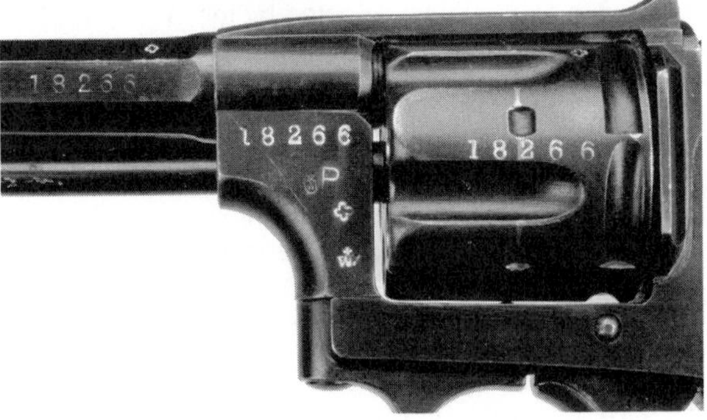

Exc.	V.G.	Good	Fair	Poor
1250	850	500	300	200

Model 1929

This is a solid frame double action revolver that is gate loaded. The round barrel is 4.5 inches long. Chambered for the 7.5x23R Swiss revolver cartridge.

Model 1929 Swiss revolver • *Courtesy Daniel Rewers collection, Paul Goodwin photo*

The fluted cylinder holds 6 rounds. Checkered bakelite grips. Weight is about 28 ozs. The grip on the Model 1929 is of a different shape than the Model 1882.

Exc.	V.G.	Good	Fair	Poor
1250	850	500	300	200

LUGER

WAFFENFABRIK BERN

Switzerland was the first country to adopt the Luger as a military sidearm with its contract purchase of the Model 1900 from DWM. Another contract for the Model 1906 soon followed. Because DWM could no longer supply Switzerland with Lugers during WWI, the Swiss firm of Waffenfabrik Bern (W+F Bern) produced its own version based on the Model 1906.

Bibliographical Note: For additional historical information, technical data, and photos, see Vittorio Bobba, ***Parabellum: A Technical History of Swiss Lugers***, Italy, 1996.

NOTE: There are a number of sub-variations of Swiss Lugers that may affect value. It is strongly suggested that thorough research of this model be undertaken prior to a sale.

Model 1906 Bern

A Swiss-made copy of the German Model 1906 Luger. Made in caliber 7.65mm, fitted with a 4.75-inch barrel, and marked "WAFFENFABRIK BERN" under the Geneva cross on top of the toggle. The grips on this pistol are unique in that most are checkered walnut with a plain border on the front and rear edges. About 17,000 of these pistols were manufactured. This model was most likely produced between 1918 and 1933, and was built for the Swiss military.

Courtesy James Rankin

Exc.	V.G.	Good	Fair	Poor
4500	3000	2000	1400	1000

Courtesy James Rankin

SWITZERLAND

Model 1929

Similar to the above, with the exception that the toggle finger pieces are smooth, the grip frame is uncurved, safety lever is a flat configuration, and the grip safety is of inordinate size. Fitted with plastic grips. Chambered for caliber 7.65mm. About 30,000 of these pistols were produced. Sold both for military and commercial use.

Exc.	V.G.	Good	Fair	Poor
3250	2000	1500	1200	900

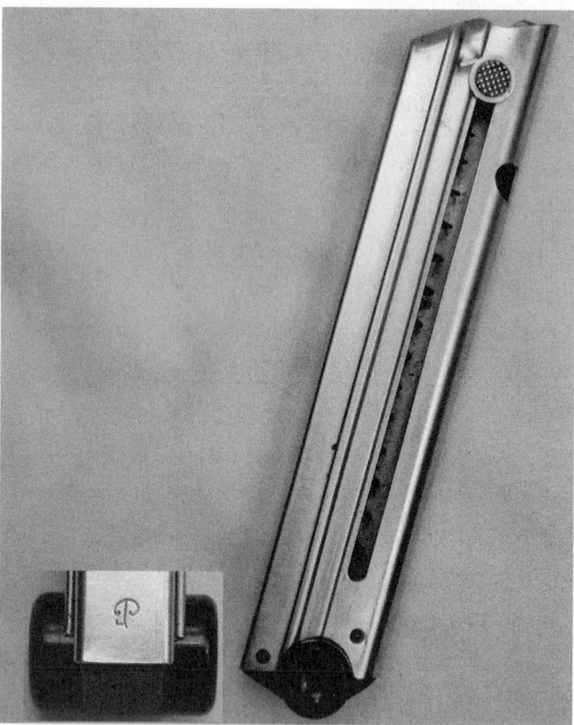

Swiss Luger magazine with script "P" marking on back. Price 150-75

SIG

Schweizerische Industrie Gesellschaft, Neuhausen am Rheinfalls, Switzerland

BIOGRAPHICAL NOTE: For historical background, technical data, and photos, see Lorenz Vetter, Das grosse Buch der SIG-Pistolen, Verlag Stocker-Schmid AG, 1995.

NOTE: The P210 pistol was designated the SP47/8 prior to 1957, when it was renamed the P210. There are a number of production changes on this pistol that follow a chronological order.

P210

A 7.65mm or 9mm semi-automatic pistol with a 4.75-inch barrel and 8-shot magazine. Fixed rear sight. Blued with plastic grips. In 1996 the 9mm version was the only one imported. Weight is about 32 oz. This model was also used by the Danish army (Model 49).

NIB	Exc.	V.G.	Good	Fair	Poor
2500	1500	1300	1100	800	500

NOTE: For 1996, a .22 caliber conversion unit serialized to the gun was available. Add $600 for this option.

P210-1

As above, with an adjustable rear sight, polished finish, and walnut grips. Imported prior to 1987. Weight is about 31 oz.

NIB	Exc.	V.G.	Good	Fair	Poor
2750	2250	1500	1150	800	—

P210-2 (Swiss Army Model 49-SP47/8)

A Swiss P 49 military version of the P210. Note the Letter prefix on the serial number; a military designation • Courtesy Simon Stoddard collection, Paul Goodwin photo

This model is similar to the P210-1 with the exception that it has a sandblasted matte finish and black plastic grips with fixed sights. Adopted by the Swiss army in 1947 and still in service.

NIB	Exc.	V.G.	Good	Fair	Poor
2250	1750	1350	1000	750	300

P210-3

Introduced in 1950, this model was issued to the Swiss police in Lausanne and Basel. Early examples are polished blue and later examples are sandblasted matte blue. Fixed sights. Production ceased in 1983. Very few of these pistols were sold on a commercial basis. Very scarce.

NIB	Exc.	V.G.	Good	Fair	Poor
N/A	—	—	—	—	—

P210-4

Special model produced for the West German Border Police. Fixed rear sight. Walnut grips on early models and black plastic grips on later models. Early models have blued finish while later models have sandblasted matte finish.

NIB	Exc.	V.G.	Good	Fair	Poor
2250	1750	1350	1000	750	300

P210-5

A commercial version as above, with an extended length barrel of 5.9 (150mm) or 7.1 inches (180mm), adjustable rear sight, target trigger, and walnut grips. Front sight is fitted to front of extended barrel, not the slide. Offered in a standard and heavy frame weight. Polished blue finish. Weight is about 35 oz. for standard weight frame.

NIB	Exc.	V.G.	Good	Fair	Poor
3750	2750	1750	1200	800	400

P210-6

A commercial version as above, with a 4.75-inch barrel. Front sight is fitted to slide. Adjustable rear sight on some of these variations, fixed sight on others. Polished blue finish.

SIG P210-6 Commercial Version • Courtesy SIGARMS

NIB	Exc.	V.G.	Good	Fair	Poor
2750	2250	1500	1250	800	400

P210-7

This model is chambered for the .22 rimfire cartridge and fitted with a 4.75-inch barrel. Most of the variations of this model are built for commercial and export sales except one variation, which was built for the West German Border Guards as a practice pistol. Fixed sights. Checkered plastic grips.

NIB	Exc.	V.G.	Good	Fair	Poor
N/A	—	—	—	—	—

P220-P225 (Swiss Army Model P-75)

Swiss army military sidearm. This is a high-quality, double action semi-automatic pistol chambered for .38 Super, .45 ACP, and 9mm Parabellum. It has a 4.41-inch barrel and fixed sights and features the decocking lever that was found originally on the Sauer Model 38H. There are two versions of this pistol: one with a bottom magazine release (commonly referred to as the European model) and the other with the release on the side (commonly referred to as the American model), as on the Model 1911 Colt. The frame is a lightweight alloy that is matte finished and is available in either blue, nickel, or K-Kote finish with black plastic grips. The .45 ACP magazine capacity is 7 rounds and the pistol weighs 25.7 oz.; the .38 Super magazine capacity is 9 rounds and the pistol weighs 26.5 oz.; the 9mm magazine holds 9 rounds and the overall weight is 26.5 oz. This model was manufactured from 1976 and is still in production. The 9mm version in this model is no longer in production. The prices listed below are for guns with a standard blue finish.

Swiss issue P225 with close-up of markings • Courtesy Danile Rewers collection, Paul Goodwin photo

NIB	Exc.	V.G.	Good	Fair	Poor
750	550	400	300	200	150

NOTE: For the K-Kote finish add $40, for nickel slide add $40.

SUBMACHINE GUNS

Steyr-Solothurn (Solothurn SI-100 or MP34[o])

See Austria, Submachine Guns, Steyr.

MP41/44

This model was developed by Furrer and built by W+F Bern arsenal between 1936 and 1942. Chambered for the 9mm Luger cartridge. Recoil operated with a toggle system similar to the Luger pistol but turned on its side. Slotted barrel jacket with 10-inch barrel with forward vertical handgrip and pistol grip wooden stock. Rate of fire is about 900 rounds per minute. Magazine capacity is 40 rounds. Very expensive to produce with the result that fewer than 5,000 guns were manufactured. Weight is about 11.5 lbs.

Swiss MP41 • Courtesy private NFA collection, Paul Goodwin photo

Pre-1968 (Rare)

Exc.	V.G.	Fair
19500	18500	18000

MP43/44

The Swiss version of the Suomi with a bayonet lug and flip over rear sight. Built by Hispano Suiza under license from Finland. Rate of fire is about 800 rounds per minute and weight is approximately 10.5 lbs. Magazine capacity is 50-round box type.

Swiss M43/44 • Courtesy private NFA collection, Paul Goodwin photo

Pre-1968 (Rare)

Exc.	V.G.	Fair
19500	19000	18000

RIFLES

Swiss Pre-Cartridge Era Rifles

Model 1842 Percussion Musket

Total length 58 inches. 42.5-inch barrel. Caliber 18mm. 3 bands.

Exc.	V.G.	Good	Fair	Poor
2000	1400	950	500	300

Model 1842/59

The Model 1842 with a replacement 36-inch barrel with a new type of rifling.

Exc.	V.G.	Good	Fair	Poor
2200	1600	1100	700	350

Model 1851 Federal Percussion Carbine

Total length 49.6 inches with a 32-inch barrel. Caliber .41/10.4mm. Features double set triggers and a stutzen style butt plate.

Exc.	V.G.	Good	Fair	Poor
2000	1450	900	600	350

Model 1863 Percussion Rifle

Similar to the M1842/59 but in 10.5mm.

Exc.	V.G.	Good	Fair	Poor
2500	1700	1250	650	350

Model 1867 Milbank-Amsler Rifle

A conversion of the M1851, 1859 and 1863 rifles to breech loading cartridge. Forward hinge trapdoor system similar to the U.S. M 1873. Both the 18mm and 10.4mm rifles were converted. Add 25% for 18mm version.

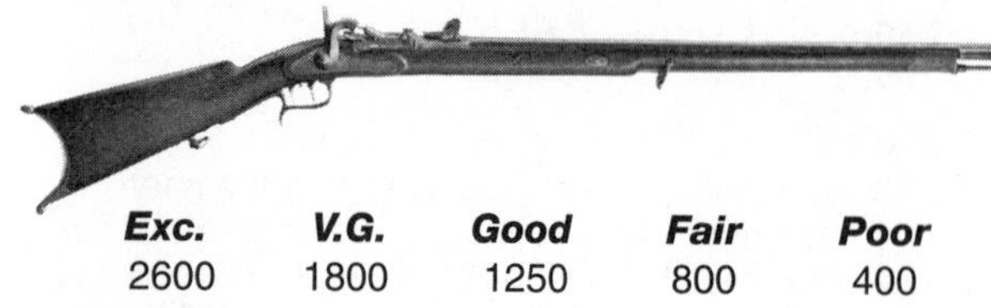

Exc.	V.G.	Good	Fair	Poor
2600	1800	1250	800	400

PEABODY

Swiss Rifle (1867)

Chambered for the .41 Swiss rimfire cartridge, this rifle was fitted with a 31.625-inch barrel. Full stock with two barrel bands. The barrel is blued and the furniture casehardened. On the left side of the receiver are a cross and "W" inside an oval. "Peabody" stamped on left side of receiver. About 15,000 rifles were sold to the Swiss. Serial number range: 5500 to 21000.

Exc.	V.G.	Good	Fair	Poor
1500	1250	750	600	400

VETTERLI

This rifle was invented by Friderich Vetterli at Neuhausen, Switzerland, in 1867. This was the first bolt action repeating rifle to be used as a military service weapon. It was adopted on January 8, 1869, and predated the Fruwirth by three years. It is chambered for the .41 Swiss rimfire cartridge (10.4mm). It has a 12-round tubular magazine that is loaded through a side gate similar to a Winchester lever action. There is a swinging cover on the loading gate. The finish is blue, with a full-length walnut stock secured by one barrel band and an endcap. There is a full-length cleaning rod located under the barrel. The receiver has a round configuration and the trigger guard has a rear spur. The rifle and its variations were built between 1869 and 1881.

Model 1869 Infantry Rifle

The first production model of the Vetterli series was made by nine contractors:

- 1869-1874 SIG, Neuhausen (total 59,000)
- 1869-1875 Eidgenössische Montier-Werstätte, Bern (total 8900)
- 1875-1879 Eidgenössische Waffenfabrik, Bern (total 36,000)
- 1869-1873 Cordier & Cie, Bellefontaine (total 4000)
- 1869-1874 W. von Steiger, Thun (total 15,200)
- 1869-1874 Ost-Schweizerische Büchsenmacher, St. Gallen (total 8700)
- 1869-1873 Rychner & Keller, Aarau (total 9700) 1869-1873 Valentin Sauerbrey, Basel (total 7000)
- 1869-1874 Zürich Zeughaus (total 1500)

Barrel length is 33 inches. Cleaning rod. A swing-down loading gate is on the right side of the receiver. Magazine capacity is 12 rounds. Weight is about 10.25 lbs. Price is for an original Model 1869 with loading gate cover and magazine cut off.

Exc.	V.G.	Good	Fair	Poor
900	750	500	350	200

Model 1870 Cadet Rifle

Same action as the Model 1869 but single shot only. Barrel length is 26.75 inches. Weight about 7 lbs.

Bayonet for Vetterli M 1871

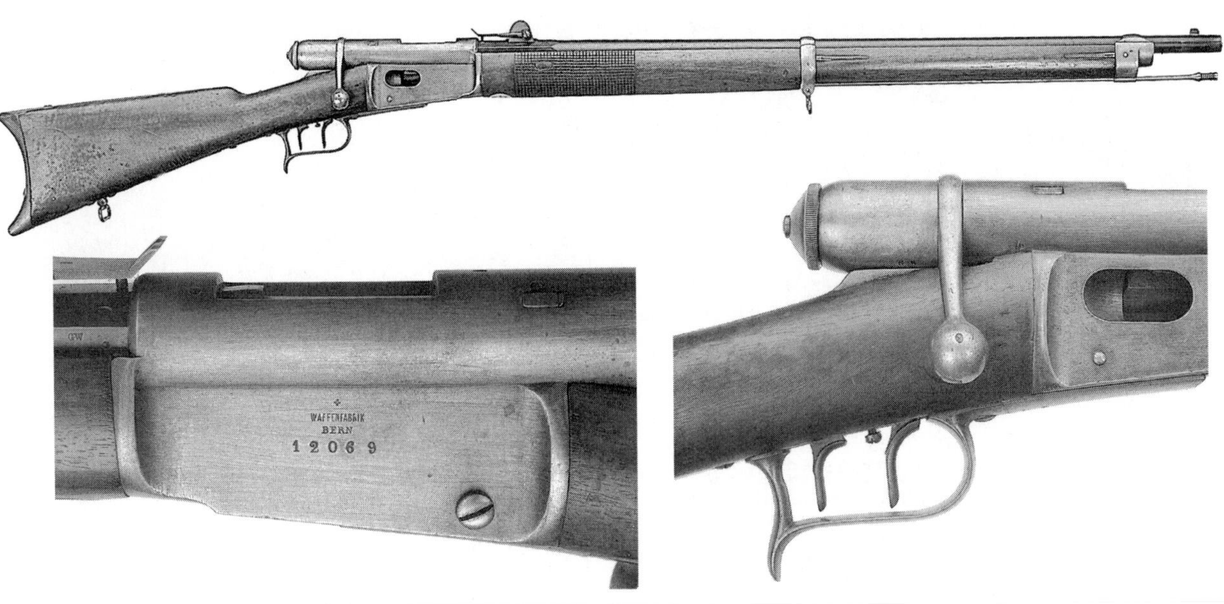

Model 1878 Sharpshooter • Private collection, Paul Goodwin photo

Exc.	V.G.	Good	Fair	Poor
900	750	500	350	200

Model 1869/71 Rifle

This rifle is fitted with a 33-inch barrel. Sights calibrated from 200 to 1,000 meters. Magazine capacity is 11 rounds. Weight is about 10.25 lbs. Most model 1869 Vetterlis were converted to this pattern by removal of the loading gate cover and magazine cut off.

Paul Goodwin photo

Exc.	V.G.	Good	Fair	Poor
400	275	200	150	100

Bayonet for Vetterli M1871

Socket type. 19-inch quadrangular blade. Opening at the rear of socket has a triangular slot to clear the front sight. Price range 150 – 85.

Model 1871 Stuzer (Short Rifle) (Sharpshooter)

This short rifle was fitted with two barrel bands on its 30-inch barrel. 9-round magazine. Fitted with a curved buttplate. Double set trigger. Weight is about 10 lbs.

Exc.	V.G.	Good	Fair	Poor
1000	800	650	400	250

Model 1871 Carbine

The carbine has an 18.5-inch barrel with no bayonet fittings. Full stock with 6-round tube magazine. Rear sling swivel behind triggerguard. Weight is about 7 lbs.

Exc.	V.G.	Good	Fair	Poor
900	750	500	350	200

Model 1878 Rifle

This model was a modified version of the Model 1878. Fitted with a full-length stock with curved buttplate and chambered for the 10.4x42R rimfire cartridge. The rear sight is graduated to 1,200 meters. Barrel length is 33-inch with an 11-round tube magazine in the forend. Built at SIG, Neuhausen, and Bern. Weight is about 10 lbs.

Exc.	V.G.	Good	Fair	Poor
450	300	250	200	100

NOTE: There is some disagreement as to production of a Model 1878 Carbine. As a rule it is thought that some M1878 rifle barrels were cut to 18.5 inches. These are thought to be arsenal conversions. These cut-down "carbines" are worth less than original rifles.

Pioneer bayonet for Vetterli M 1878

Checkered hard rubber grips. Muzzle ring. 18.7-inch single edge blade with saw teeth on top. Steel tipped leather scabbard. This bayonet resembles the M 1911 Pioneer bayonet for the Schmidt Rubin. Price range 225 – 125.

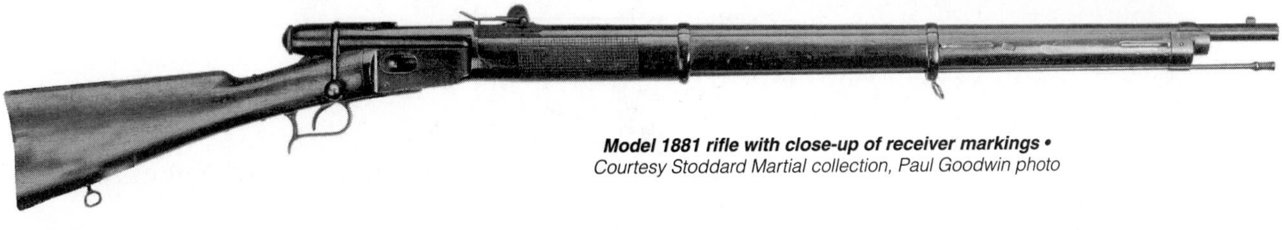

Model 1881 rifle with close-up of receiver markings •
Courtesy Stoddard Martial collection, Paul Goodwin photo

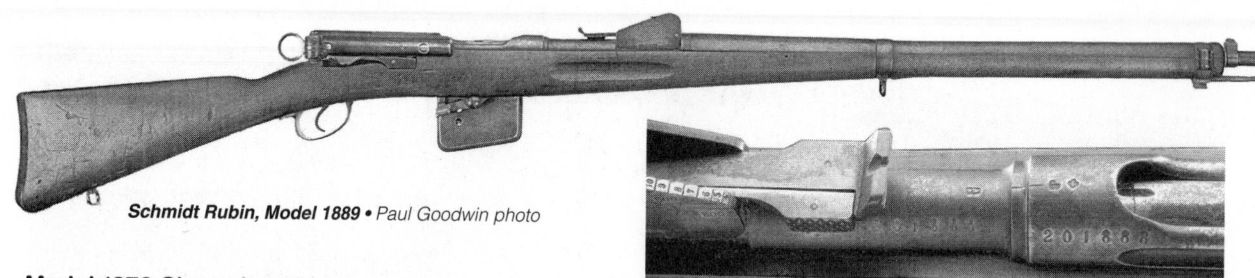

Schmidt Rubin, Model 1889 • Paul Goodwin photo

SWITZERLAND

Model 1878 Sharpshooter

Similar to the Model 1878 rifle but fitted with double set triggers and crescent butt.

Exc.	V.G.	Good	Fair	Poor
1000	800	650	400	250

Model 1881 Rifle

This model is the same as the Model 1878 above with the exception of a 1,600 meter graduated rear sight. Weight is about 10 lbs.

Exc.	V.G.	Good	Fair	Poor
500	400	250	200	100

Model 1881 Sharpshooter

Similar to the Model 1881 but fitted with double set triggers.

Exc.	V.G.	Good	Fair	Poor
1000	800	650	400	250

SCHMIDT RUBIN

Eidgenossische Waffenfabrik Bern

Bern, Switzerland (1875-1993)

Model 1889

A 7.5mm straight pull bolt action rifle with a 30.75-inch barrel and 12-shot magazine. Blued with a full-length walnut stock secured by two barrel bands. Approximately 212,000 were manufactured.

Exc.	V.G.	Good	Fair	Poor
650	475	350	250	150

Model 1889/96

Similar to the Model 1889 with a shortened action. The locking lug is moved forward 2-1/2 inches on the bolt sleeve. There were approximately 127,000 made between 1897 and 1912.

Exc.	V.G.	Good	Fair	Poor
450	325	250	180	125

Model 1897 Cadet Rifle

A single shot Cadet Rifle with reduced overall size. Barrel length is 23.3 inches. These rifles were sighted for a reduced charge cartridge for target use and to reduce recoil. Sights calibrated for 200 to 400 meters. Weight is about 7.75 lbs. Approximately 7,900 were manufactured between 1898 and 1927.

Exc.	V.G.	Good	Fair	Poor
1200	1000	700	500	350

Model 1900 Short Rifle

A shortened version of the Model 1896, with a 6-shot magazine and 23.3-inch barrel. Weight is about 8.25 lbs. Approximately 18,750 were manufactured between 1901 and 1911.

Exc.	V.G.	Good	Fair	Poor
650	400	250	175	125

Model 1900/11 Short Rifle

Modified between 1911 and 1920 to more closely resemble the Model 1911 Carbine with new barrel and sights.

Exc.	V.G.	Good	Fair	Poor
500	375	275	175	125

Model 1905 Carbine

Adopted in 1905 as a replacement for the Mannlicher 1893. Barrel length is 21.5-inch. Weight is about 8 lbs. Magazine capacity is 6 rounds. Approximately 7,900 were manufactured between 1906 and 1911.

Exc.	V.G.	Good	Fair	Poor
850	700	550	400	250

Model 1905/11 Cavalry Carbine

Modified between 1911 and 1920 to more closely resemble the Model 1911 Carbine with new barrel and sights.

Exc.	V.G.	Good	Fair	Poor
550	400	275	150	100

Model 1896/11

Updated version of the 1896 rifle to more closely resemble the Model 1911 rifle. Changes included

Model 1896/11 with barrel and receiver markings • Courtesy Stoddard Martial collection, Paul Goodwin photo

Model 1911 rifle • *Courtesy Paul S. Scarlata*

new barrel and sight, and an inlet pistol grip into the straight 1896 stock. Modification program took place between 1911 and 1920.

Exc.	*V.G.*	*Good*	*Fair*	*Poor*
425	350	250	175	125

Model 1911 Rifle

Straightened and redesigned bolt to better handle the higher performance 1911 cartridge. Barrel length is 30.7 inches. Magazine capacity was reduced from 12 to 6 rounds in the Model 1911. Other changes included a pistol grip and flat buttplate on the stock. Approximately 133,000 were manufactured between 1913 and 1919.

Exc.	*V.G.*	*Good*	*Fair*	*Poor*
425	350	250	175	125

Model 1911 Carbine

Same action as the Model 1911 rifle with a 23.25-inch barrel. Approximately 185,000 were manufactured between 1914 and 1933.

Exc.	*V.G.*	*Good*	*Fair*	*Poor*
500	400	275	200	150

Charger clip for Schmidt Rubin rifles in 7.5x55mm. Price 10-4

Engineer Bayonet for Swiss M 1911 Carbine

Sometimes called a Pioneer bayonet. Wood handle. 18.75-inch single edge blade with saw teeth on the top. Very popular with collectors. Will also fit the K-31 short rifle. Does not fit the Schmidt Rubin long rifles as the muzzle opening is not large enough. Price range 175 – 75.

Bayonets for Schmidt Rubin Series

Wood grips. Muzzle ring. Bayonets made for the long rifles have a smaller muzzle opening than the carbines. 11.7" blade. The Model 1889 and 1911 versions have a single edge. They differ in the retaining ridge or stud in the fuller. The Model 1918 has a double edge. Makers name on the ricasso: Elsner Schwyz Victoria or Waffenfabrik Neuhausen. All use the same steel scabbard.

NOTE: The model 1918 is the correct bayonet for the K-31 rifle, although the other types fit as well. Price range 175 – 80.

Model 1931 Short Rifle K-31

Similar to the above, with a redesigned lock work, 25.7-inch barrel, and 6-shot magazine. This was the final version of the Schmidt-Rubin design. Instead of locking lugs into the receiver, the lugs were

Engineer Bayonet for Swiss M 1911 Carbine

SWITZERLAND

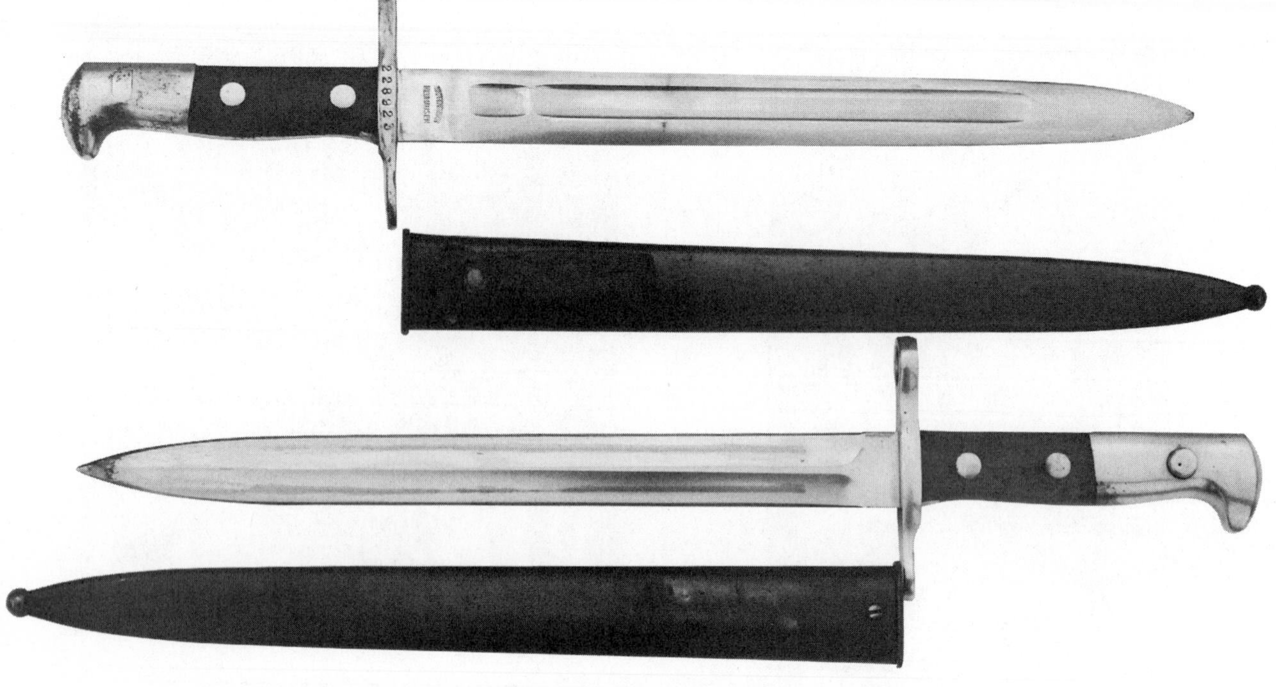

Bayonets for Schmidt Rubin Series

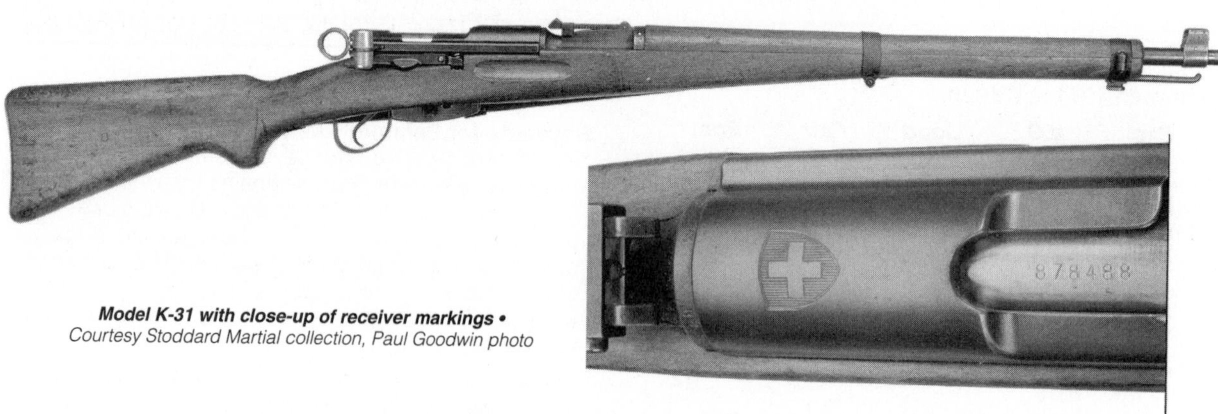

Model K-31 with close-up of receiver markings • *Courtesy Stoddard Martial collection, Paul Goodwin photo*

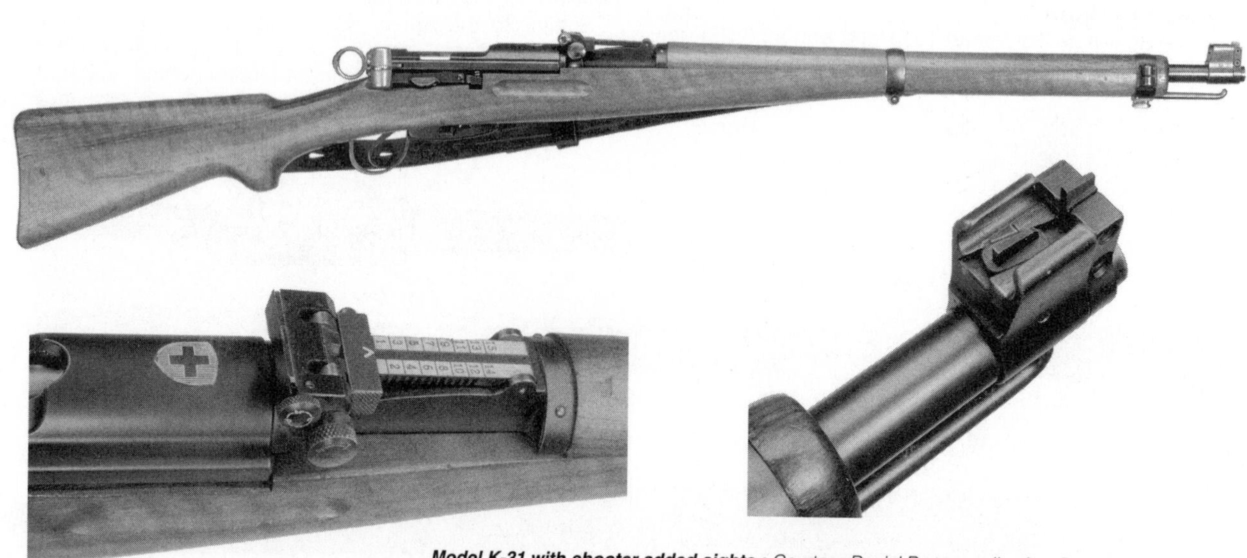

Model K-31 with shooter added sights • *Courtesy Daniel Rewers collection, Paul Goodwin photo*

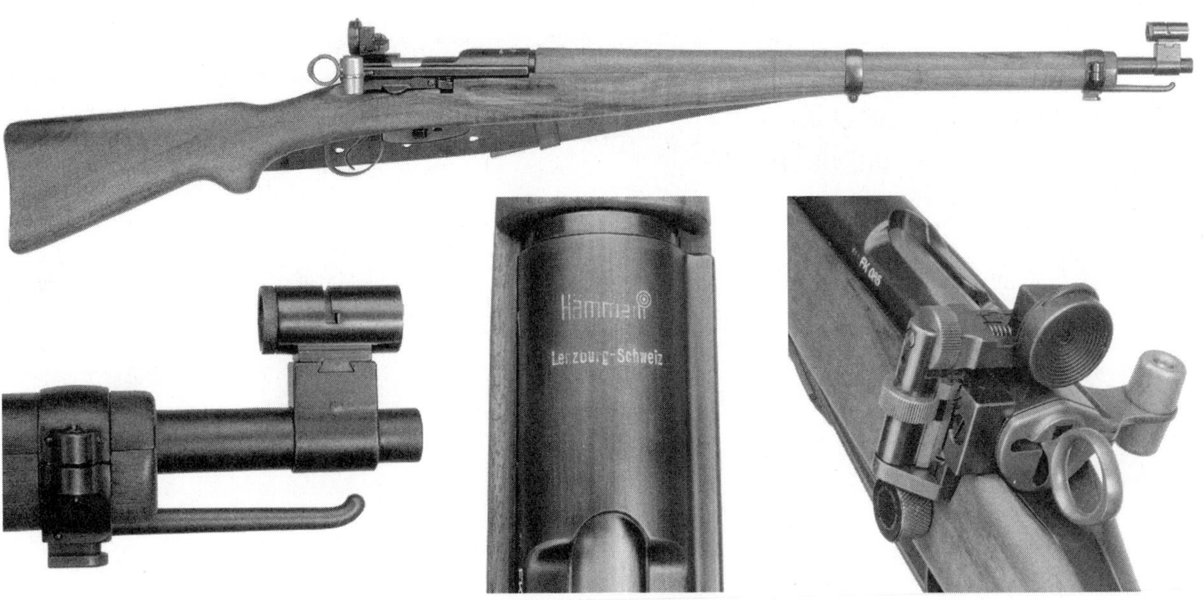

Hammerili Match K-31 with close-ups of receiver markings, and front and rear sights •
Courtesy Daniel Rewers collection, Paul Goodwin photo

Model 1931 .22 training rifle. Close-up bolt shows it in the open and closed position •
Courtesy Stoddard Martial collection, Paul Goodwin photo

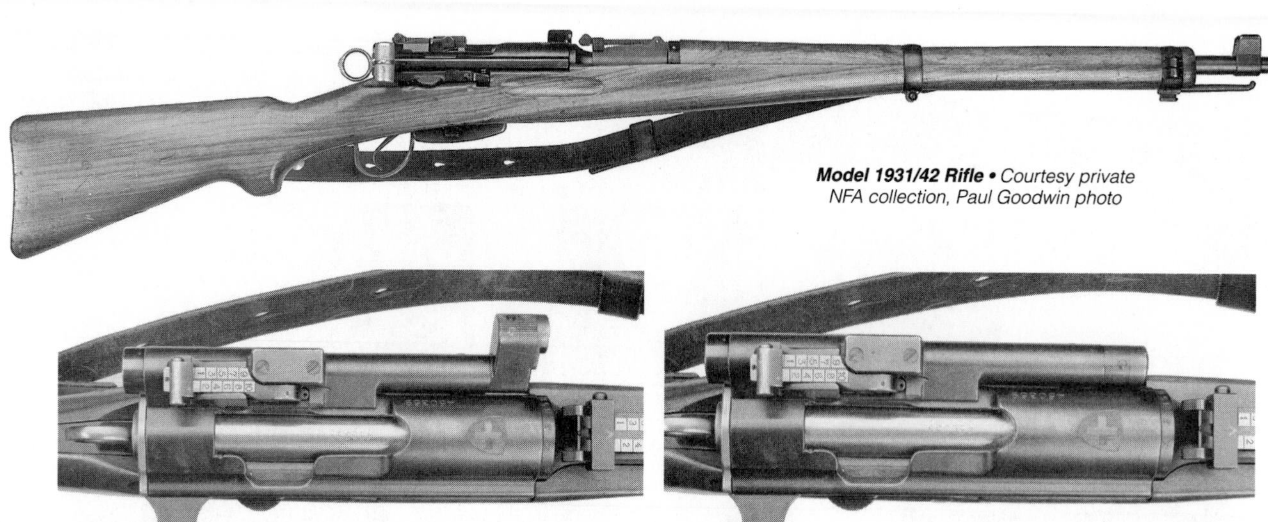

Model 1931/42 Rifle • Courtesy private NFA collection, Paul Goodwin photo

SWITZERLAND

repositioned to lock into the receiver ring thereby greatly increasing the strength of the rifle. This change also increased the length of the barrel without increasing the overall length of the rifle. Approximately 528,180 were manufactured between 1933 and 1958. Many thousands were imported in the last few years. Note: Add $25-50 for a walnut stock.

Exc.	V.G.	Good	Fair	Poor
375	300	250	125	100

Model 1931 Short Rifle with Shooter-Added Target Sights

Many shooters in Switzerland have modified Model 1931s with target sights. These can range in price due to the quality of the sights added. Prices range from $550 to $350.

Model 1931 .22 Target Rifle

This is the single-shot training version of the K31 with sights set for 50 meters. The rifle is the same overall length as the standard K31. Fitted with a highly modified bolt for the .22 caliber rimfire cartridge.

Exc.	V.G.	Good	Fair	Poor
950	750	600	350	250

Hammerili Match K31

This rifle is produced by Hammerili and is so marked on the receiver ring. These rifles have rear military sight omitted and a target sight installed at the rear of the receiver. Very limited production.

Exc.	V.G.	Good	Fair	Poor
4500	3750	3000	2000	1200

MODEL 1931 SNIPER VARIANTS

There are a number of different sniper variants to the Model 1931 rifle. The first attempt was an experimental model, the Model 1940, fitted with a Wild & Gerber scope, which was positioned high above the receiver by means of an odd looking scope mount with a forehead protector attached to it. The second experimental model was the Model 1942 with a small detachable scope fitted to the left side of the receiver. All of these rifles were manufactured in small quantities.

Model 1931/42

Built by Waffenfabrik Bern on the Model 31 action and stock. Barrel length is 25.7 inches with 6-shot magazine. Walnut stock with handguard. This variant

Model K-31/43 Sniper rifle with close-up of scope location • Courtesy Daniel Rewers collection, Paul Goodwin photo

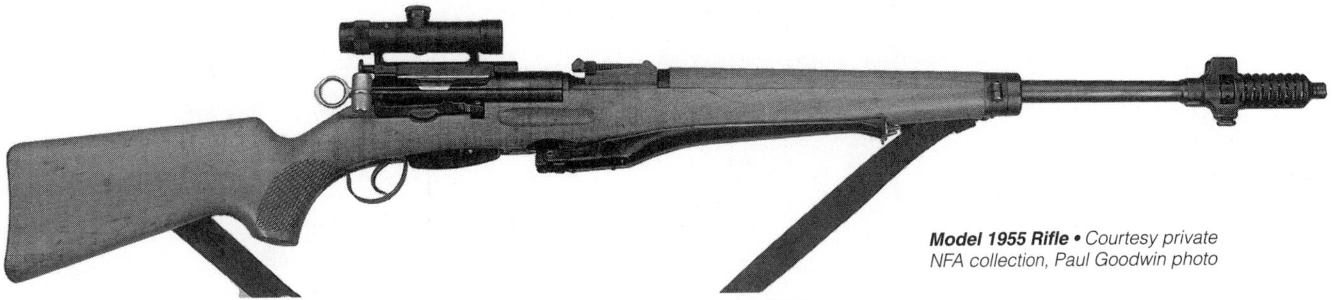
Model 1955 Rifle • *Courtesy private NFA collection, Paul Goodwin photo*

is fitted with a 1.8 power integral telescope attached to the left side of the receiver. It has a unique periscope type rotating objective. This rifle is also fitted with open sights to 1,500 meters.

Exc.	V.G.	Good	Fair	Poor
4500	3500	2500	1000	—

Model 1931/43

As above but with a 2.8 power telescope.

Exc.	V.G.	Good	Fair	Poor
4500	3500	2500	1000	—

Model 1955

This model, introduced in 1955, is built on a Model 1931 action. Barrel length is 25.7 inches. A muzzle brake is fitted. This model is fitted with a 3.5 power Kern Aarau telescope mounted on the receiver bridge. Beechwood stock is 2/3 length with handguard and checkered pistol grip. Integral bipod built into midpoint of stock. Weight is about 12 lbs.

Exc.	V.G.	Good	Fair	Poor
4500	3500	2500	1000	—

MANNLICHER

Model 1893 Carbine

This is a Mannlicher straight pull design carbine with a 21.5-inch barrel chambered for the 7.5x53.5mm cartridge. It was the only Mannlicher adopted by Switzerland. It was fitted with a full-length stock and upper handguard. No bayonet fittings. Magazine capacity was 6 rounds and it was charger loaded. The receiver ring is marked with a small Swiss cross.

Exc.	V.G.	Good	Fair	Poor
1000	800	650	350	225

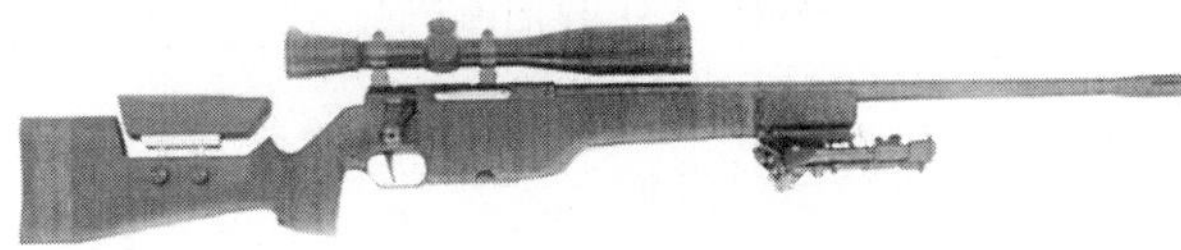

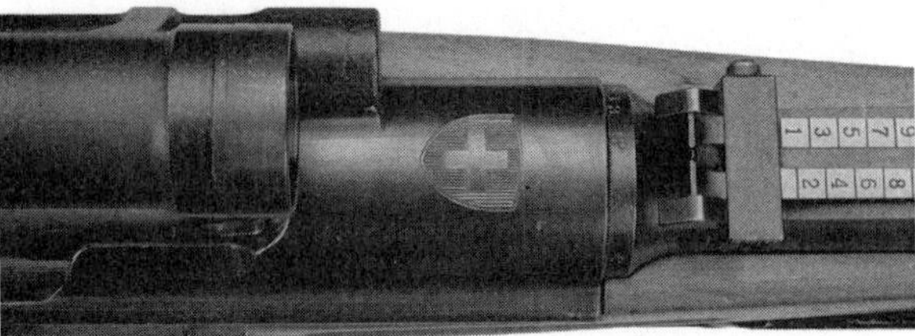

SIG

Schweizerische Industrie Gesellschaft, Neuhausen am Rheinfalls, Switzerland

SSG 2000

This is a high-grade, bolt action, sniping-type rifle chambered for .223, 7.5mm Swiss, .300 Weatherby Magnum, and .308 Winchester. It has a 24-inch barrel and was furnished without sights. It has a 4-round box magazine. The finish is matte blued with a thumbhole-style stippled walnut stock with an adjustable cheekpiece. This model was discontinued in 1986.

NIB	Exc.	V.G.	Good	Fair	Poor
8000	6000	3500	1500	—	—

SSG 3000

Chambered for the .308 Win. cartridge, this model is fitted with a 23.4-inch barrel and ambidextrous McMillian Tactical stock. Magazine capacity is 5

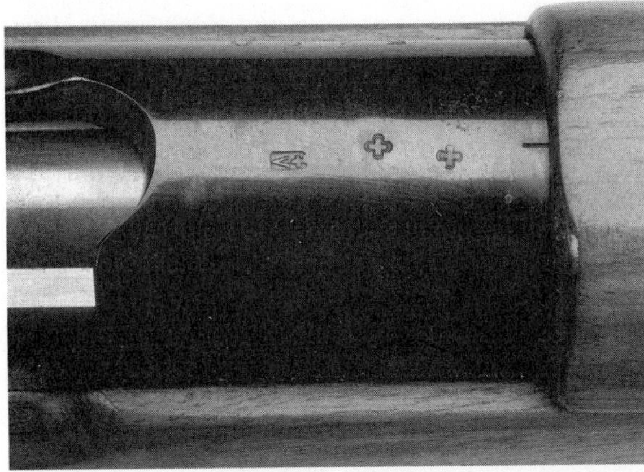

Mannlicher Model 1893 Carbine • *Courtesy West Point Museum, Paul Goodwin photo*

PE557 Assault Rifle • Courtesy Chuck Karwan

SWITZERLAND

rounds. Overall length is 46.5 inches, and approximate weight is 12 lbs. This model comes in three different packages. They are listed below.

Level I

Base model with no bipod or scope, but with carrying case.

NIB	Exc.	V.G.	Good	Fair	Poor
2600	2000	—	—	—	—

Level II

At this level a Leupold Vari-X III 3.5-10x40mm Duplex scope and Harris bipod with carrying case.

NIB	Exc.	V.G.	Good	Fair	Poor
3500	2750	—	—	—	—

Level III

Rifle is supplied with a Leupold Mark 4 M1-10x40mm Mil-Dot Scope with Harris bipod and carrying case.

NIB	Exc.	V.G.	Good	Fair	Poor
4500	3500	—	—	—	—

SIG AMT

This is a semi-automatic rifle chambered for the 7.62 NATO cartridge. Fitted with a 19-inch barrel and wooden buttstock and forearm. Folding bipod standard. Box magazine capacity is 5, 10, or 20 rounds. Weight is about 10 lbs. Built from 1960 to 1974.

NIB	Exc.	V.G.	Good	Fair	Poor
4500	3850	3250	2500	1500	1000

SIG PE57

Similar to the above but chambered for the 7.5x55 Swiss cartridge.

NIB	Exc.	V.G.	Good	Fair	Poor
4500	4100	3500	2700	1700	1300

Bern Stg 51 Assault Rifle

Developed after the end of World War II; the Swiss wanted their own version of a true assault rifle. Waffenfabrik Bern was one of the companies involved in this project. The result was the Stg 51 first built in 1951. This rifle was chambered for the 7.5mm short cartridge, a special cartridge made specifically for this rifle and no longer produced. The rifle is select fire and does so in both models in closed-bolt position. A 30-round box magazine supplies the gun that has a rate of fire of about 800 rounds per minute. The barrel is 22.5 inches in length and is fitted with a muzzle brake/flash suppressor. A mid-barrel bipod is fitted just ahead of the forend. Weight is approximately 10.5 lbs.

A second model of this rifle was also produced with internal modifications and some small external differences. Both models were issued to the Swiss army, most likely on a trial basis. Extremely rare.

Swiss Stg Model 51 (2nd Model) • Courtesy private NFA collection, Paul Goodwin photo

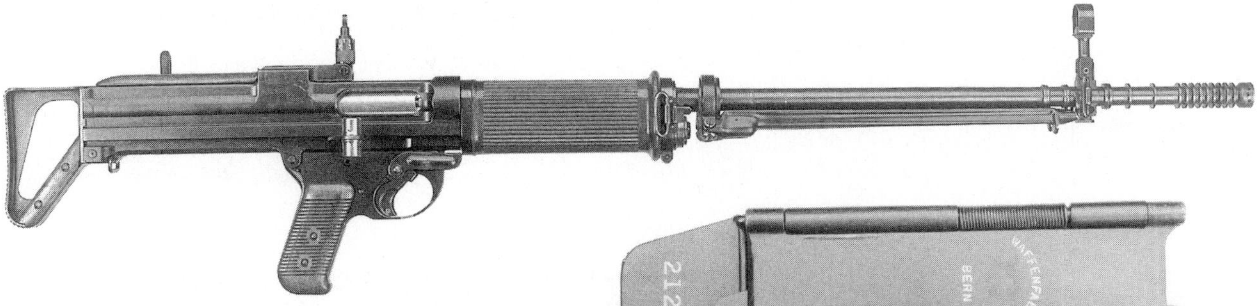

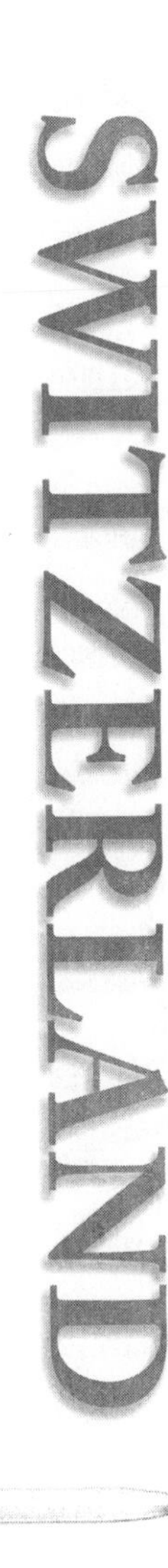

Swiss SIG Model 51 (2nd Model) • *Courtesy private NFA collection, Paul Goodwin photo*

Bern Stg 54 • *Courtesy private NFA collection, Paul Goodwin photo*

SIG Stgw 57 with close-up of receiver markings • *Courtesy Stoddard Martial collection, Paul Goodwin photo*

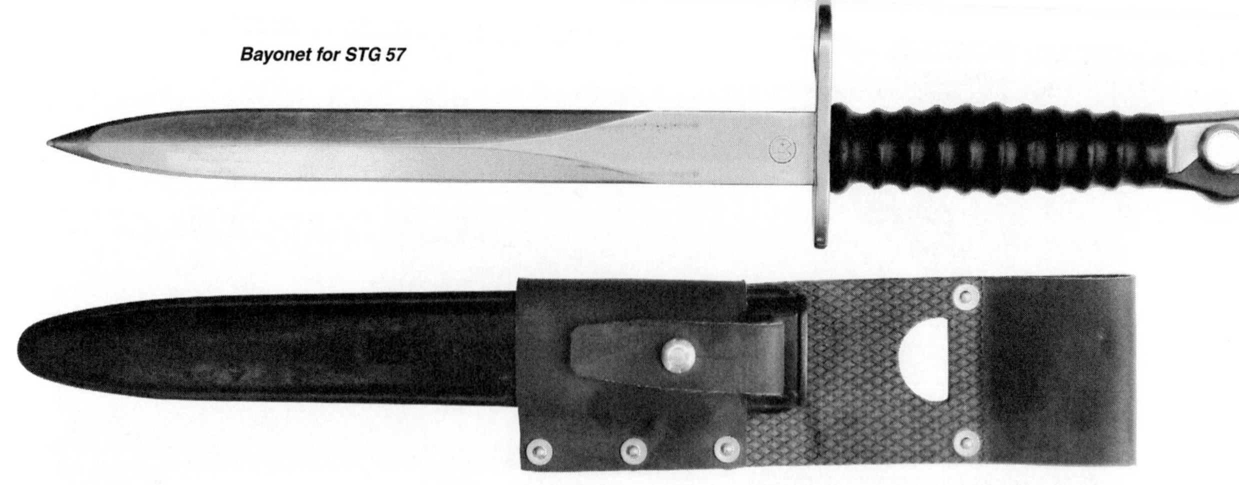
Bayonet for STG 57

SWITZERLAND

NOTE: The first model of this rifle will interchange some parts with the German FG 42. The second model will interchange all of its parts with the German FG 42.

Bern Stg 51 (First Model)
Pre-1968

Exc.	*V.G.*	*Fair*
75000+	—	—

Bern Stg 51 (Second Model)
Pre-1968

Exc.	*V.G.*	*Fair*
75000+	—	—

Bern Stg 54 (Sturmgewehr W+F 1954)

Introduced in 1954 and chambered for the 7.5mm cartridge, this assault rifle is fitted with a 28.4-inch barrel including muzzle brake. Weight is approximately 11 lbs. Rate of fire is about 800 rounds per minute. Select fire. Magazine capacity is 30 rounds. Fitted with a bipod. This was an experimental model and it was produced in a number of different variants. Extremely rare.

Pre-1968

Too Rare To Price.

SIG Stgw 57 Assault Rifle

This rifle is a select fire chambered for the 7.5x55mm Swiss cartridge. Barrel length is 23 inches. Box magazine capacity is 24 rounds. Weight is about 12.25 lbs. Adopted by the Swiss army with about 600,000 of these rifles produced between 1957 and 1983. It is based on the German StG 45. The rifle has a pressed steel receiver, folding bipod, wood butt, barrel jacket, and carry handle. The muzzle is designed to act as a grenade launcher and compensator. As with all standard issue Swiss military rifles, this rifle will remain in service for the lifetime of the soldier.

Pre-1968

Exc.	*V.G.*	*Fair*
N/A	N/A	N/A

Pre-1986 manufacture with new receiver or re-weld

Exc.	*V.G.*	*Fair*
22000	20000	18000

Bayonet for STG 57

Molded plastic handle. 9.5-inch double edge blade.

Price range 50 – 30.

SIG 550

This semi-automatic rifle is chambered for .223 cartridge and fitted with an 18" barrel.

NIB	*Exc.*	*V.G.*	*Good*	*Fair*	*Poor*
9000	7000	5500	3000	—	—

SIG 551

Same as above but fitted with a 16-inch barrel.

NIB	*Exc.*	*V.G.*	*Good*	*Fair*	*Poor*
9500	7500	6500	4000	—	—

SIG SG510-4

There are actually four different versions of this rifle. This version fires the 7.62x51mm cartridge and is fitted with a 19.7-inch barrel. A military version, adopted by the Swiss army, is called the Stgw 57(510-1). Magazine capacity is 20 rounds. Weight is 9.3 lbs. Rate of fire is 600 rounds per minute. Produced from 1957 to 1983. Markings are on left rear of receiver.

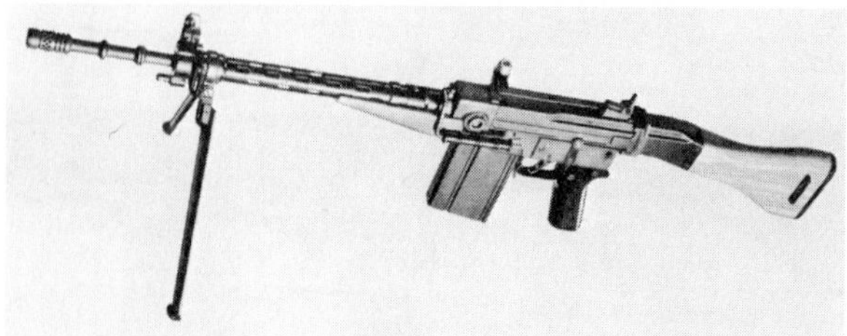

Pre-1968 (Rare)

Exc.	*V.G.*	*Fair*
N/A	N/A	N/A

Pre-1986 manufacture with new receiver or re-weld

Exc.	*V.G.*	*Fair*
20000	18000	16000

SIG 530-1

This rifle is a scaled-down version of the Stgw 57

assault rifle chambered for the 5.56x45mm cartridge. Operated by a gas piston system instead of a delayed blowback operation. Receiver is pressed steel with synthetic butt and forend. Barrel is 18 inches in length with compensator and grenade launcher rings. Magazine capacity is 30 rounds. Weight is about 7.5 lbs. Rate of fire is 600 rounds per minute. There is also a folding stock version of this rifle.

Pre-1968

Exc.	V.G.	Fair
N/A	N/A	N/A

SIG SG540

Designed by the Swiss (SIG) and built in Switzerland, and also built in France by Manurhin beginning in 1977. This 5.56x45mm rifle is in service by a number of African and South American countries. It is fitted with an 18-inch barrel, 20- or 30-round magazine and has a rate of fire of 800 rounds per minute. It is fitted with a fixed stock. Its weight is 7.8 lbs. Marked "MANURHIN FRANCE SG54X" on right side of receiver. This rifle is still in production. There are also two other variants called the SG542 and SG543.

Pre-1968

Exc.	V.G.	Fair
N/A	N/A	N/A

Bayonet for SIG Model 530 and 540 Series

Plastic tubular handle that fits over the flash hider. 7-inch double edge blade. Plastic scabbard. Price range 175 – 75.

MACHINE GUNS

The Swiss adopted the Maxim machine gun in 1894. The Swiss military also used the Maxim Model 1900. More recently the Swiss have used the FN MAG in addition to its own Swiss-built guns.

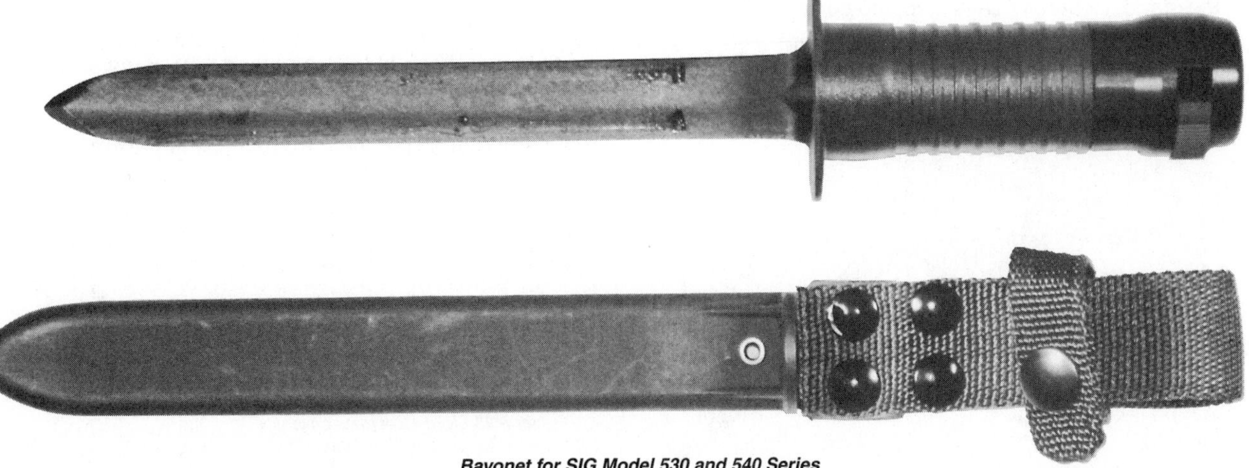

Bayonet for SIG Model 530 and 540 Series

Swiss Model 1911 Maxim • *Courtesy private NFA collection, Paul Goodwin photo*

Swiss Flab MG29 with close-up of markings • *Courtesy private NFA collection, Paul Goodwin photo*

Model 1911 Maxim (MG11)

Built by W+F Bern and chambered for the 7.5x55mm Swiss cartridge. Fitted with a plain steel water jacket, otherwise identical to the German MG 08. This was the standard Swiss heavy machine gun and remained in service until 1951.

Pre-1968

Exc.	*V.G.*	*Fair*
35000+	32500	30000

Pre-1986 manufacture with new receiver or re-weld

Exc.	*V.G.*	*Fair*
20000	18000	16000

Model Flab MG29

Developed by Adolph Furrer and built in 1929 by W+F Bern, this machine gun was chambered for the 7.5mm Swiss cartridge. Fed by metal belts. It was designed for use on armored vehicles and for anti-aircraft applications. The gun has a high rate of fire of about 1,100 rounds per minute. Weight is about 20 lbs. Too rare to price.

Model 25 Light

Introduced in 1926, this gun was designed as a light air-cooled gun chambered for the 7.5x55mm Swiss cartridge. The gun uses a toggle action that opens sideways. It is fitted with a 23-inch barrel with slotted barrel jacket, flash hider, and bipod. The buttstock is wooden. The magazine is mounted on the right side of the gun and has a capacity of 30 rounds. Rate of fire is about 450 rounds per minute. Weight is approximately 24 lbs.

Pre-1968

Exc.	*V.G.*	*Fair*
35000+	—	—

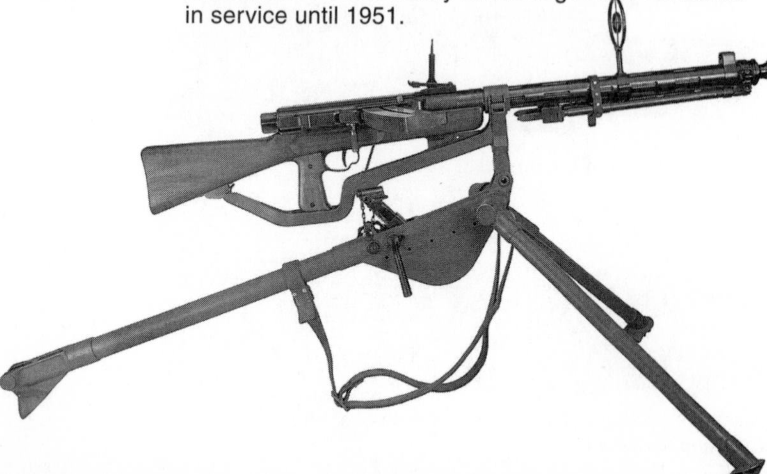

Furrer M25 Light • *Courtesy private NFA collection, Paul Goodwin photo*

The Republic of Turkey, a parliamentary democracy of the Near East located partially in Europe and partially in Asia between the Black and the Mediterranean Seas, has an area of 301,382 sq. mi. (780,580 sq. km.) and a population of *55.4 million. Capital: Ankara. Turkey exports cotton, hazelnuts, and tobacco, and enjoys a virtual monopoly in meerschaum.

The Ottoman Turks, a tribe from Central Asia, first appeared in the early 13th century, and by the 17th century had established the Ottoman Empire which stretched from the Persian Gulf to the southern frontier of Poland, and from the Caspian Sea to the Algerian plateau. The defeat of the Turkish navy by the Holy League in 1571, and of the Turkish forces besieging Vienna in 1683, began the steady decline of the Ottoman Empire which, accelerated by the rise of nationalism, contracted its European border, and by the end of World War I deprived it of its Arab lands. The present Turkish boundaries were largely fixed by the Treaty of Lausanne in 1923. The sultanate and caliphate, the political and spiritual ruling institutions of the old empire, were separated and the sultanate abolished in 1922. On Oct. 29, 1923, Turkey formally became a republic.

HANDGUNS

The Ottoman Empire purchased a number of Smith and Wesson Number 3 revolvers (see U.S. Handguns, Smith & Wesson). Handguns were not favored by Turkish military officers. Turkey also purchased Mauser C96 pistols (see Germany, Handguns, Mauser). Turkey also ordered about 70,000 Smith & Wesson Model 10 revolvers in 1980. The Turkish military also uses the Colt Model 1911A1 pistol.

Kirrikale (MKE)

Made in Ankara and Istanbul, this .380 caliber pistol is a close copy of the Walther Model PP.

Exc.	*V.G.*	*Good*	*Fair*	*Poor*
500	400	300	150	100

SUBMACHINE GUNS

Turkey uses the U.S. M3A1 submachine gun as well as the HK MP5.

RIFLES

During WWI, Turkey captured large numbers of Russian Mosin-Nagant rifles and carbines. These weapons were used by the Turks during WWI and subsequent conflicts. The Turkish crescent moon is frequently found stamped on various parts.

Over the past 40 years, Turkey has used a number of foreign-built rifles including the HK G3, the FN FAL, the M16A2, and the M1 rifle, as well as the M1 carbine.

SNAP SHOT
PEABODY-MARTINI RIFLE

If there is one military arm by which the name designations are thoroughly confusing it has to be the **Peabody Rifle**; or is it the **Peabody-Martini**? No, it has to be the **Martin-Henry** or does it? See what I mean?

The rifle developed by Henry O. Peabody should have been a resounding success with the U.S. Army. It was not. In late 1864, by the time Peabody had his side-hammer rifle, utilizing a pivoting breach block, ready for production the war was practically over. With a glut of arms at war's end, the Ordinance Dept. was more focused on modernizing the existing stockpile than acquiring new designs. However, a few National Guard units and several foreign countries adopted the **Peabody Rifle**.

A Swiss gunsmith by the name of Frederich von Martini improved the design by eliminating the side lock and incorporating a spring-loaded firing pin that was cocked upon opening the action. Martini was able to sell the design to the British who after much testing added to the rifle the Alexander Henry system of rifling. The now hammerless, self cocking rifle became what we know as the **Martini-Henry** chambered for the British .577/450 cartridge. The rifle through several model designations (Mark I – IV) took its place in the long line of Enfield-produced rifles having served the British Empire for over three decades. But, the same rifles were also produced in the United States and designated as **Peabody-Martini** rifles.

Back at the Providence Tool Company in Rhode Island, the very factory that had produced the original **Peabody rifle**, production of the Martini-Henry rifles was in full swing for the Turkish Army. The company had tried to sell the side-hammer Peabody design to the Turks but they chose the Martini improved hammerless design. Through some bizarre arrangements which even included Oliver Winchester, the Providence Tool Company produced over 600,000 exact copies of the British Martini-Henry rifles but were stamped as being **Peabody-Martini** rifles.

Now, one last tidbit of trivia to further muddy the water. Some of the original Peabody (side-hammer) rifles for the Connecticut Militia were refurbished with .45-70 barrels having Alexander Henry rifling. Were these **Peabody-Henry** rifles or what? Time for a Martini!

Kenny Durham

MARTINI

Model 1874 Peabody-Martini Rifle

This rifle was almost identical to the British Martini-Henry Mark I rifle (.45 Martini Henry cartridge). Built by the Providence Tool Company, it was not adopted by any U.S. military. About 600,000 were sold to the Turkish military and used in the Russo-Turkish War, 1877-1878. Marked "PEABODY-MARTINI PATENTS." Serial numbered in Arabic numbers. Rifle chambered for the .45 Turkish caliber and fitted with a 32.5-inch barrel with two barrel bands. Full stock. Weight is about 8.75 lbs.

Exc.	V.G.	Good	Fair	Poor
1250	950	600	400	250

Model 1874 Peabody-Martini Carbine

As above but with 21.5-inch barrel and one barrel band. Half stocked. Fitted with a saddle ring.

NOTE: Some of the rifles and carbines were sold to the Japanese Navy and exhibit both Turkish and Japanese markings. Add 25 percent for Japanese marked example.

Exc.	V.G.	Good	Fair	Poor
1600	1400	900	500	300

Bayonet for Model 1874 Peabody Martini

Checkered hard rubber grips. Muzzle ring. Hook quillon. 22.7-inch single edge yatagan style blade. Steel tipped leather scabbard. Price range 300 – 150.

MAUSER

M1887 Rifle

This model is a variation of the German Model 71/84. Differences are a smaller triggerguard, a double locking bolt handle, higher comb, and 9.5x60mm Turkish blackpowder caliber. Rear sight graduated to 1,600 meters. Markings in Turkish on the receiver ring, left side rail, and rear sight. Barrel length is 30 inches. Weight about 9.25 lbs. Tubular magazine has an 8-round capacity. About 220,000 were delivered to Turkey.

Exc.	V.G.	Good	Fair	Poor
750	650	500	300	150

M1890 Rifle

Chambered for the smokeless powder 7.65x53mm cartridge and fitted with a 29-inch barrel. Rear sight graduated to 2,000 meters. Weight is approximately 8.75 lbs. Markings in Turkish. Full length stock with short upper handguard. Box magazine has a 5-round capacity. About 280,000 rifles were produced for the Turkish government. Most were heavily used and later rebarreled to 8x57mm It is un-certain if any quantity of early Turkish Mausers has been imported to the U.S. They rarely appear on the American market.

Exc.	V.G.	Good	Fair	Poor
750	550	400	250	150

M1890 Carbine

As above but with 19.5-inch barrel. Weight is approximately 7.75 lbs.

Exc.	V.G.	Good	Fair	Poor
750	550	400	250	150

Bayonet for 1890 Mauser

Wood grips. Muzzle ring. Hook quillon. Originally made with a 18.1" single edge blade. Many were later shortened to 10". Steel scabbard. Price range 150 – 50. Add 50 percent for an unmodified long version.

M1893 Rifle

Similar to the Spanish Model 1893 but built with a magazine cutoff. Chambered for the 7.65x53mm cartridge and fitted with a 29-inch barrel. Weight is about 9 lbs. Rear sight graduated to 2,000 meters. Markings in Turkish. Full length stock with half length upper handguard. Approximately 200,000 delivered to Turkey. Most were later converted to 8x57mm when Turkey adopted that caliber.

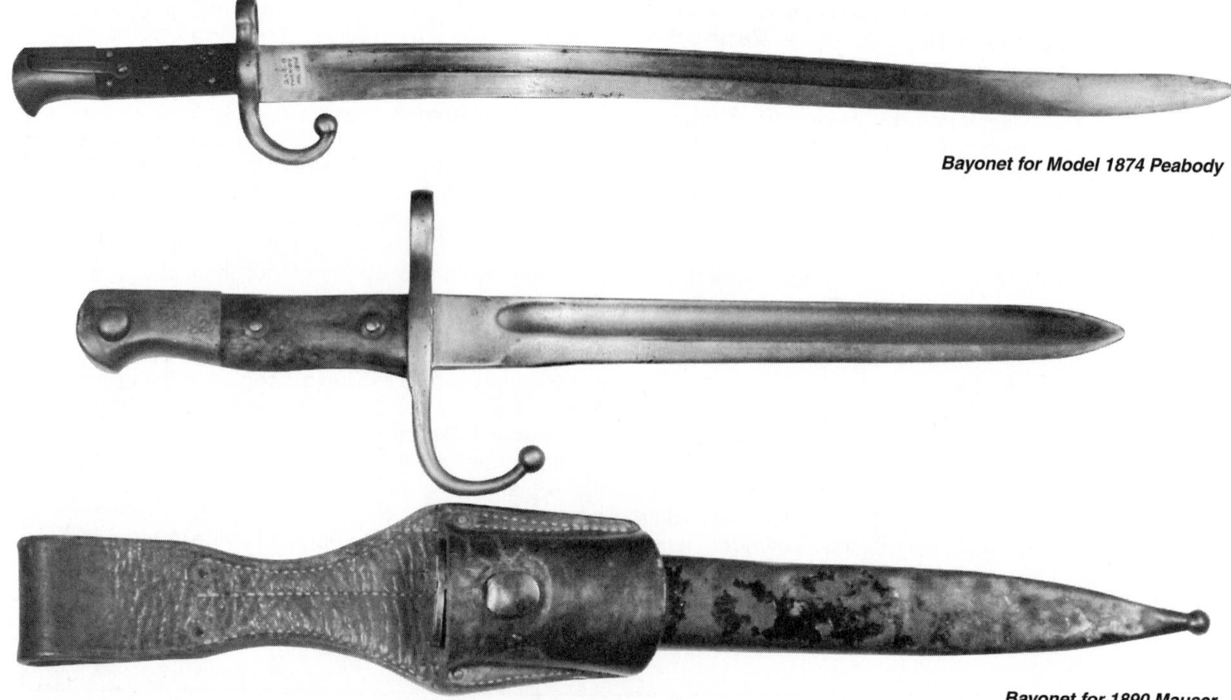

Bayonet for Model 1874 Peabody

Bayonet for 1890 Mauser

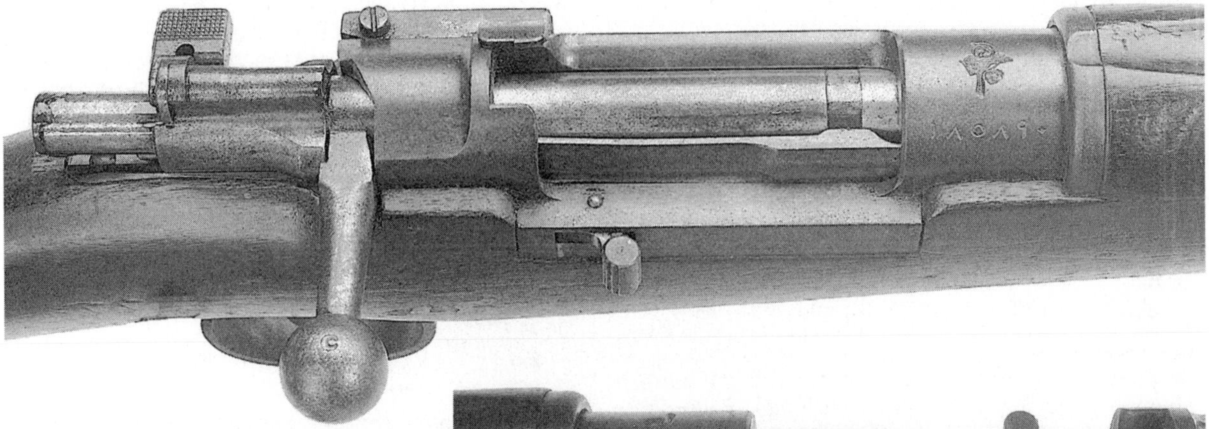

Turkish Mauser Model 1893 • *Private collection, Paul Goodwin photo*

Turkish Mauser Model 1903 • *Courtesy Paul S. Scarlata*

Exc.	V.G.	Good	Fair	Poor
550	450	300	150	100

M1893 rifle, converted to 8x57mm

Exc.	V.G.	Good	Fair	Poor
350	225	150	100	75

M1903 Rifle

Chambered for the 7.65x53mm cartridge and fitted with a 29-inch barrel, this model features a pistol grip full-length stock with half-length upper handguard. Magazine capacity is 5 rounds. Tangent rear sight graduated to 2,000 meters. Turkish crescent and star on the receiver. Weight is about 9 lbs. This model was the standard infantry rifle for the Turkish army from WW I to WWII.

Exc.	V.G.	Good	Fair	Poor
600	475	375	150	70

M1903/38 (converted to 8mm)

There have been many of these imported recently. Frequently found with a new stock. Nearly all have a mismatched bolt. Add 25-50 percent for a matching bolt.

Exc.	V.G.	Good	Fair	Poor
250	175	125	100	50

M1905 Carbine

21.5-inch barrel. Fitted with a full length stock with half length upper handguard. No bayonet mount. Chambered for the 7.65x53mm cartridge. Rear sight graduated to 1,600 meters. Magazine capacity is 5

TURKEY & OTTOMAN EMPIRE

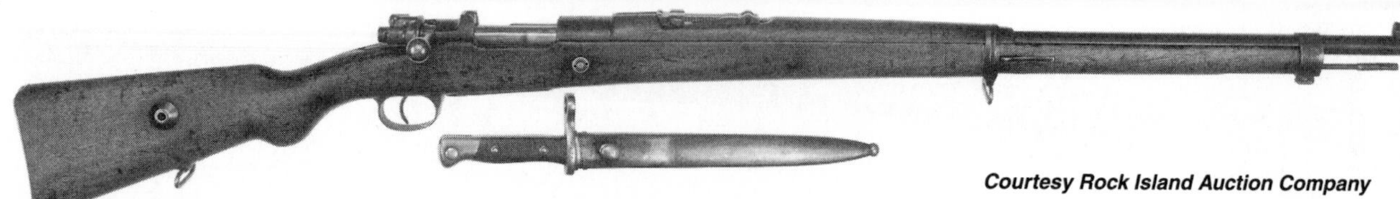
Courtesy Rock Island Auction Company

rounds. Weight is approximately 8.25 lbs. Markings in Turkish. Only about 20,000 of these carbines were produced.

Exc.	V.G.	Good	Fair	Poor
750	600	475	250	150

M98/22 Rifle

This model is a Czech Model 98/22 with Turkish or Czech markings. Many have been imported with the usual miss matched bolt. Add 50% for a rifle with matching bolt.

Exc.	V.G.	Good	Fair	Poor
250	175	150	100	75

M38 Short Rifle

This model is an arsenal-reworked rifle with 24" barrel chambered for the 7.92x37mm cartridge. Patterned after the German WW1 Kar-98a. Tangent rear sight graduated to 2,000 meters. Magazine capacity is 5 rounds. Marked with the Turkish crescent and star. Weight is about 9 lbs.

Exc.	V.G.	Good	Fair	Poor
350	250	175	100	75

Bayonets for Turkish 1903 Mausers

Turkey has used a large variety of German WWI vintage bayonets for their Mauser rifles including the ersatz type with metal handles. Many had the blades shortened to 10 inches. Some will have muzzle rings, some will not. Many of these came in with the Turkish M 1903 and 1943 Mausers recently imported. Turkey also produced its own bayonets as shown below. Wooden grips. Muzzle ring. 10-inch single edge blade. No markings except for a serial number. The modified German bayonets have a slightly higher value than the Turkish-produced specimen. Price range 50 – 20.

M38 Short Rifle with Folding Bayonet

As above but with bayonet that folds under the barrel. Rare. No known imports.

Exc.	V.G.	Good	Fair	Poor
900	750	600	200	150

MACHINE GUNS

During WWI Turkey acquired the German Maxim Model 08/15 in 7.92mm caliber. More recently Turkey has relied on the Turkish-built (under license) German MG3, the M1918A2, the M1919 A6, and the .50 M2 HB.

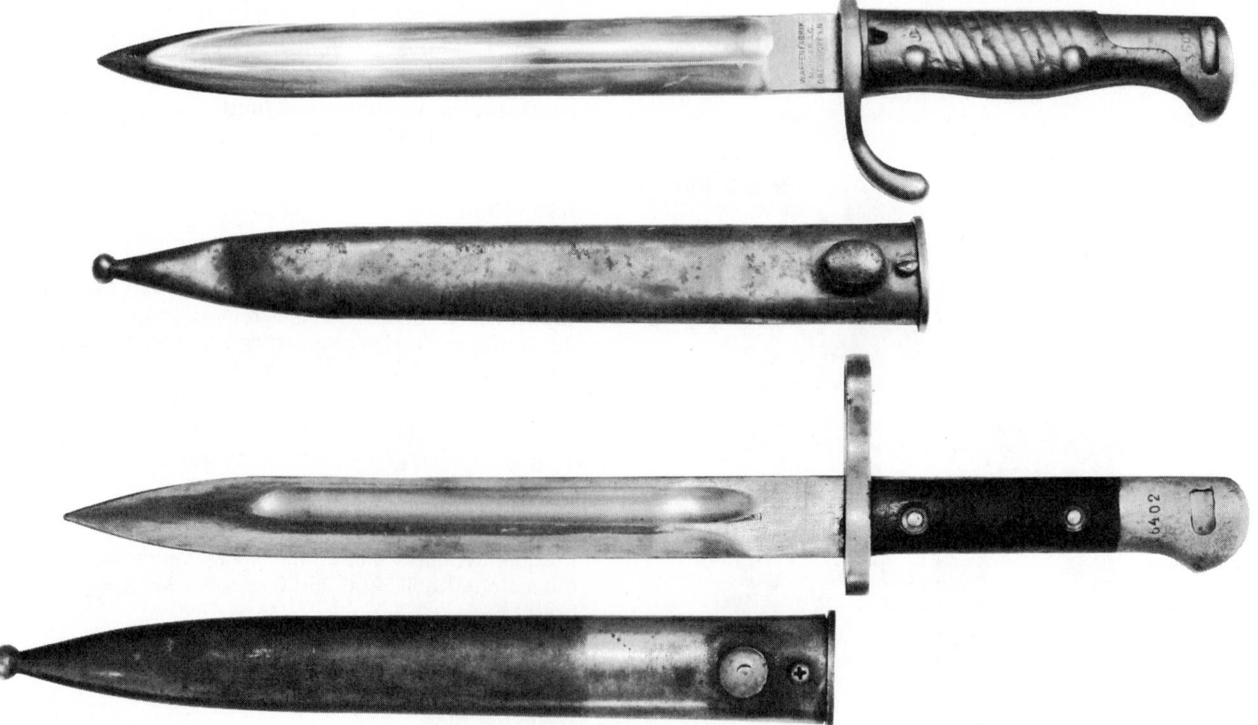

Bayonet for Turkish 1903 Mausers

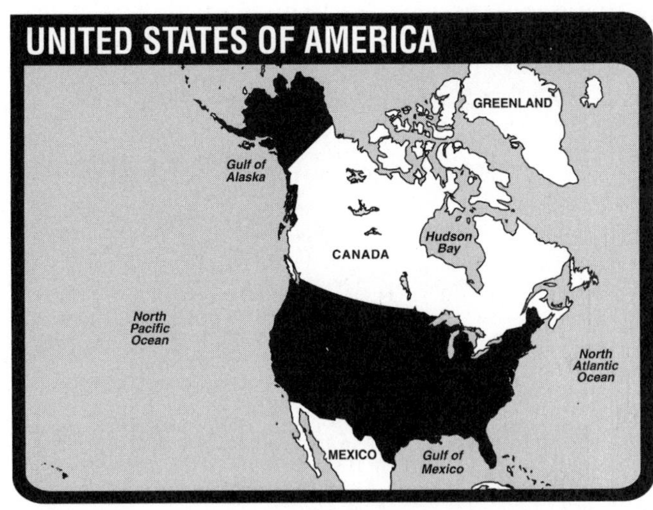

The United States of America as politically organized, under the Articles of Confederation consisted of the 13 original British-American colonies; New Hampshire, Massachusetts, Rhode Island, Connecticut, New York, New Jersey, Pennsylvania, Delaware, Virginia, North Carolina, South Carolina, Georgia and Maryland. Clustered along the eastern seaboard of North American between the forests of Maine and the marshes of Georgia. Under the Article of Confederation, the United States had no national capital: Philadelphia, where the "United States in Congress Assembled", was the "seat of government". The population during this political phase of America's history (1781-1789) was about 3 million, most of whom lived on self-sufficient family farms. Fishing, lumbering and the production of grains for export were major economic endeavors. Rapid strides were also being made in industry and manufacturing by 1775, the (then) colonies were accounting for one-seventh of the world's production of raw iron.

On the basis of the voyage of John Cabot to the North American mainland in 1497, England claimed the entire continent. The first permanent English settlement was established at Jamestown, Virginia, in 1607. France and Spain also claimed extensive territory in North America. At the end of the French and Indian Wars (1763), England acquired all of the territory east of the Mississippi River, including East and West Florida. From 1776 to 1781, the States were governed by the Continental Congress. From 1781 to 1789, they were organized under the Articles of Confederation, during which period the individual States had the right to issue money. Independence from Great Britain was attained with the American Revolution in 1776. The Constitution organized and governs the present United States. It was ratified on Nov. 21, 1788.

HANDGUNS

The famous flaming bomb ordnance mark with "U.S." stamp.

Bibliographical Note: There are a number of comprehensive publications on U.S. military handguns, some of which are: *U.S. Handguns of World War II, The Secondary Pistols and Revolvers*, Charles W. Pate, Mowbray, 1999. *U.S. Military Automatic Pistols, 1894-1920*, Scott Meadows, Ellis Publications, 1993.

COLT

Bibliographical Note: There are a number of excellent books on Colt firearms, many of which cover Colt's military models. A few of these books are: John W. Brunner, *The Colt Pocket Hammerless Automatic Pistols*, Phillips Publications, 1996. Keith Cochrane, *Colt Cavalry, Artillery and Militia Revolvers*, South Dakota, 1987. Kopec, Graham, and Moore, *A Study of the Colt Single Action Army Revolver*, California, 1976. For the Colt Model 1911 references see *Colt Model 1911* section.

NOTE: It should be pointed out that the U.S. military purchased and used a number of different Colt pistols and revolvers over the years. In some cases these handguns will be marked with military acceptance stamps or inspector's stamps. In other cases there may be no markings. The following models are some of the most often encountered military marked Colt handguns.

Single Action Army, Early Military Model 18731877

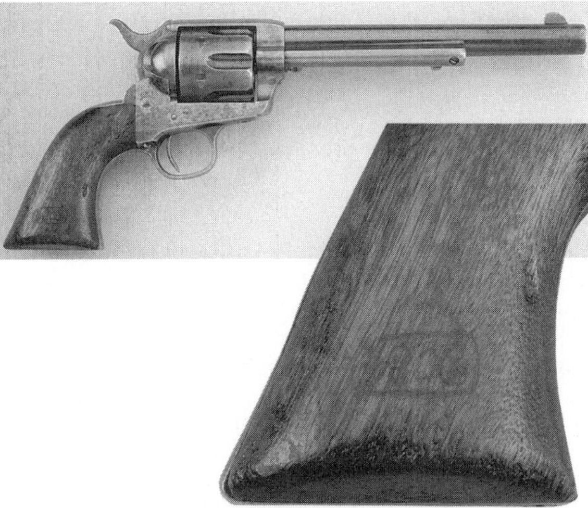

Paul Goodwin photo

The serial number range on this first run of military contract revolvers extends to #24000. The barrel address is in the early script style with the # symbol preceding and following. The frame bears the martial marking "US," and the walnut grips have the inspector's cartouche stamped on them. The front sight is steel as on all military models; the barrel length, 7.5". The caliber is .45 Colt, and the ejector rod head is the bull's-eye or donut style with a hole in the center of it. The finish features the military polish and case colored frame, with the remainder blued. Authenticate any potential purchase; many spurious examples have been noted. The Sioux Indian Campaign of 1876 saw its first use in a major military operation. In the Battle of the Little Bighorn, 1976, Custer's troops were armed with the Model 1873 revolver.

Exc.	*V.G.*	*Good*	*Fair*	*Poor*
35000	25000	15000	10000	5000

NOTE: Certain 3-digit and 4-digit serial numbers will command a substantial premium. Seek an expert appraisal prior to sale.

Single Action Army, Late Military Model 18781891

The later Military Models are serial numbered to approximately #136000. They bear the block-style barrel address without the number prefix and suffix. The frames are marked "US," and the grips have the inspector's cartouche. The finish is the military-style polish, case colored frame, and the remainder, blued. Grips are oil-stained walnut. On the military marked Colts, it is imperative that potential purchases be authenticated, as many fakes have been noted. This was the standard sidearm during the Indian campaigns up to 1890.

Exc.	*V.G.*	*Good*	*Fair*	*Poor*
20000	15000	8000	4000	2500

NOTE: Revolvers produced from 1878 to 1885 will command a premium. Seek an expert appraisal prior to sale.

Single Action Army, Artillery Model 1895-1903

A number of "US" marked SAAs were returned either to the Colt factory or to the Springfield Armory, where they were altered and refinished. These revolvers have 5.5" barrels and any combination of mixed serial numbers. They were remarked by the inspectors of the era and have a case colored frame and a blued cylinder and barrel. Some have been noted all blued within this variation. This model, as with the other military marked Colts, should definitely be authenticated before purchase. Some of these revolvers fall outside the 1898 antique cutoff date that has been established by the government and, in our experience, are not quite as desirable to investors. They are generally worth approximately 20 percent less.

Courtesy Rock Island Auction Company

Courtesy Rock Island Auction Company

Exc.	*V.G.*	*Good*	*Fair*	*Poor*
12500	8500	5000	3000	2000

Model 1902 (Philippine/Alaskan)

This is a U.S. Ordnance contract Model 1878 double-action. It has a 6" barrel and is chambered for .45 Colt. The finish is blued, and there is a lanyard swivel on the butt. This model bears the U.S. inspector's marks. It is sometimes referred to as the Philippine or the Alaskan model. The triggerguard is quite a bit larger than standard. About 4,600 produced in serial number range 43401 to 48097.

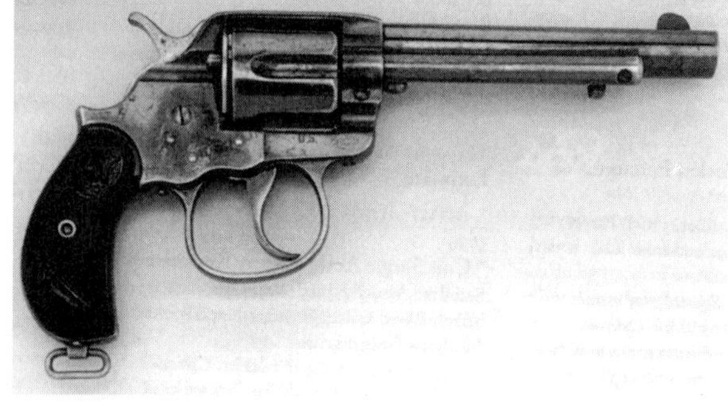

Courtesy Butterfield & Butterfield

Exc.	*V.G.*	*Good*	*Fair*	*Poor*
5500	3500	1500	1000	500

Model 1889 Navy

The 1889 Navy is an important model from a historical standpoint, as it was the first double-action revolver Colt manufactured with a swing-out cylinder. They produced 31,000 of them between 1889 and 1894. The Model

1889 is chambered for the .38 Colt and the .41 Colt cartridges. The cylinder holds 6 shots. It is offered with a 3", 4.5", or 6" barrel, and the finish was either blued or nickel-plated. The grips are checkered hard rubber with the "Rampant Colt" in an oval molded into them. The patent dates 1884 and 1888 appear in the barrel marking, and the serial numbers are stamped on the butt.

Exc.	*V.G.*	*Good*	*Fair*	*Poor*
3000	1500	1000	600	300

NOTE: For 3" barrel add 20 percent. Add a premium for blued models.

Model 1889 U.S. Navy-Martial Model

This variation has a 6" barrel, is chambered for .38 Colt, and is offered in blued finish only. "U.S.N." is stamped on the butt. Most of the Navy models were altered at the Colt factory to add the Model 1895 improvements. An original unaltered specimen would be worth as much as 50 percent premium over the altered values shown.

Courtesy Butterfield & Butterfield, San Francisco, California

Exc.	*V.G.*	*Good*	*Fair*	*Poor*
9000	5000	2500	1000	500

Model 1892 "New Army and Navy"

This model is similar in appearance to the 1889 Navy. The main differences are improvements to the lockwork function. It has double bolt stop notches, a double cylinder locking bolt, and shorter flutes on the cylinder. The .38 Smith & Wesson and the .32-20 were added to the .38 Colt and .41 Colt chamberings. The checkered hard rubber grips are standard, with plain walnut grips found on some contract series guns. Barrel lengths and finishes are the same as described for the Model 1889. The patent dates 1895 and 1901 appear stamped on later models. Colt manufactured 291,000 of these revolvers between 1892 and 1907. Antiques before 1898 are more desirable from an investment standpoint.

Courtesy Butterfield & Butterfield, San Francisco, California

Courtesy Butterfield & Butterfield, San Francisco, California

Exc.	*V.G.*	*Good*	*Fair*	*Poor*
2000	1200	500	300	100

NOTE: For 3" barrel add 20 percent.

U.S. Navy Model

Exc.	*V.G.*	*Good*	*Fair*	*Poor*
3500	2750	1500	1000	750

U.S. Army Model

The initial Army purchase was for 8,000 Model 1892 revolvers, almost all of which were altered to add "Model 1894" improvements. Unaltered examples will bring a premium.

Exc.	*V.G.*	*Good*	*Fair*	*Poor*
3000	1750	800	500	250

Improved Model

Exc.	*V.G.*	*Good*	*Fair*	*Poor*
750	550	400	250	150

NOTE: On all variations of the Model 1892 revolver, add 25-50% for pre-1899 antique, SN under 91,200.

Model 1894/96/1901/1903 Army Model

This model is an improved Model 1892 with a better locking mechanism for the cylinder. Many Model 1892 models were converted in this manner. By the middle of 1897, all U.S. troops were issued the Model 1894 revolver, which was the first U.S. military handgun to use smokeless powder cartridges. Marked "U.S ARMY MODEL 1894" on the bottom of the butt. The Model 1896 was identical to the Model 1894. The Model 1901 was the same as the Model 1894 with the addition of a lanyard swivel. The Model 1903 was identical to the Model 1894 with a smaller bore diameter (9.068mm) and a modified grip.

Paul Goodwin photo

Paul Goodwin photo

Colt Model 1896 Army with cartouche • *Paul Goodwin photo*

Exc.	*V.G.*	*Good*	*Fair*	*Poor*
1900	1000	500	400	200

Model 1905 Marine Corps

Courtesy Faintich Auction Services, Inc., Paul Goodwin photo

This model is a variation of the Model 1894. It was derived from the late production with its own serial range #10001-10926. With only 926 produced between 1905 and 1909, it is quite rare on today's market and is eagerly sought after by Colt Double Action collectors. This model is chambered for the .38 Colt and the .38 Smith & Wesson Special cartridges. It holds 6 shots, has a 6" barrel, and is offered in a blued finish only. The grips are checkered walnut and are quite different than those found on previous models. "U.S.M.C." is stamped on the butt; patent dates of 1884, 1888, and 1895 are stamped on the barrel. One hundred-twenty-five of these revolvers were earmarked for civilian sales and do not have the Marine Corps markings; these will generally be found in better condition. Values are similar.

Exc.	*V.G.*	*Good*	*Fair*	*Poor*
4000	3000	1500	850	500

Military Model of 1909 (New Service)

Made both in a commercial and military version, this revolver was chambered for the .45 Colt cartridge, fitted with a 5.5" barrel and walnut grips with lanyard swivel. Total military procurement was approximately 20,000 revolvers.

U.S. Army Model 1909, #30000-#50000

Marked "U.S. ARMY MODEL 1909" on butt. A total of about 18,000 were produced for the U.S. Army.

Courtesy Faintich Auction Services, Inc., Paul Goodwin photo

Exc.	*V.G.*	*Good*	*Fair*	*Poor*
3000	1500	800	300	200

U.S. Navy Model 1909, #30000-#50000

Same as above with "U.S.N." on butt. About 1,000 were produced for the U.S. Navy.

Exc.	*V.G.*	*Good*	*Fair*	*Poor*
3500	2000	1000	350	250

U.S. Marine Corps Model 1909, #30000-#50000

Checkered walnut grips. "U.S.M.C." on butt. About 1,200 were built for the Marine Corps.

Exc.	*V.G.*	*Good*	*Fair*	*Poor*
4500	2750	1350	650	450

U.S. Army Model 1917, #150000-#301000

Smooth walnut grips, 5.5" barrel, .45 ACP, model designation stamped on butt and barrel. The Model 1917 differed from the Model 1909 in that it had a shorter cylinder for half-moon clips for the .45 ACP cartridge, a wider cylinder stop lug on the sideplate, and a tapered barrel instead of a straight barrel. Blued, unpolished finish. Approximately 150,000 were purchased by the U.S. military.

Exc.	*V.G.*	*Good*	*Fair*	*Poor*
1150	750	500	300	225

Leather holster for 1917 Revolvers

This pattern holster was used for the Colt 1909 and 1917 and S&W Model 1917 revolvers. Most will bear a makers name and date on back. A similar but slightly smaller holster was used for the Colt 1899-1901 series of revolvers. Value is about the same.

Exc.	V.G.	Good	Fair	Poor
200	160	125	75	50

Official Police (Martially marked)

This model was purchased by the military during WWII in barrel lengths of 4", 5", and 6". It has a polished blue finish. Chambered for the .38 Special cartridge. Checkered walnut grips. About 5,000 were purchased by the U.S. Army during WWII. The Defense Supply Corporation also purchased about 5,000 revolvers from Colt as well.

Exc.	V.G.	Good	Fair	Poor
750	600	400	300	150

Commando Model (martially marked)

This model, for all intents and purposes, is an Official Police chambered for .38 Special, with 2" and 4" barrels.

Courtesy Richard M. Kumor Sr.

This model has a matte blue finish, no checkering on the cylinder latch or trigger and matte finish on top of the frame. Checkered plastic grips. Stamped "Colt Commando" on the barrel. There were approximately 50,000 manufactured from 1942 to 1945 for use in World War II.

Exc.	V.G.	Good	Fair	Poor
850	750	400	250	N/A

NOTE: Add 100 percent for 2" barrel.

Detective Special (Martially marked)

Chambered for the .38 Special cartridge and fitted with a 2" barrel. Blued finish with checkered cylinder latch and trigger. Checkered walnut grips. Approximately 5,000 were purchased by armed forces, mostly for military intelligence and police units.

Exc.	V.G.	Good	Fair	Poor
850	550	400	150	100

Aircrewman Special (Martially marked)

This model was especially fabricated for the Air Force to be carried by their pilots for protection. It is extremely lightweight at 11 oz. The frame and the cylinder are made of aluminum alloy. It has a 2" barrel and is chambered for a distinctive .38 Special "M41" military cartridge with a chamber pressure of 16,000 pounds per square inch. The finish was blued, with checkered walnut grips. There were approximately 1,200 manufactured in 1951 with special serial numbers A.F. 1 through A.F. 1189.

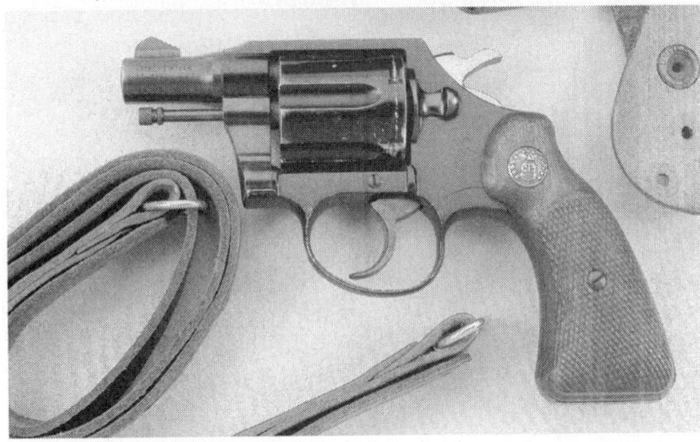

Air Crewman • *Courtesy Little John's Auction Service, Paul Goodwin photo*

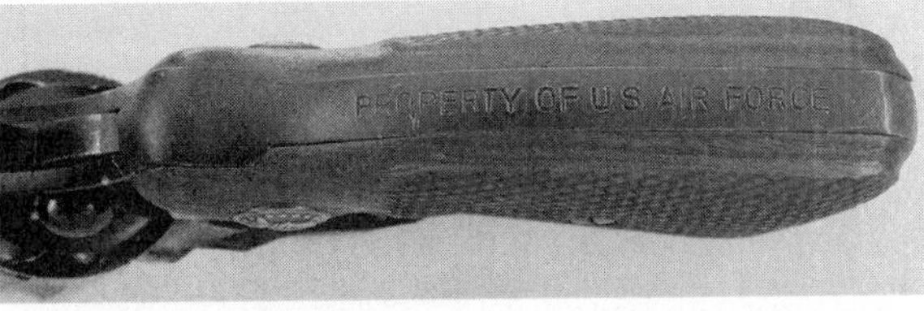

Air Crewman • *Courtesy Little John's Auction Service, Paul Goodwin photo*

Exc.	V.G.	Good	Fair	Poor
4000	2500	1800	800	N/A

COLT SEMI-AUTOMATIC PISTOLS

The Colt Firearms Co. was the first of the American gun manufacturers to take the advent of the semi-automatic pistol seriously. This pistol design was becoming popular among European gun makers in the late 1880s and early 1900s. In the United States, however, the revolver was firmly ensconced as the accepted design. Colt realized that if the semi-auto could be made to function reliably, it would soon catch on. The powers that be at Colt were able to negotiate with some of the noted inventors of the day, including Browning, and to secure or lease the rights to manufacture their designs. Colt also encouraged the creativity of their employees with bonuses and incentives and, through this innovative thinking, soon became the leader in semi-auto pistol sales. The Colt semi-automatic pistols represent an interesting field for the collector of Colt handguns. There were many variations with high enough production to make it worthwhile to seek them out.

Model 1900

This was the first of the Colt automatic pistols. It was actually a developmental model with only 3,500 being produced. The Model 1900 was not really a successful design. It was quite clumsy and out of balance in the hand and was not as reliable in function as it should have been. This model is chambered for the .38 rimless smokeless cartridge. It has a detachable magazine that holds seven cartridges. The barrel is 6" in length. The finish is blued, with a case-colored hammer and safety/sight combination. The grips are either plain walnut, checkered walnut, or hard rubber. This pistol is a Browning design, and the left side of the slide is stamped "Browning's Patent" with the 1897 patent date. Colt sold 250 pistols to the navy and 300 to the army for field trials and evaluation. The remaining 3,300 were sold on the civilian market. This model was manufactured from 1900-1903.

Standard Civilian Production

Exc.	*V.G.*	*Good*	*Fair*	*Poor*
7500	5000	3000	1250	750

NOTE: Civilian model with sight/safety combination add 40 percent.

U.S. Navy Military Model

Colt serial numbers 1001 to 1250 with navy numbers, "U.S.N. 1" to "U.S.N. 250" on the left side of frame. 250 built.

Model 1900 Navy model with sight safety • Paul Goodwin photo

Exc.	*V.G.*	*Good*	*Fair*	*Poor*
7500	6000	5000	2500	1000

U.S. Army Military Model

1st contract

100 built.

Exc.	*V.G.*	*Good*	*Fair*	*Poor*
22000	18000	10000	4000	2000

2nd contract

200 built.

Exc.	*V.G.*	*Good*	*Fair*	*Poor*
20000	16000	8000	3000	1500

Model 1902 Military Pistol

This model is a somewhat larger, heavier pistol than the 1902 Sporting Pistol. It has the same .38 ACP chambering and 6" barrel, detachable magazine holding 8 rounds. The grip of this model is larger and squared off to accommodate the larger magazine, and it has a lanyard swivel on the butt. There were approximately 18,000 manufactured between 1902 and 1929. The vast majority of these pistols were commercial models.

Early Model with Front of Slide Serrated

Model 1902 U.S. military with early front slide serrations • Paul Goodwin photo

Exc.	*V.G.*	*Good*	*Fair*	*Poor*
3500	2250	1250	750	450

Standard Model with Rear of Slide Serrated

Exc.	*V.G.*	*Good*	*Fair*	*Poor*
2500	1750	1000	500	400

Model 1902 military with rear slide serrations • Paul Goodwin photo

U.S. Army Marked

#15001-#15200 with front serrations, 200 built.

Exc.	V.G.	Good	Fair	Poor
15000	12500	5000	2000	600

Model 1903 Hammerless, .32 Pocket Pistol

This was the second pocket automatic Colt manufactured. It was another of John Browning's designs, and it developed into one of Colt's most successful pistols. This pistol is chambered for the .32 ACP cartridge. Initially the barrel length was 4"; this was shortened to 3.75". The detachable magazine holds 8 rounds. The standard finish is blue, with quite a few nickel plated. The early model grips are checkered hard rubber with the "Rampant Colt" molded into them. Many of the nickel-plated pistols had pearl grips. In 1924 the grips were changed to checkered walnut with the Colt medallions. The name of this model can be misleading as it is not a true hammerless but a concealed hammer design. It features a slide stop and a grip safety. Colt manufactured 572,215 civilian versions of this pistol and approximately 200,000 more for military contracts. This model was manufactured between 1903 and 1945.

NOTE: A number of these pistols were shipped to the Philippine army as well as other foreign military forces, but no clear record of these shipments exists. However, about 24,000 Colt Hammerless pistols were sold to Belgium between 1915 and 1917. Serial numbers for these pistols are available (see Brunner, *The Colt Pocket Hammerless Automatic Pistols*). In addition, several thousand Colt .32 pocket pistols, as well as Colt .25 and .380 pocket models, were shipped to England during WWI. During World War II, Colt supplied about 8,000 Colt pocket pistols in various calibers to England in blued and parkerized finish marked "U.S. PROPERTY." (See Brunner.)

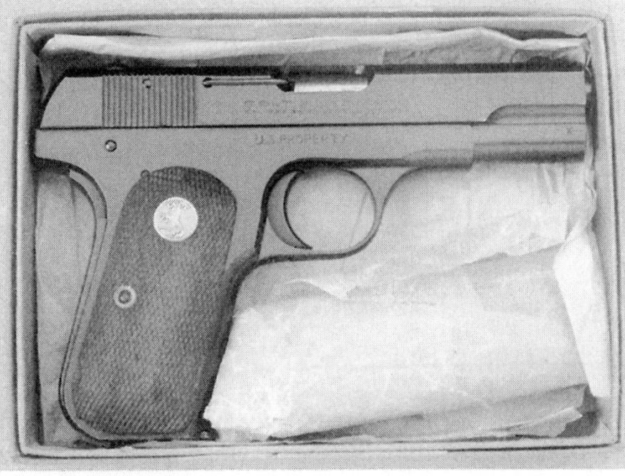

Model 1903 Hammerless with 4" barrel • *Courtesy Richard M. Kumor Sr.*

NOTE: Early Model 1897 patent date add 40 percent. Nickel plated with pearl grips add $100. 4" barrel to #72000 add 20 percent.

U.S. Military Model

Chambered for .32 caliber only and some of them marked "U.S. Property" on frame. Blue or parkerized finish.

NOTE: Pistols issued to General Officers will command a premium. Also, blued pistols will command a premium.

Model 1903, U.S. marked, issued to Gen. Ahee • *Courtesy Richard M. Kumor Sr.*

Exc.	V.G.	Good	Fair	Poor
2200	1500	900	500	300

Model 1908 Hammerless .380 Pocket Pistol

This model is essentially the same as the .32 Pocket Pistol, chambered for the more potent .380 ACP, also known as the 9mm Browning Short. Other specifications are the same. Colt manufactured approximately 138,000 in this caliber for civilian sales. An unknown number were sold to the military.

Standard Civilian Model

Exc.	V.G.	Good	Fair	Poor
800	650	500	350	250

NOTE: Nickel with pearl grips add $100.

Military Model M

Some have serial prefix "M," marked "U.S. Property" on frame, blued finish.

NOTE: None of these pistols was originally parkerized.

Exc.	V.G.	Good	Fair	Poor
2500	1750	750	500	300

Model 1908 Hammerless .25 Pocket Pistol

This was the smallest automatic Colt made. It is chambered for the .25 ACP cartridge, has a 2" barrel, and is 4.5" long overall. It weighs a mere 13 oz. This is a true pocket pistol. The detachable magazine holds 6 shots. This model was offered in blue or nickel-plate, with grips of checkered hard rubber and checkered walnut on later versions. This model has a grip safety, slide lock, and a magazine disconnector safety. This was another Browning design, and Fabrique Nationale manufactured this pistol in Belgium before Colt picked up the rights to make it in the U.S. This

Courtesy Orvel Reichert

was a commercial success by Colt's standards, with approximately 409,000 manufactured between 1908 and 1941.

NOTE: A small number of these pistols were bought by the OSS during WWII from retailers or distributors. These pistols are probably not martially marked. Beware of fakes that are marked by an engraving tool.

Civilian Model

Exc.	*V.G.*	*Good*	*Fair*	*Poor*
500	375	250	200	100

Military Model

"U.S. Property" stamped on right frame. Very rare.

Exc.	*V.G.*	*Good*	*Fair*	*Poor*
3750	3000	1000	450	300

Model 1905 .45 Automatic Pistol

The Spanish American War and the experiences with the Moros in the Philippine campaign taught a lesson about stopping power or the lack of it. The United States Army was convinced that they needed a more powerful handgun cartridge. This led Colt to the development of a .45-caliber cartridge suitable for the semi-automatic pistol. The Model 1905 and the .45 rimless round were the result. In actuality, this cartridge was not nearly powerful enough to satisfy the need, but it led to the development of the .45 ACP. Colt believed that this pistol/cartridge combination would be a success and was geared up for mass production. The Army actually bought only 200 of them, and the total production was approximately 6,300 from 1905 to 1911. The pistol has a 5" barrel and detachable 7-shot magazine and is blued, with a case-colored hammer. The grips are checkered walnut. The hammer was rounded on the first 3,600 pistols and was changed to a spur hammer on the later models. The right side of the slide is stamped "Automatic Colt/Calibre 45 Rimless Smokeless." This model was not a commercial success for Colt—possibly because it has no safety whatsoever except for the floating inertia firing pin. The 200 military models have grip safeties only. A small number (believed to be fewer than 500) of these pistols were grooved to accept a shoulder stock. The stocks were made of leather and steel and made to double as a holster. These pistols have been classified "Curios and Relics" under the provisions of the Gun Control Act of 1968.

Civilian Model

Exc.	*V.G.*	*Good*	*Fair*	*Poor*
6000	4500	2750	950	400

Military Model, Serial #1-201

Known as the 1907 Contract Pistol, it has a lanyard loop, a loaded chamber indicator, spur hammer, and a grip safety and bears the inspector's initials "K.M."

Exc.	*V.G.*	*Good*	*Fair*	*Poor*
18000	16000	8500	2500	950

COLT 1911

Model designations by Karl Karash

There are four reference books on the Colt .45 Auto Pistol so indispensable to collecting .45s that they will be mentioned by name: *Colt .45 Service Pistols, Models of 1911 and 1911A1, Colt .45 Government Models (Commercial Series)*, and *Collectors Guide to Colt .45 Service Pistols, Models of 1911 and 1911A1* all by Charles Clawson. And *U.S. Military Automatic Pistols 1894-1920* by Edward S. Meadows. Of the four books, only the "*Collectors Guide to Colt .45 Service Pistols*" third edition, by Charles Clawson is available and collectors new and old alike are urged to obtain a copy before the supply dries up. It contains the latest information as well as serial number data. One book reviewer who should probable confine his efforts to the rompings of the Royal Family has labeled Mr. Clawson's monumental work as "required reading for beginning collectors and those who need to refresh themselves on the most rudimentarly details fo the subject." This is total nonsense. Few collectors expect to be spoon fed. Some beginners who initially expect that the overlap of features between variations and exceptions should be expicitly detailed in a book, will eventually realize that most variations have overlap and that no one will ever examine more than a smattering of examples.

Colt Model 1905 • *Courtesy Rock Island Auction Company*

Consequently, no textbook will ever list all exceptions and overlaps. Most collectors who have experience in other fields of manufactured items take it for granted that "there is often the exception to the rule, and that overlap is a part of collecting." 1911/1911A1 pistols are remarkably free of the overlap and exceptions seen in other areas of collecting. To seek out and examine the overlap and the exceptions is what makes this field especially interesting for new and experienced collectors alike.

Note that since these pistols are primarily collector's items, and since originality and condition are the two factors that determine a pistol's value, the condition categories here differ from the stated categories in the front of this book. All prices are for pistols having all original parts and all finish present is factory-original finish. Broken parts, replaced parts, gun-smithing, and cold blue touch-ups will require appropriate deductions from all categories. Refinished pistols can be considered to be in or below POOR condition or as non-collectible shootable pistols. This is because once refinished, all traces of originality disappear and it becomes impossible to differentiate between a refinished pistol and a complete fake. Arsenal reworks are generally refinished, and while they are considered collectible pistols, they have their own categories that have values much lower than original pistols. The few cases of Arsenal marked but original finish pistols should probably be considered similar to original pistols but with British markings applied, and an appropriate deduction taken because the markings make the pistol less desirable than a plain pistol.

We define the condition categories in terms of the percentage of original finish remaining: Excellent = 96 percent to 98 percent original finish, VG = 90 percent to 95 percent original finish, Good = 70 percent to 89 percent original finish, Fair = 45 percent to 69 percent original finish, and Poor condition = less than 45 percent original finish.

The amount of original finish can be accurately estimated by comparing the amount and thickness of the remaining finish on each part of the pistol's surface with its portion (in percent) of the total surface area. Then, add up the percents remaining. Thinning finish only counts for a portion of area covered. For example, if the finish on the front strap covers the entire surface, but the finish is only half as dense or thick as new finish, the contribution to the total is half of 7.6 percent, or 3.8 percent, and if the remainder of the pistol was as new, the pistol would have 96.2 percent finish.

The U.S. Military Model of 1911 was developed by a combination of the genius of John Browning plus a lot of interaction and feedback from the Ordnance Department. John T. Thompson, Lt. Colonel of the Ordnance Department, informed Colt's Patented Firearms Manufacturing Company on March 29, 1911, that the (M1911) self loading pistol had passed all prescribed tests [Editor's note: And by doing so, was adopted by The Department.] and the Department requested a quote on 30,262 pistols. The price that was finally agreed on was $14.25 per pistol and one magazine. Additional magazines were to be 50 cents each. The first 40 pistols were assembled on December 28, 1911, with an additional 11 pistols assembled the next day. The first shipment, a single wooden case of M1911 pistols serial numbered from 1 to 50, was made on January 4, 1912, from the Colt factory in Hartford, Conn., to the Commanding Officer, Springfield Armory. This single crate, marked on the outside "Serial Numbers 1 Through 50," has become "the stuff that (M1911 collectors') dreams are made of." The M1911 pistol was the most advanced self loading pistol of its time and in the eyes of many, it has remained so to this date. Yet while this is probably an exaggeration, elements of its design have become adopted in most subsequent self-loading designs. While hundreds of minor manufacturing and ergonomic changes have been made, only one functional change was made to the M1911 during its manufacture from 1911 to 1945. Removal of the original dimpled magazine catch required pushing the entire catch body into the frame far enough that the fingers could grasp and turn the protruding portion until the tooth of the catch lock left its groove in the receiver. Upon coming free, the catch lock and spring (propelled by the energy stored in the spring), often flew out of sight and landed in a mud puddle. At about serial number 3190, the design was changed and a slot was cut in the magazine catch body as well as in the head of the magazine catch lock. This greatly facilitated the disassembly of the pistol, as well as reduced the chances of losing a part. Yet Colt's manufacturing changes, Ordnance Department mandated changes (including 1911/1911A1 improvements), marking, commercial derivatives, and part variations used during manufacture by the various suppliers, amounted to over 200 variations; enough to keep even the most ardent collector in pursuit for decades.

COLT FOREIGN CONTRACT 1911 PISTOLS

NOTE: These foreign contract pistols are included as military pistols despite their commercial serial numbers. The majority of these pistols were used by foreign governments as military, police, or other government agency sidearms.

First Argentine Contract C6201-C6400

These pistols were delivered to the two Argentine battleships under construction at two U.S. shipyards. Rarely seen better than Good. Many of these pistols have been reblued and parts changed. Reblue = Fair/Poor.

Courtesy Karl Karash collection

Exc.	V.G.	Good	Fair	Poor
N/A	1200	700	525	350

Second Argentine Contract C20001-C21000

Most of these pistols have been reblued and had parts changed. Reblue = Fair/Poor.

Exc.	V.G.	Good	Fair	Poor
1800	1200	750	450	300

Subsequent Argentine 1911 Contracts after C21000

Many of these pistols have been reblued and parts changed. Reblue = Fair/Poor.

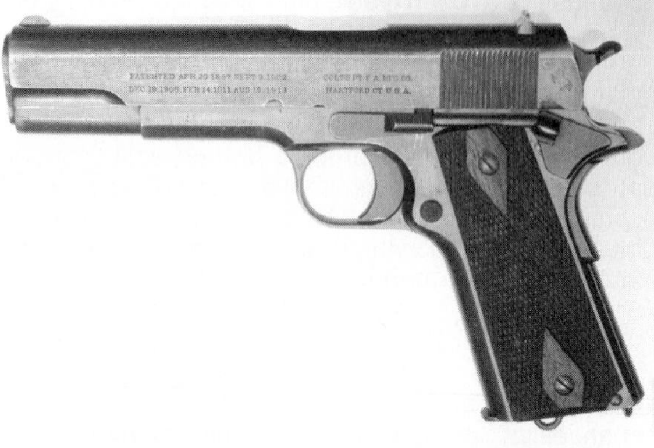

Courtesy Karl Karash collection

Exc.	V.G.	Good	Fair	Poor
1500	1000	750	450	275

Canadian Contract (About 5,000 pistols from C3000 to C14000)

Many pistols have owner's markings applied. (Condition 99-100 percent add 20-30 percent)

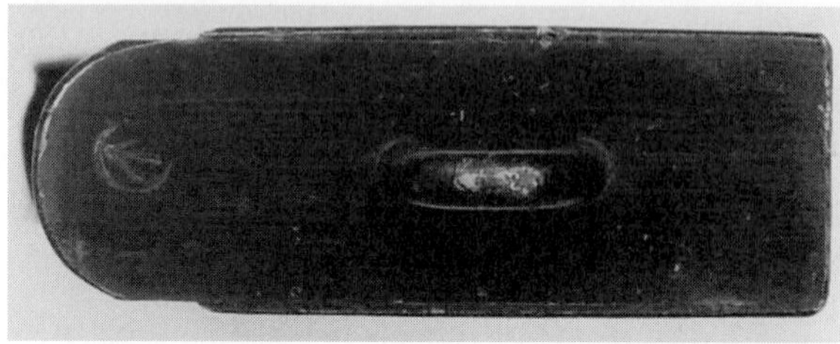

Exc.	V.G.	Good	Fair	Poor
2500	1800	950	550	400

First and Second British .455 Contract (200 pistols from W19000 to W19200) and 400 from W29001 to W29444

All "JJ" marked. Many pistols have owner's markings applied. (Condition 99-100 percent add 20-30 percent)

Exc.	V.G.	Good	Fair	Poor
3400	2100	1000	750	600

NOTE: Many of the .455 caliber pistols have been converted to .45 caliber by replacing their barrels. Converted pistols are usually considered no better than Good condition.

WWI British Contracts

This series is chambered for the British .455 cartridge and is so marked on the right side of the slide. The British "Broad Arrow" property mark will often be found. These pistols were made from 1915 to 1918. Some pistols are RAF marked on the left side of the frame (add 30 percent for RAF). RAF pistols normally have an endless welded steel ring through the lanyard loop. Many of these pistols have been reblued. Reblued=Fair/Poor. (Condition 99-100 percent add 20-30 percent)

Left side of frame stamped "RAF" • *Courtesy Karl Karash collection*

Right side of slide stamped "caliber .455" • *Courtesy Karl Karash collection*

Exc.	V.G.	Good	Fair	Poor
2500	1700	1200	900	700

French Contract (5,000 pistols between C17800 and C28000)

Very seldom seen. (Condition 99-100 percent add 20-30 percent)

Exc.	V.G.	Good	Fair	Poor
4500	3000	1500	900	700

1911 Russian Order

This variation is chambered for .45ACP and has the Russian version of "Anglo Zakazivat" stamped on the frame (English Order). There were about 51,100 pistols between serial C21000 and C89000 shipped. This variation is occasionally encountered today, and a few have been recently imported from Russia. At least one example is known that bears the Finnish arsenal mark "SA." This pistol may have been captured by the Finns as Russia invaded Finland prior to WWII. One should be extra cautious if contemplating a purchase, as fakes have been noted. However, original pistols in V.G. or better condition are in high demand despite the market uncertainties. (Condition 99-100 percent add 20-30 percent)

Courtesy Karl Karash collection

Exc.	*V.G.*	*Good*	*Fair*	*Poor*
5500	4225	3100	2000	1400

Kongsberg Vapenfabrikk Model M/1912 (Norwegian) Contract SN 1-96

(Rarely seen) (Condition 99-100 percent add 20-30 percent)

Exc.	*V.G.*	*Good*	*Fair*	*Poor*
7500	4600	2800	2000	1500

Norwegian-Kongsberg Vapenfabrikk Pistol Model 1914

Serial number 97-32854 (99-100 percent add 20-50 percent)

Exc.	*V.G.*	*Good*	*Fair*	*Poor*
1500	1200	900	700	600

Kongsberg Vapenfabrikk Model 1914 (Norwegian) Waffenamt Marked

Serial number 29615-30535 Waffenamt marked on slide and barrel (99-100 percent) add 20-30 percent) CAUTION: Fakes have been reported. Any waffenamt-marked pistol outside this serial range is probably counterfeit.

Exc.	*V.G.*	*Good*	*Fair*	*Poor*
4500	3500	2500	2000	1500

MODEL 1911 AUTOMATIC PISTOL, U.S. MILITARY SERIES

Colt Manufacture

Marked "MODEL OF 1911 U.S. ARMY" or "MODEL OF 1911 U.S. NAVY" on right slide, "UNITED STATES PROPERTY" on left front frame until about Serial Number 510000, then above trigger right. Serial number located on right front frame until Serial Number 7500, then above trigger right. Pistols have high polish and fire blue small parts until Serial Number 2400, then finish changed to non-reflective dull blue. Double diamond grips throughout. Dimpled mag catch from 1-3189, dimpled/slotted mag catch from Serial Number 3190 to about 6500, and slotted thereafter. Lanyard loop magazine (3 types) until about Serial Number 127000. Type 1 (stepped base until about Serial Number 4500, Type 2 (keyhole until about Serial Number 35000), and Type 3 (plain). Thereafter, two-tone non-looped magazine used through end of 1911 production. Add 5 percent if type I (Step Base) magazine is present (up to SN 4500). NOTE: as there were many variations in the early pistols which affect their rarity and value, several valuation groups follow.

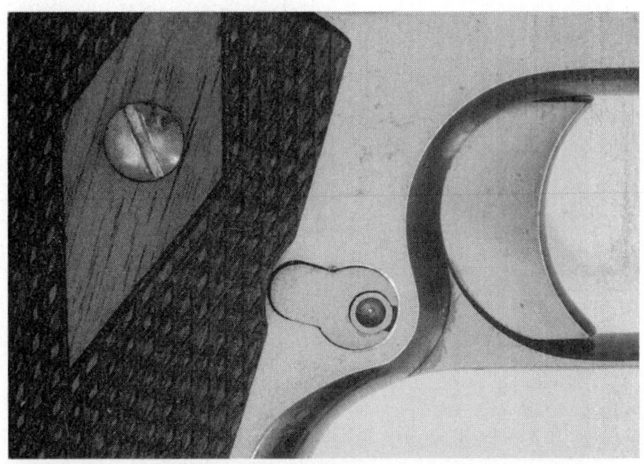

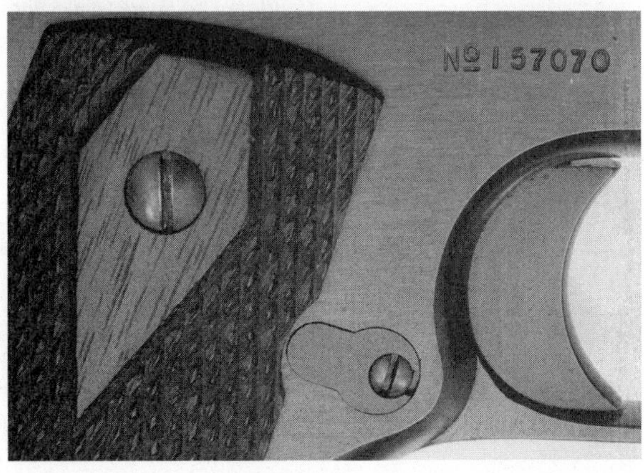

Mag catches • *Courtesy Karl Karash collection*

UNITED STATES OF AMERICA

***Serial Number 43 was shipped in first case of 50 pistols on January 4, 1912** • Courtesy Karl Karash collection*

***Model 1911 U.S. Army marked** • Paul Goodwin photo*

Below SN 101 "LARGE" "UNITED STATES PROPERTY" and other unique features

High polish mirror finish with brilliant fire blue parts. Unmarked fully blued barrel. (Condition 99-100 percent add 20-70 percent)

Courtesy Karl Karash collection

Courtesy Karl Karash collection

Courtesy Karl Karash collection

Exc.	V.G.	Good	Fair	Poor
37500	20000	15000	10000	6000

Three Digit "MODEL OF 1911 U.S. ARMY" marked slide. SN 100 through SN 500

High polish mirror finish with brilliant fire blue parts. Unmarked fully blued barrel until SN 400. H (with serifs) marked on back of the barrel hood (sometimes called "barrel overhang" or "barrel extension") until SN 500. (Condition 99-100 percent add 20-70 percent)

Exc.	V.G.	Good	Fair	Poor
16500	11000	6500	4000	3000

Three-Digit "MODEL OF 1911 U.S. NAVY" marked slide. SN 501 through SN 1000

Extremely rare in original condition. High polish mirror finish with brilliant fire blue parts. H (with serifs) marked on back of the barrel hood (sometimes called "barrel overhang" or "barrel extension") (fully blued). Some seemingly original early NAVY pistols have been observed with the later dull finish. Note that below SN 2400, pistols with the later "Fine" finish are likely to have

Three Digit "MODEL OF 1911 U.S. ARMY" marked slide

been refinished. Buyers should be very wary. However, most (or all) of the small number of observed NAVY pistols in this first batch are reported to have the later dull (fine) finish and do not have fire blue parts. (Later dull finish in this range where mirror and fire blue is expected, equal to Poor condition. (Condition 99-100 percent add 30-100 percent)

Exc.	*V.G.*	*Good*	*Fair*	*Poor*
18000	12500	8000	5000	3500

Early magazines for Colt M1911; note the two-tone finish with folded base. These are scarce. Price 250-100

***Model 1911 U.S. Navy marked** • Paul Goodwin photo*

Four Digit "MODEL OF 1911 U.S. ARMY" marked slide with fire blue parts

Very rare in original condition. SN 1001 to 1500 and 2001 to 2400 only. High polish mirror finish with brilliant fire blue parts. Barrel is H marked (with serifs) on rear of barrel hood. The only documented original early pistols (below SN 2400) with the later dull ("fine") finish are a very small group of test pistols in the SN 1201 to about SN 1600 range. Pistols below SN 2400 with the later "fine" finish are likely to have been refinished. Buyers should be exceptionally wary. (Later dull finish in this range less 65 percent. Unless documented test pistol then less 25 percent.) (Condition 99-100 percent add 20-70 percent)

Exc.	*V.G.*	*Good*	*Fair*	*Poor*
10000	7500	4000	2500	1200

Four-Digit "MODEL OF 1911 U.S. ARMY" marked slide without fire blue parts

Five groups SN 2401 to 2500, SN 3801 to 4500, SN 5501 to 6500, SN 7501 to 8500, SN 9501 to 9999. Dull (fine) no fire blue small parts. An H with serifs was marked on the rear of the barrel hood until SN 7500. After 7500 no serifs. Condition 99-100 percent add 20-50 percent)

Exc.	*V.G.*	*Good*	*Fair*	*Poor*
6000	4550	3400	2450	1675

1913 production USMC SN 3501 to 3800

Rarely seen and often well used. (Condition 99-100 percent add 20-50 percent)

Courtesy Karl Karash collection

Exc.	*V.G.*	*Good*	*Fair*	*Poor*
12000	8000	6000	3500	3000

Four-Digit "MODEL OF 1911 U.S. NAVY" marked slide with fire blue parts

Extremely rare in original condition. Fire blue parts and high polish from SN 1501 to SN 2000 only. Barrel is fully blued and H with serifs marked on rear of hood. The only documented original pistols (below SN 2400) with the later dull ("fine") finish are a very small group of test pistols in the SN 1201 to about SN 1600 range. However most or all of the reported pistols of this second NAVY batch (SN 1501 to SN 2000) have the high polish and fire blue parts. Below SN 2400, pistols with the later dull ("fine") finish are likely to have been refinished. Buyers should be exceptionally wary. Later dull finish in this range where mirror and fire blue are expected equal to Poor condition. (Unless documented test pistol then less 25 percent.) (Condition 99-100 percent add 20-100 percent)

Exc.	*V.G.*	*Good*	*Fair*	*Poor*
17500	12000	5000	3500	1500

Four-Digit "Model of 1911 U.S. NAVY" marked slide without fire blue parts

Barrel is fully blued and H marked on rear of hood (H has serifs until SN 7500, then no serifs). Five groups: SN 2501 to 3500, SN 4501 to 5500, SN 6501 to 7500, and SN 8501 to 9500. All pistols should have the later dull finish. (Condition 99-100 percent add 20-30 percent)

Exc.	*V.G.*	*Good*	*Fair*	*Poor*
8500	6000	3500	1800	900

SERIAL NUMBERS ASSIGNED TO M1911 AND 1911A1 CONTRACTORS

Year	Serial No.	Manufacturer
1912	1-500	Colt
	501-1000	Colt USN
	1001-1500	Colt
	1501-2000	Colt USN
	2001-2500	Colt
	2501-3500	Colt USN
	3501-3800	Colt USMC
	3801-4500	Colt
	4501-5500	Colt USN
	5501-6500	Colt
	6501-7500	Colt USN
	7501-8500	Colt
	8501-9500	Colt USN
	9501-10500	Colt
	10501-11500	Colt USN
	11501-12500	Colt
	12501-13500	Colt USN
	13501-17250	Colt
1913	17251-36400	Colt
	36401-37650	Colt USMC
	37651-38000	Colt
	38001-44000	Colt USN
	44001-60400	Colt
1914	60401-72570	Colt
	72571-83855	Springfield
	83856-83900	Colt
	83901-84400	Colt USMC
	84401-96000	Colt
	96001-97537	Colt
	97538-102596	Colt
	102597-107596	Springfield
1915	107597-109500	Colt
	109501-110000	Colt USN
	110001-113496	Colt
	113497-120566	Springfield
	120567-125566	Colt
	125567-133186	Springfield
1916	133187-137400	Colt
1917	137401-151186	Colt
	151187-151986	Colt USMC
	151987-185800	Colt
	185801-186200	Colt USMC
	186201-209586	Colt
	209587-210386	Colt USMC
	210387-215386	Colt Frames
	215387-216186	Colt USMC
1917	216187-216586	Colt
	216587-216986	Colt USMC
1918	216987-217386	Colt USMC
	217387-232000	Colt
	232001-233600	Colt USN
	233601-594000	Colt
	1-13152	Rem-UMC
1919	13153-21676	Rem-UMC
	594001-629500	Colt
	629501-700000	Winchester (Assigned)
1924	700001-710000	Colt
1937	710001-711605	Colt
	711606-712349	Colt USN
1938	712350-713645	Colt
1939	713646-717281	Colt USN
1940	717282-721977	Colt
1941	721978-756733	Colt
1942	756734-793657	Colt
	793658-797639	Colt USN
	797640-800000	Colt
	S800001-S800500	Singer
	H800501-H801000	H&R (Assigned, none delivered)
	801001-856100	Colt
1943	*856405-916404	Ithaca
	*916405-1041404	Remington-Rand
	*1041405-1096404	Union Switch
	1088726-1092896	Colt
	1096405-1208673	Colt
	1208674-1279673	Ithaca
	1279674-1279698	Replacement numbers
	1279699-1441430	Remington-Rand
1944	1441431-1471430	Ithaca
	1471431-1609528	Remington-Rand
	1609529-1743846	Colt
	1743847-1816641	Remington-Rand
	1816642-1890503	Ithaca
	1890504-2075103	Remington-Rand
	2075104-2134403	Ithaca
1945	2134404-2244803	Remington-Rand
	2244804-2380013	Colt
	2380014-2619013	Remington-Rand
	2619014-2693613	Ithaca

* Colt duplicated other manufacturers' serial numbers

Five-Digit Colt "MODEL OF 1911 U.S. ARMY" marked slide

No fire blue, and dull finish. Circled horse on left rear of slide until about SN 20000. H (without serifs) marked on rear of barrel hood until somewhere below about SN 24xxx. P (without serifs) marked on rear of barrel hood and H visible through ejection port from about SN 24200 to about SN 24900. H P (horizontal) visible through eject port from SN 24900 to SN about 110,000. (There is considerable uncertainty as to the barrel marking in the SN 19xxx to SN 242xx range as too few original pistols have been examined.) H on back of hood add serial range 15 percent. P on back of hood serial range add 30 percent. (Condition 99-100 percent add 20-30 percent)

Exc.	V.G.	Good	Fair	Poor
3500	2200	1750	2000	1150

1913 production SN 36401 to 37650 USMC shipment

Slide marked "MODEL OF 1911 U.S. ARMY" on all original USMC shipped pistols. (Any "USMC"-marked 1911 pistol should be considered a FAKE. Rarely seen and often well used. Extremely rare in high condition. (Condition 99-100 percent add 20-100 percent)

Courtesy Karl Karash collection

Exc.	V.G.	Good	Fair	Poor
6000	4500	3000	1800	1000

Five-Digit "MODEL OF 1911 U.S. NAVY" marked slide

4 groups: SN (10501-11500, 12501-13500, 38001-44000, 96001-97537) (Condition 99-100 percent add 20-30 percent)

Exc.	V.G.	Good	Fair	Poor
6500	4000	2500	1700	1000

Six-Digit "MODEL OF 1911 U.S. NAVY" marked slide

SN (109501-110000). These 500 NAVY marked pistols were shipped to the Brooklyn Navy Yard for the Naval Militia and are more often found than most other batches. These are the only NAVY marked pistols to bear the JMG cartouche. (Condition 99-100 percent add 20-30 percent)

Exc.	V.G.	Good	Fair	Poor
6000	4500	2800	1700	1000

Springfield Armory "MODEL OF 1911 U.S. ARMY"

Dull (Rust Blued) finish, ALL external parts are identifiable as Springfield manufactured by the shape. Most pistols have a combination of "S" marked and unmarked parts. Made in four SN groups: 72571-83855, 102597-107596, 113497-120566. Springfield Armory SN 72571 to about 75000 with short stubby hammer add 15 percent. (Condition 99-100 percent add 20-30 percent)

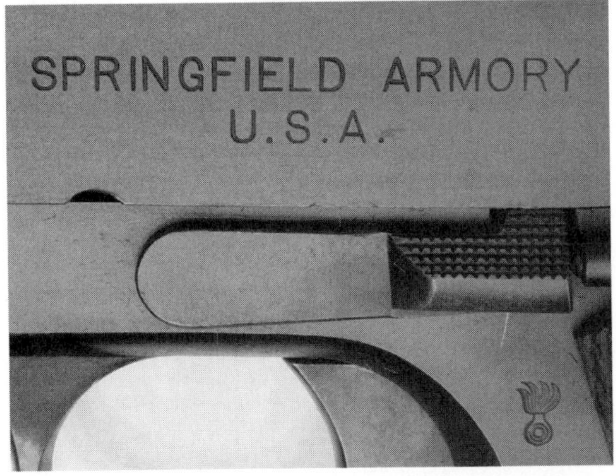

Courtesy Karl Karash collection

Exc.	V.G.	Good	Fair	Poor
6500	5000	3500	1800	1000

Remington UMC "MODEL OF 1911 U.S. ARMY"

Dull finish, ALL parts MUST be Remington made. Most examples seem to have a deteriorated finish, probably due to poor surface preparation. EEC accepted and marked. Mainspring housing "E" marked, barrels "P" marked. Most pistols show thinning finish as well as flaking with little apparent wear. Pistols numbered in their own block of numbers from 1 to 21676 in large gothic letters. Almost never seen in better than Excellent condition. Beware of refinished pistols masquerading as original. Very late pistols show a one-line right side marking (add 15 percent). (Condition 99-100 percent add 20-30 percent)

Remington U.S. Model 1911, marked "Remington/UMC" • Paul Goodwin photo

Courtesy Karl Karash collection

Exc.	V.G.	Good	Fair	Poor
5000	3200	2500	1700	1000

1911 Colt "NRA" marked pistol

An unknown number of shipped Colt 1911 pistols were taken from stores and sold to NRA members. These pistols ranged from about SN 70000 to the high 150000 range. Pistols were marked N.R.A. under the serial or at the right front of the frame. The number is unknown, perhaps 300. Both crude and clever fakes abound. (Condition 99-100 percent add 20-30 percent) So few of these rare pistols have been sold publicly that these prices are intended as a rough guide only.

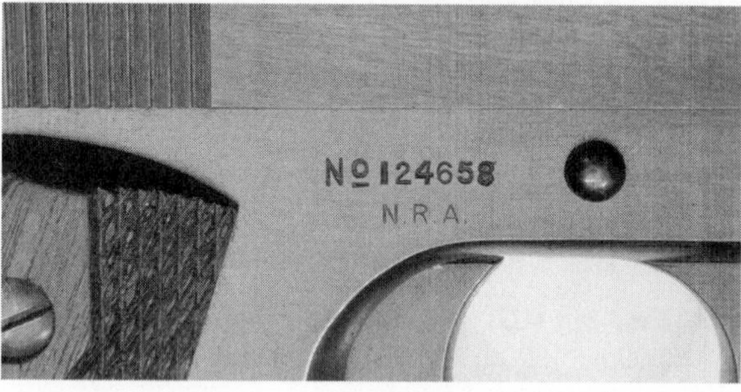

Courtesy Karl Karash collection

Exc.	V.G.	Good	Fair	Poor
6600	4200	2700	1800	1400

1911 Springfield "NRA" marked pistol

An unknown number of shipped Colt 1911 pistols were taken from stores and sold to NRA members. These pistols ranged from about SN 70000 to the high 129000 range. Pistols were marked N.R.A. under the serial or at the right front of the frame. The number of N.R.A. marked Springfields is unknown, but based on observed pistols, it is perhaps 600. Both crude and clever fakes abound. (Condition 99-100 percent add 20-30 percent) Note that at one time these NRA marked pistols sold for about twice what a normal Springfield sold for, but lately, the very few examples sold seem to have sold for about the same price as a normal Springfield. This trend may reflect the undocumentability of the NRA marking as well as the ease with which the mark can be counterfeited.

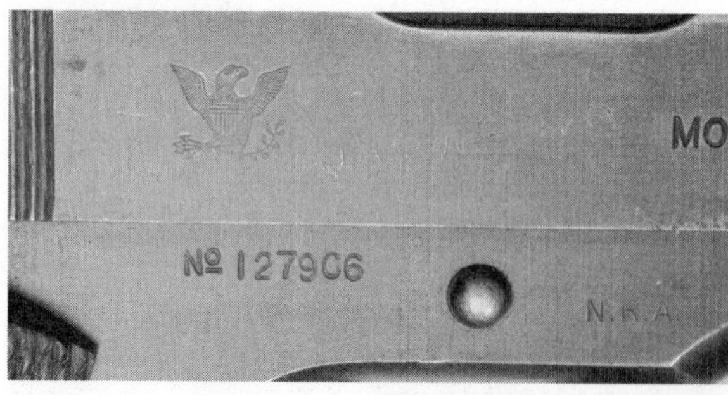

Courtesy Karl Karash collection

Exc.	V.G.	Good	Fair	Poor
7250	6100	3600	2500	1500

1915-1918 Springfield Suspended Serial Numbers Reassigned to Colt

These receiver were apparently shipped as replacement parts (incomplete pistols) because they lack an Ordnance acceptance mark. Springfield's unused assigned serial numbers (SN 128617 to SN 133186) were re-assigned to Colt when Springflield ceased production of 1911 pistols. These receivers were apparently numbered and used as needed until late 1917 when a new series of serial numbers were assigned (SN 210387 through SN 215386) These receivers are found with most any post 1911 slide. (Condition 99-100 percent add 20-30 percent.)

Exc.	V.G.	Good	Fair	Poor
4500	3250	2500	1700	1000

Six-Digit Colt 1915-1918 "MODEL OF 1911 U.S. ARMY" marked slide.

Dull blue finish. Vertically oriented "P H" or "H P" marked on barrel, visible through eject port from about SN 110000 to SN 425000. Slides marked "MODEL OF 1911 U.S. ARMY" on all original USMC shipped pistols. Any "USMC" marked 1911 pistol should be considered a fake. (Condition 99-100 percent add 20-30 percent.)

Exc.	V.G.	Good	Fair	Poor
2800	1750	1200	750	500

The following categories are listed relative to the pricing of the previous "Six-Digit" SN Colt 1915-1918 "MODEL OF 1911 U.S. ARMY" marked slide:

1916 production with "S" marked frame, slide, and barrel add 60 percent

1916 production with partial "S" marked frame, slide, or barrel add 35 percent

1916 production with normally marked frame, slide, and barrel add 20 percent

1916 production 151187 to 151986 USMC shipment add 45 percent (Often well used)

1917 production 185801 to 186200 USMC shipment add 45 percent (Often well used)

1917 production 209587 to 210386 USMC shipment add 45 percent (Often well used)

1917 production 210387 to 215386 replacement frames add 45 percent (Rarely seen)

1917 production 215387 to 216186 USMC shipment add 45 percent (Rarely seen)

1917 production 216187 to 216586 ARMY transferred from USMC add 15 percent (Rarely seen)

1917 production 216587 to 217386 USMC shipment add 45 percent (Rarely seen)

1917 production 223953 to 223990 NAVY (ARMY marked) add 15 percent

1917 production 232001 to 233600 NAVY (ARMY marked) add 15 percent

1918-1919 production with eagle over number acceptance mark

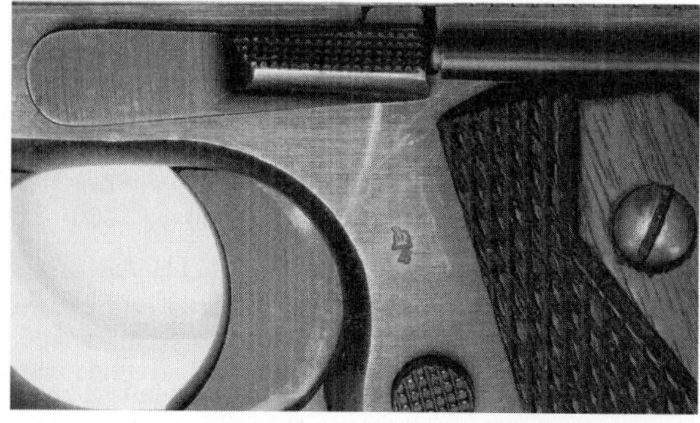

Courtesy Karl Karash collection

Often called the Black Army because the coarse wartime finish appeared almost black. The black finish started about SN 375000. No inspector's cartouche from about serial number 302000 to end of 1911 production (SN 625000). Barrel marked with letters H and P through about SN 425000. "HP" with a common leg, horizontal orientation visible through ejection port from about SN 425000 to end of 1911 production. (If flaking present deduct 25 percent, watch out for reblue if no flaking present.) (Condition 99-100 percent add 20-30 percent)

Exc.	*V.G.*	*Good*	*Fair*	*Poor*
5000	3500	2200	1250	900

Typical pre-WWII vintage lanyard loop magazine with tw- tone blue finish. Price 150-75

North American Arms of Montreal QB "1911"

Made for U.S. but none delivered to Army. Less than 100 pistols assembled from parts. Rarely seen. Numbered on trigger under left grip and on left rear slide. Similar to five-digit Colt "ARMY" marked slide, but add 500 percent. (Condition 99-100 percent add 20-30 percent) So few of these pistols have been sold publicly that these prices are intended as a rough guide only.

1911 North American Arms of Montreal •
Courtesy Karl Karash collection

Exc.	*V.G.*	*Good*	*Fair*	*Poor*
26000	20000	16000	10000	7300

Four-Digit X Numbered Rework

These pistols were renumbered when their original serial numbers were either defaced, obliterated, or became too light to read during rebuilding or refinishing. The four-digit X prefix serial numbers (X1000 through X4385) were assigned after WWI (1924) and were used by Springfield through 1953. All are considered "Arsenal Refinished."

Exc.	*V.G.*	*Good*	*Fair*	*Poor*
1350	1100	800	750	600

"Military to Commercial Conversions"

Some 1911 military pistols that were brought home by GIs were subsequently returned to the Colt factory by their owners for repair or refinishing. If the repair included a new barrel, the pistol would have been proof fired and a normal verified proofmark affixed to the triggerguard bow in the normal commercial practice. If the pistol was refinished between 1920 and 1942, the slide would probably be numbered to the frame again in the normal commercial practice. Slides were numbered on the bottom disconnector rail during part of 1920, and after that they were numbered under the firing pin stop plate. These pistols are really a remanufactured Colt pistol of limited production and should be valued at least that of a contemporary 1911A1 commercial pistol. (Pistols without VP or numbered slide usually cannot be authenticated, deduct 60 percent). Very seldom seen. (Condition 99-100 percent add 30 percent).

Exc.	*V.G.*	*Good*	*Fair*	*Poor*
2100	1500	1200	950	750

MODEL 1911A1 AUTOMATIC PISTOL MILITARY MODEL

COLT FOREIGN CONTRACT 1911A1 PISTOLS

These foreign contract pistols are included as military pistols despite their commercial serial numbers. These pistols were supplied by Colt to foreign governments as military, police, or other government agency sidearms. Many of these pistols have recently been imported into the USA, but only a few have been in "collectible, original" condition. Most have been refinished and sold at utility prices. The prices that the handful of original pistols sell for have been kept down by their poorer brothers and sisters. These original finish pistols, when found, may be some of the few remaining bargains out there. Pistols were shipped to Mexico, Philippines, Shanghai, Haiti, etc. but specific prices for these variations are not practical because they are seldom seen.

Argentine Army Modello 1927

Serial numbered 1 through 10000. Marked "EJERCITO ARGENTINO. Colts Cal.45 MOD.1927" on the right slide, and "Colts Pt. F.A. MFG. Co....etc." on the left slide. VP marked under left stock. Serial numbered on top of slide, under mainspring housing. Most of these pistols have been reblued and original finish pistols are very rare. Prices shown are for original pistols and the common reblued pistols would be equal to the Fair/Poor categories, depending on appearance.

Exc.	V.G.	Good	Fair	Poor
1800	1200	500	400	300

Argentine Navy, Coast Guard, Air Force, or Army Contract "Government Model"

Pistols serial numbered from about C130000 to about C190000. Marked "Armada Nacional," "Marina Argentina," "Aeronautica Argentina" or "Ejercito Argentina" on the right slide, and "Colts Pt. F.A. MFG. Co. [etc.]" on the left slide. VP marked on left triggerguard bow. Serial numbered and marked as were normal commercial pistols. Most of these pistols have been reblued and original finish pistols are seldom seen. Prices shown are for original pistols and the common reblued pistols would be equal to the Fair/Poor categories, depending on appearance.

Exc.	V.G.	Good	Fair	Poor
750	600	500	400	300

Argentine Navy, Coast Guard, Air Force, or Army Pistols

Serial numbered through about 112000. Marked "Armada Nacional," "Marina Argentina," "Aeronautica Argentina," or "Ejercito Argentina" on the right slide, and "D.G.F.M.-(F.M.A.P.)." on the left slide. Most of the recent imports of these pistols have been reblued and collectable original finish pistols are seldom seen except when from older collections. Prices shown are for original pistols, and the common reblued pistols would be equal to the Fair/Poor categories, depending on appearance.

Argentine Seal • *Courtesy Karl Karash collection*

Exc.	V.G.	Good	Fair	Poor
1800	1200	500	400	300

Argentine Navy "Government Model" With Swartz Safety

Serial numbered from about C199000 to about C2010001. Marked "Republica Argentina, Armada Nacional-1941" on the right slide, and "Colts Pt. F.A. MFG. Co....etc." on the left slide. VP marked on left triggerguard bow. Serial numbered and marked as were normal 1941 commercial pistols. Most or all of these pistols have the Swartz safeties. Most of these pistols have been reblued or parkerized when imported, and original finish collectable pistols are very rare. Prices shown are for original pistols, and the common reblued pistols would be equal to the Fair/Poor categories, depending on appearance. The very rare Swartz safeties (only a few thousand total were produced) in these pistols are under-appreciated by most collectors, and make this variation highly undervalued, especially for the few original finish pistols. The Swartz firing pin block safety can be observed by pulling the slide back all the way and looking at the top of the frame. A Swartz safety equipped 1911A1 pistol will have a second pin protruding up, next to the conventional disconnector pin. This second pin pushes a spring-loaded piston in the rear part of the slide that is visible when the slide is pulled back and the slide is viewed from underneath. This piston, in turn, blocks the firing pin when relaxed. A second Swartz safety (the Swartz Sear Safety) is usually built into pistols equipped with the Swartz firing pin block safety. The sear safety can sometimes be detected by the drag marks of the notched sear on the round portion of the hammer that the sear rides on. Pulling the hammer all the way back will expose these drag marks if they are visible. Presence of the drag marks however, does not insure that the Swartz modified sear safety parts are all present.

Exc.	V.G.	Good	Fair	Poor
2000	1500	900	700	500

Brazilian Army Contract "Government Model"

Pistols serial numbered from about C190000 to about C214000. Marked "Ejercito Brazilia" on the right slide, and "Colts Pt. F.A. MFG. Co....etc." on the left slide. VP marked on left triggerguard bow. Serial numbered and marked as were normal commercial pistols. Only a few of these complete pistols have made it to the USA, but many slides were sold as surplus parts when Brazil converted from .45 Cal to 9mm. Most or all of these slides have been reblued and original finish pistols are very rarely seen. Prices shown are for original pistols, and the common reblued pistols would be equal to the Poor category or below, depending on appearance. Separate slides would have the value of a high quality "after market" part.

Exc.	V.G.	Good	Fair	Poor
1800	1100	900	600	400

COLT MANUFACTURE

Service Model Ace

In 1937 Colt introduced this improved version of the Ace pistol. It utilizes a floating chamber invented by David "Carbine" Williams, the firearms designer who invented short stroke piston that is the basis of the M1 carbine while serving time on a southern chain gang. Colt advertised that this floating chamber gave the Service Model Ace the reliability and feel that the Ordnance Department wanted. However the floating chamber probably reduced the long term reliability of the pistol since it tends to lead-up with most ammunition. The serial number is prefixed by the letters "SM." The external configuration is the same as the Ace, and the slide is marked "COLT SERVICE MODEL ACE .22 LONG RIFLE." Colt sold most to the Army and a few on a commercial basis. There were a total of 13,803 manufactured before production ceased in 1945. (99-100 percent finish add 33 percent) Original boxes usually bring a healthy premium of 10 percent to 20 percent.

Blued Pistols (before serial #SM3840)

Exc.	*V.G.*	*Good*	*Fair*	*Poor*
6000	3000	2000	1600	1350

Parkerized Pistols (after about serial # SM3840)

Exc.	*V.G.*	*Good*	*Fair*	*Poor*
3000	2000	1500	1000	700

Transition Model of 1924

SN 700001 to 710000. Some very early Transition pistols (SN 700004 and SN 700009) have been observed to have matching numbered slides. The number of pistols so numbered is not known, but if enough pistols surface, the serial number range may eventually be deduced. A pistol with a matching numbered slide will probably bring a premium. Made in 1924. All were accepted by Walter T. Gordon and marked with the "G" forms the outer circle is seen through about SN 7022000. The second type has an outer circle around the "G." Brushed blue finish, all 1911A1 features (arched mainspring housing, short checkered trigger, long tang on grip safety, trigger finger cutouts, full checkered walnut grips, etc.). However, they retained the "MODEL OF 1911 U.S. ARMY" slide marking. No verified proof or final inspector's mark on triggerguard bow, interlaced "H P" and "K" marked barrel, and serifed "H" over firing pin stop plate. (Add 20-30 percent for 99-100 percent finish)

Courtesy Karl Karash collection

First Type acceptance markings • *Courtesy Karl Karash collection*

Exc.	*V.G.*	*Good*	*Fair*	*Poor*
6000	4000	2500	1600	800

First Transition Model of 1937

SN 710001 to about 711001. Numbered slide under firing pin stop plate. No "P" marking on frame or slide. Brushed blue finish, all 1911A1 features (arched mainspring housing, short checkered trigger, long tang on grip safety, trigger finger cutouts, full checkered walnut grips, etc.). However, they retained the "MODEL OF 1911 U.S. ARMY" slide marking. Verified proof and final inspector's mark on triggerguard bow. "COLT .45 AUTO" marked magazine floorplate with flattened letters and "COLT .45 AUTO" marked barrel. Extremely rare. Pistols with mis-matched number (but still second type 1937 slide) deduct 40 percent. (Add 30-40 percent for 99-100 percent finish.) So few of these pistols have sold publicly that these prices are intended as a rough guide only.

Exc.	*V.G.*	*Good*	*Fair*	*Poor*
8000	6500	5000	4000	2200

Second Transition Model of 1937

About SN 711001 to 712349. Numbered slide under firing pin stop plate. "P" marking on frame and top of slide. Brushed blue finish, all 1911A1 features (arched mainspring housing, short checkered trigger, long tang on grip safety, trigger finger cutouts, full checkered walnut grips, etc.). However, they retained the "MODEL OF 1911 U.S. ARMY" slide marking. Verified proof and final inspector's mark on triggerguard bow. "COLT .45 AUTO" marked magazine floorplate with flattened letters and "COLT .45 AUTO" marked barrel. Extremely rare. Pistols with mis-matched number (but still second type 1937 slide) deduct 40 percent. (Add 30-40 percent for 99-100 percent finish.) So few of these rare pistols have sold publicly that these prices are intended as a rough guide only.

Exc.	*V.G.*	*Good*	*Fair*	*Poor*
8000	6500	5000	4000	2200

Model of 1911A1, 1938 Production

SN 712350 to 713645. Numbered slide under firing pin stop plate. "P" marking on frame and top of slide. No markings on right side of slide. Brushed blue finish, all 1911A1 features (arched mainspring housing, short checkered trigger, long tang on grip safety, trigger finger cutouts, full checkered walnut grips, etc.). Right side of receiver is marked "M1911A1 U.S. ARMY" forward of the slide stop pin, and "United States Property" behind the slide stop pin. Verified proof and final inspector's mark on triggerguard bow. Most are "H" marked on left side by magazine catch. "COLT .45 AUTO" marked magazine floorplate with flattened letters and "COLT .45 AUTO" marked barrel. Extremely rare. Pistols with mismatched number (but still second type 1937 slide) deduct 40 percent. (Add 50 percent to 100 percent for 99-100 percent finish.) So few of these rare pistols have been sold publicly that these prices are intended as a rough guide only.

NOTE: All Military .45 cal. pistols after 710000 were officially M1911A1, although they were first called Improved M1911.

Exc.	V.G.	Good	Fair	Poor
17500	12000	7500	5000	2500

Model of 1911A1, 1939 Production (1939 NAVY)

SN 713646 to 717281. Numbered slide under firing pin stop plate. "P" marking on frame and top of slide. No markings on right side of slide. Brushed blue finish. Shortened hammer. Right side of receiver is marked "M1911A1 U.S. ARMY" forward of the slide stop pin, and "United States Property" behind the slide stop pin. Verified proof and final inspector's mark on triggerguard bow. Full checkered walnut grips. Most are "H" marked on left side by magazine catch. "COLT .45 AUTO" marked magazine floorplate with flattened letters, and "COLT .45 AUTO" marked barrel. Extremely rare. Pistols with mismatched number (but still second type 1937 slide) deduct 25 percent. (Add 20-30 percent for 99-100 percent finish)

Exc.	V.G.	Good	Fair	Poor
4500	3500	2000	1600	1000

Model of 1911A1, 1940 Production (CSR)

SN 717282 to 721977. Numbered slide under firing pin stop plate. "P" marking on frame and top of slide. No markings on right side of slide. Brushed blue finish. Shortened hammer. Right side of frame is marked "M1911A1 U.S. ARMY" forward of the slide stop pin, and "United States Property" behind the slide stop pin. Verified proof and final inspector's mark on triggerguard bow. "CSR" (Charles S. Reed) marked on left side below slide stop. "COLT .45 AUTO" marked magazine floorplate with flattened letters, and "COLT .45 AUTO" marked barrel. Full checkered walnut grips but some pistols may have early brittle plastic grips. Extremely rare. Pistols with mis-matched number (but still second type 1937 slide) deduct 25 percent. (Add 20-30 percent for 99-100 percent finish)

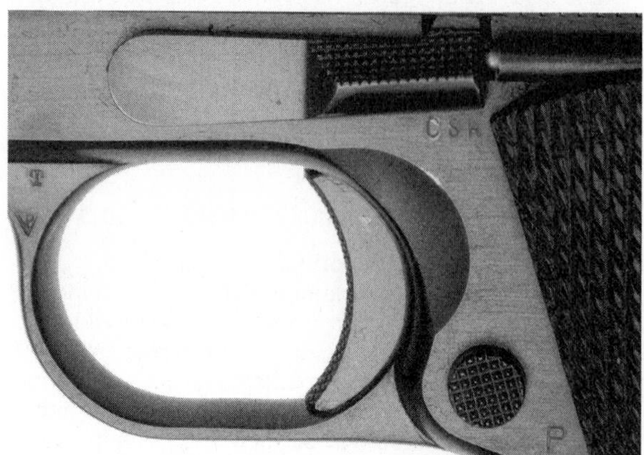

Courtesy Karl Karash collection

Exc.	V.G.	Good	Fair	Poor
4800	3500	2250	1200	1000

Model of 1911A1, 1941 Production (RS and early WB)

SN 721978 to 756733. Numbered slide under firing pin stop plate. "P" marking on frame and top of slide. No markings on right side of slide. Brushed blue finish through about SN 736000. Parkerizing was used thereafter until the end of Colt production. Any Colt pistol after about SN 737000 with a blued finish is likely to be a FAKE. Shortened hammer. Right side of frame is marked "M1911A1 U.S. ARMY" forward of the slide stop pin, and "United States Property" behind the slide stop pin. Verified proof and final inspector's mark on triggerguard bow. "RS" (Robert Sears) marked on left side below slide stop starting at about SN 723000, ending about 750500. After about SN 750500, pistols were marked "WB" (Waldemar S. Broberg). "COLT .45 AUTO" marked magazine floorplate with flattened letters, and "COLT .45 AUTO" marked barrel. Early pistols may have wood grips, later pistols have hollow back (without ribs) plastic grips. Prices are for blued finish. (Parkerized finish less 25 percent.) Extremely rare. Pistols with mis-matched number (but still second type 1937 slide) deduct 20 percent. (Subtract 5 percent to 10 percent for British proofs, most collectors prefer virgin pistols. Add 20-50 percent for 99-100 percent finish)

Exc.	V.G.	Good	Fair	Poor
3000	2200	1750	1200	700

Model of 1911A1, 1942 Production (WB)

SN 756733 to about 856100. Numbered slide under firing pin stop plate. All subsequent Colt made 1911A1 pistols have a "P" marking on frame and top of slide. No markings on right side of slide. Parkerized finish. Shortened hammer. Right side of frame is marked "M1911A1 U.S. ARMY" forward of the slide stop pin, and "United States Property" behind the slide stop pin. Colt plastic stocks with narrow concave rings and hollow backs with no ribs through SN 803000, wide rings around screws and hollow backs with ribs thereafter. A number of original in the SN 820000 range have been observed with 1911 type slide stops. This is a good example of a seemingly out of sequence part that would often be changed by someone with a hair trigger trying to make his pistol "Like the Book" when in reality they would be messing up an original rare variation. Verified proof and final inspector's mark on triggerguard bow, and "COLT .45 AUTO" marked barrel. "WB" (Waldemar S. Broberg) marked on left side below slide stop. "COLT .45 AUTO" marked magazine floorplate with flattened letters, sand blasted bottom. (Subtract 5 percent to 10 percent for British proofs, most collectors seem to prefer virgin pistols. Add 20-30 percent for 99-100 percent finish)

Exc.	V.G.	Good	Fair	Poor
2600	1700	1200	850	650

Model of 1911A1, 1942 NAVY

3982 pistols shipped to Naval supply depots, Oakland, Calif., and Sewalls Point, Va. Numbered SN 793658 to SN 797639. Numbered slide under firing pin stop plate. "P" marking on frame and top of slide. No markings on right side of slide. Parkerized finish. Shortened hammer. Right side of frame is marked "M1911A1 U.S. ARMY" forward of the slide stop pin, and "United States Property" behind the slide stop pin. Verified proof and final inspector's mark on triggerguard bow. "WB" (Waldemar S. Broberg) marked on left side below slide stop. "COLT .45 AUTO" marked magazine floorplate with flattened letters, sand blasted bottom, and "COLT .45 AUTO" marked barrel. (Subtract 5 percent to 10 percent for British proofs, most collectors seem to prefer virgin pistols. Add 20-30 percent for 99-100 percent finish)

Exc.	*V.G.*	*Good*	*Fair*	*Poor*
3100	2000	1700	1400	1000

Model of 1911A1, Singer Manufacturing Co., Educational Order 1941

Exactly 500 pistols accepted and shipped. "J.K.C." (John K. Clement) marked on left side below slide stop. At least two un-numbered (and not marked United States Property) pistols were made and retained by employees. Slightly dull blue finish, brown plastic hollow-back grips, unmarked blue magazine, wide spur hammer, checkered slide stop, thumb safety, trigger, and mainspring housing. About 100 of the original 500 are known. Very Rare and most highly desired. Exercise caution when contemplating a purchase as fakes, improved, and reblued models abound. Be extra cautious with an example that is 98 percent or better. (Add 50 percent for 99-100 percent finish. Original pistols unnumbered or numbered with out-of-sequence numbers subtract 50 percent to 70 percent. Subtract 5 percent to 10 percent for British proofs, most collectors seem to prefer virgin pistols. Reblued, restored subtract 90 percent to 95 percent)

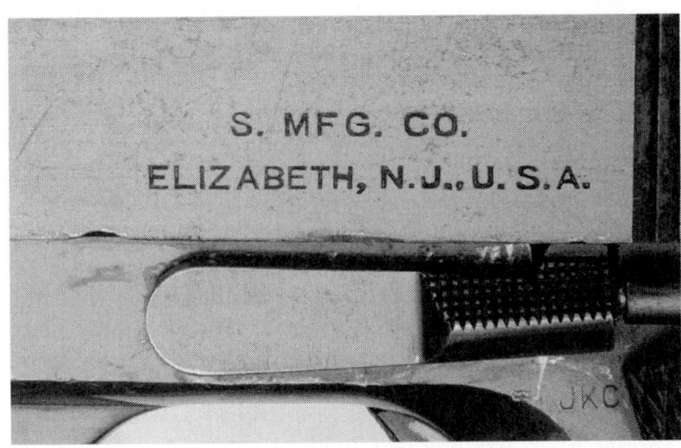

Singer Legend • *Courtesy Karl Karash collection*

Exc.	*V.G.*	*Good*	*Fair*	*Poor*
40000	28000	19500	14000	9000

Rock Island Arsenal Replacement numbers

SN 856101 to 856404. Replacement numbers issued to allow a pistol whose number had been defaced or worn away during refinishing to be numbered again. Very rare; only one known.

Exc.	*V.G.*	*Good*	*Fair*	*Poor*
1500	1200	900	750	600

Model of 1911A1, Military. 1943 Production (GHD marked)

SN 867000 to about 1155000. Colt had its own serial numbers assigned within this range, but in addition, Colt duplicated Ithaca's serial numbers between 865404, and 916404 as well as Remington Rand's between 916405 and 958100, and US&S's between 1088726 and 1092896. Numbered slide under firing pin stop plate until about SN 1140000. "P" marking on frame and top of slide. Parkerized. Right side of frame is marked "M1911A1 U.S. ARMY" forward of the slide stop pin, and "United States Property" behind the slide stop pin. Verified proof and final inspector's mark on triggerguard bow. "GHD" (Guy H. Drewry) marked on left side below slide stop. Plain blued or contract magazine, and "COLT .45 AUTO" marked barrel. Colt plastic stocks with wide rings around screws. (Subtract 5 percent to 10 percent for British proofs, most collectors prefer virgin pistols. Add 20-30 percent for 99-100 percent finish.) Colt in Ithaca or Remington Rand range add 10 percent, Colt in U.S.& S range add 20 percent.

Pre (Approx.) SN 114000 with matching slide

Exc.	*V.G.*	*Good*	*Fair*	*Poor*
2000	1500	1000	750	500

Post (Approx.) SN 114000 with matching slide

Exc.	*V.G.*	*Good*	*Fair*	*Poor*
1800	1400	925	700	500

Model of 1911A1, Commercial to Military Conversions. 1943 Production

(A few were WB marked, most were GHD marked.) SN 860003 to about 867000. Numbered slide under firing pin stop plate. "P" marking on frame and top of slide. Commercial markings on right side of slide. Parkerized finish over previously blued finish. Original Commercial SN peened and restamped with military numbers. Most have the Swartz grip safety cutouts in slide and frame but not the Swartz parts. None of the Commercial to military conversions have the Swartz "sear safety." No slides marked "NATIONAL MATCH" have been reported. If any exist, a NM slide pistol would command a premium. Shortened hammer. Right side of frame is marked "M1911A1 U.S. ARMY" forward of the slide stop pin, and "United States Property" behind the slide stop pin. Verified proof and final inspector's mark on triggerguard bow. "GHD" (Guy H. Drewry) marked on left side below slide stop. "COLT .45 AUTO" marked magazine floorplate with flattened letters, sand blasted bottom. Colt plastic stocks with wide rings around screws. (Subtract 5 percent to 10 percent for British proofs, most collectors seem to prefer virgin pistols. Add 20-30 percent for 99-100 percent finish. Add 10-30 percent for NM marked slide)

Courtesy Karl Karash collection

Exc.	*V.G.*	*Good*	*Fair*	*Poor*
2500	2000	1500	1000	600

Model of 1911A1, Military with Commercial Slide. 1943 Production (GHD marked)

SN 867000 to about 936000. Perhaps a few hundred total. Numbered slide under firing pin stop plate. "P" marking on frame and top of slide. Commercial markings on right side of slide. Parkerized finish over previously blued finish (slide only). Most have the Swartz grip safety cutouts in slide but not in frame. None have the Swartz parts. Frames are generally new military manufacture. Shortened hammer. Right side of frame is marked "M1911A1 U.S. ARMY" forward of the slide stop pin, and "United States Property" behind the slide stop pin. Verified proof and final inspector's mark on triggerguard bow. "GHD" (Guy H. Drewry) marked on left side below slide stop. May have "COLT .45 AUTO" marked magazine floorplate with flattened letters with sand blasted bottom or plain blued magazine. Colt plastic stocks with wide rings around screws. Barrels marked "COLT .45 AUTO." (Subject 5-10 percent for British proofs, most collectors seem to prefer virgin pistols) (Add 20-30 percent for 99-100 percent finish)

Exc.	V.G.	Good	Fair	Poor
2500	2000	1500	1000	600

Model of 1911A1, Canadian Broad Arrow/C marked 1943 Production

Marked with the "C" broad arrow Canadian Property mark on the left rear of the slide and left of the receiver above the magazine catch. 1515 pistols (GHD marked) SN 930000 to about 939000. Numbered slide under firing pin stop plate. "P" marking on frame and top of slide. Commercial markings on right side of slide on a few, otherwise blank. Parkerized finish. Right side of frame is marked "M1911A1 U.S. ARMY" forward of the slide stop pin, and "United States Property" behind the slide stop pin. Verified proof and final inspector's mark on triggerguard bow. "GHD" (Guy H. Drewry) marked on left side below slide stop. All appear to have British proofs except a few pistols in "Fair" condition that were recently sold at auction. These pistols without British proofs were apparently used in Canadian prisons and recently released. Beware non-British marked Canadian pistols in better than "Good" condition, as at least one of these same former prison pistols has appeared for sale in "New" condition. Barrels marked "COLT .45 AUTO." Most have plain blued magazine. Colt plastic stocks with wide rings around screws. (Add 30 percent for 99-100 percent finish. Add 25 percent for numbered commercial marked slide)

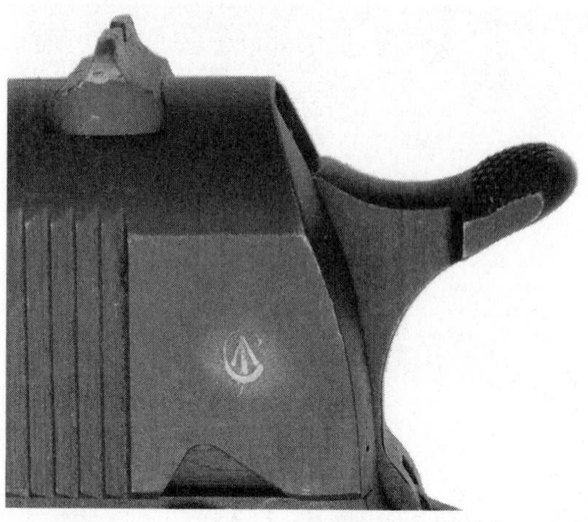

Courtesy Karl Karash collection

Exc.	V.G.	Good	Fair	Poor
2200	1500	1000	850	600

Model of 1911A1, Military. 1944 Production (GHD marked)

SN 1,155,000 to about SN 1208673, and 1609529 to 1720000. Unnumbered slide. "P" marking on frame and top of slide. Parkerized. Right side of frame is marked "M1911A1 U.S. ARMY" forward of the slide stop pin, and "United States Property" behind the slide stop pin. Verified proof and final inspector's mark on triggerguard bow. "GHD" (Guy H. Drewry) marked on left side below slide stop. Barrels marked "COLT .45 AUTO." Plain blued or contract magazine. Colt plastic stocks with wide rings around screws. (Subtract 5 percent to 10 percent for British proofs, most collectors seem to prefer virgin pistols. Add 20-30 percent for 99-100 percent finish)

Exc.	V.G.	Good	Fair	Poor
2000	1500	1100	800	600

Model of 1911A1, Military. 1945 GHD Acceptance Mark

GHD marked SN 1720000 to 1743846, and 2244804 to 2368781. Unnumbered slide. "P" marking on frame and top of slide. Parkerized. Right side of frame is marked "M1911A1 U.S. ARMY" forward of the slide stop pin, and "United States Property" behind the slide stop pin. Verified proof and final inspector's mark on triggerguard bow. "GHD" (Guy H. Drewry) marked on left side below slide stop. Plain blued or contract magazine. Early barrels marked "COLT .45 AUTO," later examples marked with a "C" in a square. Colt plastic grips with wide rings around screws. (Subtract 5 percent to 10 percent for British proofs, most collectors seem to prefer virgin pistols. Add 20-30 percent for 99-100 percent finish)

Exc.	V.G.	Good	Fair	Poor
2000	1500	1100	800	600

Model of 1911A1, Military. 1945 JSB Acceptance Mark

Around SN 2360600 a small number (perhaps a few thousand pistols) were acceptance marked under the authority of John S. Begley, a civilian employee of the Ordnance Department who had the title "Army Inspector of Ordnance". Unnumbered slide. "P" marking on frame and top of slide. Parkerized. Right side of frame is marked "M1911A1 U.S. ARMY" forward of the slide stop pin, and "United States Property" behind the slide stop pin. Verified proof and final inspector's mark on triggerguard bow. "JSB" (John S. Begley) acceptance mark on left side below slide stop. Plain blued or contract magazine. Barrels marked with a "C" in a square. Colt plastic grips with wide rings around screws. Extremely rare! Subtract 5 percent to 10 percent for British proofs, most collectors seem to prefer virgin pistols. Add 30-50 percent for 99-100 percent finish)

Exc.	V.G.	Good	Fair	Poor
3500	2500	1750	1250	900

Colt, Model of 1911A1, Military. 1945 No Acceptance Mark

(Un-inspected and usually no ordnance wheel.) Very rare and are usually found around SN 2354000. Unnumbered slide. "P" marking on frame and top of slide. Parkerized. Right side of frame is marked "M1911A1 U.S. ARMY" forward of the slide stop pin, and "United States Property" behind the slide stop pin. Verified proof and final inspector's mark on triggerguard bow. Plain blued or contract magazine. Barrels marked with a "C" in a square. Colt plastic grips with wide rings around screws. Very rare. These pistols may not have been delivered but they may have been sold commercially. Add 20-30 percent for 99-100 percent finish)

Exc.	V.G.	Good	Fair	Poor
1750	1400	950	650	450

Ithaca Gun Co. 1943-1945 Production

FJA inspected, unnumbered slide. Right side of frame is marked "M1911A1 U.S. ARMY" forward of the slide stop pin, and "United States Property" behind the slide stop pin. Plastic Keyes Fibre grips, stamped trigger, flat sided hammer, late pistols had serrated flat sided hammer, HS marked barrel, contract magazine. A few early pistols had an I prefix Serial Number. A few into the 1.28 million range had the "M1911A1 U.S. ARMY" on the right side of the slide. A few thousand early pistols were made with reclaimed WWI Colt frames ("H" marked on top of frame, and heart shaped cutouts). Add 50 percent for Colt frame. (Subtract 5 percent to 10 percent for British proofs, most collectors seem to prefer virgin pistols.) (Add 30-40 percent for 99-100 percent finish. Add 20 percent for "M1911A1 U.S. ARMY" marked slide, but only in the proper SN range. Add 15 percent for DU-LITE finish, below about SN 905000. Add 150 percent for I prefix.) Recent discovered shipping documents show certain pistols going to Navy units and Airfield orders, however it is still too early to determine the associated premium for these shipments.

Exc.	V.G.	Good	Fair	Poor
1700	1300	1000	800	600

Remington Rand Co. 1942-1943 Production

"NEW YORK" (Type I) marked slide. FJA inspected, unnumbered slide. Right side of frame is marked "M1911A1 U.S. ARMY" forward of the slide stop pin, and "United States Property" behind the slide stop pin. DU-LITE (blued over sand blasting) finish. Plastic Keyes Fibre grips with no rings around screws. Milled trigger, flat sided hammer, "COLT .45 AUTO" marked barrel, contract magazine. Fine checkered mainspring housing. (Subtract 5 percent to 10 percent for British proofs, most collectors seem to prefer virgin pistols. Add 30-50 percent for 99-100 percent finish.) (Pistols shipped after 1942 (after SN 921699) seem to be less desirable. Subtract 15 percent.

Courtesy Karl Karash collection

Exc.	V.G.	Good	Fair	Poor
2200	1500	1000	850	600

Remington Rand Co. 1943 Production

Large "N.Y." (Type II) marked slide. FJA inspected, unnumbered slide. Right side of frame is marked "M1911A1 U.S. ARMY" forward of the slide stop pin, and "United States Property" behind the slide stop pin. DU-LITE (blued over sand blasting) finish. Plastic Keyes Fibre grips with small rings around screws. Stamped trigger, flat sided hammer, "HS" marked barrel, contract magazine. Fine checkered mainspring housing. Note that there appears to be considerable overlap of features near the 1 million serial range. (Subtract 5 percent to 10 percent for British proofs, most collectors seem to prefer virgin pistols. Add 30-50 percent for 99-100 percent finish)

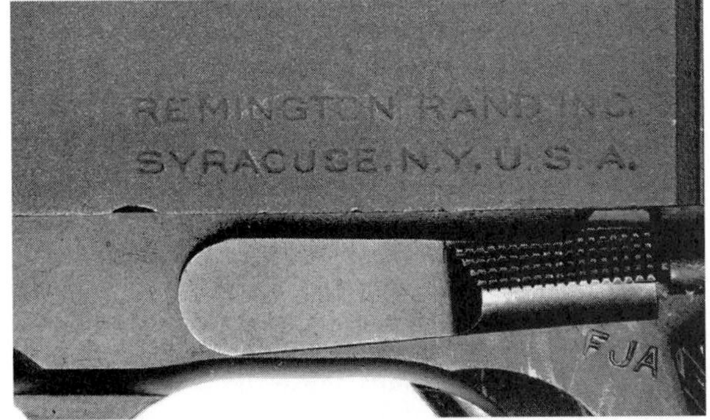

Courtesy Karl Karash collection

Exc.	V.G.	Good	Fair	Poor
1800	1250	950	650	500

Remington Rand Co. 1943-1945 Production

Small "N. Y." (Type III) marked slide. FJA inspected, unnumbered slide. Right side of frame is marked "M1911A1 U.S. ARMY" forward of the slide stop pin, and "United States Property" behind the slide stop pin. Parkerized (phosphate over sand blasting) finish. Plastic Keyes Fibre grips with small rings around screws. Stamped trigger, flat-sided hammer, "HS" marked barrel, contract magazine. Serrated mainspring housing. (Subtract 5 percent to 10 percent for British proofs, most collectors prefer virgin pistols. Add 40 percent for 99-100 percent finish)

Courtesy Karl Karash collection

Exc.	V.G.	Good	Fair	Poor
1400	1100	900	650	500

Remington Rand Co. 1942-1945 Production

Numbered Presentation pistol (all observed are Type III) marked slide. They were usually disposed of as giveaways to contracting personnel and employees, however several remained in the company safe long after WWII until they were eventually sold. No inspector, unnumbered slide. The only frame marking is a two- or three-digit number above trigger right. Parkerized (phosphate over sand blasting) finish. Plastic Keyes Fibre grips with small rings around screws. Stamped trigger, flat-sided hammer, "HS" marked barrel, contract magazine. Serrated mainspring housing. (Add 30 percent for 99-100 percent finish.) Add 10 percent to 20 percent for original box.

Exc.	*V.G.*	*Good*	*Fair*	*Poor*
3500	2500	1800	1400	1200

Remington Rand Co. 1942-1945 Production

ERRS prefix Presentation pistol (all observed are Type III) marked slide. They were usually disposed of as giveaways to contracting personnel and employees; however several remained in the company safe long after WWII until they were eventually sold. No inspector, unnumbered slide. The only frame marking is a two- or three-digit number with the "ERRS" prefix above trigger right. Parkerized (phosphate over sand blasting) finish. Plastic Keyes Fibre grips with small rings around screws. Stamped trigger, flat-sided hammer, "HS" marked barrel, contract magazine. Serrated mainspring housing. Popular wisdom seems to be that "ERRS" meant "Experimental Remington Rand"; however, there seems to be no evidence to support that notion. The true meaning of ERRS may never be known. (Add 30 percent for 99-100 percent finish.) Add 10 percent to 20 percent for original numbered box. Some ERRS pistols were DU-LITE blued and some were "P" proofed, too few to establish an accurate premium.

Exc.	*V.G.*	*Good*	*Fair*	*Poor*
3500	2800	2200	1800	1250

Union Switch Signal Co.

Swissvale, Pennsylvania. 55,000 pistols total delivered in 1943. US&S pistols have become one of the most sought after of all the 1911/1911A1 pistols.

Courtesy Karl Karash collection

Union Switch Signal Co. 1943 Production. Type I

(No "P" on frame or slide. From SN 1041405 to about 1060000 with probable overlap. RCD inspected, unnumbered slide. Right side of frame is marked "M1911A1 U.S. ARMY" forward of the slide stop pin, and "United States Property" behind the slide stop pin. DU-LITE (blued over sand blasting) finish. Plastic Keyes Fibre grips with or without rings around screws. Stamped, blued trigger, flat-sided hammer, "HS" marked barrel, contract magazine. Checkered mainspring housing. (Add 30-40 percent for 99-100 percent finish)

Courtesy Karl Karash collection

Exc.	*V.G.*	*Good*	*Fair*	*Poor*
3000	2500	1900	1250	700

Union Switch Signal Co. 1943 Production. Type II

("P" on top edge of slide.) From about SN 1060000 to about 1080000 with probable overlap. RCD inspected, unnumbered slide. Right side of frame is marked "M1911A1 U.S. ARMY" forward of the slide stop pin, and "United States Property" behind the slide stop pin. DU-LITE (blued over sand blasting) finish. Plastic Keyes Fibre grips with or without rings around screws. Stamped, blued trigger, flat sided hammer, "HS" marked barrel, contract magazine. Checkered mainspring housing. (Add 30-40 percent for 99-100 percent finish)

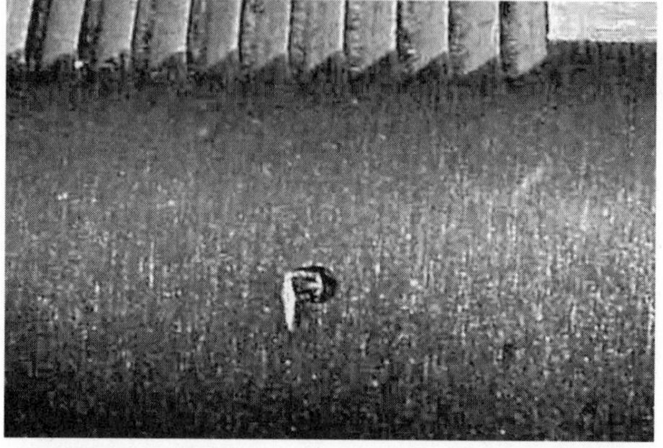

Courtesy Karl Karash collection

Exc.	*V.G.*	*Good*	*Fair*	*Poor*
3000	2500	1900	1250	700

Union Switch Signal Co. 1943 Production. Type III

"P" on frame and slide in the normal locations. From about SN 1080000 to 1096404 with probable overlap. RCD inspected, unnumbered slide. Right side of frame is marked "M1911A1 U.S. ARMY" forward of the slide stop pin, and "United States Property" behind the slide stop pin. DU-LITE (blued over sand blasting) finish. Plastic Keyes Fibre grips with or without rings around screws. Stamped, blued trigger, flat-sided hammer, "HS" marked barrel, contract magazine. Checkered mainspring housing. (Add 30-40 percent for 99-100 percent finish)

Courtesy Karl Karash collection

Exc.	V.G.	Good	Fair	Poor
3000	2500	1900	1250	700

Union Switch Signal Co. 1943 Production. Exp.

About 100 Pistols. ("EXP" followed by a one- or two-digit number on receiver partially under right grip.) These pistols usually have some apparent defect about them which may have caused them to be rejected and written off. They were believed to have been disposed of as giveaways to contracting personnel and employees. No inspector, no Ordnance mark unnumbered slide. Some pistols were finished with the DU-LITE process (blued over sand blasting) that closely resembled the finish of the delivered military pistols. The "EXP" and serial number marking was hand applied and is partially obscured by the right stock panel. Other EXP marked pistols were blued over such heavy buffing that the pistols have an amateur look about them. This, along with the crudeness of the markings, might lead one to question the authenticity of the blued EXPs. However, most evidence indicates that they are indeed genuine US&S made pistols. Popular wisdom seems to be that "EXP" meant "Experimental"; however, there seems to be no evidence to support that notion. Plastic Keyes Fibre grips with or without rings around screws. Stamped, blued trigger, flat-sided hammer, "HS" marked barrel, contract magazine. Checkered mainspring housing. (Add 30-40 percent for 99-100 percent finish. Subtract 50 percent for blued or buffed.) Most observed have type II slides.

Courtesy Karl Karash collection

Exc.	V.G.	Good	Fair	Poor
5200	3750	2800	N/A	N/A

Seven-Digit X Numbered Rework

These pistols were renumbered when their original serial numbers were either defaced, obliterated, or became too light to read during rebuilding or refinishing. The seven-digit X prefix serial numbers (X2693614 through X2695212) were assigned to various arsenals from 1949 to 1957. Some of the reworks are done in small batches and are more distinctive and collectable than the 4 digit X numbers. Each batch of pistols may have unique characteristics as they are done at different times by various arsenals. All are considered "Arsenal Refinished."

Courtesy Karl Karash collection

Exc.	V.G.	Good	Fair	Poor
1100	850	700	500	350

Military Arsenal Rework

Many 1911/1911 A1 pistols were reworked/refurbished at government arsenals such as Augusta Arsenal (AA), Rock Island Arsenal (RIA), Springfield Armory (SA), Raritan Arsenal (no mark), and others. Some arsenals applied an identification/ inspection mark to each pistol rebuilt, but others did not mark them in any way. Some of the reworks were sold through the NRA and has sales/shipping papers that identified the serial number of the pistol Most of these same pistols also had shipping boxes. An original shipping box and papers may increase the price by $200. (A fake box is worth about $2.00, and most of the boxes seen and advertised as originals are fakes.) Some reworked pistols appear to have most or all original parts but have been refinished with a Parkerized finish. A few pistols went through a rebuild facility and carry the rebuild facility's mark, but appear to be original pistols and were not refinished or rebuilt. Most rebuilt pistols have new plastic stocks as well as a new barrel. Each batch of rebuilt pistols may have unique characteristics as they are done at different times by various arsenals. Therefore it is often impossible to determine when a pistol was reworked, if it has been altered since it left the rebuild facility, or even if it was reworked in a government facility. Consequently, although reworked pistols are considered collectable, they are likely to remain at the bottom of the collectable price structure for the foreseeable future. (Add up to $100 for ORIGINAL box, add up to $100 for numbered shipping papers.) Prices shown are for government facility marked (AA, RIA, SA, etc.) reworks, equivalent to Poor condition if no Government facility markings, unless with original numbered box and papers. Add $2.00 for fake box. Completely original pistols with rework marks on them, like their original pistol category but less 20 percent.

Exc.	V.G.	Good	Fair	Poor
975	800	675	500	400

Leather holster for 1911 & 1911-A1

Sometimes referred to as a "***Sam Brown***" holster, this pattern was used for the 1911 series throughout the service life. Color was brown through WWII. Most will bear a makers name and date on the back. Post war holsters are black.

Brown holster dated 1912 - 1945

Exc.	V.G.	Good	Fair	Poor
150	100	50	35	25

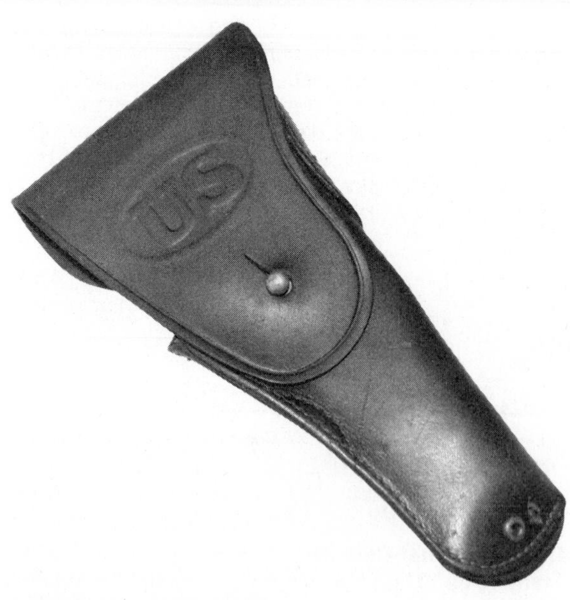

Black holster post 1945

Exc.	V.G.	Good	Fair	Poor
70	60	40	20	10

State of New York Government Model

250 pistols in the serial number range of about 255000-C to about 258000-C with factory roll mark "PROPERTY OF THE STATE OF NEW YORK" with a verified proof and "Government Model" marking. A few of the parts were leftover military. This is a state militia pistol. (99 percent to 100 percent finish add 33 percent. For the few consecutive pairs known add 15 percent premium. A few match pistols were made by Al Dinan in the early 1960s; add 15 percent.)

Courtesy Karl Karash collection

Exc.	V.G.	Good	Fair	Poor
2300	1500	1100	800	500

Military National Match

These are .45 caliber pistols rebuilt from service pistols at Springfield Armory between 1955 and about 1967. In 1968 the last year of the program, all rebuilding took place at Rock Island Arsenal. These pistols were built and rebuilt each year with a portion being sold to competitors by the NRA. Each year improvements were added to the rebuild program. Four articles in the *American Rifleman* document these pistols well: August, 1959; April, 1963; June, 1966; and July, 1966. Many parts for these pistols have been available and many "look-alike" pistols have been built by basement armorers. Pistols generally came with a numbered box or papers. Add 40 percent for numbered box and papers. When well worn these pistols offer little advantage over a standard well worn pistol. Pistols must be in original match condition to qualify as Military National Match pistols.

Courtesy Karl Karash collection

Exc.	V.G.	Good	Fair	Poor
1600	1200	950	N/A	N/A

COLT WOODSMAN

This Woodsman was cut up by the government and sold as scrap metal. The threaded section at the muzzle is probably for the Maxim type silencer, and suggest that not all of the WWII contract Match Target pistols were used exclusively for marksmanship training. Courtesy Major Robert Rayburn, USAF retired; photos by Paul Goodwin

NOTE: Colt Woodsman pistols with military markings are seldom seen. The total number used by the U.S. military is relatively small, and many of those never received any government markings. Often the only way to determine a military connection is by requesting a historical letter by serial number from Colt Firearms.

Military Woodsman Match Target with 6 5/8-inch barrel

After the United States entered World War II at the end of 1941, civilian production at Colt was stopped and the total effort was devoted to the U.S. military. Slightly more than 4000 First Series Match Target Woodsmans were delivered on U.S. Government contract from 1942-1944. Most of them, but not all, had serial numbers above MT12000. With possible rare exceptions they all had U.S. Property or U.S. military markings, standard blue finish, and extended length plastic stocks. The plastic stocks are sometimes erroneously called elephant ear stocks. The military plastic stocks are still relatively easy to find and inexpensive and, since they will fit any First Series Colt Woodsman, they are often used as replacement grips on non-military guns. Since the military guns had plastic

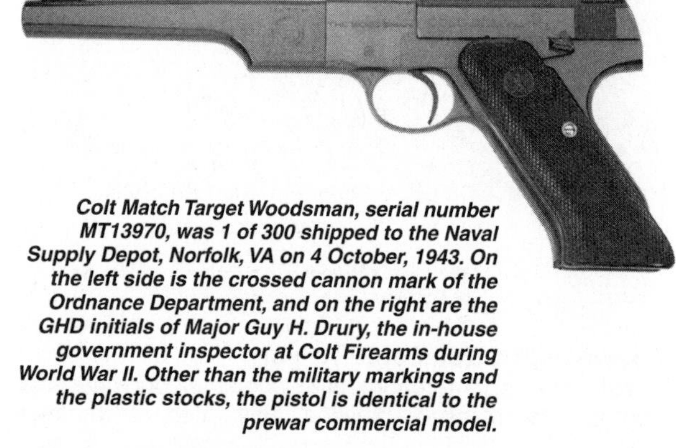

Colt Match Target Woodsman, serial number MT13970, was 1 of 300 shipped to the Naval Supply Depot, Norfolk, VA on 4 October, 1943. On the left side is the crossed cannon mark of the Ordnance Department, and on the right are the GHD initials of Major Guy H. Drury, the in-house government inspector at Colt Firearms during World War II. Other than the military markings and the plastic stocks, the pistol is identical to the prewar commercial model.

grips, rather than the costly and desirable "Elephant Ear" grips, the salvage value in the Fair and Poor condition range is less than that for the civilian model.

Exc.	*V.G.*	*Good*	*Fair*	*Poor*
2800	1600	750	450	350

U.S. Marine Corps Match Target

On December 10, 1947 Colt shipped 50 Woodsmans to the Depot Quartermaster, U.S. Marine Corp. in Philadelphia, PA. Another 50 were shipped to the same destination five days later. The 100 pistols in these two shipments were among the very first of the postwar, second series Woodsmans, and all were 6-inch Match Target models. Some bore single digit serial numbers, and all serial numbers in these shipments were under 400.

Colt Match Target Woodsman, serial number 98-S. Marked USMC PROPERTY on the right side of the receiver just below the serial number. Area has been enhanced for identification purposes.

Exc.	*V.G.*	*Good*	*Fair*	*Poor*
Too Rare To Price				

U.S. Marine Corps Sport

USMC Woodsman Sport model, serial number 130003-S

In 1953 2,500 Woodsman Sport Models were sold to the USMC, 1250 were shipped to the Marine Corps Supply Annex, Barstow, CA on June 30th, and the other 1250 to the Marine Corps Supply Depot at Camp Lejeune, NC on July 17th. Serial numbers in both shipments were around 130000-S. This version is seldom found intact, although many have turned up that have been destroyed by the government prior to being sold as scrap metal.

Exc.	*V.G.*	*Good*	*Fair*	*Poor*
Too Rare To Price				

U.S. Air Force Target

In June, 1949 Colt contracted with the U.S. government to deliver 950 Woodsman Target pistols. These were to be the standard commercial model, modified with a fixed 1/10 inch front sight blade integral with the ramp base, and a semi-fixed rear sight. In addition the following components were to be omitted: slide stop, magazine safety, lanyard loop, grip adapters, and screwdriver. 925 of these pistols were shipped to the Transportation Officer, Ogden Air Material Area, Ogden, Utah. In those cold war days the USAF was flying nuclear armed bombers over the arctic regions to provide a response should an attack come from the Soviet Union. The Colt packing list indicates that the pistols were for use in Arctic Survival Kits. The other 25 pistols in the contract were sent to the Springfield Ordnance Depot. Serial numbers of all 950 pistols were in the 64000-S and 65000-S range. Many of these were later declared surplus and sold to U.S. citizens via the DCM program. They had no military markings of any type. Almost all of these pistols are in near new condition.

Air Force Target without markings • *Courtesy Bob Rayburn*

Exc.	*V.G.*	*Good*	*Fair*	*Poor*
1900	1500	—	—	—

NOTE: For pistols in DCM box with papers in excellent condition add 25 percent.

U.S. Coast Guard Match Target

UNITED STATES OF AMERICA

Colt Match Target Woodsman, serial number MT3658, was one of eight guns of the same type shipped to the U.S. Coast Guard Academy on December 21, 1938. Colt shipping records indicate that U.S. COAST GUARD was factory engraved (NOT roll marked) on the right hand side of the receiver. It is otherwise standard in all respects.

There were at least three post-WWII Woodsman shipments to the U.S. Coast Guard: 25 pistols on June 23, 1955, 30 on December 21, 1955, and 50 on February 5, 1958. All were Match Target models with 6-inch barrels.

Exc.	*V.G.*	*Good*	*Fair*	*Poor*
Too Rare To Price				

REMINGTON

Model 1865 Navy Rolling Block Pistol

A spur trigger single-shot rolling block .50 caliber rimfire cartridge pistol with an 8.5" round barrel. Blued, case hardened with walnut grips and forend. The barrel marked "Remingtons, Ilion N.Y. U.S.A. Pat. May 3d Nov. 15th, 1864 April 17th, 1866." Examples bearing military inspection marks are worth approximately 30 percent more than the values listed below. Examples are also to be found altered to centerfire cartridge and these are worth approximately 10 percent less than the values listed below. Approximately 6,500 were manufactured between 1866 and 1870.

Exc.	*V.G.*	*Good*	*Fair*	*Poor*
9500	5000	3000	1800	750

Model 1867 Navy Rolling Block Pistol

A .50 caliber single-shot rolling block pistol with a 7" round barrel. Blued, case hardened with walnut grips and forend. The majority of these pistols were purchased by the United States government and civilian examples without inspection marks are worth approximately 30 percent more than the values listed.

Exc.	*V.G.*	*Good*	*Fair*	*Poor*
2200	1750	1500	1100	600

Model 1871 Army Rolling Block Pistol

A .50 caliber rolling block single-shot pistol with an 8" round barrel. Blued, case hardened with walnut grips and forend. The distinguishing feature of this model is that it has a rearward extension at the top of the grip and a squared butt. Approximately 6,000 were made between 1872 and 1888. Of these 6,000 approximately 5,000 were purchased by the U.S. government and are marked with inspector cartouche. Engraved ivory-stocked versions, as pictured below, will bring considerable premiums.

Exc.	*V.G.*	*Good*	*Fair*	*Poor*
2500	2000	1500	1200	700

SMITH & WESSON

NOTE: For historical information, photos, and technical data, see Jim Supica and Richard Nahas, *Standard Catalog of Smith & Wesson 4th Ed.,* Krause Publications.

Model 2 Army or Old Model

Similar in appearance to the Model 1 2nd Issue, this revolver was extremely successful from a commercial standpoint. It was released just in time for the commencement of hostilities in the Civil War. Smith & Wesson had, in this revolver, the only weapon able to fire self-contained cartridges and be easily carried as a backup by soldiers going off to war. This resulted in a backlog of more than three years before the company finally stopped taking orders. This model is chambered for .32 rimfire long and has a 6-shot nonfluted cylinder and 4", 5", or 6" barrel lengths. It has a square butt with rosewood grips and is either blued or nickel-plated. There were approximately 77,155 manufactured between 1861 and 1874.

A number of Model 2 revolvers with 6" barrels were sold to the state of Kentucky between 1862 and 1863 for the 7th Kentucky Cavalry. Most Model 2 revolvers used in the Civil War were purchased privately by individual soldiers.

NOTE: A slight premium for early two-pin model.

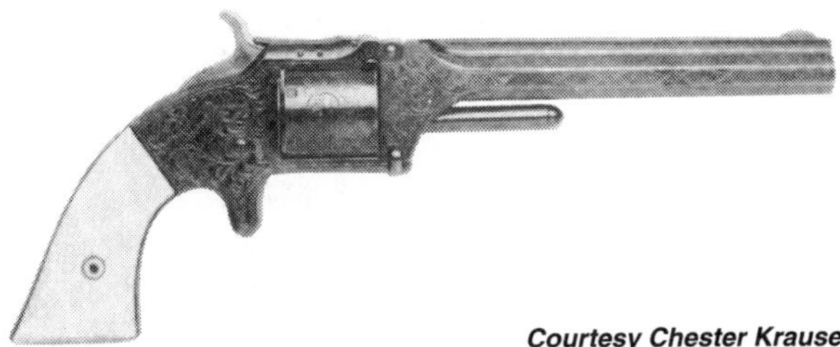

Courtesy Chester Krause

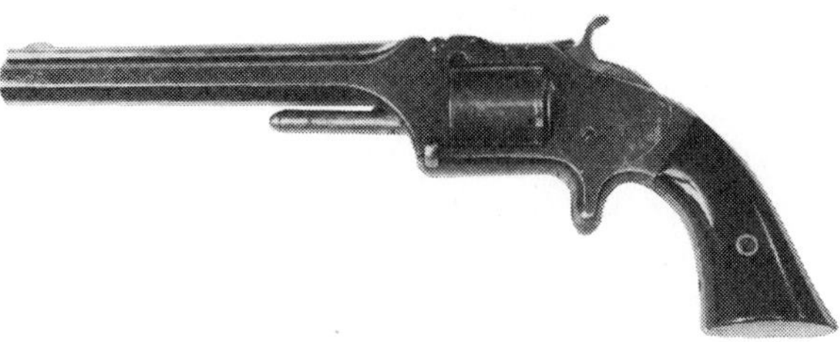

Courtesy Mike Stuckslager

5" or 6" Barrel—Standard Barrel

Exc.	V.G.	Good	Fair	Poor
—	1500	950	450	—

4" Barrel—Rare! Use Caution

Exc.	V.G.	Good	Fair	Poor
—	5000	3000	1500	—

.38 Safety Hammerless Army Test Revolver

There were 100 sold to the U.S. government in 1890. They have 3rd Model features but are in the 2nd Model serial number range, 41333-41470. Fitted with 6" barrels and marked "US."

CAUTION: Be very wary of fakes. Seek an expert appraisal prior to a sale.

Exc.	V.G.	Good	Fair	Poor
10000	7000	5000	3000	2000

Model 3 American 1st Model

This model represented a number of firsts for the Smith & Wesson Company. It was the first of the top break, automatic ejection revolvers. It was also the first Smith & Wesson in a large caliber (it is chambered for the .44 S&W American cartridge as well as the .44 Henry rimfire on rare occasions). It was also known as the 1st Model American. This large revolver is offered with an 8" round barrel with a raised rib as standard. Barrel lengths of 6" and 7" were also available. It has a 6-shot fluted cylinder and a square butt with walnut grips. It is blued or nickel-plated. It is interesting to note that this model appeared three years before Colt's Single Action Army and perhaps, more than any other model, was associated with the historic American West. There were only 8,000 manufactured between 1870 and 1872.

U.S. Army Order—Serial Number Range 1252199

One thousand (1,000) produced with "U.S." stamped on top of barrel; "OWA" on left grip.

Exc.	V.G.	Good	Fair	Poor
15000	9500	7500	3250	2500

NOTE: Add 10 percent premium for original nickel finish.

Model 3 Russian 1st Model—Cyrillic

This model is quite similar in appearance to the American 1st and 2nd Model revolvers. S&W made several internal changes to this model to satisfy the Russian government. The markings on this revolver are distinct, and the caliber for which it is chambered, .44 S&W Russian, is different. There were approximately 20,000 Russian-contract revolvers. The serial number range is 1-20000. They are marked in Russian Cyrillic letters. The Russian double-headed eagle is stamped on the rear portion of the barrel with inspector's marks underneath it. All of the contract guns have 8" barrels and lanyard swivels on the butt. These are rarely encountered, as most were shipped to Russia. The commercial run of this model numbered approximately 4,655. The barrels are stamped in English and include the words "Russian Model." Some are found with 6" and 7" barrels, as well as the standard 8". There were also 500 revolvers that were rejected from the Russian contract series and sold on the commercial market. Some of these are marked in English, some Cyrillic. Some have the Cyrillic markings ground off and the English restamped. This model was manufactured from 1871 to 1874.

Russian Contract Model—Cyrillic Barrel Address

Exc.	V.G.	Good	Fair	Poor
—	8500	6000	2000	—

Model 3 Russian 2nd Model—Foreign Contracts

This revolver was known as the "Old Model Russian." This is a complicated model to understand as there are many variations within the model designation. The serial numbering is quite complex as well, and values vary greatly due to relatively minor model differences. Before purchasing this model, it would be advisable to secure competent appraisal as well as to read reference materials solely devoted to this firearm. This model is chambered for the .44 S&W Russian, as well as the .44 rimfire Henry cartridge. It has a 7" barrel and a round butt featuring a projection on the frame that fits into the thumb web. The grips are walnut, and the finish is blue or nickel-plated. The triggerguard has a reverse curved spur on the bottom. There were approximately 85,200 manufactured between 1873 and 1878.

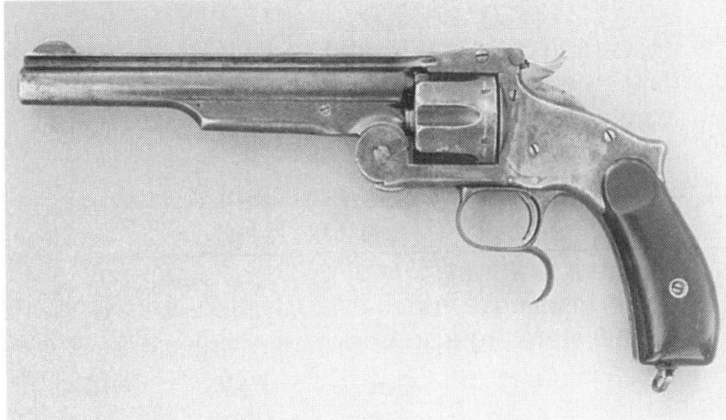

Courtesy Jim Supica, Old Town Station

Russian Contract Model

70,000 made; rare, as most were shipped to Russia. Cyrillic markings; lanyard swivel on butt.

Exc.	V.G.	Good	Fair	Poor
—	5000	3750	1500	—

1st Model Turkish Contract

.44 rimfire Henry, special rimfire frames, serial-numbered in own serial number range 1-1000.

Exc.	V.G.	Good	Fair	Poor
—	6750	4750	1750	—

2nd Model Turkish Contract

Made from altered centerfire frames from the regular commercial serial number range. 1,000 made. Use caution with this model.

Exc.	V.G.	Good	Fair	Poor
—	6500	4500	1500	—

Japanese Govt. Contract

Five thousand made between the 1-9000 serial number range. The Japanese naval insignia, an anchor over two wavy lines, found on the butt. The barrel is Japanese proofed, and the words "Jan.19, 75 REISSUE July 25, 1871" are stamped on the barrel, as well.

Exc.	V.G.	Good	Fair	Poor
—	4000	3250	1200	—

Model 3 Russian 3rd Model—Foreign Contracts

This revolver is also known as the "New Model Russian." The factory referred to this model as the Model of 1874 or the Cavalry Model. It is chambered for the .44 S&W Russian and the .44 Henry rimfire cartridge. The barrel is 6.5", and the round butt is the same humped-back affair as the 2nd Model. The grips are walnut and the finish is blue or nickel-plated. The most notable differences in appearance between this model and the 2nd Model are the shorter extractor housing under the barrel and the integral front sight blade instead of the pinned-on one found on the previous models. This is another model that bears careful research before attempting to evaluate. Minor variances can greatly affect values. Secure detailed reference materials and qualified appraisal. There were approximately 60,638 manufactured between 1874 and 1878.

Turkish Model

Five thousand made of altered centerfire frames, made to fire .44 rimfire Henry. "W" inspector's mark on butt and "CW" cartouche on grip. Fakes have been noted; be aware.

Exc.	V.G.	Good	Fair	Poor
—	4750	3000	1200	—

Japanese Contract Model

One thousand made; has the Japanese naval insignia, an anchor over two wavy lines, stamped on the bottom of the frame strap.

Exc.	V.G.	Good	Fair	Poor
—	3500	2250	1000	—

Russian Contract Model

Barrel markings are in Russian Cyrillic. Approximately 41,100 were produced.

Exc.	V.G.	Good	Fair	Poor
—	4500	3750	1500	—

Model 3 Russian 3rd Model (Loewe & Tula Copies)

The German firm of Ludwig Loewe produced a copy of this model that is nearly identical to the S&W. This German revolver was made under Russian contract, as well as for commercial sales. The contract model has different Cyrillic markings than the S&W and the letters "HK" as inspector's marks. The commercial model has the markings in English. The Russian arsenal at Tula also produced a copy of this revolver with a different Cyrillic dated stamping on the barrel.

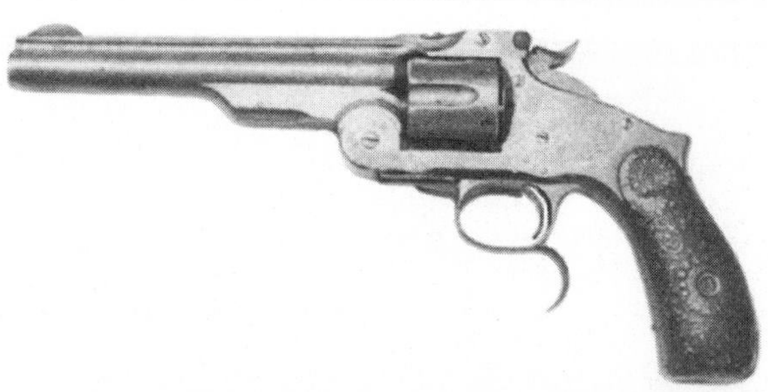

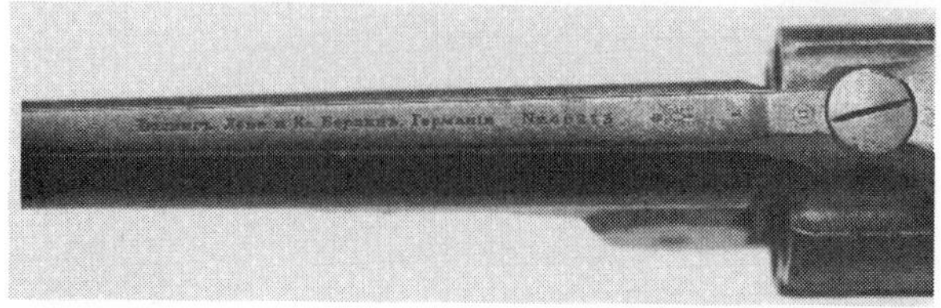

Courtesy Mike Stuckslager

Loewe

Exc.	V.G.	Good	Fair	Poor
—	3750	2500	1000	—

Tula

Exc.	V.G.	Good	Fair	Poor
—	4000	2750	1100	—

Model 3 Schofield

In 1870 Major George W. Schofield heard about the new S&W Model 3 revolver and wrote to the company expressing a desire to be an exclusive sales representative for them. At that time S&W was earnestly attempting to interest the government in this revolver and obviously felt that the Major could be of help in this endeavor, perhaps because his brother, General John Schofield, was president of the Small Arms Board. Major Schofield was sent one Model 3 revolver and 500 rounds of ammunition free of charge. After testing the revolver, Schofield felt that it needed a few changes to make it the ideal cavalry sidearm. With the company's approval, Schofield made these changes and secured patents. The company eventually began production of what became known as the Model 3 Schofield 1st Model. The Major was paid a 50-cent royalty per revolver. The eventual production of this model ran to a total of 8,969, with the last one sold in 1878. What was hoped to be the adopted government-issue sidearm never materialized—for a number of reasons. First, the Colt Single Action Army being used by the cavalry had a longer chamber than the S&W and could fire the Schofield ammunition. The Schofield could not fire the longer Colt .45 cartridges. This resulted in disastrous mix-ups on more than one occasion, when Colt ammunition was issued to troops armed with the Schofields. The company was not happy about paying the 50-cent royalty to Major Schofield. Sales of their other models were high and they simply did not care about this model, so they eventually ceased its production. It was a popular model on the American frontier and is quite historically significant.

Model 3 Schofield 1st Model

The modifications that made this model differ from the other Model 3 revolvers were quite extensive. The Schofield is chambered for the .45 S&W Schofield cartridge. The top break latch was moved from the barrel assembly to the frame. It was modified so that the action could be opened by simply pulling back on the latch with the thumb. This made it much easier to reload on horseback, as the reins would not have to be released. A groove was milled in the top of the raised barrel rib to improve the sighting plain. The extractor was changed to a cam-operated rather than rack-and-gear system. The removal of the cylinder was simplified. There were 3,000 contract Schofields and 35 commercial models. The contract revolvers were delivered to the Springfield Armory in July of 1875. These guns are stamped "US" on the butt and have the initials "L" and "P" marking various other parts. The grips have an inspector's cartouche with the initials "JFEC." There were 35 1st Models made for and sold to the civilian market; these revolvers do not have the "US" markings. The Schofield has a 7" barrel, 6-shot fluted cylinder, and walnut grips. The 1st Model is blued, with a nickel-plated original finish gun being extremely rare.

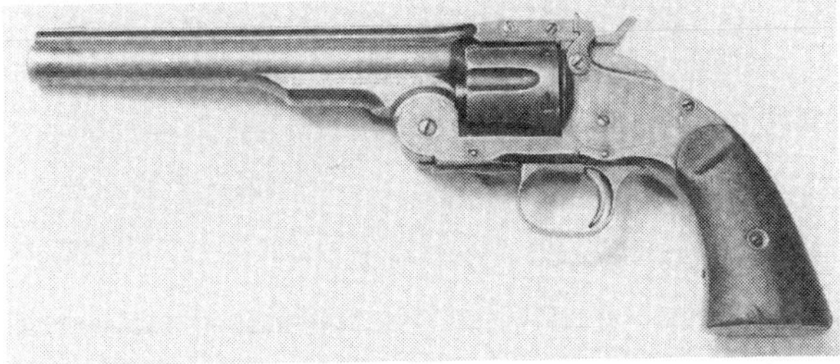

Courtesy Mike Stuckslager

"US" Contract–3,000 Issued

Exc.	*V.G.*	*Good*	*Fair*	*Poor*
12000	7500	4250	1750	1000

Civilian Model, No "US" markings

Very rare, 35 made, use caution. Unable to price. At least double the military model values. Expert appraisal needed.

Model 3 Schofield 2nd Model

The difference between the 1st and 2nd Model Schofield revolvers is in the barrel latch system. The 2nd Model latch is rounded and knurled to afford an easier and more positive grip when opening the revolver. A group of 3,000 of these revolvers was delivered to the Springfield Armory in October of 1876, and another 2,000 were delivered in 1877. These 2nd Model contract revolvers were all blued. There were an additional 649 civilian guns sold as well. The civilian models were not "US" marked and were offered either blued or nickel-plated. A total of 8,969 Model 3 Schofield 2nd Models were manufactured. The last sale was recorded in 1878.

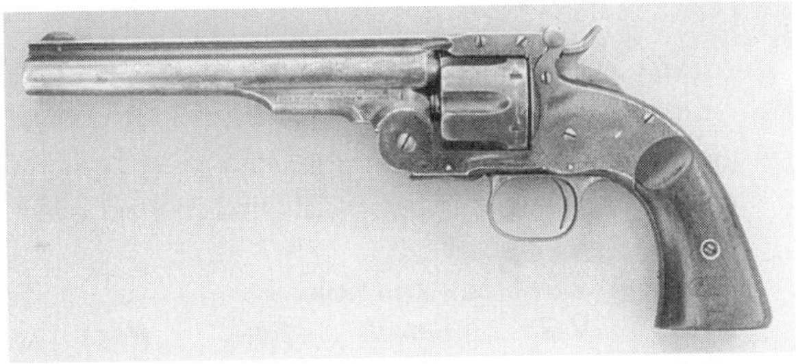

Courtesy Jim Supica, Old Town Station

"US" Contract—4,000 Issued

Exc.	*V.G.*	*Good*	*Fair*	*Poor*
—	8500	3750	1750	950

Civilian Model—646 Made

Exc.	*V.G.*	*Good*	*Fair*	*Poor*
—	8500	3750	1750	950

Model 3 Schofield—Surplus Models

Many Schofields were issued to various states under the Militia Act, some of which were used in the Spanish American War. After the government dropped the Schofield as an issue cavalry sidearm, the remaining U.S. inventory of these revolvers was sold off as military surplus. Many were sold to dealers such as Bannerman's or Schuyler, Hartley & Graham, two large gun dealers who then resold the guns to supply the growing need for guns on the Western frontier. Schuyler, Hartley & Graham sold a number of guns to the Wells Fargo Express Co. Almost all of these weapons had the barrels shortened to 5", as were many others sold during this period. Some were nickel plated. Beware of fakes when contemplating purchase of the Wells Fargo revolvers.

Wells Fargo & Co. Model

Exc.	*V.G.*	*Good*	*Fair*	*Poor*
—	5500	2500	1500	900

Surplus Cut Barrel—Not Wells Fargo

Exc.	*V.G.*	*Good*	*Fair*	*Poor*
3000	1800	1400	1100	800

New Model No. 3 Single Action

Always interested in perfecting the Model 3 revolver, D.B. Wesson redesigned and improved the old Model 3 in the hopes of attracting more sales. The Russian contracts were almost filled so the company decided to devote the effort necessary to improve on this design. In 1877 this project was undertaken. The extractor housing was shortened, the cylinder retention system was improved, and the shape of the grip was changed to a more streamlined and attractive configuration. This New Model has a 3.5", 4", 5", 6", 6.5", 7", 7.5", or 8" barrel length with a 6-shot fluted cylinder. The 6.5" barrel and .44 S&W Russian chambering is the most often encountered variation of this model, but the factory considered the 8" barrels as standard and these were kept in stock as well. The New Model No. 3 was also chambered for .32 S&W, .32-44 S&W, .320 S&W Rev. Rifle, .38 S&W, .38-40, .38-44 S&W, .41 S&W, .44 Henry rimfire, .44 S&W American, .44-40, .45 S&W Schofield, .450 Rev., .45 Webley, .455 MkI and .455 MkII. They are either blued or nickel-plated and have checkered hard rubber grips with the S&W logo molded into them or walnut grips. There are many sub-variations within this model designation, and the potential collector should secure detailed reference material that deals with this model. There were approximately 35,796 of these revolvers manufactured between 1878 and 1912. Nearly 40 percent were exported to fill contracts with Japan, Australia, Argentina, England, Spain, and Cuba. There were some sent to Asia, as well. The proofmarks of these countries will establish their provenance but will not add appreciably to standard values.

Standard Model—6.5" barrel, .44 S&W Russian

Exc.	*V.G.*	*Good*	*Fair*	*Poor*
—	3700	2000	1000	—

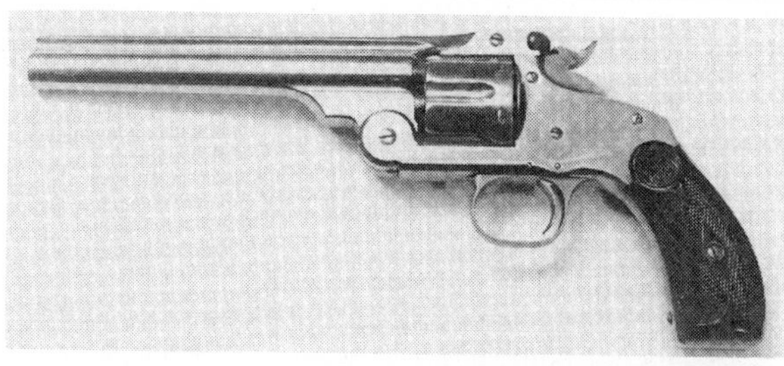

Courtesy Mike Stuckslager

Japanese Naval Contract

This was the largest foreign purchaser of this model. There were over 1,500 produced with the anchor insignia stamped on the frame.

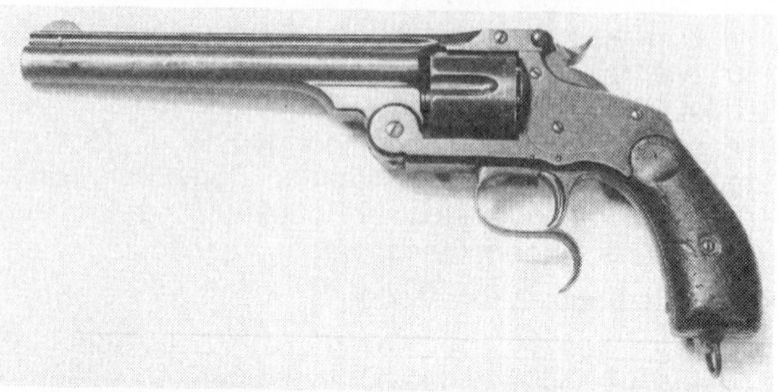

Courtesy Mike Stuckslager

Courtesy Mike Stuckslager

Exc.	*V.G.*	*Good*	*Fair*	*Poor*
—	3700	2500	1000	—

Japanese Artillery Contract

This variation is numbered in the 25,000 serial range. They are blued, with a 7" barrel and a lanyard swivel on the butt. Japanese characters are stamped on the extractor housing.

Exc.	*V.G.*	*Good*	*Fair*	*Poor*
—	6000	2500	1250	—

Maryland Militia Model

This variation is nickel-plated, has a 6.5" barrel, and is chambered for the .44 S&W Russian cartridge. The butt is stamped "U.S.," and the inspector's marks "HN" and "DAL" under the 1878 date appear on the revolver. There were 280 manufactured between serial numbers 7126 and 7405.

Exc.	*V.G.*	*Good*	*Fair*	*Poor*
—	12500	6000	3000	—

NOTE: Rarity makes valuation speculative.

Australian Contract

This variation is nickel-plated, is chambered for the .44 S&W Russian cartridge, and is marked with the Australian Colonial Police Broad Arrow on the butt. There were 250 manufactured with 7" barrels and detachable shoulder stocks. The stock has the Broad Arrow stamped on the lower tang. There were also 30 manufactured with 6.5" barrels without the stocks. They all are numbered in the 12,000-13,000 serial number range.

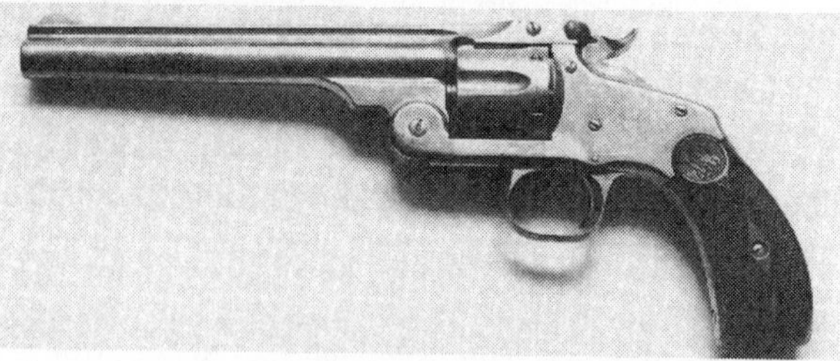

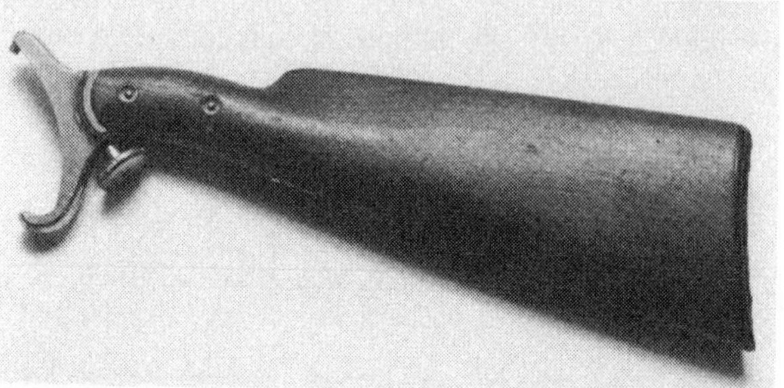

Courtesy Mike Stuckslager

BIBLIOGRAPHICAL NOTE: There are a number of excellent books on general U.S. military firearms. Some of them are Bruce Canfield's U.S. Infantry Weapons of World War I, Mowbray, 2000, and U.S. Infantry Weapons of World War II, Mowbray, 1992. Norm Flayderman's Flayderman's Guide to Antique American Firearms and Their Values, 7th edition, Krause Publications, 1998. Thomas Batha, U.S. Martial .22RF Rifles, Excalibur Publications, 2000.

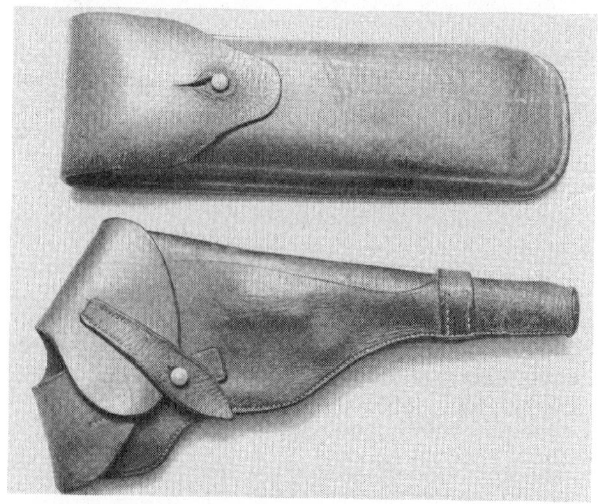

Courtesy Mike Stuckslager

NOTE: The total number of the revolvers made is greater than the number mentioned, but no exact number can be given.

Revolver with stock and holsters

Exc.	*V.G.*	*Good*	*Fair*	*Poor*
—	8000	4750	2750	—

NOTE: Deduct 40 percent for no stock.

Argentine Model

This was essentially not a factory contract but a sale through Schuyler, Hartley & Graham. They are stamped "Ejercito/Argentino" in front of the triggerguard. The order amounted to some 2,000 revolvers between the serial numbers 50 and 3400.

Exc.	V.G.	Good	Fair	Poor
—	7000	3500	1750	—

Turkish Model

This is essentially the New Model No. 3 chambered for the .44 rimfire Henry cartridge. It is stamped with the letters "P," "U" and "AFC" on various parts of the revolver. The barrels are all 6.5"; the finish, blued with walnut grips. Lanyard swivels are found on the butt. There were 5,461 manufactured and serial numbered in their own range, starting at 1 through 5461 between 1879 and 1883.

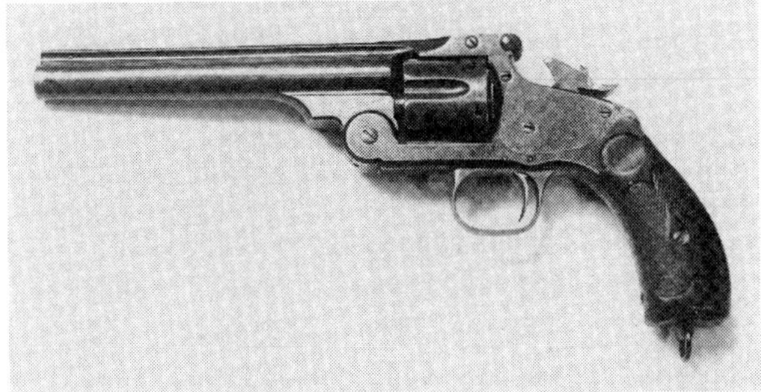

Courtesy Mike Stuckslager

Exc.	V.G.	Good	Fair	Poor
—	6500	3500	1750	—

U.S. Revenue Cutter Service (U.S. Coast Guard)

This model was issued to the U.S. Revenue Cutter Service as a standard issue sidearm. Fitted with 5", 6", or 6.5" barrels. The revolver is not marked but there are known serial numbers that identify this as a military variation. Consult an expert prior to sale, or see *Standard Catalog of Smith & Wesson* for a list of known serial numbers.

Exc.	V.G.	Good	Fair	Poor
—	8000	5000	2750	—

New Model No. 3 Frontier Single Action

This is another model similar in appearance to the standard New Model No. 3. It has a 4", 5", or 6.5" barrel and is chambered for the .44-40 Winchester Centerfire cartridge. Because the original New Model No. 3 cylinder was 1-7/16" in length this would not accommodate the longer .44-40 cartridge. The cylinder on the No. 3 Frontier was changed to 1-9/16" in length.

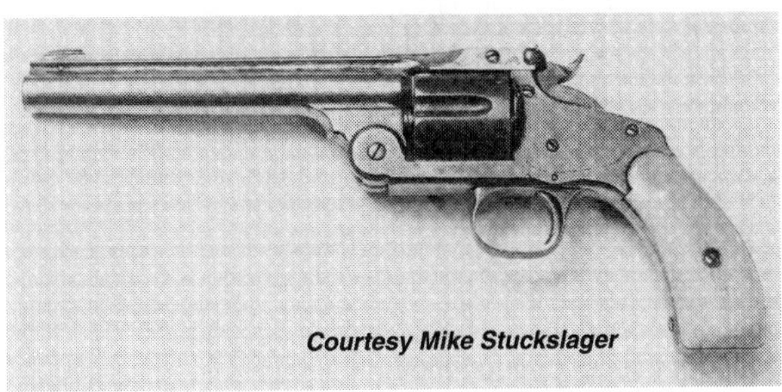

Courtesy Mike Stuckslager

Later, the company converted 786 revolvers to .44 S&W Russian and sold them to Japan. This model is either blued or nickel-plated and has checkered grips of walnut or hard rubber. They are serial numbered in their own range from 1 through 2072 and were manufactured from 1885 until 1908. This model was designed to compete with the Colt Single Action Army but was not successful.

.44-40—Commercial Model

Exc.	V.G.	Good	Fair	Poor
—	5000	2500	1250	—

Japanese Purchase Converted to .44 S&W Russian

Exc.	V.G.	Good	Fair	Poor
—	4000	2000	1000	—

.38 Hand Ejector Military & Police 1st Model or Model of 1899

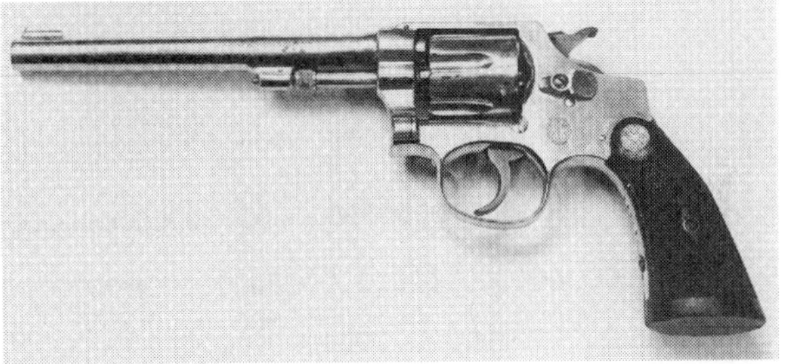

Courtesy Mike Stuckslager

This was an early swing-out cylinder revolver, and it has no front lockup for the action. The release is on the left side of the frame. This model is chambered for the .38 S&W Special cartridge and the .32 Winchester centerfire cartridge (.32-20), has a 6-shot fluted cylinder, and was offered with a 4", 5", 6", 6.5", or 8" barrel in .38 caliber, and 4", 5", and 6-1/2" in .32-20 caliber. The finish is blued or nickel-plated; the grips, checkered walnut or hard rubber. There were approximately 20,975 manufactured between 1899 and 1902 in .38 caliber; serial number range 1 to 20975. In the .32-20 caliber, 5,311 were sold between 1899 and 1902; serial number range 1 to 5311.

Commercial Model

Exc.	V.G.	Good	Fair	Poor
750	650	600	450	350

U.S. Navy Model

One thousand produced in 1900, .38 S&W, 6" barrel, blued with checkered walnut grips, "U.S.N." stamped on butt, serial number range 5000 to 6000.

Exc.	V.G.	Good	Fair	Poor
2500	1750	800	500	300

U.S. Army Model

One thousand produced in 1901, same as Navy Model

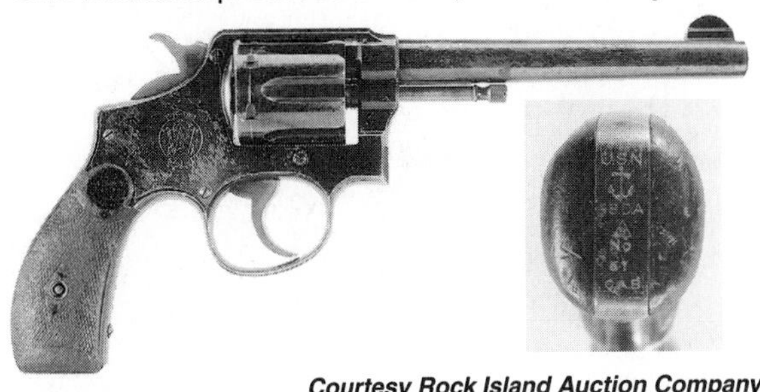

Courtesy Rock Island Auction Company

except that it is marked "U.S.Army/Model 1899" on butt, "K.S.M." and "J.T.T." on grips, serial number range 13001 to 14000.

Exc.	V.G.	Good	Fair	Poor
2750	2000	950	600	300

.38 Hand Ejector Military & Police 2nd Model or Model of 1902—U.S. Navy Model

Chambered for .38 Long Colt cartridge with Navy serial number range 1001 to 2000. Marked "u.s.n." with anchor stamped on butt. Smith & Wesson serial number stamped on front tang in the 25001 to 26000 serial range. Some 1025 revolvers were produced.

Courtesy Rock Island Auction Company

Exc.	V.G.	Good	Fair	Poor
2500	2000	900	500	300

.45 Hand Ejector U.S. Service Model of 1917

WWI was on the horizon, and it seemed certain that the United States would become involved. The S&W people began to work with the Springfield Armory to develop a hand-ejector model that would fire the .45-caliber Government cartridge. This was accomplished in 1916 by the use of half-moon clips. The new revolver is quite similar to the .44 Hand Ejector in appearance. It has a 5.5" barrel, blued finish with smooth walnut grips, and a lanyard ring on the butt. The designation "U.S.Army Model 1917" is stamped on the butt. After the war broke out, the government was not satisfied with S&W's production and actually took control of the company for the duration of the war. This was the first time that the company was not controlled by a Wesson. The factory records indicate that there were 163,476 Model 1917s manufactured between 1917 and 1919, the WWI years. After the war, the sale of these revolvers continued on a commercial and contract basis until 1949, when this model was finally dropped from the S&W product line.

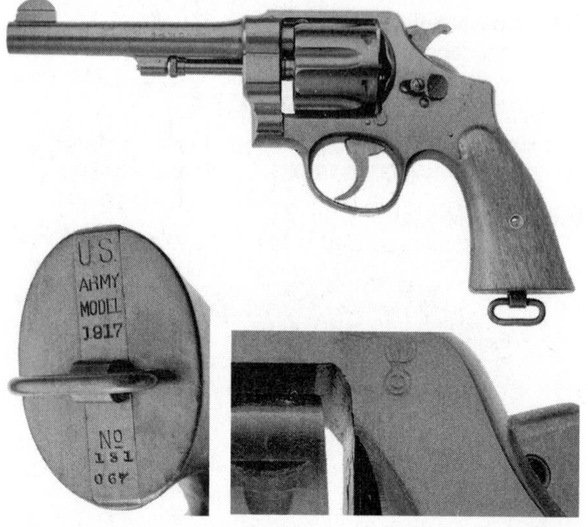

Paul Goodwin photo

Military Model

Exc.	V.G.	Good	Fair	Poor
800	600	450	300	200

Commercial Model

High gloss blue and checkered walnut grips.

Exc.	V.G.	Good	Fair	Poor
650	500	350	250	200

.455 Mark II Hand Ejector 1st Model

This model was designed the same as the .44 Hand Ejector 1st Model with no caliber stamping on the barrel. It has a barrel length of 6.4". Of the 5,000 revolvers produced and sold, only 100 were commercial guns, the rest were military. Produced between 1914 and 1915. The commercial model is worth a premium.

Exc.	V.G.	Good	Fair	Poor
1100	750	400	300	200

.455 Mark II Hand Ejector 2nd Model

Similar to the first model without an extractor shroud. Barrel length was also 6.5". Serial number range was 5000 to 74755. Manufactured from 1915 to 1917.

Exc.	V.G.	Good	Fair	Poor
650	450	300	200	150

Model 10 (.38 Military & Police)—Military Marked

This model has been in production in one configuration or another since 1899. It was always the mainstay of the S&W line and was originally known as the .38 Military and Police Model. The Model 10 is built on the K, or medium frame, and was always meant as a duty gun. It was offered with a 2", 3", 4", 5", or 6" barrel. Currently only the 4" and 6" are available. A round or square butt is offered. It is chambered for the .38 Special, .38 S&W, and .22 rimfire and is offered in blue or nickel-plate, with checkered walnut grips. The Model designation is stamped on the yoke on all S&W revolvers. This model, with many other modern S&W pistols, underwent several engineering changes. These changes may affect the value of the pistol and an expert should be consulted. The dates of these changes are as follows:

10-NONE-1957	**10-3-1961**	**10-5-1962**
10-1-1959	**10-4-1962**	**10-6-1962**
10-1961		

NIB	Exc.	V.G.	Good	Fair	Poor
550	350	250	150	125	90

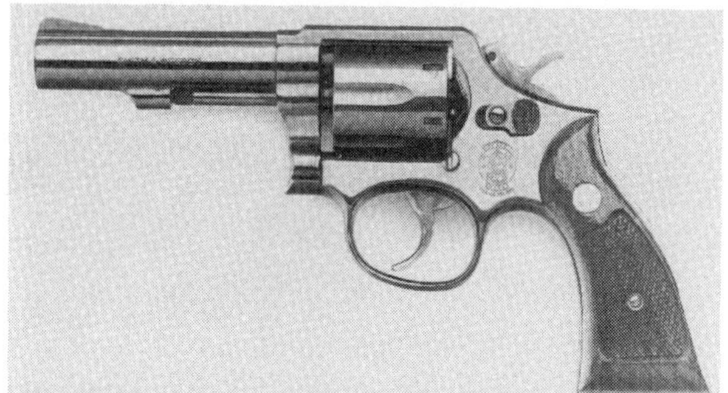

Victory Model marked "N.Y.M.I." • Courtesy Richard M. Kumor Sr.

Victory Model

Manufactured during WWII, this is a Model 10 with a sandblasted and parkerized finish, a lanyard swivel, and smooth walnut grips. The serial number has a V prefix. This model was available in only 2" and 4" barrel lengths. The Victory Model was discontinued on April 27, 1945, with serial number VS811119.

Navy marked Smith & Wesson Victory model • *Courtesy Amoskeag Auction, Co., Inc.*

Exc.	*V.G.*	*Good*	*Fair*	*Poor*
500	425	275	175	125

NOTE: Top strap marked Navy will bring a 75 percent premium. Navy variation with both top strap and side plate marked will bring a 100 percent premium. Navy variation marked "N.Y.M.I." will bring a 125 percent premium. Revolvers marked "U.S.G.C." or "U.S.M.C." will bring a premium of unknown amount. Exercise caution.

Model 11 (.38/200 British Service Revolver)

First produced in 1938, S&W manufactured these revolvers for the British Commonwealth in 4", 5", or 6" barrels. Early models are bright blue, later models are parkerized. Square butt with checkered walnut grips. Lend Lease guns marked "UNITED STATES PROPERTY." Production ended in 1945 with 568,204 built. Nicknamed the .38/200 British Service Revolver. Smith & Wesson began producing this model again in 1947 and sold many of these throughout the 1950s and 1960s when production ceased again in 1965. There are several rare variations of this model that will greatly affect its value. Consult an expert if special markings and barrel lengths are encountered.

Exc.	*V.G.*	*Good*	*Fair*	*Poor*
400	300	200	100	75

USAF M-13 (Aircrewman)

From 1952 to about 1957 the Air Force purchased a large quantity of Model 12s with alloy frames and cylinders. They were intended for use by flight crews as survival weapons in emergencies. This model was not officially designated "13" by S&W, but the Air Force requested these revolvers be stamped "M13" on the top strap. This model was rejected by the Air Force in 1960 because of trouble with the alloy cylinder.

NOTE: Beware of fakes. Seek expert advice before purchase.

Exc.	*V.G.*	*Good*	*Fair*	*Poor*
1500	1200	900	700	350

Model 39 Steel Frame

Semi-automatic pistol chambered for the 9mm cartridge. Fitted with a 4" barrel, walnut stocks, blue finish, and adjustable rear sight. Military version of this pistol has a dull blue finish, no walnut grips, with double action trigger. Manufactured from 1954 to 1966. Some of these military models are found without serial numbers. A special variation was used with a suppressor in Vietnam, and modified with a slide lock for single shot. Named the "Hush Puppy."

Exc.	*V.G.*	*Good*	*Fair*	*Poor*
1200	900	700	500	300

NOTE: Pricing does not include the suppressor.

Model 56 (KXT-38 USAF)

Introduced in 1962, this is a 2" heavy barrel built on the K frame. It is chambered for the .38 Special. There were approximately 15,000 of these revolvers built when it was discontinued in 1964. It was marked "US" on the backstrap. A total of 15,205 were produced, but most were destroyed.

NIB	*Exc.*	*V.G.*	*Good*	*Fair*	*Poor*
Too Rare To Price					

HIGH STANDARD

Model B-US

Courtesy Rock Island Auction Company

A .22 Long Rifle caliber semi-automatic pistol with a 4.5" round tapered barrel and a 10-shot magazine. A version of the Model B with slight modifications to the frame. U.S. marked Model Bs will be found in both original Model B frame and Model B-US frame. An estimated 14,000 made for the U.S. government 1942-1943. Black, monogrammed hard rubber grips. Blued finish. Black checkered hard rubber grips. Type II takedown only. Most are marked "PROPERTY OF U.S." on the top of the barrel and on the right side of the frame. Crossed cannon ordnance stamp usually found on the right side of the frame. Box with papers add premium of 20 percent. Most guns are found in serial number range from about 92344 to about 111631.

Courtesy Rock Island Auction Company

Exc.	V.G.	Good	Fair	Poor
800	650	500	300	200

Model USA—Model HD

Similar to the Model HD with 4.5" barrel and fixed sights, checkered black hard rubber grips and an external safety. Early models blued; later model parkerized. Introduced 1943; approximately 44,000 produced for the U.S. government. Most are marked "PROPERTY OF U.S." on the top of the barrel and on the right side of the frame. Crossed cannon ordnance stamp usually found on the right side of the frame. Box with papers add 20 percent premium. Most pistols are found in serial number range from about 103863 to about 145700.

Exc.	V.G.	Good	Fair	Poor
750	550	400	250	175

Model USA—Model HD-MS

A silenced variation of the USA Model HD. Approximately 2500 produced for the OSS during 1944 and 1945. 6.75" shrouded barrel. Early pistols blued; later pistols parkerized. Only a few registered with BATF for civilian ownership. All NFA rules apply. Box with papers will bring a 10 percent premium. Most guns are found in serial number range from about 110074 to about 130040.

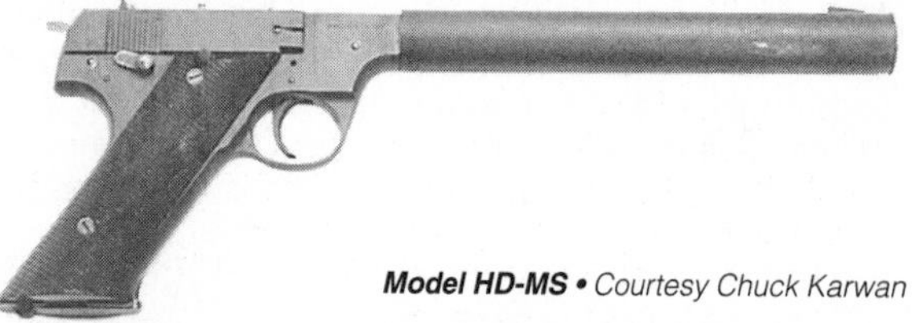

Model HD-MS • *Courtesy Chuck Karwan*

Exc.	V.G.	Good	Fair	Poor
6000	5000	—	—	—

Supermatic S-101

A .22 Long Rifle caliber semi-automatic pistol with 10-round magazine. Medium weight round barrel with blued finish, adjustable sights, brown plastic thumb rest grips. Grooved front and back straps on frame. The 6.75" barrel incorporates a muzzle brake with one slot on either side of the front sight. Marked "U.S." on the left side of the frame, above and in front of the triggerguard with characters approximately .150" high. Box with papers will bring a 13 percent premium. Most guns found in serial number range beginning at about 446,511.

Catalog # 9119—1954 to 1957.

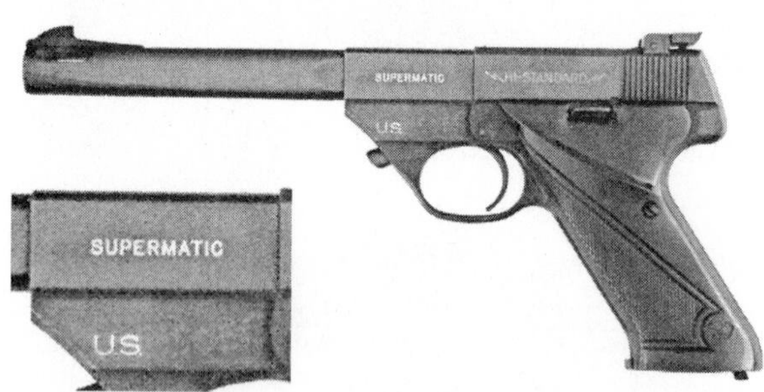

Supermatic "US" marked • *Courtesy John J. Stimson Jr.*

Exc.	V.G.	Good	Fair	Poor
700	400	275	195	150

Supermatic Citation Model 102 & 103

As above but with tapered barrel with an enlarged register at the muzzle end to hold a removable muzzle brake; adjustable sights; 2 and 3 oz. adjustable weights; checkered plastic grips, and blued finish. Grooved front and rear straps on frame. Marked "U.S." on left side of frame, above and in front of the triggerguard in characters approximately .150" high. Box with papers add 13 percent premium.

Catalog # 9260—1958 to 1963.

Supermatic Citation "US" marked • *Courtesy John J. Stimson Jr.*

Exc.	V.G.	Good	Fair	Poor
700	500	400	325	200

Supermatic Tournament 102 & 103

As above but with round tapered barrel. Blued finish, adjustable sights, checkered plastic grips. Smooth front and back straps on frame. Marked "U.S." on left side of frame, above and in front of the triggerguard in characters approximately .150" high.

Two different models catalog numbers 9271 and 9274. A contract in 1964 had mostly 9271 with some

9274. A contract in 1965 was all #9274. Catalog #9271 has a 6.75" barrel. Specifics of the #9274 are presently unknown.

Box with papers add 13 percent premium.

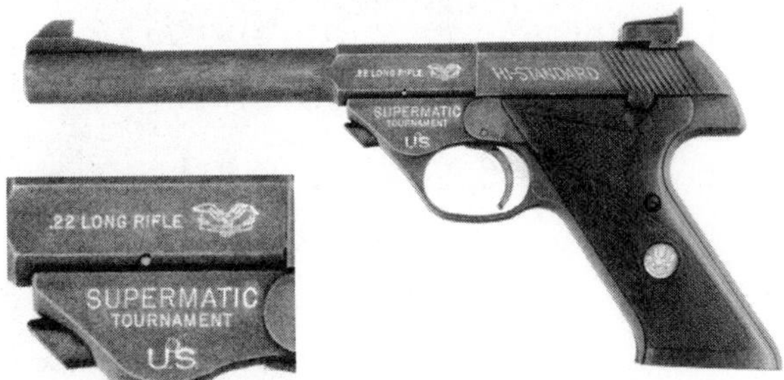

Supermatic Tournament "US" marked • *Courtesy John J. Stimson Jr.*

Catalog #9271—1958 to 1963.

Exc.	V.G.	Good	Fair	Poor
575	400	290	200	175

T-3

A semi-automatic double action pistol made under contract to the U.S. government on a development contract. All types are blowback design. A preliminary model gun exists in the white in a private collection. No serial number and no folding triggerguard. The other pistols all have folding triggerguards for use with gloved hands. These guns are also blowback design and have barrels with angular grooves in the chamber to reduce recoil. Fitted with a 4" barrel. Made in three distinct types.

Type 1 pistols were probably made in a lot of four pistols each with a 7-round single column magazine. Serial number 1 does not include the plunge to increase the trigger pull when the trigger guard is folded. The magazine release for the Type 1 is like other High Standard pistols. Grips are checkered black plastic. Serial number 2 is in the Springfield Museum. Serial numbers 1, 3, and 4 are in private collections.

T-3 Type 1 • *Courtesy John J. Stimson Jr.*

Type 2 pistols were probably built in a lot of four pistols with a 7-round single column magazine. The magazine release on Type 2 pistols is located in the frame where the triggerguard meets the front grip strap. The 2nd type incorporated a thicker triggerguard and a wider frame and slide. Serial numbers 1, 2, and 3 are in the Springfield Museum, while serial number 4 is in a private collection.

T-3-Type 2 • *Courtesy John J. Stimson Jr.*

Type 3 pistols have a 13-round double-column magazine with a Type 2 triggerguard and magazine release. The magazine is similar to the Browning High Power. The frame and slide are wider than Type 2. One is known to exist in the Rock Island Arsenal Museum and the other is in a private collection. There are two others believed to exist.

Exc.	V.G.	Good	Fair	Poor
8500	7750	—	—	—

HECKLER & KOCH

See also Germany

H&K Mark 23 Model O (SOCOM)

Very similar to H&K's U.S. government contract pistol developed for U.S. military special operation units. Chambered for the .45 ACP and fitted with a 5.87" barrel, this pistol has a polymer frame with steel slide. Magazine capacity is 10 rounds on civilian models and 12 rounds on military models. Barrel is threaded for noise suppressor. Weight is about 42 oz. Limited availability in fall 1996 to about 2,000 pistols.

NIB	Exc.	V.G.	Good	Fair	Poor
2250	1750	1250	—	—	—

Mark 23 Suppressor

This is the same suppressor as sold to the U.S. military for use on the Mark 23 pistol. This unit can be fitted to the threaded barrel of the Mark 23 and be adjusted for point of aim. With water the dB sound reduction is 33-35dB. Produced by Knight Armament Corp. of Vero Beach, Fla. This suppressor, with a different piston assembly, can be fitted to the USP Tactical.

NOTE: Suppressors require a Class III transfer tax. All NFA rules apply to the sale or purchase of these suppressors.

NIB	Exc.	V.G.	Good	Fair	Poor
1500	—	—	—	—	—

BERETTA

See also Italy

Model M9 Limited Edition

Introduced in 1995 to commemorate the 10th anniversary of the U.S. military's official sidearm, this 9mm pistol is limited to 10,000 units. Special engraving on the slide with special serial numbers. Slide stamped "U.S. 9MM M9-BERETTA U.S.A.-65490."

Standard Model

NIB	Exc.	V.G.	Good	Fair	Poor
750	600	400	N/A	N/A	N/A

Deluxe Model

Walnut grips with gold plated hammer and grip screws.

U.S. Beretta Model M9 • *Paul Goodwin photos*

NIB	Exc.	V.G.	Good	Fair	Poor
850	700	450	N/A	N/A	N/A

SAVAGE

Model 1907/10/11

Manufactured in 1905 in .45 ACP, this pistol was tested in the U.S. Army trials. A few were sold commercially. It weighs 32 oz., and has an overall length of 9". Magazine capacity is 8 rounds. Checkered two-piece walnut grips. Blued finish. An improved version was built in 1910 and another version was built in 1911. This last version was a completely redesigned pistol: the Model 1911. Some 288 pistols were built in three different versions. Once the Army trials were over, Savage refinished the pistols with a matte blue finish and sold some of them commercially.

Courtesy James Rankin

Model 1907 Test Pistol

Manufactured in 1907 in .45 ACP, this pistol was tested in the U.S. Army trials. About 290 pistols were produced for these trials. Double stack magazine held 8 rounds.

Courtesy Bailey Brower, Jr.

Exc.	V.G.	Good	Fair	Poor
12500	10000	9500	6000	2000

Model 1910 Test Pistol

This was a modified Model 1907 with a heavier slide, which was not concave like the Model 1907. There were a total of nine Model 1910s built.

Exc.	V.G.	Good	Fair	Poor
Too Rare To Price				

Model 1911 Test Pistol

This example was completely modified with a longer and thinner grip. Checkered wood grips were attached by friction instead of screws, the slide release was modified, a full grip safety was added, and a heavier serrated hammer (cocking lever) was added. Four of these pistols were built. Serial #1 has never been located.

Exc.	V.G.	Good	Fair	Poor
Too Rare To Price				

Model 1917

This semi-automatic pistol is chambered for the 7.65mm cartridge. It is fitted with an external hammer and without the grip safety. The form of the grip frame has been widened. Manufactured between 1917 and 1928. This pistol was sold to the French government during World War I and used by the French military. Approximately 27,000 of these pistols were sold to France. See also *France, Handguns, Savage.*

Exc.	V.G.	Good	Fair	Poor
300	225	175	100	75

STURM, RUGER & CO.

Mark I Target Pistol (U.S. marked)

This is a semi-automatic target pistol with 6.88" barrel and target sights. Stamped "U.S." on top of receiver. First produced in 1956. Blued finish. Rebuilt or refinished pistols may be parkerized and stamped with arsenal stamp.

Exc.	V.G.	Good	Fair	Poor
800	600	400	250	150

GUIDE LAMP

Division of General Motors

Liberator

A .45 ACP caliber single shot pistol with a 3.5" smooth bore barrel and overall length of 5.5". This pistol is made primarily of stampings and was intended to be air dropped to partisans in Europe during WWII. The hollow grip is designed to hold a packet of four extra cartridges. Originally packaged in unmarked cardboard boxes with an illustrated instruction sheet.

Courtesy Richard M. Kumor Sr.

NIB	Exc.	V.G.	Good	Fair	Poor
4000	2500	1500	650	300	175

SUBMACHINE GUNS

Bibliographical Note: For historical information, technical data, and photos, see Tracie Hill, *Thompson: The American Legend*, Collector Grade Publications, 1996.

Colt 9mm (Model 635)

Based on the M16, this submachine gun is chambered for the 9mm cartridge. It was first produced in 1990. It has the capability of semi-automatic or full automatic fire. The barrel length is 10.125" with a 20- or 32-round magazine. The gun is fitted with a retractable stock. As with the M16, this gun fires from a closed bolt. Weight is about 6.5 lbs. Rate of fire is about 900 rounds per minute. "SMG" and serial number are marked on left side of magazine housing. Used by the U.S. military, although not in any official capacity, and other countries' military forces.

This model has several other variants:

Model 634—As above but with semi-automatic fire only.
Model 639—Same as the M635 but with 3-round burst.
Model 633HB—Fitted with 7" barrel and hydraulic buffer. (Manufactured after 1986)

NOTE: See also U.S., Rifles, M16.

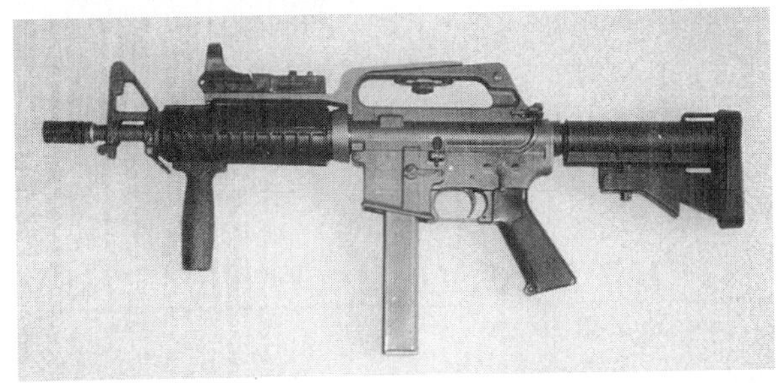

Courtesy private NFA collection

Pre-1968

Exc.	*V.G.*	*Fair*
N/A	N/A	N/A

Pre-1986 conversions, for OEM add 20 percent

Exc.	*V.G.*	*Fair*
20000	18500	17500

Ingram Model 10

Chambered for the 9mm or .45 ACP cartridge, this submachine gun is fitted with a 5.7" barrel and a 30-round magazine. It has a rate of fire of 1,100 rounds per minute. The empty weight is approximately 6.3 lbs. This submachine gun was used by various government agencies in Vietnam. A version chambered for the .380 cartridge is known as the Model 11.

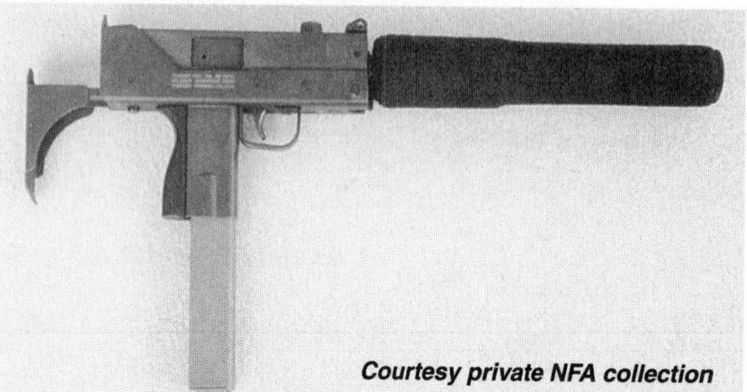

Courtesy private NFA collection

Pre-1968

Exc.	*V.G.*	*Fair*
5000	3500	2000

Reising 50/55

First built in 1941, the gun was chambered for the .45 ACP cartridge. It was first used by Marines in the Pacific but failed to be combat reliable. The Model 50 was fitted with a wooden buttstock and 10.8" barrel. Magazine capacity was 12 or 20 rounds. Rate of fire was 550 rounds per minute. The gun has a select fire mechanism for single round operation. Marked "HARRINGTON & RICHARDSON WORCESTER MASS USA" on the top of the receiver. Weight was about 6.75 lbs.

The Model 55 is the same mechanism but with a wire folding stock and no muzzle compensator. The weight of the Model 55 was 6.25 lbs. About 100,000 Reising Model 50s and 55s were built between 1941 and 1945 when production ceased.

NOTE: Commercial guns will bring less than military marked guns. Add about 25 percent for U.S. martially marked guns.

Courtesy Richard M. Kumor Sr.

Pre-1968

Exc.	*V.G.*	*Fair*
8500	7000	5000

THOMPSON SUBMACHINE GUNS

Text by Nick Tilotta

Thompson Model 1921AC/21A, 1921/28 Navy

The first Thompsons to come to market were the Model 1921s, manufactured by Colt Patent Firearms for Auto Ordnance Corporation in New York, New York. Between March 1921 and April 1922 15,000 guns were built. Of those 15,000 manufactured, only about 2,400 weapons exist in a transferable state today, "transferable" meaning weapons that can be bought, sold, or traded legally within the U.S. Three models of the Model 1921 were produced. The Model 1921A had a fixed front sight and a rate of fire of 800 rounds per minute. The Model 1921AC has a Cutts compensator instead of a fixed front sight and an 800-rounds-per-minute rate of fire. The Model 1928 Navy was fitted with a Cutts compensator and a heavier actuator that reduced the rate of fire to 600 rounds per minute. All of these Navy models had the number "8" stamped crudely over the number "1" on the left side of the receiver. Of the 15,000 Colt Model 1921s produced, approximately 25 percent were Model 1921As, 33 percent were Model 1921ACs, and 41 percent were 1928 Navys. A handful of Model 1927s were manufactured by Colt and left the factory as semi-automatics. However, the ATF considers these guns machine guns and requires that all NFA rules apply. These Model 1927s are quite rare and represent only about 1 percent of total production. They do not seem to sell for the same dollar figures that the machine guns do.

All Colt-manufactured Thompsons were bright blued; none were parkerized. All had walnut stocks, grips, and forearms manufactured by Remington. With the exception of a few prototypes, all Colt Thompsons were chambered for the .45 ACP cartridge. All internal parts were nickel plated and all barrels were finned. All weapons had a Lyman rear sight assembly. A removable rear stock was standard. All weapons were marked with a "NEW YORK, USA" address on the right side of the receiver. "COLT PATENT FIREARMS" was marked on the left side of the receiver. These Colt Thompsons would accept a 20- or 30-round box magazine as well as a 50-round "L" drum or 100 round "C" drum. Weight is about 10.75 lbs. Prices below are for original Colt guns with original parts and finish.

NOTE: Model 1921As, early serial numbers, previous ownership, and documentation can dramatically add to the prices below. In addition, missing components, re-barreled weapons, etc, will see a substantial reduction in price, as these original components are almost extinct. Re-finishing or re-bluing will result in a substantial reduction in value by as much as 50 percent.

Pre-1968

Exc.	*V.G.*	*Fair*
35000	25000	20000

PRICING NOTE: For Thompsons with historical background such as Texas Ranger or gangster guns prices can exceed 50 percent to 100 percent of above with documentation.

Thompson Model 1928 Commercial/1928A1 Military

The next limited run of Thompsons came just before and right at the beginning of WWII. This version is called the Model 1928AC or Commercial model. These weapons were assembled by Savage Arms in Utica, New York, using original Colt internal components. The receivers were still marked with the New York address but void of any "Colt" markings. Most weapons were simply marked "MODEL 1928." The first of these guns have blued receivers and blued

Thompson Model 1921 with close-up of receiver stamping • *Paul Goodwin photo*

barrels. The second run had parkerized receivers and blued barrels. These guns are quite rare and command premium prices.

At the outbreak of WWII, the demand for the Thompson gun soared. A brake lining facility in Bridgeport, Conn., was acquired to accommodate the increased demand for production. Three models of Thompsons were born in this WWII era. The first was the Model 1928A1 Thompson. This version was a copy of the Model 1928 Navy Colt Thompson. Most were parkerized with much less detail paid to fine machining. This gun was assembled in two locations: Utica, N.Y., and Bridgeport, Conn. Receivers produced in Utica were marked with an "S" prefix in front of the serial number. Receivers marked with an "AO" prefix were produced in Bridgeport. Receivers were marked on the right side "AUTO ORDNANCE CORPORATION, BRIDGEPORT, CT," no matter where the receiver was manufactured. The Utica, N.Y., plant concentrated its efforts on manufacturing components while the Bridgeport facility concentrated on assemblies. As production increased, the Model 1928A1 lost many of its "unnecessary" components such as the finned barrel, the costly Lyman sight, and finely checkered selector switches. Approximately 562,000 Thompsons were produced in the Model 1928A1 configuration. All of the weapons were parkerized, and some have finned barrels and some have smooth barrels. Some of these guns were also fitted with Lyman sights, some have a stamped "L" type sight that may or may not have protective ears. As a general rule of thumb, most Model 1928 Commercial guns were fitted with a vertical foregrip while most Model 1928A1 guns were fitted with a horizontal forearm, and all had removable butt stocks. Used by Allied forces during WWII. Used both 20- or 30-round box magazines and 50- or 100-round drum magazines.

Thompson Model 1928 Commercial

Pre-1968

Exc.	*V.G.*	*Fair*
35000	25000	20000

Thompson Model 1928A1 Military

Pre-1968

Exc.	*V.G.*	*Fair*
28000	22000	18500

Thompson M1/M1A1

In April 1942, the M1 Thompson was introduced. It was a simplified version of the Model 1928 with a smooth barrel, stamped rear "L" sight, and a fixed rear stock. The expensive Model 1928-type bolt assembly was modified to simplified machining procedures. The result was a repositioned cocking knob on the right side of the receiver. Some 285,000 M1s were produced before being replaced by an improved version, the "M1A1," in April 1942. This version of the Thompson has a fixed firing pin machined into the bolt face, and had protective ears added to the rear sight assembly. All M1 Thompsons were fitted with a horizontal forearm and fixed butt stock. Approximately 540,000 M1A1 Thompsons were produced before the end of WWII. All M1 and M1A1 Thompsons used stick or box magazines only.

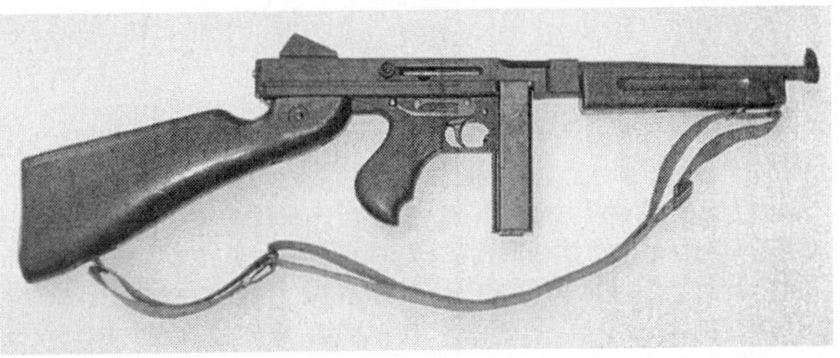

Courtesy Richard M. Kumor, Sr.

NOTE: Many of these weapons were reworked by a military arsenal during the war and may have been refinished; however, it does not significantly reduce the value of the gun. In addition to the rework, many of the serial numbered lower assemblies were not assembled with the correct serial numbered receiver. Although this may disturb some collectors, it should not significantly devalue the weapon. A very small percentage of these weapons were marked "US PROPERTY" behind the rear sight and this increases the value by as much as $1,000.

Pre-1968

Exc.	*V.G.*	*Fair*
25000	22500	18500

Third Generation Thompsons

In 1975, the Auto Ordnance Corp., West Hurley, New York, began production of the new Model 1928 Thompson. It was an attempt to produce a version of the Thompson for the civilian collector as well as a limited number of law enforcement sales. The early weapons were manufactured from surplus WWII components and were quite acceptable in quality. As time wore on, however, many of the components were of new manufacture and lesser quality. Between 1975 and 1986, approximately 3,200 models of the 1928 were produced. Some of these guns were commemorative models. The weapons had finned barrels, flip-up rear leaf sights, removable stocks, and blued finish. In 1985 and 1986, approximately 600 versions of the M1 Thompson were built. These were actually a version of the M1A1 military Thompson with blued finish. With the exception of a short production run for export in 1992, production of these weapons was banned in May 1986 by Federal law. All receivers were marked "AUTO-ORDNANCE WEST HURLEY, NEW YORK" on the right side of the receiver and "THOMPSON SUB-MACHINE GUN, CALIBER .45 M1" on the left side. All serial numbers carried the letter "A" suffix. A very limited number of .22 caliber models were produced in the Model 1928 configuration, but had limited success in the market. Auto-Ordnance is now (2007) owned by Kahr Arms; export production of the Thompson SMG has apparently been discontinued.

Thompson Model 1928—West Hurley

Pre-1986 manufacture

Exc.	*V.G.*	*Fair*
17500	12500	N/A

Thompson Model M1—West Hurley

Pre-1986 manufacture

Exc.	*V.G.*	*Fair*
12500	10000	N/A

Thompson Model 1928 .22 caliber—West Hurley

Pre-1986

Exc.	*V.G.*	*Fair*
15000	10000	6000

UD (United Defense) M42

Built by Marlin for U.S. military forces beginning in 1942. Designed by Carl Swebilius, founder of High Standard. Well constructed of excellent materials. Chambered for the 9mm Parabellum cartridge. Select fire with rate of fire of 700 rounds per minute. Barrel length was 10.8". Weight is about 9 lbs. Markings on left side of receiver are "UNITED DEFENSE SUPPLY CORP/ US MODEL 42/MARLIN FA CO NEW HAVEN." Magazine capacity is 20 rounds. Limited quantities produced with an estimate of about 15,000 produced. It seems that the majority were built to be sold to the Netherlands during WWII but, because of the war, they could not be delivered, so most were shipped to the American OSS for use in Europe and the Far East. These guns saw a lot of action during the war.

Private NFA collection, Gary Gelson photo

Pre-1968

Exc.	*V.G.*	*Fair*
20000	15000	12500

Pre-1986 conversions

Exc.	*V.G.*	*Fair*
12000	10000	9000

US M3

First produced in the U.S. in 1942, this submachine gun was chambered for the .45 ACP or 9mm cartridge (special conversion kit). It is similar in concept to the British Sten gun. It was fitted with an 8" barrel and folding metal stock. The box magazine capacity was 30 rounds. The rate of fire was 400 rounds per minute. Weight of the M3 was about 8 lbs. It was produced until 1944. Marked "GUIDE LAMP DIV OF GENERAL MOTORS/US MODEL M3" on top of the receiver. Approximately 600,000 M3s were produced. Built by the Guide Lamp Division of General Motors.

NOTE: A suppressed version of this gun was built for the OSS in World War II, and used for covert operations in Vietnam as well. Too rare to price.

US M3 • *Courtesy Richard M. Kumor Sr.*

Pre-1968

Exc.	*V.G.*	*Fair*
22500	19000	15000

Pre-1986 manufacture with new receiver

Exc.	*V.G.*	*Fair*
15000	12000	N/A

U.S. M3 with silencer • *Courtesy Chuck Karwan*

US M3A1

Similar to the M3 but with significant changes and improvements. This model has a larger ejection port, the retracting handle has been eliminated, a finger hole is used for cocking, disassembly grooves were added, a stronger cover spring was installed, a larger oil can is in the grip, a stock plate and magazine filler were added to the stock, and a guard was added for the magazine catch. First produced in 1944. Approximately 50,000 M3A1s were built. This version was built by Guide Lamp and Ithaca.

US M3A1 • *Courtesy private NFA collection*

Pre-1968

Exc.	*V.G.*	*Fair*
22500	17500	15000

Pre-1986 manufacture with new receiver

Exc.	*V.G.*	*Fair*
15000	12000	N/A

RIFLES

U.S. Pre-Cartridge Era Rifles

The United States military issued dozens of models of flintlock and percussion long arms through 1867 when the first cartridge loading arms were adopted. There is not nearly enough space in this guide to provide listings of the countless sub variations and experimental models that were produced in this era. We suggest the reader consult ***Flayderman's Guide to Antique American Firearms*** for more complete information on U.S. Military Weapons.

HARPERS FERRY ARMORY MUSKETS AND CARBINES

Harpers Ferry, Virginia

Established at Harpers Ferry, Virginia, in 1798 as the new nation's "Southern Armory," production finally began in 1800 and continued at the "musket works" until the facilities were seized by Virginia state militia in April 1861. With the signing of a contract in 1819 between the government and J.H. Hall, the latter was permitted to construct a separate facility for the production of his patent breechloading rifles, which continued to be known as the "rifle works" after the discontinuation of Hall production until it, too, was seized by Virginia militia in 1861. The machinery of the former was sent to Richmond to be used in the manufacture of the "Richmond rifle musket" while the rifle machinery was sent to Fayetteville, North Carolina, where it was employed in making "Fayetteville rifles."

Harpers Ferry U.S. M1816 Muskets (Types I to III)

Overall length 57-3/4 inches; barrel length 42 inches; caliber .69. Markings: on lockplate eagle over "US" forward of cock, "HARPERS/FERRY/(date) on tail. Barrel tang also bears the date, and barrel should show proofmarks on upper left side near breech. The 45605 (type 1) muskets produced at Harpers Ferry from 1817 through 1821 were made with a lower sling swivel that was attached to a separate lug extending from the forward strap of the trigger guard. In 1822, this piece was eliminated and the balance of the production (216,116) officially known as the M1822 musket, incorporated the lower sling swivel directly to the trigger guard bow. Until 1832, these muskets were manufactured with a "browned" barrel to inhibit rusting. The brown barrels of these 107,684 muskets distinguish them as Type II production. The balance of production until 1844 (98,432) were made with bright barrel, distinguishing Type III muskets. Despite the large numbers produced, most were altered to percussion during the 1850s. Most by the "cone-in-barrel" (so called arsenal) method. Many of these

UNITED STATES OF AMERICA

were altered again during the American Civil War, usually with a "Patent Breech," and were then rifled and sighted.

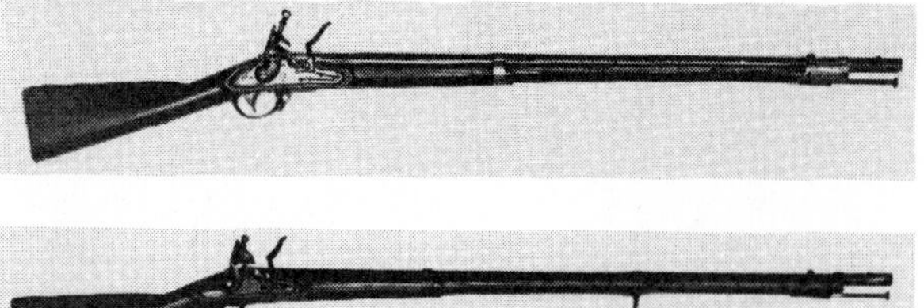

In flintlock

Exc.	V.G.	Good	Fair	Poor
—	3000	2000	1500	500

Altered to percussion

Exc.	V.G.	Good	Fair	Poor
—	900	500	350	200

NOTE: Add 100 percent for Type III flintlock muskets (Rare).

Harpers Ferry U.S. M1819 Hall Rifle (Types I and II)

Overall length 52-3/4 inches; barrel (bore) length 32-5/8 inches; caliber.52. Markings: on top of receiver, either "J.H. HALL/H.FERRY/(date)/U.S." or "J.H. HALL.S./(date)." The 2,000 rifles manufactured between 1824 and 1826 (Type I) are distinguished by having their barrel bands retained by band springs on the right side of the stock. The balance of production (17,680), made between 1828 and 1840, have pins driven through the bands and the stock, distinguishing Type II production. Many of these rifles were altered to percussion just before and in the early months of the American Civil War. Those with evidence of having been altered in the South will command a premium.

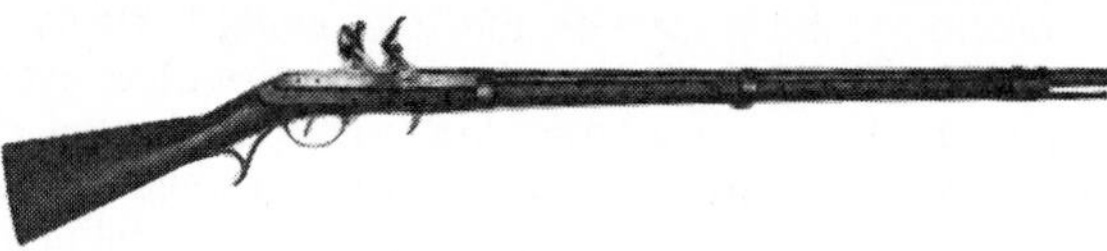

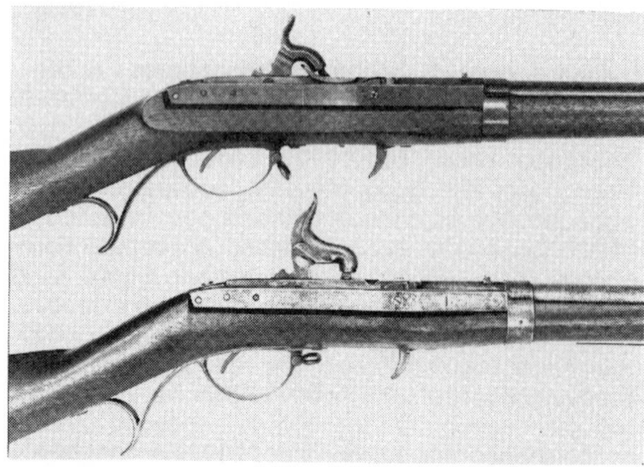

In flintlock

Exc.	V.G.	Good	Fair	Poor
—	3850	2200	1250	500

Altered to percussion

Exc.	V.G.	Good	Fair	Poor
—	2550	1500	750	350

NOTE: For Type I flintlocks add 250 percent.

Harpers Ferry U.S. M1841 Hall Rifle

Overall length 52-3/4 inches; barrel (bore) length 32-5/8 inches; caliber .52. Markings: on top of receiver, either "J.H. HALL/H.FERRY/US/ (date)." With the general adoption of the percussion system of ignition, the manufacture of Hall's rifles was changed to conform to the new system, a cone tapped directly into the breechblock substituting for the frizzen and pan, and a hammer replacing the flint cock. The newly made percussion arms also incorporated the newly adopted "fishtail" latch for levering the breechblock. Two-thirds of the 4,213 rifles made were still in storage at the arsenal when it was burned in 1861, enhancing the rarity of the arm.

Exc.	V.G.	Good	Fair	Poor
—	3500	2250	950	500

Harpers Ferry U.S. M1836 Hall Carbine (Types I & II)

Overall length 43"; barrel (bore) length 23"; caliber .64. Markings: on top of receiver, "J.H. HALL/U.S./[date]." To furnish the newly raised 2nd Regiment U.S. Dragoons raised in 1836, Harpers Ferry Armory was directed to construct 1,003 Hall carbines, differing in length and caliber over the M1833 model produced by the North for the 1st Regiment, but were not ready when the unit was sent to Florida. Another 1,017 were made during 1839-1840 with the addition of a tool compartment in the buttstock, distinguishing type II production.

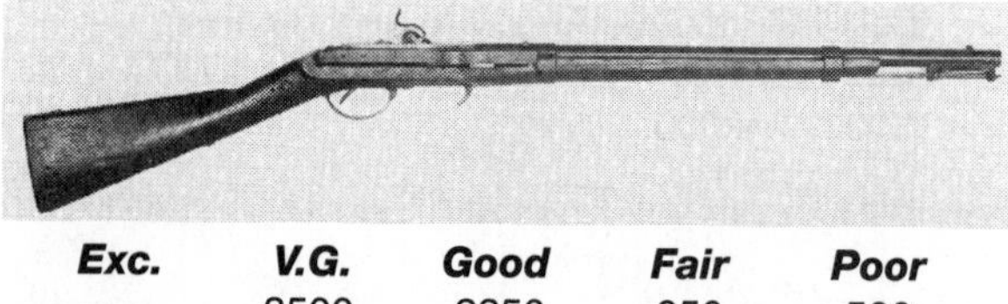

Exc.	V.G.	Good	Fair	Poor
—	3500	2250	950	500

Harpers Ferry U.S. M1842 Hall Carbine

Overall length 40 inches; barrel (bore) length 21 inches; caliber .52. Markings: on top of receiver, "H. FERRY/U S/1842." To meet the needs of the U.S. Dragoons for replacement carbines, Harpers Ferry manufactured 1,001 carbines in 1842, differing only from the North M1840 (Type II—"fishtail lever") carbine by being brass instead of iron mounted.

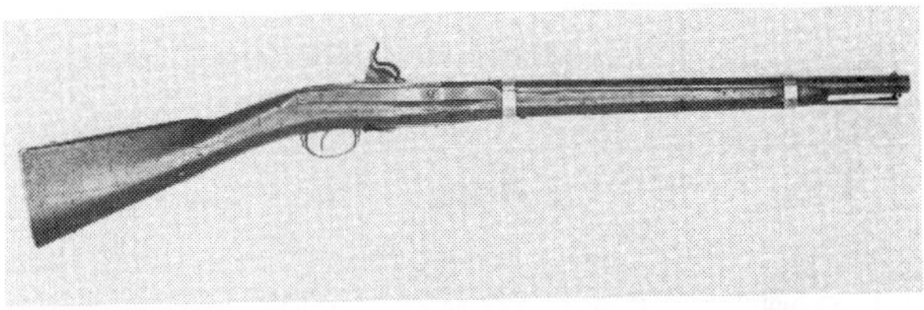

Exc.	V.G.	Good	Fair	Poor
—	6000	4500	2000	800

Harpers Ferry U.S. M1841 Muzzleloading Rifle—The "Mississippi Rifle"

Overall length 49 inches; barrel length 33 inches; caliber .54 (altered to .58 after 1857). Markings: on lockplate, eagle over "US" forward of hammer; "HARPERS/FERRY/(date)" on tail; date also on tang of breechplug; inspector's initials "AW/P" or "WW/P" and proofmarks (eagle's head, "V" and "P" on upper left side of barrel). With the discontinuance of production of the Hall patent arms, Hall's Rifle Works was transformed into the production of the new U.S. rifle adopted in 1841. From 1846 until 1855 a total of 25,296 were manufactured at Harpers Ferry. Approximately 10,000 of these rifles were subsequently adapted for long range firing and to saber bayonets at Harpers Ferry between 1855 and 1861. The adaptations in chronological order included the adoption of the Snell bayonet and Benton long range "screw" sight, the adoption of a saber bayonet lug with guide and the Benton sight, the adoption of the saber bayonet lug with guide and the Burton "ladder" long range sights, the adoption of the U.S. M1855 (Type 1) rifle sights and bayonet lug (first in .54 and then in .58 caliber), and finally the adoption of the U.S. M1855 (Type II) rifle sights and bayonet lug (in .58 caliber). A few thousand were also adapted to the Colt revolving rifle sights and split ring bayonet adaptor in 1861-1862, but that adaptation was not restricted to Harpers Ferry-made rifles.

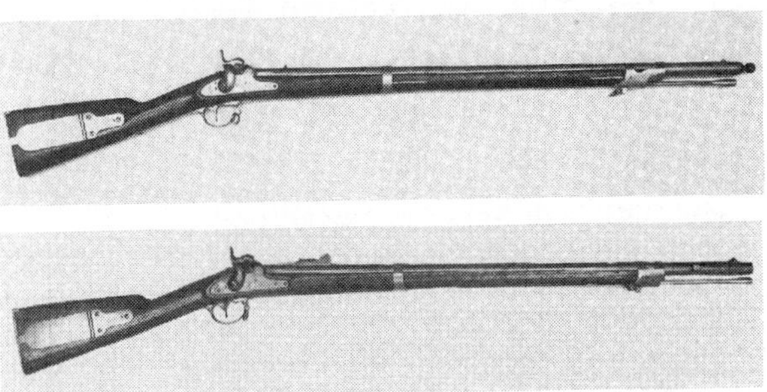

Exc.	V.G.	Good	Fair	Poor
—	3500	1750	1200	650

Harpers Ferry U.S. M1842 Musket

Overall length 57-3/4 inches; barrel length 42 inches; caliber .69. Markings: on lockplate, eagle over "US" forward of hammer; "HARPERS/FERRY/(date)" on tail; date also on tang of breechplug; inspector's initials and proofmarks on barrel near breech. Harpers Ferry manufactured a total of 106,629 of these smoothbore muskets between 1844 and 1855. Many of these muskets were subsequently rifled and sighted from 1855 to 1858 or simply rifled during the early years of the American Civil War.

Exc.	V.G.	Good	Fair	Poor
—	1850	1250	900	400

Harpers Ferry U.S. M1855 Rifle-Musket (Type I & II)

Overall length 56 inches; barrel length 40 inches; caliber .58. Markings: on lockplate, eagle on Maynard primer door; "US/HARPERS FERRY" forward of hammer; date on tail; date also on top of barrel near breech plus proofmarks (eagle's head, "V," and "P"). Between 1857 and 1858 Harpers Ferry produced 15,071 of these rifles, but many were still unsighted at the end of the fiscal year. This early production (Type I) is distinguished from the later production (1859-1860) by the absence of the iron "patchbox" on the right side of the buttstock, a long range rear sight, and a brass nosecap. The "patchbox" was added in 1859 together with a short base rear sight with leaves graduated to only 300 and 500 yards. The brass nosecaps were gradually phased out during 1859.

Exc.	V.G.	Good	Fair	Poor
—	3500	2250	1200	700

Harpers Ferry U.S. M1855 Rifles (Type I & II)

Overall length 49 inches; barrel length 33 inches; caliber .58. Markings: on lockplate, eagle on Maynard primer door; "U S/HARPERS FERRY" forward of hammer; date on tail; date also on top of barrel near breech plus proofmarks (eagle's head, "V," and "P"). Designed as the replacement of the U.S. M1841 rifle, production of the U.S. M1855 rifle began at John Hall's old "Harpers Ferry Rifle Works" in 1857. The production of 1857 and 1858 (Type I), numbering only 3,645 rifles, were all brass mounted, bore a long range rear sight on the browned barrel, and bore a "patchbox" inletted for a special crosshair figure "8" detachable front sight, though many were still without their rear sights at the end of the fiscal year due to the intervention of the Secretary of War. Most of these were never issued and were subsequently destroyed when the arsenal was set afire in April 1861 to prevent the capture of its arms by Virginia forces. The 3,771 rifles produced between 1858 and April 1861 (Type II) were all iron mounted (though a transitional period continued to utilize the brass nosecaps), eliminated

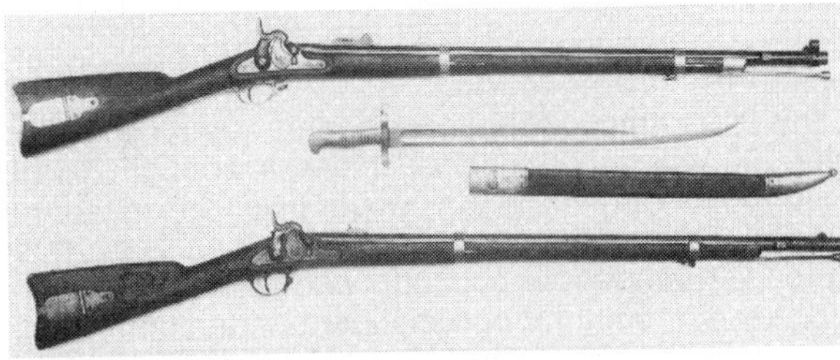

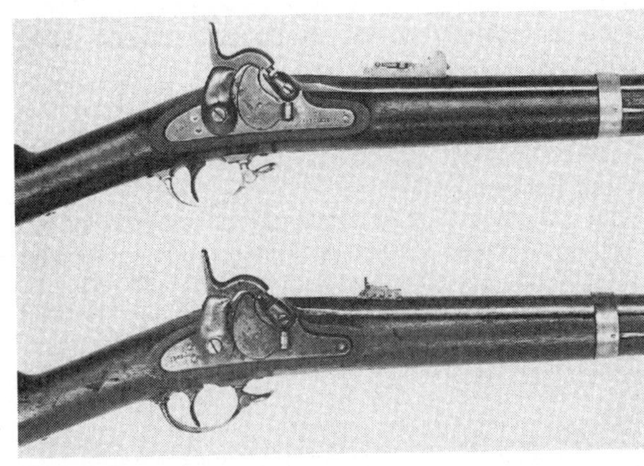

the special front sight (permitting the cavity to be enlarged for greased patches), and employed a short base long range rear sight similar to that of the Type II M 1855 rifle musket.

Type I

Exc.	V.G.	Good	Fair	Poor
—	8500	4000	2750	800

Type II

Exc.	V.G.	Good	Fair	Poor
—	4500	2650	1700	700

SPRINGFIELD ARMORY

Springfield, Massachusetts

This was America's first federal armory. It began producing military weapons in 1795. The armory has supplied military weapons to the United States throughout its history.

Model 1816 Flintlock Musket (Types I to III)

Overall length 57-3/4 inches; barrel length 42 inches; caliber .69. Markings: on lockplate eagle over "US" forward of cock, "SPRINGFIELD/(date) on tail. Barrel tang also bears the date, and barrel should show proofmarks on upper left side near breech. 325,000 total production. Despite the large numbers produced, most were altered to percussion during the 1850s. Most by the "cone-in-barrel" (so called arsenal) method. Many of these were altered again during the American Civil War, usually with a "Patent Breech," and were then rifled and sighted.

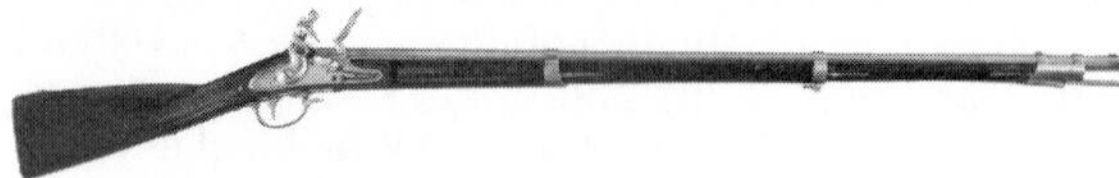

In flintlock

Exc.	V.G.	Good	Fair	Poor
—	3000	2200	1500	500

Altered to percussion

Exc.	V.G.	Good	Fair	Poor
—	900	500	350	200

Model 1841 Cadet Musket

This is a single-shot, muzzle-loading rifle chambered for .57 caliber percussion. It has a 40-inch round barrel with a full-length stock held on by three barrel bands. This rifle features no rear sight. It is browned and case-colored, with iron mountings. There is a steel ramrod mounted under the barrel. The lockplate is marked "Springfield" with the date of manufacture and "US" over an eagle motif. There were approximately 450 produced between 1844 and 1845.

Exc.	V.G.	Good	Fair	Poor
—	12500	7500	3500	1500

Model 1842 Musket

This is a single-shot muzzleloader chambered for .69 caliber percussion. It has a 42-inch round barrel and a full-length stock held on by three barrel bands. The finish is white with iron mountings and a steel ramrod mounted beneath the barrel. There were a total of approximately 275,000 manufactured between 1844 and 1855 by both the Springfield Armory and the Harper's Ferry Armory. They are so marked.

Exc.	V.G.	Good	Fair	Poor
—	1900	1500	900	400

Model 1851 Percussion Cadet Musket

This single-shot muzzleloader in .57 caliber with 40-inch round barrel is almost identical with the Model 1841 Cadet Musket, the main difference and distinguishing feature is the use of the slightly smaller Model 1847 Musketoon lock. Markings are identical as shown for the Model 1841 Cadet Musket. These weapons were made at the Springfield Armory from 1851 to 1853, with total production of 4,000 guns.

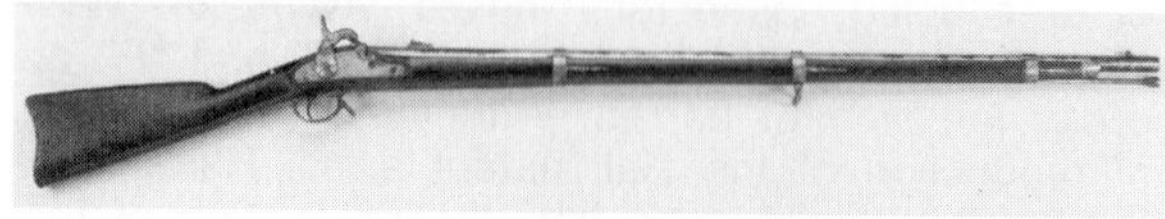

Exc.	V.G.	Good	Fair	Poor
—	1500	1000	650	400

Model 1847 Artillery Musketoon

This is a single-shot muzzleloader chambered for .69 caliber percussion. It has a 26-inch round smooth bore barrel. The finish is white, with a full-length walnut stock held on by two barrel bands. The lock is marked "Springfield." There were approximately 3,350 manufactured between 1848 and 1859.

Exc.	V.G.	Good	Fair	Poor
—	3500	2250	1500	800

Model 1847 U.S. Sappers Musketoon

Almost identical to the Model 1847 Artillery except for a lug for sword bayonet mounted on right side of upper barrel band with twin steel guides for bayonet mounted near muzzle. A total of about 830 produced. Be aware of altered Model 1847 Artillery Muskets passed as original Sappers Muskets.

Exc.	V.G.	Good	Fair	Poor
—	3800	2750	1700	900

Model 1847 U.S. Cavalry Musketoon

Similar to the Model 1847 Artillery except for a button head ramrod attached with iron swivels under the muzzle. No sling swivels. As many as 6,700 were manufactured.

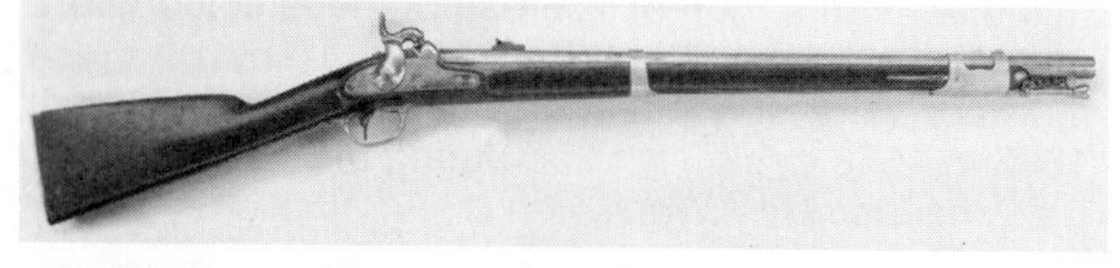

Exc.	V.G.	Good	Fair	Poor
—	3500	2250	1500	850

Model 1855 Rifled Carbine

This is a single-shot muzzleloader chambered for .54 caliber percussion. It has a 22-inch round barrel with a 3/4-length stock held on by one barrel band. The finish is white with iron mountings and a ramrod mounted under the barrel. The lock is marked "Springfield" and dated. There were approximately 1,000 manufactured between 1855 and 1856.

Exc.	V.G.	Good	Fair	Poor
—	15000	9500	4500	2000

Model 1855 Rifle Musket

This is a single-shot muzzleloader chambered for .58 caliber percussion. It has a 40-inch round barrel with a full-length stock held on by three barrel bands. It has iron mountings and a ramrod mounted under the barrel. The front sight acts as a bayonet lug. The finish is white with a walnut stock. The lock is marked "U.S. Springfield." There was also a Harper's Ferry manufactured version that is so marked. There were approximately 59,000 manufactured between 1857 and 1861.

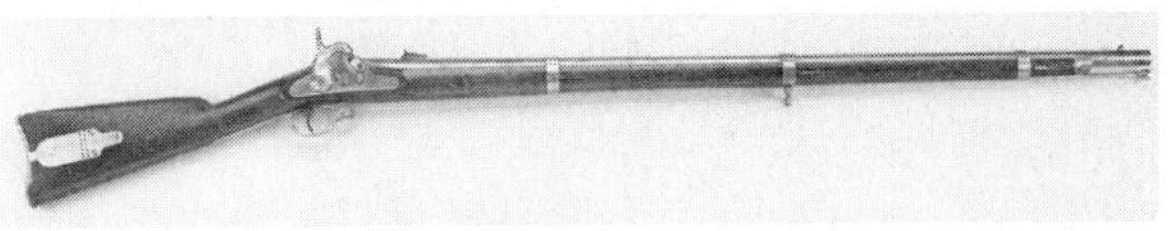

Exc.	V.G.	Good	Fair	Poor
—	3000	1750	1100	600

Model 1858 U.S. Cadet Rifle Musket

Similar to the Model 1855 Rifled Musket but with a 38-inch barrel and shorter stock. The buttstock is 1 inch shorter than the musket and the forearm is 2 inches shorter. About 2,500 were built.

Exc.	V.G.	Good	Fair	Poor
—	3500	2250	1500	900

Model 1861 Percussion Rifle Musket

The Model 1861 was the standard musket in use during the Civil War. This .58 caliber single-shot muzzleloader has a 40-inch barrel with three barrel bands and all iron mountings; all metal parts are finished bright (some rear sights are blued) and the stock is walnut. On the lock there is an eagle motif forward of the hammer, US/SPRINGFIELD, beneath the nipple bolster, and the date at the rear section of the lock. About 256,129 of these muskets were made at the Springfield Armory, while almost 750,000 more were made under contract.

NOTE: See entries in Flayderman's Guide for contract variations.

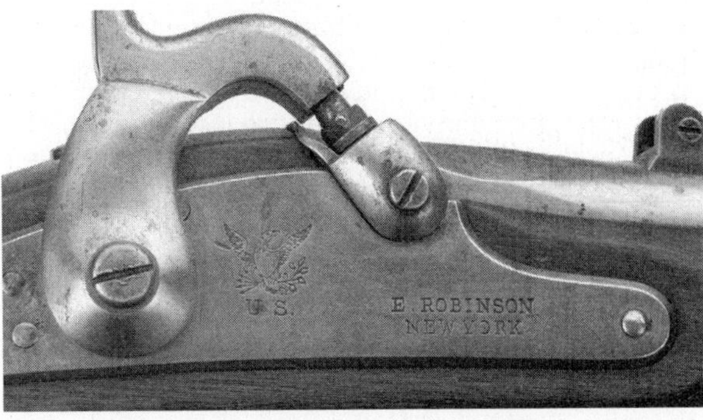

Exc.	V.G.	Good	Fair	Poor
4500	2250	1650	850	500

Model 1863 Rifle Musket, Type I

This is a single-shot muzzleloader chambered for .58 caliber percussion. It has a 40-inch round barrel and a full-length stock held on by three barrel bands. The finish is white with iron mountings, and the lock is marked "U.S. Springfield" and dated 1863. There were approximately 275,000 manufactured in 1863.

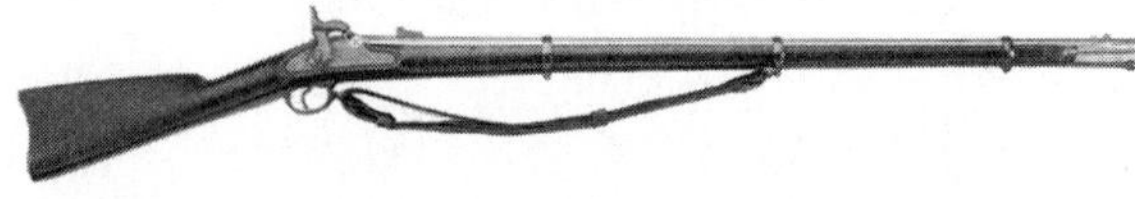

Exc.	V.G.	Good	Fair	Poor
4500	2250	1650	900	500

Model 1863 Rifle Musket, Type II, aka Model 1864

This was the last U.S. martial regulation arm of muzzleloading design, and it was widely used during the latter part of the Civil War. Produced at the Springfield Armory between 1864 and 1865, with total production of 25,540 pieces. This weapon is identical to the Type I with the exception of the dating of the lock, which is either 1864 or 1865, a single leaf rear sight, and solid barrel bands secured by flat springs mounted in the stock. The ramrod was either the tulip head type, or the new knurled and slotted design.

Exc.	V.G.	Good	Fair	Poor
4500	2250	1650	1000	600

PEABODY

Providence, Rhode Island

These rifles were made by the Providence Tool Company from 1866 to 1871. Total production for all models was approximately 112,000. These rifles were produced in a wide variety of calibers and used by military forces in Canada, Spain, Switzerland, and others. They were also issued to three state militias: Connecticut, Massachusetts, and South Carolina.

NOTE: U.S. and Canadian marked will bring a premium over foreign marked rifles of about 20 percent.

Rifle

This is a lever-action, top-loading rifle with side hammer. Full stocked with two barrel bands. The front sight also serves as a bayonet fitting. Weight is about 10 lbs. The .45-70 caliber is the most sought-after chambering. Also chambered for the .50-60 Peabody Musket rimfire. In general, European calibers denote foreign military contracts.

NOTE: Canada acquired 3,000 rifles in .50-60 caliber in 1865. Switzerland acquired 15,000 rifles in .41 Swiss rimfire in 1867. Romania acquired 25,000 rifles in .45 Romanian centerfire. France acquired 39,000 rifles during the Franco-Prussian War. Some rifles were chambered for the .43 Spanish centerfire cartridge and some were chambered for the .50-70 cartridge.

Exc.	V.G.	Good	Fair	Poor
2800	2000	1150	700	400

Carbine

This version has the same action but is half stocked with a single barrel band. Chambered for the .45 Peabody

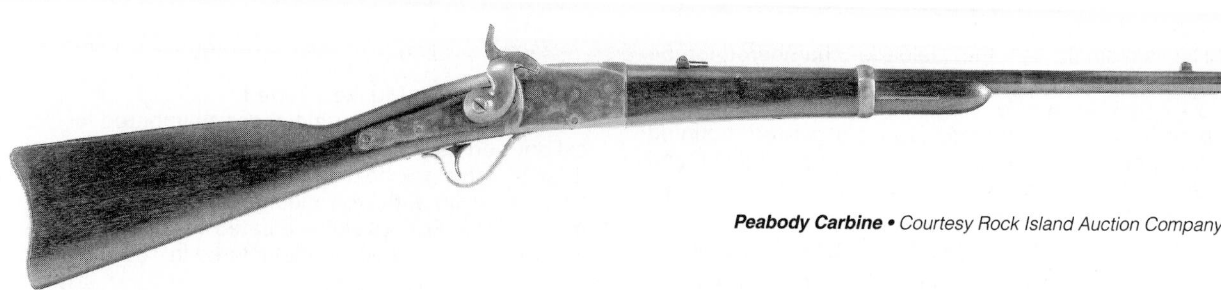

Peabody Carbine • *Courtesy Rock Island Auction Company*

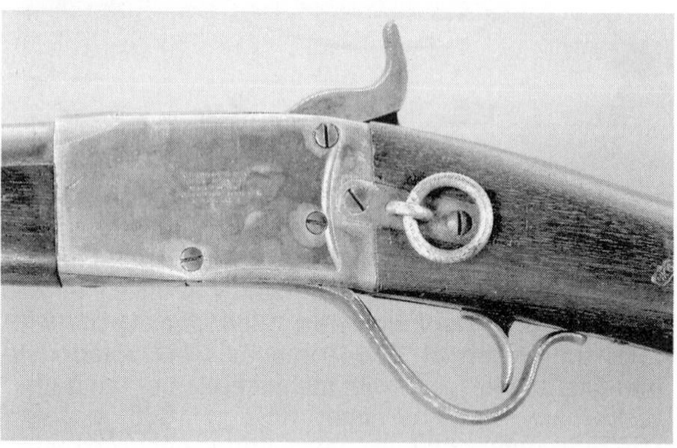

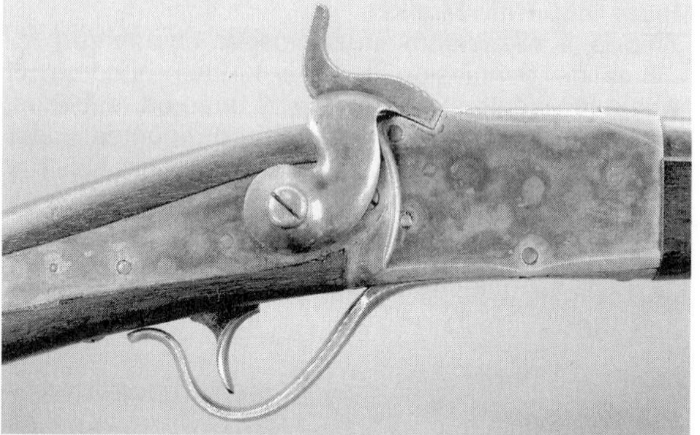

rimfire cartridge. Fitted with a 20" barrel. Weight is about 8.5 lbs.

Exc.	*V.G.*	*Good*	*Fair*	*Poor*
3000	2750	1500	750	300

Model 1874 or 1879 Peabody-Martini Rifle

See Turkey, Rifle, Peabody-Martini or Romania, Rifle, Peabody-Martini.

SPENCER

Boston, Massachusetts

Spencer Model 1860 Carbine

This was one of the most popular firearms used by Union forces during the Civil War. It is chambered for a metallic rimfire cartridge known as the "No. 56." It is actually a .52 caliber and was made with a copper case. The barrel is 22" in length. The finish is blued, with a carbine-length walnut stock held on by one barrel band. There is a sling swivel at the butt. There were approximately 45,733 manufactured between 1863 and 1865. Cartouche marked.

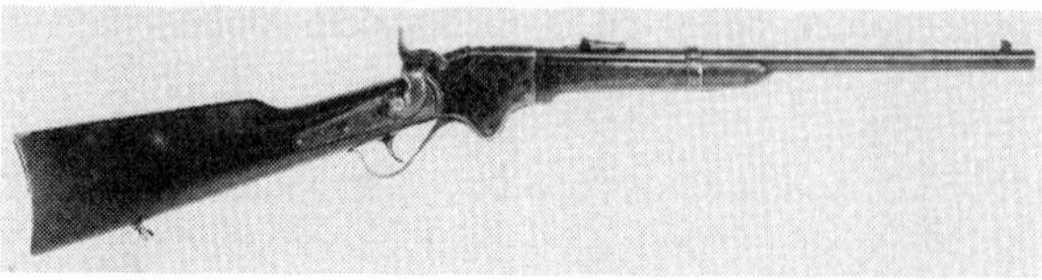

Courtesy Butterfield & Butterfield, San Francisco, California

Exc.	*V.G.*	*Good*	*Fair*	*Poor*
—	—	4750	2000	800

Military Rifle–Navy Model

This model is similar to the carbine, with a 30" round barrel and a full-length walnut stock held on by three barrel bands. It features an iron forend tip and sling swivels. The Civil War production consisted of two models. A Navy model was manufactured between 1862 and 1864 (there were approximately 803 of these so marked).

Exc.	*V.G.*	*Good*	*Fair*	*Poor*
—	—	5000	2250	600

Military Rifle–Army Model

There were approximately 11,471 produced for the army during the Civil War. They are similar to the navy model except that the front sight doubles as a bayonet lug. They were manufactured in 1863 and 1864. There were also, according to Marcot, about 200 built for the navy. Cartouche marked, "MMJ" or "DAP" or both.

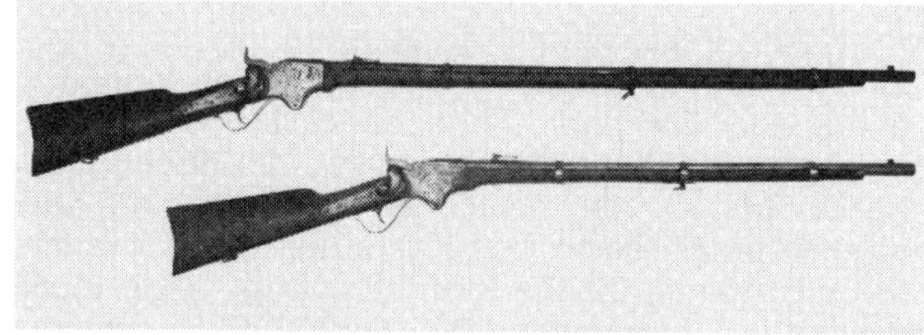

Courtesy Milwaukee Public Museum, Milwaukee, Wisconsin

Exc.	*V.G.*	*Good*	*Fair*	*Poor*
7500	6000	4000	2500	900

Springfield Armory Post-War Alteration

After the conclusion of the Civil War, approximately 11,000 carbines were refurbished and rechambered for .50 caliber rimfire. The barrels were sleeved, and a device known as the "Stabler cut-off" was added to convert the arm to single-shot function. Often they were refinished and restocked. The inspector's marks "ESA" will be found in an oval cartouche on the left side of the stock. These alterations took place in 1867 and 1868.

Exc.	*V.G.*	*Good*	*Fair*	*Poor*
—	—	3750	1500	500

Burnside Model 1865 Spencer Carbine Contract

This model was manufactured by the Burnside Rifle

UNITED STATES OF AMERICA

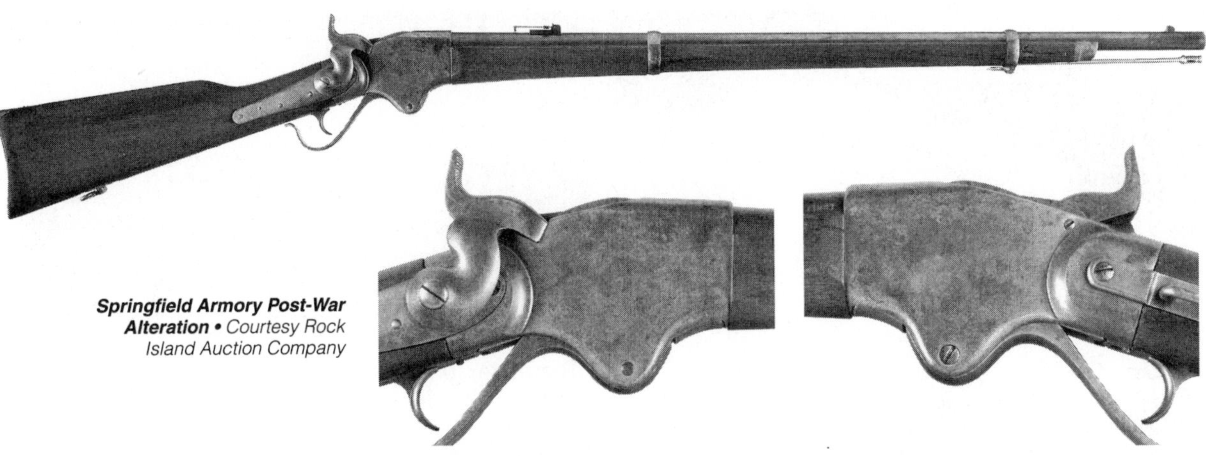
Springfield Armory Post-War Alteration • Courtesy Rock Island Auction Company

Company in 1865. They are similar to the Civil War-type carbine and are marked "By Burnside Rifle Co./Model 1865". Cartouche marked "HEV and GC" or "LH and GC".There were approximately 30,502 manufactured for the U.S. Army, and 19,000 of these had the Stabler cut-off device.

NOTE: There were a number of other variations in the Spencer line. This is a complex model with many subtle variations. The best place to begin is with Roy Marcot's book, *Spencer Repeating Firearms*, 1983.

Exc.	*V.G.*	*Good*	*Fair*	*Poor*
—	—	3750	1500	800

SHARPS RIFLE MANUFACTURING COMPANY

Metallic Cartridge Conversions (1867)

In 1867 approximately 32,000 Model 1859, 1863 and 1865 Sharps were altered to .52-70 rimfire and centerfire caliber. These conversions are cartouche marked in the middle of the left side of the butt stock.

Carbines (.52-70 CF—27,000 converted)

Exc.	*V.G.*	*Good*	*Fair*	*Poor*
—	—	3500	2000	600

Rifles (.50-70 centerfire—1,086 converted)

Exc.	*V.G.*	*Good*	*Fair*	*Poor*
—	—	4500	2500	600

Model 1869

A .40-50 to .50-70 caliber model produced in a military form with 26", 28", or 30" barrels; as a carbine with 21" or 24" barrels and in a sporting version with various barrel lengths and a forend stock fitted with a pewter tip. Approximately 650 were made.

Carbine

.50-70, saddle ring on frame.

Exc.	*V.G.*	*Good*	*Fair*	*Poor*
—	—	4750	2000	500

Military Rifle

.50-70, 30" barrel with three barrel bands.

Exc.	*V.G.*	*Good*	*Fair*	*Poor*
—	—	5500	2250	800

Model 1870 Springfield Altered

Chambered for .50-70 caliber and fitted with a 35.5" barrel with two barrel bands, walnut stock, case hardened lock and breechlock. Buttplate stamped "US". Also built for Army trials with 22" barrel converted to centerfire.

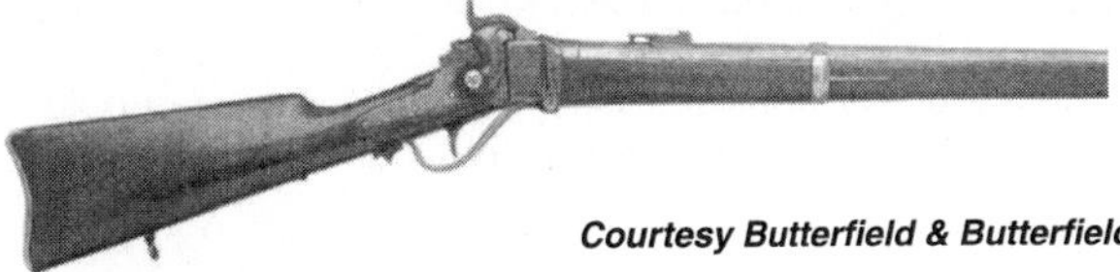
Courtesy Butterfield & Butterfield

First Type

Most common, straight breech.

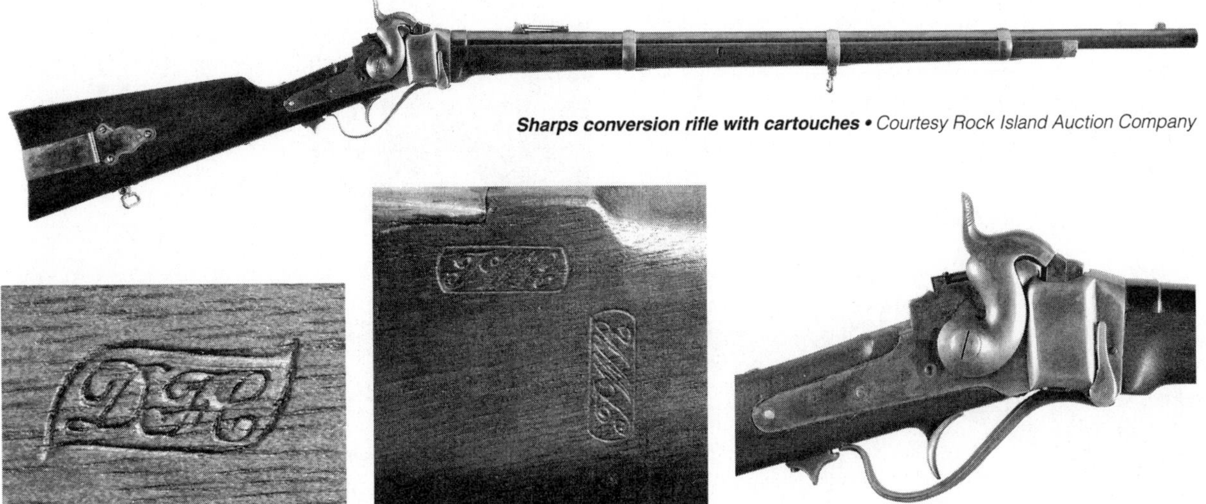
Sharps conversion rifle with cartouches • Courtesy Rock Island Auction Company

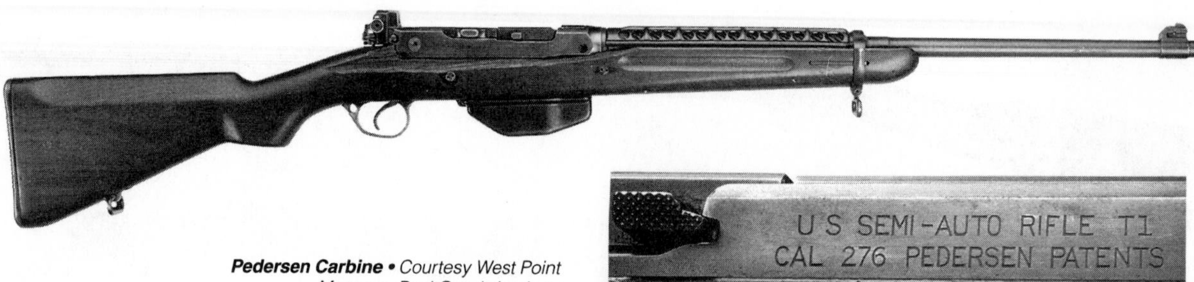

***Pedersen Carbine** • Courtesy West Point Museum, Paul Goodwin photo*

Exc.	V.G.	Good	Fair	Poor
—	—	4000	1750	500

Second Type

Model 1874 action, serial #1 to 300.

Exc.	V.G.	Good	Fair	Poor
—	—	6750	3000	750

Carbine

22" barrel converted to centerfire.

Exc.	V.G.	Good	Fair	Poor
—	—	8250	5000	1250

PEDERSEN, JOHN D.

Denver, CO & Jackson, WY

NOTE: Thanks to Jim Supica for his research into the Pedersen rifle and carbine that appeared for sale in his Old Town Station Dispatch.

John D. Pedersen was the inventor and designer of the Pedersen device that consisted of a conversion unit to be installed in a modified Springfield .30-06 bolt action rifle. This device allowed the rifle to function as a semi-automatic. At the end of World War I the idea was discarded. During the 1920s, Pedersen and John Garand began working on a new semi-automatic military rifle for U.S. forces. Pedersen's design was chambered for the .276 caliber and his rifle eventually lost out to Garand's rifle, the M1. The Pedersen rifles and carbines appear to be part of a test group for military trials. Total number built is unknown.

NOTE: Most Springfield-manufactured Pedersen rifles are so rare as not to be available to the collector. Therefore, only those rifles made by Vickers are listed.

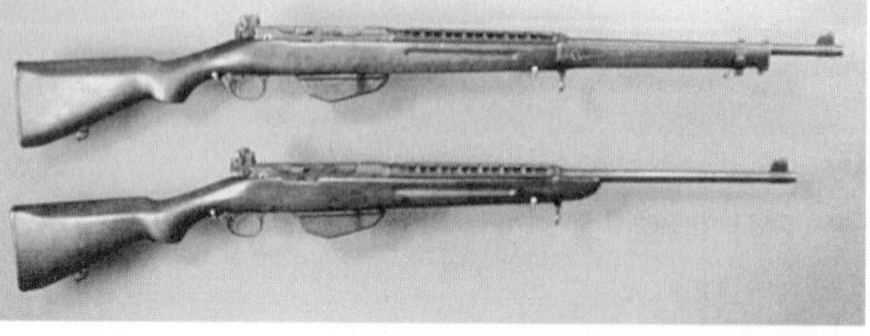

***Pedersen rifle at top, carbine at bottom** • Courtesy Jim Supica, Old Town Station*

Pedersen Rifle

Chambered for .276 Pedersen cartridge. Marked "PEDERSEN SELF LOADER PA/VICKERS-ARMSTRONG LTD." on the left side of the receiver. In oval over chamber marked "C/2." Rare.

Exc.	V.G.	Good	Fair	Poor
17500	9500	—	—	—

Pedersen Carbine

Same caliber and markings as rifle, but with 23" barrel. Rare.

Exc.	V.G.	Good	Fair	Poor
19000	10000	—	—	—

SPRINGFIELD ARMORY

This was America's first federal armory. It began producing military weapons in 1795 with the Springfield Model 1795 musket. The armory has supplied famous and well-known military weapons to the United States military forces throughout its history. The armory was phased out in 1968. The buildings and its collections are now part of the National Park Service.

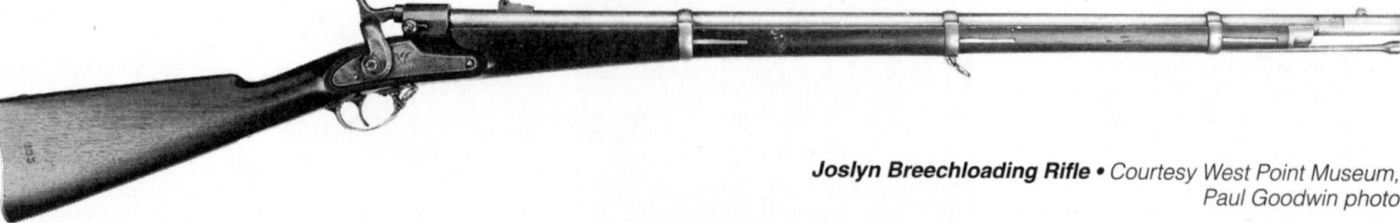

***Joslyn Breechloading Rifle** • Courtesy West Point Museum, Paul Goodwin photo*

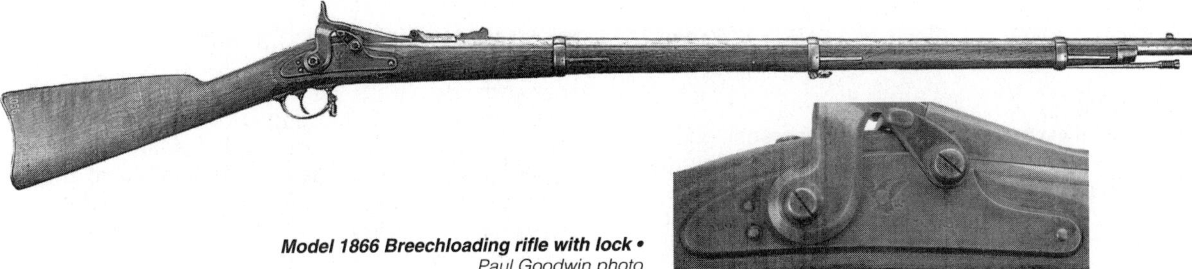

Model 1866 Breechloading rifle with lock • *Paul Goodwin photo*

Bibliographical Note: For further information, technical data, and photos, see the following: Robert W.D. Ball, *Springfield Armory Shoulder Weapons, 1795-1968*, Antique Trader Books, 1997. Blake Stevens, *U.S. Rifle M14 From John Garand to the M21,* Collector Grade Publications. William S. Brophy, *The Springfield 1903 Rifles*, Stackpole Books, 1985. Bruce Canfield, *A Collector's Guide to the '03 Springfield*, Andrew Mowbray Publishers, 1991.

Joslyn Breech-Loading Rifle

Until recently, this rifle was considered a post-Civil War breechloading conversion of a muzzleloading musket, but information developed since the 1970s indicates that this was the first true breechloading cartridge rifle to be made in quantity by a national armory, circa 1864. Actions were supplied to the Springfield Armory by the Joslyn Firearms Co. where they were assembled to newly made rifles designed for the action. Chambered for the .50-60-450 Joslyn rimfire cartridge, with a 35.5" barrel with three barrel bands, the uniquely shaped lock with eagle ahead of the hammer, "U.S./Springfield" on the front of the lock, with "1864" at the rear. Walnut stock specially made for the barreled action and lock. Converted to 50-70 centerfire will command approximately $100 more.

Exc.	*V.G.*	*Good*	*Fair*	*Poor*
—	2500	1200	700	400

Model 1865 U.S. Breech-Loading Rifle, Allin Conversion, aka First Model Allin

Designed in .58 caliber rimfire, with a 40" barrel with three flat barrel bands. The breechlock is released by a thumb latch on the right side, pivoted upward, with the firing pin contained within the breechblock. 5,000 Model 1861 percussion muskets were altered using this method at the Springfield Armory circa 1865. The breechblock is unmarked, while the lock is marked with the eagle ahead of the hammer, as well as "U.S./ Springfield," with all specimens dated 1865 at the rear.

Exc.	*V.G.*	*Good*	*Fair*	*Poor*
—	5000	3000	1500	1200

Model 1866 U.S. Breech-Loading Rifle, Allin Conversion, aka Second Model Allin

Produced in .50 caliber centerfire, with a 40" barrel with a .50 caliber liner tube inserted and brazed, walnut stock with three barrel bands with band springs. Differences between the First and Second Model Allin include a lengthened bolt, a firing pin spring, and a stronger internal extraction system. The breechblock is marked with "1866" over an eagle, while the lock bears standard Springfield markings with either an 1863 or 1864 date. A total of 25,000 Model 1863 percussion muskets were thus altered at the Springfield Armory around 1866.

Exc.	*V.G.*	*Good*	*Fair*	*Poor*
—	4000	2200	800	500

Model 1867 U.S. Breech-Loading Cadet Rifle

This model is a .50 caliber centerfire, 33" barrel, two band, scaled down version of the Model 1866 Second Model Allin "trapdoor." No sling swivels; a narrow triggerguard. The breechblock has a blackened finish, with deeply arched cut-outs on both sides of the underside, leaving a narrow flat ridge in the center. The breechblock is marked 1866/eaglehead. The lock plate was made especially for this rifle and is noticeably thinner. The plate is marked with the usual eagle and "US/ Springfield," with the date "1866" behind the hammer. About 424 rifles were produced at the Springfield Armory between 1876 and 1868.

Exc.	*V.G.*	*Good*	*Fair*	*Poor*
—	10000	7500	3000	800

Model 1868 Rifle

This is a single shot Trapdoor rifle chambered for the .50 caliber centerfire cartridge. It features a breechblock that pivots forward when a thumblatch at its rear is depressed. It has a 32.5" barrel and a full-length stock held on by two barrel bands. It has iron mountings and a cleaning rod mounted under the barrel. It features an oil-finished walnut stock. The lock is marked "US Springfield." It is dated either 1863 or 1864. The breechblock features either the date 1869 or 1870. There were approximately 51,000 manufactured between 1868 and 1872.

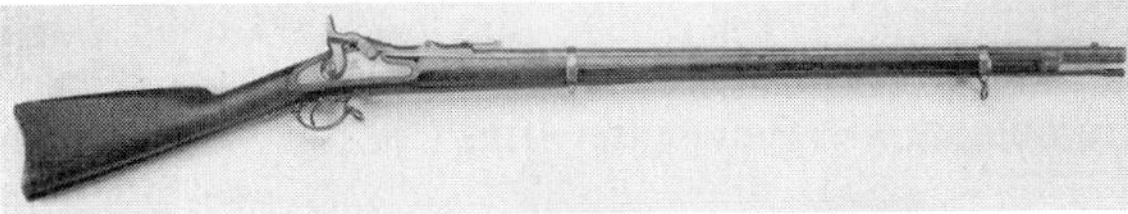

Courtesy Little John's Auction Service, Inc., Paul Goodwin photo

Exc.	*V.G.*	*Good*	*Fair*	*Poor*
—	2500	1250	500	350

Model 1869 Cadet Rifle

This is a single shot trapdoor rifle chambered for .50 caliber centerfire. It is similar to the Model 1868 with a 29.5" barrel. There were approximately 3,500 manufactured between 1869 and 1876.

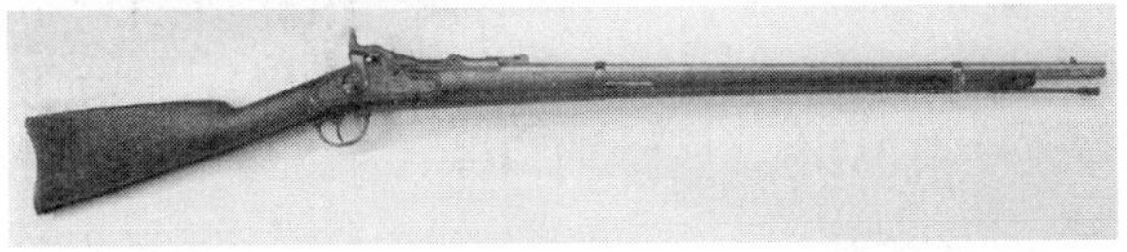

Courtesy Little John's Auction Service, Inc., Paul Goodwin photo

Exc.	V.G.	Good	Fair	Poor
—	3250	1500	500	200

Model 1870

There are two versions of this Trapdoor breechloader—a rifle with a 32.5" barrel and a carbine that features a 22" barrel and a half-stock held on by one barrel band. They are both chambered for .50 caliber centerfire and feature the standard Springfield lock markings and a breechblock marked "1870" or "Model 1870." There were a total of 11,500 manufactured between 1870 and 1873. Only 340 are carbines; they are extremely rare.

Rifle

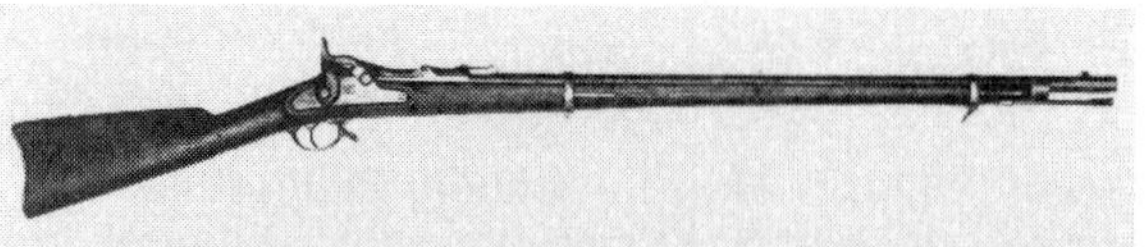

Courtesy Milwaukee Public Museum, Milwaukee, Wisconsin

Exc.	V.G.	Good	Fair	Poor
—	3750	1750	800	500

Carbine

Very rare.

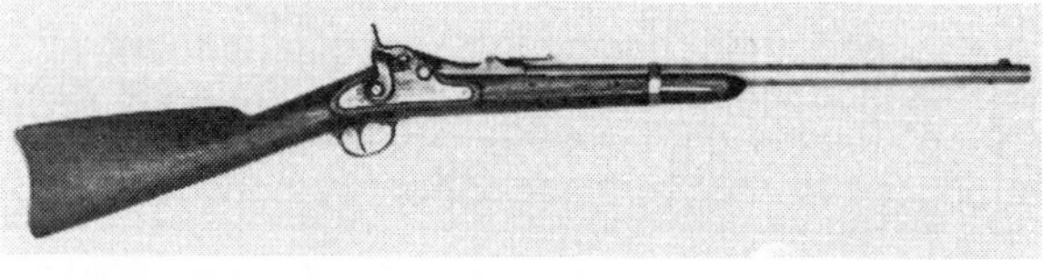

Exc.	V.G.	Good	Fair	Poor
—	16500	9500	3500	1500

Model 1871 Rolling Block U.S. Army Rifle

This model is a .50 caliber centerfire, 36" barrel, with two barrel bands, and rolling block action. Sights, sling-swivels, and most other details as for the Model 1870 Remington U.S. Navy rifle. Case-hardened frame, bright finished iron mountings. Two piece walnut stock. Known as the "locking action" as the hammer went to half cock when the breechblock was closed. No serial numbers. Left side of frame marked "Model 1871." Right side marked with eagle over "U.S./Springfield/1872." On the tang, marked "REMINGTON'S PATENT. PAT.MAY 3D, NOV. 15TH, 1864, APRIL 17TH, 1868." About 10,000 rifles were produced between 1871 and 1872 under a royalty agreement with Remington Arms Co.

Exc.	V.G.	Good	Fair	Poor
7000	4500	2000	750	500

Model 1871 Ward-Burton U.S. Rifle

A .50 caliber centerfire, 32.63" barrel secured by two barrel bands. This is an early bolt action, single shot rifle, with the cartridge loaded directly into the open action, with cocking on the closing of the bolt. Walnut stock, sling swivels on the forward barrel band and the front of the triggerguard. Not serially numbered. The top of the bolt marked, "WARD BURTON PATENT DEC. 20, 1859-FEB. 21, 1871." Left side of the action marked with American eagle motif and "US/SPRINGFIELD." 1,011 rifles (32.625" barrel) and 316 carbines (22" barrel) produced at the Springfield Armory basically as a trial weapon.

Rifle

Courtesy Greg Martin Auctions

Close-up of Ward-Burton action • *Courtesy George Hoyem*

Exc.	V.G.	Good	Fair	Poor
—	4500	2800	1250	700

Carbine

Exc.	V.G.	Good	Fair	Poor
—	6800	3500	1250	750

Model 1873

This is a Trapdoor breechloading rifle chambered for the .45-70 cartridge. The rifle version has a 32.5" barrel with a full-length stock held on by two barrel bands. The carbine features a 22" barrel with a half-stock held on by a single barrel band, and the cadet rifle features a 29.5" barrel with a full length stock and two barrel bands. The finish of all three variations is blued and case-colored, with a walnut stock. The lock is marked "US Springfield 1873." The breechblock is either marked "Model 1873" or "US Model 1873."

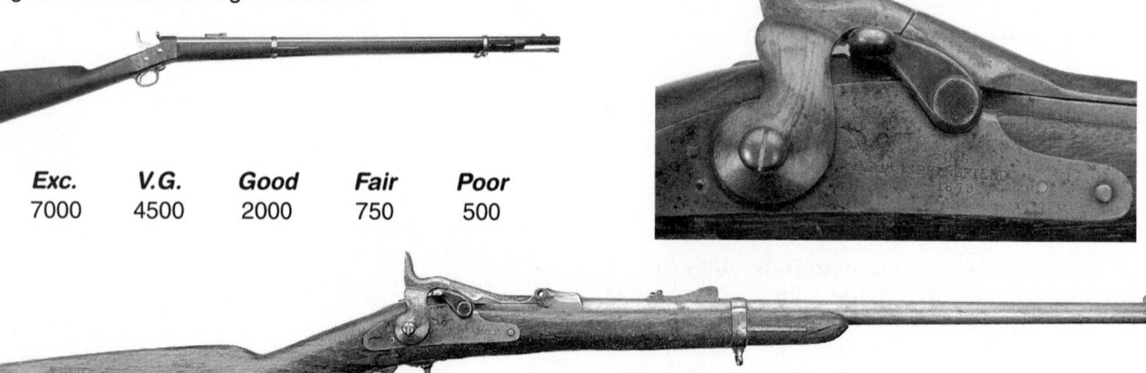

Springfield Model 1873 Carbine with lock • *Paul Goodwin photo*

There were approximately 73,000 total manufactured between 1873 and 1877.

NOTE: Prices listed are for rifles in original configuration.

Rifle

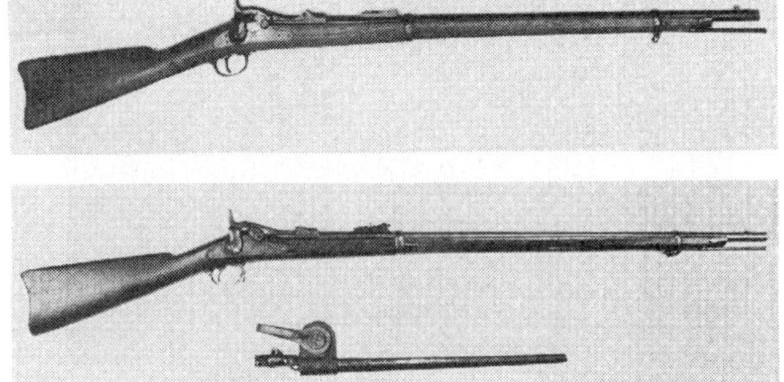

Courtesy Milwaukee Public Museum, Milwaukee, Wisconsin

50,000 manufactured.

Exc.	*V.G.*	*Good*	*Fair*	*Poor*
2500	1800	1000	500	250

Carbine

20,000 manufactured.

Exc.	*V.G.*	*Good*	*Fair*	*Poor*
3000	2200	1500	850	500

Cadet Rifle

3,000 manufactured.

Exc.	*V.G.*	*Good*	*Fair*	*Poor*
2200	1750	750	600	300

Bayonet for Model 1873 Springfield

Socket type. 18" blade. Marked "U.S." on blade. Steel scabbard. Leather frog has brass U.S. or state militia button. Price range 175 – 60.

Trowel Bayonet for Model 1873 Springfield

Socket type. 10" trowel shaped blade. This was designed to be used as a hand shovel. The bayonet application was an afterthought. Not intended to put on the rifle to use as a shovel as it could bend the barrel. Wood plug in socket is to provide a handle while digging. There have been reproductions made of this model. Price range 1000 – 450.

Model 1875 Officer's Rifle

This is a high-grade Trapdoor breechloader chambered for the .45-70 cartridge. It has a 26" barrel and a half-

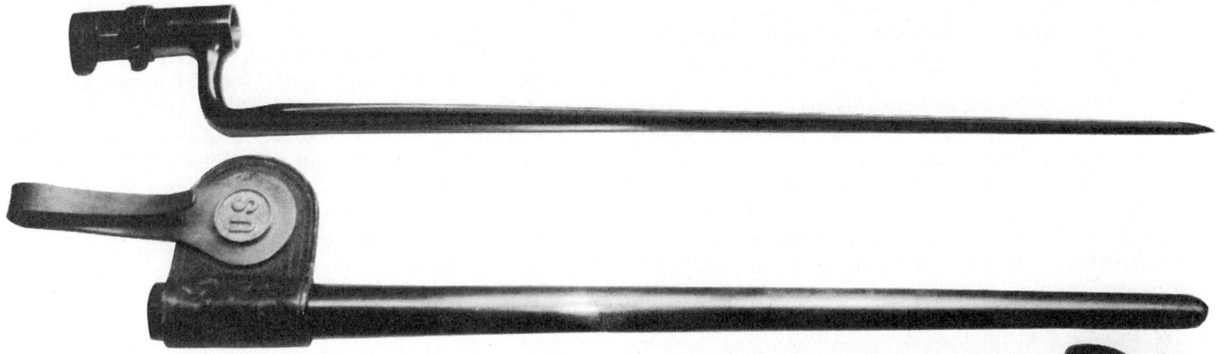

Bayonet for Model 1873 Springfield

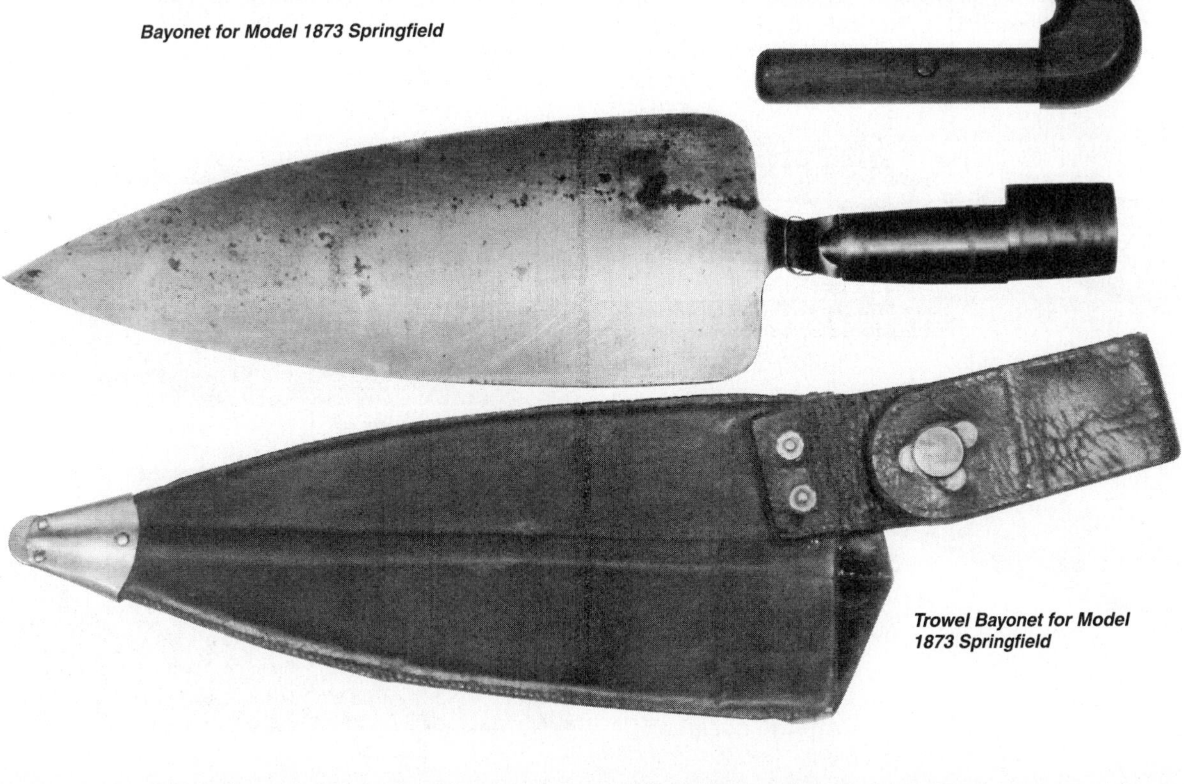

Trowel Bayonet for Model 1873 Springfield

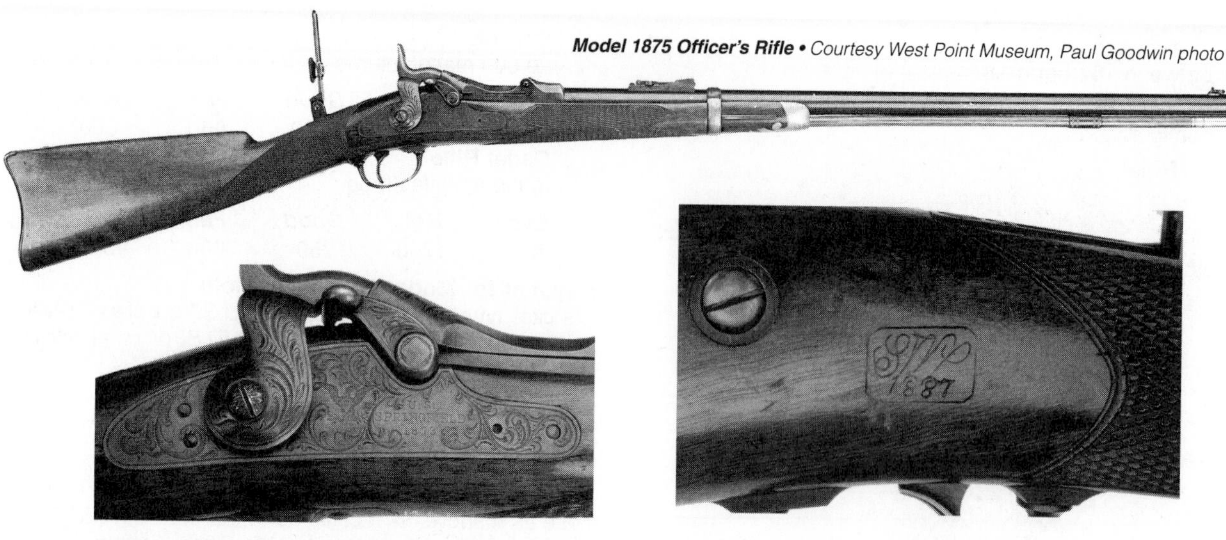

Model 1875 Officer's Rifle • Courtesy West Point Museum, Paul Goodwin photo

stock fastened by one barrel band. It is blued and case-colored, with a scroll engraved lock. It has a checkered walnut pistol grip stock with a pewter forend tip. There is a cleaning rod mounting beneath the barrel. This rifle was not issued but was sold to army officers for personal sporting purposes. There were only 477 manufactured between 1875 and 1885.

Exc.	V.G.	Good	Fair	Poor
35000	25000	10000	7000	3500

Model 1875 Lee Vertical Action Rifle

A .45-70 centerfire, 32.63" barrel secured by two barrel bands. Martini-style dropping block action, with a unique, centrally mounted hammer with an exceptionally long spur. In order to open the breech, the hammer must be given a sharp blow with the heal of the hand; the insertion of a cartridge will automatically close the breech, while the hammer is cocked by hand. All blued finish. Stacking and sling swivel on upper band, with sling swivel on triggerguard. Serially numbered 1 through 143 on the internal parts only. Upper tang marked, "U.S. PAT. MAR 16, 1875," no barrel proofmarks; inspector's initials "ESA" in an oval on the stock. 143 rifles produced in 1875 at the Springfield Armory, basically as a trials weapon.

Exc.	V.G.	Good	Fair	Poor
8500	5500	2500	1500	1000

Model 1877

This is a Trapdoor breechloading rifle chambered for the .45-70 cartridge. It was issued as a rifle with a 32" barrel and a full-length stock held on by two barrel bands, a cadet rifle with a 29.5" barrel, and a carbine with a 22" barrel, half-stock, and single barrel band. This version is similar to the Model 1873. In fact, the breechblock retained the Model 1873 marking. The basic differences are that the stock is thicker at the wrist and the breechblock was thickened and lowered. This is basically a mechanically improved version. There were approximately 12,000 manufactured in 1877 and 1878.

Rifle

3,900 manufactured.

Exc.	V.G.	Good	Fair	Poor
2500	1800	1000	550	350

Cadet Rifle

1,000 manufactured.

Model 1875 Lee Vertical Action Rifle with patent stamp on upper tang • Paul Goodwin photo

Model 1877 Cadet Rifle • Paul Goodwin photo

Exc.	V.G.	Good	Fair	Poor
—	3500	1750	1250	650

Carbine

4,500 manufactured.

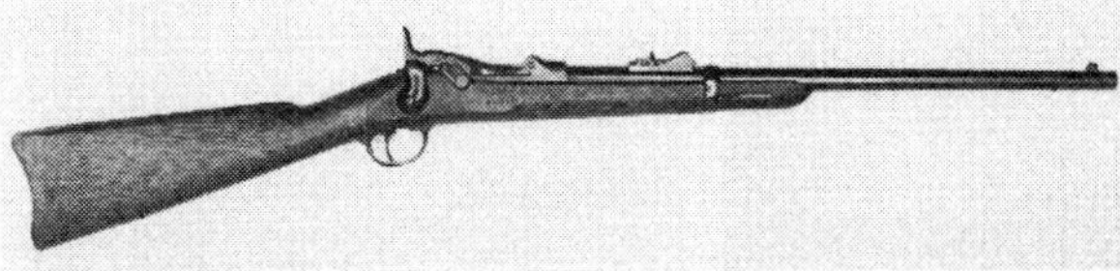

Courtesy Milwaukee Public Museum, Milwaukee, Wisconsin

Exc.	V.G.	Good	Fair	Poor
5000	3500	2000	1250	850

Model 1879 (Model 1873/1879)

This is essentially a Model 1873 with 1879 improvements. The most noticeable improvement is that the receiver is wider and thicker so that it is no longer flush with the barrel, which results in a two-step junction between barrel and receiver. These guns are found in the 100,000 to 280,000 serial number range.

Exc.	V.G.	Good	Fair	Poor
1800	1400	750	500	250

Model 1880

This version features a sliding combination cleaning rod/bayonet that is fitted in the forearm under the barrel. It retained the 1873 breechblock markings. There were approximately 1,000 manufactured for trial purposes in 1880.

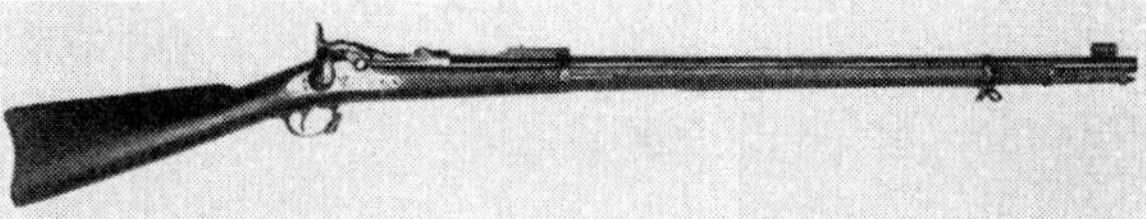

Courtesy Milwaukee Public Museum, Milwaukee, Wisconsin

Exc.	V.G.	Good	Fair	Poor
3000	2200	1000	700	500

Model 1881 Marksman Rifle

This is an extremely high-grade Trapdoor breechloading rifle chambered for the .45-70 cartridge. It has a 28" round barrel and is similar to the Model 1875 Officer's Rifle in appearance. It features a full-length, high grade, checkered walnut stock held on by one barrel band. It has a horn Schnabel forend tip. The metal parts are engraved, blued, and case-colored. It has a vernier aperture sight as well as a buckhorn rear sight on the barrel and a globe front sight with a spirit level. There were only 11 manufactured to be awarded as prizes at shooting matches.

CAUTION: This is perhaps the supreme rarity among the Trapdoor Springfields, and one should beware of fakes.

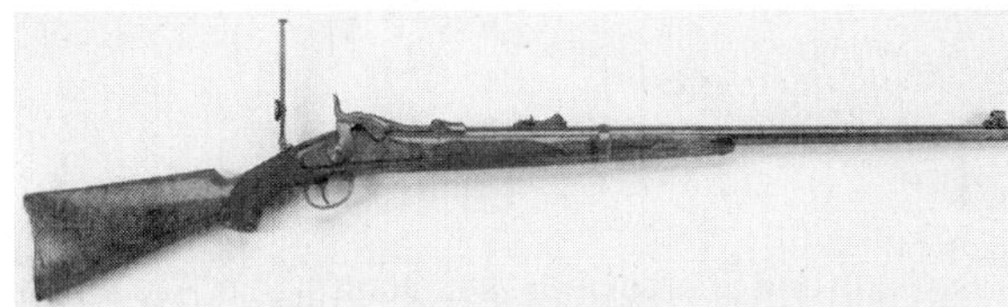

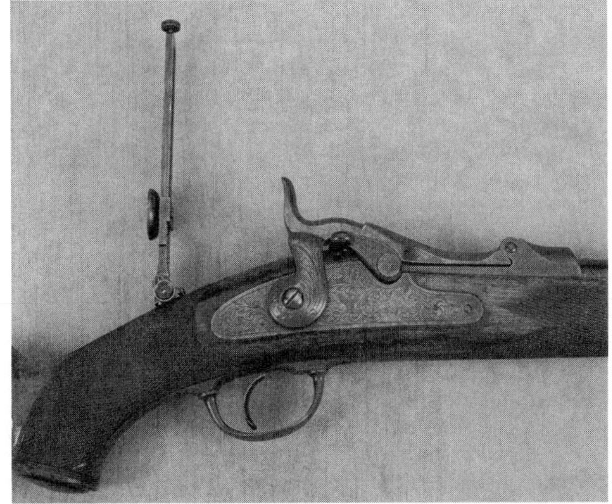

Exc.	V.G.	Good	Fair	Poor
—	75000	60000	20000	5000

Model 1881 Long Range Rifle

This model is a Model 1879 chambered for the .45-80 cartridge. The barrel has six groove rifling. The stock has a shotgun butt with Hotchkiss buttplate. Some of these rifles had uncheckered walnut stock with detachable

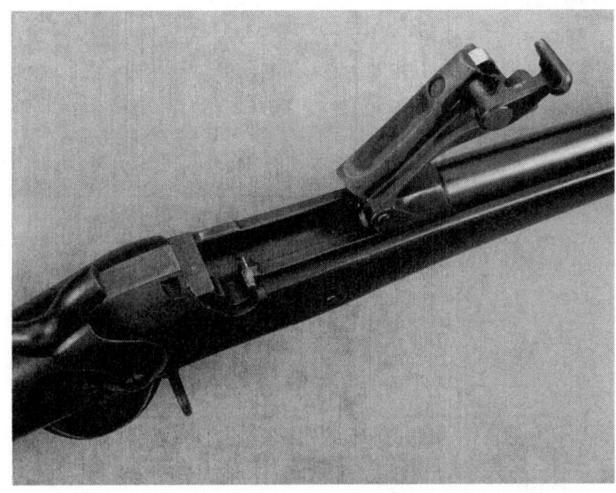

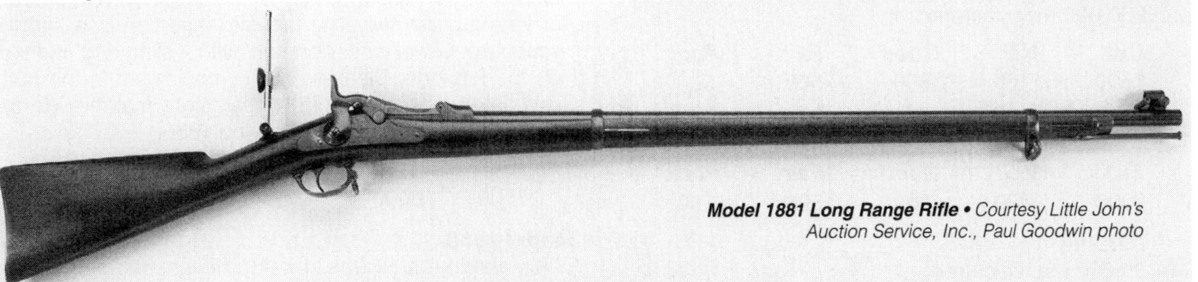

Model 1881 Long Range Rifle • *Courtesy Little John's Auction Service, Inc., Paul Goodwin photo*

Model 1882 U.S. Magazine rifle, Chaffee-Reese • Paul Goodwin photo

pistol grip and Sharps peep and globe sights. According to Flayderman, this rifle falls between serial numbers 162000 and 162500. It is estimated that less than 200 were produced between 1897 and 1880.

Exc.	V.G.	Good	Fair	Poor
—	27500	12500	5000	2000

Model 1882 U.S. Magazine Rifle, Chaffee-Reese

A .45-70 caliber centerfire, 27.78" barrel secured by two barrel bands. One of the early bolt action repeaters, with the cartridges carried in a tubular feed in the butt. Iron mountings, with a blued finish, walnut stock, stacking swivel and sling swivel on the upper barrel band, and a sling swivel on the front of the triggerguard. Not serially numbered. Left side of breech marked "US SPRINGFIELD, 1884," the barrel marked "V.P." with eagle head proof. Unfortunately, most rifles found are lacking the feed mechanism in the butt, which lowers the value approximately 15 percent. 753 rifles were produced at the Springfield Armory in 1884.

Courtesy Rock Island Auction Company

Exc.	V.G.	Good	Fair	Poor
5000	3500	2500	900	750

Model 1884

This is also a breechloading Trapdoor single shot rifle chambered for the .45-70 cartridge. It was issued as a standard rifle with a 32.75" barrel, a cadet rifle with a 29.5" barrel, and a military carbine with a 22" barrel. The finish is blued and case-colored. This model features the improved Buffington rear sight. It features the socket bayonet and a walnut stock. There were approximately 232,000 manufactured between 1885 and 1890.

Courtesy Bob Ball

Rifle

200,000 manufactured.

Exc.	V.G.	Good	Fair	Poor
1500	1100	800	500	300

Cadet Rifle

12,000 manufactured.

Exc.	V.G.	Good	Fair	Poor
2000	1400	850	500	250

Carbine

20,000 manufactured.

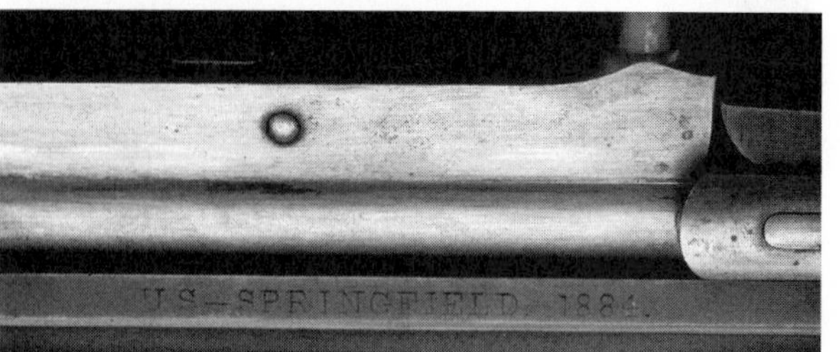

Springfield Model 1884 • Paul Goodwin photo

Exc.	V.G.	Good	Fair	Poor
3000	2500	1750	800	500

Model 1886 Experimental "Trapdoor" Carbine, aka Experimental Model 1882 third/fourth type

Apparently both of these designations are misnomers, as the weapon was officially referred to as the "24" Barrel Carbine. Collectors now call it the Model 1886 to conform to the year of manufacture. The most outstanding feature is the almost full length stock with uncapped, tapered forend. The single upper barrel band is fitted with a bent, or wraparound swivel to facilitate insertion in a saddle scabbard. Lower swivel on butt, with a sling ring and bar on the left side. Cleaning rod compartment in the butt. Buffington-type Model 1884 rear sight marked XC on leaf. About 1,000 produced during 1886.

Exc.	V.G.	Good	Fair	Poor
7500	6000	4500	2500	1000

Model 1888

This version is similar to its predecessors except that it features a sliding, ramrod-type bayonet that was

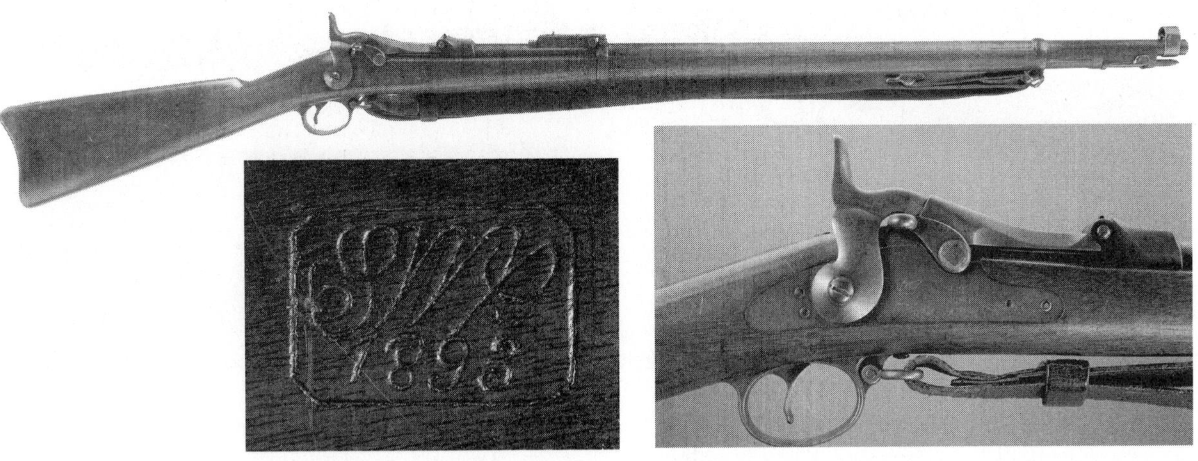

Model 1888 Rifle with bayonet • Courtesy Rock Island Auction Company

improved so that it stays securely locked when in its extended position. The breechblock was still marked "Model 1884." This was the last Springfield Trapdoor rifle produced. There were approximately 65,000 manufactured between 1889 and 1893.

Exc.	V.G.	Good	Fair	Poor
1800	1250	850	500	250

Rod Bayonet for Model 1888 Springfield

A 35.5" straight steel rod that tapers to the back end. Stored under the barrel. Not a popular design. They were prone to bending during use. Teddy Roosevelt was vehement in his criticism of this style. Price range 150 – 75.

Trapdoor Fencing Musket

This is a non-gun that was used by the army in teaching bayonet drills. They had no desire to damage serviceable rifles during practice, so they produced this version to fill the bill. There were basically four types produced.

Type I

This version is similar to the Model 1873 rifle without a breech or lock. The finish is rough, and it is unmarked. It was designed to accept a socket bayonet. There were 170 manufactured in 1876 and 1877.

Exc.	V.G.	Good	Fair	Poor
—	1500	750	400	300

Type II

This version is basically a Model 1884 with the hammer removed and the front sight blade ground off. It accepted a socket bayonet that was covered with leather and had a pad on its point.

Exc.	V.G.	Good	Fair	Poor
—	850	300	250	200

Type III

This version is similar to the Type II except that it is shortened to 43.5" in length. There were approximately 1,500 manufactured between 1905 and 1906.

Rod Bayonet for Model 1888 Springfield

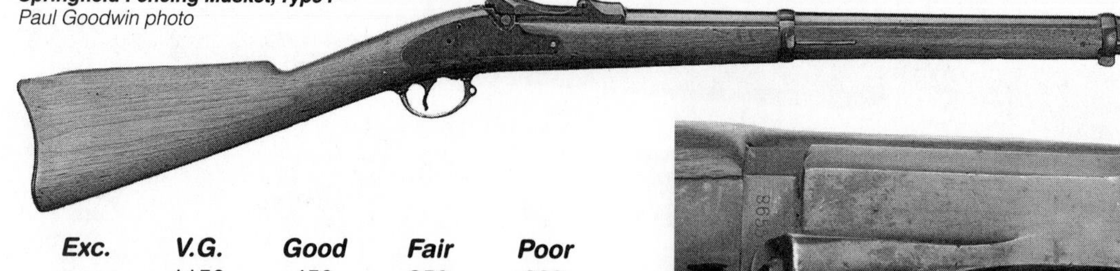

Springfield Fencing Musket, Type I • *Paul Goodwin photo*

Exc.	V.G.	Good	Fair	Poor
—	1150	450	350	300

Type IV

This version is similar to the Type III except that the barrel was filled with lead. There were approximately 11,000 manufactured between 1907 and 1916.

Exc.	V.G.	Good	Fair	Poor
—	650	300	250	200

Model 1870 Rolling Block

This is a single shot breechloading rifle with a rolling-block action. It is chambered for .50 caliber centerfire and has a 32.75" barrel. It has a full-length forend held on by two barrel bands. The finish is blued and case-colored, with a cleaning rod mounted under the barrel. The stock and forend are walnut. The frame is marked "USN Springfield 1870." There is an anchor motif marked on the top of the barrel. It also features government inspector's marks on the frame. This rifle was manufactured by Springfield Armory under license from Remington Arms Company for the United States Navy. The first 10,000 produced were rejected by our navy and were sent to France and used in the Franco-Prussian War. For that reason, this variation is quite scarce and would bring a 20 percent premium. There was also a group of approximately 100 rifles that were converted to the .22 rimfire cartridge and used for target practice aboard ships. This version is extremely rare. There were approximately 22,000 manufactured in 1870 and 1871.

Courtesy Milwaukee Public Museum, Milwaukee, Wisconsin

Standard Navy Rifle

Exc.	V.G.	Good	Fair	Poor
—	2800	2200	1250	800

Rejected Navy Rifle

Exc.	V.G.	Good	Fair	Poor
—	2000	700	400	200

.22 Caliber

Exc.	V.G.	Good	Fair	Poor
—	6000	2500	900	600

U.S. Krag Jorgensen Rifle

NOTE: This firearm will be found listed in its own section of this text.

SPRINGFIELD MODEL 1903 & VARIATIONS

These rifles were built by Springfield, Remington, Rock Island Arsenal, and Smith-Corona.

Model 1903

This rifle was a successor to the Krag Jorgensen and was also produced by the Rock Island Arsenal. It was initially chambered for the .30-03 Government cartridge and very shortly changed to the .30-06 cartridge. Its original chambering consisted of a 220-grain, metal jacket soft-point bullet. The German army introduced its spitzer bullet so our government quickly followed suit with a 150-grain, pointed bullet designated the .30-06. This model has a 24" barrel and was built on what was basically a modified Mauser action. It features a 5-round integral box magazine. The finish is blued, with a full length, straight-grip walnut stock with full handguards held on by two barrel bands. The initial version was issued with a rod-type bayonet that was quickly discontinued when President Theodore Roosevelt personally disapproved it. There were approximately 74,000 produced with this rod bayonet; and if in an unaltered condition, these would be worth a great deal more than the standard variation. **It is important to note that the early models with serial numbers under 800,000 were not heat treated sufficiently to be**

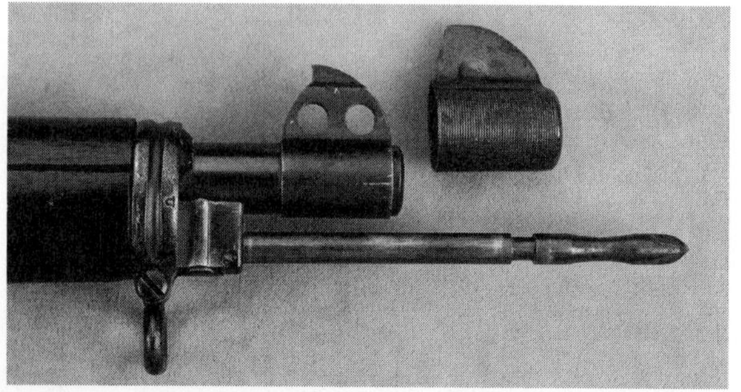

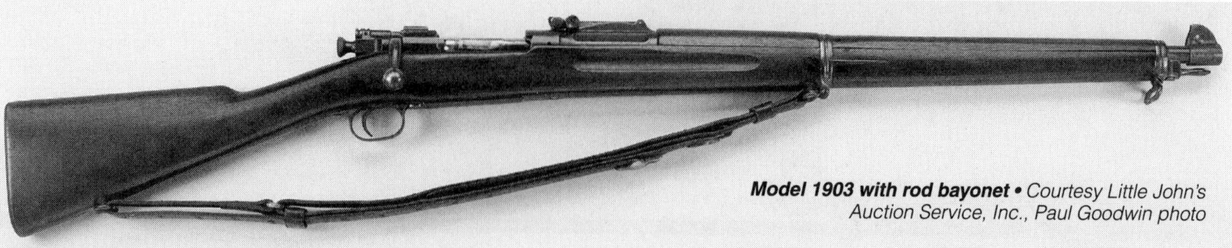

Model 1903 with rod bayonet • *Courtesy Little John's Auction Service, Inc., Paul Goodwin photo*

Model 1903 with Model 1905 modifications • *Courtesy Little John's Auction Service, Inc., Paul Goodwin photo*

safe to fire with modern ammunition. There were a great many produced between 1903 and 1930. The values represented reflect original specimens; WWII alterations would be worth approximately 15 percent less.

Rod Bayonet Version (Original & Unaltered)

Exc.	V.G.	Good	Fair	Poor
35000	20000	15000	12500	10000

NOTE: For rifles restored to Rod Bayonet configuration but in original condition deduct 85 percent.

Rod Bayonet Model 1903 (Altered to Model 1905 in .30-03)

Exc.	V.G.	Good	Fair	Poor
25000	15000	7500	4000	1500

Rod Bayonet Model 1903 (Altered to Model 1905 in .30-06)

Exc.	V.G.	Good	Fair	Poor
4750	3000	1500	850	500

Model 1903 Rifle with 1905 Modifications

This model was built in Springfield between 1905 to 1906. Chambered for .30-03 cartridge. Overall barrel length is 24.206" (chamber & bore length is 23.949"). These rifles were newly manufactured and therefore are unaltered. No ramrod bayonet. Model 1905 front and rear sight. Front barrel band is a double strap with bayonet stud and stacking swivel. There is a Model 1905 knife bayonet designed for this model. Rear sight graduated to 2,400 yards with a silver line above and below peep sight aperture. Very Rare.

Original & Unaltered Examples

Exc.	V.G.	Good	Fair	Poor
17500	10000	5000	3000	1000

Altered to .30-06

Exc.	V.G.	Good	Fair	Poor
4000	2500	1200	800	400

Model 1903 Rifle (Altered from Model 1905 in .30-06)

This model was altered to accept a new pointed bullet that required a shortened cartridge case. This required a shorter chamber. The barrel was shortened by setting it deeper into the receiver by .200" therefore making the overall barrel length 24.006" in length (chamber & bore length is 23.749"). This new cartridge was adopted in 1906 and called the "Cartridge, Ball, Caliber 30, Model Of 1906." or more commonly known as the .30-06. The rear sight base was also moved forward .200" of an inch and a new graduated rear sight up to 2,700 yards was installed. According to Flayderman the easiest way to determine a Model 1905 altered rifle "... is to remove the upper barrel band to see if a plugged hole appears 1/4" forward of the present upper band screw hole."

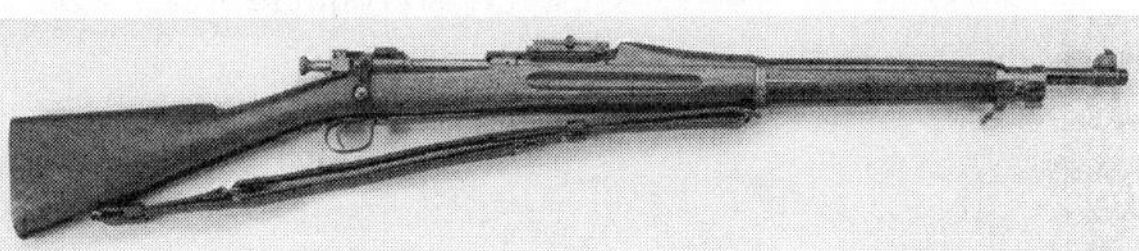
Model 1903 altered from Model 1905 • *Courtesy Little John's Auction Service, Inc., Paul Goodwin photo*

Exc.	V.G.	Good	Fair	Poor
3750	2750	1000	700	500

Model 1903 Rifle (1907-1910 in .30-06)

This variation was built both by Springfield and Rock Island. It features a stock with a square corner beside the receiver ring on the right side, a smooth and pointed trigger, smooth buttplate, the bolt handle is not bent back, blued metal. The receiver has a black or mottled finish. Early examples do not have a cross bolt in the stock while rifles built after 1908 have a single cross bolt. About 130,000 were produced in serial number range 269000 to 400000. Original examples are rare as most were arsenal rebuilt with parkerized finish and new features.

Model 1903 dated 1909 • *Courtesy Little John's Auction Service, Paul Goodwin photo*

Exc.	V.G.	Good	Fair	Poor
3750	2750	1250	750	500

Model 1903 Rifle (1910-1917 in .30-06)

This variation features a stock with tapered rather than square corner on right side of receiver ring. The trigger is serrated and not pointed. Checkered buttplate, bolt handle is not bent back, and metal is blued. Stock has a single cross bolt. Most were arsenal rebuilt. About 250,000 were manufactured between serial numbers 385000 to 635000. Between 1910 and 1913, these rifles were also built by Rock Island.

NOTE: A small number of these rifles were sold to civilians through the DCM program. They are marked "NRA" on the triggerguard. These examples are worth approximately 20 percent more.

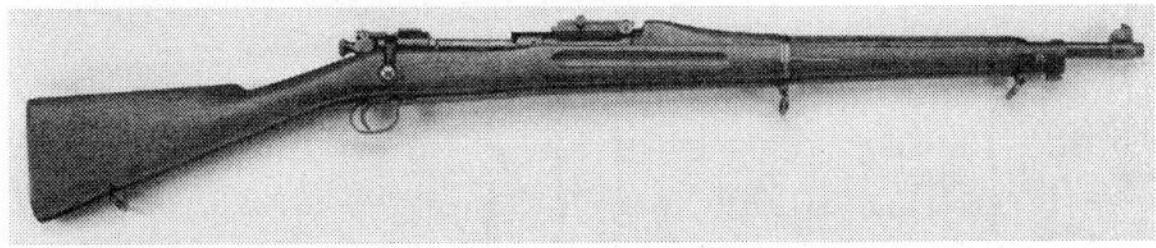
Courtesy Little John's Auction Service, Inc. • *Paul Goodwin photo*

Exc.	V.G.	Good	Fair	Poor
3750	2750	1000	700	500

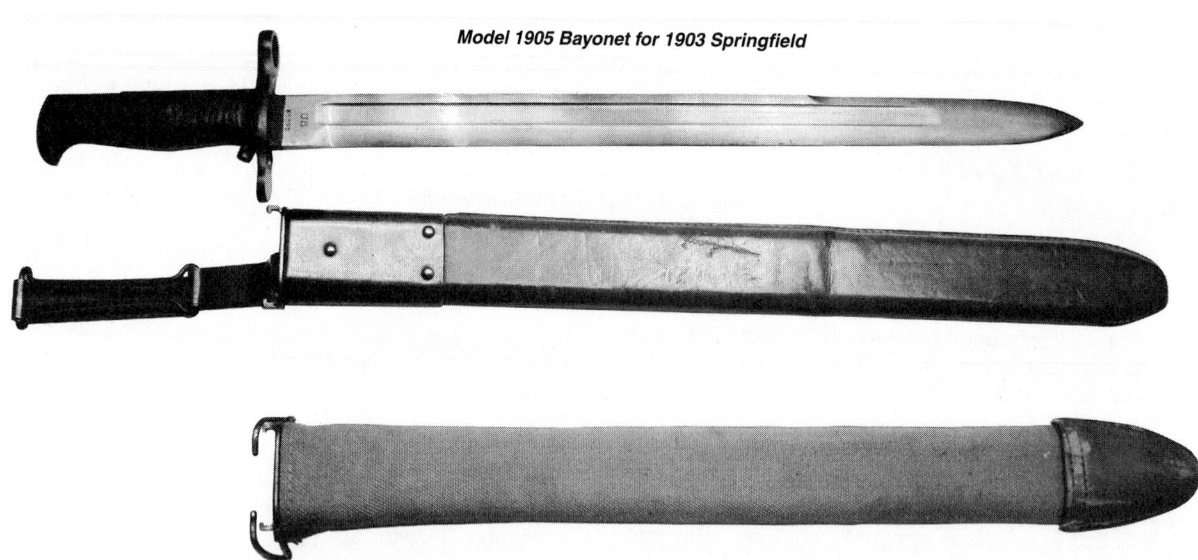
Model 1905 Bayonet for 1903 Springfield

Model 1903 Rifle (1917-1921 in .30-06)

This variation features a parkerized finish with smooth buttplate, many have smooth triggers that have a thick contour. Two cross bolts in stock. This particular variation does not have the attention to detail and finish that peacetime rifles have. Many of these rifles were arsenal rebuilt. About 590,000 of this variation were manufactured between serial numbers 635000 to 1225000.

Exc.	V.G.	Good	Fair	Poor
2500	1800	1000	700	500

NOTE: Rifles built between 1917 and 1918 will bring a 20 percent premium.

Model 1903 Rifle (1921-1929)

This variation features parkerized metal finish with checkered buttplate and serrated triggers. Stock have grasping grooves and straight grips. Many of these rifles were arsenal refinished and reassembled with different combinations of parts. About 80,000 were manufactured between serial numbers 1200000 and 1280000.

Exc.	V.G.	Good	Fair	Poor
2500	1500	800	700	500

Model 1905 Bayonet for 1903 Springfield

Wood grips. Muzzle ring. 16" single edge blade. Polished steel or blued finish. Some refinished for service in WWII have a parkerized finish. Marked with "SA" or "RIA" and production date on ricasso. The early scabbards are wood with leather covering. Later scabbards have a olive drab cloth with leather tip. There are several minor variations to in the scabbards. The value of unaltered 1905 bayonets has risen sharply in recent years. There are reproductions on the market. Price range 500 – 300.

Model 1903 Rifle Stripped for Air Service

Special 29" stock, 5.75 upper handguard specially made for this rifle, solid lower barrel band retained by screw underneath, rear leaf sight shortened and altered to open sight with square notch. 25-round extension magazine used. Some 910 rifles produced during the first half of 1918, with serial numbers ranging between 857000 and 863000; all barrels dated in first half of 1918. A very rare and desirable rifle, with the magazine almost impossible to find. Values shown include magazine.

Model 1903 with Air Service magazine • Courtesy Richard M. Kumor Sr.

Exc.	V.G.	Good	Fair	Poor
20000	12500	7500	3500	1000

Model 1903 Mark 1

This version is similar to the original except that it was cut to accept the Pedersen device. This device allows the use of a semi-automatic bolt insert that utilizes pistol cartridges. The rifle has a slot milled into the receiver that acts as an ejection port. The device was not successful and was scrapped. Approximately 102,000 rifles were produced with this millcut between 1918 and 1920.

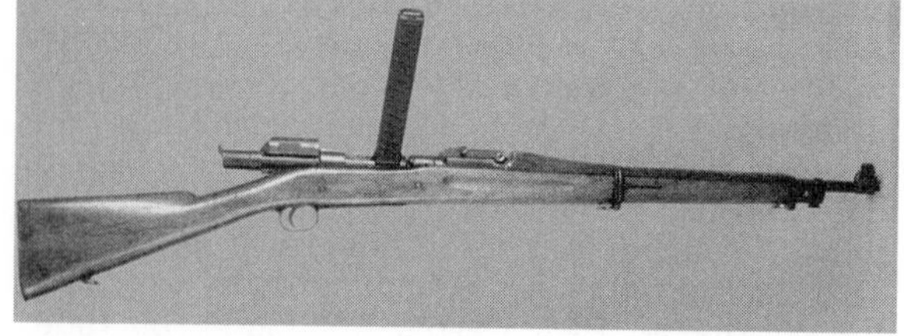
Paul Goodwin photo

Exc.	V.G.	Good	Fair	Poor
1800	1250	950	600	300

NOTE: The values given are for the rifle alone—not for the device. Rifle must contain all original Mark I parts. For rifles with the device and magazine add $35,000; for rifles with the device but no magazine add $30,000; for the metal carrying scabbard add $7,500.

Pedersen Device • *Paul Goodwin photo*

Model 1903 Sniper Rifle

Selected Model 1903 rifles were fitted with telescopic sights from 1907 to 1919; apparently 25 rifles so equipped in 1906, but the type of scope has not been definitely identified. If proven original to the period, specimens would be worth more than shown in the values guide. 400 rifles were fitted with the Warner-Swasey Model 1906, 6-power telescope sight in 1911, with the sights marked Model 1908, as well as with the full Warner-Swasey markings. Scope numbers do not match the rifle numbers. Rifles fitted with this Model 1908 scope will bring approximately 30 percent more than the values shown. Approximately 5,000 rifles were fitted with the Model 1913 Warner-Swasey telescopic sight up to 1919; similar to the Model 1908, they were only 5.2 power. When originally fitted, the scopes were numbered to the rifles; however, scopes were sold separately from the rifles as surplus and were never numbered. These were later fitted to other weapons and the chance of finding matching numbers greatly decreases. Values shown are for original guns with original, matching telescopes.

The U.S. Marine Corps also had its own versions of the Model 1903 Sniper. Early rifles were fitted with a Winchester A5 5X scope or a Lyman 5A 5X scope. Later examples were fitted with a Unertl 8X scope marked "USMC." All Marine Corps scopes had target bases.

Courtesy Bob Ball

Exc.	*V.G.*	*Good*	*Fair*	*Poor*
7000	5500	4000	2500	1500

NOTE: A few Model 1903 and 1903A1 rifles will have barrels marked "USMC" and the date. These barrels were installed by the Sedgley Company. Add a premium of about 15 percent for these barrels.

Model 1903 A1

This version is a standard Model 1903 rifle that was fitted with a Type C, semi-pistol grip stock. All other specifications were the same except for a checkered butt and serrated trigger.

Exc.	*V.G.*	*Good*	*Fair*	*Poor*
1800	950	650	500	400

World War II Model 1903s

For a complete explanation, with photos and technical data see Bruce Canfield's *U.S. Infantry Weapons of World War II*.

According to Canfield, the majority of World War II Model 1903 rifles were rebuilt. The extent varied from rifle to rifle. Look for the following alterations:

1. Refinished metal with greenish parkerizing.
2. Stock and handguard replaced or refinished. Replacement stock lacked finger grooves.
3. Replacement barrels were made by Springfield, Sedgley, and High Standard. Two-digit date stamped on new barrels.
4. A gas escape hole was added, but not to all WWII receivers.
5. Component parts were sometimes of a later vintage.

Model 1903 (Remington, WWII)

Remington began production of the Model 1903 in November 1941. These very early rifles are identical to the Rock Island Model 1903. About 1,273 of these early rifles were produced. The balance of Remington Model 1903 rifles were built using less expensive methods. Tolerances were eased and more stamped parts were employed. These rifles were stamped "Remington Model 1903," and small parts were stamped "R." These early Remington rifles will be found in serial number range 3000 to about 3050000.

Exc.	*V.G.*	*Good*	*Fair*	*Poor*
750	600	500	250	150

NOTE: Very early Remington rifles, the first 1,273, will bring a premium over the later rifles.

Model 1903 (Remington, WWII, Modified)

This version of the Model 1903 was a further attempt to reduce cost and increase production. The right gas escape hole was eliminated, and a number of machining operations were omitted. This version is known as the Model 1903 Modified. These rifles are found in serial number range 3050000 to about 3365000.

Exc.	*V.G.*	*Good*	*Fair*	*Poor*
750	500	500	300	150

Model 1903 A3

This version was introduced in May of 1942 for use in WWII. It basically consisted of improvements to simplify mass production. It features an aperture sight and various small parts that were fabricated from stampings; this includes the triggerguard, floorplate, and barrel band. The finish is parkerized. Receiver ring is marked "03-A3." This model was manufactured by Remington and Smith-Corona.

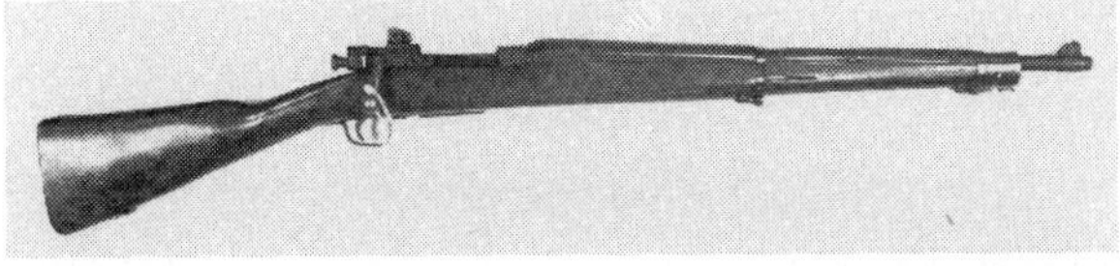

Courtesy Bob Ball

Exc.	*V.G.*	*Good*	*Fair*	*Poor*
800	650	500	350	250

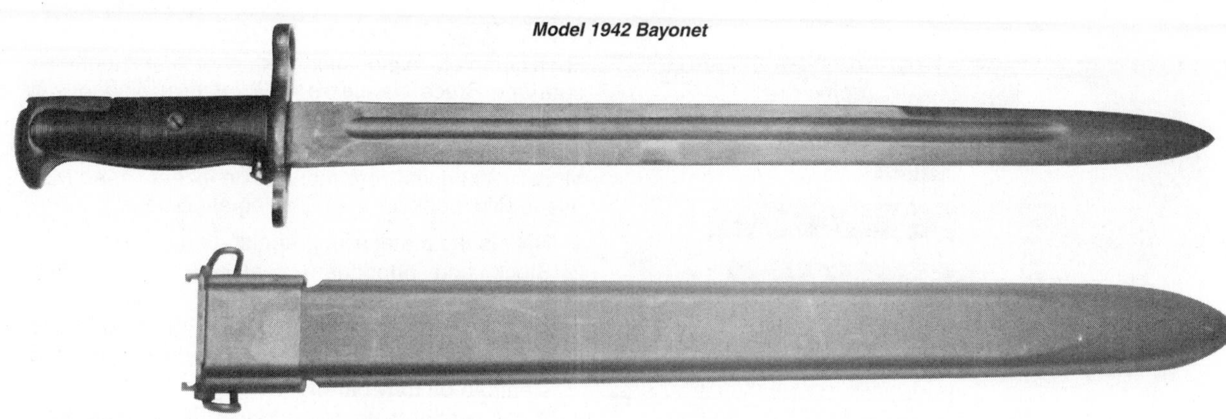

Model 1942 Bayonet

WWII-Issue Bayonets for M 1903, 1903-A3 and M-1 Garand

Model 1942

Ribbed black or brown grips. Muzzle ring. 16" single edge blade. Parkerized finish. This bayonet is the same as the U.S. 1905 design. Dated on ricasso 1942 or 43, with the initials of the manufacturer. Made by six contractors: OL-Oneida Ltd., UFH - Union Fork & Hoe, PAL – Pal Blade co., WT – Wilde Tool, AFH – American Fork & Hoe, U.C. – Utica Cutlery Co. Green plastic scabbard with U.S. ordnance bomb marking. Price range 350 – 200.

U.S. M-1

Ribbed black or brown grips. Muzzle ring. 10" single edge blade. Made by the same contractors as the M 1942. Price range 200 – 125.

1905-E1

This is a 1905 or 1942 bayonet with the blade shortened to 10". The fuller groove will run to the tip. There are two tip types. Price range 200 – 125.

Model 1903 A4

Most of these rifles were marked "A3" and not "A4." The markings were rotated to the side in order not to be covered by the scope mount. This is a sniper-rifle version of the Model 1903. It is fitted with permanently mounted scope blocks and furnished with a telescopic sight known as the M73B1. This scope was manufactured by Weaver in El Paso, Texas, and was commercially known as the Model 330C. The rifle has

Model 1905-E1 Bayonet

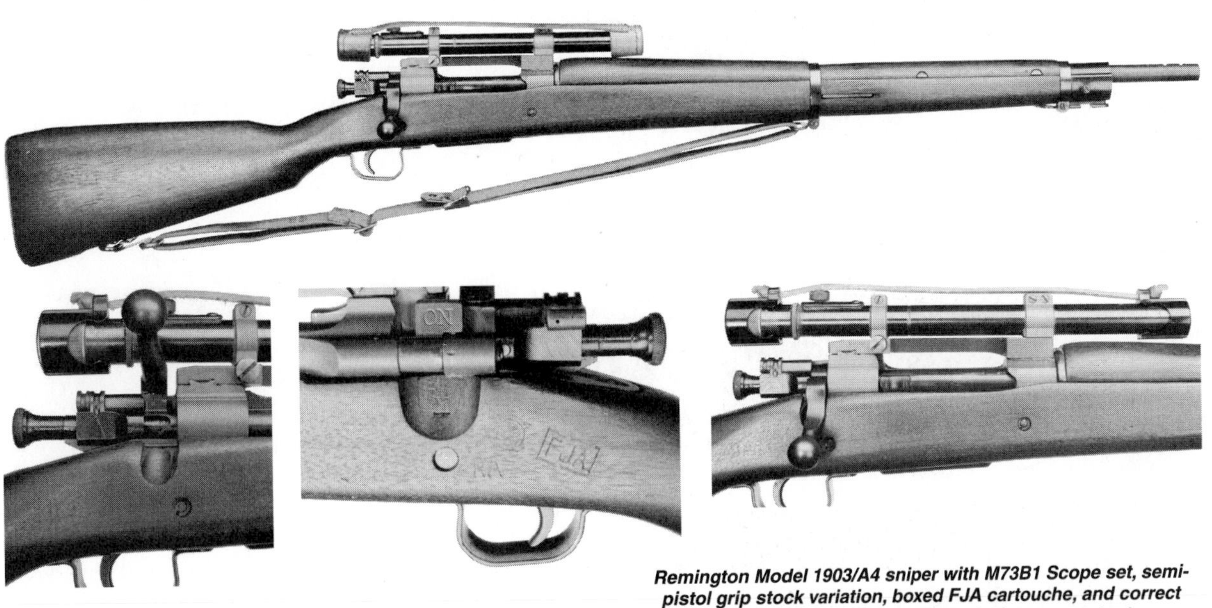

Remington Model 1903/A4 sniper with M73B1 Scope set, semi-pistol grip stock variation, boxed FJA cartouche, and correct factory original bolt handle stock clearance cutout •
Courtesy Michael Wamsher, Paul Goodwin photo

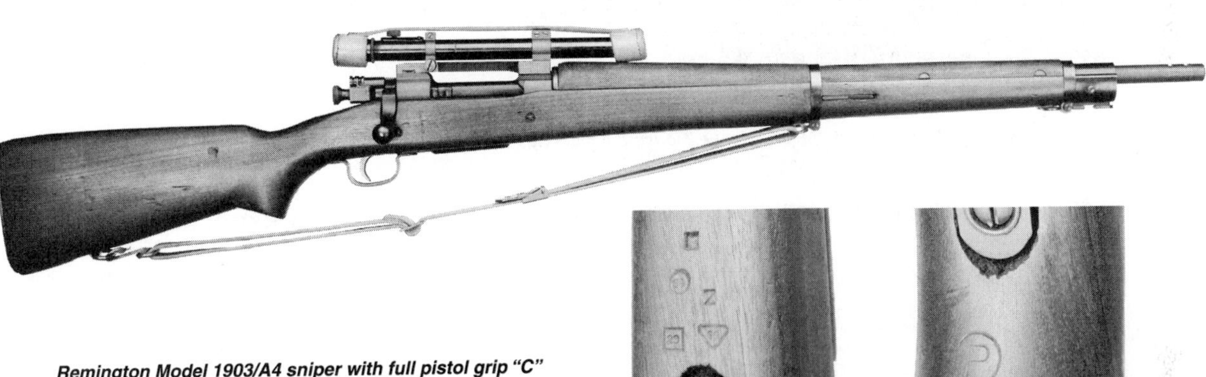

Remington Model 1903/A4 sniper with full pistol grip "C" stock variatio. "FJA" cartouche without box, factory assembly markings and "Circle P" proof markings •
Courtesy Michael Wamsher, Paul Goodwin photo

Examples of different scopes and their markings used on the Model 1903/A4 rifle. From right to left: Early Weaver Model 330 scope M73B1 scope, and MB2 scope •
Courtesy Michael Wamsher, Paul Goodwin photo

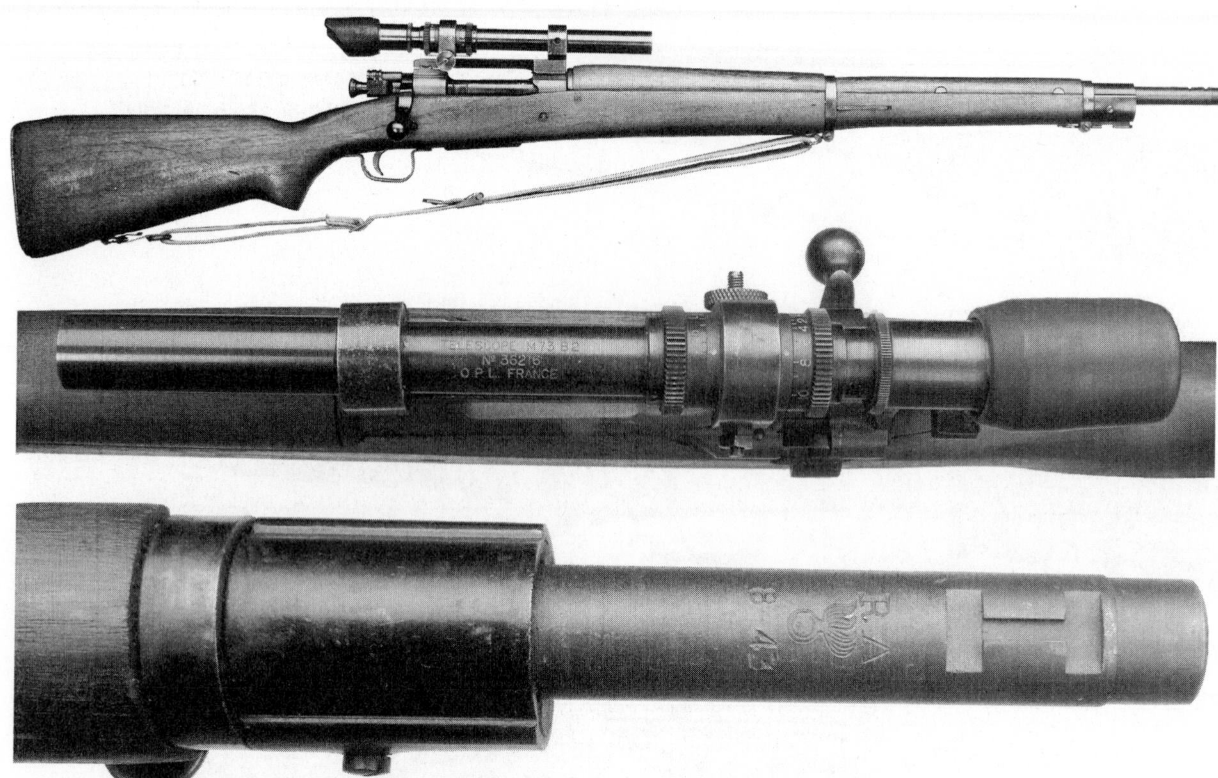

Rifle with WWII rare "French" M73B2 scope. Notice the markings and characteristics of front sight removal •
Courtesy Michael Wamsher, Paul Goodwin photo

no conventional iron sights mounted. This model was built by Remington.

Model 82 scope circa post-Korean War •
Courtesy Richard M. Kumor Sr.

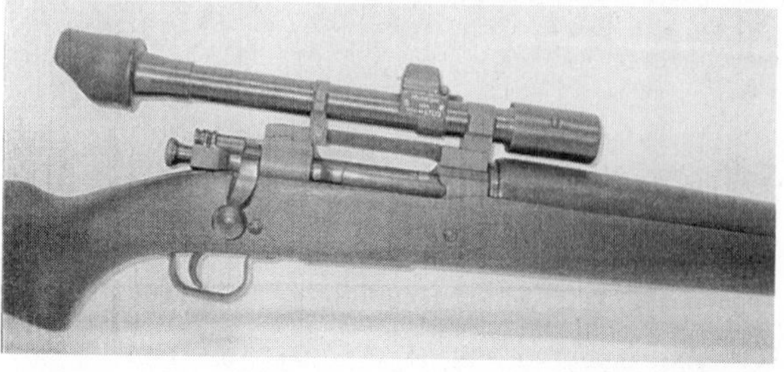

Model 84 scope circa Korea and Vietnam wars •
Courtesy Richard M. Kumor Sr.

Exc.	V.G.	Good	Fair	Poor
3000	2500	1750	650	350

NOTE: For those few rifles marked "A4" add a premium of 10 percent.

NOTE: For rifles with M84 scope deduct $250.

Model 1903 NRA National Match

This version was based on a standard 1903 service rifle that was selected for having excellent shooting qualities. The parts were then hand-fit, and a special rifled barrel was added that was checked for tolerance with a star gauge. The muzzle of this barrel was marked with a special star with six or eight rays radiating from it. These NRA rifles were drilled and tapped to accept a Lyman No. 48 rear sight. They are marked with the letters "NRA" and have a flaming bomb proofmark on the triggerguard. There were approximately 18,000 manufactured between 1921 and 1928.

Exc.	V.G.	Good	Fair	Poor
3750	2400	2000	1400	800

NOTE: Prices are for verifiable samples.

Model 1903 A1 National Match

Basically the same as the Model 1903 National Match rifle except for the "C" type, or pistol grip stock, without grasping grooves. Bolts and stocks numbered to the receiver. "P" in a circle proof on the underside of the pistol grip, with either a "DAL" in a rectangular cartouche, or S.A./SPG in a square cartouche. Rifles will be found with either a regular or reversed safety. Approximately 11,000 produced with a serial number range from 1285000 to 1532000.

Exc.	V.G.	Good	Fair	Poor
4500	3000	2000	1200	600

NOTE: Prices are for verifiable samples.

Model 1903 Style National Match Special Rifle

This rifle is identical to the National Match, but with a completely different buttstock configuration identical to the Model 1922 NRA. Large shotgun type steel buttplate; full pistol grip. About 150 rifles produced during 1924.

Model 1903 "NB" National Match showing markings • *Paul Goodwin photo*

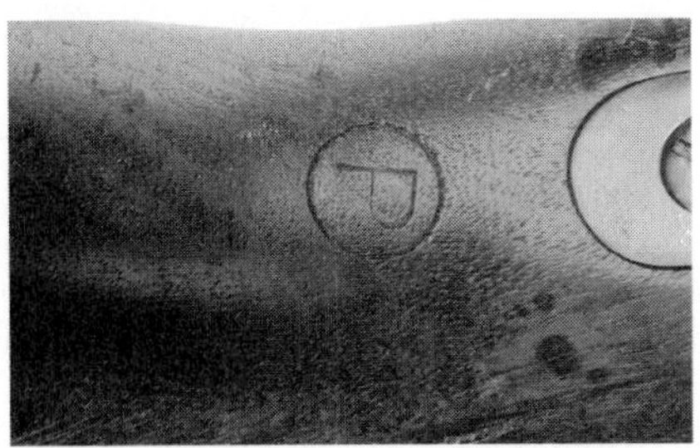

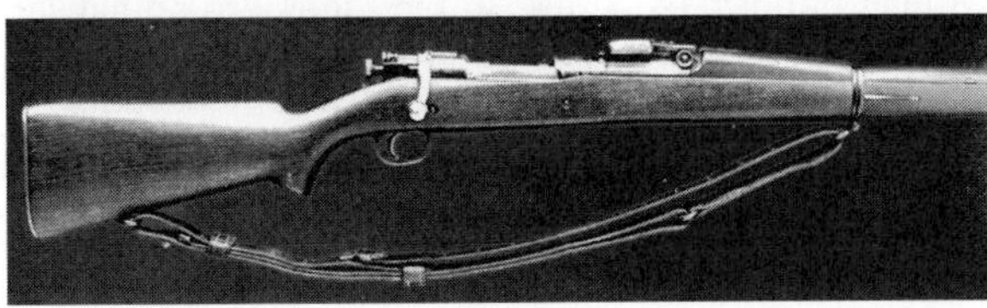

Model 1903 National Match Special Rifle • *Courtesy Butterfield & Butterfield*

Exc.	*V.G.*	*Good*	*Fair*	*Poor*
8500	6500	5500	3500	2500

NOTE: Prices are for verifiable samples.

Model 1903 Style "NB" National Match Rifle

This rifle produced with the "B" type stock with more drop than standard, suitable only for off-hand shooting; pistol grip configured with a noticeably squared profile. Deep checkered buttplate. Circle "P" proof in underside of pistol grip. About 195 rifles built between 1925 and 1926.

Exc.	*V.G.*	*Good*	*Fair*	*Poor*
8500	6500	5500	3500	2500

NOTE: Prices are for verifiable samples.

Model 1903 NRA Sporter

This version is similar to the National Match rifle but features a half-length, Sporter-type stock with one barrel band. It also features the Lyman No. 48 receiver sight. This version was produced for commercial sales. There were approximately 6,500 manufactured between 1924 and 1933.

Exc.	*V.G.*	*Good*	*Fair*	*Poor*
3000	2200	1800	1400	800

NOTE: Prices are for verifiable samples.

Model 1903 NBA Sporter Rifle

The barrel, action, and sights of this rifle are identical to the Model 1903 NRA Sporter rifle above. However it is fitted with a "B" type stock. Grasping grooves and squared pistol grip profile. Circle "P" proof in the underside of the pistol grip. 589 rifles produced at the Springfield Armory during 1925 and 1926.

Exc.	*V.G.*	*Good*	*Fair*	*Poor*
8500	6500	5500	3500	2500

NOTE: Prices are for verifiable samples.

Model 1903 Heavy Barreled Match Rifles

These rifles were made in a bewildering number of types and variations. Commonly encountered are the style "T" with NRA type stocks. Barrels, which came in three lengths, 26", 28", and 30", measured .860" at the muzzle and 1.250" at the breech. Lyman 48 rear sight; Winchester globe front sight on a modified B.A.R. front band, telescope blocks on the receiver and barrel. Some fitted with adjustable hook type buttplates, set triggers, Garand speed locks, as well as cheekpieces (all commanding premium dollars). INTERNATIONAL MATCH rifles (worth at least double the values shown) have many variant features which were changed annually at the request of the individual shooter. These features include palm rests, double set triggers, beaver-tail forends, checkered pistol grips, Swiss style buttplates, etc. Generally the Winchester 5A telescopic sight was used. These rifles are considered rare. Another variation is the 1922 MATCH SPRINGFIELD RIFLE with NRA type stock with grasping grooves, a 24" barrel with service type front sight mount and small base integral with the barrel, as well as telescopic blocks on the barrel. 566 rifles produced at the Springfield Armory between 1922 and 1930.

Model 1903 NRA Sporter • *Courtesy Little John's Auction Service, Inc., Paul Goodwin photo*

Springfield Model 1903 Heavy Barrel Match Rifle •
Courtesy Greg Martin Auctions

Exc.	*V.G.*	*Good*	*Fair*	*Poor*
7000	5500	4000	2500	1500

NOTE: Values shown are for the standard heavy barrel match rifle without any special features.

Model 1903 .22 Caliber Gallery Practice Rifle "HofferThompson"

This practice rifle differed from the standard issue '03 as follows: the barrel bored and rifled to .22 caliber, the breech chambered for the Hoffer-Thompson cartridge holder, the rear sight graduated to 240 yards, the mainspring shortened, the stocks generally found without cross bolts or the circle "P" on the underside of the pistol grip. Receivers produced after 1901 usually are marked with ".22" on the top of the bridge. About 15,525 rifles were produced at the Springfield Armory between 1907 and 1918.

Exc.	*V.G.*	*Good*	*Fair*	*Poor*
4000	3250	2500	1500	800

Model 1917

In 1917, when the United States entered WWI, there was a distinct rifle shortage. There were production facilities set up for the British pattern 1914 rifle. This "Enfield" rifle was redesigned to accept the .30-06 cartridge and was pressed into service as the U.S. rifle Model 1917. This rifle appears similar to the British pattern 1914 rifle. In fact, they are so similar that in WWII, when over a million were sold to Britain for use by their Home Guard, it was necessary to paint a 2" stripe around the butt so that the caliber was immediately known. The barrel length is 26", and it has a 6-round integral box magazine. The finish is matte-blue, with a walnut stock. Towards the end of production parkerized parts were added. The breech is marked "U.S. Model 1917." This was a

Model 1903 .22 Caliber Gallery Practice Rifle "HofferThompson" with markings

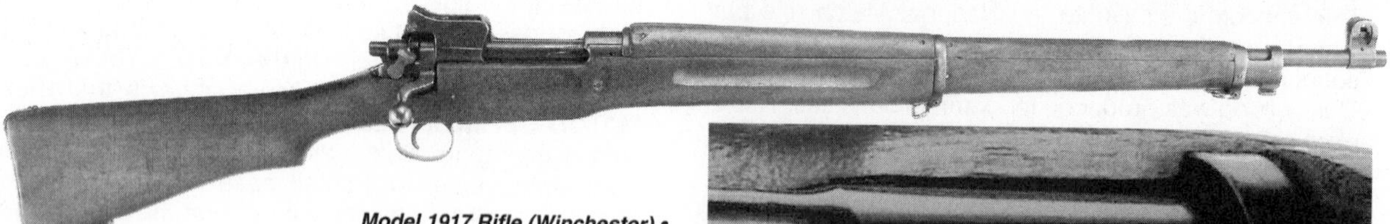

Model 1917 Rifle (Winchester) •
Courtesy Rock Island Auction Company

Remington Model 1917 receiver markings •
Courtesy Karl Karash

robust and heavy-duty rifle, and many are used in the manufacture of large-bore custom rifles to this day. There were approximately 2,200,000 manufactured by Remington, Winchester, and Eddystone between 1917 and 1918. The majority were produced at Eddystone, Pennsylvania.

During World War II all parts were parkerized, and barrels were supplied by the Johnson Automatics Company as a result of the rebuild.

Exc.	*V.G.*	*Good*	*Fair*	*Poor*
750	600	450	250	150

NOTE: Add 30 percent for Winchester model.

French troops with the Model 1917 • *Courtesy Paul S. Scarlata*

Model 1917 Bayonet

Wood grips with two notches. Muzzle ring. 16" single edge blade. Marked on ricasso "Remington" (in a circle) or "W" (Winchester) with a production month and year. They should also have the U.S. eagle head property mark. Some 1914/17 bayonets made for Great Britain were diverted for U.S. use and will have English markings as well. Steel tipped leather scabbard. This bayonet was also used on military issue shotguns. See listing in shotgun section. Price range 200 – 75. Note: The Winchester made bayonets will bring up to 50 percent more than Remington.

Model 1922

This is a bolt-action training rifle chambered for the .22 rimfire cartridge. It appears similar to the Model 1903 but has a 24.5" barrel and a half-length stock without hand guards, held on by a single barrel band. It has a 5-round detachable box magazine. The finish is blued, with a walnut stock. The receiver is marked "U.S. Springfield Armory Model of 1922 Cal. 22." It also has the flaming bomb ordnance mark. There were three basic types of the Model 1922: the standard issue type, the NRA commercial type, and the models that were altered to M1 or M2. There were a total of approximately 2,000 manufactured between 1922 and 1924. The survival rate of the original-issue types is not large as most were converted.

Issue Type

Exc.	*V.G.*	*Good*	*Fair*	*Poor*
1950	1500	1250	600	400

Altered Type

Exc.	*V.G.*	*Good*	*Fair*	*Poor*
700	500	350	200	150

NRA Type—Drilled and Tapped for Scope

Exc.	*V.G.*	*Good*	*Fair*	*Poor*
1200	850	550	300	150

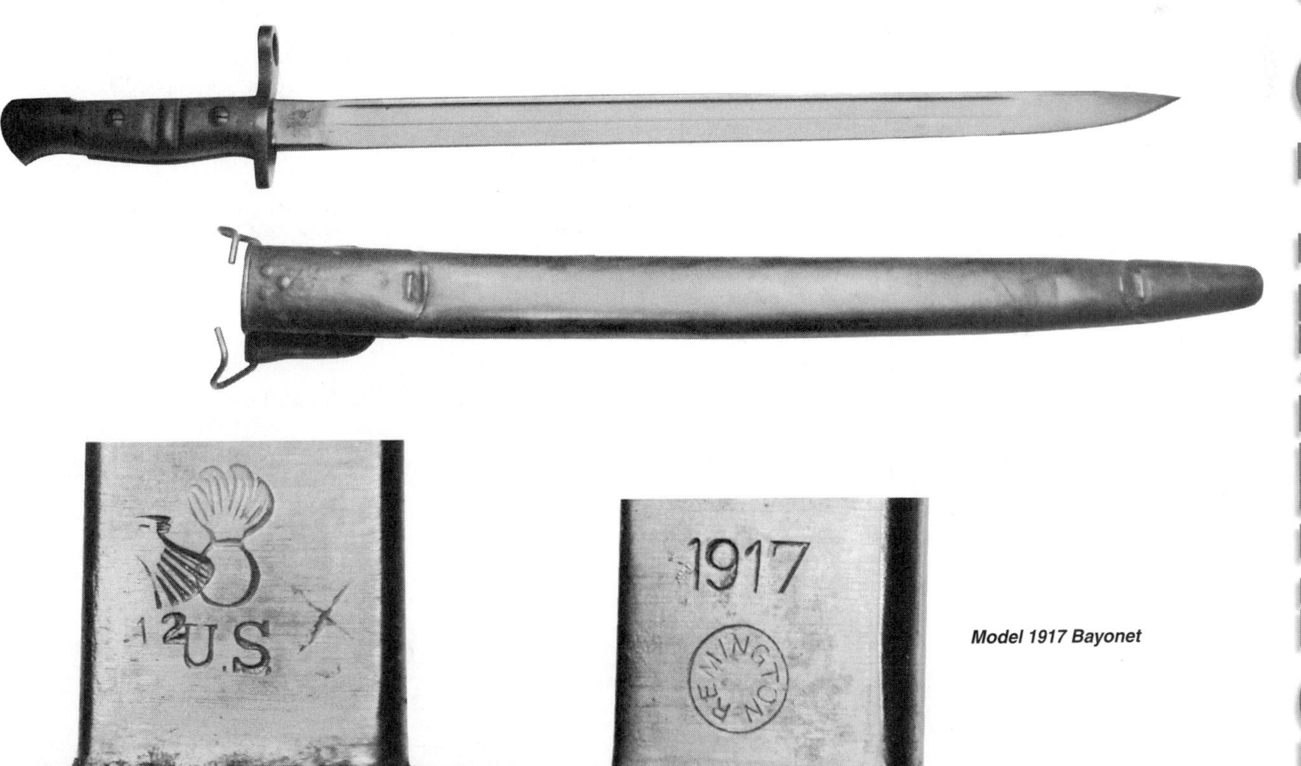

Model 1917 Bayonet

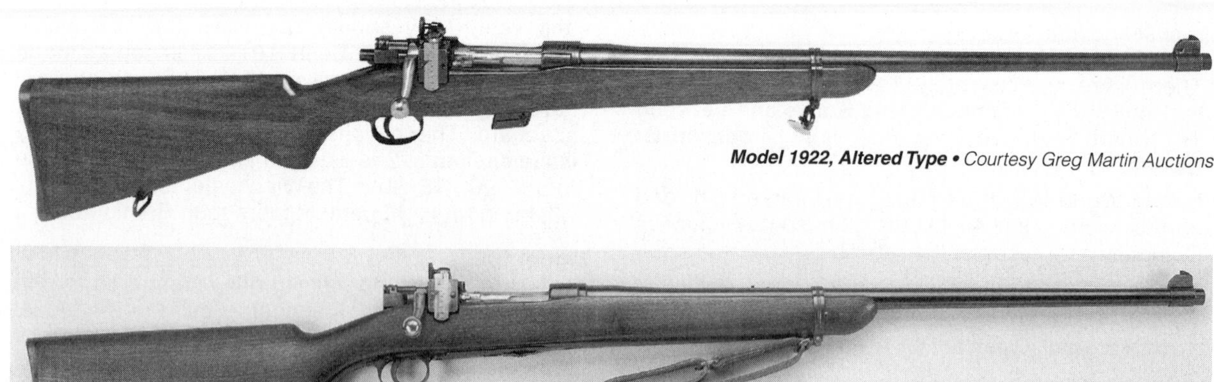

Model 1922, Altered Type • *Courtesy Greg Martin Auctions*

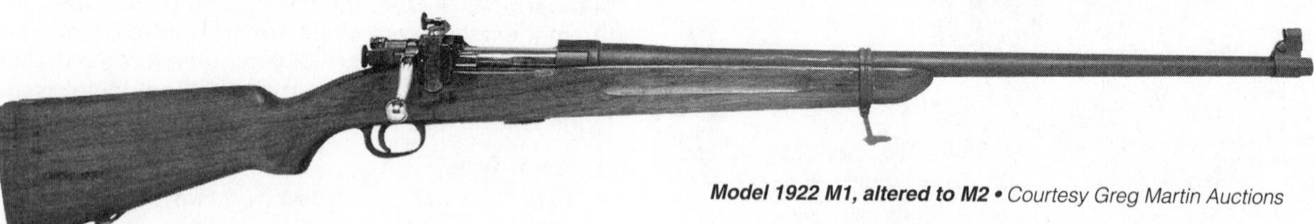

Model 1922 M1 • *Courtesy Little John's Auction Service, Inc., Paul Goodwin photo*

Model 1922 M1, altered to M2 • *Courtesy Greg Martin Auctions*

Model 1922 M1

This version is quite similar to the Model 1922, with a single-point striker system and a detachable box magazine that does not protrude from the bottom of the stock. The finish is parkerized and the stock is made of walnut. There were approximately 20,000 manufactured between 1924 and 1933.

Unaltered Type

Exc.	*V.G.*	*Good*	*Fair*	*Poor*
1750	1400	1000	600	300

Altered to M2

Exc.	*V.G.*	*Good*	*Fair*	*Poor*
1200	800	650	350	200

Unaltered NRA Type

Exc.	*V.G.*	*Good*	*Fair*	*Poor*
950	750	500	300	250

NRA Type Altered to M2

Exc.	*V.G.*	*Good*	*Fair*	*Poor*
700	500	400	300	250

Magazines for the U.S. M1922 (left) and 1922 M2 rifles (right) in .22LR. Price 1922, 300-150; 1922 M2, 175-80

Model M2

This is an improved version of the Model 1922 M1 that features an altered firing mechanism with a faster lock time. It has a knurled cocking knob added to the bolt and a flush-fitting detachable magazine with improved feeding. There were approximately 12,000 manufactured.

Exc.	*V.G.*	*Good*	*Fair*	*Poor*
1200	900	750	450	300

Model 1922 M2 Rifle • *Paul Goodwin photo*

U.S. Rifle M1 (Garand)

Springfield Armory was one of the manufacturers of this WWII service rifle. It is listed in the Garand section of this text.

Springfield M21 Sniper Rifle

This is the sniper rifle version of the M14 rifle with ART II scope. Early models were fitted with an M84 scope and Griffin & Howe mounts. This scope was followed by the ART I and finally the ART II scope in the early 1970s.

M21 with ART II scope and case • *Courtesy Richard M. Kumor Sr.*

Exc.	*V.G.*	*Good*	*Fair*	*Poor*
7000	5500	4000	—	—

NOTE: Prices are for verifiable and registered samples.

KRAG JORGENSEN

The first smallbore, bolt-action repeating rifle that used smokeless powder that was adopted by the U.S. government as a service rifle. It was adopted as the Model 1892 and was similar to the rifle being used by Denmark as a service rifle. All of the Krag-Jorgensens were manufactured at the Springfield Armory. There are 11 basic variations of Krag Rifles, and all except one are chambered for the .30-40 Govt. cartridge. They are bolt actions that hold 5 rounds in the unique side-mounted hinged magazine. All of the Krags have walnut stocks and handguards that are oil-finished. They all have dark gray case-hardened receivers and blued barrels. See also *Denmark, Rifles, Krag Jorgensen.*

Bibliographical Note: For historical information, technical data, and photos, see Lt. Col. William Brophy's, *The Krag Rifle*, Gun Room Press, 1985.

NOTE: One should be aware that there have been many alterations based on the Krag rifle by many gunsmiths through the years, and the one consistency is that all of these conversions lowered the value of the rifle and rendered it uncollectible. Proceed with caution. Prices listed are for original rifles as they left the factory.

Model 1892

Approximately 24,500 of these rifles produced, dated 1894, 1895, and 1896. They have 30" barrels and are serial numbered from 1-24562. Nearly all were converted to the latter Model 1896, and the original 1st Type is extremely scarce.

1st Type

Serial numbered from 1-1500 and is dated 1894 only. It features a wide upper barrel band and a brass tipped one-piece cleaning rod mounted under the barrel. There is no compartment in the butt, and the muzzle is not crowned and appears flat. The upper handguard does not extend over the receiver, and the buttplate is flat, without a compartment. Be wary of fakes. Unaltered specimens are extremely rare.

Exc.	*V.G.*	*Good*	*Fair*	*Poor*
—	20000	12500	6500	3000

2nd Type

Similar to the 1st Type, with a front barrel band that is cut out in the center and does not appear solid. The cleaning rod is a one piece steel type. The serial number range is 1500-24562, and the dates 1894 or 1895 are stamped on the receiver and the stock. Again be wary of fakes. This is a rare rifle.

Exc.	*V.G.*	*Good*	*Fair*	*Poor*
—	10000	7500	4000	2500

Model 1922 M2 Rifle • *Paul Goodwin photo*

Model 1892 Altered to 1896 Model

Encompassed nearly the entire production run of the Model 1892 Krag rifle. They still bear the dates 1894, 1895, and 1896 on the receiver; but they do not have a one piece cleaning rod under the barrel, but instead a three-piece type inserted into the buttstock, and the hole in the stock has been plugged. The front barrel band was changed. The top handguard covers the receiver, and the buttplate is curved at the bottom. The muzzle is crowned.

Exc.	V.G.	Good	Fair	Poor
1800	950	750	450	300

Model 1895 Carbine (Variation)

Marked "1895" and "1896" on the receiver—without the word "Model." They were produced before the Model 1896 was officially adopted, and they are serial numbered from 25000 to 35000. They are similar to the Model 1896 Carbine, with a smaller safety and no oiler bottle in the butt.

Model 1895 Carbine • *Courtesy Rock Island Auction Company*

Exc.	V.G.	Good	Fair	Poor
2500	1800	1250	650	300

Model 1896 Rifle

Similar to the altered Model 1892 and has a 30" barrel with the cleaning kit in the butt. The rear sight was improved, and the receiver is marked "U.S. Model 1896" and "Springfield Armory." Lightening cuts were made in the barrel channel to reduce weight. A total of about 62,000 Model 96 rifles were produced in the same serial number range as the Model 1896 carbine of 37240 to 108471. The stock is dated 1896, 1897, and 1898. There were many of these altered to the later stock configurations—in the field or at the Springfield Armory. These changes would lower the value, and one should secure expert appraisal on this model.

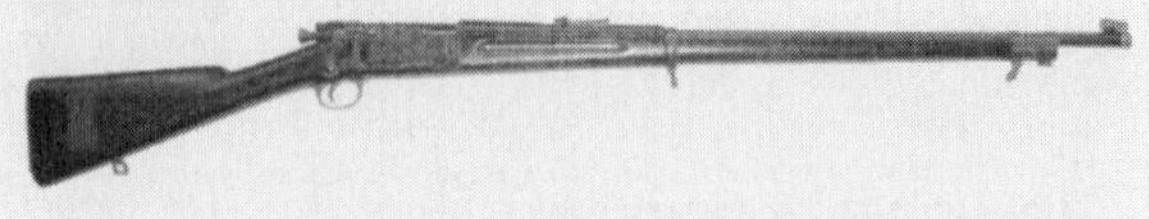

Courtesy Richard M. Kumor Sr.

Exc.	V.G.	Good	Fair	Poor
2750	2000	1600	750	400

Model 1896 Carbine

Similar to the 1896 Rifle, with a 22" barrel and half-length stock held on by one barrel band. There were approximately less than 20,000 manufactured between 1896 and 1898, and the serial number range is 35000-90000. There were many rifles cut to carbine dimensions—be wary of these alterations!

Courtesy Jim Supica, Old Town Station

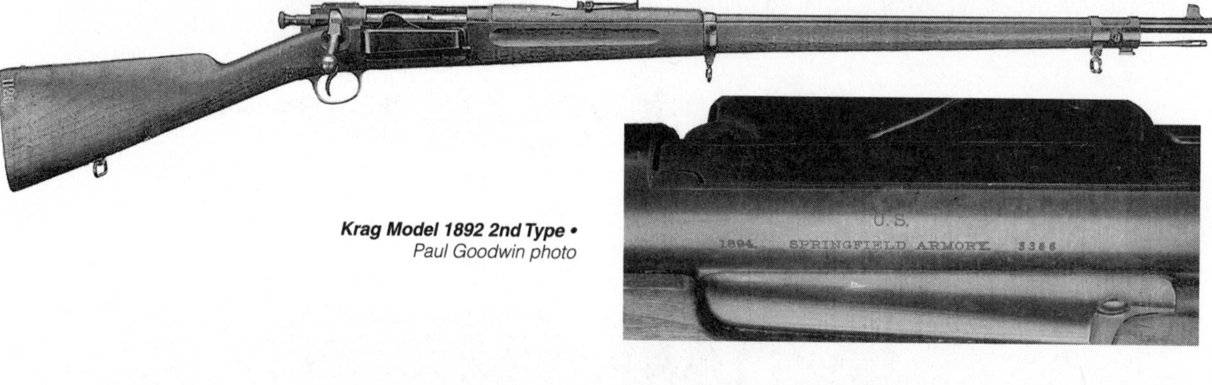

Krag Model 1892 2nd Type •
Paul Goodwin photo

Model 1896 Cadet Rifle •
Courtesy West Point Museum,
Paul Goodwin photo

Exc.	V.G.	Good	Fair	Poor
3000	2250	1500	950	600

Model 1896 Cadet Rifle

A rare variation produced for use by the Military Academy at West Point. The dimensions are the same as the 1896 Rifle with a one-piece cleaning rod under the barrel and the 1896-type front band. There were 400 manufactured, and most were altered to standard configuration when they were phased out in 1898. Extremely rare in original and unaltered condition.

Exc.	V.G.	Good	Fair	Poor
—	—	37500	15000	—

Model 1892 Bayonet for Krag Jorgensen Rifles

Wood grips. Muzzle ring. 11.6" single edge blade. Marked with "SA" and production date on ricasso. Steel scabbard. The first knife bayonet issued by the U.S. It is a close copy of the Swiss M 1889 bayonet. Used on all the Krag models that take a bayonet. Price range 250 – 125.

Krag Rifle • Courtesy Paul S. Scarlata

Model 1898 Rifle

This model is similar to the Model 1896 in appearance except that the receiver is marked "U.S./Model 1898." The bolt handle was modified, and the sights and handguards were improved. There were 330,000 manufactured between 1898 and 1903, and the serial number range is 110000-480000.

Exc.	V.G.	Good	Fair	Poor
1250	900	650	450	300

Model 1898 Carbine

Similar to the rifle, with a 22" barrel and a bar and ring on the left side of the receiver. There were approximately 5,000 manufactured in 1898 and 1899. The serial range is 118000-134000. Again, be aware that many of the rifles have been converted to carbine dimensions over the years. When in doubt, secure an independent appraisal.

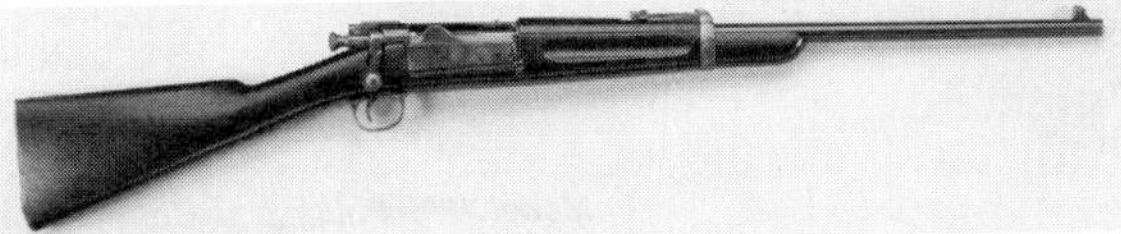

Courtesy Little John's Auction Service, Inc., Paul Goodwin photo

Exc.	V.G.	Good	Fair	Poor
2750	2000	1500	750	500

Model 1898 Carbine 26" Barrel

An attempt to satisfy both the infantry and the cavalry. There were 100 manufactured for trial, and the serial number range is between 387000-389000. Be wary of fakes.

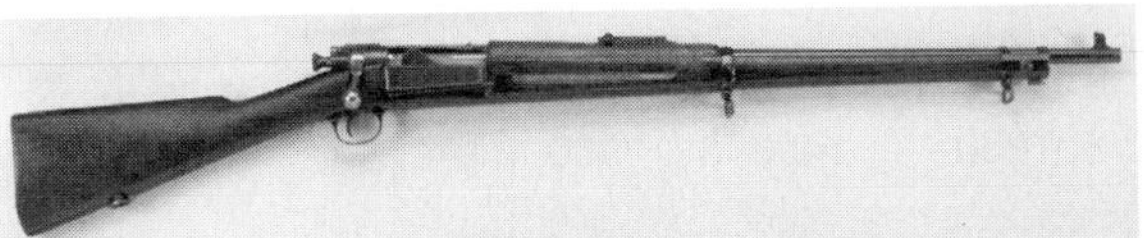

Courtesy Little John's Auction Service, Inc., Paul Goodwin photo

Exc.	V.G.	Good	Fair	Poor
—	17500	7500	2500	900

Model 1898 Practice Rifle

The only Krag not chambered for the .30-40 cartridge. It is chambered for the .22 rimfire and was designed as a target-practice rifle. It has a 30" barrel and is identical in exterior appearance to the Model 1898 Rifle. The receiver is marked the same as the standard model—with "Cal .22" added. There were approximately 840 manufactured in 1906 and 1907. Serial numbers are above 475,000.

Exc.	V.G.	Good	Fair	Poor
—	4500	2000	850	300

Model 1899 Carbine

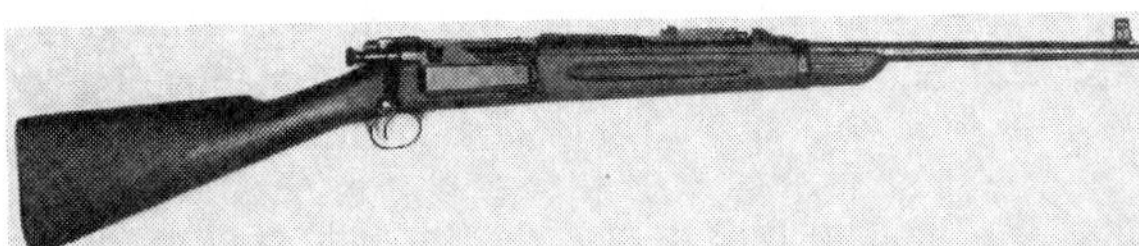

Courtesy Milwaukee Public Museum, Milwaukee, Wisconsin

The last of the Krags. It is similar to the 1898, with the "Model 1899" stamped on the receiver and a

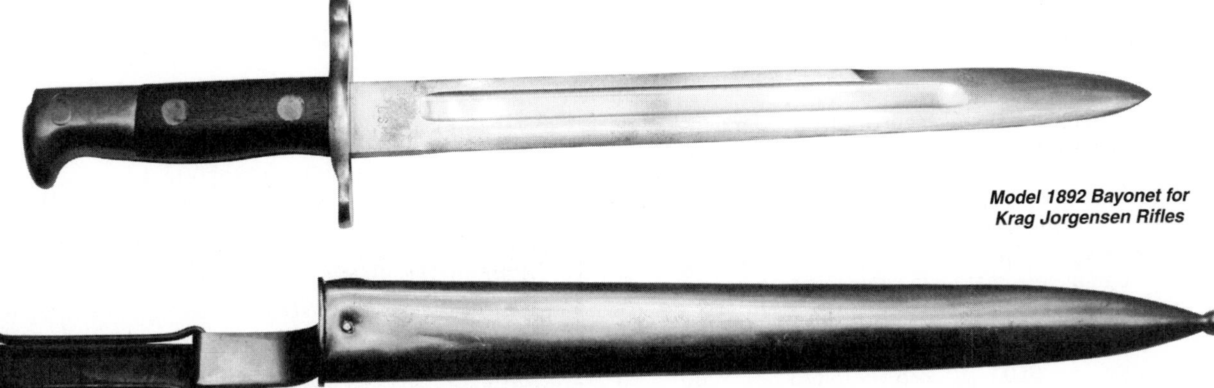

Model 1892 Bayonet for Krag Jorgensen Rifles

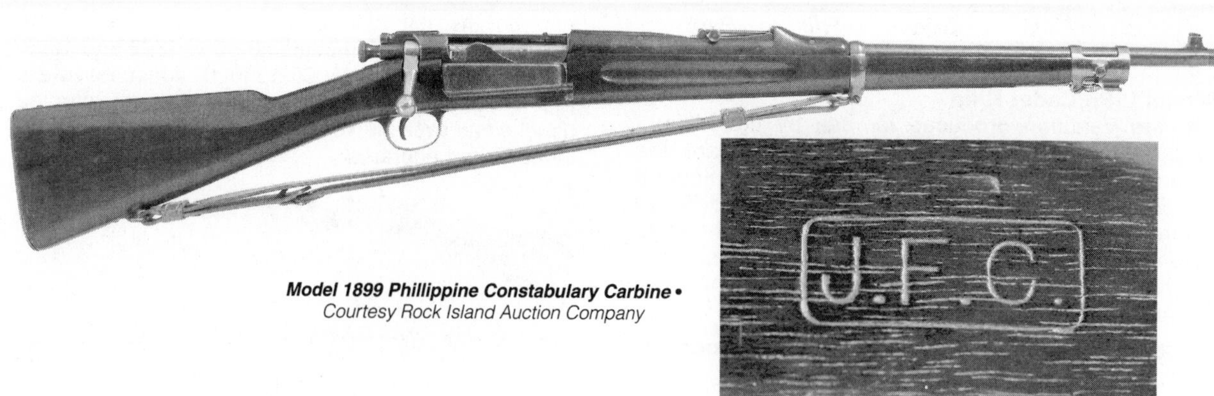

Model 1899 Phillippine Constabulary Carbine • Courtesy Rock Island Auction Company

2" longer stock. There were approximately 36,000 manufactured between 1900 and 1903. Serial numbers observed are between 222609 and 362256. These numbers are part of the Model 1898 rifle series.

Exc.	V.G.	Good	Fair	Poor
1850	1400	900	750	500

Krag Carbine • Courtesy Paul S. Scarlata

Model 1899 Philippine Constabulary Carbine

Approximately 8,000 modified to accept the knife bayonet at the Springfield Armory and the Rock Island Arsenal. The Springfield pieces are marked "J.F.C." on the stock. This model has a 22" barrel with the full, but shortened, stock of the rifle held on with two barrel bands. One must exercise extreme care as many rifles were altered in a similar manner at later dates.

Exc.	V.G.	Good	Fair	Poor
2750	2000	1500	750	500

NOTE: Prices are for verifiable samples.

Arsenal Conversions

In the 1920s, the Department of Civilian Marksmanship had a number of Krag rifles converted for their use. These are Model 1898 rifles shortened to 24" and fitted with Model 1899 Carbine stocks. Some of these rifles were also fitted with rifle stocks shortened to carbine length. These conversions are beginning to be regarded as legitimate variations by some collectors of Krag rifles.

Exc.	V.G.	Good	Fair	Poor
500	350	275	175	100

COLT

NOTE: For historical information, technical details, and photos, see Blake Stevens' and Edward Ezell's, *The Black Rifle: M16 Retrospective*, Collector Grade Publications, 1994.

Berdan Single Shot Rifle (M.1870)

This is a scarce rifle on today's market. There were approximately 30,200 manufactured, but nearly 30,000 of them were sent to Russia. This rifle was produced from 1866-1870. It is a trapdoor-type action chambered for .42 centerfire. The standard model has a 32.5" barrel; the carbine, 18.25". The finish is blued, with a walnut stock. This rifle was designed and the patent held by Hiram Berdan, Commander of the Civil War "Sharpshooters" Regiment. This was actually Colt's first cartridge arm. The 30,000 rifles and 25 half-stocked carbines that were sent to Russia were in Russian Cyrillic letters. The few examples made for American sales have Colt's name and Hartford address on the barrel.

NOTE: For information on Russian-built Berdan rifles, see *Russia, Rifles, Berdan.*

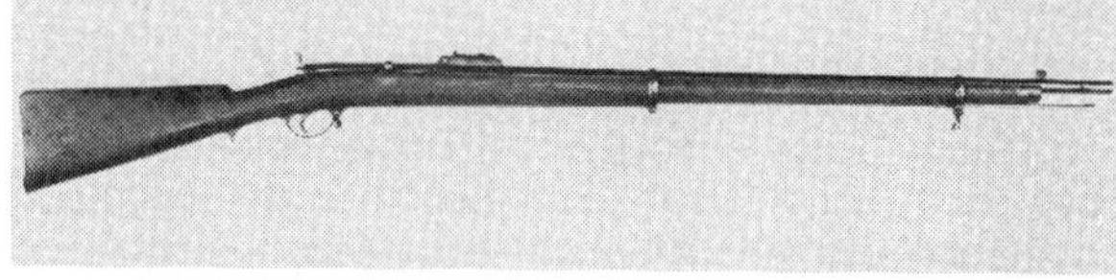

Courtesy Milwaukee Public Museum, Milwaukee, Wisconsin

Rifle Russian Order

30,000 manufactured.

Exc.	V.G.	Good	Fair	Poor
3500	2500	1200	450	—

Carbine Russian Order

25 manufactured.

Exc.	V.G.	Good	Fair	Poor
—	6000	3000	1250	—

Rifle U.S. Sales

100 manufactured.

Exc.	V.G.	Good	Fair	Poor
—	5000	2250	1250	—

Carbine U.S. Sales

25 manufactured.

Exc.	V.G.	Good	Fair	Poor
—	9500	4500	2000	—

M-6 Bayonet for M-14 Rifle

Colt-Franklin Military Rifle

This is a rifle that was not a successful venture for Colt. The patents were held by William B. Franklin, a vice-president of the company. This was a bolt-action rifle with a primitive, gravity-fed box magazine. It is chambered for the .45-70 government cartridge, has a 32.5" barrel, and is blued, with a walnut stock. The rifle has the Colt Hartford barrel address and is stamped with an eagle's head and U.S. inspector's marks. There were only 50 of these rifles produced, and it is believed that they were prototypes intended for government sales. This was not to be, and production ceased after approximately 50 were manufactured in 1887 and 1888.

Exc.	*V.G.*	*Good*	*Fair*	*Poor*
—	8500	4500	2000	—

Lightning Slide Action, Medium Frame

This was the first slide action rifle Colt produced. It is chambered for .32-20, .38-40, and .44-40, and was intended to be a companion piece to the SAAs in the same calibers. The rifle has a 26" barrel with 15-shot tube magazine; the carbine, a 20" barrel with 12-shot magazine. The finish is blued, with case-colored hammer; the walnut stock is oil-finished; and the forend is usually checkered. The Colt name and Hartford address are stamped on the barrel along with the patent dates. There were approximately 89,777 manufactured between 1884 and 1902. The military variant is listed below.

Military Rifle or Carbine

Chambered for .44-40 caliber, fitted with short magazine tube, bayonet lug, and sling swivels. These guns are fitted with various barrel lengths.

Exc.	*V.G.*	*Good*	*Fair*	*Poor*
—	4500	2000	1000	600

U.S. M14/M14E2

Based on the famous M1 Garand design this select fire rifle is chambered for the 7.62x51mm cartridge. It has a 21.8" barrel and a 20-round magazine. It weighs approximately 11.2 lbs. Rate of fire is about 750 rounds per minute. Marked "US RIFLE 7.62MM M14" on the rear top of the receiver. Production began in 1957 and ceased in 1963. Produced by Harrington & Richardson (537,512 total production) stamped "HRA," Springfield (167,172 total production) stamped "SA," Winchester (356,510 total production) stamped "66118" or "OM," and TRW (319,163 total production) stamped "TRW." The M14E2 version is a light machine gun variant with bipod, folding forward hand grip, and muzzle compensator.

NOTE: A sniper version of this rifle was designated the M21 and fitted with a Leatherwood telescope sight. *See that listing.*

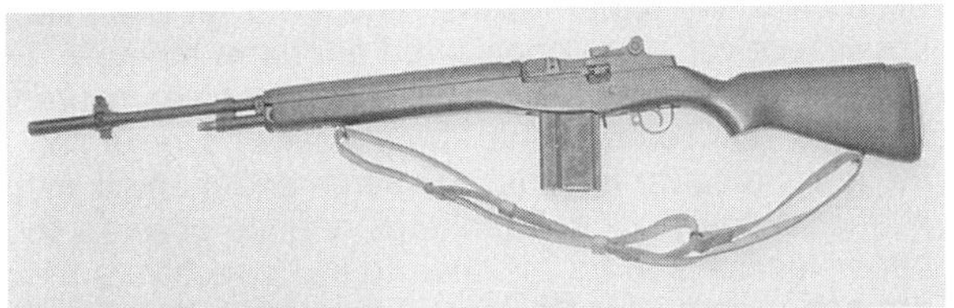

Courtesy Richard M. Kumor Sr.

Pre-1968

Exc.	*V.G.*	*Fair*
18000	14000	N/A

Pre-1986 conversions (or U.S. manufacture/M1A Springfield Armory)

Exc.	*V.G.*	*Fair*
8000	6000	N/A

The M14 in Vietnam

M16A1 with Colt AR-15 markings with M203 grenade launcher • *Paul Goodwin photo*

M-6 Bayonet for M-14 Rifle

Checkered black plastic grip. Muzzle ring. 6.7" single edge blade. Issued in the M8A1 scabbard. Price range 125 – 50.

M16 ASSAULT RIFLE

The M16 rifle has a great many variations and configurations. Some of these variations are available to the collector and others are so rare as to be, for practical purposes, unavailable to the collector. Nevertheless, we think it important to include as many variations as may be encountered by the collector. Some of the more common ones will be priced while others, because of their rarity, will not show a value. Keep in mind that the M16 series of rifles is comprised of two main parts: the upper receiver and lower receiver. The upper receiver is not considered a firearm by the ATF and is not registered. Nor is the upper receiver marked or serial numbered to the lower receiver. Conversely, the lower receiver is serial numbered and marked with its model designation. It is therefore quite possible for upper receivers to be matched to lower receivers that are not in an original factory configuration. In order to be factory original, both upper and lower receivers must be configured at the factory prior to shipment. This is sometimes impossible to determine. It is therefore highly recommended that an expert be consulted prior to a sale to help determine originality.

M16A2 MODIFICATIONS:

1. Flash suppressor is now a muzzle brake.
2. Barrel is heavier with rifle twist changed from 1 in 12 to 1 in 7.
3. Front sight is a square post adjustable for elevation.
4. Handguards are interchangeable ribbed top and bottom halves.
5. The circumference of the slip ring is now canted for a better grip.
6. Upper receiver is strengthened at the front attachment point to the lower receiver, as well as a fired case deflector behind the ejection port.
7. Completely redesigned fully adjustable rear sight.
8. Forward assist is now a round button type.
9. Pistol grip has a thumb swell and is made from stronger nylon with checkering on both sides.
10. Change lever is now, SAFE, SEMI, and BURST on most but not all A2 models.
11. The stock is stronger and 5/8" longer.
12. Buttplate is squared and checkered with internal storage cavity.

MODEL NOTE: On early models, the "A" suffix usually means it has a forward assist and the "B" suffix usually means it has a burst mechanism. Model numbers began with the 600 series, then the 700 series, which are based on the M16A2. The 800 series models are grenade launchers (M203). The 900 series models have flat top upper receivers and removable carry handles. The following are model designations with Colt nomenclature:
XM16 became the M16
XM16E1 became the M16A1
M16A1E1 became the M16A2
M16A2E4 became the M16A4

GRENADE LAUNCHER NOTE: M203 launchers will retail for about $4,500 NIB, Launchers made by AAI will bring $15,000 because of their rarity.

NOTE: As a general rule of thumb, "U.S. Property" marked guns will bring a premium, in some cases a substantial one, depending on model and configuration. These premiums will be so stated where applicable. The M16 was also produced by GM's Hydramatic division and Harrington & Richardson, Inc. Production began in late 1968. M16s from either manufacturer are rarely encountered. Rifles made by H&R will bring about 85 percent of a comparable Colt M16, while the Hydramatic rifles will bring almost double that of a Colt M16. This premium does not apply to rifles that have been re-welded.

Colt M16 NOTE: The Colt M16 comes in a variety of configurations (upper receivers), some of which are mentioned here. It is important to note that these configurations are based on the same lower receiver. In the case of civilian ownership, the lower receiver is the registered part of the firearm as far as the BATF is concerned. Therefore, it is possible, with a registered lower receiver, to interchange upper receiver components to a wide variety of different configurations from 9mm to .223 LMG uppers. Be aware that this interchangeability works best with Colt parts.

Early AR-15 Model 01 • Paul Goodwin photo

Bibliographical Note: For a full and complete description with photos, see Dan Shea's *Machine Gun Dealers Bible*, 4th edition, Moose Lake Publishing. See Blake Stevens and Edward Ezell, *The Black Rifle, M16 Retrospective*, Collector Grade Publications, for an in-depth examination of the history and development of the M16. Since the 2nd edition of this book a new publication by Christopher R. Bartocci, *Black Rifle II:The M16 into the 21st Century*. Collector Grade Publications, 2004 is highly recommended.

600 Series

Colt/Armalite AR-15/M16 Model 601

This rifle was first produced in 1960 with many variants following. Chambered for the 5.56x45mm cartridge it has a 20.8" barrel with flash hider. Magazine capacity is 20 or 30 rounds. Weight is 7 lbs. Rate of fire is 800 rounds per minute. Used extensively in Vietnam and now throughout the world. Some were marked "COLT AR-15 PROPERTY OF US GOVT.M16 CAL 5.56MM" on left side of magazine housing, but early guns were not marked "US Property." There is a wide variation in prices and models. Prices listed below are for the standard Colt/Armalite rifle.

NOTE: For Armalite only marked rifles no price given because of rarity. For Colt only marked rifles deduct $2,000.

AR-15 markings • Courtesy James Alley

Pre-1968

Exc.	*V.G.*	*Fair*
20000	18500	17500

Colt Model 602

This U.S. ("US Property") model was fitted with a 20" barrel. It has no forward assist. Select fire in full or semi-auto.

Colt Model 603 (M16A1)

This U.S. ("US Property") model has a 20" barrel with forward assist. Barrel has a 1 in 12 twist rate. Select fire in full or semi-auto.

Pre-1968

Exc.	*V.G.*	*Fair*
18500	17000	15000

Colt Model 604 (M16)

This U.S. ("US Property") Air Force model has a 20" barrel with a 1 in 12 twist. No forward assist. Select fire in full and semi-auto.

Pre-1968

Exc.	*V.G.*	*Fair*
18000	17000	15000

Colt Model 605A CAR-15 Carbine

This U.S. ("US Property") version is the short barrel (10") version of the rifle with a forward assist. A select fire in full and semi-auto.

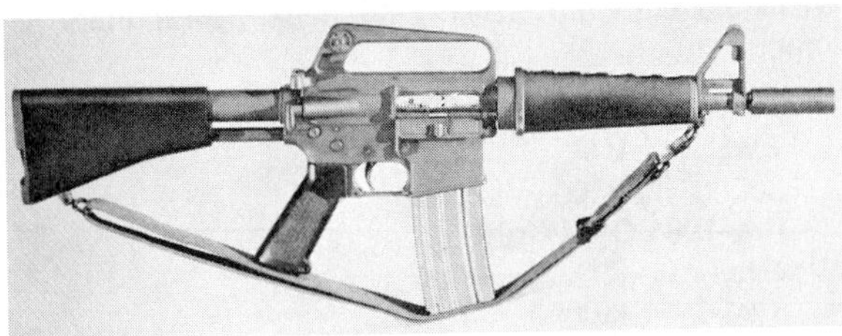

CAR-15 • Courtesy James Alley

Pre-1968

Exc.	*V.G.*	*Fair*
22000	20000	18500

Pre-1986 OEM/Colt

Exc.	*V.G.*	*Fair*
N/A	N/A	N/A

Colt Model 605B

This U.S. ("US Property") version is the same as above but with semi-auto, full auto, and burst (3-round) select fire. No forward assist.

Colt Survival Rifle Model 608 • *Courtesy James Alley*

Pre-1968

Exc.	V.G.	Fair
22000	20000	18500

Colt Model 606

This is the export version of the Model 616.

Pre-1968

Exc.	V.G.	Fair
18000	17000	16500

Colt Model 606B

As above, but with burst version.

Pre-1968

Exc.	V.G.	Fair
18000	17000	16500

Colt Model 607

This U.S. ("US Property") version is an SMG with sliding buttstock and 10" barrel. Designed for use by tank, helicopter, and APC crews. Length with stock closed is 26", with stock extended about 28.7". Weight is about 5.3 lbs.

Pre-1968

Exc.	V.G.	Fair
20000	18000	17500

Colt Model 608 Survival Rifle

This rifle was built in prototype only and its design was for use by aviation personnel. Fitted with a 10" barrel, cone shaped flash suppressor, short fixed buttstock, round handguard, no forward assist, no bayonet lug, and short pistol grip. Overall length is 29". Weight was slightly more than 4.7 lbs. Designed to be broken down to fit the standard USAF seat pack. Fewer than 10 manufactured.

Pre-1968

Exc.	V.G.	Fair
30000	29000	28500

Pre-1986 OEM/Colt

Exc.	V.G.	Fair
N/A	N/A	N/A

Colt Model 609 (XM177E1)

This is a U.S. Army version of the Commando with an 11.5" barrel with a 1 in 12 twist rate. This model has a forward assist. Select fire in full auto or semi-auto.

Pre-1968

Exc.	V.G.	Fair
25000	22500	21500

Colt Model 610 (GAU-5/A)

This is the U.S. Air Force version of the XM177 Commando with 10" barrel with 1 in 12 twist and no forward assist. Select fire in full auto or semi-auto.

Pre-1968

Exc.	V.G.	Fair
25000	22500	21500

Colt Model 613

This is export version of the 603.

Pre-1968

Exc.	V.G.	Fair
15000	12500	10500

Colt Model 614

This is the export version of the Model 604.

Pre-1968

Exc.	V.G.	Fair
15000	12500	10500

Colt Model 616

This U.S. ("US Property") version is fitted with a 20" heavy barrel with 1 in 12 twist rate. No forward assist. Select fire in full auto or semi-auto.

Pre-1968

Exc.	V.G.	Fair
20000	18500	17500

Colt Model 619

This is the export version of the 609.

Pre-1968

Exc.	V.G.	Fair
20000	18500	17500

Markings for U.S. property for Commando model • *Courtesy James Alley*

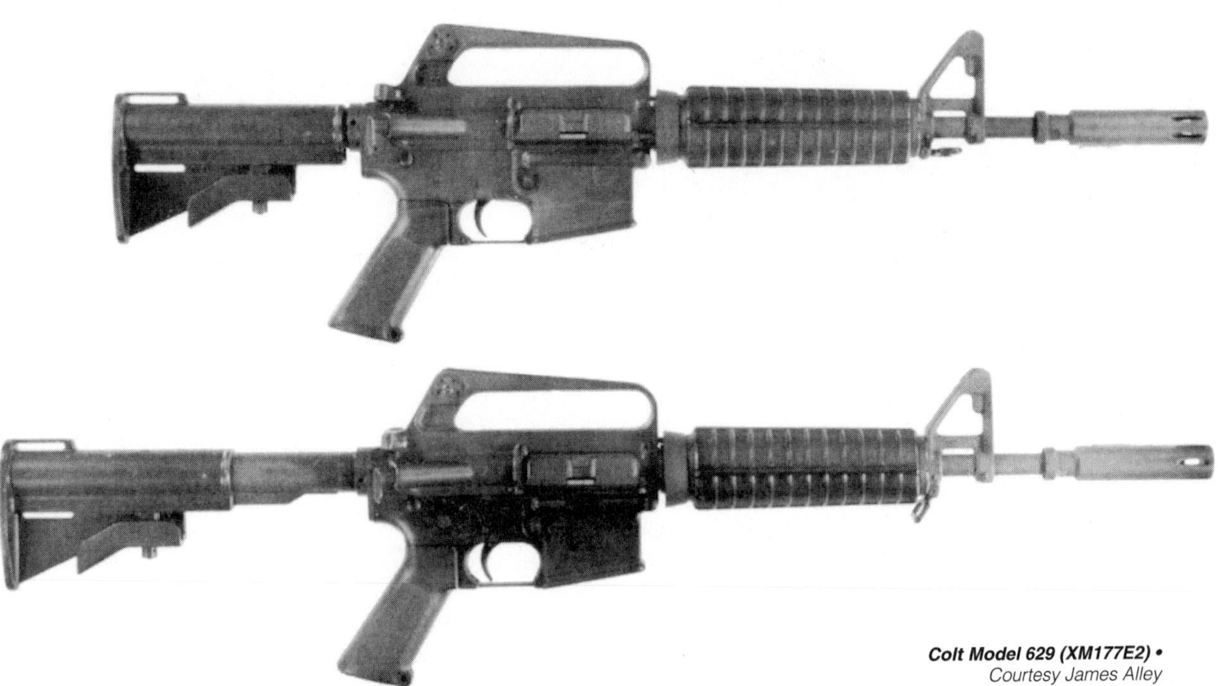

***Colt Model 629 (XM177E2)** • Courtesy James Alley*

Colt Model 621

This U.S. ("US Property") version is fitted with a 20" heavy barrel with 1 in 12 twist. It is fitted with a forward assist. Select fire in full auto or semi-auto.

Pre-1968

Exc.	*V.G.*	*Fair*
20000	18500	17500

Colt Model 629 (XM177E2)

This is the U.S. Army version of the Commando with 11.5" barrel with 1 in 12 twist. Sliding butt stock. Fitted with a forward assist. Select fire in full auto or semi-auto. Equipped with a 4.5" flash suppressor. Weight is about 6.2 lbs without magazine.

Pre-1968

Exc.	*V.G.*	*Fair*
25000	22500	21000

Colt Model 630 (GAU-5/A/B)

This is the U.S. Air Force version of the XM177E1 with 11.5" barrel with 1 in 12 twist. No forward assist. Select fire in full auto or semi-auto.

Pre-1968

Exc.	*V.G.*	*Fair*
25000	22500	21000

Colt Model 639

This is the export version of the Model 629.

Pre-1968

Exc.	*V.G.*	*Fair*
20000	18500	17500

Colt Model 645 (M16A2)

This model is an improved variation of the M16A1 Standard rifle with a 1 in 7 barrel twist and a heavier 20" barrel. A case deflector is mounted on the right side. Sights are an improved version of the standard M16 type. Forward assist. Improved flash suppressor, buttstock, and pistol grip. First produced in 1982. *See list of M16A2 modifications on prior page.*

Pre-1968

Exc.	*V.G.*	*Fair*
N/A	N/A	N/A

Pre-1986 OEM/Colt

Exc.	*V.G.*	*Fair*
16000	15000	14000

Colt Model 646 (M16A3)

This is the U.S. ("US Property") version of the M16A3 except that there is no 3-round burst but full auto and semi-auto.

Colt Model 649 (GAU-5/A/A)

This is the U.S. Air Force version of the XM177E2 with 11.5" barrel with 1 in 12 twist rate and no forward assist. Select fire with full auto and semi-auto. Equipped with a 4.5" flash suppressor.

Pre-1968

Exc.	*V.G.*	*Fair*
25000	22500	21500

Colt Model 651

This is the export version of the rifle with 14.5" barrel.

Pre-1968

Exc.	*V.G.*	*Fair*
20000	18500	17500

Colt Model 652

This is the export version of the rifle with 14.5" barrel and no forward assist.

Pre-1968

Exc.	*V.G.*	*Fair*
15000	14000	13000

Colt Model 653

This is the export version of the rifle with 14.5" barrel and sliding buttstock.

Pre-1968

Exc.	*V.G.*	*Fair*
15000	14000	13000

Model 711 • Courtesy James Alley

Colt Model 655 (Sniper)

This was a U.S. ("US Property") prototype version with a 20" barrel with a 1 in 9 twist rate. It has a forward assist. The upper receiver has a high profile scope mount and was to have been fitted with a Leatherwood Realist scope and Sionics suppressor. Select fire with full auto or semi-auto.

Colt Model 656 (Sniper)

Same as above but with a special low profile upper receiver with no carry handle and low profile scope mount.

700 Series–Export Versions of the M16A2

NOTE: A2 Military serial number are in the 6000000 range and A2 Civilian models are in the 8000000.

Colt Model 701 Export Rifle

This is the M16A2 with 20" barrel and all the A2 features. Weight is about 7.5 lbs.

Colt Model 703 Test Model

This is a test model with a gas piston designated the M703/16A2. Test model used an AK type bolt and carrier. Test model is not priced.

Colt Model 703 Export Rifle

(There are two different types of 703s. Colt used the same model designation twice. See above.) Select fire with semi, 3-round burst, and full auto. The Export Model is an M16A2 style rifle.

Pre-1968

Exc.	*V.G.*	*Fair*
N/A	N/A	N/A

Pre-1986 OEM/Colt

Exc.	*V.G.*	*Fair*
18500	17500	16500

Colt Model 707 Export rifle

This is a M16A2 with 20" A1 style barrel with 1-in-7 twist rate. Select fire with semi, 3-round burst. Weight is about 7.5 lbs.

Pre-1968

Exc.	*V.G.*	*Fair*
N/A	N/A	N/A

Pre-1986 conversions

Exc.	*V.G.*	*Fair*
18500	17500	16500

NOTE: For OEM A1 add 40 percent.

Colt Model 711 Export Rifle

This model is the same as the M16A2 but fitted with M16A1 sights and standard weight M16A1 barrel.

Pre-1968

Exc.	*V.G.*	*Fair*
N/A	N/A	N/A

Pre-1986 conversions

Exc.	*V.G.*	*Fair*
16500	15500	15000

NOTE: For OEM A1 add 40 percent.

Colt Model 713 Export Rifle

This model is fitted with an M16A1 upper receiver with case deflector 20" A1 barrel with 1 in 7 twist. Buttstock is A2 type. The compensator is A2 type with A2 lower receiver with select fire in semi and 3-round burst. Weight is about 7 lbs.

Pre-1968

Exc.	*V.G.*	*Fair*
N/A	N/A	N/A

Pre-1986 conversions

Exc.	*V.G.*	*Fair*
16500	15500	15000

NOTE: For OEM A1 add 40 percent.

Colt Model 723 Export Carbine

This model is an M16A2 carbine with lightweight 14.5" barrel, M16A1 sights, and telescoping stock. Select fire in semi-auto and full auto.

Pre-1968

Exc.	*V.G.*	*Fair*
N/A	N/A	N/A

Pre-1986 conversions

Exc.	*V.G.*	*Fair*
18500	17500	16500

NOTE: For OEM A1 add 40 percent.

Colt Model 725 Export Carbine

Same as the Model 723 but with semi-auto and three-round burst select fire.

Pre-1968

Exc.	*V.G.*	*Fair*
N/A	N/A	N/A

Pre-1986 conversions

Exc.	*V.G.*	*Fair*
17500	16500	15500

NOTE: For OEM A1 add 40 percent.

M16A2 Model 723 and Model 733 • Courtesy James Alley

Colt Model 727 Carbine

This is the M16A2 version of the M4 Carbine. Fitted with a 14.5" barrel capable of accepting the M203 grenade launcher. Rifling twist is 1 in 7. Sliding buttstock. Rate of fire is 700 to 950 rounds per minute. Select fire in semi-auto and full auto. Weight is about 5.65 lbs without magazine.

Pre-1968

Exc.	*V.G.*	*Fair*
N/A	N/A	N/A

Pre-1986 conversions

Exc.	*V.G.*	*Fair*
18500	17500	16500

NOTE: For OEM A1 add 40 percent.

Colt Model 733 Export Commando

This model is the M16A2 Commando with an 11.5" barrel, M16A1 sight, telescoping butt.

Pre-1968

Exc.	*V.G.*	*Fair*
N/A	N/A	N/A

Pre-1986 OEM/Colt

Exc.	*V.G.*	*Fair*
20000	18500	17500

Colt Model 741 Export Heavy Barrel

This is an M16A2 with 20" heavy barrel that is magazine fed. Designed as a SAW (Squad Automatic Weapon). Weight is about 10 lbs.

Pre-1968

Exc.	*V.G.*	*Fair*
N/A	N/A	N/A

Pre-1986 conversions

Exc.	*V.G.*	*Fair*
18500	17500	16500

NOTE: For OEM A1 add 40 percent.

M16A2 Model 727 • Courtesy James Alley

Colt Model 750 LMG (See *U.S., Machine Guns*)

Colt Model 720 M4 (Original Version)

This is a short barrel version of the M16 with collapsible stock. Chambered for 5.56x45mm cartridge. It is fitted with a 14.5" barrel and has a magazine capacity of 20 or 30 rounds. Its rate of fire is 800 rounds per minute. Weight is about 5.6 lbs. Marked "COLT FIREARMS DIVISION COLT INDUSTRIES HARTFORD CONN USA" on the left side of the receiver, with "COLT M4 CAL 5.56MM" on the left side of the magazine housing. In use with American military forces as well as several South American countries.

Courtesy private NFA collection

Pre-1968

Exc.	*V.G.*	*Fair*
N/A	N/A	N/A

Pre-1986 conversions or OEM/Colt (Rare)

Exc.	*V.G.*	*Fair*
25000	22500	21500

900 Series

Colt Model 920—M4

This model is the current U.S. ("US Property") version of the flat top carbine with 14.5" barrel with a 1 in 7 twist rate, forward assist, sliding buttstock, and A2 improvements. Select fire with 3-round burst and semi-auto.

Colt Model 921—M4A1

This U.S. ("US Property") model is the same as the Model 920, except it is full auto with no burst feature.

Copyright by Colt Defense LLC. used with permission, all rights reserved, Courtesy Blake Stevens,* Black Rifle II*, Collector Grade Publications

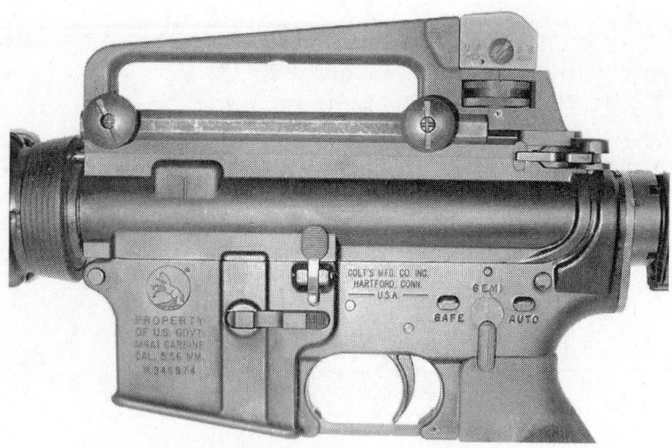

Close-up of Colt M4A1 carbine • *Copyright by Colt Defense LLC. used with permission, all rights reserved, Courtesy Blake Stevens,* Black Rifle II*, Collector Grade Publications*

Colt Model 945—M16A4

This U.S. ("US Property") version is the flat top version of the M16A2.

Specialty Series

Colt CAR-15 Model M1 Heavy Assault Rifle

This was a prototype with a heavy AR-15 20" barrel. Fires from a closed bolt. Uses standard M16 magazines. Weight without magazine is about 7.6 lbs. Semi or full auto fire. Rate of fire is approximately 800 to 850 rounds per minute.

Colt CAR-15 Model M2 Belt-fed Heavy Assault Rifle

Similar to the M1 version with the addition of a removable belt feeding mechanism designed by Rob Roy. Weight is about 8.3 lbs. Also feeds from standard M16 magazines. Less than 20 M2s were built.

Pre-1968

Exc.	*V.G.*	*Fair*
N/A	N/A	N/A

Pre-1986 OEM/Colt

Exc.	*V.G.*	*Fair*
35000+	—	—

Colt M231 Firing Port Weapon

This gun was never assigned a Colt model number but was fitted with a 15.6" barrel and a 1 in 12 twist rate. It fired from an open bolt in full auto only. It had no sights

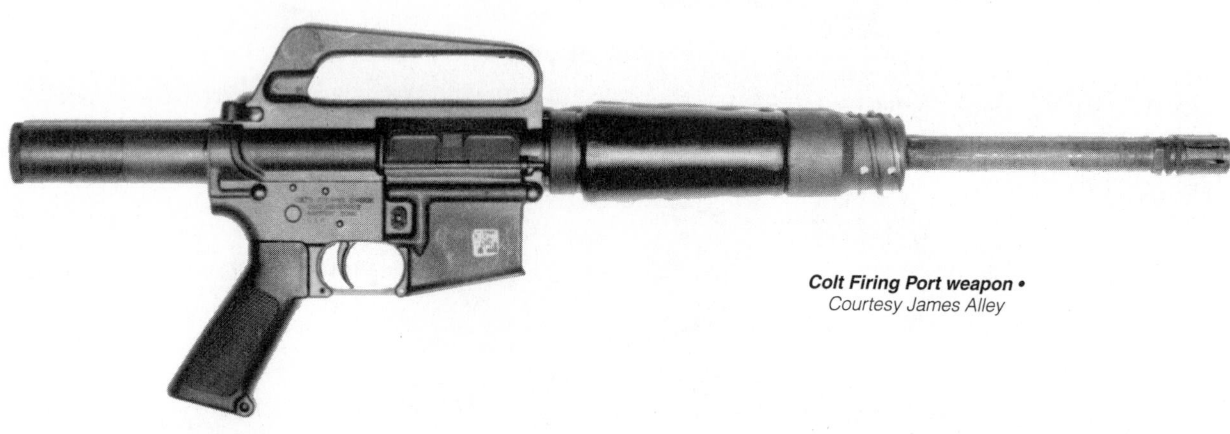

Colt Firing Port weapon • *Courtesy James Alley*

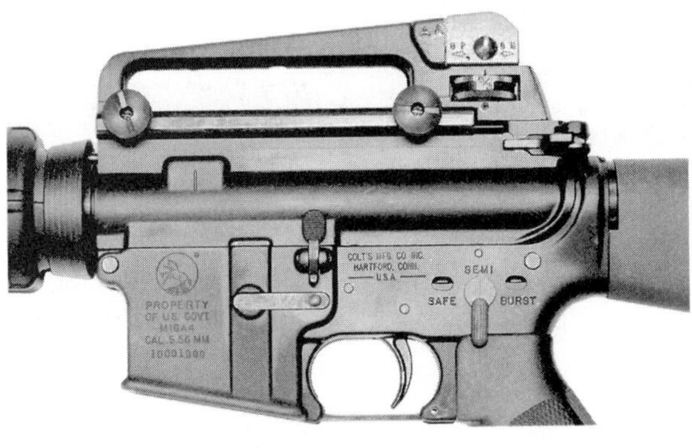

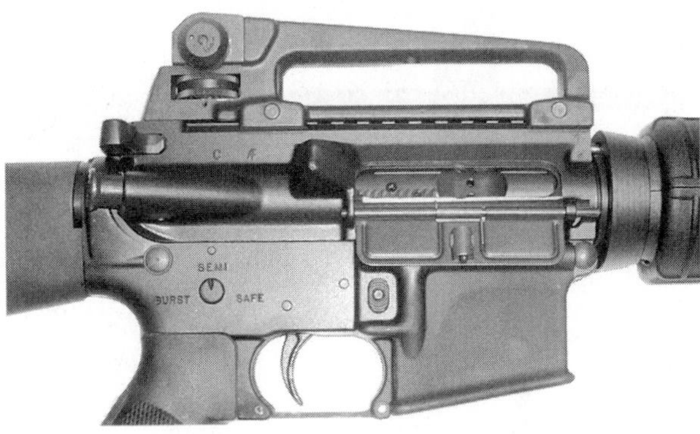

Close-up of left side of M16A4 receiver • *Copyright by Colt Defense LLC. used with permission, all rights reserved, Courtesy Blake Stevens,* ***Black Rifle II****, Collector Grade Publications*

Model M1 Heavy Assault Rifle • *Courtesy James Alley*

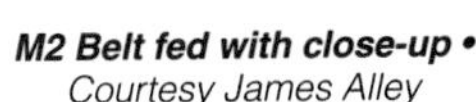

M2 Belt fed with close-up • *Courtesy James Alley*

UNITED STATES OF AMERICA

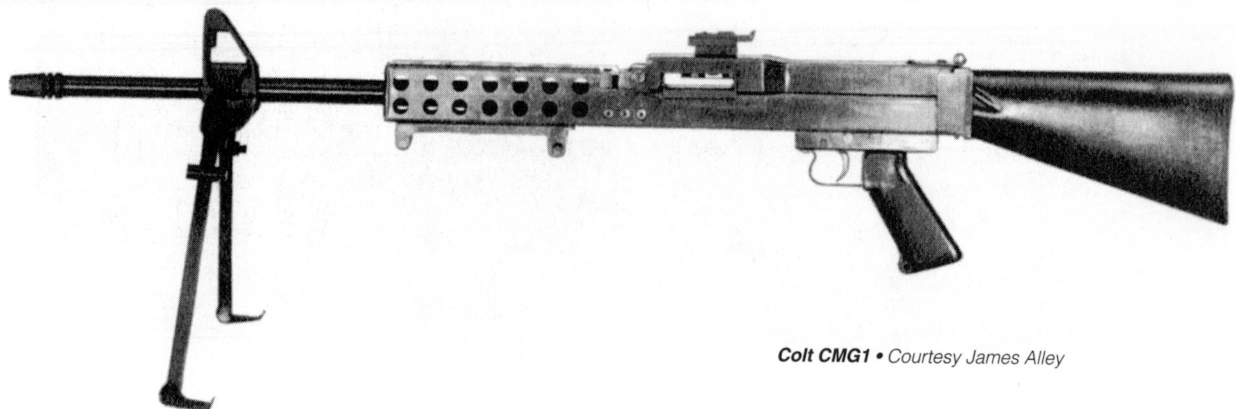

Colt CMG1 • Courtesy James Alley

or buttstock. All original Colt firing port guns have an "F" prefix as part of the serial number and are marked "US PROPERTY."

Pre-1968

Exc.	*V.G.*	*Fair*
N/A	N/A	N/A

Pre-1968 OEM/Colt

Exc.	*V.G.*	*Fair*
22000	20000	18500

Colt ACR Advanced Combat rifle

This model was built in prototype only and was designed to fire special duplex cartridges. It was fitted with a 20" barrel, flattop receiver with special rib designed by Aberdeen Human Engineering Labs. It has a sliding buttstock with a hydraulic buffer. Select fire in full auto or semi-auto.

Pre-1968

Exc.	*V.G.*	*Fair*
N/A	N/A	N/A

Pre-1986 OEM/Colt

Exc.	*V.G.*	*Fair*

Too Rare To Price

Colt CMG-1

One prototype was built of this model. It was a belt-fed light machine gun designed by Rob Roy and fitted with a 20" barrel with a 1-in-12 twist. Rate of fire of 650 rounds per minute. Weight is about 12.5 lbs. Fires from an open bolt. Designed to be used as a tripod mount, bipod mount, vehicle mount, or solenoid fixed machine gun.

Colt CMG-2

This was an improved version of the CMG-1 designed by George Curtis and Henry Tatro. Approximately 6 were produced, 5 in 5.56 NATO and 1-in-7.62 NATO. It was fitted with a 20" quick change barrel with a 1 in 8.87" twist for the 68 grain GX-6235 bullet. Hydraulic buffer in buttstock. Bipod. Weight was about 15 lbs. Cycle rate is about 650 rounds per minute. It is fed by a 150-round belt fed drum magazine. These prototypes were built by Colt between 1967 and 1969.

Pre-1968

Exc.	*V.G.*	*Fair*
N/A	N/A	N/A

Pre-1986 OEM/Colt

Exc.	*V.G.*	*Fair*
40000+	—	—

NOTE: There is little in the way of sales history, though there have been guns offered for sale in the $40,000 to $75,000 range on rare occasions.

M16 Rimfire Conversion Kits

There are several different conversion kits featuring different designs both adapted by the U.S. military. Both of these kits use a 10-round magazine but are not interchangeable with each other. The first is the Rodman design, known as the Air Force Model, built by OK Industries, New Britain, CT and the second is the M261 built by the Maremont Corp., Saco, ME. TM 9-6920-363-12 was issued with the M261 conversion kit. The Atchisson Mark I and Mark II kits and the Atchisson Mark III made by Jonathan Ciener, Inc., are

Colt CMG2 • Courtesy James Alley

M-7 Bayonet marked "Colt"

also used by military forces in the U.S. as well as by foreign governments. The Ciener kit was introduced about 1988 and is designed to be used in both the M16 and AR15 rifles, both semi-automatic fire and full auto fire. Rate of fire is between 700 and 800 rounds per minute in the M16.

NOTE: Colt built a conversion kit produced for commercial sale but this kit was not adopted by the military.

Ciener Kit Mark III

Exc.	*V.G.*	*Good*	*Fair*	*Poor*
200	150	—	—	—

M-7 Bayonet for M-16 Rifle

Checkered black plastic grip. Large muzzle ring to fit over flash hider. 6.5" single edge blade. Made by several contractors. Issued in the M8A1 scabbard. Price range 50 – 25.

M-7 Bayonet Marked "Colt"

As above, but made in Germany by Carl Eickhorn for Colt. Made for commercial sales of the M-16 series. Not military issue. Price range 250 –150.

M-9 Bayonet for M-16A2

Metal handle. Muzzle ring. 7.2" single edge blade. Plastic scabbard has sharpening stone on back. There is a wire cutting feature like that on the Russian AKM series. Price range 200 – 100125.

AR-15 Series

AR-15 Sporter (Model #6000)

A semi-automatic rifle firing from a closed bolt was introduced into the Colt product line in 1964. Similar in appearance and function to the military version, the M-16. Chambered for the .223 cartridge. It is fitted with a standard 20" barrel with no forward assist, no case deflector, but with a bayonet lug. Weighs about 7.5 lbs. Dropped from production in 1985.

NIB	*Exc.*	*V.G.*	*Good*	*Fair*	*Poor*
2100	1500	1100	700	600	400

M-9 Bayonet for M-16A2

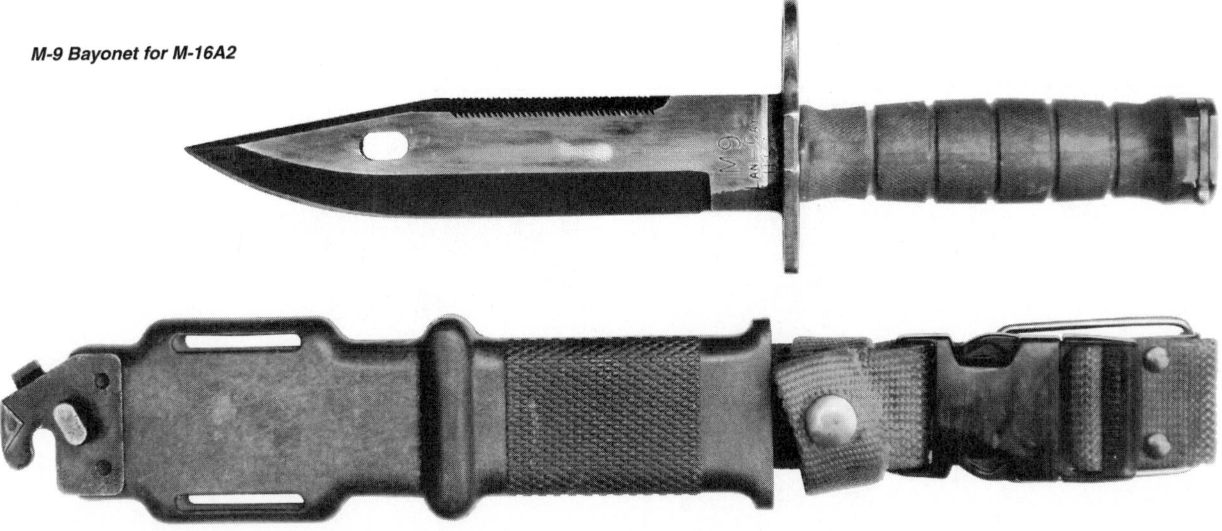

Copyright by Colt Defense LLC. used with permission, all rights reserved, Courtesy Blake Stevens, *Black Rifle II*, Collector Grade Publications

AR-15 Sporter w/Collapsible Stock (Model #6001)

Same as above but fitted with a 16" barrel and sliding stock. Weighs approximately 5.8 lbs. Introduced in 1978 and discontinued in 1985.

NIB	Exc.	V.G.	Good	Fair	Poor
2150	1600	1200	800	600	400

AR-15 Carbine (Model #6420)

Introduced in 1985 this model has a 16" standard weight barrel. All other features are the same as the previous discontinued AR-15 models. This version was dropped from the Colt product line in 1987.

NIB	Exc.	V.G.	Good	Fair	Poor
1600	1250	1000	800	N/A	N/A

AR-15 9mm Carbine (Model #6450)

Copyright by Colt Defense LLC. used with permission, all rights reserved, Courtesy Blake Stevens, *Black Rifle II*, Collector Grade Publications

Same as above but chambered for 9mm cartridge. Weighs 6.3 lbs.

NIB	Exc.	V.G.	Good	Fair	Poor
1600	1250	1000	800	N/A	N/A

AR-15A2 (Model #6500)

Introduced in 1984, this was an updated version with a heavier barrel and forward assist. The AR sight was still utilized. Weighs approximately 7.8 lbs.

NIB	Exc.	V.G.	Good	Fair	Poor
1500	1100	900	800	N/A	N/A

AR-15A2 Govt. Model Carbine (Model #6520)

Added to the Colt line in 1988, this 16" standard barrel carbine featured for the first time a case deflector, forward assist, and the improved A2 rear sight. This model is fitted with a 4-position telescoping buttstock. Weighs about 5.8 lbs.

NIB	Exc.	V.G.	Good	Fair	Poor
1600	1250	1000	800	N/A	N/A

AR-15A2 Gov't. Model (Model #6550)

This model was introduced in 1988; it is the rifle equivalent to the Carbine. It features a 20" A2 barrel, forward assist, case deflector, but still retains the bayonet lug. Weighs about 7.5 lbs. Discontinued in 1990.

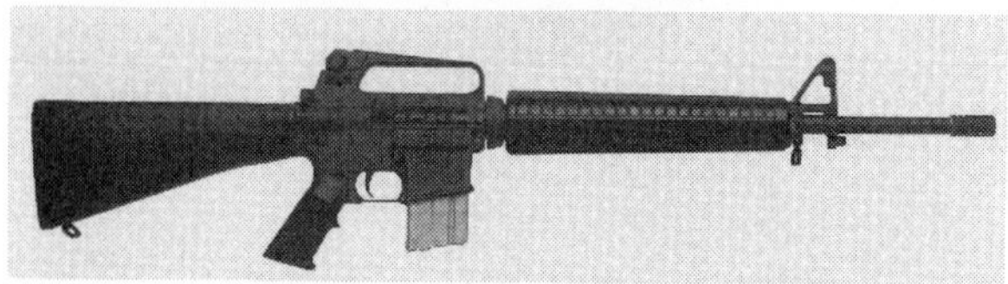

NIB	Exc.	V.G.	Good	Fair	Poor
1600	1250	1000	800	N/A	N/A

AR-15A2 H-Bar (Model #6600)

Introduced in 1986, this version features a special 20" heavy barrel. All other features are the same as the A2 series of AR15s. Discontinued in 1991. Weighs about 8 lbs.

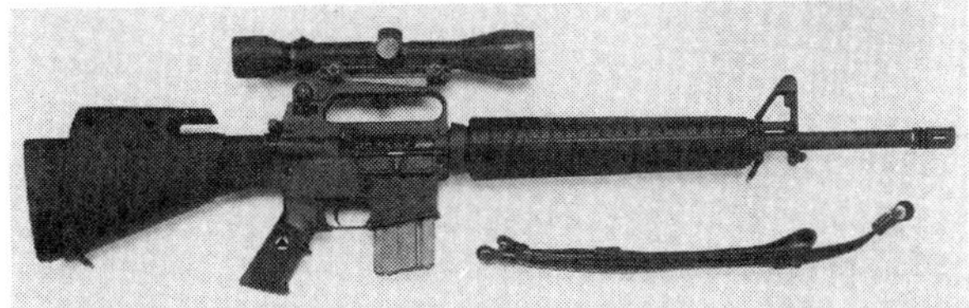

NIB	Exc.	V.G.	Good	Fair	Poor
1600	1250	1000	800	N/A	N/A

AR-15A2 Delta H-Bar (Model #6600DH)

Same as above but fitted with a 3x9 Tasco scope and detachable cheekpiece. Dropped from the Colt line in 1990. Weighs about 10 lbs. Equipped with a metal carrying case.

NIB	Exc.	V.G.	Good	Fair	Poor
2000	1800	1500	1250	N/A	N/A

Sporter Lightweight Rifle

This lightweight model has a 16" barrel and is finished in a matte black. It is available in either a .223 Rem. caliber (Model #6530) that weighs 6.7 lbs., a Model #6430 w/A1 sights, 9mm caliber weighing 7.1 lbs., or a Model #6830 7.65x39mm that weighs 7.3 lbs. The .223 is furnished with two five-round box magazines as is the 9mm and 7.65x39mm. A cleaning kit and sling are also supplied with each new rifle. The buttstock and pistol grip are made of durable nylon and the handguard is reinforced fiberglass and aluminum lined. The rear sight is adjustable for windage and elevation. These newer models are referred to simply as Sporters and are not fitted with a bayonet lug and the receiver block has different size pins.

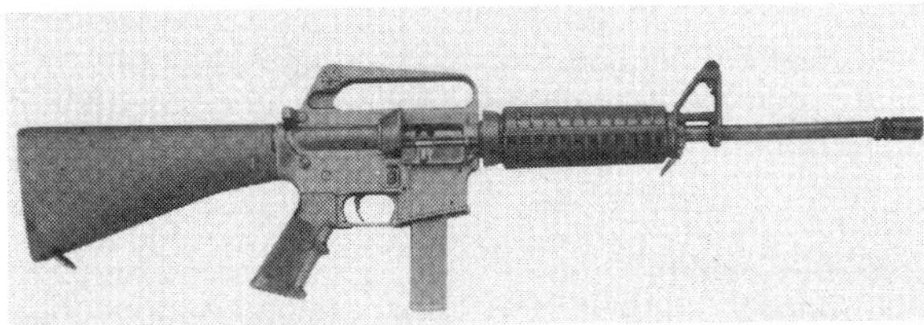

NIB	Exc.	V.G.	Good	Fair	Poor
1100	900	750	600	N/A	N/A

Sporter Target Model Rifle (Model #6551)

This 1991 model is a full size version of the Lightweight Rifle. The Target Rifle weighs 7.5 lbs. and has a 20" barrel. Offered in .223 Rem. caliber only with target sights adjustable to 800 meters. New rifles are furnished with two 5-round box magazines, sling, and cleaning kit. Same as the Model 6550 except for a rib around the magazine release.

NIB	Exc.	V.G.	Good	Fair	Poor
1350	1200	850	700	N/A	N/A

Copyright by Colt Defense LLC. used with permission, all rights reserved, Courtesy Blake Stevens,* Black Rifle II, *Collector Grade Publications

Sporter Match H-Bar (Model #6601)

This 1991 variation of the AR-15 is similar to the Target Model but has a 20" heavy barrel chambered for the .223 caliber. This model weighs 8 lbs. and has A2 sights adjustable out to 800 meters. Supplied with two 5-round box magazines, sling, and cleaning kit.

NIB	Exc.	V.G.	Good	Fair	Poor
1350	1200	850	700	N/A	N/A

Sporter Match Delta H-Bar (Model #6601 DH)

Same as above but supplied with a 3x9 Tasco scope. Has a black detachable cheekpiece and metal carrying case. Weighs about 10 lbs. Discontinued in 1992. Deduct 150 if there is no scope or hard case.

NIB	Exc.	V.G.	Good	Fair	Poor
1500	1350	1200	1000	N/A	N/A

Match Target H-BAR Compensated (Model MT6601C)

Same as the regular Sporter H-BAR with the addition of a compensator.

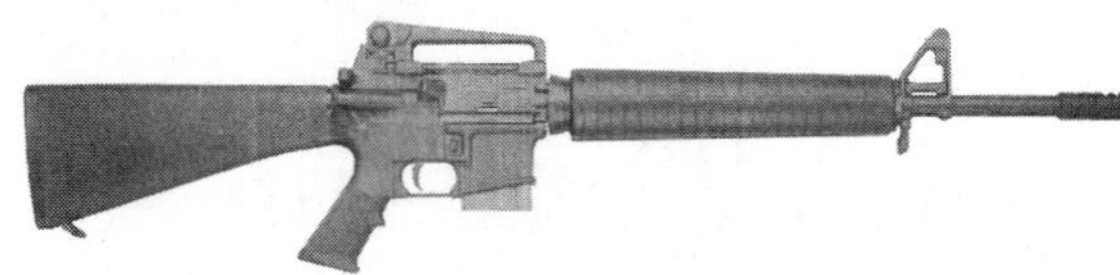

NIB	Exc.	V.G.	Good	Fair	Poor
1350	1200	850	700	N/A	N/A

Sporter Competition H-Bar (Model #6700)

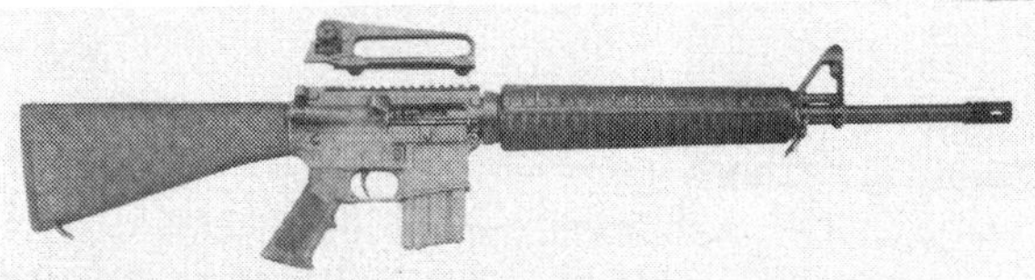

Introduced in 1992, the Competition H-Bar is available in .223 caliber with a 20" heavy barrel counterbored for accuracy. The carry handle is detachable with A2 sights. With the carry handle removed the upper receiver is dovetailed and grooved for Weaver-style scope rings.

Colt AR-15 and Colt Sporter Terminology

There are three different and distinct manufacturing cycles that not only affect the value of these rifles but also the legal consequences of their modifications.

Pre-Ban Colt AR-15 rifles (Pre-1989): Fitted with bayonet lug, flash hider, and stamped AR-15 on lower receiver. Rifles that are NIB have a green label. It is legal to modify this rifle with any AR-15 upper receiver. These are the most desirable models because of their pre-ban features.

Colt Sporters (Post-1989-pre-September, 1994): This transition model may or may not have a bayonet lug, but it does have a flash hider. There is no AR-15 designation stamped on the lower receiver. Rifles that are NIB have a blue label. It is legal to modify this rifle with upper receivers made after 1989, i.e., preban. These rifles are less desirable than pre-ban AR15s.

Colt Sporters (Post-September, 1994): This rifle has no bayonet lug, no flash hider, and does not have the AR-15 designation stamped on the lower receiver. Rifles that are NIB have a blue label. It is legal to modify this rifle only with upper receivers manufactured after September 1994. These rifles are the least desirable of the three manufacturing periods because of their lack of pre-ban military features and current manufacture status.

This model weighs approximately 8.5 lbs. New rifles are furnished with two 5-round box magazines, sling, and cleaning kit.

NIB	Exc.	V.G.	Good	Fair	Poor
1200	1100	950	850	N/A	N/A

Sporter Competition H-Bar Select w/scope (Model #6700CH)

This variation, also new in 1992, is identical to the Sporter Competition with the addition of a factory mounted scope. The rifle has also been selected for accuracy and comes complete with a 3-9X Tasco rubber armored variable scope, scope mount, carry handle with iron sights, and nylon carrying case.

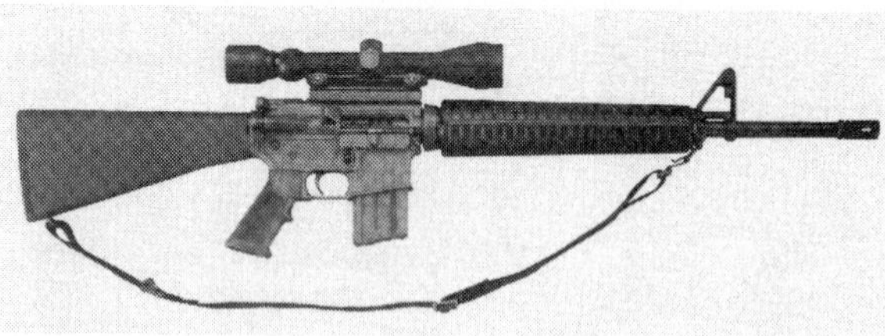

NIB	Exc.	V.G.	Good	Fair	Poor
1350	1200	850	700	N/A	N/A

Match Target Competition H-BAR Compensated (Model MT6700C)

Same as the Match Target with a compensator.

NIB	Exc.	V.G.	Good	Fair	Poor
1350	1200	850	700	N/A	N/A

AR-15 Carbine Flat-top Heavyweight/Match Target Competition (Model #6731)

This variation in the Sporter series features a heavyweight 16" barrel with flat-top receiver chambered for the .223 cartridge. It is equipped with a fixed buttstock. Weight is about 7.1 lbs.

NIB	Exc.	V.G.	Good	Fair	Poor
1350	1200	850	700	N/A	N/A

AR-15 Tactical Carbine (Model #6721)

This version is similar to the above model with the exception of the buttstock which is telescoping and adjusts to 4 positions. Chambered for the .223 cartridge with a weight of about 7 lbs. A majority of these guns were for law enforcement only.

NIB	Exc.	V.G.	Good	Fair	Poor
1850	1600	1300	1100	N/A	N/A

Colt Accurized Rifle CAR-A3 (Model CR6724)

This variation was introduced in 1996 and features a free floating 24" stainless steel match barrel with an 11-degree target crown and special Teflon coated trigger group. The handguard is all-aluminum with twin swivel studs. Weight is approximately 9.26 lbs.

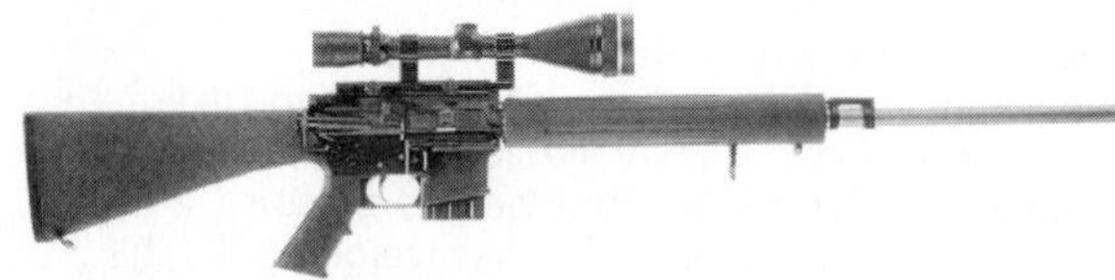

NIB	Exc.	V.G.	Good	Fair	Poor
1150	1000	900	850	N/A	N/A

U.S. Caliber .30 Carbine

Bibliographical Note: There are a number of variations, sights, stock configurations, etc., that are too numerous to cover in this publication. It is strongly recommended that for additional historical information, technical data, and photos see Larry L. Ruth's, *War Baby!, The U.S. Caliber .30 Carbine*, Collector Grade Publications, 1992.

This carbine was designed by William Roemer, Edwin Pugsley, and others at the Winchester Repeating Arms Company in late 1940 and early 1941. The only feature that can be credited to David Marsh "Carbine" Williams is the short stroke piston design. The U.S. M1 Carbine was produced by a number of manufacturers as listed below. The M1 A1 version was produced by Inland. The selective fire version is known as the Model M2. The exact number of carbines produced is unknown but approximately 6,000,000 carbines were built during WWII.

U.S. M1 Carbine

Introduced in 1941, this is a semi-automatic, gas operated carbine with a 18" barrel and a magazine capacity of 15 or 30 rounds. Half stocked with upper handguard and single barrel band. Bayonet bar located on barrel. Flip up rear sight. Later production has an adjustable sight. Chambered for the .30 U.S. Carbine cartridge. Weight is about 5.25 lbs. Widely used by U.S. military forces during World War II.

NOTE: Prices are for carbines in World War II factory original configuration. Any M1 Carbine with the earliest features such as "I" oiler cut stock, high wood, flip rear sight, and narrow barrel band will bring more than the later variations. Very few M-1 carbines survived the last sixty years with all the original parts. Carbine parts bear unique makers codes. Records

Early Underwood cartouche with large square box with WRA over GHD • Courtesy Michael Wamsher, Paul Goodwin photo

Early National Postal Meter cartouche with NPM over FJA in large square box • Courtesy Michael Wamsher, Paul Goodwin photo

German infantry during Battle of the Bulge, the rear man is carrying a U.S. M1 carbine • *Courtesy John M. Miller*

were kept that state which coded parts were installed on which makers guns. The information on these codes is available from several sources, including the book listed above. It is common for "matching" carbines to be assembled using the correctly marked parts. It will be up to the buyer to decide weather a "restored" M-1 carbine has the same value as an original speciman. It is frequently impossible to tell if a gun has been re-built using the correct parts or is originally matching.

Inland

Exc.	*V.G.*	*Good*	*Fair*	*Poor*
1500	1200	600	425	350

Underwood

Exc.	*V.G.*	*Good*	*Fair*	*Poor*
1600	1250	600	425	350

S.G. Saginaw

Exc.	*V.G.*	*Good*	*Fair*	*Poor*
1800	1300	600	425	350

IBM

Exc.	*V.G.*	*Good*	*Fair*	*Poor*
1800	1100	600	425	350

Quality Hardware

Exc.	*V.G.*	*Good*	*Fair*	*Poor*
1700	1100	600	425	350

National Postal Meter

Exc.	*V.G.*	*Good*	*Fair*	*Poor*
1800	1100	600	425	350

Standard Products

Exc.	*V.G.*	*Good*	*Fair*	*Poor*
1900	1200	650	450	375

Rockola

Exc.	*V.G.*	*Good*	*Fair*	*Poor*
2000	1400	700	450	375

Courtesy Blake Stevens, *War Baby,* **Collector Grade Publications**

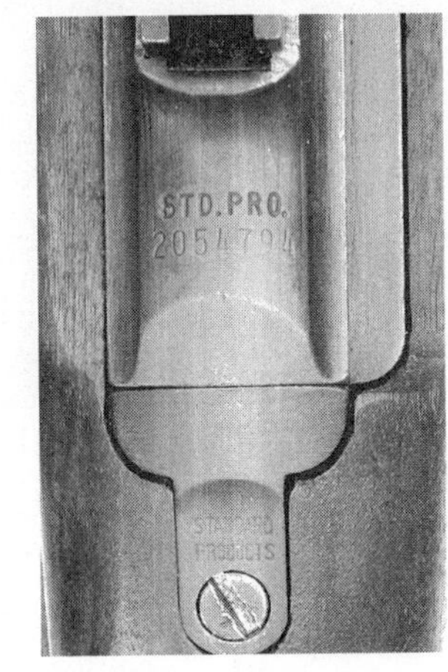

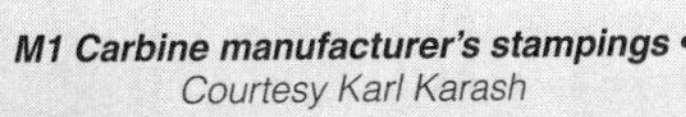

M1 Carbine manufacturer's stampings •
Courtesy Karl Karash

SG Saginaw (Grand Rapids)

Exc.	V.G.	Good	Fair	Poor
2000	1400	700	450	375

Winchester

Early Winchester cartouche • *Courtesy Michael Wamsher, Paul Goodwin photo*

Exc.	V.G.	Good	Fair	Poor
2500	1800	900	450	375

Irwin Pedersen-Rare

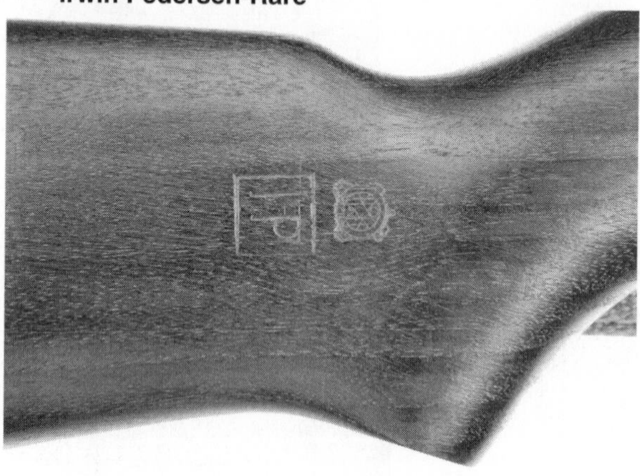

Irwin Pedersen cartouche with boxed IP and Ordnance Wheel Crossed Cannons • *Courtesy Michael Wamsher, Paul Goodwin photo*

Exc.	V.G.	Good	Fair	Poor
4000	2200	950	650	500

Rebuilt Carbine, any manufacture

Many M-1 carbines offered for sale should be considered to to be rebuilt and may have mixed parts from any of the manufacturers. This would be considered a "shooter" by most collectors. This category includes any M-1 carbine that has an import marked barrel. Several thousand carbines were imported from Korea in the late 1980's. These are US. made guns that we gave them during the cold war, they were not made in Korea. Other batches of carbines have been imported from West Germany, Israel and other nations. All post 1986 imports will have an importer stamp on the barrel or receiver. The most common are *Blue Sky Productions* and *Arlington Ordnance*. There is no longer a major price difference with the import marked rifles, as this model is so much in demand. Bore condition is the main factor to consider when examining an rebuilt carbine.

Exc.	V.G.	Good	Fair	Poor
700	575	450	350	N/A

M1 Carbine Cutaway

Used by factories and military armorers to facilitate training. Examples with documentation will bring a substantial premium.

M1 Carbine Cutaway • *Courtesy Richard M. Kumor Sr.*

Exc.	V.G.	Good	Fair	Poor
2500	1500	900	600	500

M1 Carbine Sniper (T-3)

This is an M1 carbine with a M84 scope mounted with forward vertical grip. Used in Korea.

This is a WWII "T-3" receiver markings with the Winchester variation that show the style of the one piece machined receiver • *Courtesy Michael Wamsher, Paul Goodwin photo*

Exc.	V.G.	Good	Fair	Poor
1500	1000	800	500	350

U.S. M1A1 Paratrooper Model

The standard U.S. M1 Carbine fitted with a folding stock. Approximately 110,000 were manufactured by Inland between 1942 and 1945. Weight is about 5.8 lbs. There are three variations of this carbine.

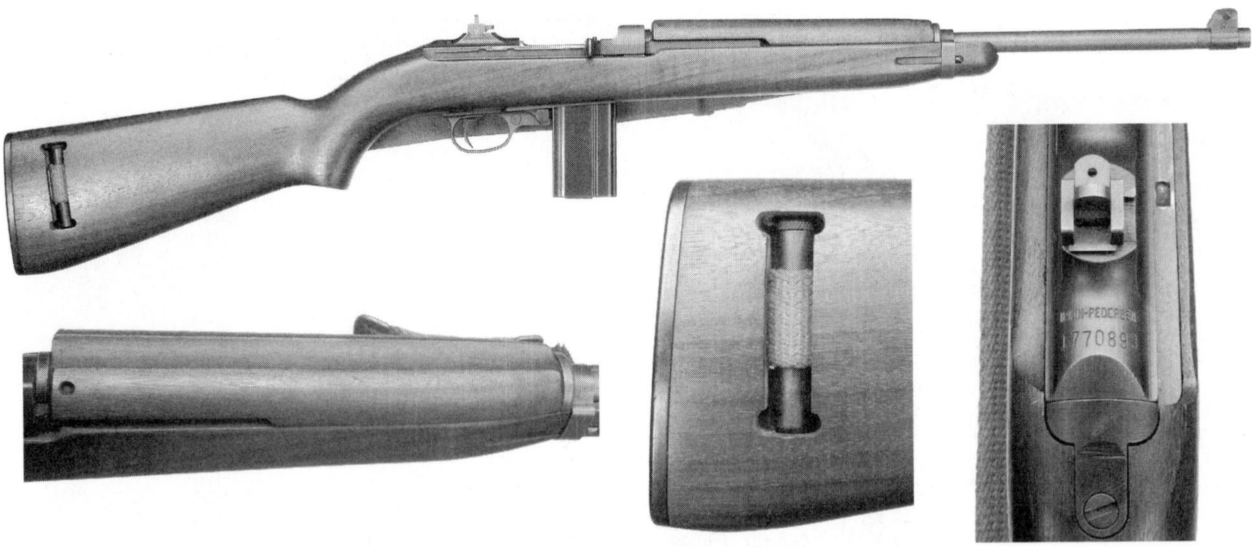

Earliest M1 stock variation with "I" oiler slot cut-out, high wood are over operating rod arm and wide groove hand guard and flip up rear sight • *Courtesy Michael Wamsher, Paul Goodwin photo*

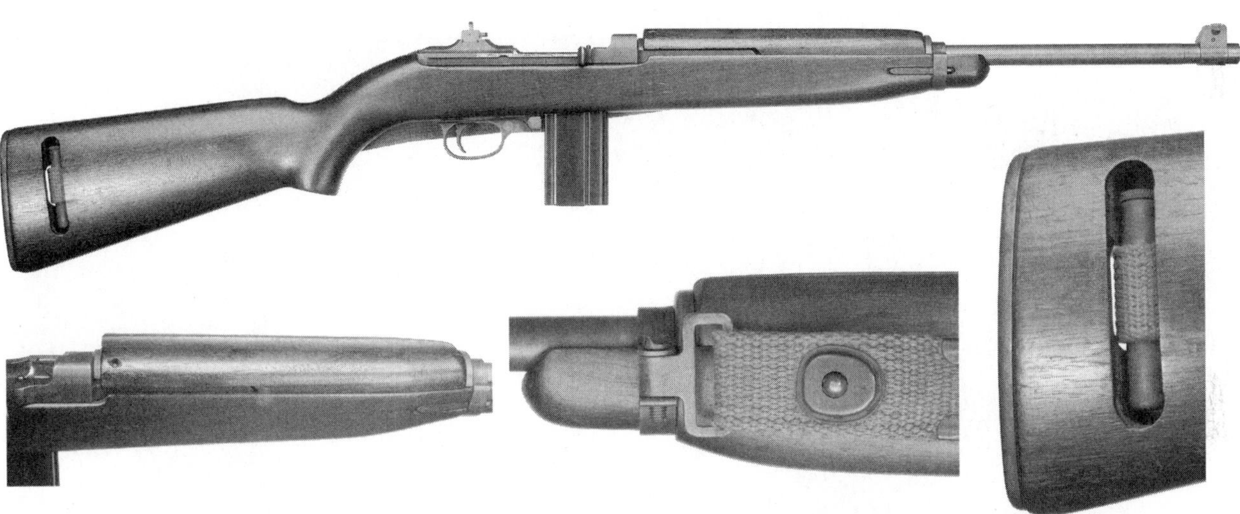

Second variation M1 stock configuration with "oval" oiler slot cut, high wood over operating arm and wide groove hand guard • *Courtesy Michael Wamsher, Paul Goodwin photo*

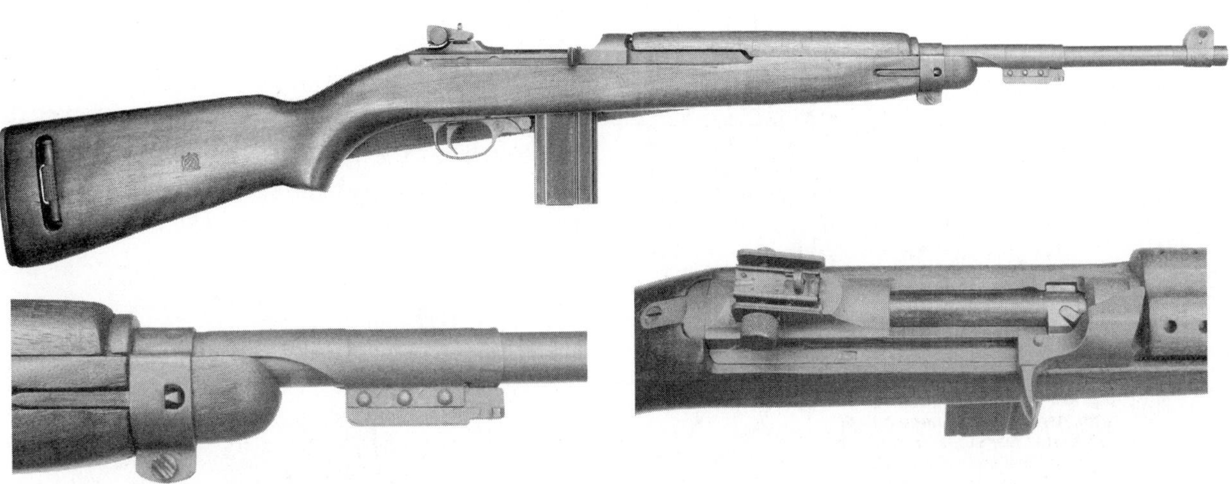

Last variation of the M1 stock configuration. Oval oiler slot cut, low wood over operating rod arm and narrow groove hand guard. Notice rear sight change • *Courtesy Michael Wamsher, Paul Goodwin photo*

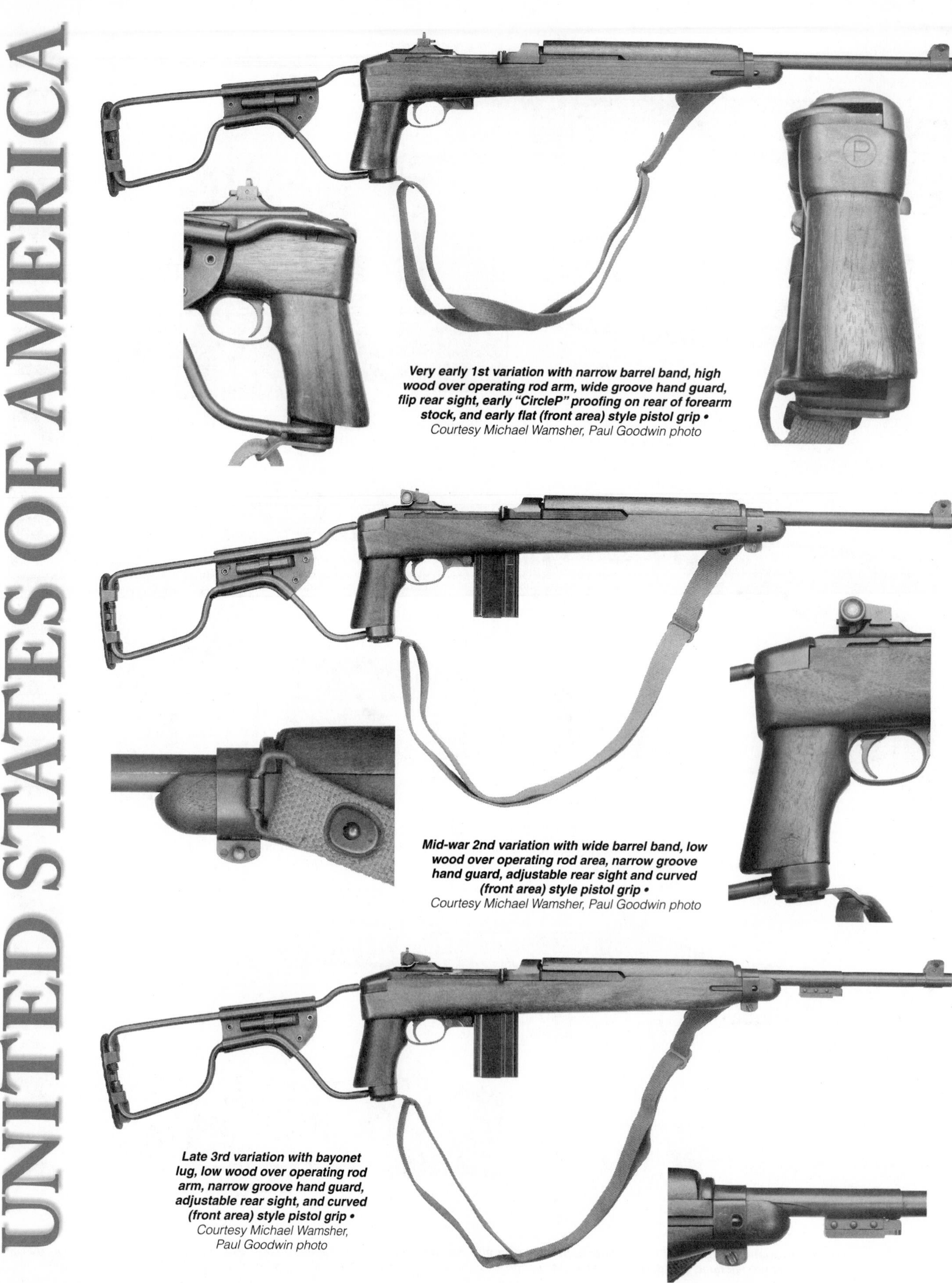

Very early 1st variation with narrow barrel band, high wood over operating rod arm, wide groove hand guard, flip rear sight, early "CircleP" proofing on rear of forearm stock, and early flat (front area) style pistol grip •
Courtesy Michael Wamsher, Paul Goodwin photo

Mid-war 2nd variation with wide barrel band, low wood over operating rod area, narrow groove hand guard, adjustable rear sight and curved (front area) style pistol grip •
Courtesy Michael Wamsher, Paul Goodwin photo

Late 3rd variation with bayonet lug, low wood over operating rod arm, narrow groove hand guard, adjustable rear sight, and curved (front area) style pistol grip •
Courtesy Michael Wamsher, Paul Goodwin photo

Variation I

Earliest variation with flip rear sight, narrow barrel band, and high wood. These were produced in late 1942 and 1943. Carbines in original condition are very rare.

Exc.	*V.G.*	*Good*	*Fair*	*Poor*
4500	3500	2250	—	—

Variation II

Manufactured in 1944 with no bayonet lug and low wood.

Exc.	*V.G.*	*Good*	*Fair*	*Poor*
3500	2500	1250	—	—

Variation III

Manufactured in late 1944 and 1945 with bayonet lug.

Exc.	*V.G.*	*Good*	*Fair*	*Poor*
3000	2400	1200	—	—

NOTE: Original jump cases sell for between $150 and $300.

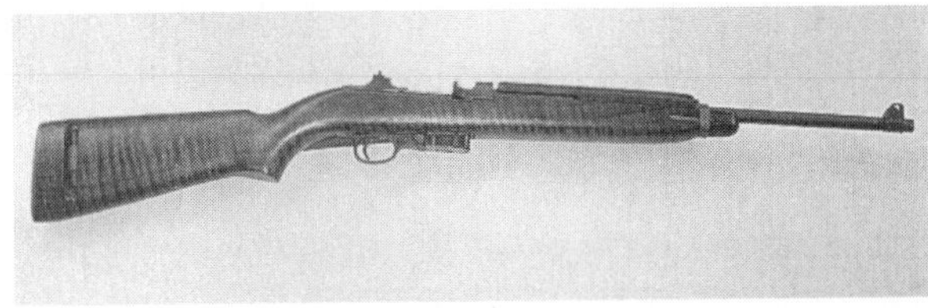

***An example of a U.S. M1 Presentation Carbine** • Courtesy Richard M. Kumor Sr.*

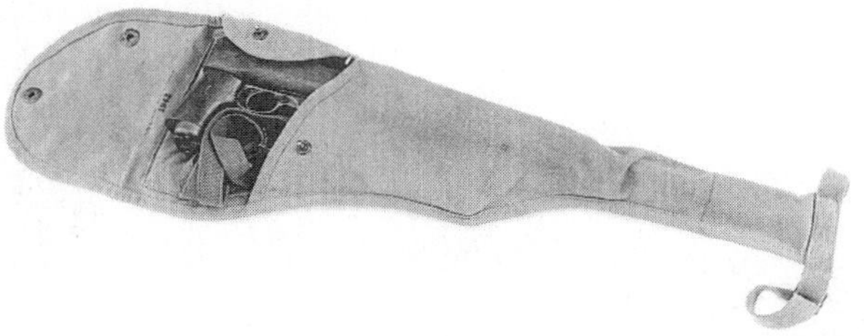

***M1A1 Carbine in its jump case** • Courtesy Chuck Karwan*

U.S. M2 Carbine

First produced in 1944 this select fire rifle is the automatic version of the famous M1 carbine. It has a 17.8" barrel and a 15- or 30-round magazine. It is chambered for the .30 Carbine cartridge (7.62x33mm). Its rate of fire is 750 rounds per minute. Weight is about 5.25 lbs. Marked "U.S.CARBINE CAL .30 M2" on top of chamber. Saw limited use in WWII but was widely used by American forces during Korea.

Pre-1968 with M-2 marked receiver

Exc.	*V.G.*	*Fair*
12500	10000	7000

Pre-1986 conversions on M-1 receiver

Exc.	*V.G.*	*Fair*
7500	6000	N/A

U.S. M3 Carbine

This model is identical to the select fire M2 carbine with the exception of no rear sight and the scope mount to support a variety of scopes for specific uses.

***M3 Carbine with scope** • Courtesy Richard M. Kumor Sr.*

U.S. M3 Carbine • Paul Goodwin photo

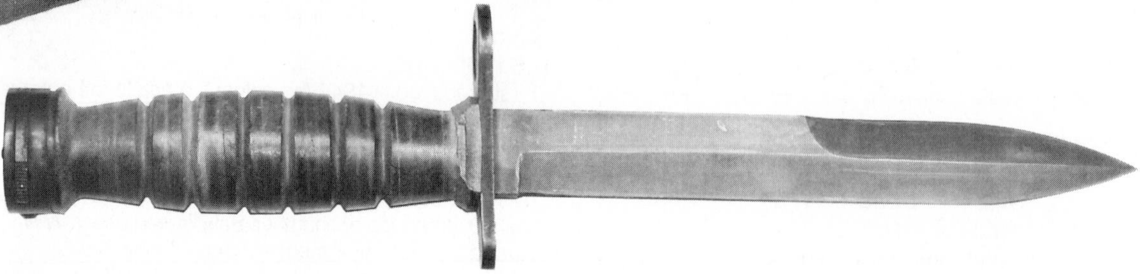

Pre-1986

Exc.	*V.G.*	*Fair*
12500	10000	7000

Pre-1986 conversions

Exc.	*V.G.*	*Fair*
7500	6000	N/A

NOTE: For M3 Carbines with infrared scope add $1,000.

M-4 Bayonet for M-1 Carbine, WW2 Production

Leather grip. Muzzle ring. 6.7" single edge blade. Makers name marked on face of cross piece. Manufactured by Case, Arial Cutlery Co. (ACC), Camillus, Imperial, Pal, Utica, Kinfolks Inc. (K.I.). Also made in occupied Japan by Kiffe. Green plastic sbabbard with metal top marked U.S. M8. There have been a few companies making reproductions of this bayonet. Original specimans will have a small ordnance bomb marking on top of the

U.S. M2 Carbine, with selector switch and cartouche • Paul Goodwin photo

pommel or on the cross piece. Price range 300 – 125.

M-4 Bayonet, Post WW2 Production

The same as the war time M-4 but has a black plastic grip. The later scabbards are green plastic with a steel tip. Marked "U.S. M8A1." This scabbard is used on several bayonets through the 1970s. Price range 150 – 50.

GARAND

(U.S. M1 Rifle)

U.S. Rifle, CAL. M1 (Garand)

Bibliographical Note: For further information, technical, and photos see Bruce Canfield, *Complete Guide to the M1 Garand and the M1 Carbine.* Andrew Mowbray, Inc.

An Introduction to the U.S. M1 Rifle by Simeon Stoddard

Adopted in 1936, the M1 remained the standard issue rifle of the United States until it was replaced by the M14 in 1957. It was designed by John C. Garand, who worked for Springfield Armory from 1919 until his retirement in 1953. During this time, Garand concentrated his efforts on the development of a semi-automatic shoulder weapon for general issue to the U.S. armed forces. The M14 rifle, the replacement for the M1, was a compilation of his design work as well.

With the exceptions noted, all values given are for rifles which are in original, as produced condition. Development of the M1 was an ongoing project until it was replaced, as Garand never finished perfecting his basic design. Over 5,400,000 M1 rifles were built, with the majority of them going through a rebuilding process at least once during their service life. During rebuilding, rifles were inspected and unserviceable parts replaced. Parts used for replacement were usually of the latest revision available or what was on hand.

Major assemblies and parts were marked with a government drawing size/part number. This number is often followed with the revision number (see photo above). Barrels were marked, with the exception of early Springfield Armory and all Winchester production, with the month and year of manufacture. It must be remembered that this date only refers to when the barrel was produced, and has nothing to do with when the receiver was produced or the rifle was assembled. This barrel date on "original as produced" rifles should be from 0 to 3 months, before the receiver was produced.

Restored rifles, defined as ones with parts added/replaced, to more closely match what they might have been originally, are worth less money than "original as produced" rifles. This difference should be on the order of 30-40 percent of the values shown, and is due to the low number of rifles of this type. When in doubt, get an appraisal. To tell what parts should be correct, study chapters 5 & 6 of *"The M1 Garand: WWII"* and chapters 7 & 8 of *"The M1 Garand: Post WWII"* by Scott A. Duff.

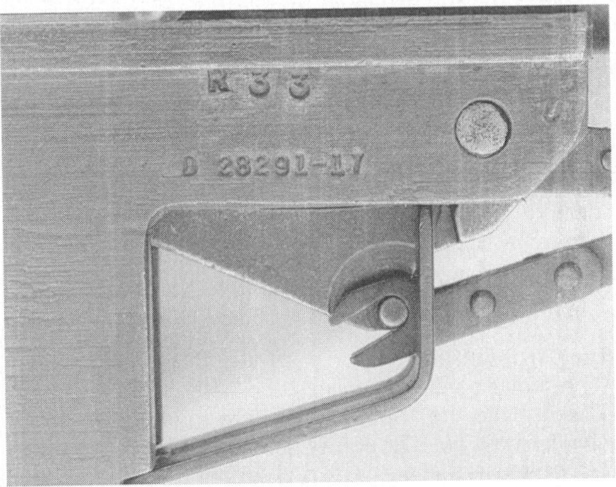

Rebuilt Rifle, any manufacture

Many of the M-1 Garands seen on the market today fit into this category. Value shown is for rifles with a majority of its parts mixed/replaced. Depending on the type of rebuilding that a rifle went through, rifles could be completely disassembled with no attempt to put parts together for the same rifle. Valued mainly for shooting merits. Bore condition, gauging and overall appearance are important factors.

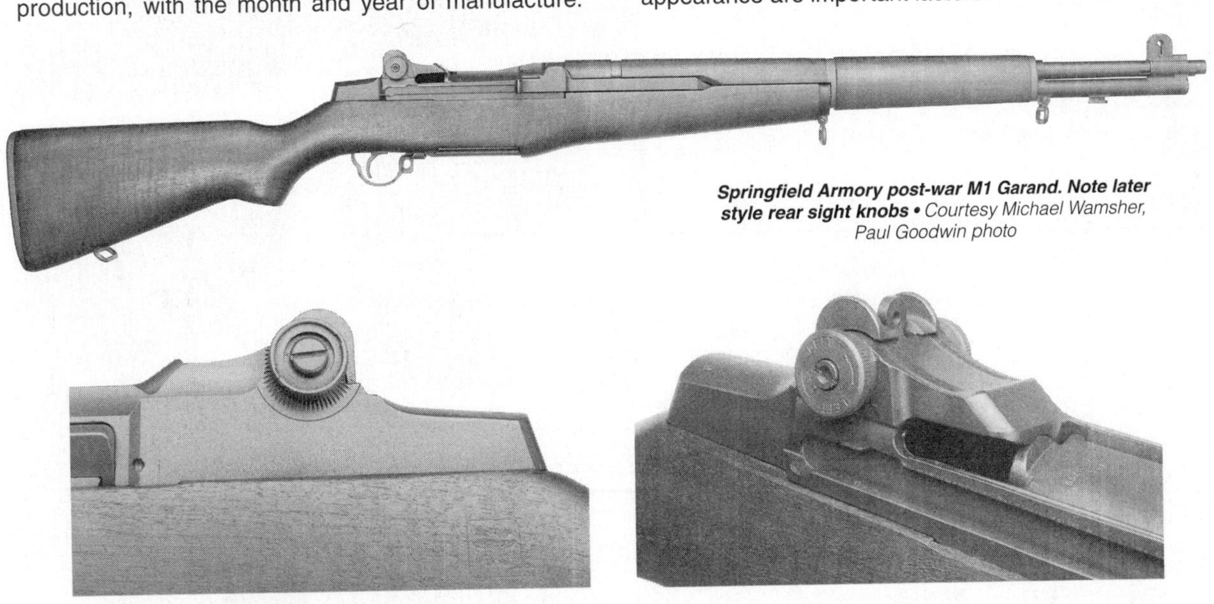

Springfield Armory post-war M1 Garand. Note later style rear sight knobs • *Courtesy Michael Wamsher, Paul Goodwin photo*

Note: There were some M-1 Garands imported from Korea in the 1990's. These will be import stamped on the barrel. Most are *Blue Sky Productions* or *Arlington Ordnance*. These import marked rifles fit in the rebuilt category. There is no longer a major price difference with the import marked rifles, as this model is so much in demand. Bore condition is the main factor to consider when examining an imported rifle.

Exc.	*V.G.*	*Good*
900	750	500

NOTE: Rifles built by Winchester will bring a small premium.

CMP or DCM Rifles

The *Civilian Marksmanship Program,* formerly known as *Director of Civilian Marksmanship*, is operated by the U.S. government to promote shooting skills. It sells surplus rifles to qualified buyers. CMP M-1 Garands are offered in several grades, currently including some rifles that were used and rebarreled by Denmark. The Danish rifles have a crown mark on the barrel. These rifles should have the correct paperwork and shipping boxes to receive the prices listed. Contact the CMP for current pricing, availibility and requirements for purchase. Web site: www.odcmp.com.

Exc.	*V.G.*	*Good*
1000	800	600

Navy Trophy Rifles

The Navy continued to use the M1 rifle as its main rifle far into the 1960s. They were modified to shoot the 7.62x51 NATO (.308 Winchester) round. This was accomplished at first with a chamber insert, and later with new replacement barrels in the NATO caliber. The Navy modified rifles can be found of any manufacture, and in any serial number range. As a general rule, Navy rifles with new barrels are worth more due to their better shooting capabilities. Paperwork and original boxes must accompany these rifles to obtain the values listed.

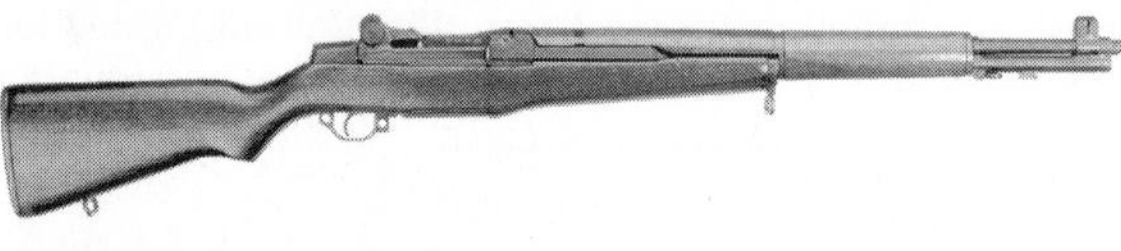

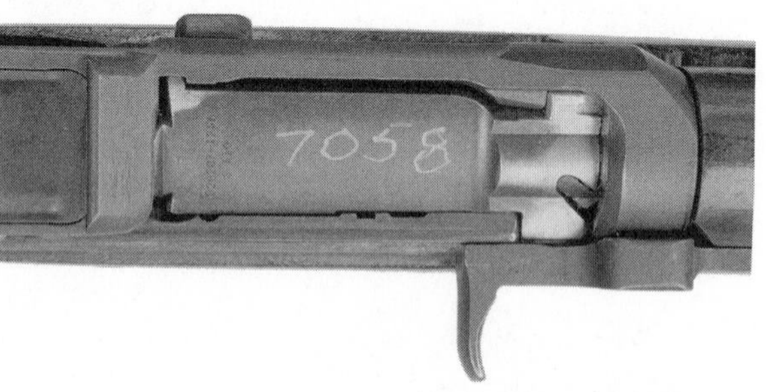

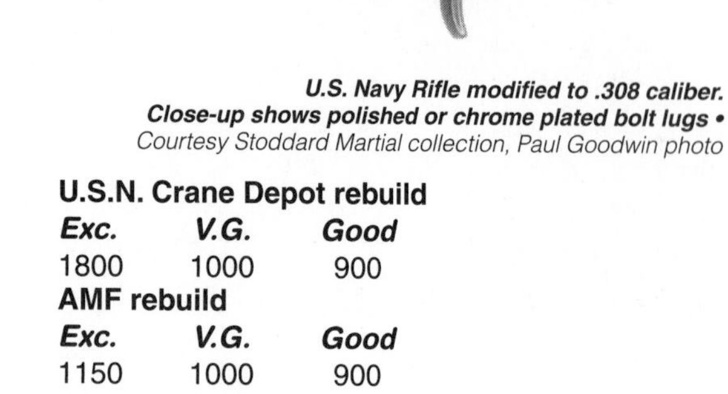

U.S. Navy Rifle modified to .308 caliber. Close-up shows polished or chrome plated bolt lugs • *Courtesy Stoddard Martial collection, Paul Goodwin photo*

U.S.N. Crane Depot rebuild

Exc.	*V.G.*	*Good*
1800	1000	900

AMF rebuild

Exc.	*V.G.*	*Good*
1150	1000	900

H&R rebuild

Exc.	*V.G.*	*Good*
1000	900	800

Springfield Armory Production

Exc.	*V.G.*	*Good*
1250	1000	900

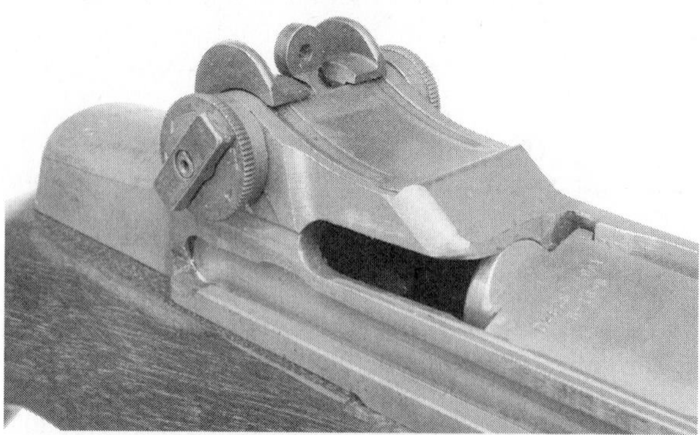

Springfield Armory M1 later style rear sight with bar type rear sight knob • *Courtesy Michael Wamsher, Paul Goodwin photo*

Springfield Armory M1 with front sight without protective screw cap • *Courtesy Michael Wamsher, Paul Goodwin photo*

Gas Trap sn: c. 81-52000

Values shown for original rifles. Most all were updated to gas port configuration. Look out for reproductions being offered as original rifles! Get a professional appraisal before purchasing.

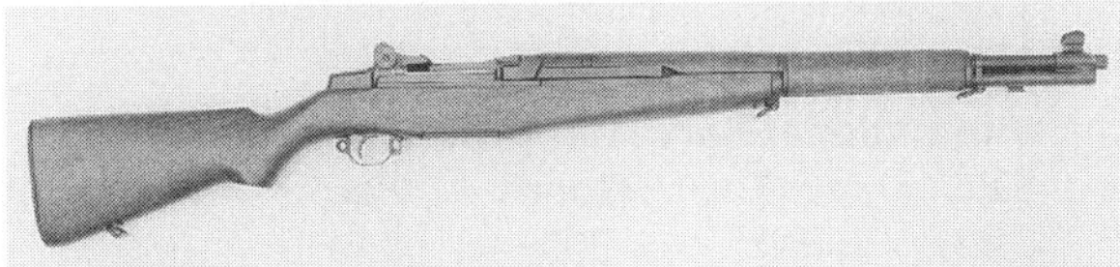

Exc.	*V.G.*	*Good*
40000	35000	25000

M1 Garand Gas Trap close-up • *Courtesy Chuck Karwan*

Gas Trap/modified to gas port

These rifles should have many of their early parts. Must be original modifications and not restored.

Exc.	*V.G.*	*Good*
5000	3500	2500

Pre-Dec. 7, 1941 gas port production sn: ca 50000-Appx. 410000

Exc.	*V.G.*	*Good*	*Fair*	*Poor*
4000	2200	1300	750	650

NOTE: Rifles built in 1940 in excellent and original condition will bring a premium of $1,500+.

WWII Production sn: ca 410000-3880000

SA/GHS Cartouche

Exc.	*V.G.*	*Good*	*Fair*	*Poor*
3500	1500	900	750	500

SA/EMF Cartouche

Exc.	*V.G.*	*Good*	*Fair*	*Poor*
3200	1500	900	750	500

SA/GAW Cartouche

Exc.	*V.G.*	*Good*	*Fair*	*Poor*
3100	1500	900	750	500

SA/NFR Cartouche

Exc.	*V.G.*	*Good*	*Fair*	*Poor*
2900	1200	900	750	500

POST WWII Production sn: c. 4200000-6099361

SA/GHS Cartouche

Exc.	*V.G.*	*Good*	*Fair*	*Poor*
2800	1200	650	500	400

National Defense Stamp

Exc.	*V.G.*	*Good*	*Fair*	*Poor*
2500	1000	650	500	400

Very Late 6000000 sn

Exc.	*V.G.*	*Good*	*Fair*	*Poor*
2500	1000	650	500	400

Winchester Production

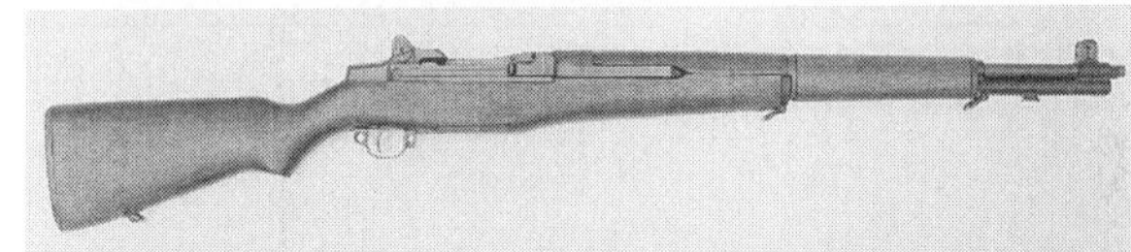

Winchester produced around 513,000 M1 rifles during WWII. Their first contract was an educational order in 1939. This contract was for 500 rifles and the gauges and fixtures to produce the rifles. Winchester's second contract was awarded during 1939 for up to 65,000 rifles. Winchester M1's are typified by noticeable machine marks on their parts, and did not have the higher grade finish that is found on Springfield Armory production. Watch for fake barrels, and barrels marked "Winchester" which were produced in the 1960s as replacement barrels.

Winchester Educational Contract sn: 100000100500

Exc.	*V.G.*	*Good*	*Fair*	*Poor*
10000	6000	4500	3000	2000

Winchester sn: 100501-165000

Rifles of this serial number range were produced from Jan. 1941 until May 1942.

Exc.	V.G.	Good	Fair	Poor
6500	4500	2000	1500	750

Winchester sn: 1200000-1380000

Rifles in this serial number range were produced from May 1942 until Aug. 1943.

Exc.	V.G.	Good	Fair	Poor
4500	2500	1800	1000	750

NOTE: Add a premium of $1,000 for earlier rifles.

Winchester sn: 2305850-2536493

Rifles in this serial number range were produced from Aug. 1943 until Jan. 1945.

Exc.	V.G.	Good	Fair	Poor
3000	2000	1250	900	550

NOTE: Add a premium of $500 for earlier rifles.

Winchester sn: 1601150-1640000

Rifles in this serial number range were produced from Jan. 1945, until June 1945. These are often referred to as "**Win-13's**" because of the revision number of the right front receiver leg.

Exc.	V.G.	Good	Fair	Poor
3500	2500	2000	1500	850

Harrington & Richardson Production

Between 1953 and 1956, Harrington & Richardson produced around 428,000 M1 rifles.

Exc.	V.G.	Good	Fair	Poor
1800	1200	900	500	350

International Harvester Corp. Production

Between 1953 and 1956, International Harvester produced around 337,000 M1 rifles. International at several different times during their production purchased receivers from both Harrington & Richardson and Springfield Armory. Always check for Springfield Armory heat lots on the right front receiver leg.

International Harvester Production

Exc.	V.G.	Good	Fair	Poor
2200	1500	800	450	350

International Harvester/with Springfield Receiver (postage stamp)

Exc.	V.G.	Good
2800	1500	900

International Harvester/with Springfield Receiver (arrow head)

Exc.	V.G.	Good
2800	1500	1000

International Harvester/with Springfield Receiver (Gap letter)

Exc.	V.G.	Good
2500	1300	900

International Harvester/with Harrington & Richardson Receiver

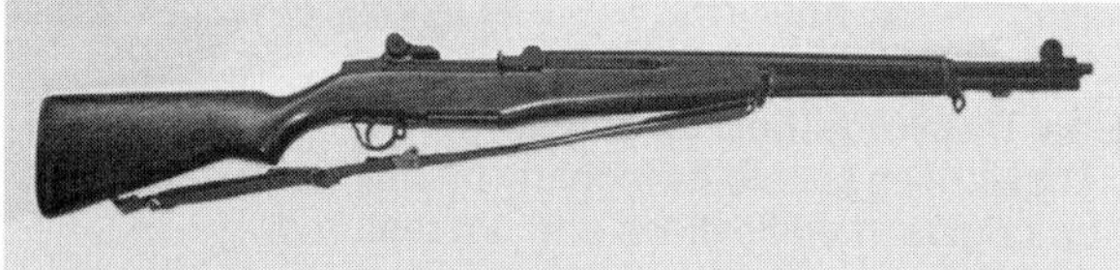

M1 Experimental with one-piece upper handguard made of fiberglass • *Courtesy Richard M. Kumor Sr.*

Exc.	V.G.	Good
1900	1200	850

British Garands (Lend Lease)

In 1941 and 1942, the U.S. sent a total of 38,000 M1 Garands to England under the Lend Lease program. These rifles were painted with a red band around the front of the handguard with the numerals "30" or "300" in black. The buttstock is stamped with a U.S. Ordnance cartouche and the initials "GHS" under "SA."

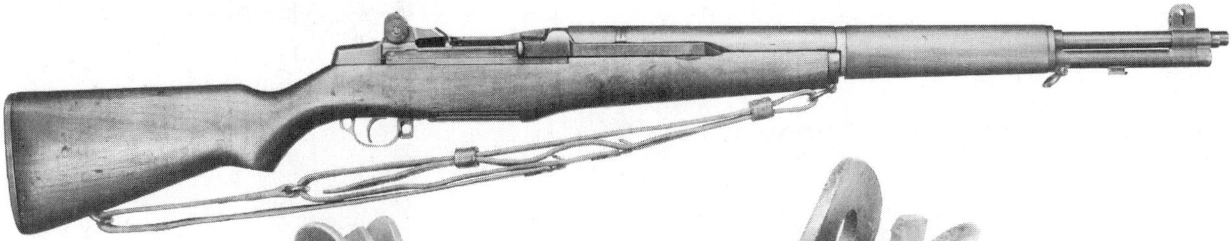

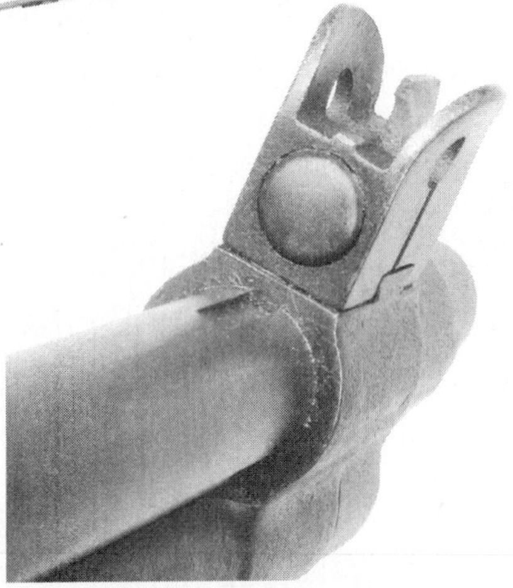

U.S. Springfield M1 Garand Lend Lease. Barrel date SA 9-41. Notice British proof marks on left rear barrel, early gas cylinder end plug, front sight with early protective cap over front sight screw, and 1st variation rear sight knob • *Courtesy Michael Wamsher, Paul Goodwin photo*

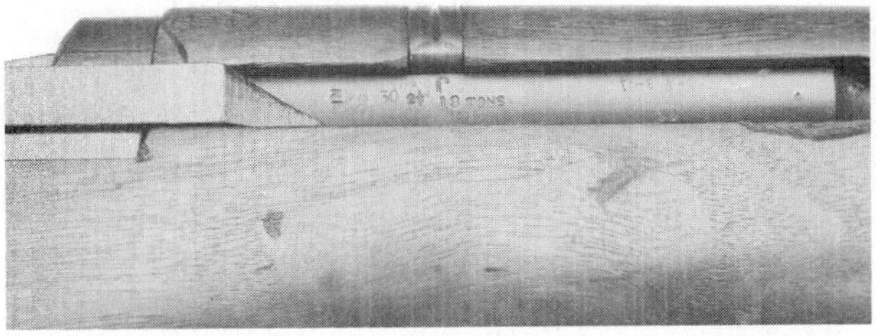

Most known examples are found in the serial number range 3000000 to 600000. When these rifles were sold and imported back into the U.S., they were stamped with either London or Birmingham proof stamps.

Exc.	V.G.	Good	Fair	Poor
2250	2000	1500	1000	750

M1 Garand Cutaway

Used by factories and military armorers to facilitate training.

M1 Garand cutaway • *Courtesy Richard M. Kumor Sr.*

Exc.	V.G.	Good	Fair	Poor
3000	2500	1000	600	500

NOTE: For examples with documentation add 300 percent.

M-5 Bayonet for M-1 Garand

Checkered black plastic grip. Cross piece has a metal stud that fits in the M-1's gas plug. 6.7" single edge blade. Issued in the M8A1 scabbard. The final bayonet issued for the M-1 Garand. Exported to several nations who got the M-1 from the U.S. Price range 85 – 40.

SCOPE VARIANTS (SNIPER RIFLES)

M1C

Springfield Armory production only. Serial number range is between ca 3200000 and 3800000. This variant is very rare with only around 7,900 produced. Should be mounted with M81, M82 or M84 scope with 7/8" scope rings. The scopes alone are worth $700 to $800 alone. Ask for government relicense paperwork, and have a serial number check run before purchase is made. If provenance cannot be established, then rifles are worth the value of their individual parts, under $2000.

NOTE: Prices listed are for the usual re-arsenaled examples with documentation. Rifles with all matching numbers and factory original condition are *extremely* rare, and would bring a substantial premium.

Exc.	V.G.	Good
10000	8000	5000

MC 1952 (USMC Issue) (sn. 10000-15000)

Same production range as above. Should be equipped with 1" scope mount and Kollmorgen scope. These rifles will command a premium. This is the rarest of the M-1 Snipers.

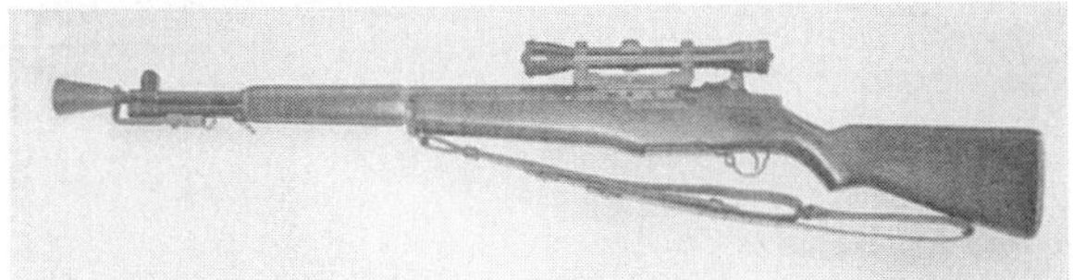

Courtesy Richard M. Kumor Sr.

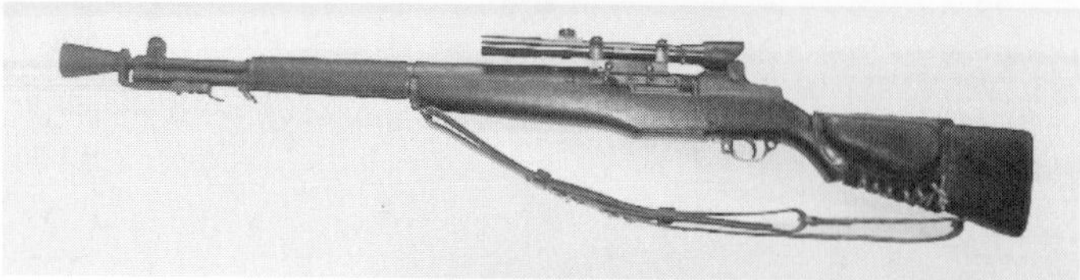

M1C serial number markings and cartouche • *Paul Goodwin photo*

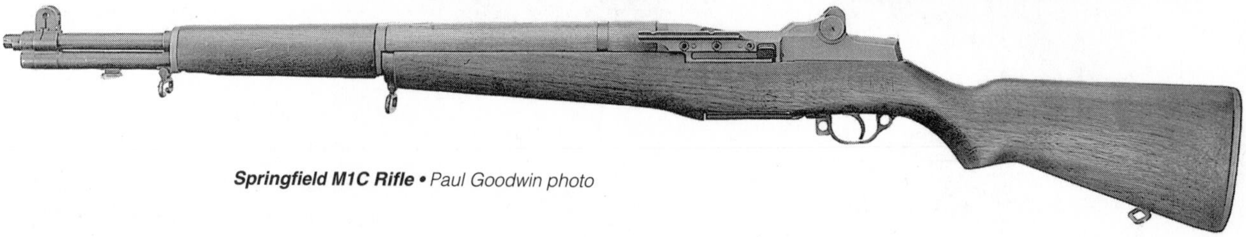

Springfield M1C Rifle • *Paul Goodwin photo*

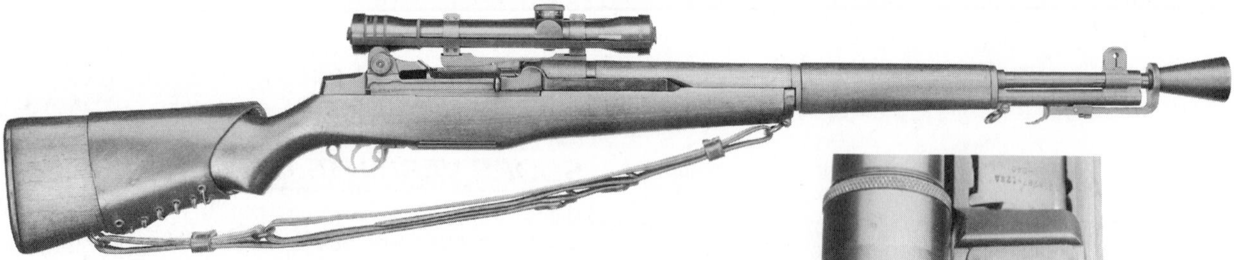

Springfield M1C Sniper rifle with Kolmorgan 4x scope set and original Storm Queen lens covers • *Courtesy Michael Wamsher, Paul Goodwin photo*

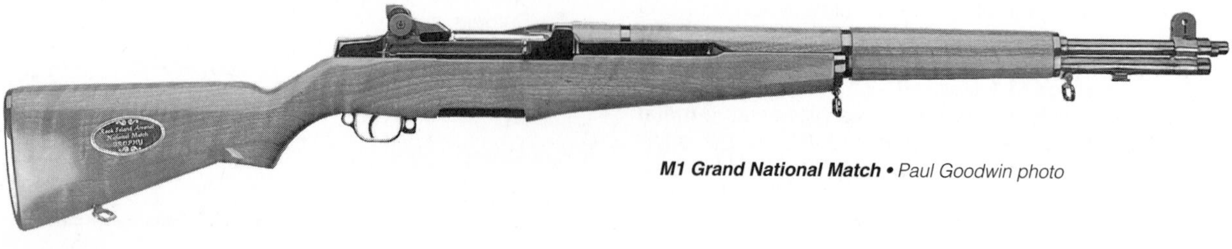

M1 Grand National Match • *Paul Goodwin photo*

Garand M1 cutaway • *Paul Goodwin photo*

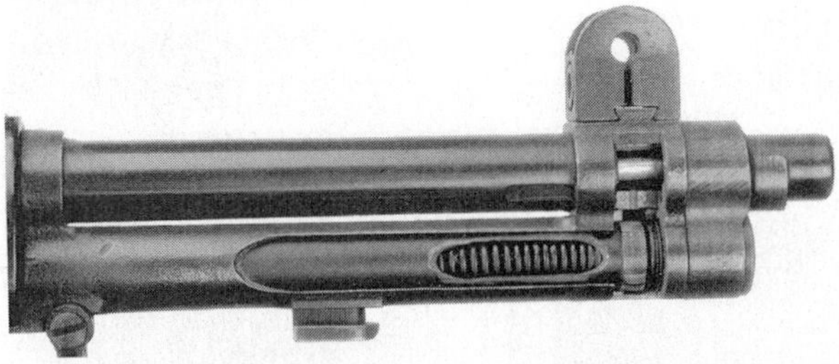

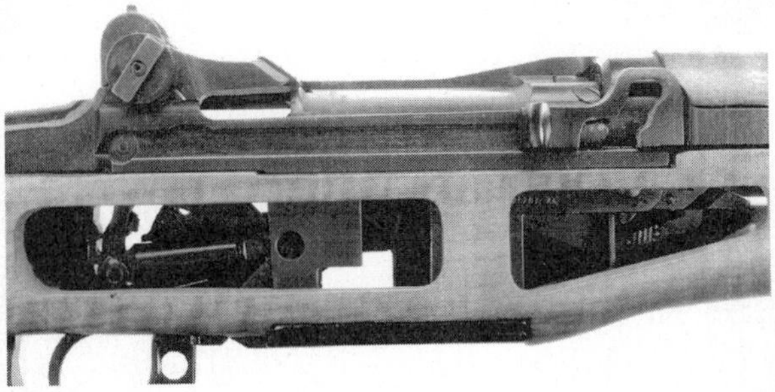

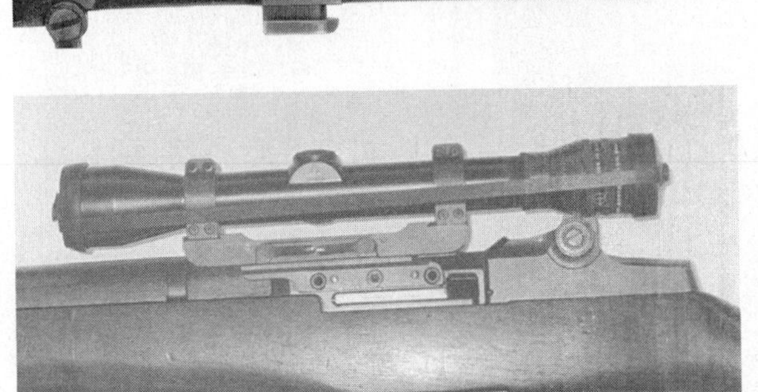

Close-up of MC 1952 scope and mount • *Courtesy Richard M. Kumor Sr.*

M1D

This model can be found by any manufacturer and in any serial number range. This mounting system was designed by John Garand, and consists of a mounting block on the rear of the barrel. The rear hand guard is shortened and the mount attaches with a large single screw system. The modification could be made on the field repair level. It is not known how many rifles were modified, but it is very likely that they numbered into the tens of thousands. If the rifle does not come with paperwork, it is only worth the value of its parts alone, under $1200. The Model 82 scope is worth between $500 and $700. With Kolmorgan scope set prices may bring up to $15,000.

SA mfr.

Exc.	*V.G.*	*Good*
3800	3000	2000

WRA mfr.

Exc.	*V.G.*	*Good*
4000	3000	2000

IHC mfr.

Exc.	*V.G.*	*Good*
4200	3000	2000

HRA mfr.

Exc.	*V.G.*	*Good*
4000	3000	2000

National Match Type I

Produced on Springfield Armory receivers and in serial number ranges from ca 5800000 to around 6090000. All parts are available to reproduce both types of national match rifles. To obtain values listed these rifles must come with original paperwork.

Exc.	*V.G.*	*Good*
4500	3000	1800

National Match Type II

Produced on Springfield Armory receivers, they can be found in any serial number range. These rifles should come with papers to receive values listed.

NOTE: Type I rifles are more rare than Type II.

Exc.	*V.G.*	*Good*
3200	2200	1500

M-5 Bayonet for M-1 Garand

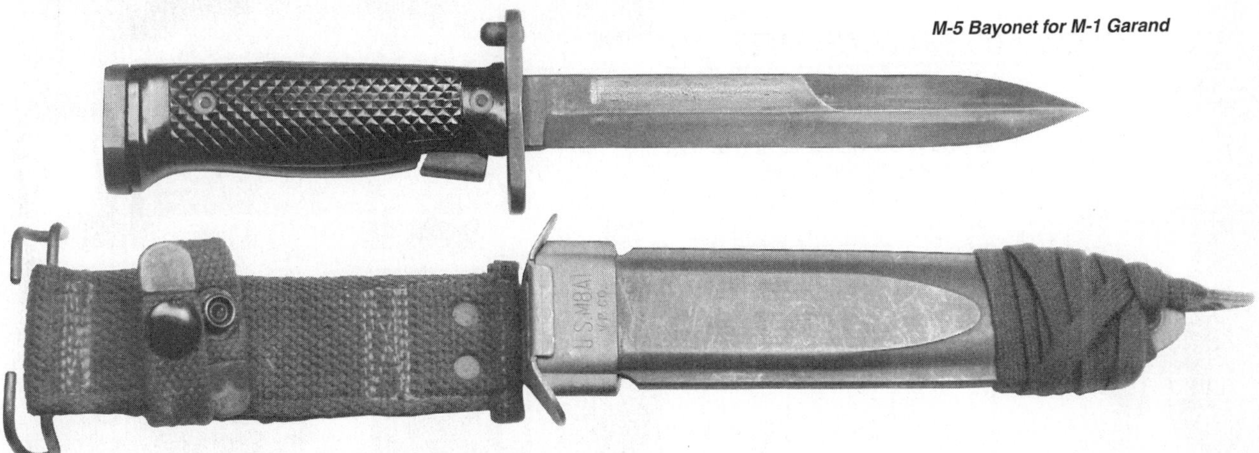

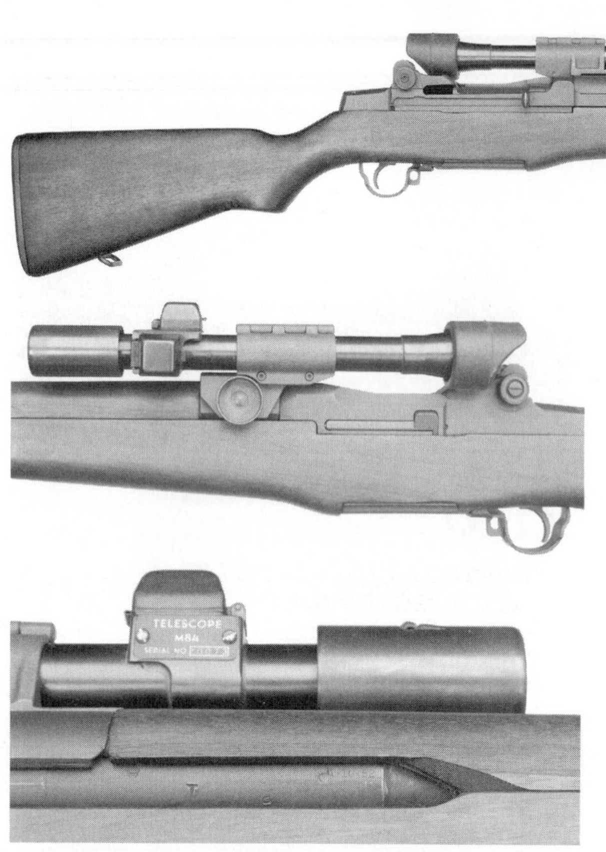

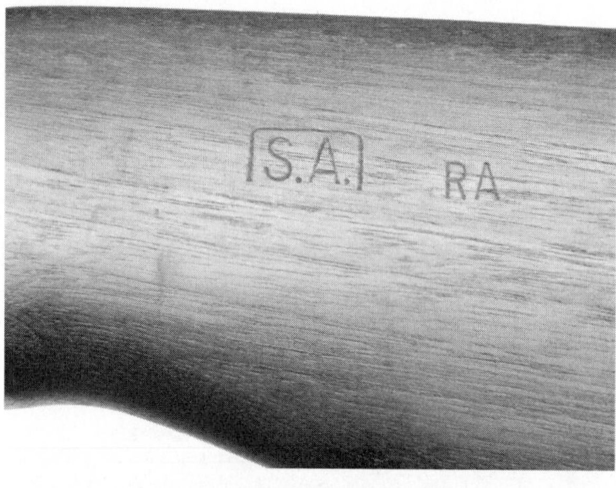

U.S. M1D Sniper with M84 scope and "RA" and open boxed "SA" cartouche • *Courtesy Michael Wamsher, Paul Goodwin photo*

KNIGHT'S MANUFACTURING CO.

SR-25 Lightweight Match (U.S. Navy, Mark 11 Model O)

This .308 rifle is fitted with a 20" free floating barrel. No sights. Weight is about 9.5 lbs. Adopted by U.S. Navy. Commercial version is the same except for the markings on the receiver.

NIB	Exc.	V.G.	Good	Fair	Poor
3250	2250	1500	900	—	—

JOHNSON AUTOMATICS MFG. CO.

Model 1941

This is a recoil-operated semi-automatic rifle chambered for the .30-06 cartridge and fitted with a rotary 10-round magazine. It has a half stock with perforated handguard. Used by the U.S. Marines, Dutch Colonial forces, and U.S. special forces during World War II. Fitted with a 22" barrel and chambered for the .30-06 cartridge. Right side of the receiver is marked "CRANSTON ARMS CO." Parkerized finish. Checkered metal buttplate. Adjustable rear sight is graduated in meters. Barrel is easily removed which was a plus for airborne Marine units. Weight is about 9.5 lbs.

Exc.	V.G.	Good	Fair	Poor
4500	3500	2000	1000	500

NOTE: Rifles with a verifiable U.S. Marine Corp provenance will bring a premium.

Bayonet for 1941 Johnson

7.75" triangle shaped blade. No grips. Steel handle with muzzle ring. Spring catch riveted in place. Leather

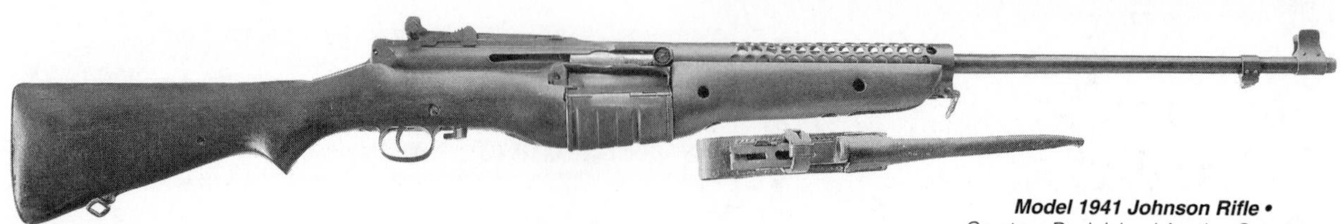

Model 1941 Johnson Rifle • *Courtesy Rock Island Auction Company*

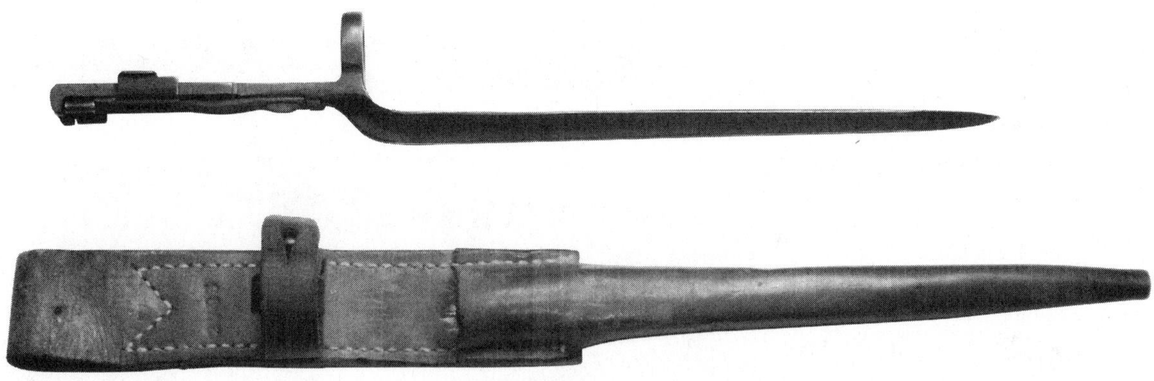

Bayonet for 1941 Johnson

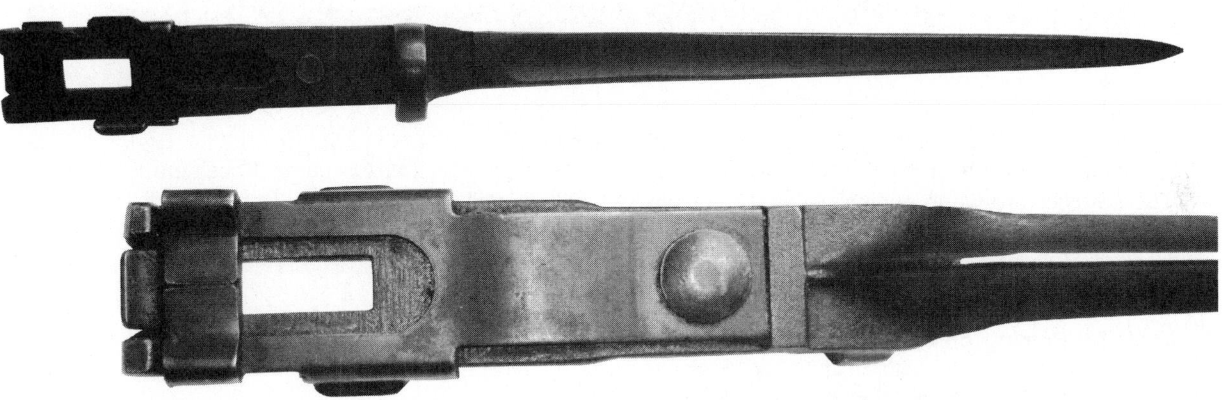

scabbard. Made to be very lightweight as the Johnson has a barrel that recoils when fired. A heavy bayonet would interfere with function. There are reproductions available. Price range 600–300.

REMINGTON ARMS COMPANY, INC.

Split-Breech Cavalry Carbine

A .46 or .50 rimfire single-shot rolling block carbine with a 20" barrel. Blued, case hardened with a walnut stock. The tang marked "Remington's Ilion, N.Y. Pat. Dec. 23, 1863 May 3 & Nov. 16, 1864." The .50 caliber version is worth approximately 15 percent more than the .46 caliber. Approximately 15,000 .50-caliber variations were made, most of which were sold to France. Approximately 5,000 carbines were made in .46 caliber. Manufactured from 1864 to 1866.

Paul Goodwin photo

Exc.	V.G.	Good	Fair	Poor
—	—	4250	2000	500

U.S. Navy Rolling Block Carbine

A .50-70 caliber single shot rolling block carbine with a 23.25" round barrel. A sling ring is normally fitted to the left side of the frame and sling swivels are mounted on the barrel band and the bottom of the butt. Inspector's markings are to be found on the right side of the frame as well as the stock. Blued, case hardened with a walnut stock. The barrel is marked "Remington's Ilion, N.Y. U.S.A." along with the patent dates. Approximately 5,000 were manufactured in 1868 and 1869.

Exc.	V.G.	Good	Fair	Poor
—	—	3500	1250	550

Model 1867 Navy Cadet Rifle

A .50-45 caliber single shot rolling block rifle with a 32.5" barrel and full length forend secured by two barrel bands. Markings identical to the above with the exception that "U.S." is stamped on the buttplate tang. Blued, case hardened with a walnut stock. Approximately 500 were made in 1868.

Exc.	V.G.	Good	Fair	Poor
—	—	2750	1200	400

Rolling Block Military Rifles

Courtesy Milwaukee Public Museum, Milwaukee, Wisconsin

Between 1867 and 1902 over 1,000,000 rolling block military rifles and carbines were manufactured by the Remington Company. Offered in a variety of calibers and

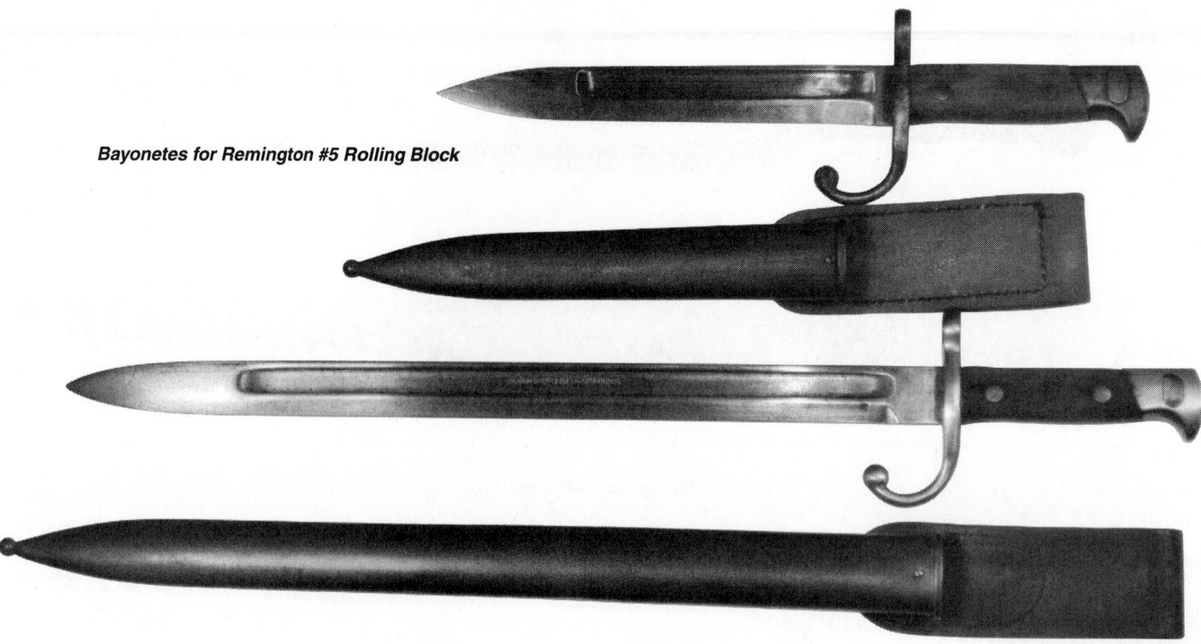

Bayonetes for Remington #5 Rolling Block

barrel lengths, the values listed below are for full length rifles. Foreign contract models are listed under country.

NOTE: Carbines are worth approximately 40 percent more.

Exc.	V.G.	Good	Fair	Poor
—	—	750	400	100

Bayonets for Remington #5 Rolling Block

Wood grip. Muzzle ring. Hook quillon. 8.25" or 15" single edge blade. Marked "Remington Arms Co. Ilion NY' in the fuller groove. Steel scabbard. These bayonets were sold with the #5 rolling blocks. Price range 275 – 150.

Remington-Keene Magazine Rifle

A bolt-action rifle chambered for the .40, .43, and .45-70 centerfire cartridges with 22", 24.5", 29.25", or 32.5" barrels. It is readily identifiable by the exposed hammer at the end of the bolt. Blued, case hardened hammer and furniture, with a walnut stock. The receiver marked "E. Remington & Sons, Ilion, N.Y." together with the patent dates 1874, 1876, and 1877. The magazine on this rifle was located beneath the barrel and the receiver is fitted with a cut-off so that the rifle could be used as a single shot. Approximately 5,000 rifles were made between 1880 and 1888 in the following variations:

Sporting Rifle

24.5 barrel.

Exc.	V.G.	Good	Fair	Poor
—	2250	1200	500	200

Army Rifle

Barrel length 32.5" with a full-length stock secured by two barrel bands. Prices are for martially marked examples.

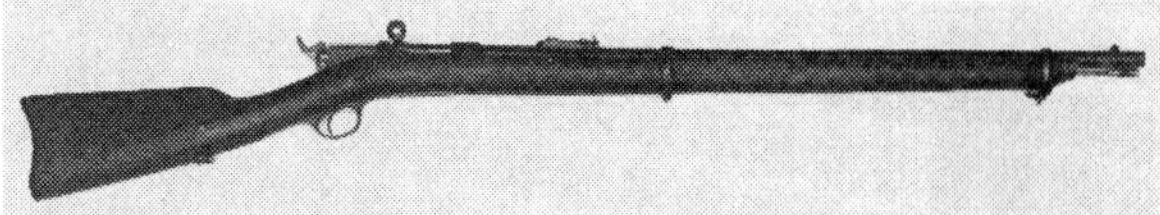

Courtesy Milwaukee Public Museum, Milwaukee, Wisconsin

Exc.	V.G.	Good	Fair	Poor
—	3500	2000	850	300

Navy Rifle

As above, with a 29.25" barrel. Prices are for martially marked examples.

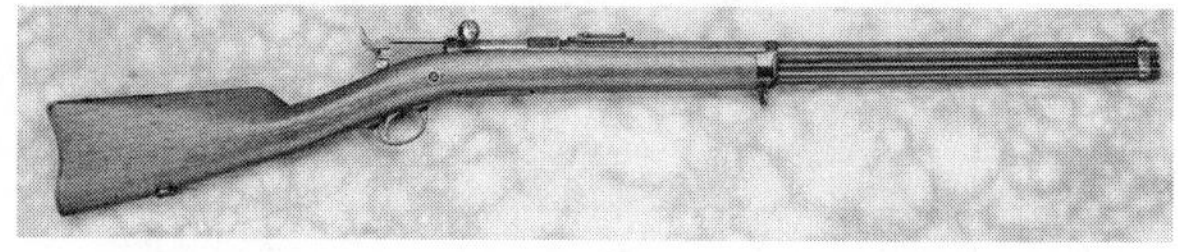

Paul Goodwin photo

Exc.	V.G.	Good	Fair	Poor
—	4750	3000	1500	750

Carbine

As above, with a 22" barrel and a half-length forend secured by one barrel band.

Courtesy Milwaukee Public Museum, Milwaukee, Wisconsin

Exc.	V.G.	Good	Fair	Poor
—	3250	1500	750	350

Frontier Model

As above, with a 24" barrel and half-length forend secured by one barrel band. Those purchased by the United States Department of the Interior for arming the Indian Police are marked "U.S.I.D." on the receiver.

Exc.	V.G.	Good	Fair	Poor
—	—	5500	3000	850

Remington-Lee Magazine Rifle

Designed by James Paris Lee, rifles of this type were originally manufactured by the Sharps Rifle Company in 1880. The Remington Company began production of this model in 1881 after the Sharps Company ceased operations. Approximately 100,000 Lee magazine rifles were made between 1880 and 1907. Their variations are as follows:

Model 1879 U.S. Navy Model

Barrel length 28", .45-70 caliber with a full-length stock secured by two barrel bands. The barrel is marked with the U.S. Navy inspector's marks and an anchor at the breech. The receiver is marked "Lee Arms Co. Bridgeport, Conn. U.S.A." and "Patented Nov. 4, 1879." Approximately 1300 were made.

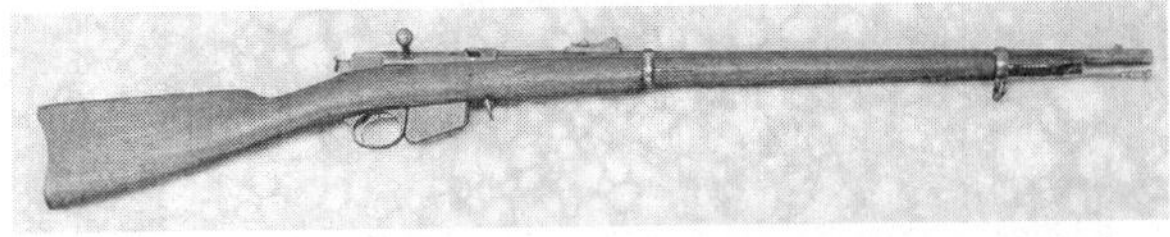

Paul Goodwin photo

Exc.	V.G.	Good	Fair	Poor
—	4500	2000	750	250

Model 1882 Army Contract

This model is identifiable by the two grooves pressed into the side of the magazine. The receiver is marked "Lee Arms Co. Bridgeport Conn., U.S.A." and on some examples it is also marked "E. Remington & Sons, Ilion, N.Y. U.S.A. Sole Manufactured & Agents." Barrel length 32", caliber .45-70, full-length stock secured by two barrel bands. U.S. Inspector's marks are stamped on the barrel breech and the stock. Approximately 750 were made.

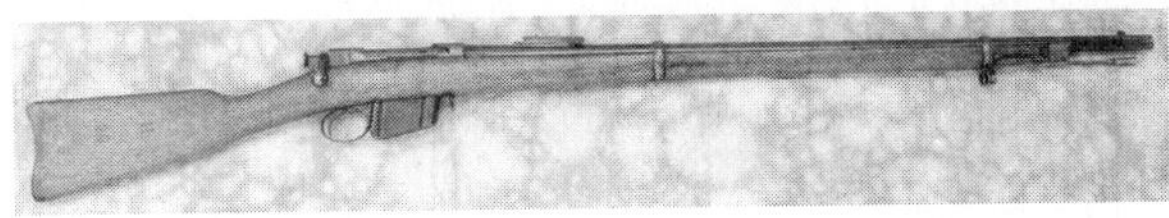

Paul Goodwin photo

Exc.	V.G.	Good	Fair	Poor
—	4500	2000	750	300

Model 1885 Navy Contract

As above, with the inspection markings (including an anchor) on the receiver ring and the left side of the stock. Approximately 1,500 were made.

Exc.	V.G.	Good	Fair	Poor
—	4500	2000	850	400

Model 1882 & 1885 Military Rifles

Barrel length 32", full-length stock secured by two barrel bands, chambered for .42 Russian, .43 Spanish, .45 Gardner or .45-70 cartridges. The values for those rifles not in .45-70 caliber would be approximately 25 percent less than those shown below. Approximately 10,000 Model 1882 rifles were made and 60,000 Model 1885 rifles. The two models can be differentiated by the fact that the cocking piece on the bolt of the Model 1885 is larger. The majority of these rifles were made for foreign contracts and commercial sales.

Exc.	V.G.	Good	Fair	Poor
—	3000	1200	600	400

Model 1899

Designed for use with smokeless and rimless cartridges, this model is marked on the receiver "Remington Arms Co. Ilion, N.Y. Patented Aug. 26th 1884 Sept. 9th 1884 March 17th 1885 Jan 18th 1887." Produced from 1889 to 1907 in the following variations:

Military Rifle

Barrel length 29", 6mm USN, .30-40, .303, 7x57mm or 7.65mm caliber with a full-length stock secured by two barrel bands.

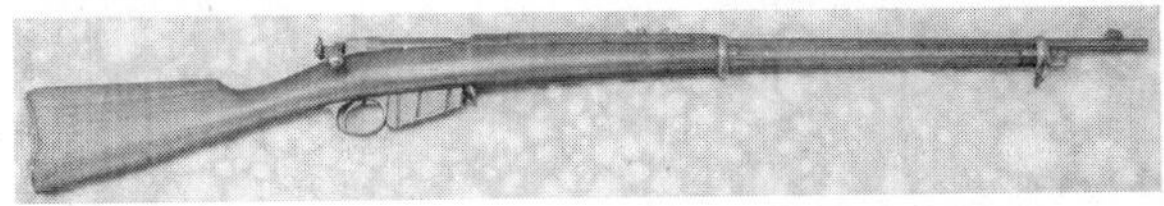

Paul Goodwin photo

Exc.	V.G.	Good	Fair	Poor
—	1500	1200	800	400

NOTE: Add $250 if U.S. marked.

Military Carbine

As above, with a 20" barrel and a 3/4-length carbine stock secured by one barrel band.

Exc.	V.G.	Good	Fair	Poor
—	2000	1500	800	500

Remington-Mannlicher Berthier Bolt-Action Rifle Model 1907/15

Produced for the French government, this rifle has a 31.5" barrel of 8mm Lebel caliber and a full-length

Model 1882 Military Rifle • *Courtesy West Point Museum, Paul Goodwin photo*

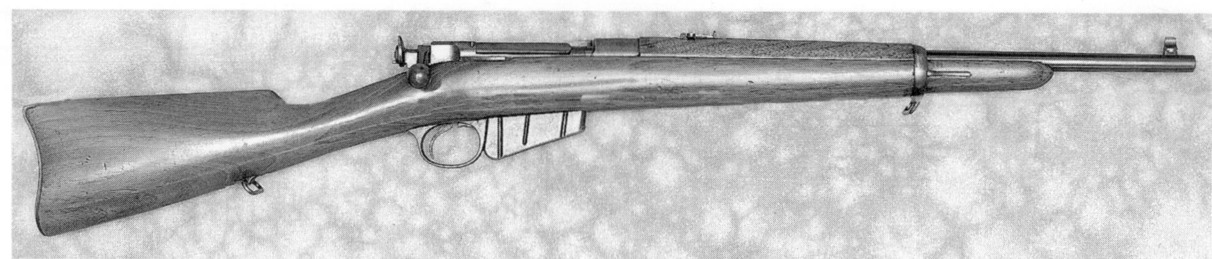

Remington Model 1899 Military Carbine • *Paul Goodwin photo*

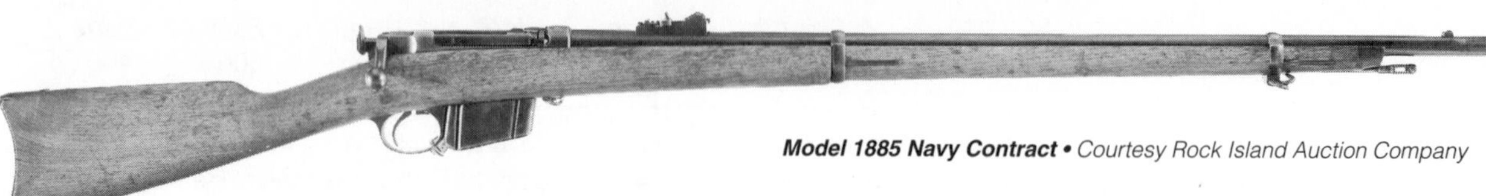

Model 1885 Navy Contract • *Courtesy Rock Island Auction Company*

stock secured by two barrel bands. The barrel marked "RAC 1907-15" and the left side of the receiver marked "Remington M'LE 1907-15." Several thousand were manufactured, however the French government inspectors rejected most of them as being of inferior quality. They were later sold through the NRA. Many are found in excellent condition.

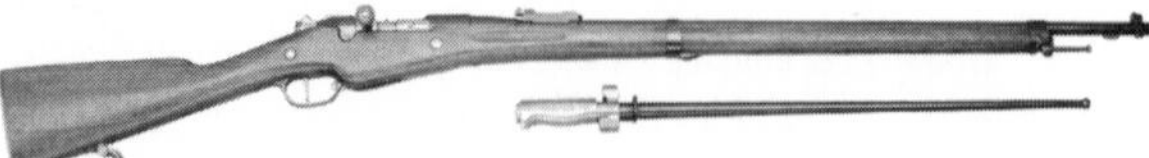

Paul Goodwin photo

Exc.	*V.G.*	*Good*	*Fair*	*Poor*
950	800	500	350	250

Remington-Mannlicher Berthier Bolt-Action Carbine Model 1907/15

As above but 24.5" barrel. Half stock with one barrel band.

Exc.	*V.G.*	*Good*	*Fair*	*Poor*
1250	1100	500	200	125

Remington/Westinghouse Model 1891 MosinNagant Bolt-Action Rifle

Produced for the Imperial Russian government, this rifle has a 32" barrel of 7.62x54mm R caliber with a full-length stock secured by two barrel bands. The barrel is marked "Remington Armory" with the date of manufacture and the receiver ring is stamped with the Russian coat-of-arms. Approximately 3,000,000 were made between 1916 and 1918. Many Remington Model 1891's were never shipped to Russia due to the Bolshevik revolution. Some were used by the U.S. as training rifles during WW1. These were later sold through the NRA. Many are in excellent condition. The stock will be marked " U.S." and have an ordnance bomb cartouche. Many of the parts have a small circle with "R" mark. Many of the Remington rifles that did get shipped to Russia ended up in Finland. These will have the "SA" in box Finnish mark on the barrel. Finland rebuilt most of the Mosin Nagants they got from Russia. These Finnish rifles were imported to the U.S. in the 1990's. Deduct 50 percent for Finnish marked rifle.

Paul Goodwin photo

Exc.	*V.G.*	*Good*	*Fair*	*Poor*
800	650	500	350	75

Model 513-T

This is a bolt action .22 caliber training rifle with oil finished walnut stock and checkered steel butt. Barrel length is 26.75" and detachable magazine capacity is 6 rounds. Rear sight is an adjustable

Model 513-T • *Paul Goodwin photo*

Redfield Model 75 RT. Most, but not all, of these rifles are drilled and tapped for telescope mounting blocks. Receiver is stamped "us property". Some of these rifles will have the arsenal rebuilder stamped on the barrel. About 70,000 of these rifles were produced under government contract from 1942 to 1944.

Exc.	V.G.	Good	Fair	Poor
750	550	400	300	200

Model 700 (M40)

This is a military version of the commercial Remington bolt action rifle. It was issued without sights and a 10x scope, chambered for the .308 (7.62x51 NATO) cartridge. Barrel length is 24". Magazine capacity is 5 rounds. Walnut stock with oil finish. Scope is a Redfield 3-9X Accu-Range. Buttplate, triggerguard and floorplate are aluminum. Weight is about 14 lbs with scope. Marked, "US RIFLE M40" with the serial number over the chamber. First issued in 1966. Weight is about 9.25 lbs. Primarily used by the U.S. Marine Corp.

In 1977, an improved version of this rifle was issued known as the M40A1. Same barrel length and scope butt-fitted with a synthetic McMillan camouflage stock, Pachmayr brown recoil pad and steel triggerguard and floorplate. In 1980, the Marine Corp began using Unertl 10X scope with mil-dot reticle with Unertl base and rings.

Exc.	V.G.	Good	Fair	Poor
5000	3500	2500	1500	1000

NOTE: Prices listed are for verifiable samples.

Remington Model 700P Rifles

Remington's line of law enforcement rifles are also used by a variety of military forces. Rifles purchased under contract will be marked for the country and service of origin. Models purchased by commercial means will not be marked.

Model 700 Police LTR (Lightweight Tactical Rifle)

Fitted with a fluted 20" barrel and chambered for the .308 or .223 cartridge this rifle weighs about 7.5 lbs. Synthetic stock.

NIB	Exc.	V.G.	Good	Fair	Poor
700	550	—	—	—	—

Model 700 Police

This model is fitted with a 26" barrel and chambered for the .308 and .223 cartridges in a short action or 7mm Rem. Mag., .300 Win. Mag., or .300 Rem. Ultra Mag. in a long action. Weight is about 9 lbs. Synthetic stock.

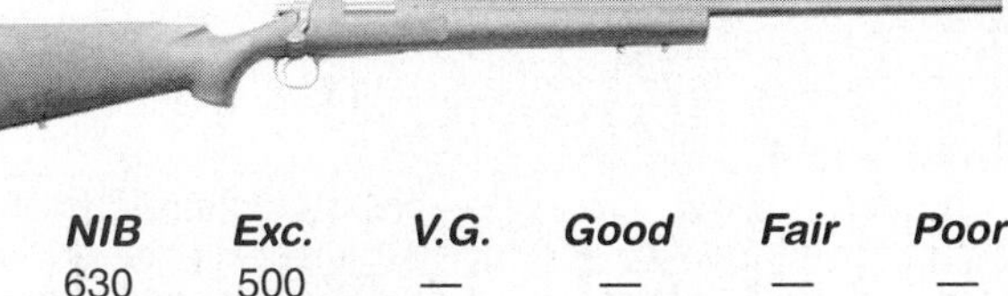

NIB	Exc.	V.G.	Good	Fair	Poor
630	500	—	—	—	—

Model 700 TWS (Tactical Weapons System)

Chambered for the .308 cartridge and fitted with a 26" barrel this model also features a Leupold Vari-X II 3.5x10 scope, a Harris bipod, quick adjustable sling, and a Pelican hard case. Weight of rifle is about 10.5 lbs.

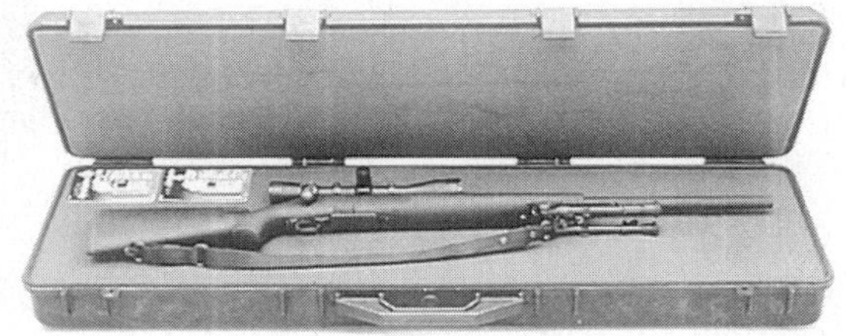

Courtesy Remington Arms

NIB	Exc.	V.G.	Good	Fair	Poor
N/A	—	—	—	—	—

Model 700 VS LH

This model is a left hand version of the Model 700m Police.

NIB	Exc.	V.G.	Good	Fair	Poor
650	500	—	—	—	—

Model 40-XB KS

Two versions of this rifle are offered. In the single shot version it is chambered for the .223, .308, and .300 Win. Mag calibers. In the repeating version it is chambered in the .223 or .308 calibers. All versions are fitted with a 27.25" barrel. Weight is about 10.25 lbs. Martially marked rifles will command a premium over retail prices.

NOTE: Retail prices range from $1,200 to $1,500 depending on configuration and finish.

PARKER-HALE

Model 85 Sniper

Built by the Gibbs Rifle Co. in Martinsburg, West Virginia, this Parker-Hale designed bolt-action rifle is chambered for the .308 cartridge and fitted with a 27.5" barrel with a telescope and bipod. Box magazine capacity is 10 rounds. Weight is about 12.5 lbs. First produced in 1986.

NIB	Exc.	V.G.	Good	Fair	Poor
4000	3000	2500	—	—	—

SAVAGE

Model 1899-D Military Musket

Courtesy Amoskeag Auction Company

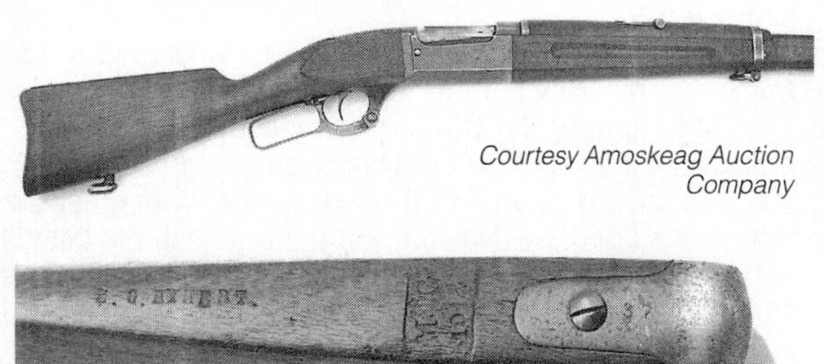

UNITED STATES OF AMERICA

Chambered for .303 Savage only with 28" barrel. Fitted with full military stocks. Produced from 1899 to 1915. Several hundred produced for Canadian Home Guard during WWI. These will have rack numbers on the buttplate.

Exc.	V.G.	Good	Fair	Poor
3250	2000	1500	700	300

WINCHESTER REPEATING ARMS COMPANY

NOTE: The U.S. government purchased many different Winchester rifles over the years for a wide variety of purposes. During World War I, the Model 1894 carbine was purchased by the government as well as small numbers of the Model 1907 and the Model 1910 self loading rifles. There is evidence that the U.S. Coast Guard purchased several thousand of Model 1906 .22 caliber rifles for use during World War I. The Model 52 bolt action rifle was first designed by Winchester in hopes of a government contract as a military training rifle, but the end of World War I precluded that goal. During World War II, the U.S. government purchased the Winchester Model 74 .22 caliber rifles from 1941 to 1943. It is possible that many Winchester rifles were purchased by the U.S. military for assorted purposes from guard duty to pest control. Many of these rifles will be martially marked and their value has increased over the standard civilian rifle.

Bibliographical Note: For more historical information, technical data, and photos see Bruce Canfield's *A Collector's Guide to Winchesters in the Service.* Also Thomas Henshaw, *The History of Winchester Firearms*, 1866-1992, Winchester Press, 1995. George Madis, *The Winchester Book*, 1985.

Martially Inspected Henry Rifles

Beginning in 1863 the Federal Government ordered 1,730 Henry Rifles for use in the Civil War. Most of these government-inspected rifles fall into serial number range 3000 to 4000 while the balance are close to this serial-number range. They are marked "C.G.C." for Charles G. Chapman, the government inspector. These Henry rifles were used under actual combat conditions and for that reason it is doubtful that there are any rifles that would fall into the excellent condition category. Therefore no price is given.

NOTE: There are many counterfeit examples of these rifles. It is strongly advised that an expert in this field be consulted prior to a sale.

Exc.	V.G.	Good	Fair	Poor
—	—	60000	25000	12000

Model 1866

In 1866 the New Haven Arms Company changed its name to the Winchester Repeating Arms Company. The first firearm to be built under the Winchester name was the Model 1866. This first Winchester was a much-improved version of the Henry. A new magazine tube developed by Nelson King, Winchester's plant superintendent, was a vast improvement over the slotted magazine tube used on the Henry and its predecessor. The old tube allowed dirt to enter through the slots and was weakened because of it. King's patent, assigned to Winchester, featured a solid tube that was much stronger and reliable. His patent also dealt with an improved loading system for the rifle. The rifle now featured a loading port on the right side of the receiver with a spring-loaded cover. The frame continued to be made from brass. The Model 1866 was chambered for the .44 caliber Flat Rimfire or the .44 caliber Pointed Rimfire. Both cartridges could be used interchangeably.

The barrel on the Model 1866 was marked with two different markings. The first, which is seen on early guns up to serial number 23000, reads "HENRY'S PATENT-OCT. 16, 1860 KING'S PATENT-MARCH 29, 1866." The second marking reads, "WINCHESTER'S-REPEATING-ARMS.NEW HAVEN, CT. KING'S-IMPROVEMENT-PATENTED MARCH 29, 1866 OCTOBER 16, 1860." There are three basic variations of the Model 1866:

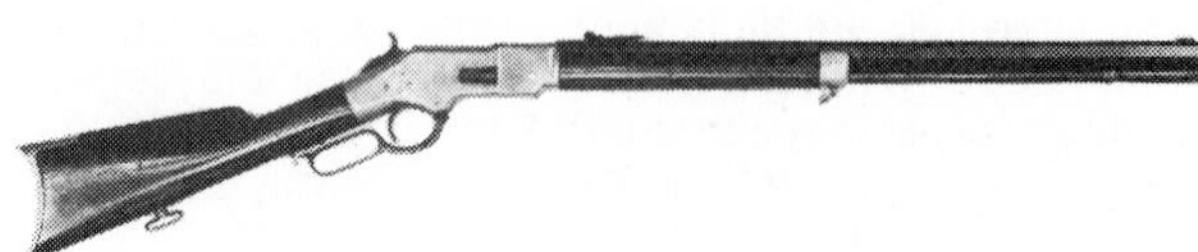

Courtesy Milwaukee Public Museum, Milwaukee, Wisconsin

1. Sporting Rifle round or octagon barrel. Approximately 28,000 were produced.
2. Carbine round barrel. Approximately 127,000 were produced.
3. Musket round barrel. Approximately 14,000 were produced.

The rifle and musket held 17 cartridges, and the carbine had a capacity of 13 cartridges. Unlike the Henry, Model 1866s were fitted with a walnut forearm. The Model 1866 was discontinued in 1898 with approximately 170,000 guns produced. The Model 1866 was sold in various special order configurations, such as barrels longer or shorter than standard, including engraved guns. The prices listed below represent only standard-model 1866s. For guns with special-order features, an independent appraisal from an expert is highly recommended.

NOTE: The Model 1866 Musket was not adopted by the U.S. military. It was sold to Mexico and Prussia. A large order of 46,000 muskets was delivered to the Turkisk goverment in 1870 and 1871. A few muskets, about 3,000, were sold to France.

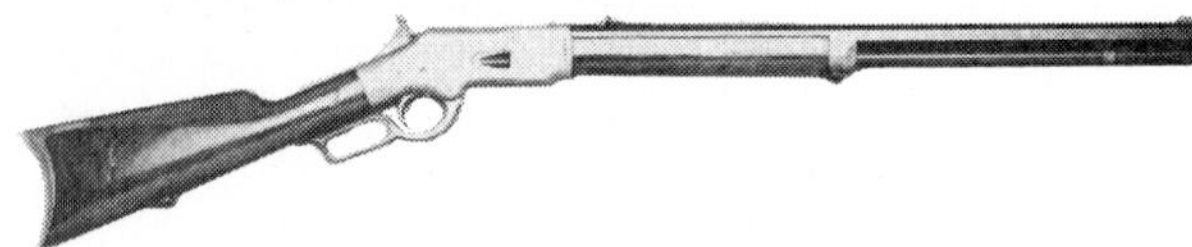

Courtesy Butterfield & Butterfield, San Francisco, California

Third Model

The third style's most noticeable characteristic is the more moderately curved receiver shape at the rear of the frame. The serial number is now stamped in block numerals behind the trigger, thus allowing the numbers to be seen for the first time without removing the stock. The barrel marking is stamped with the Winchester address. The Third Model is found between serial numbers 25000 and 149000. For the first time, a musket version was produced in this serial-number range.

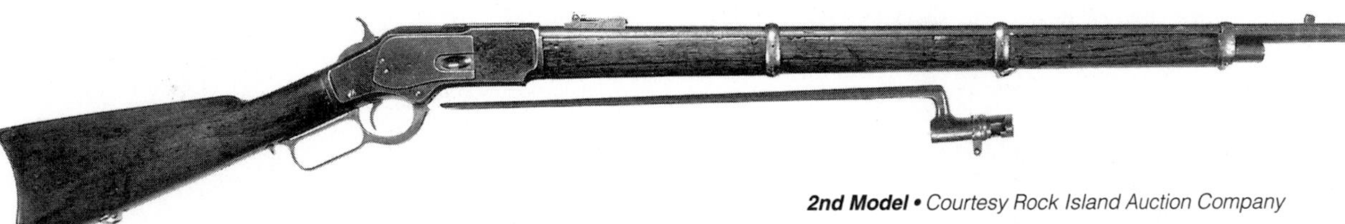

2nd Model • Courtesy Rock Island Auction Company

Musket

Exc.	V.G.	Good	Fair	Poor
—	11000	8000	3500	2500

Fourth Model

The fourth style has an even less pronounced drop at the top rear of the frame, and the serial number is stamped in script on the lower tang under the lever. The Fourth Model is seen between serial number 149000 and 170100 with the late guns having an iron buttplate instead of brass.

Musket

Exc.	V.G.	Good	Fair	Poor
—	12000	9000	3500	2500

Model 1866 Iron Frame Rifle Musket

Overall length 54-1/2"; barrel length 33-1/4"; caliber .45 c.f. Walnut stock with case hardened furniture, barrel burnished bright, the receiver case hardened. The finger lever catch mounted within a large bolster at the rear of the lever. Unmarked except for serial numbers that appear externally on the receiver and often the buttplate tang. Approximately 25 made during the early autumn of 1866. Prospective purchasers are strongly advised to secure an expert appraisal prior to acquisition. Due to the recent identification of this model pricing schedules have yet to be established.

Exc.	V.G.	Good	Fair	Poor
N/A	—	—	—	—

Model 1866 Iron Frame Swiss Sharpshooters Rifle

As above, but in .41 Swiss caliber and fitted with a Scheutzen style stock supplied by the firm of Weber Ruesch in Zurich. Marked Weber Ruesch, Zurich on the barrel and serial numbered externally. Approximately 400 to 450 manufactured in 1866 and 1867. This musket was most likely built for Swiss military trials. Prospective purchasers are strongly advised to secure an expert appraisal prior to acquisition. Due to the recent identification of this model pricing schedules have yet to be established.

Exc.	V.G.	Good	Fair	Poor
N/A	—	—	—	—

Model 1873 Musket

This rifle was fitted with a 30" round barrel and chambered for a variety of calibers at the customer's request. Nominal calibers are: .44-40, .38-40, and .32-20. Magazine capacity was 17 rounds. Muskets were fitted with almost full length wooden stocks with cleaning rod and bayonet fittings. Many of these muskets were sold under contract to foreign governments. Survival rate is very low.

1st Model

Exc.	V.G.	Good	Fair	Poor
—	—	8500	4000	1000

2nd Model

The dust cover on the Second Model operates on one central guide secured to the receiver with two screws. The checkered oval finger grip is still used, but on later Second Models this is changed to a serrated finger grip on the rear of the dust cover. Second Models are found in the 31000 to 90000 serial number range.

Exc.	V.G.	Good	Fair	Poor
7500	4000	2000	1250	9000

3rd Model

The central guide rail is still present on the Third Model, but it is now integrally machined as part of the receiver. The serrated rear edges of the dust cover are still present on the Third Model.

Exc.	V.G.	Good	Fair	Poor
6000	3500	1250	850	500

Model 1876

Musket, 32" round barrel with full-length forearm secured by one barrel band and straight grip stock. Stamped on the barrel is the Winchester address with King's patent date. The caliber marking is stamped on the bottom of the receiver near the magazine tube and the breech end of the barrel.

First Model

As with the Model 1873, the primary difference in model types lies in the dust cover. The First Model has no dust cover and is seen between serial number 1 and 3000.

Musket

Exc.	V.G.	Good	Fair	Poor
15000	12000	6500	3000	1500

Second Model

The Second Model has a dust cover with guide rail attached to the receiver with two screws. On the early Second Model an oval finger guide is stamped on top of the dust cover while later models have a serrated finger guide along the rear edge of the dust cover. Second Models range from serial numbers 3000 to 30000.

Musket

Exc.	V.G.	Good	Fair	Poor
—	—	9500	4000	1500

Northwest Mounted Police Carbine

The folding rear sight is graduated in meters instead of yards.

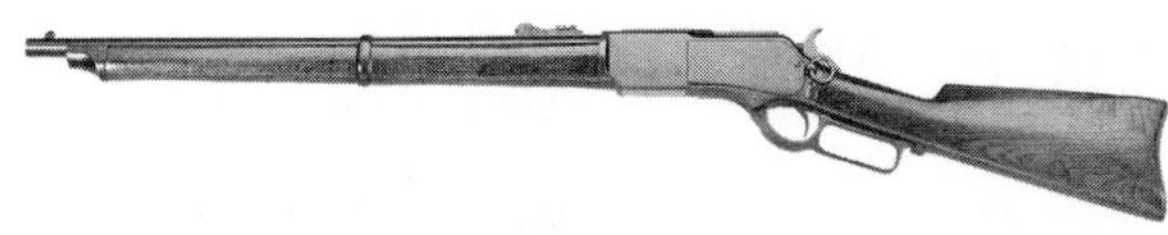

Courtesy Little John's Auction Service, Inc., Paul Goodwin photo

Exc.	V.G.	Good	Fair	Poor
15000	9000	4500	2000	1250

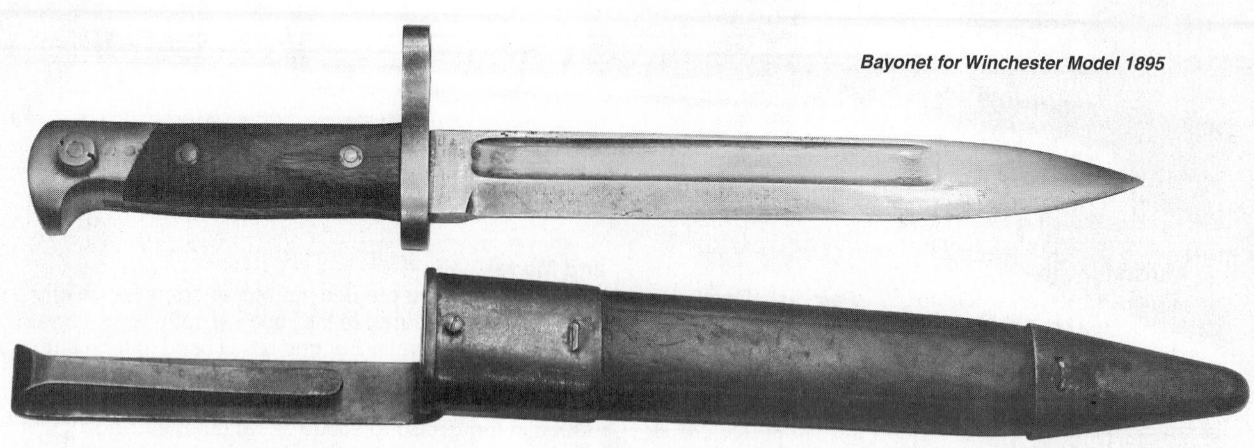
Bayonet for Winchester Model 1895

NOTE: Deduct 50 percent from prices if factory records do not confirm NWP use. A Model 1876 NWP in excellent condition is very rare. Proceed with caution.

Musket

Exc.	*V.G.*	*Good*	*Fair*	*Poor*
18000	9000	5000	1750	1000

Third Model

The dust cover guide rail on Third Model 76s is integrally machined as part of the receiver with a serrated rear edge on the dust cover. Third Model will be seen from serial numbers 30000 to 64000.

Musket

Exc.	*V.G.*	*Good*	*Fair*	*Poor*
9500	4750	3000	1250	1000

Model 1886

Based on a John Browning patent, the Model 1886 was one of the finest and strongest lever actions ever utilized in a Winchester rifle. Winchester introduced the Model 1886 in order to take advantage of the more powerful centerfire cartridges of the time.

Musket, 30" round barrel, musket style forearm with one barrel band. Military style sights. About 350 Model 1886 Muskets were produced. This is the most rare variation of all Winchester lever action rifles.

Musket

Exc.	*V.G.*	*Good*	*Fair*	*Poor*
—	18000	9000	3500	1500

Model 1895 U.S. Army Musket

U.S. Army Musket, 28" round barrel chambered for the .30-40 Krag. Came equipped with or without knife bayonet. These muskets were furnished to the U.S. Army for use during the Spanish-American War and are "US" marked on the receiver.

Exc.	*V.G.*	*Good*	*Fair*	*Poor*
5000	3500	1800	850	450

Bayonet for Winchester Model 1895

Wood grips. Muzzle ring. 8.3" single edge blade. Marked "Winchester Repeatings Arms Co." inside face of cross piece beside ricasso. Steel tipped leather scabbard. Price range 500 – 250.

Model 1885 (Single Shot)

The High Wall musket most often had a 26" round barrel chambered for the .22 caliber cartridge. Larger calibers were available as were different barrel lengths. The High Wall Musket featured an almost full length forearm fastened to the barrel with a single barrel band and rounded buttplate.

The Low Wall musket is most often referred to as the Winder Musket named after the distinguished marksman, Colonel C.B. Winder. This model features a Lyman receiver sight and was made in .22 caliber.

U.S. and Ordnance markings will appear on rifles purchased by the government.

High Wall Musket

Exc.	*V.G.*	*Good*	*Fair*	*Poor*
4000	3000	2000	1500	900

Low Wall Musket (Winder Musket)

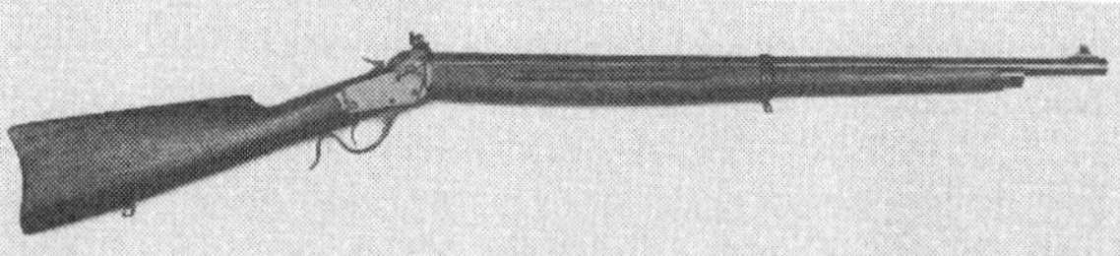
Courtesy Buffalo Bill Historical Center, Cody, Wyoming

Exc.	*V.G.*	*Good*	*Fair*	*Poor*
3500	2000	1200	750	400

Winchester Hotchkiss Bolt Action Rifle

This model is also known as the Hotchkiss Magazine Gun or the Model 1883. This rifle was designed by Benjamin Hotchkiss in 1876, and Winchester acquired the manufacturing rights to the rifle in 1877. In 1879, the first guns were delivered for sale. The Hotchkiss rifle was a bolt-action firearm designed for military and sporting use. It was the first bolt-action rifle made by Winchester. The rifle was furnished in .45-70 Government, and although the 1884 Winchester

Winchester Model 1895 Musket •
Courtesy Greg Martin Auctions

Close-up of Hotchkiss 1st Model action • *Courtesy George Hoyem*

Close-up of Hotchkiss 2nd Model action • *Courtesy George Hoyem*

Close-up of Hotchkiss 3rd Model action • *Courtesy George Hoyem*

catalog lists a .40-65 Hotchkiss as being available, no evidence exists that such a chamber was ever actually furnished. Two different types of military configurations will be seen:

1. Carbine, 24" round or 22-1/2" round barrel with military style straight grip stock. Chambered for the 45-55 cartridge.
2. Musket, 32" or 28" round barrel with almost full length military-style straight grip stock. Winchester produced the Model 1883 until 1899, having built about 85,000 guns. Chambered for the 45-70 cartridge.

First Model

This model has the safety and a turn button magazine cut-off located above the triggerguard on the right side. The carbine has a 24" round barrel with a saddle ring on the left side of the stock. The musket has a 32" round barrel with two barrel bands, a steel forearm tip, and bayonet attachment under the barrel. The serial number range for the First Model is between 1 and about 6419.

Army Rifle

These Army models are marked with the inspector stamping of "ESA/1878" on the left side of the stock. Production total of 513 rifles.

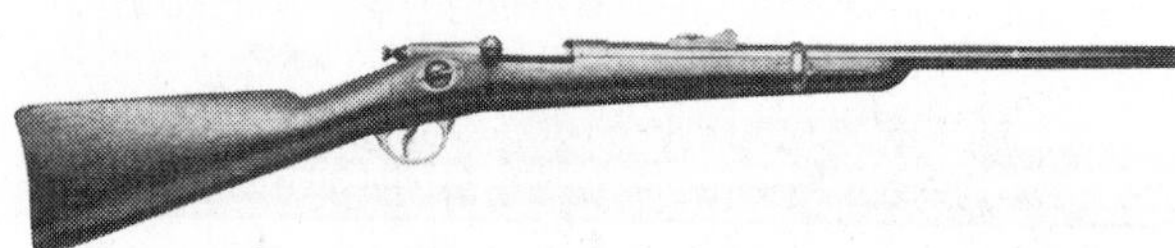

Courtesy Butterfield & Butterfield, San Francisco, California

Exc.	*V.G.*	*Good*	*Fair*	*Poor*
—	6000	3500	900	500

Carbine

501 carbines produced.

Exc.	*V.G.*	*Good*	*Fair*	*Poor*
—	5000	2750	900	500

Navy Rifle

1,474 produced.

Exc.	*V.G.*	*Good*	*Fair*	*Poor*
—	4500	2250	900	500

Musket

Exc.	*V.G.*	*Good*	*Fair*	*Poor*
—	3000	1500	700	300

Second Model

On this model the safety is located on the top left side of the receiver, and the magazine cutoff is located on the top right side of the receiver to the rear of the bolt handle. The carbine has a 22-1/2" round barrel with a nickeled forearm cap. The musket now has a 28" barrel. Serial number range for the Second Model runs from 6420 to 22521.

Carbine

400 produced.

Exc.	*V.G.*	*Good*	*Fair*	*Poor*
—	6000	3000	900	500

Musket

Exc.	*V.G.*	*Good*	*Fair*	*Poor*
—	3500	1750	750	350

Third Model

The Third Model is easily identified by the two-piece stock separated by the receiver. The carbine is now fitted with a 20" barrel with saddle ring and bar on the left side of the frame. The musket remains unchanged from the Second Model with the exception of the two-piece stock. Serial numbers of the Third Model range from 22552 to 84555.

Army Rifle

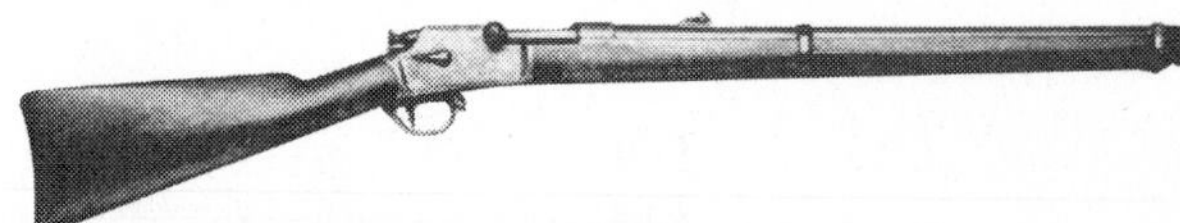

Courtesy Butterfield & Butterfield, San Francisco, California

Exc.	*V.G.*	*Good*	*Fair*	*Poor*
—	3500	1750	750	350

Musket

Exc.	*V.G.*	*Good*	*Fair*	*Poor*
—	3500	1750	750	350

Winchester-Lee Straight Pull Rifle

This rifle was a military firearm that Winchester built for the U.S. Navy in 1895. The Navy version was a musket type with a 28" round barrel and musket style forearm and plain walnut pistol grip stock. In 1897, Winchester offered a commercial musket version for public sale as well as a Sporting Rifle. All of these guns were chambered for the 6mm Lee (.236 Caliber) cartridge. The Sporting Rifle featured a 24" round barrel with plain walnut pistol grip stock and finger grooves in the forearm. Built from 1895 to 1905, Winchester sold about 20,000 Lee rifles; 15,000 were sold to the U.S. Navy, 3,000 were sold in the commercial version, and 1,700 were Sporting Rifles.

NOTE: Commercial and Sporting rifles will not have martial markings, inspector markings, or bayonet fittings.

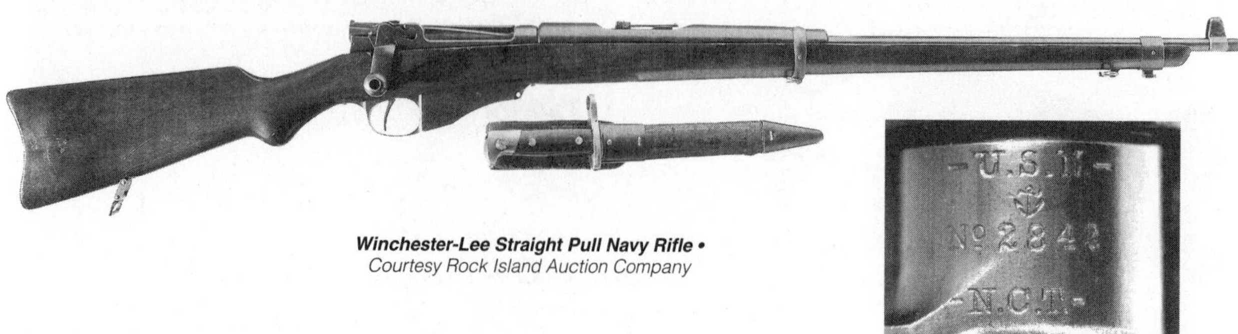

Winchester-Lee Straight Pull Navy Rifle •
Courtesy Rock Island Auction Company

U.S. Navy Musket

Exc.	*V.G.*	*Good*	*Fair*	*Poor*
4000	2500	1500	700	500

NOTE: Some of these muskets were stored on the U.S. battleship Maine. Records of serial numbers exist to authenticate these muskets. Add a premium of 50 percent for these examples.

HARRINGTON & RICHARDSON, INC.

Reising Model 60

A .45 ACP caliber semi-automatic rifle with an 18.25" barrel and a 12- or 20-round detachable magazine. Blued, with a walnut stock. It operates on a retarded blowback system and was developed to be used as a police weapon. Manufactured between 1944 and 1946.

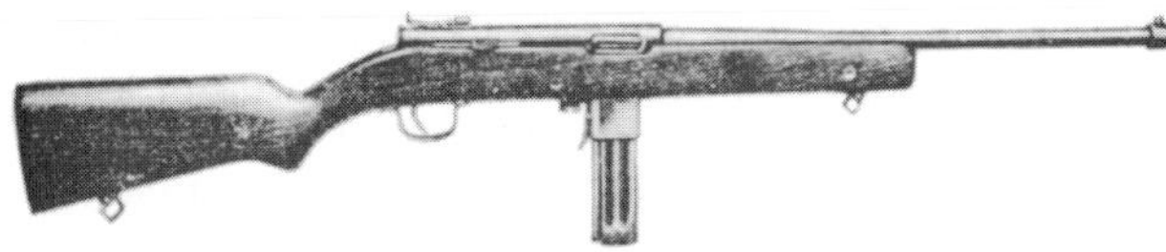

Courtesy Richard M. Kumor Sr.

Reising receiver markings •
Courtesy Stoddard Martial collection, Paul Goodwin photo

Exc.	*V.G.*	*Good*	*Fair*	*Poor*
2000	1600	1100	750	400

Model 65 Military

A .22 l.r. caliber semi-automatic rifle with a 23" barrel and Redfield peep sights. Blued, with a walnut stock. Manufactured between 1944 and 1956.

Exc.	*V.G.*	*Good*	*Fair*	*Poor*
500	300	200	125	90

NOTE: Add 100 percent if USMC marked.

BARRETT F.A. MFG. CO.

Model 95 (M 107 Sniper Weapon System)

Introduced in 1995, this .50 caliber BMG bolt action model features a 29" barrel and a 5-round magazine. Scope optional. Weight is 22 lbs. Adopted by the U.S. Army in 2000 as an anti-material weapon out to 1,500 plus meters. This model differs from the commercial version in that it breaks down into two smaller sections; it is fitted with an 11.5" optical rail, has one takedown pin, detachable bipod with spiked feet, is fitted with front and rear iron sights, and has adjustable scope rings.

Exc.	*V.G.*	*Good*	*Fair*	*Poor*
5500	4500	4000	N/A	N/A

Model 82A1 (SASR)

The US Marine Corp. traded to Barrett 112 Model 82A1 .50 caliber rifles, 100 of which were used in Desert Storm. Of the 112 rifles only 34 are in private hands. Barrett offers these rifles in very good condition with "US" stamped receivers and USMC camo finish. Serial number verification certificate.

NIB	*Exc.*	*V.G.*	*Good*	*Fair*	*Poor*
—	—	25000	—	—	—

SHOTGUNS

For a more detailed historical and technical account of U.S. military shotguns see Bruce Canfield's, *A Collectors Guide to United States Combat Shotguns*, Andrew Mobray, 1999. Also Thomas F. Swearengen, *The World's Fighting Shotguns*, Vol. IV, Ironside International Publishers, 1978.

NOTE: U.S. Military shotguns made through WWII that have a bayonet mount used the Model 1917 Bayonet.

WINCHESTER

Model 1897 Trench Gun (Model 1917)

Slide action hammer gun 12 gauge, 20" barrel bored to shoot buckshot, plain walnut modified pistol grip stock with grooved slide handle. Solid frame (WWI) or takedown (WWII). Fitted with barrel handguard and bayonet. This model was furnished to the U.S. Army for trench work in WWI. It was not listed in Winchester catalogs until 1920. This model was also used in large numbers in WWII, Korea, and Vietnam. Prices below are for U.S. marked guns.

Model 97 Solid Frame-World War I

Exc.	*V.G.*	*Good*	*Fair*	*Poor*
5000	3500	2000	1000	700

Model 97 Take Down-World War II

Exc.	*V.G.*	*Good*	*Fair*	*Poor*
4500	3000	1800	800	650

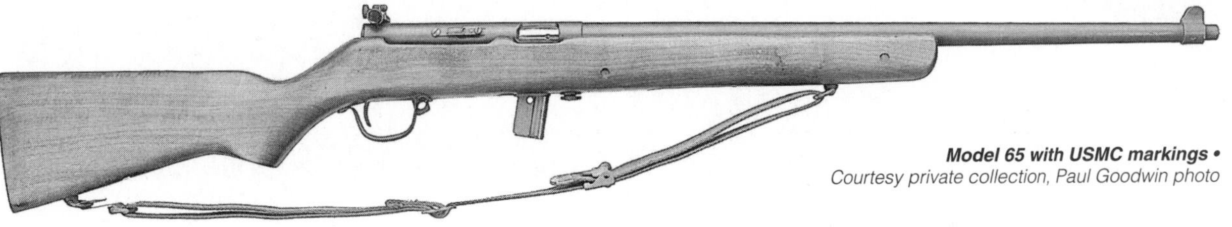

Model 65 with USMC markings •
Courtesy private collection, Paul Goodwin photo

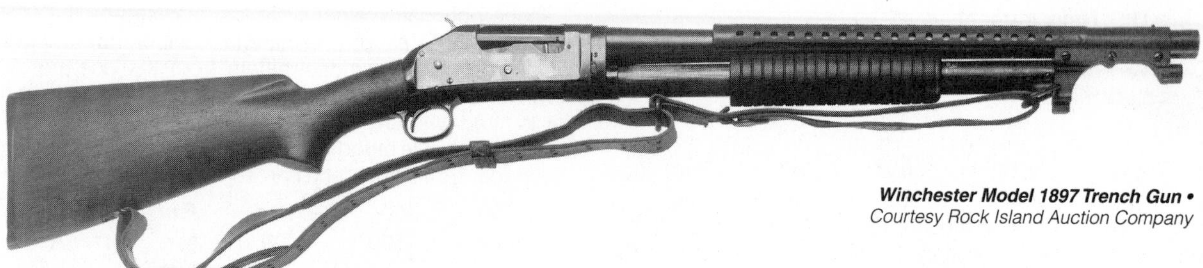

Winchester Model 1897 Trench Gun • *Courtesy Rock Island Auction Company*

NOTE: Add about $200 for Winchester marked bayonet.

Model 12 Trench Gun

Slide action hammerless gun 12 gauge, 20" barrel bored to shoot buckshot, plain walnut modified pistol grip stock with grooved slide handle. Solid frame or takedown. Fitted with barrel hand guard and bayonet. Finish is blued. This model was furnished to the U.S. Army for trench work in WWI and WWII. Prices below are for U.S. marked guns.

Exc.	*V.G.*	*Good*	*Fair*	*Poor*
5000	3500	2000	800	650

NOTE: Add about $200 for Winchester marked bayonet.

Model 1200

In 1968 and 1969 the U.S. military purchased a quantity of Model 1200 shotguns with 20" cylinder bored barrels, Type W bayonet adapter for the Model 1917 bayonet. Stocks were plain and uncheckered with oil finish.

Exc.	*V.G.*	*Good*	*Fair*	*Poor*
2500	1750	1200	600	300

Model 1400

The U.S. military purchased a small quantity of Model 1400 semi-automatic shotguns. These were fitted with a plain 20" barrel and choked cylinder. Scarce.

Exc.	*V.G.*	*Good*	*Fair*	*Poor*
N/A	—	—	—	—

REMINGTON

Model 10 Trench Gun

Slide action 12 gauge shotgun with 23" round barrel. No checkering on buttstock. Wooden handguard and bayonet lug. Prices below for shotgun only with military markings.

Exc.	*V.G.*	*Good*	*Fair*	*Poor*
15000	12500	10000	7500	5000

Model 11 Military Riot Gun

This is a 12 gauge 20" barrel shotgun used during WWI. Most were blued, some were Parkerized when rebuilt. Military markings with stock cartouche. Many thousands were sold to the military and are often encountered.

Exc.	*V.G.*	*Good*	*Fair*	*Poor*
1050	750	500	400	150

NOTE: A long barrel version of the Model 11 was used by the military for aerial gunnery practice. These examples will bring less.

Model 31 Military Riot Gun

This model was to replace the Model 10. Built in a short barrel (20") riot configuration, there were about 15,000 of these shotguns bought by the military but most were in the longer barrel lengths used for training. Stocks were not checkered. Martially marked.

Exc.	*V.G.*	*Good*	*Fair*	*Poor*
1500	1000	750	500	350

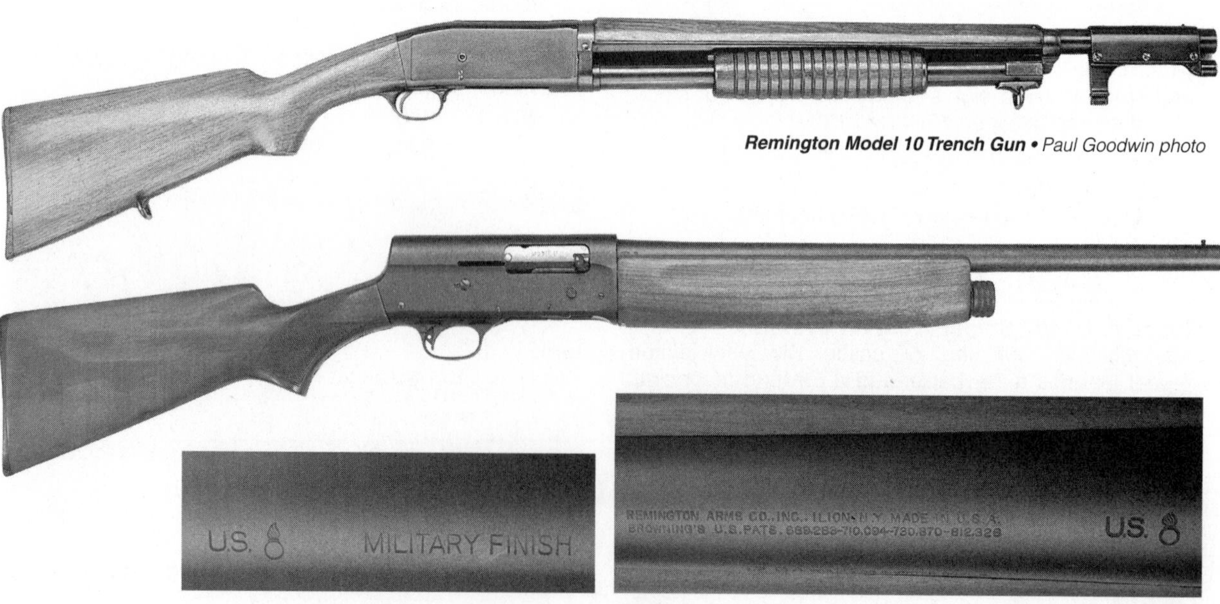

Remington Model 10 Trench Gun • *Paul Goodwin photo*

Model 11 Military Riot Gun • *Courtesy West Point Museum, Paul Goodwin photo*

Model 870 Mark I

This is a slide action 12 gauge shotgun with Parkerized finish. Fitted with an 18" round barrel. Prices are for military marked guns.

Exc.	*V.G.*	*Good*	*Fair*	*Poor*
5000	3500	2000	1250	850

NOTE: The Model 870 is still purchased by the U.S. military in a number of different configurations. The key to the correct designation of these more current shotguns lies with the military markings.

Model 11-87P

This is a semi-automatic 12 gauge shotgun with an 18" barrel and 7-round magazine extension. Fitted with synthetic stock. Purchased by various branches of the U.S. military, this shotgun may be found in a number of different configurations. All will be military marked.

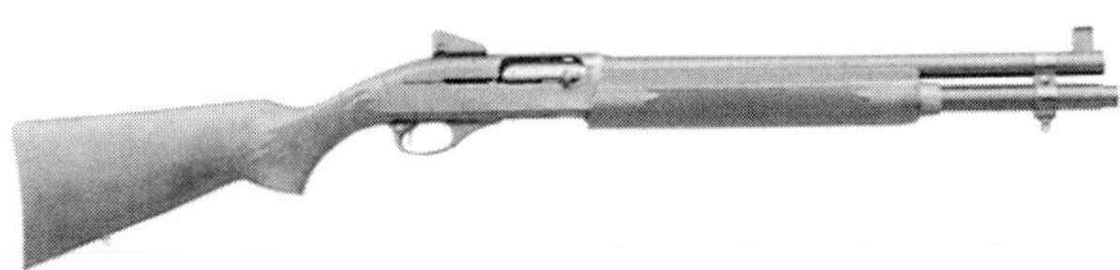

Exc.	*V.G.*	*Good*	*Fair*	*Poor*
750	600	400	300	150

SAVAGE

Model 720 Military Riot Gun

A semi-automatic 12 gauge shotgun similar in design to the Remington 11 and the Browning A-5. Some 15,000 of these shotguns were sold to the military during WWII. Martially marked. One of the more rare WWII shotguns.

Exc.	*V.G.*	*Good*	*Fair*	*Poor*
2500	1850	1500	850	500

STEVENS

Model 520 U.S. Marked Trench Gun

A slide action shotgun manufactured from 1930 to 1949. Chambered for the 12 gauge shell and fitted with a 20" barrel with cylinder choke. Fitted with a metal handguard and Stevens designed bayonet adapter. Used extensively in WWII. About 35,000 of these guns were purchased by the government during the war. Blued finish. Trench guns were fitted with metal handguards and bayonet adapters. There is also a military version without handguard called a Riot Gun. These models will also have military markings. Riot guns will bring less than Trench Guns.

Exc.	*V.G.*	*Good*	*Fair*	*Poor*
2500	1500	850	500	350

Model 620 U.S. Marked Trench Gun

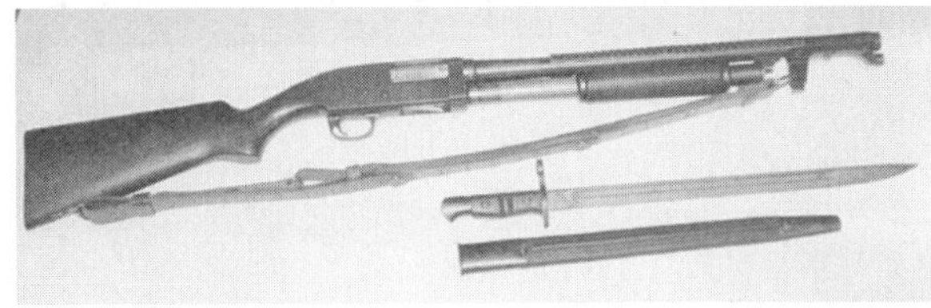

Courtesy Richard M. Kumor Sr.

Exc.	*V.G.*	*Good*	*Fair*	*Poor*
2000	1600	1100	600	300

Stevens .22/.410 Shotgun-Rifle Combination

This was the precursor to the Model 24. First made in 1940 with a Tenite stock, this combination gun was used by some bomber crews during WWII. According to Savage records the U.S. government purchased about 10,000 of these guns during the war as well as some years after as some of these guns were marked "USAF."

Exc.	*V.G.*	*Good*	*Fair*	*Poor*
N/A	—	—	—	—

MOSSBERG

Model 590 Special Purpose (ATP8)

Fitted with a 20" shrouded barrel, bayonet lug, parkerized or blued finish. Speed feed stock and ghost ring sights. Introduced in 1987. Weight is about 7.25 lbs. Military marked. This gun is also offered in a commercial version.

Model 520 Trench Gun • *Courtesy West Point Museum, Paul Goodwin photo*

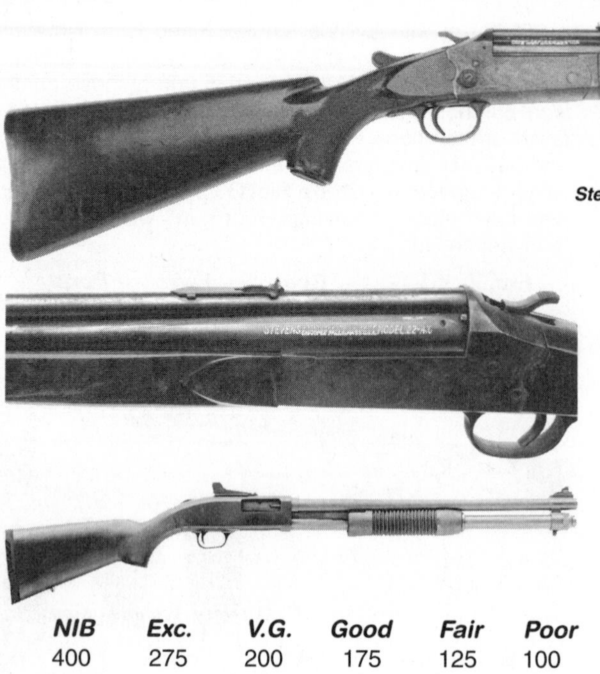

Stevens .22/.410 Shotgun-Rifle Combination

NIB	Exc.	V.G.	Good	Fair	Poor
400	275	200	175	125	100

Model 590A1

A 12 gauge slide action shotgun fitted with an 18" barrel. This model differs from the commercial one by having an aluminum trigger housing instead of plastic, an aluminum safety instead of plastic, and a heavy walled barrel. The finish is Parkerized and military marked.

Exc.	V.G.	Good	Fair	Poor
450	300	250	200	100

Model RI 96

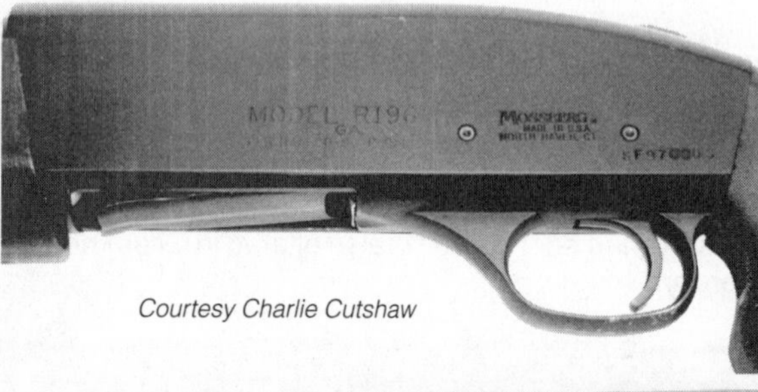

Courtesy Charlie Cutshaw

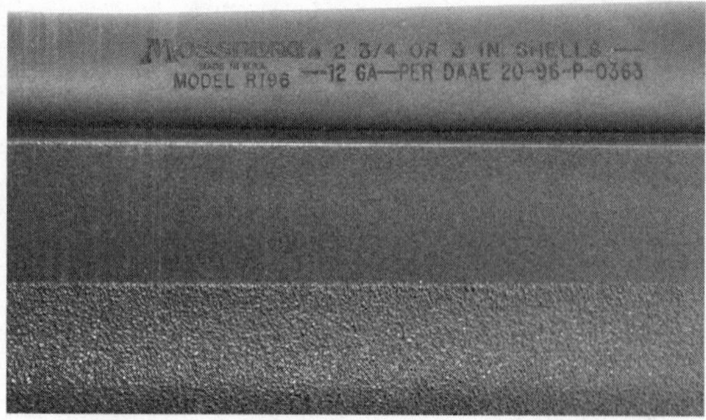

Essentially a modified Mossberg Model 9200 semi-auto gas operated 12 gauge shotgun with 3" chamber fitted with an 18" barrel thicker than standard. Five round magazine. Military contract number on barrel and receiver with "US" suffix to serial number. Black phosphate finish. Issued to army special operations units in South America.

Exc.	V.G.	Good	Fair	Poor
N/A	—	—	—	—

ITHACA

For a more detailed description of Ithaca military shotguns see Walter Snyder's book, *Ithaca Featherlight Repeaters...the Best Gun Going: A Complete History of the Ithaca Model 37 and the Model 87*, Cook and Uline Publishing, 1998.

Model 37 Military Marked Trench Gun (WWII)

This is one of the scarcest military shotguns. It was built in three different configurations; 30" barrel, 20" barrel, and 20" barrel with handguard and bayonet lug (Trench Gun). A scarce shotgun, proceed with caution.

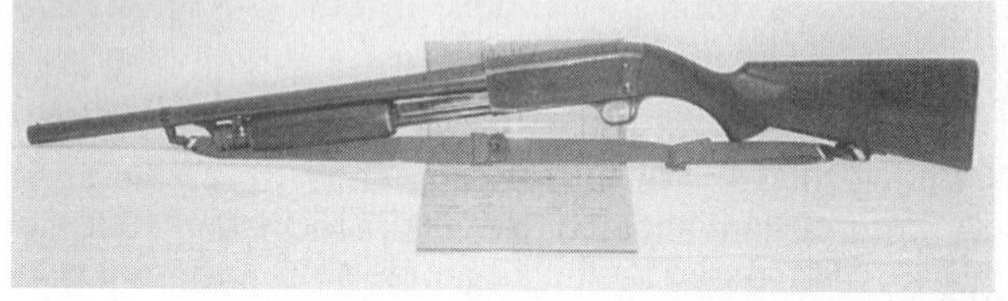

Model 37 with 20" barrel and release papers •
Courtesy Richard M. Kumor Sr.

Exc.	V.G.	Good	Fair	Poor
10000	7500	5000	2500	1500

NOTE: Add $200 for government release papers and 150 percent for Trench Gun configuration.

Model 37 Military Marked Trench Gun (Vietnam)

Same as above but built from 1962 to 1963. Fitted with 20" barrel. Stock was not checkered and had oil finish. Receiver had "US" stamped. Highest serial number reported is S23710.

Exc.	V.G.	Good	Fair	Poor
3500	2500	1800	900	750

Model 37 Military Marked Trench Gun (Navy Contract)

Similar to the Model 37 Trench gun but built in 1966-1967 for the U.S. Navy Ammunition Depot. About 3,000 were built. Based on the Model 37 M&P model.

Exc.	V.G.	Good	Fair	Poor
5000	3500	2500	1250	900

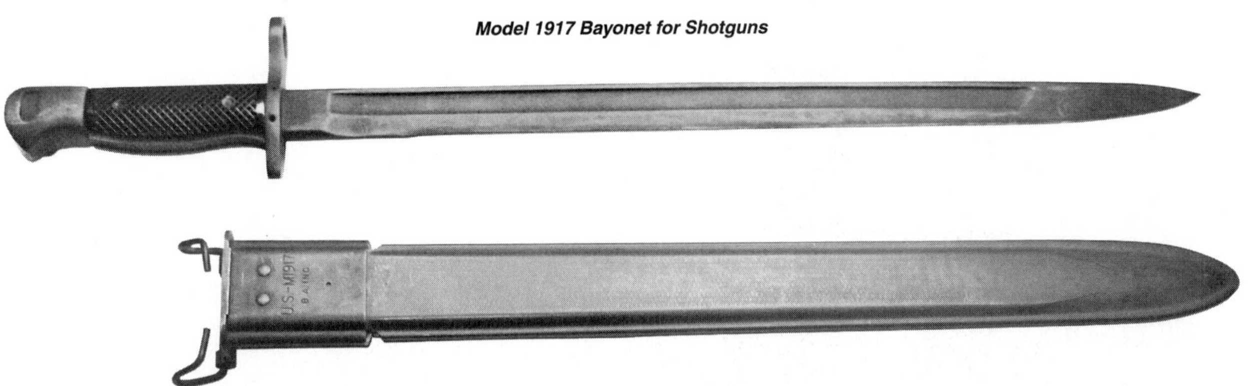

Model 1917 Bayonet for Shotguns

BENELLI

M4 Super 90 (M1014)

Adopted by the U.S. Marine Corps this 12-gauge shotgun features a choice of three modular buttstock and two barrel configurations. Action is semi-auto or slide action. Top mounted Picatinny rail. Barrel length is 18.5". Magazine capacity is 6 rounds. Ghost-ring sights. Black MILSPEC finish. Weight is about 8.4 lbs. Matte black finish. Deliveries in 2000. This model will be available in a modified form for commercial sale after military and law enforcement contracts are filled.

NIB	Exc.	V.G.	Good	Fair	Poor
1450	1150	—	—	—	—

Model 1917 Bayonet for Shotguns

Checkered black plastic grips. Cross piece held in place by two roll pins. Marked on cross piece "Gen-cut" Ring fits bayonet stud on military issue shotguns. This is the same design as the earlier M 1917 bayonet. Made in the 1960s. Green plastic scabbard marked "U.S. M-1917." Price range 275 – 125.

MACHINE GUNS

Bibliographical Note: For historical information, technical data, and photos see James Ballou, *Rock in a Hard Place; The Browning Automatic Rifle*, Collector Grade Publications, 2000. Wahl and Toppel, *The Gatling Gun*, New York, 1965.

Colt Gatling Gun

First invented by American Dr. Richard J. Gatling in 1861, this is a multi-barrel (6 to 10 barrels) hand-cranked machine gun. Several different models were developed and built in the 1860s with some were used in the American Civil War. Some of these early guns were chambered for the .58 caliber, while a few others were chambered for the 1" shell. The classic Gatling gun is the Model 1874 chambered for the .45-70 cartridge. There are several other models such as the Model 1879, Model 1881, the Model 1892, Model 1895, and the Model 1903. Some of these guns were tripod-mounted while others were mounted on gun carriages, and still others were deck-mounted for ship-board use. Some of the Gatling guns have exposed barrels while others are enclosed in a brass jacket. The Model 1877 bulldog is fitted with five 18" barrels enclosed in a brass jacket. The Model 1893 Police has six 12" barrels in .45-70 and weighs about 75 lbs. These guns are marked with a brass plate on top of the receiver, "GATLING'S/BATTERY/GUN 9 (PATENT DATES) MADE BY COLT'S/PT. FIRE ARMS MFG. CO./HARTFORD, CONN.U.S.A."

NOTE: As an interesting aside, Gatling guns are still in use by military forces but are now electrically powered (GEC M134/ GAU-2B Minigun) and capable of a rate of fire of 6,000 rounds per minute using the 7.62x51 cartridge.

Values for these guns are difficult to establish. Gatling guns in excellent condition in .45-70 caliber can bring between $75,000 to $200,000 and even more.

Colt Model 1895

Designed by John Browning and built by Colt, this is a gas operated air-cooled belt-fed gun chambered for the .30-03, 6mm U.S.N., and .30-40 cartridges as well as the .30-06 (called the Model 1906 cartridge) in later applications. Rate of fire is about 450 rounds per minute. Called the "potato digger" because of its back and forth motion and proximity to the ground. This was the first non-mechanical firing machine issued to the U.S. military. It saw limited use during the Spanish-American War, the Boxer Rebellion, and as a training gun during WWI.

NOTE: See also Colt/Marlin Model 1914/1915.

NOTE: The .30-03 cartridge was the original and earlier version of the .30-06 cartridge. Guns chambered for

Colt Model 1895 • *Courtesy Butterfield & Butterfield*

Colt Gatling Model 1883 •
Courtesy Butterfield & Butterfield

the older .30-03 cartridge will function and fire the .30-06 cartridge (accuracy suffers) *but the reverse is not true.* Sometimes the .30-03 cartridge is referred to as the .30-45. Both of these cartridges replaced the older .30-40 Krag as the official military round.

Pre-1968 (rare)

Exc.	*V.G.*	*Fair*
25000	23000	21000

Pre-1986 manufacture with new receiver or reweld

Exc.	*V.G.*	*Fair*
18000	16000	15000

Colt Maxim 1904

This belt-fed machine gun was originally chambered for the .30-03 cartridge and then altered to the .30-06. Built on the standard Maxim M1900 pattern. Barrel length is 28.5". Rate of fire is about 500 rounds per minute. Fed by a 250-round cloth belt. Primarily used as a training gun during World War I. A total of 287 of these guns were produced. Weight is approximately 75 lbs.

Pre-1968 (very rare)

Exc.	*V.G.*	*Fair*
50000	38000	30000

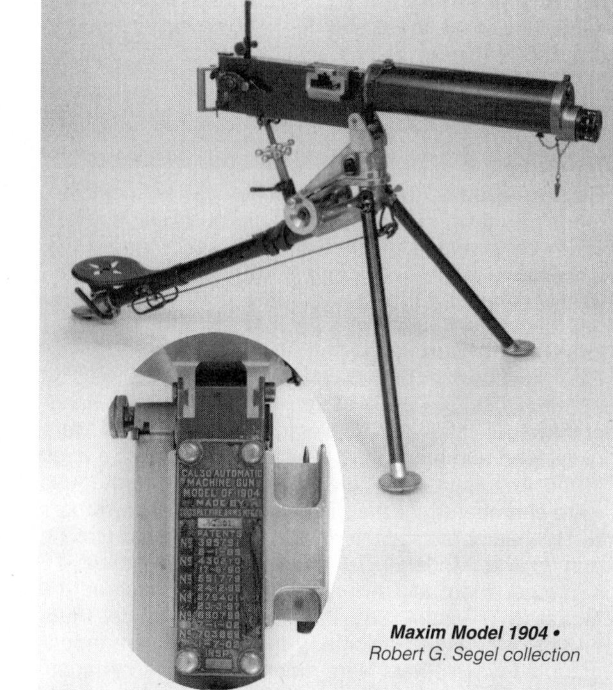

Maxim Model 1904 •
Robert G. Segel collection

Pre-1986 manufacture with new side plate

Exc.	*V.G.*	*Fair*
30000	27500	25000

Maxim Model 1904 name plate • *Robert G. Segel collection*

Model 1909 Benet-Mercie Machine Rifle

Developed by the French firm Hotchkiss and built in the U.S. by Colt's and Springfield Armory, this air-cooled gas-operated automatic rifle is fed by a 30-round metal strip. Chambered for the .30-06 cartridge. Rate of fire was about 400 rounds per minute. Weight of gun was approximately 27 lbs. This gun was equipped with a Model 1908 Warner & Swasey telescope. This model was used against Mexican bandits in 1915 and 1916 by the U.S. Army and in France during the early stages of WWI. However, it did not prove to be reliable and was soon replaced by the Hotchkiss and Vickers guns. About 670 were produced by both Colt and Springfield.

Model 1909 Benet-Mercie • *Robert G. Segel collection*

Model 1909 Benet-Mercie Warner & Swasey telescope sight • *Robert G. Segel collection*

Pre-1968 (Rare)

Exc.	*V.G.*	*Fair*
25000	18500	15000

Browning M1917 & M1917A1

Based on John M. Browning's original automatic weapon design it was chambered for the .30-06 cartridge. This water-cooled gun is fitted with a 23.8" barrel and has a rate of fire of 500 rounds per minute using a cloth belt. Its empty weight for the gun only is 33 lbs. The M1917A1 tripod weighs about 53 lbs. Marked "US INSP BROWNING MACHINE GUN US CAL 30 MODEL OF 1917." This gun was produced by various manufacturers from 1917 to 1945.

About 56,000 were built prior to the end of WWI although few saw actual combat service. In the mid 1930s, a few minor modifications were made to the gun and it became known as the Model 1917A1. These modifications follow.

Browning Model 1917A1 • *Robert G. Segel collection*

The most important legacy of the Model 1917 Browning is that it led to the use of this gun as the air-cooled Model 1919. During its production life the gun was built by Colt, Remington, and Westinghouse.

Pre-1968

Exc.	*V.G.*	*Fair*
35000	32500	30000

Pre-1986 Non-martial U.S. manufacture

Exc.	*V.G.*	*Fair*
25000	20000	N/A

A gunner's view of the Browning Model 1917 during World War II in Germany • *Courtesy John M. Miller*

Browning Model 1917 (Westinghouse) (The ID number on the side plate is a Numrich Arms registered serial number, not an original factory Model 1917 number) • *Courtesy private NFA collection, Paul Goodwin photo*

Browning .30 Aircraft M1918

This was a modified M1917 water-cooled gun to air-cooled for aircraft use. The water jacket was removed and replaced with a slotted barrel jacket and spade grips. This model is referred to as the M1918M1.

Browning .30 Aircraft M1918 Fixed

As above but made as new in the same configuration with spade grips.

Browning .30 Aircraft M1919 Flexible

Same as M1918 but newly made with spade grips.

Browning M1919 A1

First utilized in 1931, this gun was a M1919 tank gun modified for ground use. It was fitted with a removable butt with a hand grip under the receiver. The barrel jacket was slotted. The front sight was mounted on the front of the receiver. Chambered for the .30-06 cartridge. Barrel length is 18". Fed with a 250-round cloth belt. Cycle rate of about 600 rounds per minute. Weight is about 40 lbs. with tripod.

Browning M1919 A2

Introduced in 1931, this gun was intended for cavalry use. The front sight was mounted on the barrel jacket. There was no butt stock. The gun was issued with the M2 tripod. Otherwise, this model is an improved M1919 A1.

Browning M1919 A3

There were 72 trial samples built. This gun was

essentially a M1919 A2 with the front sight moved back to the receiver.

Browning M1919 A4

This air-cooled gun is chambered for the .30-06 cartridge and fitted with a 23.8" barrel. It has a rate of fire of 500 rounds per minute and is fed with a cloth belt. Weight is about 31 lbs. Marked "BROWNING M1919A4 US CAL .30" on the left side of the receiver. First produced in 1934, it is still in use today. There were a number of earlier variations of this model beginning with the M1919 aircraft gun and several improvements leading to the A4 version.

The Model 1919 was used in WWII as an infantry weapon, tank gun, and even in aircraft (M2). It has seen service all over the world in untold conflicts. Many arms experts think of the A4 version as the definitive .30 caliber machine gun.

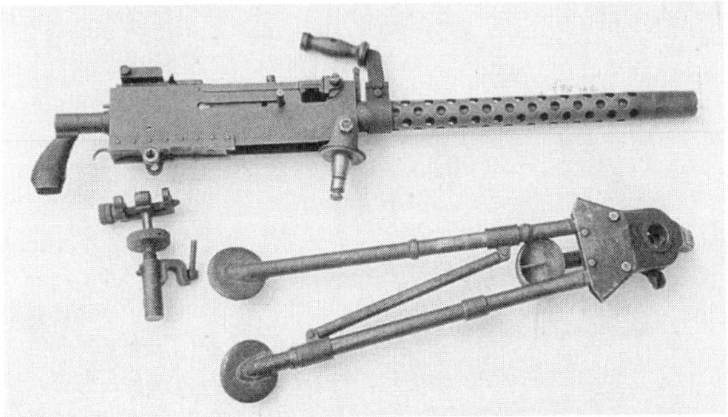

Courtesy Richard M. Kumor, Sr.

Pre-1968

Exc.	*V.G.*	*Fair*
25000	22500	20000

Pre-1986 Non-martial U.S. manufacture

Exc.	*V.G.*	*Fair*
18500	15000	N/A

Browning M1919 A5

This gun is an modified version of the M1919A4 for use with the M3 light tank. It was fitted with a special bolt retracting slide. Weight is about 30 lbs.

Browning M1919 A6

This model is a M1919 A4 fitted with a shoulder stock, flash hider, and bipod. Its weight is 32 lbs. Produced from 1943 to 1954. Marked "US INSP BROWNING MACHINE GUN US CAL 30" on the left side of the receiver.

Pre-1968

Exc.	*V.G.*	*Fair*
30000	27500	20000

Pre-1986 manufacture with new side plate

Exc.	*V.G.*	*Fair*
18000	15000	N/A

Browning .30 Aircraft M2

This gun was designed for airplane use in 1931. Its rate of fire is higher than the ground gun version: 1,000 to 1,200 rounds per minute. Chambered primarily for the .30-06 cartridge but some were chambered for the .303 British round for that country's use. The gun is fed from either the left or right side as determined by the situation. It was originally designed in two configurations; as a flexible gun (for an observer) with hand grips and hand trigger or as a fixed or wing type with a back plate without hand grips. The recoil buffer in the flexible type is horizontal while the fixed gun has a vertical type buffer. Weight is about 21 lbs. Barrel length is 23.9".

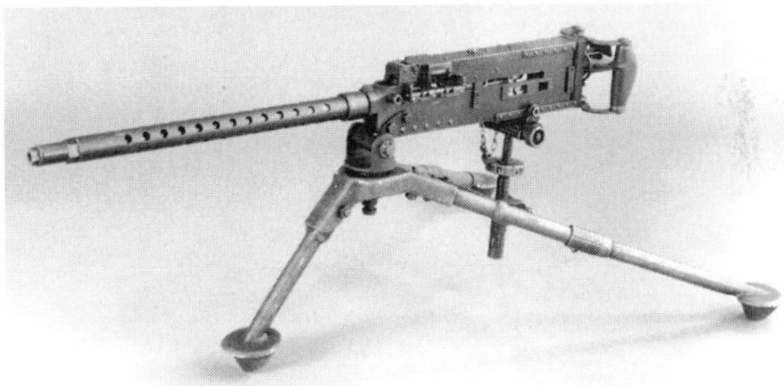

***Browning M2 machine gun (tripod used for photo purposes)** • Courtesy Robert G. Segel*

Pre-1968

Exc.	*V.G.*	*Fair*
30000	25000	18000

Pre-1986 manufacture with new side plate

Exc.	*V.G.*	*Fair*
22000	18500	N/A

Browning Tank M37

This gun is a version of the M1919 A4 adopted for tank use. Feed mechanism was designed to be used from either side.

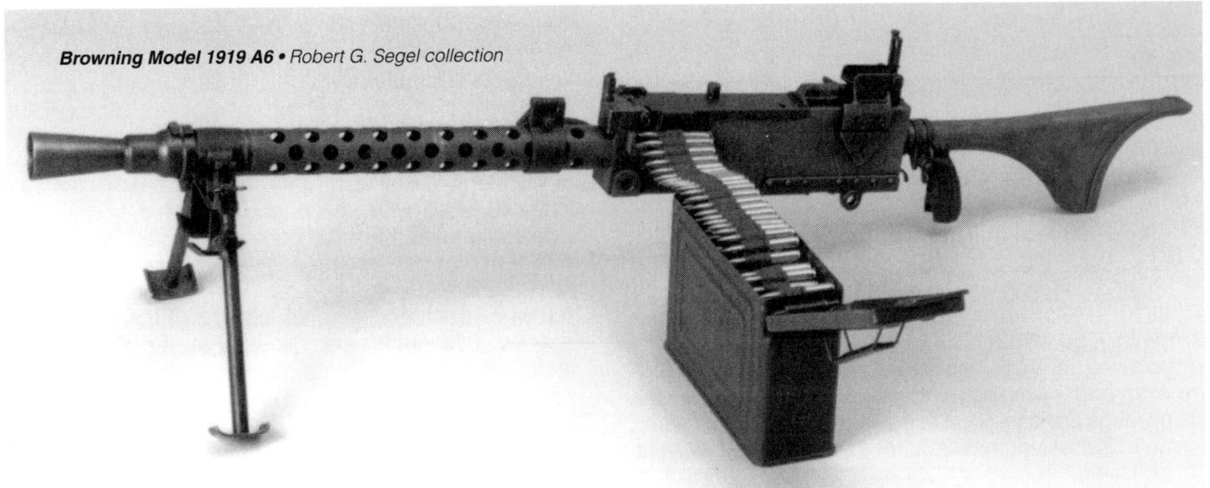

***Browning Model 1919 A6** • Robert G. Segel collection*

Pre-1968

Exc.	*V.G.*	*Fair*
25000	22500	20000

Pre-1986 Non-martial U.S. manufacture

Exc.	*V.G.*	*Fair*
17000	15000	12500

MG 38

Similar in appearance to the Model 1917 (water cooled) but with several modifications such as an improved bolt handle. The MG 38 is fitted with a pistol grip back plate while the MG 38B has a double grip (spade type) black plate. Fed from a 250-round belt. Weight of MG 38 is about 35 lbs, while the MG 38B weighs about 36.5 lbs. Barrel length is 24". This gun was utilized for several different purposes and therefore has different tripods depending on the application. Rate of fire is between 400 and 650 rounds per minute.

Courtesy Robert E. Naess

Model 1924

A commercial version of the Model 1917. Some interior modifications.

Model 1928

A commercial version of the Model 1917 with interior modifications.

Pre-1968

Exc.	*V.G.*	*Fair*
35000	32500	30000

Pre-1986 Non-martial U.S. manufacture

Exc.	*V.G.*	*Fair*
25000	20000	N/A

MG 40

This is the commercial version of the M2 .30 caliber aircraft gun.

Pre-1968

Exc.	*V.G.*	*Fair*
22000	20000	18500

Pre-1986 Non-martial U.S. manufacture

Exc.	*V.G.*	*Fair*
20000	17500	N/A

Browning .50 M1921

Introduced in 1925, this heavy machine gun is water cooled and recoil operated. Chambered for the .50 Browning cartridge. Rate of fire is about 450 rounds per minute. Barrel length is 36". Fed by a cloth belt. Weight of gun is 66 lbs.

Browning M2 water-cooled anti-aircraft gun • *Robert G. Segel collection*

Browning .50 M1921 A1

An improved version of the M1921 with a compound leverage cocking handle.

Browning .50 M2

Introduced in 1933, this gun is an improved version of the M1921 with a water jacket that extends past the muzzle. Fitted with spade grips and fed from either side. Early guns had a 36" barrels later guns were fitted with a 45" barrel. Intended for anti-aircraft use with a special mount for that purpose. Weight of gun was 100 lbs. while the tripod weighed about 375 lbs. Cycle rate is about 650 rounds per minute. Fed by a 110-round metal link belt.

Browning M2/M2HB .50

This is an air-cooled .50 caliber machine first produced in 1933. It has a 44.5" barrel and weighs about 84 lbs.

Its rate of fire is 500 rounds per minute. It is belt fed. Marked "BROWNING MACHINE GUN CAL 50 M2" on the left side of the receiver. Approximately three million were produced. The gun was produced by Colt, FN, Ramo, Saco, and Winchester.

It is one of the most widely used and successful heavy machines ever produced. Besides being utilized as an aircraft, ground and vehicle weapon, the M2 is also used as an antiaircraft gun in single, twin, and four-barrel configurations. The M2 was additionally configured as a water-cooled gun for sustained fire. The commercial designation for this model was the MG 52A. Widely used throughout the world and is still in use today and still in production in the UK, USA, and Belgium.

Browning M2HB • *Courtesy Greg Martin Auctions*

The .50 caliber cartridge was first adopted in 1923 after extensive research by John M. Browning, Winchester, and Colt. The cartridge, like many with military applications, has a wide variety of variations.

Pre-1968

Exc.	*V.G.*	*Fair*
38000	30000	25000

Pre-1986 Non-martial U.S. manufacture

Exc.	*V.G.*	*Fair*
25000	22500	20000

NOTE: For original M2 water-cooled guns add $10,000 to pre-1968 prices.

Browning Automatic Rifle (BAR)

This is gas-operated machine gun chambered for the .30-06 cartridge. Fitted with a 23.8" barrel and a 20-round magazine, it weighs about 16 lbs. Its rate of fire is 500 rounds per minute. Marked "BROWNING BAR M1918 CAL 30" on receiver it was produced from 1917 until 1945, but saw service in the Korean War.

This Browning-designed rifle was built by Colt, Marlin, and Winchester. It has several variations from the original M1918 design. About 50,000 Model 1918 BARs saw service in Europe during World War I. The M1918A1 was first built in 1927 and has the buttplate hinged shoulder support. The bipod has spiked feet and is attached to the gas cylinder. It too is select fire. Weight for the M1918A1 is 18.5 lbs. The M1918 A2 was first built in 1932 and is fitted with a bipod with skid feet attached to the flash hider. There is a monopod beneath the buttstock. The rear sight is from a Browning M1919A4 machine gun and is adjustable for windage. This version has a rate of fire regulator that sets the rate between 450 and 650 rounds per minute. Weight for this variation is 19.5 lbs. During World War II approximately 188,000 Model 1918A2 BARs were produced. The last version is called the M1922 and was built in limited numbers. It is similar to the M1918 but with a heavy finned barrel. The bipod is attached to the barrel. Barrel length is 18" with rate of fire of 550 rounds per minute.

Courtesy Jim Thompson

Marine Raider with his BAR, 1942 • *Courtesy Blake Stevens, Rock in a Hard Place, Collector Grade Publications*

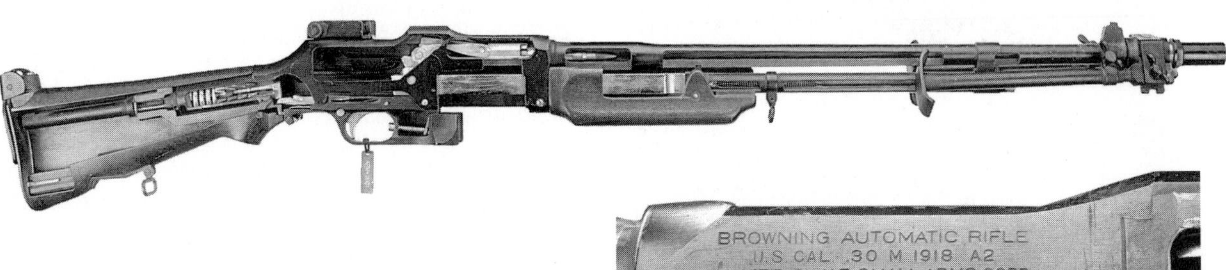

Browning Automatic Rifle cutaway with markings •
Paul Goodwin photo

Browning BAR in action, January 30, 1951, Korean front • *U.S. Army photograph*

Pre-1968

Exc.	*V.G.*	*Fair*
30000	25000	20000

Pre-1986 commercial manufacture or re-weld receiver

Exc.	*V.G.*	*Fair*
25000	20000	N/A

Johnson M1941 & 1944

Johnson Model 1941

Chambered for the .30-06 cartridge, the Model 1941 was fitted with a wooden buttstock while the Model 1944 had a metal stock. Barrel length was 21.8". The M1941 had a rate of fire of 600 rounds while the M1944 had an adjustable rate of fire between 200 and 900 rounds per minute. Fed by a side mounted 20-box magazine. Weight is about 14 lbs. Produced for the Marine Corps until 1945. Marked "LIGHT MACHINE GUN JOHNSON AUTOMATICS MODEL OF 1941" above the magazine housing. About 10,000 Model 1941 guns were built.

This is an interesting model because it fires from an open bolt for full auto fire and a closed bolt for single shots. The M1941 was built by Cranston & Johnson and the M1944 was built by Johnson.

Pre-1968

Exc.	*V.G.*	*Fair*
25000	22500	20000

Stoner Model 63/63A

Developed in 1963 as a further evolution to the Model 63 with an improved stainless steel gas system and different style safety per U.S. Marine Corp specifications. This machine gun is chambered for the 5.56x45mm cartridge. It has an overall length of 40.24", a barrel length of 21", and a weight of approximately 11 lbs. Its rate of fire is 700 rounds per minute. It can function as a belt feed gun or can be fed by a top mounted magazine. It was used by both the U.S. Navy and Marine Corps during the Vietnam conflict. Production stopped in the early 1970s. The gun was produced by Cadillac Gage Co.

NOTE: This model is really a weapons system that is capable of a number of different configurations from carbine to machine gun. Also note that Model 63 components will not always interchange with Model 63A guns.

Johnson Model 1944 • *Courtesy private NFA collection, Paul Goodwin photo*

Stoner Model 63 Carbine • *Courtesy West Point Museum, Paul Goodwin photo*

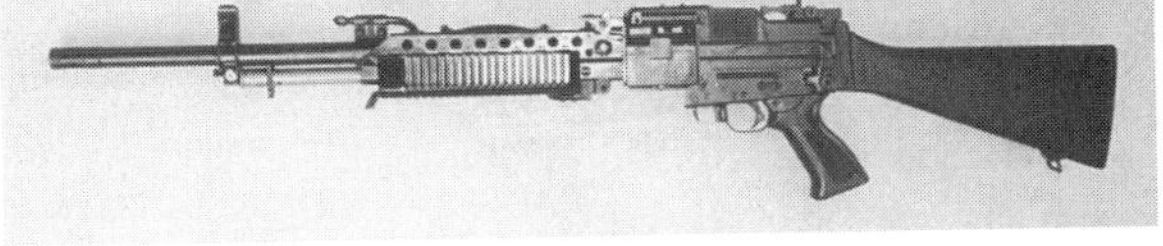

Stoner Model 63A • *Courtesy private NFA collection*

Pre-1968 (Very rare, fewer than 6 known)

Exc.	*V.G.*	*Fair*
70000	60000	50000

Pre-1986 Non-martial U.S. manufacture

Exc.	*V.G.*	*Fair*
50000	45000	N/A

NOTE: Deduct 33 percent for Stoner Model 63. There are more Model 63s availabe (transferable) than Model 63As.

U.S. M60

Chambered for the 7.62x51mm cartridge, this machine gun entered U.S. service in the late 1950s. It was fitted with a 22" barrel and a rate of fire of 550 rounds per minute using a disintegrating link belt system. The weight of the gun is 24.4 lbs. Used extensively by U.S. forces in Vietnam. Still in production and still in service with U.S. forces (Marine Corp) and many others around the world. The early M60 guns were built by Bridge & Inland.

U.S. Marines with M60 in Vietnam

Pre-1986 OEM/Maremont manufacture

Exc.	*V.G.*	*Fair*
38000	35000	30000

Pre-1986 manufacture

Exc.	*V.G.*	*Fair*
28000	25000	N/A

U.S. M60E3

This is an improved version of the M60 with a lightweight shorter 17" barrel. The forearm is replaced with a forward pistol grip with heat shield. The feed system has been modified to allow the cover to be closed when the bolt is forward. The gas system has been modified as well. Weight has been reduced to about 18 lbs. This model was in service with the U.S. Marine Corp, Navy, and Air Force. Built by both Maremont and Saco.

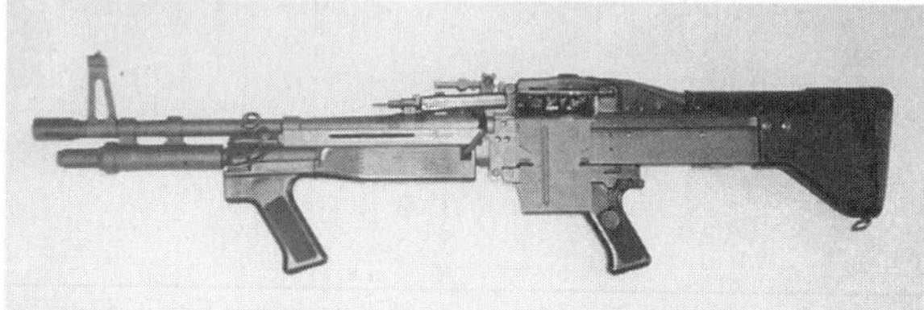

M60-E3 • *Courtesy private NFA collection*

Pre-1986 OEM/Maremont manufacture

Exc.	*V.G.*	*Fair*
40000	35000	32500

Armalite AR-10

Chambered for the 7.62x51mm cartridge, this select fire machine gun was fitted with a 19.8" barrel and had a 20-round magazine. Rate of fire is 700 rounds per minute. Weight is 9 lbs. Marked "ARMALITE AR10 MANUFACTURED BY AL NEDERLAND" on left side of magazine housing. Produced from 1958 to 1961. This gun was adopted by Burma, Portugal, Nicaragua, and Sudan. It was produced in limited numbers.

Pre-1968 (Very rare)

Exc.	*V.G.*	*Fair*
28000	20000	15000

Pre-1986 conversions of semi-automatic version

Exc.	*V.G.*	*Fair*
20000	17500	N/A

Armalite AR-15

Introduced in 1957, this select fire rifle was fitted with a plastic butt and handguard. The rear sight also acted as a carry handle. The cocking handle was located at the rear of the receiver. The 20" barrel was fitted with a flash hider. It was a gas operated mechanism with rotating bolt. This design eventually became the U.S. military M16 rifle. Weight is about 6.25 lbs. Rate of fire was about 800 rounds per minute.

Pre-1968

Exc.	*V.G.*	*Fair*
30000	25000	20000

Armalite AR-18

First produced in 1964 and chambered for the 5.56x45mm cartridge. Side-hinged plastic butt stock. Gas operated and select fire. Rate of fire is about 800 rounds per minute. Barrel length is 18.25". Weight is about 7 lbs. Magazine capacity is 20, 30, or 40 round detachable magazines. Designed to be a less expensive alternative to the AR-15. Built by ArmaLite. Rare.

Pre-1968 (Very rare)

Exc.	*V.G.*	*Fair*
25000	20000	15000

Pre-1986 conversions of semi-automatic version

Exc.	*V.G.*	*Fair*
15000	12500	N/A

Armalite AR-18 • *Courtesy West Point Museum, Paul Goodwin photo*

Marlin Model 1914

Marlin Model 1917 Tank Gun •
Courtesy private NFA collection, Paul Goodwin photo

Colt/Marlin Model 1914/1915

This was a Browning design that was first produced in 1895. Nicknamed the "Potato Digger" because of its swinging arm bolt driver. It was air cooled and fired a variety of calibers both for the military and commercial sales. The Model 1914 was converted to fire the .30-06 cartridge. Rate of fire was about 450 rounds per minute. Barrel length was 28". Belt-fed by 250-round cloth belt. The Model 1915 had cooling fins added to the barrel. The gun was built from 1916 to 1919.

Canadian soldiers on the firing line with the "Potato Digger" • *Robert G. Segel collection*

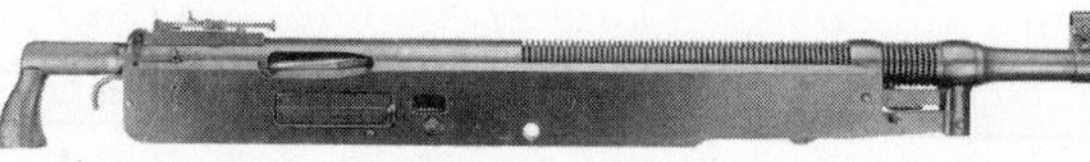

Marlin Model 1914 • *Paul Goodwin photo*

Pre-1968

Exc.	***V.G.***	***Fair***
28000	25000	20000

Pre-1986 manufacture with new receiver or reweld

Exc.	***V.G.***	***Fair***
20000	17500	N/A

Marlin Model 1917

This model is an improved Potato Digger with a gas pistol and cylinder fitted underneath the barrel. Chambered for the .30-06 cartridge. Designed for use in aircraft with long finned aluminum radiator around the barrel, and in tanks with a heavy armored barrel jacket. Barrel length is 28". Fed by a 250-round cloth belt with a rate of fire of approximately 600 rounds per minute. Weight is about 22 lbs.

Pre-1968

Exc.	***V.G.***	***Fair***
25000	20000	17500

Pre-1986 manufacture with new receiver or reweld

Exc.	***V.G.***	***Fair***
18000	15000	N/A

Savage-Lewis Model 1917

This a .30-06 caliber Lewis gun made by Savage during WWI. About 6,000 of these guns were chambered for the .30-06 caliber cartridge and used by the U.S. Marines and Navy until World War II. The U.S. Army purchased 2,500 of the guns but most of these Army guns were used for training purposes. See *Great Britain, Machine Guns, Lewis 0.303 in., Mark I.*

Savage-Lewis Gun • *Robert G. Segel collection*

Colt Vickers Model 1915 with markings • *Paul Goodwin photo*

Colt Vickers Model 1915 • *Robert G. Segel collection*

Pre-1968

Exc.	*V.G.*	*Fair*
35000	30000	25000

Pre-1986 manufacture with new receiver or reweld

Exc.	*V.G.*	*Fair*
20000	17500	N/A

Colt-Vickers Model 1915

This gun is similar to the British Vickers but built by Colt in Hartford, CT. Many of these Colt Model 1915 guns were rebuilt aircraft guns. About 12,000 were produced by Colt during the period 1915 to 1918 but few of these were original Colt-built ground guns and many of those were destroyed after the war. Therefore, original Colt-Vickers ground guns are very rare and quite desirable. See also *Great Britain, Machine Guns, Vickers.*

Pre-1968 (original Colt ground gun)

Exc.	*V.G.*	*Fair*
38000	35000	27500

Pre-1968 (Colt rebuilt aircraft gun)

Exc.	*V.G.*	*Fair*
25000	20000	17500

Pre-1986 manufacture with new side plate

Exc.	*V.G.*	*Fair*
25000	20000	N/A

Colt LMG (RO-750)

First introduced in early 1986, this M16A2 light machine gun was designed as a squad automatic weapon (SAW). SAWs are designed to provide a more sustained fire capability than the standard M16 rifle. Similar in appearance to the M16A2 rifle, this model features a 20" heavy hammer forged barrel upper made by Diemaco with square handguard and vertical handgrip. The lower receiver fires from an open bolt full auto only and is marked, "SAFE AND FIRE." The fixed stock houses a hydraulic buffer and special spring to reduce the rate of fire to about 650 rounds per minute. Weight is 12.75 lbs. Fed by a standard 30-round M16 magazine or other high capacity devices such as the 100 round Beta C magazine. In use by the U.S. Marine Corp. and other military forces in Central and South America and the Middle East. The Colt LMG was also utilized by the Canadian forces supplied by Colt licensee Diemaco of Canada. Still in production, but under the reintroduced name of Colt Automatic Rifle with changes to the bipod, removal of the front carry handle, and improvements in the handguard heat shield as well as a flat top upper. It is estimated by knowledgeable sources that there are fewer than 20 transferable examples in this country.

Pre-1968

Exc.	*V.G.*	*Fair*
N/A	N/A	N/A

Pre-1986 OEM (Very rare)

Exc.	*V.G.*	*Fair*
28000	25000	N/A

Colt LMG (RO-750)

The Federal Republic of Yugoslavia, formerly the Socialist Federal Republic of Yugoslavia, a Balkan country located on the east shore of the Adriatic Sea, has an area of 39,450 sq. mi. (102,173 sq. km.) and a population of 10.5 million. Capital: Belgrade. The chief industries area agriculture, mining, manufacturing and tourism. Machinery, nonferrous metals, meat and fabrics are exported.

Yugoslavia was proclaimed on Dec. 1, 1918, after the union of the Kingdom of Serbia, Montenegro and the South Slav territories of Austria-Hungary; and changed its official name from the Kingdom of the Serbs, Croats and Slovenes to the Kingdom of Yugoslavia on Oct. 3, 1929.The republic was composed of six autonomous republics - Serbia, Croatia, Slovenia, Bosnia-Herzegovina, Macedonia and Montenegro - and two autonomous provinces within Serbia: Kosovo-Melohija and Vojvodina. The government of Yugoslavia attempted to remain neutral in World War II but, yielding to German pressure, aligned itself with the Axis powers in March of 1941; a few days later it was overthrown by revolutionary forces and its neutrality reasserted. The Nazis occupied the country on April 6, and throughout the remaining war years were resisted by a number of guerrilla armies, notably that of Marshal Josip Broz Tito. After the defeat of the Axis powers, a leftist coalition headed by Tito abolished the monarchy and, on Jan. 31, 1946, established a "People's Republic". The collapse of the Federal Republic during 1991-1992 has resulted in the autonomous republics of Croatia, Slovenia, Bosnia-Herzegovina and Macedonia declaring their respective independence. Bosnia-Herzegovina is under military contest with the Serbian, Croat and Muslim populace opposing each other. Besides the remainder of the older Serbian sectors, a Serbian enclave in Knin located in southern Croatia has emerged called REPUBLIKE SRPSKEKRAJINE or Serbian Republic - Krajina whose capital is Knin and has also declared its independence in1992 when the former Republics of Serbia and Montenegro became the Federal Republic of Yugoslavia.

HANDGUNS

At the end of WWI, Yugoslavia acquired a large number of Austrian Model 12 Steyr pistols in 9mm. The Yugoslavians have also used the FN-built M1935 pistol in 9x19 caliber.

Model 1875

This is a double action solid frame with fixed cylinder and mechanical rod ejection. Cylinder holds 6 rounds and is chambered for the 11mm cartridge. Checkered wood grips with lanyard loop. Octagon barrel is 6.2 inches long. Built by Auguste Francotte in Liege, Belgium. In use from 1875 to 1919.

Courtesy Geschichte und Technik der europaischen Militarrevolver, Journal-Verlag Schwend GmbH with permission

Exc.	V.G.	Good	Fair	Poor
1100	700	450	250	125

Model 1876

This model is built on a modified Lefaucheux-Chaineux solid frame with swing-out cylinder. The non-fluted cylinder is chambered for the 11mm cartridge. The half-round half-octagon barrel is 4.4 inches. Checkered wood grips with lanyard loop. Built by Manufacture d'Ares, St. Etienne, France. In service with the Serbian army from 1876 to 1919.

Exc.	V.G.	Good	Fair	Poor
950	600	425	250	125

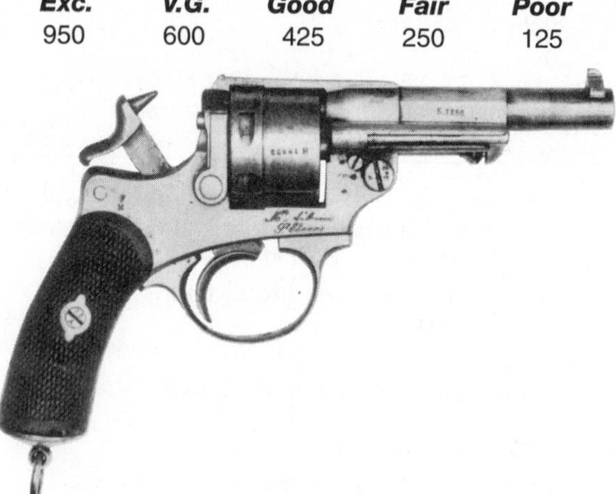

Model 1876 • *Courtesy Geschichte und Technik der europaischen Militarrevolver, Journal-Verlag Schwend GmbH with permission*

Model 1891

Built on the Nagant-Model 1887 frame, this double action model is chambered for the 7.5mm cartridge. Fluted cylinder. The 4.5-inch barrel is 3/4 octagon and 1/4 round. Checkered grips with lanyard loop. Built by

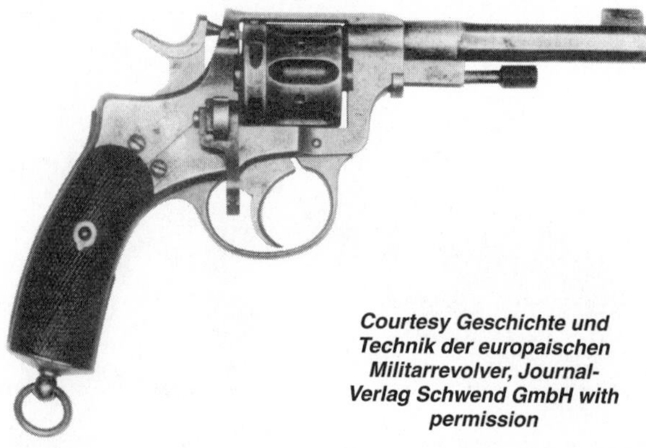

Courtesy Geschichte und Technik der europaischen Militarrevolver, Journal-Verlag Schwend GmbH with permission

the Nagant brothers in Liege, Belgium. The Serbian army used this revolver from 1891 to 1945. Revolver has cyrillic markings on the frame.

Exc.	V.G.	Good	Fair	Poor
2000	1000	500	350	225

Model 1898

This revolver is the same as the Austrian Model 1898, built by Rast & Gasser in Wien (Vienna), Austria. This model was built on the Schmidt-Galand double action solid frame with swing-out 8-round cylinder with multiple ejection. Chambered for the 8mm cartridge and fitted with a 4.5-inch round barrel. Checkered wooden grips with lanyard loop. Weight is about 33 oz.

Courtesy Geschichte und Technik der europaischen Militarrevolver, Journal-Verlag Schwend GmbH with permission

Exc.	V.G.	Good	Fair	Poor
750	500	300	150	100

Model 1910 FN Browning

Adopted by Serbia and used in WWI. Chambered for 7.65mm cartridge and fitted with a 3.5-inch barrel. Magazine capacity is 7 rounds. Weight about 21 oz. The principal difference between this model and its predecessors is that the recoil spring on the Model 1910 is wrapped around the barrel. This gives the slide a more graceful tubular appearance instead of the old slab-sided look. This model has the triple safety features of the 1906 Model 2nd variation and is blued with molded plastic grips. The pistol has the Yugoslavian crest on the slide and cyrillic lettering on the slide. This model was adopted by police forces and some military units around the world. It was manufactured between 1912 and 1954.

Courtesy Orvel Reichert

Exc.	V.G.	Good	Fair	Poor
550	400	275	150	125

Model 1922 FN Browning

Adopted by Yugoslavia in the 1930s in 9mm short (.380). Fitted with a 4.5-inch barrel and a magazine capacity of 9 rounds. Fitted with a grip safety. Yugoslavian crest on top of slide. Weight is about 25 oz. Approximately 60,000 of these pistols were produced for the Yugoslavian military between 1922 and 1925. These pistols were also used by the German occupation forces, but are not marked with German acceptance or proof stamps.

Exc.	V.G.	Good	Fair	Poor
600	500	400	300	150

Tokarev copy (Model 70)

This is a Yugoslavian copy of the Soviet TT33 in 9x19mm.

Exc.	V.G.	Good	Fair	Poor
550	400	300	200	100

Model 57

This is a Yugoslavian copy of the Soviet Tokarev, but with a 9-round magazine in 7.62x25mm.

Exc.	V.G.	Good	Fair	Poor
1200	850	700	500	200

Model 57 import

In 2008 and 2009 several thousand Model 57 pistols were imported to the U.S. In order to comply with current regulations they had a thumb safety added to the left side of the handle as well as the importer marking stamped on the frame.

Exc.	V.G.	Good	Fair	Poor
350	300	250	175	n/a

Tokarev copy (Model 65 for export)

This is a copy of the Tokarev in 9mm Parabellum.

Exc.	V.G.	Good	Fair	Poor
550	400	300	200	100

SUBMACHINE GUNS

Prior to WWII, Yugoslavia adopted the Erma submachine gun. After the war, Yugoslavia used the German Mp38 and Mp40. The Yugoslavian army also used British Sten guns and Beretta submachine guns as well. As a communist state, the Yugoslavians were supplied with Soviet PPDs and PPSh41 guns.

Yugoslav Model 49

Similar in appearance to the Soviet PPSh41 this gun is chambered for the 7.62 Soviet cartridge. Barrel is 10.5 inches and the rate of fire is 700 rounds per minute. It is fitted with a wooden stock. Weight is approximately 9.4 lbs.

Courtesy private NFA collection

Pre-1968

Exc.	V.G.	Fair
18000	15000	12000

YUGOSLAVIA & SERBIA

Pre-1986 manufacture with new receiver or re-weld

Exc.	V.G.	Fair
7500	5000	N/A

Yugoslav Model 56

The Model 56 is chambered for the 7.62 cartridge, and is fitted with a metal folding stock and 9.8-inch barrel. Magazine capacity is 35 rounds. Weight is about 6.6 lbs. Rate of fire is 600 rounds per minute.

Courtesy private NFA collection

Pre-1968

Exc.	V.G.	Fair
12500	10000	8000

Pre-1986 manufacture with new receiver or re-weld

Exc.	V.G.	Fair
6500	5500	N/A

RIFLES

MAUSER

NOTE: Most of these early Mauser rifles were used by the Serbian armed forces through WWI. The Model 24 was adopted by Yugoslavia.

M78/80 Rifle

A modified G 71 rifle with 30.7-inch barrel with two barrel bands. Turn bolt action. Single shot in 10.15x62.8mm caliber. Weight is about 10 lbs. Fitted with a long receiver tang to support rearward bolt travel. Marked in cyrillic or German on left side rail.

Exc.	V.G.	Good	Fair	Poor
1000	800	650	400	250

M1884 Koka Carbine

Chambered for 10.15mm black powder cartridge and fitted with an 18.375-inch barrel with turn bolt action. Tubular magazine holds 5 rounds. Full-length stock with front sling swivel on left side of barrel band and real swivel on bottom on buttstock near wrist. Weight is about 8 lbs. Marked "model 1884" on right side of butt. About 4,000 were built by Mauser at its Oberndorf factory.

Exc.	V.G.	Good	Fair	Poor
1250	800	650	400	250

M1899 Rifle

Produced by DWM with a full-length stock with straight grip. Barrel length is 29 inches. Chambered for 7x57mm cartridge. Adjustable rear sight graduated to 2000 meters. Serbian crest marked on receiver ring. Magazine capacity is 5 rounds. Weight is about 9 lbs.

Exc.	V.G.	Good	Fair	Poor
900	650	500	350	250

M1899c Rifle

Chambered for either the 7.92x57mm cartridge or the 7.65x53mm cartridge and fitted with a 23.25-inch barrel with full-length stock with pistol grip with finger grooves. Magazine capacity is 5 rounds. Weight is about 8.5 lbs. Straight bolt handle. Marked with Serbian crest on receiver ring. A few of these were imported in the early 1990's. Most were in fair-poor condition.

Exc.	V.G.	Good	Fair	Poor
850	650	450	300	175

M1908 Carbine

This 7x57mm caliber model is fitted with a full-length pistol grip with finger grooves. Barrel length is 17-inch. Upper handguard extends to the lower barrel band. Bolt handle is bent. No bayonet fittings. Weight is about 6.8 lbs.

Exc.	V.G.	Good	Fair	Poor
850	650	500	350	250

M1910 Rifle

This is the standard export German Model 1910 rifle. Fitted with a 29.13-inch barrel and full-length stock with pistol grip. The nose cap has a bayonet lug on its bottom. Chambered for the 7x57mm cartridge. Weight is about 9 lbs. Marked with Serbian crest on receiver ring.

Exc.	V.G.	Good	Fair	Poor
850	650	500	350	250

M90 (t) Short Rifle

A Yugoslavian model that was received from the Turks following WWI. Rebarreled for 7.92x57mm and cut to 23.25 inches. Magazine capacity is 5 rounds. Tangent rear sight graduated to 2000 meters. Weight is about 8.5 lbs.

Exc.	V.G.	Good	Fair	Poor
425	250	200	130	80

M03 (t) Short Rifle

Turkish Model 1903 converted to 7.92x57 caliber.

Exc.	V.G.	Good	Fair	Poor
400	250	200	110	70

M24 Short Rifle

This model has a full-length stock with pistol grip. Upper handguard goes from the receiver to upper barrel band. Fitted with 23.25-inch barrel and chambered for the 7.92x57mm cartridge. Tangent rear sight graduated to 2,000 meters. Weight is about

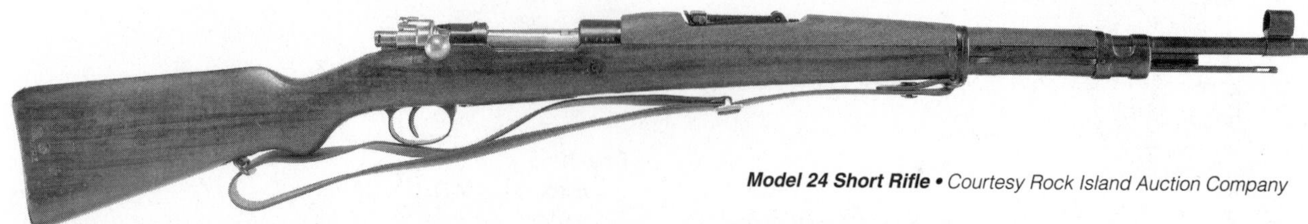

Model 24 Short Rifle • *Courtesy Rock Island Auction Company*

8.5 lbs. Yugoslavian crest over model designation on left side of receiver.

Exc.	V.G.	Good	Fair	Poor
600	450	300	175	125

M24 Carbine

Similar to the above model but with 16.75-inch barrel. Bayonet fittings are on nose cap. Weight is about 7.25 lbs.

Exc.	V.G.	Good	Fair	Poor
600	450	300	175	125

Bayonets for Model 1924 Mauser

Wood grips. Muzzle ring. 15- or 9.5-inch single edge blade. The ricasso bears the Kragiyervac arsenal mark, a triangle with "BT3" inside. Steel scabbard. This bayonet is the same as the Belgian M 1924 long and short export. Price range 85 – 50.

FN M30 Short Rifle

This model has a full-length stock with pistol grip. Straight bolt handle. This model is the standard FN Model 1930 configuration.

Exc.	V.G.	Good	Fair	Poor
600	450	250	150	100

FN M24 Carbine

Full stock with pistol grip and 17.5-inch barrel. Caliber is 7.92x57mm. Turn bolt action. Tangent leaf sight graduated to 1,400 meters. Yugoslavian crest of top of receiver ring. Weight is about 8 lbs.

Exc.	V.G.	Good	Fair	Poor
600	450	300	175	125

M1948 98k Short Rifle

This model is similar to the German 98k carbine. Almost full-length stock with pistol grip and short upper handguard. Hooded front sight with tangent leaf sight to 2000 meters. Chambered for 7.92x57mm with 5-round magazine. Weight is about 10 lbs. Communist Yugoslavian crest on receiver ring. One of the most common Mausers on the U.S. market for the last few years.

Exc.	V.G.	Good	Fair	Poor
350	225	150	125	100

M24/52C or M24/47 Short Rifle

This is an arsenal reconditioned Model 24 short rifle with communist Yugoslavian crest on the receiver ring. Another common variation recently on the U.S. market.

Exc.	V.G.	Good	Fair	Poor
250	175	125	100	75

Bayonet for M1948, 24/52C or 24/47 Short Rifle

These were usually sold with the reworked Yugoslavian Mauser rifles. Many have a cyrillic marking and the number 44 on the blade. Some were reworked from the M1924 bayonets and have the Kragiyervac arsenal mark. Wood handle. 10-inch single edge blade. Muzzle ring. Serial number on crosspiece and scabbard. Price range 45 – 20.

Steyr M1895M

Between the two world wars, many Austrian Model 1895s were converted to 8x57mm and fitted with 24-inch barrels. These rifles have a modified Steyr clip permanently installed in the magazine. Receivers were marked "M95M" and "M95/24". These were sold to Yugoslavia. Many stocks bear the triangle BT3 mark of the Kragiyervac arsenal. Some experts consider these rifles unsafe to fire with full power 8x57mm ammunition.

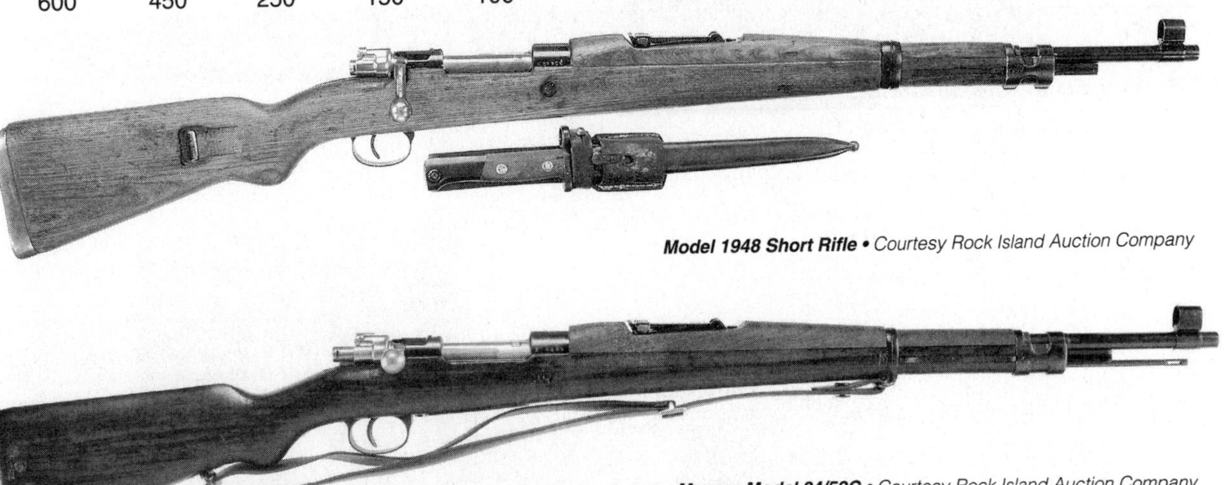

Model 1948 Short Rifle • *Courtesy Rock Island Auction Company*

Mauser Model 24/52C • *Courtesy Rock Island Auction Company*

Exc.	V.G.	Good	Fair	Poor
475	350	250	150	100

Model 59

This is an exact copy of the Russian SKS made under license in Yugoslavia by Zastava. Only the markings are different.

Exc.	V.G.	Good	Fair	Poor
375	250	175	125	100

Model 59/66

This is a Yugoslavian copy of the Soviet SKS rifle. The major difference between the two is a gas shut-off valve on the gas cylinder and an integral grenade launcher fitted to the barrel. Recently imported by the thousands.

Exc.	V.G.	Good	Fair	Poor
350	225	175	125	100

Model 64

This is a Yugoslavian copy of the Soviet AK-47, but with a 19.7-inch barrel with built-in grenade launcher sights that pivots on the barrel.

Pre-1968

Exc.	V.G.	Fair
16000	14000	12000

NOTE: Add 20 percent for folding stock.

Zastava M70B1

This Yugoslavian copy of the AK-47 rifle was first produced in 1974. It is chambered for the 7.62x39mm cartridge and is fitted with a 16.2-inch barrel. Its rate of fire is 650 rounds per minute. Weight is about 8 lbs. This model features a folding grenade sight behind the front sight. When raised, it cuts off the gas supply to the cylinder redirecting it to the launcher. This is the standard Yugoslav service rifle. Still in production.

Pre-1968

Exc.	V.G.	Fair
N/A	N/A	N/A

M70B1 (Semi-automatic version)

Exc.	V.G.	Good	Fair	Poor
2350	2150	1850	900	500

M70AB2

Copy of the Soviet AKM-S. See Russia, Rifles.

M76 Sniping Rifle

This is a copy of a Soviet AKM with a 21.5-inch barrel and wooden butt. The rifle is fitted with iron sights and a telescope mount. Semi-automatic operation. Chambered for the 8x57mm cartridge. Weight is about 9.5 lbs. Prices listed below are for rifles with correct matching military scope. Some of these have been assembled recently from original parts on a U.S. made receiver.

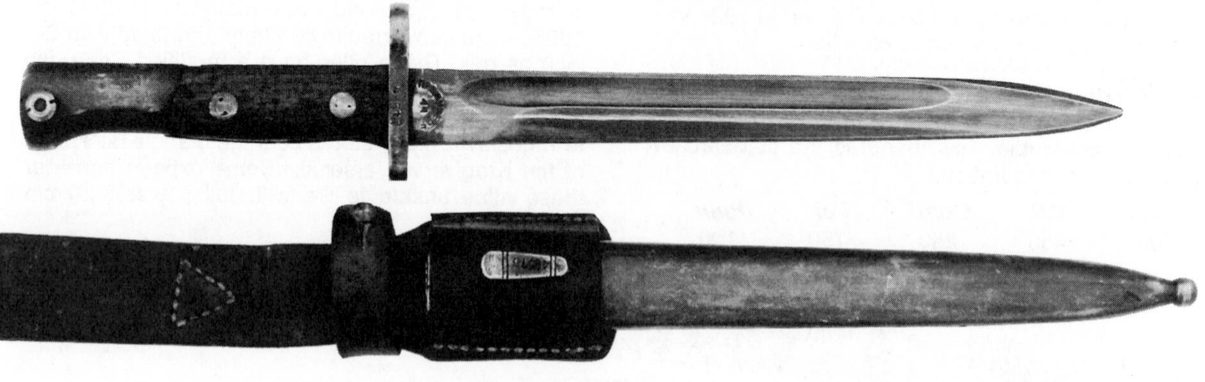

Bayonet for M1948, 24/52C or 24/47 Short Rifle

M76 with correct military scope • *Courtesy Chuck Karwan*

Exc.	*V.G.*	*Good*	*Fair*	*Poor*
2500	2000	1500	—	—

NOTE: For rifles without scope deduct $1,500. For rifles with commercial scopes but marked M76B deduct $1,000. For rifles in .308 caliber without scope deduct 70 percent.

M77B1 (Semi-automatic)

Copy of the Soviet AKM with a fixed wooden butt, straight 20-round magazine, and 16.4-inch barrel. Weight is about 8.5 lbs. Prices listed are for semi-automatic version.

Exc.	*V.G.*	*Good*	*Fair*	*Poor*
2250	1650	1100	800	300

M77 B1 Assault Rifle

Copy of the Soviet AKM with a fixed wooden butt, straight 20-round magazine, and 16.4-inch barrel. Rate of fire is about 700 rounds per minute. There are examples in this country chambered for .308 and .223. Weight is about 8.5 lbs.

NOTE: For rifles chambered for .223 add 75 percent premium.

Pre-1968

Exc.	*V.G.*	*Fair*
N/A	N/A	N/A

MACHINE GUNS

Between the two world wars, Yugoslavia used the Schwarzlose M07/12, the Maxim 08, and the Madsen. After WWII, Yugoslavia used the MG34 and MG42 as well as some Soviet machine guns. The principal Yugoslavian machine is its own produced MG 42 designated the Model 53.

Yugoslavia also acquired several thousand U.S.-made Browning Model 1919 machine guns prior to 1964 as well as the .50 M2HB Browning heavy machine gun.

ZB30J

This was the primary light machine gun used by Yugoslavian forces prior to WWII. It is a modified copy of the Czech ZB30 gun chambered for the 7.92mm cartridge. The primary difference between the ZB30 and ZB30J is the knurled barrel ring in front of the receiver on the ZB30J.

Pre-1968

Exc.	*V.G.*	*Fair*
25000	22000	17000

Pre-1986 manufacture with new receiver or re-weld

Exc.	*V.G.*	*Fair*
18500	15500	N/A

APPENDIX

FIREARMS CLASSIFIED AS CURIOS OR RELICS UNDER 18 U.S.C. CHAPTER 44 (1972-MAY 2006)

The BATF has determined that the following firearms are curios or relics as defined in 27 CFR 178.11 because they fall within one of the categories specified in the regulations.

Such determination merely classifies the firearms as curios or relics and thereby authorizes licensed collectors to acquire, hold, or dispose of them as curios or relics subject to the provisions of 18 U.S.C. Chapter 44 and the regulations in 27 CFR Part 178. They are still "firearms" as defined in 18 U.S.C. Chapter 44.

A

- Alkartasuna, semiautomatic pistol, caliber .32.
- All Original military bolt action and semiautomatic rifles mfd. between 1899 and 1946.
- All properly marked and identified semiautomatic pistols and revolvers used by, or mfd. for, any military organization prior to 1946.
- All shotguns, properly marked and identified as mfd. for any military organization prior to 1946 and in their original military configuration only.
- Argentine D.G.F.M. (FMAP) System Colt Model 1927 pistols, marked "Ejercito Argentino" bearing S/Ns less than 24501.
- Argentine D.G.F.M. - (F.M.A.P.) System Colt model 1927, cal. 11.25mm commercial variations.
- Armand Gevage, semiautomatic pistols, .32ACP cal. as mfd. in Belgium prior to World War II.
- Astra, M 800 Condor model, pistol, caliber 9mm parabellum
- Astra, model 1921 (400) semiautomatic pistols having slides marked Esperanzo Y Unceta.
- Astra, model 400 pistol, German Army Contract, caliber 9mm Bergmann-Bayard, S/N range 97351-98850.
- Astra, model 400 semiautomatic pistol, cal. 9mm Bergmann-Bayard, second German Army Contract, in S/N range 92851 through 97350.
- Auto-Mag pistols, calibers .44 AMP and .357 AMP, mfd. and/or assembled by Auto-Mag Corporation, TDE, OMC, High Standard, Lee Jurras, or AMT from 1969 to 1985.
- Auto Ordnance, West Hurley, NY, Korean War Commemorative Thompson semiautomatic rifle, caliber .45.
- Auto Ordnance, West Hurley, NY, World War II Commemorative Thompson semiautomatic rifle, caliber .45.
- Auto Ordnance Thompson, cal. 45 semiautomatic rifle, Vietnam Commemorative, S/N's V0001-V1500, issued by the American Historical Foundation, Richmond VA.

B

- Baker Gun and Forging Company, all firearms mfd. from 1899 to 1919.
- Bannerman model 1937, Springfield rifle, caliber .30-06.
- Bayard, model 1923 semiautomatic pistol, cal. 7.65mm or .380, Belgian manufacture.
- Beretta, M 1951 pistol Israeli Contract, caliber 9mm parabellum.
- Beretta, model 1915 pistols, cal. 6.35mm, 7.65mm, and 9mm Glisenti.
- Beretta, model 1915/1919 (1922) pistol (concealed hammer), caliber 7.65mm.
- Beretta, model 1919 pistol (without grip safety), caliber 6.35mm.
- Beretta, model 1923 pistol, caliber 9mm Glisenti.
- Beretta, model 1932 pistol, having smooth wooden grips w/"PB" medallion, cal. 9mm.
- Beretta, model 1934 pistol, light weight model marked "Tipo Alleggerita" or "All" having transverse ribbed barrel, cal. 9mm.
- Beretta, model 1934 pistols, cal. 9mm post war variations bearing Italian Air Force eagle markings.
- Beretta, model 1934 pistols, cal. 9mm produced during 1945 or earlier and having S/Ns within the ranges of 500000-999999, F00001-F120000, G0001-G80000, 00001AA-10000AA, 00001BB-10000BB. The classification does not include any post war variations dated subsequent to 1945 or bearing post war Italian proof marks.
- Beretta, model 1935 pistol, Finnish Home Guard Contract, marked "SKY" on the slide, cal. 7.65mm.
- Beretta, model 1935 pistol, Rumanian Contract, marked "P. Beretta - cal. 9 Scurt - Mo. 1934 - Brevet." on the slide, cal. 9mm.
- Beretta, model 1935 pistols, cal. 7.65mm, produced during 1945 and earlier and having S/Ns below 620799.
- Beretta, M1951 pistol, Egyptian Contract, caliber 9mm parabellum.
- Beretta semiautomatic pistol, Model 92F, 9mm Luger caliber, slide engraved in gold "North Carolina Highway Patrol 60th Anniversary 1929-1989," serial numbers NCHPC 0001 through NCHPC 1313 inclusive.
- Bergmann-Bayard, M1908 pistol, cal. 9mm Bergmann-Bayard.
- Bern Arsenal, Experimental Gas Locked pistol, cal. 9mm parabellum.
- Bern Arsenal, Experimental 16 shot pistol, cal. 9mm parabellum.
- Bernardelli, model 1956, experimental pistol, cal. 9mm parabellum.
- Brazilian copy of German G43 semiautomatic rifle, M954, cal. .30, mfd. at the Itajuba Arsenal, S/Ns G43-1 to G43-95.
- British Enfield L42A1, bolt action sniper rifle, 7.62 NATO caliber.
- British Enfield No. 8 Mk.1, bolt action target rifle, caliber .22.
- British "Enforcer" model Lee Enfield, bolt action Sniper rifle, caliber 7.62mm.

- British "Envoy" model Lee Enfield, bolt action rifle, cal. 7.62mm.
- British Lee Enfield No. 4, bolt action service rifle, cal. .303, in original military configuration, produced prior to 1958.
- British Lee Enfield, Number 9, training rifles, caliber .22.
- British Rifle No.7 MkI, cal. .22, bolt action, training rifle.
- British SMLE XL42E1 Bolt action sniper rifle, cal. 7.62 NATO
- FN Browning, model 1902 (usually known as the model 1903) semiautomatic pistol, caliber 9mm Browning long.
- Browning .22 caliber, semiautomatic rifles, Grade II, mfd. by Fabrique Nationale in Belgium from 1956 to 1976.
- Browning, .22 caliber, semiautomatic rifles, grade III, mfd. by Fabrique Nationale in Belgium.
- Browning .22 pump Centenary rifle.
- Browning .22 semiautomatic Centenary rifle.
- Browning Arms Company "Renaissance" engraved FN Hi Power pistol, cal. 9mm, 1954 to 1977.
- Browning Auto 5, 2 Millionth Commemorative, Ltd. Edition, semiautomatic shotgun.
- Browning FN "Renaissance" engraved .25 cal. semiautomatic pistols.
- Browning FN "Renaissance" engraved Model 10\71 semiautomatic pistol, caliber .380.
- Browning FN Challenger Gold Line and "Renaissance" engraved semiautomatic pistols, cal. .22.
- Browning FN Hi Power pistol, caliber 9mm, marked "Browning Arms Company", with tangent sight and originally slotted for shoulder stock, mfd. 1968 through 1973.
- Browning FN Medalist Gold Line and "Renaissance" engraved semiautomatic pistols, caliber .22.
- Browning FN Model 1910 semiautomatic pistols, calibers .32 and .380, marked "Browning Arms Company".
- Browning Superposed Bi-Centennial Ltd. Edition, shotgun.
- Browning, "Baby" model pistol, Russian Contract, caliber 6.35mm.
- Browning, Centennial model High Power Pistol, cal. 9mm parabellum.
- Browning, Centennial model 92 lever action rifle, cal. .44 Magnum.
- Browning, model 1906 Pocket Pistol if more than 50 years old.
- Browning, model 1922 pistol, cal. 7.65mm or 9mm Kurz, marked "C.P.I.M." denoting issue to the Belgian Political Police.
- Browning, model 1922 pistol, cal. 7.65mm, bearing German NSDAP or RFV markings.
- Browning, M1935 Hi Power pistol, Canadian, Congolese, Indian and Nationalist Chinese Contracts, cal. 9mm parabellum.
- Browning Hi Power, Classic Edition, 9mm caliber pistol, having S/Ns 245BC0001 through 245BC5000.
- Browning High Power D-Day Commemorative, 9mm caliber pistol, having S/Ns 245DD0001 through 245DD00150.
- Browning High Power, Gold Classic Edition, 9mm caliber pistol, having S/Ns 245GC0001 through 245GC0500.
- Browning, Superposed Centennial, consisting of a 20 gauge superposed shotgun, supplied with an extra set of .30-06 cal. superposed barrels.
- Budischowsky, model TP70, semiautomatic pistol, cal. .25 ACP, with custom S/N DB1.

C

- Campo-Giro, model 1913 and 1913/16 pistol, cal. 9mm Largo.
- Chinese Communist, types 51 and 54 (Tokarev) pistols, cal. 7.62mm.
- Chinese, Peoples Republic of China, copy of German Walther PPK .32 ACP cal. w/Chinese proof marks, Type I and II.
- Chinese, Peoples Republic of China, copy of Japanese Type Sigiura Shiki semiautomatic pistol, caliber 7.65mm.
- Chylewski, semiautomatic pistol mfd. by S.I.G. Switzerland, cal. 6.35mm (.25 ACP).
- Clement, pistol, Belgian manufacture, cal. 5mm Clement.
- Colt, Model 1911A1, cal. .45, semiautomatic pistols, Famous Generals of WWII, S/N's WWIIG001 - WWIIG200.
- Colt .38 National Match semiautomatic pistol, all S/Ns and in their original configuration.
- Colt .38 Special Kit semiautomatic pistols, mfd. from 1964-1970, S/Ns 00100H-00434H.
- Colt .45 ACP Kit semiautomatic pistols, mfd. from 1964-1970, S/Ns 001000-011640.
- Colt, factory engraved for "Dr. Ramon Grau San Martin," President of Cuba, .45 cal. pistol with 5" barrel and blue steel finish; S/N C231769.
- Colt, "Duke," Commemorative, .22 caliber revolver.
- Colt, Ace semiautomatic pistol, cal. .22, mfd. by Colt from 1931 to 1947, S/N range from 1 to 10935 including those marked "UNITED STATES PROPERTY" on the right side of the frame.
- Colt, Ace Service model semiautomatic pistol, cal. .22, mfd. by Colt from 1935 to 1945, S/N range from SM1 to SM13803 including those marked "UNITED STATES PROPERTY" on the right side of the frame.
- Colt, Age of Flight 75th Anniversary semiautomatic pistols, cal. .45.
- Colt, Aircrewman revolver produced between 1951 and 1959, cal. .38 Special, marked "Property of U.S. Air Force" on back strap, having Air Force issue numbers of 1 - 1189 and in the S/N range 1902LW - 90470LW.
- Colt, Alabama Sesquicentennial, .22.
- Colt, Alamo, .22 and .45.
- Colt, American Combat Companion Officers model, cal. .45ACP pistol marked "1911 American Combat Companion 1981, 70 Years at America's Side."
- Colt, American Combat Companion, Enlisted Man's model, cal. .45ACP pistol marked "1911 American Combat Companion 1981, 70 Years at America's Side."
- Colt, American Combat Companion, General Officers model, cal. .45ACP pistol marked "1911 American Combat Companion 1981, 70 Years at America's Side." S/Ns 1 STAR, 2 STAR 3 STAR, 4 STAR, and 5 STAR.
- Colt, Appomattox Court House Centennial, .22 and .45.
- Colt AR-15 Sporter "The Viet Nam Tribute Colt Special Edition" .223 cal. semiautomatic rifle, bearing the American Historical Foundation registry numbers of VT0001 through VT1500.
- Colt, Argentine model 1927, pistols, cal. .45, commercial variations.
- Colt, Arizona Ranger model commemorative, .22 Revolver.
- Colt, Arizona Territorial Centennial, .22 and .45.
- Colt, Arkansas Territory Sesquicentennial, .22.
- Colt, Army Model double action revolver, any cal., mfd. between 1899 and 1907.
- Colt Army Special Model revolver, .32-20 cal., having a barrel length of 4'1/2", with factory engraving, S/N 329653.
- Colt, ATF Special Edition, Deluxe model automatic pistol, cal. .45 ACP.
- Colt, ATF Special Edition, Python Revolver, caliber .357 magnum.
- Colt, ATF Special Edition, Standard model automatic pistol, cal. .45 ACP.
- Colt, Abilene, .22 (Kansas City-Cow Town).
- Colt, Bat Masterson, .22 and .45 (Lawman Series).
- Colt, Battle of Gettysburg Centennial, .22.
- Colt, Belleau Wood, .45 Pistol, (World War I Series).
- Colt, Border Patrol model Revolver, .38 Special Heavy Duty, Police Positive (D) style frame, S/Ns within the range 610000 through 620000.

- Colt, Buffalo Bill Historical Center, Winchester Museum, Special Issue, Colt Single Action revolver, cal. .44-40, S/N 21BB.
- Colt, Buffalo Bill Wild West Show single action army .45 caliber.
- Colt, California Bicentennial, .22.
- Colt, California Gold Rush, .22 and .45.
- Colt, Camp Perry Single Shot Target Pistols, .22 long rifle or .38 Special caliber.
- Colt, Carolina Charter Tercentenary, .22 and .22/.45.
- Colt, Chamizal Treaty, .22 and .45.
- Colt, Chateau Thierry, .45 Pistol, (World War I Series).
- Colt, Cherry's Sporting Goods 35th Anniversary, .22/.45.
- Colt, Chisholm Trail, .22 (Kansas Series-Trails).
- Colt, Civil War Centennial Single Shot, .22.
- Colt, Coffeyville, .22 (Kansas Series-Cow Town).
- Colt, Colorado Gold Rush, Colt, Colonel Samuel Colt, Sesquicentennial, .45.
- Colt, Colt's 125th Anniversary, .45.
- Colt, Columbus (Ohio) Sesquicentennial, .22.
- Colt, Custom Gun Shop's "Custom Edition Sheriff's model" Single Action Revolver, cal. .45 Colt, S/Ns 1 to 35.
- Colt, DA .38, New Army and Navy Revolver, made from 1899 to 1907.
- Colt, Dakota Territory, .22. Colt, Des Monies, Reconstruction of Old Fort, .22 and .45.
- Colt, Detective Special revolver, cal. .38, S/N 418162, owned by Colonel Charles A. Lindbergh.
- Colt, Detective Special revolvers, 2" barrels, marked "R.M.S. P.O. DEPT" or "U.S.P.O. DEPT."; S/Ns above 467000.
- Colt, Dodge City, .22 (Kansas Series-Cow Town).
- Colt, European Theater, .45 Pistol (World War II Series).
- Colt, First model, Match Target Woodsman, cal. .22, semiautomatic pistol, mfd. from 1938 to 1944, S/Ns MT1 to MT15,000.
- Colt, Florida Territory Sesquicentennial, .22.
- Colt, Fort Findlay (Ohio) sesquicentennial, .22.
- Colt, Fort Hays, .22 (Kansas Series-Forts).
- Colt, Fort Larned, .22 (Kansas Series-Forts).
- Colt, Fort McPherson (Nebraska) Centennial Derringer, .22.
- Colt, Fort Scott, .22 (Kansas Series-Forts).
- Colt, Fort Stephenson (Ohio) sesquicentennial, .22.
- Colt, Fourth model Derringer, cal. .22 short rimfire, cased as a set of two pistols in a leather book titled "Colt Derringer, Limited Edition Colt, General George Meade, Pennsylvania, by Colt," on the spine of the book and "A Limited Edition by Colt," on the cover.
- Colt, Forty-Niner Miner, .22.
- Colt, General George Meade, Pennsylvania Campaign, .22 and .45.
- Colt, General Hood, Tennessee Campaign Centennial, .22.
- Colt, General John Hunt Morgan, Indiana Raid, .22.
- Colt, General Nathan Bedford Forrest, .22.
- Colt, Geneseo (Illinois) 125th Anniversary, Derringer, .22.
- Colt, Golden Spike Centennial, .22.
- Colt, Government model pistols in cal. .45 ACP, BB series.
- Colt, H. Cook, "1 to 100," .22/.45.
- Colt, Idaho Territorial Centennial, .22.
- Colt, Indiana Sesquicentennial, .22.
- Colt, J frame, Officers model Match, .38 Special revolver mfd. from 1970-1972, identified by J S/N prefix.
- Colt, Joaquin Murrieta, "1 of 100," .22/.45.
- Colt, John M. Browning Commemorative, .45 cal., semiautomatic pistol, S/Ns JMB 0001 - JMB 3000, and numbers GAS O JMB, PE CEW JMB, and 0003JMB.
- Colt, John Wayne, Commemorative, .45 long Colt caliber revolver.
- Colt, Kansas Centennial, .22.
- Colt, Lightning model double action revolver, any cal. mfd. between 1899 and 1909.
- Colt, Lightning rifles mfd. in 1899 through 1904.
- Colt, Lord and Lady Derringer, .22 cal., as mfd. by Colts Patent Firearms Manufacturing Co., Hartford, CT.
- Colt, Los Angeles Police Department (L.A.P.D.) Special Edition .45 cal. Government model semiautomatic pistol.
- Colt, Maine Sesquicentennial, .22 and .45.
- Colt, Mark IV, Government Model, commemorative "Michigan State Police 60th Anniversary, 1917-1977". The left side of slide engraved with scroll pattern and depicts 4 modes of transportation; Horse, Motorcycle, Auto and Helicopter, S/Ns 1 to 1608.
- Colt, Match Target Woodsman Semiautomatic Pistol, cal. .22LR., S/N 128866S, owned by Ernest Hemingway.
- Colt, Meuse Argonne, .45 Pistol, (World War I Series).
- Colt, Missouri Sesquicentennial single action army .45 caliber.
- Colt, Missouri Sesquicentennial, .22.
- Colt, Mk IV Series 70 semiautomatic pistols in all cals., which were incorrectly marked at the factory with both Colt Government model markings and Colt Commander markings.
- Colt, model 1873 Peacemaker Centennial 1973, single action revolver, .44/.40 or .45.
- Colt, model 1900 semiautomatic pistol, cal. .38, in original configuration.
- Colt, model 1902 semiautomatic pistol, military model, cal. .38, in original configuration.
- Colt, model 1902 semiautomatic pistol, sporting model, cal. .38, in original configuration.
- Colt, model 1903 Pocket (exposed hammer), semiautomatic pistol cal. .38 ACP.
- Colt, model 1903 Pocket (hammerless), semiautomatic pistol, cal. .32.
- Colt, model 1908 Pocket (hammerless), semiautomatic pistol, cal. .380.
- Colt, model 1908, cal. .25 ACP, hammerless semiautomatic pistol, having a grip safety, in S/N range 1 - 409061.
- Colt, model 1911, commercial semiautomatic pistols, cal. .45 ACP, S/Ns Cl - C130000.
- Colt, model 1911-A, commercial model, in cal. .45 and bearing Egyptian inscription meaning police, on the upper forward right-hand side of the trigger guard and having S/Ns within the range of C186000 to C188000.
- Colt, 50th Anniversary of the Battle of the Bulge, Model 1911A1, .45 caliber, semiautomatic pistol, having serial numbers between BB001 and BB300.
- Colt, Montana Territory Centennial, .22 and .45.
- Colt, National Match semiautomatic pistols, all serial numbers, in original configuration.
- Colt, Nebraska Centennial, .22.
- Colt, Ned Buntline Commemorative, cal. .45 revolver.
- Colt, Nevada Centennial "Battle Born," .22 and .45.
- Colt, Nevada Centennial, .22. and .45.
- Colt, New Frontier .22 LR Revolvers, "Kit Carson" Commemorative, Colt model GB275.
- Colt, New Frontier and Single Action Army model revolvers originally ordered & shipped with factory engraving, accompanied by a letter from the manufacturer confirming the authenticity of the engraving.
- Colt, New Frontier, .357 magnum cal., single action revolver, barrel length 4-3/4" S/N 4411NF.
- Colt, New Frontier, .45 cal., Abercrombie and Fitch, "Trailblazer."
- Colt, New Jersey Tercentenary, .22 and .45.
- Colt, New Mexico Golden Anniversary, .22.
- Colt, New Police revolvers, .32 Colt cal., S/Ns 1 through 49,50.

- Colt, New Service revolvers as mfd. between 1899 - 1944, all variations, all calibers.
- Colt, NRA Centennial, Gold Cup National Match pistol, in cal. .45.
- Colt, NRA Centennial, single action revolver, in cals. .357 Magnum and .45.
- Colt, Officers model (1904-1930), .38 cal. revolver.
- Colt, Officers model (1930-1949), .22 cal. revolver.
- Colt, Officers model Match (1953-1969), .22 and .38 cal. revolvers.
- Colt, Officers model Special (1949-1952), .22 and .38 cal. revolvers.
- Colt, Officers model Target (1930-1949), .32 and .38 cal revolvers.
- Colt, Officer's Model, .38 caliber revolver, serial number 535472, 585683.
- Colt Official Police Model revolver, cal. .32-20, having a barrel length of 5 inches, with factory engraving by Wilbur Glahn, S/N 554399.
- Colt Official Police Model revolver, .38 Colt Special cal., having a barrel length of 6 inches, with factory engraving by Wilbur Glahn, S/N 554445.
- Colt, Official Police Revolver, cal. .38, Silver Inlaid and Engraved by Wilbur A. Glahn, S/N 583469.
- Colt, Oklahoma Territory Diamond Jubilee, .22.
- Colt, Oregon Trail, .22 (Kansas Series-Trails).
- Colt, Pacific Theater, .45 Pistol (World War II Series).
- Colt, Pat Garrett, .22 and .45 (Lawman Series).
- Colt, Pawnee Trail, .22 (Kansas Series-Trails).
- Colt, Peacemaker Commemorative, .22 and .45 revolver.
- Colt, Pocket Positive revolver, .32 cal.
- Colt, Pocket Positive revolver, S/N 6164.
- Colt, Police Positive .38 cal. revolvers, 2" barrels, marked "R.M.S. P.O. DEPT." or "U.S.P.O. DEPT."; S/Ns above 383000.
- Colt, Police Positive revolver (1909); "St. L.P.D. #466" on butt; S/N 24466.
- Colt, Pony Express Centennial, .22.
- Colt, Pony Express, Russell, Majors and Waddell, Presentation model .45.
- Colt, Python Model revolver, .357 cal., having a barrel length of 3 inches, with factory Type A engraving by Denise Thirion, in a presentation case with accessories, S/N T21895.
- Colt, Python Revolver, cal. .357 Magnum, engraved and inlaid with the Crest of the United Arab Emirates.
- Colt, Revolver, cal. .38, Police Positive, S/N 139212.
- Colt, Rock Island Arsenal Centennial Single Shot, .22.
- Colt, Santa Fe Trail, .22 (Kansas Series-Trails).
- Colt model San Jacinto Special edition single action army revolver, .45 caliber, marked "THE BATTLE OF SAN JACINTO, APRIL 21, 1836" and "REMEMBER GOLIAD", 200 produced.
- Colt, Second (2nd) Marne, .45 Pistol (World War I Series).
- Colt, Shawnee Trail, .22 (Kansas Series-Trails).
- Colt, Sheriffs model revolver, cal. .44 and .45.
- Colt, Single Action Army (Bisley, Standard, and target variations), all original, mfd. from 1899 to 1946, S/N range from 182000 to 357869.
- Colt, Single Action Army revolver, cal. .45, S/N 85163A, engraved and inlaid with a bust of President Abraham Lincoln.
- Colt, Single Action Revolvers, cal. .45, engraved & silver inlaid for presentation to Chuck Connors, S/Ns CC1 and CC2.
- Colt, St. Augustine Quadricentennial, .22.
- Colt, St. Louis Bicentennial, .22 and .45.
- Colt Government model Texas Battleship Special Edition, .45 caliber pistols marked "BATTLESHIP EDITION - USS TEXAS", 500 produced.
- Colt, Texas Ranger, .45.
- Colt, Texas Sesquicentennial Standard and Premier model single action army, .45 cal.
- Colt, the Liege Number 1 Colt Single Action Army Revolver, cal. .45, S/N Liege No. 1.
- Colt, "The Right to Keep and Bear Arms" commemorative, .22 cal. Peacemaker Buntline, single action revolver having a 7-1/2" barrel with the inscription, "The Right to Keep and Bear Arms" inscribed on the barrel and a S/N range of G0001RB - G3000RB.
- Colt, Theodore Roosevelt single action army .44-40 cal.
- Colt, United States Bicentennial Commemorative, Python revolver, caliber .357.
- Colt, United States Bicentennial Commemorative single action army revolver cal. .45.
- Colt, West Virginia Centennial, .22 and .45.
- Colt, Wichita, .22 (Kansas Series-Cow Town).
- Colt, Wild Bill Hickok, .22 and .45 (Lawman Series).
- Colt model Wisconsin State Patrol, 45th Anniversary, Special Edition Commemorative, 70 series, .45 government model pistols, consecutively numbered 1 through 126.
- Colt, Woodsman, cal. .22, semiautomatic target pistol, mfd. from 1915 to 1943, S/Ns 1 to 157000.
- Colt, Woodsman, First Model Match Target, .22 cal. semiautomatic pistols mfd. in or before 1944, and having S/Ns MT1 through MT15100.
- Colt, Wyatt Earp, .22 and .45 (Lawman Series).
- Colt, Wyatt Earp, Buntline Special, .45 (Lawman Series).
- Colt, Wyoming Diamond Jubilee, .22
- Colt XIT Special Edition Single Action Army revolver, .45 caliber, barrel chemically etched with a covered wagon scene and "XIT RANCH", and marked "1 of 500".
- Colt, 150th Anniversary single action army buntline, .45 cal.
- Czechoslovakian, CZ27, 7.65mm semiautomatic pistol with Nazi markings.
- Czechoslovakian, CZ38, pistol cal. .380ACP.
- Czechoslovakian, CZ50 pistol, cal. 7.65mm.
- Czechoslovakian, CZ52 pistol, cal. 7.62mm.
- Czechoslovakian, model 1952 and 1952/57, 7.62 x 45mm and 7.62 x 39mm cal., semiautomatic rifles.

D

- * Daisy, Model V/L, .22 caliber caseless rifle, manufactured during 1968-1969.
- Danish, M1910/1921 Bayard, pistol, cal. 9mm Bergmann-Bayard.
- Davis Warner, Infallible, semiautomatic pistol, cal. .32.
- Dreyse, semiautomatic pistols, all calibers.

E

- Egyptian Raschid, semiautomatic rifle, cal. 7.62 x 39mm, original Egyptian military production.
- Egyptian, Hakim (Ljungman) 7.92mm semiautomatic rifle as mfd. in Egypt.
- Erma-Werke, Model EL 24, cal. .22, rifle, mfd. prior to 1946.
- Esser-Barraft, English manufacture, slide action rifle, cal. .303.

F

- Fabrique Nationale 1889-1989 Centenary High Power pistols, cal. 9mm.
- Fabrique Nationale, Model 1906, .25 caliber semiautomatic pistol, all serial numbers.
- Fabrique Nationale, model SAFN49 semiautomatic rifles, any caliber.

- FN F.A.L. G and GL series, semiautomatic rifles, imported by Browning Arms Company, Arnold, MO from 1959 to 1963, with the following S/Ns: G Series: G492, G493, G494, G537-G540, G649-G657, G662-G673, G677-G693, G709-G748, G752-G816, G848-G1017, G1021, G1033, G1035, G1041, G1042, G1174-G1293, G1415-G1524, G1570-Gl784, G1800-Gl979, G1981-G1995, G2247-G2996, G3035-G3134. GL Series: GL749, GL835, GL1095-GL1098, GL1163,GL1164, GL1165, GL2004-GL2009, GL3135-GL3140.
- French Military Rifle Model 1949/56, in 7.62 x 51mm (NATO) cal. French, model 1949, cal. 7.5mm, semiauto. rifle (Fusil Mle. 1949 (MAS) 7.5mm).
- French, model 1949/56 (Fusil Mle (MAS 7.5mm)) semiautomatic rifle.
- A.H. Fox, Double barrel shotguns, all gauges, all grades, mfd. By Ansley H. Fox, Philadelphia, PA, and Savage Arms, Utica, NY, from approx. 1907 - 1947.

G

- Geha and Remo, shotguns made from Mauser rifles after World War I prior to 1946.
- German military training rifles, cal. .22, single shot and repeaters, all manufacturers, in their original military configuration, marked "Kleinkaliber Wehersportsgewehr" (KKW), mfd. prior to 1946.
- German sporting rifles, cal. .22, sporting rifles, single shot and repeaters, all manufacturers, in original configuration, marked "Deutsche Sportmodell" (DSM), prior to 1946.
- German, model 1916 Grenatenwerfer original spigot type mortars.
- German, P38 pistols, cal. 9mm parabellum mfd. prior to 1947.
- Greener, Martini action, 14 gauge shotgun.
- Gustloff, semiautomatic pistol in cal. 7.65mm mfd. by Gustloff Werke, Suhl, Germany.

H

- Hammond or Grant Hammond, pistols, all models, variations or prototypes, made by Grant Hammond Corporation, New Haven, CT.
- Hammond/Hi-Standard, semiautomatic pistols, in caliber .45.
- Harrington and Richardson "Reising" Model 60 semiautomatic rifles, .45 ACP caliber, manufactured between 1944 and 1946.
- Harrington and Richardson (H&R), Abilene Anniversary, .22 revolver.
- Harrington and Richardson (H&R) Handy Gun, pistols with original rifled barrel, mfd. at Worcester, MA, all calibers, all barrel lengths, without shoulder stock.
- Harrington and Richardson (H&R) Handy guns, mfd. at Worcester, MA, with shoulder stock, having an original smoothbore barrel 18 inches in length or greater, or original rifled barrel 16 inches in length or greater.
- H&R, Centennial Officer's model Springfield rifle .45-70 Government.
- H&R, Centennial Standard model Springfield rifle .45-70 Government.
- H&R, model 999, revolver, cal. 22 Long rifle, barrel 6", 110th year commemorative, S/Ns from 001 to 999.
- H&R, self loading semiautomatic pistol, caliber .32.
- Hartford Arms and Equipment Company, single shot target pistol, caliber .22LR.
- Hartford Arms and Equipment Company, repeating pistol, cal. .22LR.
- Hartford Arms and Equipment Company, model 1928 pistol, cal. .22LR.
- Hi-Standard, experimental electric free pistol, cal. .22 long rifle.
- Hi-Standard, experimental electric free pistol, cal. .38 special.
- Hi-Standard, experimental electric free pistol, cal. .38 special.
- Hi-Standard, model P 38, semiautomatic pistol, cal. .38 SPL.
- Hi-Standard, experimental model T-3 semiautomatic pistol, cal. 9mm Luger.
- Hi-Standard, experimental ISU rapid fire semiautomatic pistol, caliber .22 short.
- High Standard, Second Model Olympic pistol, cal. .22 short, mfd. between 1951 - 1953, S/N's 330,000 - 439,999.
- High Standard, Crusader Commemorative, Deluxe Pair, .44 Magnum and .45 Colt revolvers.
- High Standard, model A pistol, caliber .22LR.
- High Standard, model B pistol, caliber .22LR.
- High Standard, model C pistol, caliber .22 Short.
- High Standard, model D pistol, caliber .22LR.
- High Standard, model E pistol, caliber .22LR.
- High Standard, model H-A pistol, caliber .22LR.
- High Standard, model H-B pistol, first model, caliber .22LR.
- High Standard, model H-B pistol, second model, caliber .22LR.
- High Standard, model H-D pistol, caliber .22LR.
- High Standard, model H-E pistol, caliber .22LR.
- High Standard, model USA-HD pistol, caliber .22LR.
- High Standard, model HD-Military pistol, caliber .22LR.
- High Standard, model G-380 pistol, caliber .380.
- High Standard, model G-B pistol, caliber .22LR.
- High Standard, model G-D pistol, caliber .22LR.
- High Standard, model G-E pistol, caliber .22LR.
- High Standard, model G-O (First model Olympic) pistol, caliber .22 Short.
- High Standard, Supermatic Trophy model 107, .22 pistol Olympic Commemorative model.
- High Standard, 1980 Olympic Commemorative, .22 caliber semiautomatic pistols, S/Ns USA1 - USA1000.
- Holland and Holland, Royal Double Barrel Shotgun, .410 Gauge, S/N 36789.
- Hopkins and Allen, model 1901, "FOREHAND," caliber .32 S&W long.
- Hopkins and Allen, Revolver, .32 cal., S/N G 9545.
- Hungarian Model 48 (Mosin Nagant M44 type) carbine, caliber 7.62 X 54R, manufactured in Hungary, and identified by the manufacturer code 02 on the chamber area and marked with the date of manufacture in the 1950's or earlier.

I

- Italian, Brixia, M1906, pistol, cal. 9mm Glisenti.
- Italian, Glisenti, M1910, pistol, cal. 9mm Glisenti.
- * Ithaca, Bicentennial Model 37, pump action shotguns, serial numbered USA0001 to USA1976.
- Ithaca, double barrel shotguns actually mfd. in NY by the Ithaca Gun Co. Ithaca, NY. All gauges and all models, having barrels at least 18" in length and an overall length of at least 26", mfd. before 1950.
- Ithaca Gun Co., single barrel trap guns, break open all gauges, all models actually mfd. at Ithaca, NY, before 1950.
- Ithaca, St. Louis Bicentennial, model 49, .22 rifle.
- Iver Johnson Arms, Pistol, cal. .380, U.S. Border Patrol 60th Anniversary commemorative, S/N's USBP 0001 to USBP 5000.
- Iver Johnson Arms, model M 1 Carbine, cal. .30, Korean War commemorative, S/Ns KW0001 to KW2500.
- Iver Johnson Arms, model M 1 Carbine, cal. .30, Airborne commemorative, S/Ns KW0001 - KW2500.

J

- Jieffeco, pistol, Belgian manufacture, caliber 7.65mm.
- Jieffeco, semiautomatic pistol, cal. .25 ACP, marked "Davis Warner Arms Corp., N.Y."

K

- Kimball, pistols, all models, all calibers.
- Kolibri, pistols, cals. 2.7mm and 3mm Kolibri.

L

- L. C. Smith, Shotguns mfd. by Hunter Arms Co. and Marlin Firearms Co. from 1899 to 1971.
- Langenhan, semiautomatic pistols, all calibers.
- Lahti, L-35 pistol, Finnish manufacture, caliber 9mm parabellum.
- Lahti Swedish Model M40 pistols, cal. 9mm, all variations, mfd. prior to 1968.
- Lee Enfield, No. 1 Mk III bolt action rifle, cal. .303, mfd. in Ishapore, India between 1946 and 1960. Original military configuration only.
- Lefever, shotguns made from 1899 to 1942.
- Luger, Model 1902 Cartridge Counter, Mauser commercial, semiautomatic pistol, cal. 9mm, mfd. 1982.
- Luger, pistol, all models and variations mfd. prior to 1946.
- Luger, Mauser commercial manufacture, semiautomatic pistol, 70 Jahre, Parabellum-Pistole, Kelsoreich Russiand, commemorative, cal. 9mm.
- Luger, Mauser commercial manufacture, semiautomatic pistol, 76 Jahre, Parabellum-Pistole, 1900-1975, commemorative, cal. 7.65mm.
- Luger, Mauser commercial manufacture, semiautomatic pistol, 75 Jahre, Parabellum-Pistole, Konigreich Bulgarian, commemorative, caliber 7.65mm.
- Luger, Mauser Parabellum, semiautomatic pistol, 7.65mm or 9mm Luger, 4 and 6" barrel, Swiss pattern with grip safety and the American Eagle stamped on the receiver; made from 1970 to 1978.

M

- MAB, model R pistol, caliber 9mm parabellum.
- Makarov, pistol, Russian and East German, caliber 9mm Makarov.
- Mannlicher, pistol, M1900, M1901, M1903 and M1905, caliber 7.63mm Mannlicher.
- Marlin, Model 336 TS carbine, cal. 30-30, Powell Wyoming 75th anniversary commemorative, having PW S/N prefix.
- Marlin, 90th Anniversary, model 39-A, .22 rifle.
- Marlin, 90th Anniversary, model 39-A, .22 carbine.
- Mauser, semiautomatic pistols mfd. prior to 1946, any caliber.
- Mauser, Congolese model 1950 rifles marked FP 1952 on the receiver, caliber .30/06.
- Mauser, model 1935 rifle 7 x 57mm cal. with Chilean Police Markings.
- Mauser, P 38, pistols caliber 9mm, marked SVW46.
- Mauser, rifles, bolt action and semiautomatic any caliber, commercially produced by Waffenfabrik Mauser, Oberndoff, Germany prior to 1945.
- MBA Gyrojet Carbine, S/N B5057.
- MBA Gyrojet semiautomatic pistols, cal. 12mm or smaller, all models.
- Menz, Liliput, German manufacture caliber 4.25mm.
- Menz, PB III, in cal. 7.65mm, mfd. by August Menz, Suhl, Germany.
- Menz, PB IIIA, in cal. 7.65mm, mfd. by August Menz, Suhl, Germany.
- Menz, PB IV, in cal. 7.65mm, mfd. by August Menz, Suhl, Germany.
- Menz, PB IVa, in cal. 7.65mm, mfd. by August Menz, Suhl, Germany.
- Menz, Special, in cal. 7.65mm, mfd. by August Menz, Suhl, Germany.
- Mexican, Obregon, pistol, caliber .45 ACP.
- Mexican Model 1954 bolt action Mauser rifles and carbines, caliber .30-06 (original military configuration only).
- Mossberg, Model 40, cal. .22 tubular fed, bolt action rifles mfd. From 1933-1935.
- Mossberg, Model 42TR Targo, cal. .22 smoothbore, bolt action rifles, mfd. From 1940-1942.
- Mossberg, Model 479RR "Roy Rogers" limited edition, cal. .30-30 lever action rifles, total number mfd. In 1983 only.
- Mossberg, Model 25, .22 caliber bolt action rifles.
- Mugica, model 120, pistol, caliber 9mm parabellum.

N

- Navy Arms, Oklahoma Diamond Jubilee Commemorative, Yellow Boy Carbine.
- North Korean Type 1964, pistol, caliber 7.62mm Tokarev.
- North Korean, Type 68, 7.62 x 25mm caliber semiautomatic pistols.

O

- O.F. Mossberg Model 472SBAS "American Indian Commemorative" .30-30 and .35 Remington caliber lever action rifles, having Indian scenes etched on receiver, manufactured in 1974 only.
- Ortgies, semiautomatic, caliber .25, with S/N 10073.
- Ortgies, semiautomatic, caliber .32, with S/N 126314. OWA, semiautomatic pistol, caliber .25.

P

- PAF, "Junior" semiautomatic pistol, caliber .25, mfd. by the Pretoria Arms Factory Ltd. of South Africa.
- PAF, pistol, marked "BRF," caliber .25, mfd. by the Pretoria Arms Factory Ltd. of South Africa.
- Parker-Hale, Model T-4, cal. 7.62mm, bolt action target rifles, mfd. prior to 1975.
- Parker, shotguns, all grades, all gauges, produced by Parker Brothers, Meridan, CT, and Remington Arms, Ilion, NY, from 1899 through 1945.
- Pedersoli, 120th Anniversary of the Remington Creedmore, .45/70 caliber, single shot rolling block rifle, having S/Ns between CR001 and CR300.
- Pedersoli, 125th Anniversary of the Springfield, Model 1873 Trapdoor rifle, .45/70 caliber, having serial numbers between 125th-001 through 125th-125.
- Pedersoli, Sharps Creedmoor, single shot rifles, caliber .45-70, S/Ns SCR001 through SCR300.
- * Pedersoli, Springfield Officer's Model trapdoor rifle, .45-70 caliber, having serial numbers 2NFM001 through 2NFM250.
- Phoenix, (U.S.A.), pistol, caliber .25 ACP.
- Polish Mosin Nagant M44 type carbines, caliber 7.62 X 54R, manufactured in Poland, identified by the manufacturer code "11" in an oval on the chamber area, and marked with the actual date of manufacture during the 1950's or earlier.
- James Purdey, Over & Under shotgun, 12 gauge, S/N 26819, engraved and gold inlaid.

R

- Reising, .22 caliber, semiautomatic pistol.
- Remington, No. 1, Mid Range Rolling Block target rifle reproduction, caliber .45-70, S/N's beginnning with "RB97".
- Remington, Model 31, pump action shotguns, 12, 16, and 20 gauge, mfd. 1931 - 1950.
- Remington Rolling Block firearms, all models mfd. from 1899 - 1935.
- Remington, over/under Derringer, caliber .41 rim fire, Remington Arms Company, Ilion, NY, made between 1898 and 1935.
- Remington, Canadian Territorial Centennial, model 742, rifle.
- Remington, model 12, rifle, cal. .22 short, long rifle, and .22 Remington Special mfd. by Remington Arms, Union Metallic Cartridge Co., Remington Works, Ilion, NY, from 1909 to 1936.
- Remington, model 30 rifles.
- Remington, model 720 rifles.

- Remington, model 51, semiautomatic pistol, cals. .32 ACP or .380 ACP. Remington, Montana Territorial Centennial, model 600, rifle.
- Remington, 150th Anniversary model Nylon 66 semiautomatic rifle, caliber .22LR.
- Remington, 150th Anniversary model 1100SA semiautomatic shotgun, caliber 12 gauge.
- Remington, 150th Anniversary model 552A semiautomatic rifle, caliber. 22LR.
- Remington, 150th Anniversary model 572A slide action rifle, caliber .22LR.
- Remington, 150th Anniversary model 742ADL semiautomatic rifle caliber .30/06.
- Remington, 150th Anniversary model 760ADL slide action rifle caliber .30/06.
- Remington, 150th Anniversary model 870SA slide action shotgun, caliber 12 gauge.
- Rheinmetal, semiautomatic pistols, caliber .32.
- Rhode Island Arms Co., Morrone Model 46, shotgun.
- Rifle, caliber 7.62 2A "INDIA", all variations, originally mfd. at Ishapore Arsenal, India prior to 1965.
- * Romanian Model 56 semiautomatic carbine (SKS), caliber 7.62x39mm in original configuration as manufactured at Uzina
- Mechanica Cugir, Romania, from 1956 through 1962, having original Romanian serial numbers consisting of two letters followed by up to four digits. The right side of the receiver is also marked with the year of production and the manufacturer's trademark consisting of an unfletched arrow within a triangle.
- Roth Steyr, 1907, semiautomatic pistol, caliber 8mm.
- Ruger, Blackhawk .44 with 6-1/2" barrel, revolver with S/Ns 1 to 29860.
- Ruger, Blackhawk .44 with 7-1/2" barrel, revolver with S/Ns 17000 to 29860.
- Ruger, Blackhawk .44 with 10" barrel, revolver with S/Ns 18000 to 29860.
- Ruger, Blackhawk .357 with 4-5/8" barrel, revolver with S/Ns 1 to 42689.
- Ruger, Blackhawk .357 with 6-1/2" barrel, revolver with S/Ns 20000 to 42689.
- Ruger, Blackhawk .357 and 9mm stainless steel revolver with S/Ns 32-56000 - 32-59000.
- Ruger, Blackhawk .357 magnum with 10" barrel, revolver with S/Ns 20000 - 38000.
- Ruger, Canadian Centennial, Matched No. 1 Rifle Sets, Special Deluxe.
- Ruger, Canadian Centennial, Matched No. 2 Rifle Sets.
- Ruger, Canadian Centennial, Matched No. 3 Rifle Sets.
- Ruger, Canadian Centennial, model 10/22, carbine.
- Ruger, l0/22 Canadian Centennial, carbine with S/Ns Cl to C4500.
- Ruger, Falling Block Long Range Creedmore rifle, cal. .45 (Sharps), S/N 130-06888, The Amber Silver Jubilee.
- Ruger, flattop, "Blackhawk" revolvers, cals. .44 Magnum and .357 magnum, all barrel lengths, made from 1955 through 1962.
- Ruger, flattop, single-six, .22 cal. revolvers with flat side loading gate, all barrel lengths, made from 1953 through 1956.
- Ruger, Hawkeye, pistol with S/Ns 1 to 3296.
- Ruger, Lightweight Single Six, Revolver with S/Ns 200000 to 212630.
- Ruger, Mark I "U.S." stamped medallion, pistol with S/Ns 76000 - 79000.
- Ruger, Single Six, engraved revolver with S/Ns 5100 - 75000.
- Ruger, Standard Auto with red eagle, pistol with S/Ns 1 - 25000.
- Ruger, Super Black Hawk, revolvers having a barrel length of 6½ inches with S/Ns 24000 - 26000.
- Ruger, Super Single Six stainless with 4" barrel, revolver with S/Ns 62-07500 - 64-650000.
- Ruger, Super Single Six stainless with 9" barrel, revolver with S/Ns 62-07500 - 63-40000.
- Ruger, Super Single Six chrome with 4-5/8" barrel, revolver with S/Ns 504000 - 505000.
- Ruger, "21 Club" No. 1, rifle with random S/Ns.
- Ruger, 44 Deerstalker, carbine with S/Ns 1 to 5000.
- Ruger, S47 Code, Model Super Blackhawk, 7 ½ inch barrel, .44 magnum revolvers, in S/N range 196 to 3111, with long grip frame, micro rear sight, and in mahogany wood case, approximately 500 manufactured.
- Rumanian Mosin Nagant 1944 type carbines, caliber 7.62 X 54R, manufactured in Romania, and manufactured from 1952 to 1956.
- Russian (U.S.S.R.), Nagant revolver, model 1895, cal. 7.62 Nagant and .22 cal. all variations, mfd. by the Tula Arsenal, Tula, Russia, after 1898.
- Russian (U.S.S.R.), Tokarev, model TT, 1930, pistol, cal. 7.62, mfd. at the Tula Arsenal, Tula, U.S.S.R., from 1939 through 1956.
- Russian (U.S.S.R.), Tokarev, model TT, 1933, pistol, cal. 7.62, mfd. at the Tula Arsenal, Tula, U.S.S.R., from 1933 through 1956.
- Russian (U.S.S.R.) Tokarev, model TT R-3, .22 cal., pistol.
- Russian (U.S.S.R.) Tokarev, model TT R-4, .22 cal., pistol.
- Russian (U.S.S.R.), Tula Korovin, Tk, .25 ACP cal., semiautomatic pistol.
- Russian (U.S.S.R.), model 1891, Mosin-Nagant rifles, cal. 7.62 x 54R and .22 cal., all models and all variations, mfd. after 1898 (i.e., M1891/30, M1910, M1938, and M1944).
- Russian (U.S.S.R.), Tokarev, semiautomatic rifle, model 1938 (SVT38), cal. 7.62 x 54R, of Soviet manufacture.
- Russian (U.S.S.R.), Tokarev, semiautomatic rifle, model 1940 (SVT40), cal. 7.62 x 54R, of Soviet manufacture.
- Russian (U.S.S.R.), Tokarev, semiautomatic carbine, model 1932 (nonstandard), cal. 7.62 x 54R, of Soviet manufacture.
- Russian (U.S.S.R.), Tokarev, semiautomatic carbine, model 1940 (SVT40), cal. 7.62 x 54R, of Soviet manufacture.
- Russian (U.S.S.R.), Simonov, semiautomatic rifle, model SKS, cal. 7.62 x 39, of Soviet manufacture.
- Russian (U.S.S.R.), Dragunov, semiautomatic rifle, model SVD, cal. 7.62 x 54R, of Soviet manufacture, Soviet military issue only.

S

- * Sako, Anniversary Model, 7mm Remington magnum caliber, bolt action rifle.
- J. P. Sauer & Sohn pistols, mfd. prior to 1946.
- Sauer, 38(h), pistol, cal. 7.65mm marked w/Third Reich police acceptance stamps of Eagle C, F, K, or L.
- Savage Arms, semiautomatic pistols, cal. .45 ACP, all models.
- Savage Arms, model 99, lever action, centerfire rifles, mfd. in Utica, NY prior to World War II with S/Ns below 450000.
- Savage, Prototype pistols, cal. .25, .32 and .38 made between 1907 and 1927.
- Savage model 1907 pistol, caliber .32 and .380.
- Savage model 1915 pistol, caliber .32 and .380.
- Savage model 1917 pistol, caliber .32 and .380.
- Schwarzlose, pocket model 1908 in 7.65mm, pistol mfd. by A.W. Schwarzlose, G.m.b.h., Berlin, Germany and those assembled or made by Warner Arms.
- Smith and Wesson, Model 624 revolver, First Issue, cal. .44 Target, engraved year "1985" over the issue number (1-25) on the right sideplate.
- Smith & Wesson Collector's Association, 25th Anniversary Commemorative revolver 1970-1995, Model 29, .44 Magnum caliber, S/Ns SWC 0001 through SWC 0184.

- Smith & Wesson, 125th anniversary Commemorative, model 25, revolver, cal. .45, marked "Smith & Wesson 125th Anniversary" and mfd. in 1977.
- Smith & Wesson, 150th anniversary Texas Ranger Commemorative model 19 revolver.
- Smith & Wesson, 1st model, Ladysmith revolver, cal. .22 rimfire long.
- Smith & Wesson, .22/32 Kit Gun, cal. .22LR, S/Ns 525670 - 534636 (no letter).
- Smith & Wesson, 2nd model, Ladysmith revolver, cal. .22 rimfire long.
- Smith & Wesson, 2nd model, single shot pistol, cals. .22 rimfire, .32 S&W and .38 S&W.
- Smith & Wesson, .32 Double Action Top Break, cal. .32 S&W, S/Ns 209302 and higher.
- Smith & Wesson, .32 Safety Hammerless Top Break (New Departure), cal. .32 S&W, S/Ns 91401 and higher.
- Smith & Wesson, .357 Magnum Hand Ejector, cal. .357 Magnum, S/Ns 45768 to 60000 (no letter).
- Smith & Wesson, .38 Double Action Top Break Perfected model, cal. .38 S&W.
- Smith & Wesson, .38 Double Action Top Break, cal. .38 S&W, S/Ns 382023 and higher.
- Smith & Wesson, .38 Hand Ejector Military and Police, cal. .38, S/Ns 1 to 241703 (no letter).
- Smith & Wesson, .38 Safety Hammerless Top Break (New Departure), cal. .38 S&W, S/Ns 19901 and higher.
- Smith & Wesson, .38/44 Outdoorsman & Heavy Duty, cal. .38, S/Ns 36500-62023 (no letter).
- Smith & Wesson, 3rd model, Ladysmith revolver, cal. .22 rimfire.
- Smith & Wesson, 3rd model, single shot pistol, cals. .22 rimfire, .32 S&W and .38 S&W.
- Smith & Wesson, 4 screw side plate revolvers, old style N-frame series, with no model designation stamped in the yoke cut, in cal. .44 magnum, all barrel lengths, falling within the S130000- Sl60350 block of serial numbers, of which a total of 6,500 units were produced from 1956 to 1958.
- Smith & Wesson, .44 Hand Ejector, all cal., S/Ns 1-62488 (no letter).
- Smith & Wesson, .455 Mark II Hand Ejector, caliber .455.
- Smith & Wesson, California Highway Patrol Commemorative model 19 revolver, cal. .357. Smith & Wesson, City of Los Angeles 200th Anniversary Commemorative model 19 revolver, cal. .357.
- Smith & Wesson, K-22 Hand Ejector, cal. .22 LR, S/Ns 632132-696952 (no letter).
- Smith & Wesson, K-32 Hand Ejector (K-32 Masterpiece), cal. .32 S&W Long, S/Ns 653388 to 682207 (no letter).
- Smith & Wesson, Mercox Dart Gun, cal. .22 rimfire, blank.
- Smith & Wesson, Model 16 (K-32 Masterpiece), cal. .32 S&W Long, "K" S/N series.
- Smith & Wesson, model 21, .44 Special caliber, also known as the".44 Hand Ejector Fourth Model" and the "1950 Model Military", having serial number S75,000 - S263,000.
- Smith & Wesson, Model .22/32 Hand Ejector (Bekeart model), cal. .22LR, S/Ns 138220 to 534636 (no letter).
- Smith & Wesson, Model 29 "Elmer Keith Commemorative" .44 magnum revolvers, S/N EMK1 - EMK2500.
- Smith & Wesson, Model 39, Connecticut State Police 75th Anniversary 1903-1978, pistols, S/Ns CSP001 - CSP704.
- Smith & Wesson, Model 39, steel frame pistol, cal. 9mm parabellum.
- Smith & Wesson, Model 39-1 (52-A), pistol, cal. 9mm parabellum.
- Smith & Wesson, Model 53, Remington Jet Center Fire Magnum, cal. .22.
- Smith & Wesson, Model 41-1 .22 short cal. semiautomatic pistols.
- Smith & Wesson, Model 42 Centennial Airweight .38 Special 5-shot revolvers, with aluminum alloy frames and cylinders.
- Smith & Wesson, Model 45 Military & Police .22LR cal. revolvers.
- Smith & Wesson, Model 46 .22LR caliber semiautomatic pistols.
- Smith & Wesson, Model 56 U.S. Air Force contract .38 Special 6-shot revolvers, S/N K500001 through K515001.
- * Smith & Wesson Model 66 Bureau of Alcohol, Tobacco & Firearms 1933 - 1983 50th Anniversary Commemorative .357 magnum caliber revolvers, having a "BATF" prefix serial number and miniature replica of an agent's badge engraved into the frame.
- Smith & Wesson Model 66 Distinguished Combat Magnum, caliber .357 magnum revolver, marked with the Texas Sheriff's Assoication badge and "TEXAS LAWMAN" on the right side of the frame, commemorating 150 years of law enforcemnent in Texas 1836- 1986.
- Smith & Wesson model 66, Dallas Police Department Commemorative Edition 1881-1981.
- Smith & Wesson, Model 66, "Naval Investigative Service Commemorative" .357 6-shot revolvers.
- Smith & Wesson, Model 147-A, 9mm 14-shot semiautomatic pistols.
- Smith & Wesson, Model 544, "Texas Wagon Train Commemorative" .44/40 cal. 6-shot revolvers, S/N TWT001 through TWT7800.
- Smith & Wesson, .45 hand ejector model of 1950 Military, .45 caliber, having serial numbers between S76000 and S263000.
- Smith & Wesson, Model 1917 revolver, cal. .45 ACP, produced for Brazil.
- Smith & Wesson, Model Straight Line, single shot pistol, cal. .22 rimfire long rifle.
- Smith & Wesson, pistol, caliber .32 ACP.
- Smith & Wesson, pistol, caliber .35, all variations.
- Smith & Wesson Registered Model 27 revolvers, cal. .357-magnum, 50 Yr. Commemorative, 5" barrel, S/Ns REG0001 through REG2500, inclusive.
- Smith & Wesson U.S. Air Force contract M13 Aircrewman .38 Special 5-shot J frame and 6-shot K frame revolvers.
- Smith & Wesson, U.S. Border Patrol 50th Anniversary Commemorative, model 66, stainless steel, cal. .357 Magnum, revolvers.
- Sosso, pistols, mfd. by Guilio Sosso, Turin, Italy, or Fabrica Nationale D'Armi, Brescia, Italy, cal. 9mm.
- Springfield Armory, Inc., Korean War Commemorative .30 cal., MI Garand Rifle S/Ns from KW0001 to KW1000.
- Standard Arms Co., rifle/shotgun combination, U.S., model "Camp," slide action cal. .50.
- Standard Arms Co., rifle model G, slide action or gas operated, any caliber.
- Standard Arms Co., rifle model M, slide action caliber .25-.35, .30 Rem. and .35 Rem.
- * Stevens, Models 425, 430, 435, and 440 High-Power Repeating Rifles in calibers .25 Remington, .30 Remington, .32 Remington, and .35 Remington.
- Stevens, Model 77E, 12 gauge, military riot type shotguns, properly marked and identified as mfd. for the U.S. Military, from 1963 to 1969, in original configuration.
- Steyr, model 1909, .25 ACP cal. semiautomatic pistol.
- Steyr-Hahn, M1912, pistol, cal. 9mm Steyr.
- Steyr-Hahn, M1912, pistol, cal. 9mm parabellum marked with Third Reich police acceptance stamps of Eagle C, F, K, or L.
- Stock, semiautomatic pistols, all cals. mfd. by Franz Stock.
- Swiss Model 1931/55 rifles, cal. 7.5 mm, S/Ns 1001 to 5150.
- Swiss Schmidt Rubin, Model 1911, rifle made into a harpoon gun, caliber 12mm.

- Swiss self loading rifle, test 1947, cal. 7.5mm, all variations.

T

- Tauler, model military and police pistol.
- Thompson/Center 25th Anniversary Contender, cal. .22LR pistol, 10 inch barrel, S/N's 25 001-25 536.
- Thompson Center Contender Pistol, cal. .30 Herrett, Steve Herrett Commemorative, S/Ns SH-001 to SH-500.
- Thompson Center Contender Pistol, cal. 7mm TCU, IHMSA 10th anniversary commemorative, S/Ns IHMSA 10-001 to IHMSA 10-200.
- Tokagypt 58, pistol, caliber 9mm parabellum.
- Trejo, semiautomatic pistols, cal. .22, .32, and .380. mfd. in Mexico, circa 1952 to 1972.

U

- * Uberti, 125th Anniversary of the Winchester, Model 1873 lever action rifle, .44/40 caliber, having serial numbers between A125th001 through A125th125.
- Uberti Model 1866 lever action rifles, "An Engraver's Tribute to Gustave Young", .44/40 caliber,S/Ns GY001 through GY300.
- Uberti model 1866 L.D. Nimschke, lever action rifles, caliber .44-40, serial numbers LDN001 through LDN300.
- Uberti, Single action revolver, cal. .45, General George S. Patton Commemorative, S/Ns P0001 to P2500.
- United States Patent Fire Arms Manufacturing Company, Artillery Model single action revolver,100th anniversary of The Charge Up San Juan Hill, .45 caliber, with a 5 ½ - inch barrel and having S/N's from NFM001 through NFM500.
- U.S, model 1911-A-1, .45 cal. pistol, mfd. by Union Switch and Signal Company, prototype model, with S/Ns US&S Exp. 1 to US&S Exp. 100.
- U.S., model 1911-A1, semiautomatic, pistol, cal. .45, mfd. by the Singer Manufacturing Company in 1942, S/N range from S800001 to S800500.
- U.S., model 1911-A1, semiautomatic pistol, cal. .45, mfd. by Remington Rand, bearing S/N prefix of ERRS.
- U.S., model 1911-A1 semiautomatic pistol, cal. .45, produced as original factory cut-a-ways.
- U.S., Rifle, cal. .30 M1, original military issue only, produced prior to 1956.
- U.S., Rifle, cal. .30, MC-1952, equipped with telescopic sight mount MC, telescopic sight MC1, marked U.S.M.C. or Kollmorgan.
- U.S. Repeating Arms, Wyoming Centennial, Winchester Commemorative Model 94 Carbines, cal. .30-30, S/Ns WYC001 through WYC500.
- UZI, Model A, semiautomatic carbine, cal. 9mm, having a satin nickel finish applied at the factory, S/Ns SA 0001 to SA 0100.

W

- Walther, bolt action and semiautomatic rifles, all cals., mfd. prior to 1946.
- Walther, model PP and PPK semiautomatic pistols, in all cals., mfd. in France and marked "MANHURIN".
- Walther, Model PP pistol, 50 Jahre 1929-1959 Commemorative, caliber .22 and .380.
- Walther, Model TP and TPH pistols, cal. .22 and .25 ACP, original German manufacture only.
- Walther, Olympic bolt action single shot match rifle, in cal. .22 made by Waffenfabrik Walther, Zella-Mehlis (thur.) prior to World War II.
- Walther, pistols, mfd. at Zel1a-Mehlis prior to 1946, all models, any caliber.
- Walther, rifles, model 182, cal. .22 made by Waffenfabrik Walther, Zelia-Mehlis (thur.) prior to World War II.
- Watson Brothers, Lee-Speed type, custom sporting rifle, cal. .303, S/N 7738.
- Webley and Scott, model 1910 and 1913 high velocity pistols, cal. .38 ACP.
- Webley and Scott, M1913, Navy or Commercial, self loading pistol, cal. .455.
- Webley-Fosbury, semiautomatic revolvers, all cals., all models.
- Webley, model 1909, pistol, cal. 9mm Browning Long.
- Whitney, "Wolverine" and "Lighting" .22 cal. automatic pistols as mfd. by Whitney Firearms Company, Hartford, CT between 1955 - 1962.
- Winchester, Model 1894, Florida Sesquicentennial carbine, cal. .30-30, S/N's FL001-FL500.
- Winchester, Apache Commemorative carbine, commemorative edition of model 1894 Winchester with S/N prefix of A.
- Winchester, Comanche Commemorative carbine, commemorative edition of model 1894 Winchester with S/N prefix of CC.
- Winchester, "Ducks Unlimited" shotgun, model 12, bearing S/Ns DU-001 through DU-800 (Commemorative).
- Winchester, Kentucky Bicentennial Model 94 carbines, cal. .30-30, S/N range KY001-KY500.
- Winchester, "Matched Set of 1000," a cased pair consisting of a Winchester model 94 rifle, cal. .30-30 and a Winchester model 9422 rifle, cal. .22.
- Winchester, Model 12, pump action shotguns, mfd. from 1912 through 1963, S/Ns 1 through 1962017.
- Winchester, Model 12, Shotgun, 12 gauge, prototype, for Ducks Unlimited Commemorative, S/N Y2002214.
- * Winchester, Model 12 Y, pump action shotguns, all variations, manufactured between 1972 and 1979, S/Ns Y2000100 through Y2026399.
- Winchester, Model 21, double barrel shotguns, all gauges, all grades, mfd. by Winchester and U.S. Repeating Arms.
- Winchester, Model 21, Grand American Double Barrel Shotgun, cal. 20 and 28 gauge, S/N 32984, Engraved Custom Built by Winchester for Philip S. Rane.
- Winchester, Model 37, single barrel shotguns, all gauges, manufactured between 1936 and 1963.
- Winchester, Model 42, .410 gauge shotguns.
- Winchester, Model 52, rifle, bearing S/Ns 1 to 6500.
- Winchester, Model 53, all original, mfd. from 1924 to 1947 with 16" or longer barrel, and 26" or longer overall length.
- Winchester, Model 54 rifles.
- Winchester, Model 54, rifle, speed lock variation, cal. .270.
- Winchester, Model 55, .22 caliber, single shot rifle.
- Winchester, Model 61, cal. .22 rimfire, slide action repeater, hammerless.
- Winchester, Model 62, cal. .22 rimfire, slide action repeater.
- Winchester, Model 63, self loading rifles, cal. .22 rimfire.
- Winchester, Model 64 and 65, lever action rifles.
- * Winchester, Model 70, .300 Winchester Magnum, 50th Anniversary bolt action rifle, serial numbers 50 ANV 1 through 50 ANV 500.
- Winchester, Model 70, bolt action rifle, all cals., mfd. in or before 1963 having S/Ns less than 581472.
- Winchester, Model 70, rifle, cal. .308 rifle, 19" barrel and Mannlicher type stock, made from 1968 to 1971.
- Winchester, Model 70, rifles, .308, .270 Winchester, and 30-06 cal., 19" barrel and Mannlicher type stock, made from 1968 to 1971.
- Winchester, Model 70, Ultra Match Target Special Grade rifle, cal. .308.
- * Winchester, Model 70, XTR Featherweight Ultra Grade, .270 caliber, bolt action rifle, 1 of 1,000.
- Winchester, Model 71, all original, mfd. from 1936 to 1958 with 16"or longer barrel and 26" or Longer overall length.
- Winchester, Model 85, (single shot rifle), all original, mfd. from 1899 to 1920, with 16" or longer barrel and 26" or longer overall length.

- Winchester, Model 86, all original, mfd. from 1899 to 1935, with 16" or longer barrel and 26" or longer overall length.
- Winchester, Model 88, carbine, cal. .243, .284, .308, or .358 mfd. by Winchester Western Division, Olin Corporation, New Haven, CT.
- Winchester, Model 88 rifles, all calibers.
- Winchester, Model 92, all original, mfd. from 1899 to 1947, with 16" or longer barrel and 26" or longer overall length.
- Winchester, Model 94, Alaskan Purchase Centennial, carbine.
- Winchester, Model 94, American Bald Eagle Commemorative Carbine.
- Winchester, Model 94, Arapaho Commemorative carbines, caliber .30-30, S/Ns ARAPA001 - ARAPA500.
- Winchester, Model 94, Bat Masterson commemorative.
- Winchester, Model 94, Bicentennial 76, carbine.
- Winchester, Model 94, Buffalo Bill, carbine.
- Winchester, Model 94, Buffalo Bill, rifle.
- Winchester, Model 94, C.M. Russell, Great Western Artist Commemorative Carbine.
- Winchester, Model 94, cal. .30-30, Antlered Game Commemorative, carbine.
- Winchester, Model 94, cal. .30-30, Legendary Lawman Commemorative, carbine.
- Winchester, Model 94, Calgary Stampede Commemorative, carbine, cal. .32 Winchester Special.
- Winchester, Model 94, Canadian 1967, Centennial carbine.
- Winchester, Model 94, Canadian 1967, Centennial rifle.
- Winchester, Model 94, carbine, Canadian Pacific Centennial, cal. .32 Winchester Special.
- Winchester, Model 94, carbine, Oklahoma Diamond Jubilee Commemorative.
- Winchester, Model 94, carbines, Chevrolet Outdoorsman sets, .30-30 cal., having S/Ns between 5130000 and 5466000.
- Winchester, Model 94, "Chief Crazy Horse," commemorative lever action rifle, cal. .38-55, mfd. by U.S. Repeating Arms Co., New Haven, CT.
- Winchester, Model 94, Colt Commemorative Set, Winchester Signature model "Oliver F. Winchester" carbine, cal. 44-40, Lever Action, as mfd. by U.S. Repeating Arms Co., New Haven, CT.
- Winchester, Model 94, Cowboy Commemorative, carbine.
- Winchester, Model 94 rifle, Custom Limited Edition Centennial, .30 WCF cal., S/Ns CNTL 01 through CNTL 94.
- Winchester, Model 94, Frederick Remington, Great Western Artist Commemorative Carbine.
- Winchester, Model 94, Illinois Sesquicentennial, carbine.
- Winchester, Model 94, in cal. .38/55, 1980, Alberta Diamond Jubilee Commemorative, carbine.
- Winchester, Model 94, John Wayne Commemorative (Canadian Issue), carbine, cal. .32-40.
- Winchester, Model 94, John Wayne commemorative, cal. .32-40, carbine.
- Winchester, Model 94, Klondike Gold Rush Commemorative carbine.
- Winchester, Model 94, Legendary Frontiersman rifle, cal. .38-55.
- Winchester, Model 94, "Limited Edition I".
- Winchester, Model 94, "Limited Edition II" rifle, cal. .30-30.
- Winchester, Model 94, Limited Edition, carbine, cal. .30-30, S/Ns 77L1 - 77L1500.
- Winchester, Model 94, Limited Edition Centennial, .30 WCF rifles, S/Ns CN10,001 - CN10,250, mfd. by the USRAC Custom Gun Shop for the Winchester Arms Collectors Association, having a replica Lyman No. 2 tang sight and with the WACA medallion placed in the buttstock.
- Winchester, Model 94, Little Big Horn Centennial, carbine.
- Winchester, Model 94, Lone Star Commemorative, carbine.
- Winchester, Model 94, Lone Star Commemorative, rifle, .30-30.
- Winchester, Model 94, model NRA Centennial, carbine.
- Winchester, Model 94, Mounted Police, carbine.
- Winchester, Model 94, Nebraska Centennial, carbine.
- Winchester, Model 94, NRA Centennial rifle, .30-30.
- Winchester, Model 94, One of One Thousand European Rifle commemorative.
- Winchester, Model 94, Ontario, Canada Conservation Office, 100th Anniversary Commemorative carbines, caliber.30-30.
- Winchester, Model 94, rifles and carbines mfd. prior to January 2, 1964, and having a S/N of less than 2,700,000, provided their barrel length is at least 16" and their overall length at least 26".
- Winchester, Model 94, Royal Canadian Mounted Police Centennial carbine.
- Winchester, Model 94, Saskatchewan Diamond Jubilee Carbine commemorative.
- Winchester, Model 94, Sioux Commemorative carbines, cal. 30-30, with S/Ns beginning with "SU".
- Winchester, Model 94, The Oliver F. Winchester commemorative.
- Winchester, Model 94, Theodore Roosevelt, Carbine.
- Winchester, Model 94, Theodore Roosevelt, Rifle.
- Winchester, Model 94, United States Border Patrol Commemorative carbine cal. .30-30.
- Winchester, Model 94, Wild Bill Hickok Commemorative, Caliber .45, S/Ns WBH001 - WBH350.
- Winchester, Model 94, Wells Fargo and Company Commemorative, carbines.
- Winchester, Model 94, Wyoming Centennial Commemorative carbines, caliber .30-30, S/Ns WYC001 - -WYC500.
- Winchester, Model 94, Wyoming Diamond Jubilee, carbine.
- Winchester, Model 94, Yellow Boy Indian, carbine.
- Winchester, Model 94, 125th Anniversary Commemorative carbines, caliber .30-30, S/Ns WRAC001 - -WRAC125.
- Winchester, Model 94, 150th Anniversary Texas Ranger Commemorative, carbine.
- Winchester, Model 95, all original, mfd. from 1899 to 1938, with 16" or longer barrel and 26" or longer overall length.
- Winchester, Model 1866, Centennial, carbine.
- Winchester, Model 1866, Centennial, rifle.
- Winchester, Model 1873, all original, mfd. from 1899 to 1925, with 16" or longer barrel and 26" or longer overall length.
- Winchester Model 1890 rifles.
- Winchester, Model 1894, Golden Spike, carbine.
- Winchester, Model 1894 Nez Perce Commemorative carbine, cal. .30-30, mfd. by U.S. Repeating Arms Co., S/Ns NEZ001-NEZ600.
- Winchester, Model 1894, Texas Sesquicentennial rifle and carbine, cal. .38-55.
- Winchester, Model 1897, pump action shotguns, all gauges, manufactured between 1899 and 1957, S/N's 1 through 1,024,700.
- Winchester, Model 1897 or 97 riot guns, 12 gauge, 20" barrels with original RIC (Royal Irish Constabulary) markings.
- * Winchester, Model 1902, .22 caliber bolt action rifles.
- Winchester, Model 1903 .22 cal. semiautomatic rifles.
- Winchester, model 1906 rifles.
- Winchester, Model 9422, Annie Oakley Commemorative Carbine .22 cal.
- Winchester, Model 9422, "Eagle Scout Commemorative" rifle, .22 cal.
- Winchester, Northwest Territories Centennial rifle.

Y

- Yugoslavian M1948 (M48) bolt action rifles, 7.92 x 57mm caliber, produced at the Kragujevac Arsenal, original military configuration only.

CURIOS OR RELICS UPDATE MARCH 2001 THROUGH MAY 2005

Section II – Firearms classified as curios or relics, still subject to the provisions of 18 U.S.C. Chapter 44, the Gun Control Act of 1968.

- Albanian SKS semiautomatic rifles, caliber 7.62x39, manufactured in Albania from 1964 to 1978.
- Bren Ten pistol, all models and variants manufactured by Dornaus and Dixon Enterprises, Inc. prior to 1986.
- Colt Model "Courier" double action revolver, .32 caliber, with 3-inch barrel.
- Colt Model "Marshal" double action revolver, .38 special caliber, 2-inch and 4-inch barrels.
- Colt, Single Action Army (2nd Generation) revolvers, having serial numbers from 0001SA to 82000SA, all calibers, made between 1956 and 1976.
- Colt, Woodsman, .22 caliber semiautomatic pistols, all models, all series, all serial numbers, (to include Match Target, Challenger, Huntsmen, and Targetsman), made prior to 1978.
- Harrington & Richardson Trapdoor Springfield carbine, .45-70 caliber, 100th Anniversary Little Big Horn Commemorative, manufactured between 1973-1981.
- Lee Enfield Rifle, caliber 7.62 2A and 2A1 "India" all variations, originally manufactured at Ishapore Arsenal, India, through 1973.
- Mauser Luger, serial number 11.010034, 9mm, special engraving and ivory grips.
- Mauser Luger, serial number RG 900/1001, 9mm, special engraving and walnut grips.
- Norinco (Chinese) AK47S, 5.56x45mm caliber, serial number 403876.
- Norinco (Chinese) AK47S84S-1, 5.56x45mm caliber, serial number 303052.
- Norinco (Chinese) AK47S, 7.62x39mm caliber, serial number 1620127.
- Poly Tech (Chinese) AK 47S (386), 7.62x39mm caliber, serial number P47-11545.
- Romanian AK 74S, 5.45x45mm caliber, serial number 3-040053-97.
- Tippmann Arms Company Models 1919 A-4, 1917, and .50 HB 1/2 scale, .22 caliber semi-automatic firearms, manufactured in Fort Wayne, Indiana, from 1986-1987.
- U.S. Rifle, caliber .30, M1, original issue only, produced prior to 1958.
- Winchester Model 94 "Trapper," .357 magnum caliber saddle ring carbine, 100th Anniversary Commemorative 1894-1994.
- Winchester, Model 9422, Cheyenne Commemorative rifles, .22 caliber.
- Yugoslavian manufactured rifles M59 and M59/66, 7.62 x 39mm caliber, all semiautomatic variations and having a fixed magazine, manufactured from 1947 to 1992.

Section III – Firearms removed from the provisions of the National Firearms Act and classified as curios or relics, still subject to the provisions of 18 U.S.C. Chapter 44, the Gun Control Act of 1968.

- Chinese, Jingal rifle, caliber .60, serial number IRS 9083H.
- Colt, Model New Service revolver, caliber .44 WCF, serial number 55125, having a barrel with a smooth bore.
- Colt, Single Action Army revolver, caliber .44 WCF (.44-40), serial number 324477, with blue finish, 5-1/2 inch barrel and smooth bore presented by Colt Firearms to Mr. John W. Garrett.
- Harrington & Richardson Handy Gun, Model 122, .22 Rimfire caliber, with original shoulder stock, having a barrel length of 12-3/4 inches, serial number 157.
- High Standard, Model "S" smoothbore pistol, caliber .22 L.R., serial number 59493.
- Japanese, 20mm Single-Barrel Variant, flare pistol.
- Marlin, Model 1893, caliber .30-30, serial number C2231, with 15-inch barrel.
- Marlin, Model 1893, caliber .32-40, serial number 405878, with 15-inch barrel.
- Marlin, Model 1893, caliber .32 H.P.S., serial number 432920, with 15-inch barrel.
- Marlin, Model 1893, caliber .38-55, serial number C3394, with 15-inch barrel.
- Marlin, Model 1894, caliber .32-20, serial number 435220, with 15-inch barrel.
- Marlin, Model 1894, caliber .44-40, serial number 375792, with 15-inch barrel.
- Marlin, Model 1894, caliber .44-40, serial number 376768, with 15.25-inch barrel.
- Marlin, Model 1894, caliber .44-40, serial number 386485, with 15-inch barrel.
- Marlin, Model 1894, caliber .44-40, serial number 398492, with 15-inch barrel.
- Marlin, Model 1894, caliber .44-40, serial number 398586, with 15-inch barrel.
- Marlin, Model 1894, caliber .44-40, serial number 407596, with 15-inch barrel.
- Marlin, Model 1894, caliber .44-40, serial number 421436, with 15-inch barrel.
- Marlin, Model 1894, caliber .44-40, serial number 427022, with 15-inch barrel.
- Marlin, Model 93, caliber .32-H.P.S., serial number 3375, with 15-inch barrel.
- Mauser Parabellum 75th Year Commemorative Luger Karabiner with accompanying shoulder stock.

- ▲ Winchester, Model 1873, caliber .44 WCF, serial number 718977B, with 14-inch barrel.
- ▲ Winchester, Model 1885, caliber .44 WCF, serial number 103509, with 15-inch barrel.
- ▲ Winchester, Model 1892, caliber .25-20 WCF, serial number 295206, with 15-inch barrel.
- ▲ Winchester, Model 1892, caliber .25-20 WCF, serial number 692609, with 15-inch barrel.
- ▲ Winchester, Model 1892, caliber .25-20 WCF, serial number 800432, with 14-inch barrel.
- ▲ Winchester, Model 1892, caliber .25-20 WCF, serial number 801232, with 14-inch barrel.
- ▲ Winchester, Model 1892, caliber .25-20 WCF, serial number 801389, with 14-inch barrel.
- ▲ Winchester, Model 1892, caliber .25-20 WCF, serial number 836858, with 14-inch barrel.
- ▲ Winchester, Model 1892, caliber .25-20 WCF, serial number 852773, with 15-inch barrel.
- ▲ Winchester, Model 1892, caliber .25-20 WCF, serial number 853241, with 15-inch barrel.
- ▲ Winchester, Model 1892, caliber .25-20 WCF, serial number 942997, with 14-inch barrel.
- ▲ Winchester, Model 1892, caliber .32-20, serial number 472150, with 15-inch barrel.
- ▲ Winchester, Model 1892, caliber .32 WCF, serial number 840518, with 14-inch barrel.
- ▲ Winchester, Model 1892, caliber .32 WCF, serial number 841245, with 14-inch octagonal barrel.
- ▲ Winchester, Model 1892, caliber .32 WCF, serial number 874184, with 14-inch barrel.
- ▲ Winchester, Model 1892, caliber .32 WCF, serial number 928023, with 14-inch barrel.
- ▲ Winchester, Model 1892, caliber .32 WCF, serial number 939107, with 14-inch barrel.
- ▲ Winchester, Model 1892, caliber .35 Winchester S.L., serial number 686515, with 15-inch barrel, marked .25-20 W.C.F.
- ▲ Winchester, Model 1892, caliber .38 WCF, serial number 675600, with 14-inch barrel.
- ▲ Winchester, Model 1892, caliber .38 WCF, serial number 686204, with 14-inch barrel.
- ▲ Winchester, Model 1892, caliber .38 WCF, serial number 842774, with 14-inch barrel.
- ▲ Winchester, Model 1892, caliber .38 WCF, serial number 848416, with 14-inch barrel.
- ▲ Winchester, Model 1892, caliber .38 WCF, serial number 848742, with 14-inch barrel.
- ▲ Winchester, Model 1892, caliber .38 WCF, serial number 998336, with 14-inch barrel.
- ▲ Winchester, Model 1892, caliber .44 WCF, serial number *58732, with 15-inch barrel.
- ▲ Winchester, Model 1892, caliber .44 WCF, serial number 172068, with 15-inch barrel.
- ▲ Winchester, Model 1892, caliber .44 WCF, serial number 325125, with 14-inch barrel.
- ▲ Winchester, Model 1892, caliber .44 WCF, serial number 325412, with 14-inch barrel.
- ▲ Winchester, Model 1892, caliber .44 WCF, serial number 326732, with 14-inch barrel.
- ▲ Winchester, Model 1892, caliber .44 WCF, serial number 374202, with 14-inch barrel.
- ▲ Winchester, Model 1892, caliber .44 WCF, serial number 407490, with 14-inch barrel.
- ▲ Winchester, Model 1892, caliber .44 WCF, serial number 407735, with 14-inch barrel.
- ▲ Winchester, Model 1892, caliber .44 WCF, serial number 408070, with 12-inch barrel.
- ▲ Winchester, Model 1892, caliber .44 WCF, serial number 410488, with 14-inch barrel.
- ▲ Winchester, Model 1892, caliber .44 WCF, serial number 414816, with 14-inch octagonal barrel.
- ▲ Winchester, Model 1892, caliber .44 WCF, serial number 449861, with 15-inch barrel.
- ▲ Winchester, Model 1892, caliber .44 WCF, serial number 492863, with 14 inch barrel.
- ▲ Winchester, Model 1892, caliber .44 WCF, serial number 507295, with 14-inch barrel.
- ▲ Winchester, Model 1892, caliber .44 WCF, serial number 600075, with 14-inch barrel.
- ▲ Winchester, Model 1892, caliber .44 WCF, serial number 659956, with 14-inch barrel.
- ▲ Winchester, Model 1892, caliber .44 WCF, serial number 676111, with 14-inch barrel.
- ▲ Winchester, Model 1892, caliber .44 WCF, serial number 688571, with 14-inch barrel.
- ▲ Winchester, Model 1892, caliber .44 WCF, serial number 697497, with 15 inch barrel.
- ▲ Winchester, Model 1892, caliber .44 WCF, serial number 742128, with 14-inch barrel.
- ▲ Winchester, Model 1892, caliber .44 WCF, serial number 742128, with 14-inch barrel.
- ▲ Winchester, Model 1892, caliber .44 WCF, serial number 742330, with 14-inch barrel.
- ▲ Winchester, Model 1892, caliber .44 WCF, serial number 767088, with 14-inch barrel.
- ▲ Winchester, Model 1892, caliber .44 WCF, serial number 820970, with 15-inch barrel.
- ▲ Winchester, Model 1892, caliber .44 WCF, serial number 821110, with 15-inch barrel.
- ▲ Winchester, Model 1892, caliber .44 WCF, serial number 835806, with 15-inch barrel.
- ▲ Winchester, Model 1892, caliber .44 WCF, serial number 842869, with 15-inch barrel.
- ▲ Winchester, Model 1892, caliber .44 WCF, serial number 852145, with 14-inch barrel.
- ▲ Winchester, Model 1892, caliber .44 WCF, serial number 853128, with 14-inch barrel.
- ▲ Winchester, Model 1892, caliber .44 WCF, serial number 870893, with 14-inch barrel.
- ▲ Winchester, Model 1892, caliber .44 WCF, serial number 871544, with 15-inch barrel.
- ▲ Winchester, Model 1892, caliber .44 WCF, serial number 880098, with 14-inch barrel.
- ▲ Winchester, Model 1892, caliber .44 WCF, serial number 882743, with 14-inch barrel.
- ▲ Winchester, Model 1892, caliber .44 WCF, serial number 889143, with 14-inch barrel.
- ▲ Winchester, Model 1892, caliber .44 WCF, serial number 894524, with 14-inch barrel.
- ▲ Winchester, Model 1892, caliber .44 WCF, serial number 895290, with 14-inch barrel.
- ▲ Winchester, Model 1892, caliber .44 WCF, serial number 895861, with 15-inch barrel

- ▲ Winchester, Model 1892, caliber .44 WCF, serial number 905438, with 14-inch barrel.
- ▲ Winchester, Model 1892, caliber .44 WCF, serial number 908502, with 15-inch barrel.
- ▲ Winchester, Model 1892, caliber .44 WCF, serial number 934212, with 14 inch barrel.
- ▲ Winchester, Model 1892, caliber .44 WCF, serial number 940138, with 14-inch barrel.
- ▲ Winchester, Model 1892, caliber .44 WCF, serial number 979529, with 14-inch barrel.
- ▲ Winchester, Model 1892, caliber .44 WCF, serial number 981253, with 14-inch barrel.
- ▲ Winchester, Model 1892, caliber .44 WCF, serial number 982703, with 14-inch barrel.
- ▲ Winchester, Model 1892, caliber .44 WCF, serial number 987936, with 14-inch barrel.
- ▲ Winchester, Model 1892, caliber .44 WCF, serial number 996120, with 14-inch barrel.
- ▲ Winchester, Model 1892, caliber .44 WCF, serial number 996327, with 15-inch barrel.
- ▲ Winchester, Model 1892, caliber .44 WCF, serial number 997543, with 15-inch barrel.
- ▲ Winchester, Model 1892, caliber .44 WCF, serial number 998995, with 15-inch barrel.
- ▲ Winchester, Model 1892, caliber .44 WCF, serial number 999036, with 15-inch barrel.
- ▲ Winchester, Model 1894, caliber .25-35 WCF, serial number 427187, with 14-inch barrel.
- ▲ Winchester, Model 1894, caliber .25-35 WCF, serial number 815238, with 15-inch barrel.
- ▲ Winchester, Model 1894, caliber .30 WCF, serial number 442920, with 15-inch barrel.
- ▲ Winchester, Model 1894, caliber .30 WCF, serial number 463348, with 15-inch barrel.
- ▲ Winchester, Model 1894, caliber .30 WCF, serial number 554548, with 15-inch barrel.
- ▲ Winchester, Model 1894, caliber .30 WCF, serial number 639534, with 15-inch barrel.
- ▲ Winchester, Model 1894, caliber .30 WCF, serial number 639534, with 15-inch barrel.
- ▲ Winchester, Model 1894, caliber .30 WCF, serial number 820363, with 15-inch barrel.
- ▲ Winchester, Model 1894, caliber .30 WCF, serial number 844538, with 15-inch barrel.
- ▲ Winchester, Model 1894, caliber .30 WCF, serial number 846610, with 15-inch barrel.
- ▲ Winchester, Model 1894, caliber .30 WCF, serial number 847112, with 15-inch barrel.
- ▲ Winchester, Model 1894, caliber .30 WCF, serial number 862579, with 15-inch barrel.
- ▲ Winchester, Model 1894, caliber .30 WCF, serial number 885359, with 15-inch barrel.
- ▲ Winchester, Model 1894, caliber .30 WCF, serial number 921311, with 15-inch barrel.
- ▲ Winchester, Model 1894, caliber .30 WCF, serial number 921754, with 15-inch barrel.
- ▲ Winchester Model 94, caliber .30 WCF, serial number 992289, with 15-inch barrel.
- ▲ Winchester, Model 1894, caliber .30 WCF, serial number 959632, having a 15-inch barrel.
- ▲ Winchester, Model 1894, caliber .30 WCF, serial number 986535, with 15-inch barrel.
- ▲ Winchester, Model 1894, caliber .30 WCF, serial number 1004929, with 15-inch barrel.
- ▲ Winchester, Model 1894, caliber .30 WCF, serial number 1005373, with 15-inch barrel.
- ▲ Winchester, Model 1894, caliber .30 WCF, serial number 1009473, with 15-inch barrel.
- ▲ Winchester, Model 1894, caliber .30 WCF, serial number 1017950, with 15-inch barrel.
- ▲ Winchester, Model 1894, caliber .30 WCF, serial number 1044205, with 15-inch barrel.
- ▲ Winchester, Model 1894, caliber .30 WCF, serial number 1050280, with 15-inch barrel.
- ▲ Winchester, Model 1894, caliber .30 WCF, serial number 1057984, with 15-inch barrel.
- ▲ Winchester, Model 1894, caliber .30 WCF, serial number 1058915, with 15-inch barrel.
- ▲ Winchester, Model 94, caliber .30 WCF, serial number 1065744, with 15-inch barrel.
- ▲ Winchester, Model 94, caliber .30 WCF, serial number 1086186, with 15-inch barrel.

Section IIIA — Firearms manufactured in or before 1898, removed from the provisions of the National Firearms Act and classified as antique firearms not subject to the provisions of 18 U.S.C. Chapter 44, the Gun Control Act of 1968.

- ♦ Marlin, Model 1889, caliber .44, serial number 44335, with 15-inch barrel.
- ♦ Winchester, Model 1873, caliber .44 WCF, serial number 131592A, with 15-inch barrel.
- ♦ Winchester, Model 1885, caliber .44 WCF, serial number 73593, with 15-inch barrel.
- ♦ Winchester, Model 1892, caliber .38 WCF, serial number 102645, with 15 inch barrel.

Section IV – NFA firearms classified as curios or relics, still subject to the provisions of 26 U.S.C. Chapter 53, the National Firearms Act, and 18 U.S.C. Chapter 44, the Gun Control Act of 1968.

- ✷ Auto Ordnance, Thompson Model 1928, .22 caliber machinegun in original configuration as manufactured at the West Hurley, NY facility between 1980 and 1981.
- ✷ Colt, CMG-2, serial number 012.
- ✷ SS1-Sidewinder machinegun, serial number Ex-016
- ✷ US machinegun, Model T161, caliber 7.62, Serial numbers EXP21, EXP25, EXP26, EXP27, EXP30, EXP32, EXP34, EXP35, 3XP37, EXP38, EXP42, EXP45, EXP47, EXP51, EXP53, EXP56, EXP57, EXP60.

Section II – Firearms classified as curios or relics, still subject to the provisions of 18 U.S.C. Chapter 44, the Gun Control Act of 1968.

- ✣ Czechoslovakian, VZ-54 sniper rifle, manufactured from 1954 through 1957, caliber 7.62x54R, all S/N's with scope mount and 2.5 power telescope

Section III – Firearms removed from the provisions of the National Firearms Act and classified as curios or relics, still subject to the provisions of 18 U.S.C. Chapter 44, the Gun Control Act of 1968.

- ★ Marlin, Model 1892, caliber .44-40, S/N 386485, with 15-inch barrel
- ★ Winchester, Model 1885, caliber .44WCF, S/N 103509, with 15-inch barrel
- ★ Winchester, Model 1892, caliber .25-20WCF, S/N 686515, with 15-inch barrel
- ★ Winchester, Model 1892, caliber .25-20WCF, S/N 914301, with 15-inch barrel
- ★ Winchester, Model 1892, caliber .30WCF, S/N 211284, with 14-inch barrel
- ★ Winchester, Model 1892, caliber .38WCF, S/N 545168, with 15-inch barrel
- ★ Winchester, Model 1892, caliber .44WCF, S/N 693360, with 12-inch barrel
- ★ Winchester, Model 1892, caliber .44WCF, S/N 410015, with 14-inch barrel
- ★ Winchester, Model 1892, caliber .44WCF, S/N 661061, with 14-inch barrel
- ★ Winchester, Model 1894, caliber .30WCF, S/N 1004427, with 15-inch barrel
- ★ Winchester, Model 1894, caliber .30WCF, S/N 1032419, with 15-inch barrel
- ★ Winchester, Model 1894, caliber .30WCF, S/N 1054200, with 15-inch barrel
- ★ Winchester, Model 1894, caliber .30WCF, S/N 612946, with 15-inch barrel
- ★ Winchester, Model 1894, caliber .30WCF, S/N 746707, with 14-inch barrel
- ★ Winchester, Model 1894, caliber .30WCF, S/N 780670, with 15-inch barrel
- ★ Winchester, Model 1894, caliber .30WCF, S/N 885127, with 15-inch barrel
- ★ Winchester, Model 1894, caliber .30WCF, S/N 921922, with 15-inch barrel
- ★ Winchester, Model 1894, caliber .30WCF, S/N 958505, with 15-inch barrel

Section IV – NFA firearms classified as curios or relics, still subject to the provisions of 26 U.S.C. Chapter 53, the National Firearms Act, and 18 U.S.C. Chapter 44, the Gun Control Act of 1968.

- ✤ Browning, Automatic Rifle M1918A2, S/N 00229, mfd. Group Industries

INDEX

ARGETINA

HANDGUNS

RIFLES

REMINGTON

MAUSER

SHOTGUNS

MACHINE GUNS

AUSTRAILIA

HANDGUNS

SUBMACHINE GUNS

RIFLES

MACHINE GUNS

AUSTRIA

HANDGUNS

STEYR

SUBMACHINE GUNS

CHINA

HANDGUNS

MAUSER

CHINA STATE ARSENALS

SUBMACHINE GUNS

RIFLES

MAUSER

ARISAKA

MACHINE GUNS

CZECHOSLOVAKIA

HANDGUNS

SUBMACHINE GUNS

RIFLES

MAUSER

CZECH STATE

DENMARK

HANDGUNS

SUBMACHINE GUNS

RIFLES

REMINGTON ROLLING BLOCK

MAUSER

KRAG JORGENSEN

MADSEN

MACHINE GUNS

EGYPT

HANDGUNS

SUBMACHINE GUNS

RIFLES

AKM

FINLAND

HANDGUNS

SUBMACHINE GUNS

RIFLES

MODEL 38 AND 38-H

TYPE THREE 38-H MODEL

TYPE FOUR 38-H MODEL

TYPE FIVE MODEL 38

WALTHER

MAUSER

GERMAN SNIPER RIFLES

RIFLES

ENGLISH PRE-CARTRIDGE ERA RIFLES

SNIDER

MARTINI-HENRY

LEE-METFORD TRIALS RIFLES

ENFIELD ROYAL SMALL ARMS FACTORY

NO. 1 SMLE SERIES

NO. 4 SERIES

JUNGLE CARBINES

SNIPER RIFLES

LEE-ENFIELD .22 RIFLES

7.62X51MM CONVERSIONS & MANUFACTURE

OTHER BRITISH RIFLES

SMITH & WESSON

STERLING

ACCURACY INTERNATIONAL

PARKER-HALE

MACHINE GUNS

HUNGARY

HANDGUNS

STEYR

MANNLICHER

FEGYVERGYAR

STEYR

HUNGARIAN AK CLONES

ISRAEL

HANDGUNS

MAUSER

ITALY

HANDGUNS

BERETTA, PIETRO

VETTERLI

CARCANO

JAPAN

HANDGUNS

NORWAY

HANDGUNS

NAGANT

POLAND

HANDGUNS

RADOM

SUBMACHINE GUNS

RIFLES

MAUSER

MACHINE GUNS

PORTUGAL

HANDGUNS

SUBMACHINE GUNS

RIFLES

STEYR

WINCHESTER

TOKAREV

DRAGUNOV

SIMONOV

KALASHNIKOV

MACHINE GUNS

SPAIN

HANDGUNS

CAMPO GIRO

ASTRA-UNCETA SA

ASTRA 900 SERIES

MODEL 1911A1 AUTOMATIC PISTOL MILITARY MODEL

REMINGTON

SMITH & WESSON

HIGH STANDARD

HECKLER & KOCH

BERETTA

SAVAGE

STURM, RUGER & CO.

GUIDE LAMP

THOMPSON SUBMACHINE GUNS

HARPERS FERRY ARMORY MUSKETS & CARBINES

SPRINGFIELD ARMORY

PEABODY

SPENCER

SHARPS RIFLE MANUFACTURING COMPANY

PEDERSEN, JOHN D.

SPRINGFIELD ARMORY

SPRINGFIELD MODEL 1903 & VARIATIONS

KRAG JORGENSEN

COLT

(U.S. M1 RIFLE) U.S. RIFLE, CAL. M1 (GARAND)

SCOPE VARIANTS (SNIPER RIFLES)

KNIGHT'S MANUFACTURING CO.

JOHNSON AUTOMATICS MFG. CO.

PARKER-HALE

SAVAGE

WINCHESTER REPEATING ARMS COMPANY

HARRINGTON & RICHARDSON, INC.

BARRETT F.A. MFG. CO.

WINCHESTER

REMINGTON

SAVAGE

STEVENS

MOSSBERG

ITHACA

BENELLI

YUGOSLAVIA

HANDGUNS

SUBMACHINE GUNS

RIFLES

MAUSER

MACHINE GUNS